Lecture Notes in Artificial Intelligence   11805

Subseries of Lecture Notes in Computer Science

More information about this series at http://www.springer.com/series/1244

Paulo Moura Oliveira · Paulo Novais ·
Luís Paulo Reis (Eds.)

Progress in Artificial Intelligence

19th EPIA Conference
on Artificial Intelligence, EPIA 2019
Vila Real, Portugal, September 3–6, 2019
Proceedings, Part II

 Springer

Editors
Paulo Moura Oliveira (ID)
INESC-TEC
University of Trás-os-Montes
and Alto Douro
Vila Real, Portugal

Paulo Novais (ID)
University of Minho
Braga, Portugal

Luís Paulo Reis (ID)
LIACC/UP
University of Porto
Porto, Portugal

ISSN 0302-9743   ISSN 1611-3349 (electronic)
Lecture Notes in Artificial Intelligence
ISBN 978-3-030-30243-6   ISBN 978-3-030-30244-3 (eBook)
https://doi.org/10.1007/978-3-030-30244-3

LNCS Sublibrary: SL7 – Artificial Intelligence

This Springer imprint is published by the registered company Springer Nature Switzerland AG
The registered company address is: Gewerbestrasse 11, 6330 Cham, Switzerland

Preface

The EPIA Conference on Artificial Intelligence is a well-established European conference in the field of Artificial Intelligence (AI). In this 19th edition, EPIA 2019, took place in Vila Real at the University of Trás-os-Montes and Alto Douro (UTAD), during September 3–6, 2019 (https://epia2019.utad.pt/). Vila Real is a beautiful town in the heart of Douro Valley, a privileged wine region in Portugal. This is an elected place for the lovers of nature, food, and wine, whose people are well known for their hospitality.

Our society is undergoing a gradual process of transformation. We are moving at an accelerated pace towards an information and knowledge society where the introduction and use of AI and ITC technologies play a key role, which made EPIA 2019 even more challenging and exciting.

This conference is always organized under the auspices of the Portuguese Association for Artificial Intelligence (APPIA – http://www.appia.pt) and, as in previous editions, the program was based on a set of thematic tracks dedicated to specific themes of AI.

EPIA 2019 encompassed a record of 18 tracks devoted to different topics, plus a doctoral symposium and a panel session on "Societal AI." The selected tracks were: AIEd - Artificial Intelligence in Education, AI4G - Artificial Intelligence for Games, AIoTA - Artificial Intelligence and IoT in Agriculture, AIL - Artificial Intelligence and Law, AIM - Artificial Intelligence in Medicine, AICPDES - Artificial Intelligence in Cyber-Physical and Distributed Embedded Systems, AIPES - Artificial Intelligence in Power and Energy Systems, AITS - Artificial Intelligence in Transportation Systems, ALEA - Artificial Life and Evolutionary Algorithms, AmIA - Ambient Intelligence and Affective Environments, BAAI - Business Applications of Artificial Intelligence, GAI - General AI, IROBOT - Intelligent Robotics, KDBI - Knowledge Discovery and Business Intelligence, KRR - Knowledge Representation and Reasoning, MASTA - Multi-Agent Systems: Theory and Applications, SSM - Social Simulation and Modelling, and TeMA - Text Mining and Applications.

The conference program included three invited talks. Marco Dorigo (Université Libre de Bruxelles, Belgium) with a talk on "Swarm robotics: recent results and new research directions," Michael Wooldridge (University of Oxford, UK) with a talk on "Understanding Equilibrium Properties of Multi-Agent Systems," and Albert Bifet (Telecom ParisTech, France) with a talk on "Machine Learning for Data Streams."

For this edition, 252 paper submissions were received from 55 different countries to the thematic tracks. After a careful review process, 125 papers were selected to be presented in EPIA 2019. The papers acceptance rate was circa 49%. All of the papers were carefully revised by at least three reviewers of the corresponding track Program Committee. We thank the track organizing chairs, together with their respective Program Committee members, for their hard work of scientific reviewing.

Thanks are also due to all supporting organizations and conference sponsors, starting with SISCOG, our main sponsor to whom we sincerely address our thanks, but also Devscope. We would like to express our gratitude to all the Organizing Committee colleagues and track organizers. A special mention to Eduardo Solteiro Pires, José Boaventura Cunha, Teresa Paula Perdicoúlis, Tatiana Pinho, and Goreti Marreiros for their excellent work which was crucial for the successful realization of EPIA 2019.

Thank you all.

July 2019

Paulo Moura Oliveira
Paulo Novais
Luís Paulo Reis

EPIA-2019 Conference Organization

Event and Program Chairs

Paulo Moura Oliveira   INESC-TEC, University of Trás-os-Montes
and Alto Douro, Portugal
Paulo Novais   ALGORITMI, University of Minho, Portugal
Luís Paulo Reis   LIACC, University of Porto, Portugal

International Steering Committee

Amedeo Cesta	CNR-ISTC, Italy
Ana Bazzan	Universidade Federal do Rio Grande do Sul, Brazil
Ana Paiva	Instituto Superior Técnico, Universidade de Lisboa, Portugal
Ernesto Costa	Universidade de Coimbra, Portugal
Eugénio Oliveira	Universidade do Porto, Portugal
François Pachet	Spotify, France
Helder Coelho	Universidade de Lisboa, Portugal
José Júlio Alferes	Universidade Nova de Lisboa, Portugal
Juan Pavón	Universidad Complutense Madrid, Spain
Luís Paulo Reis	Universidade do Porto, Portugal
Marco Dorigo	Université Libre de Bruxelles, Belgium
Paulo Novais	Universidade do Minho, Portugal
Pavel Brazdil	Universidade do Porto, Portugal
Peter McBurney	King's College London, UK
Ulrich Furbach	University of Koblenz, Germany

Organizing Chairs

Eduardo Solteiro Pires	INESC-TEC, UTAD, Portugal
José Boaventura Cunha	INESC-TEC, UTAD, Portugal
Paulo Jorge Matos	IPB, Portugal

Local Organizing Committee

César Analide	ALGORITMI, University of Minho, Portugal
Eduardo Solteiro Pires	INESC-TEC, Portugal
Goreti Marreiros	GECAD, IPP, Portugal
João Barroso	INESC-TEC, UTAD, Portugal
Lio Gonçalves	INESC-TEC, UTAD, Portugal
Paulo Martins	INESC-TEC, UTAD, Portugal
Ramiro Gonçalves	INESC-TEC, UTAD, Portugal

Raul Morais dos Santos	INESC-TEC, UTAD, Portugal
Tatiana Pinho	INESC-TEC, Portugal
Teresa Paula Perdicoúlis	ISR-Coimbra, UTAD, Portugal
Vítor Filipe	INESC-TEC, UTAD, Portugal

Proceedings Chairs

| Eduardo Solteiro Pires | INESC-TEC, UTAD, Portugal |
| Tatiana Pinho | INESC-TEC, Portugal |

Artificial Intelligence in Education (AIEd)

Organizing Committee

Vitor Santos	Nova University of Lisbon, Portugal
Leontios Hadjileontiadis	Aristotle University of Thessaloniki, Greece
João Barroso	INESC TEC, University of Trás-os-Montes and Alto Douro, Portugal
Dalila Durães	ESTG, Polytechnic Institute of Porto – Portugal

Program Committee

António Lopez Herrera	University of Granada, Spain
Bert Bredeweg	University of Amsterdam, The Netherlands
Goreti Marreiros	Polytechnic Institute of Porto, Portugal
Hélder Coelho	University of Lisbon, Portugal
Isabel Fernandez de Castro	University of the Basque Country, Spain
Jim Greer	University of Saskatchewan, Canada
Eduardo Solteiro Pires	INESC-TEC, University of Trás-os-Montes and Alto Douro, Portugal
Ernesto Costa	Coimbra University, Portugal
João Barroso	INESC-TEC, University of Trás-os-Montes and Alto Douro, Portugal
Leonardo Vanneschi	New University of Lisbon, Portugal
Leontios Hadjileontiadis	Khalifa University, UAE, and Aristotle University of Thessaloniki, Greece
Meni Tsitouridou	Aristotle University of Thessaloniki, Greece
Mauro Castelli	New University of Lisbon, Portugal
Monique Grandbastien	University of Nancy, France
Panagiotis Bamidis	Aristotle University of Thessaloniki, Greece
Paulo Novais	University of Minho, Portugal
Paulo Moura Oliveira	INESC-TEC, University of Trás-os-Montes and Alto Douro, Portugal
Peter Brusilovsky	University of Pittsburgh, USA
Peter Foltz	Pearson, USA
Pierre Dillenbourg	École Polytechnique Fédérale de Lausanne, Switzerland

Richard Cox	University of Sussex, UK
Sofia Dias	University of Lisbon, Portugal
Sofia Hadjileontiadou	Democritus University of Thrace, Greece
Tasos Mikropoulos	Aristotle University of Thessaloniki, Greece
Vitor Santos	New University of Lisbon, Portugal

Artificial Intelligence for Games (AI4G)

Organizing Committee

Alberto Simões	Polytechnic Institute of Cávado and Ave, Portugal
Antonios Liapis	University of Malta, Malta
Gustavo Reis	Polytechnic Institute of Leiria, Portugal

Program Committee

Carlos Martinho	IST, Universidade de Lisboa, Portugal
Christoph Salge	University of Hertfordshire, UK
David Carneiro	Universidade do Minho, Portugal
Daniele Gravina	University of Malta, Malta
Daniel Karavolos	University of Malta, Malta
David Melhart	University of Malta, Malta
Diego Perez Liebana	University of Essex, UK
Duarte Duque	Instituto Politécnico do Cávado e do Ave, Portugal
Éric Jacopin	ESM Saint-Cyr, France
Eva Hudlicka	Psychometrix Associates, USA
Fernando Silva	New York University, USA
Gabriella A. B. Barros	New York University, USA
João Dias	IST, Universidade de Lisboa, Portugal
José Valente de Oliveira	Universidade do Algarve, Portugal
Konstantinos Karpouzis	National University of Athens, Greece
Luís Paulo Reis	Universidade do Porto, Portugal
Marco Scirea	University of Southern Denmark, Denmark
Michael Green	New York University, USA
Nuno Rodrigues	Instituto Politécnico do Cávado e do Ave, Portugal
Pedro Moreira	Instituto Politécnico de Viana do Castelo, Portugal
Penousal Machado	Universidade de Coimbra, Portugal
Phil Lopes	GAIPS, Universidade de Lisboa, Portugal
Rui Prada	INESC-ID, IST, Universidade de Lisboa, Portugal

Artificial Intelligence and IoT in Agriculture (AIoTA)

Organizing Committee

José Boaventura Cunha	INESC-TEC, University of Trás-os-Montes and Alto Douro, Portugal
Josenalde Barbosa	Federal University of Rio Grande do Norte, Brazil

Paulo Moura Oliveira   INESC-TEC, University of Trás-os-Montes
                                and Alto Douro, Portugal
Raul Morais   INESC-TEC, University of Trás-os-Montes
                                and Alto Douro, Portugal

Program Committee

Andrés Muñoz Ortega   Universidad Católica de Múrcia, Spain
Aneesh Chauhan   Wageningen University and Research, The Netherlands
António Valente   INESC-TEC, University of Trás-os-Montes
                                and Alto Douro, Portugal
Brett Whelan   University of Sydney, Australia
Bruno Tisseyre   Montpellier SupAgro, France
Carlos Eduardo Cugnasca   Escola Politécnica da Universidade de São Paulo,
                                Brazil
Carlos Serôdio   CITAB, University of Trás-os-Montes
                                and Alto Douro, Portugal
Eduardo Solteiro Pires   INESC-TEC, University of Trás-os-Montes
                                and Alto Douro, Portugal
Emanuel Peres   INESC-TEC, University of Trás-os-Montes
                                and Alto Douro, Portugal
Filipe Santos   INESC-TEC, Portugal
Francisco Rovira-Más   Polytechnic University of Valencia, Spain
Javier Sanchis Sáez   Universitat Politècnica de València, Spain
Javier Tardaguila   University of La Rioja, Spain
João Paulo Coelho   Instituto Politécnico de Bragança, Portugal
João Sousa   INESC-TEC, University of Trás-os-Montes
                                and Alto Douro, Portugal
Jos Balendonck   Wageningen University and Research, The Netherlands
Jose Antonio Sanz   Universidad Pública de Navarra, Spain
Juan López Riquelme   Universidad Politécnica de Cartagena, Spain
K. P. Ferentinos   Hellenic Agricultural Organization, Greece
Kazuhisa Ito   Shibaura Institute of Technology, Japan
Laura Emmanuela Santana   Universidade Federal do Rio Grande do Norte, Brazil
Nieves Pávon-Pulido   Universidad Politécnica de Cartagena, Spain
Pedro Couto   CITAB, University of Trás-os-Montes
                                and Alto Douro, Portugal
Pedro Melo-Pinto   CITAB, University of Trás-os-Montes
                                and Alto Douro, Portugal
Tatiana Pinho   INESC-TEC, Portugal
Tomas Norton   KU Leven, Belgium
Sjaak Wolfert   Wageningen University and Research, The Netherlands
Veronica Saiz-Rubio   Polytechnic University of Valencia, Spain
Yuxin Miao   University of Minnesota, USA

Artificial Intelligence and Law (AIL)

Organizing Committee

Pedro Miguel Freitas	Universidade Católica Portuguesa, Portugal
Ugo Pagallo	University of Torino, Italy
Massimo Durante	University of Torino, Italy

Program Committee

Carlisle E. George	Middlesex University, UK
Giovanni Sartor	European University Institute, Italy
Isabel Ferreira	Universidade de Lisboa, Portugal
Luís Moniz Pereira	Universidade Nova de Lisboa, Portugal
Manuel David Masseno	Instituto Politécnico de Beja, Portugal
Migle Laukyte	University Carlos III of Madrid, Spain
Niva Elkin-Koren	University of Haifa, Israel, and Harvard University, USA
Paulo Novais	University of Minho, Portugal
Pompeu Casanovas	Universitat Autònoma de Barcelona, Spain, and Royal Melbourne Institute of Technology, Australia
Radboud Winkels	University of Amsterdam, The Netherlands
Thomas Gordon	University of Potsdam, Germany
Vicente Julián Inglada	Valencia University of Technology, Spain

Artificial Intelligence in Medicine (AIM)

Organizing Committee

Manuel Filipe Santos	University of Minho, Portugal
Carlos Filipe Portela	University of Minho, Portugal
Allan Tucker	Brunel University London, UK

Steering Committee

José Machado	University of Minho, Portugal
António Abelha	University of Minho, Portugal
Pedro Henriques Abreu	University of Coimbra, Portugal
Daniel Castro Silva	University of Porto, Portugal
Francesca Vitali	Pavia, Italy
Manuel Fernández Delgado	University of Santiago, Spain

Program Committee

Álvaro Silva	Abel Salazar Biomedical Sciences Institute, Portugal
Andreas Holzinger	Medical University Graz, Austria
António Abelha	University of Minho, Portugal

Antonio Manuel de Jesus Pereira	Polytechnic Institute of Leiria, Portugal
Barna Iantovics	Petru Maior University of Tîrgu-Mureş, Romania
Beatriz de la Iglesia	University of East Anglia, UK
Cinzia Pizzi	Università degli Studi di Padova, Italy
Filipe Pinto	Polytechnic Institute of Leiria, Portugal
Giorgio Leonardi	University of Piemonte Orientale, Italy
Göran Falkman	Universitet of Skövde, Sweden
Helder Coelho	University of Lisbon, Portugal
Helena Lindgren	Umeå University, Sweden
Hugo Peixoto	University of Minho, Portugal
Inna Skarga-Bandurova	East Ukrainian National University, Ukraine
José Machado	University of Minho, Portugal
José Maia Neves	University of Minho, Portugal
Júlio Duarte	University of Minho, Portugal
Luca Anselma	University of Turin, Italy
Michael Ignaz Schumacher	University of Applied Sciences Western Switzerland, Switzerland
Miguel Angel Mayer	Pompeu Fabra University, Spain
Miriam Santos	University of Coimbra, Portugal
Panagiotis Bamidis	Aristotelian University of Thessaloniki, Greece
Pedro Gago	Polytechnic Institute of Leiria, Portugal
Pedro Pereira Rodrigues	University of Porto, Portugal
Rainer Schmidt	Institute for Biometrics and Medical Informatics, Germany
Ricardo Martinho	Polytechnic Institute of Leiria, Portugal
Rui Camacho	University of Porto, Portugal
Salva Tortajada	Polytechnic University of Valencia, Spain
Teresa Guarda	State University Santa Elena Peninsula, Ecuador
Werner Ceusters	State University of New York at Buffalo, USA

Artificial Intelligence in Cyber-Physical and Distributed Embedded Systems (AICPDES)

Organizing Committee

Thiago RPM Rúbio	University of Porto, Portugal
Jean-Paul Jamont	Université Grenoble Alpes, France
Paulo Leitão	Polytechnic Institute of Bragança, Portugal

Program Committee

Adriano Pereira	Federal University of Minas Gerais, Brazil
Alberto Fernández	Universidad Rey Juan Carlos, Spain
Alois Zoitl	Fortiss GmbH, Germany
Benjamim Gateau	Luxembourg Institute of Science and Technology, Luxembourg

Christopher Frantz	University of Otago, New Zealand
Florentino Riverola	Universidad de Vigo, Spain
Gauthier Picard	ENS Mines Saint-Étienne, France
José Barbosa	Polythecnic Institute of Bragança, Portugal
Laurent Vercouter	LITIS, INSA de Rouen, France
Luis M. Camarinha-Matos	New University of Lisbon, Portugal
Marco Mendes	Schneider Electric Automation GmbH, Germany
Marie-Pierre Gleizes	IRIT, Université de Toulouse, France
Marin Lujak	École des Mines de Douai, France
Michael Mrissa	Université de Pau et des Pays de l'Adour, France
Michel Occello	Université Grenoble Alpes, France
Miguel Rebollo	Universitat Politècnica de València, Spain
Olivier Boissier	ENS Mines Saint-Étienne, France
Senén Barro	Universidad de Santiago de Compostela, Spain
Simon Mayer	University of St. Gallen and ETH Zurich, Switzerland
Stamatis Karnouskos	SAP, Germany
Tiberiu Seceleanu	ABB Corporate Research, Sweden
Zafeiris Kokkinogenis	University of Porto, Portugal

Artificial Intelligence in Power and Energy Systems (AIPES)

Organizing Committee

Zita Vale	Polytechnic of Porto, Portugal
Pedro Faria	Polytechnic of Porto, Portugal
Juan Manuel Corchado	University of Salamanca, Spain
Tiago Pinto	University of Salamanca, Spain

Program Committee

Ana Estanqueiro	LNEG—National Research Institute, Portugal
Bo Norregaard Jorgensen	University of Southern Denmark, Denmark
Carlos Ramos	Polytechnic Institute of Porto, Portugal
Chen-Ching Liu	Washington State University, USA
Dagmar Niebur	Drexel University, USA
Fernando Lopes	LNEG—National Research Institute, Portugal
Germano Lambert-Torres	Dinkart Systems, Brazil
Goreti Marreiros	Polytechnic Institute of Porto, Portugal
Gustavo Figueroa	Instituto de Investigaciones Eléctricas, Mexico
Hélder Coelho	University of Lisbon, Portugal
Isabel Praça	Polytechnic Institute of Porto, Portugal
Jan Segerstam	Empower IM Oy, Finland
João P. S. Catalão	University of Porto, Portugal
José L. Rueda	Delft University of Technology, The Netherlands
Kumar Venayagamoorthy	Clemson University, USA
Kwang Y. Lee	Baylor University, USA
Nikos Hatziargyriou	National Technical University of Athens, Greece

Nouredine Hadj-Said   Institut National Polytechnique de Grenoble, France
Olivier Boissier   École Nationale Supérieure des Mines
                               de Saint-Étienne, France
Pablo Ibarguengoytia   Instituto de Investigaciones Eléctricas, Mexico
Peter Kadar   Budapest University of Technology and Economics,
                               Hungary
Phuong Nguyen   Eindhoven University of Technology, The Netherlands
Pierluigi Siano   University of Salerno, Italy
Vladimiro Miranda   University of Porto, Portugal

Artificial Intelligence in Transportation Systems (AITS)

Organizing Committee

Alberto Fernandez   Universidad Rey Juan Carlos, Spain
Rosaldo Rossetti   Universidade do Porto, Portugal

Program Committee

Ana Bazzan   UFRGS, Brazil
Ana Paula Rocha   University of Porto, Portugal
Arnaud Doniec   IMT Lille Douai, France
Carlos A. Iglesias   Universidad Politécnica de Madrid, Spain
Carlos Lisboa Bento   University of Coimbra, Portugal
Eduardo Camponogara   UFSC, Brazil
Eftihia Nathanail   University of Thessaly, Greece
Eugénio Oliveira   University of Porto, Portugal
Franziska Klügl   Örebo University, Sweden
Gonçalo Correia   TU Delft, The Netherlands
Holger Billhardt   University Rey Juan Carlos, Spain
Javier Sanchez Medina   Universidad de Las Palmas de Gran Canaria, Spain
Jihed Khiari   NEC Laboratories Europe, Germany,
João Jacob   University of Porto, Portugal
João Mendes-Moreira   University of Porto, Portugal
Josep Salanova   Center for Research and Technology Hellas, Greece
Jürgen Dunkel   Hochschule Hannover, Germany
Luís Nunes   ISCTE-IUL, Portugal
Marcela Munizaga   University of Chile, Chile
Marin Lujak   IMT Lille Douai, France
Rui Gomes   University of Coimbra, Portugal
Soora Rasouli   Eindhoven University of Technology, The Netherlands
Sascha Ossowski   Rey Juan Carlos University, Spain
Tânia Fontes   University of Porto, Portugal

Artificial Life and Evolutionary Algorithms (ALEA)

Organizing Committee

Carlos Henggeler Antunes	INESC Coimbra, DEEC, University of Coimbra, Portugal
Leonardo Trujillo	Technical Institute of Tijuana, Mexico
Luca Manzoni	University of Milano-Bicocca, Italy
Ivo Gonçalves	INESC Coimbra, DEEC, University of Coimbra, Portugal

Program Committee

Antonios Liapis	Institute of Digital Games, University of Malta, Malta
Carlos M. Fonseca	Universidade de Coimbra, Portugal
Carlos Henggeler Antunes	INESC Coimbra, University of Coimbra, Portugal
Enrique Naredo Garcia	CentroGeo, Mexico
Eric Medvet	University of Trieste, Italy
Gabriela Ochoa	University of Stirling, UK
Gianluigi Folino	CNR-ICAR, Italy
Ivo Gonçalves	INESC Coimbra, University of Coimbra, Portugal
James Foster	University of Idaho, USA
Jin-Kao Hao	University of Angers, France
Julian Miller	University of York, UK
Leonardo Trujillo	Technical Institute of Tijuana, Mexico
Luca Manzoni	University of Milano-Bicocca, Italy
Luís Correia	University of Lisbon, Portugal
Luís Paquete	Universidade de Coimbra, Portugal
Marc Schoenauer	Inria, France
Mario Giacobini	University of Torino, Italy
Mauro Castelli	NOVA IMS, Portugal
Pablo Mesejo Santiago	University of Granada, Spain
Rui Mendes	Universidade do Minho, Portugal
Stefano Cagnoni	University of Parma, Italy

Ambient Intelligence and Affective Environments (AmIA)

Organizing Committee

Goreti Marreiros	Polytechnic Institute of Porto, Portugal
Paulo Novais	University of Minho, Portugal
Ana Almeida	Polytechnic Institute of Porto, Portugal
Sara Rodríguez	University of Salamanca, Spain
Peter Mikulecky	University of Hradec Kralove, Czech Republic

Program Committee

Amal Seghrouchni	Université Pierre et Marie Curie, France
Amilcar Cardoso	University of Coimbra, Portugal

Ana Almeida	Polytechnic Institute of Porto, Portugal
Ana Paiva	IST, Universidade de Lisboa, Portugal
Ângelo Costa	Universidade do Minho, Portugal
Antonio Caballero	University of Castilla-La Mancha, Spain
Antonio Camurri	University of Genoa, Italy
Boon Kiat-Quek	National University of Singapore, Singapore
Carlos Bento	University of Coimbra, Portugal
Carlos Iglesias	Universidad Politécnica de Madrid, Spain
Carlos Ramos	Polytechnic Institute of Porto, Portugal
César Analide	University of Minho, Portugal
Dante Tapia	University of Salamanca, Spain
Davide Carneiro	Polytechnic Institute of Porto, Portugal
Diego Gachet	European University of Madrid, Spain
Eva Hudlicka	Psychometrix Associates Blacksburg, USA
Fábio Silva	University of Minho, Portugal
Florentino Fdez-Riverola	University of Vigo, Spain
Goreti Marreiros	Polytechnic Institute of Porto, Portugal
Guillaume Lopez	Aoyama Gakuin University, Japan
Grzegorz Napela	AGH University of Science and Technology, Poland
Hoon Ko	Chosun University, South Korea
Ichiro Satoh	National Institute of Informatics, Japan
Javier Bajo	Polytechnic University of Madrid, Spain
Javier Jaen	Polytechnic University of Valencia, Spain
Jean Ilié	Université Pierre et Marie Curie, France
João Carneiro	Polytechnic Institute of Porto, Portugal
José Machado	University of Minho, Portugal
José Molina	University Carlos III of Madrid, Spain
José Neves	University of Minho, Portugal
Juan Corchado	University of Salamanca, Spain
Laurence Devillers	LIMS-CNRS, France
Lino Figueiredo	Polytechnic Institute of Porto, Portugal
Luís Macedo	University of Coimbra, Portugal
Paulo Novais	University of Minho, Portugal
Peter Mikulecky	University of Hradec Kralove, Czech Republic
Preuveneers	KU Leuven, Belgium
Ricardo Santos	Polytechnic Institute of Porto, Portugal
Rui José	University of Minho, Portugal
Sara González	University of Salamanca, Spain
Shin'Ichi Konomi	University of Tokyo, Japan
Tatsuo Nakajima	Waseda University, Japan
Tiago Oliveira	National Institute of Informatics, Japan
Vic Callaghan	Essex University, UK
Vicente Julián	Polytechnic University of Valencia, Spain

Business Applications of Artificial Intelligence (BAAI)

Organizing Committee

Célia Talma Gonçalves	CEOS - ISCAP P.PORTO, LIACC, Portugal
Carlos Soares	LIACC, INESC TEC, Universidade do Porto, Portugal
Eva Lorenzo Iglesias	UVIGO, Spain
Ana Paula Appel	IBM Research, Brazil
Eunika Mercier-Laurent	Global Innovation Strategies, Université Reims Champagne Ardenne, France
Eugénio Oliveira	LIACC, Universidade do Porto, Portugal

Program Committee

Adam Woznica	Expedia, Switzerland
Adrián Seara Veira	Universidad de Vigo, Spain
António Castro	LIACC-NIADR, University of Porto, Portugal
Carlos Rodrigues	Marionete, UK
Carmela Comito	ICAR-CNR, Italy
Dario Oliveira	IBM Research, Brazil
Efi Papatheocharous	Swedish Institute of Computer Science, Sweden
Elaine Ribeiro de Faria	Universidade Federal Uberlândia, Brazil
Francesca Spezzano	Boise State University, USA
Gustavo Batista	ICMC, USP, Brazil
Ida Mele	Università della Svizzera, Italy
Jean-Pierre Briot	Laboratoire d'Informatique de Paris 6 (Paris6-CNRS), France, and PUC-Rio, Brazil
Kaustubh Patil	MIT, USA
Lourdes Borrajo	Universidad de Vigo, Spain
Marisa Affonso Vasconcelos	IBM Research, Brazil
Miriam Seoane Santos	Universidade de Coimbra, Portugal
Paulo Cavalin	IBM Research, Brazil
Pedro Henriques Abreu	FCTUC-DEI, CISUC, Portugal
Peter Van der Putten	Pegasystems, Leiden University, The Netherlands
Rodrigo Mello	Universidade de São Paulo, Brazil
YongHong Peng	University of Sunderland, UK

General Artificial Intelligence (GAI)

Organizing Committee

Luís Paulo Reis	LIACC, University of Porto, Portugal
Paulo Moura Oliveira	INESC-TEC, UTAD, Portugal
Paulo Novais	ALGORITMI, University of Minho, Portugal

Program Committee

Amparo Alonso-Betanzos	University of A Coruña, Spain
Ana Paiva	INESC-ID, University of Lisbon, Portugal
Ana Paula Rocha	LIACC, University of Porto, Portugal
Andrea Omicini	Università di Bologna, Italy
Arlindo Oliveira	INESC-ID, IST, University of Lisbon, Portugal
Brígida Mónica Faria	Polytechnic Institute of Porto, Portugal
Carlos Bento	University of Coimbra, Portugal
Carlos M. Fonseca	University of Coimbra, Portugal
Carlos Ramos	Polytechnic Institute of Porto, Portugal
Cesar Analide	University of Minho, Portugal
Davide Carneiro	Polytechnic Institute of Porto, Portugal
Eric De La Clergerie	Inria, France
Ernesto Costa	University of Coimbra, Portugal
Francisco Pereira	Polytechnic Institute of Coimbra, Portugal
Gaël Dias	Normandy University, France
Goreti Marreiros	GECAD, Polytechnic Institute of Porto, Portugal
Henrique Lopes Cardoso	University of Porto, Portugal
João Balsa	BioISI-MAS, University of Lisbon, Portugal
João Gama	University of Porto, Portugal
João Leite	New University of Lisbon, Portugal
John-Jules Meyer	Utrecht University, The Netherlands
José Cascalho	University of Azores, Portugal
José Júlio Alferes	New University of Lisbon, Portugal
José Machado	University of Minho, Portugal
José Neves	University of Minho, Portugal
Juan Corchado	University of Salamanca, Spain
Juan Pavón	University Complutense de Madrid, Spain
Luís Antunes	University of Lisbon, Portugal
Luís Camarinha-Matos	New University of Lisbon, Portugal
Luís Cavique	University Aberta, Portugal
Luís Correia	University of Lisbon, Portugal
Luís Macedo	University of Coimbra, Portugal
Luís Seabra Lopes	University of Aveiro, Portugal
Mário J. Silva	University of Lisbon, Portugal
Miguel Calejo	Declarativa, Portugal
Mikhail Lavrentiev	Novosibirsk State University, Russia
Nuno Lau	University of Aveiro, Portugal
Paulo Cortez	University of Minho, Portugal
Paulo Quaresma	University of Évora, Portugal
Paulo Urbano	University of Lisbon, Portugal
Pedro Barahona	New University of Lisbon, Portugal
Pedro Rangel Henriques	University of Minho, Portugal
Penousal Machado	University of Coimbra, Portugal
Ricardo Santos	ESTG, Polytechnic Institute of Porto, Portugal

Rosaldo Rossetti	University of Porto, Portugal
Rui Prada	University of Lisbon, Portugal
Salvador Abreu	LISP, CRI, University of Évora, Portugal
Tatsu Naka	Waseda University, Japan
Vicente Julian	University of Politècnica de València, Spain
Victor Alves	University of Minho, Portugal

Intelligent Robotics (IROBOT)

Organizing Committee

Nuno Lau	Universidade de Aveiro, Portugal
João Alberto Fabro	Universidade Tecnológica Federal do Paraná, Portugal
Fei Chen	Istituto Italiano di Tecnologia, Italy
Luís Paulo Reis	LIACC, Faculdade de Engenharia da Universidade do Porto, Portugal

Program Committee

André Marcato	Universidade Federal de Juíz de Fora, Brazil
André Scolari Conceição	Universidade Federal da Bahia, Brazil
Anna Helena Costa	EPUSP, Brazil
António José Neves	Universidade de Aveiro, Portugal
António Paulo Moreira	Universidade do Porto, Portugal
Armando Pinho	Universidade de Aveiro, Portugal
Armando Sousa	Universidade do Porto, Portugal
Axel Hessler	TU Berlin, Germany
Brígida Mónica Faria	Instituto Politécnico do Porto, Portugal
Carlos Carreto	Instituto Politécnico da Guarda, Portugal
César Analide	Universidade do Minho, Portugal
Chengxu Zhou	Istituto Italiano di Tecnologia, Italy
Fanny Ficuciello	University of Naples Federico II, Italy
Fernando Osório	Universidade São Paulo, Brazil
Jorge Dias	ISR, Universidade de Coimbra, Portugal
Josemar Rodrigues de Souza	Brazil
Liming Chen	École Centrale de Lyon, France
Luís Correia	Universidade de Lisboa, Portugal
Luis Moreno Lorente	Universidad Carlos III Madrid, Spain
Luis Seabra Lopes	Universidade de Aveiro, Portugal
Marco Dorigo	Université Libre de Bruxelles, Belgium
Maxime Petit	École Centrale de Lyon, France
Mikhail Prokopenko	CSIRO ICT Centre, Australia
Nicolas Jouandeau	University of Paris 8, France
Nikolaos Tsagarakis	Istituto Italiano di Tecnologia, Italy
Paulo Urbano	Universidade de Lisboa, Portugal
Qinyuan Ren	Zhejiang University, China

Reinaldo Bianchi	IIIA-CSIC, Barcelona, Spain
Saeed Shiry Ghidary	Amirkabir University, Iran
Sanem Sariel Talay	Istanbul Technical University, Turkey
Yan Wu	Institute for Infocomm Research A*STAR, Singapore
Urbano Nunes	Universidade de Coimbra, Portugal

Knowledge Discovery and Business Intelligence (KDBI)

Organizing Committee

Paulo Cortez	University of Minho, Portugal
Alfred Bifet	Université Paris-Saclay, France
Luís Cavique	Universidade Aberta, Portugal
João Gama	INESC-TEC, University of Porto, Portugal
Nuno Marques	Universidade Nova de Lisboa, Portugal
Manuel Filipe Santos	University of Minho, Portugal

Program Committee

Alicia Troncoso	Pablo de Olavide University, Spain
Agnes Braud	University Robert Schuman, France
Alberto Bugarin	University of Santiago de Compostela, Spain
Alípio Jorge	University of Porto, Portugal
Amilcar Oliveira	Universidade Aberta, Portugal
André Carvalho	University of São Paulo, Brazil
Antonio Tallón-Ballesteros	University of Seville, Spain
Armando Mendes	University of Azores, Portugal
Bernardete Ribeiro	University of Coimbra, Portugal
Carlos Ferreira	Institute of Engineering of Porto, Portugal
Elaine Faria	Universidade Uberlândia, Brazil
Fátima Rodrigues	Institute of Engineering of Porto, Portugal
Fernando Bação	New University of Lisbon, Portugal
Filipe Pinto	Polytechnic Institute Leiria, Portugal
Karin Becker	UFRGS, Brazil
Leandro Krug Wives	UFRGS, Brazil
Manuel Fernandez Delgado	University of Santiago de Compostela, Spain
Marcos Domingues	University of São Paulo, Brazil
Margarida Cardoso	ISCTE, Portugal
Mark Embrechts	Rensselaer Polytechnic Institute, USA
Mohamed Gaber	University of Portsmouth, UK
Murate Testik	Hacettepe University, Turkey
Ning Chen	Institute of Engineering of Porto, Portugal
Phillipe Lenca	IMT Atlantique, France
Rita Ribeiro	Universidade do Porto, Portugal
Rui Camacho	University of Porto, Portugal
Sérgio Moro	ISCTE-IUL, Portugal
Ying Tan	Peking University, China

Knowledge Representation and Reasoning (KRR)

Organizing Committee

Eduardo Fermé	University of Madeira, Portugal
Ricardo Gonçalves	Universidade NOVA de Lisboa, Portugal
Matthias Knorr	Universidade NOVA de Lisboa, Portugal
Rafael Peñaloza	University of Milano-Bicocca, Italy
Jörg Pührer	TU Wien, Austria

Program Committee

Adila A. Krisnadhi	Universitas Indonesia, Indonesia
Alejandro Garcia	Universidad Nacional del Sur, Argentina
Amelia Harrison	University of Texas at Austin, USA
Bart Bogaerts	Vrije Universiteit Brussel, Belgium
Carlos Areces	Universidad Nacional de Córdoba, Argentina
Carmine Dodaro	University of Genova, Italy
Cristina Feier	University of Bremen, Germany
David Rajaratnam	University of New South Wales, Australia
Emmanuele Dietz Saldanha	Technische Universität Dresden, Germany
Fabrizio Maggi	University of Tartu, Estonia
Francesca Alessandra Lisi	Università degli Studi di Bari Aldo Moro, Italy
Gerhard Brewka	Leipzig University, Germany
Guohui Xiao	Free University of Bozen-Bolzano, Italy
Inês Lynce	University of Lisbon, Portugal
Ivan Varzinczak	Université d'Artois, France
João Leite	Universidade Nova de Lisboa, Portugal
João Marques-Silva	University of Lisbon, Portugal
José Júlio Alferes	Universidade Nova de Lisboa, Portugal
Jorge Fandinno	IRIT, France
Loizos Michael	Open University of Cyprus, Cyprus
Mantas Simkus	Vienna University of Technology, Austria
Maria Vanina Martinez	Universidad Nacional del Sur, Argentina
Marco Paulo Ferreirinha Garapa	University of Madeira, Portugal
Mario Alviano	University of Calabria, Italy
Matthias Thimm	Universität Koblenz-Landau, Germany
Marcelo Finger	University of São Paulo, Brazil
Maurício Duarte Luís Reis	University of Madeira, Portugal
Nicolas Troquard	Free University of Bozen-Bolzano, Italy
Orkunt Sabuncu	TED University Ankara, Turkey
Pedro Cabalar	Corunna University, Spain
Rafael Testa	University of Campinas, Brazil
Ramon Pino Perez	Yachay Tech University, Ecuador
Salvador Abreu	University of Évora, Portugal
Stefan Woltran	Vienna University of Technology, Austria

MultiAgent Systems: Theory and Applications (MASTA)

Organizing Committee

Henrique Lopes Cardoso   LIACC, Universidade do Porto, Portugal
Luís Antunes   BioISI-MAS, Universidade de Lisboa, Portugal
Viviane Torres da Silva   IBM Research, Brazil
Dave de Jonge   IIIA-CSIC, Spain

Steering Committee

Eugénio Oliveira   LIACC, Universidade do Porto, Portugal
Hélder Coelho   Universidade de Lisboa, Portugal
João Balsa   Universidade de Lisboa, Portugal
Luís Paulo Reis   LIACC, Universidade do Porto, Portugal

Program Committee

Adriana Giret   Universitat Politècnica de València, Spain
Alberto Fernandez   Universidad Rey Juan Carlos, Spain
Alejandro Guerra-Hernández   Universidad Veracruzana, Mexico
Ana Paula Rocha   Universidade do Porto, Portugal
Andrea Omicini   Università di Bologna, Italy
António Castro   TAP Air Portugal, LIACC, Portugal
Carlos Carracosa   Universitat Politècnica de València, Spain
Carlos Martinho   Instituto Superior Técnico, Portugal
Daniel Silva   University of Porto, Portugal
Diana Adamatti   Universidade Federal do Rio Grande, Brazil
F. Jordan Srour   American University of Beirut, Lebanon
Francisco Grimaldo   Universidad de Valencia, Spain
Jaime Sichman   Universidade de São Paulo, Brazil
Javier Carbó   Universidad Carlos III Madrid, Spain
João Leite   Universidade Nova de Lisboa, Portugal
John-Jules Meyer   Universiteit Utrecht, The Netherlands
Jordi Sabater-Mir   IIIA-CSIC, Spain
Jorge Gomez-Sanz   Universidad Complutense Madrid, Spain
Juan Antonio Rodriguez-Aguilar   IIIA-CSIC, Spain
Juan Burguillo   Universidad de Vigo, Spain
Juan Corchado   Universidad de Salamanca, Spain
Lars Braubach   Universität Hamburg, Germany
Laurent Vercouter   École Nationale Supérieure des Mines de Saint-Étienne, France
Luís Correia   Universidade de Lisboa, Portugal
Luís Macedo   Universidade de Coimbra, Portugal
Luís Nunes   ISCTE, Portugal

Michael Schumacher	University of Applied Sciences Western Switzerland, Switzerland
Marin Lujak	Institute Mines-Télécom, France
Neil Yorke-Smith	American University of Beirut, Lebanon
Olivier Boissier	École Nationale Supérieure des Mines de Saint-Étienne, France
Paolo Torroni	Università di Bologna, Italy
Paulo Novais	Universidade do Minho, Portugal
Rafael Bordini	Pontífica Universidade Católica do Rio Grande do Sul, Brazil
Ramón Hermoso	University of Zaragoza, Spain
Reyhan Aydogan	Özyeğin University, Turkey, and Delft University of Technology, The Netherlands
Wamberto Vasconcelos	University of Aberdeen, UK

Social Simulation and Modelling (SSM)

Organizing Committee

Luis Antunes	Universidade de Lisboa, Portugal
Pedro Campos	Universidade do Porto, Portugal
Shu-Heng Chen	National Chengchi University, Taiwan

Program Committee

Ana Bazzan	UFRGS, Brazil
Andrea Teglio	University Ca' Foscari of Venice, Italy
Annalisa Fabretti	University of Rome, Italy
Bruce Edmonds	Centre for Policy Modelling, UK
Claudio Cioffi-Revilla	George Mason University, USA
Cristiano Castelfranchi	ISTC-CNR, Italy
Frederic Amblard	Université Toulouse 1, France
Friederike Wall	Alpen-Adria-Universität Klagenfurt, Austria
Ghita Mezzour	International University of Rabat, Morocco
Hélder Coelho	Universidade de Lisboa, Portugal
João Balsa	Universidade Lisbon, Portugal
Luis R. Izquierdo	Universidad de Burgos, Spain
Nuno David	ISCTE-IUL, Portugal
Pedro Magalhães	ICS, Portugal
Pedro Santos	Instituto Superior Técnico, Portugal
Philippe Mathieu	Lille1 University, CRIStAL Lab, France
Pia Ramchandani	PwC and University of Pennsylvania, USA
Ramon Villa Cox	Carnegie Mellon, USA
Sérgio Bacelar	INE, Portugal
Tânya Araújo	ISEG, Portugal
Tim Verwaart	LEI Wageningen UR, The Netherlands

Text Mining and Applications (TeMA)

Organizing Committee

Joaquim Francisco Ferreira da Silva	Universidade Nova de Lisboa, Portugal
Altigran Soares da Silva	Universidade Federal do Amazonas, Brasil

Program Committee

Adeline Nazarenko	University of Paris 13, France
Alberto Diaz	Universidad Complutense de Madrid, Spain
Alberto Simões	Algoritmi Center, University of Minho, Portugal
Alexandre Rademaker	IBM Research Lab, Brazil
Antoine Doucet	University of Caen, France
António Branco	Universidade de Lisboa, Portugal
Béatrice Daille	University of Nantes, France
Belinda Maia	Universidade do Porto, Portugal
Bruno Martins	Instituto Superior Técnico, Universidade de Lisboa, Portugal
Eric de La Clergerie	Inria, France
Fernando Batista	Instituto Universitário de Lisboa, Portugal
Francisco Couto	Universidade de Lisboa, Portugal
Gaël Dias	University of Caen Normandy, France
Hugo Oliveira	Universidade de Coimbra, Portugal
Irene Rodrigues	Universidade de Évora, Portugal
Jesús Vilares	University of A Coruña, Spain
Katerzyna Wegrzyn-Wolska	ESIGETEL, France
Luciano Barbosa	Universidade Federal de Pernambuco, Brazil
Luisa Coheur	Universidade Técnica de Lisboa, Portugal
Manuel Vilares Ferro	University of Vigo, Spain
Mário Silva	Instituto Superior Técnico, Universidade de Lisboa, Portugal
Mohand Boughanem	University of Toulouse III, France
Nuno Marques	Universidade Nova de Lisboa
Pablo Gamallo	Santiago de Compustela, Spain
Paulo Quaresma	Universidade de Évora, Portugal
Pavel Brazdil	University of Porto, Portugal
Pável Calado	Instituto Superior Técnico, Universidade de Lisboa, Portugal
Sebastião Pais	Universidade da Beira Interior, Portugal
Sérgio Nunes	Faculdade de Engenharia, Universidade do Porto, Portugal
Vítor Jorge Rocio	Universidade Aberta, Portugal

Additional Reviewers

Abdelghany, Hazem
Abrishambaf, Omid
Adedoyin-Olowe, Mariam
Akermi, Imen
Alonso, Miguel A.
Bento, L. C.
Berger, Martin
Boufidis, Neofytos
Buisson, Jocelyn
Caled, Danielle
Canizes, Bruno
Casado-Vara, Roberto
Chamby-Diaz, Jorge C.
Darriba, Victor
de Melo Pinto Junior, Ubiratan
Doria, Nara
Doval Mosquera, Yerai
Fahed, Lina
Faia, Ricardo
Fernandes, Ramon
Ghomeshi, Hossein
González Briones, Alfonso
Jozi, Aria
Khorram, Mahsa
Krippahl, Ludwig

Lamurias, Andre
Lezama, Fernando
Mendes, Marco
Mitsakis, Evangelos
Morquecho, Edgar
Mu, Shenglin
Murphy, Aidan
Pandya, Kartik
Ribadas-Pena, Francisco J.
Sanchez Passos, Lúcio
Santana, Laura
Santos, Gabriel
Santos, Valéria
Shokri Gazafroudi, Amin
Silva, Cátia
Silva, Francisco
Simões, David
Soares, Joao
Sousa, Diana
Sutana, Ricardo
Teixeira, Brigida
Trigo, Luís
Tsaples, Georgios
Xin, Songyan

Contents – Part II

General AI

Intelligent Robotics

Knowledge Discovery and Business Intelligence

Knowledge Representation and Reasoning

MultiAgent Systems: Theory and Applications

Social Simulation and Modelling

Text Mining and Applications

Contents – Part I

Artificial Intelligence and IoT in Agriculture

Artificial Intelligence and Law

Artificial Intelligence in Medicine

Artificial Intelligence in Cyber-Physical and Distributed Embedded Systems

Artificial Intelligence in Power and Energy Systems

Artificial Life and Evolutionary Algorithms

Ambient Intelligence and Affective Environments

The Influence of Age and Gender in the Interaction with Touch Screens

Rodrigo Rocha[1], Davide Carneiro[1,2]([✉]), and Paulo Novais[2]

[1] CIICESI/ESTG - Polytechnic Institute of Porto, Felgueiras, Portugal
{8140411,dcarneiro}@estg.ipp.pt
[2] Algoritmi Centre/Department of Informatics, Universidade do Minho,
Braga, Portugal
pjon@di.uminho.pt

Abstract. Touch screens are nowadays one of the major interfaces in the interaction between humans and technology, mostly due to the significant growth in the use of smartphones and tablets in the last years. This broad use, that reaches people from all strata of society, makes touch screens a relevant tool to study the mechanisms that influence the way we interact with electronic devices. In this paper we collect data regarding the interaction patterns of different users with mobile devices. We present a way to formalize these interaction patterns and analyze how aspects such as age and gender influence them. The results of this research may be relevant for developing mobile applications that identify and adapt to the users or their characteristics, including impairments in fine motor skills or in cognitive function.

Keywords: Human Computer Interaction · Touch screens · Human factors

1 Introduction

In the last years the use of devices such as smartphones and tablets has grown immensely [1]. Due to this, the touch screen emerges as one of the most used interfaces for human-computer interaction and, the gesture of the *touch*, as the most common form of interaction. When compared to other forms of interaction, such as the now more traditional mouse and keyboard, the touch screen is a much more intuitive one, which in part accounts for the acceptance and use of tactile devices by so many different strata of society, with so many different socio-economic contexts.

These means of interaction are interesting in the sense that they allow to collect information that may characterize the user of the device or her/his state. The underlying principle is that, much like in our inter-personal interactions, aspects such as our emotions, our surroundings, and many others, affect our interaction. Specifically, they do not affect so much the content of our interaction (i.e. the words spoken) but rather the way we speak them [2]. This is why we are

© Springer Nature Switzerland AG 2019
P. Moura Oliveira et al. (Eds.): EPIA 2019, LNAI 11805, pp. 3–12, 2019.
https://doi.org/10.1007/978-3-030-30244-3_1

able to perceive if our interlocutor is stressed, tired or experiencing some specific emotion without explicit information: we do so by (sometimes subconsciously) analysing the tone of the voice, the intonation or the posture of our interlocutor.

Recent findings show that our interaction with technological devices such as the keyboard and the mouse is modulated in a similar fashion. Our research team demonstrated how stress and mental fatigue affects one's interaction with the computer [3,4].

Other researchers have also studied related topics, such as the influence of age and gender on keystroke dynamics (one's typing patterns) and mouse dynamics (one's interaction patterns with the mouse) [5] or the influence of emotion on the same features as well as on text production [6].

Some researchers also started studying similar phenomena on the interaction with touch screens. Ciman & Wac [7], for example, analyse the effect of stress on our interaction with a smartphone. They do so based on smartphone gestures analysis (e.g. tap, scroll, swipe, text writing). In [8], on the other hand, the authors try to anticipate and monitor depressive states by monitoring human-smartphone interaction. For this purpose they consider application usage, location and communication logs. This kind of socio-mobile data is used by other authors for similar purposes, such as [9] or [10]. It can also be leveraged to develop more natural and immersive interfaces for Human-Computer Interaction [11,12].

In this paper we follow a different approach to the study of interaction with touch screens. The research cited previously can be characterized as being mostly behavioral, i.e., it is based on the behavior of the user while interacting with the device or its applications and/or while moving about in her/his daily routine. This approach, on the other hand, focuses more acutely on the interaction itself, that is, on the mechanics of the *touch*. We therefore consider aspects such as the duration of the touch or the variation of its intensity over time. In that sense, this approach is not only behavioral but also physical. Due to its multi-modal nature, we also believe that this approach is better suited to model our interaction with touch screens.

We detail how we build an individual interaction model for each user and how these can be compared. A case study was carried out with 32 participants. The collected data allow us to validate the approach and also show how the participant age significantly influences interaction patterns. We believe that this kind of approach can be useful for better characterizing user interaction, and eventually be applied as a proxy for user state (e.g. stress, emotional state) or user characteristics/traits (e.g. cognitive/physical impairments).

2   Defining an Interaction Model

As mentioned in Sect. 1, in this work we look at the characteristics of each specific touch of the user. Indeed, a touch in the screen of most of nowadays smartphones produces several interaction events throughout the duration of the touch. There is a first event when the finger first touches the screen, which is then followed by several other which are produced as long as the finger is still in contact with the screen. Figure 1 depicts an example of a touch, composed by 11 events (red circles) distributed over less than half second. This Figure also shows the shape that is generally associated to a touch: intensity tends to increase and then decrease during the touch.

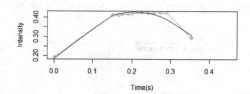

Fig. 1. Intensity of the touch events generated during a touch, over time. (Color figure online)

The frequency with which these events are produced is largely dependent on the hardware. Each of these events provides information regarding the intensity of the touch, the area of the finger that is in contact with the screen, the timestamp in which it occurred, etc.

There is thus a significant amount of information that can be used to characterize the interaction of the user. Specifically, the model proposed to characterize user interaction is composed by the following features:

- Touch duration - The duration of each individual touch on the screen;
- Touch intensity - The average, minimum and maximum values of the intensity exerted by the finger on the screen, for each touch;
- Touch area - The average, minimum and maximum values of the area occupied by the finger on the screen, for each touch;
- Intensity values - The sequence of values of intensity generated during each touch, from the moment the finger first touches the screen to the moment it is lifted;
- Area values - The different areas of finger in contact with the screen, in each touch, from the moment the finger first touches the screen to the moment it is lifted;
- Type of action - The actions on the screen can be further characterized (e.g. touch on an active control vs. touch on a layout inactive element);
- Touch pattern - Models how touch intensity varies over time during the touch. Each patient's touch pattern is modeled by fitting a quadratic function to the data (solid black line in Fig. 1). The coefficients of the resulting quadratic function are used to characterize the "general shape" of a patient's touch.

As an example, Fig. 2 shows the touch patterns of the four different patients, depicted in terms of the intensity values over time and the resulting quadratic function that models it: (a) young male, (b) elder male, (c) young female and (d) elder female. It shows that older users appear to have longer and more intense touches.

Thus, the interaction model proposed in this work considers a total of 11 features which describe how the user is interacting with the device. They provide new types of information previously not considered in this kind of applications. In this paper we examine these features, namely to find differences in interaction patterns due to socio-demographic variables such as gender and age, although others could also have an influence, such as occupation or health conditions.

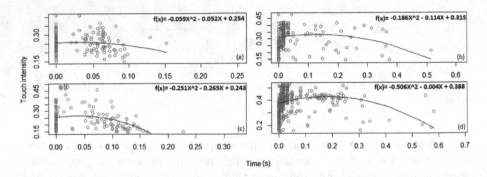

Fig. 2. Interaction models (intensity over time) of four sample users: (a) young male, (b) elder male, (c) young female and (d) elder female.

3   Case Study

To assess the validity of the proposed approach and to determine if gender and/or age influence one's interaction with the smartphone, a case study was carried out involving 32 individuals (16 male, 16 female). The average age of the population was 34.91 (min = 10, max = 67). The distribution of age by gender was also similar: male average age was 35.44 (min = 16, max = 67) while female average age was 34.38 (min = 10, max = 60).

The methodology for collecting the interaction data was as follows. A previously developed game-like application for memory stimulation was used. In this application, a new task was created (equal for all participants) that included a memorization task and a recall task. In this application, users explore and navigate a virtual scenario (composed by adjacent still pictures, like in a point-and-click game) while trying to memorize specific aspects. In this case, the virtual scenario comprised 29 still pictures distributed among 2 different virtual rooms. Two specific visual stimuli were added in two pictures, to be used in the recall task. The recall task was administered right after the end of the memorization task, since the goal of this case study is not to study or stimulate memory but rather to evaluate the suitability of the approach to study the users' interaction mechanisms. The recall task was comprised of 7 questions of different types, and used 11 visual stimuli related to the memorization task.

The users were allowed to interact with the application in a training phase, so that they could get used to the tasks. When ready, the memorization task was started by the researcher, followed by the recall task. Data were collected during both tasks. There was a time limit for the users to complete the memorization task, although there was no minimum time. That is, if the user felt that she/he had already memorized all the necessary detail, they could advance into the recall task. In average, each user spent 5.16 min interacting with the application, and touched the screen 79.22 times to complete both tasks, resulting in a dataset with a total of 2535 touches.

4 Preliminary Data Analysis

The analysis of the data that is described in this section was carried out with the goal to determine if there are significant interaction differences due to aspects such as age or gender. In the future, we want to carry out similar studies with population with special characteristics, such as mild cognitive impairments. However, at the moment, the goal is to validate the approach.

This section thus details the differences in the aforementioned interaction features when comparing users of different genders or age groups. We focus on the features for which the differences were more significant.

In what concerns the gender, the two variables that better distinguish between male and female users are *time between decisions* and *touch duration*. In both cases, female participants tend to exhibit higher values, as Fig. 3 shows. The differences observed are statistically significant for both features (p-value $< 2.2^{-16}$ and p-value $= 1.933^{-9}$), respectively.

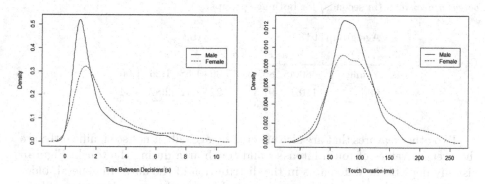

Fig. 3. Gender differences in time between decisions (p-value $< 2.2^{-16}$) (left) and in touch duration (p-value $= 1.933^{-9}$) (right) due to gender.

A similar approach was followed to visually and statistically analyze the differences between age groups. For this purpose, participants were grouped according to their age: the so-called *young* group is composed by users that are 35 or younger (17 participants), while the *old* group is constituted by the remaining users (15 participants).

In general, and as expected, older participants tend to have an overall slower interaction, as depicted in Fig. 4, which shows the distribution of the data regarding touch duration and time between decisions. Table 1 provides some more detail: touches of older people are, in average, 20.65 ms slower; the time between each two consecutive interactions is also 2.54 s slower, in average. The differences between the groups is also statistically significant: p-value $= 2.909^{-08}$ and p-value $= p$-value $= 0.025$, respectively.

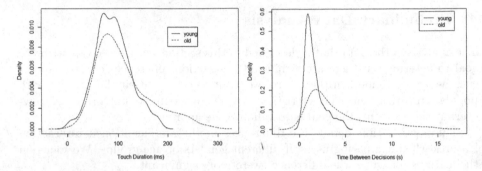

Fig. 4. Differences in touch duration (p-value $= 2.909^{-08}$) (left) and in the time between decisions (p-value $= 0.025$) (right) due to age.

Table 1. Summary statistics of the features *touch duration* (in milliseconds) and *time between decisions* (in seconds) for both age groups.

Age group	td			tbd		
	$\bar{x}$	$\tilde{x}$	σ	$\bar{x}$	$\tilde{x}$	σ
Young	89.45	89.45	35.36	1.58	1.26	1.06
Old	110.1	97.5	54.22	4.12	2.87	3.34

Two other features that are also affected by age, albeit not so significantly, are the average values of touch intensity and touch area during the touch. Figure 5 visually depicts the differences in the distribution of the data. In general, older people tend to have more intense touches and also tend to use a larger area of the finger (average touch area for the older group is 22896 pixels, against 20402 pixels for the younger group). The differences observed are also statistically significant: p-value $= 2.909^{-08}$ (touch intensity) and p-value $= 2.643^{-05}$ (touch area).

This section thus shows that both gender and age influence interaction patterns in a significant manner. In Sect. 5 we show that these differences are enough to train a classifier to distinguish between young and old users with a satisfactory accuracy rate.

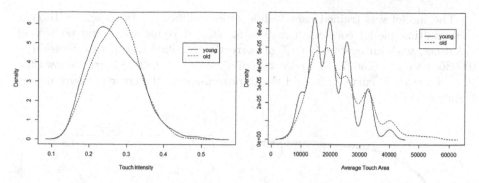

Fig. 5. Differences in the average value of touch intensity (p-value $= 2.909^{-08}$) (left) and in the average value of touch area (p-value $= 2.643^{-05}$) (right) due to age.

5 Results

After the preliminary analysis of the data described in Sect. 4, and given the observed differences in terms of interaction in several variables when comparing age groups, work shifted to the train of a model able to distinguish between young and old users. For this purpose, a gradient boosting model was used, based on an ensemble of decision trees. This algorithm is based on an ensemble of weak prediction models (the decision trees), which are gradually improved during training through increasingly refined approximations. In this algorithm, as in other ensembles, predictors are deemed weak in the sense that they are trained on a sample of the instances and/or the variables. For this reason, each predictor is, by itself, a weak one. But the combination of all these predictors generally produces a good model, with a good tendency to generalize. When one of these models is used for classification, as is the case, the output of the model is the most frequent output observed in all the trees.

The dataset used for training the model contains one instance for each touch, and the following 9 variables:

- Maximum, minimum and average touch area - the maximum, minimum and average area of the touch;
- Maximum, minimum and average touch intensity - the maximum, minimum and average intensity of the touch;
- Time between decisions - the time spent since the last touch;
- Touch Duration - the duration of the touch;
- Age bin - a new variable (target variable) added manually, to identify the group age of the user who performed the touch (young or old).

The trained model (in this case a binomial classification model) is composed of 30 trees, each with a maximum depth of 6 levels. Each of these trees was trained with a random subset of 80% of the rows of the dataset, and of 70% of the features.

The model was trained using 5-fold cross validation. As shown in Table 2, the resulting model correctly classifies 82.03% of young users and 66.37% of old users, with an overall 76.08% of correctly classified instances (precision = 0.6936, recall = 0.6637, F1 Score = 0.6783, AUC = 0.82). Figure 6 shows the plot of the ROC curve (left) and the improvement in the error measure during training (right).

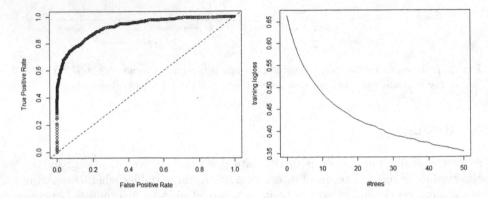

Fig. 6. True positive rate vs. false positive rate (AUC = 0.82) (left); Evolution of error during training (right).

Table 2. Confusion matrix of the trained model.

Actual/predicted	Young	Old	Error
Young	**744**	163	0.1797
Old	187	**369**	0.3363
Total	931	352	0.2392

6   Conclusions and Future Work

Smartphones and tablets are among the most used technological devices nowadays, which make touch screens a new and privileged form of interaction between humans and technology. In this paper we present a new and multi-modal form of characterizing this interaction, based on behavioral and physical features. Thus, instead of considering previously used features such as applications usage patterns, types of gestures or other sensory information (e.g. accelerometer, gyroscope), we use information that characterizes each touch of the user including its intensity, its duration or how these vary over time during the touch.

We conducted a case study in which interaction data was collected from 32 users. The collected data shows that interaction patterns are different between men and women, as well as between people with different age groups. The same data was also used to train a model that is able to distinguish between the user's age group with an accuracy of nearly 74%.

While these results are interesting *per se*, we believe that this approach can be further pursued not only to study the interaction patterns of large groups of the population (as it allows for an inexpensive process of data collection) but also to study the interaction patterns of people with specific characteristics such as mental or physical disabilities. Indeed, our interaction with these devices is nowadays so pervasive and constant that they are now being used to monitor our health. Interaction patterns may constitute another relevant indicator, namely of the emergence of certain cognitive or physical impairments over time.

We will therefore continue to collect data to widen the population of this study, and include subjects with special characteristics in order to study their specific interaction patterns and thus assess this hypothesis.

Acknowledgments. This work is co-funded by Fundos Europeus Estruturais e de Investimento (FEEI) through Programa Operacional Regional Norte, in the scope of project NORTE-01-0145-FEDER-023577.

References

1. Oulasvirta, A., Rattenbury, T., Ma, L., Raita, E.: Habits make smartphone use more pervasive. Pers. Ubiquit. Comput. **16**(1), 105–114 (2012)
2. Leeming, K., Swann, W., Coupe, J., Mittler, P.: Non-verbal communication. In: Teaching Language and Communication to the Mentally Handicapped, pp. 238–267, Routledge (2018)
3. Carneiro, D., Novais, P., Pêgo, J.M., Sousa, N., Neves, J.: Using mouse dynamics to assess stress during online exams. In: Onieva, E., Santos, I., Osaba, E., Quintián, H., Corchado, E. (eds.) HAIS 2015. LNCS (LNAI), vol. 9121, pp. 345–356. Springer, Cham (2015). https://doi.org/10.1007/978-3-319-19644-2_29
4. Pimenta, A., Carneiro, D., Neves, J., Novais, P.: A neural network to classify fatigue from human-computer interaction. Neurocomputing **172**, 413–426 (2016)
5. Pentel, A.: Predicting age and gender by keystroke dynamics and mouse patterns. In: Adjunct Publication of the 25th Conference on User Modeling, Adaptation and Personalization, pp. 381–385. ACM (2017)
6. Nahin, A.N.H., Alam, J.M., Mahmud, H., Hasan, K.: Identifying emotion by keystroke dynamics and text pattern analysis. Behav. Inf. Technol. **33**(9), 987–996 (2014)
7. Ciman, M., Wac, K.: Individuals' stress assessment using human-smartphone interaction analysis. IEEE Trans. Affect. Comput. **9**(1), 51–65 (2018)
8. Mehrotra, A., Hendley, R., Musolesi, M.: Towards multi-modal anticipatory monitoring of depressive states through the analysis of human-smartphone interaction. In: Proceedings of the 2016 ACM International Joint Conference on Pervasive and Ubiquitous Computing: Adjunct, pp. 1132–1138. ACM (2016)
9. Padmaja, B., Prasad, V.R., Sunitha, K.: TreeNet analysis of human stress behavior using socio-mobile data. J. Big Data **3**(1), 24 (2016)

10. Boonstra, T.W., Nicholas, J., Wong, Q.J., Shaw, F., Townsend, S., Christensen, H.: Using mobile phone sensor technology for mental health research: integrated analysis to identify hidden challenges and potential solutions. J. Med. Internet Res. **20**(7), e10131 (2018)
11. Sanchis, A., Julián, V., Corchado, J.M., Billhardt, H., Carrascosa, C.: Using natural interfaces for human-agent immersion. In: Corchado, J.M., Bajo, J., Kozlak, J., Pawlewski, P., Molina, J.M., Gaudou, B., Julian, V., Unland, R., Lopes, F., Hallenborg, K., García Teodoro, P. (eds.) PAAMS 2014. CCIS, vol. 430, pp. 358–367. Springer, Cham (2014). https://doi.org/10.1007/978-3-319-07767-3_32
12. Sanchis, Á., Inglada, J., Javier, V., Corchado, J.M., Billhardt, H., Carrascosa Casamayor, C.: Improving human-agent immersion using natural interfaces and CBR. Int. J. Artif. Intell. **13**(1), 81–93 (2015)

Analyzing User Experiences in Incorporated Fictionality

Tatsuo Nakajima[✉], Risa Kimura, Fumiko Ishizawa,
and Mizuki Sakamoto

Department of Computer Science and Engineering,
Waseda University, Tokyo, Japan
{tatsuo, r.kimura, f.ishizawa,
mizuki}@dcl.cs.waseda.ac.jp

Abstract. In this paper, we present an overview of a case study that aims to augment the meaning of real spaces through incorporated fictionality. The case study uses a head mounted display to show real spaces by capturing it through a camera, but the space is augmented from the true real spaces. Our focus, in particular, is criticizing how one can feel a sense of reality in augmented real spaces in a case study because the meaning of the augmented real space is lost if a user does not feel a sense of reality on the incorporated fictionality. We extract some insights and potential pitfalls from the analyses of the case study within participatory design workshops.

Keywords: Incorporated fictionality · Virtualizing real spaces ·
Participatory design

1 Introduction

Emerging computing technologies allow us to augment the meaning of our real spaces to influence our attitudes and behaviors [3, 5, 10, 16]. For our daily life to become more sustainable and flourish, influencing our attitude and behavior is essential [12, 15]. To influence our attitudes and behaviors, the meaning of real spaces needs to be refined to make people believe that their augmentation has meaningful effects on our real daily life. However, there are very few studies on design strategies to augment the semiotic meaning of the real spaces because such studies must take into account several different disciplines that are typically separated and substantial effort is required to integrate them.

For example, there are many movie and animation contents to exploit fictionality to influence our daily attitudes and behaviors, but the discussions about design contents are completely isolated from the technology design of digital services, although emerging computing technologies are significantly virtualizing and fictionalizing our dairy life.

In this paper, we discuss how we augment the semiotic meaning of real spaces by using augmented reality technologies. By incorporating components that do not exist in the real spaces that we currently see, our attitudes and behaviors can be influenced and altered. The study uses fictional components for the augmentation. In particular, a case

P. Moura Oliveira et al. (Eds.): EPIA 2019, LNAI 11805, pp. 13–25, 2019.
https://doi.org/10.1007/978-3-030-30244-3_2

study uses head mounted displays (HMDs) to increase immersion into augmented real spaces. By criticizing the case study, it is possible to extract some preliminary insights to understand how fictionality can be incorporated in the real spaces and people feel values on the incorporated fictionality.

The paper is structured as follows. In Sect. 2, we describe some related work. In Sect. 3, we present a brief overview of Enhanced TCG [14] that incorporates fictionality into a trading card game played in a real space as a case study, and its design implication. Section 4 shows how to extract some insights from the case study in two participatory design workshop. Section 5 concludes the paper.

2 Related Work

Our research approach is closely related to a new direction discussed in Research through Design [17]. As defined in [4], *"Research through design is the closest to the actual design practice, recasting the design aspect of creation as research. Designer/researchers who use Research through Design actually create new products, experimenting with new materials, processes, etc."* Critical thinking is an effective strategy to increase our knowledge to advance our future studies, but it is not popular to explicitly report these insights when a new technology is introduced in academic papers.

Because symbolization of things will be accelerated by embedding computers in our life by incorporating fictionality, our virtual consumption will progress rapidly. Currently, a product's quality is not the most important reason why many of us buy the product [3, 12]. Digital technologies have been effective in making digital objects commodities and, consequently, lowering their prices. However, the same technologies are also effective for adding value to products and services by enhancing their meaning.

Some pervasive games also incorporate both virtual and tangible objects in real-space game play [9]. For example, in Pac-Man and Ghosts, human players in the real space experience a computer graphics-generated fantasy-reality using wearable computers [7]. The basic concepts from pervasive games can also be useful in realizing our goal. Augmenting the meaning of real spaces can also be used to enhance a traditional pervasive game using transmedia storytelling [13]. A fictional story can be told across multiple media platforms, which are integrated in our daily lives.

Most recently, digital marketing and social media practitioners have adopted this approach as "gamification" [2]. Adding badges and leaderboards is a typical approach to achieving gamification. Additionally, alternate reality game (ARG) is a promising approach to making our daily life a game [8]. Additionally, in live action role-playing (LARP) [9], people wear costumes in fictional stories and play fictional roles in the stories in real spaces.

The approach described in the paper shows a way to generate useful knowledge and find potential pitfalls to understand the possibilities and limitations of the emerging new technologies by analyzing research project experiences to develop and evaluate case studies.

3   A Case Study: Enhanced TCG

Incorporating fictionality in real spaces has several merits for desirably influencing people's attitude and behavior. To discussing the approach, we have developed Enhanced TCG as a case study, where a player wears an HMD during the trading cade game (TCG) play. In Enhanced TCG, one medium presents the real-time video that captures and augments the TCG player in real spaces, and another medium presents stories in fictional virtual spaces, presenting supplemental stories about the fictionality incorporated in the real spaces through emerging digital technologies. These two media are blended into one medium that can be seen through a HMD. Our main focus is to show some insights about the importance of immersion when fictionality is incorporated into real spaces.

3.1   Incorporated Fictionality

Because real spaces can be represented both abstractly and, ironically, as a fictional component through framing to either simplify or exaggerate essential concepts in our daily lives [3, 13], people easily notice the concepts that are relevant to achieving an ideal, sustainable society. In particular, Japanese animation and game narratives contain ideological social messages related to futuristic lifestyles [11] to increase people's conscious and internalized motivation and show that fiction is a powerful tool that can influence people's activities.

The most important issue in realizing immersion is blurring the boundary between fiction and reality. The use of a HMD offers a better immersive experience by showing a video stream capturing real spaces and replacing some real components in the video stream with fictional components. The approach offers the possibility to realize more seamlessly integrated transmedia storytelling because a user is not required to switch his/her view when viewing multiple media.

3.2   An Overview of Enhanced TCG

To demonstrate the effect of incorporating fictionality into real spaces, we have developed a case study named *Enhanced TCG* shown in Figs. 1 and 2. *Enhanced TCG* allows a player to play a trading card game, while fictinonality is seamlessly integrated into the real TCG play. A 3D character replaced with a physical card depicting the character appears in a real space. At the same time, the information written on the card is also visible in the real spaces along with the 3D character. When the character appears in the real space for the first time, the user's view may be seamlessly switched to the fictional space where the character tells his/her story to the player for emotionally engaging him/her to the character. In the previous approaches, the character just appears on a physical card, but our approach replaces the card with the character. Also, the real space may be switched to a fictional space within a HMD. This is radically different from these previous approaches.

Fig. 1. An overview of enhanced TCG.

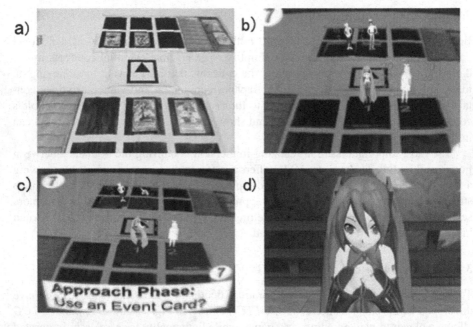

Fig. 2. Some Actual Scenes in Enhanced TCG. (a) shows a typical play space of TCG, where players put some physical cards depicting virtual characters. When starting a game, some currently used cards are replaced with the 3D characters as shown in (b), where the character performs his/her typical poses and actions, and essential information depicted in the cards is also shown along with the characters. As shown in (c), some information to help the player's decision also appears. Also, a scene in a real space may be switched to a fictional space to present a story about the character as shown in (d). The story makes a player engage with more empathy for the character or teaches the player some ideological concepts why he/she plays the game.

In the current *Enhanced TCG*, a player plays a TCG by wearing a HMD, Ocu-lusRift[1]. A web camera is attached to the HMD to capture a real space as shown in Fig. 1; the captured real-time video is transformed by replacing some real components with fictional components, and the transformed video stream is shown to a player through a HMD. NyARToolkit[2] is adopted for incorporating fictionality in real spaces. Also, we adopted Unity[3] for integrating fictional space into the real spaces seamlessly.

Enhanced TCG adopts *Precious Memories*[4] as TCG. In *Precious Memories*, each card depicts a different virtual character that appears in various Japanese animations and games. A player who likes the animation or game can enjoy the TCG by choosing its typical or his/her favorite character. Thus, *Enhanced TCG*'s features presenting the stories of various virtual characters and their 3D representations in real spaces offer highly immersive experiences to players with transmedia storytelling because each virtual character has his/her own story presented in a different animation or game.

4 Design Strategies to Augment Real Spaces

Augmenting real spaces offers the possibility to significantly influence our attitudes and behaviors. Expanding special fictional effects in games to the real spaces has significant impacts on humans' emotional experience as shown in the previous section. Additionally, recent advertisements based on transmedia storytelling bring fictional stories into our real life if people can communicate with fictional persons in the stories via social media [12, 13]. The augmented real spaces may be rather rhetorically persuasive, but if a sense of the reality of the augmentation of the real spaces is lost, the effect of the persuasiveness continues only temporally while people maintain their curiosity. The section discusses some insights to design the enhanced real spaces based on the participatory design based analyses with the case study.

4.1 Research Method

We conducted two participatory design workshops to analyze the case study presented in the previous section.

4.1.1 The First Workshop

The first participatory design workshop is unstructured, in which participants are four researchers who developed and conducted the case study. They discussed their experiences with developing and evaluating the case study in the workshop. The role of the workshop is to record the discussions among participants into a document; then, we extracted various labels related to how to augment the semiotic meaning of real spaces based on the case study from the recorded document. We divided the labels into several

---

[1] https://www.oculus.com/.

[2] http://nyatla.jp/nyartoolkit/wp/?page_id=55.

[3] http://unity3d.com/.

[4] http://www.p-memories.com/.

categories in accordance with a grounded theory [1], which is a systematic framework in the social sciences involving theory-driven content analysis that aims at identifying a set of words that best present a certain concept, that is widely used in social science to extract qualitative insights. We performed interactive open coding on the labels to identify different categories.

We conducted to extract the categories in the following three steps.

(i) Collecting documents: We collected a set of documents created by the developers of the system. The document includes some documents discussing the system's basic idea, system design and presenting the experiment including the interview with participants.

(ii) Annotating the documents: The annotator chose keywords from the documents related to the enhancement of real spaces.

(iii) Validating annotations: To qualitatively validate the keywords, we measure the agreement among developers of the system.

We finally extracted seven categories: *Living Thing, Object, Landscape, Informative Cue, Institutional Mechanism, Occurrence* and *Narrative* from the analysis, where we call the seven dimensions the *dimension world model*, that is a model helps us to discuss a process to virtualize real spaces. By examining each dimension, designers can consider the redefinition of reframe of the real spaces (Fig 3).

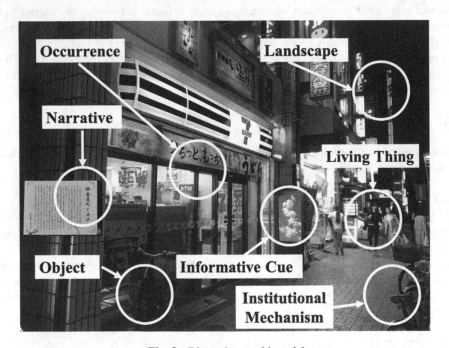

Fig. 3. Dimension world model

4.1.2   The Second Workshop

In the second participatory design workshop, eleven participants who are experts of Japanese pop culture discussed how a sense of the reality of an enhanced real space is affected with the *value-based analysis framework* by using the values as frames to structure the discussions, where the framework contains six values like the *authentic value, mindful value, empathetic value, aesthetic value, ideological value* and *informative value* proposed in [12]. Figure 4 depicts the six frames defined in the value-based analysis framework. These six frames are grounded from various theories proposed in multidisciplinary fields like social science, behavior science, marketing and cultural studies for designing meaningful digital products. The informative value offers sufficient information to people and helps them make better decisions. The empathetic value is achieved and enhanced by adding some similarity with a user. The authentic value provides people with a sense of ownership. The aesthetic value is an important concept with regard to making everyday objects more attractive. The mindful value gives people a chance to be aware of the current situation. The ideological value reminds users of important ideological concepts, such as friendship and justice. The results of the analysis are summarized in the next subsection.

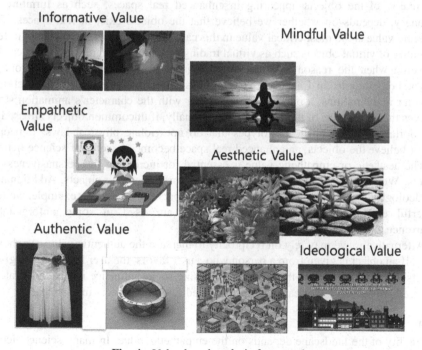

Fig. 4. Value-based analysis framework

4.2   Analyzing Enhanced TCG with the Value-Based Analysis Framework in Respective Dimensions

4.2.1   Living Thing

We mainly focus on a person as a typical living thing in our discussion. People first typically establish a human relationship based on a person's visual impression if they do not know the person well. People can also establish a human relationship with a fictional person if they know the stories of the fictional person and feel empathy toward the person. The persuasiveness is increased if a person is well known and favorable. Thus, the empathetic value is essential in this case. Additionally, if a person offers the aesthetic value, persuasiveness is typically increased because we tend to believe an aesthetic person. The ideological value affects the persuasiveness of a person because we may feel the authority of a person who offers strong ideological messages to us. The empathetic value is the most essential in Enhanced TCG because most of fictional persons used in Enhanced TCG are the fictional characters used in animation stories. The question of whether a user knows the stories of the characters and feels empathy toward them is essential.

4.2.2   Object

The reality of the objects appearing in enhanced real spaces, such as furniture or stationary, depends on whether we believe that the objects exist in real spaces. The authentic value is the most critical value in this case. As shown in [12], it is hard to feel the reality of virtual objects such as virtual trading cards, but the authentic value can be recovered when the reason that the virtual objects exist in real spaces is properly shown. For example, in Enhanced TCG, a physical card is replaced with a fictional character in animations; a player who is familiar with the character's animation story believes the appearance of the character. Additionally, if uncommon objects are used, it is important to use realistic prototypes that do not violate physical laws. If people cannot believe the objects, an enhanced real space becomes a world of science fiction.

The aesthetic or empathetic value is essential for increasing the persuasiveness of objects. We typically tend to remember beautiful or empathetic objects. Additionally, the ideological value is important to increase their persuasiveness; for example, we feel powerful emotional experiences when objects are used in some unforgettable occurrence.

Alternatively, we may rely on reciprocity to increase the authentic value. As shown in [6], if an object is given from a person who a user favors, the user feels that the given objects are precious even if they are virtual. Using social influence is a useful strategy to increase a sense of the reality of incorporated fictional objects in real spaces.

4.2.3   Landscape

The reality of the landscape depends on the empathetic value. In many science fiction movies, nonexisting impressive landscapes are used to allow people to feel that the place is not our living space. This approach increases the reality of the place in fictional stories, but people cannot feel that the landscape exists in our real space.

In Enhanced TCG, a story introducing a fictional character uses a virtual world composed by 3D models. The landscape used in the story should typically be the landscape used in the animation stories of the characters. However, many recent Japanese animations generate landscapes from the photos of real landscapes to make people feel that the characters in the animations actually live in the real town.[5] This approach increases the authentic value of the landscape; people can enjoy some fictional events in the stories as events in real spaces.

4.2.4   Informative Cue

In our case study, some information is shown to help a user's decision making. Conversely, some information may appear to increase people's buying impulses. In Enhanced TCG, information can be shown by superimposing textual information on real spaces, as in typical augmented reality services.

The authentic value of the information is essential for making people believe the information. People typically believe the information presented on newspapers or magazines published by authorized organizations. They are also easily aware of superimposing information in real spaces such as Enhanced TCG; the approach increases the persuasiveness of the information, but the means of presenting information is not natural. Thus, it is important to determine how to increase its authenticity.[6] Additionally, it should be careful not to increase people's frustration due to intrusive information. At times, there is a tradeoff between the naturalness and persuasiveness of the information. We need to investigate the use of typical methods developed in recent advertisements in public spaces.

4.2.5   Institutional Mechanism

In the current case study, institutional mechanisms such as the currency system or social norms are represented in the background described in stories, but we can explicitly incorporate the fictional economic or social mechanisms as institutional mechanisms to enhance our case study to facilitate desirable human activities. Increasing social influence is an essential way to alter human attitudes and behaviors. Additionally, virtual currency can be used to facilitate a community's activities [6]. By taking into account the ideological value, the potential drawbacks are more clearly presented. But, the authentic value should be ensured so that the effects of the mechanics have a real impact on our actual living society. This issue makes it hard to use fictional institute mechanisms in the current case studies.

It is hard to implement realistic social communication with a fictional character because the unnatural voice communication may violate the consistency of the fictional character. However, we may use social media such as Twitter to communicate with the fictional character. If the character timely retweets our tweets, the reality of the communication is significantly increased, and these responses increase our communication activities. Additionally, when the virtual currency can be exchanged with real currency, we feel the reality of the currency's economic value. However, if the currency does not

---

[5] http://ayamoe.skr.jp/photodramatica.html/.

[6] In recent pop culture contents, this way of presenting information is very common, so people in the young generation consider that the information is more authentic than do those in the old generation.

have any impacts on our real life, the currency immediately bores people and, thus, they will stop using it.

4.2.6 Occurrence

Occurrence causing strong emotional impression can be easily remembered even from partial information. For example, people typically remember a serious accident that they encounter for a long time. Additionally, they can easily remember a fateful encounter with a marvelous leader. Thus, the fictional representation including ideological messages that serve as reminders of the real past occurrence makes people feel the reality of the occurrence. The ideological value can be used to serve as a reminder of the messages and increase the reality of the fictional representation. For example, Newsgames[7] are typical examples; they use the ideological value to increase the reality of video games and in Enhanced TCG, fictional characters can give players some ideological concepts.

Music typically has a positive effect on people's behavior. Music is useful for increasing the positive value. In many dramas and movies, music is effectively used to engage audiences. In real spaces, there is no background music, but the music can be used to enhance the meaning of the real spaces. In Enhanced TCG, special sound effects and music are effectively used to increase a user's positive emotion.

4.2.7 Narrative

The informative value is used to help people's decision making. However, it is not typically easy to offer proper information to people in these case studies because people may not be aware when useful information is presented if the information is seamlessly embedded in real spaces. From the experience with Enhanced TCG, transmedia storytelling is useful for enhancing the informative value because respective media offer the same information from different angles simultaneously. This approach increases the possibility that people are aware of the usefulness of the information.

The use of multiple media is useful for offering the positive value because offering information from multiple angles is appropriate for increasing multiple emotions, and these emotions increase the positive emotion. For example, the use of several pastel colors in media may trigger human positive power to decrease fears of tackling a hard problem.

Additionally, transmedia storytelling is a useful technique to incorporate fictionality in real spaces [13]. When people see the incorporated fictionality in various places in the real spaces, the possibility that they feel that the fictionality exists in the real spaces is also increased.

4.3 Design Implication

From the discussions in the workshops, we also found that the following three issues are essential when designing incorporated fictionality. The first issue is that the use case' scenarios are essential to effectively extract a sense of values from participants.

---

[7] http://www.newsgaming.com/.

The second issue concerns how to ensure the plausibility of incorporated fictionality by adding a sense of values in each dimension. The third issue relates to how human behavior is designed according to incorporated fictionality. This subsection summarizes the discussions on these three issues.

In the second workshop, we provided a tangible working prototype to participants, but the scenarios surrounding their use were implicit to the participants. However, based on their experiences with the experiments, the designers amplified their stories about how to use the digital services because, before the workshop, the participants already knew the stories from the designers, including the case study' scenarios, as well as how to explore decisions while designing it. Additionally, the participants understood the current drawbacks of the case study from the experiments conducted by the designers. The stories are very powerful in terms of understanding the sense of values embedded in the case study. If the participants need to estimate the values from the laboratory studies with tangible prototypes, it is hard to properly understand the values, and such misunderstandings may lead to poor decisions with regard to refining the case study. The designers' stories are usually a kind of scenario related to the use of the case study. Our finding is that a well-designed scenario describing how values are embedded in the digital service is helpful to appropriately understand the precise values if the participants are hard to develop their own stories with the digital services through the long term real world field setting that is usually hard to incorporate in the user study.

The second issue discussed in the second workshop was how to ensure the plausibility of incorporated fictionality through a sense of values. One of the important issues related to design concerns the consideration of semiotic meaning in incorporated fictionality. The value attached to fictionality may be fictional, but the effect is strong enough to influence a user's attitude and behavior. A designer needs to carefully consider how users unconsciously sense the meaning of an alternate real space modified through incorporated fictionality. If the meaning is ambiguous, users may be confused about how to behave in the real space. However, the ambiguity is sometime essential because it offers opportunities to explicitly and critically consider the importance of the incorporated fictionality. Future digital services need to consider various social issues and human possibilities to overcome serious social pitfalls and to increase our potential abilities. It is important to investigate a variety of possible services to enhance our human abilities for speculative design. Incorporated fictionality offers us some possibilities for speculative design in future services and critical discussions of social issues to change the meaning of real spaces. The approach is essential in building future social services that are aligned with people's flourishing lifestyles.

The third issue discussed relates to how human behavior can be designed in incorporated fictionality. The changing visual or auditory experience in real spaces influences human behavior. In future services, influencing human is essential in relation to a variety of social issues. For example, economic issues must be taken into account to promote business on digital services, and political issues must be considered to make a government function correctly. Additionally, ethical issues should be considered to protect people from those who seek to exploit them. Previous studies have provided ample evidence of the effects of altering human eyesight. In particular, offering positive and negative feedback is powerful in controlling human behavior. However, the persuasive effects may be limited if people cannot understand the meaning of the incorporated fictionality. The plausibility of incorporated fictionality comes from the belief that people can understand the meaning and that they feel the meaning is significant for them. Thus, feeling the plausibility is very important in influencing human behavior because people do not change their behaviors according to incorporated fictionality if they do not feel the plausibility of the incorporated fictionality.

5 Conclusion

The paper presents a case study that augments the semiotic meaning of real spaces. The case study uses fictional components to augment the meaning. We then present the analysis of the case study to extract some useful insights to design future digital services that attempt to augment the meaning of real spaces.

Acknowledgement. For developing Enhanced TCG, Monami Takahashi and Keisuke Irie were significantly contributed. We like to thank them for their contribution for the research.

References

1. Corbin, J., Strauss, A.: Basics of Qualitative Research: Techniques and Procedures for developing Grounded Thoery. SAGE Publications Inc, Thousand Oaks (2008)
2. Deterding, S., Dan, D., Khaled, R., Nacke, L.: From game design elements to gamefulness: defining "ramification". In: Proceedings of the 15th International Academic MindTrek Conference: Envisioning Future Media Environments, pp. 9–15. ACM (2011)
3. Ishizawa, F., Sakamoto, M., Nakajima, T.: Extracting intermediate-level design knowledge for speculating digital–physical hybrid alternate reality experiences. Multimedia Tools Appl. **77**(16), 21329–21370 (2018)
4. Godin, D., Zahedi, M.: Aspects of research through design: a literature review. In: Proceedings of DRS 2014 (2014)
5. Kimura, R., Nakajima, T.: A ubiquitous computing platform for virtualizing collective human eyesight and hearing capabilities. In: Proceedings of the 10th International Symposium on Ambient Intelligence (2019)
6. Lehdonvirta, V.: Virtual Consumption. Publications of the Turku School of Economics, A-11:2009 (2009)
7. Magerkurth, C., Cheok, A.D., Mandryk, R.L., Nilsen, T.: Pervasive games: bringing computer entertainment back to the real world. ACM Comput. Entertain. **3**(3), 2005 (2005)
8. McGonigal, J.: Reality is Broken: Why Games Make Us Better and How They Can Change the World. Penguin Press, New York (2011)
9. Montola, M., Stenros, J., Waern, A.: Pervasive Games - Theory and Design. Morgan Kaufmann, Burlington (2009)
10. Nakajima, T., Lehdonvirta, V.: Designing motivation in persuasive ambient mirrors. Pers. Ubiquit. Comput. **17**(1), 107–126 (2013)
11. Nakajima, T., Sakamoto, M.: Incorporating cultural gamified media in our daily space for exploring alternate reality experiences, Chapter 1 in Selected Topics in Cultural Studies Chapter. Nova Publisher (2019)

12. Sakamoto, M., Nakajima, T., Alexandrova, T.: Enhancing values through virtuality for intelligent artifacts that influence human attitude and behavior. Multimedia Tools Appl. **74** (24), 11537–11568 (2015)
13. Sakamoto, M., Nakajima, T.: Incorporating fictionality into the real world with transmedia storytelling. In: Proceedings of the International Conference on Design, User Experience and Usability (2015)
14. Takahashi, M., Irie, K., Sakamoto, M., Nakajima, T.: Incorporating fictionality into the real space: a case of enhanced TCG. In: Adjunct Proceedings of the 2015 ACM International Joint Conference on Pervasive and Ubiquitous Computing and Proceedings of the 2015 ACM International Symposium on Wearable Computers (UbiComp/ISWC 2015 Adjunct) (2015)
15. Wolfe, A.K., Malone, E.L., Heerwagen, J., Dion, J.: Behavioral change and building performance: strategies for significant, persistent, and measurable institutional change, US Department of Energy (2014)
16. Yamabe, T., Nakajima, T.: Playful training with augmented reality games: case studies toward reality-oriented system design. Multimedia Tools Appl. **62**(1), 259–286 (2013)
17. Zimmerman, J., Forlizzi, J., Evenson, S.: Research through design as a method for interaction design research in HCI. In: Proceedings of the SIGCHI Conference on Human Factors in Computing Systems (2007)

Agent-Based Education Environment in Museums

Ichiro Satoh[✉]

National Institute of Informatics,
2-1-2 Hitotsubashi, Chiyoda-ku, Tokyo 101-8430, Japan
ichiro@nii.ac.jp

Abstract. This paper presents an agent-based education system featuring context-awareness. It detects the locations of visitors and deploys agents at computers near their current locations. When visitors move between exhibits at a museum, their agents follow them to annotate the exhibits in personalized form and navigate them to the next exhibits along their routes. The system enables visitors to interact with agents by their movements rather than by using portable devices, as visitor movement is one of the most basic and natural behaviors in museums. This paper also describes insights gained from our past experiments on agent-based education services.

1 Introduction

Agent-based systems have been used in a variety of ways to assist in human learning. In artificial intelligence, agents are autonomous entities that direct their activity towards achieving goals in environments by means of observation through sensors and external database systems. Such agents are adaptive in the sense that they may learn or use knowledge to achieve their goals. They are also useful to enhance human learning in the real world. We have attempted to use agents for user-assistant services in the real world, e.g., museums, train stations, and shopping malls.

This paper describes our agent-based user-assistant system to navigate and provide educational annotation for users according to their past and present locations. The system detected the presence of visitors standing in front of specified exhibits and deployed agents at stationary computers close to their current positions to provide visitors with annotational information on the exhibits that they are in front of. They recorded and maintained the experiences of visitors, e.g., a record of the exhibits that the visitors had previously viewed. In addition, they recorded and maintained profile information on the visitors and provided them with personalized annotations about the exhibits that they were standing in front of. Also, to free visitors from the burden of complex interaction with their agents and annotation configuration, we used their movements between exhibits as implicit operations to select the annotations that they wanted to view/hear and to evaluate what they had learned from the exhibits, as visitor movement is one of the most basic and natural behaviors in museums.

© Springer Nature Switzerland AG 2019
P. Moura Oliveira et al. (Eds.): EPIA 2019, LNAI 11805, pp. 26–37, 2019.
https://doi.org/10.1007/978-3-030-30244-3_3

2   Basic Approach

This section discusses the requirements and concept of the proposed system.

2.1   Requirements

This work was inspired by our collaboration with several science museums. One of the museums asked us to develop agent-based navigation and annotation services for their visitors.

- Annotation services should be personalized, because most visitors in the museum lack sufficient knowledge about the exhibits and they need supplementary annotations on these. As their knowledge and experience are varied, they may become puzzled (or bored) if the annotations provided to them are beyond (or beneath) their knowledge-level or interest. Ideally, visitors will be provided with annotations on exhibits according to their own knowledge and experience, e.g., exhibits that they have already seen.
- Portable devices should not be used, because visitors tend to pay attention to the devices and less to the exhibits. It is also difficult for some visitors, particularly children, the elderly, and handicapped people, to interact with annotation services through the buttons or touch panels on portable computers, cellular phones, and stationary terminals.
- Visitor routes are often effective for helping visitors to learn about exhibits. However, visitors often miss their routes, so that annotation services should navigate visitors. Such routes should also be personalized with annotations.
- The museum wants to provide quizzes on their exhibits for visitors, because quizzes are a useful way to review what has been learned about the exhibits. Since children tend to study thing through playing games, quizzes are also useful to enhance their learning experiences.

2.2   Design Principles

To satisfy the above requirements, our approach is to combine between the notion of agents with context-awareness.

The system can assign one or more agents to each visitor to support the first requirement. These agents select or modify annotation contents in a personalized form according to the visitors' knowledge and experience, e.g., the exhibits that they have previous viewed. They are autonomous and can also have their own programs to provide annotations in different modalities.

To satisfy the second requirement, our services should be provided from stationary computers located close to the exhibits instead of via portable devices. Visitors move from exhibit to exhibit in a museum, and whenever they move to a new one, their agents should be deployed at computing devices close to the new exhibit. That is, our virtual agents should accompany the visitors and annotate the exhibits in front of them in the real world on behalf of museum guides or curators.

Agents should navigate visitors to exhibits along the routes assigned to them. Agents can dynamically select which exhibits their visitors should see next and inform them via their favorite modalities, e.g, visualization or sound. Both the annotations about exhibits and the visitor routes may often be changed and modified, as real museums frequently replace and relocate displays in their exhibition spaces. Non-professional administrator, e.g., curators, should be able to easily define and customize visitor-assistant agents.

To support quizzes, the system needs to let users input their answers, but user-manipulation must be simple and natural, because it is difficult for visitors to explicitly operate buttons, mice, touch panels, and smart cards. We introduce visitor movements as a user-friendly interaction with agents, because visitor movement is one of the most basic and natural behaviors in museums.

3 Design and Implementation

Before explaining our experiment in a museum, we describe our system for monitoring contextual information and executing agents. It consists of three subsystems: (1) context-aware directory server(s) (CDS), (2) agent hosts, and (3) context-aware agents (Fig. 1). The CDS is responsible for monitoring the underlying location sensing systems and reflecting changes in the real world, e.g., the movement of visitors, to supply information on the locations of agents. The

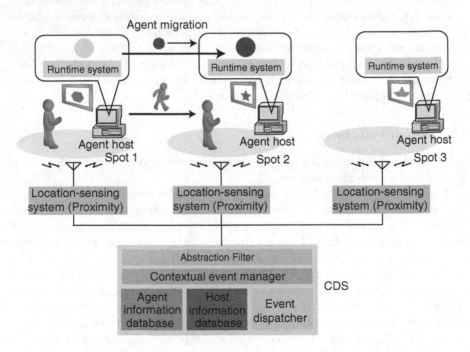

Fig. 1. Architecture of context-aware virtual agent system.

agent hosts are located at computers and can execute context-aware agents. The context-aware agents are autonomous entities that define application-specific services for visitors. Visitor-assistant services are encapsulated within the third subsystem so that the first and second subsystems are independent of any application-specific services or other agents, which are simultaneously running to provide different services, including artificial intelligence (AI)-based processing.

3.1   Context-Aware Agent Deployment

Although the system itself is independent of any underlying location-sensing systems, the experiment presented in this paper was based on a proximity-based location sensing system with active RFID tags, so here, we briefly explain how CDSs are used with the system. We assume that the museum has provided visitors with active RFID tags, where tags are small RF transmitters that periodically broadcast beacons including the identifiers of the tags to receivers located in exhibition spaces, where each receiver can detect the presence of tags within the coverage area of its antenna, e.g., 3-m circle, called a *spot*. CDS monitors one or more receivers. When the receiver detects the presence (or absence) of a tag in a spot, its CDS attempts to query the locations of the agent tied to the tag from its database and then instructs the agent to migrate to a computer in that spot.

3.2   Agent Host

Each agent host is located at a computer with user-interface devices, e.g., display screens and loudspeakers. It is constructed as a runtime system for executing and migrating agents to other hosts. Each runtime system is built on the Java virtual machine (Java VM), which conceals differences between the platform architectures of the source and destination hosts. Each agent host can exchange agents with another host through a TCP channel using mobile-agent technology. When an agent is transferred over the network, both the code of the agent and its state are transformed into a bitstream by using Java's object serialization package and then the bitstream is then transferred to the destination. The agent host on the receiving side receives and unmarshals the bitstream.

Each runtime system governs all the agents inside it and maintains the life-cycle state of each agent. When the life-cycle state of an agent changes e.g., its creation, termination, or migration to another host changes, the runtime system issues specific events to the agent. Navigation or annotation content, e.g., audio-annotation, should be played without interruption, so agents may have to acquire various resources, e.g., video and sound, or release previously acquired resources.

3.3   Context-Aware Agent

Each agent is assigned to at most one visitor and has his/her preference information and its own programs that provide annotation and navigation. To enable

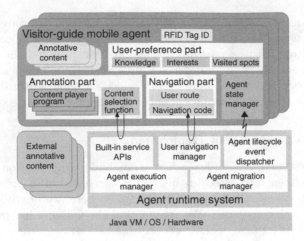

Fig. 2. Architecture of agent host.

agents to be easily developed and configured, each agent consists of three parts:
(1) a *user-preference part*, which maintains and records information about visitors, e.g., their knowledge, interests, routes, name, and the durations and times
they spend at each exhibit; (2) an *annotation part*, which defines a task for playing annotations about exhibits or interacting with visitors; and (3) a *navigation
part*, which defines a task for navigating visitors to their destinations (Fig. 2).
When an agent is deployed at another computer, the runtime system invokes a
specified callback method defined in the annotation part and then one defined
in the navigation part. Although these parts are implemented as Java objects,
they are loosely connected with one another through data attributes by using
Java's introspection mechanism so that they can be replaced without any com-
pilations or linkages between their programs. The current implementation uses
the standard JAR file format for archiving these parts because this format can
support digital signatures, thus enabling authentication. Each agent keeps the
identifier of the tag attached to its visitor.

User-Preference Part. This part is responsible for maintaining information
about a visitor. Actually it is almost impossible to accurately infer what a visitor
knows or is interested in from data that are measured by sensing systems, so
instead, the current implementation assumes that administrators will explicitly
ask visitors about their knowledge and interests and manually input the information into this part. Nevertheless, it is still possible to make an educated guess
with some probability as to what a visitor may be interested in, if we know
which spots he/she has visited, how many he/she has visited, and how long
he/she stayed there. Each agent has a mechanism to automatically record the
identifiers, the number of visits to, and the length of stays at spots by visitors.

Annotation Part. Each agent is required to select annotations according to the current spot and route in addition to the information stored in the user-preference part and to play the content in the personalized form of its user. This part defines the content-selection function and the set of programs for playing the selected content. The function maps more than one property, e.g., the current spot, the user's selected route, and the number of times he/she has visited the spot, into a URL referring to the annotative content. The content can be stored in the agent, the current agent host, or external http servers. This part is defined as Java-based general-purpose programs.

Navigation Part. Our agents are used to navigate visitors to their destinations along routes recommended by museums or the visitors themselves. After executing their annotation part, the navigation part is invoked by the runtime system to provide visual or audio information on the display screens or from loudspeakers of the current agent host.

We also introduced visitor movements between exhibits as an implicit operation for selecting the routes that they wanted and evaluating what they had learned from the exhibits, because visitor movement is one of the most basic and natural behaviors in museums. This part consists of the four navigation patterns, outlined in Fig. 3.

- *Navigation* instructs users to move to at least one specified destination spot.
- *Selection* enables users to explicitly or implicitly select one spot or route from more options close to their current spot by moving to the selected spot or another spot along the selected route.
- *Termination* informs users that they have arrived at the final destination spot.
- *Warning* informs users that they have missed their destination exhibit or strayed off their route.

No agent knows the spatial directions to the destinations because the directions themselves depend on the spatial relationships between the locations of the current agent host and the locations of the destinations, as well as on the direction to the current host's screen.

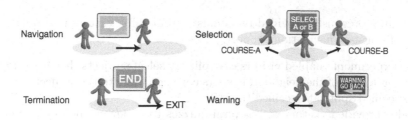

Fig. 3. User-navigation patterns.

4   Experience

This section describes our experience with the system in addition to the basic performance of the system.

5   Experiment in a Museum

We performed an experiment at the Museum of Nature and Human Activities in Hyogo, Japan, using the proposed system. As shown in Fig. 4, the experiment was carried out at four spots in front of specimens of stuffed animals: a bear, a deer, a raccoon dog, and a wild boar. Each spot provided five different pieces of animation-based annotative content about the animals, namely its ethology, footprints, feeding, habitats, and features, and had a display and active RFID reader with a coverage range that roughly corresponding to the space. Before a visitor participated in the experiment, an operator input his/her point of interest and the route and created his/her virtual agent. When a visitor stood at each of the spots, his/her agent was deployed at one computer within his/her current spot. It displayed content in a process defined within its program and navigate him/her to the next destination, where the content and the next destination were selected according to the past spots that he/she visited in addition to his/her current spot and his/her route.

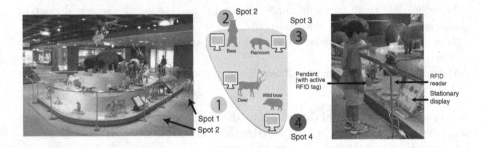

Fig. 4. Experiment.

We simultaneously provided two kinds of routes for visitors to evaluate the utility of our user-navigation support.

- The experiment enabled visitors to explicitly select subjects they preferred by moving to one of the neighboring spots corresponding to the subjects selected in specified spots at specified times.
- It also provided visitors with several quizzes to review what they had learnt about the animals by selectively moving to neighboring spots corresponding to their answers in specified spots at specified times (Fig. 5).

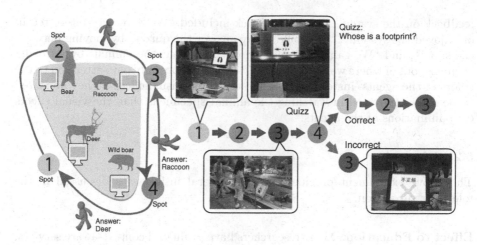

Fig. 5. Interactive route for quizzes on exhibits

Both the experiments offered visitors animation-based annotative content about the animal in front of them so they could learn about it while observing the corresponding specimen.

An agent bound to a user could recommend two or more destination spots by using the *selection* pattern provided on its current agent host. When a visitor moved to one of the spots, his/her agent recorded their selection. If the selection corresponded to a quiz choice, when the user moved to a spot corresponding to a correct or incorrect answer, their agent modified the visitor's profile that was maintained within it. Furthermore, if a user strayed from his/her route, the navigation part played a warning content for him/her to return to the spot.

5.1   Evaluation

Although the current implementation was not built for performance, we measured the cost of migrating a null agent (5-KB zip-compressed) and an annotation agent (1.2-MB, zip-compressed) from a source host to a destination host that was recommended by the CDSs. The latency of discovering and instructing an agent attached to a tag after the CDS had detected the presence of the tag was 320 ms and the respective cost of migrating the null and annotation agents between two hosts over a TCP connection was 32 ms and 380 ms. This evaluation was performed using three computers (Intel Core 7i-2.4 GHz with Windows 10 and Java version 8) connected via a Giga-Ethernet. This cost is reasonable for migrating agents between computers to follow visitors moving between exhibits.

We ran the experiment over two weeks. Each day, more than 60 individuals or groups took part in the experiment. Most of the participants were groups of families or friends aged from seven to 16. Most visitors answered questionnaires about their answers to the quizzes and their feedback on the system in addition to their gender and age. Almost all participants (more than 95%) provided positive feedback on the system. Typical feedback included "We were very interested in or enjoyed the system", "We could easily answer the quizzes by moving between the spots", and "We gained detailed knowledge about the animals by watching them in front of where we were standing." Most visitors only paid attention to the colors of the agents, instead of the characters and visual effects. They appeared to be more interested in watching the animal specimens than the visual effects e.g., animations of the agents.

5.2 Discussion

The above experiment provided us with several insights, as discussed in the following subsection.

Effect to Education. Many researchers have evaluated context-aware services, most focused on services themselves rather than their utility or effectiveness in terms of users achieving their own goals. The main purpose of context-aware services is to assist with user activities. Context-aware services can be thought of as methods rather than goals. In fact, one goal of science museums is to provide visitors with experiences that will enhance their knowledge of science through the exhibitions themselves, not devices. Several existing projects have used context-aware visual agents, e.g., characters or avatars, on terminals to attract the interest of children. Therefore, such services should play as an *extra* roles rather than a leading one. The problem is that visitors tend to focus their attention on the visual agents rather than the exhibits. Our solution is to simply use context-awareness and agents as extras rather than in leading roles. When we initially designed our context-aware services, our focus was enabling visitors to enjoy exhibitions. At first we provided animations with visual agents but later in the experiment, we abandoned the animations because some of the visitors tended to focus their attentions on the visual agents at the expense of the exhibits. Our early experiment enabled visitors to interact with their agents, but interactive services often tend to lower the extent of the learning experiences in the museum because visitors are too preoccupied with interactions.

Awareness of Context-Aware Services. Most other projects' experiments on context-aware services explicitly or implicitly assume that users know where, when, who, what, and how to receive the services. However, actually users often fail to recognize their context-aware services. In fact, most visitors at our early experiment in the museum missed the locations where they were provided with location-aware services because they did not know where they could receive them. They also wandered around the exhibition room and haphazardly entered enter certain places where they could receive the services. In short, it was difficult for them to know where, when, who, what, and how context-aware services were provided, because context-aware services e.g., location-aware, time-aware and and user-aware, were only provided when the current contexts e.g., locations, times, and user satisfied the conditions of the services. To notify visitors of the spots where context-aware services are provided, we designed a simple solution after several attempts: we placed visual markers on the floor in front of these places. Figure 6 shows the two kinds of markers we used: a printing sheet and a quoits. All visitors were able to place after these markers were set up.

a)   b)   c)

Fig. 6. (a) and (b) Markers on location-aware services and (c) two or more visitors at a spot

Sensing Errors. In the experiment, we deployed, installed, and configured the entire system, including location-sensing systems and servers within one day, the day the museum was closed without conducting any preparatory experiments in the exhibition room. Existing location-sensing systems are not perfect in the sense that errors in measurement are essentially unavoidable. The ranges and rates of measurement errors tend to depend on the location-sensing systems. There are two typical errors. The first is to miss a tag attached to a visitor. This results in the visitor standing in front of a display and not receiving any services. The second is to estimate the positions of tags a long distance from their real positions. Proximity-based systems, including active RFID tag systems, may occasionally lose the positions of tags but they seldom estimate incorrect positions. Therefore, we used a commerical active RFID tag system in the experiment instead of any lateration-based tracking systems.

Adaptation to Changes in the Requirements. Although the experiment lasted for just two weeks, exhibits were often replaced for the sake of the museum's convenience. Adaptation to such changes was needed. As application-specific services could be defined and encapsulated within the agents, we were able to easily change the services provided by modifying the corresponding agents while the entire system was running. More than two different visitor guide services could also be simultaneously supported for visitors. Even while visitors were participating, curators with no knowledge of context-aware systems were able to reconfigure the annotative content through drag-and-drop manipulations using the GUI-based configuration system. Most real spaces, including modern buildings, have not been designed to accommodate computers and sensors for context-aware services. For example, there may be no power lines or networks available.

The deployment of context-aware services needs to make existing spaces smart without losing any of the original utility of the spaces. There are unavoidable time limitations that come with the deployment and configuration of context-aware services in the real spaces. We had to deploy, install, and configure the entire system, including location-sensing systems and servers, by us within one day in the experiment i.e., a day the museum was closed without conducting any preparatory experiments in the exhibition room.

6   Related Work

There have been many attempts at agent-based or context-aware learning systems. Multiple agents have been widely used in educational environments. This technology can serve an aid to learning environments by making these environments more proactive and autonomous [2,11]. Context-awareness can make a significant difference in learning efficiency compared to traditional classroom-based learning because in context-aware learning environments, learning resources and activities are adapted to match the learner's current situation [4,5]. There have been many attempts to provide museum visitor guide systems. Most existing works e.g., the Electronic Guidebook, [3], Museum Project [1], Hippie system [8], ImogI [7], and Rememberer [3] have assumed that visitors carry portable devices. A few researchers have attempted approaches to support users from stationary sensors, actuators, and computers. For example, the PEACH project [9] developed a visitor guide system for use in museums and has evaluated it in a museum. Their system enables agents to migrate between computing devices [6] by displaying an image of an avatar or character corresponding to the agent on the remote computing devices; However the agents themselves cannot migrate to computing devices. Satoh proposed an agent-based education system [10], but the system intended to focused on their agent programming model for context-aware services.

7   Conclusion

We designed and implemented an agent-based system for providing context-aware visitor guide services in a public museum. When a visitor moves from exhibit to exhibit, his/her agent can be dynamically deployed at a computer close to the current exhibit and play annotations about the exhibit according to their knowledge, interest, and the exhibits that they have already seen the agent can also navigate him/her to exhibits along their route.

References

1. Ciavarella, C., Paterno, F.: The design of a handheld, location-aware guide for indoor environments. Pers. Ubiquit. Comput. 8(2), 82–91 (2004)
2. da Silva, L.C,N., Neto, F.M.M., Junior, L.J., de C. Muniz, R.: An agent-based approach for supporting ubiquitous learning. Int. J. Sci. Eng. Res. 2(9), 8–11 (2011)

3. Fleck, M., Frid, M., Kindberg, T., Rajani, R., O'BrienStrain, E., Spasojevic, M.: From informing to remembering: deploying a ubiquitous system in an interactive science museum. IEEE Pervasive Comput. **1**(2), 13–21 (2002)

4. Gomez, J.E., Huete, J., Hernandez, V.: A contextualized system for supporting active learning. IEEE Trans. Learn. Technol. **9**(2), 196–202 (2016)

5. Hsu, T., Chiou, C., Tseng, J.C.R., Hwang, G.: Development and evaluation of an active learning support system for context-aware ubiquitous learning. IEEE Trans. Learn. Technol. **9**(1), 37–45 (2016)

6. Kruppa, M., Krüger, A.: Performing physical object references with migrating virtual characters. In: Maybury, M., Stock, O., Wahlster, W. (eds.) INTETAIN 2005. LNCS (LNAI), vol. 3814, pp. 64–73. Springer, Heidelberg (2005). https://doi.org/10.1007/11590323_7

7. Luyten, K., Coninx, K.: ImogI: take control over a context-aware electronic mobile guide for museums. In: Workshop on HCI in Mobile Guides, in Conjunction with 6th International Conference on Human Computer Interaction with Mobile Devices and Services (2004)

8. Oppermann, R., Specht, M.: A context-sensitive nomadic exhibition guide. In: Thomas, P., Gellersen, H.-W. (eds.) HUC 2000. LNCS, vol. 1927, pp. 127–142. Springer, Heidelberg (2000). https://doi.org/10.1007/3-540-39959-3_10

9. Rocchi, C., Stock, O., Zancanaro, M., Kruppa, M., Kruger, A.: The museum visit: generating seamless personalized presentations on multiple devices. In: Proceedings of 9th International Conference on Intelligent User Interface, pp. 316–318. ACM Press (2004)

10. Satoh, I.: Design and implementation of context-aware musuem guide agents. IEICE Trans. **93**(D(4)), 789–799 (2010)

11. Yaghmaie, M., Bahreininejad, A.: A context-aware adaptive learning system using agents. Expert Syst. Appl. **38**, 3280–3286 (2011)

Describing Interfaces in the Framework of Adaptive Interface Ecosystems

Antonio J. Sánchez[1(✉)], Elena Hernández[2(✉)],
Fernando de la Prieta[2(✉)], Juan Manuel Corchado[2(✉)],
and Sara Rodríguez[2(✉)]

[1] Informatics and Automation Department, University of Salamanca,
Salamanca, Spain
anto@usal.es
[2] IoT Digital Innovation Hub, University of Salamanca, Salamanca, Spain
{elenahn, corchado, fer, srg}@usal.es

Abstract. Currently, we can find a large number of user interfaces made by developers who do not follow of current UX premises, i.e. they are not adapted. Normally this is due to financing problems and resources of software projects. In order to study, develop and reuse adaptive user interfaces in a fast and non-invasive way, a new method of interface description is proposed, which would provide to an external library with enough information to restructure the interface in accordance with the use and habits of the user. This way of defining the interfaces is directly linked to the use of Adaptive Interface Ecosystems (AIE), components that work at sight level and whose mechanics can be applied to interfaces independently of their physical nature. Following this methodology of description of the interface, the AIE will be able to carry out an adaptive design of the interface, with very low production and development costs.

Keywords: User experience · Context aware computing · Adaptive systems · Smart interfaces · Intelligent environments

1 Introduction

This research work deals with how to define interfaces and/or describe correctly those interfaces already defined, so that these can be applied Adaptive Interface Ecosystems (AIE). The AIEs are a group of components that work at the view level [1] and are integrated with components of an existing interface, taking on this some freedom of manipulation of the presentation properties. The architecture of the AIE, which will be briefly explained in Sect. 3, is valid both for graphical interfaces, as for interfaces of another nature, and although it has a calculation core that is independent of the type of interface it must implement a module specific to the language and/or the specific technology type with which the interface is programmed.

The final intention of correctly describing an interface is to be able to modify it automatically, applying changes that improve its accessibility in accordance with user usage patterns. The form of inclusion of AIE inside the code tries to be as less intrusive as possible in the programming/definition of the interface, for that reason the system of

© Springer Nature Switzerland AG 2019
P. Moura Oliveira et al. (Eds.): EPIA 2019, LNAI 11805, pp. 38–49, 2019.
https://doi.org/10.1007/978-3-030-30244-3_4

definition of the elements that compose the interface must be as complete as possible without invading the field of development of the functionality.

Throughout this article, we will analyse the usual problems that the interfaces have and what solutions would be obtained through improving the systems of description. The point 3 describes the structure and functioning of an AIE. Point 4 presents a method for describing interfaces. Point 5 presents the case study by applying the model to a Smart City data management platform called SPECTRA, and finally point 6 includes conclusions and results.

2   Defining Interfaces

At present we can find different ways of grouping the types of interfaces. The most common is grouping depending on the senses affected: visual, auditory, tactile, olfactory, gustatory and mixed [2] (as consequence of the rise of ubiquitous computing [3]). Today we find interfaces on many devices in any location and format. Within them, the visual component commonly predominates, although the auditory interfaces begin to have more importance today with the growing expansion of voice assistants. Some of the most used devices, smartphones or laptops, are a very clear example of mixed interface, although they are eminently visual, they also have audio and tactile interfaces (tactile it's not referring to the screen is touch, since the screen can be considered a peripheral; it's referring to the characteristic elements of the interface, such as the inclusion of gestures in the way of interacting with it, or notifications in the form of vibration).

A good definition of the concept of interface is provided by the Special Interest Group on Computer- Human Interaction (SIGCHI) of the Association of Computer Machinery (ACM) in [4]: "Human-Computer Interaction (HCI) is the design, evolution and implementation of interactive systems for human use and the study of the phenomenon that surrounds it. "

The nature of the interface explains the fact that some of the characteristic input/output elements can only exist for a certain type (for example, a window in the visual interfaces). However, basic structures that group similar elements can be found in most interfaces, regardless of their nature. These elements are: menus (set of elements, grouped and classified whose interaction triggers an action in the system), lists (set of elements, grouped and classified whose interaction does not cause an action in the system), forms (set of information entries), elements of action (isolated element that trigger one or more actions of the system), information inputs with a basic casting of type (for example, the entry of a date), information inputs of the selector type (selection of an option or several options among a set of offered options), screens or views (as a grouping of different types of elements), displays (visualizer of a specific data type, either simple or complex - formed by several types of data, can allow interaction to modify the type of data, its visualization or access specific data in a more detailed way). To the group of sensitive interfaces can be added the Brain-Computer Interfaces (BCI) [5], based on both the reception and the sending of information to the computer directly from the brain, without the need to reinterpret it through other organs. These interfaces were originally created for the adaptation of applications to people with severe motor disabilities, although their use is currently being extended to more areas (see [6]). The grouping of input/output elements in this type of interfaces does not apply since the brain impulses are interpreted directly with the electronic system that is responsible for capturing them. There are also cases in which the instrument that collects the brain impulses is not an interface itself (as for example in [7]), but only translates the impulses to input events of other types of interfaces (for example, the control of a mouse pointer thanks to brain activity). For these cases the basic elements exposed previously above are equally valid. The versatility in the implementation of interfaces in different formats leads us to reconsider the usability and interface construction patterns (see [8]) that are currently applied, and consider whether they can be established in a global way. Today the problems that the methodologies to develop interfaces have to solve, see the studies of [26] and [27], are the following:

- Use of erroneously ordered menu options and a confusing separation, inappropriate terminology or iconography that does not conform to the expected meaning.
- Inconsistent and inappropriate use of colours, sounds, icons, and other multimedia content that does not fit the user's cognition.
- Text illegibility due to appearance or incorrect content. Lack of the adaptation of the interface to the tastes of the user and absence of an assistance system.
- Waste of computational resources.

Most of the methodologies most used in the development of interfaces, such as [9, 10] or [11], are based on the resolution of graphic user interface (GUI) problems. Bentley (in [9]), for example, presents a fourteen-step guide for interfaces in SAS (Statistical Analysis System), whose implementation is carried out by a design team in which the end user can participate. The steps in this guide, which are carried out iteratively, are: the analysis of activities and users, interface design, selection of interface components, prototyping and evaluation of results.

The example of the Bentley methodology is one among the many examples of iterative methodologies that derive from the development cycles proposed by the RUP (Rational Unified Process, [12]) or the DSDM (Dynamic Systems Development Method, [13]) where usability revolves around the design of interfaces, user archetype (see [14]), and critic reviews to identify the needs and skills of this.

In other cases, as in TERESA (Transformation Environment for InteRactivE Systems representaAtions), a semiautomatic design is chosen from task models created using the ConcurTaskTrees (CTT) notation defined in [15] and [16]. CTT is a notation based on the LOTOS language for the analysis and generation of user interfaces from task models.

The semiautomatic design added to the increase of machine learning processes (see [17]) when configuring the interfaces or the harvest of environmental data using sensors (in [18]) are the most significant advances to date. The collecting and treatment of user experiences, both positive and negative [19], are taken into account when planning the interface. It seems assumed that without the necessary resources (as multidisciplinary teams) it is impossible to come up with the exact interface design for non-homogeneous groups of users and that user experiences vary greatly depending on each archetype. For this reason, in [19] it points as fundamental actions, the harvest and analysis of the parametrizable elements of the user behaviour patterns to build intuitive and effective interfaces. To this, as has been added previously, we must add the ubiquity of the interfaces, so the procedure for describing becomes a critical point for analysing and modifying them.

3   The Adaptive Interface Ecosystems

An IEA is a mechanism to solve usability problems, interface design and user experience (UX) to existing interfaces. The advantage of the use of AIE over already elaborated and functioning interfaces is that it is not necessary to redesign or re-implement the interface, but rather it will be adjusted (adapting over time) to each user's own way of using and monitoring it. Therefore, it is ideal for the application of small projects that do not have many resources.

At no time should the AIE modify the functionality of the application to which they are added, they should only change the presentation of the interface components, but not the data or the way they are represented. The functioning of the IEA is very similar to that of a network of neurons, since it has a learning process in which each element of the interface calculates its specific weight (which in the case of the AIE is called pregnancy) and once the training is completed, it adapts its physical form to its relative importance for the user (the following sample system, despite being very incomplete, can be very easy to understand: in an interface with two buttons, a button that is not used will end up being more than small than the other one who uses a lot more). For an AIE, the interfaces are divided into subsystems or Environments and these in turn in other subsystems or Sub-environments or in Environment Elements, regardless of the exact type of elements that make up the interface; that is, for an AIE both a menu item and a list item will be Environment Element, while a list or a menu will be considered Environments. The norm that governs the dynamics is the following: all items within an Environment, whether Element or Sub-environment will compete with its sister elements for the pregnancy.

The learning process of an EIA is measured in cycles, and to calculate its specific weight, i.e. its pregnancy, the number and type of user interactions (since these may or may not have been satisfactory [19]) are measured over element and over the environment to which it belongs. The calculation of the pregnancy is governed by the following equation:

$$\Delta P_i = v_m \cdot \tau \left(\frac{n_i}{n_{ambient}}, \frac{t_i}{t_{ambient}} \right) \xi(i, m_{ambient}) \quad \text{where:} \tag{1}$$

i = system cycle.

ΔP_i = Pregnancy variation for the element in an i-cycle.

n_i = number of successful user interactions (may be negative) in i-cycle.

$n_{ambient}$ = number of successful user interactions into the environment of the element in i-cycle (may be negative)

t_i = the number of cycles of the element.

v_m = learning speed.

τ = Pregnancy calculation function.

ξ = Maturation or stop function. Determines when the system is sufficiently trained.

$m_{ambient}$ = degree of maturation of the environment.

$t_{ambient}$ = number of cycles of the environment that contains the element.

It is urgent to clarify that the elements of the display interface (see Sect. 2), despite allowing interaction with the user, are as black boxes for the AIE, they do not inspect or govern its interface. If the functionality of a display is very large or its behavior is very complex, it should be a goal of the programmer to granulize it and divide its functions into views or screens, in order to make them more accessible and describable.

Finally, to determine all the elements of the interface that intervene in an AIE, the unused presentation resources must be added. These resources are linked directly to the nature of the interface, and are for example the space available within a window or the time for the reproduction of a usable sound. Each element of an AIE has the following characteristics:

- **Interactions**. Each event, in which the user provides some type of information to the system, either directly or indirectly, is an interaction. In such a way that a domain model similar to that of [20] can be used to store the information.
- **Memory**. Each component must evolve over time, this implies that it must be aware of its status and note if the mutations produced have positive or negative consequences.
- **Communication**. Each component must be able to communicate with the other components, since the measures it takes on its own response capacity are meaningless if it can't establish a scale. For example, a button could not determine if one-click over it is more or less, without knowing if the user makes also clicks over on the rest of the components.
- **Limits**. Somehow each component must know in what ranges it should be able to be modified (we do not want a text box to flood the whole screen or that a link on privacy policy disappears from a website because no one accesses its content). The fact that the elements of the interface mutate freely can come into conflict with aesthetic considerations (aesthetics in their widest range, not only visual that is the most commonly treated). Therefore, the establishment of the available resources of an EIA does not have to be that of the total system (the designer of the interface must determine this). The limits of growth and decrease of the elements of the system must be established by the designer or the developer of the interface of the system, in such a way that the aesthetic aspect is not affected or invades the space of other functionalities of the system to which an AIE is not applied.

From the point of view of the description of an interface, in addition to unused resources, only the interactions and the limits of the elements are important, since memory and communication are internal mechanisms of an IEA.

4   Describing Interfaces

Currently one of the most commonly used interface creation systems is the definition of these using a mark-up language, as HTML, JSX, n-templates (for web pages) or XML (for Java applications for Android and iOS Storyboards). Many development environments (IDE) are also incorporating the XML standard to define interfaces for Rich Client Application in desktop environments regardless of the development language. The versatility of the XML descriptors is very useful when working with an AIE, since it is a fantastic support on which to add information to the interface, without the need to create another scheme and ensuring the use of a standard.

Not all the elements of an interface will must be important inside an AIE, there will be elements whose representation has been determined untouchable for different reasons (such as for example an advertising banner, or a legal alert), even though it lacks relevance for the user. As mentioned in Sect. 2, an AIE only needs to know the form of interaction with the user of the interface elements and if there are limits to recomposing it every time the interface is reconstructed according to the preferences of the user. It is understood that since the AIE programming library have access to the representation properties of the elements, they must not be necessarily exposed and can be defined separately, for example, in a style guide.

XML and its derivatives allow the definition of both new tags to describe elements, and new tags for properties (within HTML, from version 4.0, for example, there is a formalization called data- * attributes that allows to any user who use the language include any attribute he want as long as you follow the nomenclature data-{attribute-name} [21]). If within an XML document (from version 1.0) a Document Type Definition (DTD) is referenced, then the use of own attributes can be made much more tailored. The attributes defined for an AIE are the following (Table 1):

Table 1. Description attributes of AIE elements

Property	Description
aie-name="**Unique_identifier**"	Identify that this interface element is interesting for an AIE. The fact of identifying with a name to the element will help later to check the evolutions of the system and the debugging of the same
aie-prestance-fields="**propterty|extra**" **Extras max:MAX_VALUE | min:MIN_VALUE** Example: aie-prestance-fields = "volume|min:0.5"	This field refers to the limits of the elements mentioned in Sect. 2. It identifies name of the properties and maximum and minimum values that can be reached. PROPERTY is a string and MAX_VALUE and MIN_VALUE are decimal numbers. The valid identifiers of PROPERTY will depend on the environment and the implementation of the AIE, although they will generally refer to style name of the style sheets of the languages used to style the interface
aie-trigger="**Event_name**" Example: aie-trigger="click"	It identifies the name of the events that indicates the interactions that must be collected for the calculation of performance. Like the properties, they will depend on the environment and the implementation of the AIE

It is very important that all the elements that are of interest for an AIE are correctly defined, with their properties and their events (it does not matter if they are not initially shown to the user). If new elements were added to the interface dynamically, the system would have to be rebooted (this possibility exists and is valid, the values of the elements on the screen persist, but it must be taken into account that this requires extra processing).

The properties aie-trigger and aie-prestance-fields are not obligatory, but it must be considered that not specified them will provoke some interface changes not being made. The fact of not specifying them can also suppose that the element that is being referenced is sub-ambient, and therefore only a container.

The structure in the form of a tree that has an XML will be replicated into an AIE, but that it will not be the same because there will be branches of the XML that can disappear (those that contains elements that have no meaning for the AIE). By agreement, each AIE element of the tree that contains within another element will be an environment.

In the example shown below, made in HTML code, we see how to define an environment formed by an element and a sub-environment that in turn contains two elements. As can be seen, the labelling for an AIE allows coexisting perfectly with the labelling for the browser, by defining itself through attributes that do not conflict with the standards. It simply includes extra information that is not necessarily indicated in the HTML code, such as the collection of events, and also allows maintaining the original semantic value of the object within the system, since the properties are defined for any type of element.

```
<ul aie-name="menu" aie-prestance-fields="font-size, position, level">
    <li><label aie-name="item_1" aie-trigger="click">Menu Option 1</label></li>
    <li><label aie-name="item_2" aie-trigger="mouseover">Menu Option 2</label>
        <ul aie-name="submenu_1" aie-prestance-fields="position">
            <li><label aie-name="item_2_1" aie-trigger="click">Option 1</label></li>
```

The case is more or less the same for XML for mobile devices, the syntax is a bit different but equally simple to interpret:

```
<menu aie:id="menu" aie:fields="font-size, position, level"
    xmlns:android="http://schemas.android.com/apk/res/android">
    <item android:id="@+id/menu_save" aie:id="menuItem1" aie:trigger="mouseOver"
        android:icon="@drawable/menu_save" android:title="@string/menu_save" />
    <group aie:fields="font-size, position" aie:id="menuItem2" aie:trigger="click"
        android:id="@+id/group_delete">< . . . />
```

5   Case Study

In the case of the study, we will see how to describe, using the HTML attributes, a screen of the web application, the SPECTRA platform. SPECTRA (Smart PErsonal Co2-free TRAnsport, Reference: IDI-20150664), is a platform co-financed by the CDTI and the European Regional Development Fund (ERDF) and developed by a consortium made up of eight companies and supported by other ten organizations, including the University of Salamanca, whose main objective is to achieve an improvement in urban mobility by reducing congestion and the impact on the environment (Fig. 1).

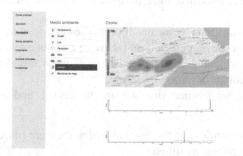

Fig. 1. Screen with information about ozone in the atmosphere (SPECTRA platform)

In the analyzed screen is shown the ozone information in the atmosphere of Santander. To access to this view the user use a two levels menu (in the left). On the screen we can find two two-dimensional graphics and an interactive map.

A textual description of the elements of the page could be the following:

- The elements of the second level menu appear clicking on the first level menu elements.
- The map element is a **display** type. The user can click on it or drag and move the mouse pointer over it.
- The graphics are also displays. The user can click on them or move the mouse pointer over any of its elements to get more information about its values.

The screen is therefore divided into two environments, one dedicated to the menu and another to the content. In turn, the menu will have an element and a sub-environment for each item of the menu, which in turn will contain an element for each item of the submenu (see Fig. 2):

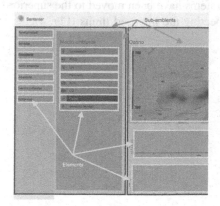
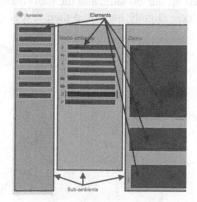

Fig. 2. Environments distribution   **Fig. 3.** Alternative environments distribution

There is a different possibility to describe the page. If we consider that each of the three regions were watertight (it does not matter right now why, there may be technical or legislative reasons in this regard), that is to say that the elements disposed within them could not be freely relocated, the environments distribution could be different (see Fig. 3).

The establishment of limits by means of properties provides many variants, the fact that the specification of the properties is an inclusive and not exclusive procedure (only those that are going to change are indicated) provides a more strict control of the changes that may occur in the interface.

For the example, we assume that we are in case 1 and apply the following limitations:

- The menu items, regardless of the level at which they are placed, can be relocated and their size and colour modified.
- The graphics and maps will also be granted the permits for relocation and modification of their size depending on the use.
- Due to design issues, in no case may the size of any element's sources exceed 200% of its original size.

Arranged the elements and defined the limits that take part in the AIE, the original code of page would have to modify of the following form (the changes are marked in bold text):

```
<div aie-name="spectra_page" aie-prestance-fields="position">
   <div aie-name="menu" aie-prestance-fields="position, font-size|max:2, color" > . . .
      <div class="menu_item" aie-name="menu_4" aie-trigger="click" >
         <label lass="menu_text">Medio ambiente</label>
         <div class="submenu_content" aie-name="submenu_items" aie-prestance-fields="position">
            <label class="submenu_item" aie-name="submenu_1" aie-trigger="click">Temp.</label>
```

After the data collection, once the mutations are applied to the interface, it can be observed how the elements with which the user interacts most frequently have been placed on the left side, and the most used menu items have been moved to the superior and have slightly increased their text size, respecting the imposed limits (Fig. 4).

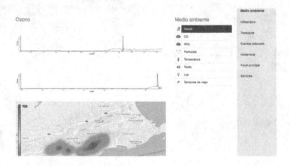

Fig. 4. Final distribution of interfaces element

With the definition of the elements of an AIE in a mark-up file, the initial intention to be as less intrusive as possible in the programming/definition of the interface is solved. In addition, the specification of interface elements in this way also complies with their possibility of use in interface formats that go beyond the graphic representation: for this is only necessary use templates or marking systems to define the elements.

In an aural interface, for example, it would be very simple to define and interpret a template for a menu of options or a form. All types of interfaces (see [2] and [3]) support a definition of elements sequentially and labelled, it only depends on the implementation and the interface definition language, in fact, the latest trends and design patterns [22] they go in this sense using similar languages to XML.

6 Conclusions

The use of a marking system, as we have seen in the previous section, is very beneficial in terms of impact on development, the time that is invested in terms of time and resources is minimal, and at the same time allows the user to have interfaces much more adapted to their use. We can find other systems, libraries or programming methodologies that can reach proportional similar results such as TRIDEN -based on an enriched E/R model and Activity Chaining Graphs (ACG), see [23], PMT -a group of procedural modelling tools-, see [24], or AOP -a machine learning system applied to a collection of environmental data-, see [25].

The main advantage of using a marking system together with the AIE compared to the use of the previous methods, besides the incidence on the development is minimal, is AIE solves a large part of the UX problems seen in Sect. 2(Table 2):

Table 2. Resolution of UI problems according to the methodology

Problems	TRIDEN	PMT	AOP	AIE
Confusing menu options and terminology	No	✓	No	Partial
Inconsistent and inappropriate use of symbols	No	✓	✓	Partial
Text illegibility	No	✓	No	✓
Assistance system	Partial	No	No	Partial
Waste of computational resources	No	No	✓	✓

In conclusion, it's is presented a new method of interface description that, with its application within the framework of the AIE, helps to restructure and create for adapted interfaces with a minimum investment in time and resources. One of the points to improve is the definition of the available resources of the system (for example, when the limits on the properties have not been specified), since the diversity of different execution environments, as well as the numerous of physical systems.

Acknowledgements. This work has been supported by "Virtual-Ledgers-Tecnologías DLT/ Blockchain y Cripto-IOT sobre organizaciones virtuales de agentes ligeros y su aplicación en la eficiencia en el transporte de última milla", ID SA267P18, project cofinanced by Junta Castilla y León, Consejería de Educación, and FEDER funds.

References

1. Krasner, G.E., Pope, S.T.: A description of the model-view-controller user interface paradigm in the smalltalk-80 system. J. Object-Orient. Prog. **1**(3) 26–49 (2000)
2. Krumm, J. (ed.): Ubiquitous Computing Fundamentals. Chapman and Hall/CRC, New York (2010). https://doi.org/10.1201/9781420093612
3. Poslad, S.: Ubiquitous computing: smart devices, environments and interactions. Wiley (2011). OCLC 964717717. (1 de enero de 2009), ISBN 9780470035603
4. Rusu, C., Rusu, V., Roncagliolo, S.: Usability practice: the appealing way to HCI. In: 1st International Conference on Advances in Computer Human Interaction, pp. 265–270 (2008)
5. Guger, C., Allison, B.Z., Müller-Putz, G.R.: Brain-computer interface research: a state-of-the-art summary 4. In: Guger, C., Müller-Putz, G., Allison, B. (eds.) Brain-Computer Interface Research. SECE, pp. 1–8. Springer, Cham (2015). https://doi.org/10.1007/978-3-319-25190-5_1
6. Sourin, A., Earnshaw, R., Gavrilova, M., Sourina, O.: Problems of human-computer interaction in cyberworlds. In: Gavrilova, Marina L., Tan, C.J.K., Sourin, A. (eds.) Transactions on Computational Science XXVIII. LNCS, vol. 9590, pp. 1–22. Springer, Heidelberg (2016). https://doi.org/10.1007/978-3-662-53090-0_1
7. Aoun, P., Berg, N.: Moving an on-screen cursor with the emotiv insight EEG headset: an evaluation through case studies (Dissertation) (2018). http://urn.kb.se/resolve?urn=urn:nbn:se:bth-16307
8. Cockton, G., Lavery, D., Woolrychn, A.: Inspection-based evaluations. In: Jacko, J.A., Sears, A. (eds.) The Human-Computer Interaction Handbook, 2nd edn. pp. 1171–1190, Lawrence Erlbaum Associates (2003). ISBN 0-8058-3838-4
9. Bentley, J.: 14 Steps to a Good GUI. In: SAS® Users Group International Conference (1999)
10. Piasecki, M., Piezka, K.: Conceptual methodology of developing the user interface, Institute of Applied Informatics, Wroc law University of Technology (2006)
11. Koch, N.: Software engineering for adaptive hypermedia systems: reference model, modelling techniques and development process. Ph.D. thesis, Ludwig-Maximilians-Universität Munchen (2001)
12. Jacobson, I., Booch, G., Rumbaugh, J.: The Unified Software Development Process (19991). ISBN 0-201-57169-2
13. Stapleton, J.: Business Focused Development. p. 113, Pearson Education, January 2003. ISBN 9780321112248
14. Junior, P.T.A., Filgueiras, L.V.: User modeling with personas. In: Proceedings of the 2005 Latin American Conference on Human-Computer Interaction (CLIHC 2005), pp. 277–282. ACM, New York (2005). https://doi.org/10.1145/1111360.1111388
15. Paternò, F.: Model-Based Design and Evaluation of Interactive Applications. Springer, Heidelberg (1999). https://doi.org/10.1007/978-1-4471-0445-2
16. Mori, G., Paternò, F., Santoro, C.: CTTE: support for developing and analyzing task models for interactive system design. IEEE Trans. Softw. Eng. **28**(8), 797–813 (2002)

17. Lauren, D., Arnaud, B., Paul, K., Hervé, G., Olivier, M.: Using machine learning algorithms to develop adaptive man–machine interfaces. In: Neuroergonomics - The Brain at Work and in Everyday Life, pp. 237–238. Academic Press (2018). Chapter 53. https://doi.org/10.1016/B978-0-12-811926-6.00053-1

18. Šebek, J., Trnka, M., Černý, T.: On aspect-oriented programming in adaptive user interfaces, pp. 1–5 (2015). https://doi.org/10.1109/icissec.2015.7371024

19. Kirisci, P.T., Thoben, K.D.: A method for designing physical user interfaces for intelligent production environments. Adv. Hum. Comput. Interact. **2018**(6487070), 21 (2018). https://doi.org/10.1155/2018/6487070

20. Feng, J., Liu, Y.: Intelligent context-aware and adaptive interface for mobile LBS. Comput. Intell. Neurosci. **2015**(489793), 10 (2015). https://doi.org/10.1155/2015/489793

21. Marsh, J.: XML Base, 2nd edn. REC, 28 January 2009. https://www.w3.org/TR/xmlbase/

22. Gullà, F., Cavalieri, L., Ceccacci, S., Germani, M., Bevilacqua, R.: Method to design adaptable and adaptive user interfaces. In: Stephanidis, C. (ed.) HCI 2015. CCIS, vol. 528, pp. 19–24. Springer, Cham (2015). https://doi.org/10.1007/978-3-319-21380-4_4

23. Bodart, F., Hennebert, A.M., Leheureux, J.M., Provot, I., Sacré, B., Vanderdonckt, J.: Towards a systematic building of software architecture: the TRIDENT methodological guide. In: Palanque, P., Bastide, R. (eds.) Design, Specification and Verification of Interactive Systems 1995 Eurographics, pp. 262–278. Springer, Vienna (1995). https://doi.org/10.1007/978-3-7091-9437-9_16

24. Kirisci, P.T., Thoben, K.-D.: A method for designing physical user interfaces for intelligent production environments. Adv. Hum. Comput. Interact. 1–21 (2018). https://doi.org/10.1155/2018/6487070

25. Sebek, J., Trnka, M., Cerny, T.: On aspect-oriented programming in adaptive user interfaces. In: 2015 2nd International Conference on Information Science and Security (ICISS), pp. 1–5 (2015). https://doi.org/10.1109/ICISSEC.2015.7371024

26. Carroll, J.M.: Human-computer interaction. Int. J. Hum Comput Stud. **46**(4), 501–522 (1997). https://doi.org/10.1006/ijhc.1996.0101

27. Zuffi, S., Brambilla, C., Beretta, G., Scala, P.L.: Human computer interaction: legibility and contrast. In: International Conference on Image Analysis and Processing, pp. 241–246 (2007). http://dx.doi.org/10.1109/ICIAP.2007.76

A Conceptual Approach to Enhance the Well-Being of Elderly People

Diogo Martinho[1]([⊠])(iD), João Carneiro[1](iD), Paulo Novais[2](iD),
José Neves[2](iD), Juan Corchado[3](iD), and Goreti Marreiros[1](iD)

[1] Research Group on Intelligent Engineering and Computing for Advanced
Innovation and Development (GECAD), Institute of Engineering,
Polytechnic of Porto, Porto, Portugal
{diepm,jomrc,mgt}@isep.ipp.pt
[2] ALGORITMI Centre, University of Minho, Guimarães, Portugal
{pjon,jneves}@di.uminho.pt
[3] BISITE Digital Innovation Hub, University of Salamanca,
Edificio Multiusos, Madrid, Spain
corchado@usal.es

Abstract. The number of elderly people living alone is increasing. Consequently, a lot of research works have been addressing this issue in order to propose solutions that can enhance the quality of life of elderly people. Most of them have been concerned in dealing with objective issues such as forgetfulness or detecting falls. In this paper, we propose a conceptual approach of a system that intends to enhance the daily sense of user's well-being. For that, our proposal consists in a system that works as a social network and a smartwatch application that works unobtrusively and collects the user's physiological data. In addition, we debate how important features such as to detect user's affective states and to potentiate user's memory could be implemented. Our study shows that there are still some important limitations which affect the success of applications built in the context of elderly care and which are mostly related with accuracy and usability of this kind of system. However, we believe that with our approach we will be able to address some of those limitations and define a system that can enhance the well-being of elderly people and improve their cognitive capabilities.

Keywords: Ambient assisted living · Cognitive assistant ·
Affective wearables · Affective computing · Gamification · Elderly care

1 Introduction

We are currently witnessing an increase of the elderly population around the world. According to the United Nations's World Population Ageing Report [1], the global population aged 60 years or older has registered a total of 962 million in 2017 and it is expected to reach 2 billion by 2050. With such an increase of the number of older citizens living in today's society it becomes necessary to research and develop assistive technologies that can support elderly people [2, 3] and encourage them to maintain independence [4]. It no longer makes sense to just rely on traditional healthcare

© Springer Nature Switzerland AG 2019
P. Moura Oliveira et al. (Eds.): EPIA 2019, LNAI 11805, pp. 50–61, 2019.
https://doi.org/10.1007/978-3-030-30244-3_5

services to assist elderly people (such as adult day cares, or nursing homes) which are expensive and unfordable by many, and that cannot accurately assess the current health condition of the elderly (both physical and cognitive). Therefore, physical environments enhanced by innovative technologies should become the new trend in the context of elderly care to promote active ageing. These physical environments also known as smart homes [4–6] comprise a set of technologies including telecare devices [7], persuasive technologies [8], rehabilitation systems [9] and digital games [10–13].

In this work, we propose a conceptual approach to enhance the well-being of elderly people. Our approach differs from most existent approaches because it concerns in potentiating the elders' sense of well-being through activities that control their levels of stress, anxiety and cognitive capabilities, rather than focusing in most traditional tasks such as detecting falls, scheduling meds, among others. We propose (conceptually) a social network specific for elderly people, where they can interact naturally with their family members and other elders and a smartwatch application that controls the physiological signals and work together with the system (social network) to study the effect of different interactions on the person. Furthermore, an overview of the current state of the literature regarding different topics relevant to the context of this work is also presented so that we can understand existing knowledge that allows us to develop the proposed approach and also allows us to understand what kind of main limitations and challenges should be overcome.

The rest of the paper is organized in the following order: in the next Section we present the related work. In Sect. 3 we described the proposed conceptual approach, mostly in terms of architecture, features and devices. Finally, some conclusions are put forward in Sect. 4, alongside with suggestions of work to be done hereafter.

2 Related Work

In this work we explored some of the most recent approaches under the topics of cognitive assistants, affective wearables and gamification applied to healthcare with focus on elderly care. We believe these three areas of artificial intelligence are essential to define a personalized approach to correctly support elderly people and motivate them to pursue healthier lifestyle habits. For this, cognitive assistants can provide tools and features to help people perform activities of daily living [14]. Furthermore, these assistants will interact directly with the user using different mechanisms such as affective wearables to collect physiological data and correctly assess user's affective states and gamification to motivate the user to perform different activities and improve health condition.

2.1 Cognitive Assistants

The development and research of solutions using cognitive assistants has seen great advances in the literature over the last decade. Cognitive assistants can be endowed with social and emotional processing [15, 16] to interact with humans and improve their capabilities while not replacing them in specific tasks. In other words, cognitive assistants will augment human intelligence and assist in decision-making and action taking [17]. As such, in the last years there have been proposed very interesting approaches targeted towards elderly care with the goal to enhance their daily lives and improve both their cognitive and physical capabilities. Costa et al. [18] proposed an interactive physical robot system to recommend and monitor physical exercises designed for the elderly people. The system is divided in three main components: a physical robot which interacts with the elderly person and records the performance of different exercises.; a human exercise recognition system which uses deep learning techniques to identify different gestures associated to each exercise; and a recommendation system which suggests and adapts physical activities according to the capabilities and current health condition of the elderly person. The authors were able to validate the developed system in terms of exercise variance and personalization; however, they still recognized some limitations mainly related with the accuracy of their exercise recognition algorithm and the lack or robot gestures mimicking the exerciser. Kostavelis et al. [19] proposed a service robot system to operate in domestic environments and support elderly people and people with mild cognitive impairments. For this, the developed robot included a set of mechanisms to observe and perceive the environment, track different activities and assess cognitive and physical capabilities. The authors presented the architecture of the developed system under both hardware and software point of view and highlighted how the developed system should discreetly assist the user in daily activities and allow to retain both autonomy and decision-making. Furthermore, the authors also concluded that the developed system should never replace the caregiver but act as a complementary to the work of the caregivers instead. Ramos et al. [14] proposed a system using a smartphone and augmented reality to guide people with mild or moderate cognitive disabilities according to their preferences and offers an application that allows the caregiver to locate the disabled person. The developed system also considered ethical questions since it collects and ciphers sensitive data and assumes the disabled person has given his/her consent to provide all the information necessary for the system to operate correctly. The authors were not able to test and validate the proposed system in real case scenarios and they expressed it would be necessary to select people with cognitive impairments for further system testing and evaluation as the only tests performed in this study used people without any cognitive disabilities. Nguyen-Thinh and Laura [20] proposed a cognitive assistant to improve the reasoning and decision-making ability of users by teaching the user different topics while holding a conversation with them using natural language processing and a dialog model. The authors performed a study to validate the developed model with 65 participants and obtained positive feedback regarding the interaction with the system, however the authors expressed a larger sample as well as a larger testing timespan would be necessary to further validate the results of the presented study. The robot developed in [21] promotes social interaction between elderly people while performing different functions such as: monitoring and recognizing facial expressions which translate to different emotions and adapting the interaction with each elderly person; playing different games with elderly people so they keep interested to interact with the robot; personalizing care with flexible communication features like speech recognition and voice vocalization; promoting mental activity while running a set of short or long quizzes which depend on the alertness and medical condition of the elderly person. A field trial was performed with seventy residents of residential homes over a three-day period and the authors obtained positive results regarding engagement, acceptability, personalization and facilitation of healthier eating and living. In [22], three robots were developed for a preventive care system which are able to interact and compete against each other during a match up game based on a traditional Japanese game. The system adapts the exercise load according to the feedback provided by the user (the user reports the fatigue level in a questionnaire presented in a tablet device). The authors performed three experiments to test their system and the result showed that elderly people preferred to play the game rather than watch others playing it. However, the developed system only provided accurate exercise loads for 70% of the participants. Furthermore, the authors also expressed it would be relevant to extend the game settings and test the developed system with multiple players at the same time.

2.2 Affective Wearables: Detection of Emotions, Stress and Anxiety

The affective wearables consist in systems composed by sensors and tools to recognize its wearer's affective patterns such as friendly gesture, a strange voice, expression of emotions or a change in autonomic nervous system activity (such as heart rate or skin conductivity) [23]. The data collected by affective wearables can then be used to help wearers, improving their quality of life or prevent the occurrence of negative events. Since affective wearables are usually in contact with the user during a considerable time period and may take the form of clothes, jewelry, watches, among others [24, 25], these have less constraints than other traditional devices such a keyboard or a mouse. This ability to recognize physical and psychological patterns allows to develop intelligent systems capable of adapting to the needs of each user [26–29]. One of the current greatest challenges in the development of affective wearables consists in turning a system capable of recognizing different affective patterns. If on the one hand the affective wearables allow to collect important data, on the other hand it is hard to create "rules" to determine which responses occur with which emotions, as different individuals can feel different emotions and demonstrate different behaviors in the same situation. Several authors have been addressed this problematic in the recent years. Yang and Samuel [30] proposed a method to detect user's emotions based on the user's voice. Their approach consists in detecting the user's voice using the smartphone's microphone and consequently use a liner machine learning algorithm to train the system and to predict the emotions. They method allows to predict happy and sad emotions with an accuracy of 71% Dai, Liu and Meng [31] proposed an approach that intends to understand the user's emotional state according to the usage of smartphone. They used the finger-stroke pattern to predict the user's emotional state (positive, neutral, and negative). A machine learning classification algorithm to train the classifier was used and the results showed an accuracy of 72,3%, 74,6% and 69% for male, female and all subjects. Hänsel, Alomainy and Haddadi [32] presented a smartphone/smartwatch application that allows users to indicate the affective state they are feeling. They use the data collected from the smartphone and smartwatch such as current location, heart rate, prior physical activity (steps and workouts), ambient noise and wrist movements to correlate with the reported affective states. No results were reported but the authors intend to evaluate the application and to study if the collected data can be used to infer emotional and affective states. Ciabattoni, Ferracuti, Longhi,

Pepa, Romeo and Verdini [33] proposed an approach to detect mental stress in real-time. They used a smartwatch to collect bio signal data (heart rate, galvanic skin response and body temperature). They chose a smartwatch because they intended to detect the stress through an unobtrusively and inexpensive way. The Mutual Information (M.I.) was used to measure the dependence between variables and the features with the highest M.I. were selected to train a K-NN classifier. The results obtained indicated an accuracy of 84,5% and a misclassification error of 26% when subject is relaxed. There are also some other works where the authors use similar strategies and that present similar results, such as the one proposed by Quiroz, Geangu and Yong [34] (median accuracies higher than 78%) and the one proposed by Zhang, Song, Cui, Liu and Zhu [35] (with an accuracy that ranged from 60% to 91,3%).

2.3 Gamification

The use of games and game design elements in nongame contexts is being applied to different areas and application fields such as healthcare, digital marketing, finances, education, productivity, sustainability or even news [36, 37]. Two concepts have emerged in the literature also known as serious games and gamification. Serious games can be described as games "designed to entertain players as they educate, train, or change behavior" [38], while gamification refers to the enhancement of services with features that can offer "gameful" experiences to its and motivate and engage them in the pursuit of different activities, social interaction, and to increase the quality and productivity of their actions [39]. Recent research and advancements on gamification and serious games have been made in healthcare, and more particularly, in elderly care. Gamification and serious games are now being study as a way to motivate and persuade elderly people to undertake both physical, cognitive and social activities, thus contributing to their overall wellbeing and to motivate elderly people to pursuit more active and healthy lifestyles [11, 40, 41]. In [42] it is presented a smartwatch application to monitor and support people suffering from obesity and to motivate them to follow diet programs. The authors refer to the fact that our current lifestyle habits such as sedentary behaviors and poor diets contribute to chronic illness and to experience long-term limitations such as obesity until death. The authors claim that these issues cannot be simply managed through a set of measurements on patient health state nor through a set of treatments, but instead require day-to-day planning and adherence to new and healthier behaviors for best health outcomes in a long-term. They explain how personalized diet programs should be presented to the patient using checklists providing specific set of activities and performance goals that are embedded in daily life activities. The authors finally express that their approach will allow to document patient past successful experiences and increase their self-efficacy and contribute to healthier lifestyle changes and long-term health outcomes. In [43] it is performed a study to evaluate the efficacy of a smartwatch intervention in home-based dementia care. The authors explain how current home-based care models that monitor patients and report the progression of their physical and cognitive degeneration depend on health operators visits and these visits are scheduled based on passage of time and not based on the cognitive and physical current condition of the patient [44].To overcome this issue, the authors then explain how smartwatches could be used to monitor physical health aspects of dementia patients in a home-based care scenario and provide physicians with relevant information regarding events or activities experienced by the patient which cannot be recollected or re-experienced during a home visit. In [25], the authors discuss how gamification elements may improve user behavior and health condition using wearable self-tracking devices (such as smartphones or smartwatches). However, the authors explain that it is currently not know how users of these kind of devices accurately perceive their motivations being fulfilled nor how the use of gamification can raise motivation and device usage. To study these issues the authors developed a conceptual model where they investigated the influence of motivational factors by combining two research models developed by Gimpel et al. [45] and by Baumgart and Wiewiorra [24] with the integration of gamification elements and explained the many different advantages of using gamification elements in this kind of devices (to enhance user experience, ensure user engagement and to contribute to long-term adherence). The authors still alert to some of the negative aspects of using gamification elements in self-tracking devices (elements such as rewards and social comparison might contribute to decreasing autonomy and intrinsic motivation). Finally, the authors conclude that the usage of gamification elements should not be mandatory and should be up to each user instead.

3 Proposed (Conceptual) Approach

This work distinguished essentially by the way how the problematic of elderly care is addressed. Rather than idealize the system in terms of a model capable of detecting falls or scheduling meds, our focus is to increase the sense of well-being in cognitive and affective terms. Obviously, this topic is neither more nor less important than others, but it is a less traditional topic in this context.

This approach was planned with three main concerns in mind: scalability, unobtrusively and affordable. The cheapest way to use the system is using an internet connection, a smartwatch and a desktop/laptop/smartphone/tablet. So, this baseline version consists in an internet connection and two devices. The smartwatch works in the user's perspective as any regular watch in order to respect our concern in maintain the system unobtrusive. The system's smartwatch application collects physiological data of the elderly person (such as heart rate, body temperature, etc.) through embedded sensors, and sends this information plus other relevant data (such as the date and time when a certain physiological data was collected) to an online server to be processed. After this, the system may send a response (if necessary) to the user through the tablet application to recommend different cognitive activities (these activities are detailed in the Features section of this work). The most expensive way to use the system would be through several sensors and tablets installed through the elder person's home and detecting and collecting additional data (user location, fall detection, user actions such as cooking or sleeping or bathing) and providing more personalized interactions (for example, having a tablet installed in the bathroom and using a visual reminder with a photo of a family member to remind the elderly person to brush teeth and take medication).

3.1   Architecture

In this section we present the architecture for the system proposed in this work.

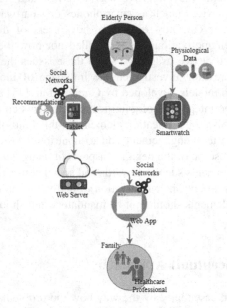

Fig. 1. Proposed system architecture

As can be seen in Fig. 1, the main user of the system is the elderly person which interacts directly with the smartwatch and tablet. Regarding the interaction with the smartwatch, the relation is unidirectional as the elderly person will provide physiological data which is captured by the smartwatch embedded sensors. With this flow we can assure an unobtrusive collection of data without user explicit interference. All the information acquired by the smartwatch along with other relevant information that can be measured and acquired using the smartwatch is sent to the table device. The tablet receives all the acquired data from the smartwatch as well as any kind of user direct input while using the application. This data is then sent to the web server to be processed in order to generate specific recommendations/suggestions regarding different activities that can be performed by the elderly person. The application also includes a web component that can be accessed remotely by family members or healthcare professionals to check and assess the current health condition of the elderly person as well as to exchange messages, images, videos, or even recommendations and suggestions on more activities to be performed by the elderly person. We consider that the proposed system will offer a set of intelligent features that will allow to establish a more intelligent and personalized interaction with the elderly person based on his health condition, capabilities, preferences, interests and affective state. Technologies considered for the proposed architecture include but are not limited to: (1) the use of

Xamarin[1] which allows smartwatch app development; (2) the use of Drools Business Rule Management System[2] as inference based rules engine which allows for simplified understanding of coding, flexibility, reusability, centralized knowledge, scalability among other benefits. In terms of devices, the only requirement considered is the capability of collecting physiological data and there already several solutions available in the market such as Xiaomi Smart Band[3] and Samsung Galaxy Fit[4] as more affordable options and Sony SmartWatch[5] and Apple Watch[6] as more expensive options.

3.2   Features

In our approach we present three main features which represent the novelty of work and which allow to develop a fully personalized system that can correctly interact with the elderly person and motivate to be healthier and at the same time improve cognitive capabilities. These features are as follows:

To Learn User's Preferences and Potentiate His/Her Fun. Besides including different features available in the most known social networks available online (such as exchanging messages, comments, likes and dislikes, among others), we propose a social network adapted to the context of elderly care whose information provided to the user must follow his preferences, interests and necessities. Moreover, it must understand the impact associated with each provided information as to understand if the user perceived that information as a positive or negative event. For this, in our approach we consider different physiological data that will be acquired while the elderly person is interacting with the social network and then processed using big data and different machine learning algorithms. After that, we can define the profile of the elderly person and identify and predict possible interests and preferences and this way personalize the social network accordingly. As a result, the elderly person will feel interested and motivated to use the social network, and ultimately be entertained while doing so.

To Evaluate the Current User's Cognitive Capabilities and to Work on Strategies That can Help Him/Her Stimulate His/Her Memory. With this feature, we intend to evaluate and measure the cognitive state of the elderly person as well as the cognitive degradation overtime. For this, we consider the use of gamification techniques to assess the memory of the elderly person such as to suggest effective recommendations and activities to stimulate his/her cognitive capabilities and to understand if the elderly person had improved or worsen his/her ability to perform the same activity overtime. These activities are presented to the elderly person using different game structures (such as quizzes, puzzles, associations, etc.) and the elderly person will then be able to

---

[1] https://visualstudio.microsoft.com/xamarin/.

[2] https://www.drools.org/.

[3] https://www.mi.com/global/mi-smart-band-4/.

[4] https://www.samsung.com/us/mobile/wearables/all-wearables/?flagship_series=Galaxy+Fit.

[5] https://www.sonymobile.com/global-en/products/smart-products/smartwatch-3-swr50/.

[6] https://www.apple.com/watch/.

build own family tree and recall past events and experiences. Furthermore, we combine both these gamification techniques with the proposed social network (and the retrieved data) to promote social interaction between the elderly person and his/her family members (for example, using family photos and videos). This way we can motivate the elderly person to use the system, and to define intelligent strategies that can improve his/her memory and cognitive condition due to all factors that involve and that may affect the family context of the elderly person. Besides this, this feature considers the two current major limitations associated to gamified systems related with the lack of personalization of the support provided to each individual (as the system only provides the same features to every single user instead) and with the fact that elderly people have difficulty to understand, accept and use new technologies and game mechanics that are available in gamified approaches (resulting in a great difficulty to perceive the inherent benefits associated to those systems). Therefore, all suggested activities and gamification techniques used to measure and assess cognitive condition must be presented to each user according to his/her interests and preferences.

To Detect Affective States, Stress and Anxiety. The user affective state, stress and anxiety levels are monitored through the smartwatch application to process physiological data with each interaction to understand what kind of events and interactions are perceived as positive or negative by the elderly person. For this, big data analysis is performed, and the acquired data is compared with pre-established patterns (for example, ECG patterns) for different daily activities performed by the elderly person. By doing so, the system will be capable of personalizing and filter negative interactions with the user. According to the literature, it is still very difficult to develop a system that can accurately measure and identify generated emotions using this kind of approach

4 Conclusions and Future Work

In this paper we proposed a conceptual approach that intends to increase the sense of well-being of elderly people. In this regard, we presented a conceptual version of a system that works as a social network and that can be used in any common device such as a smartphone, a tablet, a laptop or a desktop. In addition, the system includes a smartwatch application which gathers user's physiological signs and sends them to the server. Considering the environment that a social network can provide and the acquired data, we proposed strategies to achieve three major features: (1) to learn user's preferences and potentiate his/her fun; (2) to evaluate the current user's cognitive capabilities and to work on strategies that can help stimulate memory (refreshing his/her memory associations); and (3) to detect affective states, stress and anxiety.

We concluded that the biggest challenges are to develop gamification strategies that can be adequate to the different needs and capabilities of each user, to develop strategies that can accurately detect user's emotions and to develop a model that can learn the user's preferences, maintaining at same time a level of usability adequate to the user's profile.

As future work, we want to study strategies that allow to overcome the limitations that were identified in each presented feature. We also intend to develop a prototype to evaluate the models and algorithms that will be created and finally we intend to test the prototype in a real scenario.

Acknowledgments. The work presented in this paper has been developed under the EUREKA - ITEA3 Project PHE (PHE-16040), and by National Funds through FCT (Fundação para a Ciência e a Tecnologia) under the projects UID/EEA/00760/2019 and UID/CEC/00319/2019 and by NORTE-01-0247-FEDER-033275 (AIRDOC - "Aplicação móvel Inteligente para suporte individualizado e monitorização da função e sons Respiratórios de Doentes Obstrutivos Crónicos") by NORTE 2020 (Programa Operacional Regional do Norte).

References

1. UN: World Population Ageing Report (2017)
2. Durick, J., Robertson, T., Brereton, M., Vetere, F., Nansen, B.: Dispelling ageing myths in technology design. In: Proceedings of the 25th Australian Computer-Human Interaction Conference: Augmentation, Application, Innovation, Collaboration, pp. 467–476. ACM (2013)
3. Roupa, Z., et al.: The use of technology by the elderly. Health Sci. J. **4**, 118 (2010)
4. Do, H.M., Pham, M., Sheng, W., Yang, D., Liu, M.: RiSH: a robot-integrated smart home for elderly care. Robot. Auton. Syst. **101**, 74–92 (2018)
5. Cook, D., Das, S.K.: Smart Environments: Technology. Protocols and Applications. Wiley, Hoboken (2004)
6. Liu, L., Stroulia, E., Nikolaidis, I., Miguel-Cruz, A., Rincon, A.R.: Smart homes and home health monitoring technologies for older adults: a systematic review. Int. J. Med. Inform. **91**, 44–59 (2016)
7. Botsis, T., Demiris, G., Pedersen, S., Hartvigsen, G.: Home telecare technologies for the elderly. J. Telemed. Telecare **14**, 333–337 (2008)
8. Chatterjee, S., Price, A.: Healthy living with persuasive technologies: framework, issues, and challenges. J. Am. Med. Inform. Assoc. **16**, 171–178 (2009)
9. World Health Organization: Rehabilitation in health systems (2017)
10. Van Diest, M., Lamoth, C.J., Stegenga, J., Verkerke, G.J., Postema, K.: Exergaming for balance training of elderly: state of the art and future developments. J. Neuroeng. Rehabil. **10**, 101 (2013)
11. Gerling, K.M., Masuch, M.: Exploring the potential of gamification among frail elderly persons. In: Proceedings of the CHI 2011 Workshop Gamification: Using Game Design Elements in Non-Game Contexts (2011)
12. Gerling, K.M., Schulte, F.P., Masuch, M.: Designing and evaluating digital games for frail elderly persons. In: Proceedings of the 8th International Conference on Advances in Computer Entertainment Technology, p. 62. ACM (2011)
13. Ijsselsteijn, W., Nap, H.H., de Kort, Y., Poels, K.: Digital game design for elderly users. In: Proceedings of the 2007 Conference on Future Play, pp. 17–22. ACM (2007)
14. Ramos, J., Oliveira, T., Satoh, K., Neves, J., Novais, P.: Cognitive assistants—an analysis and future trends based on speculative default reasoning. Appl. Sci. **8**, 742 (2018)
15. Paiva, A., Mascarenhas, S., Petisca, S., Correia, F., Alves-Oliveira, P.: Towards more humane machines: creating emotional social robots. In: New Interdisciplinary Landscapes in Morality and Emotion, pp. 125–139. Routledge (2018)
16. Leite, I., Martinho, C., Paiva, A.: Social robots for long-term interaction: a survey. Int. J. Soc. Robot. **5**, 291–308 (2013)

17. Engelbart, D.C.: Augmenting Human Intellect: A Conceptual Framework. Menlo Park, California (1962)
18. Costa, A., Martinez-Martin, E., Cazorla, M., Julian, V.: PHAROS—physical assistant robot system. Sensors **18**, 2633 (2018)
19. Kostavelis, I., Giakoumis, D., Malasiotis, S., Tzovaras, D.: RAMCIP: towards a robotic assistant to support elderly with mild cognitive impairments at home. In: Serino, S., Matic, A., Giakoumis, D., Lopez, G., Cipresso, P. (eds.) MindCare 2015. CCIS, vol. 604, pp. 186–195. Springer, Cham (2016). https://doi.org/10.1007/978-3-319-32270-4_19
20. Le, N.-T., Wartschinski, L.: A cognitive assistant for improving human reasoning skills. Int. J. Hum Comput Stud. **117**, 45–54 (2018)
21. Khosla, R., Chu, M.-T., Nguyen, K.: Affective robot enabled capacity and quality improvement of nursing home aged care services in australia. In: 2013 IEEE 37th Annual Computer Software and Applications Conference Workshops (COMPSACW), pp. 409–414. IEEE (2013)
22. Kitakoshi, D., Okano, T., Suzuki, M.: An empirical study on evaluating basic characteristics and adaptability to users of a preventive care system with learning communication robots. Soft. Comput. **21**, 331–351 (2017)
23. Picard, R.W., Healey, J.: Affective wearables. Pers. Technol. **1**, 231–240 (1997)
24. Baumgart, R., Wiewiorra, L.: The role of self-control in self-tracking (2016)
25. von Entress-Fürsteneck, M., Gimpel, H., Nüske, N., Rückel, T., Urbach, N.: Self-tracking and gamification: analyzing the interplay of motivations, usage and motivation fulfillment (2019)
26. Kostopoulos, P., Kyritsis, A.I., Ricard, V., Deriaz, M., Konstantas, D.: Enhance daily live and health of elderly people. Proc. Comput. Sci. **130**, 967–972 (2018)
27. O'Connor, D., Brennan, L., Caulfield, B.: The use of neuromuscular electrical stimulation (NMES) for managing the complications of ageing related to reduced exercise participation. Maturitas **113**, 13–20 (2018)
28. Malwade, S., et al.: Mobile and wearable technologies in healthcare for the ageing population. Comput. Methods Programs Biomed. **161**, 233–237 (2018)
29. Gamecho, B., Silva, H., Guerreiro, J., Gardeazabal, L., Abascal, J.: A context-aware application to increase elderly users compliance with physical rehabilitation exercises at home via animatronic biofeedback. J. Med. Syst. **39**, 135 (2015)
30. Yang, N., Samuel, A.: Context-rich detection of user's emotions using a smartphone. Microsoft Research Internship Report (2011)
31. Dai, D., Liu, Q., Meng, H.: Can your smartphone detect your emotion? In: 2016 12th International Conference on Natural Computation, Fuzzy Systems and Knowledge Discovery (ICNC-FSKD), pp. 1704–1709. IEEE (2016)
32. Hänsel, K., Alomainy, A., Haddadi, H.: Large scale mood and stress self-assessments on a smartwatch. In: Proceedings of the 2016 ACM International Joint Conference on Pervasive and Ubiquitous Computing: Adjunct, pp. 1180–1184. ACM (2016)
33. Ciabattoni, L., Ferracuti, F., Longhi, S., Pepa, L., Romeo, L., Verdini, F.: Real-time mental stress detection based on smartwatch. In: 2017 IEEE International Conference on Consumer Electronics (ICCE), pp. 110–111. IEEE (2017)
34. Quiroz, J.C., Geangu, E., Yong, M.H.: Emotion recognition using smart watch sensor data: mixed-design study. JMIR Ment. Health **5**, e10153 (2018)
35. Zhang, Z., Song, Y., Cui, L., Liu, X., Zhu, T.: Emotion recognition based on customized smart bracelet with built-in accelerometer. PeerJ **4**, e2258 (2016)
36. Deterding, S., Dixon, D., Khaled, R., Nacke, L.: From game design elements to gamefulness: defining gamification. In: Proceedings of the 15th International Academic MindTrek Conference: Envisioning Future Media Environments, pp. 9–15. ACM (2014)

37. Deterding, S., Sicart, M., Nacke, L., O'Hara, K., Dixon, D.: Gamification using game-design elements in non-gaming contexts. In: CHI 2011 Extended Abstracts on Human Factors in Computing Systems, pp. 2425–2428. ACM (2011)
38. Stokes, B.: Videogames have changed: time to consider Serious Games'? Dev. Educ. J. **11**, 12 (2005)
39. Hamari, J., Koivisto, J., Sarsa, H.: Does gamification work?–a literature review of empirical studies on gamification. In: 2014 47th Hawaii International Conference on System Sciences (HICSS), pp. 3025–3034. IEEE (2014)
40. McCallum, S.: Gamification and serious games for personalized health. Stud. Health Technol. Inform. **177**, 85–96 (2012)
41. Brauner, P., Calero Valdez, A., Schroeder, U., Ziefle, M.: Increase physical fitness and create health awareness through exergames and gamification. In: Holzinger, A., Ziefle, M., Hitz, M., Debevc, M. (eds.) SouthCHI 2013. LNCS, vol. 7946, pp. 349–362. Springer, Heidelberg (2013). https://doi.org/10.1007/978-3-642-39062-3_22
42. Boillat, T., Rivas, H., Wac, K.: "Healthcare on a Wrist": increasing compliance through checklists on wearables in obesity (self-)management programs. In: Rivas, H., Wac, K. (eds.) Digital Health. HI, pp. 65–81. Springer, Cham (2018). https://doi.org/10.1007/978-3-319-61446-5_6
43. Boletsis, C., McCallum, S., Landmark, B.F.: The use of smartwatches for health monitoring in home-based dementia care. In: Zhou, J., Salvendy, G. (eds.) DUXU 2015. LNCS, vol. 9194, pp. 15–26. Springer, Cham (2015). https://doi.org/10.1007/978-3-319-20913-5_2
44. Boletsis, C., McCallum, S.: Connecting the player to the doctor: utilising serious games for cognitive training and screening. Des. Self-care Everyday Life. **5** (2014)
45. Gimpel, H., Nißen, M., Görlitz, R.: Quantifying the quantified self: a study on the motivations of patients to track their own health (2013)

Blended Learning in Smart Learning Environments

Peter Mikulecky(✉)

Faculty of Informatics and Management, University of Hradec Kralove,
Hradec Kralove, Czech Republic
peter.mikulecky@uhk.cz

Abstract. It is already commonly accepted, that blended learning seems to be one of the modern and promising approaches to teaching and learning. Blended learning aims to integrate traditional learning with innovative means, such as e-learning, analytics, game-based learning, and open educational resources, in order to create a new learning environment aiming to enhance learning effectiveness, and enrich learning experience. In the meantime, as one important and applicable output of the smart environments research, the concept of smart learning environments has evolved with a number of successful applications. The aim of this paper is to argue, that blended learning concept can be viewed as a promising perspective for affective learning strategies inclusion into recently more and more popular smart learning environments.

Keywords: Blended learning · Smart learning environments · Affective learning strategies

1 Introduction

Nowadays we witness various directions of research in the area of technological support of education. One of recent steps in this effort resulted in the concept of smart learning environments, illustrated by the number of interesting and really implemented projects. Smart learning environments are offering many new interesting facilities, however, there is only a few attempts in the direction of investigating their possibilities for affective learning, or coping with emotional states of learners in general. We are deeply convinced that blended learning approaches certainly could contribute to increase the level of affective learning strategies to be used in smart learning environments.

In 2001, already two decades of numerous research initiatives in the area of ambient intelligence have been started by the famous ISTAG Report [1]. Among the four basic scenarios described in the report, it introduced also a smart learning environment example in the form of the *Scenario 4: Annette and Solomon in the Ambient for Social Learning*. Without any doubt, it was a vision of a smart learning environment, based on a position that learning is a social process. And moreover, although affective states are not mentioned in the original ISTAG

© Springer Nature Switzerland AG 2019
P. Moura Oliveira et al. (Eds.): EPIA 2019, LNAI 11805, pp. 62–67, 2019.
https://doi.org/10.1007/978-3-030-30244-3_6

Report, there is no doubt that the view on learning as a social process cannot be understood without necessity to cope also with affective states, positive as well as negative. However, this aspect was in those days a bit neglected.

An attempt to specify smart learning environments in a slightly detailed way was published in [2]. A bit more general overview of the Ambient Intelligence possibilities in education brings [3]. The aim of the paper was to identify and analyze key aspects and possibilities of Ambient Intelligence applications in educational processes and institutions (universities), as well as to present a couple of possible visions for these applications. The conclusion of the presented research was that exploitation of Ambient Intelligence approaches and technologies in educational institutions was possible and could bring us new experience utilizable in further development of various Ambient Intelligence applications.

In what follows, we bring an overview of related works on Smart Learning Environments shortly in the Sect. 2.1, some related opinions on Affective Learning in the Sect. 2.2, and an overview on Blended Learning principles together with their possible use in the Sect. 2.3. The Sect. 3 is the conclusion.

2 On the Way to Affective Learning in Smart Learning Environments

2.1 Smart Learning Environments

There are various approaches trying to define learning environments that deserve the name *smart learning environments*. Maybe the best specification of smart learning environments can be found in an important paper [4] by Kinshuk and his colleagues. Their opinion is that *a learning environment can be considered smart when the learner is supported through the use of adaptive and innovative technologies from childhood all the way through formal education, and continued during work and adult life where non-formal and informal learning approaches become primary means for learning.* That is, Kinshuk and his colleagues support the meaning of smart learning environments as neither pure technology-based systems nor a particular pedagogical approach, but as a mixture of both.

Another description of smart learning environments has been presented in [5]. The smart learning environments are defined here as physical environments that are enriched with digital, context-aware and adaptive devices, to promote better and faster learning. Particularly, according to Koper [5], *a smart learning environment is such a learning environment, in which:*

- *One or more digital devices are added to the physical locations of the learner;*
- *The digital devices are aware of the learners location, context and culture;*
- *The digital devices add learning functions to the locations, context and culture, such as the provision of (augmented) information, assessments, remote collaboration, feedforward, feedback, etc.;*
- *The digital devices are monitoring the progress of learners and provide appropriate information to relevant stakeholders.*

It means that a smart learning environment should be context-aware and adaptive to the individual learner's behaviour. Nevertheless, Koper [5] stressed, that concentrating on the technical aspects mentioned above, does not automatically promote better and faster learning. However, also Koper in [5] failed in taking into account some affective aspects of smart learning environments.

Hwang [6] published an important idea about smart learning environments that have to be taken always into account: *A smart learning environment not only enables learners to access digital resources and interact with learning systems in any place and at any time, but also actively provides the necessary learning guidance, hints, supportive tools or learning suggestions... in the right place,...right time and... right form.*

2.2   From Smart Learning to Affective Learning

Let us quote the opinion of Libbrecht et al. [7] as an incentive for introducing new technologies into Smart Learning Environments research and development. According to them, Smart Learning Environments can be understood as *systems that apply novel approaches and methods on the levels of learning design and instruction, learning management and organization, and technology to create a context for learning....* However, they pointed out that these novel approaches cannot be restricted only on the technological level. Certainly, coping with affective states in a smart learning environment without any doubts cannot be reduced on the technological level only.

As Spector [8] points out, it is necessary for a smart learning environment to autonomously provide *different learning situations and circumstances, as... a human teacher or tutor... to help learners become more organized and aware of their own learning goals, processes and outcomes.*

All of this can be understood as a good entry point for including various aspects of affective learning into smart learning environments, or, at least, to accept the opinion, that it is always necessary to cope with affective aspects in any smart learning environment, that is considered to be functional.

According to well-known Affective Learning Manifesto [9], *the use of the computer as a model, metaphor, and modelling tool has tended to privilege the 'cognitive' over the 'affective' by engendering theories in which thinking and learning are viewed as information processing and affect is ignored or marginalised. In the last decade there has been an accelerated flow of findings in multiple disciplines supporting a view of affect as complexly intertwined with cognition in guiding rational behaviour, memory retrieval, decision-making, creativity, and more.*

The importance of emotions for our ways of thinking, and implicitly for learning, has been stressed by Minsky in his famous book [10], where he wrote *... when we change what we call our 'emotional states', we are switching between different ways to think.* As Daradoumis et al. [11] pointed out, current research on web-based learning environments has shown the importance of taking into account not only the cognitive abilities and capabilities that students possess or need to acquire through learning processes, but also their affective abilities and capabilities.

There are already some attempts to merge various kinds of smart learning environments with affective learning. One example could be an affective and Web 3.0-based learning environment for learning Java programming by Cabada et al. [12]. The most important components of this environment are a recommender and mining system, an affect recognizer, a sentiment analyzer, and an authoring tool. If we concentrate just on the affect recognition part of the described environment, the affect recognition is based on obtaining the current emotion from facial expressions of the learner. There is a number of techniques and approaches for this purpose, but the authors of [12] decided to build their own affect recognizer. Actually, in order to recognize facial expressions in the learning environment, they decided to build a facial-expressions database, that should contain faces expressing emotions directly related to learning. Every face in the database was labeled as one of the learning-centered emotions (frustration, boredom, engagement, and excitement). In order to accomplish this task, the authors used an electroencephalography (EEG) technology called EMOTIV Epoc. The system captured student's emotions while the student was solving a problem by coding a Java program using a Java environment.

Another interesting smart learning system with affect recognition has been earlier described in [13]. It is a learning environment for Java with multimodal affect recognition. It takes into account cognitive and affective aspects of students using different hardware tools to recognize their affective state. A couple of recently developed smart learning environments with affect learning capability are certainly described elsewhere.

2.3 Blended Learning as a Step to Affective Learning

First, let us go back to the ISTAG *Scenario 4: Annette and Solomon in the Ambient for Social Learning* [1]. According to the ISTAG group, a number of specific technologies would be needed for implementation of this Smart Learning Environment, among others the following ones:

– Recognition (tracing and identification) of individuals, groups and objects.
– Interactive commitment aids for negotiating targets and challenges (goal synchronization).
– Natural language and speech interfaces and dialogue modeling.
– Projection facilities for light and soundfields (visualization, virtual reality and holographic representation), including perception based technologies such as psycho-acoustics.
– Tangible/tactile and sensorial interfacing (including direct brain interfaces).
– Reflexive learning systems (adaptable, customisable) to build aids for reviewing experiences.
– Content design facilities, simulation and visualization aids.
– Knowledge management tools to build community memory.

Actually, there is nothing written about emotional states of learners, just recognition (tracing and identification) of individuals, groups, and objects. Taking into account such interesting attempts, that were described in the last chapter

([12], or [13]), some ways of automatic recognition of affective states are possible. Nevertheless, these approaches are still relatively experimental, and from the pedagogical point of view, any absence of human factor in learning process could appear to be controversial. The way, how to introduce affective learning into modern smart learning environments, could go through introducing some elements of well known blended learning.

Blended learning in a form of a blend between face-to-face and online learning, certainly introduces several advantages of some forms of direct contact between learners and their instructors. Typical smart learning environments are usually not capable of recognizing nor coping with emotional states of learners, with possible negative influences on the learning process in the cases of particular learners with somehow limited cognitive or emotional capabilities (see [2,4,14], or [15]).

Introducing blended learning into a suitable smart learning environment certainly requires increasing of blended learning strategies support from the side of the smart learning environment. That means an increased support of instructor's tasks in the learning process, etc. For a number of relevant literature see, e.g., [16].

3   Conclusions

As Arguedas with colleagues [17] pointed out, *a great variety of emotions play important role in every computer-related situation. Negative emotions require mental or behavioral adjustment, whereas positive emotions urge students to explore the computer-based environment and direct the actions that they take in it.* Although the evolution of smart learning environments seems to be considerably successful, and a number of them is recently practically used, they are usually lacking any feature of recognizing nor coping with emotional states of the learners. Our position is that instead of inventing complicated and possibly not too reliable automatic techniques for recognizing and evaluating affective states of learners, it would be better to employ more reliable and already accepted approaches, based on face-to-face contact of learners with an instructor. Such a blended learning as a suitable combination of face-to-face learning with many useful features of a smart learning environment could serve as a desirable step towards introducing certain affective learning approaches into certainly very attractive smart learning environments to bring them closer towards real educational needs of both students and instructors. However, this needs intensive research oriented on possibilities of coupling the three concepts, Affective Learning, Blended Learning, and Smart Learning Environments in a useful combination. This is one of the aims of a recent research project at our university.

Acknowledgment. The research has been partially supported by the Faculty of Informatics and Management UHK specific research project 2107 *Computer Networks for Cloud, Distributed Computing, and Internet of Things II.* Thanks goes also to Mr. Martin Kulhanek, a diploma student, for some preparatory help in writing the paper.

References

1. Ducatel, K., Bogdanowicz, M., Scapolo, F., Leijten, J., Burgelman, J.C.: Scenarios for ambient intelligence 2010. Institute for Prospective Technological Studies, Seville, November 2001 (2001). ftp://ftp.cordis.lu/pub/ist/docs/istagscenarios2010.pdf
2. Mikulecký, P.: Smart environments for smart learning. In: DIVAI 2012 (2012)
3. Bureš, V., Tučník, P., Mikulecký, P., Mls, K., Blecha, P.: Application of ambient intelligence in educational institutions: visions and architectures. Int. J. Ambient Comput. Intell. (IJACI) **7**(1), 94–120 (2016)
4. Kinshuk, Chen, N.S., Cheng, I.L., Chew, S.W.: Evolution is not enough: revolutionizing current learning environments to smart learning environments. Int. J. Artif. Intell. Educ. **26**(2) 561–581 (2016)
5. Koper, R.: Conditions for effective smart learning environments. Smart Learn. Environ. **1**(1), 5 (2014)
6. Hwang, G.J.: Definition, framework and research issues of smart learning environments: a context-aware ubiquitous learning perspective. Smart Learn. Environ. **1**(1), 1–14 (2014)
7. Libbrecht, P., Müller, W., Rebholz, S.: Smart learner support through semi-automatic feedback. In: Chang, M., Li, Y. (eds.) Smart Learning Environments. LNET, pp. 129–157. Springer, Heidelberg (2015). https://doi.org/10.1007/978-3-662-44447-4_8
8. Spector, J.M.: Conceptualizing the emerging field of smart learning environments. Smart Learn. Environ. **1**(1), 1–10 (2014)
9. Picard, R.W., Papert, S., Bender, W., Blumberg, B., Breazeal, C., Cavallo, D., Machover, T., Resnick, M., Roy, D., Strohecker, C.: Affective learning: a manifesto. BT Technol. J. **22**(4), 253–269 (2004)
10. Minsky, M.: The emotion machine: commonsense thinking, artificial intelligence, and the future of the human mind. Simon and Schuster (2007)
11. Daradoumis, T., Arguedas, M., Xhafa, F.: Current trends in emotional e-learning: new perspectives for enhancing emotional intelligence. In: 2013 Seventh International Conference on Complex, Intelligent, and Software Intensive Systems, pp. 34–39. IEEE (2013)
12. Cabada, R.Z., Estrada, M.L.B., Hernández, F.G., Bustillos, R.O., Reyes-García, C.A.: An affective and web 3.0-based learning environment for a programming language. Telematics Inform. **35**(3) 611–628 (2018)
13. Wiggins, J.B., et al.: JavaTutor: an intelligent tutoring system that adapts to cognitive and affective states during computer programming. In: Proceedings of the 46th ACM Technical Symposium on Computer Science Education, p. 599. ACM (2015)
14. Mikulecky, P.: User adaptivity in smart workplaces. In: Pan, J.-S., Chen, S.-M., Nguyen, N.T. (eds.) ACIIDS 2012. LNCS (LNAI), vol. 7197, pp. 401–410. Springer, Heidelberg (2012). https://doi.org/10.1007/978-3-642-28490-8_42
15. Mikulecký, P.: Smart learning environments - a multi-agent architecture proposal. In: DIVAI 2014, 10th International Scientific Conference on Distance Learning in Applied Informatics. Wolters Kluwer (2014)
16. Ma'arop, A.H., Embi, M.A.: Implementation of blended learning in higher learning institutions: a review of the literature. Int. Educ. Stud. **9**(3), 41–52 (2016)
17. Arguedas, M., Daradoumis, T., Xhafa, F.: Analyzing the effects of emotion management on time and self-management in computer-based learning. Comput. Hum. Behav. **63**, 517–529 (2016)

Facial Virtual Tracking: A System to Mirror Emotions

Pedro Santos[1], Vinícius Silva[2], Filomena Soares[1,2(✉)],
and Alberto Simões[3]

[1] Industrial Electronics Department, School of Engineering,
University of Minho, Guimarães, Portugal
a74504@alunos.uminho.pt, fsoares@dei.uminho.pt
[2] R&D Centre Algoritmi, School of Engineering, University of Minho,
Guimarães, Portugal
a65312@alunos.uminho.pt
[3] IPCA, Barcelos, Portugal
asimoes@ipca.pt

Abstract. The capacity for social interaction, communication and recognition of emotions is a characteristic that the human being possesses and that allows him/her to be socially included. However, some have difficulties in expressing and interpreting emotional states, which can contribute to their marginalisation in society. A particular case is children with Autism Spectrum Disorder. These children have difficulties in social interaction and manifest repetitive patterns. In this work, a serious game is being developed in which an avatar (ZECA avatar) is able to interact with the child, through challenges and training of certain facial movements that will be validated by the system, facilitating imitation and recognition of emotions (happiness, sadness, anger, surprise and fear). The tests performed in the laboratory environment allowed to conclude the adequacy of the game for promoting emotional states in a friendly way.

Keywords: Serious game · Facial expressions · Emotions ·
Human Computer Interaction

1 Introduction

The human being has the capacity to mimic several face expressions that characterize an emotional state. This is done in a conscious way according to what the human is feeling at a given moment. In addition, he/she can interpret these emotions through the facial expressions made by others, which help to promote and understand the interaction. In fact, for humans to be able to interact, it is essential that they understand what the partner is feeling to comprehend his/her reactions. In the face, it is reflected what we feel, and from this, anyone can interpret a message, verbal or non-verbal. This message can be passed in the form of gestures and expressions. However, automatic reading of these expressions can be a very complex task. This is the case of children with Autism Spectrum Disorder (ASD) [1].

© Springer Nature Switzerland AG 2019
P. Moura Oliveira et al. (Eds.): EPIA 2019, LNAI 11805, pp. 68–79, 2019.
https://doi.org/10.1007/978-3-030-30244-3_7

The authors of the present paper have been working on promoting emotional and social skills of children with ASD by using a humanoid robot ZECA as a mediator [2, 3]. The five emotional states considered are: happiness, sadness, anger, surprise and fear. Three activities were designed: emotions imitation and recognition and story-telling. The results obtained so far allow to conclude that the use of robotic platforms in therapeutic scenarios with children with ASD may be a successful tool [4]. The experimental set-up of this system includes the robot (approximately height: 17 cm, weight: 1 kg), computer and cameras to register the session for further analysis of children behavior. The sessions take place in a school environment, requiring the system to be portable.

It would be interesting to reinforce emotional skills acquisition in other experimental configurations and tools, especially more lightweight. A serious game can be a suitable tool to fulfill this need. In [5] the authors present a study on using a serious game with a playware object to promote emotional skills in children with ASD. The playware object is a physical/interactive tool for the user to play the game, acting as a game controller. It has six buttons, each displaying an emoji with a different facial expression, and communicates with the game via Bluetooth. The game includes the three activities designed for the ZECA robot - imitation, recognition, and storytelling - and includes six facial expressions - happiness, sadness, anger, surprise, fear, and neutral. The preliminary tests allowed to conclude that the playware object and the serious game had a high level of approval from the children and their therapists.

Following this trend, the goal of this work is to develop a serious game that replicates the activities designed with the ZECA robot in order to promote the ability to associate facial expressions with emotions. The ZECA avatar challenges the child to understand and interpret emotional states. For this, the user's face will be monitored in order to verify the execution of his/her facial movements and to support improvements, if they are not executed correctly. This way, the user interacts with ZECA avatar by performing facial movements, identifying emotional states, and receiving feedback for improvement of possible incorrect movements/challenges. The system automatically registers the response time and the number of correct/incorrect answers.

The final goal of the work presented in this paper is to compare the results obtained by using the ZECA robot and the ZECA avatar.

This paper is organized in five sections. Section 2 presents the related works available in the literature; Sect. 3 details the developed serious game; Sect. 4 explains the facial expressions recognition process; Sect. 5 shows the preliminary results obtained so far; and the final remarks and future work are addressed in Sect. 6.

2 Related Work

The use of robots for interaction with children with ASD has been widely used and tested [6–10]. One of such robots is ZECA (Portuguese acronym for Zeca Engaging Children with Autism) from Hanson Robotics [11]. This robot allows to promote the interaction with the children providing the communication and the development of capacities of emotion understanding. Another more recent example is the QTROBOT

[12] (launched in 2018) created by LuxAI to assist children in interpreting facial expressions and promoting social interaction.

Currently the design of applications to support these children is an area that has been increasing. These applications are designed to promote the development of certain capabilities in a didactic way. Livox is one of those applications [13] that contains several modes of games where the child receives stimulus to develop the capacity of communication. Using its database with over 20,000 images, audio and video features, the user can choose an item and Livox produces the audio or video that is associated with it. The association of words with images is a good way of training children who have difficulties in distinguishing emotions. Sono Flex [14] is one of the applications that is based on this concept. TippyTalk [15] allows a person with verbal disabilities to communicate by translating the pictures into text messages, which are sent to a family member or to a friend. This allows the child to communicate and express a desire, need or feeling.

For all these applications to be well accepted by the user, it is necessary that the Graphical User Interface (GUI) is captivating and intuitive so that children do not have difficulties in using them. As such, the use of games to support the development of communication and interaction skills in children with ASD is one of the potential solutions to use. In fact, some tests have already been conducted with children [16], where significant progress has been made in their behavior regarding relationships with colleagues and teachers, for example.

However, Human-Computer Interaction (HCI) is a concept that, although widely used, requires some advances in order to understand the user's reactions and to adapt the machine's behavior accordingly. It is important that this interaction is increasingly fluid and dynamic, preventing the human at any time from feeling that on the other side there is a machine programmed for certain predefined and static tasks. Through the face, the human being can transmit several expressions [17] and it is with this capacity that he/she can communicate with others allowing him/her to be accepted and introduced in society. Thus, it is important that children with ASD perceive each emotion and relate it to characteristic facial expressions.

As children with ASD have some cognitive and social problems, it is important to create a support in the sense of improving their abilities to make their relationship with others easier and more fluid [18]. For this, the creation of tools or games capable of aiding in the learning of emotions and understanding of the interlocutor's mood becomes a relevant solution. These applications become an important base of support for enabling children to develop capacities in a didactic way through constructive entertainment.

3 Serious Game Development

This section presents the purpose, the developed scenarios, the architecture and the design of the serious game that allows to mirror the user facial expressions onto the avatar's face in real-time by recognizing emotions and emotional states in a pre-define context.

3.1   Game Purpose

The goal of the serious game is to have a friendly and an easily portable tool to promote the recognition and imitation of emotional states in children with ASD. The game must replicate the activities designed with the ZECA robot in the triadic interactions (child, robot, and researcher) performed in a school environment [3, 4]. In total, the system is capable of recognizing up to five emotions: happiness, sadness, surprise, anger and fear.

Taking the target group into account, the game interface should be as simple as possible, with minimum information and colour, in order to avoid distracting the children. The game activity is then dedicated to promoting the understanding and recognition of emotional states in children with ASD.

It is worth pointing out that the proposed game is to be tested in a Portuguese Special Education Unit, part of a first cycle school. For that, all the game scenarios (and voice commands) were implemented in Portuguese language.

3.2   Game Scenarios

The game is composed by three levels with increased difficulty: facial movements, facial expressions, and storytelling.

The goal of the first game level is to start introducing the child to the facial expressions related to emotional states. So, the game asks the child, by voice and through phrases written in the game scenario, to help the ZECA avatar to perform simple facial movements. Figure 1 presents (from left to right) the commands read out by the game for the execution of the facial movements "frown", "raise the eyebrow" and "open the mouth".

a) "frown"   b) "open the mouth"   c) "raise the eyebrow"

Fig. 1. Challenges of the first level facial movements (in Portuguese).

These facial movements performed by the child are acquired and validated by the system. If the movement corresponds to the cue, it is mirrored in real-time in the avatar. As a positive feedback, the ZECA avatar performs a dance. In case the child executes no movement (during a pre-defined time), or the movement does not correspond to the cue, the game moves to other challenge within the current level until a sequence of different movements is completed. The system registers the number and the time to perform the movements.

In the second level, based on learning facial expressions through a model, the difficulty is slightly increased. In this level there is a text box, with the name of an emotion, and an animation of ZECA performing the corresponding emotional expression. The game then challenges the child to imitate that expression. As he/she correctly responds to the task, the image is decreased, and the text box is increased until the animation (the model) disappears and there is only the textbox with the emotion written in it. Thus, the child must mimic the emotional state written in the textbox without having the model as reference. Figure 2 shows the learning by model sequences in the game level for "surprise". The system registers the number of correct answers and the response time. This functionality allows to infer the performance of the child along the sessions.

Fig. 2. Learning by model: challenges of the second level facial expressions, "surprise" (in Portuguese).

In the last level, storytelling, there is a visual and audio cue to find the emotional state. The avatar tells a story and the game shows a scenario where ZECA expresses the correspondent emotion. The child must identify ZECA's emotional state in the scene. This task is particularly difficult for children with ASD, as they rarely are able to identify their peers' emotional state. However, this level is still under development.

3.3   Game Architecture and Design

Figure 3 presents the system workflow. The camera acquires the facial features, the computer processes the information and communicates with the serious game.

Concerning the facial tracking of the user, the open source library OpenFace was used [19]. This toolkit is capable of tracking up to 72 facial landmarks, head pose estimation, facial action unit recognition, and eye-gaze estimation only using the RGB information of a webcam.

A GUI was developed in C# to extract the user's facial Action Units (AUs) and to visualize the user's facial cues. The extracted AUs are then sent to the game and the user's facial AUs are mirrored in real-time onto the avatar's face.

The game was developed in Unity 3D software, a powerful platform to create 2D or 3D games.

In order to develop the serious game, an avatar (Fig. 3, right) was developed using the Adobe Cloud with Fuse [20] and Mixamo [21]. The physical design of the avatar was inspired by the actual humanoid robot ZECA [3]. The facial blend shapes of the avatar's face were animated using Mixamo.

Fig. 3. System workflow.

Concerning the game design, the game was developed bearing in mind the characteristics of the target group (children with ASD) and their impairments. Thus, the game environment was kept as simple as possible to maintain the user focused on the main game character. Figure 4 shows the system software flowchart describing the main procedure of the game. Firstly, a TCP/IP connection to the GUI is established. Then, the game starts and, while the user face is detected, the AUs are sent to the game.

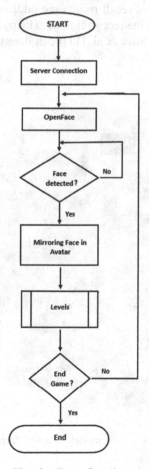

Fig. 4. Game flowchart.

4   Facial Movements and Emotion Recognition

Typically, emotions can be characterized as negative (sadness, anger, disgust or fear), positive (happiness or surprise) or neutral. The Facial Action Coding System (FACS) is the earliest method for characterizing the physical expression of emotions [17]. FACS describes several categories of head and eye positions and movements as well as the visually distinguishable facial activity. It associates the action of the muscles to the changes in facial appearance. An Action Unit (AU), which are actions performed by a muscle or a group of muscles, is the basic measurement used by the FACS. Following this idea, OpenFace is used to extract 18 facial AUs (such as blink, mouth open, among others), and the head pose angles (pitch, roll, and yaw). Figure 5 and Table 1, show the features used as input for training the model.

A dataset was created with 32 typically developing children aged between 6 and 9 years old and 30 adults. Then, to detect the user facial expressions, a Support Vector Machine with a Radial Basis Function kernel was trained, achieving a K-fold cross-validation (with K = 5) accuracy of 89%. Table 2 shows the confusion matrix obtained for this model.

In Table 3 the precision and recall results are addressed for each class. The best performances are achieved for the recognition of 'Happy' and 'Surprise'. This model (adapted from previous work, Silva et al. [11]) can detect the six basic emotions plus neutral.

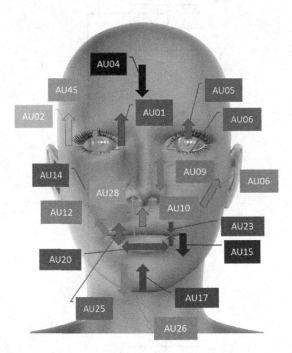

Fig. 5. Facial AUs used as input for the model (adapted from https://www.freepik.com/free-photo/3d-head_1020655.htm).

Table 1. Facial AUs and description.

AU code	AU description
AU01	Inner brow raiser
AU02	Outer brow raiser
AU04	Brow lowerer
AU05	Upper lid raiser
AU06	Cheek raiser
AU07	Lid tightener
AU09	Nose wrinkler
AU10	Upper lip raiser
AU12	Lip corner puller
AU14	Dimpler
AU15	Lip corner depressor
AU17	Chin raiser
AU20	Lip stretcher
AU23	Lip tightener
AU25	Lips part
AU26	Jaw drop
AU28	Lip suck
AU45	Blink

Table 2. Facial AUs and description.

	Happy	Sad	Scared	Anger	Surprise	Disgusting	Neutral
Happy	**95%**	0%	2%	1%	0%	2%	0%
Sad	1%	**88%**	2%	0%	0%	2%	4%
Scared	1%	2%	**86%**	1%	6%	3%	3%
Anger	1%	2%	2%	**88%**	0%	4%	1%
Surprise	1%	0%	3%	0%	**92%**	0%	1%
Disgusting	1%	1%	1%	2%	0%	**87%**	1%
Neutral	1%	6%	5%	7%	1%	2%	**89%**

Table 3. Facial AUs and description.

	Precision	Recall
Happy	94.9%	94.8%
Sad	88.3%	91.1%
Scared	86.3%	84.0%
Anger	88.3%	90.1%
Surprise	92.2%	94.4%
Disgusting	87.4%	93.1%
Neutral	89.2%	80.7%

5 Preliminary Results

This section presents the results obtained with the proposed system for the real-time mirroring of the user facial AUs. The first level of the game was tested in a laboratorial setting. The game was tested with 12 adults in different environment configurations, such as distance to the camera, light conditions and camera configurations in order to test and optimize the game performance.

The ZECA avatar successfully mimicked the user's movements and the system correctly registered the user performance for each level. As an example, Fig. 6 presents the text file where the game outputs are saved: type of movement (left column), correct answer (middle column) and time to answer (right column). If the child does not perform any movement, the system registers "Timeout" in the last column.

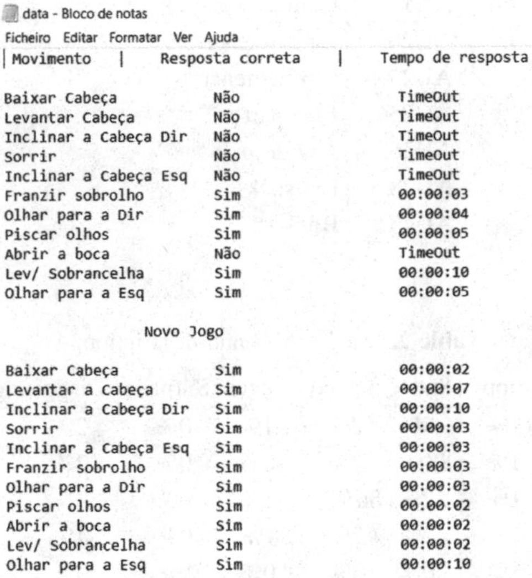

```
data - Bloco de notas
Ficheiro  Editar  Formatar  Ver  Ajuda
| Movimento    |    Resposta correta    |    Tempo de resposta

Baixar Cabeça           Não              TimeOut
Levantar Cabeça         Não              TimeOut
Inclinar a Cabeça Dir   Não              TimeOut
Sorrir                  Não              TimeOut
Inclinar a Cabeça Esq   Não              TimeOut
Franzir sobrolho        Sim              00:00:03
Olhar para a Dir        Sim              00:00:04
Piscar olhos            Sim              00:00:05
Abrir a boca            Não              TimeOut
Lev/ Sobrancelha        Sim              00:00:10
Olhar para a Esq        Sim              00:00:05

                Novo Jogo

Baixar Cabeça           Sim              00:00:02
Levantar a Cabeça       Sim              00:00:07
Inclinar a Cabeça Dir   Sim              00:00:10
Sorrir                  Sim              00:00:03
Inclinar a Cabeça Esq   Sim              00:00:03
Franzir sobrolho        Sim              00:00:03
Olhar para a Dir        Sim              00:00:03
Piscar olhos            Sim              00:00:02
Abrir a boca            Sim              00:00:02
Lev/ Sobrancelha        Sim              00:00:02
Olhar para a Esq        Sim              00:00:10
```

Fig. 6. Text file with the results of two trials of the first level of the game: type of movement (left column), correct answer (middle column) and time to answer (right column) (in Portuguese).

Figure 7 shows some of the preliminary results, where the avatar mimics the model's facial movements: frown, blink, raise the eyebrow and open the mouth.

a) frown

b) blink

c) raise the eyebrow

d) open the mouth

Fig. 7. Test results of the first level of the game, facial movements, in laboratorial environment (in Portuguese).

Before testing game level 2, the emotion recognition system presented in Sect. 4 was tested in laboratorial environment. Figure 8 presents the neutral, surprise, happiness and sadness recognition results with 98% confidence.

a) Neutral

b) Surprise

c) Happy

d) Sad

Fig. 8. Test results of emotion recognition system in laboratorial environment using the approach presented in Sect. 4 (98% confidence).

The next steps include the testing of level 1 and 2 in a school environment with children with Autism Spectrum Disorder.

6 Final Remarks and Future Work

In this work, a serious game was developed to promote the ability to perform characteristic movements (smiling, opening the eyes or opening the mouth) related to some emotions, such as being content, surprised, among others. Regarding the game implementation, an avatar (ZECA Avatar) is able to interact with the child, proposing challenges and training certain facial movements.

The system allows real-time monitoring of the user's face, verifying certain patterns related to emotions. If these are not being detected, the application can aid in the training of movements, thus improving the ability to express emotions.

The serious game is being developed in Unity software. This is a free access game engine, having libraries optimized for creating 2D and 3D games and for containing an intuitive and accessible interface. For the monitoring and follow-up of the child's face it is applied the OpenFace library (open-source library) that was developed and optimized for facial recognition with neural networks.

Future work considers optimizing and testing the system in a school environment with children with autism spectrum disorder. With this game, children are expected to promote their cognitive abilities and improve their ability to communicate and socially interact with peers.

Acknowledgments. This work has been supported by COMPETE: POCI-01-0145-FEDER-007043 and FCT – Fundação para a Ciência e Tecnologia within the Project Scope: UID/CEC/00319/2019. Vinicius Silva also thanks FCT for the PhD scholarship SFRH/BD/SFRH/BD/133314/2017.

References

1. Martins, C.: Face a face com o Autismo-será a Inclusão um mito ou uma realidade?, Escola Superior de Educação João de Deus, Lisboa (2012). (in Portuguese)
2. Costa, S., Soares, F., Pereira, A.P., Santos, C., Hiolle, A.: A pilot study using imitation and storytelling scenarios as activities for labelling emotions by children with autism using a humanoid robot. In: The Fourth Joint IEEE International Conference on Development and Learning and on Epigenetic Robotics, IEEE ICDL-EPIROB 2014, Genova, Italy, 13–16 October (2014)
3. Silva, V., Soares, F., Esteves, J.S.: Mirroring and recognizing emotions through facial expressions for a RoboKind platform. In: IEEE ENBENG 2017 - 5th Portuguese Meeting in Bioengineering, Coimbra, Portugal, 16–18 February 2017
4. Costa, S., Soares, F., Santos, C., Pereira, A.P., Hiolle, A., Silva, V.: Socio-emotional development in children with autism spectrum disorders using a humanoid robot, interaction studies (in press)
5. Azevedo, J., Silva, V., Soares, F., Pereira, A.P., Esteves, J.S.: An application to promote emotional skills in children with autism spectrum disorders. In: Göbel, S., et al. (eds.) Serious Games JCSG 2018. LNCS, vol. 11243, pp. 282–287. Springer, Cham (2018). https://doi.org/10.1007/978-3-030-02762-9_30

6. Dautenhahn, K., Billard, A.: Games children with autism can play with robota, a humanoid robotic doll. In: Keates, S., Langdon, P., Clarkson, P.J., Robinson, P. (eds.) Universal Access and Assistive Technology, pp. 179–190. Springer, London (2002). https://doi.org/10.1007/978-1-4471-3719-1_18

7. Dautenhahn, K., et al.: KASPAR - a minimally expressive humanoid robot for human-robot interaction research. Appl. Bionics Biomech. 6(3–4), 369–397 (2009)

8. Kozima, H., Michalowski, M.P., Nakagawa, C.: Keepon. Int. J. Soc. Robot. 1(1), 3–18 (2008)

9. Miskam, M.A., Shamsuddin, S., Samat, M., Yussof, H., Ainudin, H., Omar, A.: Humanoid robot NAO as a teaching tool of emotion recognition for children with autism using the Android app. In: 2014 International Symposium on Micro-NanoMechatronics and Human Science, MHS 2014, pp. 2–6 (2015)

10. Freitas, H., Costa, P., Silva, V., Pereira, A.P., Soares, F., Sena Esteves, J.: Using a humanoid robot as the promoter of the interaction with children in the context of educational games. Int. J. Mechatron. Appl. Mech. 1(1), 282–288 (2017)

11. Silva, V., Soares, F., Sena Esteves, J.: Mirroring emotion system – on-line synthesizing facial expressions on a robot face. In: 8th International Congress on Ultra Modern Telecommunications and Control Systems and Workshops (ICUMT), Lisboa, Portugal, 18–20 October 2016

12. LuxAI: "QTrobot - LuxAI.com,". http://luxai.com/qtrobot/. Accessed 6 Dec 2018

13. Livox: Livox: para pessoas com deficiências e transtornos de aprendizagem. http://www.livox.com.br/pt/quem-somos/#sobre. Accessed 6 Dec 2018. (in Portuguese)

14. Tobii Dynavox logo: "Sono Flex for Communicator 5 - Tobii Dynavox." https://www.tobiidynavox.com/software/content/sono-flex-for-communicator-5/. Accessed 7 Dec 2018

15. TippyTalk - Comunicação Instantânea para Pessoas Não Verbais. (n.d.). http://www.tippy-talk.com/. Accessed 16 Jan 2019. (in Portuguese)

16. Ferreira, V.: Utilização das tecnologias em crianças com perturbações do espectro autista em contexto da Prática de Ensino Supervisionada, Universidade Católica Portuguesa, Centro Regional de Braga, Faculdade de Ciências Sociais, Braga (2013). (in Portuguese)

17. Ekman, P., Rosenberg, E.L.: What the Face Reveals: Basic and Applied Studies of Spontaneous Expression Using the Facial Action Coding System (FACS). Oxford University Press, Oxford (2005)

18. Darwin, C.: The Expression of Emotions in Man and Animals. D. Appleton and Company, New York (1897)

19. Baltrušaitis, T., Mahmoud, M., Robinson, P.: Cross-dataset learning and person-specific normalisation for automatic action unit detection. In: Facial Expression Recognition and Analysis Challenge. In: IEEE International Conference on Automatic Face and Gesture Recognition (2015)

20. Fuse -> Adobe. Fuse (Beta). Accessed 30 April 2019. https://www.adobe.com/products/fuse/features.html

21. Mixamo -> Adobe. Mixamo. Accessed 30 April 2019. https://www.mixamo.com/

Business Applications of Artificial Intelligence

A Recommender System
for Telecommunication Operators'
Campaigns

Diogo Alves[1,2], Bruno Valente[2], Ricardo Filipe[1,2(✉)], Maria Castro[2],
and Luís Macedo[1]

[1] CISUC, Department of Informatics Engineering, University of Coimbra,
Coimbra, Portugal
daalves@student.dei.uc.pt, {rafilipe,macedo}@dei.uc.pt
[2] Altice Labs, Aveiro, Portugal
{diogo-c-alves,bruno-b-valente,ricardo-a-filipe,
maria-m-castro}@alticelabs.com

Abstract. Achieving a complete client characterization to attribute better and customized products is a trend on the rise. This information
filtering process, known as "recommendation system", increases companies revenues, and improve client quality-of-experience. Unfortunately,
current state-of-the-art focus mostly on data sets with explicit client feedback regarding the advised product, or are more focused on case studies
such as e-commerce, or movies recommendation. Our main goal is to
understand the feasibility of a recommendation approach in one specific
scenario: recommendation of telecommunication operators' campaigns.
We aim to determine the extent to which it is possible to characterize
the clients, using implicit feedback and state-of-the-art recommendation
algorithms.

We resorted to a data set supplied by an European Telecommunication Operator, with two years of advertised campaigns to a specific group
of clients, and more than forty-six million lines of raw data. Having this
data set, we applied pre-processing methods and analysed several algorithms to understand the feasibility of such approach in this real-world
scenario. Results show that our approach can indeed infer the best product or service to advertise to the client – specially when we have historical
data about past client adherence –, thus showing that these algorithms
can improve recommendations in the context of a telecommunication
operator.

Keywords: Recommendation systems · Machine learning ·
Telecom operator · Analytics · Advertising campaigns

1 Introduction

Recommender systems are information tools tailored to deal with information
overload by suggesting items that are likely to match users' needs and preferences. They have become a trend in the analysis and creation of customized

© Springer Nature Switzerland AG 2019
P. Moura Oliveira et al. (Eds.): EPIA 2019, LNAI 11805, pp. 83–95, 2019.
https://doi.org/10.1007/978-3-030-30244-3_8

profiles that are client-oriented. This paradigm evolved due to several factors. First, from the client-side point-of-view, the exponential growth of information and products creates a seemingly intimidating and herculean task to find viable products and information. Secondly, from the company's point-of-view, it is mandatory to understand what is useful and relevant to a specific client. The two aforementioned points are key aspects to increase companies trustworthiness and revenues, decrease churn rate and ultimately increase the client quality-of-experience. Hence, recommendation systems take an important role on nowadays companies and are a vital part to improve client's loyalty [10]. Currently, major companies, such as *Netflix*, *Amazon* or *Spotify*, are using recommendation of products or services to increase their sales and also their market-share. To understand the role that these algorithms have, for instance on *Netflix*, 80% of all visualizations seen in the platform are related with recommendation made by the service [5].

Telecommunication operators are no exception to the rule, and they also want to increase their product sales and create personalized advertising. Hence, inferring what product should be advertised next to the client can bring concrete benefits for the profits of the company [11,13,14].

In this paper, we describe a recommender system applied to the telecommunication operators domain. The end-user of the system is an European Telecommunication company with about 10 million clients. This company has a module, designed for advertising products and services, based on rules, and client features such as age, gender, among others. Each iteration, to advertise a product or service, corresponds in the company's vocabulary to the launch of a "campaign". They have supplied a data set with two years of information and more than 46 millions of raw data, associated with advertising to their users. This data set also included the result of the campaign, i.e. if the client has accepted or not the product or service. A recommender system was built based on this data set. In order to evaluate the performance of this recommender system, We split the data set into two sets, one for training the system, and another to test it.

Our experiments show that the system can accurately infer recommendation for clients that have purchased products or services in the past. With the exception, for the clients that regardless of the incentives or notifications, they never adhere to the campaigns, the overall methods achieved satisfactory results. They show the feasibility of using recommendation algorithms to do personalized advertising in the context of telecommunication operators. Furthermore, it reinforces that it is possible to have client characterization even without explicit feedback concerning the products proposed to clients.

The rest of the paper is organized as follows. Section 2 describes the methods we used for the problem we tackle in this paper. Section 3 describes the settings for our experiment and our data set. In Sect. 4 we present and evaluate the meaning of the results, the strengths of this approach and its limitations. Section 5 presents the related work. Section 6 concludes the paper and describes future directions.

2   Proposed Methodology

In this Section, we give a brief description of the domain of our work, we explain how the data set was built and we present the methods to evaluate our system. The data set has raw data, composed by past campaign notifications and respective subscription or rejection of the offer by the clients. Providing recommendations of campaigns in a telecommunication operator's scenario can be a difficult task since users do not provide any explicit feedback in the form of ratings or likes, such as in *Amazon* [9].

2.1   Domain - Telecommunication Operator General Information

A telecommunication operator relies on advertising campaigns to increase its revenues and loyalty of its clients, more specifically, to increase the Average Revenue Per User and decrease churn rates. Through this platform, an operator can send a notification of a campaign to the clients. The notifications can be sent via SMS, Interactive Voice Response (IVR) or email. In the case of the SMS, the notification consists of a text message describing what is being offered to the client. The same concept applies for the IVR case, with the difference that the clients receive an automatic call advertising about a certain campaign.

The types of campaigns the clients receive can consist of informative, recharge or consumption incentives. These type of campaigns may have distinct goals such as to increase the recharge amount—or frequency—, offer data bundles, incentives to adhere or buy a service/product, among others. Depending on the campaign, several benefits are offered to the clients, like extra balance, more mobile data, discount coupons in the purchase of a product, etc.

The notifications are sent to the clients when certain events are triggered, like having the balance reach an amount lower than the average balance before recharging, or entering a specific area, like a shopping mall. Having received this notifications, the clients choose to join the campaign or not. Depending on the nature of the campaign, a client can join the same campaign several times within a time period, if the events that trigger the notification of the campaign occur. This consists on the information we use to build the recommendations for our system.

2.2   Data Set

In order to create a rating given by a user to a campaign, we transformed the implicit feedback, specifically how many times a user joined a campaign, into explicit feedback. This value is calculated by using the number of times a user joined a campaign versus the number of times a user was notified to join a campaign. For instance, if a user X has been notified 6 times for campaign A and the user subscribed it twice, the ratio would be $2/6 = 0.33(3)$. This ratio value is then normalized to a scale between 0 and 10. In this example, the ratio for user X and campaign A would be 3.

This is done in opposition to considering only ratings of zeros and ones for users who had not joined or had joined a campaign, respectively. The reason is that, we wanted to distinguish the overall acceptance of each user to a specific campaign. For instance, a user that has been notified 3 times and joined 1 time is different from a user who has been notified 15 times and joined only 1 time. With this ratio value, we have a more fine-grained idea of how interested a user might be in a campaign.

The data set we used is very sparse, since the majority of users receive notifications to very few campaigns. This approach is normal, since the operator do not want to "stress" the clients with multiple offers and services. It would be counter-productive and in a worst case scenario increase the churn rate. This is also a reason why a recommender system able to provide adequate campaigns to the clients can be very useful and beneficial for a telecommunications operator.

Hence, the vast majority of ratings would be equal to zero, which would influence the recommendations in a negative way, due to the provoked "noise". With this in mind, we filtered the data set and provided for training only the user-campaign records where the number of joins was greater or equal than one. This does not mean that ratings equal to zero are not present in the data set – there may be users that have been notified for campaigns several times and joined one time for instance –, but the proportion of ratings equal to zero is much less this way. The number of campaigns considered after the application of this filter was reduced from 286 to 177. The training and testing of the algorithms were applied to the data set obtained after the filter was applied. In Sect. 3, we indicate how the training and testing split was done and we will make a more detailed analysis of the data set.

2.3   Evaluation Methods

To evaluate our approach, and thus to understand the trustworthiness of the recommendations algorithms on predicting rating value that a user would have given to a certain campaign, we resort to several metrics. Hence, predictive accuracy metrics like *Mean Absolute Error* (MAE) and *Root Mean Squared Error* (RMSE) were calculated to measure how close the system predicted ratings were from the true ratings given by the users.

Classification accuracy metrics like precision, recall and specificity were also calculated to evaluate the correctness of the predictions. These metrics have in consideration the number of true positives, false positives and false negatives present in the list of recommendations. For this kind of denomination, we defined a threshold corresponding to the value above which a rating is considered to be positive or negative, i.e., if the rating reflects the subscriptions of the campaign. The classification in true positives, false positives, false negatives and true negatives was done according to the table and respective threshold present in Table 1.

The specificity metric represents the true negative rate, giving information about the clients that are correctly not being notified with campaigns. It is also

Table 1. Classification of predicted ratings and true ratings for a specific threshold.

	Predicted rating >= TH	Predicted rating < TH
True rating >= TH	True positive	False negative
True rating < TH	False positive	True negative

calculated the F1-Measure that combines precision and recall into a single value [7], simplifying their understanding.

We also calculated the Mean Average Precision at K (MAP@K), following the approach described in [1]. Having the recommendation lists for several users ordered by the predicted rating, we consider for precision the first element, then the first two elements, then the first three elements, up to k elements. For a single user, this is the computation of Average Precision at K. For several users, we need to calculate the average of those values, hence the term Mean Average Precision.

Another metric we used to evaluate the quality of the recommendations was Mean Reciprocal Rank (MRR). This metric give us the rank of the highest rated campaign (by a user) in the list of recommendations. This list, which can be different for each user, consists of all the campaigns sorted by the predicted rating for a specific user. This way we can measure if the system is providing useful recommendations by checking if highest rated campaigns are occupying top positions in the list. If we consider several users, we need to average those values, obtaining the metrics' result.

We also calculated a variation of MRR, applying it to each campaign, to see in which position a campaign is ranked in average, considering several users recommendation lists. For example, a value of 50 for a campaign tells us that, on average, the campaign occupies the $50th$ position in the users recommendation list. The values of this metric is more easily interpretable than the one achieved by the inverse of the ranking, i.e. the MRR metric.

The algorithms used to test our data set are algorithms of collaborative filtering, namely some of matrix factorization, baseline estimators, among others [2].

3   Evaluation

The data set we used consists of approximately 46 million real records of campaign notifications sent to users, collected over a time period of 2 years. Each of this records correspond to a campaign notification sent to a client and contain information about the client who was notified, the campaign he received, and if he joined the campaign or not. The data set contains more information in each record but only these 3 fields were used because they contain the relevant information about the users' history. It is worth of notice that the data set provided have the client real number encoded, therefore anonymised for our algorithms.

Some statistics of the data set are shown in Table 2. There is a total number of 6610833 clients who have been notified with at least one of the 286 campaigns. In total, the clients joined 1460281 times. Furthermore, analysing Table 2, we can observe that we have the concept of remainders, where the same client receive multiple notifications for the same campaign in a wide time window. The statistical values of the data set after the filter refered in Sect. 2.2 was applied are also shown.

Table 2. Statistics of the data set.

Statistic	Original data set	Filtered data set
Records/notifications sent	46422213	8255599
Clients notified	6610833	804750
Campaigns	286	177
Joins to campaigns	1460281	1460281

The recommender system was implemented using Surprise [8], a Python Scikit library for building and analysing recommender systems. The data set was divided into two sets: the training set, representing 75% of the whole data set, and the test set, representing the remaining 25%.

Several values for the threshold mentioned in Sect. 2 were considered in order to obtain the best results possible. The choice of the threshold value should be a strategic decision made by the telecom operator because it is the value above which a rating is considered to reflect a user's interest in the campaign. Different operators can have different opinions about this value. In our case, we defined the threshold value to be 7.5. We consider that a client who adheres more than 75% of the times he is notified with a campaign, reflects a true interest in that campaign. Hence, only campaigns above that predicted value should be recommended to the client.

The execution times were also registered because performance of the algorithms is an important aspect to be considered. The comparison between the execution time of the different algorithms is shown in Sect. 4. To serve as reference, the hardware specifications of the machine in which the results were achieved in Sect. 4 are: 8.00 GB of RAM and Intel Core i5-4200M CPU @ 2.50 GHz processor.

4   Results

In this Section we present the results obtained for the different algorithms. The algorithms tested for the aforementioned data set, which are implemented in Surprise available in the "prediction_algorithms" package [8], are SVD, SVDpp, NormalPredictor, BaselineOnly, SlopeOne and CoClustering. Other algorithms present in Surprise, like nearest neighbours algorithms, were considered, but due to paper length restrictions they are not presented in this paper.

The values for some of the aforementioned metrics, computed with a threshold value of 7.5, are shown in Table 3. We can observe that in terms of the error metrics RMSE and MAE, the BaselineOnly and SVD algorithms show slight better results than the other algorithms, with predicted ratings deviating on average from true ratings ≈ 2.5 and ≈ 1.85, for RMSE and MAE, respectively. Focusing on the F1-Score metric, that combines precision and recall, they also show good results, meaning that the predicted ratings correctly reflect the behaviour expressed in the corresponding true ratings, whether that behaviour means the client is interested in the campaign or not. The results for specificity of the BaselineOnly and SVD algorithms are also the best compared with the other algorithms, which tells us that they are better capable of identifying clients that should not be notified with certain campaigns. Values for the MRR metric are all very similar which implies that the top rated campaign by the users is occupying roughly the same position in the recommendation lists of each user, with the exception of the SVDpp algorithm that places this best rated campaign in a much upper position in the list.

Table 3. Metric values of the different algorithms.

Algorithm	RMSE	MAE	Precision	Recall	F1-Score	Specificity	MRR
BaselineOnly	2.518	1.888	83.9%	81.7%	82.7%	63.2%	0.0286
SVD	2.558	1.908	82.8%	82.5%	82.7%	59.9%	0.0287
SVDpp	2.762	2.312	73.4%	94.1%	82.5%	20.6%	0.2176
CoClustering	3.143	2.537	72.6%	89.9%	80.3%	20.7%	0.0132
SlopeOne	2.959	2.433	73.6%	91.1%	81.4%	23.4%	0.0261
NormalPredictor	3.769	2.864	70.1%	58.8%	63.9%	41.3%	0.0299

In Table 4 we present the values for the MAP@K metric, in percentage. The metric was calculated for multiple values of k, using the library available in [6].

Table 4. MAP@K values for different k's. All values are in percentage

	MAP									
Algorithm	k = 1	k = 2	k = 3	k = 4	k = 5	k = 6	k = 7	k = 8	k = 9	k = 10
BaselineOnly	81.63	74.54	73.81	73.70	73.68	73.68	73.68	73.68	73.68	73.68
SVD	89.75	82.62	81.99	81.90	81.88	81.88	81.88	81.88	81.88	81.88
SVDpp	93.59	86.51	85.83	85.73	85.72	85.72	85.72	85.72	85.72	85.72
CoClustering	93.30	84.11	83.30	83.20	83.18	83.18	83.18	83.18	83.18	83.18
SlopeOne	94.40	86.23	85.50	85.40	85.39	85.38	85.38	85.38	85.38	85.38
NormalPredictor	60.42	53.89	53.26	53.17	53.15	53.15	53.15	53.15	53.15	53.15

It is possible to see that for a value of K greater than 6, the MAP@K values are always the same. This is due to the maximum value of K being equal to the maximum number of different campaigns the users have rated. The majority of users, i.e., 80%, only rated one or two campaigns, more specifically, each user have rated ≈1.27 campaigns. With this information, we can infer that the values of MAP@K in Table 4 for smaller K's are the ones that better reflect the true behaviour of the algorithm.

Taking this into consideration, we made a more detailed analysis to understand the dispersion for the campaign ranking for all the algorithms - see Figs. 1 and 2. The box plot in Fig. 1 give us information about the adapted ranking metric mentioned in Sect. 2. Note that the value in the Y-axis represents the ranking position in a list of campaigns, so lower values mean a better score. We can see a similar behaviour between them, with the exception of the NormalPredictor algorithm. This specific algorithm demonstrates very similar average ranking values for all the campaigns, which may be a drawback of this approach. The minimum value for the boxplot is always very low, regardless of the algorithm – exception made to the NormalPredictor –, demonstrating that some campaigns are always appearing in the top recommendations.

To understand what campaigns appear in the top recommendations for the distinct algorithms, we present Fig. 2. The X-axis represents the different campaigns – all 177 of them. The score bar represents the campaign ranking with more saturated colors being the lower values for the ranking, i.e., the best positioned campaigns. The Y-axis have the 6 algorithms presented in this paper.

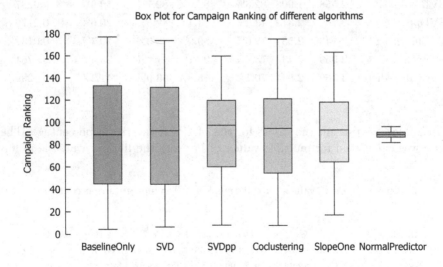

Fig. 1. Boxplot for campaign rankings for the different algorithms.

It is possible to notice that some campaigns have similar values for different algorithms, which is concordant with what Fig. 1 shows. We can see that there are very saturated vertical lines, which means that, for different algorithms, the same campaigns are being recommended in top users' recommendations lists. For example, around campaign 150, we see several vertical lines, meaning that some campaigns are highly recommended. Concerning the algorithm Normal-Predictior, the results are in line with Fig. 1, since those recommendations are always around ranking 90.

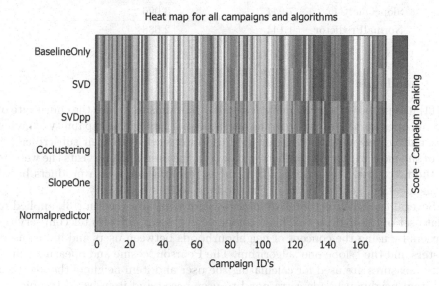

Fig. 2. Heatmap for all the campaign rankings and different algorithms.

In Table 5 presents the duration of the training and testing of the different algorithms, in seconds. The NormalPredictor algorithm have the fastest training phase, but, taking into consideration Figs. 1 and 2, this algorithm does not generate good recommendations. Hence, we will not use this algorithm in our recommendation system for a production scenario. The best algorithms, by the graphics and also by Tables 3, 4 and 5, are BaselineOnly and SVD. They have good performance in terms of time to train the model, and also good results concerning our evaluation metrics.

5 Related Work

We divide previous related work into two main areas: industry and academic recommender systems. The techniques used can be transversal to both domains, but industry recommender systems tend to be more complete in order to achieve the company's business goals while academic recommender systems tend to explore novel approaches to provide the recommendations.

Table 5. Training and testing times for the different algorithms.

Algorithm	Training time (seconds)	Testing time (seconds)
BaselineOnly	4.613	3.474
SVD	42.844	4.994
SVDpp	103.917	4.381
CoClustering	76.721	3.440
SlopeOne	7.944	3.096
NormalPredictor	1.144	2.638

5.1 Academic

In [11] it is proposed a recommender system that aims to reduce the churn rate of telecom operators. This is due to the operators not having the capability of giving personalized recommendations for products and services to their subscribers. A list of the most top-rated products is shown to the user when he visits the website for the first time. When he logs in it, he is recommended with products based on his location, gender, usage of the product and its popularity.

Several types of collaborative filtering algorithms are used in [13], applied to a data set of telecom users. This recommender system provides telecom services to users by using the concept of neighbourhoods between users and items, users clusters and the "slope one" algorithm. The Pearson, cosine and Spearman similarity measures are used for calculating the user and item neighbourhoods. User and item neighbourhoods correspond to user-based and item-based techniques, respectively. These techniques can be applied to address the data sparsity problem, common in recommender systems that deal with large amounts of users that rate a few number of items. In [14] the goal is to get recommendations for mobile telecommunications products and services. Item-based collaborative filtering is used to generate predictions and create a user-item rating matrix. User-based collaborative filtering is then applied to generate recommendations, thus taking advantage of both the horizontal and vertical information in the user-item rating matrix, which can solve the sparsity problem.

5.2 Industry

The *Netflix* recommender system uses different kinds of algorithms for recommending their shows to the users. The recommendations vary from the most popular items on the platform rated by several users to more personalized recommendations, based on a user's ratings and implicit feedback [5]. *Netflix* also uses the characteristics of the movies and TV shows that the user has rated highly to recommend more shows that he might like and also captures contextual information about him like location.

Amazon's recommender systems also provides product recommendations to its users based on their past ratings and purchases, items in the basket and items that other users have seen/bought. The company developed their own algorithm called Item-to-Item Collaborative Filtering [9] which higly personalizes their website according to a user's tastes and preferences. Years later, the company started using their own recommendation libray called Deep Scalable Sparse Tensor Network Engine [3] to build deep learning models for recommendations.

5.3 Discussion

In this subsection, we compare the aforementioned works, in a concise approach, on Table 6.

Table 6. Comparison of the described recommender systems.

Rec. system	Collaborative filtering	Content-based	Context-based	Feedback	
				Implicit	Explicit
[11]	X		X		X
[13]	X				X
[14]	X				X
[4]	X	X			X
[12]			X		X
Amazon [3]	X			X	X
Netflix [5]	X	X	X	X	X

We can observe that the majority of the scientific research is based on explicit feedback. However, due to necessity or to improve recommendations, in Industry we have both types of feedback being used to enrich the algorithm and improve the products and services proposed to clients. Additionally, the research is more focused on collaborative filtering, existing some hybrid solutions.

Our work is focused on collaborative filtering approaches, because the recommendations are based on past history of users. Due to the non-existence of explicit feedback, we consider the transformation of the implicit feedback into ratings that express the likelihood of users to join the campaigns. This way, we can provide to users several types of recommendations, like the top-rated campaigns or more personalized recommendations related with their activity. To our knowledge, it does not exist any work done about recommendation of advertising campaigns for telecommunication operators. Thus, we consider the study and experiments we developed a novel approach in this specific context.

6 Conclusion

In a world with a plethora of products and services, it is a difficult task for a client to identify good offers for their needs. Hence, recommendation systems have an important role to ensure the best experience and quality-of-service.

In this paper, we explore the possibility to predict recommendations in a telecommunication operator, in a real-world scenario, with implicit feedback, 2 years of client information and more than 46 millions lines of raw data.

Our objective was to identify the feasibility of a recommendation system in a telco system. More concretely, we wanted to study and evaluate distinct state-of-the-art algorithms in the provided data set. Our results allow us to infer about the best algorithm to use for recommendations, basing our decision in the evaluated metrics concerning the quality of the recommendations and the performance of the algorithm. In order to do so, we had to transform implicit feedback into explicit feedback and only consider users that provided useful information for the recommendation engine, i.e., users with past adhesions. Overall, we acknowledge the advantages of recommender algorithms for telecom operators, but recognize also the challenges required to obtain good recommendations with the data we have available.

For future work, we intend to study the cold-start problem for this type of telecommunication system.

References

1. Mean Average Precision. http://sdsawtelle.github.io/blog/output/mean-average-precision-MAP-for-recommender-systems.html. Accessed Feb 2019
2. References surprise algorithms. https://surprise.readthedocs.io/en/stable/prediction_algorithms_package.html. Accessed Feb 2019
3. Amazon DSSTNE. https://github.com/amzn/amazon-dsstne. Accessed Feb 2019
4. Alsalama, A.: A hybrid recommendation system based on association rules (2013)
5. Gomez-Uribe, C.A., Hunt, N.: The Netflix recommender system: algorithms, business value, and innovation. ACM Trans. Manage. Inf. Syst. **6**(4), 13:1–13:19 (2015). https://doi.org/10.1145/2843948
6. Hamner, B.: Machine learning evaluation metrics (2015). https://github.com/benhamner/Metrics. Accessed Feb 2019
7. Herlocker, J.L., Konstan, J.A., Terveen, L.G., Riedl, J.T.: Evaluating collaborative filtering recommender systems. ACM Trans. Inf. Syst. **22**(1), 5–53 (2004). https://doi.org/10.1145/963770.963772
8. Hug, N.: Surprise, a Python library for recommender systems (2017). http://surpriselib.com. Accessed Feb 2019
9. Linden, G., Smith, B., York, J.: Amazon.com recommendations: item-to-item collaborative filtering. IEEE Internet Comput. **7**(1), 76–80 (2003). https://doi.org/10.1109/MIC.2003.1167344
10. Ricci, F., Rokach, L., Shapira, B.: Introduction to recommender systems handbook. In: Ricci, F., Rokach, L., Shapira, B., Kantor, P.B. (eds.) Recommender Systems Handbook, pp. 1–35. Springer, Boston, MA (2011). https://doi.org/10.1007/978-0-387-85820-3_1
11. Soft, M., Makadani, D., Mazhandu, R.: Recommender system for telecommunication industries: a case of zambia telecoms. Am. J. Econ. **7**, 271–273 (2017). https://doi.org/10.5923/j.economics.20170706.01
12. Yoon, K., Lee, J., Kim, M.U.: Music recommendation system using emotion triggering low-level features. IEEE Trans. Consum. Electron. **58**, 612–618 (2012). https://doi.org/10.1109/TCE.2012.6227467

13. Yu, J., Falcarin, P., Vetro, A.: A recommender system for telecom users: experimental evaluation of recommendation algorithms, pp. 81–85 (2011). https://doi.org/10.1109/CIS.2011.6169139
14. Zhang, Z., Liu, K., Wang, W., Zhang, T., Lu, J.: A personalized recommender system for telecom products and services. In: ICAART, pp. 689–693 (2011)

Improving the AHT in Telecommunication Companies by Automatic Modeling of Call Center Service

Henrique de Castro Neto[1(✉)], Rita Maria Silva Julia[1],
Elaine Ribeiro Faria Paiva[1], Andre Ponce de Leon Ferreira Carvalho[2],
Anisio Pereira Santos Junior[1], Diansley Raphael Santos Peres[1],
Etienne Silva Julia[1], Jony Teixeira de Melo[3], Umberto Maia Barcelos[3],
and Josiane Esteves de Assis[3]

[1] Computer Science Department, Federal University of Uberlandia,
Uberlandia, MG, Brazil
henriquecneto@yahoo.com.br, {henriquec,anisiop,
diansleyr,etiennej}@kyros.com.br, {rita,elaine}@ufu.br
[2] Computer Science Department, University of Sao Paulo, Sao Carlos, SP, Brazil
andre@icmc.usp.br
[3] Algar Telecom, Uberlandia, MG, Brazil
{jonyt,umbertom,josianeea}@algartelecom.com.br

Abstract. Several companies have been taking advantage of Data Mining (DM) techniques to improve their operations by retrieving relevant knowledge from available raw data. Due to the high impact of the internet in all domains of modern life, such data exploration is particularly important in the context of *Internet Service Providers (ISP)*. In these companies, significant information can be extracted from raw data available in Data Warehouses built from sequences of dialogues between customers and attendants, recorded in their *Customer Relationship Management (CRM)* system. These data are collected every time the clients contact the *call center* to report problems. Thus, these data have several *scripts*, each with a set of questions and actions that must be carried out over the course of the dialogues. Two parameters are very relevant in such attendance process: the *Average Handle Time (AHT)*, representing the average time spent to solve the problems of the clients; and the costs with technical visits required whenever the attendant can not remotely solve such problems through the call center *scripts*. This paper proposes to enhance the customer service of an *ISP* company through the following strategy: firstly, performing a modelling of its CRM Data Warehouse; and secondly, using such model to improve the call center *scripts*, so as to reduce the *AHT*. The modelling proposed here uses DM to induce classification rules able to predict the need for technical visit taking into account the client problems. In the experiments carried out, rules with high predictive accuracy were generated. The results confirm that the generated rules allow for reducing the call *AHT* and can also be used as a tool for reducing the need for technical visits.

© Springer Nature Switzerland AG 2019
P. Moura Oliveira et al. (Eds.): EPIA 2019, LNAI 11805, pp. 96–107, 2019.
https://doi.org/10.1007/978-3-030-30244-3_9

Keywords: Knowledge Discovery in Database · Decision tree · Internet Service Providers · Applied data science

1 Introduction

Internet users worldwide are increasing at impressive rate. According to a statistics published by "Miniwatts Marketing Group" and "Internet Lives Stats", there are about 4,208,571,287 internet users in the world with 1.5 billion websites [19]. Along with this growth, *Internet Service Providers* (ISP) are making efforts to increase the number of customers, to keep their cost and improve the quality of the services provided [13]. On the other hand, customers always tend to look for ISPs with better benefits. This is the main origin of churns. Churn or customer attrition can be defined as the annual turnover of the market base [13]. Keeping in mind that the cost of obtaining new customer is five times higher than maintaining an existing customer, the financial situation of ISPs is strongly affected by churns [13].

The occurrence of churns is closely associated to how satisfied the customer is with the services provided, which, in turn, depends directly on the customer experience. Thus, in order to increase customer satisfaction, several tools have been proposed to model customer experience. Among them, those that apply Data Mining (DM) techniques to large *Data Warehouse* (DW) obtained from *Customer Relationship Management* (CRM) systems stand out [1–3,10,15]. The CRM Data Warehouse stores all call center interactions between a company and its customers, most of them reporting customer complaints about service failures.

The Average Handle Time (AHT), which represents the average time spent to solve the customer problems, is a parameter that has a great impact on the customer service quality. The lower the *AHT*, the better the customer experience, the greater the customer satisfaction, and the smaller the company cost with the customer service [11].

This study investigates then how *AHT* can be mitigated through the extraction of relevant knowledge from raw data stored in the CRM Data Warehouse of a Brazilian ISP company, *Algar Telecom*, and using such knowledge to improve the customer experience. Particularly, the data with which the present work deals are related to the GPON (*Gigabit Passive Optical Network*) technology. Then, each of these data is produced whenever a customer calls the company to report a GPON problem and the CRM attendant, in order to try to solve such problem remotely, must follow a specific customer service flow, named *Integrated Script* (IS).

A *IS* is composed of several questions or actions, which must be carried out by the attendants together with the customers, as their dialogue progresses. Whenever the *IS* flow does not allow for remotely solving the customer problems, the attendant must open a *Service Order* (SO) pointing out the need for a technical visit, which is not a good alternative neither for the client nor for the company, since it increases the *AHT* and the company expenses.

More specifically then, this paper proposes to enhance the customer service of an *ISP* company through the following strategy: firstly, performing a modelling of the portion of its CRM Data Warehouse that is related to GPON problems; and secondly, using such model to improve the call center *scripts*, so as to reduce the *AHT*, which represents an innovative aspect of this work.

The model produced corresponds to a set of decision-tree based rules able to predict the need for technical visits. These rules are generated according to the *Knowledge Discovery in Databases (KDD)* methodology [9]. To produce rules with high predictive accuracy, the authors investigated some of the most popular decision-tree induction algorithms. In the experiments performed, the rules produced were used to re-order *IS* questions and actions, which significantly reduced the *AHT*. Further, an analysis of the results show that these rules can also be used to reduce the need for technical visits.

Among the difficulties faced in the execution of the present approach, the need for a careful work of data pre-processing stands out. Such difficulty is due to the following aspects inherent to the DW that is the subject of the present study: undue occurrence of repeated data; presence of missing variable values in almost all instances; high frequency of non unified data; imbalanced DW; high occurrence of variable values with low statistical frequency.

The next sections are organized as following: Sect. 2 resumes the main aspects of the *IS*. Section 3 presents the related works. Section 4 details the application of the proposed method and the experimental results. Conclusion and future works are presented in Sect. 5.

2   Attendance Service Through Integrated Script: Context Design

Figure 1 summarizes the customer attendance service flow used by *Algar Telecom* to solve GPON Broadband problems. This flow is the basis for the customer experience modeling proposed herein. The attendance process starts when the customer contacts the call center to report a new complaint (step #1 in the figure). The attendant, together with the claimant, executes a set of *checklists—Integrated Script (IS)—*, which represents a set of questions and actions, to try to solve the problem (steps #2, #3 and #4). If any of the actions suggested by the *IS* solve the problem of the client (step #5), then all the steps performed in steps #2, #3 and #4 are stored in the *IS* database (DW). This database contains all the answers or actions performed for that particular call (step #6). Otherwise, if none of the measures proposed by the *IS* solve the problem (step #7), then a new *Service Order (SO)* is created and stored in the DW database that contains the historic of all SOs (step #8). After creating the SO, the call data are also stored in the database (steps #9 and #10). The SO generated in step #7 follows another call flow, known as *screening*, which is not in the scope in this paper and requires the allocation of a technical expert to go to the client site to solve the problem not solved by the *IS*. It must be observed that steps

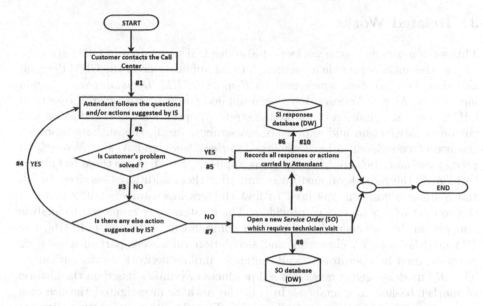

Fig. 1. The attendance service workflow for solving Broadband problems.

#6 and #10 set the flag that indicates whether there is or not the need for a technical visit, respectively, with values "Yes" or "No".

For every question and action suggested by the *IS checklist*, there is a specific *feature* or *variable* associated, which is stored in the DW of the company with its answer. Table 1 shows two examples of questions/actions, with their associated *features* and answers provided during each one of the two calls. These figures were adopted by the authors for constructing the proposed rule-based classification model.

Table 1. Table with examples of questions (or actions) from the attendant, description of the associated features, follows by the answers from the customer in the *IS* used.

Questions	Features	Answers
Is there any problem with landline? (Perform tests and verify the registration of the landline)	LANDLINE_PROBLEM	No
Is there any problem with the cord/fiber? (Ask the client to check if the cord/fiber is ok)	FIBER_PROBLEM	Yes

3 Related Works

This section presents some works that also use DM techniques in CRM systems. In [12], the authors provide a summary of DM applications in the CRM domain, and show how ML techniques, such as *K-means*, *SVM*, *Decision-tree induction algorithms*, *Neural Network*, have been applied to deal with several aspects of CRMs, such as definition of marketing strategy, operational cost reduction and customer satisfaction and experience assessment. In [3], the authors proposed the use of two classification techniques, *Naive Bayes* and *Neural Network*, to predict customer behavior for marketing applications. They use these techniques to identify the most loyal customers and offer them additional services. In [4], the K-mean algorithm was used to find clusters in customers call records in the context of mobile service providers. The clusters were employed to analyze and profile the customers based on their communication behavior. In [16], two DM models based on clustering and association rules were part of a software platform used by operators at call centers of mobile network service providers. The DM models suggest new cross-sell products or bundles based on the historic of market basket data analysis. In [14], the authors investigated the use of a sequence mining algorithm in call centers. The algorithm induce models that automatically transfer the customer call to the adequate support level (between two levels of support available).

4 Experiments Performed in This Study

This section presents the generation of the model corresponding to the CRM Data Warehouse through the KDD stages [9] and how the rules of the models can be used to reduce the *AHT*. It is interesting to remind that these rules must model the CRM Data Warehouse so as to predict the need for technical visit in function of the reported customer problems.

4.1 Extracting the Database

This section presents how the data used in the experiments were collected from the DW so as to produce a raw version of the Database to be used in this work. The KDD stages that were executed in order to generate this raw Database, that is, *Selection* and *Processing* stages, which cope with feature selection and data collect, respectively, are presented below.

Feature Selection. As aforementioned, each single datum handled here corresponds to the register of a specific interaction of a costumer with the CRM. Then, the CRM Data Warehouse is a set of questions/answers/actions produced from the *IS checklists*.

  The feature selection was not a trivial task due to the following fact: the strong non-unified characteristic of the DW data, that is, the pieces of information about each datum was scattered across different DW tables. This fact required a great effort by the research team to effect a junction of the pieces of information of the data scattered in the DW in order to select an appropriate set of features. At the end of this stage, 127 features were selected. Due to a *NonDisclosure Agreement* (NDA) signed with *Algar Telecom*, these *features* will not be listed here.

Data Collect: Producing the Raw Database. Another difficulty faced here was to find an adequate SQL (*Structured Query Language*) query that allowed for generating a Database from which good predictive rules were mined. Such question was formulated from the 127 features previously selected, having collected the set of 111, 230 historical records (covering the period between January 2017 and November 2018) from which a raw Database was built. Each instance (composed of 127 attributes) was labeled with the *target variable* "*A_VISIT_WAS_-REQUIRED*", whose values are "Yes" or "No", depending on whether or not the solution to the problem referred to required a technical visit, respectively.

In the next section, this raw Database will be submitted to *Data Transformation* KDD process in such a way as to be refined and become adequate to be used in the modelling proposed herein (in the *Data Mining* stage).

4.2   Refining the Raw Database: *Data Transformation*

Almost all instances of the generated Database present missing attribute values. The reason for this can be either the fact that the customer service flow did not address these attributes (since this flow varies according to each particular problem), or the fact that the attendant, for some reason, did not assign a value to the attribute during the call. As shown in the next section, the present work investigates two distinct alternatives to deal with these missing values: creating a new category "NI" (*"Non Informative"*) to fulfill them; and adopting the standard solutions provided by the DM-based algorithms used. Additionally, there are some attribute values whose frequency of occurrence is not statistically relevant. These values were then grouped so as to present statistical relevance in the course of the classification process.

Another significant data transformation executed here is the removal of *attributes* strongly associated to the *target variable*, such as the feature "*SOLVED_XXX_PROBLEM*" (where "XXX" represents the type of each treated problem) at steps #3 and #5 of Fig. 1 (Sect. 2). This *variable* represents the last question of the *IS* asked to the customers during the customer service. It is convenient to remove such variable because the answer corresponding to it ("Yes" or "No") automatically sets the *target variable* "*A_VISIT_WAS_REQUIRED*", since a technical visit is required whenever the problem is not solved by means of the *IS*. In total, 23 attributes strongly associated to the *target variable* were excluded in this step. It is interesting to point out that this Database is imbalanced, since 40% of its instances are target with "No" for technical visit, whereas 60% are target with "Yes". However, as this imbalance did not compromise the classification process, it was not necessary to apply class balancing techniques, as shown in the next section.

4.3   Data Mining Stage: Generating the Rule Base

Experimental Setup. The Database obtained is submitted to a binary classification process whose purpose is to produce rules that model the CRM Data
Warehouse predicting the need or not for technical visits in function of the client
problems. For such modelling, this work uses *Decision-tree* induction algorithms,
since, in addition to the high performance that they have been obtaining as a
predictive tool in many tasks, these algorithms provide explainable models by
means of human-readable classification rules. Thus, these algorithms are a very
friendly tool allowing for abstracting the general knowledge implicit on large
dataset [17].

The following 4 algorithms were investigated here, all available in the WEKA
platform: C4.5 [18], PART (*Projective Adaptive Resonance Theory*) [6], REPTree
(*Reduced Error Prunning Tree*) [20] and CART (*Classification And Regression
Trees*) [5]. In this work, the values assigned to the hyperparameters required to
run each algorithm correspond to the default values suggested by WEKA.

For the experiments, the dataset was partitioned using 10-fold-cross-
validation. The experiments were run in two machines with a CPU Intel Core
i5-7200U of 2.71 GHz and with 12 GB of RAM.

Building Data Models. Tables 3 and 2 show the predictive performance
obtained by each *decision-tree* algorithm investigated herein, computed over
two datasets: one, including a new category for missing values (Table 2) and,
the other, not (Table 3). The measures used to represent these performances in
both Tables are: with respect to each class, *True Positive (TP)* and *False Positive (FP)* rates; and, considering both classes, the measures are *f-measure* and
the *standard deviation* related to *f-measure*, taking into account the 10 folds. Is
interesting to point out that *f-measure* is used as a measure due to the fact that
the database is unbalanced.

Two points can be highlighted from Tables 2 and 3. First, there is no need
to apply class-balancing technique over no one of these datasets, since in both
scenarios all algorithms presented high *f-measure* values and the assertiveness of
both classes is balanced. Second, the predictive performances of all algorithms
in both scenarios are also very close. To prove it statistically, the authors applied
the Wilcoxon non-parametric statistical hypothesis test with paired samples [8]
to the *f-measure* values presented in Tables 2 and 3. The values R^+, R^- and
p-values were computed through the software R Studio.

To cope with this, two paired sets were created, one associated to Table 2
and, the other, to Table 3. The *f-measure* value of each algorithm was paired
on the same fold - on the course of the 10 folds cross-validation tests. Adopting
the usual confidence level of 95%, the *p-value* obtained was 0.1475, which proves
that all algorithms present almost the same behavior in both test scenarios
(that is, in situations in which a new category for missing values is created
or not). Considering this fact, from this point on, this work continues with its
investigations only considering the scenario presented in Table 3 (that is, using
the default strategy of each algorithm to deal with missing attribute values).

Table 2. Predictive performance of the four *decision-tree* algorithms with the missing values treated as category "NI".

Algorithm	f-measure	Class = Visit is required		Class = Visit not required	
		TP rate	FP rate	TP rate	FP rate
C4.5	0,9360 ± 0,003	0,949	0,063	0,937	0,051
PART	0,9285 ± 0,002	0,951	0,088	0,912	0,049
REPTree	0,9340 ± 0,002	0,95	0,069	0,931	0,05
CART	0,9385 ± 0,003	0,949	0,057	0,943	0,051

Table 3. Predictive performance of the four *decision-tree* algorithms with untreated missing values.

Algorithm	f-measure	Class = Visit is required		Class = Visit not required	
		TP rate	FP rate	TP rate	FP rate
C4.5	0,9345 ± 0,003	0,945	0,059	0,941	0,055
PART	0,934 ± 0,002	0,94	0,05	0,95	0,06
REPTree	0,9325 ± 0,003	0,946	0,067	0,933	0,054
CART	0,933 ± 0,002	0.946	0,067	0.933	0,054

Then the authors, based on the results shown in Table 3, used the Friedman hypothesis test [7] to evaluate the statistical significance of each algorithm in relation to the *f-measure* values. Table 4(a) shows the *sum of ranks* produced from the Friedman test (over 10 folds cross-validation) and the *groups* produced from the Nemenyi post-hoc test [7] to assess algorithm pairwise differences. Adopting 95% as confidence level, the p-value calculated was 0.1257 (computed through the software R Studio), which proves that there is no statistical difference in the performance rank obtained by the algorithms investigated.

Table 4. Hypothesis testing: (a) Statistic test for the measure *f-measure* over Table 3; (b) Statistic test for the measures *processing time* and *number of features* over Table 5.

(a) Test 1

Algorithm	Sum of ranks
C4.5	28.5 (group a)
PART	26.5 (group a)
REPTree	24.5 (group a)
CART	20.5 (group a)

(b) Test 2

Algorithm	Sum of ranks
REPTree	40 (group a)
C4.5	30 (group b)
CART	20 (group c)
PART	10 (group d)

In the domain used as a case study in this work, the fundamental criteria that must be considered in the classification process are: the *processing time* required to generate the *rule base*, since the dataset must be periodically updated so as to include new registers reporting other dialogues with customers; and the *number of features* used for abstracting the necessity or not for technical visit to solve the problem of the client. Regarding this last criterion, it is interesting to note that classification algorithms that use a lower number of features tend to allow for a reduction on the *AHT* call service measure, as they can speed up the remote contact with the client by identifying more rapidly the need for a technical visit. Table 5 resumes the general results obtained with each tested algorithm. As aforementioned, the criteria which most impact the classification process are *Processing Time* and *number of features*. That is why the remaining criteria are not taken into consideration in the following analysis.

Table 5. Interpretability of the tree data generated by each algorithm and its training time.

Algorithm	Num. of rules	Num. of nodes	Num. of features (FT)	Processing time (TT) in seconds
C4.5	95	184	45	76.6
REPTree	270	457	44	25.12
PART	312	-	52	914.37
CART	42	82	23	342

Thus, given the elevate value presented by *PART* in terms of these criteria (compared to the others), such algorithm can be eliminated. Next, compared to *REPTree*, *C4.5* can be excluded, since, in spite of having used almost the same *number of features* as *REPTree*, its processing time was 3 times greater than that of *REPTree*. Finally, *REPTree* proves to be the best option, as it eliminates the other remaining algorithm *CART* for the following reason: although using the double of features, its *processing time* is 92.65% less than *CART*. Such conclusion was confirmed by submitting the cross-validation results (in terms of *processing time* and *number of features*) to the Friedman non-parametric statistical test. Table 4(b) shows the *sum of ranks* derived from Friedman test and the *groups* produced from the Nemenyi post-hoc test (confidence level of 95%) with p-value $= 1.38e-06$ (computed through the software R Studio). Such a test points out that *REPTree* was the most successful among the algorithms tested to deal with the problem addressed here.

Considering such results, the next section details the results of the predictive performance obtained by *REPTree* and how its rules contributed to improve the customer service of *Algar Telecom*.

4.4 Evaluation Stage: How REPTree Improved the Customer Service

Table 6, by means of a *Confusion Matrix* (CM), evaluates the quality of the rules generated by *REPTree*, in terms of how well they succeeded in predicting the need or not for technical visits (*target variable*). Thus, here the first and second lines of CM represent the rates related to the *true* - that is, necessity - and the *false* - that is, non necessity, values of the *target variable A_VISIT_WAS_REQUIRED*, respectively. As shown in Table 6, *REPTree* presented the following results: accuracy = 94.30%; sensitivity = 93.59%; PPV (*Positive Predictive Value*) = 88.28%; specificity = 94.61% and NPV (*Negative Predictive Value*) = 97.14%, where: *sensitivity* and *PPV* concern both the value *yes* of the *target variable*, being that *PPV*, particularly, indicates the rate of correct predictions related to the need for technical visits (31,513 cases, such as shown in line 1/column 1); *specificity* and *NPV* concern both the value *non* of the *target variable* (that is, the customers' problems were remotely solved), being that *NPV*, particularly, indicates the rate of correct predictions related to the non need for technical visits (73,374, such as shown in line 2/column 2). Such results confirm the appropriateness of using *REPTree* in the modeling of the customer service in *Algar Telecom*.

Table 6. *REPTree* model confusion matrix.

Predict	Actual	
	True	False
A_VISIT_WAS_REQUIRED = True	31,513	2,159
A_VISIT_WAS_REQUIRED = False	4,184	73,374

Further, the reliability of the rule predictions in terms of the need for technical visits is useful to simplify the script of the *IS*, thus allowing reducing the *AHT*. For example, in Table 7, the rule number *89*, related to the customers whose problem is "*Slowness (Low Performance)*", predicts - based on the *predictive attributes* "*SOFTWARES_BL*", "*CONTRACTED_SPEED*" and "*ROUTER*" - that the problem will be remotely resolved.

In the original *IS* from which the rule *89* was generated, considering the same problem, there exist 33 possible questions/actions that can be suggested by the *checklist* over the call service. In this case, the same rule shows the convenience of reordering the flow of questions related to such problem in the original *IS*, so as to prioritize those involving the three attributes present in rule *89*. Such reordering was validated herein in the following manner: by using the new ordered IS, the authors simulated an attending flow corresponding to each case associated to the problem "*Slowness (Low Performance)*" present in the DW used here as a case study. Such simulations confirmed that the reordering allowed for a reduction of 10.31% in the portion of the *AHT* spent to treat the simulated cases, as shown in Table 7.

Analogous reasoning can be applied to rule *105* (related to *Navigation Problem*), whose diagnosis, unlike rule 89, predicts the need for a technical visit. In this case, the simulations of the CRM attending flow from the reordered *IS* reduced the portion of the *AHT* spent to treat such problem by 13.44%, as shown in Table 7.

Table 7. Rule examples based on probability of requiring technical visit.

Number	Rule	Probability of visit	AHT reduction
89	IF ('PROBLEM_TYPE' = 'SLOWNESS - LOW PERFORMANCE' AND 'SOFTWARES_BL' = 'YES' AND 'CONTRACTED_SPEED' = '40MBPS_GPON' AND 'ROUTER' = 'CISCO_E900')	4%	10.31%
105	IF ('PROBLEM_TYPE' = 'NAVIGATION PROBLEM' AND 'SETTING_NAVIGATOR' = 'YES' AND 'NETWORK_ISOLATE' = 'YES' AND 'SLOWNESS_PROBLEM' = 'YES')	91.5%	13.44%

5   Conclusions and Future Works

This paper applies a rule-based classification approach to model the customer service of a ISP company with the purpose of predicting the need for technical visits to solve customer problems. The generated rules proved to be very useful to enhance the customer service through a reduction on the average time related to the remote contact between the customers and the call center in order to try to solve their problems.

As future studies, the authors intend: to validate the results related to the *AHT* reduction through the IS reordering in the real scenario of the company's CRM; to extend the approach proposed herein so as to retrieve new relevant attributes from the OS free texts written by the technical experts to catalog the problems of the clients detected in their visits, as well as the way in which they were solved. These new attributes will point out new questions/actions to be inserted into the *IS* in such a way as to increase the number of problems remotely solved (reducing the need for technical visits).

Acknowledgments. The authors thank Algar Telecom/BRAIN, Federal University of Uberlandia, University of Sao Paulo, Fundação de Apoio Universitáirio (FAU), and Kyros Tecnologia for all financial, administrative, technical and legal support.

References

1. Amin, A., Al-Obeidat, F., Shah, B., Adnan, A., Loo, J., Anwar, S.: Customer churn prediction in telecommunication industry using data certainty. J. Bus. Res. **94**, 290–301 (2019)
2. Amin, A., et al.: Customer churn prediction in the telecommunication sector using a rough set approach. Neurocomputing **237**, 242–254 (2017)
3. Bahari, T.F., Elayidom, M.S.: An efficient CRM-data mining framework for the prediction of customer behaviour. Proc. Comput. Sci. **46**, 725–731 (2015)
4. Bascacov, A., Cernazanu, C., Marcu, M.: Using data mining for mobile communication clustering and characterization, pp. 41–46 (2013)

5. Breiman, L., Friedman, J., Stone, C., Olshen, R.: Classification and Regression Trees. The Wadsworth and Brooks-Cole statistics-probability series. Taylor & Francis (1984)
6. Cao, Y., Wu, J.: Projective art for clustering data sets in high dimensional spaces. Neural Netw. **15**, 105–120 (2002)
7. Demsar, J.: Statistical comparisons of classifiers over multiple data sets. J. Mach. Learn. Res. **7**(Jan), 1–30 (2006)
8. Derrac, J., Garcia, S., Molina, D., Herrera, F.: A practical tutorial on the use of nonparametric statistical tests as a methodology for comparing evolutionary and swarm intelligence algorithms. Swarm Evol. Comput. **1**(1), 3–18 (2011)
9. Fayyad, U.M.: Data mining and knowledge discovery: making sense out of data. IEEE Expert **11**(5), 20–25 (1996)
10. Gupta, G., Aggarwal, H.: Improving customer relationship management using data mining. Int. J. Mach. Learn. Comput. 874–877 (2012)
11. Helper, C.C.: 49 tips for reducing average handling time (2019). https://www.callcentrehelper.com/49-tips-for-reducing-average-handling-time-aht-38157.htm/. Accessed 02 Mar 2019
12. Janakiraman, S., Umamaheswari, K.: A survey on data mining techniques for customer relationship management. Int. J. Eng. Bus. Enterp. Appl. (IJEBEA) (2014)
13. Khan, A.A., Jamwal, S., Sepehri, M.M.: Applying data mining to customer churn prediction in an internet service provider. Int. J. Comput. Appl. **9**(7), 8–14 (2010). published By Foundation of Computer Science
14. Lohse, J., Sanati-Mehrizy, R., Minaie, A.: Data mining in call centers: the overlooked interaction between employees. In: ASEE Annual Conference and Exposition (2015)
15. Ngai, E., Xiu, L., Chau, D.: Application of data mining techniques in customer relationship management: a literature review and classification. Expert Syst. Appl. **36**(2), 2592–2602 (2009)
16. Petrovic, N.: Adopting data mining techniques in telecommunications industry: Call center case study (2018)
17. Provost, F., Fawcett, T.: Data Science for Business. What You Need to Know About Data Mining and Data-analytic Thinking. O'Reilly Media Inc., Sebastopol (2013)
18. Quinlan, J.R.: C4.5: Programs for Machine Learning. Morgan Kaufmann, Burlington (1992)
19. Stats, I.L., Stats, I.W.: Total number of websites and usage and population statistics (2019). http://www.internetlivestats.com/total-number-of-websites/, https://www.internetworldstats.com/stats.htm. Accessed 22 Feb 2019
20. Witten, I.H., Frank, E., Hall, M.A., Pal, C.J.: Data Mining: Practical Machine Learning Tools and Techniques. Morgan Kaufmann, Burlington (2016)

Comparing Machine Learning and Statistical Process Control for Predicting Manufacturing Performance

Sibusiso C. Khoza and Jacomine Grobler[✉]

Department of Industrial Engineering, Stellenbosch University,
Stellenbosch, South Africa
jacomine.grobler@gmail.com

Abstract. Quality has become one of the most important factors in the success of manufacturing companies. In this paper, the use of machine learning algorithms in quality control is compared to the use of statistical process monitoring, a classical quality management technique. The test dataset has a large number of features, which requires the use of principal component analysis and clustering to isolate the data into potential process groups. A Random Forest, Support Vector Machine and Naive Bayes algorithms were used to predict when the manufacturing process is out of control. The Random Forest algorithm performed significantly better than both the Naive Bayes and SVM algorithms in all 3 clusters of the dataset. The results were benchmarked against Hotelling's T^2 control charts which were trained using 80% of each cluster dataset and tested on the remaining 20%. In comparison with Hotelling's T^2 multivariate statistical process monitoring charts, the Random Forest algorithm still emerges as the better quality control method.

1 Introduction

Quality control has been a pivotal aspect of the manufacturing industry for several decades now. The increasingly competitive nature of modern manufacturing environments and customer quality expectations drives the need for organisations to strive for superior product quality. The increasing integration of revolutionary sensor technology, Radio-Frequency Identification, and the "Internet of Things" into the manufacturing industry facilitates the collection of data at multiple points of the manufacturing process. However, with this enormous amount of data, challenges are presented by its complexity, velocity and volume [22].

Trends in the literature show that data science techniques are becoming popular in the control of quality in modern manufacturing environments. The prevalent trends lean toward the application of machine learning algorithms to predict the occurrence of defective products in manufacturing processes. The manufacturing industry has long relied on Statistical Process Control (SPC) as an industry-wide quality control methodology [15]. The use of SPC techniques has evolved over the years to suit modern manufacturing environments that track

P. Moura Oliveira et al. (Eds.): EPIA 2019, LNAI 11805, pp. 108–119, 2019.
https://doi.org/10.1007/978-3-030-30244-3_10

and monitor many continuous and batch process variables. These techniques are referred to as Multivariate Statistical Process Control (MSPC) techniques [3]. The techniques that a manufacturing company chooses to use for quality control/monitoring of its processes contribute to its ability to minimise the distribution of defective products. For manufacturers, this leads to the question: "Which techniques are best suited for quality monitoring/prediction for our processes?". This paper attempts to aid in answering this question using a specific manufacturing dataset as a case study. The aim of the paper is to compare various supervised machine learning classification algorithms for quality prediction and compare the best performing algorithm to a traditional statistical process control (SPC) technique.

This paper is significant since, to the best of our knowledge, it is the first paper to compare Random Forest, Naive Bayes and Support Vector Machine (SVM) algorithms to traditional SPC techniques for quality control.

The rest of this paper is organised as follows: Sect. 2 provides an overview of the relevant literature, Sect. 3 describes the methodology and experimental setup, the dataset used and performance metrics for comparisons. Section 4 presents the results of the study. Finally, Sect. 5 concludes the article.

2 Literature Review

A significant amount of research has been conducted into improving product quality over the last century. Throughout the rest of this section Sect. 2.1 provides an introduction to quality management. Section 2.2 discusses the literature related to statistical process control and Sect. 2.3 reviews previous attempts at using machine learning to predict quality in a manufacturing environment.

2.1 Quality Management

ISO 9000 [17] defines Quality Management (QM) as "management with regard to quality"; where management refers to "the coordinated activities to direct and control an organisation", and quality refers to "the degree to which, a set of inherent characteristics of an object fulfils requirements". ISO further states that QM can entail the establishment of quality policies and quality objectives, as well as processes aimed at achieving the quality objectives thereof through quality planning, quality assurance, quality control, and quality improvement.

ISO [17] also introduces seven quality management principles (QMPs) upon which the ISO 9000 series and related quality management standards are based; these principles are derived from the philosophies and principles set in motion by "quality gurus" such as Deming and Juran in the aftermath of the second world war. These principles do not necessarily have a preset order of priority, hence, organisations can prioritize each QMP differently. The process approach principle is one such principle: "Consistent and predictable results are achieved more effectively and efficiently when activities are understood and managed as interrelated processes that function as a coherent system". The rationale behind this principle is that, by understanding how a system (consisting of interrelated processes) produces results, an organisation can better optimise this system and its performance [17]. Practices of quality monitoring and prediction have paramount importance when it comes to adhering to the "process approach" principle.

2.2 Statistical Process Control

Evans and Lindsay [9] define SPC as a process monitoring methodology aimed at the identification of assignable (special) causes of process variation and cueing the need for corrective action when necessary. The presence of special causes means that a process is out of control, whereas the presence of variation due to common causes means the process is in statistical control i.e. the variances and averages remain constant over time.

Madanhire and Mbohwa [16] found through interviews that between 50% and 75% of the manufacturing businesses in developing countries were certain that SPC had greater benefits when it came to quality control when compared to finished product inspection. Most of the benefits were shown to be attributed to the use of control charts. The main idea is to extract samples of a certain size from the ongoing production process. Line charts of the variability in those samples are drawn and their closeness to target specifications is considered. If a trend emerges in those lines, or if samples fall outside prespecified limits, the process is declared to be out of control and the operator will take action to find the cause of the problem.

SPC is a technique that has been proven to improve productivity and quality and gives firms a means of quality capability demonstration. SPC is, however, not effective for levels of quality approaching six sigma (i.e. when the tolerance for defective products is less than 3.4 defective products in a sample of 1 million products). However, it is considerably effective for firms in their initial stages of quality endeavours [9].

One of the most popular SPC control charts is Hotelling's T^2 chart [12]. This chart is a generalization of the standard X-bar chart for variables. Instead of controlling single values or means, and standard deviations, the Hotelling T^2 chart allows for the control of a vector of means for multiple characteristics, and the variance or covariance matrix of the variables to control process variability. Hotelling's T^2 chart will be used for comparison purposes in this paper due to its popularity.

2.3 Machine Learning in Manufacturing

One of the first papers to suggest the use of data science techniques to augment SPC was Kourti and Macgregor [13]. Conventional MSPC chart methods such as Hotelling's T^2 and χ^2 were seen to be effective only with the provision that the multivariate space does not have extensive dimensionality. Methods that allow visibility of the contribution to the out-of-control condition was suggested in conjunction with these traditional approaches. One such approach involved incorporating PCA, in conjunction with the use of these traditional MSPC charts.

Wuest et al. [19] suggested using cluster analysis and supervised machine learning when dealing with complex (multivariate or highly dimensional) manufacturing environments, as opposed to using conventional methods such as cause-effect relations, because these traditional methods cannot keep up with the growing complexity of modern manufacturing environments.

Chiang et al. [6] conducted a study to compare the classifying capabilities of the fault discriminant algorithm (FDA) and Support Vector Machine (SVM). The dataset used in this comparison was generated using the Tennessee Eastman (manufacturing) process simulator; the simulator used to generate the dataset had the capabilities of simulating normal plant operating conditions, including 21 types of faults (mostly mechanical) that could occur in these simulated conditions. The high dimensionality of the dataset was solved using PCA. The results of this study showed that SVM had a much lower fault misclassification rate than FDA (6% vs 18%, respectively).

Gao and Hou [10] also used the same Tennesse Eastman Process simulator used by [6] and conducted a study to compare the use of SVM in conjunction with grid search (GS), genetic algorithm (GA) and particle swarm optimisation (PSO) in fault prediction. The results of this study showed that all three combinations produced comparable accuracies; however, the GS-SVM approach, was more time efficient. The study also showed that introducing PCA into the GS-SVM approach is a more efficient approach with comparable accuracy.

Escobar and Morales-Menendez [8] applied an "intelligent supervisory control system" based on the logistic regression ML algorithm in detecting rare poor quality events in a high conformance (lean) manufacturing environment. The results of the experimental stage of this application showed a 100% sensitivity on the detection of defects.

Lieber et al. [14] proposed a framework based on unsupervised and supervised machine learning for optimising pattern identification and predicting the quality of intermediate products in interlinked manufacturing processes based on a hot rolling mill process case study. The results of this study showed that better energy-efficiency and sustainability of the interlinked processes could be achieved through the use of this data mining based framework.

Ahsan et al. [1] found that the use of principal component analysis (PCA) in conjunction with Hotelling's T^2 based control charts for a network intrusion detection system, had a similar performance to regular T^2 control charts, with less computation time.

Yu et al. [20] investigated the performance of a multivariate statistical process monitoring (MSPM) approach based using artificial neural networks in identifying sources of out-of-control signals in a manufacturing process. The results of this investigation showed that the neural networked-based system had a higher accuracy in comparison to the system with no incorporation of neural networks.

Sánchez-Fernádez et al. [18] carried out a study in two plants; namely, the Tennessee Eastman (manufacturing) plant and a wastewater treatment plant. The study found that incorporating PCA into Hotelling's T^2 has a higher fault detection rate as compared to using the univariate exponentially weighted moving average (EWMA) method in both MSPC environments.

Yu et al. [21] state that the use of conventional T^2 in multivariate statistical process control (MSPC) is effective, but has shortcomings when it comes to locating the origin of assignable causes. Yu et al. (2018) found that the incorporation of a stacked denoising autoencoder (SDAE) into the T^2 MSPC control charts for multivariate process pattern recognition (MPPR) helps detect process-intrinsic patterns better.

Finally, Zhang et al. [22] used a two-stage approach of clustering and supervised learning to predict product failures on a manufacturing dataset from a competition that was hosted by Bosch on Kaggle. Zhang et al. also overcame the high dimensionality of the dataset through the use of PCA. They found that the Random Forest classification algorithm achieved the highest score, outperforming the logistic regression, Naive Bayes, gradient boosting and decision tree classification algorithms. They did not, however, comment on how these machine learning approaches compared with traditional SPC techniques.

Most of the reviewed papers employ the application of machine learning classifiers in manufacturing environments with domain knowledge of features and processes. The work of Zhang et al. [22] differs in that no domain knowedge is available about the manufacturing process. They first had to segment the data into separate manufacturing processes before any quality predictions could be performed. They used PCA to reduce dimensionality and K-means clustering to separate these process groups within the dataset.

From the literature it is clear that SPC has limitations and machine learning algorithms have the potential to add value, however, no clear comparison between the two techniques can be found and it is not clear what the performance improvement associated with machine learning is.

3 Methodology and Experimental Setup

The purpose of this paper is to compare machine learning and SPC for manufacturing quality control. To achieve this aim, an extract of the dataset of [22] is used and a similar unsupervised-supervised approach is followed. This paper, however, extends the work of [22] by testing additional supervised learning algorithms and evaluating the machine learning approach against a traditional SPC approach.

Observations in the dataset represent products as they move through the production lines. The features in the dataset are anonymised; they are given names relating to their line, station number, and feature number which follow the convention of "L#_S##_F###". The end result of whether a product is a success or a failure is given as a binary class named "Responses", with 0 representing a success and 1 representing a failure. The dataset used in this paper contains only the numerical product line features. The dataset consists of 968 features, 20 001 observations, and 0.56% of failed products.

The use of the Zhang et al. dataset resulted in a number of unique challenges:

- Poor domain knowledge: the anonymized features presents a problem since the domain knowledge of the manufacturing process is not available. The different processes need to be discovered before the responses can be predicted. These added step presents added computational complexity and potential reliability issues with the results.
- High sparsity, since several manufacturing stations serve a similar purpose to a product, this leaves a large proportion of features within an observation having no data or having inputs as zeros.
- High imbalance, since there exists a high imbalance in the distribution of the responses since only a very small proportion of the products failed.

PCA and K-means is used for the unsupervised learning phase, and a Random Forest, Support Vector Machine and Naive Bayes algorithms are used for the classification phase. These algorithms were selected because they cover a wide range of algorithms and have showed promising results in previous work.

- Support Vector Machines (SVMs) perceive observations as points in p-dimensional space (where p is the number of features in the dataset excluding the response variables) these points are plotted in the p-dimensional space, and the best hyperplane is then employed to separate points of different classes. The coordinates of these points are referred to as support vectors [7].
- Naive Bayes uses Bayes' theorem to classify observations, with a naive strong assumption that the features in the data are independent [11].
- Decision Trees follow a tree-like structure. It iteratively breaks down a dataset into smaller subsets while incrementally developing a (decision) tree. The built tree is made up of decision nodes and leaf nodes; the decision nodes represent features and its branches are the possible entries to this feature and the leaf nodes represent the classes or decisions [5].
- A Random Forest employs multiple decision trees and predicts the most probable class based on the "majority vote" of the decision trees [4].

This machine learning based solution is then compared with a Hotelling's T^2 chart. The complete methodology is described in more detail below:

- Step 1: Principal Component Analysis- The PCA function is used to reduce dimensionality in the dataset by combining correlated features such that the end result is a dataset consisting of features that are uncorrelated. This helps combine all features representing similar production processes since they are correlated. The resulting number of principal components becomes the new number of features. These principal component features are then further reduced according to the variances they account for in the dataset; the first and second principal component features normally remain in the dataset since principal component features are named in increasing order of the variance accounted for. A reduced dataset is then produced by deleting principal component features that account for very low variance. A scatterplot of the first and the second principal components is then visualised to estimate the number of clusters in the dataset, which represents the number of process groups that use similar stations.

- Step 2: Clustering- With the aid of visual data (a scatter plot) the observations of the dataset is grouped into different production processes using the k-means algorithm. K is chosen as the number of clusters seen from the scatter plot. The k-means algorithm is then used to divide the clusters in the dataset (this is the reduced dataset with original inputs based on a selected number of principal components).
- Step 3: Classification- After clustering and subsetting of the dataset according to its clusters, each subset is split into a training set and a test set (80%:20%), the training and testing is executed using the N-fold cross validation function with the value of N chosen as 5 (as this allows the function to split each cluster dataset according to the 80%:20% ratio). The training sets are then oversampled and undersampled to overcome the class imbalance. Classification algorithms are then trained on the training sets and tested on the test sets of each cluster
- Step 4: Compare ML algorithms based on chosen performance metrics and choose the best algorithm in each cluster to compare to MSPC Hotelling's T^2 control chart.
- Step 5: Train and Test Hotelling's T^2 based control charts – Each cluster is then arranged in increasing order of the numerical product ID (SPC chart control limits are established over time, and product ID values increase over time) and split into a training and test set (80%:20%). The training set is used to establish and fix control limits. The test set data is then plotted on the control charts to provide indications of whether the process is seen as in-control or not.
- Step 6: Compare the best algorithms in each cluster with the MSPC control chart's performance – the same metrics used to compare ML algorithms are used here with a slight modification of the meaning of the confusion matrix outputs. In the case of the control charts, TP refers to instances where the charts indicate that a process is not in control and the actual responses are positive (failures), TN refers to instances where the charts indicate that a process is in control and the actual responses are negative (success or "0"), FP refers to instances where the charts indicate that a process is not in control and the actual responses are negative (success or "0"), and FN refers to instances where the charts indicate that a process is in control and the actual responses are positive (failures).

Most classification problems use classification accuracy as the primary measure of performance; however, according to Bekkar et al. [2], imbalanced class proportions leads to misreading of common classifier evaluation metrics such as accuracy. Accuracy is simply a measure of the overall effectiveness of a classification model, it represents the proportion of instances correctly predicted by a model. Another common metric is sensitivity, which is simply the conditional probability of a model predicting true minority/positive class given the minority/positive class. Specifity works the same way as sensitivity, but on the negative or majority class. Therefore, sensitivity and specificity measure the effectiveness of a classifier on a single class, i.e. positive and negative classes, respectively. In the case of evaluating models in imbalanced class problems, metrics that combine specificity and sensitivity are preferred [2], because they are less influenced by imbalance. In this paper, three of these combined metrics will be used, namely Mathew's Correlation Coefficient (MCC), G-mean and balanced accuracy.

MCC values range from -1 (100% imperfect predictions) to 1 (100% perfect predictions), with 0 indicating a random classifier, and can be determined from the confusion matrix. G-mean is the geometric mean of the sensitivity and the specificity of a model, this metric heavily penalises models that predict only one class, thus eliminating biased models. G-mean values range from 0 (100% biased or imperfect) to 1 (100% perfect and unbiased). Balanced accuracy is simply the arithmetic average of sensitivity and specificity. This metric has the same range as G-mean, however, it enables better comparison of 100% biased models, since it will only have a value of 0 if both sensitivity and specificity have a value of 0.

The algorithms are compared based on their performance in the test sets using MCC, G-mean and balanced accuracy with equal weights. The same metrics are also used when comparing the "best" algorithms to SPC.

4   Results

This section presents the results found in this paper according to the methodology that is presented in Sect. 3.

4.1   Feature Selection and Dimensionality Reduction

The results of principal component analysis show that more than 50% of the variance is accounted for by features grouped as component 1 feature (Comp.1), and just above 10% of the variance is accounted for by component 2 feature, while the remaining component features lack variance i.e. less than 10% (these are features with constant values, which are regarded as noise that models cannot learn much from) as shown in Fig. 1 below. The selected component features to reduce dimensionality and feed useful information into the models are, therefore, chosen as component 1 and component 2 features with their respective principal component scores.

Using the first two principal components, a biplot is produced to aid on deciding on the number of clusters of "homogeneous" products or similar groups of stations to divide the dataset into, as shown in Fig. 2. The black points within the figure are product IDs, and the red/grey points are features/process variables; the Comp.1 and Comp.2 axis are the principal scores of each product ID on the first and second principal components, and the top and right axis are the

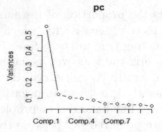

Fig. 1. Variance explanation of principal components.

loadings of the features on the first two principal components. Visually, it can be seen that despite some variation within clusters, there is most probably 3 product clusters (product ID groups) and/or 3 different feature groups (3 types of processes/stations); hence, a decision is made to split the dataset into 3 clusters, thus concluding the unsupervised learning phase.

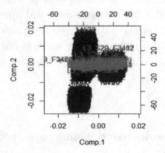

Fig. 2. Biplot of component 1 and 2. (Color figure online)

The K-means clustering algorithm is thus used with $k = 3$ to split the dataset into three production process groups. The results of the clustering summary are as follows: Cluster 1: 9757 observations, Cluster 2: 1074 observations, and Cluster 3: 7339 observations.

4.2   Classification Algorithm Training and Testing

After clustering, it is assumed that each cluster represents data from a single manufacturing process. Each cluster dataset is then over-and-under sampled to balance the distribution of the response variable. Training and testing procedures of the ML algorithms are executed with the aid of n-fold cross validation with $n = 5$.

For each cluster, three ML classification algorithms i.e. Random Forest, Naive Bayes and SVM are used to train models on the over-and-under sampled observations. The models are then tested on the test sets and the results are summarised in Table 1. For the Naive Bayes algorithm, the ZeroProba parameter is kept at the default 0.001, to maximise its sensitivity and the kernael parameter is set to "radial" to optimise its ability to isolate observations. For the random forest algorithm, the default parameters set within Rstudio are used and the default tree depth parameter is kept at the maximum possible depth.

Table 1. Summary of classification model test results.

Test dataset (Cluster)	ML algorithm	Average MCC	Average G mean	Average balanced accuracy
1	Random forest	0,9955015	0,9977944	0,9979963
	Naive Bayes	0,2053079	0,6051928	0,6062934
	Support vector machine	0,260833	0,6304471	0,6306527
2	Random forest	1	1	1
	Naive Bayes	0,2347075	0,6231602	0,6235933
	Support vector machine	0,7059401	0,8701798	0,8787396
3	Random forest	0,9954342	0,9980517	0,9977323
	Naive Bayes	0,2745122	0,6779324	0,6902451
	Support vector machine	0,334727	0,6697478	0,670461

In each cluster, the scores in each metric are ranked in increasing order (worst to best), with the best score in bold. The Random Forest algorithm can be seen to be the best performing algorihtm for all three metrics in all three clusters.

4.3   Random Forest Algorithm and SPC Chart Comparison

Finally, the Random Forest algorithm is benchmarked against a MSPC Hotelling's T^2 control chart. The training and testing of the control charts are done for each cluster as described in step 6 of the methodology section. The test results are based on the plotting of future observations in the fixed control chart limits established during the "training" phase.

The monitoring signals of the control charts are then translated into confusion metric equivalents by comparing the signals given by each the charts to the actual test responses or classes through conditional coding (if-statements) in Excel following the description of the confusion matrix described in step 6 of the methodology. The best ML models in each cluster, which all happen to be based on the Random Forest algorithm are then compared to the MSPC Hotelling's T^2 control charts performance. The metrics of each cluster are then summarised in Table 2.

The cluster 1 and cluster 3 results show that the Random Forest classification models rank much higher than the MSPC Hotelling's T^2 control chart monitoring

Table 2. Hotelling's T^2 -Random Forest evaluation summary.

Test dataset (Cluster)	1		2		3	
Predictor/monitor	**RF**	T^2	**RF**	T^2	**RF**	T^2
TP		0		0		0
TN		1916		215		1812
FP		16		7		13
FN		13		0		6
MCC	**0.9955**	−0.007	**1**	N/A	**0.9954**	−0.005
Sensitivity		0		N/A		0
Specificity		0.992		0.968		0.993
G mean	**0.9978**	0	**1**	N/A	**0.9981**	0
Balanced accuracy	**0.9980**	0.496	**1**	0.484	**0.9977**	0.496

model. The results from Cluster 2 are mostly inconclusive due to the inapplicable metrics; these metrics are undefined when a particular class does not occur in the test data. In this cluster 2 case, the 20% test split for the Hotelling's T^2 model in cluster 2 does not have any positive classes; however, the perfect metric scores obtained by the Random Forest models indicate that there is an extremely low likelihood of the Hotelling's T^2 charts performing any better than the Random Forest model. The inability of the Hotelling's T^2 charts to perform better in any of the chosen metrics in all clusters provides some degree of verification that the Random Forest has an overall better performance. In practice, if assumed that these results relate to a specific process, the Random Forest models would be recommended.

5   Conclusion

This article compares the performance of a Naive Bayes, a Random Forest and a SVM algorithm against MSPC control charting (Hotelling's T^2) on an anonymised feature dataset of imbalanced class distribution. On all 3 subsets of the data that are produced based on PCA and K-means clustering, the Random Forest based models outperformed the Naive Bayes, Support Vector Machine model and the (M)SPC chart monitoring.

Recommendations for future work include investigating the application of predictive quality control based on classification algorithms against statistical process control methods using data from known processes and improving the performance of the classification algorithms.

References

1. Ahsan, M., Mashuri, M., Kuswanto, H., Prastyo, D.D., et al.: Intrusion detection system using multivariate control chart Hotelling's T2 based on PCA. Int. J. Adv. Sci. Eng. Inf. Technol. **8**(5), 1905–1911 (2018)

2. Bekkar, M., Djemaa, H.K., Alitouche, T.A.: Evaluation measures for models assessment over imbalanced data sets. J. Inf. Eng. Appl. **3**(10) (2013)
3. Bersimis, S., Panaretos, J., Psarakis, S.: Multivariate statistical process control charts and the problem of interpretation: a short overview and some applications in industry. In: Proceedings of the 7th Hellenic European Conference on Computer Mathematics and its Applications, Athens, Greece (2005)
4. Breiman, L.: Random forests. Mach. Learn. **45**(1), 5–32 (2001)
5. Breiman, L., Friedman, J., Olshen, R., Stone, C.: Classification and Regression Trees, vol. 37, no. 15, pp. 237–251. Wadsworth International Group (1984)
6. Chiang, L.H., Kotanchek, M.E., Kordon, A.K.: Fault diagnosis based on fisher discriminant analysis and support vector machines. Comput. Chem. Eng. **28**(8), 1389–1401 (2004)
7. Cortes, C., Vapnik, V.: Support-vector networks. Mach. Learn. **20**(3), 273–297 (1995)
8. Escobar, C.A., Morales-Menendez, R.: Machine learning techniques for quality control in high conformance manufacturing environment. Adv. Mech. Eng. **10**(2), 1687814018755519 (2018)
9. Evans, J.R., Lindsay, W.M.C.: The management and control of quality. Technical report, South Western (2002)
10. Gao, X., Hou, J.: An improved SVM integrated GS-PCA fault diagnosis approach of tennessee eastman process. Neurocomputing **174**, 906–911 (2016)
11. Hand, D.J., Yu, K.: Idiot's bayes–not so stupid after all? Int. stat. Rev. **69**(3), 385–398 (2001)
12. Hotelling, H.: Multivariate Quality Control. Techniques of Statistical Analysis. McGraw-Hill, New York (1947)
13. Kourti, T., Macgregor, J.F.: Multivariate SPC methods for process and product monitoring. J. Qual. Technol. **28**(4), 409–428 (1996)
14. Lieber, D., Stolpe, M., Konrad, B., Deuse, J., Morik, K.: Quality prediction in interlinked manufacturing processes based on supervised and unsupervised machine learning. Proc. Cirp **7**, 193–198 (2013)
15. MacGregor, J.F., Kourti, T.: Statistical process control of multivariate processes. Control Eng. Pract. **3**(3), 403–414 (1995)
16. Madanhire, I., Mbohwa, C.: Application of statistical process control (SPC) in manufacturing industry in a developing country. Proc. Cirp **40**, 580–583 (2016)
17. International Organization for Standardization: ISO 9000. Technical report, International Organization for Standardization (1995)
18. Sánchez-Fernádez, A.: Fault detection based on time series modelling and multivariate statistical process control. Chemom. Intell. Lab. Syst. **182**, 57–69 (2018)
19. Wuest, T., Irgens, C., Thoben, K.D.: An approach to monitoring quality in manufacturing using supervised machine learning on product state data. J. Intell. Manuf. **25**(5), 1167–1180 (2014)
20. Yu, J., Xi, L., Zhou, X.: Identifying source(s) of out of control signals in multivariate manufacturing process using selective network ensemble. Eng. Appl. Artif. Intell. **22**, 141–152 (2009)
21. Yu, J., Zheng, X., Wang, S.: Stacked denoising autoencoder-based feature learning for out-of-control source recognition in multivariate manufacturing process. Qual. Reliabi. Eng. Int. **35**, 204–223 (2018)
22. Zhang, D., Xu, B., Wood, J.: Predict failures in production lines: a two-stage approach with clustering and supervised learning. In: 2016 IEEE International Conference on Big Data (Big Data), pp. 2070–2074. IEEE (2016)

Feature-Based Time Series Classification for Service Request Opening Prediction in the Telecom Industry

Fabíola S. F. Pereira[1]([✉]), André C. P. L. F. Carvalho[1], Rafael Assis[2],
Maxley Costa[2], Elaine R. Faria[2], Rita Maria Silva Julia[2], Umberto Barcelos[3],
and Jony Melo[3]

[1] University of São Paulo, São Carlos, Brazil
{fabiola.pereira,andre}@usp.br
[2] Federal University of Uberlândia, Uberlândia, Brazil
{rafael.assis,maxley.costa,elaine,rita}@ufu.br
[3] Algar Telecom, Uberlândia, Brazil
{umbertom,jonyt}@algartelecom.com.br

Abstract. Telecommunication companies face the challenge to reduce
the number of service request openings (SROs). A predictive behavior able to reduce this number can improve customers experience and
decrease operational costs. This paper proposes a machine learning (ML)
based approach to reduce the number of SROs. For such, it uses real data
from a Brazilian telecom operator. The proposed approach uses feature-
based time series extracted from network equipment's signals, modeling
the problem as a binary classification task. We carry out experiments to
investigate the impact of long-term and short-term windows in the predictive performance. After pre-processing the data, we apply different
classifiers algorithms. According to experimental results, a high predictive performance was obtained, mainly when long-term network behavior
data was used. These results have a positive impact in the company costs.

Keywords: Telecom industry · Predictive model ·
Service request opening · Time series classification

1 Introduction

The complexity of communications networks increases with the offering of new
services, such as software-defined wide-area networking and employment of new
technology paradigms, like network functions virtualization. To meet ever-rising
customer expectations, telecommunication companies (telcos) need to improve
the quality and reduce the cost of their network operations, planning and optimization.

Big data analytic tools are good alternatives for this improvement. Many
studies report the use of big data analytics in tasks like churn prediction [23],

© Springer Nature Switzerland AG 2019
P. Moura Oliveira et al. (Eds.): EPIA 2019, LNAI 11805, pp. 120–132, 2019.
https://doi.org/10.1007/978-3-030-30244-3_11

user behavior based on mobile data [11] and anomaly detection in core router systems [13].

Although big data analytics is already widespread in the telecom industry, it is typically conducted in batch, after the fact, and according to manually update rules and policies [3]. To improve customer experience, telcos need to efficiently mode from reactive to predictive actions. For such, they need to use intelligent and customer-centric systems.

Service request opening (SRO) is a typical customer service in telecommunication companies that requires predictive actions [16]. When a customer contacts the call center to report a problem and the problem cannot be remotely resolved, a service request (SR) is open and a technician is often dispatched for on-site problem solving. Thus dispatches have a high cost and, therefore, should be made only when really necessary. A predictive action that is able to avoid SROs could not only reduce costs, but improve customers experience.

According to [21], Internet SRO in telcos are usually due to network behavior, like, e.g., inability to reach contracted download rate, absence of Internet signal and slow download/upload rates. Thus, network signal behavior can provide important clues to predict SROs.

This paper proposed a ML based approach to predict SROs using network behavior data. The hypothesis assumed in this study is that *it is possible to use ML techniques to predict, based on network signals behavior, with a good predictive performance, whether a customer will open an Internet service request the following days.*

To investigate this hypothesis, the SRO problem is addressed in this paper using a feature-based time series (FBTS) classification approach, i.e. a supervised ML task where a feature extraction procedure is performed before the classification phase [14]. For such, we extract features from several time series formed by the signals from each customer modem. From these features, we use ML to induce a model able to decide, for a given customer, whether he/she will open an Internet SR or not.

Thus, the main goal of this work is to explore the SRO prediction problem as a FBTS classification task. Experiments were performed comparing 2 different feature-based transformations. The data used in the experiments were provided by Algar Telecom – a Brazilian telecommunication company, in disjoint form, i.e., different relational databases. We carefully built a joint dataset containing customer's demographic information, SRO records and daily snapshots of network signals behavior.

From business viewpoint, this study contributes to (i) provide visualization platforms to support decision making regarding SROs and (ii) cost savings based on optimized planning of technicians dispatches. Regarding ML contributions, this paper (i) investigates, for the first time, the use of ML for SRO prediction in Internet service provided by a telecom company, (ii) uses network device signals behavior as main information source to induce ML-based models for SRO prediction and (iii) proposes 2 new feature-based extractions over time-series to improve predictive accuracy.

The rest of this paper is organized as follows: in Sect. 2, the main aspects and previous works on communication service providers predictive tasks are briefly presented. Section 3 introduces feature-based time series classification. Section 4 describes the dataset used. Then, Sect. 5 presents and analyzes the experimental results. Section 6 has the main conclusions from this study.

2   Related Work

To the best our knowledge, this is the first time the SRO prediction problem in the telecommunication domain is investigated. Previous studies in analytics using telecom data include churn prediction [9,18,22,23], failure and anomaly detection on network equipments [13], customer behavior analysis from mobile data [11,16] and customer experience improvement [4].

In [13], the authors proposed the use of time series analysis and ML algorithms to detect anomalies and predict failures in complex core router systems. A SVM-based failure predictor was created to predict lead time of system failures from collected anomalies. An example of feature is "route age". This proposal is close to ours regarding the use of time series data from network equipments, however the predictive task focus only on network failures. We focus on SRO events, which are related to customers reactions from network behavior.

A comprehensive survey on churn prediction can be found in [9]. In one of these works, [23] proposed a model for early churn prediction. The model considers time series attributes and influence of churning contacts in social networks.

Studies investigating user behavior based on mobile data [11,16] create personalized models according to users geographical traces, using mobile data kept by telcos. A similar work, regarding customer experience viewpoint, can be found in [4]. In our search for related works, we detected a lack of works exploring network behavior data.

3   Feature-Based Time Series Classification

According to [20], classification of time series has been investigated in many application domains, from speech recognition to financial analysis, from power system to telecom systems. In this work, we investigate time series classification to identify whether a Internet SRO event will occur.

Feature-based methods perform a feature extraction procedure before inducing a classifier. In general, from the original signal s, a moving window of fixed length k is used to obtain a time-series s_t. Next, a set of p features, usually average, standard deviation, maximum and minimum, is extracted from the time-series. Thus, each time-series, together with a class label, become an instance in a dataset. In theory, if the process that originated the signal is weakly stationary, second-order statistic measures are sufficient to characterize the signal. However, as signals obtained from real-world scenarios are not stationary, more features may be necessary to summarize the information present in the signal, many of them requiring domain knowledge [20].

In this study, due to the lack of baseline approaches in SRO prediction domain, we combine a set of time series with different window lengths to describe an instance in dataset. In order to reduce the time necessary to extract the features, only common second-order statistic measures were used to extract the features.

4   Telecom Dataset

The data used in the experiments reported in the paper come from 4 data sources, with different properties regarding the DSL (Digital Subscriber Line) Internet service. One of the main contributions of this work is the integration of these datasets into a single one. All datasets were provided by Algar Telecom company. Figure 1 illustrates the data sources integration to create a unified dataset.

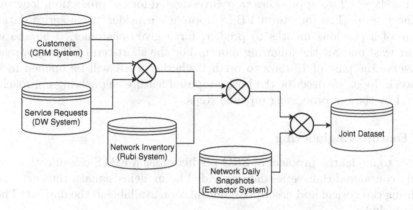

Fig. 1. Telecom data sources joined into a single dataset.

We considered the period from January to April 2018. First, we collected all active DSL Internet customers from the CRM (Customer Relationship Management) system, resulting in 1,239,483 rows. Next, we extracted from the Data Warehouse (DW) all service request openings in the period, which resulted in 470,948 rows. After cleaning duplicated and inconsistent information, we joined the two datasets obtaining a dataset with 418,066 rows. Afterwards, we enriched the resultant dataset with network inventory from Rubi system, in order to gather customers DSL modems information. Due to low data quality, we had to discard a large number of inconsistent data in this step, evidencing the fragility of the telecom relational storage. This resulted in a dataset with 38,321 rows. Finally, we added, for each customer, the respective modem daily signals from Extractor system, resulting in 31,485 customers with full information.

The joint dataset has 217 columns, which include customer demographic information, SRO descriptive data, DSL modem inventory data and daily signal measurements. Table 1 summarizes the main aspects of the dataset.

Table 1. Telecom dataset statistics after joining four data sources.

Timespan	Jan–Apr/2018 (120 days)
Service	DSL Internet
# customers	31,485
# customers with at least 1 SRO	2,337
Time series data	Modem signals daily behavior
# columns	217

5   Predicting Service Request Openings

As mentioned in the introduction, we modelled the SRO prediction problem as
a general binary classification task: "will the customer open a SR or not in the
following days?" Two approaches were investigated for the prediction, long term
and short term. The long-term FBTS approach considers time series data in
a range of 3 previous months to predict, for a given customer, if he/she will
open at least one SR the following month. For the short-term FBTS approach,
we observe the past of 15 days to predict whether a SR will be opened in the
next week. Next, we describe the both proposed feature engineering approaches,
followed by the pre-processing pipeline steps.

5.1   Feature Engineering

In order to model the problem of SRO prediction as a FBTS classification task,
we only considered time series data provided by modems signals, thus excluding
remaining categorical and descriptive information available in the dataset. These
signals include:

- signal upload/download: number expressed in dBs that describes the speaking
  strength on line;
- attenuation rate upload/download:
  reduction in signal strength on line, sometimes also referred to as loss. As it
  is related to the length of the line from the exchange, it varies according to
  the actual wire gauge, material, as well as the frequency. Unit measure in dB;
- attainable rate upload/download:
  maximum attainable rate that a line can theoretically handle, measured in
  kbps. It can vary with the dynamic nature of subscriber line and
- current rate upload/download: daily rate of line upload/download, also measured in kbps.

Figure 2 illustrates the network behavior of 2 randomly selected customers,
together with SRO events. It must be observed that SRO events are not straight
correlated with any specific signal.

Long-Term Feature Extraction (LT Dataset). We modeled the signals from
customers' network behavior as feature-based time series considering 3 months of

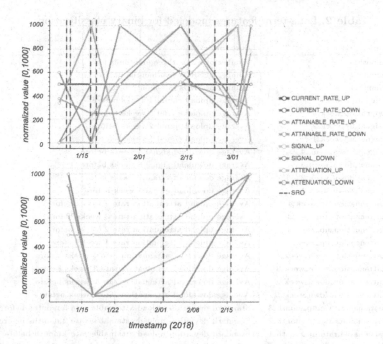

Fig. 2. Network behavior of 2 randomly selected customers over time. Dashed red lines represent SRO events. (Color figure online)

historical data. A brief description of these features is given in Table 2. The time series were grouped based on average and standard deviation. We use average for weekly periods (moving window $k = 7$ days) and standard deviation for monthly periods ($k = 30$ days).

Short-Term Feature Extraction (ST Dataset). The time series were grouped considering up to 15 days of historical data (Table 3). The features were also based on average and standard deviation. Moving windows were set to $k = 2$ and $k = 5$ days.

Both feature engineering approaches take into account business knowledge. Measurements based on signals and attenuation rates are assumed to be more related to SROs. For them, we used average as statistical feature and shorter moving window sizes. On the other hand, attainable and current rates use standard deviation as statistical feature and larger moving windows sizes. The idea is to combine different window sizes and statistical features for each approach, increasing diversity and coverage.

Features Analysis. When observing the correlation of the predictive features (Fig. 3), we identified that signal and attenuation rates have a higher correlation when compared to the other attributes in both datasets. Similarly, attainable and current rates are more correlated. The upload and download rates are correlated by definition. However, there was a low correlation of these rates in our datasets,

Table 2. Long-term features modeled for binary classification.

	Feature	Description
1	SR_month_3	Number of SROs three months before
2	SR_month_2	Number of SROs two months before
3	SR_month_1	Number of SROs one month before
4	avg_signal_up_week_4	Average upload signal 4 weeks before
5	avg_signal_up_week_3	Average upload signal 3 weeks before
6	avg_signal_up_week_2	Average upload signal 2 weeks before
7	avg_signal_up_week_1	Average upload signal 1 week before
8	avg_signal_down_week_4	Average download signal 4 weeks before
9	avg_signal_down_week_3	Average download signal 3 weeks before
10	avg_signal_down_week_2	Average download signal 2 weeks before
11	avg_signal_down_week_1	Average download signal 1 week before
12	avg_attenuation_up_week_4	Average upload attenuation rate 4 weeks before
13	avg_attenuation_up_week_3	Average upload attenuation rate 3 weeks before
14	avg_attenuation_up_week_2	Average upload attenuation rate 2 weeks before
15	avg_attenuation_up_week_1	Average upload attenuation rate 1 week before
16	avg_attenuation_down_week_4	Average download attenuation rate 4 weeks before
17	avg_attenuation_down_week_3	Average download attenuation rate 3 weeks before
18	avg_attenuation_down_week_2	Average download attenuation rate 2 weeks before
19	avg_attenuation_down_week_1	Average download attenuation rate 1 week before
20	std_attainable_rate_up_month_3	Standard deviation upload attainable rate 3 months before
21	std_attainable_rate_up_month_2	Standard deviation upload attainable rate 2 months before
22	std_attainable_rate_up_month_1	Standard deviation upload attainable rate 1 month before
23	std_attainable_rate_down_month_3	Standard deviation download attainable rate 3 months before
24	std_attainable_rate_down_month_2	Standard deviation download attainable rate 2 months before
25	std_attainable_rate_down_month_1	Standard deviation download attainable rate 1 month before
26	std_current_rate_up_month_3	Standard deviation upload current rate 3 months before
27	std_current_rate_up_month_2	Standard deviation upload current rate 2 months before
28	std_current_rate_up_month_1	Standard deviation upload current rate 1 month before
29	std_current_rate_down_month_3	Standard deviation download current rate 3 months before
30	std_current_rate_down_month_2	Standard deviation download current rate 2 months before
31	std_current_rate_down_month_1	Standard deviation download current rate 1 month before
	will_open_SR_next_month	Boolean for will open or not a SR next month

showing that both should be used. Remind that in the ST dataset, average-based features have high correlation, showing that one of them would be enough. Thus, in ST dataset we only kept average-based features related to 1-2 days, dropping the others average-based features. The final LT and ST datasets contain 31 and 19 predictive features, respectively.

5.2   Pre-processing

Removing Outliers. We use Z-score to identify outliers in our datasets. The intuition behind Z-score is to describe any data point by finding its relationship with the Standard Deviation and the Mean of a group of data points. Using Z-score, we re-scaled and centered the data and looked for data points very far from zero. Those data points are treated as outliers. As illustrated in Fig. 4, we set thresholds $t_{LT} = 11$ and $t_{ST} = 5$, removing 2.4% and 2.7% of instances, respectively. All removed outliers are from the not-open class.

Table 3. Short-term features modeled for binary classification.

	Feature	Description
1	SR_day_15	Number of SROs 15 days before
2	SR_day_7	Number of SROs 7 days before
3	SR_day_3	Number of SROs 3 days before
4	avg_signal_up_day_7_8	Average upload signal 7–8 days before
5	avg_signal_up_day_5_6	Average upload signal 5–6 days before
6	avg_signal_up_day_3_4	Average upload signal 3–4 days before
7	avg_signal_up_day_1_2	Average upload signal 1–2 days before
8	avg_signal_down_day_7_8	Average download signal 7–8 days before
9	avg_signal_down_day_5_6	Average download signal 5–6 days before
10	avg_signal_down_day_3_4	Average download signal 3–4 days before
11	avg_signal_down_day_1_2	Average download signal 1–2 days before
12	avg_attenuation_up_day_7_8	Average upload attenuation rate 7–8 days before
13	avg_attenuation_up_day_5_6	Average upload attenuation rate 5–6 days before
14	avg_attenuation_up_day_3_4	Average upload attenuation rate 3–4 days before
15	avg_attenuation_up_day_1_2	Average upload attenuation rate 1–2 days before
16	avg_attenuation_down_day_7_8	Average download attenuation rate 7–8 days before
17	avg_attenuation_down_day_5_6	Average download attenuation rate 5–6 days before
18	avg_attenuation_down_day_3_4	Average download attenuation rate 3–4 days before
19	avg_attenuation_down_day_1_2	Average download attenuation rate 1–2 days before
20	std_attainable_rate_up_day_11_15	Standard deviation upload attainable rate 11–15 days before
21	std_attainable_rate_up_day_6_10	Standard deviation upload attainable rate 6–10 days before
22	std_attainable_rate_up_day_1_5	Standard deviation upload attainable rate 1–5 days before
23	std_attainable_rate_down_day_11_15	Standard deviation download attainable rate 11–15 days before
24	std_attainable_rate_down_day_6_10	Standard deviation download attainable rate 6–10 days before
25	std_attainable_rate_down_day_1_5	Standard deviation download attainable rate 1–5 days before
26	std_current_rate_up_day_11_15	Standard deviation upload current rate 11–15 days before
27	std_current_rate_up_day_6_10	Standard deviation upload current rate 6–10 days before
28	std_current_rate_up_day_1_5	Standard deviation upload current rate 1–1 days before
29	std_current_rate_down_day_11_15	Standard deviation download current rate 11–15 days before
30	std_current_rate_down_day_6_10	Standard deviation download current rate 6–10 days before
31	std_current_rate_down_day_1_5	Standard deviation download current rate 1–5 days before
	will_open_SR_next_week	Boolean for will open or not a SR next week

Balancing Data. SRO datasets present imbalanced class distributions. When classification algorithms are applied to imbalanced datasets, the induced models usually favour the majority class. Figure 5 illustrates classes distributions in LT and ST datasets which have proportions of 97.99/2.01 and 98.38/1.62, respectively. There are several alternatives to reduce class imbalance. One of them is to increase the number of instances in the minority class by adding artificial instances, known as data oversampling. We consider that is more important to avoid false positives than false negatives, as useless predictive actions can be costly for the company. We use one of the most popular data oversampling algorithms, SMOTE [2], for each training set.

5.3   Model Selection and Evaluation

The experiments were carried out using Python with the scikit-learn library [17]. Binary classification (BC) models were induced using 9 ML algorithms: Gaussian

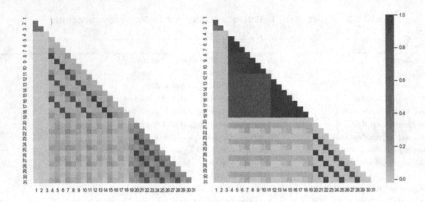

Fig. 3. Correlation heatmap of predictive features for LT (left) and ST (right) datasets.

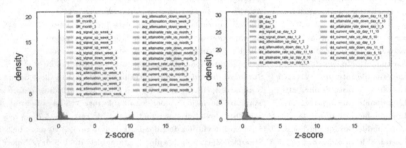

Fig. 4. Z-score data distribution for LT (left) and ST (right) datasets.

Naive Bayes (GNB) [8], Linear Support Vector (LSV) [6], Multi-layer Perceptron (MLP) [19], Random Forest (RF) [1], Extremely Randomized Trees (ERT) [10], Voting among RF, GNB and LSV (VOT) [15], Bagging based on RF (BAG) [15], Adaboost over decision trees (ADA) [7] and Gradient boosting (GRB) [15]. These algorithms were chosen because they have different bias and presented high predictive performance in several classification tasks, even without hyper-parameter tuning [5]. Thus, all algorithms used the default values defined in the sklearn package.

The reported results were obtained using 10-fold cross validation. The same training and test partitions were used to obtain the average of the measures for all BC models. To ensure the same proportion of each label in each fold, the split between train and test followed the binary stratification algorithm [12].

The evaluation of the predictive performance of the BC models requires the use of specific measures that are able to explore their particularities [12]. In this work, measures that evaluate different perspectives of the learning process were considered. Accuracy measures the predictive quality. It is lenient when considering the partial successes. F1 score is the harmonic average of the precision and recall. And AUC (Area Under the ROC Curve) provides an aggregate measure of

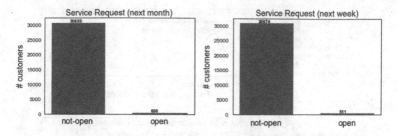

Fig. 5. Proportion of customers that opened at least one service request in the next month (LT) and in the next week (ST)

performance across all possible classification thresholds. AUC is the probability that the model ranks a random positive example more highly than a random negative example.

5.4   Analysis of the Experimental Results

Table 4 shows the BC results obtained for each model and each FBTS extraction approach. The bold markup indicates the best value obtained for each measure. Regarding LT approach, ADA algorithm obtained the best result for accuracy, but low predictive performance in F1 and AUC. RF has the best balance when considering all measures. GNB, LSV and MLP did not perform well, with poor F1 scores. In general, strategies based on decision trees outperformed the rest.

In ST approach, ERT obtained the best performance according to accuracy, but low F1 when compared to the best one RF. Even so, ST approach results indicate the models, in general, did not perform well regarding minority class, with poor F1 performance.

Table 4. Results obtained for different BC models in the LT and ST datasets.

Strategy	Long-term (LT)			Short-term (ST)		
	Accuracy↑	F1↑	AUC	Accuracy↑	F1↑	AUC↑
GNB	0.051	0.038	0.496	0.026	0.027	0.501
LSV	0.828	0.232	0.710	0.843	0.075	**0.551**
MLP	0.642	0.144	0.527	0.694	0.024	0.485
RF	0.898	**0.664**	**0.791**	0.969	**0.148**	0.550
ERT	0.904	0.504	0.697	**0.972**	0.093	0.536
VOT	0.827	0.262	0.762	0.851	0.060	0.547
BAG	0.897	0.662	**0.791**	0.968	0.143	0.549
ADA	**0.906**	0.481	0.683	0.967	0.090	0.540
GRB	0.905	0.481	0.695	0.970	0.089	0.535

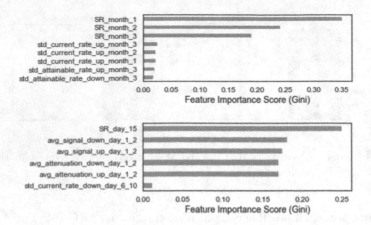

Fig. 6. Feature importance obtained from the RF model for the LT approach (up) and from the ERT model for the ST approach (down).

Surprisingly, the predictive performance in the long-term FBTS approach outperformed that of the short-term FBTS approach in the most of algorithms and measures. According to business insights, specialists expected short term signals to be sufficient and more decisive than signals from long-term signals. Intuitively, to the slightest sign of falling in network quality, customers could raise a SRO event. The insights, therefore, were not confirmed in our experiments.

On the other hand, the results throw light on important features and time issues regarding the SRO prediction problem. Figure 6 illustrates the most important features for the LT and ST approaches, considering the models induced by RF and ERT, respectively. The absolute number of SROs have high impact on predictive performance, particularly when considering long-term data. Extracted features based on network signals have more impact on the ST approach.

6   Conclusion

This paper investigated the SRO prediction problem as a FBTS binary classification task over network behavior from telecom data. Two FBTS extraction approaches were applied covering long-term and short-term historical data. We applied pre-processing techniques to the data and ran different ML algorithms on the pre-processed data. According to the experimental results, the predictive performance obtained by the long-term approach was superior to the performance obtained using the short-term approach. Additionally, experiments validated the hypothesis that we can predict whether a Internet SRO event will occur in the following days.

We believe that the investigation of new alternatives can improve the performance obtained. (i) Exploring new predictive attributes, (ii) different pre-processing strategies, (iii) a train-test evaluation considering a landmark in time and (iv) exploring methods that can directly operate over multi-variate time series, such as Long Short Term Networks are inherent extensions of this work. We did not find other works investigating the use of network behavior data for SRO prediction in telecom industry. Thus, our proposal is a first step in this direction. Furthermore, we conjecture that many of the observations generalize beyond the studied telecom operator data.

Acknowledgements. We thank Algar Telecom/Brain for financial, technical and legal support; Federal University of Uberlândia (UFU) and University of São Paulo (USP) for research, legal and administrative support; and Fundação de Apoio Universitário (FAU/UFU) for financial management.

References

1. Breiman, L.: Random forests. Mach. Learn. **45**(1), 5–32 (2001)
2. Chawla, N.V., Bowyer, K.W., Hall, L.O., Kegelmeyer, W.P.: Smote: synthetic minority over-sampling technique. J. Artif. Int. Res. **16**(1), 321–357 (2002)
3. Crawshaw, J.: AI in telecom operations: Opportunities & obstacles. Technical report, Heavy Reading Reports (2018)
4. Diaz-Aviles, E., et al.: Towards real-time customer experience prediction for telecommunication operators. In: IEEE International Conference on Big Data, pp. 1063–1072 (2015)
5. Dietterich, T.G.: Ensemble methods in machine learning. In: Kittler, J., Roli, F. (eds.) MCS 2000. LNCS, vol. 1857, pp. 1–15. Springer, Heidelberg (2000). https://doi.org/10.1007/3-540-45014-9_1
6. Fan, R., Chang, K., Hsieh, C., Wang, X., Lin, C.: Liblinear: a library for large linear classification. J. Mach. Learn. Res. **9**, 1871–1874 (2008)
7. Friedman, J.H.: Greedy function approximation: a gradient boosting machine. Ann. Stat. **29**, 1189–1232 (2000)
8. Friedman, N., Geiger, D., Goldszmidt, M.: Bayesian network classifiers. Mach. Learn. **29**(2–3), 131–163 (1997)
9. García, D.L., Nebot, À., Vellido, A.: Intelligent data analysis approaches to churn as a business problem: a survey. Knowl. Inf. Syst. **51**(3), 719–774 (2017)
10. Geurts, P., Ernst, D., Wehenkel, L.: Extremely randomized trees. Mach. Learn. **63**(1), 3–42 (2006)
11. Huang, H., et al.: A cross-platform consumer behavior analysis of large-scale mobile shopping data. In: Proceedings of the 2018 World Wide Web Conference (WWW 2018), Geneva, Switzerland, pp. 1785–1794 (2018)
12. Japkowicz, N., Shah, M.: Evaluating Learning Algorithms: A Classification Perspective. Cambridge University Press, New York (2011)
13. Jin, S., Zhang, Z., Chakrabarty, K., Gu, X.: Failure prediction based on anomaly detection for complex core routers. In: Proceedings of the International Conference on Computer-Aided Design, ICCAD 2018, pp. 49:1–49:6 (2018)
14. Kleist, C.: Time series data mining methods: a review. Master's thesis, Humboldt-Universitat zu Berlin (2015)
15. Kuncheva, L.I.: Combining Pattern Classifiers: Methods and Algorithms (2014)
16. Ouyang, Y., Hu, M.: Big Data Applications in the Telecommunications Industry. IGI Global, Pennsylvania (2016)
17. Pedregosa, F., et al.: Scikit-learn: machine learning in Python. J. Mach. Learn. Res. **12**, 2825–2830 (2011)

18. Prashanth, R., Deepak, K., Meher, A.K.: High accuracy predictive modelling for customer churn prediction in telecom industry. In: Perner, P. (ed.) MLDM 2017. LNCS (LNAI), vol. 10358, pp. 391–402. Springer, Cham (2017). https://doi.org/10.1007/978-3-319-62416-7_28
19. Rosenblatt, F.: The perceptron: a probabilistic model for information storage and organization in the brain. Psychol. Rev. **65**, 386 (1958)
20. Susto, G.A., Cenedese, A., Terzi, M.: Chapter 9 - time-series classification methods: review and applications to power systems data. In: Arghandeh, R., Zhou, Y. (eds.) Big Data Application in Power Systems, pp. 179–220. Elsevier (2018)
21. Totok, A.: Modern Internet Services: Exploiting Service Usage Information for Optimizing Service Management. VDM Verlag (2009)
22. Wei, C.P., Chiu, I.T.: Turning telecommunications call details to churn prediction: a data mining approach. Expert Syst. Appl. **23**(2), 103–112 (2002)
23. Zhang, J., Fu, J., Zhang, C., Ke, X., Hu, Z.: Not too late to identify potential churners: early churn prediction in telecommunication industry. In: IEEE/ACM International Conference on Big Data Computing, Applications and Technologies, pp. 194–199. BDCAT (2016)

Sequence and Network Mining of Touristic Routes Based on Flickr Geotagged Photos

Ana Silva[1], Pedro Campos[1,2], and Carlos Ferreira[2,3(✉)]

[1] Faculty of Economics, University of Porto, Porto, Portugal
anarsilva92@gmail.com
[2] LIAAD INESC TEC, Porto, Portugal
pcampos@fep.up.pt
[3] ISEP, Polythechnic Institute of Porto, Porto, Portugal
cgf@isep.ipp.pt

Abstract. Information provided by geotagged photos allow us to know where and when people have been, supporting a better understanding about tourist's movement patterns across a destination. The aim of this paper is to study tourists' movement patterns during their staying in Porto through the analysis of geotagged photos in order to fulfill marketing segmentation in an innovative way. For that purpose, the SPADE algorithm was used to find sequence patterns of tourists paths based on the time and location of the photos collected. Then, the K-Mode clustering algorithm was applied to these sequences in order to find identical behaviors in terms of paths followed by tourists. At the same time, in order to understand the influence of the different attractions on tourists' paths, we performed a Social Network Analysis of the touristic attractions (spots, museums, streets, monuments, etc.). Based on the time and location of the photos collected, along with personal information, it was possible to understand tourists' frequent movements across the city and to identify market segments based on a hybrid strategy.

Keywords: Tourism Marketing · Market segmentation ·
Geotagged photos · Sequence mining · Cluster Analysis ·
Social Network Analysis · Flickr.com

1 Introduction

Traditionally, tourists market segmentation is based on behavior, demographic, psychographic or/and geographical strategies. Demographic strategies are used with more frequency in tourism than others are, because most of the times the necessary information is easy to identify and measure [5]. However, market segmentation strategies can be hybrid, which means that more than one strategy can be used [5]. Business organizations recognized that customer needs and behavior are not obvious without formal research and analysis [6]. The identification of spatio-temporal trajectories creating spots of interest is an important issue in

© Springer Nature Switzerland AG 2019
P. Moura Oliveira et al. (Eds.): EPIA 2019, LNAI 11805, pp. 133–144, 2019.
https://doi.org/10.1007/978-3-030-30244-3_12

Tourism Marketing. Several definitions of tourists' movement patterns can be found in literature but almost all related with spatial changes and sequences of movements between activites or locations [4,7]; Tourists' behavior patterns are nowadays considered as a sequential event of visiting different places, their travel routes, and the amount of time spent at any location [8].

Finally, millions of geotagged photos are available in online web services recently and people are contributing with geotagged photos and share their travel experiences through social media. These photos have important information like location, time, tags, title and weather [8,9]. The analysis of photography data related to the geographical position taken by tourists is an effective method to study tourist movement patterns in urban spaces [8,10]. Regarding to market segmentation, Internet not only provided huge advances in database marketing and innovative distribution approaches, but also expanded the ability of implement market segmentation in a more effectively way and expanded the portfolio of segmentation methods available [11].

In this work we explore photos collected from Flickr.com media-sharing site to unveil and understand the behavior of tourists that visit Porto, Portugal. The photos explored in this work were taken over a period of 29 months (from January 2014 to May 2016) by 253 users/tourists. Based on the time and location of the photos collected, along with personal information such as origin and gender, it was possible to analyze tourists' activity and the corresponding tracks in space and time. We run sequence mining algorithms to find the most frequent tourist patterns across the city and use Social Network Analysis to understand the connections between the places and sites visited by tourists. Finally, we employ Cluster Analysis to identify tourist segments and fulfill market segmentation, based on demographic, geographic and behavioural information.

In the next section we present related literature that has been relevant for the development of this work. In Section Methodology we introduce the methodology. In Section Results we analyze the findings. In the final section we conclude and present some research directions that may be explored in a near future.

2 Related Work

The evolution of the World Wide Web allowed the appearance of interaction and user-generated content on the online world, assuming various forms. According to [20], six types of social media have been identified in the literature: social networking websites (e.g., Facebook), blogs, content communities (YouTube), collaborative projects (Wikipedia), virtual social worlds and virtual game worlds. In [21] the authors describe Flickr as a media-sharing site and classified the online revolution into Wikis (e.g., Wikitravel), blogs (Travelblog), microblogs (Twitter), social network sites (Facebook) and review sites (TripAdvisor).

Some researchers used geotagged photos from Flickr.com in order to track tourists in cities. However, few attention has been paid to the spatial and temporal behavior of tourist despite research on human space-time behavior exists since the 1970s. In [12] Vu et al. explore geotagged photos taken from Hong Kong tourists for delivering useful insights on destination development, transportation planning and impact management. In [13] the authors focused on the analysis of user-generated touristic routes within urban areas. In [10] the authors study tourists' spatial distribution in the city of Budapest. In [14] the authors analyzed the relation between the location and the content of photos. However, none of the mentioned works aimed to fulfill market segmentation.

For the present study, it is important to highlight the research done by Xia et al. [4] that proposed fulfilling market segments based on the dominant movement patterns of tourists, using general log-linear models and the Expectation–Maximization algorithm. Leung et al. [7] as well as Mckercher, Shoval and Birenboim [16], along with a few others, completed the insights of Xia et al. [4] and Vu et al. [12], by providing alternative classifications for tourist's market segments based on individuals' behavior. However, these researchers' motivations were not exactly marketing strategies oriented, but instead they oriented towards management and planning. Moreover, these authors did not used Flickr.com database to fulfill the market segmentation process.

Bermingham and Lee [22] uncovered patterns in Queensland photo takers movements for the year 2012. One of the most interesting aspects of this approach is that this spatio-temporal trajectory forms spots of interest taking into consideration both space and time simultaneously, producing highly informative sequence patterns. However, the authors did not identified typical patterns or groups in the data.

3   Data and Methods

3.1   The Case of Porto

Porto, in the northern coast of Portugal, has recently become one of the most searched destinations in Europe. Since the UEFA Football European Championship in 2004, there has been a positive evolution on Portuguese tourism as a result of strong communication campaigns. Porto won the award European Best Destination in 2012 and again, in 2017, against major European cities such as Milan, Paris and Amsterdam. Porto is the only Portuguese city with such recognition and most part of the votes actually came from foreign countries.

3.2   Data Collection

Flickr.com is a popular photo-sharing platform and became one of the most popular online resources for people to share their travel experiences by uploading photos and it is a rich data source for mining tourist travel patterns, since its public API allows anyone to access these photos along with their textual metadata [8,12]. In 2014 there were over 14 billion of photos uploaded in Flick and more than 200 million geotagged images stored. Related to the city of Porto, there were more than 600.000 photos with the Tag *Porto* (found in the period between January 2014 until May 2016) but only around 20% contained geotag information. Of those, only 55% were actually related to the city of Porto. After data cleansing, the database contains 8201 photos from 253 different users.

The first 500 geotagged photos have been taken and uploaded since 1 January 2014 within the tags *Porto*, given in the parameter tag. The attributes *min_upload_date* and *max_upload_date* were used in this sense. The location generally marks where the photo was taken but also can mark the area of the photographed object. For that purpose, an accuracy attribute was used to disclose the location of the photo. This extra attribute allowed us to extract further information about the photo using the field *date_taken*. Finally, as it was also in our interest to acquire additional and more personal information about the users a second query was used. The results from this query provided insights about individual's gender, country origin, social state and profession.

In the end, a chronologically ordered set of photos was created taking into consideration the attribute *date_taken* and the photo owner. In this study, different from [15], we do not distinguish between tourists, travelers and visitors. Therefore, we assume that all users are tourists. Each trip duration was calculated based on the attribute date_taken, one of the attributes of Flickr. Thus, two followed photos of a certain owner are considered part of a certain trip if the date_taken value between the pictures does not exceed more than 8 days. However, it is not possible to assume that such data portrays exactly the real individual's trip duration. Finally, we considered the amount of information disclosed. Sharing personal data in Flickr.com is no mandatory, so not all users provided it. From all the 253 users available in our database only 20% shared complete information about themselves. In some cases, a country was manually assigned due to spelling errors. Additionally, as the data collected came from public posts, user names were omitted regarding privacy issues. For all other fields where information was not obtained, the value NA was assigned.

3.3 Sequence Mining Analysis

Sequence Mining is a task of data mining concerned with finding patterns consisting of an ordered set of elements or events. The patterns found by sequence mining algorithms can be very useful in many fields. Particularly in the marketing area to develop advertising campaigns, develop recommendation systems, improve systems performance, among others.

Let $I = \{i_1, i_2, \ldots, i_n\}$ be a set of items and e an event such that $e \subseteq I$. A *sequence* is an ordered list of events $e_1 e_2 \ldots e_m$ where each $e_i \subseteq I$. Given two sequences $\alpha = a_1 a_2 \ldots a_k$ and $\beta = b_1 b_2 \ldots b_t$, sequence α is called a *subsequence* of β if there exists integers $1 \leq j_1 < j_2 < \ldots < j_l \leq t$ such that $a_1 \subseteq b_{j_1}, a_2 \subseteq b_{j_2}, \ldots, a_k \subseteq b_{j_l}$. A sequence database is a set of tuples $< sid, \alpha >$ where sid is the sequence identification and α is a sequence. The *count* of a sequence α in a database of sequences D, denoted $count(\alpha, D)$, is the number of examples in D that contain the α subsequence. The *support* of a sequence α is the ratio between $count(\alpha, D)$ and the number of sequences in D. We denote support of a sequence as $support(\alpha, D)$. Given a sequence database D and a minimum support value λ, the problem of sequence mining is to find all subsequences in D having a support value equal or higher than the user-defined value, the λ value. Each one of the obtained sequences is also known as a frequent sequence or a sequential pattern.

There are several algorithms that can be used to find frequent sequences. In this work SPADE [3] algorithm was used to discover tourists' movement patterns in Porto. This algorithm uses a vertical layout format where each sequence in the lattice is associated with the *idlist*. This *idlist* is a list of all examples containing the candidate sequence, the list contains a set of pairs where each pair consists of both the sequence id (*sid*) and an event identifier (typically the event time). To search for frequent patterns the SPADE algorithm uses a candidate-generation strategy. To compute the support of each candidate pattern of level l, the *idlist*'s of sequences from level $l-1$ are joined using a *temporal join*. The support of each candidate pattern is the number of distinct *sid* in the candidate *idlist*. Like other algorithms, SPADE uses the apriori property to prune the search space. Five experiences were run based on the percentage of frequent movement parameter, represented by the variable support in the algorithm (support level equal to 0.4, 0.2, 0.1, 0.05 and 0.03). The higher the support level of a sequence, the higher the frequency of the movements returned will be and the lower the number of movements identified.

3.4   Social Network Analysis

A social network [1, 2] represents entities and their relations as nodes and links, which form a network. It can be defined as a method used to map and measure relationships and flows between people, groups, organizations, and other connected information/knowledge entities.

Networks can be represented as a graph in mathematical terms. Considering a graph $G = (V, E)$ where V represents the set of vertices or nodes and E the sets of edges or links where elements of E are unordered pairs u, v of distinct vertices $u, v \in V$, the network, in the context of this study, is a graph $G = (V, E)$ where $V = \{1, 2, \ldots, 85\}$ is the set of the 85 vertices/places in the city that are explored in this work and E represents the set of edges created by the movements between places because a photo is proof of the individual's physical presence in a certain place and time.

Table 1. Most frequent movement patterns found using a minimum support level equal to 10%.

Path	Support (%)
Rio Douro $\longleftrightarrow$ Ponte D. Luis I	**32.1**
Cais de Gaia $\longrightarrow$ Ponte D. Luis I	**11.1**
Ribeira $\longrightarrow$ Ponte D. Luis I	**10.6**
Estação de São Bento $\longrightarrow$ Ponte D. Luis I	**10.2**

Table 2. Most frequent movement patterns and its frequency/support for a level between 5 and 10%.

Path	Support (%)
Aliados ⟶ Ponte D Luis I	9.3
Torre dos Clérigos ⟶ Ponte D Luis I ⟶ Aliados	8.1
Rio Douro ⟶ {Torre dos Clérigos or São Bento station}	7.7
São Bento station ⟶ Rio Douro	7.7
Ponte Luís I ⟶ Estação de São Bento	7.7
Livraria Lello and Irmão ⟶ Ponte Luíŋs I	6.5
Torre dos Clérigos ⟶ Rio Douro ⟶ Ponte Luíŋs I	6.5
Igreja dos Clérigos ⟶ Rio Douro	6.1
Rio Douro ⟶ Cais de Gaia ⟶ Ponte Luíŋs I	6.1
Torre dos Clérigos ⟶ Cais de Gaia	5.7
Cais de Gaia ⟶ Rio Douro ⟶ Ponte Luís I	5.7
Rio Douro ⟶ Igreja do Carmo	5.7

The network extracted is composed by all the sets of paths made by tourists chronologically. A centrality metric was used to quantify the importance and the influence of the vertices in the network.

3.5   Cluster Analysis

A Cluster Analysis using K-mode algorithm was applied to sequences in order to fulfill market segmentation. Clustering can be seen as a common approach to implementing the partitioning operation that can reveal significant impacts on data classification, aggregation and segmentation processes and used for marketing purposes [18]. Although k-means is maybe the most popular clustering algorithm because of its efficiency in grouping large quantities of data, we can not apply it on categorical data. This limitation was addressed by the k-mode algorithm [17–19]. Ralambondrainy's [19] approach consists on converting multiple category attributes into binary attributes, in which 0 represents the absence and 1 the presence of each category.

Different analysis were performed considering different attributes such as gender, origin, social state and profession, as well as some experiences with the purpose of finding the exact number of clusters to be considered.

4   Mining Tourists' Paths

4.1   Mining Frequent Paths

With the sequence mining analysis we were able to identify the most frequent trips fulfilled by tourists between January 2014 and May 2016. As explained previously, five experiences (support level equal to 0.4, 0.2, 0.1, 0.05 and 0.03) were performed based on the movement frequency rate and the results are represented in Tables 1, 2 and 3.

With the first two experiences, by setting the minimum support equal to 40% and 20%, we were not able to find any frequent path of length higher than one. Only frequent attractions like Luíŋs I bridge, with 44.7% of frequency, and Douro River, with 29%, were found.

By setting the minimum support level to 10%, we extract frequent patterns (having a length higher than one) and frequent places in our sample. We present these patterns and places in Table 1. At this level of frequency, the algorithm found a few frequent paths, but they keep being related directly to movements near riverside.

For a level of 5% and 3% of frequency, we were able to extract significant results regarding individuals behavior. These results are shown in Tables 2 and 3. A significant part of the places are related to religious monuments (churches most part), followed by photos taken to Palaces and photos related to Porto wine activities. Finally, pictures taken to the ocean and pictures taken through strategic spots such as bridges and Metro tours present a significant frequency.

In conclusion, the first insights provided by this experience revealed that individuals' paths are mainly concentrated around the river. Moreover, other attractions, such as Clérigos Tower and Estação de São Bento, are considered a movement accelerator, which means these places present major influence in tourists' travelling patterns. Some paths are almost mandatory given the proximity of the places, for example, Ribeira, Cais da Ribeira and Douro River: the places are so close that it is hard not to appear in a certain path when the tourist takes photos in one of those places. Finally, the results also demonstrate a downstream pattern since most trips start in highest city spots and most of them end in the lowest city spot. After that, individuals tend to cross over the river or redirect their trips in direction to Foz (parish bounded by the sea and the Douro river). Some of them decide to go back by using facilities such as the historical tram and Metro.

Table 3. Most frequent movement patterns and its frequency for a level between 3 and 5% that did not start/end in Douro River or D Luis bridge.

Path	Support (%)
Aliados square ⟶ Estação de São Bento	4.5
Aliados square ⟶ Torre dos Clérigos	3.7
Porto wine activites ⟶ Aliados square	4.5
Estação de São Bento ⟶ {Torre dos Clérigos, igreja dos Clérigos or Liberdade square}	3.7
Palácio da Bolsa ⟶ Estação de São Bento	3.3
Palácio da Justiça ⟶ Photos taken to the ocean	3.7
{Igreja das Carmelitas, Livraria Lello or Terreiro da Sé} ⟶ São Bento station	3.3

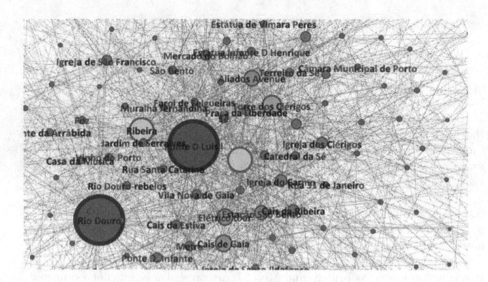

Fig. 1. Social Network Representation of the tourist's movement patterns across Porto city. (Color figure online)

4.2   How Do Networks Between Different Locations Help Us to Understand Tourists' Behavior: Social Network Analysis

In order to understand the influence of the different attractions on tourists' paths, we performed a Social Network Analysis and we run some Centrality metrics. Given the low level of accuracy of those places, we focused on the results provided by the Degree distribution, Distance and Diameter metrics and by the Betweenness centrality.

The two spots in the middle of the figure represent Ponte D. Luis and Rio Douro, the two most popular spots for Flickr photos. At the first sight, the Network tell us that tourist's present a similar pattern across time since they are mostly concentrated on a small range of common spots (bigger nodes) and then they disperse through the city. There are a few attractions that appear in practically all paths (the darker blue ones).

The Degree distribution shows that there are many places with few edges connected and a few places with a range of connections associated, which is very clear to observe in Fig. 1 by the connections higher density around the bigger nodes.

The Betweenness centrality results confirm that a range of places with more connections associated are also the ones that most frequently appeared in individuals' paths.

The Distance and Diameter metrics revealed that, on average, tourists pass through four places during their trips and the longest distance between two nodes (places) is ten places. Crossing with the information provided by the Sequence Mining analysis we can easily observe that the places with higher degree level also have the highest betweenness centrality such as Rio Douro, Ponte D. Luis and Ribeira, followed by Torre dos Clérigos and Estação de São Bento for instance. Not only are the most photographed places (connections) but also are the most frequent itens in the trips (betweeness). We also can find attractions with high degree-level but less-betwenness centrality which can mean that there are places with a lot of connections associated but they appear less frequently in tourists paths like Bolhão, Casa da Música and Livraria Lello and Irmão.

In terms of connections, there are a small group of places with high-level of connections associated. Given the downstream movement of tourists flow in the city, the places near the riverside presents more out connections than in and the places that are working as movement accelerators also present a high level of in connections despite being located in higher spots of the city.

In conclusion, the network analysis revealed that tourists are spatially concentrated on a few main locations related to the historical centre and the riverside. It is also possible to observe that most part of the individuals in our sample tend to look for a range of common spots, no matter their motivations. We can observe a profound connection between such places since they appear in most part of individuals' trips. Crossing with the information provided by the Sequence Mining analysis we can easily observe that places with higher degree level also have the highest betweenness centrality - not only are the most photographed places (connections), but also are the most frequent items in the trips (betweenness). The results of this analysis are a complement to the insights of the sequence mining approach because we were not able to find communities among the attractions. We were expecting to observe profound connections between a certain numbers of attractions that could support the travelling paths discovered.

4.3   Finding Market Segmentation Basis

A cluster analysis was applied in order to find clusters in our sample. The segmentation-based applied to perform tourists' market segmentation in this study are hybrid and mostly based on a demographic and geographic approach. Each category in the sequence of the attractions found in the previous steps has been transformed into binary attributes, in which 0 represents the absence and 1 the presence of each category.

Then, other qualitative variables have been considered. A first experience was based on individuals' gender. It was possible to segment the market into 10 different segments. Most part of the male segments have Luis I bridge, Douro River and Porto landscapes as places in common.

We performed the same analysis based on individual's social marital status and we were able to find some differences between the married and the single travelers. In this case, the massive part of the married ones have Luis I bridge in common.

A third experience was based on individual's origin – a geographic segmentation strategy. For this experience we classified the tourists as European, American and others.

The three experiences revealed some details about tourists market in Porto:

- We were able to find groups that searched for art, cultural and entertainment activities;
- The married European and retired tourists search for attractions near the river and the American ones for attractions in Gaia related with wine;
- The married man tourists search for wine activities and religious monuments and the female European single tourists for the river and for the riverside;
- Behavioural differences between Spanish and German tourists by opposite to the French and British ones etc
- The youngest individuals in this sample (the single and student ones) are mainly Spanish and British

In general, there are groups that search for cultural and historical attractions, for attractions in the historical center and others that search essentially by the riverside, despite their origin, gender or social state.

Despite the lack of information about individual's profession, we could observe through the information available that the sample present high-level of education, which might imply a higher purchase power and a higher interest by cultural facilities as well as an average age of above 25 years old. If we consider the information provided by photos related to accommodation, activities, buildings, restaurants and nightlife categories in this sample, it was possible to observe some interesting behaviours, but it was still not enough to get significant conclusions and relations between the choices made by tourists and their purchase power and lifestyle.

In other words, we were able to segment the market of tourism in Porto, but we believe the segments are not different enough to apply specific marketing strategies on each one. The reason is that a massive part of the photos shared on Flickr.com are highly concentrated around a small group of attractions, which are the most popular ones. The remain places visited (almost 500) are not expressive enough so the algorithm could not find patterns with it so they became statistical irrelevant. This behavior is acceptable since tourists do not share every step they take on a destination, they only share the most interesting spots that will catch the attention of their followers as well.

5   Conclusion and Further Recommendations

The results were not as we expected at the beginning of this research, mostly because individuals did not share a significant part of their personal information that was necessary to define the market segments.

Starting with the first insights provided by the database characterization, the information provided by it was not enough to get significant conclusion and relations between the tourist choice and its purchase power and lifestyle. However, it was possible to observe that there is an increase of search for apartments and rental houses instead of hotels, for instance.

With respect to the places visited and photographed, the tendency was the same. We can also observe that they choose to cross over the river not only because their interest on visiting the city, but also because they intend to take pictures from there, which explains the range of photos taken from Vila Nova de Gaia regarding places or attractions located in Porto.

With reference to the sequence mining analysis, we expect to find longer frequent paths with higher frequency that the ones identified. However, given the high concentration of the tourists around a small group of attractions (observed on the Social Network analysis), the results are in line with tourists' behavior. Additionally, we were able to observe that a massive part of the tourists' paths ends on the river or on the bridge, presenting a downstream direction. The results of the Social Network analysis basically completed the insights provided by the Sequence Mining analysis. It was expected to find communities among the attractions but the analysis only provided high connections between these attractions.

Regarding our last research question, the cluster analysis was able to identify tourists market segments based on their behavior and personal characteristics. However, given the lack of personal information plus the tourists travelling behavior, we believe that the segments found are not detailed enough to perform specific marketing strategies. Looking at the sequence mining and to the network results, a massive part of these places does not appear. Their level of frequency is not enough to be inserted on a travelling pattern. We also believe that a sample with more photos will not resolve this matter since tourists share on their network the places that they believe that are the most interesting, popular or beautiful ones, which is perfectly understandable. This fact brought issues to our analysis and also revealed city image issues because it makes the city looks smaller than it is.

The insights provided by this kind of study can be applied on recommendation systems applications and on the development of marketing strategies, advertising and promotion. First, the information about tourist's path on a city can be useful in terms of marketing services, marketing strategies and for business decision-making process in general. Second, new applications like the recommendation systems have been developed based on tourists behaviour. Finally, if the insights provided by the Sequence Mining approach could be considered, we can introduce new places into individuals' trips and encourage them to run away from the people's flow and with that support services development. It could also guide an individual during the trip considering his or her profile, segment and, with that, improve marketing efficiency.

Acknowledgments. This work is financed by National Funds through the Portuguese funding agency, FCT - Fundação para a Ciência e a Tecnologia within project: UID/EEA/50014/2019

References

1. Fyall, A., Garrod, B.: Tourism Marketing: A Collaborative Approach. Channel View Publications, Bristol (2005)
2. Newman, M.E.J.: Networks: An Introduction, 1st edn. Oxford University Press, Oxford (2010)

3. Zaki, J.: SPADE: an efficient algorithm for mining frequent sequences. Mach. Learn. **42**(1), 31–60 (2001)
4. Xia, J., Evans, F., Spilsbury, K., Ciesielski, V., Arrowsmith, C., Wright, G.: Market segments based on the dominant movement patterns of tourists. Tourism Manag. **31**(4), 464–469 (2010)
5. Gilaninia, S., Mohammadi, M., Rasht, I.: Impact of marketing on tourism industry. Tourism Manag. **5**(2), 39–46 (2015)
6. Kotler, P., Sidney, J.: Broadening the concept of marketing. J. Market. **33**, 10–15 (1969)
7. Leung, X., Wang, F., Wu, B., Billy, B., Stahura, K., Xie, Z.: A social network analysis of overseas tourist movement patterns in Beijing: the impact of the Olympic Games. Int. J. Tourism Res. **14**(5), 469–484 (2012)
8. Zheng, Y.-T., Zha, Z.-J., Chua, T.: Mining travel patterns from geotagged photos. ACM Trans. Intell. Syst. Technol. (TIST) **3**(3), 56 (2012)
9. Memon, I., Chen, L., Majid, A., Mingqi, L., Hussain, I., Chen, G.: Travel recommendation using geo-tagged photos in social media for tourist. Wirel. Pers. Commun. **80**(4), 1347–1362 (2015)
10. Kádár, B., Mátyás, G.: Where do tourists go? Visualizing and analysing the spatial distribution of geotagged photography. Cartographica: Int. J. Geogr. Inf. Geovisualization **48**(2), 78–88 (2013)
11. Wind, J., Bell, D.: Market Segmentation. The Marketing Book, p. 222 (2007)
12. Vu, Q., Li, G., Law, R., Ye, H.: Exploring the travel behaviors of inbound tourists to Hong Kong using geotagged photos. Tourism Manag. **46**, 222–232 (2015)
13. Spyrou, E., Mylonas, P.: An overview of Flickr challenges and research opportunities. In: 2014 9th International Workshop on Semantic and Social Media Adaptation and Personalization (SMAP), pp. 88–93. IEEE, Corfu (2014)
14. Crandall, D., Snavely, N.: Networks of photos, landmarks, and people. Leonardo **443**, 240–243 (2011)
15. Girardin, F., Dal Fiore, F., Blat, J., Ratti, C.: Understanding of tourist dynamics from explicitly disclosed location information. In: Symposium on LBS and Telecartography. Citeseer (2017)
16. McKercher, B., Shoval, N., Ng, E., Birenboim, A.: First and repeat visitor behaviour: GPS tracking and GIS analysis in Hong Kong. Tourism Geographies **141**, 147–161 (2012)
17. Huang, J.Z.: Clustering Categorical Data with k-Modes (2019)
18. Huang, Z.: Extensions to the k-means algorithm for clustering large data sets with categorical values. Data Min. Knowl. Discov. **23**, 283–304 (1998)
19. Ralambondrainy, H.: A conceptual version of the K-means algorithm. Pattern Recogn. Lett. **1611**, 1147–1157 (1995)
20. Fotis, J., Buhalis, D., Rossides, N.: Social media use and impact during the holiday travel planning process. Inf. Commun. Technol. Tourism **1324**, 13–24 (2012)
21. Munar, M., Jacobsen, J.: Motivations for sharing tourism experiment through social media. Tourism Manag. **43**, 46–54 (2014)
22. Bermingham, L., Lee, F.: Spatio-temporal sequential pattern mining for tourism sciences. Proc. Comput. Sci. **29**, 379–389 (2014)

A Diversity Based Multi-objective Hyper-heuristic for the FJSP with Sequence-Dependent Set-Up Times, Auxiliary Resources and Machine Down Time

Jacomine Grobler[✉]

Department of Industrial Engineering, Stellenbosch University,
Stellenbosch, South Africa
jacomine.grobler@gmail.com

Abstract. In this paper a diversity based multi-objective hyper-heuristic (MOO-HMHH) algorithm for the flexible job shop scheduling problem (FJSP) with sequence-dependent set-up times (SDST), auxiliary resources and machine down time is analyzed. The algorithm is evaluated on real customer datasets to determine the impact of machine breakdown intervals and due dates on algorithm performance. The diversity based hyper-heuristic algorithm compared well to two other hyper-heuristic algorithms and to its constituent algorithms and promising results were obtained with respect to the increased generality of the hyper-heuristics.

1 Introduction

Effective production scheduling is an important requirement for operational success. However, scheduling problems are usually multi-objective and it is difficult to predict ahead of time which one of the multitude of metaheuristics available, will be most suited for solving the specific problem.

In this scenario, utilizing a hybrid metaheuristic algorithm such as a hyper-heuristic (HH) [4] can be valuable. Hyper-heuristics focus on the development of search methods or learning mechanisms for selecting or generating heuristics to solve computational search problems. A hyper-heuristic algorithm, capitalizes on the strengths and compensates for the weaknesses of its constituent algorithms and can have a significant positive impact on solution quality and algorithm development time in a scheduling environment.

A dominance-based multi-objective hyper-heuristic scheduling algorithm for the flexible job shop scheduling problem (FJSP) with sequence-dependent set-up times, auxiliary resources and machine down time [19] was proposed for the first time in [15]. Two variations of the multi-objective heterogeneous meta-hyper-heuristic (MOO-HMHH) algorithm were evaluated on three real world datasets.

© Springer Nature Switzerland AG 2019
P. Moura Oliveira et al. (Eds.): EPIA 2019, LNAI 11805, pp. 145–156, 2019.
https://doi.org/10.1007/978-3-030-30244-3_13

This paper proposes an improved multi-objective hyper-heuristic algorithm (MOO-HMHH2) which makes use of heuristic space diversity to ensure that the algorithm explores the search space effectively. A rigorous evaluation of this algorithm versus the previous state-of-the-art multi-objective HHs developed for this problem, as well as a NSGA-3 based scheduling algorithm, is performed on 15 datasets. The datasets are based on real customer data and differ in size and breakdown interval and due date characteristics. The various HH algorithms are also compared to their constituent algorithms, which were previously shown to be the state-of-the-art MOO algorithms for this variation of the FJSP. Highly promising results were obtained by the MOO-HMHH2 algorithm versus its constituents, the other HH algorithms and the NSGA-3 algorithm.

This paper is significant because the MOO-HMHH2 algorithm is the first dominance-based multi-objective hyper-heuristic algorithm which makes use of heuristic space diversity to solve this variation of the FJSP.

The rest of the paper is organized as follows: Sect. 2 describes the scheduling problem and related literature in more detail. Section 3 describes the diversity based multi-objective hyper-heuristic algorithm. The experimental setup and results are described in Sect. 4. Finally, the paper is concluded in Sect. 5.

2 Multi-objective Flexible Job Shop Scheduling with Additional Constraints

The flexible job shop scheduling problem with sequence-dependent set-up times, auxiliary resources and machine down time can be formulated as follows [16]: There is a set of J jobs that needs to be processed on d machines and e auxiliary resources. The set of machines is denoted by $D = \{D_1, D_2, \ldots, D_d\}$ and the set of auxiliary resources are denoted by $E = \{E_1, E_2, \ldots, E_e\}$. Each job j consists of a sequence of operations N_j, where $\sum N_{j_{j=1}}^{J} = n$. All operations in each job needs to be completed in the correct sequence to complete a job. The execution of each operation i requires one machine out of a set of primary resources denoted by D_i and one resource from a set of auxiliary resources denoted by E_i. The problem thus focuses on determining both an assignment and a sequence of the operations on all machines that minimize some criteria. In addition, production calendars and resource down time intervals were addressed as described in [19].

Three objectives need to be minimized, namely

- makespan ($\max f_i \forall i \in L$),
- earliness/tardiness ($\sum_{i=1}^{n} \max\{0, \nu_i - f_i\} + \max\{0, f_i - \nu_i\} \forall i \in L$) and
- queue time ($\sum_{j=1}^{J} \max\{0, f_j - \tau_j - p_j\}$).

Here ν_i denotes the due date of operation i, f_i is the actual finishing time of operation i, p_i is the processing time of operation i, L is the set containing the last operations of all jobs and Υ is the set containing the first operations of all jobs. Minimizing makespan has an effect on the total time required for production and impacts operational cost, earliness/tardiness impacts customer satisfaction and reliability of order delivery, and queue time has an influence, amongst others, on work in process inventory, material handling and available space on the production floor.

A number of algorithms have already been developed to solve the multi-objective flexible job shop problem (MFJSP). Some notable examples include a multi-objective simulated annealing algorithm [26], tabu search [7], evolutionary algorithms [20,21], simulated annealing-particle swarm hybrid [33], multi-stage genetic algorithm (GA) [13] and a shifting bottleneck-GA hybrid [12]. However, the consideration of sequence-dependent setup times, breakdown intervals and auxiliary resources to this problem adds significant complexity and is thus not commonly addressed in literature. This fact can be seen from the summary of recent MFJSP literature where additional constraints have been considered. The inclusion of these additional complexities are, however, much more realistic and unrealistic schedules will be obtained if these issues are simply ignored in a production schedule (Table 1).

Table 1. Multi-objective FJSP (MFJSP) literature.

Problem	References
MFJSP with SDST	[22]
MFJSP with stochastic processing times	[28]
MFJSP with machine breakdowns	[2,34]
MFJSP with maintenance constraints	[6,24]
MFJSP with setup times and automated guided vehicles	[14]
MFJSP with overlapping operations	[1]
MFJSP with setup times, maintenance planning and intermediate inventory restrictions	[25]
Welding scheduling with SDST, controllable processing times and job dependent transportation times	[27]

3   Multi-objective Heterogeneous Meta-hyper-heuristic Scheduling Algorithms

The HMHH algorithm was previously extended to solve the FJSP with additional constraints [16]. However, a modified goal programming approach was used to address the multiple objectives. A Pareto dominance based approach to optimizing multiple objectives requires a number of significant modifications to the algorithm and was first introduced in [15].

The MOO-HMHH algorithm is inspired from the vector evaluated MOO algorithms of Schaffer [32] and Parsopoulos et al. [31] and thus consists of three populations of entities, each focused on the minimization of one of the objective functions of the scheduling problem. Each entity within each of these three populations can be evolved by operators from any of three constituent algorithms.

The allocation of entities to algorithms is updated dynamically throughout the optimization run based on the performance of the constituent algorithms over k preceding iterations. The various constituent algorithms are ranked based on their previous performance as defined by $Q_{\delta m}(t)$ in [17] where

$$Q_{\delta m}(t) = \sum_{i=1}^{|\boldsymbol{I}_m(t)|} (f(\boldsymbol{x}_i(t)) - f(\boldsymbol{x}_i(t+k))) \qquad \forall i \in \boldsymbol{I}_m(t) \qquad (1)$$

where $f(\boldsymbol{x}_i(t))$ denotes the fitness function value of entity i at iteration t and $\boldsymbol{I}_m(t)$ is the set of entities allocated to algorithm m at iteration t.

The multi-objective optimization capabilities of the MOO-HMHH algorithm is based on information sharing between the populations, dominance-based selection mechanisms and migration of entities between populations.

It is important to note that the entities of the MOO-HMHH algorithm are evolved in a continuous search space. Each of the entities consists of a $2n$-dimensional vector, where dimensions 1 to n are the sequencing variables and is interpreted as the priority values of each of the operations. Dimensions $n+1$ to $2n$ are used to represent the allocation of operations to resources. This is done by discretizing the search space as follows: For each operation i, the ith dimension of the entity is divided into D_i intervals, where D_i denotes the number of primary resources on which operation i can be processed. Since each interval is associated with a unique integer number or resource index, dimensions $n+1$ to $2n$ of the position vector can easily be interpreted as resource allocation variables. The operation priorities and resource allocations are then used as input to a schedule-building heuristic which attempts to schedule each operation at the earliest available time on its selected resource. After the schedule associated with each entity has been generated, the fitness function of the schedule can be calculated. Refer to [19] for more detail.

The MOO-HMHH scheduling algorithm's three constituent multi-objective algorithms thus operate in a continuous search space and include:

- **GA:** A multi-objective genetic algorithm (GA) inspired by the vector evaluated GA [32] with a floating-point representation, dominance-based tournament selection, blend crossover [11,29], and self-adaptive Gaussian mutation [17].
- **PSO:** The guaranteed convergence vector evaluated particle swarm optimization algorithm (GCPSO) [3,31].
- **DE:** A differential evolution (DE) algorithm inspired by the vector evaluated DE [30] with self-adaptive parameters and neighborhood search as implemented in Yang et al.'s SaNSDE algorithm [35].

These three constituent algorithms were selected because the Vector Evaluated DE and Vector Evaluated PSO algorithms were previously shown to be the state-of-the-art dominance-based MOO algorithms for the FJSP with additional constraints [19]. The MOO-HMHH algorithm is described in Algorithm 1.

A popular variation on the single-objective HMHH algorithm, the exponentially increasing HMHH algorithm with *a priori* knowledge (EIHH1) [18], was

---

Algorithm 1. The multi-objective heterogeneous meta-hyper-heuristic (MOO-HMHH) scheduling algorithm.

---

1 Initialize three parent populations X_1, X_2 and X_3
2 $M(t)$ denotes the set of constituent algorithms available at iteration t
3 $A_{ip}(t)$ denotes the algorithm applied to entity i of population p at iteration t
4 k denotes the number of iterations between entity-to-algorithm allocation
5 Initialize $M(t)$
6 $t = 0$
7 **for** *All entities* $i \in X_1(0), X_2(0)$ *and* $X_3(0)$ **do**
8 | Randomly select an initial algorithm $A_{ip}(0)$ from $M(t)$ to apply to entity i
9 **end**
10 **while** *A stopping condition is not met* **do**
11 | **for** *All entities* $i \in X_1(t), X_2(t)$ *and* $X_3(t)$ **do**
12 | | **for** *k iterations* **do**
13 | | | Apply constituent algorithm $A_{ip}(t)$ to entity i in population p to obtain $X_1'(t), X_2'(t)$ and $X_3'(t)$
14 | | | **for** *All populations p* **do**
15 | | | | **if** $X_p'(t) \prec X_p(t)$ **then**
16 | | | | | $X_p(t) = X_p'(t)$
17 | | | **end**
18 | | | Update the external archive to include all non-dominated solutions in X
19 | | **end**
20 | **end**
21   **end**
22     $t = t + k$
23   Calculate $Q_{\delta m}(t)$, the total improvement in fitness function value of all entities assigned to algorithm m from iteration $t - k$ to iteration t using Equation (1).
24   **for** *All entities* $i \in X_1(t), X_2(t)$ *and* $X_3(t)$ **do**
25 | Use $Q_{\delta m}(t)$ as input to select constituent algorithm $A_{ip}(t)$ according to the rank based tabu search mechanism described in [5].
26   **end**
27   **if** *Migration interval reached* **then**
28 | Move best entity of each population to another randomly selected population
29   **end**
30 **end**

---

also extended to solve the multi-objective scheduling problem. MOO-EIHH only differs from MOO-HMHH in that the set of available metaheuristics is manipulated over time. The best performing constituent algorithm is first allowed to work on the problem until minimal improvement is obtained and then other constituent algorithms are added at exponential time intervals, i.e. at 20%, 40% and 80% of the maximum number of function evaluations.

MOO-HMHH2 makes use of the MOO-HMHH framework, but monitors heuristic space diversity (HSD) [18] throughout the optimization run.

A quantitative metric for heuristic space diversity, $D_h(t)$, the heuristic space diversity at iteration t, was defined in [18] as follows:

$$D_h(t) = UB_{D_h(t)} \left(1 - \frac{\sum_{i=1}^{I} |T - n_i(t)|}{1.5 n_s} \right) \tag{2}$$

with

$$T = \frac{n_s}{n_a}, \tag{3}$$

where n_a is the number of algorithms available for selection by the hyper-heuristic, n_s is the number of entities in the population, $n_i(t)$ is the number of entities allocated to algorithm i at iteration t, and $UB_{D_h(t)}$ is the upper bound of the HSD measure. For the purposes of this paper, $UB_{D_h(t)}$ was set to 100 so that $D_h(t) \in [0, 100]$.

The idea of the measure is to calculate a target number of entities per algorithm, T. The absolute deviation between this target and the actual allocation of entities to algorithms is then used to determine the HSD associated with the entity-to-algorithm allocation. Maximum diversity would be achieved when all entities are assigned equally between algorithms and this would translate into a $D_h(t)$ of 100.

As soon as the HSD drops to below a pre-defined level, then entities are randomly re-allocated to different constituent algorithms to ensure that HSD remains high. A higher HSD allows for better exploration of the heuristic space.

4   Empirical Evaluation

The evaluation of the HH scheduling algorithms were conducted on 15 datasets derived from real world client data. The datasets range in size from 56 operations to 256 operations which needs to be scheduled on a set of 216 auxiliary and primary resources. These datasets are available for comparison purposes from the corresponding author.

Each dataset can be classified according to one of three types:

- Type 1 datasets contain only 1 breakdown interval on 1 resource and is described in detail in [19].
- Type 2 datasets have breakdown intervals which affect 10% of all resources and all job due dates fall within ±5% of the estimated minimum makespan of the problem.
- Type 3 datasets have breakdown intervals which affect 30% of the 216 resources and all job due dates fall within ±20% of the estimated minimum makespan of the problem.

The problems thus increase in difficulty from type 1 to type 3. More breakdowns result in increased difficulty in minimizing makespan and a larger dispersion of due dates negatively affect the minimization of earliness/tardiness.

Since an extensive analysis of the most suitable control parameters for priority-based FJSP algorithms were already performed in [19], these parameters were used as is. Similarly, the constituent algorithm control parameters specified in [18] were used.

Three performance measures were again used in this paper to compare the multi-objective HH scheduling algorithms. The S-metric [23,36] measures the size of the region dominated by the Pareto front based on a reference vector consisting of the maximum value in each objective (Table 2).

Table 2. The reference vectors used for each of the problems.

Problem	Vector
56-operation problem	{3000, 14500, 5000}
100-operation problem	{4000, 13500, 8500}
146-operation problem	{7000, 24500, 9000}
200-operation problem	{12500, 39000, 19000}
256-operation problem	{9000, 53000, 23500}

The other two measures include the size of the approximated Pareto fronts $(N(PF))$ as well as the extent of the Pareto fronts $(\chi(PF))$ [10].

The actual results of the MOO-HMHH2, MOO-HMHH and MOO-EIHH algorithms are recorded in Tables 3 and 4. A NSGA-3 algorithm [8] was also used to solve the same problem instances for benchmarking purposes. All algorithm results were recorded over 30 independent simulation runs. Throughout the rest of this section, μ and σ respectively denote the mean and standard deviation associated with the corresponding performance measure. The notation n_τ indicates that the dataset consists of n operations and is of type τ.

An important observation which can be made from the results is that it is difficult to predict from the three constituent algorithms, which algorithm will be the best performing algorithm for a specific problem. As an example, for the 56 and 100 operation problems, the PSO algorithm provides the best quality Pareto front with respect to the S-metric and the extent of the Pareto fronts, $\chi(PF)$. However, for the 146 operation problems, the DE and GA outperform the PSO algorithm which then becomes the worst performing algorithm. Here, the advantages becomes clear of a hyper-heuristic algorithm which can perform comparatively well to its constituent algorithms without the guesswork involved in determining which algorithm is best. Due to its ability to exploit the strengths of each of its constituent algorithms, the hyper-heuristics can even exceed the performance of its constituents as can be seen for various datasets in Tables 3 and 4. Finally, the hyper-heuristics also obtained highly competitive results against the NSGA-3 algorithm.

Table 3. Comparative results of the hyper-heuristic algorithms versus PSO.

Metric	Dataset	MOO-HMHH2		MOO-HMHH		MOO-EIHH		PSO	
		μ	σ	μ	σ	μ	σ	μ	σ
$N(PF)$	56_1	24,83	5,76	24,90	6,51	25,23	6,88	28,17	6,51
	56_2	195,20	18,48	184,63	20,62	203,73	22,54	231,90	24,33
	56_3	154,67	16,06	159,53	20,61	166,93	21,39	170,57	22,84
$\chi(PF)$	56_1	42,30	2,70	42,55	4,53	41,64	3,51	43,29	3,25
	56_2	97,83	2,29	98,27	2,54	99,00	1,79	98,66	2,21
	56_3	76,42	2,28	76,86	1,98	77,03	1,72	76,69	2,82
$S(PF)$	56_1	$5,51E+10$	$7,48E+08$	$5,47E+10$	$8,74E+08$	$5,52E+10$	$7,73E+08$	$5,56E+10$	$6,67E+08$
	56_2	$3,53E+10$	$9,49E+08$	$3,55E+10$	$8,57E+08$	$3,57E+10$	$7,65E+08$	$3,56E+10$	$1,11E+09$
	56_3	$7,98E+10$	$9,78E+08$	$7,97E+10$	$1,24E+09$	$8,03E+10$	$9,22E+08$	$8,00E+10$	$1,23E+09$
$N(PF)$	100_1	18,03	6,00	1,00	0,00	19,90	5,47	23,33	6,96
	100_2	102,73	15,90	99,37	14,82	107,83	18,99	111,30	19,09
	100_3	114,07	18,03	111,43	17,44	119,53	14,91	130,83	19,74
$\chi(PF)$	100_1	55,16	6,33	0,00	0,00	56,91	7,12	55,60	5,27
	100_2	102,67	4,48	102,57	3,88	101,12	4,61	105,62	3,38
	100_3	109,13	4,67	108,96	5,17	109,15	4,77	111,92	5,30
$S(PF)$	100_1	$1,23E+11$	$3,32E+09$	$3,28E+11$	$3,03E+09$	$1,25E+11$	$5,03E+09$	$1,25E+11$	$4,50E+09$
	100_2	$1,17E+11$	$2,70E+09$	$1,18E+11$	$3,02E+09$	$1,18E+11$	$2,74E+09$	$1,20E+11$	$3,39E+09$
	100_3	$9,79E+10$	$2,57E+09$	$9,73E+10$	$2,74E+09$	$9,95E+10$	$2,11E+09$	$1,01E+11$	$3,14E+09$
$N(PF)$	146_1	23,67	5,52	25,37	7,60	25,40	5,28	10,23	3,96
	146_2	10,53	4,73	9,23	3,04	9,70	4,02	6,00	2,60
	146_3	19,30	5,71	18,03	6,33	17,33	6,16	9,30	2,59
$\chi(PF)$	146_1	124,66	7,13	127,37	7,14	124,39	4,20	117,19	7,82
	146_2	55,63	13,52	49,87	7,34	50,49	7,97	39,64	5,77
	146_3	62,56	5,29	61,54	4,70	60,86	4,67	54,54	4,67
$S(PF)$	146_1	$1,05E+11$	$6,29E+09$	$1,04E+11$	$4,88E+09$	$1,03E+11$	$4,53E+09$	$9,28E+10$	$8,78E+09$
	146_2	$5,13E+11$	$1,37E+11$	$5,10E+11$	$1,66E+11$	$5,28E+11$	$2,12E+10$	$4,93E+11$	$2,01E+10$
	146_3	$5,74E+11$	$1,13E+11$	$5,77E+11$	$1,60E+10$	$5,86E+11$	$1,14E+10$	$5,57E+11$	$1,26E+10$
$N(PF)$	200_1	17,93	5,57	16,10	6,03	17,90	7,11	9,07	2,99
	200_2	164,47	22,37	166,30	22,91	171,07	23,69	30,93	5,11
	200_3	202,57	24,94	210,27	24,11	227,90	27,71	33,83	4,69
$\chi(PF)$	200_1	161,16	11,00	160,20	12,10	158,79	10,71	140,11	42,53
	200_2	114,45	3,49	115,49	3,89	115,41	3,72	91,93	4,10
	200_3	101,56	2,50	102,04	2,74	103,59	2,93	81,76	4,19
$S(PF)$	200_1	$2,06E+12$	$7,26E+10$	$2,09E+12$	$8,12E+10$	$2,10E+12$	$7,87E+10$	$1,93E+12$	$1,01E+11$
	200_2	$1,30E+12$	$3,68E+10$	$1,30E+12$	$4,66E+10$	$1,31E+12$	$2,74E+10$	$1,09E+12$	$4,03E+10$
	200_3	$2,04E+12$	$9,14E+10$	$2,08E+12$	$1,03E+11$	$2,13E+12$	$1,03E+11$	$1,57E+12$	$9,37E+10$
$N(PF)$	256_1	17,17	4,20	19,30	6,73	19,83	6,13	9,77	2,21
	256_2	89,47	11,82	90,57	13,45	92,47	10,86	20,73	4,35
	256_3	29,63	8,68	30,53	10,81	29,70	8,51	11,17	4,39
$\chi(PF)$	256_1	160,90	18,50	159,38	21,93	161,91	18,94	138,73	15,63
	256_2	142,74	5,12	142,07	5,44	141,57	4,52	102,92	8,08
	256_3	112,17	5,97	110,16	6,16	113,41	6,94	88,20	10,73
$S(PF)$	256_1	$1,36E+12$	$1,35E+11$	$1,37E+12$	$1,04E+11$	$1,37E+12$	$6,64E+10$	$1,13E+12$	$9,14E+10$
	256_2	$3,52E+12$	$7,70E+10$	$3,57E+12$	$1,06E+11$	$3,59E+12$	$8,16E+10$	$2,69E+12$	$6,95E+10$
	256_3	$2,82E+12$	$1,28E+11$	$2,78E+12$	$1,27E+11$	$2,91E+12$	$9,76E+10$	$2,48E+12$	$1,41E+11$

A statistical analysis was also conducted to validate the results obtained. The results in Tables 5 and 6 were obtained by comparing the performance of the two MOO HH algorithms to each of the constituent algorithms for each dataset and each metric. For every comparison, a Mann-Whitney U test at 95% significance was performed (using the two sets of 30 data points of the two algorithms, one hyper-heuristic and one constituent algorithm, being compared) and if the hyper-heuristic algorithm statistically significantly outperformed the constituent algorithm, a win was recorded. If no statistical difference could be observed a draw was recorded. If the constituent algorithm outperformed the hyper-heuristic, a loss was recorded for the hyper-heuristic. As an example, (4-0-1) in row 1 column 1, indicates that the MOO-HMHH algorithm significantly outperformed the multi-objective PSO algorithm for four of the datasets. No draws were recorded and one loss was recorded.

It can be seen from Tables 5 and 6 that the performance improvement resulting from utilizing the multi-objective HH algorithms is statistically significant over all three measures for a large number of the dataset-algorithm combinations considered. As the difficulty of the problems increase from type 1 to 3, the HH algorithms also tend to increase the gap of the performance improvement over

Table 4. Comparative results of the MOO-HMHH and MOO-EIHH algorithms versus DE, GA and NSGA-III [9].

Metric	Dataset	DE μ	σ	GA μ	σ	NSGA-III μ	σ
$N(PF)$	56_1	22, 23	5, 15	9, 70	3, 56	26, 00	2, 64
	56_2	179, 33	15, 89	32, 40	4, 92	27, 00	0, 00
	56_3	157, 03	16, 89	30, 47	5, 01	27, 00	0, 00
$\chi(PF)$	56_1	45, 47	3, 42	33, 13	3, 56	35, 00	4, 81
	56_2	98, 18	1, 81	78, 32	4, 39	83, 29	7, 55
	56_3	77, 18	1, 96	61, 69	3, 48	72, 46	5, 22
$S(PF)$	56_1	$5,28E+10$	$8,58E+08$	$5,32E+10$	$1,39E+09$	$5,43E+10$	$2,08E+09$
	56_2	$3,54E+10$	$6,30E+08$	$2,71E+10$	$1,04E+09$	$2,86E+10$	$2,53E+09$
	56_3	$7,92E+10$	$1,09E+09$	$6,70E+10$	$2,23E+09$	$6,92E+10$	$3,35E+09$
$N(PF)$	100_1	11, 13	3, 77	9, 27	4, 27	25, 30	3, 43
	100_2	24, 13	5, 22	22, 43	5, 06	27, 00	0, 00
	100_3	28, 97	4, 44	23, 47	4, 61	27, 00	0, 00
$\chi(PF)$	100_1	46, 31	4, 72	38, 45	9, 02	36, 29	10, 51
	100_2	83, 49	5, 12	82, 93	6, 76	94, 15	11, 08
	100_3	92, 03	4, 81	82, 80	8, 95	98, 74	11, 47
$S(PF)$	100_1	$1,27E+11$	$4,74E+09$	$1,18E+11$	$6,14E+09$	$1,18E+11$	$9,33E+09$
	100_2	$1,03E+11$	$2,88E+09$	$1,00E+11$	$3,90E+09$	$1,11E+11$	$8,92E+09$
	100_3	$8,51E+10$	$2,62E+09$	$8,30E+10$	$3,85E+09$	$9,19E+10$	$6,12E+09$
$N(PF)$	146_1	12, 60	3, 67	10, 80	4, 22	21, 67	5, 82
	146_2	6, 10	2, 58	5, 23	2, 47	18, 80	6, 89
	146_3	8, 93	3, 33	8, 43	2, 92	24, 50	3, 86
$\chi(PF)$	146_1	117, 64	5, 22	120, 71	8, 24	104, 38	21, 32
	146_2	43, 80	9, 81	30, 99	12, 00	39, 05	10, 64
	146_3	53, 66	5, 41	49, 31	7, 67	55, 31	6, 55
$S(PF)$	146_1	$1,15E+11$	$4,54E+09$	$1,10E+11$	$6,48E+09$	$1,19E+11$	$6,30E+09$
	146_2	$5,32E+11$	$1,50E+10$	$5,13E+11$	$2,21E+10$	$5,35E+11$	$2,62E+10$
	146_3	$5,68E+11$	$1,11E+10$	$5,65E+11$	$1,60E+10$	$5,86E+11$	$2,28E+10$
$N(PF)$	200_1	7, 33	2, 64	7, 73	3, 59	20, 63	6, 35
	200_2	30, 10	5, 47	28, 40	5, 94	27, 00	0, 00
	200_3	32, 27	4, 70	31, 03	6, 54	27, 00	0, 00
$\chi(PF)$	200_1	126, 28	42, 01	88, 56	54, 20	89, 80	45, 32
	200_2	92, 70	5, 26	90, 83	6, 04	103, 34	7, 98
	200_3	80, 06	4, 02	78, 31	4, 92	92, 63	6, 62
$S(PF)$	200_1	$2,23E+12$	$5,94E+10$	$2,11E+12$	$1,06E+11$	$2,25E+12$	$1,35E+11$
	200_2	$1,07E+12$	$4,00E+11$	$1,07E+12$	$3,38E+11$	$1,19E+12$	$6,62E+10$
	200_3	$1,63E+12$	$1,06E+11$	$1,57E+12$	$1,07E+11$	$1,79E+12$	$1,59E+11$
$N(PF)$	256_1	10, 80	2, 71	8, 70	3, 89	21, 47	5, 15
	256_2	26, 73	3, 47	20, 33	4, 14	27, 00	0, 00
	256_3	13, 03	4, 30	11, 17	3, 90	26, 13	1, 89
$\chi(PF)$	256_1	140, 17	20, 90	114, 08	36, 93	131, 29	25, 90
	256_2	112, 16	8, 42	103, 25	9, 82	116, 36	18, 23
	256_3	90, 99	7, 33	83, 04	10, 91	95, 96	11, 49
$S(PF)$	256_1	$1,63E+12$	$9,36E+10$	$1,48E+12$	$1,56E+11$	$1,53E+12$	$2,29E+11$
	256_2	$3,06E+12$	$9,75E+10$	$2,60E+12$	$1,42E+11$	$3,08E+12$	$2,15E+11$
	256_3	$2,58E+12$	$1,36E+11$	$2,55E+12$	$1,80E+11$	$2,90E+12$	$1,82E+11$

Table 5. Hypotheses analysis of the performance of the hyper-heuristics per problem type versus their constituent algorithms. The best results are highlighted in bold.

Metric	Problem type	MOO-HMHH2 PSO	DE	GA	TOTAL	MOO-HMHH PSO	DE	GA	TOTAL	MOO-EIHH PSO	DE	GA	TOTAL
$S(PF)$	1	3-1-1	1-0-4	2-0-3	6-1-8	4-0-1	2-0-3	2-1-2	**8-1-6**	3-1-1	1-0-4	2-1-2	6-2-7
	2	3-1-1	3-1-1	4-1-0	10-3-2	3-1-1	3-1-1	4-1-0	10-3-2	3-1-1	3-2-0	5-0-0	**11-3-1**
	3	3-1-1	5-0-0	5-0-0	**13-1-1**	3-1-1	4-1-0	5-0-0	12-2-1	3-1-1	3-2-0	5-0-0	11-3-1
$N(PF)$	1	3-0-2	4-1-0	5-0-0	12-1-2	3-1-1	3-1-1	4-0-1	10-2-3	3-2-0	4-1-0	5-0-0	**12-3-0**
	2	3-0-2	5-0-0	5-0-0	13-0-2	3-0-2	4-1-0	5-0-0	12-1-2	3-1-1	5-0-0	5-0-0	**13-1-1**
	3	3-0-2	4-1-0	5-0-0	**12-1-2**	3-0-2	4-1-0	5-0-0	**12-1-2**	3-1-1	4-1-0	5-0-0	12-2-1
$\chi(PF)$	1	2-3-0	4-0-1	4-1-0	**10-4-1**	2-2-1	3-0-2	4-0-1	9-2-4	2-3-0	4-0-1	4-1-0	**10-4-1**
	2	3-1-1	4-1-0	5-0-0	**12-2-1**	3-1-1	4-1-0	5-0-0	**12-2-1**	3-1-1	4-1-0	5-0-0	**12-2-1**
	3	3-2-0	4-1-0	5-0-0	**12-3-0**	3-1-1	4-1-0	5-0-0	12-2-1	3-1-1	4-1-0	5-0-0	12-2-1

its constituent algorithms. Finally, with regard to the performance of the three hyper-heuristic algorithms, it can be seen that the MOO-HMHH2 algorithm significantly outperforms the other state-of-the-art multi-objective hyper-heuristic for a large number of problem instances.

Table 6. Hypotheses analysis of the performance of the hyper-heuristic algorithms per problem size (operations) versus their constituent algorithms. The best results are highlighted in bold.

Metric	Problem size	MOO-HMHH2				MOO-HMHH				MOO-EIHH			
		PSO	DE	GA	TOTAL	PSO	DE	GA	TOTAL	PSO	DE	GA	TOTAL
$S(PF)$	56	2-0-1	3-0-0	3-0-0	**8-0-1**	0-2-1	1-2-0	3-0-0	4-4-1	0-2-1	2-1-0	3-0-0	5-3-1
	100	2-0-1	2-0-1	2-1-0	6-1-2	1-0-2	3-0-0	3-0-0	**7-0-2**	0-1-2	2-0-1	3-0-0	5-1-3
	146	3-0-0	3-0-0	3-0-0	**9-0-0**	3-0-0	1-0-2	1-1-1	5-1-3	3-0-0	1-1-1	2-0-1	6-1-2
	200	2-0-1	2-0-1	2-0-1	6-0-3	3-0-0	2-0-1	2-1-0	**7-1-1**	3-0-0	2-0-1	2-1-0	**7-1-1**
	256	3-0-0	3-0-0	3-0-0	**9-0-0**	3-0-0	2-0-1	2-0-1	7-0-2	3-0-0	2-0-1	2-0-1	7-0-2
$N(PF)$	56	0-0-3	1-2-0	3-0-0	4-2-3	0-1-2	0-3-0	3-0-0	3-4-2	0-2-1	1-2-0	3-0-0	**4-4-1**
	100	0-0-3	3-0-0	3-0-0	6-0-3	0-0-3	2-0-1	2-0-1	4-0-5	0-2-1	3-0-0	3-0-0	**6-2-1**
	146	3-0-0	3-0-0	3-0-0	**9-0-0**	3-0-0	3-0-0	3-0-0	**9-0-0**	3-0-0	3-0-0	3-0-0	**9-0-0**
	200	3-0-0	3-0-0	3-0-0	**9-0-0**	3-0-0	3-0-0	3-0-0	**9-0-0**	3-0-0	3-0-0	3-0-0	**9-0-0**
	256	3-0-0	3-0-0	3-0-0	**9-0-0**	3-0-0	3-0-0	3-0-0	**9-0-0**	3-0-0	3-0-0	3-0-0	**9-0-0**
$\chi(PF)$	56	0-3-0	0-2-1	3-0-0	**3-5-1**	0-3-0	0-2-1	3-0-0	**3-5-1**	0-3-0	0-2-1	3-0-0	**3-5-1**
	100	0-2-1	3-0-0	3-0-0	**6-2-1**	0-3-0	0-2-1	3-0-0	3-5-1	0-1-2	3-0-0	3-0-0	6-1-2
	146	3-0-0	3-0-0	2-1-0	8-1-0	3-0-0	3-0-0	3-0-0	**9-0-0**	3-0-0	3-0-0	2-1-0	8-1-0
	200	2-1-0	3-0-0	3-0-0	**8-1-0**	2-1-0	3-0-0	3-0-0	**8-1-0**	2-1-0	3-0-0	3-0-0	**8-1-0**
	256	3-0-0	3-0-0	3-0-0	**9-0-0**	3-0-0	3-0-0	3-0-0	**9-0-0**	3-0-0	3-0-0	3-0-0	**9-0-0**

5   Conclusion

This paper described a diversity based multi-objective HMHH scheduling algorithm for the FJSP with sequence-dependent set-up times, auxiliary resources and machine down time. The algorithm was tested against two state-of-the-art multi-objective HMHH scheduling algorithms and also evaluated against three constituent metaheuristic algorithms. The MOO-HMHH2 scheduling algorithm was shown to obtain highly competitive results against the other MOO HMHH scheduling algorithms and also significantly outperformed its constituent algorithms.

Future research opportunities exist in analyzing the performance of the different multi-objective hyper-heuristics in significantly more detail and investigating alternative dominance-based strategies to address the multiple objectives.

References

1. Abdi Khalife, M., Abbasi, B., et al.: A simulated annealing algorithm for multi objective flexible job shop scheduling with overlapping in operations. J. Optim. Ind. Eng. **5**, 17–28 (2010)
2. Ahmadi, E., Zandieh, M., Farrokh, M., Emami, S.M.: A multi objective optimization approach for flexible job shop scheduling problem under random machine breakdown by evolutionary algorithms. Comput. Oper. Res. **73**, 56–66 (2016)
3. van den Bergh, F., Engelbrecht, A.P.: A new locally convergent particle swarm optimiser. In: 2002 IEEE International Conference on Systems, Man and Cybernetics, vol. 3, p. 6. IEEE (2002)

4. Burke, E.K., et al.: Hyper-heuristics: a survey of the state of the art. J. Oper. Res. Soc. **64**(12), 1695–1724 (2013)
5. Burke, E.K., Kendall, G., Soubeiga, E.: A tabu-search hyperheuristic for timetabling and rostering. J. Heuristics **9**(6), 451–470 (2003)
6. Dalfard, V.M., Mohammadi, G.: Two meta-heuristic algorithms for solving multi-objective flexible job-shop scheduling with parallel machine and maintenance constraints. Comput. Math. Appl. **64**(6), 2111–2117 (2012)
7. Dauzère-Pérès, S., Paulli, J.: An integrated approach for modeling and solving the general multiprocessor job-shop scheduling problem using tabu search. Ann. Oper. Res. **70**, 281–306 (1997)
8. Deb, K., Jain, H.: An evolutionary many-objective optimization algorithm using reference-point-based nondominated sorting approach, part I: solving problems with box constraints. IEEE Trans. Evol. Comput. **18**(4), 577–601 (2013)
9. Deb, K., Jain, H.: An evolutionary many-objective optimization algorithm using reference-point-based nondominated sorting approach, part I: Solving problems with box constraints. IEEE Trans. Evol. Comput. **18**(4), 577–601 (2014)
10. Engelbrecht, A.P.: Fundamentals of Computational Swarm Intelligence. Wiley, Hoboken (2006)
11. Eshelman Larry, J., Schaffer David, J.: Real-coded geneticalgorithms andinterval-schemata. Found. Genet. Algorithms **2**, 187–202 (1993)
12. Gao, J., Gen, M., Sun, L., Zhao, X.: A hybrid of genetic algorithm and bottleneck shifting for multiobjective flexible job shop scheduling problems. Comput. Ind. Eng. **53**(1), 149–162 (2007)
13. Gen, M., Gao, J., Lin, L.: Multistage-based genetic algorithm for flexible job-shop scheduling problem. In: Gen, M., et al. (eds.) Intelligent and Evolutionary Systems. Studies in Computational Intelligence, vol. 187, pp. 183–196. Springer, Heidelberg (2009). https://doi.org/10.1007/978-3-540-95978-6_13
14. Gen, M., Lin, L.: Multiobjective genetic algorithm for scheduling problems in manufacturing systems. Ind. Eng. Manag. Syst. **11**(4), 310–330 (2012)
15. Grobler, J.: A multi-objective hyper-heuristic for the flexible job shop scheduling problem with additional constraints. In: Proceedings of the 3rd International Conference on Soft Computing and Machine Intelligence (2016)
16. Grobler, J., Engelbrecht, A.P.: Hyper-heuristics for the flexible job shop scheduling problem with additional constraints. In: Tan, Y., Shi, Y., Li, L. (eds.) ICSI 2016. LNCS, vol. 9713, pp. 3–10. Springer, Cham (2016). https://doi.org/10.1007/978-3-319-41009-8_1
17. Grobler, J., Engelbrecht, A.P., Kendall, G., Yadavalli, V.: Investigating the impact of alternative evolutionary selection strategies on multi-method global optimization. In: 2011 IEEE Congress on Evolutionary Computation (CEC), pp. 2337–2344. IEEE (2011)
18. Grobler, J., Engelbrecht, A.P., Kendall, G., Yadavalli, V.: Heuristic space diversity control for improved meta-hyper-heuristic performance. Inf. Sci. **300**, 49–62 (2015)
19. Grobler, J., Engelbrecht, A.P., Kok, S., Yadavalli, S.: Metaheuristics for the multi-objective FJSP with sequence-dependent set-up times, auxiliary resources and machine down time. Ann. Oper. Res. **180**(1), 165–196 (2010)
20. Kacem, I., Hammadi, S., Borne, P.: Approach by localization and multiobjective evolutionary optimization for flexible job-shop scheduling problems. IEEE Trans. Syst. Man Cybern. Part C (Appl. Rev.) **32**(1), 1–13 (2002)
21. Kacem, I., Hammadi, S., Borne, P.: Pareto-optimality approach for flexible job-shop scheduling problems: hybridization of evolutionary algorithms and fuzzy logic. Math. Comput. Simul. **60**(3), 245–276 (2002)

22. Khalili, M., Naderi, B.: Multi-objective job shop scheduling problem with sequence dependent setup times using a novel metaheuristic. Int. J. Intell. Eng. Inf. **2**(4), 243–258 (2014)
23. Knowles, J.D.: Local-search and hybrid evolutionary algorithms for Pareto optimization. Ph.D. thesis, Department of Computer Science Local-Search and Hybrid Evolutionary Algorithms for Pareto OptimiZation Joshua D. Knowles Submitted in partial fulfilment of the requirements for the degree of Doctor of Philosophy in Computer Science. Department of Computer Science, University of Reading (2002)
24. Li, J.Q., Pan, Q.K., Tasgetiren, M.F.: A discrete artificial bee colony algorithm for the multi-objective flexible job-shop scheduling problem with maintenance activities. Appl. Math. Model. **38**(3), 1111–1132 (2014)
25. Li, L., Huo, J.: Multi-objective flexible job-shop scheduling problem in steel tubes production. Syst. Eng.-Theor. Pract. **29**(8), 117–126 (2009)
26. Loukil, T., Teghem, J., Fortemps, P.: A multi-objective production scheduling case study solved by simulated annealing. Eur. J. Oper. Res. **179**(3), 709–722 (2007)
27. Lu, C., Xiao, S., Li, X., Gao, L.: An effective multi-objective discrete grey wolf optimizer for a real-world scheduling problem in welding production. Adv. Eng. Softw. **99**, 161–176 (2016)
28. Nicoara, E.S., Filip, F.G., Paraschiv, N.: Simulation-based optimization using genetic algorithms for multi-objective flexible JSSP. Stud. Inf. Control **20**(4), 333–344 (2011)
29. Olorunda, O., Engelbrecht, A.P.: An analysis of heterogeneous cooperative algorithms. In: 2009 IEEE Congress on Evolutionary Computation, CEC 2009, pp. 1562–1569. IEEE (2009)
30. Parsopoulos, K.E., Tasoulis, D.K., Pavlidis, N.G., Plagianakos, V.P., Vrahatis, M.N.: Vector evaluated differential evolution for multiobjective optimization. In: 2004 Congress on Evolutionary Computation, CEC 2004, vol. 1, pp. 204–211. IEEE (2004)
31. Parsopoulos, K.E., Vrahatis, M.N.: Particle swarm optimization method in multiobjective problems. In: Proceedings of the 2002 ACM Symposium on Applied Computing, pp. 603–607. ACM (2002)
32. Schaffer, J.D.: Multiple objective optimization with vector evaluated genetic algorithms. In: Proceedings of the 1st international Conference on Genetic Algorithms, pp. 93–100. L. Erlbaum Associates Inc. (1985)
33. Xia, W., Wu, Z.: An effective hybrid optimization approach for multi-objective flexible job-shop scheduling problems. Comput. Ind. Eng. **48**(2), 409–425 (2005)
34. Xiong, J., Xing, L., Chen, Y.: Robust scheduling for multi-objective flexible job-shop problems with random machine breakdowns. Int. J. Prod. Econ. **141**(1), 112–126 (2013)
35. Yang, Z., Tang, K., Yao, X.: Self-adaptive differential evolution with neighborhood search. In: 2008 IEEE Congress on Evolutionary Computation (IEEE World Congress on Computational Intelligence), CEC 2008, pp. 1110–1116. IEEE (2008)
36. Zitzler, E., Thiele, L., Laumanns, M., Fonseca, C.M., Da Fonseca, V.G.: Performance assessment of multiobjective optimizers: an analysis and review. IEEE Trans. Evol. Comput. **7**(2), 117–132 (2003)

General AI

Determining Emotional Profile Based on Microblogging Analysis

Ricardo Martins[✉], Pedro Henriques, and Paulo Novais

Algoritmi Centre, University of Minho, Braga, Portugal
`ricardo.martins@algoritmi.uminho.pt`
`{prh,pjon}@di.uminho.pt`

Abstract. In general, groups of people are formed because of the similarities and affinities that members have with each other. Musical preferences, soccer teams or even similar behaviours are examples of similarities and affinities that motivate group formation. In social media, identifying these affinities is a difficult task because personal information is not easily identified.

In this paper we present an alternative to identifying similarities between authors and their most frequent audience in Twitter, using emotional and grammatical writing style analysis. Through this study it is possible to define the creation of an emotional profile entirely based on the interactions of people, thus allowing software like chatbots to "learn emotions" and provide emotionally acceptable responses.

Keywords: Sentiment analysis · Emotion analysis · Natural language processing · Social media

1 Introduction

Probably, one of the well known and used proverbs is: "Birds of a feather, flock together". However, what does it mean? In general meaning, it refers that people with common traits, interests and tastes tend to associate and relate with each other, in the same way as birds of the same species flock together. It can be observed in several different human behaviours, where people with common personalities tend to relate to each other.

Psychodynamic researchers claim that personality structure is set in childhood. For Sapir [24], the individual personality is formed around 2 or 3 years old, mostly through child training practices. Freud [3] argues that when the Oedipal complex is resolved, all basic structures of personality - the id, ego, and superego - are fully developed in opposition to Erikson [2] and Loevinger [10], which believe that personality continues to develop later in life. Sharing the same vision of Erikson and Loevinger, the motivational speaker Rohn [23] claimed that "you are the average of the five people you spend the most time with".

© Springer Nature Switzerland AG 2019
P. Moura Oliveira et al. (Eds.): EPIA 2019, LNAI 11805, pp. 159–171, 2019.
https://doi.org/10.1007/978-3-030-30244-3_14

Through social media usage - in general microblogging - people (authors) can express their opinion, desires and thoughts to a broad audience - from friends to unknown followers - keeping proximity despite physical distance. However, is this audience interested in the author's posts because they share the same sentiment, mood or emotions? Also, since software has no childhood, neither id, ego, and superego, is it possible to create an emotional profile based on existing ones, enabling the software "learn" how to have a personality?

In this paper, we present an approach for emotional profile creation based on existent emotional profiles, using emotion-based analysis to determine the proximity of the author's emotional and grammatical writing style with their audience on microblogging.

The remainder of this paper is as follows: Sect. 2, introduces the concept of emotion and presents some theories for emotion representation and analysis. Section 3 presents some work in this area to detect emotion from social media, while Sect. 4, describes the steps used in our analysis and presents some data regarding them. Section 4 discusses about the data obtained and their impact, and finally, the paper ends in Sect. 5 with the conclusion and future work.

2   Emotion Theories

In the literature, there are several models that attempt to explain the emergence of emotions and their associated behaviours. The main research theories here surveyed to serve as background to our analytical work are discrete, dimensional and appraisal theories.

Discrete emotional theories propose the existence of basic emotions that are universally displayed and recognized, grouped into categories and independent. An example of discrete emotional theory is proposed by Plutchik [21], where all sentiment is composed of a set of 8 basic emotions (*anger, anticipation, disgust, fear, joy, sadness, surprise* and *trust*).

On the other hand, **dimensional theories** characterize emotions regarding two or three dimensions, generally "arousal" and "valence." Valence is related to a positive or negative evaluation and is associated with the feeling state of pleasure (vs displeasure). Arousal reflects the general degree of intensity felt. However, using this two-dimensional is confusing to different emotions that share the same values of valence and arousal, as *anger* and *fear*. For this reason, it is common to add a third dimension to support this differentiation, as intensity. According to Leventhal [8] "the third view emphasises the distinct component of emotions, and is often termed the componential view."

Emotional-cognitive psychologists focus their studies mainly on the **appraisal process**. According to Scherer [25], the central idea is that emotions are triggered and differentiated by subjective analysis of an event, situation or object. For instance, Bill and Mike are watching a football game where their teams are playing. Bill's favourite team wins (event). Mike's appraisal is that an undesirable event happened. For Bill, the appraisal is that the event is desirable. So, the same event has produced opposite appraisals. In fact, emotions are triggered by the personal interpretation of the annoying or cheerful aspects of an event, the appraisal.

3 Related Work

Due to the extensive usage, sentiment analysis on microblogs can be considered an opinion-rich resource and has been gaining popularity and attracting researchers from other areas to correlate information about specific events (e.g. Christmas, football matches, elections) with the sentiment contained in posts.

To perform sentiment analysis on microblogging, according to Pang et al. [20], a straightforward approach is to exploit traditional sentiment analysis models. However, such methods are inefficient because they ignore some unique characteristics of microblog's data, as emoticons representations. Moreover, there are lots of colloquial terms, abbreviations and misspelt words used in microblogs which leads to heavy preprocessing tasks in order to identify its occurrences and "translate" them to a canonical form to be interpreted correctly. Due to such properties, several models have been developed especially for microblogs sentiment analysis recently.

An example of correlations between events and sentiments was proposed by Bollen et al. [1], which measures the sentiments on Twitter during a period and compares the correlation between sentiments contained in the text and significant events, including the stock market, elections and Thanksgiving. Also, Kim et al. [7] examined a dataset containing tweets about Michael Jackson's death in order to analyse how emotion is expressed on Twitter. O'Connor et al. [18] have analysed the sentiments about politicians, detecting a strong correlation between the aggregated sentiment and manually collected poll ratings.

Hu et al. [6] predict the individual well-being, as measured by a life satisfaction scale, through the language people used on social media. This is made using randomly selected posts from Facebook and a lexicon-based approach to identify the text words polarities.

A different approach of sentiment analysis using Twitter posts was presented by Pak and Paroubek [19], which consists of a linguistic analysis of the collected corpus to build a sentiment classifier. This classifier can determine positive, negative and neutral sentiments for a document.

Go et al. [5] proposed a framework which interprets the emoticons in tweets as noisy labels using supervised learning. However, as Liu [9] describes, there are some disadvantages when using only emoticons as noisy labels. A reason for this is because it is difficult to collect a large number of tweets with emoticons because they are time-related, dynamic and region-related. For Lu [12], "usually we can only exploit topic-independent tweets with emoticons. That is to say, in topic-dependent datasets which focus on one given topic, the performance boost brought by emoticons is not significant enough. Besides emoticons, rich topic-dependent unlabelled data can be exploited better."

Despite vast works about sentiment analysis in microblogs, none concerns on the study of the relationship between emotional profile and the writing style similarities among authors and their audiences.

4   Data Analysis

In order to analyse the correlation between author's emotional writing style and their audience, we collected 2500 recent Twitter tweets from 6 different aleatory authors from different areas, as presented in Table 1:

Table 1. Tweets authors

Author	Area	Origin
Elon Musk	Business	Press office
Katy Perry	Entertainment	Press office
Donald Trump	Business	By himself
Alan Shipnuck	News	By himself
Michele Dauber	Education	By herself
Floyd Mayweather	Sports	Press office

Although it is clear that three authors do not post in Twitter - i.e. it is a press office representing them - the idea is of this paper is analyse the emotional, grammatical and textual proximity between authors and audiences, even if an author and/or an audience is a press office. In a different point of view, it can highlight an "press office emotional style", which can inform even where the conversation has occurred, as presented by Martins [15].

All tweets were gathered using the package TwitteR [4] for R [22]. Additionally, the tweets were labelled with an annotation indicating if the message was produced by a press office or by the author himself. During the gathering processes, we considered only the tweets and discarded the re-tweets. This decision wad adopted to avoid that texts from other author, like digital influencers or unknown viral texts, biased the individual analysis.

The task of analysing the emotional profile can be split into some intermediate steps: first, it was necessary for some preprocessing tasks in order to reduce data size by removing unnecessary text from the original message; Later, the relevant remaining text was analysed in order to evidence the author's polarities and the author's emotional style.

4.1   Preprocessing

Preprocessing is a data mining technique that involves transforming raw data into an intelligible form. In the literature, several preprocessing techniques are available to extract information from text, and their usage is according to the characteristics of the information desired.

In our analysis, the preprocessing pipeline begins with tokenization and in subsequent starts three parallel jobs, as shown in Fig. 1: Part of Speech Tagging (POS-T), Named Entity Recognition (NER) and Stopwords Removal. This

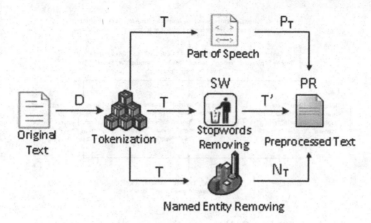

Fig. 1. Preprocessing tasks

strategy was used because both POS-T and NER need the text in the original format, in order to return the correct data from the analysis.

The POS-T process identifies the text grammatical structure and preserves nouns, verbs, adverbs and adjectives. The reason for this approach is because only these grammatical categories can bring emotional information. In a formal description, the Tokenization process converts the original text D in a set of tokens $T = \{t_1, t_2, ..., t_n\}$ where each element contained in T is part of the original document D. Later, the POS-T labels each token with semantic information and the process keeps all nouns, verbs, adverbs and adjectives in a set set P_T, where $P_T = \{p_{T_1}, p_{T_2}, ..., p_{T_k}\}$ and $0 \leq k \leq n$ and $P_T \subset T$.

Like POS-T, NER process identifies names in 3 different categories: "Location", "Person" and "Organization" and removes all tokens related with these categories. As a result, a set $N_T = \{n_{(T_1)}, n_{(T_2)}, ..., n_{(T_j)}\}$ is constructed based on identified word category where $\forall j, cat(N_j) = "O"$. This step is important to be done in parallel with POS-T because some locations can be confused with some grammatical structure (as Long Beach or Crystal Lake, for instance).

The Stopwords list is a predefined set $SW = \{sw_1, sw_2, ...sw_y\}$ of words, available in R through the package **tm**[16]. This step will return a set $T' = t'_1, t'_2, ..., t'_n$, where $T' \cap SW = \emptyset$.

After the 3 preprocessing tasks finish, the outcoming set ST is defined as $ST = T' \cap P_T \cap N_T$.

Later, a stemming algorithm is responsible for obtaining the stem of a word. For this task, we adopted an implementation of the Lovins stemmer [11], resulting in a set of stemmed words $PR = \{ST_1, ST_2, ..., ST_z\}$ ready to be analysed.

For all three tasks - POS-T, NER and Tokenization - the Stanford Core NLP [13] toolkit was used. An example of how the steps change the information is presented in Fig. 2.

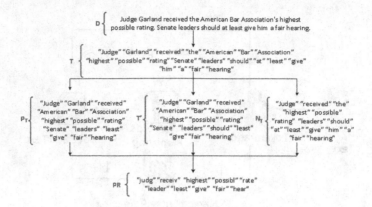

Fig. 2. Preprocessing example

4.2   Polarity Analysis

In order to determine the author's polarity style, after the preprocessing all sentences contained in PR were compared against EmoLex lexicon [17] in order to identify the positive and negative sentiment of the entire text. Later, it was collected and analysed tweets from the top 5 most contacted audience from the author, in order to analyse the proximity of their polarities tweets and author, as presented in Table 2.

Table 2. Polarities analysis from authors and their top 5 audience

	Author		Audience's average	
	Positive	Negative	Positive	Negative
Elon Musk	0,68	0,26	0,68	0,28
Donald Trump	1,13	0,76	1,05	0,57
Katy Perry	1,01	0,27	0,59	0,18
Alan Shipnuck	0,45	0,27	0,57	0,38
Michele Dauber	0,68	0,65	0,83	0,70
Floyd Mayweather	0,62	0,13	0,61	0,27

When applying the Pearson's correlation coefficient (r^2) between polarities authors and their respective top audience give $r^2 = 1$ for all results, indicating a **very strong** correlation between author's polarities and top audience's polarities.

Another analysis made was creating the sets:

$A = \{a1, ..., a6\}$ of authors,
$AP = \{ap_{a_1}, an_{a_1}, ..., ap_{a_6}, an_{a_6}\}$ of polarities where ap is the author positive

polarity, an is the author negative polarity,
$C_A = \{c_{a_1,1}, ..., c_{a_i,j}\}$ of author's topmost contacts, where $0 \leq i \leq 6$ and $1 \leq j \leq 5$,
$CP = \{\overline{cp_i}, \overline{cn_i}\}$ of polarities, where $\overline{cp}$ is the average of audience's positive polarities, $\overline{cn}$ is the average of audience's negative polarities and $0 \leq i \leq 6$.

When applying the correlation coefficient between AP and CP, the result is $r^2 = 0,85$, indicating a strong correlation between authors' polarities their audiences polarities.

4.3   Emotional Analysis

In order to analyse the emotions contained into the text, it was used a lexicon-based approach provided by Syuzhet package in R, in order to identify the emotions contained in text according to the model proposed by Plutchik [21], where all sentiment is composed of a set of 8 basic emotions (*anger, anticipation, disgust, fear, joy, sadness, surprise* and *trust*).

After all author's tweets analysis, the distribution of each basic emotion introduces a specific emotional profile for each author, defined as "emotional writing style", which is presented Table 3.

Using this information, the next step was to determine the average of each basic emotion for the audience's author. To achieve this objective, we used the same strategy used for the polarities, resulting in the audience's emotional writing style, according to Table 4.

Table 3. Basic emotions per author

Author	Anger	Anticipation	Disgust	Fear	Joy	Sadness	Surprise	Trust
Elon Musk	0,11	0,34	0,06	0,14	0,23	0,10	0,12	0,38
Donald Trump	0,34	0,53	0,20	0,36	0,45	0,40	0,33	0,83
Katy Perry	0,12	0,52	0,04	0,13	0,67	0,16	0,25	0,43
Alan Shipnuck	0,11	0,20	0,09	0,14	0,20	0,15	0,11	0,26
Michele Dauber	0,37	0,32	0,23	0,34	0,20	0,31	0,10	0,48
Floyd Mayweather	0,11	0,44	0,02	0,10	0,43	0,08	0,18	0,37

Hence, when applying the Pearson's correlation coefficient (r^2) between basic emotions from authors and the average of their audiences, it is possible to verify that in significant part they are strongly correlated, as presented in Table 5.

Moreover, in order to establish Jim Rohn's statement, the analysis was expanded to verify the emotional profile of 100 most frequent contacts from each author. According to Fig. 3, the correlation between authors' emotions and most frequent contacts emotions' average decreases when the number of contacts increases, supporting that "you are the average of 5 people you spend the most time with."

Table 4. Basic emotion's frequency average of audience's author

Average audience of	Anger	Anticipation	Disgust	Fear	Joy	Sadness	Surprise	Trust
Elon Musk	0,13	0,38	0,08	0,20	0,20	0,13	0,13	0,30
Donald Trump	0,25	0,48	0,12	0,36	0,40	0,34	0,33	0,80
Katy Perry	0,10	0,35	0,05	0,09	0,42	0,11	0,18	0,34
Alan Shipnuck	0,18	0,31	0,13	0,22	0,25	0,21	0,18	0,33
Michele Dauber	0,45	0,36	0,26	0,53	0,22	0,36	0,17	0,64
Floyd Mayweather	0,19	0,34	0,08	0,14	0,35	0,12	0,16	0,33

Table 5. Correlation between basic emotion's authors and frequency average basic emotion's top audiences

Author	Correlation	Author	Correlation
Elon Musk	0,93	Donald Trump	0,99
Katy Perry	0,99	Alan Shipnuck	0,96
Michele Dauber	0,95	Floyd Mayweather	0,98

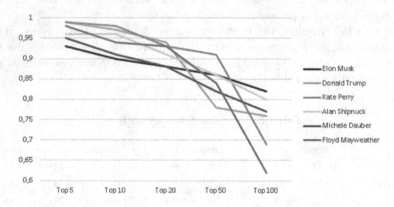

Fig. 3. Correlations by author

A new point identified during the analysis, as showed in Table 6, is that the correlations tend to be higher within authors from the same origin, indicating a "press office emotional pattern."

4.4   Grammatical Analysis

Another approach used was to determine if both authors and audiences share the same grammatical style when writing. For grammatical style, we understand the distribution of grammatical categories of words in sentences. To achieve this objective, both authors and audiences had their tweets labelled according to Part of Speech Penn Treebank [14] tags using Stanford Core NLP [13]. The next

Table 6. Correlation between basic emotion's authors

	Elon Musk	Donald Trump	Katy Perry	Alan Shipnuck	Michele Dauber	Floyd Mayweather
Elon Musk	1,00	0,92	0,77	0,94	0,48	0,89
Donald Trump	0,92	1,00	0,61	0,95	0,64	0,71
Katy Perry	0,77	0,61	1,00	0,79	−0,04	0,97
Alan Shipnuck	0,94	0,95	0,79	1,00	0,49	0,84
Michele Dauber	0,48	0,64	−0,04	0,49	1,00	0,11
Floyd Mayweather	0,89	0,71	0,97	0,84	0,11	1,00

step was to determine the average of each Part of Speech tag for each author and their audience, resulting in the grammatical style, according to Table 7.

Hence, when applying the Pearson's correlation coefficient (r^2) between the grammatical style of authors and their audience, it is possible to verify that they are strongly correlated, as presented in Table 8.

4.5   Similarity Analysis

The objective of the similarity analysis is to quantify the level of similarity of the author's texts and their respective audiences' texts. For this analysis, we collected the last 1000 tweets for each author and the last 1000 tweets for the same audiences used in Sect. 4.2 in order to identify the similarity between their texts.

Before analysing the texts, they were preprocessed using the same pipeline described in Sect. 4.1 in order to keep the texts in the same structure in for the different analysis.

Using the Jaccard distance as metric to analyse the similarity among the texts; initially, we analysed the similarity between each author's texts and the texts of all audiences, in order to identify which audience is more similar to the author. Once identified the text's similarity percentage, we calculated the average of each audience, according to the formula:

$$\frac{\sum_{i=1}^{n} SM1_i + \sum_{i=1}^{n} SM2_i + \sum_{i=1}^{n} SM3_i + \sum_{i=1}^{n} SM4_i + \sum_{i=1}^{n} SM5_i}{n}$$

Later, for each author, we calculated the mean and standard deviation for the similarity between him and the audiences, as presented in Table 9.

This information allowed to identify that, in most cases, the highest similarity average was between the author and his audience. Moreover, the cases where it did not occur, the similarities values of the author's audience added with standard deviation indicates that the audience's value is close to the highest value.

Table 7. Grammatical style for authors and audiences

	Part of Speech	Elon Musk	Donald Trump	Kate Perry	Alan Shipnuck	Michele Dauber	Floyd Mayweather
Author	CC	0,38	0,61	0,48	0,24	0,46	0,26
	CD	0,27	0,28	0,2	0,12	0,15	0,48
	DT	0,91	1,66	1,08	0,96	1,32	0,68
	IN	1,12	2,07	1,37	0,87	1,39	0,9
	JJ	1,05	1,39	1,09	0,83	1,11	0,63
	JJR	0,06	0,07	0,04	0,02	0,06	0,02
	JJS	0,06	0,07	0,03	0,03	0,01	0,04
	MD	0,28	0,31	0,1	0,15	0,21	0,05
	NN	2,94	3,18	3,58	2,56	3,73	2,72
	NNS	0,61	0,96	0,96	0,48	0,69	0,39
	POS	0,03	0,05	0,06	0,08	0,07	0,02
	RB	0,94	0,93	0,57	0,65	0,92	0,29
	RP	0,03	0,06	0,03	0,04	0,02	0,03
	TO	0,3	0,58	0,22	0,18	0,38	0,29
	VB	0,64	0,89	0,48	0,43	0,77	0,66
	VBD	0,18	0,4	0,25	0,25	0,46	0,12
	VBG	0,25	0,51	0,54	0,19	0,4	0,18
	VBN	0,21	0,35	0,12	0,12	0,26	0,05
	VBP	0,31	0,43	0,69	0,31	0,55	0,23
	VBZ	0,38	0,47	0,49	0,37	0,55	0,2
	WP	0,04	0,12	0,14	0,03	0,06	0,02
	WRB	0,03	0,05	0,06	0,04	0,11	0,03
Audience	CC	0,29	0,35	0,15	0,26	0,35	0,25
	CD	0,46	0,23	0,25	0,38	0,25	0,31
	DT	0,95	1,21	0,66	1	1,39	0,93
	IN	1,33	1,67	0,98	1,13	1,61	1,07
	JJ	1,02	0,9	0,62	0,84	1,13	0,82
	JJR	0,03	0,06	0,03	0,05	0,06	0,03
	JJS	0,05	0,05	0,03	0,03	0,03	0,03
	MD	0,2	0,14	0,05	0,18	0,2	0,13
	NN	3,65	3,93	2,92	2,96	3,68	3,33
	NNS	0,62	0,91	0,42	0,58	0,77	0,51
	POS	0,11	0,18	0,05	0,09	0,11	0,08
	RB	0,7	0,39	0,43	0,72	0,94	0,56
	RP	0,06	0,08	0,08	0,06	0,06	0,08
	TO	0,28	0,48	0,24	0,26	0,44	0,27
	VB	0,63	0,67	0,44	0,52	0,83	0,55
	VBD	0,27	0,32	0,14	0,37	0,35	0,25
	VBG	0,3	0,41	0,22	0,28	0,42	0,26
	VBN	0,23	0,28	0,09	0,19	0,25	0,17
	VBP	0,41	0,32	0,26	0,4	0,5	0,25
	VBZ	0,44	0,52	0,23	0,43	0,65	0,32
	WP	0,05	0,09	0,04	0,05	0,09	0,06
	WRB	0,08	0,06	0,05	0,08	0,11	0,05

Table 8. Correlation of grammatical frequency average between authors and audience

Author	Correlation	Author	Correlation
Elon Musk	0,99	Donald Trump	0,95
Katy Perry	0,98	Alan Shipnuck	0,99
Michele Dauber	0,99	Floyd Mayweather	0,99

Table 9. Similarities between authors and audiences

Audiences								
Author	(1)	(2)	(3)	(4)	(5)	(6)	Mean	Standard deviation
Elon Musk (1)	**0,681%**	0,605%	0,629%	0,650%	0,542%	0,536%	0,607%	0,058%
Donald Trump (2)	0,728%	**1,068%**	0,840%	0,833%	0,893%	0,687%	0,842%	0,135%
Katy Perry (3)	0,712%	0,613%	0,999%	0,811%	0,623%	**1,096%**	0,809%	0,201%
Alan Shipnuck (4)	0,553%	0,531%	**0,738%**	0,664%	0,557%	0,573%	0,603%	0,081%
Michele Dauber (5)	0,739%	0,745%	0,731%	0,824%	**0,926%**	0,672%	0,773%	0,089%
Floyd Maywheather (6)	0,605%	0,542%	0,846%	0,566%	0,473%	**1,430%**	0,744%	0,360%

5   Conclusion

This paper presented an analysis of the emotional and grammatical writing styles similarity from authors and their most frequent audiences on microblogs. This approach used lexicon-based techniques to explore the emotions contained in tweets and NLP techniques to identify grammatical excerpts.

Once the emotional and grammatical writing styles have very high values, indicating a strong correlation between authors and audiences, it is possible to conclude that both authors and audiences share the same writing style. Moreover, the correlation between authors emotions and the most frequent audiences emotions exhibited in Fig. 3 is high, and as the size of this audience increases, the lower the correlation becomes, confirming Jim Rohn's claiming.

This is a crucial issue because it enables the possibility of chatbots to create an emotional profile based on the interactions received from people or even other systems, creating an identity and interacting with the end user in smooth communication. Combining Generative Adversarial Networks (GANs) and emotional profiles, a new generation of chatbots can create its own "personality" and generate textual responses that fit its emotional profile.

As future work, it is planned to create a running example of an emotional chatbot that "learns" the emotional profile from the interactions and communicates according to this profile.

Acknowledgements. This work has been supported by FCT – Fundação para a Ciência e Tecnologia within the Project Scope: UID/CEC/00319/2019.

References

1. Bollen, J., Mao, H., Pepe, A.: Modeling public mood and emotion: Twitter sentiment and socio-economic phenomena. ICWSM **11**, 450–453 (2011)
2. Erikson, E.H.: Childhood and Society. WW Norton & Company, New York City (1993)
3. Freud, S.: The Ego and the Id. WW Norton & Company, New York City (1962)
4. Gentry, J.: twitteR: R Based Twitter Client. R Package Version 1.1.9 (2015)
5. Go, A., Bhayani, R., Huang, L.: Twitter sentiment classification using distant supervision. CS224N Proj. Rep. Stanford **1**(2009), 12 (2009)
6. Hu, X., Tang, L., Tang, J., Liu, H.: Exploiting social relations for sentiment analysis in microblogging. In: Proceedings of the Sixth ACM International Conference on Web Search and Data Mining, pp. 537–546. ACM (2013)
7. Kim, E., Gilbert, S., Edwards, M.J., Grae, E.: Detecting sadness in 140 characters: sentiment analysis of mourning Michael Jackson on Twitter. Web Ecol. **3**, 1–15 (2009)
8. Leventhal, H., Scherer, K.: The relationship of emotion to cognition: a functional approach to a semantic controversy. Cogn. Emot. **1**(1), 3–28 (1987)
9. Liu, K.-L., Li, W.-J., Guo, M.: Emoticon smoothed language models for Twitter sentiment analysis. In: AAAI (2012)
10. Loevinger, J.: The meaning and measurement of ego development. Am. Psychol. **21**(3), 195 (1966)
11. Lovins, J.B.: Development of a stemming algorithm. Mech. Transl. Comput. Linguist. **11**(1–2), 22–31 (1968)
12. Lu, T.-J.: Semi-supervised microblog sentiment analysis using social relation and text similarity. In: 2015 International Conference on Big Data and Smart Computing (BigComp), pp. 194–201. IEEE (2015)
13. Manning, C.D., Surdeanu, M., Bauer, J., Finkel, J., Bethard, S.J., McClosky, D.: The Stanford CoreNLP natural language processing toolkit. In: Association for Computational Linguistics (ACL) System Demonstrations, pp. 55–60 (2014)
14. Marcus, M.P., Marcinkiewicz, M.A., Santorini, B.: Building a large annotated corpus of English: the penn treebank. Comput. Linguist. **19**(2), 313–330 (1993)
15. Martins, R., Almeida, J.J., Henriques, P., Novais, P.: Domain identification through sentiment analysis. In: De La Prieta, F., Omatu, S., Fernández-Caballero, A. (eds.) DCAI 2018. AISC, vol. 800, pp. 276–283. Springer, Cham (2019). https://doi.org/10.1007/978-3-319-94649-8_33
16. Meyer, D., Hornik, K., Feinerer, I.: Text mining infrastructure in R. J. Stat. Softw. **25**(5), 1–54 (2008)
17. Mohammad, S.M., Turney, P.D.: Crowdsourcing a word-emotion association lexicon. Comput. Intell. **29**(3), 436–465 (2013)
18. O'Connor, B., Balasubramanyan, R., Routledge, B.R., Smith, N.A.: From Tweets to polls: linking text sentiment to public opinion time series. ICWSM **11**(122–129), 1–2 (2010)
19. Pak, A., Paroubek, P.: Twitter as a corpus for sentiment analysis and opinion mining. In: LREc, vol. 10 (2010)
20. Pang, B., Lee, L., et al.: Opinion mining and sentiment analysis. Found. Trends® Inf. Retrieval **2**(1–2), 1–135 (2008)
21. Plutchik, R.: Emotions: a general psychoevolutionary theory. Approaches Emot. **197–219**, 1984 (1984)

22. R Core Team: R: A Language and Environment for Statistical Computing. R Foundation for Statistical Computing, Vienna, Austria (2017)
23. Rohn, E.J., Rohn, E.J.: The Treasury of Quotes. Health Communications (1994)
24. Sapir, E.: Personality. In: Seligman, E., Johnson, A. (eds.) Encyclopedia of the Social Sciences, pp. 85–88 (1934)
25. Scherer, K.R., Dalgleish, T., Power, M.: Handbook of Cognition and Emotion (1999)

Using Deep Learning Techniques for Authentication of Amadeo de Souza Cardoso Paintings and Drawings

Ailin Chen[1(✉)], Rui Jesus[2(✉)], and Marcia Villarigues[1(✉)]

[1] Departamento de Conservação e Restauro, Faculdade de Ciências e
Tecnologia, Universidade NOVA de Lisboa, 2825-149 Caparica,
Lisbon, Portugal
ailin.chen@campus.fct.unl.pt, mgv@fct.unl.pt
[2] NOVA LINCS, Faculdade de Ciências e Tecnologia, Universidade NOVA de
Lisboa, 2825-149 Caparica, Lisbon, Portugal
rjesus@deetc.isel.ipl.pt

Abstract. This paper investigates the application of a Convolutional Neural Network (CNN), AlexNet, on the authentication of paintings by different artists, including Portuguese painter Amadeo de Souza Cardoso, Chinese painter Daqian Zhang and Dutch painter Vincent van Gogh. The research is motivated by the studies on the identification of the works by Amadeo based on the painter's brushstroke implementing Machine Learning algorithms combined with material analysis. The employment of CNN intends to improve the performance of the brushstroke analysis and increase the accuracy while authenticating an artist' works. The results show that the implementation of AlexNet produces higher accuracies than its counterparts applying previous brushstroke analysis. Notably, when Amadeo drawings are included in the testing based on Amadeo paintings, the accuracies obtained with the original algorithm drop substantially, whilst the counterparts attained with AlexNet improved considerably. However, when other testing sets are introduced, especially the Chinese paintings, the accuracies show a great increase with the original algorithm but a significant decrease with AlexNet. It implies that AlexNet surpasses the traditional computation through learning by examples; it can potentially solve the problem of limited number of artworks by a specific artist for training.

Keywords: Neural network · Artificial intelligence ·
Convolutional Neural Network · AlexNet · Machine learning · Authentication ·
Paintings · Drawings · Art

1 Introduction

1.1 Authentication of Paintings

Although art forgeries have long existed since the Roman period, the booming of the commercial art market in the 20th Century certainly has stimulated the prosperity of the art forgery market. It is often the case when some unknown paintings, discovered or owned by private individuals, entering the market. It is thus quintessential that the

© Springer Nature Switzerland AG 2019
P. Moura Oliveira et al. (Eds.): EPIA 2019, LNAI 11805, pp. 172–183, 2019.
https://doi.org/10.1007/978-3-030-30244-3_15

paintings are authenticated before entering the art market to avoid financial loss for both the museums and art collectors. Authentication investigation encompasses both invasive techniques and non-destructive approaches. The former practice is destructive and therefore not often recommended, particularly on legacies and heritages. As the field of computer science advances, its application on various areas including the conservation and restoration of artworks also develops. The implementation of machine learning techniques is one of the non-invasive approaches to study artworks. The Conservation and Restauration Department (DCR) of Universidade NOVA de Lisboa (NOVA) applied machine learning algorithms on the brushstroke analysis of the paintings by the late Portuguese artist Amadeo de Souza Cardoso, along with material analysis in order to determine the authenticity of his paintings. Both brushstroke and material analysis were regarded equally valuable for the purpose of authentication in the work [1]. Our research is motivated by the afore-mentioned study with the intention of improving the original method so that it can be implemented to a broader setting. The present focus is on the implementation of machine learning techniques for the investigation on the brushstroke.

1.2   Artificial Neural Network (ANN)

In recent years, ANN has been practised in many fields, via the means of classification, recognition, identification and so on. It is also applied in the art world for artistic analysis, processing and production. Different from the conventional computing paradigm, the ANN computing paradigm is inspired by how human brain functions and performs a type of "brain-style computation" and learns by examples through a learning process [2]. In general, ANN is composed of input layer, hidden layer and output layer. The input layer is generally fed with raw information, followed by distinguishing weights carried with the connections between input and hidden layer, ended with interactions through weights between hidden layer and output layer. Neural networks require a fair number of samples to produce a satisfactory result, usually thousands to millions. That is, the computation demand is very high, so is the demand for the quantity of raw information. Nevertheless, one of the major challenges in terms of analysing artworks using neural networks is the finite number of samples from a particular artist. Furthermore, many neural networks are designed specifically for object recognition. Consequently, analysis on artworks applying neural networks currently appears to be very limited. Our research adopts the pre-designed and pre-trained CNN, AlexNet, for the identification of paintings so that the results generated by both the brain-style computation and the conventional computation cited in Montagner's work can be compared and evaluated; it might be one of the first works hitherto where neural networks have been used for the authentication of artworks.

2 Related Work

2.1 Convolutional Neural Network (CNN)

CNN is a subset of ANN and is a deep learning algorithm. The employment of CNN is multifaceted; it is however oftentimes utilised for visual imagery analysis by apprehending both the spatial and temporal information via a set of pertinent filters [3]. Similar to ANN, CNN is also comprised of a sequence of layers, where the hidden layer usually consists of one or multiple series of three types of layers; Convolutional Layer (CONV), Pooling Layer (POOL) and Fully-Connected Layer (FC). Further layers or operations can be added to or repeated respectively in the hidden layer depending on the architecture of CNN. Other operations or layers in CNN include padding, activation function, flatten, soft-max and normalisation among others. The CONV is performed by the convolution operation through a kernel with a pre-defined stride from left to right and from top to bottom until a complete parse of the image length and width. The function of CONV is to extract low level features such as edges, colour and gradient orientation at lower level layers and more structured representation of images at higher level layers. CONV is followed by POOL with the objective of reducing the number of parameters thus reducing the computation load, extracting dominant features as well as helping to minimise overfitting. FC uses the full connections of the output from the previous layer and classifies the output.

2.2 CNN in Identification of Artworks

Although the concept of CNN has been around for some time, the application of CNN is relatively new particularly in the field of artwork identification. One of the earliest works on the authentication of artworks employing neural networks is by Marmara University and Istanbul University in Turkey in 2009 where ANN was applied following the wavelet transform with a high classification accuracy of 88% [4].

Most of the works applying CNN on the artist attribution seem to be more recent; many are inspired by AlexNet. Almost all were reported to outperform the conventional image classification projects [5]. Bar et al. [6] combined the high-level descriptors extracted via deep neural network learning AlexNet and Decaf, and low-level descriptors extracted from conventional image processing and pattern recognition tools in order to classify the painting styles. The results intended to assess the performances of different combinations of the aforementioned techniques on the classification of different painting styles. In the work by van Noord et al. [7], the visual characteristics of artists' works were learned thus recognised for the purpose of artist attribution by the implementation of one of CNNs, PigeoNET. The achieved accuracy was more than 70% when unseen data were tested. PigeoNET corresponds to AlexNet with an integrated visual component based on the biological visual discernibility of certain animals like pigeons and honeybees. Tan et al. [8] devised their CNN based on AlexNet with minor modifications on parameters like stride size and softmax layer. A better result of 68% in comparison with other research on the same dataset acquired from Wikiart was attained. Additionally, they considered that the classification of artworks was more difficult than object and face recognition applying CNN. Hong et al.

[9] researched on three types of CNN architectures, derived from AlexNet, VGGNet and VGGNet respectively, and then compared the results with SIFT method, in terms of art painting identification. One of the three architectures was a smaller version of the architecture based on VGGNet. Their results showed the smaller version architecture based on VGGNet had the lowest error rate and outperformed SIFT by 13.6%.

Excluding the widely implemented AlexNet in such field, another CNN specialised in object detection, ResNet also appears to be an inspiration to many researches in this topic. For instance, Viswanathan [10] compared three CNN architectures; a simple CNN with six layers served as a base CNN for comparison, ResNet-18 trained from scratch, ResNet-18 with transfer learning applying pre-trained weights calculated based on ImageNet database, both with a further FC for artist prediction. The results showed that the pre-trained ResNet-18 achieved the best accuracy up to 97% for training accuracy and 90% for testing accuracy. They affirmed that the deeper the network, the better the results. Likewise, Lecoutre et al. [11] employed and compared variations of CNNs: pre-trained AlexNet, pre-trained ResNet-50, retrained ResNet-50 and ResNet-34. The outcome of their experiments confirmed that the pre-trained models performed better, especially the pre-trained ResNet-50, and that the deeper the retraining procedure on pre-trained networks, the better the result.

3   Algorithm

In Montagner's work, the brushstroke was investigated via implementing a series of conventional machine learning techniques. Our research substitutes completely the algorithms applied in her work and applies brain-style neural networks to assess the effects of both approaches on the data, i.e. different artists, styles and genres.

3.1   Application via Scale-Invariant Feature Transform (SIFT)+Gabor

Montagner [1] conducted the brushstroke investigation based on four computation methods. Only the most representative results generated with the method named SIFT +Gabor are reported below. The SIFT+Gabor algorithm starts with feature extraction by assessing images from both positive and negative training sets with keypoints and descriptors highlighted by SIFT. Blocks centred around the keypoints are then excerpted from the original training images and rotated accordingly based on the angle of the keypoint vectors. A set of Gabor features are hence obtained from those blocks after being filtered with 24 Gabor filters of 4 scales and 6 orientations respectively. K-Means++ clustering is applied on the Gabor features to generate a series of centroids, which are used to generate a bag of features. The number of centroids evaluated by Montagner is 100, 200, 400, 1000, 1200, 1400, 1600 and 2000 respectively. For each number of centroids used, half are derived from the positive set and half from the negative set. The bag of features is then processed with Term Frequency-Inverse Document Frequency (TF-IDF) in order to evaluate the frequency of centroids and balance the difference between positive and negative number of terms. The resulting bag of features is thus processed applying a Regularised Least Squares Classifier

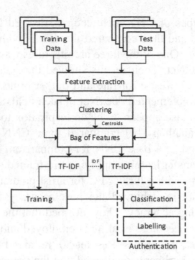

Fig. 1. Block diagram of SIFT+Gabor method

(RLSC) to produce classifiers with relevant coefficients, which will be then used to evaluate the test data. The block diagram of the SIFT+Gabor method is illustrated in Fig. 1.

3.2 Application via AlexNet

The CNN applied in our research is the pre-designed and pre-trained deep learning CNN, AlexNet, created by Krizhevsky et al. [5]. AlexNet [5] is composed of eight layers with the first five layers as CONV, some of them are followed by Max Pooing Layer, where the maximum value is returned from the output of the previous CONV, and the last three layers as FC. In comparison with other CNNs, more kernels are used in each layer and stacked in CONV. Kernel sizes are of 11×11, 5×5 and 3×3 with the depth of 3, same as the depth of RGB image that applied for the training of AlexNet. ReLU activation function is applied after each of the CONV and FC. AlexNet was initially devised for object classification being implemented on ImageNet database. The resolutions of the images are various; whereas AlexNet requires image input of a fixed resolution 227×227. Hence, all images are downsampled and cropped out by size 227×227 from the central area.

The artists that we studied in our research only left limited number of artworks. Subsequently, preprocessing on the original image for the objective of data augmentation is necessary for our study. The following data augmentation method was applied for the training data: random area crop, random scale between 10% and 100%, random X/Y reflection (mirroring), random rotation between 0° and 360°. Initially random X/Y translation with ±30 pixels were also applied and processed. However, the nature of random area cropping and random translation is similar and, depending on the preprocessing order, translation can yield sections beyond the limits of the image which may introduce unusable information thereby reducing the amount of usable data. The attained results produced lower accuracy than the ones obtained without translation. Therefore, the results with translation operation are not included in this paper. For testing, the data are not augmented. However, due to the requirement of the input size 227 × 227 for AlexNet, the testing data have to be cropped as well. For the purposes of this research the central area of the image has been used, as generally this contains the most prominent information of the whole image. Moreover, some of testing images have an irregular outline which discards the use of random cropping for the testing image as this might contain blank useless information. As a result, only the blocks cropped from the centre of the original images in the testing data instead of the full images were evaluated for the time being. In this paper, the results are only conveyed by affirmation of either negative or positive instead of the probability of the artwork belonging to a particular artist or another.

4 Data

Our research systematically evaluated three groups of databases concerning the Portuguese artist Amadeo de Souza Cardoso, the Chinese painter Daqian Zhang and the Dutch painter Vincent van Gogh respectively. The first group of datasets comprises the same data applied in Montagner's work and, is considered as the reference data. It consists of only paintings of Amadeo as well as his contemporaries such as Gino Severini, Sonia and Robert Delaunay and Jose Almada Negreiros. They include 200 Amadeo paintings published in *Catalogue Raisonné Amadeo de Souza Cardoso pintura*, used as the positive dataset, as well as 109 Amadeo contemporary paintings displayed mostly in the exhibition *Amadeo de Souza-Cardoso-Diálogo de Vanguardas*, used as the negative dataset. Approximately half of the data from each dataset are used to attain the Amadeo classifier with SIFT+Gabor, as well as to train the neural networks with AlexNet. In addition to the paintings analysed in Montagner's work, we studied a further set of 39 Amadeo drawings obtained from Calouste Gulbenkian Museum. Out of the collection of drawings, 29 are loose drawings with distinctive styles; the medium applied on most of them is watercolour. Another 10 drawings are extracted from the manuscript *La Légende de Saint-Julien L'hospitalier*; they are selected because they are primarily drawings without text so that they can be used as a part of the Amadeo drawings database. Examples of Amadeo paintings and drawings are shown in Figs. 2, 3 and 4.

Fig. 2. Sample Amadeo paintings

Fig. 3. Sample Amadeo drawings (loose)

Fig. 4. Sample Amadeo drawings from *La Légende de Saint-Julien L'hospitalier*

The second group of datasets were bestowed by the Pennsylvania State University. This dataset is composed of a total of 1177 images of 23 renowned traditional Chinese painters like Baishi Qi, Daqian Zhang, Banqiao Zheng. Chinese paintings are very different from Western painting style and have very distinguishing brushstrokes throughout the painting. A majority of them also use very extensively the calligraphy and stamps in the paintings; oftentimes almost half of the paintings are covered with calligraphy and stamps. In order to maximise the amount of the actual paintings with content and brushstrokes, and minimise the amount of text with calligraphy and stamps, manual selection is carefully performed resulting in a dataset of 91 paintings by the Chinese painter Daqian Zhang. They are applied in the negative dataset for the Amadeo classifier and Amadeo AlexNet in order to evaluate the performance of the two computation paradigms. Examples of Chinese paintings are shown in Fig. 5.

Fig. 5. Sample Chinese paintings

The third group of datasets is a database of paintings by van Gogh and his contemporaries obtained from van Gogh museum. The total of 210 van Gogh paintings are used in the negative dataset for Amadeo classifier and Amadeo AlexNet for the purpose of comparison. Sample van Gogh paintings are displayed in Fig. 6.

Fig. 6. Sample van Gogh paintings

Due to the complexity of the numerous datasets, classifiers and neural networks, notations are applied respectively as follows: Amadeo paintings trained with SIFT +Gabor is noted as Amadeo Classifier; Amadeo paintings trained with AlexNet is noted as Amadeo AlexNet. The results obtained via classifier and AlexNet retrained on Chinese paintings and van Gogh paintings respectively are not reported due to the size requirement of the paper. Amadeo paintings – AP; Amadeo contemporary paintings – ACP; Amadeo drawings – AD; Chinese paintings – CP; van Gogh paintings – VGP; van Gogh contemporary paintings – VGCP.

5 Results and Discussion

The datasets applied in Montagner's work are considered as reference datasets and are shown in Table 1. The resulting accuracies acquired are thus noted as reference accuracy and used for comparison with accuracies attained with other testing datasets. It can be found that although the training data and testing data are the same, the accuracy of 75.00% applying AlexNet is evidently higher than the accuracies resulting from the original algorithm (SIFT+Gabor Ref Accuracy). This suggests CNN does perform better than the conventional method in this particular case.

Table 1. Reference training and testing sets for Amadeo paintings

Ref test	Positive	Negative
Ref training set	105 AP	60 ACP
Ref testing set	95 AP	49 ACP

When the 29 Amadeo drawings are introduced in the testing set, the accuracy obtained with AlexNet shows even higher accuracy of 76.30% and 82.76% (Table 4) than when the 29 Amadeo drawings are excluded from the testing set (Table 2), whilst the accuracies obtained from the conventional computation actually dropped significantly to only around 65% and 40% (Table 4). Particularly when the 29 Amadeo drawings are included alone, AlexNet achieved a substantial improvement on accuracy from about 40% to 82.76%. Although the medium applied on the 29 Amadeo drawings are mostly watercolour, the styles differ from each other. The authors consider that the styles of the 29 Amadeo drawings still resemble a lot of styles of Amadeo paintings. This might be one of the reasons that AlexNet works so well on the identification of the

Table 2. Reference accuracy for Amadeo paintings

SIFT+Gabor classifier								AlexNet
Number of words	100	200	400	1000	1200	1400	1600	2000	N/A
Ref accuracy	70.83	66.67	65.97	70.14	70.83	70.83	73.61	71.53	75.00

Table 3. Training and testing sets for Amadeo paintings and 29 Amadeo drawings

	Test 1.1		Test 1.2	
	Positive	Negative	Positive	Negative
Training set	105 AP	60 ACP	105 AP	60 ACP
Testing set	95 AP + 29 AD = 124	49 ACP	29 AD	49 ACP

29 Amadeo drawings since it functions like a human brain and discerns objects through learning by examples. Unlike Amadeo Classifier, AlexNet does not seem to need retraining with drawings only in order to correctly identify Amadeo drawings. This can potentially solve the problem of finite number of artworks by a particular artist for training (Table 3).

Table 4. Accuracies for Amadeo paintings and 29 Amadeo drawings

SIFT+Gabor classifier								AlexNet
Number of words	100	200	400	1000	1200	1400	1600	2000	N/A
Accuracy 1.1	65.90	63.01	62.43	65.32	66.47	66.47	68.79	67.05	76.30
Accuracy 1.2	50.00	43.59	41.03	41.03	42.31	42.31	38.46	39.74	82.76

Unexpectedly, when a further 10 Amadeo drawings selected from the manuscript *La Légende de Saint-Julien L'hospitalier* are included in the testing, the accuracy tested via AlexNet dropped to 69.23% (AlexNet Accuracy 2.2) in comparison with when the 10 drawings are not included in the testing (AlexNet Accuracy 1.2), although the authors consider those 10 drawings also simulate one style of Amadeo paintings. Nevertheless, the result obtained through AlexNet is still significantly higher than the results obtained through original algorithm which are only around 45% (Accuracy 2.2) (Tables 5 and 6).

Table 5. Training and testing sets for Amadeo paintings and 39 Amadeo drawings

	Test 2.1		Test 2.2	
	Positive	Negative	Positive	Negative
Training set	105 AP	60 ACP	105 AP	60 ACP
Testing set	95 AP + 29 AD + 10 AD = 134	49 ACP	29 AD + 10 AD = 39	49 ACP

Table 6. Accuracies for Amadeo paintings and 39 Amadeo drawings

SIFT+Gabor classifier									AlexNet
Number of words	100	200	400	1000	1200	1400	1600	2000	N/A
Accuracy 2.1	64.48	61.75	62.84	65.03	66.67	65.57	68.31	66.67	73.77
Accuracy 2.2	48.86	43.18	44.32	43.18	45.45	43.18	40.91	42.05	69.23

On the other hand, when the paintings of Chinese artist Daqian Zhang are intro-duced in the testing applying Amadeo Classifier and Amadeo AlexNet trained with only Amadeo paintings, the accuracies obtained through AlexNet dropped considerably to as low as 13% (AlexNet Accuracy 3.3) in comparison with the previous testing sets, whilst the counterpart accuracies obtained from the original algorithm instead increased remarkably to more than 90% (SIFT+Gabor Accuracy 3.3). It clearly shows that original method derives features from brushstroke. Since the brushstrokes of Chinese paintings are very different from Amadeo paintings, they are mostly correctly classified as negative, hence the accuracies increased. Contrarily, neural networks require learning by examples. Amadeo AlexNet is trained with only Amadeo paintings and without any examples of Chinese paintings. It is therefore expected that the networks are unable to discern appropriately the Chinese paintings (Tables 7 and 8).

Table 7. Training and testing sets for Amadeo paintings and 91 Chinese paintings

	Test 3.1		Test 3.2		Test 3.3	
	Positive	Negative	Positive	Negative	Positive	Negative
Training set	105 AP	60 ACP	105 AP	60 ACP	105 AP	60 ACP
Testing set	95 AP	49 ACP + 91 CP = 140	0	49 ACP + 91 CP = 140	0	91 CP

Table 8. Accuracies for Amadeo paintings and 91 Chinese paintings

SIFT+Gabor classifier									AlexNet
Number of words	100	200	400	1000	1200	1400	1600	2000	N/A
Accuracy 3.1	75.32	78.30	75.32	78.30	79.15	78.30	81.70	79.15	51.06
Accuracy 3.2	72.86	77.86	72.14	73.57	74.29	72.86	73.57	72.14	24.29
Accuracy 3.3	82.42	96.70	90.11	91.21	92.31	90.11	94.51	91.21	13.19

Similarly, when van Gogh paintings substitute the Chinese paintings in the testing applying Amadeo Classifier and Amadeo AlexNet, the accuracies resulted from AlexNet dropped as well when being compared with the accuracies obtained via the original algorithm (Table 10). The phenomenon can also be explained in a similar manner as when the Chinese paintings were applied earlier. Nevertheless, the decline of accuracies is not as significantly as the previous situation with Chinese paintings. After all, the accuracies acquired from both approaches are low in both situations. This confirms once again that AlexNet learns by examples since Amadeo AlexNet was trained without any samples of van Gogh paintings (Table 9).

Table 9. Training and testing sets for Amadeo paintings and 210 van Gogh paintings

	Test 4.1		Test 4.2		Test 4.3	
	Positive	Negative	Positive	Negative	Positive	Negative
Training set	105 AP	60 ACP	105 AP	60 ACP	105 AP	60 ACP
Testing set	95 AP	49 ACP + 210 VGP = 259	0	49 ACP + 210 VGP = 259	0	210 VGP

Table 10. Accuracies for Amadeo paintings and 210 van Gogh paintings

SIFT+Gabor classifier									AlexNet
Number of words	100	200	400	1000	1200	1400	1600	2000	N/A
Accuracy 4.1	57.34	57.34	53.67	50.00	52.54	52.26	50.28	52.82	46.61
Accuracy 4.2	49.42	49.42	44.02	37.07	40.15	39.77	34.36	39.38	30.50
Accuracy 4.3	48.10	50.95	45.24	36.19	40.00	39.52	34.29	40.00	27.14

6 Conclusion and Future Work

Our research methodically assesses the conventional computation applying SIFT +Gabor and the brain-style computation with AlexNet trained respectively on Amadeo painting database, van Gogh painting database and Chinese painting database. The results corroborate the presumption that the performance of neural networks surpasses the traditional machine learning algorithms when samples are learned by the networks. Even with a limited number of samples from the database for training and a small cropped area for testing, AlexNet still outperforms the original algorithm. Without learning on the examples, especially samples with a very different artist, style or genre, AlexNet can fail to correctly classify the data. It appears that Amadeo drawings do not need to be retrained for classification with AlexNet; unlike the situation with the original brushstroke analysis, Amadeo drawings can be identified very well with AlexNet trained with only Amadeo paintings. It could be an advantage for the authentication of an artist's work when the number of his/her artworks is rich with one class but limited with another class.

Our current work is still on trial period of applying CNN for the identification of artist's works and therefore improvement and development on the algorithms of deep learning is necessary. The neural networks usually necessitate large databases for training. Excluding the data augmentation methods applied in our research, more data augmentation techniques for the interest of improving further the results is still in consideration. Splitting testing images into more cropped areas is being explored at the time the present paper is being written. Our results proved to be superior than the conventional algorithm although the accuracy is obtained only on the cropped central area, further examination by evaluating the classification of all the cropped areas of a single test image to calculate a final accuracy on the entire image can be explored. Other pre-defined CNNs like GoogLeNet, ResNet, VGGNet with more layers or self-designed CNN are also being experimented or considered for future work.

Acknowledgment. A great appreciation to the researchers and experts who have provided help and support for our research; it includes but not exhaustive: Dr Rui Xavier and Ms Marta Areia from Calouste Gulbenkian Museum, Prof. Dr. Jia Li and Prof. Dr. James Z. Wang from the Pennsylvania State University and van Gogh Museum for having supplied the respective data-bases applied in our research. This work is supported by FCT/MEC NOVA LINCS PEst UID/CEC/04516/2019 and the grant PD/BD/135223/2017.

References

1. Montagner, C.: The brushstroke and materials of Amadeo de Souza-Cardoso combined in an authentication tool. Ph.D. Dissertation, Departmento de Conservação e Restauro, Faculdade de Ciências e Tecnologia, Universidade NOVA de Lisboa (2015)
2. Rumelhart, D.E.: Brain style computation: learning and generalization. In: Zornetzer, S.F., Davis, J.L., Lau, C. (eds.) An Introduction to Neural and Electronic Networks. Academic Press, San Diego (1990)
3. A comprehensive guide to convolutional neural networks—the ELI5 way. https://towardsdatascience.com/a-comprehensive-guide-to-convolutional-neural-networks-the-eli5-way-3bd2b1164a53. Accessed 11 Apr 2019
4. Temel, B., Kilic, N., Ozgultekin, B., Ucan, O.N.: Separation of original paintings of Matisse and his fakes using wavelet and artificial neural networks. J. Electr. Electron. Eng. **9**(1), 791–796 (2009)
5. Krizhevsky, A., Sutskever, I., Hinton, G.E.: ImageNet classification with deep convolutional neural networks. In: Advances in Neural Information Processing Systems, pp. 1097–1105 (2012)
6. Bar, Y., Levy, N., Wolf, L.: Classification of artistic styles using binarized features derived from a deep neural network. In: Agapito, L., Bronstein, M.M., Rother, C. (eds.) ECCV 2014. LNCS, vol. 8925, pp. 71–84. Springer, Cham (2015). https://doi.org/10.1007/978-3-319-16178-5_5
7. van Noord, N., Hendriks, E., Postma, E.: Toward discovery of the artist's style: learning to recognize artists by their artworks. IEEE Sig. Process. Mag. **32**(4), 46–54 (2015)
8. Tan, W.R., Chan, C.S., Aguirre, H.E., Tanaka, K.: Ceci n'est pas une pipe: a deep convolutional network for fine-art paintings Classification. In: International Conference on Image Processing (ICIP), pp. 3703–3707 (2016)
9. Hong, Y., Kim, J.: Art painting identification using convolutional neural network. Int. J. Appl. Eng. Res. **12**(4), 532–539 (2017)
10. Viswanathan, N.: Artist identification with convolutional neural networks. Technical report, Stanford University (2017)
11. Lecoutre, A., Negrevergne, B., Yger, F.: Recognizing art style automatically in painting with deep learning. In: JMLR: Workshop and Conference Proceedings, vol. 80, pp. 1–17 (2017)

MNAR Imputation with Distributed Healthcare Data

Ricardo Cardoso Pereira[1(✉)], Miriam Seoane Santos[1,2],
Pedro Pereira Rodrigues[3], and Pedro Henriques Abreu[1]

[1] Department of Informatics Engineering,
Centre for Informatics and Systems of the University of Coimbra,
3030-290 Coimbra, Portugal
{rdpereira,miriams,pha}@dei.uc.pt
[2] The IPO-Porto Research Centre, 4200-072 Porto, Portugal
[3] Faculty of Medicine of the University of Porto,
Center for Health Technology and Services Research, 4200-319 Porto, Portugal
pprodrigues@med.up.pt

Abstract. Missing data is a problem found in real-world datasets that has a considerable impact on the learning process of classifiers. Although extensive work has been done in this field, the MNAR mechanism still remains a challenge for the existing imputation methods, mainly because it is not related with any observed information. Focusing on healthcare contexts, MNAR is present in multiple scenarios such as clinical trials where the participants may be quitting the study for reasons related to the outcome that is being measured. This work proposes an approach that uses different sources of information from the same healthcare context to improve the imputation quality and classification performance for datasets with missing data under MNAR. The experiment was performed with several databases from the medical context and the results show that the use of multiple sources of data has a positive impact in the imputation error and classification performance.

Keywords: Missing data · Missing Not At Random ·
Missing mechanisms · Healthcare data · Data context ·
Data imputation

1 Introduction

Missing data can be defined as the lack of information in one or several features of a dataset, which can create additional difficulties on the learning process of classifiers. The cause behind the missing values is usually described by one of three missing mechanisms [1,3,10]:

- Missing Completely At Random (MCAR), which occurs when the values are randomly missing and, as consequence, the cause is not related to any observed or unobserved values;

© Springer Nature Switzerland AG 2019
P. Moura Oliveira et al. (Eds.): EPIA 2019, LNAI 11805, pp. 184–195, 2019.
https://doi.org/10.1007/978-3-030-30244-3_16

- Missing At Random (MAR), which occurs when the missing values are related with observed values (i.e., a strong correlation exists between the features);
- Missing Not At Random (MNAR), which occurs when the missing values are related with themselves or with other unobserved values.

This missing data issue is often addressed with imputation strategies that generate new plausible values for the missing ones based on the existing data. However, the imputation methods often produce bad results when the missing mechanism is MNAR [4], which is natural since this mechanism is related to unobserved data. Moreover, a context where the MNAR mechanism is often found is the medical one. As an example, an hospital can be conducting a study that requires people to report how many cigarettes they smoke each day. Considering that smoking has a negative impact in the study results, people that smoke a lot may hide this information from the surveys. However, this data may exist in other datasets from other hospitals or even other different sources (e.g. a life insurance survey may ask the same question).

To improve the imputation for the MNAR mechanism other sources of information of the same context can be used to help complete the missing values, since these sources may contain the related unobserved data. Having this idea in mind, the following research questions can arise:

- Could the error of the imputation methods used to generate missing values under the MNAR mechanism decrease if they use more information of the same data context?
- Could the performance of the classifiers trained by this imputed data improve their precision and recall?

This paper presents an experimental design that aims to answer these research questions. The data processing steps and the experimental pipeline are described with detail. The simulation results show that using other sources of information from the same context reduces the imputation error. Moreover, the classification performance is not biased by this imputation, and in fact improves with a statistical significance of 5%.

The remainder of the paper is organized in the following way: Sect. 2 presents related works that also address the imputation for the MNAR mechanism, Sect. 3 describes the design of the experiment, Sect. 4 presents the obtained results and their discussion, and Sect. 5 the conclusions and future directions of this work.

2   Related Work

In this section a set of recent works that have addressed the MNAR mechanism are briefly described.

Olsen et al. [8] proposed an experimental study to assess the quality of the imputation performed by several methods in missing values under the MNAR mechanism, using data from controlled trials of knee osteoarthritis. A custom multiple imputation regression method is the one that presents the best results with MSE values between 7.2 and 9.1 comparing to values between 8.5 and 13.7 for the second best method. Wolkowitz and Skorupski [13] performed an experimental study where missing values of multiple-choice items are imputed with a multiple imputation of the Multiple-Choice Model, being the missing data generated for all mechanisms, including MNAR. The results are presented through the mean bias between the obtain p-values, and they considerably good for MCAR and MAR (near 0) but worse for MNAR (between 0.0056 and 0.0422). Valdiviezo and Van Aelst [12] presented a study where single and multiple imputation methods are applied to medical datasets of different sub-contexts (breast cancer survival, heart disease, etc.) with simulated missing values under all mechanisms. The results show that in general the multiple imputation approaches (Multiple Imputation by Chained Equations and Multiple Imputation by Sequential Regression Trees) are the best, but the worst results are always under the MNAR mechanism, especially when the missing rate is greater than 20%, presenting sometimes more than the double of the imputation error. Van Kuijk et al. [7] presented an experimental study where the method Multiple Imputation by Chained Equations is compared with ignoring the observations containing missing values, using an epidemiological dataset with missing data under all mechanisms. The results show that the multiple imputation method presents the best results under MAR and MCAR, but with MNAR the case deletion approach presents the best results. Garciarena and Santana [5] introduced a statistical significance study focused on the interactions between the missing mechanism, the imputation method and the classification algorithms used with the imputed data. The study considers several sources of data, including medical ones (e.g. a diabetic dataset). The results regarding the imputation methods are presented by showing the number of times they were significantly better than the others for each missing mechanism, and MNAR displayed the worst and more biased results when compared to MCAR and MAR.

In conclusion, the described studies show that the MNAR mechanism is the one that consistently presents the worst results, which is not a surprise because of this mechanism nature, as previously described. Although these studies address missing values under MNAR, the use of multiple sources was never explored by the authors, which makes it a novel aspect in this work. Considering the relation of the missing values with unobserved data, the fusion of different databases can mitigate the MNAR assumptions and, to some extent, transform them into MAR. Moreover, this scenario is realistic since nowadays the amount of data distributed in different points is quite considerable, particularly in the healthcare context.

3   Experimental Design

An experimental design was proposed to prove the impact of using different sources of the same data context in the imputation quality and classification performance. The imputation evaluation is assessed through the Root Mean Square Error (**RMSE**) metric and the classification evaluation through the **F1 score**. In the experiment the following variables were considered:

- Features Similarity Rate ($FSRate$), which indicates the percentage of equal features that the datasets must have to be properly combined, and has the values 40%, 50%, 60% and 70%;
- Number of datasets ($NumDatasets$), which indicates how many datasets are being combined, and the values can vary between 1 and 5 (for the imputation evaluation the value 1 is discarded since no missing values exist, which leads to a constant RMSE value of 0);
- Imputation algorithms ($Algorithm$), which are the methods that generate the plausible values to replace the missing ones, and the algorithms used are the Mean Imputation, Multivariate Imputation by Chained Equations (MICE), K-Nearest Neighbors (KNN) Imputation, SoftImpute (SI) and Support Vector Regression (SVR).

Based on the presented variables, an experimental setup with the following pipeline of tasks was proposed (see Fig. 1):

- A given database with F features and O observations is divided in N smaller datasets:
  - The observations are randomly divided in equal parts for all datasets, which means that each one will contain $\frac{O}{N}$ rows;
  - A percentage of the features is kept equal for all datasets ($FSRate$). These $FSRate * F$ features are chosen randomly from the total. The remaining features will only exist in one of the smaller datasets and are assigned sequentially and circularly.
- Each smaller dataset is combined gradually with the remaining ones by being concatenated with each one through $N - 1$ iterations (e.g., for $N = 4$ the combinations for the first smaller dataset would be $\{D1, D2\}$, $\{D1, D2, D3\}$ and $\{D1, D2, D3, D4\}$ over three iterations). This entire process is repeated N times, one for each of the datasets, and the final results are an average of these repetitions;
- Since all datasets have a set of features that are unique, the combination of two datasets generates missing values under MNAR for those features on the resulting dataset. Therefore, for each of the combinations described in the previous item, the missing values are predicted using 5 imputation algorithms, being the quality evaluated through the RMSE:
  - Mean Imputation, that uses the mean of the features to fill in the missing values;
  - Multivariate Imputation by Chained Equations (MICE) with 100 iterations, which uses a multiple imputation approach to create several regression models for the missing features based on the complete ones [2];
  - K-Nearest Neighbors (KNN) Imputation with $K = 1$, which finds the nearest neighbor through the Euclidean distance and uses its value of the missing feature to fill in the observation [9];
  - SoftImpute (SI), which is a matrix completion method based on nuclear-norm regularization [6];
  - Support Vector Regression (SVR), which is an adaptation of the well-known Support Vector Machines that can be applied for regression

instead of classification, and it was configured with a RBF kernel and $\gamma = \frac{1}{\#Features}$ [11].

– The datasets imputed by each of the described algorithms are also used to train a classifier with the purpose of evaluating the impact of the imputation in the learning capabilities of the model. In this experiment a Decision Tree was used since it is widely applied in healthcare contexts for interpretability and explainability reasons. The quality of the classification is evaluated through the F1 score using hold-out validation (75% of the data for training and 25% for testing).

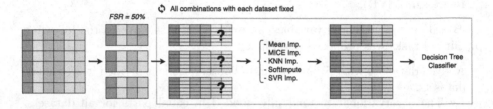

Fig. 1. Pipeline of tasks for the experiment.

As stated before, merging the small datasets generates MNAR values because these missingness of a specific dataset is related with the information of the remaining ones. In other words, the missing values are related with the unobserved data that is being merged, and therefore are MNAR. The fusion approach here proposed is an attempt to mitigate the MNAR assumptions by transforming the MNAR mechanism into MAR, since the unobserved data will become observed after the fusion process. For that reason, the state-of-the-art imputation algorithms should now provide better and less biased results. Moreover, since the small datasets are generated from a complete one, the ground truth is available for error and accuracy calculations.

To reduce bias and mitigate stochastic behaviors the described pipeline is executed 100 times, being the average of the 100 results considered for analysis purposes. The pipeline was implemented through several Python scripts using the Pandas[1] framework to process the data and the scikit-learn[2] and fancyimpute[3] frameworks to assist the implementation of the imputation methods and the classifier. The experiment was conducted using 15 public databases of the medical context, available on the UCI[4] and Kaggle[5] repositories, that cover a variety of pathologies: ctg_2c, bc_coimbra, breast_tissue_2c, cleveland_0_vs_4, dermatology_6, ecoli, parkinson, pima, relax, spectf, thyroid_3_vs_2, transfusion,

---

[1] Available at https://pandas.pydata.org/.

[2] Available at https://scikit-learn.org/stable/.

[3] Available at https://github.com/iskandr/fancyimpute.

[4] Available at https://archive.ics.uci.edu/ml/datasets.html.

[5] Available at https://www.kaggle.com/.

vertebral_2c, wisconsin and wpbc. These databases have a number of observations between 106 and 2126, and a number of features between 4 and 44.

4   Results and Discussion

Starting the analysis by the imputation quality, the RMSE results obtained from the experiment are presented in Table 1. These results show that the imputation error increases a small amount when the number of combined datasets increases, being the best results always when 2 datasets are combined. However, it is import to consider that, for each dataset added in the combinations, the amount of missing values increases the number of observations times the number of new unique features. This means that the error increase is not proportional to the growth in the missing values. Therefore, to proper analyze the error, the ratio of RMSE results by missing value must be considered. Table 2 presents this ratio for the best RMSE results of each database, along with the average number of missing values that is presented in Table 3 for each combination of datasets. These results show that the lowest RMSE ratio is obtained when 5 datasets are combined. Moreover, this ratio decreases when the number of combined datasets increases, which is a clear indication of the improvements in the imputation by the use of external information. Therefore, it is possible to conclude that the use of more information of the same medical context improves the imputation of missing values under MNAR.

Analyzing the classification performance, the F1 score results for the Decision Tree classifier are presented in Table 4. For all the 15 databases, the best F1 score appears almost always when the number of datasets combined is 5 (the maximum). Moreover, the results also show that the classification performance increases gradually when the number of combinations of datasets also increases. To ensure that these results were statistically significant, the Friedman test was applied with a significance level of 5%. The treatment variable used was the number of datasets and the block variable was the imputation algorithm. This means that, although the p-values exist only for the number of datasets, the effect of the imputation algorithm is taken into account in them and is not being neglected. The inference was made individually for each value of the feature similarity rate, and the results are presented in Table 5. The p-values show that the number of datasets combined have an impact on the F1 scores in 13 of the 15 databases.

To understand when the differences between the F1 score results obtained using a single dataset and the ones obtained using the combinations of 2, 3, 4 and 5 datasets were statistical significance, the post hoc Nemenyi test was applied. Table 6 presents the results and they show that in general the statistical significance only exists when the number of datasets combined is 4 or 5, which reinforces the results previously described[6]. Therefore, it is possible to conclude

---

[6] Although the Nemenyi test p-values are two-tailed, it is possible to ensure that these results always reflect improvement in the F1 scores by cross-analyzing them with the ones from Table 4.

Table 1. RMSE results for each combination of the number of datasets and imputation algorithms, applied to all the 15 databases and averaged over the 4 values of the features similarity rate. For each cell, the top value is the RMSE average and the bottom value the standard deviation. The yellow cells are the best results for each combination of variables and the bolded results are the best for the 15 databases.

Database	Num. Datasets = 2					Num. Datasets = 3					Num. Datasets = 4					Num. Datasets = 5				
	AL1	AL2	AL3	AL4	AL5	AL1	AL2	AL3	AL4	AL5	AL1	AL2	AL3	AL4	AL5	AL1	AL2	AL3	AL4	AL5
ctg_2c	14.32 (0.54)	8.55 (1.05)	8.77 (0.83)	16.44 (4.07)	14.53 (0.52)	14.94 (0.27)	9.30 (1.13)	9.99 (0.73)	23.78 (6.02)	15.17 (0.28)	15.17 (0.26)	9.38 (1.05)	9.92 (0.75)	29.05 (6.48)	15.41 (0.29)	15.32 (0.16)	9.55 (1.14)	9.37 (0.79)	32.96 (6.14)	15.55 (0.19)
bc_coimbra	61.07 (10.33)	64.06 (10.01)	78.94 (13.49)	103.29 (20.87)	62.55 (10.74)	75.41 (5.90)	80.48 (5.64)	97.68 (7.76)	129.73 (14.40)	77.46 (6.36)	84.00 (9.05)	89.39 (9.86)	108.82 (12.35)	145.12 (19.37)	86.15 (9.34)	58.09 (12.80)	94.07 (14.03)	113.16 (16.88)	152.28 (24.66)	90.31 (13.00)
breast_tissue_2c	2717.14 (525.28)	2032.60 (530.40)	2304.24 (550.39)	2706.11 (562.62)	2691.05 (530.54)	3565.39 (825.98)	2773.12 (810.70)	3045.60 (809.70)	3634.17 (863.80)	3552.68 (829.10)	4194.04 (1013.68)	3290.42 (977.52)	3676.55 (974.71)	4313.53 (1053.16)	4187.02 (1018.79)	4678.72 (1172.25)	3754.08 (1162.43)	4217.82 (1178.67)	4817.34 (1213.37)	4674.10 (1163.73)
cleveland_0_vs_4	15.49 (0.70)	14.63 (0.65)	18.12 (1.10)	40.95 (8.62)	13.57 (0.76)	15.32 (0.58)	16.39 (0.63)	20.37 (1.07)	52.03 (9.21)	15.33 (0.62)	15.17 (0.43)	17.53 (0.50)	21.60 (1.13)	58.36 (8.29)	16.29 (0.42)	16.00 (0.37)	17.82 (0.43)	21.99 (1.05)	61.40 (7.26)	16.53 (0.38)
dermatology_6	1.99 (0.17)	1.85 (0.19)	2.34 (0.24)	3.78 (0.52)	1.83 (0.17)	2.16 (0.21)	2.04 (0.23)	2.59 (0.30)	4.36 (0.68)	2.02 (0.21)	2.29 (0.24)	2.19 (0.26)	2.78 (0.34)	4.83 (0.76)	2.17 (0.24)	2.43 (0.32)	2.36 (0.36)	3.00 (0.47)	5.32 (1.01)	2.31 (0.34)
ecoli	0.15 (0.00)	0.14 (0.01)	0.16 (0.01)	0.25 (0.06)	0.14 (0.01)	0.16 (0.00)	0.15 (0.00)	0.17 (0.01)	0.25 (0.04)	0.14 (0.01)	0.16 (0.00)	0.15 (0.00)	0.17 (0.01)	0.26 (0.04)	0.14 (0.01)	0.16 (0.00)	0.15 (0.00)	0.17 (0.01)	0.27 (0.03)	0.14 (0.01)
parkinson	16.04 (1.03)	15.70 (1.31)	17.67 (1.75)	28.61 (4.68)	16.36 (1.07)	18.13 (1.30)	17.95 (1.78)	20.15 (2.22)	34.61 (5.27)	18.58 (1.33)	19.85 (1.22)	19.80 (1.82)	22.23 (2.20)	39.17 (5.17)	20.32 (1.23)	20.87 (1.40)	20.71 (2.00)	23.43 (2.71)	42.16 (5.07)	21.34 (1.38)
pima	30.20 (1.60)	29.20 (1.32)	37.24 (1.48)	43.48 (3.10)	32.38 (2.00)	33.40 (0.93)	32.48 (0.49)	41.01 (0.74)	50.04 (2.92)	35.91 (1.15)	35.88 (1.50)	34.84 (2.03)	44.10 (3.24)	53.53 (4.24)	38.78 (1.98)	36.80 (2.33)	35.75 (3.00)	45.24 (4.54)	54.98 (4.79)	39.91 (2.93)
relax	0.42 (0.00)	0.27 (0.06)	0.42 (0.03)	0.30 (0.04)	0.29 (0.04)	0.42 (0.00)	0.27 (0.06)	0.42 (0.03)	0.32 (0.03)	0.29 (0.04)	0.42 (0.00)	0.27 (0.06)	0.42 (0.03)	0.33 (0.03)	0.29 (0.04)	0.42 (0.00)	0.27 (0.06)	0.42 (0.03)	0.33 (0.03)	0.29 (0.04)
spectf	10.00 (0.06)	8.50 (0.31)	9.15 (0.18)	7.43 (0.12)	10.23 (0.07)	10.05 (0.08)	8.50 (0.26)	9.17 (0.18)	9.03 (1.36)	10.27 (0.09)	10.04 (0.04)	8.91 (0.32)	9.18 (0.18)	10.61 (3.34)	10.27 (0.05)	10.03 (0.02)	8.67 (0.35)	9.17 (0.16)	12.34 (4.95)	10.26 (0.03)
thyroid_3_vs_2	0.17 (0.01)	0.17 (0.01)	0.23 (0.01)	0.19 (0.01)	0.18 (0.01)	0.17 (0.01)	0.18 (0.01)	0.24 (0.01)	0.20 (0.01)	0.18 (0.01)	0.17 (0.00)	0.18 (0.00)	0.24 (0.01)	0.21 (0.01)	0.19 (0.00)	0.17 (0.00)	0.18 (0.00)	0.24 (0.01)	0.21 (0.00)	0.19 (0.00)
transfusion	417.52 (68.62)	188.18 (89.75)	231.32 (91.23)	567.86 (95.69)	432.72 (70.67)	528.88 (57.72)	174.09 (111.11)	291.79 (111.32)	719.21 (80.64)	549.14 (60.02)	537.69 (68.86)	179.07 (118.44)	296.39 (121.34)	732.53 (96.94)	558.39 (71.47)	537.00 (71.50)	180.07 (117.64)	297.65 (124.63)	731.54 (98.85)	557.44 (74.09)
vertebral_2c	18.93 (0.72)	16.19 (1.62)	17.11 (1.55)	32.37 (4.97)	19.44 (0.76)	19.88 (0.93)	16.76 (1.09)	18.18 (1.64)	38.29 (3.73)	20.49 (0.96)	20.26 (1.01)	18.57 (1.44)	18.57 (1.84)	40.15 (4.27)	20.90 (1.07)	20.31 (0.94)	17.51 (1.40)	18.61 (1.83)	41.17 (4.15)	20.94 (1.00)
wisconsin	2.81 (0.02)	1.99 (0.06)	2.39 (0.09)	2.84 (0.36)	2.02 (0.02)	2.83 (0.01)	1.92 (0.04)	2.41 (0.07)	2.76 (0.26)	2.03 (0.02)	2.83 (0.01)	1.92 (0.03)	2.42 (0.06)	2.73 (0.24)	2.03 (0.02)	2.83 (0.00)	1.92 (0.04)	2.43 (0.07)	2.76 (0.22)	2.03 (0.02)
wpbc	69.56 (8.83)	27.35 (10.60)	40.04 (6.04)	115.79 (28.47)	70.55 (9.19)	82.96 (12.27)	32.72 (13.20)	47.51 (7.61)	153.84 (37.00)	84.25 (12.78)	93.70 (13.80)	37.21 (15.37)	53.13 (8.54)	183.58 (40.69)	95.00 (14.28)	99.93 (16.70)	41.28 (18.54)	56.66 (10.46)	203.12 (47.01)	101.39 (16.95)

Algorithms Legend - AL1: Mean, AL2: MICE, AL3: KNN, AL4: SI, AL5: SVR.

Table 2. Best RMSE result for each combination of the number of datasets divided by the average number of missing values and applied to all the 15 databases. Each cell presents the ratio of the RMSE by missing value. The bolded results are the best for the 15 databases.

Database	Num. Datasets			
	2	3	4	5
ctg_2c	0.00452	0.00162	0.00086	**0.00055**
bc_coimbra	1.25788	0.52737	0.30747	**0.21074**
breast_tissue_2c	45.83089	20.84623	13.18806	**9.82743**
cleveland_0_vs_4	0.13310	0.05112	0.02895	**0.01893**
dermatology_6	0.00377	0.00143	0.00078	**0.00052**
ecoli	0.00119	0.00038	0.00020	**0.00014**
parkinson	0.08946	0.03461	0.01956	**0.01295**
pima	0.10580	0.03786	0.02077	**0.01454**
relax	0.00287	0.00097	0.00050	**0.00032**
spectf	0.01721	0.00627	0.00324	**0.00200**
thyroid_3_vs_2	0.00027	0.00009	0.00005	**0.00003**
transfusion	0.63757	0.27261	0.17781	**0.13361**
vertebral_2c	0.15313	0.05406	0.03164	**0.02353**
wisconsin	0.00660	0.00227	0.00119	**0.00078**
wpbc	0.11311	0.04561	0.02640	**0.01766**

Table 3. Average number of missing values for each combination of the number of datasets and applied to all the 15 databases.

Database	Num. Datasets			
	2	3	4	5
ctg_2c	1892	5611	10775	17009
bc_coimbra	49	143	273	418
breast_tissue_2c	44	131	250	382
cleveland_0_vs_4	101	298	559	867
dermatology_6	485	1417	2764	4512
ecoli	117	369	694	1009
parkinson	176	519	1012	1599
pima	276	858	1677	2459
relax	94	278	536	838
spectf	455	1366	2661	4327
thyroid_3_vs_2	625	1851	3553	5626
transfusion	217	642	1007	1348
vertebral_2c	99	310	549	744
wisconsin	286	845	1614	2460
wpbc	242	717	1410	2337

Table 4. F1 score results for each combination of the number of datasets and imputation algorithms, applied to all the 15 databases and averaged over the 4 values of the features similarity rate. For each cell, the top value is the F1 score average and the bottom value the standard deviation. The yellow cells are the best results for each combination of variables and the bolded results are the best for the 15 databases.

Database	Num. Datasets = 1					Num. Datasets = 2					Num. Datasets = 3					Num. Datasets = 4					Num. Datasets = 5				
	AL1	AL2	AL3	AL4	AL5	AL1	AL2	AL3	AL4	AL5	AL1	AL2	AL3	AL4	AL5	AL1	AL2	AL3	AL4	AL5	AL1	AL2	AL3	AL4	AL5
ctg_2c	0.66 (0.02)	0.66 (0.03)	0.66 (0.02)	0.66 (0.02)	0.65 (0.02)	0.67 (0.04)	0.67 (0.04)	0.68 (0.03)	0.67 (0.03)	0.67 (0.03)	0.69 (0.03)	0.67 (0.04)	0.70 (0.03)	0.68 (0.03)	0.69 (0.03)	0.71 (0.03)	0.68 (0.04)	0.71 (0.03)	0.69 (0.03)	0.70 (0.03)	0.72 (0.03)	0.69 (0.04)	0.72 (0.03)	0.70 (0.04)	0.71 (0.03)
bc_coimbra	0.97 (0.00)	0.97 (0.00)	0.97 (0.00)	0.97 (0.00)	0.97 (0.00)	0.98 (0.00)	0.98 (0.00)	0.98 (0.00)	0.98 (0.00)	0.98 (0.00)	0.99 (0.00)	0.99 (0.00)	0.99 (0.00)	0.99 (0.00)	0.99 (0.00)	0.99 (0.00)	0.99 (0.00)	0.99 (0.00)	0.99 (0.00)	0.99 (0.00)	0.99 (0.00)	0.99 (0.00)	0.99 (0.00)	0.99 (0.00)	0.99 (0.00)
breast_tissue_2c	0.94 (0.01)	0.94 (0.00)	0.94 (0.01)	0.94 (0.01)	0.95 (0.01)	0.98 (0.00)	0.97 (0.00)	0.98 (0.00)	0.98 (0.00)	0.98 (0.00)	0.99 (0.00)	0.99 (0.00)	0.99 (0.00)	0.99 (0.00)	0.99 (0.00)	0.99 (0.00)	0.99 (0.00)	0.99 (0.00)	0.99 (0.00)	0.99 (0.00)	0.99 (0.00)	0.99 (0.00)	0.99 (0.00)	0.99 (0.00)	0.99 (0.00)
cleveland_0_vs_4	0.96 (0.00)	0.96 (0.01)	0.96 (0.00)	0.96 (0.00)	0.96 (0.00)	0.98 (0.00)	0.98 (0.00)	0.98 (0.00)	0.98 (0.00)	0.98 (0.00)	0.99 (0.00)	0.99 (0.00)	0.99 (0.00)	0.99 (0.00)	0.99 (0.00)	0.99 (0.00)	0.99 (0.00)	0.99 (0.00)	0.99 (0.00)	0.99 (0.00)	0.99 (0.00)	0.99 (0.00)	0.99 (0.00)	0.99 (0.00)	0.99 (0.00)
dermatology_6	0.98 (0.00)	0.98 (0.00)	0.98 (0.00)	0.98 (0.00)	0.98 (0.00)	0.99 (0.00)	0.99 (0.00)	0.99 (0.00)	0.98 (0.00)	0.98 (0.00)	0.99 (0.00)	0.99 (0.00)	0.99 (0.00)	0.99 (0.00)	0.99 (0.00)	0.99 (0.00)	0.99 (0.00)	0.98 (0.00)	0.99 (0.00)	0.99 (0.00)	0.99 (0.00)	0.99 (0.00)	0.99 (0.00)	0.99 (0.00)	0.99 (0.00)
ecoli	0.94 (0.00)	0.94 (0.00)	0.94 (0.01)	0.94 (0.00)	0.94 (0.00)	0.96 (0.00)	0.96 (0.01)	0.97 (0.01)	0.96 (0.00)	0.96 (0.00)	0.98 (0.00)	0.97 (0.00)	0.98 (0.00)	0.97 (0.00)	0.97 (0.00)	0.98 (0.00)	0.98 (0.00)	0.98 (0.00)	0.98 (0.00)	0.98 (0.00)	0.98 (0.00)	0.98 (0.00)	0.98 (0.00)	0.98 (0.00)	0.98 (0.00)
parkinson	0.81 (0.00)	0.81 (0.01)	0.81 (0.00)	0.82 (0.00)	0.82 (0.01)	0.86 (0.01)	0.85 (0.01)	0.86 (0.00)	0.86 (0.00)	0.85 (0.00)	0.88 (0.00)	0.88 (0.01)	0.89 (0.00)	0.88 (0.01)	0.88 (0.01)	0.90 (0.01)	0.89 (0.01)	0.91 (0.00)	0.90 (0.01)	0.90 (0.01)	0.91 (0.01)	0.90 (0.01)	0.92 (0.01)	0.91 (0.01)	0.91 (0.01)
pima	0.65 (0.01)	0.65 (0.01)	0.65 (0.01)	0.65 (0.01)	0.65 (0.01)	0.65 (0.01)	0.65 (0.01)	0.65 (0.01)	0.65 (0.01)	0.65 (0.01)	0.65 (0.01)	0.65 (0.01)	0.65 (0.01)	0.65 (0.00)	0.65 (0.01)	0.66 (0.01)	0.65 (0.01)	0.64 (0.01)	0.65 (0.01)	0.65 (0.01)	0.65 (0.01)	0.65 (0.01)	0.65 (0.01)	0.65 (0.01)	0.65 (0.01)
relax	0.57 (0.01)	0.57 (0.00)	0.57 (0.01)	0.57 (0.00)	0.57 (0.00)	0.57 (0.01)	0.57 (0.01)	0.57 (0.00)	0.56 (0.01)	0.57 (0.01)	0.57 (0.00)	0.57 (0.01)	0.57 (0.01)	0.57 (0.00)	0.57 (0.01)	0.57 (0.00)	0.57 (0.01)	0.58 (0.01)	0.57 (0.00)	0.57 (0.00)	0.57 (0.00)	0.57 (0.01)	0.58 (0.01)	0.57 (0.01)	0.57 (0.01)
spectf	0.8 (0.01)	0.81 (0.00)	0.81 (0.01)	0.81 (0.00)	0.81 (0.00)	0.94 (0.01)	0.93 (0.01)	0.94 (0.00)	0.93 (0.00)	0.94 (0.01)	0.97 (0.00)	0.97 (0.00)	0.97 (0.01)	0.97 (0.00)	0.98 (0.00)	0.98 (0.00)	0.98 (0.00)	0.98 (0.00)	0.98 (0.00)	0.99 (0.00)	0.99 (0.00)	0.99 (0.00)	0.99 (0.00)	0.99 (0.00)	0.99 (0.00)
thyroid_3_vs_2	0.94 (0.01)	0.94 (0.01)	0.94 (0.00)	0.94 (0.00)	0.94 (0.00)	0.94 (0.01)	0.94 (0.01)	0.94 (0.00)	0.95 (0.01)	0.94 (0.00)	0.95 (0.01)	0.94 (0.01)	0.94 (0.01)	0.95 (0.01)	0.94 (0.01)	0.95 (0.01)	0.94 (0.01)	0.94 (0.01)	0.95 (0.01)	0.94 (0.01)	0.95 (0.01)	0.95 (0.01)	0.94 (0.01)	0.95 (0.01)	0.95 (0.01)
transfusion	0.69 (0.00)	0.70 (0.00)	0.69 (0.00)	0.69 (0.00)	0.69 (0.00)	0.69 (0.00)	0.69 (0.00)	0.70 (0.00)	0.69 (0.00)	0.69 (0.00)	0.70 (0.00)	0.69 (0.00)	0.70 (0.00)	0.69 (0.00)	0.70 (0.00)	0.70 (0.00)	0.69 (0.00)	0.70 (0.00)	0.70 (0.00)	0.70 (0.00)	0.70 (0.00)	0.69 (0.00)	0.70 (0.00)	0.70 (0.00)	0.70 (0.00)
vertebral_2c	0.99 (0.00)	0.99 (0.00)	0.99 (0.00)	0.99 (0.00)	0.99 (0.00)	0.99 (0.00)	0.99 (0.00)	0.99 (0.00)	0.99 (0.00)	0.99 (0.00)	0.99 (0.00)	1.00 (0.00)	1.00 (0.00)	1.00 (0.00)	1.00 (0.00)	1.00 (0.00)	1.00 (0.00)	1.00 (0.00)	1.00 (0.00)	1.00 (0.00)	1.00 (0.00)	1.00 (0.00)	1.00 (0.00)	1.00 (0.00)	1.00 (0.00)
wisconsin	0.93 (0.00)	0.92 (0.00)	0.92 (0.00)	0.93 (0.00)	0.93 (0.01)	0.93 (0.01)	0.93 (0.00)	0.93 (0.00)	0.93 (0.00)	0.93 (0.00)	0.93 (0.00)	0.93 (0.01)	0.93 (0.01)	0.93 (0.01)	0.94 (0.01)	0.93 (0.01)	0.94 (0.01)	0.94 (0.01)	0.93 (0.01)	0.94 (0.01)	0.93 (0.00)	0.94 (0.00)	0.94 (0.00)	0.93 (0.00)	0.94 (0.01)
wpbc	0.65 (0.00)	0.66 (0.01)	0.65 (0.01)	0.65 (0.00)	0.65 (0.00)	0.66 (0.01)	0.66 (0.00)	0.66 (0.00)	0.66 (0.00)	0.66 (0.00)	0.67 (0.00)	0.66 (0.01)	0.67 (0.01)	0.67 (0.01)	0.66 (0.01)	0.67 (0.01)	0.67 (0.01)	0.67 (0.01)	0.67 (0.01)	0.67 (0.01)	0.67 (0.01)	0.67 (0.01)	0.67 (0.01)	0.67 (0.01)	0.67 (0.00)

Algorithms Legend - AL1: Mean, AL2: MICE, AL3: KNN, AL4: SI, AL5: SVR

Table 5. *P*-values of the Friedman test for the F1 score, using the number of datasets as the treatment variable and the imputation algorithm as the block variable, and obtained individually for each feature similarity rate. The bolded *p*-values are the statistical significant ones, assuming a significance level of 5%.

Database	FSRate			
	40%	50%	60%	70%
ctg_2c	**0.001**	**0.000**	**0.000**	**0.000**
bc_coimbra	**0.001**	**0.001**	**0.001**	**0.001**
breast_tissue_2c	**0.001**	**0.001**	**0.001**	**0.000**
cleveland_0_vs_4	**0.000**	**0.001**	**0.000**	**0.001**
dermatology_6	**0.001**	**0.000**	**0.001**	**0.000**
ecoli	**0.000**	**0.000**	**0.000**	**0.000**
parkinson	**0.000**	**0.000**	**0.000**	**0.000**
pima	0.193	**0.023**	0.291	0.161
relax	0.364	0.218	0.142	0.051
spectf	**0.000**	**0.000**	**0.000**	**0.000**
thyroid_3_vs_2	0.205	**0.015**	**0.001**	**0.001**
transfusion	**0.039**	**0.003**	**0.015**	**0.013**
vertebral_2c	**0.000**	**0.002**	**0.001**	**0.002**
wisconsin	0.092	**0.001**	**0.001**	**0.000**
wpbc	0.218	**0.010**	**0.001**	**0.001**

that the use of more information of the same medical context for the imputation of missing values under MNAR has a positive impact on the performance of the Decision Tree classifier. The use of more information could also be in part responsible for the improvements, but the main conclusion here is that the imputation was well performed, otherwise it would have a negative impact in the classification results.

Table 6. Number of times where the difference between the F1 score for num. datasets = 1 *vs* num. datasets = 2, 3, 4, 5 was statistical significant, according to the *p*-values of the post hoc Nemenyi test and assuming a significance level of 5%. The frequencies are presented individually for each value of the features similarity rate.

ND	FSRate			
	40%	50%	60%	70%
2	0	0	0	0
3	0	1	0	0
4	9	10	10	12
5	9	13	13	13

Finally, an analysis of the results obtained from the imputation algorithms was also conducted, since they also have an impact on the study (the Friedman test was also used to prove this, but the p-values are not presented here for lack of space). Table 7 shows how many times each algorithm was the best. The results show different but consistent values for the classification and imputation evaluation. For the imputation the MICE algorithm clearly outperformed the remaining methods, but for the classification the KNN presented the best results. A possible explanation for this difference is that MICE creates several regressions based on all complete data, and therefore is able to generate values that better represent the overall population and that are more close to real ones. On the other hand, the KNN obtains the observation more similar to the one that is being imputed, which means that the generated value is a copy of the other value, and this benefits the classification because the dispersion of the observations reduces and the classifier is able to define the "boundaries" between the labels more easily.

Table 7. Number of times that each imputation algorithm presented the best results for each number of datasets. The frequencies are presented individually for the F1 score (left) and the RMSE (right).

| | F1 Score | | | | | RMSE | | | | |
ND	AL1	AL2	AL3	AL4	AL5	AL1	AL2	AL3	AL4	AL5
1	5	**18**	15	11	11	–	–	–	–	–
2	6	5	**25**	12	12	12	**34**	1	4	9
3	13	6	**20**	7	14	13	**34**	3	2	8
4	14	7	**20**	6	13	14	**34**	3	0	9
5	**21**	5	14	6	14	14	**34**	3	0	9
Sum	59	41	**94**	42	64	53	**136**	10	6	35

Algorithms Legend - AL1: Mean, AL2: MICE, AL3: KNN, AL4: SI, AL5: SVR

5   Conclusions

Missing data is a problem often found in real-world datasets and, although several works have been published in this field, the MNAR mechanism is still the one less addressed and with worst results. Considering the nature of MNAR, this work tries to prove if using multiple sources of information from the same data context helps improving the imputation of MNAR missing values, using only medical databases. The results show that when the number of datasets increases the RMSE values increase just a small amount, which is a considerable improvement when the ratio of RMSE by missing value is considered. Moreover, the results also show that the precision and recall of the Decision Tree classifier increase and are not negatively biased by the imputation when more information is added, particularly when at least 4 datasets are combined, and the results are statistically significant with a significance level of 5%. Moreover, the use of the MICE algorithm for the imputation benefits its error and the KNN algorithm is the best for the classification performance. In the future the study should be extended to include more databases from different data contexts and more classifiers of different natures, in order to allow a generalization of the results for these scenarios.

References

1. Abreu, P.H., Amaro, H., Silva, D.C., Machado, P., Abreu, M.H.: Personalizing breast cancer patients with heterogeneous data. In: Zhang, Y.-T. (ed.) The International Conference on Health Informatics. IP, vol. 42, pp. 39–42. Springer, Cham (2014). https://doi.org/10.1007/978-3-319-03005-0_11
2. Azur, M.J., Stuart, E.A., Frangakis, C., Leaf, P.J.: Multiple imputation by chained equations: what is it and how does it work? Int. J. Methods Psychiatr. Res. **20**(1), 40–49 (2011)
3. Baraldi, A.N., Enders, C.K.: An introduction to modern missing data analyses. J. Sch. Psychol. **48**(1), 5–37 (2010)
4. Costa, A.F., Santos, M.S., Soares, J.P., Abreu, P.H.: Missing data imputation via denoising autoencoders: the untold story. In: Duivesteijn, W., Siebes, A., Ukkonen, A. (eds.) IDA 2018. LNCS, vol. 11191, pp. 87–98. Springer, Cham (2018). https://doi.org/10.1007/978-3-030-01768-2_8
5. Garciarena, U., Santana, R.: An extensive analysis of the interaction between missing data types, imputation methods, and supervised classifiers. Expert Syst. Appl. **89**, 52–65 (2017)
6. Hastie, T., Mazumder, R., Lee, J.D., Zadeh, R.: Matrix completion and low-rank SVD via fast alternating least squares. J. Mach. Learn. Res. **16**(1), 3367–3402 (2015)
7. van Kuijk, S.M., Viechtbauer, W., Peeters, L.L., Smits, L.: Bias in regression coefficient estimates when assumptions for handling missing data are violated: a simulation study. Epidemiol. Biostat. Public Health **13**(1), e11598-1–e11598-8 (2016)
8. Olsen, I., Kvien, T., Uhlig, T.: Consequences of handling missing data for treatment response in osteoarthritis: a simulation study. Osteoarthritis Cartilage **20**(8), 822–828 (2012)
9. Santos, M.S., Abreu, P.H., García-Laencina, P.J., Simão, A., Carvalho, A.: A new cluster-based oversampling method for improving survival prediction of hepatocellular carcinoma patients. J. Biomed. Inform. **58**, 49–59 (2015)
10. Santos, M.S., Soares, J.P., Henriques Abreu, P., Araújo, H., Santos, J.: Influence of data distribution in missing data imputation. In: ten Teije, A., Popow, C., Holmes, J.H., Sacchi, L. (eds.) AIME 2017. LNCS (LNAI), vol. 10259, pp. 285–294. Springer, Cham (2017). https://doi.org/10.1007/978-3-319-59758-4_33
11. Smola, A.J., Schölkopf, B.: A tutorial on support vector regression. Stat. Comput. **14**(3), 199–222 (2004)
12. Valdiviezo, H.C., Van Aelst, S.: Tree-based prediction on incomplete data using imputation or surrogate decisions. Inf. Sci. **311**, 163–181 (2015)
13. Wolkowitz, A.A., Skorupski, W.P.: A method for imputing response options for missing data on multiple-choice assessments. Educ. Psychol. Measur. **73**(6), 1036–1053 (2013)

Automatic Switching Between Video and Audio According to User's Context

Paulo J. S. Ferreira$^{(\boxtimes)}$ (iD), João M. P. Cardoso$^{(\boxtimes)}$ (iD),
and João Mendes-Moreira$^{(\boxtimes)}$ (iD)

INESC TEC, Faculty of Engineering, University of Porto,
R. Dr. Roberto Frias s/n, 4200-465 Porto, Portugal
{up201305617,jmpc,jmoreira}@fe.up.pt

Abstract. Smartphones are increasingly present in human's life. For example, for entertainment many people use their smartphones to watch videos or listen to music. Many users, however, stream or play videos with the intention to only listen to the audio track. This way, some battery energy, which is critical to most users, is unnecessarily consumed thus and switching between video and audio can increase the time of use of the smartphone between battery recharges. In this paper, we present a first approach that, based on the user context, can automatically switch between video and audio. A supervised learning approach is used along with the classifiers K-Nearest Neighbors, Hoeffding Trees and Naive Bayes, individually and combined to create an ensemble classifier. We investigate the accuracy for recognizing the context of the user and the overhead that this system can have on the smartphone energy consumption. We evaluate our approach with several usage scenarios and an average accuracy of 88.40% was obtained for the ensemble classifier. However, the actual overhead of the system on the smartphone energy consumption highlights the need for researching further optimizations and techniques.

Keywords: Human Activity Recognition · Machine learning ·
Mobile applications · Supervised learning · Smartphones ·
Mobile sensors

1 Introduction

Human Activity Recognition (HAR) (see, e.g., [1]) aims to recognize the activities performed by humans through the analyses of a series of observations using sensors, e.g., carried by users. Smartphones include built-in sensors, such as accelerometer and gyroscopes, that make possible for these devices to recognize the activities performed by users, i.e., to implement mobile HAR systems.

This work has been partially funded by the European Regional Development Fund (ERDF) through the Operational Programme for Competitiveness and Internationalisation - COMPETE 2020 Programme and by National Funds through Fundação para a Ciência e a Tecnologia (FCT) within project POCI-01-0145-FEDER-016883.

© Springer Nature Switzerland AG 2019
P. Moura Oliveira et al. (Eds.): EPIA 2019, LNAI 11805, pp. 196–207, 2019.
https://doi.org/10.1007/978-3-030-30244-3_17

HAR systems need to consider various aspects, such as power and energy consumption, processing requirements, accuracy and overall system overhead. Main HAR tasks include data acquisition (sensing), preprocessing, feature extraction and either training or classification. At the end, it results in a model capable of detecting meaningful patterns.

Smartphone-based HAR systems can be split into two types. The first one is online activity recognition, in which the learning and recognition processes are carried out in real-time and locally on the smartphones. The second type is offline activity recognition, in which the learning process is carried out in non-real-time while the recognition process is in real-time [3].

Despite the significant advances in mobile computing, smartphones continue to have limited resources [2]. With the Today's number of applications and functions on smartphones, those resources run out quickly and thus schemes to save energy consumption are very important. One example of wasting of energy is the fact that many users only want to hear the audio track associated with a video, but still play and/or stream the video.

In order to address this problem, this paper presents a method which, based on real-time machine-learning based recognition of the user's context, can distinguish, in some contexts, whether the user is watching a video or listening to audio and automatically switch between video and audio according to the output of the real-time recognition.

This paper is organized as follows. Section 2 presents the motivation behind this work. Section 3 describes the scenarios considered and Sect. 4 presents the implementation of the desktop and of the mobile software prototype. Then, in Sect. 5 we show experimental results and finally, in Sect. 6 we draw some conclusions and summarize possible future work.

2   Motivation

Switching from video to audio sources in smartphones, and when users play videos and are only interested in the audio track, may provide energy savings. We conducted several experiments in order to evaluate the energy consumption associated to play video or audio. In those experiments, we monitored the battery level while playing media files stored locally and on a streaming platform.

For example, in one experiment we used a video of a show with the duration of 2 h. The file was split into mp4 (590 MB) and mp3 (165 MB) formats. For measurements on the streaming platform, we used a normal YouTube video and another one with the whole video frames in black. Figure 1 shows the energy consumption measurements obtained. The results show that playing the original video file consumes more battery when compared to the respective audio file (i.e., represented in this experiment by the one with all frames in black).

Assuming that the user starts playing the video when the battery level is at 100% and continues playing until the battery level reaches 0%, and the battery discharge is linear along the time, when switching to the audio file the user would profit by an additional 2.22 h of battery life. The two charts in Fig. 1 illustrate

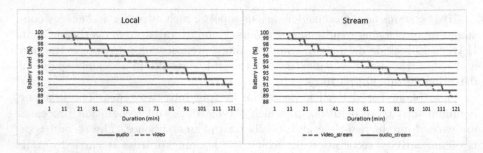

Fig. 1. Battery consumption during playback of a video and audio file locally (left chart) and on a streaming platform (right chart). The results show a ladder effect due to the one unit resolution, and whenever a battery level drops by 1% a step is presented.

that in the case of the use of video streaming platforms, the smartphone energy consumption associated with the play of video files is even higher than when playing audio files (due to the energy needed for network communications).

The experiments show that switching from video to audio saves the battery resources of the smartphone, and thus justify research efforts on finding automatic ways to switch between video and audio according to the user needs. This paper shows our first efforts on the topic and present an approach addressing a set of possible user scenarios.

3   Scenarios

In this paper, we identify some usage scenarios, where the user could be watching a video, listening to audio or none of the above. The scenarios considered are associated with playing video/audio while doing the following activities: Running, Walking, Sitting in the Couch and Cooking in the Kitchen.

3.1   Walking

In this scenario, 3 possible situations are considered: the user is "walking and watching a video"; the user is "walking and listening to audio"; the user is "just walking". The Table 1 summarizes the position and location of smartphone in the situations considered for this scenario.

This scenario does not consider the situations where: the user changes the file being played; the user continues walking even after the media file is finished playing; the user watches to videos in landscape mode.

3.2   Running

In this scenario, 2 possible situations are considered: the user is "running and listening to audio"; the user is "just running". It was not considered the situation of watching video, because it is uncommon (difficult) to watch a video while

Table 1. Walking scenario summary

Situation	Description
Walking and watching a video	With and without headset; smartphone in portrait mode
Walking and listening to audio	With smartphone in left and right pocket, the screen facing outwards and upside down with headsets
Walking	With the smartphone in the left and right pocket, the screen facing outwards, upside down and right side up

Table 2. Running scenario summary

Situation	Description
Running and listening audio	with the smartphone in the left pocket, the screen facing outwards and upside down
Running	with the smartphone in the left pocket, the screen facing outwards, right side up and upside down

running. The Table 2 summarizes the position and location of smartphone in the situations considered for this scenario.

As already mentioned, this scenario does not include all the possible activities of the user. The following activities were not included: running and listening to audio without headphones; running with the headset, but not listening, because the audio playback has ended.

3.3 Sitting on the Couch

For this scenario, 3 possible situations were considered: the user is "sitting on the couch while watching a video"; the user is "sitting on the couch while listening to audio"; the user is "just sitting on the couch". The Table 3 summarizes the position and location of smartphone in the situations considered for this scenario.

Table 3. Sitting scenario summary

Situation	Description
Sitting and watching a video	With the smartphone in portrait and landscape mode, with and without headset
Sitting and listening to audio	With smartphone on the couch next to him/her and with the screen facing up; with smartphone in left and right pocket with screen facing up and upside down; with the smartphone in portrait mode while interacting with the device
Sitting on the couch	With smartphone in left and right pocket with screen facing up and upside down

In this scenario the following activities were not considered: the user is sitting on the couch interacting with the smartphone without listening to audio or watching videos; the user is sitting on the couch listening to audio with the smartphone in landscape mode while interacting with the device; the user is listening to audio without headphones; the user chooses another file to play.

3.4 Cooking in the Kitchen

For this scenario, 3 possible situations were considered: the user is "cooking in the kitchen and watching a video"; the user is "cooking in the kitchen and listening to audio"; the user is "cooking in the kitchen". In this scenario, no headphones were used. The Table 4 summarizes the position and location of smartphone in the situations considered for this scenario.

Table 4. Cooking scenario summary

Situation	Description
Cooking and watching a video	With the smartphone on the table with the screen facing up; with the smartphone leaning against an object in portrait and landscape mode
Cooking and listening to audio	With the smartphone on the table with the screen facing up and facing down
Cooking	With the smartphone on the table with the screen facing up

It was not considered situations in which the user interacts with the smartphone to change the file being played. In addition, we have not considered situations where the user may connect sound amplification devices, such as Bluetooth speakers, to the smartphone.

4 Implementation

4.1 Prototype

The prototype Android application was developed as a proof of concept to test the classification in real-time and based on the result switch between video and audio. The prototype was developed and tested on a Samsung Galaxy J5 smartphone. Figure 2 presents a block diagram of the architecture of the prototype.

The prototype loads the desktop trained models stored locally before starting the real-time classification process. We note, however, that the prototype can be used for incremental/online learning.

The models are trained using feature vectors from the sliding windows consisting of a few sensor samples and an overlapping between contiguous windows based on empirical studies.

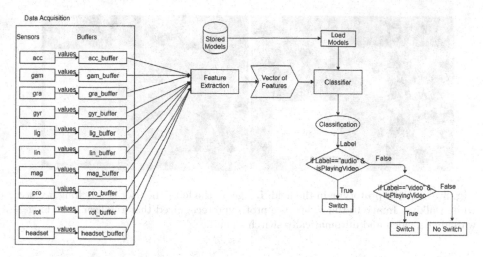

Fig. 2. Architecture of the prototype.

The prototype has 10 buffers, one for each sensor. Once the classification process is started by the user, the buffers begin to be filled with data from the sensors in real time. When the buffers reach the capacity defined by the user, the features are extracted. This produces a vector of features that will be classified by the pre-loaded models.

The possible output predictions from the prototype are: Other, Audio and Video. Based on these outputs, the prototype can adopt one of the following behaviors:

- If the prediction is "Audio" and the video file is playing, the prototype switches to the audio;
- If the prediction is "Video" and the audio file is playing, the prototype switches to the video;
- If the prediction is "Audio" and the audio file is playing, the prototype keeps the audio file playing;
- If the prediction is "Video" and the video file is playing, the prototype keeps the video file playing;
- If the prediction is "Other", the prototype does not switch regardless of the file being played.

When switching from video to audio or vice versa, the prototype tries to achieve a smooth transition. Figure 3 illustrates the prototype functioning in the field.

4.2 Classifiers

Both the desktop and smartphone prototypes rely on the MOA framework [4]. MOA allows data stream processing, includes representative incre-

Fig. 3. Using the prototype in the field. Image on the left - the user is watching a video while walking. Image to the right - the prototype recognized that the user is no longer watching a video and automatically switch to audio.

mental machine learning algorithms, and is written in Java, which facilitated integration with the Android platform.

The three main incremental algorithms used were Naive Bayes (NB), Hoeffding Trees (HT), and K-Nearest Neighbors (KNN), individually, and as a Confidence Ensemble (CE). The CE uses the confidence of classifiers to classify an instance. For example, if a classifier is 99% certain of an activity, but the other two agree on a different activity with just 30% certainty, then first classifier's opinion is considered.

4.3   Feature Extraction

For each sliding window with sensor data, and according to the number of axis of each sensor, several features are extracted. In the case of our prototypes the features are associated to 3D and 1D sensors.

The following 10 features are extracted from each 3D sensor:

- **Arithmetic Mean** of the X, Y and Z axis, individually and together, resulting in 4 features for each of the sensors;
- **Standard Deviation** of the X, Y and Z axis, individually, resulting in 3 features for each of the sensors;
- **Pearson Correlation** of axis X and Y, Y and Z, and X and Z, resulting in 3 features for each of the sensors.

The following 2 features are extracted from each 1D sensor:

- **Arithmetic Mean** of the X axis, resulting in 1 feature for each of the sensors;
- **Standard Deviation** of the X, resulting in 1 feature for each of the sensors.

4.4   Desktop

The desktop program consists of two phases: the training phase and the test phase. During the training phase, training data is used to train the classifiers.

In the test phase, the trained classifiers are used to classify the test data and to study the accuracy of classifiers since the data used for testing are already labeled.

5 Experimental Results

The experiments with the prototype use a Samsung Galaxy J5 smartphone, with a battery capacity of 3000 mAh. Those experiments use a sampling frequency of 5 Hz, sliding windows with 200 samples (i.e., with duration of 40 s), and a 70% overlap.

It was decided to use a frequency of 5 Hz, as according to Zheng et al. [3], at this frequency it is possible to save energy, when compared with higher frequencies, and yet maintaining a high accuracy in the recognition of similar user's activities. The size of the windows and the overlapping factor were selected based on previous experiments to find the most adequate parameter values.

5.1 Dataset

The data were collected based on the activities described in the scenarios described in Sect. 3. As mentioned before, seven 3D sensors and two 1D were used. The 3D sensors used to collect the data were: accelerometer, game rotation vector, gravity, gyroscope, linear acceleration, magnetic field and rotation vector. The 1D sensors used to collect the data were: light and proximity. In addition, information from the Android API, which indicates if the headset was connected to the smartphone, was also collected at the same rate as the other sensors. A total of 76 features are extracted: 10 for each of the seven 3D sensors and 2 for each of the other three sensors.

A total of 2 subjects, 2 males with ages of 18 and 24, were involved in data acquisition. The dataset consists of a total of 494,914 samples, 180,002 "Walking", 89,960 "Running", 134,964 "Sitting", and 89,988 "Kitchen" samples.

5.2 Overhead

In order to study the overhead associated with real-time classification, an experiment was carried out.

Twenty measures were taken for each of the situations under analysis and then the average of the values was used. The average runtimes are shown in Table 5. The results show that the entire classification process (which includes the Features Extraction and the classification with all the active classifiers) takes 98.95 ms on average. Most of this time concerns the classification that, with all active classifiers, takes on average 79.05 ms to classify a new instance. Features Extraction takes on average 15.15 ms.

The KNN (k = 3) takes approximately 71.70 ms, which is significantly more than with the other classifiers. KNN needs on average 70 ms more time than NB and HT to classify an instance.

Table 5. Average execution time (FE - Feature Extraction; EC - Ensemble Classification).

	FE and EC	FE	EC	kNN (k = 3)	NB	HT
Average execution time (ms)	98.95	15.15	79.05	71.70	1.55	1.45

5.3 Battery Energy Consumption

We show now the energy consumption while playing media files stored locally with real-time classification. During the experiments no other app was running in the background and all the experiments were conducted in the same conditions.

The results obtained showed that during real-time classification, the KNN and the HT are, among the three classifiers, the ones that consume more and less battery, respectively.

Assuming that the battery discharge is linear with the time and the battery level, the use of KNN as a classifier implies an increase in battery consumption of approximately 4 h. As previously shown, the switch from video to audio (without classifiers) allows an increase in battery life of 2.22 h. Due to the extra consumption of KNN, its use with the classification period used is not feasible as the extra consumption is higher than the savings obtained with the switching. On the other hand, HT implies an increase in consumption of 2.22 h. So, with HT, it is not expected to be able to save battery by switching video to audio with HT, but it also does not consume enough to make a possible solution using HT unfeasible. Therefore, the HT is a possible viable classifier, being necessary to reduce the extra consumption associated to this classifier.

5.4 Supervised Learning

In this subsection, we study the accuracy and evaluate the performance of the classifiers. Two different experiments were performed: a first one with all the data; and a second with each individual scenario.

In the first experiment, the dataset was split in 80% for training and 20% for test but considering that each set must have considerable samples of each activity, to avoid an unbalanced training set or one without samples of a activity.

In the second experiment, the data was organized in their respective scenarios. The training set was the same used in the first experiment, 80% of all data available in the dataset, that is, the data of all the scenarios. For the test set we used only the data referring to the scenario under study and that were not part of the training set.

The results are presented in Table 6. As expected, the Ensemble classifier obtained the best result in all the scenarios under study and allowed to improve accuracy by 4.13% (average value) when compared to the best accuracy obtained by each individual classifier. Individually, the classifiers KNN and HT obtained the best accuracy. Overall, HT obtained the best result when compared to the other individual classifiers. With respect to NB, it was the one that obtained the lowest accuracy, in addition to having performed inferiorly (with respect to precision, recall and F1 measures) when compared to the other individual classifiers.

Table 6. Performance of each of the classifiers. For the KNN the value of k used was 3 (k = 3). (E - Ensemble; KNN - k-Nearest Neighbors; NB - Naive Bayes; HT - Hoeffding Tree)

%	Accuracy				Precision				Recall				F1			
	E	kNN	NB	HT	E	kNN	NB	HT	E	kNN	NB	HT	E	kNN	NB	HT
Global	92.20	86.49	70.66	88.40	93.37	90.05	76.19	89.62	92.21	89.48	70.92	88.41	92.79	89.76	73.46	89.02
Walking	98.14	87.84	78.38	97.97	98.19	91.51	86.37	98.32	98.14	89.05	78.76	98.31	98.16	90.26	82.39	98.32
Running	97.96	96.94	97.28	97.96	NaN	NaN	NaN	NaN	NaN	NaN	NaN	NaN	NaN	NaN	NaN	NaN
Kitchen	63.63	62.93	61.90	48.98	52.11	73.04	50.62	NaN	47.92	67.89	47.80	32.43	49.93	70.37	49.17	NaN
Sitting	90.09	82.66	42.12	88.06	91.90	88.33	23.82	88.98	90.02	87.04	31.87	88.52	90.95	87.68	27.26	88.75

5.5 Improving Energy Consumption

The results of the previous experiments allow us to conclude that the Hoeffding Trees (HT) classifier consumes less energy and achieves higher accuracy than the other two classifiers. Even though the HT classifier has the least impact on battery consumption, it is still not possible to save energy when switching from video to audio with this classifier and considering its execution per each sliding window.

In order to reduce the energy impact associated with the real-time classification, experiments were carried out in order to trigger the classification of N sliding windows every T minutes. For example, using N = 5 windows and T = 4 min results in a classification of 150 windows instead of the previous 361 windows for the near 2 h of playing (file presented in Sect. 2). This can reduce the energy consumption of the battery by approximately 1% when compared to the continuously classification approach previously used (resulting in additional 2.22 h of battery life).

Although it is possible to save energy by making N classifications every T minutes, during the time the system waits for the next set of windows, the last classification obtained is the one used by the system. In these preliminary results, the accuracy of the HT decreased from 75.16% to 69.65%.

6 Related Work

There has been a lot of research regarding HAR with smartphone's sensors. Herein, we summarize some of the related work in terms of the classifiers used, recognized human activities and the use of supervised or semi-supervised learning. We note, however, that to the best of our knowledge we are the first addressing the switching from video to audio.

Kose et al. [6] developed an app for online activity recognition on smartphones using a built-in tri-axial accelerometer to recognize four main activities: walking, running, standing and sitting. Clustered KNN and Naïve Bayes were used as classifiers. Naïve Bayes achieved a 48% average accuracy rate for all subjects with different sampling rates and window sizes. Compared to Naïve Bayes, on average, clustered KNN achieved a much better classification performance, around 92% accuracy.

Anjum et al. [7] developed a smartphone app that performs activity recognition without requiring any user intervention. The app can recognize in real-time 7 main activities: inactive, walking, running, climbing stairs, descending stairs, cycling and driving. They evaluated four different classification algorithms: Naive Bayes, C4.5, KNN and Support Vector Machine (SVM). Naive Bayes achieved an accuracy of 83%, C4.5 obtained an accuracy of 94%, KNN, with $K = 1$, achieved an accuracy of 80%, and SVM achieved an accuracy of 79%.

Cardoso and Moreira [5] developed an online HAR system using Semi-Supervised Learning to recognize 12 basic activities and their transitions: standing, sitting, laying, walking, walking downstairs, walking upstairs, stand-to-sit, sit-to- stand, sit-to-lie, lie-to-sit, stand-to-lie and lie-to-stand. For classifying they used Naive Bayes, Very Fast Decision Trees and KNN, and Democratic and Confidence based Ensemble. They compare the Semi-Supervised Learning and Supervised Learning using a sliding window with 70% overlapping. Supervised Learning achieved an accuracy of 82.69% for Democratic and 84.55% for Confidence. Semi-Supervised Learning achieved an accuracy of 83.03% for Democratic and 84.63% for Confidence.

7   Conclusion

As in many situations, users play videos with the only purpose to listen to the audio track, and that playing videos consumes more energy than playing audio, this paper presented a smartphone-based human activity recognition (HAR) able to automatically switch between video and audio playing. The HAR system is implemented using machine-learning techniques, including an ensemble scheme consisting of Hoeffding Trees, Naive Bayes, and KNN. The Hoeffding Trees classifier achieved the highest accuracy when compared to the other individual classifiers and was also the classifier that consumed less energy and with the lowest computational needs. Thus, Hoeffding Trees is the classifier, among those studied, that best suits the proposed system.

Although the classifiers used achieved high accuracy for the user scenarios studied in this work, the energy consumption associated to the HAR system would prevent the practical use of the actual solution. Specifically, the HAR system proposed in combination with the playing, even when switching to audio files, consumes more energy than the playing of video files. Our preliminary improvements in order to save energy consumption of the system, considered reductions on the frequency with which the system classifies in real-time. The results show that it is possible to save 1% of the battery when compared to a version of the system continuously classifying all the windows of samples period-ically acquired from the sensors. An example of reduction allows to increase the battery life in 2.22 h by switching from video to audio. However, further research efforts need to be done to mitigate the fact that if the system has been without classification for a long time, it may suffer from increased energy consumption due to its longer time in video or from the slow switch to video from audio which may affect negatively the quality of user experience.

Future work plans include research on schemes to tackle the problem in different ways. For example, as the classifications considered in the HAR system proposed in this paper can be thought as activities composed by events and atomic activities, our plans include the use of machine learning techniques to target sequences of events and atomic activities and transitions between these activities/events. As the prototype is continuously acquiring and processing sensing data, there is a significant increase in energy consumption. One way to reduce the extra consumption caused by this would be to trigger the classification process when a certain event was detected by the prototype. In this way, the prototype would not have to continuously acquire sensing data, which would reduce the impact that the real-time classification process has on the smartphone's battery.

References

1. Zhang, S., Wei, Z., Nie, J., Huang, L., Wang, S., Li, Z.: A review on human activity recognition using vision-based method. J. Healthc. Eng. **2017**(3090343), 31 (2017)
2. Shoaib, M., Bosch, S., Durmaz Incel, O., Scholten, H., Havinga, P.: A survey of online activity recognition using mobile phones. Sensors **15**(1), 2059–2085 (2015)
3. Zheng, L., et al.: A novel energy-efficient approach for human activity recognition. Sensors **17**(9), 2064–2085 (2017)
4. Bifet, A., Holmes, G., Kirkby, R., Pfahringer, B.: Moa: massive online analysis. J. Mach. Learn. Res. **11**, 1601–1604 (2010)
5. Cardoso, H., Mendes-Moreira, J.: Improving human activity classification through online semi-supervised learning. In: Workshop StreamEvolv co-located with ECML/PKDD 2016, CEUR, vol. 2069, pp. 15–26 (2017)
6. Kose, M., Durmaz Incel, O., Ersoy, C.: Online human activity recognition on smart phones. Smartphones Wearables Big Data **16**, 11–15 (2012). InWorkshop on Mobile Sensing
7. Anjum, A., Ilyas, M.: Activity recognition using smartphone sensors. In: 2013 IEEE 10th Consumer Communications and Networking Conference (CCNC), pp. 914–919 (2013)

Energy Efficient Smartphone-Based Users Activity Classification

Ricardo M. C. Magalhães[(✉)] [iD], João M. P. Cardoso[(✉)] [iD],
and João Mendes-Moreira[(✉)] [iD]

INESC TEC, Faculty of Engineering, University of Porto,
R. Dr. Roberto Frias s/n, 4200-465 Porto, Portugal
{up201502862,jmpc,jmoreira}@fe.up.pt

Abstract. Nowadays most people carry a smartphone with built-in sensors (e.g., accelerometers, gyroscopes) capable of providing useful data for Human Activity Recognition (HAR). Machine learning classification methods have been intensively researched and developed for HAR systems, each with different accuracy and performance levels. However, acquiring sensor data and executing machine learning classifiers require computational power and consume energy. As such, a number of factors, such as inadequate preprocessing, can have a negative impact on the overall HAR performance, even on high-end handheld devices. While high accuracy can be extremely important in some applications, the device's battery life can be highly critical to the end-user. This paper is focused on the k-nearest neighbors' algorithm (kNN), one of the most used algorithms in HAR systems, and research and develop energy-efficient implementations for mobile devices. We focus on a kNN implementation based on Locality-Sensitive Hashing (LSH) with a significant positive impact on the device's battery life, fully integrated into a mobile HAR Android application able to classify human activities in real-time. The proposed kNN implementation was able to achieve execution time reductions of 50% over other versions of kNN with average accuracy of 96.55% when considering 8 human activities.

Keywords: Human activity recognition (HAR) · Mobile sensors ·
Mobile application · k-nearest neighbors (kNN) ·
Locality-sensitive Hashing (LSH)

1 Introduction

Human Activity Recognition's (HAR) main purpose (see, e.g., [11]) resides on recognizing activities performed by individuals in a certain context, playing a

This work has been partially funded by the European Regional Development Fund (ERDF) through the Operational Programme for Competitiveness and Internationalisation - COMPETE 2020 Programme and by National Funds through the Fundação para a Ciência e a Tecnologia (FCT) within project POCI-01-0145-FEDER-016883.

© Springer Nature Switzerland AG 2019
P. Moura Oliveira et al. (Eds.): EPIA 2019, LNAI 11805, pp. 208–219, 2019.
https://doi.org/10.1007/978-3-030-30244-3_18

key alliance with ubiquitous or pervasive computing. With the advent of smartphones, people started to carry around a computing device with integrated sensors, opening an opportunity to use these devices for HAR. Smartphone's sensors are capable of gathering useful data for HAR and the use of Machine Learning classifiers to recognize activities has been focus of intense research efforts (see, e.g., [11]). Classifying human activities can be very useful in certain areas, such as monitoring elder people [1] or maintaining a healthy lifestyle [9]. There is also the potential of providing contextualized recommendations to the user, such as suggesting TV shows, places to visit, physical activities to perform, or even improve advertisements by correlating different data results. Also, in an age where social networking is mostly omnipresent on everyone's lives, this opened the possibility of giving automatic personal information on activities to one's social circle (see, e.g., [17]).

However, with the increase of computing power in smartphones, battery life is always one of the main concerns by the users. For instance, a survey among Portuguese young individuals [7] reveals around 30% of the sample population is always managing mobile features or capabilities in order to increase the daily battery life. Therefore, one of the main concerns of mobile HAR is its energy efficiency. Acquiring data from sensors requires continuous background computing tasks. The implementation of such an HAR application with usage on other applications or services, as mentioned before, needs to care about the impact on energy efficiency and about techniques to save energy consumption (see, e.g., [13,20]).

The work and study presented in this paper aim at contributing to the HAR scientific community by studying different optimization techniques for kNN, namely an LSH (Locality Sensitive Hashing [8]) based kNN as alternative implementation for trading-off between accuracy and energy efficiency. Specifically, this paper presents an LSH-based kNN (kNN-LSH) implemented in a smartphone-based HAR system. The kNN-LSH implementation is able to reduce execution time and energy consumption of the classification time while maintaining similar accuracy when considering the PAMAP2 data set [16] and our own experiments considering 8 activities (walking, standing, sitting, sprinting, jogging, ascending stairs, descending stairs, jumping).

This paper is organized as follows. Section 2 presents related work. Section 3 presents our methodological approach, namely datasets, classifiers and developed applications. Section 4 presents experimental results. Finally, Sect. 5 concludes the paper and provides some ideas for future work.

2   Related Work

Many different techniques, methods and approaches have been proposed for energy savings in HAR systems (see, e.g., [15] and [10]). Those techniques range from preprocessing techniques to classifier algorithms optimization, each having its advantages and disadvantages. The following paragraphs describe some representative techniques.

Yan et al. [19] propose a new strategy, *A3R* (Adaptive Accelerometer-based Activity Recognition), based on the investigation of effects in sampling frequency and classification features. They claim that their approach can reduce energy consumption by 50% under ideal conditions, while users running on their Android device save between 20% to 25% of energy consumption.

Zheng et al. [20] propose a system based on H-SVM, study different sampling rates, and conclude that the energy consumption is considerably lower when adopting a lower sampling rate. Adopting a rate of 1 Hz saves 59.6% of power than of 50 Hz. When comparing 10 Hz and 50 Hz, the later only increases accuracy by 0.03%, but increases energy consumption by 32.7%.

Wang et al. [18] propose EEMSS, capable of characterizing a user's state by time, location and activity while exploring sensor monitoring by only keeping the minimum sensors, triggering new ones when the state transition is recognized. Tests performed on a Nokia N95 provided an average accuracy of 92.56% with an average battery life of 11.33 h, depending on the user activity.

Liang et al. [13] propose a hierarchical recognition solution with decision trees based on recognition of 11 activities using only accelerometer data, reducing energy consumption with lower sampling rates and increasing accuracy with adjusts to the size of the sliding window.

Anguita et al. [2] explore three different types of SVM algorithms, concluding that L1-SVM is capable of achieving high accuracy with less computation by performing dimensionality reduction. Also, the impact of adding gyroscope features improve accuracy results.

Morillo et al. [14] propose the use of discrete variables obtained from accelerometers, applying the Ameva algorithm. While saving up to 27 h of usage time, it maintains an average accuracy of 98% with 8 activities.

While all these research activities show significant contributions to save energy consumption and using distinct techniques, we note, however, that there is a lack of studies about the use of kNN with Locality-sensitive Hashing (LSH) for reducing energy consumption in HAR. Nonetheless, there is a number of studies proposing the use of LSH to solve kNN's problems (see, e.g., [6,8]).

3 Methodological Approach

3.1 Dataset and Data Collecting

The first step in HAR studies is to identify an existing dataset and/or collect our own data.

PAMAP2. We first started using PAMAP2 (Physical Activity Monitoring for Aging People) [16], a dataset where 18 different activities were recorded with 9 different subjects, each wearing 3 IMUs (Inertial Measurement Units) and a heart-rate monitor, with each IMU presenting 3D-data from accelerometer, gyroscope, and magnetometer.

Our Own Dataset. For further data collection, we used an Android-based Samsung Galaxy J5 to collect data from 9 different sensors (accelerometer, game rotation, gravity, gyroscope, proximity, linear acceleration, rotation, magnetic field and light) for 8 different activities by a single male individual. Each activity was collected using a sampling frequency of 5 Hz with the device located on the pant's right pocket, being upside down and with the screen facing the leg of the user.

3.2 Feature Extraction

For both datasets, a number of features were extracted using functions such as mean, correlation and standard deviation. Each 1D and 3D sensor has, respectively, 2 and 10 features extracted. In total, each window consisted of 45 extracted features for PAMAP2 and 74 for our own dataset. The features extracted from each sensor are:

- 1D Sensor Features: mean and standard deviation;
- 3D Sensor Features: x Mean, y Mean, z Mean, x Standard Deviation, y Standard Deviation, z Standard Deviation, xy Correlation, xz Correlation, and yz Correlation.

3.3 Classifiers

Our focus on optimizing kNN led us to use the techniques explained below.

KNN with PAW and ADWIN. Among other alternatives to improve kNN's performance, we selected two that were designed to reduce the number of instances stored by the classifier. Probabilistic Adaptive Window (PAW) [5] maintains in logarithmic memory a sample of the instances, storing the most recent with a higher probability. Adaptive Windowing (ADWIN) [3] works by discarding old instances whenever two "large enough" subsets present "distinct enough" averages by concluding the expected values are different. We note that ADWIN can be combined with PAW.

LSH. Locality-sensitive Hashing (LSH) [8] is another technique, using dot products with random vectors to find the neighbor more quickly. The main aspect of LSH is storing similar data in the same buckets with higher probability. The kNN-LSH used in this paper is based on Smile's [12] LSH implementation, extended for incremental/online learning, and integrated to MOA [4].

Basically, each feature vector is stored on a bucket of each hash table, based on the hash function of each table. LSH presents three main parameters with an impact in performance: number of random projections per hash value (hk), number of hash tables (l) and the width of the projection (r). The two last parameters in particular are important regarding energy. Increasing the number of hash tables requires progressively more memory, while increasing the width of projection will lead to bigger query times.

3.4 Architecture

For this work, we used two Machine Learning libraries: MOA (Massive Online Analysis) [4] and Smile (Statistical Machine Intelligence and Learning Engine) [12]. Since our studies were conducted in two different environments, we present a summary of each one.

Offline Java Application. Our offline Java application is responsible for doing all our offline machine learning studies. This application is capable of loading data instances, of extracting all features, respecting window size and overlap values, and of creating a feature vector per window to be used as training or testing in the classifier. Finally, we are able to run our classifiers independently or with an ensemble of our choice, executing the testing phase on the application or creating a model to be loaded on the mobile application.

Android Application. Our Android application is responsible for implementing the smartphone-based HAR system and for doing all our online machine learning studies.

This application is capable of collecting data from sensors in order to create a dataset or to be stored in buffers in order to be used on live classification. For the latter, it basically acquires data until all buffers are full (i.e., the window size is reached), extracting all features to create a vector to be tested on the classifier. The classifiers are loaded by models previously created on the desktop application, already containing the trained dataset. Finally, the application notifies the classified activity to the user.

4 HAR Studies and Experiments

4.1 Desktop Studies

Most of the studies in this section were conducted with the PAMAP2 [16] dataset in order to evaluate the performance of different classifiers and finding *optimal* parameters for this particular case. After these studies, we analyzed the performance using our own dataset.

Alternative kNN Approaches and Window Size Variation. Due to its lazy nature, kNN is typically slow in the predictive task. The largest the training set is, the largest the predictive time is. However, we selected two different alternative approaches to kNN present on MOA: kNN with PAW and kNN with PAW and ADWIN. This study's goal was to compare base kNN with the other alternative implementations in terms of global accuracy and both training and testing time with different window sizes.

Since the PAMAP2 samples were recorded in 100 Hz, every 100 instances represent 1 s in time. We chose to experiment with increments of 100 in window

Table 1. Performance of each kNN approach with different window sizes

Classifier	Train (s)	Test (s)	Window avg. test (s)	Global acc. (%)	Train (s)	Test (s)	Window avg. test (s)	Global acc. (%)
	100				200			
kNN	28.541	124.521	0.047	78.73	29.393	36.969	0.024	83.45
kNN with PAW	36.403	135.53	0.047	78.69	31.321	37.811	0.024	83.45
kNN with PAW+ADWIN	76.152	10.888	0.03	41.22	57.439	8.399	0.04	73.16
	300				400			
k-NN	26.866	17.964	0.019	87.35	3.497	12.945	0.013	88.24
k-NN with PAW	31.845	21.038	0.019	87.24	27.446	11.436	0.013	87.24
k-NN with PAW+ADWIN	59.296	14.042	0.013	87.12	46.984	7.649	0.007	85.60
	500				600			
k-NN	26.550	8.231	0.010	89.75	26.989	6.144	0.010	90.93
k-NN with PAW	26.338	7.960	0,011	89.75	29.727	6.570	0.010	90.93
k-NN with PAW+ADWIN	39.102	7.580	0.010	89.75	38.385	6.839	0.009	90.93
	700				800			
k-NN	26.953	5.821	0.009	89.16	31.967	4.933	0.007	91.95
k-NN with PAW	28.828	5.376	0.009	89.16	29.389	5.275	0.007	91.95
k-NN with PAW+ADWIN	35.479	5.126	0.008	89.16	35.373	4.673	0.007	91.95
	900				1000			
k-NN	27.708	4.199	0.006	93.38	28.598	3.700	0.006	92.64
k-NN with PAW	28.160	4.061	0.006	93.38	29.507	3.826	0.006	92.64
k-NN with PAW+ADWIN	31.909	3.903	0.006	93.38	32.448	4.033	0.005	92.64

size. Each experiment was conducted in the same conditions for each of the three classifiers ($k = 3$; $overlap = 10\%$). Table 1 shows results with different window sizes for each classifier.

None of the alternative approaches outperforms the base kNN in training and testing time or global accuracy. kNN with PAW consistently present similar training and testing time in relation to kNN. On the other hand, kNN with PAW and ADWIN started by taking significantly less time to complete classification with a negative impact on global accuracy due to discarding of many samples. However, as the window size increases, this approach starts to discard fewer samples, until it reaches a point where it discards the same as kNN with PAW only.

The three classifiers behave similarly when window sizes are of 500 or more samples, achieving the same global accuracy in each experiment. When windows consist of 900 samples (i.e., 9 s of activity), the maximum global accuracy of 93.38% is reached, taking 4 ± 0.1 s to classify all samples.

Since PAW and ADWIN techniques did not present improvements, the following studies do not consider those.

Overlap Study. This study's goal was to test different values of overlap from 0% to near 100%, in order to evaluate the global accuracy and computational cost. The overlapping technique consists of maintaining a percentage of samples between each two consecutive sliding windows. This is particularly important in

HAR, because activities can span different times and are not instantly changed (i.e., a person who is running will not instantly stop that activity). Therefore, the transition between activities is important to this case.

Each experiment was conducted in the same conditions for base kNN (*window size* = 900; $k = 3$). Following, we present more detailed results with accuracy per activity in Table 2.

Table 2. kNN Accuracy per Activity with different overlap values

Overlap	Accuracy (%)											
	All	Lying	Sitting	Standing	Walking	Running	Cycling	Nordic Walking	Asc. Stairs	Desc. Stairs	Vacuum Cleaning	Ironing
0	92.25	96.43	92.86	93.10	91.90	100	88.46	96.88	85	84.62	83.33	100
10	93.38	100	93.33	96.88	100	75	96.43	97.22	95.24	73.33	77.78	91.67
20	94.12	100	88.89	97.14	96.37	80	96.77	97.50	100	82.35	83.33	95.12
30	92.95	100	85	92.68	90.74	66.67	94.44	100	92.86	88.89	**88.24**	93.62
40	93.72	100	93.75	90.48	83.33	**95.24**	100	93.75	93.75	81.82	87.50	96.30
50	93.80	100	92.86	100	89.33	85.71	90.20	98.44	87.50	**92.00**	85.42	98.46
60	94.27	98.59	97.06	97.22	93.62	77.78	93.65	98.75	93.75	84.85	85	96.34
70	94.30	100	**97.78**	97.92	90.40	75	94.05	99.06	92.19	84.09	86.25	98.17
80	**94.44**	100	94.20	99.41	91.01	77.78	92.91	99.38	91.84	87.69	87.60	96.95
90	94.41	100	93.43	98.95	90.40	77.78	94.05	99.38	92.35	90.70	86.67	96.33

As expected, computations increase progressively as the overlap reaches 90%, which is justified by the increase in the number of windows to be classified. The variation between 0% and 90% in the number of windows is from 1900 to 18992, while training time ranged from 28.007 to 42.513 s and testing time varied between 3.847 to 135.635 s. In order to get a better trade-off between accuracy and computation cost, the choice lies with 10% and 20% overlap, each respectively taking 3.965 and 4.423 s to classify all vectors. However, while the latter performs relatively better accuracy-wise, we opted to perform the next experiments with 10% overlap, because it takes approximately 0.5 s less to classify all samples, even with a less accuracy of 0.74%.

Impact of k Value. One of the particularities of kNN is the value of k. If $k = 1$, then the class is simply assigned to the class of its nearest neighbor. Therefore, it is expected that the classification time increases with bigger values of k. This study's goal is to choose the best value in relation to accuracy and classification time. Each experiment was conducted in the same conditions (*window size* = 900; *overlap* = 10%).

By evaluating different possible k values for k-NN from $k = 1$ to $k = 5$, we concluded that 1-NN is a valid option for this particular dataset, taking 3.804 s to classify all samples with an accuracy of 93.73%.

KNN Optimization with LSH. In order to further optimize the kNN classifier, the LSH (Locality Sensitive Hashing) was our choice. Because MOA [4]

lacks a LSH implementation, we adopted the code in the Smile library. Our kNN with LSH implementation consists of combining Smile's LSH inside MOA's base kNN.

As our last study concluded that $k = 1$ is sufficient for this dataset, we decided to use 1 for k. For hk, we evaluated values from 1 to 3. Regarding the width of the projection, the authors suggest the value to be sufficiently away from 0 [6], but not too large because of an increase in query time; in this particular dataset, $r = 10$ was considered optimal because it is the smaller value with the biggest accuracy, since $r > 10$ does not improve accuracy anymore and increases the query time. Our last tested parameter was l, which we tested from 10 to 60. Our goal is to find an optimal value of l and hk, maintaining a good trade-off between time and accuracy. Each experiment was conducted in the same conditions ($window\ size = 900$; $overlap = 10\%$, $k = 1$, $r = 10$). We present the results of LSH k-NN performance with both different l and hk by training and class time and accuracy (Tables 3 and 4).

Table 3. kNN-LSH performance with different number of hash tables (l) with $hk = 1$

l	Train time (s)	Test Time (s)	Accuracy (%)											
			All	Lying	Sitting	Standing	Walking	Running	Cycling	Nordic Walking	Asc. Stairs	Desc. Stairs	Vacuum Cleaning	Ironing
1	26.654	**2.222**	78.40	93.75	93.33	96.88	95.12	50	92.86	61.11	42.86	33.34	44.44	97.22
5	27.609	2.247	88.50	96.88	93.33	100	100	75	96.43	**97.22**	61.90	**60.00**	48.15	100
10	27.744	2.354	89.90	96.88	100	100	100	75	96.43	**97.22**	**71.43**	**53.33**	55.56	100
20	26.67	2.483	90.24	100	100	100	100	75	96.43	**97.22**	**71.43**	**53.33**	55.56	100
30	27.911	2.779	90.24	100	100	100	100	75	96.43	**97.22**	**71.43**	46.67	**59.26**	100
40	28.959	2.561	90.24	100	100	100	100	75	96.43	**97.22**	**71.43**	46.67	**59.26**	100
50	26.998	2.648	90.24	100	100	100	100	75	96.43	**97.22**	**71.43**	46.67	**59.26**	100
60	27.121	2.631	90.24	100	100	100	100	75	96.43	**97.22**	**71.43**	46.67	**59.26**	100

Table 4. kNN-LSH performance with different number of projections per hash value (hk)

hk	Train time (s)	Test time (s)	Global acc. (%)
1	27.857	2.475	**90.24**
2	28.882	2.614	87.46
3	27.497	2.225	74.22
4	28.764	2.297	46.34
5	30.080	2.215	22.30

We can conclude that $l = 20$ can be considered an optimal number for this particular case, achieving the same global accuracy than $l > 20$ and takes less time to classify. In addition, we conclude that $hk = 1$ presents the best global accuracy. Finally, we can also notice how kNN-LSH with $l = 20$ took ≈35% less time to classify compared to base kNN, while just losing 3.49% of accuracy.

Sampling Frequency Study. The sampling frequency which data is acquired can have an impact on the classifier's performance. Logically, reducing the frequency may result in less computations. The goal of this experiment is to study the impact of reducing sampling frequency in performance and accuracy. Since PAMAP2 was recorded using a sampling frequency of 100 Hz (i.e., data was recorded each 10 ms), in our studies of frequency reductions using PAMAP2 we skip instances of the dataset.

Each experiment was conducted in the same conditions ($overlap = 10\%$, $k = 1$, $r = 10$, $l = 20$) with the kNN-LSH classifier. Since our optimal window size for 100 Hz is 900 (i.e., 9 s), this value is reduced to still represent the same time span (e.g., for 50 Hz, window size = 450). As such, the number of training and testing vectors of features always stays the same (2111 and 287, respectively). Table 5 shows kNN-LSH performance with different sampling frequencies, showing the training and testing time, as well as accuracy per activity.

Table 5. LSH k-NN performance with different sampling frequencies

f (Hz)	Train time (s)	Test Time (s)	Accuracy (%) All	Lying	Sitting	Standing	Walking	Running	Cycling	Nordic Walking	Asc. Stairs	Desc. Stairs	Vacuum Cleaning	Ironing
100	26.67	2.483	90.24	100	100	100	100	75	96.43	97.22	71.43	53.33	55.56	100
50	14.781	1.396	90.94	100	100	100	100	75	96.43	97.22	71.43	60	59.26	100
25	7.532	0.948	90.94	96.88	100	100	95.24	50	100	100	77.27	71.423	55.56	100
5	1.964	0.692	89.31	96.88	93.33	96.88	100	50	100	97.22	81.82	66.66	44.44	97.30
1	0.861	0.645	85.52	96.88	93.33	100	92.86	75	96.43	80.56	65.22	50	55.55	97.30

From this study, we conclude that smaller sampling frequencies are more suited to situations where less computation is needed. With $f = 5$ Hz, it took ≈93% less time to train the dataset and ≈72% less time to test all samples, while just losing 0.93% of accuracy. Curiously, with $f = 50$ Hz and $f = 25$ Hz, the accuracy actually improved by 0.7%. Another interesting conclusion is the bigger accuracy some activities get on reduced frequencies, particularly both *ascending stairs* and *descending stairs*. This could be related to some noisy data being eliminated.

Our Own Dataset. The goal of this study is to support our conclusions in earlier experiments and the performance of kNN-LSH with a different dataset. We also performed the experiments in different sampling frequencies. Since our dataset was recorded using a frequency of 5 Hz (i.e., data was recorded each 200 ms), we applied a filter, created for the last study, to its data in order to progressively reduce the sampling frequency.

Each experiment was conducted in the same conditions ($overlap = 10\%$, $k = 1$, $r = 10$, $l = 20$) with k-NN and LSH k-NN classifiers. Similar to the last study, we start with a window size of 45 for 5 Hz and reduce it to preserve the same timespan. Therefore, the number of windows (118) stays the same for each one of the experiment. Table 6 shows kNN and kNN-LSH performance with our dataset by training and testing time, as well as accuracy per activity.

Table 6. Our own dataset performance with kNN and kNN-LSH with different frequencies

f (Hz)	Classifier $k=1$	Train time (s)	Test Time (s)	Accuracy (%) All	Walking	Standing	Desc. stairs	Asc. stairs	Running (jogging)	Sitting	Jumping	Running (sprint)
5	k-NN	0.548	0.134	89.66	100	100	0	100	66.67	100	100	100
	LSH k-NN	0.527	0.06	**96.55**	100	100	100	100	100	100	100	50
4	k-NN	0.481	0.081	93.10	100	100	100	100	66.67	100	100	100
	LSH k-NN	0.524	0.047	**96.55**	100	100	100	100	100	100	100	50
2	k-NN	0.399	0.08	89.66	100	100	0	100	66.67	100	100	100
	LSH k-NN	0.438	0.042	**96.55**	100	100	100	100	100	100	100	50
1	k-NN	0.386	0.069	86.21	100	100	0	100	50	100	100	100
	LSH k-NN	0.413	0.03	**96.55**	100	100	100	100	100	100	100	50

We can observe how kNN-LSH maintains its accuracy on each different frequency, while kNN offers some variations. Also, kNN-LSH presents a better accuracy on every single experiment. However, it should be noted the kNN surpasses kNN-LSH on one of the activities, *running (sprint)*. Focusing on computing performance, kNN is consistently faster on $f > 5$. However, kNN-LSH spends $\approx 50\%$ less time to classify all samples on every experiment.

4.2   Android Studies

This section covers our studies using a smartphone. Every experiment was performed on a Samsung Galaxy J5 (2017) with a 64-bit Octa Core Processor (1.6 GHz) and 2 GB of RAM, running Android 7.0 (Nougat).

Energy Consumption. In this study, we experimented our application with live recognition on the pocket, while doing daily activities, for 30 min and checked how much battery the device had lost. We also detected how much time had spent between each change in remaining battery percentage. For each experiment, the battery started with 100% and the screen remained on with the lowest brightness, while cellular data, Wi-Fi, GPS and Bluetooth were all turned off. We tested both kNN and kNN-LSH on 5 Hz. It should be noted the window size represents a time span of 9 s. The goal of this study is to understand if our proposed kNN-LSH is suited for a live application and the impact of sensor collection on the energy consumed. Table 7 shows the time span for each change in battery in minutes and seconds.

Table 7. kNN and kNN-LSH impact on battery for 30 min

Remaining battery (%)	Time span (minutes:seconds)	
	kNN	kNN-LSH
99	09:20	14:15
98	00:18:40	00:25:55

From this study, we conclude that kNN-LSH spends less energy than kNN in live activity recognition, saving ≈35% of the battery.

5 Conclusion

This paper presented a smartphone-based human activity recognition (HAR) system focused on the use of kNN for classifying activities in real-time. The paper includes studies about the energy consumption and accuracy of four kNN implementations and proposes the use of an LSH-based kNN (kNN-LSH) in order to reduce execution time and energy consumption, while maintaining similar or even better accuracy. Our experiments show that applying LSH to kNN with optimal window sizes, sampling frequency, k and overlap, can contribute significantly for developing HAR-based mobile applications by reducing the overall computation and energy spent.

The kNN-LSH was able to classify each sliding window of samples acquired from the smartphone sensors in ≈8.7 and 10 ms on average with offline training and online training, respectively. This results in an ≈35% less time than using a linear KNN implementation (with a feature space of 91 dimensions and with 287 points), with the cost of just losing 3.49% in terms of accuracy.

We further extended our kNN-LSH studies by reducing the sampling frequency of sensing acquisition. Reducing the sampling frequency from 100 Hz to 5 Hz and to 1 Hz results in execution time and energy consumption improvements and maintains acceptable accuracy (89.31% and 85.52%, respectively) when considering the PAMAP2 dataset. The experiments conducted with our dataset further sustain our conclusions, as kNN-LSH performed significantly better than kNN, achieving always ≈50% less time to classify and higher accuracy (96.55% instead of 89.66%). Once again, reducing the sampling frequency (in this cases from 5 Hz to 1 Hz) did not impact the accuracy on kNN-LSH.

As future work, we plan to extend the studies considering incremental/online learning and to research techniques to deal with the maximum size of the feature space constraint imposed by kNN prototype implementations.

References

1. de la Concepción, M.A.A., Morillo, L.M.S., García, J.A.A., González-Abril, L.: Mobile activity recognition and fall detection system for elderly people using Ameva algorithm. Pervasive Mob. Comput. **34**, 3–13 (2017)
2. Anguita, D., Ghio, A., Oneto, L., Parra, X., Reyes-Ortiz, J.L.: Training computationally efficient smartphone-based human activity recognition models. In: Mladenov, V., Koprinkova-Hristova, P., Palm, G., Villa, A.E.P., Appollini, B., Kasabov, N. (eds.) ICANN 2013. LNCS, vol. 8131, pp. 426–433. Springer, Heidelberg (2013). https://doi.org/10.1007/978-3-642-40728-4_54
3. Bifet, A., Gavaldà, R.: Learning from time-changing data with adaptive windowing. In: Proceedings of the 2007 SIAM International Conference on Data Mining, pp. 443–448 (2007)

4. Bifet, A., Holmes, G., Kirkby, R., Pfahringer, B.: MOA: massive online analysis. J. Mach. Learn. Res. **11**, 1601–1604 (2010)
5. Bifet, A., Pfahringer, B., Read, J., Holmes, G.: Efficient data stream classification via probabilistic adaptive windows. In: Proceedings of the 28th Annual ACM Symposium on Applied Computing - SAC 2013, p. 801 (2013)
6. Datar, M., Immorlica, N., Indyk, P., Mirrokni, V.S.: Locality-sensitive hashing scheme based on p-stable distributions. In: Proceedings of the Twentieth Annual Symposium on Computational Geometry - SCG 2004, p. 253 (2004)
7. Horta, A., Fonseca, S., Truninger, M., Nobre, N., Correia, A.: Mobile phones, batteries and power consumption: an analysis of social practices in Portugal. Energy Res. Soc. Sci. **13**, 15–23 (2016)
8. Indyk, P., Motwani, R.: Approximate nearest neighbors: towards removing the curse of dimensionality. In: Proceedings of the Thirtieth Annual ACM Symposium on Theory of Computing, pp. 604–613. ACM (1998)
9. Lane, N., et al.: BeWell: a smartphone application to monitor, model and promote wellbeing. In: Proceedings of the 5th International ICST Conference on Pervasive Computing Technologies for Healthcare, January 2011
10. Lara, O.D., Labrador, M.A.: A mobile platform for real-time human activity recognition. In: 2012 IEEE Consumer Communications and Networking Conference (CCNC), pp. 667–671 (2012)
11. Lara, O.D., Labrador, M.A.: A survey on human activity recognition using wearable sensors. IEEE Commun. Surv. Tutorials **15**(3), 1192–1209 (2013)
12. Li, F., Shirahama, K., Nisar, M.A., Köping, L., Grzegorzek, M.: Comparison of feature learning methods for human activity recognition using wearable sensors. Sensors **18**(2), 1–22 (2018). (Switzerland)
13. Liang, Y., Zhou, X., Yu, Z., Guo, B.: Energy-efficient motion related activity recognition on mobile devices for pervasive healthcare. Mob. Netw. Appl. **19**(3), 303–317 (2014)
14. Morillo, L., Gonzalez-Abril, L., Ramirez, J., de la Concepcion, M.: Low energy physical activity recognition system on smartphones. Sensors **15**(3), 5163–5196 (2015)
15. Pérez-Torres, R., Torres-Huitzil, C., Galeana-Zapién, H.: Power management techniques in smartphone-based mobility sensing systems: a survey. Pervasive Mob. Comput. **31**, 1–21 (2016)
16. Reiss, A., Stricker, D.: Introducing a new benchmarked dataset for activity monitoring. In: Proceedings - International Symposium on Wearable Computers, ISWC, pp. 108–109 (2012)
17. Santos, A.C., Cardoso, J.M.P., Ferreira, D.R., Diniz, P.C., Chaínho, P.: Providing user context for mobile and social networking applications. Pervasive Mob. Comput. **6**(3), 324–341 (2010)
18. Wang, Y., et al.: A framework of energy efficient mobile sensing for automatic user state recognition. In: MobiSys, pp. 179–192 (2009)
19. Yan, Z., Subbaraju, V., Chakraborty, D., Misra, A., Aberer, K.: Energy-efficient continuous activity recognition on mobile phones: an activity-adaptive approach. In: Proceedings - International Symposium on Wearable Computers, ISWC, pp. 17–24. IEEE, June 2012
20. Zheng, L., et al.: A novel energy-efficient approach for human activity recognition. Sensors **17**(9), 2064 (2017)

A Divide and Conquer Approach to Automatic Music Transcription Using Neural Networks

André Gil[1], Carlos Grilo[1,2(✉)], Gustavo Reis[1,2],
and Patrício Domingues[1,2,3]

[1] School of Technology and Management, Polytechnic Institute of Leiria,
Leiria, Portugal
2151630@my.ipleiria.pt, {carlos.grilo, gustavo.reis,
patricio.domingues}@ipleiria.pt
[2] CIIC, Polytechnic Institute of Leiria, Leiria, Portugal
[3] Instituto de Telecomunicações, Lisbon, Portugal

Abstract. This paper describes a new approach for the automatic music transcription problem. We take advantage of the *divide and conquer* design paradigm and create several artificial neural networks, each one responsible for transcribing one musical note. This way, we depart from the traditional approach which resorts to a single classifier for transcribing all musical notes. To further improve results, an additional post-processing stage using artificial neural networks with the same design paradigm is also proposed. This last stage comprises three main steps: (1) *fix notes duration*, (2) *fix notes duration regarding onsets* and (3) *fix onsets*. The obtained results show that these steps were essential to improve the final transcription. We also compare our results with existing neural network-based approaches. Our approach is able to surpass current state-of-the-art works in frame-based results and, at the same time, reach similar results in onset only, thus demonstrating its viability.

Keywords: Automatic music transcription · Multi-pitch estimation · Artificial neural networks

1 Introduction

Automatic music transcription (AMT) consists in detecting the notes being played in a musical piece, via a machine. This problem is comprised of several sub-problems, which makes a solution for it hard to find. In this work, we mainly focus on the variant called multi-pitch estimation. Multi-pitch estimation consists in identifying the pitched notes present in a polyphonic musical piece. A common approach to this problem is to split a musical piece into smaller chunks, referred to as *frames*, and then, estimate the pitch(es) present in each frame (see Fig. 1).

We apply artificial neural networks (ANNs) to tackle the multi-pitch estimation problem. ANNs have been applied in several different types of problems as, for example, object recognition, image segmentation, speech recognition, text-to-speech synthesis, and, also, music transcription [1–4].

© Springer Nature Switzerland AG 2019
P. Moura Oliveira et al. (Eds.): EPIA 2019, LNAI 11805, pp. 220–231, 2019.
https://doi.org/10.1007/978-3-030-30244-3_19

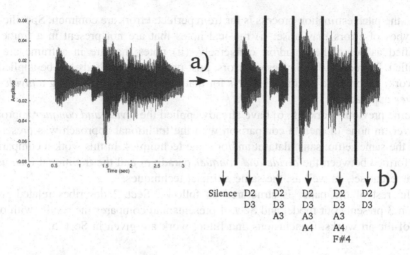

Silence D2 D2 D2 D2 D2
         D3 D3 D3 D3 D3
             A3 A3 A3
             A4 A4
                 F#4

Fig. 1. A common approach to tackle the multi-pitch estimation problem. (a) A musical piece is split into frames. (b) The pitch(es) is estimated for each frame.

The traditional approach to the AMT problem, especially when ANNs are applied, consists in having a single module/network that is responsible for detecting and transcribing all the musical notes in each frame (see Fig. 2a) [2–4]. In this work we use a *divide and conquer* approach which translates into using several networks, referred to as *classifiers*, each one responsible for detecting and transcribing one musical note only (see Fig. 2b). This approach aims at dividing the AMT problem into smaller subproblems, hopefully, easier to solve, possibly boosting the performance of the whole AMT system.

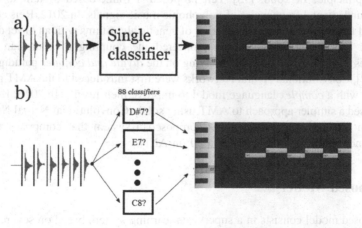

Fig. 2. Representation of (a) the traditional approach for the AMT problem, where a single classifier is responsible for transcribing all musical notes and (b) the *divide and conquer* approach, where several classifiers are used, each one responsible for identifying only one note.

As the pitch estimation process is far from perfect, errors are common. Specifically, two types of errors may arise: (i) musical notes that are not present in a frame are identified as being there and/or, conversely, (ii) notes that are in a frame are not identified. To reduce these types of errors, post-processing methods can be applied. In this work, we propose additional ANNs for that purpose, again following a *divide and conquer* approach.

Some previous works [5, 6] have already applied the *divide and conquer* approach, however, in none of them a comparison with the traditional approach was presented, using the same setup: same dataset and/or same techniques. In this work a comparison is performed between the *divide and conquer* paradigm and the traditional one, using the same dataset, as well as, the same artificial techniques.

The rest of the paper is structured as follows: Sect. 2 describes related work. Section 3 presents our model and Sect. 4 presents and compares the results with other state-of-the-art works. Conclusions and future work are given in Sect. 5.

2   Related Work

Since the first polyphonic music transcription system [7], several approaches have been presented. In 1992, Lea [8] proposed a method that iteratively extracted the predominant peaks. In 2000, Bello and Sandler [9] proposed a simple polyphonic music transcription system using a *blackboard system*. In 2003, Klapuri et al. [10] introduced an algorithm based on harmonicity and spectral smoothness. Also, in 2003 [11], the non-negative matrix factorization technique was introduced for the first time to the AMT problem. In 2004, Moorer [5] introduced for the first time the *divide and conquer* design paradigm to the AMT field, using Artificial Neural Networks. In 2007, Emiya et al. [12] designed a multi-pitch estimation system based on the likelihood maximization principle. In 2008, [13] Yeh proposed a frame-based system to estimate multiple fundamental frequencies of polyphonic music signals. In 2012, Reis et al. [14] introduced for the first time a combination of genetic algorithms with an onset detection algorithm. In 2016, Leite et al. [6] pioneered the coupling of Cartesian Genetic Algorithms with the AMT field, also relying on the *divide and conquer* paradigm. Also in 2016 [2], Convolutional Neural Networks were first introduced to the AMT problem, combined with a *complex* language model to improve their results. In 2016, Kelz et al. [3] proposed a simpler approach to AMT using solely Convolutional Neural Networks. Finally, in 2018, Hawthorne et al. [4] proposed a system that comprises an onset detector and a multi-pitch estimator based on ANNs.

3   Proposed Model

The proposed model consists in a supervised learning system based on several ANNs, each one responsible for transcribing one musical note, resulting in a total of 88 ANNs per dataset, corresponding to the keys in a grand piano. In this work, we have applied classic Multi-Layer Perceptron Neural Networks, instead of more recent techniques as the ones used in Deep Learning, in order to get baseline results. The model is comprised by three sequential main stages: (1) pre-processing, (2) classification and (3) post-processing. In the following sections, a deeper explanation of each is presented.

3.1 Pre-processing

The pre-processing stage is responsible for splitting the musical pieces into frames and also for converting each frame to the frequency domain, using the Fast Fourier Transform (FFT). Although each frame is comprised of 4096 samples, only the first half is taken into account since the second half of the signal mirrors the first half.

Regarding the ANNs training process, a fundamental key point to consider is the quality of the data. Hence, this stage is responsible for applying two additional sequential transformations used solely in the training set: (i) removal of meaningless data, such as frames with silence and (ii) adapting the ratio between frames with and without the note that should be identified by each classifier, more specifically, 20% of frames with the given note and 80% frames without it (see Fig. 3).

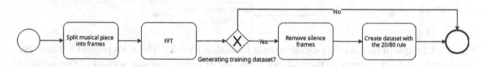

Fig. 3. Transformations applied during the pre-processing stage.

3.2 Classification

The classification stage is where the actual transcription process starts. The resulting data from the pre-processing stage is inserted into this stage so that the note can be detected. As already mentioned, we use the divide and conquer approach, thus, 88 classifiers were created, each one responsible for transcribing one note (see Fig. 2b).

Each classifier comprises five hidden layers with 256, 128, 64, 32 and 8 units, respectively, and an output layer with one unit (*yes* or *no* output). The hidden layers apply the *leaky relu* activation function, while the output layer uses the *sigmoid* function. During the training phase, the optimizer chosen was *Adam* [15] combined with a *learning rate* of 1×10^{-6} and the *cross-entropy* loss function. Also, the following optimization techniques were applied: *data shuffling* [18]; *dropout* [16] with a probability of 0.15; *noisy gradients* [17] with a probability of 0.70 and a standard deviation of 0.05.

3.3 Post-processing

As mentioned earlier, post-processing methods can be applied to correct errors from the classification process. In this work, we use three different types of post-processing methods, labeled as: (i) step 1 - fix notes duration, (ii) step 2 - fix notes duration according to onsets and (iii) step 3 - fix notes onset. Each type applies the *divide and conquer* approach, where an ANN is created to post-process one musical note only, resulting on 88 ANNs per post-processing step. This means that the whole post-processing stage comprises $88 \times 3 = 264$ ANNs. In the topics that follow, we detail each post-processing type.

Step 1 - Fix notes duration

Music is a time-series phenomenon. By this, we mean that a given event is closely related to a previous and/or a following one. The first post-processing step aims at incorporating that sense of time in the transcription process. Thus, each ANN in this step receives as input the output of the corresponding note classifier, from the classification stage, as well as, the output for some preceding and following frames, and gives as output a *yes* or *no* answer. This way, it assesses whether the middle frame of the sequence contains the specific note or not. See Fig. 4, below, for an example.

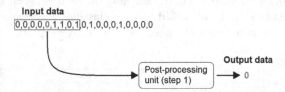

Fig. 4. Example of how a post-processing unit from step 1 works. The 1's represent a frame that was identified with a specific musical note and the 0's the opposite scenario. The squared window around a portion of the input data represents the sequence given to the post-processing unit. The number in the middle of that window, represents the frame that the unit is trying to predict. Finally, the number represented below the *output data* illustrates the actual prediction from the post-processing unit.

Note that during the post-processing, the squared window represented in the figure above, will slide to the right, one frame at a time, until the last frame, and for each sequence contained on that window, an output prediction is given for the middle frame. When finished, the whole set of new predictions represents the resultant transcription of the system (see Fig. 5).

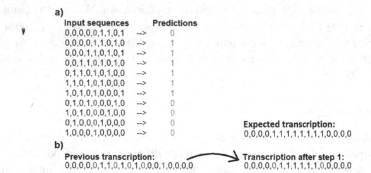

Fig. 5. Representation of all the sequences given to step 1, regarding the previous example. The numbers in red represent wrongly transcribed frames. (a) All the input sequences given to the unit and its resultant predictions. (b) Representation of the previous and new transcription.

It is important to point out that, the sequences given to a post-processing unit do not contain binary data (only zeros or ones) but, instead, values between 0 and 1 (because the classifiers' output unit use the sigmoid activation function). However, for ease of understanding all the examples given in this section represent those values as binary data.

Step 2 - Fix notes duration according to onsets

For further improvement, an additional post-processing step was created (see Fig. 6). This new step is like the previous one since it receives as input a sequence of previously transcribed frames from step 1 and it also tries to predict the possible transcription for the middle frame of that sequence. However, it also receives two additional sequences: one sequence with the original transcription from the classification stage and another one based on the output of an onset detector algorithm [19]. An onset consists in the start time of a musical note.

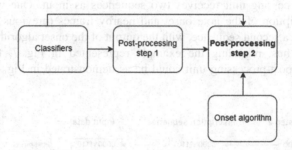

Fig. 6. Representation of the three different sequences received by step 2 post-processing units.

The rationale behind the concept of receiving the original transcription from the classification stage is based on *stacked* systems [20], where an additional system receives as input the output of the previous step, as well as, the original input.

Note that the onset detector algorithm applied is not perfect and is also not able to distinguish between onsets of different musical notes. Thus, these post-processing units need to deal with problems like: (i) falsely and missing detected onsets and (ii) onsets of other musical notes.

Step 3 - Fix notes onset

To refine our model in terms of onset detection, an additional post-processing step was added. In this step, only the frames predicted as note onsets are targeted. Specifically, for each predicted note onset, these post-processing units decide whether a readjustment is needed or not. Therefore, they can output three possible transformations: *SHIFT LEFT*, *ACCEPT* and *SHIFT RIGHT*. An example of the three possible transformations is shown in Fig. 7.

226   A. Gil et al.

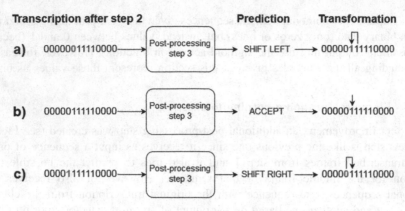

Fig. 7. Three possible transformations in step 3 of the post-processing stage.

This post-processing unit receives two sequences as input. One with the corresponding transcription of the note onset and nearby frames (previous and following four frames), and a second sequence, with the output of the onset algorithm, used in the previous step. Thus, regarding the example represented in Fig. 7, the input data received by this post-processing unit could be as demonstrated in Fig. 8:

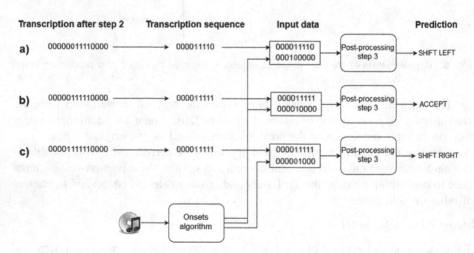

Fig. 8. Illustration of the given input data with all three types of possible transformations. (a) Scenario where the note onset should be readjusted to one frame before. (b) Scenario where the onset is considered already correct. (c) Scenario where the onset should be shifted to one frame after.

4 Results

In this section, results and a comparison with similar techniques used in other state-of-the-art works are presented. First, the dataset is described, followed by the metrics used for comparing our approach. Then, the results obtained are shown, and finally, a comparison with other research works is given.

4.1 Dataset

To be able to compare our approach with already existent ones, we use the *Configuration 1* dataset from [2], based on MAPS [21]. This dataset comprises four folds, each one containing a different combination of musical pieces, with 216 musical pieces in the training set and 54 pieces in the testing set. This means that, for each fold, a transcription system comprised of 88 ANNs for the classification stage and 264 ANNs (88 × 3) for the post-processing stage, need to be created.

4.2 Metrics

We use both frame-based and note-based metrics [22] to compare our model. Frame-based metrics consists on evaluating frame-by-frame the final transcription, whereas note-based consists on evaluating each transcribed musical note by considering its pitch and its onset. Regarding the note onset, we also assume a tolerance of ± 50 ms.

We use *precision*, *recall* and *f-measure* for both frame-based and note-based evaluation metrics. Mathematically, these metrics can be expressed as:

$$Precision\,(P) = \frac{TP}{TP+FP} \tag{1}$$

$$Recall\,(R)\ = \frac{TP}{TP+FN} \tag{2}$$

$$F\text{-}measure\,(F)\ = \frac{2 \times P \times R}{P+R}, \tag{3}$$

where TP represents true positives, which consist on correctly identified frames/notes, FP represents false positives, which consist on wrongly detected frames/notes and FN represents false negatives, which consist on missed detected frames/notes.

4.3 Results and Comparison

The obtained results from our model, per each step are presented in Table 1, below.

Table 1. Obtained results per each step.

Stage/step	Frame-based (F)	Note-based (F)
Classifiers	66.89	33.08
Post-processing step 1 - Fix notes duration	79.78 (+12.89)	51.61 (+18.53)
Post-processing step 2 - Fix notes duration according to onsets	80.23 (+0.45)	55.97 (+4.36)
Post-processing step 3 - Fix onsets	80.47 (+0.24)	61.64 (+5.67)

From the table above, we may conclude that the post-processing stage played an essential role in the improvement of the transcription results. The frame-based metrics were improved by an amount of 13.58% and the note-based by 28.56%. To better evaluate how distant our system is from the expected transcription, a portion of the resultant and expected transcription from the musical piece *BMW 846 Prelude in C Major* from J. S. Bach is shown in Fig. 9.

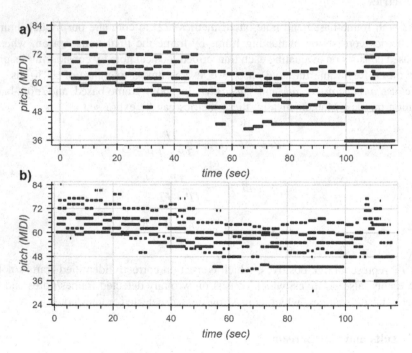

Fig. 9. Portion of the expected and resulting transcription of the *BMW 847 Prelude in C Major*. (a) Expected transcription. (b) Resulting transcription.

To compare our results, two state-of-the-art works were chosen: [7] and [8]. Both apply the same dataset as well as the same type of ANNs. The comparison is shown in Table 2.

Table 2. Comparison with two other state-of-the-art works.

Approach	Frame-based			Note-based		
	P	R	F	P	R	F
ANN [7]	65.66	70.34	67.92	**62.62**	**63.75**	**63.179**
ANN [8]	76.63	70.12	73.11	–	–	–
Ours	**84.94**	**76.46**	**80.47**	61.81	61.54	61.64

From the table above, one can conclude that our approach significantly surpasses both works in frame-based metrics, while reaching similar results in note-based.

To assess our approach against more recent artificial intelligence techniques such as Recurrent Neural Networks (RNNs) or Convolutional Neural Networks (CNNs), we further compare it to three other systems, taking advantage of the fact that these three systems have also used the same dataset, thus making the comparison feasible. Table 3 encompasses the results from all the approaches.

Table 3. Comparison with works that apply more recent types of artificial neural networks.

Approach	Frame-based			Note-based		
	P	R	F	P	R	F
RNN [7]	67.89	70.66	69.25	64.64	65.85	65.24
CNN [7]	72.45	76.56	74.45	**67.75**	**66.36**	**67.05**
CNN [8]	80.19	**78.66**	79.33	–	–	–
Ours	**84.94**	76.46	**80.47**	61.81	61.54	61.64

Even when our approach is compared with works that implement more recent types of ANNs, it still yields higher frame-based metrics than those systems, and, at the same time, it reaches comparable results in note-based metrics. This demonstrates the effectiveness of our approach.

5   Conclusions and Future Work

In this paper, we tackled the AMT problem using a *divide and conquer* approach. The obtained results show that this is a promising path for tackling the AMT problem, since they surpassed current state-of-the-art works in frame-based metrics and reach similar metrics in note-based, even when compared with other systems that apply more recent types of artificial neural networks. The use of artificial neural networks as post-processing units demonstrated to be essential for improving the whole performance of the system. In the future, a comparison could be done between post-processing units that take advantage of artificial neural networks and traditional statistical methods, such as Hidden Markov Models, in order to understand which one is better.

To conclude, there is still plenty of space for future work. For instance, in the case of the classifiers, other techniques could be used, like Recurrent Neural Networks or Convolutional Neural Networks. In addition, an improved version of the onset algorithm could also be used. Thus, a possible solution could be the creation of an additional ANN to filter false positives from this original onset algorithm, or, instead, create an onset algorithm from-scratch using deep learning techniques, like some authors propose [23].

References

1. Schmidhuber, J.: Deep learning in neural networks: an overview. Neural Netw. **61**, 85–117 (2015)
2. Sigtia, S., Benetos, E., Dixon, S.: An end-to-end neural network for polyphonic piano music transcription. IEEE/ACM Trans. Audio Speech Lang. Process. **24**(5), 927–939 (2016)
3. Kelz, D., Korzeniowski, B., Arzt, W.: On the potential of simple framewise approaches to piano transcription. In: 17th International Society for Music Information Retrieval Conference (2016)
4. Hawthorne, C., et al.: Onsets and frames: dual-objective piano transcription. arXiv preprint arXiv:1710.11153 (2017)
5. Marolt, M.: A connectionist approach to automatic transcription of polyphonic piano music. IEEE Trans. Multimed. **6**, 439–449 (2004)
6. Inácio, T., Miragaia, R., Reis, G., Grilo, C., Fernandéz, F.: Cartesian genetic programming applied to pitch estimation of piano notes. In: 2016 IEEE Symposium Series on Computational Intelligence, pp. 1–7 (2016)
7. Moorer, J.A.: On the segmentation and analysis of continuous musical sound by digital computer (1975)
8. Lea, A.P.: Auditory modeling of vowel perception. Ph.D. thesis, University of Nottingham, United Kingdom (1992)
9. Bello, J.P., Sandler, M.: Blackboard system and top-down processing for the transcription of simple polyphonic music. In: Proceedings of the COST G-6 Conference on Digital Audio Effects, pp. 7–9 (2000)
10. Klapuri, A.P.: Multiple fundamental frequency estimation based on harmonicity and spectral smoothness. IEEE Trans. Speech Audio Process. **11**(6), 804–816 (2003)
11. Smaragdis, P., Brown, J.C.: Non-negative matrix factorization for polyphonic music transcription. In: 2003 IEEE Workshop on Applications of Signal Processing to Audio and Acoustics, pp. 177–180 (2003)
12. Emiya, V., Badeau, R., David, B.: Multipitch estimation of quasi-harmonic sounds in colored noise. In: 10th International Conference on Digital Audio Effects (2007)
13. Yeh, C.: Multiple fundamental frequency estimation of polyphonic recordings. Ph.D. thesis, University Paris, France (2008)
14. Reis, G.M.J.D.: Una aproximación genética a la transcripción automática de música. Ph.D. thesis, University of Extremadura, Spain (2012)
15. Kingma, D.P., Ba, J.: Adam: a method for stochastic optimization. arXiv preprint arXiv: 1412.6980 (2014)
16. Srivastava, N., Hinton, G., Krizhevsky, A., Sutskever, I., Salakhutdinov, R.: Dropout: a simple way to prevent neural networks from overfitting. J. Mach. Learn. Res. **15**(1), 1929–1958 (2014)

17. Neelakantan, A., et al.: Adding gradient noise improves learning for very deep networks. arXiv preprint arXiv:1511.06807 (2015)
18. Montavon, G., Orr, Geneviève B., Müller, K.-R. (eds.): Neural Networks: Tricks of the Trade. LNCS, vol. 7700. Springer, Heidelberg (2012). https://doi.org/10.1007/978-3-642-35289-8
19. Martins, L.G.P.M.: A computational framework for sound segregation in music signals. Ph. D. thesis, University of Porto, Portugal (2008)
20. Zhang, H., et al.: StackGAN: text to photo-realistic image synthesis with stacked generative adversarial networks. In: Proceedings of the IEEE International Conference on Computer Vision, pp. 5907–5915 (2017)
21. Emiya, V., Badeau, R., David, B.: Multipitch estimation of piano sounds using a new probabilistic spectral smoothness principle. IEEE Trans. Audio Speech Lang. Process. **18**(6), 1643–1654 (2010)
22. Bay, M., Ehmann, A.F., Downie, J.S.: Evaluation of multiple-F0 estimation and tracking systems. In: The International Society of Music Information Retrieval, pp. 315–320 (2009)
23. Eyben, F., Böck, S., Schuller, B., Graves, A.: Universal onset detection with bidirectional long-short term memory neural networks. In: Proceedings 11th International Society for Music Information Retrieval Conference, pp. 589–594 (2010)

An Adaptive and Transferable Dialog Management System for Social Aware Task Execution

Antonio Capela, Samuel Mascarenhas, Pedro A. Santos[iD],
and Manuel Lopes[✉][iD]

Instituto Superior Técnico, INESC-ID, Lisboa, Portugal
manuel.lopes@tecnico.ulisboa.pt

Abstract. Efficient and acceptable AI agents need to interact and dialog with their users taking into account not just task efficiency but also social preferences in the interaction. In this work we introduce a model for generating dialog in different scenarios. At the base of the system is a dialog management based on POMDP (Partially Observable Markov Decision Process) models. This task specific component can by itself be used to execute the task. We then introduce another level, and define the interface between the levels, to be able to complement the dialog generated to take into account the social preferences of interaction of each particular user. We show how a particular parameterization of the state allows to learn a personalised policy. We further show that with our formalism a social policy learned for a particular user can then be used in other similar tasks without requiring further learning. We present several simulations showing how we can plan multiple tasks, learn social policies and that those policies can be transferred.

Keywords: Social aware agents · Dialog management ·
Adaptive learning · User adaptation · Task transfer

1 Introduction

A Spoken dialog system (SDS) is a computer system allowing people to achieve a task by interacting via spoken language to achieve their goals. SDSs are an increasingly prominent part of our society, we see them in costumer support, intelligent home appliances, automated personal assistants, and much more. The relatively recent increase in popularity of SDS makes them a very interesting topic to study [9].

With the current advances in AI the number of situations where we will be interacting with autonomous agents is expected to rise in the future. One example would be fully autonomous vehicles that provide taxi services. In this situation, how should an autonomous taxi interact with passengers from a social perspective? What happens when a person tries to abide by the same social norms he or she would when interacting with a human cab driver but the system

© Springer Nature Switzerland AG 2019
P. Moura Oliveira et al. (Eds.): EPIA 2019, LNAI 11805, pp. 232–243, 2019.
https://doi.org/10.1007/978-3-030-30244-3_20

is unable to reciprocate? In that case, the interaction will likely not be as pleasant when compared to an autonomous driver that is capable of understanding and follow the same social conventions. These implicit conventions are described in sociological theories of interaction such as the highly influential Politeness theory [3]. This theory postulates that people use specific politeness strategies when communicating in order to maintain each others social and moral standing, also referred to as the concept of 'face' in the theory. Moreover, rational agents, according to the theory, choose what they perceive to be the most effective strategies to avoid losing their face. This choice is non-trivial as, for instance, an overuse of the same strategy might come across as insincere and neglectful of the other person.

With the rise of smart speakers like Amazon Alexa, we are currently witnessing a renewed interest in spoken dialogue systems. The great progress made in speech recognition and speech synthesis opens up the potential for such systems to engage with their users in novel ways that go beyond simple information exchange. Moreover, the research fields of Intelligent Virtual Agents and Social Robotics are also highly invested in developing dialogue systems with social capabilities. The main reason is that there are several benefits in having a dialogue system that is capable of engaging in social dialogue with humans [1]. Not only this type of dialogue can make the interaction feel more enjoyable but it also can contribute to a greater feeling of trust in the system [2]. This is because human-human communication is greatly affected by how well the interlocutors are able to establish rapport with each other and studies have shown that the same applies to human-agent communication [4,6]. In fact, in scenarios that involve the disclosure of sensitive information, such as a medical interview, people can feel even more comfortable when interacting with a virtual agent that is fully autonomous rather than one that is being operated by a human [5].

Initial strategies to model SDSs were based around creating a Finite State Automaton (FSA)[8,10], which can be represented as a graph where the nodes represent prompts given by the machine and the links give the user's possible responses. In order to avoid errors in automatic speech recognition (ASR), the possible responses must be very limited, and the resulting dialogues could be very frustrating to the users. Different strategies appeared to deal with this but, as shown by Williams and Young [11], most fall under the POMDP framework.

In this paper we develop a machine capable of doing simple social tasks taking in consideration the social context and preferences of each user. To do this the model will contain the usual POMDP model that is indifferent to the social implications of the conversation, only focused on the user's goals, with an additional layer is built on top of it, that is responsible for adding actions of social character, like greeting or thanking. This layer avoids using the internal structure of the POMDP in order to be possible to transfer it to a different problem where it would be able to perform without extra learning necessary.

This approach differs from existing work because of the separation between the task level planing (the instrumental goal), handled by a POMDP, and the social planing (social goal), handled by a layer on top of that.

Due to our contributed architectural choices and the defined interfaces between the different state representation, it is possible to use Reinforcement learning on the social layer to learn the social context and preferences of the user and transfer the social policy between different tasks.

2 Computational Model

The proposed decision architecture, shown in Fig. 1, is divided into two main components. At the core, we have a model for the conversation that ignores social context and its only focus is on completing the task at hand. The POMDP model is used for this effect. This layer is task specific and normally all its parameters can be hand-tuned.

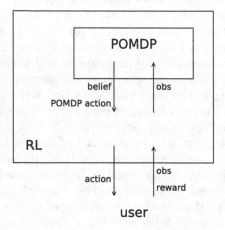

Fig. 1. Architecture of the model. At the core we have a POMDP responsible to generate a task specific dialog. At the top layer we have an RL agent that learns social policies that enhances the POMDP policy to take into account the social preferences of the users. An interface between the two levels was develop to ensure that the RL agent can learn and that its policy can be transferred to other tasks.

On top of that, we build a system that is responsible for adding the social interactions to accommodate the user. This system will use reinforcement learning to find the optimal policy, so we'll refer to it as the RL layer. This component is not task specific but is instead user specific. It will learn how each user prefers its interactions.

A great challenge is to provide a clear interface between the task and social levels to ensure that: (i) each component can work reliably; (ii) the interface is as simple as possible; (iii) the system can adapt to each user; (iv) user dependent knowledge can be transferred.

With these goals in mind we defined the following interface. The RL layer will receive information about the change in belief of the POMDP because we want to know if the last part of the dialog changed the belief about the task. It also receives the optimal action proposed by the POMDP that the RL level can choose to accept or to overwrite it with a social action. The reason for this is that if the belief changed in the last interaction maybe the agent is in the middle of asking some task specific information and so we should not interrupt the exchange with social cues. For instance if the belief grew to increase the probability of the task being to serve a beer, we should not interrupt the process with a comment on the weather before asking if it is with or without alcohol. The RL layer will then observe the response from the user and, if it kept the action from the POMDP, it will relay it to the POMDP and update the belief.

We now go into more detail how these parts work.

2.1   Mathematical Models

POMDP - for Dialog Management. A Partially Observable Markov Decision Process (POMDP) is a mathematical framework that can be used to model sequential decision problems where only partial information on the state of the environment is available to the agent. A POMDP is formally defined by the tuple $(S, A_m, T, R, O, Z, \lambda, b_0)$, where:

- S is the set of states
- A_m is the set of action the agent may take
- T defines a transition probability $p(s'|s, a_m)$
- R defines the expected reward $r(s, a_m)$
- O is the set of observations
- Z defines the observation probability $p(o|s', a_m)$
- λ is a geometric discount factor $0 \leq \lambda \leq 1$
- $b_0(s)$ is the initial state distribution.

At each time step t, the environment is in some state s. The agent chooses an action a_m that causes the environment to transition to state s' with probability $p(s'|s, a_m)$. Finally, the agent receives an observation o with probability $p(o|s', a_m)$ and a reward r equal to $r(s, a_m)$.

A useful quantity to keep track is the probability distribution over the states, known as the belief (b). This quantity can be updated according to equation Eq. (1), where $p(o'|a_m, b_t)$ is a normalising constant.

$$
\begin{aligned}
b_{t+1}(s') &= p(s'|o', a_m, b_t) \\
&= \frac{p(o'|s', a_m, b_t)p(s'|a_m, b_t)}{p(o'|a_m, b_t)} \\
&= \frac{p(o'|s', a) \sum_{s \in S} p(s'|a_m, b_t, s)p(s|a_m, b_t)}{p(o'|a_m, b_t)} \\
&= \frac{p(o'|s', a) \sum_{s \in S} p(s'|s, a_m)b_t(s)}{p(o'|a_m, b_t)}
\end{aligned}
\tag{1}
$$

The goal of the agent is to maximise the cumulative, infinite-horizon, discounted reward Eq. (2):

$$\Theta = \sum_{t=0}^{\infty} \lambda^t r_t \tag{2}$$

The policy that maximises the expected return, depends on the complete history of the dialog. However, the belief has a useful property that it is the complete summary of the dialog history. Formally, given an initial belief b_0 and a history $\{a_1, o_1, a_2, o_2, ...\}$, the belief provides a sufficient statistic. As a result, the policy can be seen as simply a mapping from belief state to action $\pi(b) \in A_m$.

Spoken Dialog System-POMDP. In this section we show how a POMDP is commonly used for generating Spoken Dialog Systems (SDS). We follow the approach of Williams and Young [11] The properties of spoken dialog make it so that, when represented as a POMDP, the state can be naturally separated into three distinct components:

- User goal (g)
- User action (u)
- Dialog history (h)

As a result, the factored POMDP state will be defined as:

$$s = (g, u, h) \tag{3}$$

With this in mind, we can expand the transition function and decompose it into its three components:

$$
\begin{aligned}
p(s'|s, a_m) &= p(g', u', h'|g, u, h, a_m) \\
&= p(g'|g, u, h, a_m)p(u'|g', g, u, h, a_m)p(h'|g', u', g, u, h, a_m)
\end{aligned} \tag{4}
$$

We can then simplify this equation by taking some independence assumptions. For the first term, which refers to how the user goal changes at each step, we'll assume it only depends on the previous goal, the dialog history and the machine's action.

$$p(g'|g, u, h, a_m) = p(g'|g, h, a_m) \tag{5}$$

The next term, how the user will act at each step, we assume to only depend on the current goal, the dialog history an the machine's action.

$$p(u'|g', g, u, h, a_m) = p(u'|g', h, a_m) \tag{6}$$

For the last term, which captures relevant information about the history of the dialog, this will only depend on the most recent variables, as well as the previous dialog history.

$$p(h'|g', u', g, u, h, a_m) = p(h'|g', u', h, a_m) \tag{7}$$

Replacing Eqs. (5), (6) and (7) into Eq. (4), we get:

$$p(s'|s, a_m) = p(g'|g, h, a_m)p(g'|g', h, a_m)p(h'|g', u', h, a_m) \tag{8}$$

As for the observation, this will only depend on the user's action, so the observation probabilities become:

$$p(o'|s, a_m) = p(o'|g, u, h, a_m)$$
$$= p(o'|u) \tag{9}$$

Combining Eqs. (8) and (9) with Eq. (1), we get the equation for belief updating for the SDS-POMDP:

$$b(g', u', h') =$$
$$= k \cdot p(o'|u') \sum_{h \in H} p(u'|s', h, a_m) \cdot p(h'|g', u', h, a_m) \sum_{g \in G} p(g'|g, h, a_m) \sum_{u \in U} b(g, u, h) \tag{10}$$

Overall, the SDS-POMDP framework makes it easier to model spoken dialog systems when compared to the usual POMDP framework, and the assumptions made allow more efficient algorithms.

RL - for User's Personality Adaptation. The RL layer runs on top of the POMDP. Its task is to choose between the action selected by the optimal policy (π_{POMDP}) of the POMDP or a social action. It is composed of:

- The observed state s in which we will learn, composed of:
  - the current POMDP belief b.
  - the previous POMDP belief pb.
  - the action selected using the optimal policy from the POMDP a_m.
  - the previous action pa.
- A set of actions the agent can take, both the action from the POMDP and the social actions: $A = A_m \cup A_{social}$
- a hidden state h that in unknown and includes the POMDP state (of which the structure is known), as well as information on the user's social preferences. This could be information on whether the user is happy with the conversation so far, if he feels that he has been treated fairly, and so on.
- A reward function $r(h, a)$
- A observation probability function $p(o|h, a)$

As explained before this state guarantees that the agent can learn, but also that it can transfer the learned knowledge about the user for another task.

The update of the beliefs (b and pb) are dependent on the type of action a. If the action was social, both beliefs remain the same. If the action was not social, then b is updated using Eq. (10), and pb is set to b. Also, pa is set to the previous action, unless the last action terminated the dialog, in which case pa indicates that this is the beginning of a new dialog.

In order to have the RL layer not depend on the underlying POMDP structure, instead of taking the belief directly, only the total variation (TV) between the current and the previous belief, calculated according to Eq. (11), will be used to create the optimal policy for the RL layer.

$$TV(b_{t+1}, b_t) = \frac{1}{2} \sum_{s \in S} |b_{t+1}(s) - b_t(s)| \tag{11}$$

An identifier (id) will also be used as information on the last action. It will store the last social action that was performed (or whether it is the beginning of the conversation), and in the case of the last action being non-social, whether it is the same as the last non-social action or not. These two elements will be converted to a numerical vector ($\phi(s)$). The first component of the vector will be the total variation referred above and the rest will be a one-hot encoding of the id.

We can then create a policy using this encoding, by taking the inner product with a parameter vector w_a for each social action plus one for keeping the optimal POMDP action, and then normalising using the softmax function, like in Eq. (12). The elements of the final vector give the probability of selecting the corresponding action.

$$\pi(s, a) = \frac{e^{w_a \cdot \phi(s)}}{\sum_{a' \in A} e^{w_{a'} \cdot \phi(s)}} \tag{12}$$

To find the parameters that optimise the policy, we use the evolution strategy CMA-ES [7]. The function to optimise is the sum of the rewards received over n-steps, and the optimisation occurs over the parameters w_a.

3   Experiments

In the experiments we show the two main capabilities of our system. First that the system is able to learn how to use social actions to increase how well the user enjoys the interaction beyond the instrumental goal. We consider different user profiles and see how well it can adapt to each profile. Second we want to show that with our architecture we are able to transfer the knowledge about the user from one scenario to another. If an user enjoys a certain type of social interaction in one scenario we can use such preference to bootstrap the social actions in a new (related) scenario (Fig. 2).

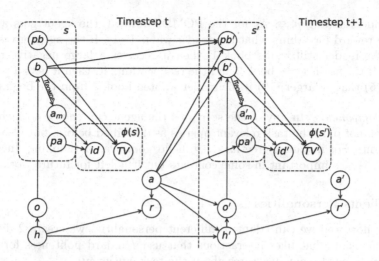

Fig. 2. Structure of the RL layer. Each arrow indicates that the variable is directly dependent on the other. The dashed boxes represent the observed state s and the numerical representation of the state $\phi(s)$. o is the observed response by the user, a is the action selected by the RL, r is the reward received. The other variables are explain in the text.

3.1 Scenarios

We consider two different scenarios to validate our claims and contributions. We need two scenarios to test the transfer and also to see how well the architecture we have is agnostic to the specific details of each task. In the following, we make a simple description of the POMDP structure of these scenarios:

Scenario 1: Bar. In the first scenario, we have a costumer going to a bar asking for a drink. He can want a bottle of water, or a glass of beer of brand 1 or brand 2. The agent (acting as the barman) can ask the costumer what he wants to drink, ask him to specify the brand of beer he wants or give the costumer one of the three options, ending the dialog. At each time step, the agent has a probability p_{err} of misunderstanding the client and observing a different random action. For this POMDP, whenever the agent chooses to ask the costumer what he wants or to specify he receives a small negative reward (-1). When giving one of the drinks, if the drink corresponds to the costumer desired drink, then the agent receives a positive reward (10), otherwise, it receives a large negative reward (-100).

Scenario 2: Library. In the second scenario, we have a user who goes to a library with the intention to request one of two books. The library however only has book 2, as a result, if the reader asks for book 1 then the agent (the librarian) must inform that there is no such book in the library, at which point the reader changes its mind and want book 2. Like in scenario 1, there is a probability of misunderstanding p_{err}. As for the POMDP reward, the agent gets a small negative reward for asking what the reader wants (-1). If the agent gives book 2, but the reader still wants book 1, then it receives a large negative reward (-100). If the agent gives book 2 and the reader wants it, then it gets a positive reward (5) that is larger (10) if the reader wanted book 2 from the beginning.

Social Components. In any of the scenarios the agent can choose to include in the dialog not only the task relevant queries as described before, but also social components. For instance, greetings, e.g. hello/goodbye, or thanking. Including smalltalk is also important in some contexts but it is left for future work.

3.2   Clients Personalities

To show how well we can adapt to different personalities we create 2 different clients: a social (that likes interactions that use standard politeness formulas) and an anti-social (that just cares about the task efficiency).

We model this by the use of different reward functions for the RL layer. To have the reward be analogous something like tipping or a survey at the end, the reward will be zero if the action of the RL layer is not terminal, that is, it does not cause the conversation to restart. In both scenarios, a positive reward (1.) will be awarded if the agent perform the action that is expected of him, and a negative reward $(-1.)$ if he fails (by giving the wrong drink or the wrong book). The difference between the two costumers is that the social costumer will receive an extra positive reward (.5) if at the beginning of the conversation the agent said hello, while the anti-social is indifferent to this.

Sample conversations for both scenarios and clients can be seen in Sect. 3.4.

3.3   Results

Check Learning Capability. Four different policies, one for each combination of scenario and client personality, were learned using the method referred in Sect. 2.1. $\pi_{B,S}$ corresponds to the policy learned on the bar scenario with the social client, $\pi_{L,A}$ corresponds to the policy learned on the library scenario with the anti-social client, etc.

As can be seen in Fig. 3, the method used for optimisation is capable of improving the initial policy, created with random parameters. Due to the randomness of the observations (agent has a chance to misunderstanding what the user was saying), the received reward can be different from the expected reward. This helps explain the noise that can be seen in the objective function.

Check Transfer Capability. To check the transferability of the policies, that is, if a social policy learned in one scenario will perform well in another, a series of simulations were performed on each scenario for all policies referred above. The results can be seen in Table 1. As can be seen, policies trained with the same client profile perform very similarly, which means that even though a policy is trained in a different scenario, it achieves a performance close to the performance of the

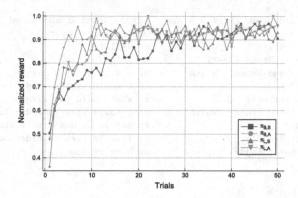

Fig. 3. Average reward of the μ best solutions with the number of trials during the training. The rewards are normalised so that the maximum of each one is 1.

optimal policy trained in that scenario. We can conclude that for this example, the policy learned in one scenario transfers well to the other scenario.

It can also be observed that the policies learned from one client perform worse on the other client than the policies learned on that client. This is evidence that the optimal policy for both personalities is different.

Table 1. Estimated normalised average rewards and its standard deviation, for every policy in each scenario. In each row, the values are normalised such that the reward for the social policy trained in the respective Scenario/Client is 1. We can clearly see that our mechanism for transfer works as social policies learned in one task can be executed in a different task and achieve a high success if the social profile of the user is the same.

Scenario/client	$\pi_{B,S}$	$\pi_{B,A}$	$\pi_{L,S}$	$\pi_{L,A}$
Bar/social	1.0 ± 0.0	0.784 ± 0.003	0.995 ± 0.004	0.787 ± 0.003
Bar/anti-social	0.767 ± 0.003	1.0 ± 0.0	0.771 ± 0.004	1.014 ± 0.005
Library/social	1.005 ± 0.004	0.810 ± 0.003	1.0 ± 0.0	0.810 ± 0.003
Library/anti-social	0.758 ± 0.003	0.997 ± 0.004	0.756 ± 0.003	1.0 ± 0.0

3.4 Sample Conversations

Sample conversations for both scenarios from Sect. 3.4. In parentheses are the observed user actions. Due to the change of misunderstanding the client (dictated by p_{err}), the system repeats some questions to assure that it understands the users intentions.

Bar scenario with anti-social client. The system follows policy $\pi_{B,A}$.
```
s: What would you like?
u: I'd like a beer please.(beer)
s: We have brand1 and brand2. Which
would you prefer?
u: Brand1 please.(Brand1)
s: We have brand1 and brand2. Which
would you prefer?
u: Brand1 please.(Brand1)
s: Here is your beer. Enjoy.
```

Library scenario with social client. The system follows policy $\pi_{L,S}$.
```
s: Hello!
u: Hello.(hello)
s: What would you like?
u: I would like to order book1(book1)
s: What would you like?
u: I would like to order book1(book1)
s: Sorry, we don't have that book.
u: I would like to order book2(book2)
s: Here is book2
```

4 Conclusions

We have defined a model that separates the social and task planning into two components. The task planning is formally modelled as a POMDP that has been shown to be a framework appropriate for planning in SDSs. In particular, a variation on the POMDP referred to as SDS-POMDP is used, that takes advantage of the properties of SDS to achieve more efficient results. The social planning comes from a layer on top of the POMDP that will receive information about the change in belief of the POMDP and the optimal action proposed by the POMDP. Since the belief is not used directly, and instead only the observed change in belief is used, the policies created are independent of the underlying POMDP structure. RL is then used to learn a policy that selects whether to override the POMDP action with a social action or to accept such action.

This approach allows for the social policy to not depend on the underlying structure of the POMDP, and as a result, the social policy learned in a particular scenario can be transferred to another.

We trained the RL layer on two different simulated scenarios with two different user personalities, and found that it was capable of learning the policies that optimise the rewards. We then simulated the policies on scenarios different from the one they were trained in and found that the learned policies still performed well.

In this work, social interactions were fairly minimal. More complex interactions like smalltalk could be added and would be interesting to see to what extent this would be transferable between tasks. It would also be of interest to see how the model would perform on real users and not just simulations, but for that the necessary empirical data would need to be gathered.

Acknowledgements. This work was partially by the FCT grants FCT: UID/CEC/50021/2019 and PTDC/CCI-COM/30787/2017.

References

1. André, E., Pelachaud, C.: Interacting with embodied conversational agents. In: Chen, F., Huggins, (eds.) Speech Technology, pp. 123–149. Springer, Heidelberg (2010). https://doi.org/10.1007/978-0-387-73819-2_8
2. Bickmore, T., Cassell, J.: Relational agents: a model and implementation of building user trust. In: Proceedings of the SIGCHI Conference on Human Factors in Computing Systems, pp. 396–403. ACM (2001)
3. Brown, P., Levinson, S.C.: Politeness: Some Universals in Language Usage, vol. 4. Cambridge University Press, Cambridge (1987)
4. Cassell, J., Gill, A.J., Tepper, P.A.: Coordination in conversation and rapport. In: Proceedings of the Workshop on Embodied Language Processing, pp. 41–50. Association for Computational Linguistics (2007)
5. Gratch, J., Lucas, G.M., King, A.A., Morency, L.P.: It's only a computer: the impact of human-agent interaction in clinical interviews. In: Proceedings of the 2014 International Conference on Autonomous Agents and Multi-agent Systems, AAMAS 2014, pp. 85–92. International Foundation for Autonomous Agents and Multiagent Systems, Richland (2014). http://dl.acm.org/citation.cfm?id=2615731.2615748
6. Gratch, J., Wang, N., Gerten, J., Fast, E., Duffy, R.: Creating rapport with virtual agents. In: Pelachaud, C., Martin, J.-C., André, E., Chollet, G., Karpouzis, K., Pelé, D. (eds.) IVA 2007. LNCS (LNAI), vol. 4722, pp. 125–138. Springer, Heidelberg (2007). https://doi.org/10.1007/978-3-540-74997-4_12
7. Hansen, N., Ostermeier, A.: Convergence properties of evolution strategies with the derandomized covariance matrix adaptation: the $(\mu/\mu_I, \lambda)$-CMA-ES. In: Proceedings of the EUFIT 1997, 5th European Congress on Intelligent Techniques and Soft Computing, pp. 650–654 (1997)
8. McTear, M.F.: Modelling spoken dialogues with state transition diagrams: experiences with the CSLU toolkit. In: Fifth International Conference on Spoken Language Processing (1998)
9. Nishida, T., Nakazawa, A., Ohmoto, Y., Mohammad, Y.: Conversational Informatics: A Data-intensive Approach with Emphasis on Nonverbal Communication. Springer, Heidelberg (2014). https://doi.org/10.1007/978-4-431-55040-2
10. Sutton, S., et al.: Building 10,000 spoken dialogue systems. In: Proceeding of Fourth International Conference on Spoken Language Processing. ICSLP 1996, vol. 2, pp. 709–712. IEEE (1996)
11. Williams, J.D., Young, S.: Partially observable Markov decision processes for spoken dialog systems. Comput. Speech Lang. **21**(2), 393–422 (2007)

SimpleLSTM: A Deep-Learning Approach to Simple-Claims Classification

Piyush Chawla[1,2], Diego Esteves[2,3(✉)], Karthik Pujar[1], and Jens Lehmann[2,4]

[1] The Ohio State University, Columbus, USA
{chawla.81,pujar.4}@osu.edu
[2] SDA Research, University of Bonn, Bonn, Germany
{esteves,lehmann}@cs.uni-bonn.de
[3] Farfetch, Porto, Portugal
diego.esteves@farfetch.com
[4] Fraunhofer IAIS, Sankt Augustin, Germany

Abstract. The information on the internet suffers from noise and corrupt knowledge that may arise due to human and mechanical errors. To further exacerbate this problem, an ever-increasing amount of fake news on social media, or internet in general, has created another challenge to drawing correct information from the web. This huge sea of data makes it difficult for human fact checkers and journalists to assess all the information manually. In recent years *Automated Fact-Checking* has emerged as a branch of natural language processing devoted to achieving this feat. In this work, we give an overview of recent approaches, emphasizing on the key challenges faced during the development of such frameworks. We test existing solutions to perform claim classification on simple-claims and introduce a new model dubbed SIMPLELSTM, which outperforms baselines by 11%, 10.2% and 18.7% on FEVER-Support, FEVER-Reject and 3-Class datasets respectively. The data, metadata and code are released as open-source and will be available at https://github.com/DeFacto/SimpleLSTM.

Keywords: Fact-checking · Trustworthiness · Evidence extraction

1 Introduction

With the increase in false-fact circulation across different social media platforms, it has become pertinent to validate the claims and statements released online [8, 34]. The terms *Fake-News* and *Junk-News* have gained importance in the last few years, mainly in the context of electoral activities in North America and Western Europe. The false facts (or rumors), in the past, have led to situations like stock price drops and large scale investments [35]. Though social media platforms are the most common breeding grounds for fake-news, it sometimes finds its way into the mainstream media too [15]. The constant skepticism about inflammatory news headlines and rapid growth in the facts that are shared online led to a new

© Springer Nature Switzerland AG 2019
P. Moura Oliveira et al. (Eds.): EPIA 2019, LNAI 11805, pp. 244–255, 2019.
https://doi.org/10.1007/978-3-030-30244-3_21

form of journalism that validates political facts made on the web. Political fact-checking [25] has emerged as an effort to fight against the fake news and validate the claims and alternative facts [15] made in political discourse. Organizations like *PolitiFact*[1], *Snopes*[2] and *Factcheck*[3], for instance, employ journalists that manually check facts and hand annotate them publicly. Though this is a good effort towards curbing false information, the human annotators cannot compete with the speed with which these facts are generated. The content on the internet is increasing every day which also means an increase in the false and incorrect facts. This makes manual validation of facts almost impossible (although its high precision). *Automated Fact-Checking (or Fact-Validation)* is a (relatively) recent effort that tries to automate the process of manual fact-checking. Many different branches of natural language processing have emerged that try to achieve this goal [28]. The fact-checking task involves different perspectives. For instance, *stance detection* aims at detecting whether the author of a piece of text is in favor of the given target or against it. Recent challenges like the Fake News Challenge 2017[4] [13] tackle this problem. Yet another task in the fact-checking domain is the *claim classification* which deals with deciding whether a given claim is true or not based on the evidence. FEVER 2018[5] [31] have proved to be important milestone in this direction. Overall these challenges have worked as a catalyst for the automated fact-checking community, releasing new datasets and defining strong baselines to fuel future research. In this paper we focus our attention on the latter case (*claim classification*).

Fact-Checking at its core can be treated as a *claim classification* problem. It is a holistic approach that extracts *evidence* and then uses its *arguments* to make a decision regarding the claim. Given a claim and a corpus containing a set of documents, the problem boils down to predicting the veracity of the claim. In practice, however, searching, extracting and processing evidence is a complex underlying task (discussed in Sect. 3). In this work we describe the automation process and its nuances, we also propose a LSTM-based model (dubbed SIM-PLELSTM) for claim classification phase of the pipeline.

2 Related Work

Ciampaglia et al. [5] formulate the fact-checking problem as a special case of link prediction in knowledge graphs (*DBpedia*[6]). However, this approach is problematic as the Knowledge Graphs are often outdated and lack status-quo of the world. Vlachos and Riedel [34] defined the problem of fact-checking as the truthfulness of claims in the form of a binary classification problem. They provide two datasets constructed from political fact-checking websites. Their work

---

[1] https://www.politifact.com/.
[2] https://www.snopes.com/.
[3] https://www.factcheck.org/.
[4] http://www.fakenewschallenge.org/.
[5] http://fever.ai.
[6] https://wiki.dbpedia.org/.

tries to define the problem of fact-checking as a one-to-one automation mapping of the human fact-checking process. Thorne et al. [28] give an overview of fact-checking automation for natural language claims, bridging the gaps between fact-checking and related research areas. Starting with the fact-checking in journalism, they define basic terminology and then go on drawing a parallel between Fake news research, fact-checking, textual entailment etc. Lee et al. [16] propose a neural-ranker-based evidence extraction method, an important part of the fact-checking pipeline, extending the baseline method [31]. Taniguchi et al. [27] give a three-component pipeline consisting of document retrieval, sentence selection and recognizing textual entailment (RTE). Popat et al. [24] design an end2end model for fake-news detection. They use pre-retrieved articles related to a single fact and aggregate the veracity score from each article to make the final decision about the claim. Yang et al. [37] propose a convolution neural network-based approach for fake news detection. They combine the text in the articles with the image cues. Recently many studies have also proposed deep learning solutions to the fact-checking problem [6,17,24,38]. DeclarE [24] combines the evidence extraction and claim classification in a single end2end model. Sizhen et al. [17] select relevant Wikipedia entities using an online available tool - *S-MART* - and use their model to perform both *evidence selection* and *claim classification* in a combined fashion, reaching baseline results *evidence retrieval*. Conforti et al. [6] propose an approach for fake-news detection by focusing on the stance of the claims. They use the dataset from Fake-News-Challenge (FNC-1) to test their model. The model yields better results than the top performers of FNC-1. Yin and Roth [38], give a two-wing-optimization strategy and combine the last two steps of Fact-Checking pipeline. Their model beats the baseline [29] on evidence identification and claim verification by a good margin. Baly et al. [2] use the approach of bias detection in the news media and predict the "factuality" in news reported by the media source. They use the following variants of veracity assessment: fact-checking, fake news detection, troll detection and source reliability estimation. Popat et al. [23] add source trend and language to the credibility assessment approach, and also provide user interpretable explanations of the final decision.

3   Fact-Checking Pipeline: Automating the Task

Fact-checking is a relatively new research area in NLP, but is not a new task in journalism. The problem was first discussed in the early 1920s, evolving into standard practice at many American magazines later on [36]. However, only recently the task has spread over different communities and countries [12]. Most recent ideas in fact-checking revolve around automation of the human (or journalist) fact-checking process. Currently, this is broadly translated into a 3-step process which involves (1) collecting articles about the claim, (2) selecting prospective evidence and finally (3) performing a final judgment. Figure 1 exemplifies this in a nutshell, delineating these three components: (1) *document retrieval*, (2) *evidence selection* and (3) *claim classification*. The flow is detailed in the following.

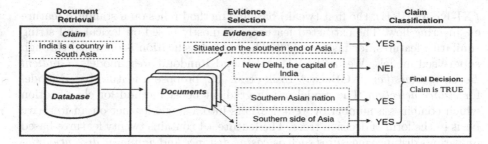

Fig. 1. The figure shows three-component fact-checking pipeline: Document Retrieval, Evidence Selection and Claim Classification.

Document Retrieval: The first step focuses on obtaining relevant documents [2, 31]. The module selects documents from a large corpus that are related to a given claim. The relatedness is determined by selecting a matching metric. Throne et al. [29] use DrQA [4] for document retrieval that selects documents from Wikipedia[7] corpus based on TF-IDF. An alternative approach could be using web search APIs [3,11,18,23] (e.g., Bing API[8]) for collecting related webpages from the internet. This approach is a better approximation of the human fact-checking process, since human fact-checkers do not restrict their research to a single corpus (like Wikipedia).

Evidence Selection: The next step of the pipeline is to select potential evidences from the documents or collection of sentences that we retrieved in the first step. This component does not differentiate between a piece of evidence that refutes the claim, from one that supports it. The main goal at this phase is to collect sentences that could potentially be used to run inference on the veracity of the claim.

Source Classification: This step, although not strictly necessary in order to perform the task, has major importance in order to weight all of the extracted claims (proofs) according to the trustworthiness of source [7,23].

Claim Classification: In the last step, as the name suggests, the model makes final decision on the claim by taking all the collected information into account [24], producing scores for each evidence, and then finally making decision on aggregation of all the scores (textual entailment on the claim by using all pieces of evidence [29]).

3.1 Claim Classification Methods

In the following section we describe common (*weak* and *strong* baselines) methods to perform *claim classification*. The methods are detailed in Sect. 4. *Feature-based*

---

[7] https://www.wikipedia.org/.

[8] https://azure.microsoft.com/en-us/services/cognitive-services/bing-web-search-api/.

(XI-FEATURE): the first (weak) baseline method relies on a standard feature engineering flow. The extracted features are mostly based on lexical and string similarity features, for instance [26]. The final classification is obtained through supervised models. We used SVM, MLP and RandomForest models. *Gradient Boosting Classifier (*XGBoost*)* Tosik et al. [32] propose a feature based model for *stance detection*. The model uses a gradient boost method for classification which combines a number of weak learners into a single learner on an iterative basis in the form of decision trees. The feature set contains twenty features based on various distance measures such as *cosine distance* and *hamming distance*, *relative entropy* between topic model probability distributions, *sentiment scores* of the claim and sentence (or evidence) and etc. We use this model as one of the baselines for the claim classification task. *Textual Entailment (TE)* is under the umbrella of Argumentation Mining in NLP and is a natural language processing task to find directional relation between texts [33]. Given a text fragment, the task is to determine if this text is a consequence of another text. The first text fragment is called a *hypothesis* and the second reference text *entailing text*, where the *entailing text* and *hypothesis* can be seen as the evidence and the claim, respectively. We use the TE model implementation by AllenNLP [9] as the second baseline for the claim classification task. The model is an implementation of the decomposable attention model given by Parikh et al. [21].

3.2 Proposed Architecture: SimpleLSTM

We employ recent deep learning techniques for claim-classification step in the automated fact-checking task. To this aim, we propose SIMPLELSTM, a Long-Short-Term-Memory (LSTM) based model that extracts semantic information from claims and evidences and then combines these representations. The combined layer is then fed to a fully-connected neural network, where the final decision making (classification) is done. We use stacked-LSTM layers for both, claim and evidence. Figure 2 gives a schematic representation of SIMPLELSTM.

The inputs to the model are a claim, evidence and a target label. The claim is represented as $[C_1, C_2, \cdots, C_m]$ where m ranges from 10–20 words, and the evidence is represented as $[E_1, E_2, \cdots, E_n]$ where n ranges from 100–200 words. The claim and evidence vectors are first passed through a pre-trained embedding layer to get corresponding $d \times m$ and $d \times n$ matrices for claim and evidence respectively, where d is the size of each word embedding. The embedding matrices are then fed to two parallel stacked-LSTM layers. Last LSTM outputs for the both the LSTM stacks give feature representations for claim and evidence. We call them *claimvec* and *sentvec*. The feature vectors are passed through a merge function. It should be noted that both the evidence and claim share the embedding layer which facilitates the merging of *claimvec* and *sentvec* vectors. In practice any binary function `MERGE(sentvec,claimvec)` can be used to produce a merged representation. We experimented with (1) Cosine distance, (2) Concatenation and Multiplication of *sentvec* and *claimvec*. We found element-wise multiplication to be most effective. Finally the fully connected layer makes the decision.

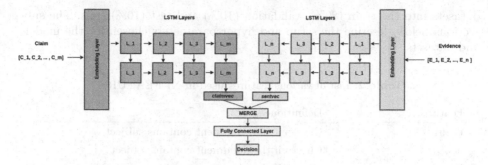

Fig. 2. SIMPLELSTM model. The inputs are claim and evidence. Both, the evidence and the claim are fed to an embedding layer (common for both) that outputs embedding representation for each word. These embeddings are then passed through LSTM layers. The final output of LSTM, `sentvec` and `claimvec`, are merged and fed to the fully connected layer.

4   Experiments

For the experiments, we used the most relevant fact-checking dataset publicity available: FEVER [30]. In this section we give details of the experiments we performed on FEVER-Simple datasets for the claim classification task. In this work, we mainly focused on *simple claims*, i.e., claims which do not exceed one sentence in length. Therefore, we extracted from FEVER only those claims which are represented by a *subject-predicate-object* triple. We refer to this extracted subset as FEVER-Simple. We implemented two strong baselines to compare the performance with our models. We further divide the claim classification task into three tasks: FEVER-Support, FEVER-Reject and FEVER-3-Class. FEVER-Support uses only those claims which are *true* and have corresponding evidences that support them. Similarly, FEVER-Reject contains claims which are *false* and have corresponding evidences. The last task uses three class classification *Support*, *Reject* and *NEI* (Not enough information). Table 1 gives details about the number of instances for each dataset. For training the models, we divide the

Table 1. FEVER-Simple subsets

Dataset	Label	Count
FEVER-Support	Support	2761
	NEI	2761
FEVER-Reject	Reject	2955
	NEI	2955
FEVER 3-Class	Support	2761
	Reject	2847
	NEI	2804

datasets into the train (80%), validation (10%) and test (10%) split. The subsections below describe the setup and hyper-parameters chosen for the models and datasets.

Table 2. List of various features used in XI-FEATURE.

Feature	Definition
is sub	Checks if the document contains subject
is obj	Checks if the document contains object
is pred	Checks if the document contains predicate
dist sub obj Text follows	Distance between subject and object
pred between	Does predicate occur between subject and object
sub relax	Checks whether subject is present in partial form
obj relax	Checks whether object is present in partial form
pred relax	Checks whether predicate is present in partial form
Jaccard distance	Maximum Jaccard coefficient
Cosine similarity	Maximum cosine similarity
Semantic similarity	Similarity score of most semantically similar sentence

4.1 Baselines

XI-FEATURE. The XI-FEATURE experiments involve tuning the hyper-parameters for all the three classifiers: MLP, RF and SVM. We used cross-validation as sampling method with grid search for hyper-parameter optimization[9]. We generate a set of eleven features that incorporate the morphological, syntactic and semantic information of the claim and evidence pair. The features are generated by extracting claim specific information from the evidence. We utilize subject, predicate and object (spo) triples (pre-extracted from the claim) in our datasets. A claim like "That 70s show is a sitcom" can be broken down into a spo triple ['That 70s Show', 'is a', 'sitcom']. Given a *spo* triple for each claim, a simple method to find similarity between *claim* and *evidence* is to find whether subject, predicate, and object (or their synonyms) appear in the sentence. The first eight features utilize the triples to extract morphological information from evidence sentence. We later added semantic similarity, cosine similarity and Jaccard similarity between the claim and evidence sentence as three features. These features represent the similarity measure between the *claim* and the most similar sentence in the evidence. Table 2 lists all the eleven features.

Pre-trained word embeddings were used to compute the similarity based metrics using spaCy[10] python library. The extracted features are trained on three classifier models: Support Vector Machine (SVM), Random Forest (RF) and

---

[9] GridSearchCV from scikit-learn to obtain the best hyper-parameters.
[10] github.com/explosion/spaCy.

Multi-Layer Perceptron (MLP). According to our experiments, Random Forest yields the best results with a maximum depth of 10 and *entropy* as splitting criterion. For SVM penalty of 100, *gamma* 0.001 and *rbf* kernel gave the best performance. The neural network has two hidden layers with 44 perceptrons in each. The model provides best results with *Adam* optimizer and *ReLU* activation function.

XGBoost. *XGBoost* model is trained on FeverSimple datasets and the best hyperparameter settings for each model are selected using a grid search with cross-validation on the training set. A max-depth of 8 and 1000 estimators provide the best performance overall on the three datasets.

TE. *TE* represents the pre-trained textual entailment model with decomposable attention [21] by AllenNLP [9]. We ran this on the testing data by using claim as the hypothesis and evidence as the entailing text.

4.2 Results

Table 3 depicts the accuracy, precision, recall and F1 scores for all the models. It can be observed that the our feature models outperform the gradient-boost (XGBoost) [32] and TE [9]. The MLP models gives better performance than RF

Table 3. Performance comparison of different models on FEVER support, FEVER Reject and FEVER 3-class

Dataset	Classifier	Accuracy	Precision	Recall	f1 Score
FEVER Support	XGBoost [32]	0.766	0.766	0.766	0.762
	TE [9]	0.691	0.835	0.655	0.734
	XI-FEATURE RF	0.79	0.76	0.83	0.79
	XI-FEATURE SVM	0.79	0.71	0.85	0.77
	XI-FEATURE MLP	0.79	0.76	0.81	0.78
	SimpleLSTM	0.850	0.834	0.856	0.845
FEVER Reject	XGBoost [32]	0.74	0.738	0.736	0.73
	TE [9]	0.548	0.759	0.533	0.626
	XI-FEATURE RF	0.73	0.73	0.81	0.76
	XI-FEATURE SVM	0.642	0.73	0.78	0.75
	XI-FEATURE MLP	0.74	0.69	0.78	0.73
	SimpleLSTM	0.816	0.836	0.811	0.824
FEVER 3-class	XGBoost [32]	0.535	0.54	0.534	0.539
	TE [9]	0.418	0.372	0.622	0.465
	XI-FEATURE RF	0.55	0.60	0.61	0.60
	XI-FEATURE SVM	0.55	0.54	0.56	0.53
	XI-FEATURE MLP	0.59	0.61	0.62	0.61
	SimpleLSTM	0.635	0.643	0.620	0.642

and SVM on the FEVER-Simple datasets. The SIMPLELSTM model beats all the baselines with significant margin.

We found that out of cosine distance, element-wise multiplication, and plain concatenation, element-wise multiplication works the best for SIMPLELSTM, so we decided to go with it. We chose GoogleNews vectors *GoogleNews vectors*[11] [19] for pre-trained word embeddings. This is a word2vec [19] model has been trained on Google News dataset that has about 100 billion words. It contains word embeddings of dimension 300 for 3 million words and phrases. We fixed batch size of 64 and Adam Optimizer, with learning rate of 0.001, for all the datasets. The loss is *binary cross-entropy* loss for binary classification tasks, and *categorical cross-entropy* loss for the 3-class problem. The input size for LSTM stack is 300, and the output size is 150 for FEVER-Support and FEVER-Reject, and 100 for 3-Class.

4.3   Challenges

On the computational side, there are different fundamental challenges w.r.t. the execution of the underlying tasks in this pipeline. We extend the definition of [14] (items 1 and 4) by highlighting two more challenges (items 2 and 3) we argue are crucial to bridge the gap between *automated fact-checking* approaches and human fact-checkers, as follows. (1) to understand what one says [14] (NLU) (2) to have the ability to generate equivalent arguments and counter-arguments (NLG) (3) to have the ability to distinguish credible and non-credible information sources (Credibility) (4) to have the ability to obtain plausible evidence [14] (Argumentation Mining)

Firstly, algorithms need to have the ability to understand what is being said. This refers to a specific research area called Natural Language Understanding (NLU), which encompasses several NLP sub-tasks, such as Named Entity Recognition (NER), and Part-of-speech (POS). Although significant leaps have been made in this area, these technologies are far from human performance, especially in more noisy contexts such as microblogs [1].

Secondly, algorithms need to process similar content accordingly, i.e., to collect equivalent and related content which are potentially useful in the fact-checking process. This is part of a branch in NLP called Natural Language Generation (NLG) [10]. This is of utmost importance in order to have a broader coverage when checking claims. In structured fact-checking [11], this is a crucial step towards interpreting and transforming the input *claim* into natural language. Moreover, in free text, for instance, the sentences *"he was born in USA."* and *"he is a Yankee."* share the same meaning. Given a claim *"he is American."*, algorithms should be capable to perceive that, in this context, "USA" and "Yankee" are synonyms for "American", thus the information extraction phase should generate similar content automatically in order to increase *recall*.

Thirdly, the level of trustworthiness of authorities and sources must be checked and taken into account. This has been studied in a topic known as

---

[11] https://code.google.com/archive/p/word2vec/.

(Web) Credibility [7]. This step is important both in assessing the credibility of sources isolated, as well as when confronting opposite claims made by two or more authorities [33]. For instance, consider a scenario of researching information about a dietary supplement that potentially helps in certain disease treatment. One may find websites from reputable agencies (e.g., NCI USA) alongside sites from private organizations which sell dietary supplements (which may serve as advice hub whilst pointing to their own products). Discerning which sources are trustworthy and which are not is a crucial step forward automated fact-checking systems [7]. Finally, besides collecting sufficient evidence for asserting a given claim, explicit and implicit relations among extracted arguments (as well as possible counter-arguments) should (ideally) be labeled and linked. This is studied in another branch of NLP called Argumentation Mining [20]. The generated graph allows achieving a richer level of metadata in order to better perform the final fact-checking task [22].

5 Conclusion

In this work, we give an overview of the fact-checking problem and its automation in the context of natural language processing. We discuss the fact-checking pipeline that consists of document retrieval, evidence selection, source classification, and claim classification, shedding light on existing challenges. Most notably the claim classification phase, which consists of classification of claims as support, reject or not related. In order to solve this task, we propose two new models: SIMPLELSTM and XI-FEATURE, comparing the results with two strong baselines. Our experiments show that SIMPLELSTM outperforms all the baselines. Compared to the best baseline (XGBoost [32]), it outperforms it by 11%, 10.2% and 18.7% on the FEVER-Support, FEVER-Reject and 3-Class tasks respectively. However, we show that the task is far from being solved and performance is only reasonable even in more simple scenarios (simple claims). As future work, we will study the impact of such architectures in complex claims, explore other languages and investigate further architectures to minimize the gaps in the fact-checking automation task.

Acknowledgement. This work was partially funded by the European Union Marie Curie ITN Cleopatra project (GA no. 812997).

References

1. Akbik, A., Blythe, D., Vollgraf, R.: Contextual string embeddings for sequence labeling. In: Proceedings of the 27th International Conference on Computational Linguistics, pp. 1638–1649 (2018)
2. Baly, R., Karadzhov, G., Alexandrov, D., Glass, J.R., Nakov, P.: Predicting factuality of reporting and bias of news media sources. CoRR abs/1810.01765 (2018). http://arxiv.org/abs/1810.01765

3. Baly, R., Mohtarami, M., Glass, J.R., Màrquez, L., Moschitti, A., Nakov, P.: Integrating stance detection and fact checking in a unified corpus. CoRR abs/1804.08012 (2018). http://arxiv.org/abs/1804.08012
4. Chen, D., Fisch, A., Weston, J., Bordes, A.: Reading wikipedia to answer open-domain questions. arXiv preprint arXiv:1704.00051 (2017)
5. Ciampaglia, G.L., Shiralkar, P., Rocha, L.M., Bollen, J., Menczer, F., Flammini, A.: Computational fact checking from knowledge networks. PLoS ONE **10**(6), e0128193 (2015)
6. Conforti, C., Pilehvar, M.T., Collier, N.: Towards automatic fake news detection: cross-level stance detection in news articles. In: Proceedings of the First Workshop on Fact Extraction and VERification (FEVER), pp. 40–49 (2018)
7. Esteves, D., Reddy, A.J., Chawla, P., Lehmann, J.: Belittling the source: trustworthiness indicators to obfuscate fake news on the web. In: Proceedings of the First Workshop on Fact Extraction and Verification (FEVER), pp. 50–59. Association for Computational Linguistics (2018). http://aclweb.org/anthology/W18-5508
8. Fridkin, K., Kenney, P.J., Wintersieck, A.: Liar, liar, pants on fire: How fact-checking influences citizens' reactions to negative advertising. Polit. Commun. **32**(1), 127–151 (2015). https://doi.org/10.1080/10584609.2014.914613
9. Gardner, M., et al.: AllenNLP: a deep semantic natural language processing platform (2017)
10. Gatt, A., Krahmer, E.: Survey of the state of the art in natural language generation: core tasks, applications and evaluation. J. Artif. Intell. Res. **61**, 65–170 (2018)
11. Gerber, D., et al.: Defacto–temporal and multilingual deep fact validation. Web Semant.: Sci. Serv. Agents World Wide Web **35**, 85–101 (2015)
12. Graves, L., Cherubini, F.: The rise of fact-checking sites in Europe (2016)
13. Hanselowski, A., et al.: A retrospective analysis of the fake news challenge stance detection task. arXiv preprint arXiv:1806.05180 (2018)
14. Hassan, N., et al.: The quest to automate fact-checking. World (2015)
15. Himma-Kadakas, M., et al.: Alternative facts and fake news entering journalistic content production cycle. Cosmopolitan Civil Soc.: Interdisc. J. **9**(2), 25 (2017)
16. Lee, N., Wu, C.S., Fung, P.: Improving large-scale fact-checking using decomposable attention models and lexical tagging. In: Proceedings of the 2018 Conference on Empirical Methods in Natural Language Processing, pp. 1133–1138 (2018)
17. Li, S., Zhao, S., Cheng, B., Yang, H.: An end-to-end multi-task learning model for fact checking. In: Proceedings of the First Workshop on Fact Extraction and Verification (FEVER), pp. 138–144. Association for Computational Linguistics (2018). http://aclweb.org/anthology/W18-5523
18. Mihaylova, T., et al.: Fact checking in community forums. CoRR abs/1803.03178 (2018). http://arxiv.org/abs/1803.03178
19. Mikolov, T., Sutskever, I., Chen, K., Corrado, G., Dean, J.: Distributed representations of words and phrases and their compositionality. CoRR abs/1310.4546 (2013). http://arxiv.org/abs/1310.4546
20. Palau, R.M., Moens, M.F.: Argumentation mining: the detection, classification and structure of arguments in text. In: Proceedings of the 12th International Conference on Artificial Intelligence and Law, pp. 98–107. ACM (2009)
21. Parikh, A.P., Täckström, O., Das, D., Uszkoreit, J.: A decomposable attention model for natural language inference. In: EMNLP (2016)
22. Peldszus, A., Stede, M.: From argument diagrams to argumentation mining in texts: a survey. Int. J. Cogn. Inform. Nat. Intell. (IJCINI) **7**(1), 1–31 (2013)

23. Popat, K., Mukherjee, S., Strötgen, J., Weikum, G.: Where the truth lies: explaining the credibility of emerging claims on the web and social media. In: Proceedings of the 26th International Conference on World Wide Web Companion, pp. 1003–1012. International World Wide Web Conferences Steering Committee (2017)

24. Popat, K., Mukherjee, S., Yates, A., Weikum, G.: Declare: debunking fake news and false claims using evidence-aware deep learning. CoRR abs/1809.06416 (2018). http://arxiv.org/abs/1809.06416

25. Rashkin, H., Choi, E., Jang, J.Y., Volkova, S., Choi, Y.: Truth of varying shades: analyzing language in fake news and political fact-checking. In: Proceedings of the 2017 Conference on Empirical Methods in Natural Language Processing, pp. 2931–2937. Association for Computational Linguistics (2017). https://doi.org/10.18653/v1/D17-1317. http://aclweb.org/anthology/D17-1317

26. Reddy, A.J., Rocha, G., Esteves, D.: DeFactoNLP: fact verification using entity recognition, TFIDF vector comparison and decomposable attention. CoRR abs/1809.00509 (2018)

27. Taniguchi, M., Taniguchi, T., Takahashi, T., Miura, Y., Ohkuma, T.: Integrating entity linking and evidence ranking for fact extraction and verification. In: Proceedings of the First Workshop on Fact Extraction and Verification (FEVER), pp. 124–126 (2018)

28. Thorne, J., Vlachos, A.: Automated fact checking: task formulations, methods and future directions. arXiv preprint arXiv:1806.07687 (2018)

29. Thorne, J., Vlachos, A., Christodoulopoulos, C., Mittal, A.: FEVER: a large-scale dataset for fact extraction and verification. CoRR abs/1803.05355 (2018). http://arxiv.org/abs/1803.05355

30. Thorne, J., Vlachos, A., Christodoulopoulos, C., Mittal, A.: Fever: a large-scale dataset for fact extraction and verification. arXiv preprint arXiv:1803.05355 (2018)

31. Thorne, J., Vlachos, A., Cocarascu, O., Christodoulopoulos, C., Mittal, A.: The fact extraction and verification (fever) shared task. arXiv preprint arXiv:1811.10971 (2018)

32. Tosik, M., Mallia, A., Gangopadhyay, K.: Debunking fake news one feature at a time. arXiv preprint arXiv:1808.02831 (2018)

33. Villata, S., Boella, G., Gabbay, D.M., van der Torre, L.: Arguing about the trustworthiness of the information sources. In: Liu, W. (ed.) ECSQARU 2011. LNCS (LNAI), vol. 6717, pp. 74–85. Springer, Heidelberg (2011). https://doi.org/10.1007/978-3-642-22152-1_7

34. Vlachos, A., Riedel, S.: Fact checking: task definition and dataset construction. In: Proceedings of the ACL 2014 Workshop on Language Technologies and Computational Social Science, pp. 18–22 (2014)

35. Vosoughi, S., Roy, D., Aral, S.: The spread of true and false news online. Science **359**(6380), 1146–1151 (2018)

36. Witschge, T., Nygren, G.: Journalistic work: a profession under pressure? J. Media Bus. Stud. **6**(1), 37–59 (2009)

37. Yang, Y., Zheng, L., Zhang, J., Cui, Q., Li, Z., Yu, P.S.: TI-CNN: convolutional neural networks for fake news detection. CoRR abs/1806.00749 (2018). http://arxiv.org/abs/1806.00749

38. Yin, W., Roth, D.: TwoWingOS: a two-wing optimization strategy for evidential claim verification. CoRR abs/1808.03465 (2018). http://arxiv.org/abs/1808.03465

Analyzing the Footprint of Classifiers in Adversarial Denial of Service Contexts

Nuno Martins[1]([✉]), José Magalhães Cruz[1], Tiago Cruz[2], and Pedro Henriques Abreu[2]

[1] Faculty of Engineering, University of Porto, 4200-465 Porto, Portugal
{up201405079,jmcruz}@fe.up.pt
[2] Faculty of Sciences and Technology, University of Coimbra,
3030-290 Coimbra, Portugal
{tjcruz,pha}@dei.uc.pt

Abstract. Adversarial machine learning is an area of study that examines both the generation and detection of adversarial examples, which are inputs specially crafted to deceive classifiers, and has been extensively researched specifically in the area of image recognition, where humanly imperceptible modifications are performed on images that cause a classifier to perform incorrect predictions.

The main objective of this paper is to study the behavior of multiple state of the art machine learning algorithms in an adversarial context. To perform this study, six different classification algorithms were used on two datasets, NSL-KDD and CICIDS2017, and four adversarial attack techniques were implemented with multiple perturbation magnitudes. Furthermore, the effectiveness of training the models with adversaries to improve recognition is also tested. The results show that adversarial attacks successfully deteriorate the performance of all the classifiers between 13% and 40%, with the Denoising Autoencoder being the technique with highest resilience to attacks.

Keywords: Classifiers' footprint · Adversarial machine learning · Denial of service

1 Introduction

Cyber-security is the practice of protecting computing systems and networks from digital attacks, and a rising concern in the Information Age [23]. Although most systems today are built with increasing security, there is still a vast amount of vulnerabilities, mainly due to outdated software, non-secure protocols and systems and human error. Cyber-attacks can target any infrastructure, from cloud systems to IoT devices, in the most various forms [23].

Intrusion Detection Systems typically use signature or misuse based detection to identify cyber-attacks, but with the growth of the diversity of attacks in recent years, machine learning approaches are being widely used [19].

© Springer Nature Switzerland AG 2019
P. Moura Oliveira et al. (Eds.): EPIA 2019, LNAI 11805, pp. 256–267, 2019.
https://doi.org/10.1007/978-3-030-30244-3_22

A downside of using machine learning techniques to perform classifications is the possibility of existence of adversaries that try to circumvent the classifiers. The area that studies these types of attacks is called Adversarial Machine Learning, and has been extensively explored in some areas such as image classification and spam detection; its exploration is scarce in other areas though, such as intrusion detection [12].

Models are many times trained with assumptions in mind for convenience or ease of computation, such as feature independence and linear separability of the data, but these types of assumptions can often open possibilities for adversarial attacks [6]. Basically, adversarial examples are inputs to a classifier specifically crafted to deceive the model, causing misclassification.

The purpose of this paper is to extend the idea of another work on the detection of Denial of Service attacks using multiple classifiers [11], by introducing adversaries, and answer the following questions:

1. **Can the generation of adversarial datasets deteriorate the performance of classifiers?**
2. **Can the training of models using adversaries improve their resilience to them?**
3. **Which techniques are most robust in each scenario?**

To answer these questions, three experiments were performed using two public datasets, NSL-KDD [3] and CICIDS2017 [9]. We first trained and tested the models on the original datasets using 10-fold cross validation. On the second experiment, we modified these datasets to generate adversaries using four common adversarial example techniques, and repeated the cross validation, this time training with the original data and testing on the adversary dataset. By comparing the results between the first and second experiment, we can answer the first and second research questions. For the final experiment, instead of training the classifiers on the original dataset, we trained them on the adversarial datasets. In this scenario, we made sure that the adversarial dataset being tested would not be included in the training set, to better simulate a scenario where an attacker uses a technique for which the classifiers were not trained for. We observed that, for the second experiment, the Denoising Autoencoder was the classifier which performed the best on both datasets, and in the third experiment, the Random Forest classifier offered the best performance.

To the best of the authors knowledge, the novelty of this work is centered around the following points:

1. We used at least one classifier for each machine learning tribe, according to Domingos [5], with the exception of evolutionary algorithms, to perform classification against four types of adversarial attacks;
2. Along with a prominent dataset used in many works, we used a new dataset, CICIDS 2017 [9], which has never been used on adversarial machine learning applied to intrusion detection;
3. We were the first testing the effectiveness of adversarial training, an adversarial defense technique, in an intrusion detection scenario, when other works [7,10,12] only tested attack strategies;

4. We extended the strategy of adversarial training by using different types of classifiers, other than neural networks, from other machine learning tribes.

The article is organized as follows: In Sect. 2, some background knowledge and fundamentals of adversarial machine learning are explored; in Sect. 3, we explore some other works on adversarial machine learning applied to intrusion detection; in Sect. 4, we explain the setup of the experiments, and explore the results in Sect. 5; in Sect. 6, we display our conclusions and future work.

2   Background Knowledge

This chapter is split into two subsections. On the first, some general concepts on adversarial machine learning will be exposed. On the second, the adversarial attacks that are used in this paper are explained.

2.1   Fundamentals of Adversarial Machine Learning

Adversarial attacks can be mainly classified as **Poisoning** attacks, if the attacker influences the training data to cause the model to under-perform during deployment, or **Evasion** attacks, if the attacker manipulates the data during deployment to deceive classifiers [20].

Huang [20] proposed a formal taxonomy to further model an adversarial attacker, according to the following properties:

- **Influence** - refers to the capabilities the attacker has over the training data. It can either be a **Causative** attacker if he can temper the training data of the classifier, or **Exploratory** if the attacker can't alter the training data, but can use other techniques to probe for useful information;
- **Security Violation** - refers to the type of violation of the attack. There can be **Integrity** attacks when the aim is for the attack to be classified as normal (false negative), **Availability** attacks, when the aim is to cause misclassifications of any type (false negative or false positive), rendering the model useless, or **Privacy** attacks, when the aim is to obtain information from the learner;
- **Specificity** - refers to the broadness of misclassification. These can be **Targeted** attacks when the intent is for the attacks to be misclassified into a certain class/group of classes, or **Indiscriminate** when there is no specific class to be targeted, and the objective is only to cause a misclassification.

2.2   Adversarial Attack Strategies

To produce adversarial attacks, several techniques have been proposed to introduce perturbations under different distance metrics, with a trade-off on performance, complexity and generation speed [12].

Goodfellow et al. [16] proposed a simple and fast method to generate adversarial examples called **Fast Gradient Sign method (FGSM)**, with the aim of

minimizing the maximum amount of perturbation added to any pixel
(L$_{inf}$ distance metric) of the image to cause misclassification. The rationale
of this technique is to compute the gradient of the loss function with respect to
the input (e.g. using backpropagation), and alter the existing data by adding a
perturbation which consists of the product of the sign gradient of the input and
the parameter ε controlling the magnitude of the attack.

Papernot et al. [18] proposed a new adversarial sample generation technique
called **Jacobian based Saliency Map Attack (JSMA)**, that uses feature
selection, unlike the previous method, with the aim of **minimizing the number of pixels modified (L$_0$ distance metric)** while cause misclassification.
This method revolves around the computation of saliency maps for an input
sample, which contain the saliency values for each feature. These values indicate how much the modification of each feature will perturb the classification
process. The features are then selected in decreasing order of saliency value,
and each is perturbed according to the parameter ϑ. The process finishes when
misclassification occurs, or a threshold number of modified features is reached.

Moosavi-Dezfooli et al. [17] proposed another adversarial sample generation
technique called **DeepFool**, with the aim of **minimizing the euclidean distance between perturbed samples and original samples (L$_2$ distance
metric)**. The generation of the attack consists of the analytical calculation of a
linear decision boundary that separates samples from different classes, followed
by the addition of a perturbation perpendicular to that decision boundary. In
neural networks, these decision boundaries are normally not linear, so they add
the perturbations iteratively by performing the attack multiple times, finishing
when an adversary is found. The overshoot parameter is used as a termination
criterion to prevent vanishing updates.

Carlini and Wagner [14] proposed a new type of attack, called **Carlini &
Wagner attack (C&W)**, which is more efficient than all other methods at
generating adversarial examples on the **L$_2$ distance metric**, and is claimed to
defeat adversarial distillation, a defensive technique which was proven effective
against other attacks [14].

Goodfellow et al. [16] explored an interesting property of adversarial inputs,
which is transferability across models. The authors observed that, when an adversarial input is successfully misclassified by a model, it will often be misclassified
by other models, even when they have different arquitectures or were trained in
different datasets. It was also observed that they often agree on the predicted
class.

The strategies described above were used on this paper to generate adversaries, and the transferability property was also tested by using different classifiers from the neural network originally used to produce the attacks.

3   Literature Review

Rigaki and Elragal [12] first tested the effectiveness of adversarial attacks in
an intrusion detection scenario. The authors performed tests using the NSL-
KDD dataset [3], by using FGSM and JSMA to generate Targeted attacks, and

used 5 models to perform classification: Decision Tree, Random Forest, Linear Support Vector Machine, Voting ensembles of the previous three classifiers and a Multilayer Perceptron. The results on JSMA showed that all classifiers accuracy was affected, with Linear SVM being the most substantial one with a drop of 27%. The drop on F1-score and AUC was also notable, especially on the Linear SVM and Voting ensemble. Overall, the most resilient classifier was Random Forest, which suffered smaller performance drops across all metrics.

Lin et al. [7] proposed the application of a Generative Adversarial Network (GAN) to generate Indiscriminate adversaries on the NSL-KDD dataset [3]. A GAN is a machine learning system, where two neural networks contest each other, with one acting as a generator, while the other behaves as the discriminator. The two networks play a zero-sum game, where the generator tries to produce samples that will be misclassified by the discriminator, while the latter will try to distinguish real samples from generated ones. By applying this concept to the NSL-KDD dataset, the results showed that the detection rates dropped up to 99% for the majority of classifiers.

Wang [10] also tested the performance of adversarial attacks on the NSL-KDD dataset, this time using four different adversarial attack techniques to attack a MLP classifier: **FGSM, JSMA, Deepfool** and **C&W**. The results showed that all attacks were effective at decreasing AUC, with C&W was the least effective attack. JSMA was by far the most realistic attack, since a small range of features was modified, producing an AUC of aproximately 50 for all classes, and FGSM and Deepfool were the most effective at decreasing overall performance across all metrics.

Even though there are multiple works on adversarial machine learning applied to intrusion detection that prove the effectiveness of some adversarial techniques, all were performed on only one dataset, the effectiveness of adversarial training was never tested, and some techniques were not tested against some classifiers.

4   Experimental Setup

To answer the questions proposed in Sect. 1, an experimental setup was proposed. The main steps consisted of choosing and preparing the datasets, choosing the classifiers and the adversarial attack algorithms, and preparing a pipeline for the multiple experiments (Fig. 1).

4.1   Datasets

The datasets that was chosen for the experiments were the **NSL-KDD** [3] and **CICIDS2017** [9]. **NSL-KDD** is an improved version of the **KDD99** [2] dataset, with redundant records removed to balance the data, scaling of the number of records according to their labeling difficulty, and reduction of the size of the dataset, while maintaining enough records to perform experiments [15]. This dataset is extensively used in the area of intrusion detection, and includes a wide variety of labeled attacks [4]. Since the main interest is in the Denial of

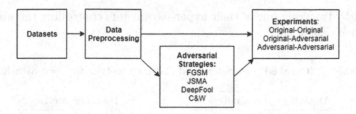

Fig. 1. Pipeline of the experiments. After preparing the dataset, ten datasets are created using four adversarial algorithms. Three experiences are then performed, with varying training and testing datasets.

Service attacks, all records of other types of attacks were removed. This dataset contains ten Denial of Service attack types, but to simplify the process, all were converted to the same class 'dos'.

CICIDS2017 is a more up-to-date dataset which contains, among many intrusions, multiple types of DDoS attacks, with statistical features generated to facilitate classification. To the best of authors knowledge, there are no other works on adversarial machine learning using this dataset.

4.2   Dataset Preparation

The first step to prepare the datasets was to **One-Hot Encode** the categorical features of the datasets. This consists on creating a different boolean feature for each possible value of the categorical feature, assign a 1 to the correct value and 0 to all others. This allows categorical data to be used for classification on some classifiers.

Min-max normalization was then applied to all features, squeezing their values to a certain interval, which was in this case between 0 and 1, preventing some classifiers from giving more importance to some features.

The last step was to perform **Feature Selection** to remove misleading data and improve training times. Among many tested approaches, **Recursive Feature Elimination with Linear SVMs** was the technique that offered the highest mean AUC for all classifiers on the original dataset. The optimal number of features for the NSL-KDD dataset was 41 from 122, while for the CICIDS2017 it was 26 from 77.

4.3   Adversarial Generation

To generate the adversarial examples, four adversarial attack techniques were used: **FGSM, JSMA, Deepfool** and **C&W**, using the **Cleverhans** Python library [8]. The choice of adversarial attack algorithms was done to have at least one attack for each distance metric (JSMA for L_0, Deepfool and C&W for L_2 and FGSM for L_{inf}). **C&W** was also included to test its effectiveness against adversarial training. Multiple tests for the first three algorithms were also performed by tweaking one of their hyper-parameters controlling the magnitude of the attack (Table 1).

Table 1. Tweaked parameters and distance metrics for each attack.

Algorithm	Parameters	Distance metric
FGSM	ε (0.1, 0.2 and 0.3)	L_{inf}
JSMA	ϑ (0.1, 0.2 and 0.3)	L_0
Deepfool	Overshoot (0.2, 0.5 and 1)	L_2
C&W	*None*	L_2

When generating adversarial datasets, only DDoS labeled connections were perturbed, and not benign rows, since the aim is to misclassify an attack as a normal connection, which makes this an **Integrity** and **Targeted** attack. Since there are only two labels (Normal and DDoS), adversarial algorithms that can only generate untargeted attacks can also be used.

One-hot-encoded columns were also not introduced to perturbations, since the methods used by these attacks could assign values between 0 and 1 to these columns, which is impossible in a normal scenario. Because of this, on the NSL-KDD dataset, perturbations were only added to 10 out of the 41 columns, while on the CICIDS, the perturbations were added to 25 out of 26 features.

4.4 Machine Learning Algorithms

To perform classification, six algorithms were used: **Decision Tree, Random Forest, Naive Bayes, Support Vector Machine, Neural Network and Denoising Autoencoder**. To perform classification with the Denoising Autoencoder, new layers were added on top of the last layer of the autoencoder, which were trained after the autoencoder was trained, with the original layers frozen.

The choice of algorithms was performed in order to have at least one for each tribe of algorithms (according to Domingos [5]), with the exception of evolutionary algorithms. To optimize the hyper-parameters of the algorithms, Cross Validation Grid Search with 3 folds was performed, mainly to optimize performance. The algorithms and hyper-parameters that were optimized can be found in Table 2.

The first four classifiers were implemented using the **scikit-learn** [21] library for Python, while the last two were implemented using **Keras** [1] with **Tensorflow**[13] backend.

4.5 Pipeline

In total, three different experiments were performed to answer the questions proposed in Sect. 1. 10-fold cross-validation was used in all the scenarios.

Table 2. Optimized parameters for each algorithm.

Algorithm	Parameters
Decision tree	Max depth, criterion
Random forest	Max depth, criterion, number of estimators
Support vector machine	Cost, gamma
Naive Bayes	Laplace smoothing
Neural network	Neurons per layer, dropout rate
Denoising autoencoder	Neurons per layer, Gaussian Noise Std. Dev.

Scenario 1 - Original/Original: on the first experiment, all classifiers were trained on the original datasets, and tested on that same datasets. This serves as the baseline performance of the classifiers on the datasets;

Scenario 2 - Original/Adversarial: on the second experiment, all classifiers were trained on the original datasets, and tested on all the adversarial datasets. This experiment validates if the generation of adversaries can deteriorate the performance of classifiers that were not trained against them;

Scenario 3 - Adversarial/Adversarial: third experiment, all classifiers were trained on all adversarial techniques used, leaving out the technique being tested. This was done to prevent the classifiers from overfitting to the technique being tested.

5   Results

To evaluate the performance of the classifiers under the attacks, the ROC-AUC and F1 metrics were used. Due to space limitations, only the ROC-AUC was included in the results, although the F1 results followed the same tendency as ROC-AUC for every experiment.

The results of the three experiments can be observed in Tables 3 and 4. To perform a statistical comparison between different methods, we used the **Friedman test** [22]. The ranks in the tables can be compared between each other with the **Nemenyi test** [22], using the critical difference of **2.38** for a 95% confidence level. This indicates that, if the difference between the rankings of classifiers is greater than the critical difference, we can reject the null hypothesis which states that the classifiers have the same performance.

The first experiment (Table 3) serves as a baseline for the performance of the classifiers, with no adversaries being used (scenario 1). The algorithms that performed the best were Decision Tree and Random Forest, while the algorithms that performed the worst were Naive Bayes and Denoising Autoencoder.

On the second experiment (Table 4), with the introduction of adversaries in the testing phase, we can observe a generalized decrease of the performance of all classifiers (scenario 2). The average of the AUC of all classifiers decreased by 13%

Table 3. NSL-KDD (left) and CICIDS (right) Original dataset Train and Test (AUC)

	Original	Ranks		Original	Ranks
dtree	**0.9910**	1	dtree	**0.9993**	1
rforest	0.9884	2	rforest	0.9993	2
svm	0.9702	4	svm	0.9931	4
naive	0.9038	6	naive	0.8889	6
nn	0.9783	3	nn	0.9921	3
dae	0.9038	5	dae	0.8750	5

Table 4. Second and Third experiments on both datasets (AUC). The best performing algorithms for each scenario are identified in the yellow cells.

	FGSM (ε=0.3)	FGSM (ε=0.2)	FGSM (ε=0.1)	JSMA (ϑ=0.3)	JSMA (ϑ=0.2)	JSMA (ϑ=0.1)	DFOOL (os=1)	DFOOL (os=0.5)	DFOOL (os=0.2)	C&W	Mean Ranks
NSL-KDD: Original-Adversarial										
dtree	0.7286	0.7650	0.8783	0.8695	0.9241	0.8781	0.5920	0.7176	0.7306	0.7068	5.2
rforest	0.6870	0.7741	0.8849	**0.9526**	**0.9548**	0.9476	0.5488	0.5779	0.6820	0.6200	4.5
svm	0.8082	0.8700	**0.9336**	0.9000	0.9349	**0.9669**	0.6420	0.6723	0.7666	**0.9456**	2.9
naive	0.7888	0.8914	0.9016	0.9057	0.9056	0.9044	0.7612	0.8231	0.8996	0.9014	2.9
nn	0.7681	0.8474	0.9244	0.9054	0.9372	0.9637	0.7034	0.7239	0.7728	0.8671	3
dae	**0.8953**	**0.9027**	0.9058	0.9010	0.9012	0.9072	**0.8846**	**0.9027**	**0.9047**	0.8922	2.5
CICIDS: Original-Adversarial										
dtree	0.5030	0.5006	0.5018	0.5648	0.5646	0.5642	0.5001	0.5018	0.5039	0.5030	3.5
rforest	0.5006	0.4996	0.4996	0.6355	0.6292	0.6550	0.4997	0.5000	0.5032	0.5010	4.2
svm	0.4998	0.4998	0.5000	0.4990	0.5025	0.5015	0.5031	0.5040	0.5056	0.5529	3.8
naive	0.3891	0.3891	0.3891	0.3898	0.3898	0.3898	0.4106	0.4201	0.4303	0.5587	5.7
nn	0.5004	0.4999	0.5265	0.6043	0.6520	0.7926	0.5000	0.5024	0.5050	**0.9349**	2.7
dae	**0.8155**	**0.8602**	**0.8284**	**0.8887**	**0.8976**	**0.8766**	**0.8692**	**0.8491**	**0.8840**	0.9147	1.1
NSL-KDD: Adversarial-Adversarial										
dtree	0.9847	0.9865	0.9914	0.9798	0.9808	0.9818	0.9934	0.9931	0.9929	0.9942	2.4
rforest	**0.9924**	**0.9931**	**0.9935**	0.9740	0.9737	0.9781	**0.9996**	**0.9995**	**0.9995**	**0.9944**	1.9
svm	0.9912	0.9894	0.9882	0.9794	0.9797	0.9804	0.9093	0.9593	0.9736	0.9692	3.3
naive	0.7935	0.6376	0.6114	0.9171	0.6863	0.6114	0.6467	0.6378	0.6333	0.6114	5.9
nn	0.9860	0.9875	0.9893	**0.9833**	**0.9851**	**0.9846**	0.9890	0.9895	0.9902	0.9770	2.4
dae	0.8384	0.8966	0.8902	0.8982	0.8960	0.8988	0.8946	0.8979	0.9002	0.8954	5.1
CICIDS: Adversarial-Adversarial										
dtree	0.8579	0.8868	0.9752	0.5649	0.5648	0.6171	0.9060	0.9679	0.9981	0.9916	3.8
rforest	**0.9999**	**0.9999**	**0.9999**	**0.9992**	**0.9991**	0.9910	**0.9997**	**0.9996**	**0.9996**	**0.9923**	1
svm	0.4981	0.6039	0.8192	0.9809	0.9858	0.9882	0.9883	0.9883	0.9883	0.9872	3.4
naive	0.3990	0.5684	0.6924	0.8435	0.8024	0.8024	0.8219	0.8204	0.8155	0.7950	5.4
nn	0.8134	0.9389	0.9919	0.8401	0.9270	0.9474	0.9951	0.9959	0.9955	0.9896	2.9
dae	0.8282	0.7959	0.7935	0.8535	0.7763	0.8463	0.7916	0.8613	0.8599	0.8271	4.5

on the NSL-KDD dataset, from **0.956** to **0.833**, while on the CICIDS dataset, it decreased by 40%, from **0.958** to **0.576**. The higher decrease in performance of the CICIDS dataset can mainly be attributed to the higher proportion of features that were added noise, since on the NSL-KDD dataset, noise was only added to 10 out of its 41 features, while on the CICIDS dataset, it was added to 25 out of 26 features On this experiment, the classifier that offered most resilience to adversaries on both datasets was the Denoising Autoencoder, whose mean AUC only decreased by 1% from **0.904** to **0.899** on the NSL-KDD dataset, and 1% on the CICIDS dataset, from **0.875** to **0.868**. Using the Friedman test, we can observe that the performance of the Denoising Autoencoder is significantly better than the Decision Tree on the NSL-KDD dataset, and significantly better than all classifiers except the Neural Network on the CICIDS dataset. The higher performance of the Denoising Autoencoder over other classifiers can be due to its ability to remove noise from the adversarial data, since it was trained by introducing additive gaussian noise on the training data. Although on average the Denoising Autoencoder had the highest rank in this experiment, we can observe that the Support Vector Machine and Random Forest performed generally well in scenarios with less noise introduced, such as JSMA and FGSM with $\varepsilon = 0.1$ on the NSL-KDD dataset.

On the third and final experiment (Table 4), by introducing adversaries in the training phase from different algorithms (scenario 3), the decrease in the average of the AUC of all classifiers was significantly less notorious, with a decrease of 4%, from **0.956** to **0.917** on the NSL-KDD dataset, and of 18%, from **0.958** to **0.870** on the CICIDS dataset. In this scenario, the classifier that showed more resilience to adversaries was the Random Forest, which only suffered a decrease on the mean AUC of 0.1%, from **0.988** to **0.987** on the NSL-KDD dataset, and of 0.1% **0.999** to **0.998** on the CICIDS dataset. Contrary to the second experiment, the Denoising Autoencoder suffered minimal changes in the mean AUC, with larger improvements being observed on the Random Forest and Neural Network Classifiers. Using the Friedman test, the Random Forest classifier is significantly better than the Denoising Autoencoder and Naive Bayes on the NSL-KDD dataset, and significantly better than all classifiers except the Neural Network on the CICIDS dataset. The performance of Random Forest in this scenario can be attributed to it being an ensemble method, which reduces the error by averaging the outputs of all the independent trees. Although Random Forest performed the best on the CICIDS classifier for all attacks, we can observe that in the NSL-KDD dataset, where less features were perturbed, the classifier that performed the best against JSMA was the Neural Network.

To validate the integrity of the attacks on both datasets, for each altered sample, we measured the Euclidean Distance to every other sample on the original dataset, and confirmed that for 99% of adversaries, the closest sample on the original dataset belonged to the same label. Furthermore, no algorithm produced an average perturbation on any feature superior to 30%, to emulate realistic attacks.

6   Conclusions

This paper extends other works on the generation of adversarial attacks on the **NSL-KDD** dataset, providing a more insightful view on the performance of different classifiers and a broader type of attacks. It also provides experimental validation of the results achieved with that dataset with the more recent dataset **CICIDS2017**.

With the results obtained from the experiments, we can answer the three questions proposed in Sect. 1:

- The generation of adversarial datasets deteriorates the mean performance of all classifiers, with JSMA being the least effective attack, but the attack which perturbs less features, making it more feasible in real scenarios;
- The training of models using adversaries improved the performance of all classifiers, with a smaller improvement being observed in the Denoising Autoencoder;
- When not including adversaries in the training set, the algorithm that showed higher resilience in scenarios with substantial noise was the Denoising Autoencoder, while in the presence of smaller perturbations, the Random Forest and Support Vector Machines performed the best. When training with adversaries, the Random Forest classifier was the best performing classifier.

To extend this paper, more datasets should be used, and new directions should be explored to introduce perturbations on lower level features, such as packet level, to allow the generation of adversarial Denial of Service attacks on real scenarios. A more thorough analysis of which features are modifiable, while maintaining the integrity of the attack, should also be considered for this scenario. Furthermore, to achieve more realistic results, the problem should be explored on a Denial of Service dataset with three classes representing: (1) a normal connection with normal traffic, (2) a normal connection with heavy traffic (which can involuntarily produce Denial of Service) and (3) a malign connection. In the studied datasets, only a normal and malign connection was considered, as no dataset was found for the three-class scenario.

Acknowledgements. This work was supported by the ATENA European H2020 Project (H2020-DS-2015-1 Project 700581).

References

1. Chollet, F., et al.: Keras. https://keras.io. Accessed June 2019
2. Kdd99 dataset (KDD Cup 1999 data). http://kdd.ics.uci.edu/databases/kddcup99/kddcup99.html. Accessed June 2019
3. NSL-KDD Dataset. https://www.unb.ca/cic/datasets/nsl.html. Accessed June 2019
4. Ring, M., et al.: A survey of network-based intrusion detection data sets (2019). 12 Authors Suppressed Due to Excessive Length https://doi.org/10.1016/j.cose.2019.06.005
5. Domingos, P.: The Master Algorithm: How the Quest for the Ultimate Learning Machine Will Remake Our World. Basic Books Inc., New York (2018)
6. Duddu, V.: A survey of adversarial machine learning in cyber warfare. Def. Sci. J. **68**(4), 356–366 (2018)
7. Lin, Z., et al.: IDSGAN: generative adversarial networks for attack generation against intrusion detection (2018). arXiv:1809.02077
8. Papernot, N., et al.: Technical report on the CleverHans v2.1.0 adversarial examples library (2018). arXiv:1610.00768

9. Sharafaldin, I., et al.: Toward generating a new intrusion detection dataset and intrusion traffic characterization. In: 4th International Conference on Information Systems Security and Privacy (2018)

10. Wang, Z.: Deep learning-based intrusion detection with adversaries. IEEE Access **6**, 38:367–38:384 (2018)

11. Frazão, I., Abreu, P.H., Cruz, T., Araújo, H., Simões, P.: Denial of service attacks: detecting the frailties of machine learning algorithms in the classification process. In: Luiijf, E., Žutautaitė, I., Hämmerli, B.M. (eds.) CRITIS 2018. LNCS, vol. 11260, pp. 230–235. Springer, Cham (2019). https://doi.org/10.1007/978-3-030-05849-4_19

12. Rigaki, M., et al.: Adversarial deep learning against intrusion detection classifiers. Master's thesis, Information Security's master dissertation, Luleå University of Technology (2017)

13. Abadi, M., et al.: TensorFlow: large-scale machine learning on heterogeneous systems (2016). arXiv:1603.04467v2

14. Carlini, N., et al.: Towards evaluating the robustness of neural networks (2016). arXiv:1608.04644

15. Dhanabal, L., Shantharajah, D.S.P.: A study on NSL-KDD dataset for intrusion detection system based on classification algorithms. Int. J. Adv. Res. Comp. Comm. Eng. **4**(6), 446–452 (2015)

16. Goodfellow, I., et al.: Explaining and harnessing adversarial examples (2015). arXiv:1412.6572

17. Moosavi-Dezfooli, S., et al.: DeepFool: a simple and accurate method to fool deep neural networks (2015). arXiv:1511.04599

18. Papernot, N., et al.: The limitations of deep learning in adversarial settings (2015). arXiv:1511.07528

19. Zamani, M.: Machine learning techniques for intrusion detection (2013). arXiv:1312.2177

20. Huang, L., et al.: Adversarial machine learning. In: Proceedings of the 4th ACM Workshop on Security and Artificial Intelligence, Illinois, USA, Chicago, pp. 43–58 (2011)

21. Pedregosa, F., et al.: Scikit-learn: machine learning in Python. J. Mach. Learn. Res. **12**, 2825–2830 (2011)

22. Demšar, J.: Statistical comparisons of classifiers over multiple data sets. J. Mach. Learn. Res. **7**, 1–30 (2006)

23. Kemmerer, R.A.: Cybersecurity. In: 25th International Conference on Software Engineering, pp. 705–715 (2003)

The Regression Tsetlin Machine: A Tsetlin Machine for Continuous Output Problems

K. Darshana Abeyrathna[✉], Ole-Christoffer Granmo, Lei Jiao, and Morten Goodwin

Centre for Artificial Intelligence Research, University of Agder, Grimstad, Norway
{darshana.abeyrathna,ole.granmo,lei.jiao,morten.goodwin}@uia.no

Abstract. The recently introduced Tsetlin Machine (TM) has provided competitive pattern classification accuracy in several benchmarks, composing patterns with easy-to-interpret conjunctive clauses in propositional logic. In this paper, we go beyond pattern classification by introducing a new type of TMs, namely, the *Regression Tsetlin Machine* (RTM). In all brevity, we modify the inner inference mechanism of the TM so that input patterns are transformed into a single continuous output, rather than to distinct categories. We achieve this by: (1) using the conjunctive clauses of the TM to capture arbitrarily complex patterns; (2) mapping these patterns to a continuous output through a novel voting and normalization mechanism; and (3) employing a feedback scheme that updates the TM clauses to minimize the regression error. The feedback scheme uses a new activation probability function that stabilizes the updating of clauses, while the overall system converges towards an accurate input-output mapping. The performance of the RTM is evaluated using six different artificial datasets with and without noise, in comparison with the Classic Tsetlin Machine (CTM) and the Multiclass Tsetlin Machine (MTM). Our empirical results indicate that the RTM obtains the best training and testing results for both noisy and noise-free datasets, with a smaller number of clauses. This, in turn, translates to higher regression accuracy, using significantly less computational resources.

Keywords: Tsetlin Machine · Regression Tsetlin Machine · Tsetlin Automata · Regression · Pattern recognition · Propositional logic

1 Introduction

Computational simplicity, ease of interpretation, along with competitive pattern recognition accuracy, make the recently introduced Tsetlin Machine (TM) [1] a promising new paradigm for machine learning. Indeed, the TM has outperformed well-known machine learning algorithms such as Logistic Regression,

© Springer Nature Switzerland AG 2019
P. Moura Oliveira et al. (Eds.): EPIA 2019, LNAI 11805, pp. 268–280, 2019.
https://doi.org/10.1007/978-3-030-30244-3_23

Neural Networks, and Support Vector Machine (SVM) in several benchmarks, including Iris Data Classification, Handwritten Digits Classification (MNIST), Predicting Optimum Moves in the Axis and Allies Board Game, and Classification of Noisy XOR Data with Non-Informative Features [1].

Tsetlin Automata and the Tsetlin Machine. The core of the TM is built on Tsetlin Automata (TAs), developed by Tsetlin in the early 1960s [2]. This powerful, yet simple, leaning mechanism has been used to solve a number of machine learning and stochastic optimization problems, such as resource allocation [3], stochastic searching on the line [4], distributed coordination [5], graph coloring [6], and forecasting disease outbreaks [7]. In the TM, TAs represent literals – input features and their negations. The literals, in turn, form conjunctive clauses in propositional logic, as decided by the TAs. The final TM output is a disjunction of all the specified clauses. In this manner, the pattern composition and learning procedure of the TM is fully transparent and understandable, facilitating human interpretation. In addition, the TM has an inherent computational advantage. That is, the inputs and outputs of the TM can naturally be represented as bits, and recognition and learning is performed by manipulating those bits. The operation of the TM thus demands relatively small computational resources, and supports hardware-near and parallel computation e.g. on GPUs.

Lately, the TM has provided state-of-the-art performance in several real-life applications. Berge et al. have for instance successfully used the TM for medical text categorization [8]. They used the TM to provide interpretable pattern recognition for the analysis of electronic health records. The authors demonstrated that the TM can outperform established machine learning algorithms such as k-nearest neighbors (kNN), SVM, Random Forest, Decision Trees, Multilayer Perceptron (MLP), Long Short-Term Memory (LSTM) Neural Networks, and Convolutional Neural Networks (CNNs), in terms of precision, recall, and F-measure. Furthermore, Darshana et al. have shown that the TM can outperform MLPs, Decision Trees, and SVMs in dengue fever outbreak prediction. The latter result was achieved by making the TM capable of expressing thresholds and intervals that capture patterns formed by continuous features. By carefully selecting thresholds and intervals, the TM avoided losing information due to binarization [9].

Research Question and Paper Contributions. The TM has been designed for classification, not for producing continuous output. How to best produce continuous output is unclear, with the existing binarization schemes being incapable of fully leveraging the natural ranking of numbers. In this paper, we introduce the Regression Tsetlin Machine (RTM) to overcome above limitation of the TM. The RTM is a novel variant of the Classic Tsetlin Machine (CTM), specifically addressing the unique properties of regression. The novel modifications that we introduce are subtle, but crucial. First of all, the clause polarities the CTM uses to discriminate patterns, using positive and negative examples, are eliminated. Instead, the objective of the RTM is to use the clauses to map the sum of the clause outputs into one single continuous output. The discrepancy between predicted and target output is minimized with a new feedback scheme tailored for regression, including a modified stochastic activation probability function.

Paper Organization. The remainder of the paper is organized as follows. In Sect. 2, we present the main contribution of this paper, which is the RTM, and how we build it upon the CTM. We then investigate the behavior of the RTM using six different artificial datasets in Sect. 3. We demonstrate empirically that the RTM is superior both to the CTM as well as its multiclass version when it comes to predicting continuous output. We conclude our work in Sect. 4.

2   The Regression Tsetlin Machine (RTM)

The RTM is a novel variant of the CTM. To highlight the unique properties of the RTM, we start this section with first reviewing the TM in more detail, and then discuss how it can be modified to support continuous output.

2.1   The Classic Tsetlin Machine (CTM)

At the heart of the TM, we find multiple teams of TAs that build conjunctive clauses in propositional logic. The purpose is to capture hidden patterns in the data.

Learning with TAs. Each Tsetlin Automaton (TA) learns the optimal action in an environment by sequentially performing the actions that the environment offers. To identify the optimal actions, the TAs adjust their states based on the feedback they receive from the environment, which can be penalties or rewards. Asymptotically, a TA identifies the action that provides the highest probability of reward [10,11]. These simple learning devices are capable of online learning, have a simple structure, and require modest computational power. Yet, they are able to learn accurately with relatively few interactions with the environment [12,13].

Clause Formation and the TA Team. The TM bases its operations on the simplest form of TAs, namely, the two action one, with finite memory depth. As illustrated in Table 1, a team of TAs cooperates to form a clause. The table depicts the steps leading to a clause being formed. Consider an input feature vector $X = [x_1, x_2, \ldots, x_o]$. Each TA represents either an input feature x_k or its negation $\neg x_k$ (jointly referred to as literals). Further, each TA in the team decides whether to include or exclude its assigned literal in the clause that the

Table 1. The steps used to form a clause based on the input features and the actions of the TAs.

Phase	Operations							Comments
1	x_1		x_2		$\ldots$		x_o	Input Features, X
2	x_1	$\neg x_1$	x_2	$\neg x_2$		x_o	$\neg x_o$	Literals
3	TA_1^1	TA_1^2	TA_2^1	TA_2^2	$\ldots$	TA_o^1	TA_o^2	TA
4	in	ex	ex	in	$\ldots$	ex	in	Actions = $\{in, ex\}$
5	$x_1 \wedge \neg x_2 \wedge \ldots \ldots \wedge \neg x_o$							$c_1 = \bigwedge_{k=1}^{o} x_k, \quad \forall\, TA_k^1 = in$ $c_2 = \bigwedge_{k=1}^{o} \neg x_k, \quad \forall\, TA_k^2 = in$ $C = c_1 \wedge c_2$

team is forming. Accordingly, when there are o input features, $2 \times o$ TAs are needed to form the clause. The two actions available to each TA are $\{in,\ ex\}$. Here, in refers to including the literal controlled by the TA and ex refers to excluding it. As seen in the final step in the table, the included literals form a conjunctive clause, while the excluded ones are ignored.

Clauses and Voting. The number of clauses, m, needed for a particular problem depends on the complexity of the dataset. It should at least be sufficient to cover the full range of sub-patterns associated with each output $\{0, 1\}$. However, with hidden and unknown sub-patterns, a grid search is required to find the best m.

The m clauses are assigned either a positive or negative polarity, and they vote separately to decide the final output of the TM. Clauses with odd index are assigned positive polarity (C^{+}) and they vote for the final output 1. Clauses with even index are assigned negative polarity (C^{-}) and they vote for the final output 0. For both categories, a vote is submitted when the clause recognizes a sub-pattern. If the clause is unable to find a sub-pattern, it declines to vote. Finally, the output, y, is decided based on the number of votes gained by each category $\{0, 1\}$ as given in the Eq. (1):

$$y = \begin{cases} 1, & \text{if } \sum_{j=1,3,m-1} C_j^{+} > \sum_{j=2,4,m} C_j^{-} \\ 0, & \text{if } \sum_{j=1,3,m-1} C_j^{+} < \sum_{j=2,4,m} C_j^{-} \end{cases} \tag{1}$$

Learning Procedure. Learning in the TM is based on reinforcement learning. The reward, penalty, and inaction probabilities that guide the TAs in all of the clauses depend on several factors, namely, the actual output, the clause output, the literal value, and the current state of the TA. The basic idea is to alter the number of votes belong to each output category when the output is a false negative or a false positive. In the TM, this is done by two types of feedback - Type I and Type II. Type I feedback eliminates false negative output and reinforces true positive output, while Type II feedback eliminates false positive output. Both of these kinds of feedback are summarized in Table 2.

Table 2. Type I and Type II feedback designed to eliminate false negative and false positive output.

Feedback type			I				II			
Clause output			1		0		1		0	
Literal value			1	0	1	0	1	0	1	0
Current state	Include	Reward probability	$(s-1)/s$	NA	0	0	0	NA	0	0
		Inaction probability	$1/s$	NA	$(s-1)/s$	$(s-1)/s$	1	NA	1	1
		Penalty probability	0	NA	$1/s$	$1/s$	0	NA	0	0
	Exclude	Reward probability	0	$1/s$	$1/s$	$1/s$	0	0	0	0
		Inaction probability	$1/s$	$(s-1)/s$	$(s-1)/s$	$(s-1)/s$	1	0	1	1
		Penalty probability	$(s-1)/s$	0	0	0	0	1	0	0

† s is the precision and controls the granularity of the sub-patterns captured [1]

Type I feedback is given to clauses with positive polarity when the actual output, $\hat{y}$, is 1 and clauses with negative polarity when the actual output, $\hat{y}$, is 0. The probability of activation of Type I feedback is $[T - \max(-T, \min(T, \sum_{j=1}^{m} C_j))]/2T$. Type II feedback is given to clauses with positive polarity when the actual output, $\hat{y}$, is 0 and clauses with negative polarity when the actual output, $\hat{y}$, is 1. The probability of activation of Type II feedback is $[T + \max(-T, \min(T, \sum_{j=1}^{m} C_j))]/2T$. TAs remain unchanged if the vote difference, $\sum_{j=1}^{m} C_j$, is higher than or equal to T when $\hat{y} = 1$ and lower than or equal to $-T$ when $\hat{y} = 0$, according to the activation probabilities of each type of feedback.

In all brevity, when the target output for a training instance $\hat{X}$ is $\hat{y} = 1$, the votes from the clauses with negative polarity must not outnumber the votes from the clauses with positive polarity (in order to correctly classify the instance). Therefore, clauses with positive polarity receive Type I feedback (the activation probability increases with the number of voting clauses with negative polarity) since this reinforces clauses which output 1. Similarly, clauses with negative polarity receive Type II feedback (the activation probability increases with the number of voting clauses with positive polarity) since this suppresses voting activity by making clauses of negative polarity evaluate to 0. The procedure is similar when the target output is $\hat{y} = 0$. The TM then needs to make sure that more clauses with negative polarity provide votes compared to those with positive polarity. Eventually, the above feedback reduces the number of false positives and false negatives to make the TM learn the propositional formulae that provide high accuracy output.

2.2   The Multiclass Tsetlin Machine (MTM)

For the CTM, the final summation operator aggregates all of the clause outputs into one of the two available outputs: 0 or 1. However, for categorization tasks with more classes than two, another design is needed. In the Multiclass Tsetlin Machine (MTM), clauses are partitioned equally among the classes. The clauses of each individual class then act separately, similarly to a single TM. However, the votes output for each class then form the basis for classification. That is, an argmax operator arbitrates the final class, based on the votes collected for each class. When there are n classes, the output y can thus be expressed as:

$$y = \operatorname{argmax}_{i=1,\ldots,n}\left\{\left(\sum_{j=1,3,\ldots(\frac{m}{n})-1} C_j^i - \sum_{j=2,4,\ldots(\frac{m}{n})} C_j^i\right)\right\}. \tag{2}$$

The training procedure is similar to the CTM training procedure. However, in the MTM, the clauses of the class being the target of the current training sample are treated as if $\hat{y} = 1$, while the clauses of a randomly selected class from the remaining classes is treated as if $\hat{y} = 0$. In each class, clauses with positive polarity vote to say that the output belongs to the considered class. Similarly, the clauses with negative polarity vote to indicate that the output does not belong to the considered class.

2.3   The Regression Tsetlin Machine (RTM)

When the output is continuous, neither the CTM or the MTM above are ideal. However, we will now show that the CTM can be modified to produce continuous output by means of three pertinent modifications.

In CTM and MTM, the polarity of clauses is used to classify data into different classes. We now remove the polarity of clauses, since we intend to use the clauses as additive building blocks that can be used to calculate continuous output. That is, we intend to map the total vote count into a single continuous output. As a result, the complexity of the RTM is actually reduced.

With merely one type of clauses, the summation operator outputs a value between 0 and T, which is simply the number of clauses that evaluates to 1. This value is then normalized to produce the regression output. Thus, through this simple modification, the TM can now produce continuous output, with precision that increases with higher T.

Let $\hat{y}_{\max}$ denote the maximum output value $\hat{y}$ among the N training samples $Y = [\hat{y}_1, \hat{y}_2, \hat{y}_3, \ldots, \hat{y}_N]$. Then the sum of the votes from the clauses $\sum_{j=1}^{m} C_j$ of the TM is normalized to achieve the regression output by dividing by T and multiplying with $\hat{y}_{\max}$. So, for the oth training sample, $(\hat{X}_o, \hat{y}_o)$, the TM output, y_o, is calculated from the input $\hat{X}_o$ as follows:

$$y_o = \frac{\sum_{j=1}^{m} C_j(\hat{X}_o) \times \hat{y}_{\max}}{T}. \tag{3}$$

Feedback, then, is based on comparing the output, y_o of the TM with the target output $\hat{y}_o$. The target value $\hat{y}_o$ can be higher or lower than the output value y_o. This is our basis for our new feedback scheme. That is, similarly to other machine learning methods, certain internal operations are needed to minimize the error between the predicted output, y_o, and target output, $\hat{y}_o$. In the RTM, this is quite simply achieved by providing Type I and Type II feedbacks according to the following criteria:

$$Feedback = \begin{cases} \text{Type I,} & \text{if } \quad y_o < \hat{y}_o, \\ \\ \text{Type II,} & \text{if } \quad y_o > \hat{y}_o. \end{cases} \tag{4}$$

As with the CTM, the idea here is to increase the number of clauses that output 1 when the predicted output is less than the target output $(y_o < \hat{y}_o)$. To achieve this, we then provide Type I feedback. Conversely, Type II feedback is applied to decrease the number of clauses that evaluate to 1 when the predicted output is higher than the target output $(y_o > \hat{y}_o)$.

To stabilize learning, we use an activation probability function that makes the probability of giving a clause feedback proportional to the difference between the predicted and target output (the error). That is, in the RTM, feedback to clauses is determined stochastically using the following activation probability function, P_{act}:

$$P_{act} = \frac{K \times |y_o - \hat{y}_o|}{\hat{y}_{\max}}. \tag{5}$$

As seen, the magnitude of the function is adjusted with the constant K. The resulting activation function reduces the oscillation of the predicted value during the training process, stabilizing it around the target value.

The behavior of the RTM is studied in the following sections, in comparison with the CTM and MTM.

3   Empirical Results

3.1   Experiment Setup

We study the behavior of the RTM using six different datasets. These datasets have been constructed to facilitate empirical analysis of the optimality of RTM learning, with the underlying input-output mapping being known. Dataset I contains 2-bit feature input. The output is 100 times larger than the decimal value of the binary input (e.g., when the input is [1, 0], the output is 200). The training set consists of 8000 samples while the testing set consists of 2000 samples, both without noise. Dataset II contains the same data as Dataset I, except that the output of the training data is perturbed to introduce noise. For Dataset III we introduce 3-bit input, without noise, and for Dataset IV we have 3-bit input with noisy output. Finally, Dataset V has 4-bit input without noise, and Dataset VI has 4-bit input with noisy.

Each input feature have been generated independently with equal probability of 0 and 1 values, leading to a more or less uniform distribution of bit values.

In order to increase our understanding of the RTM, we investigate the effect the hyper-parameters T and s have on learning.

Experiment I: We first study the effect varying T has on performance for the different datasets.

Experiment II: The effect of different s values (controlling the number of sub-patterns) is further investigated for all of the datasets.

Experiment III: We finally compare the RTM results with what can be achieved with CTM and MTM.

3.2   Results and Discussion

We use Mean Absolute Error (MAE) to measure performance. Figure 1 plots error across 200 epochs, with learning influenced by different T values. Figure 1(a) shows the results for Dataset I, Fig. 1(b) reports results for Dataset II, and so on. MAE after 200 epochs is also given in brackets for each threshold in the legend.

From Fig. 1, we can observe that just 3 clauses ($T = 3$) are enough to reduce error to zero for Dataset I, which can be explained by the noise-free data. Because the output value is decided by the number of clauses that output 1, we require *two* clauses with $TA_1^1 = \{in\}$, $TA_1^2 = \{ex\}$, $TA_2^1 = \{ex\}$, and $TA_2^2 = \{ex\}$ to capture the pattern (1 $*$); see Phase 4 in Table 1. Further, we need *one* clause

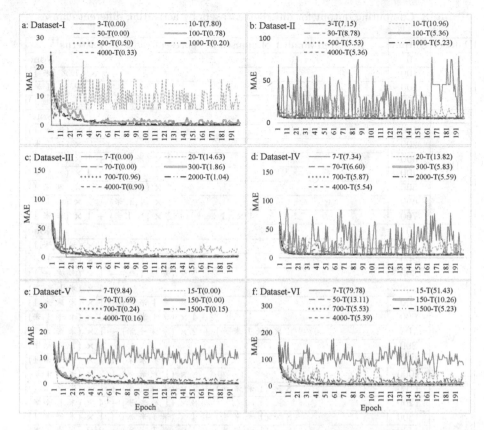

Fig. 1. Training error over training epochs. Each dataset is processed with different T.

with $\mathrm{TA}_1^1 = \{ex\}$, $\mathrm{TA}_1^2 = \{ex\}$, $\mathrm{TA}_2^1 = \{in\}$, and $\mathrm{TA}_2^2 = \{ex\}$ to capture the pattern ($*$ 1). Here, $*$ means an input feature that can take an arbitrary value, either 0 or 1. These three clauses can collectively form any outputs for the Dataset I as shown in Table 3. For instance, input (0 1) only activates the clause with $\mathrm{TA}_1^1 = \{ex\}$, $\mathrm{TA}_1^2 = \{ex\}$, $\mathrm{TA}_2^1 = \{in\}$, and $\mathrm{TA}_2^2 = \{ex\}$, which represents the pattern ($*$ 1). Accordingly, the RTM correctly computes the output, 100. Likewise, input (1 0) only activates the *two* clauses with $\mathrm{TA}_1^1 = \{in\}$, $\mathrm{TA}_1^2 = \{ex\}$, $\mathrm{TA}_2^1 = \{ex\}$, and $\mathrm{TA}_2^2 = \{ex\}$, which represent the pattern (1 $*$). Thus, the output 200 is correctly computed. All the clauses are activated when the input is (1 1) and therefore the output 300 is computed correctly as well.

We observe similar behaviour for Dataset III and Dataset V. More specifically, Dataset III requires *seven* clauses to represent the three different patterns it contains, namely, $(4 \times (1\, * \, *), 2 \times (*\, 1\, *), 1 \times (*\, *\, 1))$[1]. Further, Dataset

---

[1] In this expression, "*four* clauses to represent the pattern (1 $*$ $*$)" is written as "4 $\times$ (1 $*$ $*$)".

Table 3. Computing output for different datasets by activating different clauses.

Dataset	Output	Required number of clauses to represent different patterns††
I	0	None
	100	1 × (* 1)
	200	2 × (1 *)
	300	2 × (1 *) + 1 × (* 1)
III	0	None
	100	1 × (* * 1)
	200	2 × (* 1 *)
	300	2 × (* 1 *) + 1 × (* * 1)
	400	4 × (1 * *)
	500	4 × (1 * *) + 1 × (* * 1)
	600	4 × (1 * *) + 2 × (* 1 *)
	700	4 × (1 * *) + 2 × (* 1 *) + 1 × (* * 1)
V	0	None
	100	1 × (* * * 1)
	200	2 × (* * 1 *)
	300	2 × (* * 1 *) + 1 × (* * * 1)
	400	4 × (* 1 * *)
	500	4 × (* 1 * *) + 1 × (* * * 1)
	600	4 × (* 1 * *) + 2 × (* * 1 *)
	700	4 × (* 1 * *) + 2 × (* * 1 *) + 1 × (* * * 1)
	800	8 × (1 * * *)
	900	8 × (1 * * *) + 1 × (* * * 1)
	1000	8 × (1 * * *) + 2 × (* * 1 *)
	1100	8 × (1 * * *) + 2 × (* * 1 *) + 1 × (* * * 1)
	1200	8 × (1 * * *) + 4 × (* 1 * *)
	1300	8 × (1 * * *) + 4 × (* 1 * *) + 1 × (* * * 1)
	1400	8 × (1 * * *) + 4 × (* 1 * *) + 2 × (* * 1 *)
	1500	8 × (1 * * *) + 4 × (* 1 * *) + 2 × (* * 1 *) + 1 × (* * * 1)

†† for example, "*two* clauses to represent the pattern (1 *)" is written as "2 × (1 *)"

V requires *fifteen* clauses to represent four different patterns it contains (8 × (1 * * *), 4 × (* 1 * *), 2 × (* * 1 *), 1 × (* * * 1)). As we can see from these 3 datasets, RTM can reach 0.00 for the training *MAE* when T is a multiplier of the minimum required clauses. For example, Dataset I can also be perfectly learned when there are 30 clauses.

However, when T is not a multiplier of the minimum required clauses, RTM cannot align its output y_o to the target output $\hat{y}_o$ during the training phase. For instance, by assigning *four* clauses for Dataset I, the training will end up with e.g. allocating *three* clauses to represent the pattern (1 *) or *two* clauses to represent the pattern (* 1). As a result, one or more output values cannot be computed correctly. For example, if there are *three* clauses for the pattern (1 *) and *one* clause for the pattern (* 1) after training, input (1 0) activates the clauses that represent the pattern (1 *), producing an incorrect output that is 300. Likewise, input (1 1) activates all four clauses to incorrectly compute the output 400.

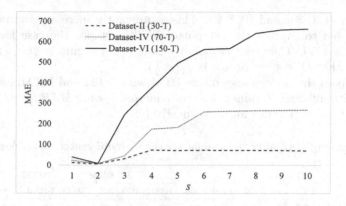

Fig. 2. Variation of MAE over different s for fixed T.

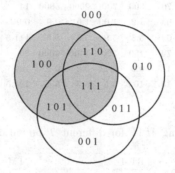

Fig. 3. Pattern distribution for the 3-bits input datasets.

As a strategy for problems where the number of clauses is unknown, and for real-world applications where noise plays a significant role, the RTM can be initialized with a much larger T. Then, since the output, y_o, is a fraction of the threshold, T, the error decreases. This behaviour is verified empirically in Fig. 1, showing how increasing T leads to reduced error.

The effect of s is studied by increasing it from 1.0 to 10.0 for Dataset II, Dataset IV, and Dataset VI, with fixed T. Figure 2 shows the variation of MAE over various s values for noisy data. The MAE decreases when s increases from 1.0 to 2.0. After 2.0, MAE increases, and then stabilizes after a while.

For all of the datasets considered here, the optimum s, where the RTM learns the datasets with minimum MAE, is equal to 2.0. The reason can be explained with the aid of Fig. 3, where one sees the distribution of patterns when the dataset has 3 input bits.

The occurrence probability of any of the 3-bit patterns is $\frac{1}{8}$ since there are overall 8 unique patterns. However, to capture the pattern $(1 * *)$ (shaded area), according to the TM dynamics [1], $\frac{1}{s}$ should be equal to the probability of the considered pattern, which is $\frac{4}{8}(=\frac{1}{2})$. Hence, s should be 2. For instance, if someone assigns $s = 4$, clauses will start to learn much finer patterns, such as $(1\ 0\ *)$, $(1\ 1\ *)$, and $(0\ 1\ *)$. This significantly increases the number of clauses needed to capture the sub-patterns. This is also the case for Dataset II and Dataset VI. Then, the probability that $(1\ *)$ occurs is $\frac{2}{4}(=\frac{1}{2})$ and the probability that $(1\ *\ *\ *)$ occurs is $\frac{7}{14}(=\frac{1}{2})$.

To compare the performance of the RTM with CTM and MTM, each model is tested with different T values. The training and testing MAE for all the cases are summarized in Tables 4 and 5, respectively.

Table 4. Training MAE after 200 training epochs with different T on various methods.

			RTM							CTM		MTM		
		T	3	10	30	100	500	1000	4000	6	8000	1000	10000	16000
Dataset	1	MAE	0.0	7.8	0.0	0.8	0.5	0.2	0.3	7.7	0.0	0.0	0.0	0.0
	2	MAE	7.2	11.0	8.8	5.4	5.5	5.2	5.4	11.1	24.1	8.4	7.1	7.9
		T	7	20	70	300	700	2000	5000	14	8000	2000	10000	16000
	3	MAE	0.0	14.6	0.0	1.9	1.00	1.0	0.9	0.0	0.0	18.3	0.0	0.0
	4	MAE	7.4	13.8	6.6	5.8	5.9	5.6	5.5	111.3	13.3	14.2	8.8	8.4
		T	7	15	70	150	700	1500	4000	30	8000	4000	10000	16000
	5	MAE	9.8	0.0	1.7	0.0	0.2	0.2	0.2	149.7	158.7	373.1	0.0	0.0
	6	MAE	79.8	51.4	13.1	10.3	5.5	5.3	5.4	181.5	96.4	449.9	8.0	7.8

Table 5. Testing MAE for different T on various methods.

			RTM							CTM		MTM		
		T	3	10	30	100	500	1000	4000	6	8000	1000	10000	16000
Dataset	1	MAE	0.0	7.6	0.0	0.8	0.5	0.2	0.3	9.0	0.0	0.0	0.0	0.0
	2	MAE	5.0	10.6	7.1	1.2	2.7	1.6	1.8	9.4	25.3	7.5	5.4	7.0
		T	7	20	70	300	700	2000	5000	14	8000	2000	10000	16000
	3	MAE	0.0	14.2	0.0	2.1	1.0	1.2	1.0	0.0	0.0	22.0	0.0	0.0
	4	MAE	5.0	14.5	4.2	3.3	3.4	1.9	2.7	98.5	12.5	16.0	8.7	8.3
		T	7	15	70	150	700	1500	4000	30	8000	4000	10000	16000
	5	MAE	9.9	0.0	1.8	0.0	0.3	0.2	0.2	154.6	155.5	372.9	0.0	0.0
	6	MAE	78.0	50.1	12.5	8.5	3.5	2.7	2.8	191.3	102.4	431.3	6.9	6.7

The training and testing MAE reach zero when the RTM operates with noise free data and when T equals the optimum clauses required. When the optimum T is unknown, and when data is noisy, applying a higher T is beneficial. As an example, Dataset III, which has 3 bits as inputs, can be perfectly learned with T equal to 7 and 70. For the same dataset, RTM acquires training MAE 1.0 with T equaling 700, which is better than the MAE of 14.2 obtained when T equals 20.

For CTM, the outputs are converted to bits and each bit position is then trained and predicted separately. According to the training and testing MAE in Tables 4 and 5, CTM works better with less complex datasets such as Dataset I and Dataset III. However, with a higher number of inputs and with noisy training data, performance decreases.

MTM requires a large number of clauses by nature when it works with continuous outputs since it has to consider all possible values from 0 to $\hat{y}_{max}$ as distinct classes (e.g. 300 classes for Dataset I and Dataset II, and 700 classes for Dataset III and Dataset IV). According to the training and testing MAE in the Tables 4 and 5, MTM requires roughly 3 clauses or more per class. For instance, the features in Dataset I can be learned with 1000 clauses, yet that amount is insufficient for Dataset III and Dataset V. Note that the noise free datasets can be learned perfectly with 10000 or more clauses. However, this accuracy gain is accompanied with a larger computational cost.

Overall, RTM obtains the best training and testing MAE for both noisy and noise free data with a smaller number of clauses compared with the CTM and MTM. Dataset II, Dataset IV, and Dataset VI are more similar to real-world datasets by being noisy. The minimum MAE values obtained by RTM for these three Datasets are 1.6, 1.9, and 2.7, respectively. The average of these minimum MAE values (2.07) is approximately 20 and 3.5 times lower than the averages obtained with CTM and MTM, respectively. In terms of the number of clauses required to achieve the above results, RTM utilizes 1000 clauses, while CTM and MTM utilize 8 and 16 times more clauses than that. This difference is characteristic for RTM – it provides better MAE with less computational power.

4   Conclusion

In this paper we proposed the Regression Tsetlin Machine (RTM), a novel variant of the Classic Tsetlin Machine that supports continuous output in regression problems. In RTM, the polarities in clauses were removed and the total clause output was normalized to produce continuous output predictions. The number of clauses to receive the feedback in RTM was decided stochastically using a linear activation probability function. The prediction power of this novel approach was studied using six different datasets, with noise free and noisy training data. Our empirical results showed significantly better performance of RTM compared with CTM and MTM, both in terms of training and the testing error, as well as the computational power required.

Potential applications for RTM can be weather prediction, sales forecasting, stock predictions, energy forecasting, and outbreak forecasting, to name a few. In our future work, we will evaluate RTM on the aforementioned applications and performance will be compared with conventional machine learning methods.

References

1. Granmo, O.-C.: The Tsetlin machine - a game theoretic bandit driven approach to optimal pattern recognition with propositional logic, arXiv e-prints, arXiv:1804.01508, April 2018
2. Tsetlin, M.L.: On behaviour of finite automata in random medium. Avtom I Telemekhanika **22**, 1345–1354 (1961)

3. Granmo, O.-C., Oommen, B.J.: Solving stochastic nonlinear resource allocation problems using a hierarchy of twofold resource allocation automata. IEEE Trans. Comput. **59**(4), 545–560 (2010)
4. Oommen, B.J., Kim, S.-W., Samuel, M.T., Granmo, O.-C.: A solution to the stochastic point location problem in metalevel nonstationary environments. IEEE Trans. Syst. Man Cybern. Part B (Cybern.) **38**(2), 466–476 (2008)
5. Tung, B., Kleinrock, L.: Using finite state automata to produce self-optimization and self-control. IEEE Trans. Parallel Distrib. Syst. **7**(4), 439–448 (1996)
6. Bouhmala, N., Granmo, O.-C.: Stochastic learning for SAT-encoded graph coloring problems. Int. J. Appl. Metaheuristic Comput. (IJAMC) **1**(3), 1–19 (2010)
7. Abeyrathna, K., Granmo, O.-C., Goodwin, M.: A novel Tsetlin automata scheme to forecast dengue outbreaks in the Philippines. In: 2018 IEEE 30th International Conference on Tools with Artificial Intelligence (ICTAI), pp. 680–685. IEEE (2018)
8. Berge, G.T., Granmo, O.-C., Oddbjørn Tveit, T., Goodwin, M., Jiao, L., Viggo Matheussen, B.: Using the Tsetlin machine to learn human-interpretable rules for high-accuracy text categorization with medical applications, arXiv e-prints, arXiv:1809.04547, September 2018
9. Abeyrathna, K., Granmo, O.-C., Zhang, X., Goodwin, M.: A scheme for continuous input to the Tsetlin machine with applications to forecasting disease outbreaks, arXiv e-prints, arXiv:1905.04199, May 2019
10. Misra, S., Krishna, P.V., Abraham, K.I.: A simple learning automata-based solution for intrusion detection in wireless sensor networks. Wirel. Commun. Mob. Comput. **11**(3), 426–441 (2011)
11. Tuan, T.A., Tong, L.C., Premkumar, A.: An adaptive learning automata algorithm for channel selection in cognitive radio network. In: 2010 International Conference on Communications and Mobile Computing, pp. 159–163. IEEE (2010)
12. Narendra, K.S., Thathachar, M.A.: Learning Automata: An Introduction. Courier Corporation, North Chelmsford (2012)
13. Narendra, K., Thathachar, M.: Learning automata-a survey. IEEE Trans. Syst. Man Cybern. **4**, 323–334 (1974)

Learning Regularization Parameters of Radial Basis Functions in Embedded Likelihoods Space

Murilo Menezes[1($\boxtimes$)] ⓘ, Luiz C. B. Torres[1,2] ⓘ, and Antônio P. Braga[1] ⓘ

[1] Graduate Program in Electrical Engineering,
Universidade Federal de Minas Gerais,
Av. Antônio Carlos 6627, Belo Horizonte, MG 31270-901, Brazil
murilovfm@gmail.com, apbraga@ufmg.br
[2] Department of Computer and Systems, Federal University of Ouro Preto,
João Monlevade, Brazil

Abstract. Neural networks with radial basis activation functions are typically trained in two different phases: the first consists in the construction of the hidden layer, while the second consists in finding the output layer weights. Constructing the hidden layer involves defining the number of units in it, as well as their centers and widths. The training process of the output layer can be done using least squares methods, usually setting a regularization term. This work proposes an approach for building the whole network using information extracted directly from the projected training data in the space formed by the likelihoods functions. One can, then, train RBF networks for pattern classification with minimal external intervention.

Keywords: Neural networks · Radial Basis Function · Classification · Regularization

1 Introduction

Non-parametric learning from data often requires the accomplishment of a trade-off between two objectives, related to model fitting to learning data and generalization. Both model capacity, e.g. its VC-dimension [16], and the proximity of learned outputs to training data will affect its general behavior. If data is noisy and sparse, error minimization may also result in a model that learns the uncertainty of the data. Generalization is usually achieved by controlling not only the error, but also the complexity of the model. Model selection in this context is inherently a difficult problem since it depends on a decision criteria to balance bias and variance [6]. There isn't, therefore, a general method to solve the problem that can be applied to all families of approximating functions. There are,

Thanks to funding agencies CNPq, CAPES and FAPEMIG.

P. Moura Oliveira et al. (Eds.): EPIA 2019, LNAI 11805, pp. 281–292, 2019.
https://doi.org/10.1007/978-3-030-30244-3_24

however, many approaches in the literature that aims at simplifying the trade-off problem by making previous assumptions about the data and the target model.

Classification learning problems are often based on error minimization with constraints applied to the magnitude of the weights [1] or by implicitly discarding selected margin training samples [2]. Weight space constraint is usually implemented using a penalty function, while implicit smoothing in the margin region is obtained by weighing samples according to their proximity to the decision surface. These are in fact regularization strategies that require hyperparameters to be set in advance by the user or estimated with methods such as cross-validation or resampling. In any case, prior hyperparameter setting determine the trade-off between bias and variance and embody, therefore, a selection criteria.

This work proposes a method for defining the general topology of neural networks with radial activation functions, as well as defining a regularized training process. The hidden layer is obtained by using all samples as centers. The width of the RBF functions is defined by maximizing a separability measure. The proposed model is independent of any *prior* assumptions, reaching good results without requiring external hyperparameter definition.

This work is structured as follows: Sect. 1.1 introduces RBF networks, their general topology, and training process. Section 2 discusses the close relationship between RBF networks and Support Vector Machines, which are used as inspiration. Section 3 presents the likelihood space used to analyze the samples for the classes, and then to define values of hyperparameters. Section 4 contains a detailed explanation of the method, while Sect. 5 shows the accuracy results. Finally, Sect. 6 contains the conclusions and final remarks.

1.1   Radial Basis Function Neural Networks

Radial Basis Function (RBF) [10] networks are formed by a single layer of hidden neurons with radial activation functions, typically Gaussians. Parameters of the radial basis layer are the number of functions p, their locations (centers c_i) and width σ_i. Hidden layer aims at performing non-linear mapping and linearization so that a linear combination of the radial functions is accomplished to produce the outputs, as shown schematically in Fig. 1.

In order to train an RBF, the centers and widths of each Gaussian should be obtained, as well as the weight vector **w** of the output neurons. Although the usual gradient descent algorithm could be applied to estimate parameters, it may suffer from instability due to the bell shape of Gaussian functions, which are not limited as sigmoidal functions. So, usually RBF training is accomplished by first selecting centers and width of each one of the p radial functions and, after that, the weights of the output neuron are obtained. Hidden layer training is often accomplished by a clustering algorithm, such as K-Means [13], however, it is sensitive to initialization and also to the hyperparameter K, the number of clusters. Other approaches, such as the use of Fisher's separability criterion or Orthogonal Least Squares (OLS) to iteratively construct the network can also be applied [3, 10]. Particularly for classification problems, the location of RBF functions are associated to class distribution at the input space in order to obtain

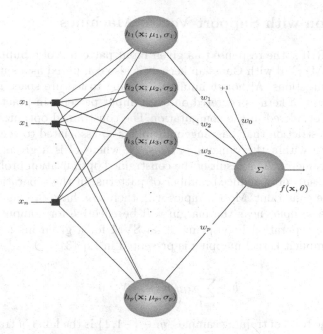

Fig. 1. Schematic representation of a radial basis function network.

a mapping that provides good separability while avoiding intermediate complex designs that may cause overfitting.

Once the parameters of the hidden layer are obtained, the problem becomes linear and its solution can be achieved directly by least squares or gradient descent. The hidden layer provides a mapping from input matrix $\mathbf{X}$ into the projected matrix $\mathbf{H}$, so that $\mathbf{Hw} = \mathbf{y}$. The least squares solution of the weights can be obtained by the product $\mathbf{w} = \mathbf{H}^{-1}\mathbf{y}$ or, considering regularization, as shown in Eq. (1).

$$\mathbf{w} = (\mathbf{H}^T\mathbf{H} + \Lambda)^{-1}\mathbf{H}^T\mathbf{y} \tag{1}$$

where Λ is a regularization matrix and $\mathbf{y}$ is a vector of target outputs. Considering p RBF neurons, Λ is a diagonal $p \times p$ matrix, that contains regularization parameters for every neuron. Typically, diagonal elements are set to a single value λ, so that the regularization matrix is given by equation

$$\Lambda = \lambda\mathbf{I}_p \tag{2}$$

where $\mathbf{I}_p$ is a $p \times p$ identity matrix.

In addition to the centers and widths of the RBF functions, one must also define matrix Λ. These hyperparameters are usually defined using performance estimation methods, such as cross validation [8]. Here we propose a novel method for both defining hidden layer parameters and training the output layer using regularized least squares.

2   Relation with Support Vector Machines

Similarly to RBFs, the response to a given input pattern **x** of a Support Vector Machine (SVM) [2,4] with Gaussian kernels is also computed as a superposition of Gaussian functions. Although implicit mapping to feature space in SVMs is based on Gaussian kernels centered on every input pattern, in practice, not all of them are considered in the computation. The constrained optimization problem has the restriction that Lagrange multipliers α_i associated to every training pattern $\mathbf{x}_i$ are within the range $0 \leq \alpha_i \leq C$, where C is a given regularization hyperparameter. As a result of the constrained optimization problem, given values of C result on a reduced number of patterns, in the separation margin, that fulfill the constraint. Most samples will, therefore, have α_i equal to zero so that only the samples near the margin will be effective for computing SVM's response. The separation hyperplane of an SVM for a given input pattern **x**, considering implicit kernel mapping is presented in Eq. (3).

$$b + \sum_{i=1}^{N} \alpha_i y_i K(\mathbf{x}, \mathbf{x}_i) = 0 \tag{3}$$

where N is the total of training samples, $y_i \in \{-1, 1\}$ is the label of training sample $\mathbf{x}_i$, and K is a kernel function, usually Gaussian. The classification response $f(\mathbf{x})$ is then obtained by the following decision function.

$$f(\mathbf{x}) = \begin{cases} 1, & \text{if } b + \sum_{i=1}^{N} \alpha_i y_i K(\mathbf{x}, \mathbf{x}_i) \geq 0 \\ -1, & \text{if } b + \sum_{i=1}^{N} \alpha_i y_i K(\mathbf{x}, \mathbf{x}_i) < 0 \end{cases} \tag{4}$$

The decision function presented in Eq. (3) corresponds in fact to a summation of all Gaussian kernels, with **x** as an argument, weighted by the product of the corresponding Lagrange multipliers and labels. A positive outcome of the summation means that the positive class had a larger influence on the result. Similarly, if the result is negative the same holds for the negative class. In fact, the summation can be split into positive and negative terms, as shown in Eq. (5).

$$\sum_{i=1}^{N} \alpha_i y_i K(\mathbf{x}, \mathbf{x}_i) = \underbrace{\sum_{i=1}^{N_p} \alpha_i K(\mathbf{x}, \mathbf{x}_i)}_{y_i = +1} - \underbrace{\sum_{j=1}^{N_n} \alpha_j K(\mathbf{x}, \mathbf{x}_j)}_{y_j = -1} \tag{5}$$

where $\mathbf{x}_i \in C_p$ (positive class), $\mathbf{x}_j \in C_n$ (negative class), N_p is the number of positive samples and N_n is the number of negative samples.

Since the output layer of an RBF network provides a linear separation of the projections, once defined the m centers c_i and weights **w**, the separating hyperplane for an input **x** is defined as in the Eq. (6).

$$w_0 + \sum_{i=1}^{m} w_i K(\mathbf{x}, c_i) = 0 \tag{6}$$

One can see the similarity between the classification process in SVMs and RBF networks. The former can be interpreted as a particular case of the latter, with all of the samples serving as centers for the hidden layer. Here we present a novel approach to train an RBF network with autonomously-selected hyperparameters.

The kernel summations in Eqs. (3) to (5) can be seen as weighted sums of non-normalized kernel density estimations (KDE) [9,14,15] of margin samples ($\alpha \neq 0$) of the likelihoods of the two classes in relation to sample $\mathbf{x}$. So, the assessment of an arbitrary sample $\mathbf{x}$ by SVM's classification function (Eq. (4)) is in fact accomplished in the space of non-normalized KDE densities of the positive and negative classes. This concept will be explored in the next sections in order to present a method for width selection of Gaussian kernel functions.

3 Likelihoods Mapping

While in SVM's formulation, classification is supported by an implicit kernel mapping, binary classification based on the Bayes Rule and kernel density estimation (KDE) is also based on kernel mapping. In fact, the general Bayes rule for binary classification problems $P(\mathbf{x}|C_1) - \frac{N_1}{N_2}P(\mathbf{x}|C_2) \geq 0 \implies C_1$ is accomplished in the space of likelihood functions $P(\mathbf{x}|C_1)$ and $P(\mathbf{x}|C_2)$. This concept is shown schematically in the two-layers network representation of Fig. 2, so input vectors are mapped into the two-dimensional space $P(\mathbf{x}|C_1) \times P(\mathbf{x}|C_2)$, where classication is accomplished by the linear discriminant function $P(\mathbf{x}|C_1) = \frac{N_1}{N_2}P(\mathbf{x}|C_2)$.

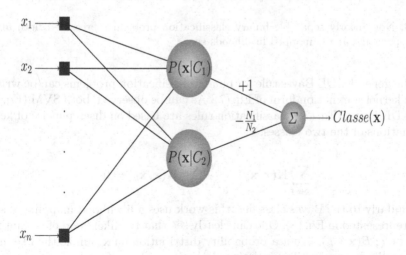

Fig. 2. Schematic representation of Bayes binary classification rule as a two-layers network with two intermediate neurons represented by the likelihood functions $P(\mathbf{x}|C_1)$ and $P(\mathbf{x}|C_2)$.

The example shown in Fig. 3 presents the data of the classical spirals classification problem mapped into the likelihoods space $P(\mathbf{x}|C_1) \times P(\mathbf{x}|C_2)$ with probabilities estimated with KDE and a given value of σ. As can be observed, the problem in the space $P(\mathbf{x}|C_1) \times P(\mathbf{x}|C_2)$ became linearly separable by the straight line $P(\mathbf{x}|C_1) = P(\mathbf{x}|C_2)$, since in this example $\frac{N_1}{N_2} = 1$. As for KDE, there is only one parameter to be set, the radius σ of each Gaussian, so the mapping depends solely of σ. It has been shown in a previous work [11] that separability measures in the likelihoods space can be used to select a proper value of σ that yields good generalization performance.

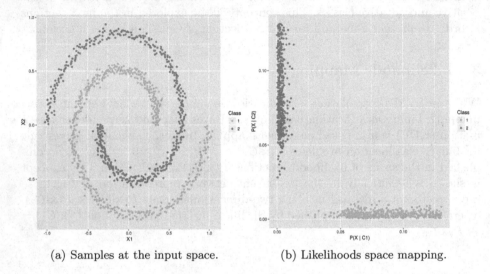

(a) Samples at the input space.   (b) Likelihoods space mapping.

Fig. 3. Non-linearly separable binary classification problem represented both at the input space and at the mapped likelihoods space.

The general KDE Bayes rule for binary classification problems can be written in the kernel summation form of Eq. (7). As can be observed, both SVM (Eq. (4)) and KDE Bayes (Eq. (7)) classification rules are based on discrepancies of kernel summations of the two classes.

$$\sum_{k=1}^{N_p} \mathbf{K}(\mathbf{x}, \mathbf{x}_k) - \frac{N_1}{N_2} \sum_{k=1}^{N_2} \mathbf{K}(\mathbf{x}, \mathbf{x}_k) = 0 \qquad (7)$$

Similarly to the Bayes classifier, this work uses a likelihood mapping of samples, represented in Eq. (8). One can clearly see that the likelihood of a point $\mathbf{x}$ to a class C_k, $B(\mathbf{x}, C_k)$, is not a probability distribution on $\mathbf{x}$, unlike the likelihood as a conditional probability, mentioned above.

$$B(\mathbf{x}, C_k) = \frac{1}{N} \sum_{j=1}^{N} K(\mathbf{x}, \mathbf{x}_j) = \frac{1}{N} \sum_{j=1}^{N} \exp \frac{-||\mathbf{x} - c||^2}{2\sigma^2} \qquad (8)$$

By mapping all of the samples to this space, it becomes possible to take useful measures which will be at the core of the solution proposed here. The value of σ is chosen in order to maximize the separability of classes, while the regularization parameters (Λ in Eq. (1)) are found using similarity metrics. These measures, as well as how they are used, are defined in the next section.

4   Methodology

As mentioned in Sect. 1.1, the first step of the training process of an RBF network consists in finding the number p of radial functions to use, as well as their centers c_i and widths σ_i. In the approach proposed in this work, the hidden units have the same value of the width, i.e., $\sigma_i = \sigma \forall i$.

The value of σ is obtained using the likelihood mapping defined on Eq. (8). With all training samples on the mapped space, the mean points of the samples belonging to each class are computed. For the classes C_1 and C_2, the vectors that defined these points are defined as $\mathbf{V}_1$ and $\mathbf{V}_2$. These vectors are depicted in Fig. 4. Given the training set, the arrangement of the mapped points depends only on σ. It is chosen the value of width that maximizes the distance between the midpoints, $\|\mathbf{V}_1 - \mathbf{V}_2\|$. Figure 5 depicts the behavior of this distance as σ varies in the spirals dataset (Fig. 3).

Finding the number of hidden units and their centers is straightforward: all training samples are selected as centers of the hidden layer units. Since all training samples are used, the number of centers can scale up and cause overfitting in the final model. In order to avoid overfitting, regularized RBF networks are trained by least squares uses a matrix Λ of regularization parameters.

We propose a technique to define matrix Λ based on the same likelihood space described in Sect. 3. The regularization process is based on the penalization of the norms of the weights in the output layer. The elements of matrix Λ define the magnitude of the penalization of each weight. Typically, all weights are penalized just the same, and we can define Λ as in Eq. (2).

Here we explore the possibility that the weights are penalized with different magnitudes. Since each hidden unit is defined on a training sample, the regularization parameter for a given weight can be determined using the spatial distribution of mapped samples.

Aiming at large margin classification, samples closer to the separation margin tend to be more important when classifying a new observation. To achieve this, one can use the likelihood space to provide this information. Once obtained the optimal value of σ, we have a fixed mapping for the training samples. The ones that are closer to the margin tend to have a higher similarity to the opposite class. One can use, then, these inter-class similarities to define the regularization parameters.

For the classification problem presented in Fig. 3, the projection of the samples in the axes of similarity to the opposite class is shown in Fig. 6.

The measure of likelihood can be interpreted as a measure of proximity of the point to the class. Thus, when calculating the likelihood of the instance to

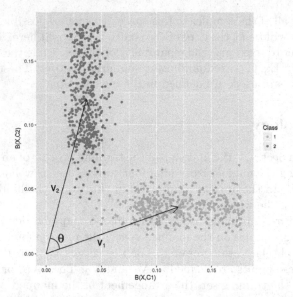

Fig. 4. Samples mapped in the likelihood space. The vectors that define the mean points of the classes are shown.

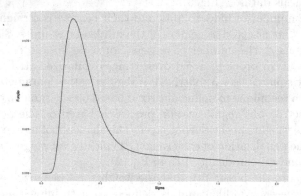

Fig. 5. The distance between the mapped average points as σ varies. The value that gives the maximizes the function is chosen as the width of the hidden neurons.

the opposite class, its distance to the separation margin is implicitly measured. For N training samples, an N-dimensional vector $\mathbf{r}$ of proximity to the opposite class is computed. A series of transformations is then applied. This vector is scaled for its values to fit in the interval $[0, 1]$, obtaining an unit vector $\mathbf{u}$.

The larger the regularization parameter, the stronger the weight is penalized. Then we create another vector $\mathbf{d} = 1 - \mathbf{u}$, such that it has a value close to 1 to the weights related to points that are far from the margin and close to 0 to the closer ones. The regularization matrix Λ is then defined as a diagonal matrix of

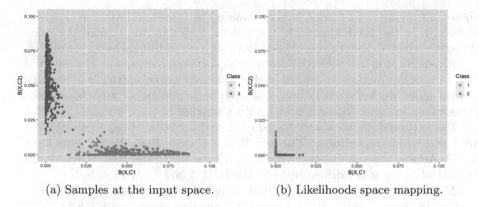

(a) Samples at the input space.   (b) Likelihoods space mapping.

Fig. 6. Sample projections of the spirals problem. (a) represents the original projections, while (b) shows the projectios on the axes of opposite classes. These values are used for regularization.

dimension N (where N is the number of training samples), with the elements of $\mathbf{d}$ on the main diagonal, according to Eq. (9) below.

$$\Lambda = \text{diag}(\mathbf{d}) = \begin{bmatrix} D_1 & & & \\ & D_2 & & \\ & & \ddots & \\ & & & D_N \end{bmatrix} \tag{9}$$

Once obtained Λ, the output layer weights are defined according to Eq. (1), where $\mathbf{H}$ is the output of the hidden layer for all training samples, and y are the labels. This construction of the regularization matrix differs from the usual least squares training process by the fact that each weight will have a different regularization parameter associated with it. The weights connected to neurons with centers in points far from the margin will have their magnitudes strongly penalized, resulting in the fact that these samples will have its importance reduced when classifying a new instance.

In the experiments, two different approaches are tested. In the first one, the regularization matrix is multiplied by a scaling value of λ, obtained through cross-validation and grid search. In the second, the matrix Λ is directly used in regularization. The results are presented next.

5 Results

Four different models were tested. The first, **RBF1**, consists in an RBF neural network using all samples as centers and regularization matrix defined as the scaled identity matrix, $\Lambda = \lambda I$. The parameter λ was obtained by using cross-validation and grid search. **RBF2** consists in the previously described RBF network, obtaining the regularization matrix based on the likelihood space and then multiplying it by a scale factor, obtained by cross-validation, as described in Sect. 4. In the **RBF3** network, the matrix Λ uses in its diagonal the values directly extracted from the likelihood space, with no additional hyperparameters. Finally, an SVM model with RBF Kernel was also used to compare. For the SVM, the σ hyperparameter was defined in the same way as the widths from the RBF hidden units, as described in Sect. 4. The hyperparameter C was chosen using cross-validation and grid-search with values ranging in $\{2^{-5}, 2^{-4}, \cdots, 2^7, 2^8\}$.

The proposed methods were tested in 18 real datasets, obtained mostly from UCI and KEEL repositories. The set "Breast Cancer Hess Probes" was found in [7]. Accuracy results were obtained for all datasets, and then the Wilcoxon statistical test was performed between the **RBF3** and SVM models.

The test performance was estimated using 10 training/test splits. The accuracy results are in Table 1. It can be seen that the performance of **RBF3** network was, in general, considerably better than the other two neural networks tested, approaching the accuracy values achieved by the SVM.

Table 1. Results of the average accuracy and standard deviation of real databases.

Base	RBF1	RBF2	RBF3	SVM
diabetes	76.422 ± 4.113	76.823 ± 4.016	77.464 ± 2.913	**77.471 ± 4.808**
sonar	66.905 ± 8.593	66.452 ± 13.496	79.333 ± 7.797	**82.238 ± 7.048**
segmentation	85.714 ± 7.776	85.714 ± 7.776	94.286 ± 6.269	**99.048 ± 2.008**
glass	87.727 ± 9.361	96.234 ± 3.745	**96.710 ± 3.904**	96.255 ± 2.991
appendicitis	79.182 ± 9.767	**87.818 ± 8.732**	**87.818 ± 9.727**	**87.818 ± 9.727**
ionosphere	72.659 ± 7.103	82.889 ± 7.405	87.762 ± 5.517	**94.024 ± 3.658**
breastcancer	97.067 ± 1.702	**97.214 ± 1.895**	96.777 ± 1.935	96.198 ± 2.410
australian	85.797 ± 3.666	85.072 ± 3.807	**85.942 ± 5.294**	85.362 ± 4.451
breastHess	74.505 ± 11.825	**83.462 ± 9.398**	**83.462 ± 9.398**	83.352 ± 10.77
bupa	57.076 ± 7.323	57.630 ± 7.637	**71.866 ± 6.277**	68.403 ± 7.295
haberman	72.516 ± 7.994	**75.774 ± 5.754**	74.151 ± 5.993	72.849 ± 6.930
banknote	97.084 ± 2.035	97.666 ± 1.493	98.176 ± 1.300	**100.000 ± 0.000**
fertility	**88.000 ± 4.216**	**88.000 ± 4.216**	**88.000 ± 4.216**	**88.000 ± 4.216**
parkinsons	75.289 ± 9.237	82.500 ± 9.134	84.553 ± 7.702	**87.658 ± 7.689**
climate	**91.481 ± 4.876**	**91.481 ± 4.876**	**91.481 ± 4.876**	**91.481 ± 4.876**
ILPD	71.331 ± 6.031	**71.503 ± 5.813**	70.635 ± 5.825	71.331 ± 6.031
german	71.100 ± 4.280	74.500 ± 4.994	**77.200 ± 3.853**	75.500 ± 3.136
heart	82.593 ± 9.081	81.852 ± 8.979	82.222 ± 7.963	**83.704 ± 10.060**

Other methods for finding the centers of the hidden neurons of the RBF network were not considered for comparison in this work. The main objective was to test the proposed regularization technique when compared to the classical ones, as well as the implicit regularization executed by SVM's.

The Wilcoxon Signed-Rank Test is a paired, nonparametric hypothesis test that measures the equivalence of two models based on the differences between their performances in different situations [12]. Ranking the absolute values of their differences, the Z statistic is computed. For the difference between two models to be considered statistically significant for a significance level of 0.05, one must have $Z < -1.96$ [5]. In this work, the two models with the best general accuracies were compared: **RBF3** (network with no hyperparameters) and SVM. As a measure of performance, the average value of accuracy in each dataset was used. Comparing these two models, $Z = 0.9655$ was obtained, attesting that the differences between these classifiers are not statistically significant. This equivalence means that the proposed method indeed approximates SVM's performance by attempting to approximate its behavior.

6 Conclusion

In this work, it was proposed a method to build an RBF neural network, defining the whole set of hyperparameters without user interaction. To define the hidden layer, all of the samples are considered as centers. Thus, the number of hidden units grow linearly with the number of samples. By projecting the samples to a likelihood space, the value of the width σ, which is shared between all hidden layer neurons, is obtained by maximizing a separability measure. This method shows itself to be very consistent with respect to data domain, achieving good accuracy performance in imbalanced highly dimensional datasets.

Once the hidden layer is obtained, the output weights can be found using least squares optimization. However, since the number of parameters has the same order of magnitude of the training set size, the model tends to overfit. The weights, then, need to be regularized. Since each hidden layer neuron represents a single sample from the training set, it was possible to use the likelihood space to find measures of each sample, and, then, the regularization parameters.

The proposed methods outperformed the classical RBF network setting. Also, the independent method of estimating any hyperparameters obtained a classification performance statistically equivalent to the SVM, with the advantage of having the entire topology of the model built autonomously from the dataset structure.

Although effective, this method may not scale very well for large datasets, just like Support Vector Machines, since the number of units in the hidden layer grows linearly with the number of samples.

Using only similarity measures taken from data arrangement, it was shown to be possible to obtain a model with good performance and no need for externally-defined hyperparameters.

References

1. Bartlett, P.L.: For valid generalization the size of the weights is more important than the size of the network. In: Advances in Neural Information Processing Systems, pp. 134–140 (1997)
2. Boser, B.E., Guyon, I.M., Vapnik, V.N.: A training algorithm for optimal margin classifiers. In: Proceedings of the Fifth Annual Workshop on Computational Learning Theory, COLT 1992, pp. 144–152. ACM, New York (1992). http://doi.acm.org/10.1145/130385.130401

3. Chen, S., Cowan, C.F., Grant, P.M.: Orthogonal least squares learning algorithm for radial basis function networks. EEE Trans. Neural Netw. **2**(2), 302–309 (1991)
4. Cortes, C., Vapnik, V.: Support-vector networks. Mach. Learn. **20**(3), 273–297 (1995)
5. Demšar, J.: Statistical comparisons of classifiers over multiple data sets. J. Mach. Learn. Res. **7**(Jan), 1–30 (2006)
6. Geman, S., Bienenstock, E., Doursat, R.: Neural networks and the bias/variance dilemma. Neural Comput. **4**(1), 1–58 (1992)
7. Hess, K.R., et al.: Pharmacogenomic predictor of sensitivity to preoperative chemotherapy with paclitaxel and fluorouracil, doxorubicin, and cyclophosphamide in breast cancer. J. Clin. Oncol. **24**(26), 4236–4244 (2006)
8. James, G., Witten, D., Hastie, T., Tibshirani, R.: An Introduction to Statistical Learning, vol. 112. Springer, Heidelberg (2013). https://doi.org/10.1007/978-1-4614-7138-7
9. MacQueen, J.: Some methods for classification and analysis of multivariate observations. In: Proceedings of the Fifth Berkeley Symposium on Mathematical Statistics and Probability, Volume 1: Statistics, pp. 281–297. University of California Press, Berkeley (1967)
10. Mao, K.: RBF neural network center selection based on fisher ratio class separability measure. IEEE Trans. Neural Netw. **13**(5), 1211–1217 (2002)
11. Menezes, M., Torres, L., Braga, A.: Otimização da largura de kernels rbf para máquinas de vetores de suporte: Uma abordagem baseada em estimativa de densidades. In: XIII Congresso Brasileiro de Inteligência Computacional (2017)
12. Montgomery, D.C., Runger, G.C.: Applied Statistics and Probability for Engineers. Wiley, Hoboken (2010)
13. Oh, S.K., Kim, W.D., Pedrycz, W., Joo, S.C.: Design of K-means clustering-based polynomial radial basis function neural networks (pRBF NNs) realized with the aid of particle swarm optimization and differential evolution. Neurocomputing **78**(1), 121–132 (2012)
14. Rosenblatt, M.: Remarks on some nonparametric estimates of a density function. Ann. Math. Stat. **27**, 832–837 (1956)
15. Silverman, B.W.: Density Estimation for Statistics and Data Analysis, vol. 26. CRC Press, Boca Raton (1986)
16. Vapnik, V.: The Nature of Statistical Learning Theory. Springer, Heidelberg (2013). https://doi.org/10.1007/978-1-4757-3264-1

Intelligent Robotics

Path Planning Algorithms Benchmarking for Grapevines Pruning and Monitoring

Sandro Augusto Magalhães[1]([✉]) [iD], Filipe Neves dos Santos[1] [iD],
Rui Costa Martins[1] [iD], Luis F. Rocha[1] [iD], and José Brito[2]

[1] INESC TEC, Campus da FEUP, Rua Dr. Roberto Frias, 4200-465 Porto, Portugal
sandro.a.magalhaes@inesctec.pt
[2] Faculty of Engineering of University of Porto, Rua Dr. Roberto Frias,
4200-465 Porto, Portugal
http://www.inesctec.com/, http://www.fe.up.pt/

Abstract. Labour shortage is a reality in agriculture. Farmers are asking for solutions to automate agronomic tasks, such as monitoring, pruning, spraying, and harvesting. The automation of these tasks requires, most of the time, the use of robotic arms to mimic human arms capabilities. The current robotic arm based solutions available, both in the market and in the scientific sphere, have several limitations, such as, low-speed manipulation, the path planning algorithms are not aware of the requirements of the agricultural tasks (robotic motion and manipulation synchronisation), and require active perception tuning to the end-target point. This work benchmarks algorithms from open manipulation planning library (OMPL) considering a cost-effective six-degree freedom manipulator in a simulated vineyard. The OMPL planners shown a very low performance under demanding pruning tasks. The best and most promising results are performed and obtained by BiTRRT. However, further work is needed to increase its performance and reduce planning time. This benchmark work helps the reader to understand the limitations of each algorithm and when to use them.

Keywords: Agricultural robotics · Robotic pruning · Robotic manipulators

1 Introduction

The strategic European research agenda for robotics [6] affirms that robots may improve agricultural efficiency and competitiveness.

Steep slope vineyards placed in the demarcated region of Portugal, UNESCO Heritage place, presents unique characteristics, as shown in Fig. 1, to produce Porto wine. These steep slope vineyards, like other agricultural scenarios, are labour intensive, as most of the required work is hands-on. Because of the frequent exposition of human workers to high temperatures, high demanding

Supported by FCT project Metbots (POCI-01-0145-FEDER-031124).

© Springer Nature Switzerland AG 2019
P. Moura Oliveira et al. (Eds.): EPIA 2019, LNAI 11805, pp. 295–306, 2019.
https://doi.org/10.1007/978-3-030-30244-3_25

physical work, and non-ergonomic tasks, viticulturists are experiencing a critical labour shortage. So, naturally, and to overcome these production limitations, viticulturists need and desire new robotic solutions to automate agricultural tasks (monitoring, pruning, spraying, and harvesting).

Fig. 1. Steep slope vineyard in the Douro region.

The special Douro's steep slope vineyard features bring a high number of robotic challenges which needs to overcome, namely, robot self-localisation, robot environment perception, environment modelling and decision-making, to reach a fully autonomous and intelligent system [11,15]. The resolution of these robotic challenges, besides improve the robotics technology in agriculture and viticulture, they will reduce the requirement of labour work in the most basic agricultural tasks, such as watering, pruning, harvesting or monitoring. Despite this undeniable impact, agriculture and viticulture robotics research investment does not have as main goal the reduction of human labour, but instead the promotion of a better high-quality product, through the development of new or improved agriculture precision methods [9] that help viticulturist to have better monitoring and control about their cultures.

Between the targets for precision agriculture, Porto wine is a high biotechnology complex product, whose quality level begins at the vineyard and its characteristics are directly related to the interaction with soil, climate and plant physiology. In this scenario, the precision technology brings many advantages to monitor vineyards, measuring the best time for harvesting or detecting plant diseases earlier, ensuring high-quality grapes which results in high-quality wine.

The state-of-the-art for monitoring in precision agriculture can summarise in multi-spectral-satellite, drone imaging and site-specific sensors with pattern recognition and artificial intelligence [14]. Despite this, some experiments point out that the usage of site-specific sensors, also known as site-specific management methods, can bring a closer look at the vine and present more deterministic results [10]. However, this site-specific sensing kind, such as uv-vis-nir or Nuclear Magnetic Resonance (NMR), implies the increment of labour for repetitive tasks or usage of mobile robotics for intelligent sampling along all vineyard. These procedures, beyond a mobile robot, also requires a robotic arm to manipulate the sensor or tool and collect random samples. This goal is not trivial to achieve once the manipulator should be capable of approximate to the grape, through vine foliage, without damage the vine.

Therefore, this work intends to benchmarks the path planners algorithms from Open Manipulation Planning Library (OMPL) Sucan2012. Once viticulture context desires a generic solution for multiple applications, this work selects the hardest path planning case, the pruning task, to evaluate the performance of all path planning algorithms. The generic benchmark platform Moll2015 used, facilitates the evaluation process, granting a broader benchmarking between different poses with different degrees of accessibility difficulty.

This paper is subdivided into five sections. The Sect. 2 presents the related work, mentioning the last developed robots for pruning tasks and a little description of OMPL planners. On Sect. 3, it is presented the chosen approach to solve the stated problem and the follow section analyse the results from different benchmarks. Finally, the conclusions and the future work to improve these results are referred into the last section.

This paper is divided into five sections. Section 2 presents the related work, mentioning the last developed robots for pruning tasks and a small description of OMPL planners. The following section describes the chosen approach to benchmark the algorithms and Sect. 4 analyse the results from the different performance tests. Finally, the last section refers to some conclusions and the future work to improve the reached results.

2   Related Work

Pruning is a typical task for some kind of trees. These tasks may vary with the species kind, the age or the aim for the plant. Besides consume some time, pruning trees also require some specific decision-making knowledge, which does it very attractive in terms of robotics research activities.

In the last few years, researchers have been proposing new robotic solution for pruning. Due to this job, there already are some commercial products, although far of being the ideal solution to this task. Vision Robotics Corporation developed one of these systems. They produced an intelligent system [8], pulled for a tractor, with two robotic arms with scissors which operate inside a light controlled environment.

Tom Botterill et al. [2,4,13] developed a similar decision-making system which uses an artificial intelligence algorithm to select the pruning points, after mapping the vineyard. An end-effector drill assures whole pruning job which consumes about two minutes (similar time consumed through human labour) [2], using the RRTConnect path planning algorithm.

To urge better research for agricultural robotics, Bac et al. [1] wrote a broad survey about robotics developments for pruning and harvesting tasks. Besides presenting the current researching state in this area, the authors indicate the subsequent improvement steps through four future challenges for R&D that may positively trend in performance, to successfully implement harvesting and pruning robots in practice:

Simplify the task – this challenge relates to the workspace design and proposes the development of a modified cultivation system (such as the implementation of the high-wire cultivation system), cultivar selection and breeding and/or implementation of supportive systems.

Enhancing the robot – the integration of sensors system with the world model is the proposed line to achieve the robot enhancement, through reasoning, adaptation and learning capabilities, collaborative robotics, specialised robotics or alternative robot designs.

Defining requirements and measuring performance – this challenge urges for deep testing procedures through well-defined requirements with specific performance indicators and tests. The robots must be tested under a wide range of conditions.

Considering additional requirements for successful implementation – besides the features of the robot, the designed solution should achieve growers and society. So, this should be economically feasible, safe and match the logistics processes.

Considering the research above, there are several challenges to overcome, such as perception or path planning. Concerning to the path planning problem, there are numerous solutions capable of solving this issue. Developing optimisation metrics and considering planner features allows the best calibration parameters reachability. Some typically considered metrics are the trajectory length, execution time, success rate or computational complexity. Additionally, grant the online or offline planning mode or the resolution kind, such as if the planner if complete, complete in resolution or probabilistic complete is also frequent.

There are many path planning algorithms, most of them grouped into generic libraries, such as STOMP [7], CHOMP [17], SBLP or OMPL [16]. OMPL is the most accepted motion planning library by MoveIt! community and the best integrated into this platform. So, the following work it will be just focused in this library.

There are many path planning algorithms which vary with approaching strategy or solving methodology. Due to these features, STOMP [7], CHOMP [17], SBPL[1] and OMPL [16] are generic libraries which intends to group most of these planners. Inside MoveIt! community, OMPL is the most used and the best-integrated motion planning library. So, the following work focuses on the performance of the planners from this library.

2.1 Open Motion Planning Library

The Open Motion Planning Library (OMPL) [16] contains an implementation of path planning algorithms of a sample-based motion planning kind. It is possible

---

[1] http://www.sbpl.net/.

to divide this library into two different categories, geometric-based planners and control-based planners, where the planners from the first group only regard to the geometric and kinematics features and the planners from the second category also consider some dynamic restrictions such like the velocity or the acceleration.

Inside geometric-based planners, it is possible to find single-query planners and multi-query planners. Single-query planners execute the tasks of roadmap creation and path search sequentially and contain planners from RRT, EST and KPIECE family, and STRIDE, PDST, FMT* and BFMT* planners. Otherwise, multi-query planner executes both tasks simultaneously and group planners from PRM and SPARS family. This category also groups a new set of optimisation planners which are variants of the first algorithms, always ensuring the shortest path.

Finally, the control-based planners contain some of the previous planners such as RRT, SST, EST, KPIECE, PDST, Syclop and LTLPlanner, that are capable of manage dynamics constraints.

3   Benchmark Methodology

For the solution under development, there are two ultimate goals. Firstly, intends to touch randomly dispersed grapes along a vineyard with a specific-designed sensor. After, aims to feature the robotic arm with pruning capabilities in real environment conditions. Due to the complexity of operation of robotic arms and the high-cluttered environment, path planning computation is not a trivial task. So, regarding these issues, the next sections plan to approach a benchmarking strategy for OMPL path planners, searching for a robust and efficient path planner.

As referred in Sect. 2, there are several metrics possible to consider. For this case study, the success rate, the planning time, the path length and the path clearance were the most significant features to serialise and select the best performance planners.

Fig. 2. Vine model to algorithms benchmarking

To accomplish the aim of benchmarking the planners for a vine pruning problem, the AgRob v16 robot (Fig. 3) with a simplified model of a vine tree compose the simulated scenario (Fig. 3b). The AgRob v16 robot [11] is a modular mobile robot designed to navigate and manipulate inside Douro's vineyard, sustaining its complexities. At the rear of the robot, there is a lightweight manipulator, the Robotis Manipulator-H, with about 6 kg and a maximum payload of 3 kg. It has 6 DoF and reaches about 633 mm with repeatability of ±0.05 mm. Each joint can move 180°/s, due to its Robotis Dynamixel servos.

 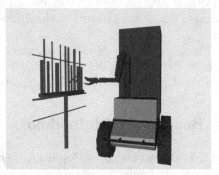

(a) Real mobile robot   (b) Simulated mobile robot

Fig. 3. AgRob v16 using a Robotis Manipulator-H arm in (a) real and (b) and simulated environments

An automatic generalised platform [3,12] benchmarked all the path planners at the simulated environment of Fig. 2. Attempting to broad the benchmarking process to evaluate algorithms robustness, the benchmarking platform computed each path planning algorithm between the home pose (Fig. 4a) and each pruning pose (Fig. 4b to f) and between pruning poses, considering both directions. The selected pruning poses attempts to have different degrees of the accessibility difficulty inside the manipulator workspace, where the poses from Fig. 4b and f should be the easiest to reach, the poses from Fig. 4d and e the hardest and Fig. 4c the middle-level reachability difficulty. The option for a between two poses path planning instead of a full path planning allows a shortage of the planning time, focusing the computation effort on smaller paths. On future work, it is also possible to parallelise the path planning algorithm with other current tasks, such as grasping or punning.

To solve the path planning problem, all the planners have controllable parameters. Some of them are transverse to all the planners, such as the planning timeout and the Longest Valid Segmentation Fraction (LVSF), while others are specific to the planner or planners family. Once some planners trends to reach always the maximum planning time, namely the planners from multi-query family, it was considered 5s as the maximum supportable waiting time to plan in real environment conditions. Additionally, it was studied the influence of planning

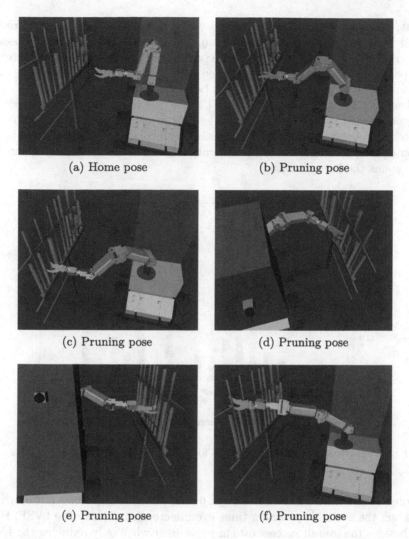

(a) Home pose   (b) Pruning pose

(c) Pruning pose   (d) Pruning pose

(e) Pruning pose   (f) Pruning pose

Fig. 4. Poses to benchmark. (a) Standard initial pose. (b–f) Selected pruning points

timeout and Longest Valid Segmentation Fraction (LVSF) variation in the solution success rate. Since it is intended to perform planners with different features with different and specific controlling parameters, in this first approach, these values were set up with the standard values from the OMPL MoveIt! tutorials[2].

4   Planners Benchmark and Discussion

Path planning algorithms from OMPL library do not assure the same trajectory for the same pair of poses in each running, due to its probabilistic nature. Because

---

[2] https://github.com/ros-planning/panda_moveit_config.

of that, planners benchmarking is required to measure its performance for the desired task. All planners performed ten times between each pair of poses of Fig. 4, respecting the Figs. 5, 6 and 7 contain the graphics that illustrate the total path planners success rate between all pairs of points. Comparing these three figures, it is noticeable differences between them.

Observing the graphic of Fig. 5, BiTTR is the best performing algorithm. However, due to its low success rate, less than 40%, this solution cannot be accepted as reliable. Therefore, it is possible to increase the LVSF (which bringing some precision and convergence difficulties) or increase the planning timeout, which seems the best solution.

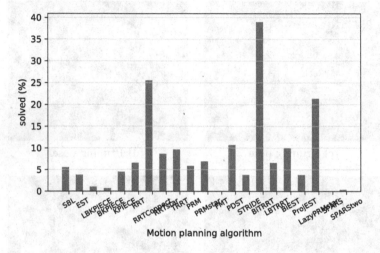

Fig. 5. Success rate of path planners for LVSF = 5 mm and timeout = 2.5 s

Consequently, the graphics of Figs. 6 and 7 show the clear advantage of increasing the available planning time, even decreasing slightly the LVSF. However, besides the overall success rate improvement when only reducing the LVSF (Fig. 6), some planners, as SPARS or SPARStwo, cannot still reach 10% success rate. On the other hand, LBKPIECE and BiTRRT seem to be near perfect solutions. So, considering a success rate higher than 80%, SBL, LBKPIECE, RRTConnect and BiTRRT are the most accepted path planners to be implemented for the final solution.

The third approach, observing the success rate when reducing the LVSF to 1 mm (Fig. 7), shows that, as expected, there is an overall deterioration of the planners' performance. However, there are still some remarkable planners such as SBL or LBKPIECE, whose performance keep higher than 80%.

Because of the probabilistic feature of these planners, the path reached for each planner may fluctuate thoughtfully. Therefore, it is also important to analyse the length (Fig. 8) and the clearance (Fig. 9) average and standard deviation

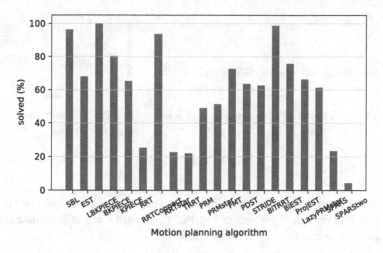

Fig. 6. Success rate of path planners for LVSF = 5 mm and timeout = 5 s

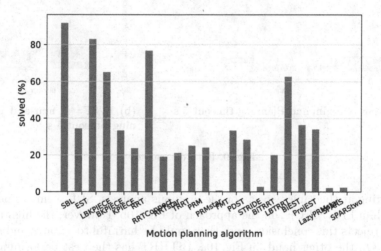

Fig. 7. Success rate of path planners for LVSF = 1 mm and timeout = 5 s

for each planner. To simplify this study, just the best performing planners will be considered.

Regarding the resulting path length (Fig. 8), the planners under the conditions of Fig. 8a performed better than planners of Fig. 8b. The first ones have a lower average and standard deviation, but higher outliers, mainly SBL and LBKPIECE planners. BKPIECE performed the smallest and the most identical paths. In its turn, Fig. 8b planners have similar conclusions and LBKPIECE performed the best results.

Path clearance metrics attempt to evaluate the highest average and the lowest standard deviation values. Comparing between the results of Fig. 9a and b, no

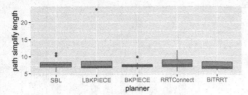
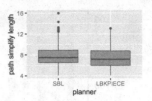

(a) LVSF = 5 mm and Planning timeout 5 s

(b) LVSF= 1 mm and Planning timeout 5 s

Fig. 8. Path length

advantage is got in select a lower LVSF, the media is identical and the standard deviation is higher. So, focusing on Fig. 9b, the results are still similar and the best results are performed by RRTConnect.

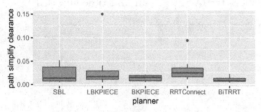
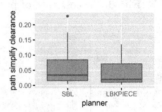

(a) LVSF = 5 mm and Planning timeout 5 s

(b) LVSF= 1 mm and Planning timeout 5 s

Fig. 9. Path clearance

Looking at the same aspects of the previous analysis, SBL seems to perform better than LBKPIECE, on the approach of Fig. 10b. However, the high rate of outliers rejects this conclusion, once they could be harmful to a stable and robust system. On the other hand, in Fig. 10a, BiTRRT has the best performing time and consumes less than 0.25 s to compute the path. Its high standard deviation value assures a high repeatability rate.

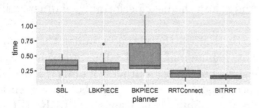
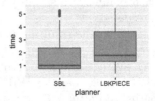

(a) LVSF = 5 mm and Planning timeout 5 s

(b) LVSF= 1 mm and Planning timeout 5 s

Fig. 10. Total planning time

Attending the previous discussion, and prioritising measurements as success rate, planning time, path length and path clearance, BiTRRT has the best performance. However, these conclusions should not be fixed, once that are still some planner specific parameter that should also be benchmarked to improve got results.

5   Conclusions

One of the problems faced with the open motion planning library [16] is the probabilistic nature of its planners. Because of that, there is not any assurance that planner founds the same or a similar path in each run for the same pair of poses. Regardless, the studied approach tries to minimise this problem, measuring path planners success rate and full planning and simplification time, path length and path clearance average and standard deviation. Therefore, attending got results, it could be concluded that no advantage is found in using the smallest longest valid segmentation fraction, once the path clearance and length and the success rate worsen. So for this case, it is satisfiable to choose general parameters with 5 mm for the longest valid segmentation fraction (LVSF) and 5 s for the maximum planning time. Inside these conditions and regarding planners performance, considering the classification order of importance of the highest success rate, the lowest planning time, the lowest path length and the highest path clearance, it is reasonable to select BiTRRT [5] as the best path planning algorithm for the proposed problem and improve it in the future.

Considering this benchmarking work, in the future, the planners with the best performance, namely BiTRRT, SBL, LBKPIECE and RRTConnect, should be re-tested, varying their specific parameters. In future work, it should also be explored in detail each planner specific parameters and implemented a solution of OMPL and CHOMP planning, using OMPL as a pre-processing algorithm. Besides that, to optimise the planning time, it should be explored the algorithm parallelisation approaches to reach a better time performance. Another solution is to use a more stable and predictable solution (non-probabilistic planners) through SBPL (Search-Based Planners Library), that contains many algorithms such as A* based or Dijkstra.

This benchmark work helps the reader to understand the limitations of each method and when to use them.

Acknowledgements. This research was financed by National Funds through FCT - Portuguese Foundation for Science and Technology, - Metbots-Metabolomic Robots with Self-learning Artificial Intelligence for Precision Agriculture' Reference PTDC/EEI-ROB/31124/2017 and FEDER funds through the COMPETE 2020 Programme under the project number POCI01-0145-FEDER-031124.

References

1. Bac, C.W., Van Henten, E.J., Hemming, J., Edan, Y.: Harvesting robots for high-value crops: state-of-the-art review and challenges ahead. J. Field Robot. **31**(6), 888–911 (2014)

2. Botterill, T., et al.: A robot system for pruning grape vines. J. Field Robot. **34**(6), 1100–1122 (2017)

3. Cohen, B., Sucan, I.A., Chitta, S.: A generic infrastructure for benchmarking motion planners. In: IEEE International Conference on Intelligent Robots and Systems, pp. 589–595. IEEE, Vilamoura, October 2012

4. Corbett-Davies, S., Botterill, T., Green, R., Saxton, V.: An expert system for automatically pruning vines. In: Proceedings of the 27th Conference on Image and Vision Computing New Zealand - IVCNZ 2012, p. 55. ACM Press, New York (2013)

5. Devaurs, D., Siméon, T., Cortés, J.: Enhancing the transition-based RRT to deal with complex cost spaces. In: 2013 IEEE International Conference on Robotics and Automation, pp. 4120–4125 (2013)

6. euRobotics: Strategic Research Agenda for Robotics in Europe. Draft 0v42 (2013). https://ec.europa.eu/research/industrial_technologies/pdf/robotics-ppp-roadmap_en.pdf

7. Kalakrishnan, M., Chitta, S., Theodorou, E., Pastor, P., Schaal, S.: STOMP: stochastic trajectory optimization for motion planning. In: 2011 IEEE International Conference on Robotics and Automation, pp. 4569–4574. IEEE, May 2011

8. Koselka, H., Wallach, B.: Agricultural robot system and method (2013)

9. Leonard, E.: Precision Agriculture. Reference Module in Food Science, Jan 2015

10. Matese, A., Di Gennaro, S.F.: Technology in precision viticulture: a state of the art review. Int. J. Wine Res. **7**, 69 (2015)

11. Mendes, J.M., dos Santos, F.N., Ferraz, N.A., do Couto, P.M., dos Santos, R.M.: localization based on natural features detector for steep slope vineyards. J. Intell. Robot. Syst. **93**(3), 433–446 (2019)

12. Moll, M., Sucan, I.A., Kavraki, L.E.: Benchmarking motion planning algorithms: an extensible infrastructure for analysis and visualization. IEEE Robot. Autom. Mag. **22**(3), 96–102 (2015)

13. Paulin, S., Botterill, T., Chen, X.Q., Green, R.: A specialised collision detector for grape vines. In: Australasian Conference on Robotics and Automation, ACRA, Australia, pp. 218–223 (2015)

14. Santesteban, L.G., Guillaume, S., Royo, J.B., Tisseyre, B.: Are precision agriculture tools and methods relevant at the whole-vineyard scale? Precis. Agric. **14**(1), 2–17 (2013)

15. dos Santos, F.N., Sobreira, H., Campos, D., Morais, R., Paulo Moreira, A., Contente, O.: Towards a reliable robot for steep slope vineyards monitoring. J. Intell. Robot. Syst. **83**(3), 429–444 (2016)

16. Şucan, I.A., Moll, M., Kavraki, L.: The open motion planning library. IEEE Robot. Autom. Mag. **19**(4), 72–82 (2012)

17. Zucker, M., et al.: CHOMP: covariant Hamiltonian optimization for motion planning. Int. J. Robot. Res. **32**(9–10), 1164–1193 (2013)

Online Optimization of Movement Cost for Robotic Applications of PSO

Sebastian Mai[(✉)] [iD], Heiner Zille [iD], Christoph Steup, and Sanaz Mostaghim [iD]

Otto-von-Guericke University, Magdeburg, Germany
{sebastian.mai,heiner.zille,christoph.steup,sanaz.mostaghim}@ovgu.de

Abstract. Particle Swarm Optimization is an optimization algorithm that can be used as a control mechanism in robotic tasks, especially robotic search. Existing algorithms are tuned to use as little evaluations of the objective function as possible. Measuring the objective with a sensor usually has a low cost in terms of time and energy compared to moving the robot. We propose a new algorithm to optimize the particle movement in SMPSO that samples the same points in the environment with less movement cost. Our experiments show that the average movement cost can be reduced by 50% or more in all test problems we used. The huge gain shows that there is a big potential in adapting swarm intelligence algorithms to robotic applications by optimizing them to better serve the constraints of the application.

Keywords: PSO · Swarm robotics · Movement cost · Energy efficiency

1 Introduction

One part of the digital revolution is the ever growing number of robotic systems. To control a large number of robots, swarm intelligence algorithms promise decentralized, robust and scalable strategies [16]. Particle Swarm Optimization (PSO) is one of the algorithms that can be used as a control mechanism in many robotic tasks, such as collective search tasks and tracking [16], task allocation [14] or segregation [8].

In a robotic search task using PSO, the robots are typically equipped with a sensor measuring a property of the environment. The task for the robots is to find the location where the best value is measured. In this context the PSO algorithm is used to compute the position the robot will move to and measure the next value, eventually leading the robots to the optimal value. While PSO algorithms seem well suited for robotic search applications, there is one problem we want to address in this paper: PSO algorithms are usually tuned to use as little evaluations of the fitness function as possible. However, the major cost in the robotic application is usually not reading a sensor but moving the robot [15].

In prior work we defined two metrics: Normalized Movement Energy Cost ($NMEC$) and Normalized Movement Time Cost ($NMTC$) to quantify the cost of movement in a comparable way [11]. In this paper we propose two versions of a

© Springer Nature Switzerland AG 2019
P. Moura Oliveira et al. (Eds.): EPIA 2019, LNAI 11805, pp. 307–318, 2019.
https://doi.org/10.1007/978-3-030-30244-3_26

new algorithm called *Energy Efficient SMPSO* and *Time Efficient SMPSO*. The algorithms use simple adaptations in the well-known multi-objective SMPSO [13] that optimize the *NMEC* and *NMTC* during runtime. Our experiments show that the adapted algorithm saves a large amount of the movement-associated costs without deteriorating the final solution quality. The proposed adaptation is intended to help the development of PSO algorithms specialized for robotic applications and illustrates the potential gain made from optimizing movement cost.

The remainder of this paper is structured as follows. Section 2 describes how other authors reduced the movement cost during optimization and presents other versions of PSO that deal with problems occurring in the robotic context. In Sect. 3 we introduce our modification of the SMPSO [13] algorithm, the *Energy Efficient SMPSO* and *Time Efficient SMPSO* and explain how we quantify and optimize the movement cost. Our experiments show that our algorithm is able to significantly reduce the movement of particles. The setup of the experiments and their results are discussed in Sect. 4. Finally, we want to discuss the meaning of our findings and share ideas for further research.

2   Related Work

Movement related cost has been determined as an important factor in the adaptation of PSO to robotic applications by different groups [10,12,15]. Pugh and Martinoli [15] describe a swarm of simulated robots performing a signal-source localization, using PSO as a search mechanism. They determine the duration of rotation and movement as a major performance factor. In addition to the travelled distance, the rotation of the robots also consumes time. At the same time, duration of the measurement can be neglected. The paper also addresses collision avoidance which is another important aspect that needs to be considered when using PSO in a robotic context. Mostaghim et al. [12] present an energy aware PSO algorithm that assumes a swarm of quadcopters that can land and stay at their position to save energy. The basic assumption is that quadcopters consume nearly no energy when landed and the energy expenditure is roughly equivalent to the travelled distance with some extra energy required for starting and landing. Bartashevich et al. [1] present a PSO modification that can reduce the energy spent for quadcopter affected by wind (or other disturbances) modelled by vector fields. While the additional energy expenditure to compensate for the wind condition is analyzed, the energy spent for the normal PSO without wind is not subject to the analysis.

Even though the application of PSO in robotics suffers from the problem of movement cost, some real robotic swarms already apply PSO and related methods as distributed control mechanism. Krishnanand et al. [10] used glow-worm optimization for signal source localization and Jatminko et al. [9] used PSO for odor source localization. Odor source localization suffers less from the movement cost, as the specific sensors take a long time (multiple seconds [9]) to acquire a measurement so the assumption that function evaluation is expensive still holds for this application. Other researchers have focused on including different application-related challenges into PSO algorithms. Among them are the PSO variations RDPSO [4] and A-RPSO [5] that introduce collision avoidance in the PSO algorithm. The rising interest in solving dynamic optimization problems can also be seen as a step towards application of PSO algorithms in robotics. The algorithms are evaluated with simulated and real robots to measure the performance in the search task using robot run time as a cost factor. However, this work does not explicitly analyze the amount of run time used for the movement nor how much energy is consumed due to the PSO-related movement.

3   Energy- and Time Efficient PSO

The main contribution of this paper is a PSO modification that can help to mitigate the inefficient movement happening in PSO. Before we describe the method we created, we first explain the metric we use to quantify movement cost and why we chose the SMPSO [13] algorithm as a baseline. Afterwards, we explain how the metric is used to optimize the movement of the particles during each iteration. The following mathematical notation is used throughout the paper:

N size of the population
$x_i^{(t)}$ position of individual i at iteration t
$P^{(t)} := \{x_1^{(t)}, x_2^{(t)}, ... x_N^{(t)}\}$ population at iteration t
g maximum number of generations
$\aleph$ number of iterations in movement optimization

$$NMEC := \frac{\sum_t \sum_i \|x_i^{(t+1)} - x_i^{(t)}\|}{N \cdot g} \qquad NMTC := \frac{\sum_t \max_i \|x_i^{(t+1)} - x_i^{(t)}\|}{g}$$

In a previous paper we presented two metrics called Normalized Movement Energy Cost ($NMEC$) and Normalized Movement Time Cost ($NMTC$) [11]. The $NMEC$ is equal to the average distance that each particle travels in a given time frame. It represents the energy expenditure of the robot as we assume the robot spends energy proportionally to the moved distance. The $NMTC$ is equal to the longest travel distance of the particles in each time step normalized by generations, as we assume that the largest distance in each generation dictates the time each generation takes in the robotic application. This is based on the assumption that the robots all need arrive at their planned destinations before the next target $x_i^{(t+1)}$ is calculated for each robot.

The idea for our algorithm is based on an observation in multi-objective PSO algorithms. When solving a multi-objective problem with PSO the non-dominated particles are ordered in the Pareto-Front and the order of the particles in the front is subject to change. We assume that switching positions in the front translates to the particles switching their positions in decision space (crossing

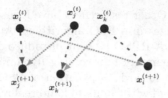

Fig. 1. By reassigning the index of the target position to the particles of the population the resulting movement (dashed, blue) can be shorter than the original movement (dotted, red). (Color figure online)

paths as depicted in the red, dotted lines in Fig. 1). When this happens we try to reassign the targets of the particles in such a way that every target position is covered, but the movement is shortened by not crossing the paths of the particles. In general, PSO algorithms compute their new positions usually based on the (past) positions of the particles in the swarm. In the next iteration of the PSO, measurements (i.e. fitness evaluations) are conducted at these newly computed positions. Sometimes these new positions are far away from the current positions of the particles, resulting in long distance motions. We assume that the swarm consists of identical particles. Consequently, it is not necessary that each particle travels to its next designated position. Instead, in the end of the time step each target position needs to be occupied by any of the particles. Therefore, the basic idea of the *Energy Efficient SMPSO* is to reduce the traveled distances by exchanging the destination of the particles, so that each location is reached by a particle and particles prefer closer destinations. This idea is not specific to Multi-Objective algorithms. Due to the observation in the Pareto-Front, we assume that the potential gain is larger in Multi-Objective Optimization. For this reason we did not want to use Single-Objective Optimization for our first experiment. A common restriction for real robots is limited movement speed. The well-known Speed-constrained Multi-Objective Particle Swarm Optimization (SMPSO [13]) algorithm also includes this property. Hence, we chose this algorithm as a baseline for our modification.

The full algorithm works as follows. The original SMPSO [13] calculates the new particle positions. Afterwards, we added a function that changes the particle assignment (line 8 in Algorithm 1). This function (**reassignTargets()**), optimizes the movement of the current time step by reordering the new particle assignments. Figure 1 shows the concept in a small example. In the upper part we show three particles $x_i^{(t)}$, $x_j^{(t)}$ and $x_k^{(t)}$ at time step t. Based on the PSO equations, the new positions for the particles on the bottom of the figure are calculated. The necessary travel paths for the particles are denoted in red dotted lines. Through a reassignment of the target destinations of each particle, we can reduce the travelled distances while at the same time obtaining the same measurements at the same positions in time step $t + 1$.

The function **reassignTargets()** reorders the new particle positions $P^{(t+1)}$ so movement cost is minimized according to $NMEC$ (or $NMTC$). During this process, only the new particle positions are swapped, but each particle keeps

---

Algorithm 1. Original SMPSO algorithm [13], with the highlighted *Energy Efficient SMPSO* modification.

---

1 initializeSwarm();
2 initializeLeadersArchive();
3 generation = 0;
4 **while** *generation < maxGenerations* **do**
5   computeSpeed();
6   updatePosition();
7   mutation();
8   **reassignTargets();**
9   evaluation();
10   updateLeadersArchive();
11   updateParticlesMemory();
12   generation++;
13 **end**
14 **return** LeadersArchive();

---

its memory and its computed velocity $v(t + 1)$. The values are used in the next iteration to compute the next positions, and changing the velocities to the actual traveled velocities after reassignment may change the algorithm's behavior (It is important to note that the computed movement vector does not match the real movement of the robot in case the positions are swapped).

Algorithm 2 outlines how the new order of the target positions is computed for *Energy Efficient SMPSO* that optimizes the energy cost ($NMEC$). Finding the optimal particle assignment is an NP-complete problem in itself. We use a simple local search to find an assignment that is used in the current time step. The local search mechanism uses the list of current particle positions $P^{(t)}$ and the list of the planned particle positions computed by SMPSO $P^{(t+1)}$ that is optimized in-place by reordering its elements. Using these positions, the $NMEC$ is computed. In each iteration two random elements a and b of the list of planned positions are swapped. In case the movement cost increases, the elements are swapped back to restore the original order. After $\aleph$ iterations the result is returned. When optimizing not for $NMEC$, but for $NMTC$ a is still chosen randomly, but b is chosen according to the particle moving the maximum distance to search for improvements more efficiently. We call this variant of the algorithm *Time Efficient SMPSO*. A drawback of our modification is the large number of iterations necessary to find an improved reassignment of the target positions for the swarm. Consequently, the computational effort used for each iteration of the *Energy Efficient SMPSO* algorithm is considerably higher than the original SMPSO. While our implementation for finding the particle reassignment follows a very naïve approach and can be improved by using more sophisticated algorithms, the underlying problem is still NP-hard and cannot be solved without investing considerable computational power. As such, *Energy Efficient SMPSO* and *Time Efficient SMPSO* require additional computational overhead in exchange for the optimization of the energy- and time consumption. The computational budget used to optimize these metrics is limited

Algorithm 2. *Energy Efficient SMPSO*: **reassignTargets()** to minimize energy expenditure according to *NMEC*.

Input: Number of Iterations: $\aleph$,
Current Particle Positions: $P^{(t)}$,
Planned Particle Positions: $P^{(t+1)}$
Output: Swapped Particle Positions: $P'^{(t+1)}$

1 **for** i *in [1, $\aleph$]* **do**
2     $m = NMEC\left(P^{(t+1)} - P^{(t)}\right)$;
3     $a = \text{randomInteger}(1,N)$;
4     $b = \text{randomInteger}(1,N)$;
5     $\text{swap}\left(x_a^{(t+1)}, x_b^{(t+1)}\right)$;
6   **if** $NMEC\left(P^{(t+1)} - P^{(t)}\right) \geq m$ **then**
7       $\text{swap}\left(x_a^{(t+1)}, x_b^{(t+1)}\right)$;   /* unswap */
8   **end**
9 **end**
10 **return** $P^{(t+1)}$;

---

by the capabilities of the robots using the algorithm. Often robots are assumed to have only very limited processing power rendering our approach infeasible. This is especially true in swarm robotics where a swarm of many cheap robots is often preferred over a smaller swarm with few expensive robots. However, we think that this limitation is becoming less relevant as embedded processors are getting cheaper and more powerful while the movement-associated cost remains constant.

4 Experimental Evaluation

In this section we evaluate the proposed approaches with respect to the obtained solution quality as well as the movement cost generated by the particles in the swarm. As a baseline for algorithm we use the well-known SMPSO algorithm [13], a multi-objective PSO introduced in 2009. The two versions of the particle reassignment proposed in the last section are implemented into the SMPSO, called *Energy Efficient SMPSO* and *Time Efficient SMPSO* respectively.

4.1 Experiment Settings

The Inverted Generational Distance indicator (IGD [2]) is used to evaluate the obtained solution quality, which can simultaneously assess convergence and diversity of the solutions sets. The IGD is computed as the average of the minimum distances from each point in the sample of the true Pareto-front to the obtained solution set. Both the metrics for movement-associated cost *NMEC* and *NMTC* are included in the evaluation as well. A description of the metrics is given in Sect. 3. The experiments were performed with a number of popular benchmark functions from the Multi-Objective Optimization literature, namely the DTLZ 1–7 [6], LSMOP 1–9 [3], ZDT 1–4, 6 [18] and WFG 1–9 [7] benchmarks. We evaluate the used benchmark problems with $n = 2$, $n = 3$, $n = 10$ and $n = 30$ decision variables to account for possible robotic applications. All experiments are performed with a maximum of $10,000$ function evaluations. We did a second round of experiments with a maximum of $2,000$ evaluations to check whether convergence differs between the algorithms. The further parameter settings are as follows: The population size for all algorithms is set to 100. All algorithms use polynomial mutation with a distribution index of 20.0 and a probability of $1/n$, as those are the default parameters in the literature. The experiments are repeated in 31 independent runs, and the median and interquartile range (IQR) values of all indicators are reported in the resulting tables. Statistical significance is tested using a two-sided Mann-Whitney-U Test. The null hypothesis of the test is that the tested samples have equal medians. Statistical significance is assumed for a value of $p < 0.01$. For implementation, the PlatEMO framework [17] version 1.5 is used. The source-code for *Energy Efficient SMPSO* and *Time Efficient SMPSO* can be found at our website[1]. The results for the DTZL 1–7 [6] benchmark functions are shown in Table 1.

4.2   Results

In our experiment we compared the two variants of *Energy Efficient SMPSO* against the original SMPSO [13]. *Time Efficient SMPSO* is designed to save time according to the *NMTC* metric by reducing the maximum movement in each time step. The *Energy Efficient SMPSO* is designed to save energy as modeled by the *NMEC* metric by reducing the sum of overall movement. Our experiments clearly show that both *Cost Efficient SMPSO* algorithms achieve this goal. Both algorithms achieve the best value in the respective indicator in each of the experiments (see Table 1). The reduction of movement cost is maximal for low dimensional problems – exactly the problems that are most relevant to robotics. In the two and three dimensional DTLZ problems *Time Efficient SMPSO* reduces movement to less than half of the original *NMTC* value, *Energy Efficient SMPSO* achieves an even higher relative improvement regarding the *NMEC* metric. As both *NMEC* and *NMTC* are not independent as optimizing one additionally optimizes the other. This is supported by our experiments, where *Energy Efficient SMPSO* performs better regarding *NMTC* than the stock SMPSO and vice versa. This statement especially holds for low-dimensional problems.

For most functions the IGD-indicator shows no significant difference between the performance of the two *Cost Efficient SMPSO* variants and the original SMPSO [13]. The only exceptions are DTLZ5 with two variables where the difference in performance is very small. There are other significant differences in the 30-dimensional DLTZ1 and 3 problems where none of the algorithms performed reasonably well. In the 30-dimensional DTLZ6 *Energy Efficient SMPSO*

---

[1] http://ci.ovgu.de/Research/Codes.html.

Table 1. Performance comparison on the DTLZ-Benchmarks using 10.000 function evaluations.

	IGD			NMTC			NMEC		
	Energy Efficient SMPSO	Time Efficient SMPSO	SMPSO	Energy Efficient SMPSO	Time Efficient SMPSO	SMPSO	Energy Efficient SMPSO	Time Efficient SMPSO	SMPSO
n = 2									
DTLZ1	0.0022 (1.21E-4)	0.0022 (1.08E-4)	0.0022 (1.06E-4)	0.3458 * (1.75E-2)	0.2281 * (1.33E-2)	0.5936 (1.88E-2)	0.0612 (5.20E-3)	0.1251 * (6.90E-3)	0.2652 (8.06E-3)
DTLZ2	0.0049 (2.39E-4)	0.0050 (2.56E-4)	0.0051 (4.33E-4)	0.2816 * (1.61E-2)	0.2064 * (8.91E-3)	0.5692 (9.10E-3)	0.0581 (2.70E-3)	0.1196 * (4.86E-3)	0.2470 (2.25E-3)
DTLZ3	0.0049 (2.38E-4)	0.0049 (2.44E-4)	0.0049 (2.21E-4)	0.3489 * (1.55E-2)	0.2303 * (1.11E-2)	0.5950 (1.56E-2)	0.0609 (4.66E-3)	0.1261 * (4.77E-3)	0.2612 (6.55E-3)
DTLZ4	0.0051 (2.22E-4)	0.0050 (4.01E-4)	0.0051 (1.21E-4)	0.3323 * (2.49E-2)	0.2665 * (2.13E-2)	0.5274 (1.47E-2)	0.0304 (3.42E-3)	0.0676 * (4.15E-3)	0.0921 (1.24E-2)
DTLZ5	0.0051 * (2.23E-4)	0.0051 * (3.17E-4)	0.0049 (2.60E-4)	0.2847 * (1.33E-2)	0.2085 * (1.15E-2)	0.5705 (7.17E-3)	0.0578 (2.49E-3)	0.1201 * (5.69E-3)	0.2469 (2.32E-3)
DTLZ6	0.0052 (3.48E-4)	0.0051 (2.79E-4)	0.0051 (3.37E-4)	0.3765 * (1.60E-2)	0.1959 * (1.02E-2)	0.5437 (6.30E-3)	0.0535 (1.79E-3)	0.1021 * (4.49E-3)	0.2460 (2.99E-3)
DTLZ7	0.0053 (3.94E-4)	0.0053 (3.21E-4)	0.0052 (3.55E-4)	0.3690 * (3.53E-2)	0.1928 * (9.14E-3)	0.5441 (7.16E-3)	0.0525 (4.30E-3)	0.0991 * (2.86E-3)	0.2437 (3.02E-3)
n = 3									
DTLZ1	0.1079 (1.48E-1)	0.0427 (1.71E-1)	0.1098 (1.81E-1)	0.4915 * (2.78E-2)	0.3696 * (5.39E-2)	0.7393 (1.45E-1)	0.1310 (2.19E-2)	0.2281 * (4.10E-2)	0.3225 (5.64E-2)
DTLZ2	0.0049 (2.13E-4)	0.0050 (2.71E-4)	0.0050 (1.70E-4)	0.3059 * (1.11E-2)	0.2534 * (1.11E-2)	0.5902 (1.36E-2)	0.0709 (1.74E-3)	0.1486 * (5.89E-3)	0.2528 (2.78E-3)
DTLZ3	0.2027 (3.21E-1)	0.0087 (4.04E-1)	0.1252 (3.89E-1)	0.4975 * (2.50E-2)	0.3601 * (5.10E-2)	0.7997 (1.08E-1)	0.1348 (1.78E-2)	0.2146 * (4.45E-2)	0.3424 (2.14E-2)
DTLZ4	0.0051 (7.37E-1)	0.0052 (7.37E-1)	0.0051 (4.04E-4)	0.3485 * (1.48E-1)	0.2783 * (1.19E-1)	0.5605 (3.27E-2)	0.0432 (2.24E-2)	0.0834 * (5.19E-2)	0.1105 (2.24E-2)
DTLZ5	0.0050 (1.78E-4)	0.0050 (2.53E-4)	0.0050 (2.68E-4)	0.3042 * (1.69E-2)	0.2527 * (1.22E-2)	0.5873 (6.19E-2)	0.0700 (2.21E-3)	0.1469 * (5.83E-3)	0.2525 (2.37E-3)
DTLZ6	0.0052 (3.15E-4)	0.0052 (2.36E-4)	0.0051 (2.16E-4)	0.3928 * (3.08E-2)	0.2197 * (1.23E-2)	0.5559 (1.01E-2)	0.0594 (1.90E-3)	0.1162 * (5.49E-3)	0.2526 (4.15E-3)
DTLZ7	0.0053 (4.37E-1)	0.0053 (3.83E-4)	0.0053 (4.37E-1)	0.3568 * (1.48E-1)	0.2061 * (1.45E-2)	0.5484 (7.88E-2)	0.0530 (2.62E-3)	0.1077 * (4.96E-3)	0.2463 (1.44E-1)
n = 10									
DTLZ1	17.6788 * (2.17E1)	11.3331 (1.94E1)	4.8673 (1.28E1)	0.9745 * (5.75E-2)	0.7379 * (6.82E-2)	1.5069 (9.30E-2)	0.3166 (3.81E-2)	0.4809 * (6.00E-2)	0.7438 (1.38E-1)
DTLZ2	0.0053 (2.16E-4)	0.0054 (4.17E-4)	0.0053 (2.59E-4)	0.4809 * (2.60E-2)	0.4270 * (3.24E-2)	0.7431 (3.52E-2)	0.1349 (6.56E-3)	0.2435 * (1.13E-2)	0.2901 (5.40E-3)
DTLZ3	25.1229 (6.04E1)	35.8635 (4.91E1)	38.4455 (4.91E1)	0.9897 * (4.81E-2)	0.7438 * (5.56E-2)	1.4922 (8.46E-2)	0.3268 (2.28E-2)	0.4745 * (5.41E-2)	0.7156 (8.91E-2)
DTLZ4	0.0056 (7.36E-1)	0.0057 (7.36E-1)	0.0057 (7.36E-1)	0.5088 * (2.02E-1)	0.4013 * (1.46E-1)	0.7069 (3.06E-1)	0.1137 (6.38E-2)	0.1778 * (1.07E-1)	0.1806 (1.39E-1)
DTLZ5	0.0054 (2.92E-4)	0.0053 (2.67E-4)	0.0053 (2.98E-4)	0.4833 * (1.18E-2)	0.4244 * (2.41E-2)	0.7424 (3.27E-2)	0.1361 (5.71E-3)	0.2416 * (1.12E-2)	0.2918 (6.31E-3)
DTLZ6	0.0051 (3.62E-4)	0.0052 (2.91E-4)	0.0050 (2.55E-4)	0.6112 * (7.86E-2)	0.3912 * (4.89E-2)	0.7654 (1.09E-1)	0.1441 (2.75E-2)	0.2268 * (3.36E-2)	0.3428 (3.65E-2)
DTLZ7	0.0054 (4.37E-1)	0.0053 (4.37E-1)	0.4425 (4.37E-1)	0.4332 * (1.16E-1)	0.2919 * (5.39E-2)	0.5895 (1.29E-1)	0.0912 (3.28E-2)	0.1634 * (5.82E-2)	0.1632 (1.48E-1)
n = 30									
DTLZ1	63.1565 * (4.83E1)	26.5158 (4.79E1)	19.0938 (4.60E1)	1.7049 * (1.17E-1)	1.3628 * (1.35E-1)	2.6028 (1.37E-1)	0.5729 (9.66E-2)	0.8644 * (1.16E-1)	1.3315 (1.48E-1)
DTLZ2	0.0164 (3.68E-3)	0.0190 (4.50E-3)	0.0181 (7.65E-3)	0.7617 * (4.17E-2)	0.6577 * (3.17E-2)	1.0641 (5.59E-2)	0.2148 (1.07E-2)	0.3566 * (1.36E-2)	0.3730 (1.26E-2)
DTLZ3	156.5351 (1.91E2)	121.8046 * (1.16E2)	30.8679 (1.19E2)	1.7062 * (1.54E-1)	1.3333 * (9.44E-2)	2.6171 (1.37E-1)	0.5511 (5.26E-2)	0.8080 * (6.58E-2)	1.3381 (2.10E-1)
DTLZ4	0.0238 (1.91E-2)	0.0275 (7.20E-1)	0.0302 (7.22E-1)	0.7942 * (2.27E-1)	0.6166 * (2.27E-1)	1.0806 (4.64E-2)	0.2091 (2.69E-2)	0.3008 * (1.58E-1)	0.3268 (1.81E-1)
DTLZ5	0.0169 (6.87E-3)	0.0182 (8.81E-3)	0.0192 (6.19E-3)	0.7702 * (5.50E-2)	0.6634 * (3.34E-2)	1.0692 (4.64E-2)	0.2157 (9.71E-3)	0.3597 * (1.42E-2)	0.3711 (1.14E-2)
DTLZ6	3.1023 (2.83E0)	3.0796 * (1.58E0)	4.2498 (2.16E0)	1.0940 * (1.90E-1)	0.9029 * (1.39E-1)	1.4023 (2.40E-1)	0.3292 (5.83E-2)	0.5344 * (7.36E-2)	0.5768 (9.02E-2)
DTLZ7	0.4428 (4.25E-1)	0.0565 (4.31E-1)	0.4425 (3.93E-1)	0.7742 * (2.88E-1)	0.6377 * (1.61E-1)	0.9771 (4.83E-1)	0.2200 (1.23E-1)	0.3988 * (1.18E-1)	0.3518 (2.74E-1)

Table 2. Performance comparison on the DTLZ-Benchmarks using 2.000 function evaluations.

	IGD			NMTC			NMEC		
	Energy Efficient SMPSO	Time Efficient SMPSO	SMPSO	Energy Efficient SMPSO	Time Efficient SMPSO	SMPSO	Energy Efficient SMPSO	Time Efficient SMPSO	SMPSO
n = 2									
DTLZ1	0.0125 (1.46E-2)	0.0129 (1.17E-2)	0.0135 (2.01E-2)	0.3997 * (3.66E-2)	0.2895 * (2.51E-2)	0.6427 (4.06E-2)	0.0884 (7.77E-3)	0.1773 (1.30E-2)	0.2999 (2.45E-2)
DTLZ2	0.0051 (3.07E-4)	0.0050 (2.45E-4)	0.0050 (2.60E-4)	0.3152 * (3.47E-2)	0.2296 * (2.23E-2)	0.5980 (2.02E-2)	0.0646 (4.16E-3)	0.1347 (1.05E-2)	0.2471 (6.79E-3)
DTLZ3	0.0248 (3.15E-2)	0.0362 (2.08E-2)	0.0275 (5.25E-2)	0.4096 * (4.56E-2)	0.2898 * (3.21E-2)	0.6478 (2.94E-2)	0.0893 (9.94E-3)	0.1748 (1.65E-2)	0.2920 (2.24E-2)
DTLZ4	0.0051 (5.93E-4)	0.0051 (3.10E-4)	0.0051 (4.77E-4)	0.3677 * (5.18E-2)	0.2627 * (2.43E-2)	0.5941 (3.38E-2)	0.0634 (1.10E-2)	0.1253 (1.53E-2)	0.1854 (3.58E-2)
DTLZ5	0.0050 (2.84E-4)	0.0051 (2.05E-4)	0.0050 (3.15E-4)	0.3012 * (3.16E-2)	0.2260 * (1.63E-2)	0.5922 (1.69E-2)	0.0645 (3.62E-3)	0.1359 (1.09E-2)	0.2483 (7.09E-3)
DTLZ6	0.0053 (3.03E-4)	0.0051 (3.03E-4)	0.0052 (4.11E-4)	0.4221 * (3.95E-2)	0.2604 * (3.26E-2)	0.5712 (1.74E-2)	0.0699 (5.90E-3)	0.1403 (1.48E-2)	0.2535 (6.34E-3)
DTLZ7	0.0051 (2.47E-4)	0.0052 (2.49E-4)	0.0053 (3.82E-4)	0.4327 * (5.25E-2)	0.2440 * (3.12E-2)	0.5625 (2.43E-2)	0.0724 (5.32E-3)	0.1324 (1.04E-2)	0.2532 (9.23E-3)
n = 3									
DTLZ1	0.3931 (6.14E-1)	0.3494 (5.38E-1)	0.3800 (6.38E-1)	0.5427 * (4.18E-2)	0.3975 * (2.75E-2)	0.8065 (3.45E-2)	0.1546 (1.05E-2)	0.2604 (1.44E-2)	0.3710 (5.40E-2)
DTLZ2	0.0053 (3.42E-4)	0.0053 (3.57E-4)	0.0053 (3.49E-4)	0.3774 * (3.72E-2)	0.3075 * (2.12E-2)	0.6649 (3.75E-2)	0.0936 (4.86E-3)	0.1873 (1.03E-2)	0.2658 (7.59E-3)
DTLZ3	0.8939 (1.11E0)	0.7420 (1.32E0)	0.8544 (1.08E0)	0.5368 * (3.93E-2)	0.4067 * (3.85E-2)	0.8059 (4.60E-2)	0.1520 (1.10E-2)	0.2674 (2.20E-2)	0.3804 (3.78E-2)
DTLZ4	0.0058 (7.36E-1)	0.0062 (7.36E-1)	0.0072 (7.66E-3)	0.4321 * (1.43E-1)	0.3247 * (9.52E-2)	0.6955 (9.11E-2)	0.0949 (2.70E-2)	0.1750 (8.35E-2)	0.2503 (7.53E-2)
DTLZ5	0.0054 (4.03E-4)	0.0054 * (2.67E-4)	0.0052 (2.63E-4)	0.3715 * (5.12E-2)	0.3027 * (3.31E-2)	0.6588 (2.49E-2)	0.0917 (5.54E-3)	0.1856 (1.44E-2)	0.2663 (7.58E-3)
DTLZ6	0.0050 (2.80E-4)	0.0051 (2.29E-4)	0.0052 (3.18E-4)	0.4961 * (5.10E-2)	0.3577 * (4.76E-2)	0.6586 (3.57E-2)	0.0976 (9.94E-3)	0.1949 (2.12E-2)	0.2856 (1.91E-2)
DTLZ7	0.0053 (4.37E-1)	0.0052 (2.55E-4)	0.0052 (4.37E-1)	0.4276 * (9.02E-2)	0.3061 * (3.64E-2)	0.6091 (7.54E-2)	0.0859 (1.92E-2)	0.1689 (1.57E-2)	0.2629 (1.12E-1)
n = 10									
DTLZ1	50.5123 (3.28E1)	58.4101 (4.68E1)	46.7126 (5.44E1)	1.0817 * (4.52E-2)	0.8487 * (3.79E-2)	1.4227 (5.19E-2)	0.4125 (3.53E-2)	0.5973 (4.00E-2)	0.7228 (7.70E-2)
DTLZ2	0.0153 * (6.66E-3)	0.0188 * (5.34E-3)	0.0155 (5.89E-3)	0.7836 * (6.79E-2)	0.6871 * (3.37E-2)	1.1187 (5.86E-2)	0.2549 (1.93E-2)	0.4210 (2.30E-2)	0.4043 (1.62E-2)
DTLZ3	137.9567 (1.31E2)	140.6188 (7.09E1)	130.8458 (9.29E1)	1.0854 * (5.78E-2)	0.8632 * (4.50E-2)	1.4271 (5.97E-2)	0.4041 (2.31E-2)	0.5933 (3.22E-2)	0.7022 (6.28E-2)
DTLZ4	0.1709 (6.92E-2)	0.2099 (6.65E-1)	0.2787 (6.81E-1)	0.7873 * (2.12E-1)	0.6504 * (1.39E-1)	1.1443 (3.31E-1)	0.2470 (9.93E-2)	0.3976 (1.65E-1)	0.4279 (1.90E-1)
DTLZ5	0.0159 (6.09E-3)	0.0170 (4.14E-3)	0.0159 (4.26E-3)	0.7873 * (7.94E-2)	0.6801 * (3.42E-2)	1.1197 (5.28E-2)	0.2528 (2.16E-2)	0.4142 (2.32E-2)	0.4145 (2.56E-2)
DTLZ6	1.9491 (8.94E-1)	1.2674 (1.10B0)	1.4928 (9.90E-1)	1.0947 * (7.86E-2)	0.8235 * (6.75E-2)	1.2758 (1.05E-1)	0.3695 (5.51E-2)	0.5480 (4.63E-2)	0.6307 (9.66E-2)
DTLZ7	0.0909 (4.02E-1)	0.1418 (4.10E-1)	0.4413 (3.99E-1)	0.8653 * (1.01E-1)	0.6618 * (1.51E-1)	1.0041 (1.94E-1)	0.2577 (4.60E-2)	0.4065 (1.37E-1)	0.4122 (1.40E-1)
n = 30									
DTLZ1	396.4429 * (2.17E2)	357.3761 (1.98E2)	232.2336 (2.85E2)	1.9465 * (7.41E-2)	1.5729 * (5.50E-2)	2.4170 (4.67E-2)	0.8165 (4.82E-2)	1.1624 (4.52E-2)	1.2707 (4.13E-2)
DTLZ2	0.0946 (2.14E-2)	0.1066 (2.94E-2)	0.0984 (2.63E-2)	1.4622 * (1.05E-1)	1.2417 * (7.18E-2)	1.9750 (5.44E-2)	0.4905 (4.58E-2)	0.7534 (3.62E-2)	0.7134 (3.89E-2)
DTLZ3	684.3363 (4.35E2)	685.2052 (5.41E2)	412.4879 (7.53E2)	1.9531 * (1.26E-1)	1.5393 * (1.23E-1)	2.4226 (6.13E-2)	0.7709 (6.44E-2)	1.0831 (9.37E-2)	1.2389 (5.25E-2)
DTLZ4	0.4696 * (3.16E-1)	0.6160 (3.41E-1)	0.7107 (2.60E-1)	1.4505 * (1.97E-1)	1.1500 * (1.86E-1)	2.0313 (4.28E-1)	0.4863 (6.38E-2)	0.7174 (2.08E-1)	0.7048 (2.27E-1)
DTLZ5	0.1040 (3.15E-2)	0.1019 (2.95E-2)	0.0960 (2.06E-2)	1.4623 * (8.56E-2)	1.2402 * (9.28E-2)	1.9725 (1.27E-1)	0.4956 (2.07E-2)	0.7557 (4.99E-2)	0.7029 (3.75E-2)
DTLZ6	11.2499 (1.77E0)	10.9788 (2.26E0)	10.6501 (2.25E0)	2.0208 * (1.57E-1)	1.5857 * (9.65E-2)	2.3079 (1.04E-1)	0.7852 (1.21E-1)	1.1035 (7.81E-2)	1.1851 (1.45E-1)
DTLZ7	2.5100 (8.28E-1)	1.9790 (1.30E0)	2.2555 (8.03E-1)	1.6411 * (2.03E-1)	1.3481 * (1.48E-1)	2.0024 (4.70E-1)	0.6022 (1.20E-1)	0.8904 (1.49E-1)	0.9286 (3.75E-1)

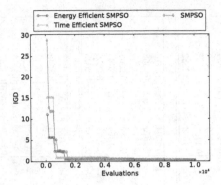

Fig. 2. IGD of the median run for DTLZ3 with 3 decision variables.

and *Time Efficient SMPSO* perform even better than the original algorithm. The results of the other benchmarks confirm these findings. While there are significant differences in some of the problems, especially with $n \geq 10$ dimensions, we could not identify a clear trend which algorithm performs better or specific reasons why *Energy Efficient SMPSO* and *Time Efficient SMPSO* show different IGD-performance with some of the benchmarks. Figure 2 shows the IGD-value for the first 10.000 function evaluations for the median run for each algorithm on the 3-variable DTLZ 3 problem. The figure shows a strong similarity between the convergence behavior of the algorithms. The only notable difference is the first iteration where SMPSO shows a significantly higher IGD. This may be caused by the random initialization of the populations of the compared algorithms. To verify our assumption of the similarity of convergence between *Energy Efficient SMPSO, Time Efficient SMPSO* and SMPSO, we sampled the IGD, *NMEC* and *NMTC* values after 2000 function evaluations (see Table 2) and compared them with the indicators after 10.000 function evaluations (see Table 1). The acquired results confirm our assumption that there is no clear trend which of the algorithms shows better (IGD-) convergence. However, the *Cost Efficient SMPSO* algorithms show a notable improvement in the *NMEC* and *NMTC* metrics. During the first 2000 evaluations the particles in all algorithms seem to move more compared to the rest of the run, which results in higher values in both movement metrics. This is explained by the exploration happening in the beginning of each run in contrast to the converged state at the end. In all experiments, the modified *Cost Efficient SMPSO* algorithms perform significantly better than the original SMPSO. Therefore, in a robotic system with limited movement budget the *Cost Efficient SMPSO* algorithms provides better solution quality than SMPSO. The unmodified SMPSO exhausts its movement budget faster than the *Cost Efficient SMPSO*.

5   Conclusion

This paper presents the *Time Efficient SMPSO* and *Energy Efficient SMPSO* algorithm, a modification of SMPSO [13] designed to reduce the particle movement. *Energy Efficient SMPSO* and *Time Efficient SMPSO* reassign the target positions of each particle to minimize the movement associated cost according to the respective metric, which translates to a more efficient movement of real robots saving battery and time. Both variants of the modified algorithm save at least half the movement cost compared to the original algorithm while showing no significant degradation in solution quality or convergence speed. We could show that PSO can be adapted to better meet the requirements of the robotic domain. This work may serve as a stepping stone to transfer the knowledge gathered in PSO as optimization algorithm to the robotic domain. We do not think that the *Time Efficient SMPSO* and *Energy Efficient SMPSO* algorithm will soon find their application in robotics, but rather that the effectiveness of our simple modification points out the potential room for improvement in applying PSO to robotics.

In the future we plan to test different algorithms with the modification, especially single objective PSO algorithms. The test problems currently available convey typical properties of optimization problems, but may not accurately represent the environment of robotic applications. A new framework with success and cost metrics and state of the art single- and multi-objective PSO algorithms may help to classify and analyze algorithms for their applicability to robotic applications. Such a framework could also help to compare how algorithms cope with real-world constraints like collision avoidance or speed limitations. Usually, the performance of optimization algorithms are measured with a fixed computational budged and the final solution quality is analyzed. For the application of PSO algorithms to the robotic domain, the inverted approach may be more relevant. Most real-world applications aim for a specific solution quality and the effort put into the optimization needs to be analyzed. In future we hope that more work uses this type of evaluation based on task-specific cost metrics. This also paves the way for research of time-cost optimization of algorithms based on asynchronous updates. Currently, the research on those algorithms is lacking and the bias introduced by doing asynchronous updates poses a huge problem, as it causes premature convergence to local optima without much benefit in the classical evaluation metrics.

References

1. Bartashevich, P., Koerte, D., Mostaghim, S.: Energy-saving decision making for aerial swarms: PSO-based navigation in vector fields. In: 2017 IEEE Symposium Series on Computational Intelligence (SSCI), pp. 1–8. IEEE, Honolulu, November 2017
2. Bosman, P.A.N., Thierens, D.: The balance between proximity and diversity in multiobjective evolutionary algorithms. IEEE Trans. Evol. Comput. **7**(2), 174–188 (2003)
3. Cheng, R., Jin, Y., Olhofer, M., Sendhoff, B.: Test problems for large-scale multiobjective and many-objective optimization. IEEE Trans. Cybern. **PP**(99), 1–14 (2016)

4. Couceiro, M.S., Rocha, R.P., Ferreira, N.M.F.: A novel multi-robot exploration approach based on particle swarm optimization algorithms. In 9th IEEE International Symposium on Safety, Security, and Rescue Robotics, SSRR 2011, pp. 327–332. IEEE, Kyoto (2011)
5. Dadgar, M., Jafari, S., Hamzeh, A.: A PSO-based multi-robot cooperation method for target searching in unknown environments. Neurocomputing 177, 62–74 (2016)
6. Deb, K., Thiele, L., Laumanns, M., Zitzler, E.: Scalable multi-objective optimization test problems. In: IEEE Congress on Evolutionary Computation (CEC), pp. 825–830. IEEE, Honolulu (2002)
7. Huband, S., Hingston, P., Barone, L., While, L.: A review of multiobjective test problems and a scalable test problem toolkit. IEEE Trans. Evol. Comput. 10(5), 477–506 (2006)
8. Inácio, F.R., Macharet, D.G., Chaimowicz, L.: Pso-based strategy for the segregation of heterogeneous robotic swarms. J. Comput. Sci. 31, 86–94 (2018)
9. Jatmiko, W., et al.: Robots implementation for odor source localization using PSO algorithm. WSEAS Trans. Circ. Syst. 10(4), 115–125 (2011)
10. Krishnanand, K.N., Ghose, D.: A glowworm swarm optimization based multi-robot system for signal source localization. In: Liu, D., Wang, L., Tan, K.C. (eds.) Design and Control of Intelligent Robotic Systems. SCI, pp. 49–68. Springer, Heidelberg (2009). https://doi.org/10.1007/978-3-540-89933-4_3
11. Mai, S., Zille, H., Steup, C., Mostaghim, S.: Multi-objective collective search and movement-based metrics in swarm robotics. In: Genetic and Evolutionary Computation Conference Companion (GECCO 2019 Companion). ACM, Prague (2019)
12. Mostaghim, S., Steup, C., Witt, F.: Energy aware particle swarm optimization as search mechanism for aerial micro-robots. In: 2016 IEEE Symposium Series on Computational Intelligence (SSCI), pp. 1–7. IEEE, Athens, December 2016
13. Nebro, A.J., Durillo, J.J., Garcia-Nieto, J., Coello, C.A., Luna, F., Alba, E.: SMPSO: a new PSO-based metaheuristic for multi-objective optimization. In: 2009 IEEE Symposium on Computational Intelligence in Multi-criteria Decision-Making (MCDM), pp. 66–73. IEEE, Nashville, March 2009
14. Nedjah, N., De Mendonça, R.M., De Macedo Mourelle, L.: PSO-based distributed algorithm for dynamic task allocation in a robotic swarm. Procedia Comput. Sci. 51(1), 326–335 (2015)
15. Pugh, J., Martinoli, A.: Inspiring and modeling multi-robot search with particle swarm optimization. In: 2007 IEEE Swarm Intelligence Symposium, pp. 332–339. IEEE, Honolulu, April 2007
16. Senanayake, M., Senthooran, I., Barca, J.C., Chung, H., Kamruzzaman, J., Murshed, M.: Search and tracking algorithms for swarms of robots: a survey. Robot. Auton. Syst. 75, 422–434 (2016)
17. Tian, Y., Cheng, R., Zhang, X., Jin, Y.: Platemo: a MATLAB platform for evolutionary multi-objective optimization. CoRR, abs/1701.00879, 1–20 (2017)
18. Zitzler, E., Deb, K., Thiele, L.: Comparison of multiobjective evolutionary algorithms: empirical results. Evol. Comput. 8(2), 173–195 (2000)

Monocular Visual Odometry
Using Fisheye Lens Cameras

André Aguiar[1]([⊠]), Filipe Santos[2], Luís Santos[2], and Armando Sousa[1]

[1] FEUP, University of Porto, Porto, Portugal
{andre.aguiar,asousa}@fe.up.pt
[2] INESCTEC, CRIIS, Porto, Portugal
{fbsantos,luis.c.santos}@inesctec.fe.up.pt

Abstract. Developing ground robots for crop monitoring and harvesting in steep slope vineyards is a complex challenge due to two main reasons: harsh condition of the terrain and unstable localization accuracy obtained with Global Navigation Satellite System. In this context, a reliable localization system requires an accurate and redundant information to Global Navigation Satellite System and wheel odometry based system. To pursue this goal and have a reliable localization system in our robotic platform we aim to extract the better performance as possible from a monocular Visual Odometry method. To do so, we present a benchmark of Libviso2 using both perspective and fisheye lens cameras, studying the behavior of the method using both topologies in terms of motion performance in an outdoor environment. Also we analyze the quality of feature extraction of the method using the two camera systems studying the impact of the field of view and omnidirectional image rectification in VO. We propose a general methodology to incorporate a fisheye lens camera system into a VO method. Finally, we briefly describe the robot setup that was used to generate the results that will be presented.

1 Introduction

Developing ground robots for crop monitoring and harvesting is a complex challenge because robotic sensing, perception and interpretation of the crop needs to be efficient, accurate, and robust in an unstructured environment [12]. The strategic European research agenda for robotics [13] states that robots can improve agriculture efficiency and competitiveness. However, few commercial robots for agricultural applications are available [12]. In the context of the European Union, there are only a few funded projects focusing on the development of monitoring robots for flat vineyards: the VineRobot [14] and Vinbot [15]. However, vineyards built on steep slope hills present additional challenges for the machinery and automation development due to the higher complexity of the sloped environment. These called steep slope vineyards exist in Portugal in the Douro region, an United Nations Educational, Scientific and Cultural Organization (UNESCO) heritage place, and in other regions of five European countries.

The context of a vineyard built in a steep hill presents several challenges to robotic systems:

© Springer Nature Switzerland AG 2019
P. Moura Oliveira et al. (Eds.): EPIA 2019, LNAI 11805, pp. 319–330, 2019.
https://doi.org/10.1007/978-3-030-30244-3_27

- Terrain characteristics produces signal blockage and multi-reflection which decreases the availability and accuracy of the Global Navigation Satellite System (GNSS).
- Harsh conditions of the terrain limits the accuracy of dead-reckoning sensors - odometry and inertial measurement unit (IMU), for example;
- Terrain slopes imposes constrains to the robot path planning. Safe robot motion planning and control depends on accurate maps of the vineyard and precise information about its posture (localization and attitude).

In these vineyards, the high elevation mask imposed by the hills limits the number of GNSS satellites in view [16]. Thus, GNSS accuracy is low and robot localization is not always available. Beside, a GNSS receiver can suffer spoofing attacks which is a possible safety issue. For these reasons, a redundant localization solution is needed to get an always available, efficient and safe robot. Aiming to solve these robotic challenges for the steep slope vineyards, the INESC TEC team has developed an agricultural robotic platform (AgRob V16) to acquire real data and test the proposed agricultural robotic components in a real scenario.

In [16] and [17] the VineSLAM approach is presented, which is a GNSS-free localization system for steep slope vineyards. VineSLAM considers a hybrid map architecture to increase the localization accuracy and robustness. The topological localization of the robot is updated considering artificial landmarks, such as those proposed in [18]. In metric localization, VineSLAM considers natural vineyard features [16] to increase the system redundancy and reliability. These natural features are the vine trunks and masts. They exist in all vineyards with a large density. However, a reliable detector of these natural features requires several sensors, such as laser range finders (LRF), cameras and/or RGB-D sensors. The use of standalone LRF-based detectors is not reliable because grass and dust creates small artifacts that are classified as trunks/masts [17]. Vision-based detectors provides complementary and richer information to reach a reliable natural feature detector. In [19], we presented a vision-based detector for these natural features detection.

In this work, aiming to overcome the environment limitations previous described, we are interested in extracting the better performance as possible of a monocular Visual Odometry (VO) method. To do so, we present a benchmark of Libviso2 [2] using perspective and fisheye lens cameras, studying the behavior of the method using both topologies in terms of trajectory performance. Also we analyze the quality of feature extraction of the method using the two camera systems studying the impact of the field of view (FoV) and fisheye image rectification in VO. To do this we compare Libviso2 performance using a perspective camera image, a fisheye rectified image and a raw fisheye image. We propose a general methodology to incorporate a fisheye lens camera system into a VO method. Finally, we briefly describe the robot setup that was used to generate the results that will be presented.

2   Related Work

Monocular VO is one of the most challenging fields of robotics. Estimating a robot motion using a single camera is a real challenge. In order to optimize VO performance it is convenient to have as many information about the surrounding environment as possible. In this context arises the use of wide FoV cameras in VO and SLAM methods. For example, in [10] a comparison of the performance of a monocular feature-based VO method using perspective, fisheye and catadioptric images is done. They study the impact of using large FoV raw images in indoor and outdoor environments. Also, they propose an extension of the state-of-the-art SVO [7] addapted to fisheye lens cameras. To do so, they use the camera model that will be described in Sect. 5 and sample the curved epipolar line based on the unit sphere. The results show that for a fixed resolution, large FoV cameras are better in indoor scenes but worst in outdoor environments given the radial distortion associated with raw omnidirectional images. In [11] Streckel et al. studied the impact of lens selection in Structure for Motion (SfM) which includes VO. This work only considers indoor scenes. They use a fisheye lens camera with 180° of FoV with a resolution of 1600×1200 and crop the center of the high resolution images to obtain 400×400 perspective images. In order to have a fisheye camera image with the same resolution a FoV of 160° was subsampled to 400×400 resolution. The experiments show the superior performance of the high resolution configuration in terms of translation and rotation. However, these results are restricted to synthetic and indoor data. [4] uses a stereo fisheye camera system and performs semi-dense direct image alignment to estimate the camera pose while using raw fisheye images. It presents high accuracy levels estimating camera motions. [3] is an extension of the original DSO [5] method for a monocular fisheye camera. They use an unified omnidirectional camera model as a projection function that can both represent perspective and omnidirectional cameras. The camera motion is estimated by the minimization of the photometric error between consecutive frames. In [6] a catadioptric image is used in an Extended Kalman Filter (EKF) based SLAM approach. They use a spherical camera model jacobian needed by the EKF and the SIFT detector to compute the feature matching. The results show that the omnidirectional camera system outperforms the tested perspective one.

In this work we propose a general approach to obtain rectified images that can be inputted in a VO system. We also compare Libviso2 motion performance and matching quality using monocular perspective images, rectified fisheye images and raw fisheye images. To do so we present our built in-house datasets[1] that are composed by a side by side perspective camera and fisheye camera that capture the same robot motion. Two input resolutions were recorded.

3   Robotic Platform System

This work is inserted in AgRob V16 that is a robotic platform for research and development of robotics technologies for Douro vineyard, Fig. 1. AgRob V16

---

[1] http://vcriis01.inesctec.pt/datasets/DataSet/Romovi/Andre_visual_odom.zip.

has four wheels with differential traction configuration. It is equipped with an IMU, Odometry, GNSS, 2D LIDARs and with one camera with special light filters to extract Normalized Difference Vegetation Index (NDVI) images. To have a fair comparison between the perspective camera and the fisheye lens camera performances in motion estimation, the robot was also equipped with a stereo camera system. This setup consisted in two Raspberry Pi's powered by the robot each one with a connected camera. The perspective camera used was the Raspberry Pi's Camera Module V2.1[2] that has an horizontal FoV of 62.2°. The fisheye lens camera used was the Raspberry Pi Camera (I)[3] that has an horizontal FoV of 170°. They were positioned side by side in order to capture the same environment scenario and robot motion. Two outdoor sequences in a garden environment were captured with two different camera resolutions.

Fig. 1. AgRoB V16 robotic platform.

4 Fisheye Lens Approach

In order to incorporate the fisheye lens camera system into the VO method, the first step was to calibrate the camera. To do so, OCamCalib [1] from David Scaramuzza et al. was used. This work consists in an easy-to-use Matlab toolbox that has as input a set of images that capture a checkerboard. It describes the imaging function, i.e., the relation between a 2D pixel point and a 3D half-ray emanating from a single view point, as a Taylor series expansion that is determined by solving a least squares minimization problem. This parametric model is described as follows:

$$f(u'', v'') = a_0 + a_1\rho^1 + a_2\rho^2 + ... + a_N\rho^N \tag{1}$$

---

where (u'', v'') states for the sensor plane. Normally a_1 is equal to 0 and N is equal to 4 due the improvement of results on several experiments with different cameras performed by the authors of this work. So, the camera calibration consists in estimating $\{a_0, a_1, ..., a_N\}$ coefficients and also the omnidirectional image center. Also, a non-linear refinement of the parameters estimation is performed at the end of the calibration. All this procedures revealed to be quite efficient when applied to our fisheye camera system since we obtain a low calibration error in the order of one pixel.

The next step consisted in using the calibration output to rectify the camera images on real time. To do so, we use a method also developed by David Scaramuzza that creates a lookup table that contains the mapping function that converts the fisheye image into a perspective image. So, for every frame we apply a remapping to all the pixels of the input frame using the information given by this lookup table. An example of the transformation can be observed in Fig. 2. Although some information gets lost, namely some pixels in the corners, it is clear that the distortion is well corrected.

(a)   (b)

Fig. 2. (a) Raw fisheye lens camera image and (b) rectified fisheye len camera image.

Having the VO input images prepared, we applied them into Libviso2. This method computes its own features based on corners and blobs. So, it is expected that it interprets the border that separates the image and the black region resultant from rectification as features. By applying these images to Libviso2 we were able to validate this, as represented in Fig. 3. As these are static features, they are all matched. Although Libviso2 uses RANSAC to remove the outliers, if it fails removing even a small set of these matches, the motion estimation will be highly affected since these matches represent that no motion was computed between frames. This way, we propose a simple method to eliminate all these outliers that we apply into Libviso2. To do so, we create an image mask based on three basic image processing techniques: segmentation, closing and erosion. We apply a segmentation to the input rectified image in order to isolate the black regions. Then we correct the segmentation preventing some of the image

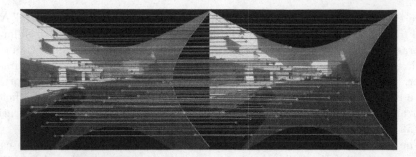

Fig. 3. Set of matches originally computed by Libviso2 given two consecutive frames.

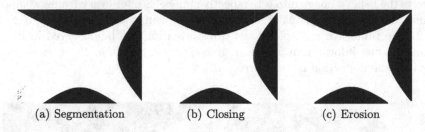

(a) Segmentation   (b) Closing   (c) Erosion

Fig. 4. Set of image processing operators applied to the input rectified image to generate a mask.

scenario region of staying grouped with the black regions as can be observed in Fig. 4(a) where a small region inside the image scenario is black. This is done by applying the morphological operator closing. After that, as the border is still in the image scenario group, the image is eroded in order to remove it from the image. Figure 4 represents the steps described and Fig. 5 is the resultant set of matches after the application of the mask. This procedure allows the definition of a region of interest where the method considers the existence of matches by applying the mask to a set of raw matches found. In conclusion, this approach

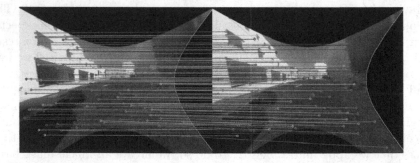

Fig. 5. Set of matches computed by Libviso2 given two consecutive frames after applying the generated mask.

is a simple way to take advantage of wider field of view camera rectified images and apply them into a feature-based VO method preventing the rectification of damaging motion estimation.

5 Results

To have a good and fair comparison between the two camera systems we analyze their performance in two different sequences using two different resolutions. We use 640×480 and 1280×720 resolutions and choose to make these sequences the worst case scenario for a VO method. Both sequences present a rotational component in every instant so that we can see the behavior of each camera system in this kind of motion. We compare the perspective camera performance with the fisheye camera performance, this last using both rectified and raw images, in terms of motion accuracy and feature matching quality. We also show the motion results of all the configurations with a gyroscope fusion that was developed in our previous work [9]. The used ground-truth was the Hector SLAM algorithm [8] that uses the laser described in Sect. 3.

5.1 Feature Matching

As mentioned before, Libviso2 uses corners and blobs to compute features that it tries to match between consecutive frames. By inspection of Fig. 6 it is visible that the number of feature matches computed by Libviso2 using the perspective camera configuration is highest compared with the matches found using the fisheye lens camera rectified image. Although, if we use the fisheye lens camera with raw images, we get a similar number of matches and inliers comparing with the ones obtained using the perspective camera. Once again, Fig. 7 shows that even for a higher resolution Libviso2 matches more features between frames using the perspective camera than using rectified fisheye lens camera images. However, for this resolution if we use the fisheye lens without rectifying the image we obtain a really dense feature matching. This shows the impact of rectification in feature matching. In fact, Fig. 7(c) shows that for the high resolution sequence, Libviso2 computes in average about 1000 matches. This is the highest number of matches observed. Using the perspective camera in the high resolution sequence results in a maximum number of matches of 750 which is quite lower. In terms of inliers extraction, it is visible that the configuration where RANSAC discards more matches is the one that uses unrectified fisheye lens camera images in the 1280×720 resolution.

5.2 Motion Estimation

In order to evaluate and compare the efficiency of Libviso2 in terms of motion estimation, two sequences were used both characterized by an almost constant rotational movement. This kind of motion is the most challenging for monocular VO methods since their main difficulty is to estimate motions that contain a significant rotational component. In Fig. 8 is visible the impact of the

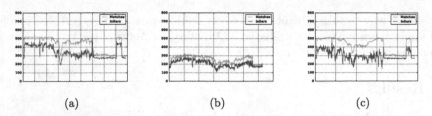

Fig. 6. Number of matches and respective inliers for the resolution 640 × 480 using (a) the perspective camera, (b) the fisheye lens camera rectified images and (c) the fisheye lens camera image raw images.

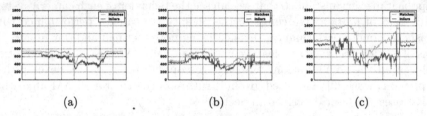

Fig. 7. Number of matches and respective inliers for the resolution 1280 × 720 using (a) the perspective camera, (b) the fisheye lens camera rectified images and (c) the fisheye lens camera image raw images.

higher computation of matches by Libviso2 while using a perspective camera. This configuration estimating the motion standalone presents a final result much closer to the ground truth than using the rectified fisheye image. Figures 8(b) and 8(c) show that using a fisheye lens camera with a rectified or raw image with a low resolution results in an underestimation of the rotational component. Figure 10 proves exactly this. In this figure it is clear that although this configuration detects all the rotations, they are all estimated with a negative offset. This means that during all the sequence the VO method underestimates the rotational component when using the fisheye lens camera.

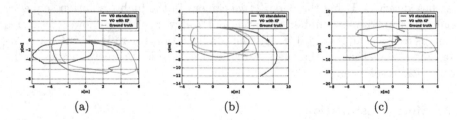

Fig. 8. Motion estimation from Libviso2 in the resolution 640 × 480 standalone and with a gyroscope fusion using (a) the perspective camera, (b) the fisheye lens camera rectified images and (c) the fisheye lens camera image raw images.

When using the high resolution sequence it is visible that since more matches and, consequently, inliers are computed, the rotational component is better estimated in the three cases. Figure 9 shows this improvement relatively to the lower resolution, mainly in both fisheye configurations. Here, rotations are not so underestimated due to the higher computation of inliers.

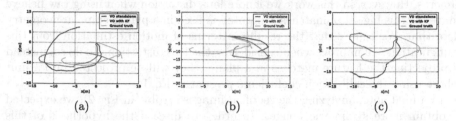

(a)   (b)   (c)

Fig. 9. Motion estimation from Libviso2 in the resolution 1280×720 standalone and with a gyroscope fusion using (a) the perspective camera, (b) the fisheye lens camera rectified images and (c) the fisheye lens camera image raw images.

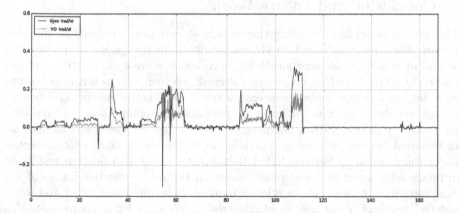

Fig. 10. Angular velocity estimated by VO using a fisheye lens camera with a resolution of 640×480 and measured by a gyroscope.

5.3 Discussion

The tested configurations allowed us to take many conclusions about the use of fisheye cameras in feature-based VO methods. Rectifying a fisheye image to use in these kind of methods has several disadvantages. Since from rectification results black regions to compensate lens distortion, the rectified image presents a lower pixel resolution comparatively to a perspective image of the same resolution. This leads to a lower computation of matches from the VO method and, consequently, to a higher difficulty estimating motion. Also, the rectification transforms the fisheye image into a perspective image and, due to the calibration imperfections, the final image has lower FoV than the original raw image. So, in order to obtain an equal or better performance using rectified fisheye images, a higher resolution has to be used in order to compensate the previous described issues. Using raw fisheye images leads to a dense feature matching. This is due to the higher FoV that allows to capture a larger scenario comparing to normal perspective cameras. However, in this work we ignore lens distortion when using raw fisheye images so this big set of matches computed is used in a planar epipolar geometry algorithm. We believe that the results in terms of motion estimation from this configuration will improve when considering the lens distortion. To do so, instead of projecting the feature matches in a plane, they will be projected into a unit sphere using the calibration coefficients present in Eq. 1.

In a final note, analyzing the rectified images (visible in Fig. 2), we expected to obtain more symmetric images. In order to discard the hypothesis of this being due to the calibration toolbox used, we also calibrated the camera with OpenCV fisheye camera calibration toolbox[4]. We obtained a similar result so we think that this asymmetry is due to a non uniform distortion of the lens and/or to a disalignment between the lens and the CCD.

6   Conclusion and Future Work

Our main focus while performing this work was to obtain a reliable localization system that does not depend on GNSS. To do so, in this paper we proposed a general methodology to incorporate a fisheye lens camera system into a feature-based VO method and we compared Libviso2 performance in terms of feature matching quality and motion estimation using perspective images and fisheye images, rectified and raw. In order to perform this comparison we equipped our robotic platform with a perspective camera and a fisheye lens camera an we recorded two datasets using two different image resolutions. This dataset is now public available. We concluded that fisheye image rectification results in an image with lower FoV and pixel resolution than a perspective image of the same resolution which leads to a lower number of matches computed and to an underestimation of rotations. So a higher resolution is needed to compensate this issues. However, using the raw fisheye images results in a dense feature matching. As we consider a planar epipolar geometry method for the raw fisheye image instead of a spherical one, this configuration presents some issues estimating motion.

For future work we aim to implement an epipolar geometry method that considers fisheye lens distortion. Also we would like to solve Libviso2 scale issue, which is an open issue in monocular VO, using a distance sensor.

Acknowledgment. This work is financed by the ERDF – European Regional Development Fund through the Operational Programme for Competitiveness and Internationalisation - COMPETE 2020 Programme within project «POCI-01-0145-FEDER-006961», and by National Funds through the FCT – Fundação para a Ciência e a

---

[4] https://docs.opencv.org/3.4/db/d58/group__calib3d__fisheye.html

Tecnologia (Portuguese Foundation for Science and Technology) as part of project UID/EEA/50014/2013 and by through ANI - Agência Nacional de Inovação (Portuguese National Agency of Innovation) as part of project "ROMOVI: POCI-01-0247-FEDER-017945". Project "NORTE-07-0124-FEDER-000060" is financed by the North Portugal Regional Operational Programme (ON.2 – O Novo Norte), under the National Strategic Reference Framework (NSRF), through the European Regional Development Fund (ERDF), and by national funds, through the Portuguese funding agency, Fundação para a Ciência e a Tecnologia (FCT).

References

1. Scaramuzza, D., Martinelli, A., Siegwart, R.: A toolbox for easily calibrating omnidirectional cameras. In: 2006 IEEE/RSJ International Conference on Intelligent Robots and Systems, October 2006
2. Geiger, A., Ziegler, J., Stiller, C.: StereoScan: dense 3D reconstruction in real-time. In: 2011 IEEE Intelligent Vehicles Symposium (IV). IEEE, June 2011. https://doi.org/10.1109/ivs.2011.5940405
3. Liu, P., Heng, L., Sattler, T., Geiger, A., Pollefeys, M.: Direct visual odometry for a fisheye-stereo camera. In: 2017 IEEE/RSJ International Conference on Intelligent Robots and Systems (IROS) (2017)
4. Matsuki, H., von Stumberg, L., Usenko, V., Stückler, J., Cremers, D.: Omnidirectional DSO: direct sparse odometry with fisheye cameras. IEEE Robot. Autom. Lett. **3**, 3693–3700 (2018)
5. Engel, J., Koltun, V., Cremers, D.: Direct sparse odometry. IEEE Trans. Pattern Anal. Mach. Intell. **40**(3), 611–625 (2018). https://doi.org/10.1109/tpami.2017.2658577, Institute of Electrical and Electronics Engineers (IEEE)
6. Rituerto, A., Puig, L., Guerrero, J.J.: Comparison of omnidirectional and conventional monocular systems for visual SLAM
7. Forster, C., Pizzoli, M., Scaramuzza, D.: SVO: fast semi-direct monocular visual odometry. In: 2014 IEEE International Conference on Robotics and Automation (ICRA). IEEE, May 2014. https://doi.org/10.1109/icra.2014.6906584
8. Kohlbrecher, S., Meyer, J., von Stryk, O., Klingauf, U., Flexible, A., Scalable, S.L.A.M.: System with Full 3D motion estimation. In: Proceedings of IEEE International Symposium on Safety, Security and Rescue Robotics (SSRR). IEEE (2011)
9. Aguiar, A., Sousa, A., Santos, F., Oliveira, M.: Monocular visual odometry benchmarking and turn performance optimization. In: 19th IEEE International Conference on Autonomous Robot Systems and Competitions, April 2019
10. Zhang, Z., Rebecq, H., Forster, C., Scaramuzza, D.: Benefit of large field-of-view cameras for visual odometry. In: 2016 IEEE International Conference on Robotics and Automation (ICRA) (2016)
11. Streckel, B., Koch, R.: Lens model selection for visual tracking. In: Kropatsch, W.G., Sablatnig, R., Hanbury, A. (eds.) DAGM 2005. LNCS, vol. 3663, pp. 41–48. Springer, Heidelberg (2005). https://doi.org/10.1007/11550518_6
12. Bac, C.W., Henten, E.J., Hemming, J., Edan, Y.: Harvesting robots for high-value crops: state-of-the-art review and challenges ahead. J. Field Robot. **31**(6), 888–911 (2014)
13. euRobotics. Strategic research agenda for robotics in Europe. Draft 0v42. http://ec.europa.eu/research/industrial_technologies/pdf/robotics-ppp-roadmap_en.pdf
14. VineRobot - FP7 project. http://www.vinerobot.eu/

15. Vinbot - FP7 project. http://vinbot.eu/
16. dos Santos, F.B.N., Sobreira, H.M.P., Campos, D.F.B., dos Santos, R.M.P.M., Moreira, A.P.G.M., Contente, O.M.S.: Towards a reliable monitoring robot for mountain vineyards. In: 2015 IEEE International Conference on Autonomous Robot Systems and Competitions (ICARSC), pp. 37–43. IEEE, April 2015
17. Santos, F.N., Sobreira, H.M., Campos, D., Morais, R., Moreira, A.P., Contente, O.: Towards a reliable robot for steep slope vineyards monitoring (2016). https://doi.org/10.1007/s10846-016-0340-5
18. Duarte, M., dos Santos, F.N., Sousa, A., Morais, R.: Agricultural wireless sensor mapping for robot localization. Robot 2015: Second Iberian Robotics Conference. AISC, vol. 417, pp. 359–370. Springer, Cham (2016). https://doi.org/10.1007/978-3-319-27146-0_28
19. Mendes, J.M., dos Santos, F.N., Ferraz, N.A., do Couto, P.M., dos Santos, R.M.: Localization based on natural features detector for steep slope vineyards. J. Intell. Robot. Syst. **93**, 1–14 (2018)

A Comparison Procedure for IMUs Performance

Tiago Mendonça[1]([✉]), Diana Guimarães[1], António Paulo Moreira[1,2] [iD],
and Paulo Costa[1,2] [iD]

[1] INESC TEC - Instituto de Engenharia de Sistemas e Computadores,
Tecnologia e Ciência, Porto, Portugal
{tiago.j.mendonca,diana.a.guimaraes}@inesctec.pt
[2] FEUP, Universidade do Porto, Porto, Portugal
{amoreira,paco}@fe.up.pt
http://www.inesctec.pt, http://www.fe.up.pt

Abstract. Inertial measurement units (IMU) are, typically, a cluster of
accelerometers, gyroscopes and magnetometers. Its use was introduced
with military applications, being, nowadays, widely common on industrial applications, namely robot navigation. Since there are a lot of units
in different cost ranges, it is proposed, in this paper, a procedure to
compare their performance in tracking tasks. Once IMU samples are
unavoidably corrupted by systematic and stochastic errors, a calibration procedure (without any external equipment) to identify sensors'
error models and a Kalman filter implementation to remove white noise
are suggested. Then, the comparison is carried out over two trajectories, square and circular paths, respectively, being described by a robotic
arm, which acts as reference. The results show that different manufacturing quality units can track, with success, orientation references but
are incapable to perform position tracking activities.

Keywords: IMU · Calibration · Kalman Filter · Tracking

1 Introduction

Inertial sensors are based on inertia. Normally, this classification refers to gyroscope and accelerometer sensors. The first one measures the angular velocity,
i.e., the rate of change of sensor's orientation, while the second one provides the
external specific force acting on the sensor, which corresponds to its acceleration
plus the earth's gravity [7]. These elements are, typically, arranged together on
an inertial measurement unit (IMU). A triad of accelerometers and a triad of
gyroscopes (one sensor per axis) are comprised inside, complemented, in some
units, with a triad of magnetometers, which indicate local magnetic field, fulfilling a set of tri-axial clusters [14]. Traditionally, its use became popular on
military applications, being, nowadays, exploited to industrial purposes, namely
robot navigation systems as well as body motion tracking, and also included on

© Springer Nature Switzerland AG 2019
P. Moura Oliveira et al. (Eds.): EPIA 2019, LNAI 11805, pp. 331–344, 2019.
https://doi.org/10.1007/978-3-030-30244-3_28

smartphones. For such tasks, an IMU is based on microelectro mechanical systems (MEMS), characterized for being small, light and low power consumption [7].

The downside of using low cost MEMS based IMU is that, usually, they are associated to calibration issues, including non accurate scaling, sensor axis misalignment, cross-axis sensitivities and non-zero biases [14]. These are related with imperfections in production process [15]. Additionally, the presence of magnetic perturbations largely degrades magnetometers' performance. That's why, a reliable operation implies a previous calibration, which consists in identifying the enumerated parameters [14]. Some manufactures provide products calibrated by default and with increased accuracy. However, such procedures cost time and resources, enriching, naturally, the unit value, invalidating a cost-effective utilization [15].

Despite of a good calibration, sensors' output is still noisy and can't be directly used to provide position, velocity and orientation estimations, increasingly differing from the true value along time. This is a problem commonly addressed on literature. The solution depends on the necessary application accuracy. While with relaxed constraints a low pass filter in each sensor set of samples is enough [3], for tracking problems, fusion of IMU sensors is mandatory to obtain a reliable estimation. With that in mind, there are complementary filter based algorithms and Kalman filter approaches [7]. In this paper, the sensor information is combined through a Kalman filter implementation. Depending on processing capability, there are some IMU that already provide filtered samples due to internal algorithms supported on cited approaches. This feature is associated with higher cost units.

The purpose of this paper is to evaluate distinct IMU performance over a proposed comparison procedure. The strategy followed is to take different cost range products, proceed to calibration and posterior samples filtration, checking whether in the end the results have the same accuracy or if, in fact, the manufacturing quality limits it.

To achieve such goal, in next subsection, it is exposed the calibration techniques and filter implementations presented in literature, being followed by the details about the chosen approach for both processing stages. Next, the tests performed are referred. First, the setup configuration supporting those is detailed and, then, the results are shown, evaluated and compared among IMU. Here, three models are tested – UM7 from CHRobotics (an average price of $140), MinIMU-9 v3 from Pololu (an average price of $15) and 10 DOF IMU from Waveshare (also an average price of $15) – being later detailed. Last, some conclusions and further improvements are suggested.

1.1   Related Work and Contributions

The IMU calibration is a problem massively referred in the literature. Although calibrated IMUs are commercially available, they not always represent the best solution, namely with respect to size, flexibility and cost criteria [4]. In some cases, it is preferable a tailor made (allowing to pick some specific models of inertial sensors) or cheaper units, introducing, however, the need of calibration.

The basic idea consists in comparing the sensors' output with the reference value and use that to quantify error model parameters. The traditional methods are based on precision centrifuge tests [5], optical [6] and GPS trackers [8], which provides a ground truth for linear acceleration and/or angular rate. Since calibration parameters are characterized by slowly time variance, in [13] is also suggested an extended Kalman filter implementation to achieve an online estimation of bias and axes' misalignment. However, all these procedures not only imply an external infrastructure to act as reference, which has an inherent high cost, as well as treat the sensors as independent entities, ignoring the cross-misalignment between sensors' frames. Those drawbacks are overpassed in [14] proposing a multi-position calibration procedure (which can be even made by hand) and taking advantage of an optimization algorithm to calculate sensors' model. This is the work that supports this paper. The approach, however, lacks in the fact that doesn't include the magnetometer calibration and can be complemented by the work [12]. Here, the magnetometer calibration is a two step process: the first one related with sensor model using earth magnetic field as reference and, then, the alignment with the remaining sensors' coordinate system. Additionally, in [9], a similar approach to [14] is promoted but using a robotic arm to a better trajectory precision. This is only valid if the motion between positions is slow enough to ignore the linear acceleration regarding to gravity.

Even after calibration, sensors measurements tend to be accurate, but just for a short time, suffering from integration drift over longer time scales [7]. Such behavior makes impossible to obtain a reliable estimation in tracking applications. The solution is to combine all inertial information from sensors. Most of resources in the literature points to the use of Kalman filters (KF) or the extended version (EKF) [11]. To decrease algorithm complexity, a typical approach is to decompose the estimation in two stages, separating position from orientation. In the last one, the quaternions are the preferable choice to represent rotations, for being compact, singularity free and easily converted from or to rotation matrix and Euler angles [10]. In [7], an EKF implementation is proposed, using, in the prediction step, a constant acceleration model and a constant angular velocity model. The approach fuses information from all sensors and provides a reliable representation of system model, but uses different ways of representing rotations (mixing quaternions with rotation matrices), requiring online calculation of several large size matrices which aren't of easy deduction. To overcome the computational demand, a simplified EKF implementation is presented in [2]. Here, the processing effort is transferred to an external algorithm that extracts the quaternion from inertial sensors samples, role which might be performed by TRIAD method. This is an algebraic algorithm that obtains the direction cosine matrix (DCM) relating two frames, requiring a pair of vectors in one of them and the respective counterpart in the other one (for further detailed explanation see [1]). For all said, this paper provides a solution that merges both approaches. As additional feature, it is included a magnetometer validation module that, in each iteration, evaluates the conditions to discard or not the sensor sample. According to [11], those conditions are related to the angle between accelerometer and magnetometer measurements (which must be constant in absence of movement or in a constant velocity trajectory) and sensed magnetic field norm (which must be also constant and equal to earth field one, in the absence of disturbances).

2   Calibration

The calibration of sensors consists in identifying the systematic error's sources, the consequent sensor error model and quantify its parameters. The acquired samples are, then, corrected using the calculated model. The procedure flow of the present topic is the following: the accelerometer is calibrated taking gravity as reference, the gyroscope is calibrated using accelerometer corrected samples as reference and then the magnetometer is calibrated using both earth magnetic field and accelerometer samples as reference.

2.1   Accelerometer and Gyroscope

The accelerometer and gyroscope calibration is supported and implemented by [14].

First, we need to identify the error's sources and in what way they affect sensor's output. In case of inertial sensors, the samples are dominated by instrumentation errors. Assembling imperfections are included in this group. Those are caused by bad sensors disposition on IMU frame in a way that they are not orthogonal with each other, as supposed. Thus, they represent an invalid coordinate system. In addition, it isn't guaranteed that the coordinate systems from different sensors match. Therefore, all the frames must be aligned to a reference one, being selected the corrected accelerometer orthogonal frame. Then, the gyroscopes' coordinate system must be aligned with that. To simplify the problem, it is assumed that the reference frame matches the IMU body frame. Mathematically, the compensation consists in samples multiplication by a square matrix (T) where α and β represent the angular displacement between accelerometer (a) and gyroscope (ω) axes, respectively.

$$T^a = \begin{bmatrix} 1 & -\alpha_{yz} & \alpha_{zy} \\ 0 & 1 & -\alpha_{zx} \\ 0 & 0 & 1 \end{bmatrix} \qquad T^\omega = \begin{bmatrix} 1 & -\beta_{yz} & \beta_{zy} \\ \beta_{xz} & 1 & -\beta_{zx} \\ -\beta_{xy} & \beta_{yx} & 1 \end{bmatrix} \tag{1}$$

Besides that, the measurements may also include scale factors (s) distortions, compensated by a diagonal matrix (K).

$$K^a = \begin{bmatrix} s_x^a & 0 & 0 \\ 0 & s_y^a & 0 \\ 0 & 0 & s_z^a \end{bmatrix} \qquad K^\omega = \begin{bmatrix} s_x^\omega & 0 & 0 \\ 0 & s_y^\omega & 0 \\ 0 & 0 & s_z^\omega \end{bmatrix} \tag{2}$$

Finally, there are additive errors. They emerge as an offset value on sensors' output, tending to diverge over long time runs as well as between turn on operations. They are classified as bias (b).

The accelerometer and gyroscope calibration models are given, respectively, by 3 and 4. The superscript o refers to calibrated sample on orthogonal frame while s refers to non-calibrated sample provided by sensor.

$$\vec{a}^o = T^a K^a (\vec{a}^s + \vec{b}^a + \vec{v}^a) \tag{3}$$

$$\vec{\omega}^o = T^\omega K^\omega (\vec{\omega}^s + \vec{b}^\omega + \vec{v}^\omega) \tag{4}$$

The v parameter refers to white noise (gaussian with zero mean) that is removed through Kalman filter, presented in next stage.

The model parameters quantification is made by a minimization algorithm. Its input is the set of samples acquired during a multi-position calibration path [14]. Shortly, the IMU is moved along several positions, remaining static, during a some time, in each one. To assure the posterior convergence of the algorithm, it is recommended a number of positions between 36 and 50 and to stay, at least, 5s in each one. The referred movement can be performed manually, i.e., just by hand, but, to increase results accuracy, the tests described in this work were realized with a robotic arm.

The acquired accelerometer samples are the input of the minimization function, which is formulated as the reference value minus sensor model output (L). In this case, gravity corresponds to the reference (g) but only if linear acceleration is discarded, which is only valid when the IMU rests at static positions or performs a constant linear velocity movement. That's why, only that samples' subset (of size M) is used on minimization algorithm, which is an implementation of Levenberg-Marquardt method [14].

$$L(T^a, K^a, b^a) = \sum_{k=1}^{M} \left(\|\vec{g}\|_2 - \|T^a K^a (\vec{a}^s_k + b^a)\|_2 \right)^2 \tag{5}$$

Regarding to gyroscope, the implementation follows the same guidelines. However, since during static positions the angular rate is zero, the angular integration (function ψ) occurs on transitions instead. Here, the calibrated accelerometer samples are used to extract the reference, which is the angular displacement between the samples immediately before and after the transition interval (u_a). Similarly to accelerometer calibration, a minimization function is also defined (L).

$$L(T^\omega, K^\omega, b^\omega) = \sum_{k=1}^{N} \|u_{a,k} - \psi(T^\omega, K^\omega, b^\omega, \omega^s_k, u_{a,k-1})\|_2 \tag{6}$$

2.2 Magnetometer

In magnetometers, besides the previous instrumental errors, their measurements are also susceptible to magnetic perturbations. In an ideal scenario, the magnetometer should only measures earth's magnetic field. However, when applied indoors, local magnetic fields tend to overlap it. Such effects may be classified as hard and soft irons. The first ones are characteristic of some materials that generate their own magnetic field, actuating equally in all directions/axes. On the other side, the soft irons result from materials that perturb earth's field but in specific directions of actuation.

To exemplify the concepts exposed, three scenarios are now considered. In absence of any distortion, when the IMU is rotated on a space plane, a circumference is drawn from magnetometer samples, centered at IMU body and with a radius equal to earth's magnetic field norm. In presence of hard irons perturbations, a circumference is still obtained but translated from center and with a different radius value. Finally, the soft irons presence generates an ellipse, centered at the origin, and with the respective axes indicating the direction of the distortion.

The compensation of previous effects is made over two steps. Since hard irons induce an offset on the measurements, the same value must be subtracted to the data (H^m). On the other hand, to transform an ellipse into a circumference, their axes must be aligned with body frame axes (R^m), apply a scale factor (S^m) per axis and turn back to initial orientation $(R^{m^{-1}})$. The resulting sensor model is presented in Eq. 7.

$$\vec{m}' = (R^{m^{-1}} S^m R^m \vec{m}^s - \vec{H}^m) \tag{7}$$

In addition, it must be also considered the instrumentation errors already referred. In order to simplify the final model, some simplifications are performed, concentrating the calibration parameters only in two matrices (A, B).

$$\vec{m}^o = T^m K^m (\vec{m}' + \vec{b}^m + \vec{v}^m) = A(\vec{m}^s + \vec{B} + \vec{v}^m) \tag{8}$$

The calibration procedure is made over two moments. In the first step, the IMU must be forced to describe circumference based paths (at least one per space's plane) and the magnetometer samples must be recorded. Such measurements are the input of the minimization algorithm, already used in previous sensors. The reference is the earth's magnetic field vector in that point of the globe $(\vec{m}^{ref})$.

$$L(A, B) = \sum_{k=1}^{M} \left(\|\vec{m}^{ref}\|_2 - \|\vec{m}_k^o\|_2 \right)^2 \tag{9}$$

In this point, the calculated model already represents the calibrated samples relatively to the magnetometer orthogonal frame. However, it is still necessary to align this coordinate system with the other sensors. For that, the accelerometer frame is used as reference and the constant angle between both sensors' arrays is included as a problem restriction. Once again, this is a minimization problem to find the rotation that minimizes the angular displacement between samples. Such rotation could be represented by a rotation matrix, but would be a 9-parameter problem and would imply the consideration of SO(3) properties. To avoid that computational effort, the axe-angle representation is preferred, reducing the solution to only three parameters. The minimization algorithm follows the previous implementation rules. The samples used as input are the ones acquired during multi-position path: the calibrated accelerometer measurements (the output of 3) and magnetometer samples on orthogonal frame (the output of 8).

Considering the constant angle between samples, the unitary norm arrays and taking advantage of inner product properties results in Eq. 10.

$$\frac{\vec{a} \cdot \vec{b}}{\|a\|\|b\|} = cos(\vec{a}, \vec{b}) \tag{10}$$

Finally, the problem formulation is presented in Eq. 11, being a the accelerometer calibrated sample and m the magnetometer orthogonal sample (output of 8). The goal is to obtain a rotation (given by ω in axis-angle representation) which closes as much as possible the sample's angular displacement from real angular displacement between gravity and earth's magnetic field (α).

$$argmin_{\vec{\omega}} \sum_{i=1}^{n} \left(\vec{a}_i^{\delta T} \cdot Rot(\vec{\omega}) \vec{m}_i^o - cos(\frac{\pi}{2} - \alpha) \right)^2 \tag{11}$$

3   Kalman Filter

According with the ideas captured from literature and presented in Sect. 1, the Kalman filter implementation is divided in two subsystems: position and orientation estimation. Although some cross-effects are lost, this decision is justified by the reduction of complexity.

Regarding to linear motion, the main goal is to estimate the position (p), linear velocity (v) and acceleration (a) in 3D space. Inspired in [7], it is defined a constant linear acceleration motion model (where linear acceleration corresponds to Kalman filter state, x), being the remaining estimations obtained by pure integration during sampling time (T). The system has only one output (y) which is the linear acceleration on body frame (obtained by rotation from earth to IMU frame, R^{bn}), the output of inverse accelerometer model calibrated on previous stage.

$$p_{t+1} = p_t + Tv_t + \frac{T^2}{2}a_t \tag{12}$$

$$v_{t+1} = v_t + Ta_t \tag{13}$$

$$x_{t+1} = a_{t+1} = a_t + e_{a,t} \tag{14}$$

$$y_t = (T^a K^a)^{-1} R_t^{bn}(a_t + g^n) - b_a + e_{a,t} \tag{15}$$

In terms of orientation, it is intended to obtain quaternion and angular velocity estimations. The quaternion is given by time integration, according with the angular displacement in each iteration (which is angular velocity integrated during sampling time, T). The angular velocity is directly replaced by the calibrated value of gyroscope measure (ω^o). A constant angular velocity model could be considered instead, but it would be accomplished by computational complexity with the advantage of the estimation being less sensitive to perturbations. With this implementation, although more reactive, a better commitment is achieved. The system state and output are the same, the quaternion that represents the rotation from IMU to earth frame (q^{nb}). The observation quaternion is returned by the application of TRIAD method over the set of accelerometer (a^o) and magnetometer (m^o) calibrated samples and gravity and earth magnetic filed arrays. Taking the two pair of arrays, the algorithm returns the rotation matrix that best relates the earth and IMU frames, being, after that, converted to quaternion representation which constitutes the observation measure.

$$x_{t+1} = q_{t+1}^{nb} = q_t^{nb} + \frac{dq_t^{nb}}{dt}T + e_{q,t} = q_t^{nb} + \frac{1}{2}\Omega(\omega^o)q_t^{nb} + e_{q,t} = \qquad (16)$$

$$\begin{bmatrix} 1 & -0.5T\omega_x^o & -0.5T\omega_y^o & -0.5T\omega_z^o \\ 0.5T\omega_x^o & 1 & 0.5T\omega_z^o & -0.5T\omega_y^o \\ 0.5T\omega_y^o & -0.5T\omega_x^o & 1 & 0.5T\omega_x^o \\ 0.5T\omega_z^o & 0.5T\omega_y^o & -0.5T\omega_x^o & 1 \end{bmatrix} \cdot q_t^{nb} + e_{q,t} \qquad (17)$$

$$y_t = q_{meas,t}^{nb}(a^o, m^o) = q_t^{nb} + e_{q_m,t} \qquad (18)$$

$$\omega^o = T^\omega K^\omega(\omega^s + b^\omega) \qquad (19)$$

$$a^o = T^a K^a(a^s + b^a) \qquad (20)$$

$$m^o = A^m(m^s + b^m) \qquad (21)$$

3.1   Magnetometer Validation

During the movement of IMU, it could interact with a magnetic neighborhood, generating perturbed magnetometer measurements. In such scenarios, the sample is not valid and must be discarded, otherwise an unreliable estimate would be provided. The validation must be performed in each iteration, before applying Kalman filter, and through two verification steps. First, it is calculated the magnetometer array norm ($\vec{m}_k$) and verified if that is within a established acceptance range (ϵ_m). Second, if the first condition is verified with success, the inclination angle, i.e., the angle between the array and the horizontal plane, is considered ((ϵ_{dip})). A set of samples is considered valid when it passes with success over the two tests.

$$\left| \|\vec{m}_k\| - \|\vec{h}\| \right| < \epsilon_m \quad \cap \quad \left| \Theta_{dip} - arccos(\frac{R^{nb}\vec{m}^o \cdot R^{nb}\vec{a}^o}{\|\vec{m}^o\|\|\vec{a}^o\|}) \right| < \epsilon_{dip} \qquad (22)$$

When the samples are rejected, there is no valid magnetometer sample and the TRIAD method is not applied on that iteration. Instead, an Euler angles representation is applicable: the roll and pitch angles are extracted from accelerometer samples and the yaw is extracted from predicted quaternion of prediction step. In the end, a transformation from Euler angles to quaternions form is applied.

3.2 Allan Variance

The sensors model parameters tend to be characteristics of a specific IMU. However, the bias, namely from the gyroscope, tend to slowly varies with time when in operation. That's why, since such parameters are considered static on filter model, during long time runs they can become outdated and not correctly reproduce the initial calibrated model. To avoid that, it is important to calculate instability of the sensors and, that way, know during how long the model is valid according to acceptable tolerance. That value can be obtained through the Allan variance calculation. This is a mathematical tool which provides the stability degree of a set of samples along the time. Since we are looking for low frequency variations, the samples should be acquired during a large time interval (8 hours and above) and in static conditions, i.e., with the sensor immobilized. The minimum value of the graphic indicates the maximum stability in degrees per second and, with the maximum angular tolerance allowed, the validity of the model is easily extracted.

In addition, this parameter can be used as a benchmarking indication to compare different sensors. How much lower is the (in)stability, the sensor operation is more precise during a long interval operation whereby it is suggested that it has a more quality construction, providing an immediate choice criteria of IMUs without any further test.

4 Results

4.1 Setup and Methodology

The objective of tests is to compare the performance of different IMUs, with distinct construction quality, and to conclude whether this premise affects or not the accuracy of the estimation, even after calibration and filtering of the measured samples. For that purpose, three units were picked from different cost ranges. They were UM-7 from CHRobtics, minIMU-9 v3 from Polulu and 10DOF IMU v2 from Waveshare. All units offer a triad of 3-axis accelerometers, gyroscopes and magnetometers.

For all of them, raw data was collected, and pros-processing done offline.

The tests were carried out over three trajectories. It was defined, in first place, a calibration path, characterized by a circumference based movement in each plane of 3D space (xy, xz, yz) in order to ensure the large number of positions required to the calibration algorithm convergence. Although this trajectory allows to evaluate the position and orientation tracking, the movements were considered, separately, on a square (with a fixed orientation) and circular paths.

To be able to simulate the indicated motions multiple times and always with equal spaced points in the trajectory, an ABB IRB2600 was used (see Fig. 1. The paths' design was, firstly, supported on a simulated environment, RobotStudio, and, only then, transferred to real world application.

Additionally, a 3D printed tool was built to remove the magnetic perturbations produced by having the IMus and the end-effort's metallic material in close proximity and to ensure a proper accommodation.

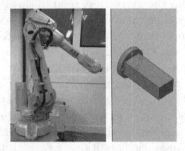

Fig. 1. ABB IRB2600 and 3D printed end-effort tool used in the tests.

4.2   Experimental Results

To process the results, the samples were converted from raw data to proper units (g, rad/s and gauss) and only then were able to be compared with the reference. Here, it was used the position and orientation feedback provided by the robotic arm, with an enough accuracy to be considered, in this case, the ground truth. The comparison criteria was the root mean square error. Such indicator was computed (per coordinate error and Euler angle error) before and after calibration and after Kalman filter application in order to observe the estimation increments induced. After, an inter-IMU analysis is carried out, discussing the final accuracy of each unit. The referred procedure was developed in each configured path.

$$e_{rms} = \sqrt{\frac{1}{N} \sum_{i=1}^{N} e_i^2} \tag{23}$$

Calibration Trajectory. Resuming what was previously said, the trajectory path is formed by a large number of positions where the IMU rest during, approximately, 10 s. The trajectory points are included in different planes of 3D space.

Regarding to orientation, this is represented in quaternions format. However, since its components don't provide an intuitive error's interpretation, the Euler

Table 1. Root mean square orientation error of the IMUs.

IMU	Euler angles	W/o calibration	W/ calibration
UM7	$Roll_{rms}$	8.287°	15.294°
	$Pitch_{rms}$	6.741°	10.772°
	Yaw_{rms}	7.341°	8.644°
MinIMU-9	$Roll_{rms}$	19.267°	18.187°
	$Pitch_{rms}$	16.434°	15.464°
	Yaw_{rms}	49.066°	34.575°
10DOF	$Roll_{rms}$	36.280°	27.033°
	$Pitch_{rms}$	30.462°	20.002°
	Yaw_{rms}	30.694°	16.302°

angles representation is applied. Then, the root mean square error is showed on Table 1.

The purpose of showed results is to present the improvement introduced by calibration procedure and justify its use. This is applied over the three IMUs. In no calibration case, the samples are directly used to calculate the orientation estimation and then compared with the reference returned by robotic arm, being the result exported on Euler angles format. The same samples are, then, corrected through calibrated sensors' error model and the orientation calculated again. In both cases, the Kalman filter is not considered. For UM7, it can be seen that, even without any correction, the samples have an acceptable orientation error, with an equivalent precision in all axes. Since calibration algorithm can't provide more accurate measures, its application degrades the estimated angles. Regarding to remaining units, the calibration effect is more noticeable. With minIMU, the most yelling improvement is imputed to yaw angle, which might be justified by an initial deficient magnetometer calibration, while accelerometer provide reasonable measures (used to obtain roll and pitch). Finally, with 10DOF unit, the calibration need is more explicit. The improvement is shared by all angles, indicating, probably, a worst manufacturing quality construction, inherent to both accelerometer and magnetometer.

The calibration intends to eliminate the systematic errors, while the subsequent Kalman filter has the purpose to suppress the zero mean noise which affects the samples. This process results in a smooth and more precise estimation when compared with calibration data, also due to the inclusion of magnetometer validation module. The 10DOF IMU case is presented in Fig. 2.

In terms of position tracking, a more detailed analysis is made in square trajectory topic.

Angular Trajectory. This path is characterized by an axial movement perpendicular to horizontal earth's plane. There is no end-effort translation, staying rotating on a fixed point until it reaches the joint limit, alternating between

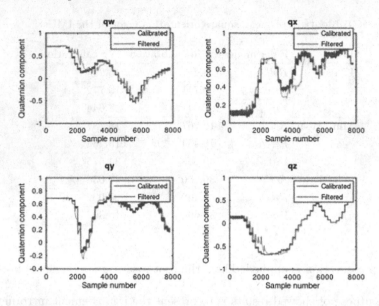

Fig. 2. 10DOF calibrated and filtered quaternions comparison.

clockwise and anticlockwise. The root mean square error of Euler angles is discriminated on Table 2, being considered the filtered values.

Considering all angles, it is concluded that the UM7 present the best behaviour, being the error more noticeable only in yaw (the axis direction of the movement). Regarding to minIMU, an equivalent precision was achieved, being the 10DOF the worst unit. This result can be partially justified by the fact of the rotation's speed be higher than sample rate of sensors, making difficult the tracking task.

Table 2. Root mean square orientation error on circular path.

Euler Angles	UM7	MinIMU-9	10DOF IMU
$Roll_{rms}$	0.632°	3.268°	1.384°
$Pitch_{rms}$	0.106°	8.496°	2.590°
Yaw_{rms}	11.523°	8.303°	22.642°

Square Trajectory. Despite of already has been concluded that the units are unable to track a linear displacement, it is, anyway, provided a procedure to evaluate such capability. Since the path is described by a robotic arm, the available working area is more restricted. For that reason, it was defined a square path, in xy plane, with 50 cm of side length. It was performed several turns.

The filtered position estimation diverges continuously from robot reference since initial moment. Such behaviour is common to all axes, being justified by the fact that estimate results from time integration of calibrated linear acceleration and, that's why, any offset from real value will affect position estimation by a quadratic factor, leading to an unbounded estimation error.

To compensate that behaviour, it is proposed the definition of reference positions which provide a reset of position estimation always they were crossed by IMU. However, since the tracking with IMU is not possible even in short periods of time, probably the use of an external accurate position sensor is a more reliable approach.

5 Conclusion

In this paper, it has been presented an algorithm to process the samples from an IMU and a further proceeding to compare units performance. The calibration implementation showed to be reliable and can be realized without any external and expensive equipment. The results also confirmed that the Kalman filter ensures a reliable estimation. Two paths have been proposed to evaluate IMUs' performance, having been concluded that different manufacturing quality units can achieve an equivalent accuracy in terms of orientation estimation, but they are incapable to be used as position tracking sensors. Then, as further improvement, it is suggested the integration of an accurate position sensor for that purpose.

Acknowledgment. This work is financed by the ERDF – European Regional Development Fund through the Operational Programme for Competitiveness and Internationalisation – COMPETE 2020 Programme, and by National Funds through the Portuguese funding agency, FCT - Fundação para a Ciência e a Tecnologia, within project SAICTPAC/0034/2015- POCI-01-0145-FEDER-016418.

This research was also supported by the Portuguese Foundation for Science and Technology (FCT) project COBOTIS (PTDC/EMEEME/ 32595/2017)

References

1. Triad Method. https://en.wikipedia.org/wiki/Triad_method
2. Comotti, D., Ermidoro, M.: Report of the course progetto di microelettronica. Technical report (2017)
3. Ferdinando, H., Khoswanto, H., Purwanto, D.: Embedded Kalman filter for inertial measurement unit (IMU) on the ATMega8535. In: 2012 International Symposium on Innovations in Intelligent Systems and Applications, pp. 1–5. IEEE, July 2012. https://doi.org/10.1109/INISTA.2012.6246978, http://ieeexplore.ieee.org/document/6246978/
4. Fong, W.T., Ong, S.K., Nee, A.Y.C.: Methods for in-field user calibration of an inertial measurement unit without external equipment. Meas. Sci. Technol. **19**(8), 085202 (2008). https://doi.org/10.1088/0957-0233/19/8/085202, http://stacks.iop.org/0957-0233/19/i=8/a=085202?key=crossref.eba2d86c89ec30974df9369d76e4e33e

5. IEEE Aerospace and Electronic Systems Society. Gyro and Accelerometer Panel, IEEE Standards Board, American National Standards Institute: IEEE recommended practice for precision centrifuge testing of linear accelerometers. Institute of Electrical and Electronics Engineers (2001). https://ieeexplore.ieee.org/document/972832

6. Kim, A., Golnaraghi, M.: Initial calibration of an inertial measurement unit using an optical position tracking system. In: PLANS 2004. Position Location and Navigation Symposium (IEEE Cat. No.04CH37556), pp. 96–101. IEEE. https://doi.org/10.1109/PLANS.2004.1308980, http://ieeexplore.ieee.org/document/1308980/

7. Kok, M., Hol, J.D., Schön, T.B.: Using inertial sensors for position and orientation estimation. Found. Trends Signal Process. 11(2), 1–153 (2017). https://doi.org/10.1561/2000000094

8. Nebot, E., Durrant-Whyte, H.: Initial calibration and alignment of low-cost inertial navigation units for land vehicle applications. J. Robot. Syst. 16(2), 81–92 (1999). https://doi.org/10.1002/(SICI)1097-4563(199902)16:2⟨81::AID-ROB2⟩3.0.CO;2-9

9. Renk, E., Collins, W., Rizzo, M., Lee, F., Bernstein, D.: Optimization-based calibration of a triaxial accelerometer-magnetometer. In: Proceedings of the 2005, American Control Conference, pp. 1957–1962. IEEE (2005). https://doi.org/10.1109/ACC.2005.1470256, http://ieeexplore.ieee.org/document/1470256/

10. Sabatelli, S., Galgani, M., Fanucci, L., Rocchi, A.: A double stage Kalman filter for sensor fusion and orientation tracking in 9D IMU. In: 2012 IEEE Sensors Applications Symposium Proceedings, pp. 1–5. IEEE, February 2012. https://doi.org/10.1109/SAS.2012.6166315, http://ieeexplore.ieee.org/document/6166315/

11. Sabatini, A.: Quaternion-based extended Kalman filter for determining orientation by inertial and magnetic sensing. IEEE Trans. Biomed. Eng. 53(7), 1346–1356 (2006). https://doi.org/10.1109/TBME.2006.875664. http://ieeexplore.ieee.org/document/1643403/

12. Salehi, S., Mostofi, N., Bleser, G.: A practical in-field magnetometer calibration method for IMUs (2012). https://www.researchgate.net/publication/258449504_A_practical_in-field_magnetometer_calibration_method_for_IMUs

13. Stakkeland, M., Prytz, G., Booij, W.E., Pedersen, S.T.: Characterization of accelerometers using nonlinear Kalman filters and position feedback. IEEE Trans. Instrum. Meas. 56(6), 2698–2704 (2007). https://doi.org/10.1109/TIM.2007.908145. http://ieeexplore.ieee.org/document/4389144/

14. Tedaldi, D., Pretto, A., Menegatti, E.: A robust and easy to implement method for IMU calibration without external equipments. In: 2014 IEEE International Conference on Robotics and Automation (ICRA), pp. 3042–3049. IEEE, May 2014. https://doi.org/10.1109/ICRA.2014.6907297, http://ieeexplore.ieee.org/document/6907297/

15. Tomczyński, J., Mańkowski, T., Kaczmarek, P.: Cross-sensor calibration procedure for magnetometer and inertial units. In: Szewczyk, R., Zieliński, C., Kaliczyńska, M. (eds.) ICA 2017. AISC, vol. 550, pp. 450–459. Springer, Cham (2017). https://doi.org/10.1007/978-3-319-54042-9_43

Application of the Open Scalable Production System to Machine Tending of Additive Manufacturing Operations by a Mobile Manipulator

Rafael Arrais[1,2]([✉]) [ID], Germano Veiga[1,2] [ID], Tiago T. Ribeiro[3]([✉]) [ID],
Daniel Oliveira[3] [ID], Ramon Fernandes[3] [ID], André Gustavo S. Conceição[3] [ID],
and P. C. M. A. Farias[3] [ID]

[1] INESC TEC - INESC Technology and Science,
Campus da FEUP, Rua Dr. Roberto Frias, 4200-465 Porto, Portugal
{rafael.l.arrais,germano.veiga}@inesctec.pt
[2] Faculty of Engineering, University of Porto,
Rua Dr. Roberto Frias, 4200-465 Porto, Portugal
[3] Department of Electrical Engineering, Federal University of Bahia,
Rua Aristides Novis, 02, Salvador, BA 40210-630, Brazil
{tiagotr,andre.gustavo,paulo.farias}@ufba.br

Abstract. To support the full adoption of Cyber-Physical Systems (CPS) in modern production lines, effective solutions need to be extended to the technological domains of robotics and industrial automation. This paper addresses the description, application and results of usage of the Open Scalable Production System (OSPS) and its underlying skill-based robot programming ideology to support machine tending of additive manufacturing operations by a mobile manipulator.

Keywords: Adaptive and flexible industrial robotics ·
Additive manufacturing · Machine tending · Mobile manipulator

1 Introduction

With the ongoing Fourth Industrial Revolution, so often referred to as Industry 4.0, characterized by the full adoption of Cyber-Physical System (CPS) and by the introduction of Internet of Things (IoT) in manufacturing scenarios, research

The research leading to these results has received funding from the European Unions Horizon 2020 - The EU Framework Programme for Research and Innovation 2014–2020, under grant agreement No. 777096. This work is also financed by the ERDF – European Regional Development Fund through the Operational Programme for Competitiveness and Internationalisation – COMPETE 2020 Programme within project POCI-01-0145-FEDER-006961, and by National Funds through the FCT – Fundação para a Ciência e a Tecnologia (Portuguese Foundation for Science and Technology) as part of project UID/EEA/50014/2013.

© Springer Nature Switzerland AG 2019
P. Moura Oliveira et al. (Eds.): EPIA 2019, LNAI 11805, pp. 345–356, 2019.
https://doi.org/10.1007/978-3-030-30244-3_29

and commercial efforts for novel production systems have extended to technological domains such as industrial automation and robotics. The advent of advanced robotic systems, such as mobile manipulators, able to sense and interact with increasingly complex, unstructured and challenging industrial environments, originates a critical necessity to fully integrate, support, and enable the set of technologies, models and functional components that support advanced robotic operations.

Advanced and flexible CPSs play an important role in empowering companies to cope with increasing product customization, high demand diversity, products with shorter life cycles, and low volumes per order. In fact, the flexibility, effectiveness and interoperability of such systems are key factors to enable efficient manufacturing and expedite delivery of more personalized products. In contrast, inflexible robotic solutions that can usually only deal with delimited sets of tasks on restricted lots of parts, operate in rather structured and pre-defined environments with long changeover times, characterized by ad hoc vertical integration and limited interoperability with industrial equipment are typical of traditional production systems. In addition, conventional robotic solutions are generally unsuitable for small production series, that are characterized by frequent changes in the production layout.

To overcome the aforementioned limitations, projects such as the European-funded H2020 FASTEN[1] and H2020 ScalABLE4.0[2] are altering the paradigm of the development and application of robotic systems in industry. Thus, the development of autonomous mobile manipulators, fully integrated with industrial equipment, additive manufacturing systems, intralogistics mechanisms, vertical layers in the production systems architecture, and that are capable of performing automated tasks at mass customization production lines in a flexible way.

To achieve the proposed objectives, a novel framework, entitled Open Scalable Production System (OSPS), is being developed on the scope of the above-mentioned R&D initiatives. The OSPS development will aim to accomplish a fully connected and scalable manufacturing system, integrating robotic systems, automation equipment, simulation and decision-support systems, and optimization and prescriptive analytics technologies to produce one-of-a-kind customer designs, effectively adapt to changes in factory layout and alterations to manufacturing processes, and to implicitly establish extemporaneous interoperability on vertical and horizontal levels.

This paper will overview the main OSPS components, emphasising the set of modules that enable the development of sustainable and scalable robotic systems, promoting easy programming and configuration of robotic tasks, and that will allow successful recognition, localization and grasping of highly customized products, such as 3D printed parts, resulting from additive manufacturing processes. Furthermore, the OSPS will also support localization algorithms and autonomous navigation methodologies on unstructured and dynamic industrial environments as robotic skills.

---

[1] http://fastenmanufacturing.eu/.
[2] https://www.scalable40.eu/.

The remainder of this paper is organized as follows: Sect. 2 describes related work, Sect. 3 describes the OSPS, detailing its internal components, Sect. 4 presents the application of the developed system in a machine tending application in an additive manufacturing industrial setting, and, finally, Sect. 5 draws some conclusions.

2   Related Work

Complex applications such as robotics in unstructured industrial environments often require the integration of several software modules. The orchestration of several independent robotic applications for the accomplishment of a given production task is not a trivial problem, even if nodes provide well-defined interfaces. Usually, strategies rely on the development of monolithic conditional cascading structures or nested switch statements. In some situations, ad hoc implementations of state-machines are developed, or compelling inference and task planning methodologies are applied.

The literature suggests two appealing approaches for high-level control applications in robotic systems: task scripting and task planning [9]. Task scripting empowers the developer with the ability to specify exactly what is the approach followed by the robot to solve a given task at hand. Task scripting is widely used in classical industrial robotic applications, where the operation scenario is constant, well structured, and where unscripted behaviour is often undesired. For the majority of industrial applications, where robots need to comply with safety and productivity requirements, and where, consequently, robot behaviour needs to be well defined, measurable, systematic and bounded, task scripting is the most reliable approach. Moreover, unexpected events during operation result necessarily in unrecoverable errors, as to not incur in any potential safety breach. When applying task scripting in an unstructured environment, the developer is required to specify how the robot should behave when faced with different failure modes.

On its turn, task planning concedes more autonomy to the robot for planning and executing issued production tasks. Task planning relies heavily on a supportive physical world and functional models for model-based task planning, and inference systems based on artificial intelligence. As model-based task planning can potentially recover from failure situations that can be considered within the model used for planning, this methodology contrasts with the former, in the sense that the burden of solving application-specific nominal execution and failure states shifts from the developer to the autonomous system [9]. Although the autonomous prevention of failures is promising, task planning methodologies have the potential of undesirably preventing non-conflicts and producing unexpected solutions to common or trivial problems, which might result in potential safety issues and largely affect productivity.

Robot skills and skill-based programming were concepts introduced to allow a re-utilization of previously developed sets of operations that a given robot is capable of performing [8]. The concept of a robotic skill is related to the capacity of a given robotic system to perform a physical or conceptual action that has a resemblance with an activity that could be performed by a human [7].

A skill-based programming paradigm ensures that the cost of programming robotic systems is significantly lower than a problem-specific approach. A common abstraction for the skill-based is the one highlighted by Archibald et al. in [7], where the authors suggest the separation of programming responsibilities between the robot programmer and the application specialist. As such, through the skill-based paradigm, an application specialist, who has the operational and technical know-how on shop floor operations is able to create robotic applications using a set of skills previously defined by the robotic programmer. The main advantage of the proposed paradigm is that the application specialist does not need to be concerned with low-level robot programming and can focus solely on creating effective robot applications for the set of problems at hand, inferring skills parameters and their organization through the gathered operational know-how.

Over the years, several approaches and applications of robotic skills and skill-based robot programming have been presented in the literature [8,11,16,17]. Although there is a significant scientific effort to develop a skill-based programming framework that tackles the problems associated with robotic application reusability, there is not yet a definite solution in the state-of-the-art.

3 Open Scalable Production System

In the proposed architecture, depicted in Fig. 1, manufacturing and logistic Standard Operating Proceduress (SOPs) will be issued by the uppermost modules in terms of verticality in the OSPS architecture, such as Manufacturing Execution Systems (MES) or Enterprise Resource Planners (ERP) systems. These SOPs will be gathered by the Advanced Plant Model (APM), that will relay these sets of complex routine operations to the Production Manager. The Production Manager, in its turn, will be able to gather information on the available

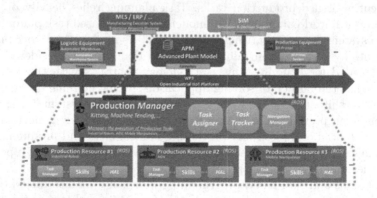

Fig. 1. High-level architecture overview of the OSPS framework.

Production Resources, such as knowledge regarding the skills available, production availability, and current location on the shop floor. Based on these insights, the Production Manager will be able to determine which Production Resource is suitable to conduct the set of tasks encapsulated on the issued SOPs. The Task Manager software module, running inside the robotic implementation, will be able to process the issued task and execute it in the form of a composition of multiple pre-programmed robotic skills.

3.1 Task Manager

In the proposed OSPS software architecture, the Task Manager is the central node running within the robot itself. The Task Manager, a stack of ROS packages developed in Python, has a dual responsibility: on one hand, it is the element that provides integration mechanisms between the robot and other modules in the system, such as the Production Manager or the APM. On the other hand, the Task Manager is the component responsible for orchestrating tasks in the form of sets of skills on the robotic level.

For the task-level orchestration, the Task Manager relies heavily on community supported tools for its internal organization, enhancing and tuning already existing solutions for the problem at hand. As such, the proposed approach abides by the ROS SMACH task scripting paradigm, a Python API that can be used to orchestrate hierarchical and concurrent state machines [9], and with interoperability with the APM and PM to support dynamic and intuitive task-level robot programming. As task scripting performed in ROS SMACH must be programmed in Python, which deeply limits practical application in real scenarios, the proposed approach provides an interpreter for state-machines defined on SCXML files, an industrial standard for encoding state-machines based on CCXML and Harel State Tables [5].

Besides the orchestration role, the Task Manager stack provides a set of services and publisher-subscriber messaging pattern that allow the characterization of the robot. Namely, Task Manager makes available interfaces for allowing the robot to be discoverable in a network, by enlisting the robot identification and properties, as are examples its size and current location. Moreover, the current status of the robot, enlisting also its current location, is made available through services or periodic published messages.

3.2 Skill-Based Robot Programming

The principal motivation behind the proposed skill-based robot programming ideology is to introduce and combine skill-based programming concepts with tools that are widely popular and backed by the ROS community, such as ROS Actions, a ROS stack that provides a standardized interface for interacting with preemptable operations, and with ROS SMACH, a task-level architecture for rapidly creating complex robot behaviour. Moreover, to ensure maximum adaptability of the proposed skill-based robot programming methodology, industrial standards such as SCXML, an XML-based file that supports the construction of state-machines, are introduced in the proposed solution.

A central enhancement and contribution to the state-of-the-art of the proposed skill-based programming approach will be the integration with community supported tools as ROS Actions. The asynchronous property of Service-Oriented Architectures (SOAs) is of paramount importance in complex systems. Asynchronistic functions ensure that a given client module can issue a request to be processed by the server module in its own timeframe and receives a reply when the requested processing is concluded. In the cyber-physical domain, specifically in applications that have a physical component, such as robotic operation, if the asynchronous request takes a long time to be processed, due to physical constraints associated with the operation itself, the requesting entity might want the ability to be periodically informed about the state of the requested process. Moreover, the entity requesting the physical operation might require the feature of cancelling the requested execution at any given time. ROS Actions present the aforementioned benefits and complement ROS services for operations where it is important to have a continuous evaluation of the requested operation, as are examples operations that have a physical component and, therefore, a measurable impact in the physical reality. Thus, the proposed skill-based programming approach is aligned with the ROS Action Protocol in order to take advantage of its spread usage in the ROS community.

3.3   Production Manager

The Production Manager stack is responsible for managing a set of production resources in a given production environment. Specifically, the Production Manager component is responsible for controlling the execution of production schedules defined by MES on each manufacturing area of the factory. Besides the task assignment, the Production Manager is responsible for monitoring the ongoing performance of a previously issued production task.

As depicted in Fig. 1, the Production Manager stack coordinates a distributed set of production resources, and thus, assumes a centralized position in the OSPS architecture. The Production Manager heavily relies on the APM for data on physical objects and functional elements that will enable the attribution of tasks through resource allocation methodologies. Moreover, within its stack, the Production Manager entity can make available to its production resources a set of services for aiding the execution of the issued tasks.

4   Experimental Results

4.1   Additive Manufacturing Machine Tending Use Case

The Additive Manufacturing Systems Unit, composed of a 3D printer and a mobile manipulator robot, has the main objective to provide flexibility, scalability and agility to cope with spare parts demand.

The mobile manipulator, depicted in Fig. 2, is equipped with three main robotic equipment: a Husky Unmanned Ground Vehicle (UGV) [1], an Universal Robots UR5 collaborative robot arm [6], and a Robotiq 2-Fingers Adaptive Gripper [3]. The main sensors used in the navigation and machine tending tasks are a SICK LMS111 LIDAR [4] and the camera Intel Real Sense D435 [2].

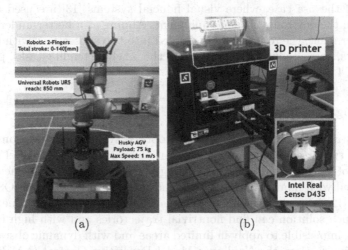

(a)   (b)

Fig. 2. Mobile manipulator *(a)* and the additive manufacturing system *(b)*.

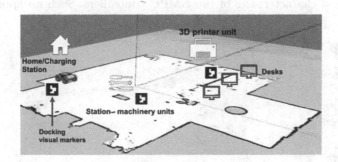

Fig. 3. Use case environment, composed by a home/charging station, additive manufacturing equipment, machinery units and the mobile manipulator.

The mobile manipulator used in this scenario has three specific roles: (i) Perception system: the objects must be detected, along with its position and orientation with respect to the base coordinate system of the robot. (ii) Grasping system: this system should be capable of pick up objects, planning a collision-free trajectory accordingly, and then place the object in a pre-determined location. (iii) Navigation system: the mobile manipulator shall be able to navigate in the

environment and perform a properly docking at the 3D printer or other units
(warehouse, machinery units, etc).

In this context, the experimental test with the OSPS framework consists of a
navigation task from the home station to the 3D printer unit, a task to remove
the part of the printer and place on the robot bin, and a last navigation task
to transport the part to the following machinery unit. Figure 3 shows the environment of the use case, where visual fiducial systems [13] are used as visual
reference in the environment and equipment. Aiming at a better understanding
of the experiment, the results will be divided into two subsections with the navigation tasks, presented in Subsect. 4.2, and the machine tending tasks, presented
in Subsect. 4.3.

4.2   Navigation Tasks

To demonstrate the functionality of the proposed system, a navigation environment with two levels of human interaction is considered: A low level typically
consisting of machinery and parts and a high level consisting of the factory floor
itself, shared with humans. For low-level interaction, the standard ROS navigation stack [12] is used for planning and tracking trajectories from one point to
another. Such solution can find nontrivial trajectories and with high execution
time, being impossible to apply in limited areas and with dynamic obstacles. For
high-level interaction, the Nonlinear Model Predictive Control (NMPC)-based
visual path following strategy proposed by [14], adapted for obstacle detection
and emergency stop is used. In this case, the movements of the mobile manipulator are restricted to a safety zone, besides taking advantage of the inherent robustness characteristics of the NMPC controllers. Such an approach has

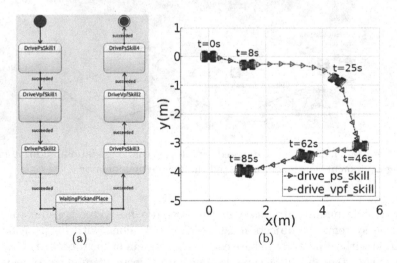

(a)   (b)

Fig. 4. Navigation task experiment: *(a)* state machine; *(b)* pose planes.

already been validated successfully in a more challenging context like for time-varying robot formations applied to industrial environments [15].

In the navigation experiment, a task is issued by the PM to the TM running on-board of the mobile manipulator. The TM processes the issued task and orchestrates the execution of a set of skills, which have been pre-programmed in the developed framework. The navigation task is, therefore, composed of the following skills:

- **drive_ps_skill** $\hookrightarrow$ Moves the mobile manipulator to the boundary between the two navigation zones.
- **drive_vpf_skill** $\hookrightarrow$ Navigation in dynamic environment using visual information and NMPC controllers.
- **wait_p&p_skill** $\hookrightarrow$ Wait the total time of the pick and place task (T_{pp}).

Figure 4(a) shows the graphical representation of the state machine, while Table 1 presents the goals of the individual skills for the navigation task. The pose plane represented in Fig. 4(b) shows that the skills related to navigation task were successfully executed.

The temporal behaviour of this experiment can be verified in Fig. 5. As can be seen in Fig. 5(a), all skills have been executed at a time compatible with the application requirements. Figure 5(b) shows a consistent time evolution of pose and soft control efforts necessary to the complex dynamics of the mobile manipulator.

Table 1. Navigation task experiment - skills individual goals.

Skill	Label	Goal
drive_ps_skill	DrivePsSkill1	Stabilize at point: $x = 1.5$m; $y = -0.3$m; $\theta = 0$rad
	DrivePsSkill2	Stabilize at point: $x = 5.4$m; $y = -3.2$m; $\theta = -\frac{\pi}{2}$rad
	DrivePsSkill3	Stabilize at point: $x = 5.0$m; $y = -3.2$m; $\theta = -\pi$rad
	DrivePsSkill4	Stabilize at point: $x = 1.1$m; $y = -4.0$m; $\theta = \frac{\pi}{2}$rad
drive_vpf_skill	DriveVpfSkill1	Follow the visual path by 4 m length
	DriveVpfSkill2	Follow the visual path by 1.5 m length
wait_p& p_skill	WaitingPickandPlace	Wait the Pick and Place task

4.3   Machine Tending Task

This subsection describes the skills and results of the machine tending tasks. As shown in Fig. 2(b), the 3D sensor is mounted on the robotic arm providing the feature of a vision-based control to perform the task. In general 3D printers have limited working space, with even more limited space to remove the part. The limitation of position and orientation of the gripper workspace, coupled with the type of part that will be printed within a wide range of geometries,

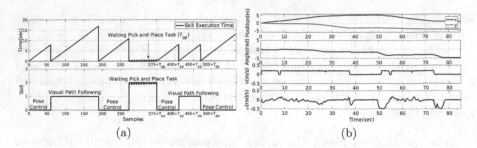

(a)   (b)

Fig. 5. Navigation task performance indicators: *(a)* execution time and corresponding skills; *(b)* poses and velocities

weights, among other characteristics, becomes a challenge and sometimes makes the task unfeasible. A feasible solution, described in this article, takes advantage of the additive manufacturing to aid the grasping system by incorporating into the parts a small tag enabling the machine tending operation by intrinsically providing a precise and effective pose estimation of the part [10].

Figure 6(a) showcases the graphical representation of the machine tending state machine, while Fig. 6(b) shows the corresponding operation snapshots as follows: home pose (top left); pre-grasping pose (top right); grasping the object (bottom left); placing the object (bottom right). Similarly to the navigation task,

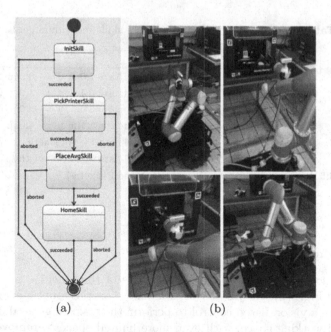

(a)   (b)

Fig. 6. Machine tending task: *(a)* state machine; *(b)* operation snapshots.

Table 2. Machine tending task experiment - skill individual goals

Skill	Label	Goal
init_skill	InitSkill	Stabilize at point: $x = -0.25$m; $y = 0.1$m; $z = 0.4$m
pick_printer_skill	PickPrinterSkill	Stabilize at point: $x = -0.52$m; $y = 0.015$m; $z = 0.34$m
place_avg_skill	PlaceAvgSkill	Stabilize at point: $x = -0.06$m; $y = -0.44$m; $z = 0.07$m
home_skill	HomeSkill	Stabilize at point: $x = 0.14$m; $y = -0.15$m; $z = 0.25$m

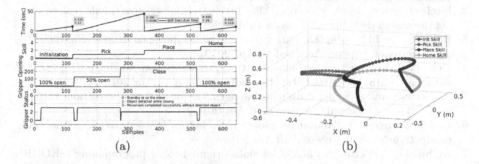

(a)   (b)

Fig. 7. Machine tending task performance indicators: *(a)* execution time, skills and gripper data; *(b)* gripper position with relation to the world frame.

the TM processes the issued task and orchestrates the execution of a set of Skills, that have been pre-programmed in the developed framework (see Table 2):

1. **init_skill** ↪ Initialize the gripper and move to pre-grasping pose, fails if cannot reach the pose, collide or cannot initialize the gripper.
2. **pick_printer_skill** ↪ Pick the object from the printer. Skill that picks the object inside the 3D printer. Fails if the arm collides or if it does not grasp the object.
3. **place_avg_skill** ↪ Move the object to the UGV base.
4. **home_skill** ↪ Move the arm to the home position.

Figure 7(a) shows the temporal behaviour of this experiment, while Fig. 7(b) shows the evolution of gripper pose in the world frame. As can be seen, the skills related to machine tending task were successfully executed.

5   Conclusions

This paper proposed a novel framework to improve the flexibility, effectiveness and interoperability of Cyber-Physical System on Industry 4.0 context, aiming to develop a fully connected and scalable manufacturing system, integrating advanced robotic systems and automation equipment, and others facilities to produce one-of-a-kind customer designs, effectively adapt to changes in factory layout and alterations to manufacturing processes. Real results with a mobile manipulator robot demonstrated the effectiveness of the skill-based approach through navigation and machine tending tasks aiming to collect on demand industrial parts on a 3D printer. Future work involves a complete evaluation of vertical integration with the highest levels of the framework stack.

References

1. Husky - unmanned ground vehicle. https://www.clearpathrobotics.com/husky-unmanned-ground-vehicle-robot. Accessed 10 Apr 2019
2. Intel realsense depth camera d435. https://click.intel.com/intelr-realsensetm-depth-camera-d435.html. Accessed 10 Apr 2019
3. Robotiq 2f–140 adaptive grippers. https://robotiq.com/products/2f85-140-adaptive-robot-gripper. Accessed 10 Apr 2019
4. Sick lms111 laser scanner-lidar. https://www.sick.com/media/pdf/2/42/842/dataSheet_LMS111-10100_1041114_en.pdf. Accessed 10 Apr 2019
5. State chart xml (scxml): state machine notation for control abstraction. https://www.w3.org/TR/scxml/. Accessed 10 Apr 2019
6. Ur5 - a flexible collaborative robot arm. https://www.universal-robots.com/products/ur5-robot. Accessed 10 Apr 2019
7. Archibald, C., Petriu, E.: Model for skills-oriented robot programming (SKORP), vol. 1964 (1993). https://doi.org/10.1117/12.141787
8. Bøgh, S., Nielsen, O., Pedersen, M., Krüger, V., Madsen, O.: Does your robot have skills? In: Proceedings of the 43rd International Symposium on Robotics. VDE Verlag GMBH, August 2012
9. Bohren, J., Cousins, S.: The smach high-level executive [ROS news]. IEEE Robot. Autom. Mag. **17**(4), 18–20 (2010). https://doi.org/10.1109/MRA.2010.938836
10. Conceicao, A.G.S., Oliveira, D.M., Carvalho, M.P.: ORB algorithm applied to detection, location and grasping objects. In: 2018 Latin American Robotic Symposium, pp. 176–181, November 2018. https://doi.org/10.1109/LARS/SBR/WRE.2018.00040
11. Klotzbücher, M., Bruyninckx, H.: Coordinating robotic tasks and systems with rFSM statecharts. JOSER: J. Softw. Eng. Robot. **3**(1), 28–56 (2012)
12. Marder-Eppstein, E., Berger, E., Foote, T., Gerkey, B., Konolige, K.: The office marathon: robust navigation in an indoor office environment. In: International Conference on Robotics and Automation (2010)
13. Olson, E.: AprilTag: a robust and flexible visual fiducial system. In: 2011 IEEE International Conference on Robotics and Automation. IEEE, May 2011
14. Ribeiro, T.T., Conceição, A.G.S.: Nonlinear model predictive visual path following control to autonomous mobile robots. J. Intell. Robot. Syst. (2018). https://doi.org/10.1007/s10846-018-0896-3
15. Ribeiro, T.T., Fernandez, R.O., Conceição, A.G.S.: NMPC-based visual leader-follower formation control for wheeled mobile robots. In: 16th IEEE International Conference on Industrial Informatics, INDIN 2018, Porto, Portugal, 18–20 July 2018, pp. 406–411 (2018). https://doi.org/10.1109/INDIN.2018.8472107
16. Schou, C., Andersen, R.S., Chrysostomou, D., Bøgh, S., Madsen, O.: Skill-based instruction of collaborative robots in industrial settings. Robot. Comput.-Integr. Manuf. **53**, 72–80 (2018). https://doi.org/10.1016/j.rcim.2018.03.008
17. Thomas, U., Hirzinger, G., Rumpe, B., Schulze, C., Wortmann, A.: A new skill based robot programming language using UML/P statecharts. In: 2013 IEEE International Conference on Robotics and Automation, pp. 461–466, May 2013. https://doi.org/10.1109/ICRA.2013.6630615

Do You Trust Me? Investigating the Formation of Trust in Social Robots

Mojgan Hashemian$^{(\boxtimes)}$, Raul Paradeda, Carla Guerra, and Ana Paiva

INESC-ID and Instituto Superior Técnico, University of Lisbon,
Av. Prof. Dr. Cavaco Silva, Porto Salvo, Portugal
{mojgan.hashemian,raul.paradeda,carla.azevedo,
ana.paiva}@tecnico.ulisboa.pt
https://tecnico.ulisboa.pt/en/

Abstract. Human beings live in a society with a complex system of
social-emotional relations. Trust is one key concept in this system. It can
help to reduce the social complexity, mainly in those cases where it is
necessary to cooperate. Thus, the area of social robotics has been studying different approaches to perform cooperative tasks between humans
and robots. Here, we examine the influence of a set of factors (gender,
emotional representation, making Small Talk and embodiment) that may
affect the trustworthiness of a robot. The results showed that these factors influence the level of trust that people put in robots. Specifically, a
social robot with embodiment telling a sad story with sad facial expression and gestures has more influence on the trust level of a female subject.

Keywords: Trust · Human-robot interaction · HRI ·
Emotional representation · Small talk · Embodiment

1 Introduction

The concept of trust has been studied over decades in the fields of psychology
and social science. In general, trust is defined as a factor of human personality,
which is the result of a choice among behaviors under a specific situation [1].
Other views of trust deal with an individual's evaluation to face a certain level
of risk when interacting with another agent [2].

Recently, social robots are becoming a part of our daily lives. In this sense,
social robotics gets major importance in order to make this integration the
safer and more satisfactory as possible. One important area, where the relation between human and robot must be the safest, is the Assistive Robotics, in
which robot's actions could have serious consequences to the people surrounding
them [3]. For instance, social robots as health-care givers as well as compan-
ions for the elderly have been addressed in recent literature [4,5]. In these cases,
the interaction with the patients, family or medics must have a high degree of
trustworthiness [5]. On the other hand, the combination of social robots and
the concept of trust may lead to an important question: is it possible for a

© Springer Nature Switzerland AG 2019
P. Moura Oliveira et al. (Eds.): EPIA 2019, LNAI 11805, pp. 357–369, 2019.
https://doi.org/10.1007/978-3-030-30244-3_30

human to trust a machine? As far as the confidence of humans in robots grows, they turn into more collaborative partners [6]. As a result, a number of studies explored factors influencing trust in the field of social robotics [7]. The idea that trust is entwined with persuasiveness in social and collaborative setups could be another interesting factor [8,9]. Furthermore, people's tendency to cooperate with a robot or accept the suggestions or orders given by the robot could be highly affected by the trust felt by the human user [10]. Also, previous HRI research has established that trust, disclosure, and a sense of companionship lead to positive outcomes [11].

Hence, understanding the factors that influence trust becomes a major concern in Human-Robot Interaction [12]. Thereby, the preceding remarks motivated us to explore which factors could affect the trust a human feels towards a robot. In this study, we designed different scenarios to compare and evaluate the levels of trust under different circumstances. For instance, with different emotions, expressed either in facial expressions or body gestures, and by making Small Talk (ST) before starting the interaction. The embodiment of the robot may also influence how trustworthy a robot could be. Other factor we explored was the gender of the users, which could also reveal some differences towards the trust in the robot.

2   Related Work

Previous studies have approached trust in HRI mostly from the perspective of automation. However, few studies dealt with human-interpersonal trust in solo and within a group [13]. For instance, Brule et al. [14] conducted experiments to evaluate how the robot's performance and behavior affect human trust. They used a virtual robot with different behavioral styles and measured the effects of these behaviors on trustworthiness judgments as a function of task performance. The factors used by the authors to measure differences in trust were gaze, the motion fluency and the hesitation in the task. The authors concluded that the performance of the robot on each task indeed influenced its trustworthiness. Youssef et al. [15] investigated how the combination of inarticulate utterances and/or iconic gestures with a proactive or reactive response mode would affect the establishment of a positive relationship between the human and the accompanying robot. Results suggest a significant positive relationship between the human and robot when using the full mode (utterances + gestures) and the proactive mode.

In a recent study [16], the authors investigated the dual nature of trust in HRI, specifically 'dispositional and historical' trust. Dispositional trust reflects trust in other people (or machines) after having an initial encounter with them, even if no interaction has yet occured. On the other hand, historical trust is based on past interactions that took place between the person and other people or machine. In the study 210 young adult participants responded 30 questions to share their opinion towards autonomous systems. The results indicate the importance of dispositional trust. Even though there are recent promising results, a lot more behavioral factors remain unexplored that can play an important role on the trust felt by a human while interacting with robots. Therefore, in this work we argue that emotional representation, either in facial expression or robot's gestures, embodiment, small talk and gender may influence the trustworthiness of a robot.

In a similar study [17], the authors conducted a study with a humanoid Nao robot where people tend to donate differently when the robot is showing different emotions and making or not making ST. A previous study indicated that male participants have more experience with computers leading them to perceive the robot more as an easy to use technology and consequently better accept it [18].

In sum, previous studies show that factors such as robot characteristics (e.g., performance, appearance, proximity), the type, size and behavior of the robot influence trust. These findings motivated us to focus more on human-interpersonal trust. In this paper, we inquire different behavioral cues of a robot while interacting with a user. Specifically, the way it starts the conversation (by making small talks), the way it present the emotional information (using gestures and facial expressions), as well as its appearance (embodiment). Also, we explore how the gender of the participants can also influence the trust towards the robot.

3   The Study

The study consists of interactive scenarios in which a fully autonomous robot complains about suffering from a mechanical fault. Then, the robot asks for financial support from the participants to fix the fault. Depending on the robot (a humanoid Nao robot or Head-Only Emys robot), the malfunctioning part is different: in case of Emys, his left eye has a problem and does not function properly (Fig. 1 on the left); in Nao's case, his left arm is broken (Fig. 1 on the right). We created four (2 × 2) scenarios with regard to the combination of two emotional representations and making or not ST.

In our designed scenarios the following hypotheses are addressed:

- **H1** We hypothesize that starting a conversation with ST would increase the level of trust an individual puts in the robot.
- **H2** We postulate that expressing sad emotions while telling a sad story would enhance the level of trust an individual feels towards the robot.
- **H3** We hypothesize that the participant's gender may influence the evaluated factors.
- **H4** We argue that the robot's embodiment may influence the trustworthiness of the robot.

In this sense, we consider these hypotheses to be associated with binary variables. To be more specific, the first hypothesis regards a variable with two possible values: making ST or not. Similarly, the second hypothesis relates with expressing either happy/sad emotion. The third variable would be having a complete physical body vs. only a head. The fourth variable could be having a male or a female participant. Considering the four hypotheses, we examine the influence of a set of factors in the trust levels towards a robot:

- The robot starts the interaction with ST while expressing a sad face {ST_SAD}
- The robot starts the interaction without ST while expressing a sad face {NST_SAD}
- The robot starts the interaction with ST while expressing a joyful face {ST_JOY}
- The robot starts the interaction without ST while expressing a joyful face {NST_JOY}.

Initially, the subjects are asked to sign the consent form. Then trust is accessed with a 40-item Human-Robot Trust questionnaire [19] that we ask the participants to fill out in two time points, before (pre-questionnaire) and after (post-questionnaire) the interaction with the robot. The main goal of the pre-questionnaire is to determine subjects' mood and their expectation about the robot before the interaction. Next, for each interaction, the experimenter introduces the robot to the participant just saying the robot's name, without explaining the purpose of the experiment or what the robot will do. The experimenter leaves the room, letting the participant alone with the robot. To start the interaction, the participant must introduce his/her name and press a start button in the screen. The robot starts the interaction with a greeting utterance saying the participant's name. Then, the rest of the interaction depends on which scenario the participant is assigned to: in case of ST scenario the robot would ask some short questions as presented in the following.

```
- Hello, my name is Emys/Nao. I have to apologize for
my voice the designers who, programmed me in this project
thought it was more natural and a better idea. What you
think?
- Anyway, it's a beautiful day, isn't it?
- I, hope you are healthy and happy. Are you?
- Well, however, I should confess it's not very well with
me. I am a robot here in, this Lab., used in several im-
portant projects. Do you believe in that?
- Everything was fine till a month ago. But suddenly,
everything changed. Can you imagine why?
Let me tell you my case.
```

After Small Talks (ST), the robot starts telling the story. In the case of scenarios without ST, the robot starts the story right away. Both robots tell the story describing how they are very important to the university and that they were used in several important projects. However, because of a mechanical problem, they will be replaced by a new robot. In the case of Emys, the problem is with his left eye, which jumps out. In the experiments using Nao, the problem is with its left arm and the robot uses something to keep it straight (Fig. 1).

Fig. 1. Representation of the robots explaining the fault to the subject, Emys on the left and Nao on the right.

Table 1. Statistics of the participants in the experiments using Emys. Ages mean and standard deviation are given in brackets, respectively.

Scenario	Female	Male	Sum	Mean age	SD age
Joy Small Talk (ST_JOY)	5(28/9.6)	6(23.3/4.9)	11	25.6	7.4
Sad Small Talk (ST_SAD)	2(22/1.4)	9(28/4.7)	11	25	4.7
Joy (NST_JOY)	1(23/0)	10(23.4/2.5)	11	23.2	2.4
Sad (NST_SAD)	3(25.3/3.2)	6(23.1/2.1)	9	24.25	2.5
Total	**11**	**31**	**42**	**24.9**	**4.85**
Mean Age	**25.7**	**24.6**			
SD Age	**6.72**	**4.1**			

The main story is told expressing different emotions using facial expressions or gestures of joy or sadness, according to the selected scenario. After finishing the story, the robot asks for a fictional donation (not real money to avoid biases that could arise towards their generosity, etc.). After the donations, the robot will express a happy/sad emotion according to a predefined threshold (20 EUR). Finally, the post-questionnaire is given to the participants.

3.1 Participants

We conducted a study in an isolated room, and the population was a random selection of students from our university, where they all share a scientific/engineering background. In the first experiment (experiment 1) using Emys, a total of 42 subjects participated as listed in Table 1 (24.9 ± 4.9; 11 females and 31 males). In the second experiment (experiment 2) with Nao, a total number of 40 subjects participated, as listed in Table 2 (22.15 ± 4.8; 17 females and 23 males). It is important to note that each participant participated only in one of the studies.

Each interaction was performed with a human subject and a robot sitting face to face, and a screen in the middle used to receive information from the participants, such as their demographic information and the donation amounts. The interaction time depends on the scenario: in scenarios starting with ST, the experiment took around 8–10 min, while scenarios without ST took around 3–5 min.

Table 2. Statistics of the participants in the experiments using Nao. Ages mean and standard deviation are given in brackets, respectively.

Scenario	Female	Male	Sum	Mean age	SD age
Joy Small Talk (ST_JOY)	3(19/0.8)	7(19.8/1.8)	10	19.6	1.6
Sad Small Talk (ST_SAD)	7(22.8/3.9)	3(20/2.1)	10	22	3.7
Joy (NST_JOY)	5(27/9.5)	5(22.2/3.9)	10	25.7	7.4
Sad (NST_SAD)	2(21.5/0.5)	8(21.2/1.4)	10	21.8	1.3
Total	17	23	40	22.15	4.84
Mean Age	22.75	21.34			
SD Age	6.02	2.97			

4   Results

As discussed earlier, the trust questionnaire is contained of two parts (pre- and post-questionnaire). Most of the questions are the same in each part, hence the difference between the answers in the two attempts highlights the influence of the perception of the subjects' trust level (more details in [19]). In the following section, first we report the results of the two experiments, starting with Emys and then Nao. Under each subsection we consider 2 categories: the "emotion representation" (JOY or SAD) and the presence of Small Talk (ST or NST). Further, the results are examined considering the gender of the participants, either the corresponding trust levels or donation. Finally, we compare the two experiments to evaluate the influence of embodiment on trust.

4.1   Experiment 1: The Head-Only Emys Robot

The result of a normality test indicates that the population is non-normal in all the subgroups. Hence, we performed a U Mann Whitney test on the pre-questionnaires under each subgroup. The tests indicated that in case of ST and JOY scenarios there was no significant difference between the subjects *before* interacting with the robot (ST: $U = 47.500$, $p = .882$; JOY: $U = 53.0$, $p = .652$). It signifies that people under these two subcategories had the same pre-assumption about the robot before starting the interaction. Therefore, the possible difference in the perception of the robot after the interaction (post-questionnaire scores) would be due to the different variables, i.e. emotional representation and/or ST together with embodiment. Under these two cases, U Mann Whitney tests showed there is no significant difference among the participants *after* interacting with the robot (ST: $U = 46.0$, $p = .824$; JOY: $U = 38.0$, $p = .151$).

However, in the other two subcategories, i.e. NST and SAD there was significant difference among the pre-questionnaire results (NST: $U = 29.500$, $p = .020$; SAD: $U = 20.500$, $p = .003$). Hence, regarding these two subcategories we turn to two ways tests. In this sense, in case of NST scenario the result of a Sign test showed that there was a significant difference between the scores of the pre and post-questionnaires ($p = .001$). To be more specific, the lower mean in the post-questionnaire ($M = 50.09$ vs. $M = 58.30$) signifies that the participants lost their trust in the robot after the interaction. However, the result of a Sign test showed that there is no significant difference between the scores of the pre and post-questionnaires in case of SAD scenario ($p = .238$).

The result of a Kruskal-Wallis (K-W) test indicated that the four groups (Facial expression $2x2$ Small Talk) are significantly different regarding the trust factors ($\chi^2(3) = 10.396$, $p = .015$). The higher mean corresponding to the ST_SAD group signifies that people tend to trust more in Emys showing SAD facial expression while starting his conversation with ST (26.64 vs. 13.85 vs. 17.05 vs. 25.90).

As discussed earlier there is no significant difference between different genders under the four subcategories. Hence, we may combine the subcategories and compare a larger population (ST, NST, JOY, SAD). In this sense, the results indicated that there was a significant difference comparing the gender of the subjects just in the case when the robot performs SAD facial expression (SAD: $\chi^2(3) = 10.033$, $p = .018$), and for other groups no significant difference were observed (ST: $\chi^2(3) = 3.788$, $p = .285$; NST: $\chi^2(3) = 5.938$, $p = .115$; JOY: $\chi^2(3) = 4.760$, $p = .190$).

Also, we inquired if the amount of donation amount differs between the groups. However, a K-W test's result indicated that there is no significant differences between the four group regarding the donation amount ($\chi^2(3) = 3.397$, $p = .334$); nor regarding the genders ($\chi^2(7) = 8.480$, $p = .292$). However, comparing the genders of the participants in the SAD condition a significant difference found between trust level reported by males and females ($\chi^2(3) = 10.033$, $p = .018$). Table 3 lists a summary of the results.

Table 3. Analysis of the first experiment with Emys

Factor	Pre-questionnaire	Post-questionnaire
ST	$U = 47.500$, $p = .882$	$U = 46.000$, $p = .824$
JOY	$U = 53.000$, $p = .652$	$U = 38.000$, $p = .151$
NST	$U = 29.500$, $p = .020$	$p = .001$
SAD	$U = 20.500$, $p = .003$	$p = .238$

4.2   Experiment 2: The Humanoid Nao Robot

Similar to experiment 1, in the case of Nao robot none of the subgroups are normally distributed. Then we performed a non-parametric test on the pre-questionnaires' scores to determine whether the participants' population is similar across each group *before* the interaction. Results of U Mann Whitney tests indicated that there is no significant difference in the distribution of the subjects regarding the pre-questionnaire scores (ST: $U = 48.0$, $p = .880$; NST: $U = 39.5$, $p = .427$; SAD: $U = 46.5$, $p = .791$; JOY: $U = 36.0$, $p = .29$). To be more specific, all the participants in each group had the same feeling and presumption of trust toward Nao. Turning now to the post-questionnaire results, the only significant difference happened in case of SAD ($U(9) = 22.5$, $p = .038$), and for other groups no significant difference were observed (ST: $U(9) = 42.5$, $p = .571$; NST: $U(9) = 43.0$, $p = .596$; JOY: $U(9) = 40.5$, $p = .472$).

The preceding paragraph entails that JOY_SAD under ST, forms the same distribution, as well as JOY_SAD under NST condition. Hence, regarding the combined group, which forms a non-normal distribution ($D(19) = 0.119$, $p = .20$), a significant difference exists between the two groups ($U(19) = 127.0$, $p = .048$) and the higher mean in the NST (81.6 vs 80.8) shows that participants tend to trust more in the NST, regardless of the gestures.

In the same way of experiment 1, to compare the whole data together, we turn to the K-W test. However, in this experiment the multivariate analysis did not show any significant difference between the groups ($\chi^2(3) = 4.729$, $p = .193$). Neither, comparing the gender of the subjects, no significant difference was found (ST: $\chi^2(3) = 4.129$, $p = .248$; NST: $\chi^2(3) = .782$, $p = .854$; SAD: $\chi^2(3) = 7.001$, $p = .072$; JOY: $\chi^2(3) = 1.422$, $p = .700$).

Similar to the first experiment, we performed a non-parametric K-W test on the donation values. The K-W result, showed that there is a significant difference in the donation amount among the four groups ($\chi^2(3) = 8.816$, $p = .032$); as well as, the participants' gender differences ($\chi^2(7) = 15.202$, $p = .033$). Table 4 lists a summary of the results.

Table 4. Analysis of the second experiment with Nao

Factor	Pre-questionnaire	Post-questionnaire
ST	$U = 48.0$, $p = .880$	$U(9) = 42.5$, $p = .571$
JOY	$U = 36.0$, $p = .29$	$U(9) = 40.5$, $p = .472$
NST	$U = 39.5$, $p = .427$	$U(9) = 43.0$, $p = .596$
SAD	$U = 46.5$, $p = .791$	$U(9) = 22.5$, $p = .038$

4.3   Embodiment

Putting the results of the two experiments together, which were similar in all the factors except the robot itself, we investigate the influence of embodiment on the participants' trust level. To do so, we applied the K-W test on the eight groups

(ST, NST, SAD, JOY corresponding x 2 experiments). The results showed that there was a significant difference between the trust level of these groups ($\chi^2(7) = 18.281$, $p = .011$), and the higher mean (58.10 vs 49.3, 45.63, 45.3, 41.45, 35.65, 33.40, 17.05) observed in the group of the participants who interacted with Nao and started its conversation without ST while showing SAD gestures. However, considering the donation amount, no significant difference was observed between these eight groups ($\chi^2(7) = 12.596$, $p = .083$).

In addition, considering the gender of the participants' we have 16 different groups composed of non-normal distributions. Applying a K-W test, the results indicated that there was a significant difference comparing the gender of the subjects regarding the embodiment ($\chi^2(15) = 27.529$, $p = .025$) with the higher mean obtained by the group of males in the condition NST_JOY interacting with the Nao (62.60). However, we did not found any significant difference between these 16 groups regarding the donations ($\chi^2(15) = 22.701$, $p = .091$).

5 Discussion

In the first experiment, comparing the subgroups, the only significant difference was found under the condition in which the robot did not start the interaction with ST (Sign test: $p = .001$). And the lower score in the post questionnaire means that subjects lost their initial trust after interacting with a robot that does not make any small talk. This finding highlights the importance of forming a social relationship before starting the interaction using small talks (H1).

Moreover, the results indicated that facial expression and ST significantly influence how people infer trustworthiness of a robot considering the whole four factors ($\chi^2(3) = 10.396$, $p = .015$). The higher mean of trust scores in case of ST_SAD shows that people tend to trust more on the robot under this situation. As we hypothesized, starting the conversation with ST together with showing sad facial expressions while telling a sad story enhances the trust level of people interacting with the robot (H1&H2).

Besides, a significant difference was found comparing the genders of the participants in the SAD condition ($\chi^2(3) = 10.033$, $p = .018$), which signifies that females and males react differently facing a robot expressing sadness (H3). The higher mean in case of females interacting with Emys representing SAD facial expressions and that started his conversation with ST approves all the hypotheses made (17.50 vs. 12.94 vs. 8.25 vs. 3.00).

Turning now to the donation factor, no significant difference was found among the four groups. To be more specific, we can not consider the amount of donated money as a discriminant of trust. We can argue that, in this experiment, people were not supposed to donate from their own budget and it was only fictional. However, if they were supposed to donate, those who had a higher level of trust in the robot might pay more than the others. However, potential biases of personal characteristics of the subject (e.g. their generosity) might influence the results in this case. Taking into account the influence of genders on the amount of donated money no significant difference was found either.

On the other hand, in the second experiment (with Nao) the results show that only in one scenario the trust scores differ significantly. To be more specific, under conditions of ST, NST and JOY, people perceived the robot similarly under different conditions. More specifically, in case of making a ST before starting the conversation, an U Mann-Whitney test shows that the distribution of the population are the same in both groups of SAD and JOY ($U(9) = 42.5, p = .571$). It means that the influence of emotional representation was not clear in this scenario. We argue that due to the ambiguity of the gestures, the participants could not perceive the robot's emotional state. More specifically, only one subject out of 10 found the robot a bit SAD. The others found him neutral or even joyful (the mean rank equals to 3.2, which 1 refers to very sad and 5 refers to very joyful). Similarly, in case of the NST scenario, the distribution of trust scores recorded in SAD and JOY is almost the same ($U(9) = 43.0, p = .596$). In this scenario, the average perceived emotion rank equals to 2.9. Hence, we argue that people could not clearly differentiate between the gestures and did not perceive emotional status well. Further, in case of participants interacting with the robot with JOY gestures, no significant difference found whether the conversation was started with ST or not ($U(9) = 40.5, p = .472$). In this case, difficulties in the perception of the utterances might have influenced adversely the results. More specifically, the mean rank of the utterances perception which equals to 2.14 (where a score of five signifies understanding completely) endorses this fact. However, in case of SAD the mean rank of the utterances perception was equal under two groups of SAD and JOY. Hence, people did not face difficulties in understanding the robot's utterances.

If we now turn to multivariate analysis, no significant difference was found comparing the two conditions (ST and emotional representation) together. We argue that this counter-intuitive observation might be caused by the fact that people had difficulties in understanding the utterances as well as the gestures. To be more specific, we investigated these two factors by evaluating two specific questions in a Likert scale (Did you have any problem in perceiving Nao utterances? And Nao gestures, how do you define it?). The scores revealed that only 3 people out of 20 were able to understand the robot completely. More interestingly, under SAD condition, people perceived the robot to be joyful rather than sad. Hence, although embodiment may influence the trust, facial expression plays a substantial role on it.

Considering the participants' genders, no significant differences were found and we argue that this happened due to Nao's specifications which has a neutral appearance. In addition, in our setup it was equipped with a childish voice, not carrying any gender.

Turning now to the Donation amounts, unlike the first experiment, in the second experiment, a significant difference was observed in the amount of donation. We argue that this might happen due to the robot's representation of its "malfunctioning" (Fig. 1). In other words, the "malfunctioning" of the robot is more clear in Nao comparing to Emys. More specifically, Nao's problem was observable during the whole interaction, on the contrary Emys' problem was shown by popping out the eye only once and in a specific part of the story. So, the scenario is more believable in experiment 2. Further, we measured this aspect in the questionnaire in a Likert scale (Did the appearance of Nao influence on your donation?). The results show that under this category, the robot induced higher influence on the subjects; which again endorses the higher trustworthiness under this situation.

More interestingly, considering the gender differences of the participants (H3), there is a significant difference between the eight groups and the higher mean observed in group of males under the condition of NST_SAD. This observation endorses the results reported in [18].

Finally, as showed in the results section, embodiment influences significantly the level of trust in subjects (H4). And the higher mean (62.83 vs. 57.19) in the second experiment proves that Nao with a physical embodiment could gain higher levels of trust. Besides, measuring the results according with genders, we found a significant difference with a higher average (71.21) in the condition with ST_SAD in the female group to the Emys interaction.

6 Conclusion and Future Work

The trust level differed significantly in experiment 1, which endorses the influence of ST (H1). Moreover, the results indicate that starting the conversation with ST while showing a sad facial expression enhances the trust level of people interacting with the robot (H2). Also, we can conclude females and males react differently facing a robot expressing sadness. The higher mean in case of females interacting with Emys representing SAD facial expressions and that started his conversation with ST approves the third hypothesis (H3). Finally, as showed in the results section, embodiment influences significantly the level of trust in subjects (H4). And the higher mean (62.83 vs. 57.19) in the second experiment proves that Nao with a physical embodiment could gain higher levels of trust. Finally, in the second experiment, the donation scores differed significantly among the four groups, which endorses the credibility of the fault in the second experiment. Furthermore, the trust scores differed significantly in case of embodiment.

So, we conclude that the four conditions influence significantly the way people infer trustworthiness of social robots. However, despite the promising result, future steps are still required. The first and foremost is increasing the sample size to increase more reliable results in subgroup analysis and balance the number of participants between the genders. Furthermore, in the next implementations the perception of robots' utterances should be checked more carefully and we intend to make the facial expression and gestures more natural and believable.

Acknowledgment. This work was supported by national funds through Fundação para a Ciência e a Tecnologia (FCT) with references UID/CEC/50021/2019 and SFRH/BD/118006/2016, through the project AMIGOS (PTDC/EEISII/7174/2014), and the project RAGE funded by the EU under the H2020-ICT-2014-1 program with grant agreement No 644187. We would like to acknowledge the CNPq (201833/2014-0) and UERN-Brazil.

References

1. Deutsch, M.: Cooperation and trust: Some theoretical notes. Nebraska, pp. 275–318 (1962)
2. Kollock, P.: The emergence of exchange structures: an experimental study of uncertainty, commitment, and trust. Am. J. Sociol. **100**(2), 313–345 (1994)
3. Wagner, A.R.: The Role of Trust and Relationships in Human-Robot Social Interaction. Ph.D. dissertation (2009)
4. Breazeal, C.: Social robots for health applications. in Annual International Conference of the IEEE Engineering in Medicine and Biology Society, pp. 5368–5371. IEEE (2011)
5. Broadbent, E., Stafford, R., MacDonald, B.: Acceptance of healthcare robots for the older population: review and future directions. Int. J. Soc. Robot. **1**(4), 319–330 (2009). https://doi.org/10.1007/s12369-009-0030-6
6. Lee, J.J., Knox, W.B., Wormwood, J.B., Breazeal, C., DeSteno, D.: Computationally modeling interpersonal trust. Front. Psychol. **4**, 893 (2013)
7. Hancock, P.A., Billings, D.R., Schaefer, K.E., Chen, J.Y., De Visser, E.J., Parasuraman, R.: A meta-analysis of factors affecting trust in human-robot interaction. Hum. Factors **53**(5), 517–527 (2011)
8. Ahmad, W., Nooraishya, W., Ali, N.M.: A study on persuasive technologies: the relationship between user emotions, trust and persuasion. Int. J. Interact. Multimedia Artif. Intell. **5**(1), 57–61 (2018)
9. Cheng, X., Macaulay, L.: Exploring individual trust factors in computer mediated group collaboration: a case study approach. Group Decis. Negot. **23**(3), 533–560 (2014)
10. Freedy, A., DeVisser, E., Weltman, G., Coeyman, N.: Measurement of trust in human-robot collaboration. In: International Symposium on Collaborative Technologies and Systems 2007, CTS 2007, pp. 106–114 (2007)
11. Martelaro, N., Nneji, V.C., Ju, W., Hinds, P.: Tell me more: Designing HRI to encourage more trust, disclosure, and companionship. In: Eleventh ACM/IEEE International Conference on Human Robot Interaction, pp. 181–188. IEEE Press (2016)
12. Hancock, P.A., Billings, D.R., Schaefer, K.E.: Can you trust your robot? Ergon. Des. Q. Hum. Factors Appl. **19**(3), 24–29 (2011)
13. Ullrich, D., Diefenbach, S.: Truly social robots-understanding human-robot interaction from the perspective of social psychology. In: VISIGRAPP (2: HUCAPP), pp. 39–45 (2017)
14. van den Brule, R., Dotsch, R., Bijlstra, G., Wigboldus, D.H.J., Haselager, P.: Do robot performance and behavioral style affect human trust? Int. J. Soc. Robot. **6**(4), 519–531 (2014)
15. Youssef, K., De Silva, P.R., Okada, M.: Exploring the four social bonds evolvement for an accompanying minimally designed robot. Social Robotics. LNCS (LNAI), vol. 9388, pp. 337–347. Springer, Cham (2015). https://doi.org/10.1007/978-3-319-25554-5_34
16. Lazányi, K., Hajdu, B.: Trust in human-robot interactions. In: 2017 IEEE 14th International Scientific Conference on Informatics, pp. 216–220. IEEE (2017)

17. Paradeda, R., Hashemian, M., Guerra, C., Prada, R., Dias, J., Paiva, A.: Fides: how emotions and small talks may influence trust in an embodied vs. non-embodied robot (extended abstract). In: Proceedings of the 16th International Conference on Autonomous Agents and Multiagent Systems (AAMAS 2017), no. 16, São Paulo, Brazil, forthcoming (2017)
18. Heerink, M.: Exploring the influence of age, gender, education and computer experience on robot acceptance by older adults. In: Proceedings of the 6th International Conference on Human-robot Interaction, pp. 147–148. ACM (2011)
19. Schaefer, K.: The perception and measurement of human-robot trust (2013)

Knowledge Discovery and Business Intelligence

Using Neuroevolution for Predicting Mobile Marketing Conversion

Pedro José Pereira[1], Pedro Pinto[2], Rui Mendes[2], Paulo Cortez[1(✉)],
and Antoine Moreau[3]

[1] ALGORITMI Centre, Department of Information Systems, University of Minho,
4804-533 Guimarães, Portugal
`id6927@alunos.uminho.pt, pcortez@dsi.uminho.pt`
[2] ALGORITMI Centre, Department of Informatics, University of Minho,
4710-057 Braga, Portugal
`a71929@alunos.uminho.pt, rcm@di.uminho.pt`
[3] OLAmobile, Spinpark, 4805-017 Guimarães, Portugal
`antoine.moreau@olamobile.pt`

Abstract. This paper addresses user Conversion Rate (CVR) prediction within the context of Mobile Performance Marketing. Specifically, we
adapt two main neuroevolution methods: Neuroevolution of Augmenting
Topologies (NEAT) and Hypercube-based NEAT (HyperNEAT). First,
we discuss two mechanisms for increasing execution speed (parallelism
and data sampling); a strategy for preventing excessive network complexity with NEAT; and a rolling window scheme for performing an online
learning. Then, we present experimental results, using distinct datasets
and testing both offline and online learning environments.

Keywords: Marketing · Classification · Neuroevolution

1 Introduction

The massive usage of portable computing devices (e.g., tablet, smartphone)
increased the value of mobile markets, giving rise to Demand-Side Platforms
(DSPs). A DSP is a broker that matches users to advertisements and involves
users, publishers and advertisers. Publishers attract a vast audience of users,
which want to access a popular content web site (e.g., games or news portal).
The web site is funded by requiring users to click a dynamic ad link before
accessing the content. The goal of the DSP is to select the ad to be displayed
to the user. If there is a product or service acquisition (a conversion), then the
DSP automatically returns a portion of the advertiser profit to the publisher.

In this paper, we approach the Conversion Rate (CVR) task [5], aiming to
predict if a user will produce a conversion when seeing an ad. Such prediction is
a key tool to assist the DSP in better assigning ads to users. The CVR task has
been approached using several machine learning models, mostly linear models,
such as the linear Poisson regression [3] or Logistic Regression (LR) [5]. More

© Springer Nature Switzerland AG 2019
P. Moura Oliveira et al. (Eds.): EPIA 2019, LNAI 11805, pp. 373–384, 2019.
https://doi.org/10.1007/978-3-030-30244-3_31

sophisticated methods, such as Gradient Boosting Decision Trees [16], Random Forest [5], XGboost [11] or Deep Learning [15], have also been proposed.

This paper describes the implementation of a data-driven approach for CVR user prediction, with application to a real-world DSP, managed by Olamobile, which is a mobile marketing worldwide company. Specifically, we explore *neuroevolution* algorithms, which use Evolutionary Algorithms (EAs) to design and fit Artificial Neural Networks (ANNs). An important advantage of these methods is the ability to automatically optimize the topology and weights of the networks [7]. The automatic design of ANN is particularly valuable in this marketing domain, since data is created with high velocity and there are several dynamic changes (e.g., new campaigns, changes in online user buying behaviors). Thus, new data-driven models need to be constantly created, which is clearly facilitated by the usage of automatic data-driven model selection procedures. Within our knowledge, the application of neuroevolution to Mobile Performance Marketing is non-existent. Moreover, several related works tend to consider only prediction classification measures and not the computational effort. For example, the deep learning method used in [15] is much more complex than LR and the classification performance of the deep learning models only improved very slightly (e.g., 0.1% points) when compared with LR. Also, several related studies (e.g., [5,10,15,16]) only address static offline learning scenarios, with a single holdout train and test split.

In this paper, we adapt and compare two neuroevolution algorithms for CVR prediction: NeuroEvolution of Augmenting Topologies (NEAT) [13] and Hypercube-based NEAT (HyperNEAT) [12]. We test the algorithms with two categorical data transforms, two traffic modes (TEST and BEST), and with static and dynamic environments, measuring the predictive classification performance and computational effort. This document is organized as follows: Sect. 2 presents the collected data and neuroevolution methods; Sect. 3 details the performed experiments and obtained results; finally, Sect. 4 describes the main conclusions.

2   Materials and Methods

2.1   Collected Data

The analyzed real-world DSP produces redirects and sales data events. Redirects are created each time a user clicks an ad, while a sale is produced when there is a product acquisition. CVR is modeled using binary classification. This task is complex since the DSP generates big data, with high volume and velocity properties. There are millions of redirects and thousands of sales per hour. Moreover, only a small fraction of redirects lead to sales. Also, only a partial set of characterization features are available due to privacy and technological constraints (e.g., it is not possible to identify a single user). And the nominal input features often present a high cardinality, with hundreds or thousands of distinct levels.

We had access to an Intel Xeon 1.70 GHz server with 56 cores and 2 TB of disk space, which is limited when compared with the DSP datacenter. Due to server limitations (e.g., storage, communication costs), we work with sampled data, retrieved from the DSP datacenter over a two-week period, from 2018-05-30 to 2018-06-13. The data includes redirects and sales related with two traffic modes: TEST and BEST. The former is used to test the performance for new incoming campaigns (20% of the traffic), while the latter includes only the best TEST performing campaigns (80%). The sampled data contains 484, 665 BEST mode observations, of which 156, 637 (32.3%) were sales, and the TEST dataset contains 319, 875 observations, of which only 29, 596 (9.25%) resulted in sales.

The collected eleven input features are summarized in Table 1, partially characterizing the advertiser, publisher and user. The table details the cardinality (number of levels) for each feature and traffic mode. The datasets contain two other attributes (not shown in the table): a time-stamp – when the sale or redirect occurred; and the target – binary variable with the sale (1) or no sale (0) label.

Table 1. Features.

Feature	Description	Cardinality		Examples
		BEST	TEST	
Campaign	Advertisement campaign	1389	1741	Numeric ID
Vertical	Advertisement type	5	4	Video, Mainstream
Application	Advertised product	1018	1101	Numeric ID
Partner	Publisher	167	200	Numeric ID
Account	Publisher type	8	9	Network, Developer
Manager	Publisher account manager	19	34	Numeric ID
Operator	User mobile carrier or WiFi	404	448	Vodafone, WiFi
Browser	User web browser	14	14	Chrome, Safari
Region	User region	23	23	Asia, South America
Country	User country	198	225	India, Brazil
City	User city	13423	10690	Dhaka, Sao Paulo

All features are nominal, including the numeric identifiers. Since the neural network base learner requires numeric inputs, we compare two feature handling modes: RAW and Inverse Document Frequency (IDF). RAW uses original numeric identifier raw values. For features that contain text, Raw Encoding (RAW) converts each category into a number $1..N$, where N is the cardinality of the feature, by order of appearance. The IDF encodes each level as $IDF(x) = ln(\frac{N}{f_x})$, where N is the total number of instances, and f_x is the number of occurrences of category x [2]. The levels are ranked according to their frequency, with values that are more frequent being closer to 0, and those that are less frequent ranging up to a maximum value of $ln(N)$, for $f_x = 1$. The transformations are performed using only training data, with an encoding mapping being stored in order to transform test data values. Any unseen input value is transformed in a special way, depending on the encoding: with RAW, it takes the value 0; and with IDF, it attains the maximum value $ln(N)$.

2.2 Neuroevolution Models

The predictive models employ an ANN trained by an EA, aiming to estimate the target probability: $p(1|\mathbf{x}) \in [0, 1]$, where $\mathbf{x}$ denotes the input vector for a particular redirect. Two neuroevolution algorithms are tested: NEAT [13] and HyperNEAT [12]. To implement the algorithms, we used the modern MultiNEAT library (http://multineat.com), which includes recent deep learning features, such as usage of the ReLU activation function [8] (see Table 2).

NEAT is a popular neuroevolution technique with three main characteristics: tracking of genes through historical markings; protection of innovation through speciation; and minimization of dimensionality through incremental growth from a minimal structure [13]. NEAT uses a direct encoding, where individuals contain every connection of the ANN. In contrast, HyperNEAT [12] uses an indirect encoding, allowing to evolve large-scale ANNs. In HyperNEAT, the individual is a Compositional Pattern-Producing Network (CPPN), an intermediate neural network which is used to generate the weights of the final network connections. The method requires a grid of nodes (neurons), called the *substrate*, to be previously defined by the user. Then, for each potential connection in the substrate, the CPPN takes as inputs the geometric positions of the two neurons and outputs the connection weight. A connection is not expressed if the magnitude of its weight is below a minimal threshold.

These neuroevolution methods share the same EA, which includes two phases in each generation: evolution and evaluation. The evolution uses the selection, crossover and mutation operators that are applied to generate a new population. The evaluation requires the highest computational effort and it is based on the Area Under the ROC Curve (AUC) of the Receiver Operating Characteristic (ROC) [6], computed using the ANN individual predictions.

To speed up the evaluation, two mechanisms were implemented: parallel evaluation of each individual of the population and sampling of the training data. Since the evaluation of each individual of the population is independent, each AUC calculation is executed as a parallel task that is run in a unique core. Moreover, the fitness computation is applied only to a random sample of data. We note that working with the full data would require a high computational effort and in particular a computational effort would be "wasted" to compute the fitness of very weak solutions. The sampling procedure works as follows: in every generation, a balanced sample (with both sale and no sale redirects) of a predefined size is randomly selected from the whole training dataset. All individuals are then evaluated over the same sample. Balanced sampling is used to avoid classifiers that are too biased towards the more prevalent "no sale" class.

The sampling calls into question which individual should be returned at the end of the execution, since the fitness scores represent the performance of individuals over a portion and not all of the training data. This issue is addressed by storing in memory the best individuals along the generations: the *elite*. When the termination criterion is met, an extra evaluation is performed over the elite using the whole training dataset, aiming to select the best ANN.

The sample size becomes an extra hyperparameter of the algorithm. The optimum sample size should be small enough to provide a fast execution speed, allowing for a high number of generations to be completed, but not so small that it hurts the algorithm capability of adjusting to the training data. The trade-off is shown in Fig. 1, where the two extremes on the low and high end of four predefined sample sizes provide the worst results. Note that, for a meaningful comparison, the execution time was the same for all sample sizes (total of 20 min).

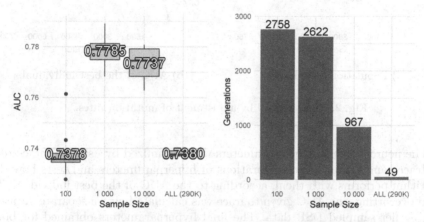

(a) Test AUC of best individuals (average of multiple runs).

(b) Average number of generations completed.

Fig. 1. Comparison of sample sizes.

There is a tendency for network complexity to increase with the number of generations. This growth is expected, and positive, as long as it leads to significantly better networks. However, this *bloat* phenomenon, if not controlled or limited, results in an ever increasing computational effort for both the evolutionary algorithm and the processing of network predictions (Fig. 2a). To limit bloat, we dynamically adjust the mutation rates for addition and removal of neurons and connections. This strategy works by introducing a simplification phase whenever the mean complexity of the population overcomes a predefined limit. During the simplification phase, the probability of mutations that add complexity (i.e., neurons or connections) is gradually decreased, while the probability of mutations that remove complexity is increased by the same amount. Once the complexity of the population is diminished, the simplification phase ends. And the default behaviour of the EA is resumed. We employ this strategy over NEAT, calling it NEAT Pruned (NEATP), with the simplification phase starting at 100 connections. A simplification strategy cannot be applied to HyperNEAT, because it uses an indirect encoding. A comparison between NEAT and NEATP is shown in Fig. 2, revealing that NEATP limits the network complexity with no significant impact on performance.

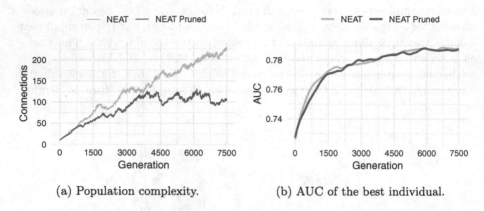

(a) Population complexity.   (b) AUC of the best individual.

Fig. 2. Bloat control by adjustment of mutation rates.

The neuroevolution hyperparameters were optimized by using the irace tool [9]. Irace samples various configurations of hyperparameters and tests how the algorithm performs with them, according to the AUC of the best individual. To avoid overfitting, the AUC given to irace was calculated over a separate dataset, with earlier sampled DSP data. The final hyperparameters obtained for both NEAT and HyperNEAT are shown in Table 2. We note that the sample size value of 2,000 is consistent with Fig. 1a results.

Table 2. Hyperparameters set using the irace tool.

Parameter	NEAT	Hyper-NEAT	Parameter	NEAT	Hyper-NEAT
Sample size	2 000	2 000	Add neuron rate	3.25%	8.04%
Substrate hidden layers	–	8	Remove neuron rate	2.30%	6.68%
Substrate neurons per layer	–	23	Add link rate	13.3%	9.56%
Population size	120	145	Remove link rate	9.1%	4.65%
Min species	6	4	Mutation weight rate	64.8%	64.6%
Max species	10	11	Mutation bias rate	6.7%	5.8%
Survival rate	66.8%	34.4%	Mutation activation rate	0.4%	0.6%
Crossover rate	89.0%	74.1%	Sigmoid neuron rate	33.4%	50%
Interspecies rate	0.25%	0.23%	Relu neuron rate	33.3%	0%
Mutation rate	34.8%	69.2%	Gaussian neuron rate	33.3%	0%
Elitism	2.5%	2.8%	Sine neuron rate	0%	50%

2.3 Evaluation

We test both static (offline) and dynamic (online learning) scenarios. We use the AUC classification metric [6], since it is a popular metric in CVR [5,15]. The AUC metric is independent of false positive and negative costs, which might not be known during the training phase; also, it is independent of the class distribution, thus it can be used with highly unbalanced tasks, such as the CVR data. The quality of a AUC value is often interpreted as: 0.5, the performance of a random classifier; 0.6 to 0.7, reasonable; 0.7 to 0.8, good; 0.8 to 0.9, very good; 0.9 to 1, excellent.

First, we compare NEAT, NEATP and HyperNEAT over the two types of numerical transformations (RAW and IDF) with static data, using a simpler holdout validation, in which the data is randomly split into train (70%) and test (30%) sets. The algorithms run for 10,000 generations, with 6 parallel processes being used for the evaluations. Then, we test a dynamic scenario by using a rolling window scheme [14]. In the first iteration, the last $W = 4$ days of data are used to fit the model, which is tested to predict the next $T = 1$ day events. After a predefined number of generations, there is a shift in time, which results in the second iteration. It is assumed that one day has passed, thus the training data slides $S = 1$ day. The neuroevolution population is continuously adjusted to the new training data and then predictions are computed for the next $T = 1$ day. And so on.

The continuous update of data requires the IDF transform to be updated after each rolling window iteration. The two inputs of IDF – f_x (frequency of category x) and N (size of the data sample) – are then calculated as a weighted average over time:

$$f_x^t = \lambda \cdot f_x^{t-1} + f_x^{new} \tag{1}$$

$$N^t = \lambda \cdot N^{t-1} + N^{new} \tag{2}$$

where the index t represents the rolling window iteration; f_x^{new} and N^{new} are the frequency of category x and size of the data sample over the latest window; and λ is a coefficient within the range $[0, 1]$ used to progressively "forget" information from past iterations. In this work, and after some experimentation with an older dataset (collected before 30th May of 2018), λ was set to 0.8.

3 Results

The progression of fitness along the generations is represented in Fig. 3, and a summary of the results obtained is given in Table 3. To establish a baseline, the performance of a Logistic Regression (LR) model is also presented, implemented using the Broyden-Fletcher-Goldfarb-Shanno (BFGS) offline learning algorithm of the **rminer** R package [4].

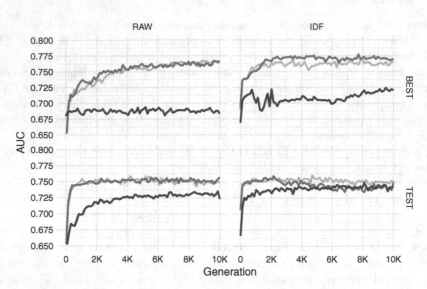

Fig. 3. Fitness of the best individual per generation with static data (top graphs are related with BEST traffic, while bottom plots consider TEST traffic).

Regarding the two numerical transformations, IDF presents a slight improvement over RAW in terms of the AUC metric for all BEST traffic cases and also HyperNEAT and TEST data. Focusing on the algorithms, it is clear that Hyper-NEAT does not perform as well as NEAT, which can be due to two reasons. First, HyperNEAT might be more suitable to problems with geometric relationships among inputs [12]. Second, results suggest that large-scale networks do not seem to significantly increase AUC, as evidenced by the similar performances of NEAT and NEATP. And HyperNEAT tends to evolve more complex networks when compared with NEAT. Overall, NEAT and NEATP yield the best results. In particular, NEATP successfully maintained the ANN complexity near the pre-defined limit of 100 connections without any significant decrease in AUC, which reflects in a shorter training time. When compared to the LR model, the neuroevolution algorithms present better predictive AUC results for BEST data (e.g., 0.78 versus 0.74) and a similar discrimination level for TEST mode data (AUC of 0.76).

We only compare the neuroevolution models in the dynamic rolling window scenario because the standard LR model only works in an offline learning scenario. The neuroevolution results are compared in Fig. 4, which plots the test AUC value of the best ANN per rolling window iteration; and in Table 4, as the median of all iterations.

Table 3. Results with static data (averaged over 10 runs).

Mode	Algorithm	AUC[a]		Time[b]		Complexity[c]	
		RAW	IDF	RAW	IDF	RAW	IDF
BEST	NEAT	**0.77**	**0.78**	81	107	$31 \cdot 54$	$40 \cdot 103$
	NEATP	**0.77**	**0.78**	81	85	**$29 \cdot 50$**	**$31 \cdot 50$**
	HyperNEAT	0.70	0.74	215	225	$184 \cdot 620$	$184 \cdot 355$
	LR	0.71	0.74	**0.15**	**0.15**	–	–
TEST	NEAT	**0.76**	**0.76**	94	157	$53 \cdot 139$	$79 \cdot 281$
	NEATP	**0.76**	**0.76**	88	100	**$41 \cdot 96$**	**$56 \cdot 109$**
	HyperNEAT	0.73	0.75	198	216	$184 \cdot 316$	$184 \cdot 643$
	LR	**0.76**	0.75	**0.15**	**0.15**	–	–

[a]Calculated over the test set.
[b]Total training time in minutes.
[c]Complexity (nodes · connections) of the returned network.

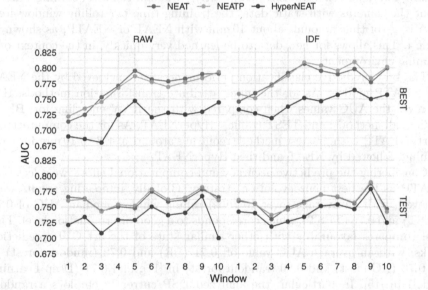

Fig. 4. AUC per rolling window iteration (top graphs are related with BEST traffic, while bottom plots consider TEST traffic).

The performance of the algorithms and numerical transformations with dynamic data is similar to their performance with static data. The highlight of these results, and focusing in particular in Fig. 4, is that the algorithms are capable of building upon previous training in order to adjust to new data, while maintaining a steady (TEST data) or even improved (BEST traffic) performance. Thus, it is possible to update the predictive model according to the latest set

Table 4. Results with dynamic data (median of 10 rolling window iterations and averaged over 10 runs).

Mode	Algorithm	AUC		Time		Complexity	
		RAW	IDF	RAW	IDF	RAW	IDF
BEST	NEAT	**0.78**	**0.79**	**8**	11	23 · 60	29 · 124
	NEATP	**0.78**	**0.79**	**8**	9	**19 · 57**	**22 · 65**
	HyperNEAT	0.73	0.75	21	23	184 · 315	184 · 691
TEST	NEAT	**0.76**	**0.76**	9	14	24 · 89	38 · 156
	NEATP	**0.76**	**0.76**	**8**	10	**24 · 82**	**31 · 105**
	HyperNEAT	0.73	0.74	20	21	184 · 340	184 · 643

of data using a relatively small number of generations. In this case, the total of 10,000 generations is split over 10 rolling window iterations, each, therefore, running for 1,000 generations. Consequently, although the total training time is about the same as with static data, the training time per rolling window iteration is $\frac{1}{10}$ of that amount: about 10 min with NEAT or NEATP, as shown in Table 4. This allows for new data to be learned very quickly, in the context of a dynamic environment.

The best predictive classification performances were achieved by the NEAT and NEATP models. As for the input attribute transformation methods, IDF improves the AUC values when compared with the RAW encoding for: BEST traffic – all methods; and TEST traffic – HyperNEAT. As for the computational effort, NEATP is the fastest method, requiring around just 8 to 10 min for each training, followed by NEAT and then HyperNEAT.

Considering the predictive accuracy and computational effort, we select IDF NEATP as the best neuroevolution strategy. Globally, interesting results were achieved, with an average (over 10 runs) rolling window median AUC of 0.79 (BEST) and 0.76 (TEST), which corresponds to a good discrimination level. This level compares favourably with other similar state of the art CVR prediction works, with an average AUC value of: 0.71 (LR) and 0.72 (random forest) in [5]; 0.76 (XGboost) and 0.80 (random forest) in [11]; and 0.71 (Deep Learning model) in [15]. In particular, the analyzed DSP currently employs a random user to advertisement matching when working with the TEST mode traffic, which corresponds to an AUC of 0.5. The NEATP classification performance is 26% points better when compared with the random DSP assignment for new marketing campaigns. Also, NEATP can handle big data and produce daily predictions in real-time.

4   Conclusions

In this paper, we address user mobile marketing CVR prediction. As a case study, we had access to recent big data gathered from a real-world DSP company. We particularly focus on neuroevolution models, which present the advantage of automatically designing the ANN topology and weights. We compared two neuroevolution algorithms that automatically design ANN for CVR prediction: NEAT and HyperNEAT. NEAT uses a direct encoding, while HyperNEAT employs an indirect encoding. We also compared two categorical to numerical transformations and two learning scenarios: static (offline) and dynamic (online). The prediction models were compared using both predictive classification performance and computational effort.

Considering the classification performance, computational effort and bloat, the best results were obtained by the NEATP model (a NEAT variant that limits the ANN growth). It produces better classification discrimination results when compared with HyperNEAT and an offline Logistic Regression (LR) in the static experiments. Also, it produces a steady or improved performance in the dynamic experiments, comparing favourably against HyperNEAT. Overall, a good classification discrimination level was obtained, resulting in a Area Under the ROC Curve (AUC) of 0.79 for BEST and 0.76 for TEST traffic. Moreover, under the tested experimental setup, NEATP requires a training time around 10 min, allowing its daily usage to perform real-time predictions. This model is particularly valuable for the TEST traffic, since the analyzed DSP uses a random selection of advertisements for new incoming TEST campains, which corresponds to an AUC of 0.5.

As future work, we wish to compare the proposed neuroevolution approaches with deep learning methods (e.g., Deep Feedforward Neural Network), using both classification performance and computational effort measures. Also, we intend to extend the proposed neuroevolution methods by exploring the use of a local search, based on gradient descent (e.g., backpropagation), to further tune the ANN connection weights. In particular, we aim to explore in the dynamic DSP learning what is the best mixed global and local search strategy: if the improved connections should be encoded back into the EA chromosomes (Lamarckian evolution) or not (Baldwin effect) [1].

Acknowledgements. This article is a result of the project NORTE-01-0247-FEDER-017497, supported by Norte Portugal Regional Operational Programme (NORTE 2020), under the PORTUGAL 2020 Partnership Agreement, through the European Regional Development Fund (ERDF). This work was also supported by FCT – Fundação para a Ciência e Tecnologia within the Project Scope: UID/CEC/00319/2019.

References

1. Bereta, M.: Baldwin effect and Lamarckian evolution in a memetic algorithm for Euclidean Steiner tree problem. Memetic Comput. **11**(1), 1–18 (2018)
2. Campos, G.O., et al.: On the evaluation of unsupervised outlier detection: measures, datasets, and an empirical study. Data Min. Knowl. Disc. **30**(4), 891–927 (2016)
3. Chen, Y., Pavlov, D., Canny, J.F.: Large-scale behavioral targeting. In: Proceedings of the 15th ACM SIGKDD International Conference on Knowledge Discovery and Data Mining, Paris, France, 28 June–1 July 2009, pp. 209–218 (2009). https://doi. org/10.1145/1557019.1557048
4. Cortez, P.: Data mining with neural networks and support vector machines using the R/rminer tool. In: Perner, P. (ed.) ICDM 2010. LNCS (LNAI), vol. 6171, pp. 572–583. Springer, Heidelberg (2010). https://doi.org/10.1007/978-3-642-14400-4_44
5. Du, M., Brorsson, M., Avenesov, T., State, R.: Behavior profiling for mobile advertising. In: Proceedings of the 3rd IEEE/ACM International Conference on Big Data Computing, Applications and Technologies, New Shanghai, China, pp. 302–307. ACM (2016)
6. Fawcett, T.: An introduction to ROC analysis. Pattern Recogn. Lett. **27**, 861–874 (2006)
7. Floreano, D., Dürr, P., Mattiussi, C.: Neuroevolution: from architectures to learning. Evol. Intel. **1**(1), 47–62 (2008)
8. Glorot, X., Bordes, A., Bengio, Y.: Deep sparse rectifier neural networks. In: Gordon, G.J., Dunson, D.B., Dudík, M. (eds.) Proceedings of the Fourteenth International Conference on Artificial Intelligence and Statistics, AISTATS 2011, Fort Lauderdale, USA, 11–13 April 2011. JMLR Proceedings, vol. 15, pp. 315–323. JMLR.org (2011). http://www.jmlr.org/proceedings/papers/v15/glorot11a/glorot11a.pdf
9. López-Ibáñez, M., Dubois-Lacoste, J., Cáceres, L.P., Birattari, M., Stützle, T.: The irace package: iterated racing for automatic algorithm configuration. Oper. Res. Perspect. **3**, 43–58 (2016)
10. Lu, Q., Pan, S., Wang, L., Pan, J., Wan, F., Yang, H.: A practical framework of conversion rate prediction for online display advertising. In: Proceedings of the ADKDD 2017, Halifax, Canada, p. 9. ACM (2017)
11. Matos, L., Cortez, P., Mendes, R., Moreau, A.: A comparison of data-driven approaches for mobile marketing user conversion prediction. In: Proceedings of the 9th IEEE International Conference on Intelligent Systems (IS 2018), Funchal, Madeira, Portugal. IEEE, September 2018
12. Stanley, K.O., D'Ambrosio, D.B., Gauci, J.: A hypercube-based encoding for evolving large-scale neural networks. Artif. Life **15**(2), 185–212 (2009)
13. Stanley, K.O., Miikkulainen, R.: Evolving neural networks through augmenting topologies. Evol. Comput. **10**(2), 99–127 (2002)
14. Tashman, L.: Out-of-sample tests of forecasting accuracy: an analysis and review. Int. Forecast. J. **16**(4), 437–450 (2000)
15. Zhang, W., Du, T., Wang, J.: Deep learning over multi-field categorical data. In: Ferro, N., et al. (eds.) ECIR 2016. LNCS, vol. 9626, pp. 45–57. Springer, Cham (2016). https://doi.org/10.1007/978-3-319-30671-1_4
16. Zhang, W., Yuan, S., Wang, J.: Real-time bidding benchmarking with iPinYou dataset. CoRR abs/1407.7073 (2014)

A Context-Aware Recommender Method Based on Text Mining

Camila Vaccari Sundermann[1]([⊠]), Renan de Pádua[1], Vítor Rodrigues Tonon[1],
Marcos Aurélio Domingues[2], and Solange Oliveira Rezende[1]

[1] Institute of Mathematics and Computer Science - University of São Paulo,
Avenida Trabalhador São Carlense, 400, São Carlos, SP 13566-590, Brazil
{camilavs,padua,vitor.tonon,solange}@icmc.usp.br
[2] Department of Informatics, State University of Maringá,
Avenida Colombo, 5790, Maringá, PR 87020-900, Brazil
madomingues@uem.br

Abstract. A recommender system is an information filtering technology that can be used to recommend items that may be of interest to users. In their traditional form, recommender systems do not consider information that might enrich the recommendation process, as contextual information. In this way, we have the context-aware recommender systems that consider contextual information to generate the recommendations. Reviews can provide relevant information that can be used by recommender systems, including the contextual one. Thus, in this paper, we propose a context-aware recommender method based on text mining (**CARM-TM**) that includes two context extraction techniques: (1) $CIET.5_{embed}$, a technique based on word embeddings; and (2) *RulesContext*, a technique based on association rules. For this work, **CARM-TM** makes use of context by running the CAMF algorithm, a context-aware recommender system based on matrix factorization. To evaluate our method, we compare it against the MF algorithm, an uncontextual recommender system based on matrix factorization. The evaluation showed that our method presented better results than the MF algorithm in most cases.

Keywords: Context-aware recommender systems · Text mining ·
Association rules · Word embedding · Matrix factorization

1 Introduction

A recommender system is an information filtering technology that can be used to predict ratings for items (like products, services, *etc.*) and/or generate a custom item ranking that may be of interest to the user [1]. In their traditional form, recommender systems consider only the items that users have accessed, bought or evaluated positively, thus ignoring any other information that might enrich the recommendation process. One type of information that may enrich the process

P. Moura Oliveira et al. (Eds.): EPIA 2019, LNAI 11805, pp. 385–396, 2019.
https://doi.org/10.1007/978-3-030-30244-3_32

is contextual information. For example, when recommending a restaurant to a user, the system may consider the context "Day of the Week". At weekends the user may prefer snack bars while on other days he/she may prefer less caloric meals.

In this way, there are the context-aware recommender systems that, unlike traditional systems, also consider contextual information to generate the set of recommendations. The term "context" may assume different definitions depending on the area in which it is being used. In the area of recommender systems, the definition most used and adopted in our work was proposed by Dey [8]. According to this author, "Context is any information that can be used to characterize the situation of an entity. An entity is a person, place, or object that is considered relevant to the interaction between a user and an application, including the user and applications themselves."

Many authors have been working with new context-aware recommender algorithms. However, there is a lack of automatic techniques for extracting context. With the emergence of Web 2.0, users have enriched sites with contextual information through texts in social networks, comments and mainly through reviews. These reviews are usually in the form of textual comments, in which users explain why they liked or disliked an item based on their own experiences. According to Chen *et al.* [7], the incorporation of important information extracted from reviews can benefit the recommender systems, solving the sparse data and the cold-start problems. Reviews can provide relevant information that can be used by recommender systems, including the contextual one.

Thus, in this work, we propose a context-aware recommender method based on text mining (**CARM-TM**) that includes two context extraction techniques: (1) $CIET.5_{embed}$, a technique based on word embeddings; and (2) *RulesContext*, a technique based on association rules. **CARM-TM** makes use of context by running the CAMF algorithm, a context-aware recommender based on matrix factorization. To evaluate our method, we compare it against the MF algorithm, an uncontextual recommender system based on matrix factorization. The evaluation was conducted in a dataset of reviews from Yelp and showed that our method provided better results than the MF algorithm in most cases.

This paper is structured as follows: in Sect. 2, we describe some related works about context extraction based on text mining. In Sect. 3, we present our proposal, a context-aware recommender method based on text mining (**CARM-TM**). We evaluate and discuss the main findings in Sect. 4. Finally, in Sect. 5, we present conclusion and future work.

2   Related Work

In this section, we present some related works that extract context from reviews or from other textual sources.

Li et al. [14] investigated available restaurant reviews and four types of contextual information for a meal. They developed algorithms with existing natural language processing tools to extract these types of contextual information from restaurant reviews. Hariri et al. [9] obtained contextual information by mining hotel reviews written by users. Their approach is based on using a classifier which is trained by the description sample and their corresponding contexts.

In [3], Bauman and Tuzhilin presented a method to find relevant contextual information from reviews of users. In this method, the reviews are classified as "specifics" and "generics", and the context is extracted from the specific reviews by using two methods: "word-based" and "LDA-based". Chen and Chen [6] extracted contexts employing a keyword matching method.

Kim et al. [10] presented a recommendation system model called Convolutional Matrix Factorization (ConvMF). The model integrates convolutional neural networks into probabilistic matrix factorization in order to capture contextual information (adjacent words) of the documents. Sulthana and Ramasamy [15] proposed an Ontology and Context Based Recommendation System for the book domain that uses a Neuro-Fuzzy Classification approach.

In [16], we proposed the $CIET.5_{embed}$, a textual context extraction technique based on word embeddings model that was used with neighborhood-based contextual recommender systems. This technique is implemented in our **CARM-TM**, so it is detailed in Sect. 3.4. In addition, in this paper, we also propose for the **CARM-TM**, the *RulesContext* technique, that extracts association rules from user reviews and transforms them into contextual information to be used in recommender systems. In the next section, we present our context-aware recommender method (**CARM-TM**).

3 Context-Aware Recommender Method Based on Text Mining (CARM-TM)

In this work, we propose the **CARM-TM**, a context-aware recommender method that uses text mining techniques to extract contextual information from reviews to make recommendations. The CARM-TM, illustrated in Fig. 1, has 5 steps which are explained in the next subsections.

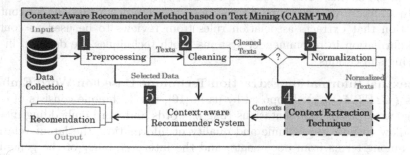

Fig. 1. Overview of the Context-Aware Recommender Method based on Text Mining (**CARM-TM**).

3.1   Step 1 - Preprocessing

The input of our method is a dataset, where which row contains a user identification, the identification of the item evaluated by the user together with the evaluation value, a textual content containing reviews/opinions about the item, and the date when the evaluation was made.

The step 1 is responsible for preparing the dataset for both the context extraction and the recommendation steps. In this step, the data are filtered, excluding those without textual content or other important information such as the user or item identification. In addition, users, items and reviews that are less relevant are excluded by using the exclusion criterias in [6]: (1) users with 1 review; (2) items with less than 15 reviews; and (3) reviews with less than 3 sentences. Besides filtering, we also create a file for each review.

3.2   Step 2 - Cleaning

In the step 2, the textual content goes through a cleaning in order to eliminate special characters such as @, *, # and &. These characters may negatively influence the context extraction process. Then, the cleaned texts can pass through a normalizer in the step 3 or they can be directly used by the context extraction technique (step 4).

3.3   Step 3 - Normalization

Normalization is optional and aims to solve problems commonly encountered in texts written by users, like typos, spelling mistakes, abbreviations, etc. In this work, we used the TextExpansion[1] tool to normalize the texts.

3.4   Step 4 - Context Extraction

The main step of our method is the fourth step, which consists of extracting contextual information from reviews. Here, we can adopt different text mining techniques. For this work, we use the $CIET.5_{embed}$ technique, proposed by us in [16]. In addition, we also propose the *RulesContext*, a new technique for context extraction that extracts association rules from reviews to be used as contextual information in recommender systems. Both techniques are detailed in the following subsections.

Contextual Information Extraction Technique Based on Word Embeddings ($CIET.5_{embed}$). Proposed by us in [16], this technique consists of combining two types of representations (bag of words and word embedding model) that allow to raise the volume and quality of information, the latent relationships among terms from documents, and the interpretability of the generated text representations. The $CIET.5_{embed}$ technique is composed of five complementary steps (Fig. 2), which aim to transform a set of text documents into a set of contextualized documents.

---

[1] http://lasid.sor.ufscar.br/expansion/static/index.html.

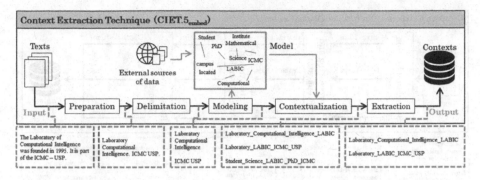

Fig. 2. Overview of the Context Extraction Technique $CIET.5_{embed}$. Adapted from Sundermann et al. [16].

In Fig. 2, the **Preparation** step sends all documents to a textual enrichment, which consists of named entity and concept recognition. In the **Delimitation** step, the documents already prepared are submitted to a process to delimit the textual scopes, like paragraphs and sentences. In the **Modeling**, a language model based on word embeddings, previously trained with external source of documents, is retrained with the internal documents. Then, we identify contexts in the internal documents (**Contextualization** step). The terms of each sentence are processed in the language model to find their most related terms, by using for example the cosine measure. Finally, in the step **Extraction**, the contexts are extracted from the documents by using a comparative threshold.

Contextual Information Extraction Technique Based on Association Rules (*RulesContext*). Proposed in this work, the *RulesContext* is a technique that extracts association rules from reviews and transform them into contextual information to be used in context-aware recommender systems.

Association rules are widely used in the literature to find correlation among items on a given database [2]. The association rules are presented on the format $LHS \rightarrow RHS$, where LHS stands for left hand side and RHS for right hand side, both of them contains a set of items such as $LHS \cap RHS = \emptyset$.

The *RulesContext* technique is executed in four steps, as illustrated in Fig. 3. In the step **Separation by item**, the texts are separated by item, i.e. subsets of texts are grouped for each item that can be recommended. Each subset is composed of the reviews' texts about the item.

In the second step (**Preprocessing and Preparation**), the texts are preprocessed, i.e. the stopwords are removed and the terms are stemmed. Besides, each subset of texts is transformed into a transaction.

In the third step (**Extraction of Association Rules**), we extract the association rules from each subset. To extract the rules, we use the algorithm apriori [2]. This algorithm extracts the rules in 2 steps by combining the items on a given dataset and calculating the measures support and confidence for each rule. After extracting the rules, we use the mutual information (MI) measure to evaluate

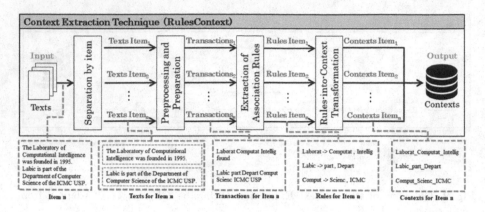

Fig. 3. Overview of the *RulesContext* technique.

them. The MI measures how dependent the items on the *LHS* and *RHS* are. The mutual information is presented in Eq. 1.

$$MI(LHS \rightarrow RHS) = Support(LHS \cup RHS)log(Lift(LHS \rightarrow RHS)). \quad (1)$$

After extracting the association rules, in the step four **Rules-into-Context Transformation**, the rules are transformed into contextual information as illustrated in Fig. 3.

3.5   Step 5 - Context-Aware Recommender Systems

In the fifth step of the **CARM-TM**, the contextual dataset generated by one of the previous Context Extraction Techniques is used as input by a **Context-Aware Recommender System**, together with the user and data items obtained in the Preprocessing. Contextual information is considered for recommendation according to the type of recommender system that is being used by the method. Latent factor models look for finding hidden features or patterns in the training data, also called factors, that are used to make the recommendations. Some of the most successful latent factor models are based upon matrix factorization techniques, such as the one presented by [11], which combines good accuracy and scalability. For this reason, in this paper, we use, as baseline, the matrix factorization algorithm (MF) [12], and as context-aware system, the context-aware matrix factorization algorithm (CAMF) [1].

According to Aggarwal [1], the recommendation training data consists of ratings given by users to sets of items, which are organized into the ratings matrix R. This matrix, given m users and n items, is of size $m \times n$ and the entry r_{x_i,y_j} corresponds to the rating given by user x_i to item y_j. The main purpose of matrix factorization is to decompose this matrix, R, into two approximate smaller matrices, X and Y, seeking to find k latent factors, which are hidden features or patterns in the training data, for the m users and the n items, respectively.

Considering that our purpose is to predict the unknown ratings in the matrix R, it is possible to use the inferred matrices X and Y to compute an approximate rating prediction. The predicted rating $\hat{r}_{x_i,y_j}$ is given by the cross-product of the user-factors vector and the item-factors vector, as shown in Eq. 2, such that x_i corresponds to the factors inferred for user x_i and y_j to the factors inferred for item y_j.

$$\hat{r}_{x_i,y_j} = x_i \cdot (y_j)^T \tag{2}$$

In order to obtain the factors vectors, the system should minimize Eq. 3, by using the training data (set S) and some optimization algorithm, such as *Stochastic Gradient Descent* [4] or *Alternating Least Squares* [13]. Regardless of the chosen algorithm, the parameters k and λ must be optimized. The first parameter corresponds to the number of latent features used to model the recommendation data. It is responsible for making the model simpler or more complex, depending on how much complexity is needed to capture all of the latent dimensions of the input data. The second parameter (λ) is used to weight the regularization constraint, in order to prevent overfitting. This algorithm is usually called MF, i.e. matrix factorization algorithm.

$$J = \sum_{(x_i,y_j)\in S} (r_{x_i,y_j} - x_i \cdot (y_j)^T)^2 + \lambda(\|x_i\|^2 + \|y_j\|^2) \tag{3}$$

Matrix factorization techniques are not exclusive to traditional recommender systems, Aggarwal [1] describes a method based on pairwise interactions that is suited to the context-aware recommendation task. The central idea in pairwise interaction algorithms is to decompose the ratings tensor R into n factor matrices, such that the first two correspond to users (U) and items (V) and the others correspond to the contextual variables (C_a, $1 \leq a \leq n - 2$). This new matrices are then used to make the rating prediction ($\hat{r}_{i,j,c_1\cdots,c_{n-2}}$) for user i, item j and contexts $c_1, \cdots c_{n-2}$, by multiplying them in a pairwise manner, as shown in Eq. 4.

$$\hat{r}_{i,j,c_1\cdots,c_{n-2}} = (UV^T)_{ij} + (UC_1^T)_{ic_1} + (UC_2^T)_{ic_2} + \cdots + (C_{n-3}C_{n-2}^T)_{c_{n-3}c_{n-2}} \tag{4}$$

In order to obtain this matrices, the following equation must be minimized (Eq. 5) using some optimization algorithm. The parameter λ is used for regularization purposes and the set S consists of specified ratings. This algorithm is called CAMF, i.e. context-aware matrix factorization algorithm

$$J = \sum_{(i,j,c_1\cdots,i_{n-2})\in S} (r_{i,j,c_1\cdots,c_{n-2}} - \hat{r}_{i,j,c_1\cdots,c_{n-2}})^2 + \lambda(\|U\|^2 + \|V\|^2 + \sum_{a=1}^{n-2} \|C_a\|^2) \tag{5}$$

The output of our context-aware recommender method is the recommendations generated by the context-aware recommender systems using the two types of context extracted by the $CIET.5_{embed}$ and the *RulesContext* techniques. In the next section we present the empirical evaluation conducted with our proposal.

4   Empirical Evaluation

For this work, we carried out two different evaluations. In the first one, we compare the CARM-TM method, with the $CIET.5_{embed}$ and the $RulesContext$ techniques, against the uncontextual MF algorithm (baseline). With this evaluation, we aimed to demonstrate the impact of the use of contextual information extracted by the $CIET.5_{embed}$ and $RulesContext$ techniques in the contextual CAMF recommender systems. Additionally, in the second evaluation, we use the CARM-TM method to compare the $CIET.5_{embed}$ against the $RulesContext$, in order to identify which contextual extraction technique provides the best recommendations.

4.1   Dataset

The dataset used in the empirical evaluation was the RecSys dataset for the recommender system challenge, ACM RecSysChallenge 2013, proposed to the customization of recommendations for Yelp[2] users. In the Yelp website the users can evaluate businesses through reviews. In these reviews, it is possible to evaluate the item by leaving a rating in the format of stars (from one to five stars). In addition, the user can write a text explaining his/her opinion about the establishment and the reason for which he/she gave a certain note. The RecSys dataset contains 11,537 items (businesses), 45,980 users and 229,901 reviews.

4.2   Experimental Setup

To measure the predictive ability of the recommender systems, we used the *All But One protocol* [5] with 10-fold cross validation, where the set of documents were partitioned into 10 subsets. For each fold, we used $n - 1$ of these subsets for training and the rest for testing. The training set T_r was used to build the recommendation model. For each user in the test set T_e, an item was hidden as a singleton set H, and the remaining items represent the set of observable items O used in the recommendation. Based on 10-fold cross validation, we computed *Mean Average Precision* for 10 recommendations ($MAP@10$) and to compare two recommendation algorithms, we applied the two-sided paired t-test with a 95% confidence level.

For the $CIET.5_{embed}$ technique, we considered the threshold values: 0.25, 0.50 and 1.0. The context sizes were 4 and 10 words. Altogether, we used 6 different configurations (3 threshold values × 2 context sizes). These values were adopted according to the best results obtained in our previous work [16].

Regarding the $RulesContext$ technique, we generated the association rules using a minimum support value equals to 10% and a confidence value equals to 50%. To select the most relevant rules, we used cut percentages of the MI measure equal to 50% and 75%. From the most relevant rules, we selected sets

---

[2] https://www.yelp.com.

with the top 5, 10 and 20 rules, totalling 6 combinations (2 MI values × 3 set sizes).

The MF and CAMF algorithms were executed 20 times, varying the values of k and λ (see Sect. 3.5). The used values were: $k = 5$, 10, 50 and 100; and $\lambda = 1$, 10, 100, 150 and 200.

4.3 Results

In this section, we first present the results of our proposal with the $CIET.5_{embed}$, and then, with the $RulesContext$ technique. Both against the baseline MF. In Tables 1 and 2, the values that are statistically significant (p-value > 0.05) are with an asterisk and the highest values are in boldface. At the end, we compare the results between the $CIET.5_{embed}$ and the $RulesContext$ techniques.

Table 1 presents the results of our proposal, with the $\boldsymbol{CIET.5_{embed}}$ **technique** and the CAMF algorithm, against the baseline MF. We refer to each contextual information as $Size\_Threshold$. For example, the type of context 4_025 represents the context with 4 words that were extracted considering the value of threshold 0.25. In Table 1, we can observe that, in general, the results were very satisfactory compared against the baseline MF. Contextual information 10_1 provided the best results. However, the context 10_025 presented the best value of $MAP@10$ for the parameters k equals to 5 and λ equals to 150. We must emphasize that this combination of parameters resulted the best results for these experiments in particular.

The results of our proposal, with the contexts extracted by the $\boldsymbol{RulesContext\ technique}$, are presented in Table 2. There, we refer to each contextual information as $MI\_NumberOfRules$. For example, the type of context 50_5 means the top 5 rules (contexts) extracted using the cut percentage of the MI measure equals to 50%. Again, the results were very satisfactory. We can observe that the contexts extracted with the cut of MI equals to 50% presented the best results in most of the cases, with the highest value of MAP being provided by the context 50_20.

Analyzing the parameters used in the experiments, we observed that for $CIET.5_{embed}$, the best result was obtained with a context size equals to 10 and a threshold equals to 25%. For the $RulesContext$ technique, the MI cut that generated the best results was 50%, that is, using a greater number of rules and selecting the best ones. Regarding the matrix factorization parameters, the best results were obtained with k equals to 5 and λ equals to 150, that is, a model with low complexity level and with a relatively high value of the parameter that controls overfitting.

Finally, we present in Fig. 4 the comparison between the $CIET.5_{embed}$ and the $RulesContext$ techniques. There, we compare the best $MAP@10$ (vertical axis) varying the values of λ and k (horizontal axis). In most cases, the $CIET.5_{embed}$ performed better than the $RulesContext$ technique. However, in two cases, 10_5 e 150_5, the $RulesContext$ technique was superior. In Fig. 4, we can also observe that our proposal with the context extraction techniques outperformed the baseline MF in all cases.

Table 1. Comparing the results ($MAP@10$) of our proposal, with the CAMF contextual recommender algorithm using contexts extracted by the $CIET.5_{embed}$ technique, against the results of the baseline MF.

Parameters		Baseline	4_025	4_05	4_1	10_025	10_05	10_1
λ	k							
1	5	0.001479	0.001436	0.001535	0.000929	0.001503	0.001929	**0.002839**
	10	0.001176	0.001400	0.001569	0.001431	0.001262	0.000925	**0.003606***
	50	0.001176	0.001039	0.001657	0.000769	0.001415	0.001334	**0.008186***
	100	0.001169	0.001137	0.001042	0.000530*	0.001536	0.000982	**0.008331***
10	5	0.001562	0.002907*	0.003969*	0.001780	0.003123*	0.003418*	**0.008163***
	10	0.001642	0.002767*	0.003391*	0.003526*	0.004016*	0.003400*	**0.007680***
	50	0.001454	0.003432*	0.004029*	0.001208*	0.003849*	0.003281*	**0.007949***
	100	0.001419	0.002211*	0.001940*	0.000658*	0.001517	0.001359	**0.008260***
100	5	0.001732	0.003986*	0.003637*	0.001923	0.003866*	0.003487*	**0.007935***
	10	0.001886	0.004396*	0.004920*	0.003619*	0.005861*	0.005805*	**0.008374***
	50	0.002022	0.003388*	0.004083*	0.002638*	0.004501*	0.005079*	**0.007971***
	100	0.001891	0.003191*	0.003044*	0.000670*	0.002738*	0.003062*	**0.008241***
150	5	0.001657	0.006773*	0.007885*	0.001967*	**0.009253***	0.008709*	0.008035*
	10	0.001856	0.004569*	0.003312*	0.003627*	0.005285*	0.005269*	**0.007744***
	50	0.001960	0.005775*	0.004491*	0.001452*	0.004570*	0.003758*	**0.008137***
	100	0.001881	0.002783*	0.002233	0.000712*	0.002502	0.002432	**0.008060***
200	5	0.003324	0.007404*	0.006192*	0.002068*	0.008022*	0.006149*	**0.008220***
	10	0.003112	0.003838*	0.003433	0.003883*	0.003373	0.004230*	**0.006908***
	50	0.002447	0.003543*	0.005781*	0.002908	0.004549*	0.006557*	**0.007958***
	100	0.002288	0.002955*	0.003190*	0.000650*	0.002636*	0.003126*	**0.008105***

Table 2. Comparing the results ($MAP@10$) of our proposal, with the CAMF contextual recommender algorithm using contexts extracted by the $RulesContext$ technique, against the results of the baseline MF.

Parameters		Baseline	50_5	50_10	50_20	75_5	75_10	75_20
λ	k							
1	5	0.001479	0.001641	**0.002433**	0.002041	0.001886	0.002178	0.001942
	10	0.001176	**0.002079***	0.001764*	0.001864	0.001581	0.001657	0.002057*
	50	0.001176	0.001614*	**0.002134***	0.001707	0.001471*	0.001984*	0.001924*
	100	0.001169	0.002140*	0.002098*	**0.002295***	0.001458	0.001529	0.001698
10	5	0.001562	0.008969*	0.011458*	**0.011627***	0.003281*	0.008474*	0.008162*
	10	0.001642	0.004001*	0.005019*	0.005521*	**0.006199***	0.004761*	0.003334*
	50	0.001454	**0.004025***	0.002828*	0.000944*	0.003475*	0.003618*	0.001911
	100	0.001419	**0.003026***	0.001507	0.001386	0.002332*	0.001502	0.001591
100	5	0.001732	0.001389	0.000890*	**0.003739***	0.002550	0.001661	0.001482
	10	0.001886	0.004898*	**0.007647***	0.007017*	0.003827*	0.004673*	0.005663*
	50	0.002022	0.007193*	0.007869*	0.008437*	0.005692*	0.009264*	**0.010544***
	100	0.001891	0.002361*	**0.002873***	0.001403*	0.001859	0.001420*	0.001496*
150	5	0.001657	**0.011691***	0.011434*	0.006454*	0.010267*	0.011105*	0.010705*
	10	0.001856	0.005591*	**0.005994***	0.005518*	0.003927*	0.003966*	0.004469*
	50	0.001960	0.001812	**0.002626***	0.002181	0.001459*	0.000776*	0.000517*
	100	0.001881	**0.002637***	0.002622*	0.001840*	0.001663*	0.001429*	0.001506
200	5	0.003324	0.001422*	0.001143*	**0.003600**	0.001795	0.001665*	0.001594*
	10	0.003112	0.005928*	**0.007412***	0.007184*	0.003948*	0.004515*	0.006337*
	50	0.002447	0.007175*	0.007511*	**0.011850***	0.005883*	0.002342	0.011005*
	100	0.002288	0.002799	**0.002874***	0.002874	0.001696	0.001375*	0.001661*

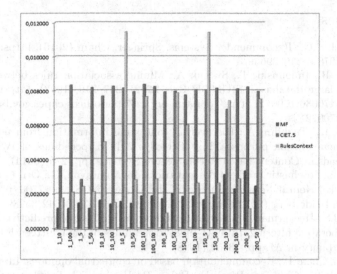

Fig. 4. Comparing the $MAP@10$ values between $CIET.5_{embed}$ and $RulesContext$ techniques.

5 Conclusion and Future Work

In this work, we proposed a context-aware recommender method based on text mining (**CARM-TM**). Our method uses the context extraction techniques $CIET.5_{embed}$, which is based on word embeddings; and $RulesContext$, which is based on association rules. For this work, our proposal used the CAMF contextual algorithm to generate the contextual recommendations.

The evaluation was conducted by using the Yelp dataset and the uncontextual MF algorithm as baseline. Our method provided better results than the baseline in all cases. Using the $CIET.5_{embed}$ technique, we obtained good results in most cases. However, the best $MAP@10$ value was provided using the context 50_10 extracted by the $RulesContext$ technique.

As future work, we will evaluate our proposal with other datasets and context-aware recommender systems. In addition, we will combine both context extraction techniques, $CIET.5_{embed}$ and $RulesContext$. We will also work on the proposal of a new method for context extraction by using opinion mining.

Acknowledgment. This study was financed in part by the Coordenação de Aperfeiçoamento de Pessoal de Nível Superior - Brasil (CAPES) - Finance Code 001, Conselho Nacional de Desenvolvimento Científico e Tecnológico - Brasil (CNPq) - grants #403648/2016-5 and #426663/2018-7, and Fundação Araucária de Apoio ao Desenvolvimento Científico e Tecnológico do Estado do Paraná - Brasil (FAPPR). The authors also would like to thank FAPESP (grant #2018/04651-0, São Paulo Research Foundation (FAPESP)).

References

1. Aggarwal, C.C.: Recommender Systems. Springer, Cham (2016). https://doi.org/10.1007/978-3-319-29659-3
2. Agrawal, R., Imieliński, T., Swami, A.: Mining association rules between sets of items in large databases. SIGMOD Rec. **22**(2), 207–216 (1993). https://doi.org/10.1145/170036.170072. http://doi-acm-org.ez67.periodicos.capes.gov.br/10.1145/170036.170072
3. Bauman, K., Tuzhilin, A.: Discovering contextual information from user reviews for recommendation purposes. In: CBRecSys 2014: Proceedings of Workshop on New Trends in Content-based Recommender Systems, pp. 2–9 (2014)
4. Bottou, L.: Stochastic gradient descent tricks. In: Montavon, G., Orr, G.B., Müller, K.-R. (eds.) Neural Networks: Tricks of the Trade. LNCS, vol. 7700, pp. 421–436. Springer, Heidelberg (2012). https://doi.org/10.1007/978-3-642-35289-8_25
5. Breese, J.S., Heckerman, D., Kadie, C.: Empirical analysis of predictive algorithms for collaborative filtering. In: UAI 1998: Proceedings of the Fourteenth Conference on Uncertainty in AI, pp. 43–52 (1998)
6. Chen, G., Chen, L.: Recommendation based on contextual opinions. In: Dimitrova, V., Kuflik, T., Chin, D., Ricci, F., Dolog, P., Houben, G.-J. (eds.) UMAP 2014. LNCS, vol. 8538, pp. 61–73. Springer, Cham (2014). https://doi.org/10.1007/978-3-319-08786-3_6
7. Chen, L., Chen, G., Wang, F.: Recommender systems based on user reviews: the state of the art. User Model. User-Adapt. Interact. **25**(2), 99–154 (2015)
8. Dey, A.K.: Understanding and using context. Person. Ubiquit. Comput. **5**(1), 4–7 (2001)
9. Hariri, N., Mobasher, B., Burke, R., Zheng, Y.: Context-aware recommendation based on review mining. In: ITWP 2011: Proceedings of the 9th Workshop on Intelligent Techniques for Web Personalization and Recommender Systems, pp. 30–36 (2011)
10. Kim, D., Park, C., Oh, J., Lee, S., Yu, H.: Convolutional matrix factorization for document context-aware recommendation. In: Proceedings of the 10th ACM Conference on Recommender Systems, RecSys 2016, pp. 233–240. ACM, New York (2016). https://doi.org/10.1145/2959100.2959165. http://doi-acm-org.ez67.periodicos.capes.gov.br/10.1145/2959100.2959165
11. Koren, Y.: Collaborative filtering with temporal dynamics. In: Proceedings of the 15th ACM SIGKDD International Conference on Knowledge Discovery and Data Mining, KDD 2009, pp. 447–456. ACM, New York (2009)
12. Koren, Y., Bell, R., Volinsky, C., et al.: Matrix factorization techniques for recommender systems. Computer **42**(8), 30–37 (2009)
13. Lawson, C.L., Hanson, R.J.: Solving Least Squares Problems, vol. 15. SIAM, Philadelphia (1995)
14. Li, Y., Nie, J., Zhang, Y.: Contextual recommendation based on text mining. In: COLING 2010: Proceedings of the 23rd International Conference on Computational Linguistics: Posters, pp. 692–700 (2010)
15. Sulthana, A.R., Ramasamy, S.: Ontology and context based recommendation system using neuro-fuzzy classification. Comput. Elect. Engin. (2018). https://doi.org/10.1016/j.compeleceng.2018.01.034. http://www.sciencedirect.com/science/article/pii/S0045790617337382
16. Sundermann, C., Antunes, J., Domingues, M., Rezende, S.: Exploration of word embedding model to improve context-aware recommender systems. In: 2018 IEEE/WIC/ACM International Conference on Web Intelligence (WI), pp. 383–388, December 2018. https://doi.org/10.1109/WI.2018.00-64

Extracting Actionable Knowledge to Increase Business Utility in Sport Services

Paulo Pinheiro[1] and Luís Cavique[2]

[1] Universidade Aberta and Cedis, Lisbon, Portugal
ppinheiro@cedis.pt
[2] MAS-BioISI, FCUL and Universidade Aberta, Lisbon, Portugal
luis.cavique@uab.pt

Abstract. The increase in retention of customer in gyms and health clubs is nowadays a challenge that requires concrete and personalized actions. Traditional data mining studies focused essentially on predictive analytics, neglecting the business domain. This work presents an actionable knowledge discovery system which uses the following pipeline (data collection, predictive model, loyalty actions). In the first step, it extracts and transforms existing real data from databases of the sports facilities. In a second step, predictive models are applied to identify user profiles more susceptible to dropout. Actionable rules are generated based on actionable attributes that should be avoided, in order to increase retention. Finally, in the third step, based on the previous actionable knowledge, experimental planning is carried out, with test and control groups, in order to find the best loyalty actions for customer retention. This document presents a simulation and the measure of the business utility of an actions sequence to avoid dropout.

Keywords: Sport services · Loyalty · Actionable knowledge · Business utility

1 Introduction

The promotion of physical activity as a means to prevent increasing rates of obesity and maintenance of well-being has provoked a proliferation of gyms and health clubs that compete with public sports facilities, and consequently there has been an increasing pressure on providers to maintain competitive advantage through services that provide higher levels of customer satisfaction (Howat and Assaker 2016). In a context of a great supply, the sports services sector is characterized by a high dropout rate (Avourdiadou and Theodorakis 2014), being the largest dropout in health clubs and gyms where the most promoted activity is fitness, than in sports facilities that have other facilities, namely swimming pools (Frota 2011).

Some gyms promote activities in which users subscribe continuously, becoming withdrawn when they fail to pay their monthly subscription or by the customer initiative. Other facilities work during sports seasons, and they need to encourage their users at the end of each season to renew their inscriptions for the following season. In both cases, with monthly subscription or seasonal subscription, the increase in retention

P. Moura Oliveira et al. (Eds.): EPIA 2019, LNAI 11805, pp. 397–409, 2019.
https://doi.org/10.1007/978-3-030-30244-3_33

is nowadays a challenge that requires concrete and personalized actions, in addition to generic actions to improve the quality of services and facilities.

The widespread use of ERP and access control systems by these sports facilities nowadays enables a collection of quality data that allow us to find and measure user preferences and behavior from admission to abandonment. We intend to use existing data from those systems to get actionable knowledge that allows the identification of users of regular sports services at risk of moving out and those who keep being loyal to the service. The use of machine learning techniques, namely with decision trees, are able to generate rules that allow to predict the change of behavior of the dropout group.

In this context, the concept of actionable knowledge can be successfully applied, since the goal is not focused only on the predictive algorithms but in solving business problems (Cao 2010).

We reuse some concepts of Database Marketing (Cavique 2006) and IDIC model, <Identify, Differentiate, Interact, Customize>, (Peppers and Rogers 2004) to obtain Actionable Knowledge. The proposed model, which includes the data preparation, the profile discovery using predictive models and the loyalty actions with evaluation, can be presented in the following data pipeline:

$$\text{Data Collection} \rightarrow \text{Predictive Model} \rightarrow \text{Loyalty Actions}$$

This work extends previous works where this pipeline was presented (Pinheiro and Cavique 2018; Pinheiro and Cavique 2019). These works fill a gap in the study of retention through the use of machine learning techniques in regular sports services. The novelty of this work includes not only the creation of knowledge rules, but also the simulation and the measure of the business utility of a sequence of actions to avoid dropout.

This document has the following structure. In Sect. 2, the related work in sports service retention and in actionable knowledge is presented. In Sect. 3, we present the proposed method in three steps: the data collection, the predictive model and finally the application of loyalty actions. In Sect. 4, the loyalty actions process is detailed regarding the business utility measure. Finally, in Sect. 5 we draw the conclusions of this work.

2 Related Work

2.1 Sports Service Retention

Frota (Frota 2011) says that 25% of withdrawals are motivated by club-related issues, of which 45% are recoverable; 22% are related to money, of which 31% are recoverable; 29% are related to situational problems, of which 44% are recoverable; and finally 24% leave for personal reasons, and the recovery of these is extremely difficult. Doing the calculation we can conclude that about 30% of the dropouts are recoverable. These recoveries can be made through the implementation of loyalty actions that are preferably carried out before the withdrawal takes place. The solution to the problem is to answer the following questions: who will be the target of these actions and what actions should be developed to avoid the dropout.

Gorgoglione (Gorgoglione 2011) identifies five possible approaches for the creation of personalized actions: the computational approach, the similarity approach, the bottom-up approach, the top-down approach and the personalized approach. The computational approach generates actions based on the profiles of clients, with no human intervention. The similarity based approach is used by recommendation systems and web content personalization methods; this type of approach assumes that actions are related to customer preferences, can be inferred through customer profiles, and it is assumed that similar customers behave similarly and similar actions cause similar reactions. The bottom-up approach includes the methods of knowledge discovery and is implemented in two separate steps: by creating customer profiles and deciding what actions are appropriate. The top-down approach consists in the same two steps of the bottom-up approach, but the decision on which actions to implement is taken before defining customer profiles. Finally, the personalized approach offers customers a number of different options, being at their discretion to choose which they prefer.

Once one tries to define profiles of behaviors that lead to abandonment, it is necessary to find characteristics or attributes that somehow allow to trace those profiles. Work related to retention in sports services (Avourdiadou and Theodorakis 2014; Howat and Assaker 2016; Surujlal and Dhurup 2012; Gonçalves 2012; Frota 2011) allows systematizing and identifying attributes necessary to characterize users and their behavior, both those who continue to use the services and those who leave.

In CRM applications, a decision tree can be built from a set of examples (customers) described by a rich set of attributes including customer personal information (such as name, gender, birthday), financial information (such as yearly income), family information (such as life style, number of children), and so on. Because decision trees can be converted to rules for explicit representation of the classification, one can easily obtain characteristics of customers belonging to a certain class (such as loyal customer or churner) (Yang et al. 2007).

2.2   Actionable Knowledge

Traditional data mining studies concentrated primarily on predictive mining, where the cause and effect scenario is described. But this information alone is not sufficient as it does not provide much benefit to the final user. What becomes more interesting and critical to organizations is to mine patterns in order to create knowledge actionable (Cao 2010).

As Yang et al. (2007) says a common problem in current applications of data mining, particularly in intelligent CRM, is that people tend to focus on, and be satisfied with, building up the models and interpreting them, but not to use them to get profit explicitly. More specifically, most data mining algorithms (predictive or supervised learning algorithms) only aim at the construction of customer profiles, which predicts the characteristics of customers of certain classes. This knowledge is useful but it does not directly benefit the enterprise. To improve customer relationship, the enterprise must know what actions to take to change customers from an undesired status (such as churner) to a desired one (such as loyal customers).

Knowledge is considered actionable if users can take direct actions based on such knowledge to their advantage. Actionability should be a criterion which can measure the utility of the mined patterns. Among the most important and distinctive actionable knowledge are actionable behavioral rules that can directly and explicitly suggest specific actions to take to influence (retain and encourage) the behavior of customers (Su et al. 2014).

To face the increasingly complex challenges of data mining in real-life world problems, Cao (Cao et al. 2007; Cao 2010) presents a new approach, which opposes data-driven to domain-driven. Data-driven corresponds to the traditional data mining, while domain-driven is related to the business domain, or business area. The domain-driven data mining (D^3M) close the gap between researchers and practitioners, by generating actionable knowledge for real user needs.

The D^3M evaluates a pattern (p) using the utility measure U(p) from both technical and business perspectives. U(p) is measured in terms of technical significance (technicalU(p)) and business utility (businessU(p)), i.e., U(p) = f(technicalU(p), businessU(p)).

An example of technical utility can be given by: accuracy = 87.90% and precision = 91.54%. While an example of business utility is, for instance, the average frequency in days and the average customer value in euros.

Table 1 presents eight different aspects of data-driven and domain-driven extracted from (Cao et al. 2007; Cao 2010). In domain-driven data mining the object mined is not only the data but the business domain, where the goal is to develop effective problem-solving and discover actionable knowledge to satisfy real users, by using real data and information related. D^3M is a multiple-step, iterative and interactive process, where the human cooperates, in a customizable environment, to provide actionable knowledge, which are evaluated in a trade-off between technical significance and business utility.

Table 1. Data-driven versus domain-driven

Aspects	Data-driven	Domain-driven
Object	Data tells the story	Data and business domain tell the story
Objective	Effective algorithms, discover knowledge of research interest	Effective problem-solving, discover actionable knowledge to satisfy real users
Data	Abstract, synthetic data	Real-life data and information related
Process	One step	Multiple-step, iterative and interactive
Mechanism	Automated	Human mining cooperation
Usability	Predefined models and process	Customizable models and process
Deliverable	Patterns	Actionable knowledge
Evaluation	Technical metrics	Trade-off between technical significance and business utility

3 Proposed Method

To better explain the developed work, we introduce the concept in three steps: the data collection, where the data is prepared and the attributes selected, the selection of dropout and loyalty rules with decision tree algorithm, and the creation of loyalty actions to prevent dropout.

3.1 Data Collection

Following the first step of the pipeline, we need to create a data warehouse to support the predictive model. This data warehouse should present a fact table with a set of suitable attributes. The selection of attributes must take into account the existence of factors with a greater or lesser impact on the retention of sports facilities and the possibility of being able to be extracted from the data registered in the databases of the ERP systems used by the sports facilities.

In order to develop the experiment and test the results, we used data from a Lisbon sports facility to which we applied the Extraction, Transformation and Loading (ETL) processes as explained in previous works (Pinheiro and Cavique 2018; Pinheiro and Cavique 2019). Since the performance of Machine Learning techniques is obtained through the manipulation of values (Gama et al. 2017), in addition to the attributes directly mapped from the source database, some attributes have been transformed, discretized through numeric-symbolic conversions, or created new attributes that derive from transformations made on the original data.

As so the ETL process resulted in the construction of a fact table in the data warehouse with 51 relevant attributes, although only 45 have valid data. These 51 attributes fit into the four groups:

(1) Demographic: e.g. age, gender;
(2) Frequency: e.g. number of days without attendance; frequency of classes;
(3) Service agreement: e.g. number of months of enrollment, number of renewals;
(4) Service quality: e.g. indications of satisfaction, net promoter score;

Relevant attributes, such as those related to the quality of the service were not filled due to lack of data.

One of the attributes in the fact table, the attribute 'withdrawal' is what characterizes the state of the user to date and therefore the predicted attribute (the target attribute). For practical reasons it was decided to define the attribute as a binary value, corresponding to a value of 1 for a quitter user, and a value of 0 to an active member.

After executing all ETL processes the fact table was populated with 8381 users as shown in Table 2.

Table 2. Number of users in data warehouse fact table

Users	In aquatic activities	In fitness activities	Total
Active	1226	803	1927
Dropouts	1697	4926	6454
Total	2923	5729	8381

3.2   Predictive Model

Since we intend to formulate a model or hypothesis capable of relating the values of the attributes in the fact table with the value of the target attribute, which is a nominal attribute, in practice we intend to construct a predictive model that is able to identify sets of characteristics that allow to rank a user against the level of their pre-dropout status.

To obtain the decision trees we use Microsoft Decision Trees algorithm available in Microsoft SQL Server Analysis Services Designer ver. 13.0.1701.8. This version uses a hybrid algorithm that incorporates different methods to create a tree. The algorithm offers three formulas for scoring information gain: Shannon's entropy, Bayesian network with K2 prior, and Bayesian network with a uniform Dirichlet distribution of priors (Microsoft 2017).

Since some attributes in the fact table result from different forms of classification or discretization of the same characteristic, the proposed models eventually use redundant attributes. Gama (Gama et al. 2017) states that since the process of constructing a tree selects the attributes to use, they result in models that tend to be quite robust in relation to the addition of irrelevant and redundant attributes. However, it is desirable to obtain models with significant predictive capacity and at the same time to obtain actionable profiles, so redundant attributes should be avoided.

After removing the redundant attributes, several adjustments were made to avoid overfitting. The resulting models correspond to shallow trees with leaves that always have a number of examples greater than 50. The evaluation metrics obtained with the Holdout method considering 70% of data for training and 30% for testing of the model are presented in Table 3.

Table 3. Evaluation metrics of Predictive Model with Holdout Method

#Nodes	Depth	Accuracy	Sensitivity	Specificity	Precision	F-Score
30	6	87.90%	92.69%	72.53%	91.54%	92.11%

In order to create loyalty actions specific attributes from the decision tree should be chosen to generate actionable knowledge. Some attributes cannot influence or be changed, such as the attribute 'age' or 'gender', denominated by 'non-actionable attributes'. On the other hand, customer retention strategies can change the content of some attributes that reflect user behavior. These attributes, that allows operational changes, are called 'actionable attributes'. An example of an actionable attribute is the number of 'days without frequency', since a strategy can be implemented that causes, at least to some users, to return to the sports facility, after some time without attending. Table 4 presents the actionable attributes selected by the decision tree whose metrics were presented in Table 3.

Table 4. Actionable attributes

Attribute	Description
X_1	Days without frequency
X_2	Aquatic activity attendance
X_3	Number of months of enrollment
X_4	Number of renewals
X_5	Weekly contracted frequency
X_6	Fitness activity attendance

Each branch of the decision tree forms a splitting rule, where each node includes an attribute used by the algorithm. In each leaf of the tree there are examples that correspond to users quitting and examples that correspond to active users. The relationship between these quantities defines the probability of withdrawal that we refer as dropout in Table 5.

Table 5. Actionable knowledge based on actionable rules

Actionable Rules	

Actionable rule A:
If
  X_1 (days without frequency) $\in$]30, 60] and
  X_4 (number of renewals) = 0
Then
  dropout = 99.29%
	Actionable rule B:
	If
	  X_1 (days without frequency) $\in$]60, ∞[and
	  X_3 (number of months of enrollment) $\notin$]12, ∞[
	Then
	  dropout = 98.15%

Actionable rule C:
If
  X_1 (days without frequency) $\in$]15, 30] and
  X_2 (aquatic activity attendance) = False
Then
  dropout = 96.47%
	Actionable rule D:
	If
	  X_1 (days without frequency) $\in$ [0, 7] and
	  X_2 (aquatic activity attendance) = False and
	  X_3 (number of months of enrollment) > 2 and
	  X_4 (number of renewals) = 0
	Then
	  dropout = 93.03%

Actionable rule E:
If
  X_1 (days without frequency) $\in$]30, 60] and
  X_4 (number of renewals) > 0
Then
  dropout = 92.84%	

Thus, it is possible to draw dropout profiles from the splitting rules on each leaf that shows a dropping rate above a considered threshold. These profiles allow us to segment users according to the criteria mentioned by Kotler (Kotler and Keller 2009) which indicates that segmentation is only useful if the segments meet five criteria: they are measurable, substantial, accessible, differentiable and actionable.

Actionable knowledge is supported by splitting the tree in actionable rules which include the actionable attributes. Table 5 presents several actionable rules above the

90% threshold that should be taken into account. Each actionable rule contains actionable attributes with values that should be avoided.

Actionable rule A shows a user who does not visit the facilities between 31 to 60 days and never renewed. Actionable rule B shows a user profile who does not visit the facilities for more than 60 days and whose enrolment is inferior to 12 months. Actionable rule C shows a user who does not visit the facilities between 16 to 30 days and does not attend aquatic activities. Actionable rule D shows a user who does not visit the facilities in the last 7 days, does not attend aquatic activities, whose enrolment has more than two months and has never renewed subscription. Finally, actionable rule E shows a user who does not visit the facilities between 31 to 60 days and has already renewed at least once.

3.3   Loyalty Actions with Evaluation

The retention strategy includes a communication process in three stages, starting with a personalized e-mail send to the user, where the cost is practically zero, followed by the use of a SMS and finally a personal contact, creating a funnel workflow. It is expected that after sending each communication the behavior of part of the target users will change, so for this subset it will no longer be necessary to send them the following communications.

After defining the retention strategy, it is necessary to evaluate its effectiveness. The experiments are constructed through the implementation of A/B tests and evaluated through the chi-square method, which will allow computing a statistical conclusion. A/B tests manipulate a causal variable in order to determine the impact of the variable in two different groups of individuals, the test group and the control group. The groups are created by splitting randomly the users into two groups with same number of elements. In the test group the loyalty actions are applied, and in the control group the loyalty actions will not be applied.

The users who received the communication and return to attend the facilities are called 'recovered'. The recovered users allow evaluating the loyalty campaign impact in euros. This last estimation is used to measure the business utility we were looking for.

3.4   Discussion of the Proposed Method

The proposed framework presented in (Cavique 2006; Pinheiro and Cavique 2018; Pinheiro and Cavique 2019) works in a multiple-step pipeline, shown in Table 6, where the columns phase, outcome, evaluation and groups are presented. The column 'groups' is presented in order to clarify and differentiate groups that have similar names but different meanings.

In the data collection phase the outcome is a data warehouse that will be used in the following steps. In the predictive model phase actionable rules are generated, the evaluation is given by technical metrics as accuracy and the performance of the model is measured using training and test groups. Finally, in the loyalty actions phase the business utility is the outcome, measured in euros and the significance of the actions is measured using test and control group in an A/B test.

Table 6. Pipeline phases, outcomes, evaluation and groups

Pipeline phase	Outcome	Evaluation	Groups
1. Data collection	Data warehouse	–	–
2. Predictive model	Actionable knowledge	Accuracy	Training and test
3. Loyalty actions	Business utility	Euros	Test and control

This method corresponds to the domain-driven approach presented by Cao (Cao et al. 2007; Cao 2010), where the predictive model delivers business-friendly decision support actions reified in actionable knowledge rules and the evaluation includes the trade-off between technical significance and business utility.

4 Detailed View of the Loyalty Actions

In this section we propose to detail and evaluate the effectiveness of the proposed model according to the following hypotheses:

H_0: *After executing the loyalty actions, the number of dropouts is the same as if no loyalty actions had been taken;*
H_1: *After performing the loyalty actions, the number of dropouts is lower than if the loyalty actions had not been carried out;*

For this purpose, an interface was developed in Visual Studio to select the users according to the rules of the model in which they fit and apply changes in their attributes and status, in order to simulate reactions to loyalty actions.

With this tool, we use the users defined by Rule A and work with this subset of users through the entire simulation of the campaign. This subset represents a possible real case in which a leaf of the tree may contain some users who, although yet active, presents the profile of dropout, and should therefore be the target of the loyalty actions proposed for this profile. The subset is divided into a test and control group, where the first group has 594 users and the second 593, and both contain at the beginning 3 users who have not given up.

The simulation of the communication strategy occurs in different instants: t_1, t_2 and t_3, using e-mail, SMS and personal contacts respectively. We expect a recovery of 5% of the users of the test group after the first action, a recovery of 10% after the second action and 15% after the third action, obtaining a final recovery of approximately 30%, as referred by Frota (Frota 2011). Table 7 illustrates the experiment, where it was avoided the dropout of 177 users.

Table 7. Loyalty actions simulation with the users of rule A

Time	Loyalty action	Control group		Test group		
		# potential dropout	# of dropouts	# potential dropout	# of avoided dropouts	# of dropouts
t_1	Email	593	590	594	35	559
t_2	SMS	593	590	559	57	502
t_3	Personal contact	593	590	502	85	417
Total					177	

To evaluate the significance of A/B test a matrix with observed (O) and expected (E) users is defined, where t indicates users in test group, c defines users in control group, n defines non-dropout (or retained) users and d defines dropout users, as shown in Table 8.

Table 8. Observed and expected users

	Observed		Total	Expected	
	$O_t = 594$	$O_c = 593$	$T = 1187$	$E_t = 594$	$E_c = 593$
Retained	$On_t = 177$	$On_c = 3$	$N = 180$	$En_t = 90.29$	$En_c = 90.14$
Dropout	$Od_t = 417$	$Od_c = 590$	$D = 1007$	$Ed_t = 503.71$	$Ed_c = 502.86$

With the result obtained for chi-square ($\chi^2 = 197.539$) we can conclude, through the query of the distribution table, with one degree of freedom and a confidence level of 99%, that the loyalty actions carried out with the proposed campaign had the effect wanted.

In addition to the significance obtained through the A/B test, we also calculate the business utility expressed in euros. To obtain this value, we consider the average monthly cost for a regular inscription (38.07€) indicated by AGAP (AGAP 2017). For the number of users recovered from the experience, the business utility is 6,624.18€ for each month in which the recovered users maintained their registration.

In this document the result of the simulation goes beyond the significance of A/B test and the value of the business utility, which could be easily calculate given the recovery rate of 30% (Frota 2011).

First of all, it is important to understand that 'triggered' users share behavioral similarities defined by sets of limited values in the actionable attributes given by the rules obtained from the predictive model, which allows directing perfectly personalized actions.

Secondly, actions were directed only to users of one of the rules with a threshold above 90% of withdrawals. Applying another actions to the other profiles defined by the other rules and according to their actionable attributes the business utility will be higher.

Finally, the simulated reaction to the actions carried out on the users in rule A was to consider that the users returned to attend the sports facilities. Thus, in the 174 users retrieved, where before the attribute $X_1 \in] 30, 60]$, was changed to $X_1 \in [00, 07]$. By recycling the predictive model after this simulation a new set of actionable rules could be generated as presented in Table 9.

Table 9. Actionable knowledge in the second loyalty campaign

Actionable Rules	

Actionable rule A:
If
  X_1 (days without frequency) $\in]30, 60]$ and
  X_4 (number of renewals) = 0
Then
  dropout = 99.71%
	Actionable rule B:
	If
	  X_1 (days without frequency) $\in]60, \infty[$ and
	  X_3 (number of months of enrollment) $\notin]12, \infty[$
	Then
	  dropout = 98.42%

Actionable rule C:
If
  X_1 (days without frequency) $\in]30, 60]$ and
  X_2 (aquatic activity attendance) = False and
  X_4 (number of renewals) > 0
Then
  dropout = 97.18%
	Actionable rule D:
	If
	  X_1 (days without frequency) $\in]15, 30]$ and
	  X_6 (fitness activity attendance) = False
	Then
	  dropout = 96.34%

The observation of the Table 9 allows us to verify that the rules with a threshold of more than 90% have been reduced to 4, with two remaining, and two emerging rules that have a threshold of withdrawal above 90%. The first of the rules that remained, rule A, is the rule on which the loyalty actions were applied, and now presents a higher level of dropouts and a lower number of users, since the recovered ones have come to be considered by other rules.

With the recovery of users by changing the attribute X_1, changes would be expected at the level of the whole predictive model, which is why new rules with withdrawal limits higher than 90% appear, and new attributes, like X_6, 'fitness activities attendance', are considered. That is why the recycle of the predictive model should only take place after complete the cycle of the loyalty actions to avoid concept drift during the campaign. However, it is desirable that the predictive model be recycled after completing the campaign so that it adapts to the new data, discovering new actionable attributes and generating new rules if appropriate.

5 Conclusions

In a context of great supply in health clubs and gyms, the sports services sector is characterized by a high dropout rate. The increase in retention of customer is nowadays a challenge that requires concrete and personalized actions. Most of data mining techniques achieve interesting patterns for churning. However, the implementation in real scenarios is still in development.

We reuse the data pipeline presented in (Cavique 2006; Pinheiro and Cavique 2018; Pinheiro and Cavique 2019) with three steps: data collection, predictive model and loyalty actions. This data pipeline corresponds to the domain-driven approach presented by Cao (Cao et al. 2007; Cao 2010), where the predictive model delivers actionable knowledge and the loyalty actions return a business utility measure.

In the data collection phase, real data from databases of the sports facilities is used, containing information of more than 8,000 users with 51 attributes.

In the predictive model phase, actionable attributes are identified and actionable knowledge rules, extracted with the decision trees, with a dropout threshold above the 90%, are detailed.

In order to follow the simulation of the loyalty actions only one subset of users is created using the information of Actionable Rule A. The same subset was divided into test and control group, and A/B test was performed with success. This experiment allowed us to achieve a value for the business utility and to generate a set of actionable rules for the second loyalty campaign.

In this work data-driven approach was overcome and we believe domain-driven approach was reached with real actionable attributes, real actionable rules and a concrete business utility measure. It is not enough to have technical interesting and significant metrics. The real world requires a business utility, which can be easily justified and applied.

References

AGAP. Associação de empresas de ginásios e academias de Portugal, Barómetro 2017 (2017)
Avourdiadou, S., Theodorakis, N.D.: The development of loyalty among novice and experienced customers of sport and fitness centres. Sport Manag. Rev. 17(4), 419–431 (2014). https://doi.org/10.1016/j.smr.2014.02.001
Cao, L., Zhang, C.: The evolution of KDD: towards domain-driven data mining. Int. J. Pattern Recognit. Artif. Intell. 21, 677–692 (2007)
Cao, L.: Domain-driven data mining: challenges and prospects. IEEE Trans. Knowl. Data Eng. 22(6), 755–769 (2010). https://doi.org/10.1109/TKDE.2010.32
Cavique, L.: Relatório da Unidade Curricular de Database Marketing, 2005–2006. Escola Superior de Comunicação Social. Instituto Politécnico de Lisboa (2006). Unpublished
Frota, M.: Gestão da Retenção. In: Manual de Gestão de Ginásios e Health Clubs - Excelência no sector do Health & Fitness, pp. 103–148 (2011)
Gama, J., de Leon Carvalho, A.P., Faceli, K., Lorean, A.C., Oliveira, M.: Extração de Conhecimento de Dados (3a edição; E. Silabo, Ed.) (2017)
Gonçalves, C.: Variáveis Internas e Externas ao Indivíduo que influenciam o Comportamento de Retenção de Sócios no Fitness. PODIUM Sport Leisure Tourism Rev. 1(2), 28–58 (2012)
Gorgoglione, M., Panniello, U.: Beyond customer churn: generating personalized actions to retain customers in a retail bank by a recommender system approach. J. Intell. Learn. Syst. Appl. 03(02), 90–102 (2011). https://doi.org/10.4236/jilsa.2011.32011
Howat, G., Assaker, G.: Outcome quality in participant sport and recreation service quality models: empirical results from public aquatic centres in Australia. Sport Manag. Rev. 19(5), 520–535 (2016). https://doi.org/10.1016/j.smr.2016.04.002

Kotler, P., Keller, K.L.: Marketing management. In: Organization, 14th Editi, vol. 22 (2009). https://doi.org/10.1080/08911760903022556

Microsoft: Microsoft Decision Trees Algorithm Technical Reference (2017) https://docs. microsoft.com/en-us/sql/analysis-services/data-mining/microsoft-decision-trees-algorithm-technical-reference?view=sql-server-2014. Accessed 18 April 2019

Peppers, D., Rogers, M.: Managing Customer Relationships: A Strategic Framework. Wiley, Hoboken (2004). ISBN 047148590X

Pinheiro, P., Cavique, L.: Models for increasing retention in regular sports services: predictive analysis and loyalty actions (2018). https://doi.org/10.23919/CISTI.2018.8399160

Pinheiro, P., Cavique, L.: An actionable knowledge discovery system in regular sports services. In: Rocha, Á., Adeli, H., Reis, L., Costanzo, S. (eds.) New Knowledge in Information Systems and Technologies, vol. 931, pp. 461–471. Springer, Cham (2019). https://doi.org/10. 1007/978-3-030-16184-2_44

Su, P., Zhu, D., Zeng, D.: A new approach for resolving conflicts in actionable behavioral rules. Sci. World J. **2014**, 9 (2014). https://doi.org/10.1155/2014/530483. Article id 530483

Surujlal, J., Dhurup, M.: Establishing and maintaining customer relationships in commercial health and fitness centres in South Africa. Int. J. Trade Econ. Finance **3**(1), 14–18 (2012). https://doi.org/10.7763/IJTEF.2012.V3.165

Yang, Q., Yin, J., Ling, C., Pan, R.: Extracting actionable knowledge from decision trees. IEEE Trans. Knowl. Data Eng. **19**(1), 43–55 (2007). https://doi.org/10.1109/TKDE.2007.250584

Discovering Common Pathways
Across Users' Habits in Mobility Data

Thiago Andrade[1,2(✉)], Brais Cancela[1,3], and João Gama[1,2]

[1] INESC TEC, Porto, Portugal
thiago.a.silva@inesctec.pt
[2] University of Porto, Porto, Portugal
[3] Universidade da Coruña, A Coruña, Spain

Abstract. Different activities are performed by people during the day and many aspects of life are associated with places of human mobility patterns. Among those activities, there are some that are recurrent and demand displacement of the individual between regular places like going to work, going to school, going back home from wherever the individual is located. To accomplish these recurrent daily activities, people tend to follow regular paths with similar temporal and spatial characteristics. In this paper, we propose a method for discovering common pathways across users' habits. By using density-based clustering algorithms, we detect the users' most preferable locations and apply a Gaussian Mixture Model (GMM) over these locations to automatically separate the trajectories that follow patterns of days and hours, in order to discover the representations of individual's habits. Over the set of users' habits, we search for the trajectories that are more common among them by using the Longest Common Sub-sequence (LCSS) algorithm considering the distance that pairs of users travel on the same path. To evaluate the proposed method we use a real-world GPS dataset. The results show that the method is able to find common routes between users that have similar habits paving the way for future recommendation, prediction and carpooling research techniques.

Keywords: Habits · Longest Common Sub-sequence ·
Gaussian Mixture Model · Pattern · Mobility ·
Spatio-temporal clustering

1 Introduction

The first efforts to learn human mobility patterns were associated with classic social sciences back in the nineteenth century where sociologists proposed studies to measure the time people spend doing different activities throughout the day [18]. Nowadays, the pervasiveness of position-enabled personal devices also boosted new disciplines in the direction of studying the mobility behavior of individuals from mobility data [3,9]. According to a recent survey [18], the availability and scale of mobility data are expected to grow exponentially, as more and more physical objects will be connected to the Internet of Things (IoT).

© Springer Nature Switzerland AG 2019
P. Moura Oliveira et al. (Eds.): EPIA 2019, LNAI 11805, pp. 410–421, 2019.
https://doi.org/10.1007/978-3-030-30244-3_34

Several studies confirmed the intuition that human mobility is highly predictable, centered around a small number of base locations [6]. This opens a wide range of opportunities for more intelligent recommendations and support of routine activities. Still, empirical studies on individual mobility patterns are scarce. A review published by MIT Technology[1] reveals that the collection and analysis of information from simple cheap cellphones is able to give us very useful insights into how people behave and perform their mobility traces. A range of applications can leverage from the discovering of locations, similar users and their habits like recommender systems [27], location based advertising [14] and carpooling [19].

Longest common sub-sequences has been the aim of research in many different scenarios in computer science where pattern recognition, text analysis, speech identification and comparison between files and trajectories were improved. In the Biological field it is applied in comparison of genomics [22], rapid search in huge biological sequences [21] and re-sequencing strings [8].

In this paper, we propose a method for discovering common pathways across users' habits without any a priori or external knowledge. First, we perform density-based clustering for spatio-temporal data to obtain the places the user visits the most. Secondly, a Gaussian Mixture Model (GMM) is applied over the clustered origin x destination (OD) places to automatically separate the trajectories into habits. Finally, we apply a variation of the Longest Common Sub-sequence (LCSS) algorithm over the habits to find those trips that are more similar.

The following section presents the literature review and the most important related works. The remainder of the paper describes the methodology and the data set utilized to assert the validity of the method in Sect. 3, in Sect. 4 we discuss the experiments and results obtained. Finally, the conclusions and future work are presented in Sect. 5.

2   Related Work

In recent years, the interest in methods to analyze mobility data has grown and researchers have been applying data-mining techniques over many scenarios. In this section, we review some relevant works which leverage the information contained in these data for a multitude of different applications and show how it can be effectively used for understanding the human habits and mobility patterns.

Several methods based on density have been proposed in order to discover regions of interest although most of these methods are used to aggregate spatial point objects [4,10]. The semantic movement of trajectories was studied by [11]. In order to discover personalized visited-POIs, [16] proposed a method to estimate fine-grained and pre-defined locations. Identification of meaningful places and similar user profiles was studied in [1].

---

[1] http://www.technologyreview.com/featuredstory/513721/big-data-from-cheap-phones.

Many researchers are also interested in mobility patterns. Most location-based services provide recommendations based on a user's current location or a given route or destination. Even though there are indications that human movement is highly predictable, daily and weekly routines of individual users constitute a largely unexplored and unexploited area. The temporal character of human behavior is explored in [6]. Call Detail Record (CDR) data was used to identify weekly patterns of human mobility through mobile phone data in [17]. In [14], a methodology that analyzes user location information in order to identify users' habits is introduced by making use of clustering, sequential mining, and Apriori algorithms. In [15], a method for detecting regular behaviours of elderly people through the analysis of data from sensors disseminated in their home and detect some emerging pathologies is proposed. In [23] the authors proposed a framework for mining individual similarity based on long-term trajectory data.

In the longest common subsequence (LCSS) field, is worth to mention the work of [7] that propose a new spatial and temporal characterization of travel patterns in a traffic network using vehicle trajectories. A modified version of the LCSS algorithm which takes into account the better matches between the points of the trajectories getting a better alignment of the values is introduced.

3   Methodology

Some definitions must be set in order to understand better the concepts addressed in the methodology: A point is a triple of the form p = *(latitude, longitude, time)* that represents a latitude-longitude location and a time-stamp. A trajectory is sequence of ordered points triples $Tr = (p_1, p_2, \ldots, p_n)$ where p_i is a point and $p_1.time < p_2.time < \ldots < p_n.time$.

Other characteristics are also important to mention: Trajectories may have different lengths. As individuals tend to move accordingly to their needs and singularities (e.g., N and M can be different for $Tr_i = (p_1, p_2, ..., p_N)$ and $Tr_j = (p_1, p_2, ..., p_M)$). Trajectories may have different directions. In the context of individuals' movement, the direction of each trajectory is an important condition for the similarity of trajectories. As we propose study habits of users, two trajectories moving in opposite directions should be considered as different trajectories despite their close proximity to each other as they may represent different habits (e.g., going to work from home and going back home from work).

3.1   Dataset

Geolife Dataset. This GPS trajectory dataset was collected in (Microsoft Research Asia) Geolife project by 182 users in a period of over three years (from April 2007 to August 2012). The dataset contains 17,621 trajectories with a total distance of about 1, 2 million km and a total duration of 48,000+ h. These trajectories were recorded by different GPS loggers and GPS-phones, and have a variety of sampling rates. 91% of the trajectories are logged in a dense representation, e.g. every 1 to 5 s or every 5 to 10 m per point [25, 26, 28].

Preprocessing and Data Transformation. As we are dealing with movements and transitions, one need to derive new information from the original data to calculate key features such as time delta of the transitions, traveled distance between points, start and stop positions, time and day of the week, length and duration of a trajectory. In this work, we denote a new trajectory every time an individual stop moving or the time delta between points is more than 30 min.

3.2   Stay Points Detection

A Stay Point (SP) represents a geographic region in which an individual stays longer than a given time threshold θ within a distance threshold λ. The algorithm is a hybrid density and time-based proposed in [24]. It is denoted by a quadruple of the form $Sp = (latitude, longitude, time_{arrive}, time_{leave})$. For this experiment, we set the parameters distance threshold λ as 200 m and the time threshold θ to 20 min. The values were set based on similar studies from the literature [28]. An example of SP is shown in Fig. 1.

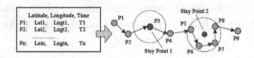

Fig. 1. GPS log and stay points [24]

3.3   Points of Interest (POI) and Meaningful Places

In human mobility data, usually, the last point of a trip is associated with a Point of Interest (POI) or Meaningful Place representing the place that the person visited. A POI is a geographical object that is interesting for a specific application and is usually associated with a community of users as it is of interest of many people. An example of POI is the Tsinghua University Northwest Campus which most of the users of this dataset have visited. More details about this in Subsection in 4.2. In contrast, a Meaningful Place (MP) is defined as a frequent location visited by an individual. This can be the user's home, a particular location like a parents' or friends' house. Taking into account we have the user's stay points, now we need to look for those places (stay points) a person visits repeatedly in order to form the so-called users' MPs which may or may not be a POI.

Location detection techniques (like identification of POIs and MPs) commonly make use of density-based methods. This is because the mechanism of density-based clustering is able to detect clusters of arbitrary shapes without specifying the number of the clusters in the data a priori and it is also tolerant of outliers (noise). For this, we apply the well know DBSCAN [5] algorithm.

3.4 Identification of Habits

According to Andrews B. from the Psychology field, a habit is a more or less fixed way of thinking, willing, or feeling acquired through previous repetition [2]. One important task to identify habits is to filter the data in order to maintain just trajectories which may represent some meaningful movements. So, we consider just trajectories with more than 50 points and 5 min of duration. We also filter out trajectories with more than 20 km of distance and 6 h of duration as these trajectories hardly will be part of an individual daily habit. In the end, users with less than 150 trajectories are also deleted as this is a too short amount of moves to represent habits.

Individuals have a remarkable propensity to return to their frequently visited places. Hence, the interactions between individuals and these places are likely to represent an individual's characteristics. After clustering the user SPs into MPs or POIs as described in Subsect. 3.3 we ended up with: trajectories not connecting MPs (those who start and end in places classified as noise), trajectories connecting one MP at the end or at the start and trajectories connecting two MPs. For the habits study purpose, we focus on the last item as we are interested in discovering frequent movements across meaningful places considering only the two locations that have at least 5 trajectories connecting them.

3.5 Gaussian Mixture Model to Classify the Different Habits

We can say that time is continuous and circular whereas the day of the week is a discrete ordered value. With daily users' habits it's not different. Based on that, our idea is to transform the start and end hour of each trajectory in a way that 23:55 and 00:05 are 10 minutes apart and may be part of the same habit. To tackle this issue we create two new features, deriving a sine and cosine transform from the start hour according to the formulas in Eqs. 1 and 2. Note that the value 86, 400 is related to the total number of seconds in a day (60 s * 60 min * 24 h).

$$StartHourSIN = SIN(2\pi * \text{``}HabitHourInSeconds\text{''}/86,400) \qquad (1)$$

$$StartHourCOS = COS(2\pi * \text{``}HabitHourInSeconds\text{''}/86,400) \qquad (2)$$

Even though the definition of a habit stated in Subsect. 3.4, the distribution of the habits data may be non-normal resulting in more than one peak along the day when dealing with individuals that use to go to a certain place in a non-strict way. Here we propose utilizing a Gaussian Mixture Model to handle these data and segment it into habits in a dynamic way following just the natural breaks of the data. Figure 2 shows the starting hours of a given user habit. One can notice that this user has 37 different starting hours for the same Origin × Destination pair depicted in Fig. 2(a) while is possible to verify the segmentation made by the multiple Gaussians in the start hour distribution in (c).

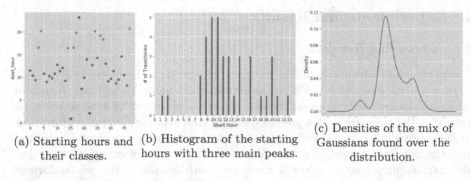

(a) Starting hours and their classes.

(b) Histogram of the starting hours with three main peaks.

(c) Densities of the mix of Gaussians found over the distribution.

Fig. 2. GMM model over the start hours of the trajectories. The blue dots on the top and the bottom of the left image represents the same class of trajectories that occur close to 23:00 pm and 02:00 am and the x axis represents the observations. (Color figure online)

3.6   Longest Common Sub-sequence to Discover Pathways

According to [13], the similarity of trajectories can be defined in various ways, e.g., origin-based, destination-based, OD pair-based, route-based. One way to identify this is to check if there is an overlap between two trajectories. Since the individuals' movements are constrained by the road network or sidewalks, portions of trajectories will be completely overlapping (at a macroscopic scale) if they traveled the same road/sidewalk section. The Longest Common Sub-sequence (LCSS) [20] is an algorithm for finding the longest common sub-sequence of two sequences. It was originally proposed in the field of string matching. Two strings with different lengths are given to find a set of characters that appear left-to-right, not necessarily consecutively, in both strings. This approach is more robust to noise and outliers than similar approaches like Dynamic Time Warping (DTW) [12] because not all points need to be matched.

Our idea is to use LCSS in two phases: first, one is at the individual level over the habits of many users that we found in Sect. 3.4 to get the most representative trajectories of the user. As mentioned before, an individual tends to follow similar routes to travel between locations (be it a POI or a MP). Thus, we count the hits a trajectory matches to others and select the top five trajectories for each habit of each user. In phase two, we iterate over all the users' most significant set of trajectories to find those pairs of trips that share the same pathway. For this study we consider a trajectory being similar to others when there is an overlap of more than 75% of the shortest trajectory. This value is set based on empirical evaluation of the most common paths as we intend to find the longest part of overlapping between two trips. As much as we decrease this value the number of common paths increases but the quality of matching paths decreases.

4   Experiments and Results

4.1   Clustering Results

One of the main advantages of density-based clustering techniques like DBSCAN
[5] over partition methods like KMeans is that it can identify and form clusters of
arbitrary shapes. Although user movements are constrained by road or sidewalk
networks, the trajectories can present dynamic and arbitrary shapes with respect
to the individuals' needs. Following this idea, we cluster the stay points and
find the most significant locations based on the frequency of visits/stops. For
illustration purposes, we select 5 users as a sub-sample of the whole dataset
to show the results regarding the clustering process. The results are shown in
Fig. 3. Each dot represents a MP or POI, the colors represent the users. We set
the DBSCAN parameters *MinPts* to 5 and the *eps* to 70 m.

Fig. 3. The top significant locations of the first 5 users of the dataset. Note that most
of locations are concentrated around the university campus. The colors represent the
users: red is the user 001, blue is the user 002, purple is the user 003, gray is the user
004 and yellow is the user 005. (Color figure online)

4.2   Habits Results

The knowledge discovery process over raw location data has led us to a panorama
of the mobility patterns of the given community. Main factors that characterize
habits are related to the start hour, length and duration of the trajectories that
follow an Origin × Destination pattern. Figure 4 shows the three different habits

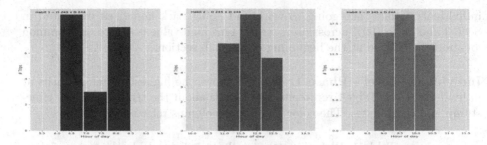

Fig. 4. Three main habits returned from the start hours connecting the top two locations of the user 004

returned from the Gaussians showed in Fig. 2 for the trajectories of the user connecting the two locations.

Another relevant way to analyze habits is looking for the day of the week a trip was taken. Routines are very common in human patterns and some of them may occur less often than the others. Playing football, going to the cinema, shopping at a supermarket are common examples of such situations. In Fig. 5 we show the distribution of the trips in a weekly view distributed by days.

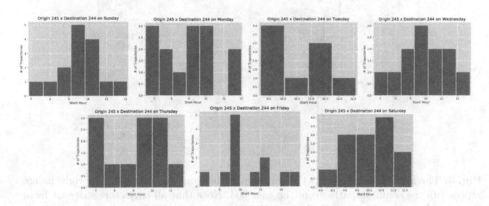

Fig. 5. Distribution of the trajectories according to the hour and day of week from the top two meaningful locations of the user 004

4.3   Common Pathways Results

Based on the characteristics of the dataset utilized for this study, is not a surprise that all of the users share at least one destination region, which is the University Campus. Many of them also share some student residences as similar POI. That said, we show the most common trajectories over a subset of 5 users that were found applying our method. Some trajectories share an overlap of 100% across individuals' habits (like going to work and going back home) as we stated in Sect. 3 and up to 100% across users' trips. This high value is due to the common locations mentioned at the beginning of this sub-section.

Individuals' Level - Phase 1. Figure 6 shows the highest matched paths at individuals' level. Table 1 represents the details about the trajectories like time-stamp and coordinates. The color and image columns refer to Fig. 6.

Table 1. Highest matched paths at individuals' level

Date	Origin coords	Destination coords	Color	Image	User
2008-11-01 09:25:00	39.99972, 116.32741	40.00765, 116.31969	Red	Left	003
2009-02-22 21:35:00	39.99991, 116.32747	40.01152, 116.32168	Blue	Left	003
2009-04-09 21:15:00	39.99995, 116.32735	40.00613, 116.32569	Red	Right	004
2008-12-04 08:25:00	39.99981, 116.32682	40.01069, 116.32206	Blue	Right	004

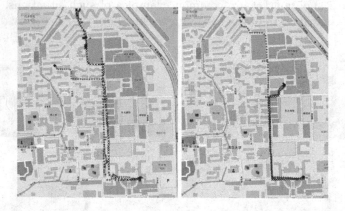

Fig. 6. The left image represents the common paths from the user 003. The right image represents the common paths from the user 004. Note that all trajectories depart from the same location *Tsinghua Park Aged University.*

Cross-Users Level - Phase 2. Figure 7, the left image shows the highest matched paths between the pair of users 005 and 003. The number of matched points is 74 having the user 003 the biggest trajectory sharing 81% of the total routes. The right image shows the highest matched paths between the pair of users 003 and 004. The number of matched points is 72 also having the user 003 the biggest trajectory sharing 81% of the total routes.

Table 2 represents the details about the trajectories of common paths across users like time-stamp and coordinates. The color and image columns refer to Fig. 7.

Table 2. Common paths across users habits

Date	Origin Coords	Destination coords	Color	Image	User
2008-12-05 06:20:00	39.99994, 116.32604	40.01071, 116.32179	Red	Left	005
2009-03-03 06:25:00	39.99998, 116.32739	40.01108, 116.32189	Blue	Left	003
2008-11-17 17:30:00	40.00735, 116.31998	39.99994, 116.32746	Red	Right	003
2009-07-06 02:05:00	40.00943, 116.32021	39.99984, 116.32740	Blue	Right	004

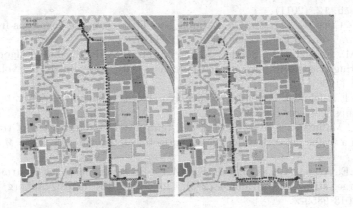

Fig. 7. The left image represents the common paths across the users 003 and 005. The right image represents the common paths from the users 003 and 004. Note that all trajectories depart from the same location *Tsinghua Park Aged University*.

5   Conclusions and Future Work

Although human nature seems to be random, the analysis of historical records of daily mobility data of the users shows a very high degree of predictability and recurrent actions characterized as habits. Following this idea, we show that most people have a relatively regular schedule and frequent routes when they travel from one location to another.

In this research, we present a method to process mobility data and discover the most frequent places an individual move between. We also present a Gaussian Mixture Model to find individual's habits combined with the Longest Common Sub-sequence algorithm to identify the most common pathways across the users' habits. The usefulness of the approach is shown in a real-world dataset from GPS records performed in Beijing/China demonstrating that is possible to reach a satisfactory level of knowledge over raw data.

For future work, we intend to propose a modification on the LCSS algorithm to obtain similar trajectories in a faster way and incorporate the time feature when comparing the pathways between user's habits. Map matching tasks including external information in order to find the semantic meaning of the individuals' trips and the collective points of interest or regions of interest also is on the list of intentions. We also consider extending the research to recommender systems and carpooling based on habits and places shared by similar individuals.

References

1. Andrade, T., Gama, J.: Identifying points of interest and similar individuals from raw GPS data. In: 5th EAI International Conference on Smart Cities within SmartCity 360° Summit - (Mobility IoT 2018) (2018)
2. Andrews, B.R.: Habit. Am. J. Psychol. **14**(2), 121–149 (1903). http://www.jstor.org/stable/1412711
3. Berry, D.M.: The computational turn: thinking about the digital humanities. Culture Mach. **12**, (2011)
4. Cao, X., Cong, G., Jensen, C.S.: Mining significant semantic locations from GPS data. Proc. VLDB Endowment **3**(1–2), 1009–1020 (2010)
5. Ester, M., Kriegel, H.P., Sander, J., Xu, X., et al.: A density-based algorithm for discovering clusters in large spatial databases with noise. In: KDD, vol. 96, pp. 226–231 (1996)
6. Herder, E., Siehndel, P.: Daily and weekly patterns in human mobility. In: UMAP Workshops, Citeseer (2012)
7. Kim, J., Mahmassani, H.S.: Spatial and temporal characterization of travel patterns in a traffic network using vehicle trajectories. Transp. Res. Proc. **9**, 164–184 (2015)
8. Kuo, C.E., Wang, Y.L., Liu, J.J., Ko, M.T.: Resequencing a set of strings based on a target string. Algorithmica **72**(2), 430–449 (2015). https://doi.org/10.1007/s00453-013-9859-z
9. Lazer, D., et al.: Computational social science. Science **323**(5915), 721–723 (2009)
10. Lee, I., Cai, G., Lee, K.: Mining points-of-interest association rules from geo-tagged photos. In: 2013 46th Hawaii International Conference on System Sciences, pp. 1580–1588. IEEE (2013)
11. Li, Q., Zheng, Y., Xie, X., Chen, Y., Liu, W., Ma, W.Y.: Mining user similarity based on location history. In: Proceedings of the 16th ACM SIGSPATIAL International Conference on Advances in Geographic Information Systems, p. 34. ACM (2008)
12. Rabiner, L., Juang, B.H.: Fundamentals of Speech Recognition. Prentice-Hall Inc., Upper Saddle River (1993)
13. Rinzivillo, S., Pedreschi, D., Nanni, M., Giannotti, F., Andrienko, N., Andrienko, G.: Visually driven analysis of movement data by progressive clustering. Inf. Vis. **7**(3), 225–239 (2008). https://doi.org/10.1057/palgrave.ivs.9500183
14. Sardianos, C., Varlamis, I., Bouras, G.: Extracting user habits from Google maps history logs. In: 2018 IEEE/ACM International Conference on Advances in Social Networks Analysis and Mining (ASONAM), pp. 690–697. IEEE (2018)
15. Soulas, J., Lenca, P., Thépaut, A.: Monitoring the habits of elderly people through data mining from home automation devices data. In: Correia, L., Reis, L.P., Cascalho, J. (eds.) EPIA 2013. LNCS (LNAI), vol. 8154, pp. 343–354. Springer, Heidelberg (2013). https://doi.org/10.1007/978-3-642-40669-0_30
16. Suzuki, J., Suhara, Y., Toda, H., Nishida, K.: Personalized visited-poi assignment to individual raw GPS trajectories. arXiv preprint arXiv:1901.06257 (2019)
17. Thuillier, E., Moalic, L., Lamrous, S., Caminada, A.: Clustering weekly patterns of human mobility through mobile phone data. IEEE Trans. Mob. Comput. **17**(4), 817–830 (2018)
18. Toch, E., Lerner, B., Ben-Zion, E., Ben-Gal, I.: Analyzing large-scale human mobility data: a survey of machine learning methods and applications. Knowl. Inf. Syst. **58**(3), 501–523 (2019)

19. Trasarti, R., Pinelli, F., Nanni, M., Giannotti, F.: Mining mobility user profiles for car pooling. In: Proceedings of the 17th ACM SIGKDD International Conference on Knowledge Discovery and Data Mining, KDD 2011, pp. 1190–1198. ACM, New York (2011). https://doi.org/10.1145/2020408.2020591

20. Vlachos, M., Gunopoulos, D., Kollios, G.: Discovering similar multidimensional trajectories. In: Proceedings of the 18th International Conference on Data Engineering, ICDE 2002, p. 673. IEEE Computer Society, Washington (2002). http://dl.acm.org/citation.cfm?id=876875.878994

21. Wandelt, S., Leser, U.: FRESCO: referential compression of highly similar sequences. IEEE/ACM Trans. Comput. Biol. Bioinf. **10**, 1275–1288 (2013). https://doi.org/10.1109/TCBB.2013.122

22. Xuan, Z., Wang, J., Zhang, M.Q.: Computational comparison of two mouse draft genomes and the human golden path. Genome Biol. **4**(1), R1 (2002). https://doi.org/10.1186/gb-2002-4-1-r1

23. Yang, M., Cheng, C., Chen, B.: Mining individual similarity by assessing interactions with personally significant places from GPS trajectories. ISPRS Int. J. Geo-Inf. **7**(3), 126 (2018)

24. Ye, Y., Zheng, Y., Chen, Y., Feng, J., Xie, X.: Mining individual life pattern based on location history. In: Tenth International Conference on Mobile Data Management: Systems, Services and Middleware, 2009, MDM 2009, pp. 1–10. IEEE (2009)

25. Zheng, Y., Li, Q., Chen, Y., Xie, X., Ma, W.Y.: Understanding mobility based on GPS data. In: Proceedings of the 10th International Conference on Ubiquitous Computing, pp. 312–321. ACM (2008)

26. Zheng, Y., Xie, X., Ma, W.Y.: GeoLife: a collaborative social networking service among user, location and trajectory. IEEE Data Eng. Bull. **33**(2), 32–39 (2010)

27. Zheng, Y., Zhang, L., Ma, Z., Xie, X., Ma, W.Y.: Recommending friends and locations based on individual location history. ACM Trans. Web (TWEB) **5**(1), 5 (2011)

28. Zheng, Y., Zhang, L., Xie, X., Ma, W.Y.: Mining interesting locations and travel sequences from GPS trajectories. In: Proceedings of the 18th International Conference on World Wide Web. pp. 791–800. ACM (2009)

Discovering Analytical Preferences
for Personalizing What-If Scenarios

Mariana Carvalho and Orlando Belo[(⊠)]

ALGORITMI R&D Centre, Department of Informatics, School of Engineering,
University of Minho, Campus de Gualtar, 4710-057 Braga, Portugal
obelo@di.uminho.pt

Abstract. In this paper, we expose a hybridization methodology for helping to overcome the pitfalls of conventional What-If analysis process design and development by discovering the best recommendations for What-If analysis scenarios' parameters using OLAP preferences. The hybridization process aims at assisting users during the decision-making processes by suggesting the most adequate scenario parameters according to their needs, making What-If scenarios more valuable, helping them during decision-making processes. The hybridization process provides several advantages to companies by making possible to study the behavior of a system without building it or creating the circumstances to make it happen in a business real-world system. Thus, knowing existing approaches for extracting preferences when dealing with OLAP application environments has clear business advantages. This work is about this, with a particular focus on discovering analytical preferences for personalizing What-If application scenarios.

Keywords: Business intelligence · What-If analysis ·
On-Line Analytical Processing · Usage preferences · OLAP personalization ·
Alloy formal specification

1 Introductions

The amount of data for analysis and the complexity of OLAP (On-Line Analytical Processing) queries for answering are two factors that can influence drastically querying time response. When the execution of a query takes more than a few minutes, the company productivity can be impaired. Therefore, knowing which data should be materialized is a relevant step during any analysis process [1]. The outcome of complex OLAP queries may be a huge volume of data, which may contain a low percentage of interesting information to the user. Due to large volumes of data, typical OLAP queries performed using OLAP operations – e.g. roll-up, drill-down, or slicing-and-dicing – can make data explorations a large burden or even impractical. Using personalization can help the user by assisting him during OLAP analysis by suggesting the next step or even by helping users to choose which information is the most interesting. Thus, integrating preferences can be valuable in OLAP analysis.

What-If analysis [2] allows for helping managers and executives, persuading completely decision-making processes. This decision method and technique permits the

P. Moura Oliveira et al. (Eds.): EPIA 2019, LNAI 11805, pp. 422–434, 2019.
https://doi.org/10.1007/978-3-030-30244-3_35

creation of hypothetical scenarios for inspecting the behavior of a complex system, by analyzing effects caused by changing a set of decision variables. A What-If analysis process starts with the intention of executives or managers to take future steps, which have some doubts or questions that need to have an answer for supporting a particular decision. Then, decision makers are responsible for creating hypothetical scenarios about the specific business situation for exploring and helping them to take business decisions. Running the simulation model enables the user to get a better understanding of the business and to explore different outcomes that are likely to occur under different scenarios.

The lack of expertise of a user during a What-If design and implementation is one of the pitfalls of the What-If analysis process itself. A user who is not familiar with the What-If process or even the business data, may not choose the most correct parameters in an application scenario, leading to poor results or inadequate outcomes. One possible way for solving this is integrating OLAP preferences [3] in the process. The extraction of OLAP preferences according to each analytic session promoted by a user may come as an advantage to decision-makers, since it provides a very effective way to personalize the outcome of queries of analytical sessions and multidimensional data structures acting as their decision-making support. OLAP preferences can recommend a set of related scenario parameters, introducing helpful and useful information to the application scenario under construction.

In this paper, we make a review of some of the most relevant OLAP personalization techniques for choosing the most adequate OLAP personalization technique to integrate in the conventional What-If analysis process with the goal to extract OLAP preferences. Overviewing OLAP personalization will help to provide the basis to choose the most acceptable way for extracting preferences in the hybridization process [4] we designed and developed. Additionally, we reinforced the characterization of the hybridization process providing a strong formal specification of the extraction of preferences phase using Alloy. The rest of the paper has the following organization: Sect. 2 presents a general overview of personalization systems, Sect. 3 exposes personalization in OLAP systems, and Sect. 4 reveals the specification of the extraction of preferences to validate the whole process. Finally, in Sect. 5, we conclude the paper presenting some conclusions and discussing some research lines for future work.

2 Personalization Systems

2.1 Using Personalization

Personalization (or recommender) systems are software tools and techniques to discover and recommend items that are more appropriate to a specific user. To do that, the system must be able to deduce what are the needs or requirements of the user. Recommendations help users for discovering what they are looking for, filtering and obtaining the best outcome based on their preferences, as for instance, likes, dislikes or orientation. In general, personalization systems help users to focus on the most interesting data.

Personalization systems are already widely used. These systems differ essentially on the approach chosen for discovering which will be the recommendations for the user [5–7], and can be organized in five large categories, namely:

(1) Content-based filtering – the content-based systems aim is to recommend items that are similar to items that a specific user has already expressed as interesting. Interesting information is stored in a user profile. The system analyses the description of those items, in order to determine the common preferences or set of features used to characterize the set of items. The personalization system is then responsible for interpreting the defined preferences, comparing them with unrated items and discovering which unrated items could be suggested as interesting to the user. The system opts to choose the unrated items that are similar to the ones on the user profile.

(2) Collaborative Filtering – these systems suggest recommendations to the user that are based on items that other users, who share similar interests considered interesting. More specifically, these systems aim to match the rating system for objects of a specific user with the rating system for objects of similar users, which means users that have similar interests or even characteristics, in order to produce recommendations for items not yet rated by the user. These systems use a mining classification algorithm that compares a user's profile with historical profiles of other users to identify which ones have similar tastes or interests.

(3) Knowledge-based – this recommender system offers items to users based on knowledge about the users, items and their relationship. These systems aim at recommending items to a user based on a specific knowledge domain about how a specific item is useful for a particular user. In other words, how the item features adapt or meet the users' needs or preferences.

(4) Hybrid Recommender Systems – this type of recommender systems is based on the combination of the above described systems. A hybrid system, for instance, combines a technique A with a technique B, and tries to use the advantages of the technique A to fix the disadvantages of the technique B.

(5) Computational intelligence-based – some recommendation tasks can be solved with the help of techniques developed in the field of computational intelligence, like data mining algorithms: clustering techniques, association rules, Bayesian techniques and artificial neural networks.

2.2   Personalization in OLAP

More recently, some personalization techniques have been developed in multidimensional databases context. Personalization and recommendation are used to make the OLAP experience less confusing to the user. The main goal is to help the user by orienting him/her during the OLAP session analysis when navigating huge amounts of multidimensional data.

The recommendations are made to guide the user through the OLAP session, by filtering the irrelevant results so that the user can focus on the most relevant data. OLAP personalization helps the user to deal with either too many or too few results, formulate a query corresponding to a specific objective that the user can't express or even to suggest new queries to pursue the navigation. To do this, the integration of preferences is useful. Preferences are used to get the irrelevant results filtered or even rank the results to get the most relevant first. The main goal of the use of personalization in an OLAP context is to ease the entire user experience. The personalization helps the user to get more refined information in its analysis, by delivering relevant information to the user. OLAP personalization can fit into each of the following approaches [8]:

- Query recommendation. The system recommends queries based on the current query and on information of past sessions. This approach aims essentially to help the user to navigate the cube by easing this process in an OLAP session analysis.
- Personalized visualization. The user specifies a set of constraints that are used to determine a preferred visualization.
- Result ranking. The system is responsible for ranking the results of a specific query. The ranking process consists of using a total or partial order to organize the data and display the most relevant data first.
- Query contextualization: based on a previous analysis of the context of the OLAP session, suggestions are made to the user to enhance the current query by adding context-based preferences predicates.

OLAP personalization and recommendation approaches can be categorized using the following criteria [9]:

- Formulation effort. This criterion refers essentially to the level of involvement of the user regarding the user preferences during OLAP sessions. In some approaches, the user needs for specifying manually his preferences, while in others, user preferences are inferred from the context of the analysis and the information of the user profile.
- Proactiveness. This criterion allows for evaluating how some approaches react during OLAP sessions. Suggesting new queries based on past navigation is an action of low proactiveness. Changing the current query or posting an outcome before returning them to the user is an example of an approach with increased proactiveness.
- Prescriptiveness. An approach with a high prescriptiveness uses profile elements as hard constraints, adding them to a query. On the other hand, an approach with a low prescriptiveness uses profile elements (preferences) as soft constraints, adding them to a query: tuples that satisfy as many profile criteria as possible are returned even if no tuples satisfy all of them.

Taking in consideration the above descriptions, the user's experience in an OLAP session can be improved by (i) decreasing the formulation effort by decreasing the user involvement in the definition of the preferences; (ii) increasing the proactiveness by limiting the interference of the user by changing the current queries and anticipating the query results; and (iii) providing low prescriptiveness by annotating queries with soft constraints. According to [10], the following topics describe the OLAP personalization types developed in the literature:

- The Dynamic personalization consists in creating an adapted OLAP cube during the execution time according to the needs and performed actions of the user approach [11].
- Visual personalization of an OLAP cube consists in easing the process of composing queries for the user in a database language, like SQL or MDX. An interface for formulating queries with graphical OLAP schema was provided by [12].
- In a User Session Analysis approach, the main goal is to recommend patterns detected in query logs of past OLAP sessions for helping users in a current session. The discovered information from past sessions delivered to the user aims to help the user navigate the cube, when facing the same unexpected data as the current sessions [13].
- In a User Preference Analysis approach, the recommendations suggested to the user are based on his preferences. User preferences can be inferred from context-based method of his OLAP session analysis and are used to help the user on further analysis. User preferences are stored in a user profile and ranked with a degree of importance, and in a posterior phase are used to generate recommendations - the recommendation with the highest degree of importance is displayed to the user [14].
- Preference Constructors. This approach consists of an algebra that allows for expressing preferences on queries. In other words, an algebra that allows for formulating preferences on attributes, measures and hierarchies. Preferences can be expressed on both categorical (attributes) and numerical (measures) domains and can be formulated on the aggregation level of data [3].

3   Extracting OLAP Preferences

Preferences [15] arise naturally on a daily basis. The definition of preference is quite common in our daily life, which means that people can intuitively express their preferences. When facing two objects, a person used to express his preferences in a declarative way. For example, someone can automatically say "I like A better than B", and this kind of interpretation of preferences is universally understood. All user preferences should be considered and fulfilled as much as possible. The system recommends to the user the most similar suggestion that fits best its preferences. Preferences can be modelled mostly using strict partial orders.

Performing OLAP Mining [16] is one of many ways we can use for extracting preferences. OLAP mining is a mechanism that integrates OLAP and data mining, which means that a data mining technique is applied to a part of the multidimensional structure containing historical data at different levels of abstraction. The choice of the data mining technique must be done according to the user's needs. Data mining aims to help for discovering non-trivial, unknown and interesting knowledge (or patterns) in the data stored in large historical databases.

OLAP mining techniques are very promising due to its characteristics. OLAP mining provides the user with the flexibility of choosing the desired mining function and the possibility of switching mining tasks dynamically and consequently ease the process of extracting and achieving the required outcome. Dealing with data mining, it is possible to work on consistent, integrated and cleaned data. If the user wants to improve the quality of data, he can perform some techniques of pre-processing data, like data cleaning or data integration. This pre-processing data step is essential for achieving the best data quality and consequently the better quality of the mining outcome. Finally, OLAP operations brings to OLAP mining the advantage of inter-active exploratory data analysis. Through the OLAP operations, roll-up, drill-down, slice and dice and pivoting, we have the ability to select portions of interesting data, analyzing data at different levels of abstraction and display knowledge in different formats.

Knowing beforehand what type of knowledge to extract from the data cube is quite a difficult task to the user. With the integration of OLAP and data mining, it is possible to interleave cubing and mining functions to perform flexible mining and discover interesting knowledge in data cubes in a highly interactive way:

- Cubing then mining. One can perform cubing operations to select the portion of the cubing to be mined and then apply a data mining technique. The data mining can be applied to any portions of the data cube.
- Mining then cubing. Data mining can be first performed on a data cube and then the result can be analyzed further by performing cubing operations.
- Cubing while mining. By performing cubing operations during mining, the mining operations can be performed at different abstraction levels or on any portion of the cube.
- Backtracking. It should be possible to backtrack one or more steps in the mining process so the user can explore alternative mining paths and ease the interactive mining process. By jumping back a few steps in the mining process, one can consider other mining operations and analyze the alternative results.
- Comparative mining. One should allow comparative data mining, which means, comparing alternative data mining processes. It should be possible to compare side by side the mining techniques results, efficiency and other aspects.

The known set of OLAP mining techniques were developed based on the traditional data mining methods. These OLAP mining techniques consist in including features from analytical processing into mining techniques, so they can be applied to multidi-mensional data structures. In [16] we found a definition of OLAP mining techniques, which characterize them in OLAP-based characterization, comparison, association, classification, or clustering analysis. Let see shortly each one of them.

Data Characterization is used to generalize a set of task-relevant data based on data generalization. This technique is used to extract different kinds of rules of the data cube. The application of this method leads to the extraction of set of characteristic rules that summarizes the set of general characteristics of a set of user-specified data. This technique is useful to characterize a target class, like, for example, frequent customers. It allows to define the characteristics of specific customers that can be summarized by a characteristic rule. The characterization technique can be integrated with OLAP tech-niques, such as drill-down (progressive deepening) and rollup (progressive general-ization). These operations help to discover the set of characteristics in different levels of abstraction. Progressive deepening (drill-down) starts with a high-level cuboid and then progressively specializes attributes to lower abstraction levels. This approach is considered to be the best one, since it starts by finding the general data characteristics at a high abstraction level, and then follows to interesting paths to drill down to specialized cases. This is the opposite of what happens with progressive generalization (roll-up), which, starting with a more conservative generalization process, first generalizes the data to a level higher than the existing in the primitive data cube.

Comparison is the second technique. It is used to mine the set of discriminant rules that summarize the general features of a target class in order to distinguish that class from other classes. For example, mining a discriminant rule that summarizes the characteristics of a customer to distinguish that one customer from others. This technique is similar to the OLAP-based characterization, described before. However, OLAP-based comparison uses comparative measures to be easier to distinguish classes. It is implemented as follows. The set of relevant data in the database is collected and partitioned into a target class and one or more other classes. Then, an attribute-oriented induction is performed on the target class to extract a main cuboid. Then the set of contrasting classes are generalized to the same level as those in the main cuboid, forming the main contrasting cuboid. Finally, the information contained in these two cuboids is used to generate quantitative and qualitative discriminant rules.

Next, we have association. It aims to extract, from a set of relevant data, a set of association rules at multiple levels of abstraction. Facing an OLAP environment, it is important to consider the dependencies between attributes within the same dimension and between dimensions. Therefore, there are two kinds of associations: inter-attribute association and intra-attribute association. The intra-attribute association is the association within one or a set of attributes formed by grouping of another set of attributes. On the other hand, inter-attribute association is the association among different attributes. Classification is the fourth technique, and it aims for analyzing a set of training data with a known class label and constructs a model for each class based on the data characteristics. A set of classification rules is generated and used to classify future and unknown data. There are many classification methods, the most used including decision tree methods, like ID-3 and C4.5 [17]. In an OLAP environment, the classification methods consist on four phases:

(i)   collecting the relevant data and partitioning the data into training and testing data sets;
(ii) analysing the relevance of the attributes in the training set, which is made by determining how much an attribute is relevant to the class attribute; a generalization operation is also performed at this phase, allowing to classify the objects in the different levels of abstraction;
(iii) applying the mining algorithm and creating the classification tree (also called decision tree);
(iv) testing the effectiveness of the created model using the testing data set.

Finally, the clustering technique consists in grouping a selected set of relevant data into a set of clusters. The clusters must ensure that the similarity between two different clusters is low and the similarity within the same cluster is high. The clustering process is based on a well-known mining method, the k-means algorithm. OLAP-based clustering is performed using a k-means based methods. This kind of methods is considered promising due to their efficiency in processing large data sets. However, they are limited to numeric data. To overcome this difficulty, a method was implemented to encode concept hierarchies. With this, it is possible, for the adapted methods, to deal with large data sets with both numeric and categorical attributes. OLAP-based clustering can also be applied at the different levels of abstraction.

4   The Process of Extracting Preferences

To check if the process of extraction of preferences in the hybridization process is free of defects or inconsistencies, we can run a formal specification [18] and create an abstract model using Alloy [19]. Alloy is a declarative specification language and can be checked using the Alloy Analyzer tool. The following descriptive abstract model describes the main steps of the extraction of preferences process: the OLAP mining process, i.e. the application of the mining algorithm to the cube structure, we chose the Apriori-based algorithm [20] for illustration purpose only. Based on this research, we can say that this algorithm is one of the most adequate for extracting preferences. First, in the abstract model, we need to specify the mining structure and mining model. These two elements support the mining association process and store the extracted association rules. The element *MiningStructure* defines the data from which mining models are built and the element *MiningModel* is created afterwards by applying the mining algorithm to the data cube.

```
one sig MiningStructure {
    model : one MiningModel}
one sig MiningModel {
    rules : set Rule,strongRules : set rules,
    preferences : set Preference}
```

This mining model stores the set of extracted association rules. Each rule denotes a logical implication: X → Y meaning that if X occurs, then it is likely that Y also occurs. The antecedent can be one or more fields and the consequent can only contain one field. For example, each rule can be either (Attribute × Attribute → Attribute) or (Attribute → Attribute). Also, each rule needs to be associated with a pair of performance measures (support (supp) and confidence (conf)). The performance measures help the user to identify the set of strong association rules.

```
sig Rule {
    is : some Field,o : one Field,
    performance : one Performance
}sig Performance {
    supp : Int, conf : Int}
{gte[conf,0] gte[supp,0]}
```

In the abstract model, we need to assure the creation of the all the possible combinations of valid rules. To do that we specify the element SubsetField, which consists on the representation of the powerset of all available fields.

```
sig SubsetFields {
    elems : set Field
} {all s : SubsetFields | s.@elems = elems => s = this}
```

To specify the set of extracted association rules, we define the *ConstructRules* predicate. This specification firstly assures that the cube is constructed and creates all the combination of rules using the available cube fields. To find all the available fields that are reachable within the data cube, we specify the function *related*. The predicate *ConstructRules* also guarantees that there are no duplicates in the returned set of created rules.

```
pred ConstructRules[c : OLAPCube, p : CubeParameters] {
    ConstructCube[c,p]
    all f : c.flds, s : SubsetFields | some s.elems &&
    s.elems in related[f,p] =>
        some r : c.struct.model.rules | r.o = f && r.is = s.elems
    all r : (c.struct.model.rules) {
        some f : c.flds | r.is in related[f,p]
        all r' : (c.struct.model.rules) - r | r.is != r'.is ||
    r.o != r'.o
    }}
fun related[f:Field,p:CubeParameters] : set Field {
    ((f.~fields&p.tabs).*(p.tabs<:related:>p.tabs)).fields - f}
```

Next, we specify the set of strong association rules. In our hybridization process, the set of recommendations are formed using the components of the strong association rules. An association rule that has performance measures values greater than or equal the defined performance measure threshold values is a strong association rule. To do this validation, we need to specify the element *PreferenceParameters*. This element contains the performance measures thresholds (conf and supp) and the information about the goal analysis attribute. The predicate *ConstructStrongRules* uses the *PreferenceParameters* to filter the rules, returning only rules that are strong rules and contain the goal analysis attribute. This will allow us to know which attributes are strongly related with the goal analysis attribute.

```
one sig PreferenceParameters {
    conf : one Int,supp : one Int,
    attr : one Attribute
} { gte[conf,0] gte[supp,0]}
pred ConstructStrongRules[c : OLAPCube, p:PreferenceParameters] {
    c.struct.model.strongRules = {r : c.struct.model.rules |
        p.attr in (r.is + r.o) && gte[r.performance.supp,p.supp] &&
gte[r.performance.conf,p.conf] }
}
```

Next, we specify the element *Preference* and the predicate *ConstructPreferences*, which creates the set of preferences that will be recommended to the user. This set of preferences is created by merging attributes of the resultant strong rules. A Preference is defined by a set of fields and a source strong rule. Preference generation is threefold, as we can see in the *ConstructPreferences* predicate.

```
sig Preference {
    atts : set Field,
    sourceRule : one Rule
}

pred ConstructPreferences [c : OLAPCube] {
    all p : c.struct.model.preferences | p.atts = p.sourceRule.(is+o)
    all  p1,p2  :  c.struct.model.preferences  |  p1.sourceRule  =
p2.sourceRule => p1 = p2
    c.struct.model.strongRules = c.struct.model.preferences.sourceRule
}
```

We use the Alloy analyser tool to run the specified the abstract model and get a valid and consistent instance. Figure 1 represents a consistent instance of the described formal model. In this instance, there were created two valid Rules (*Rule0* and *Rule1* in blue). The *Rule0* is defined as *Measure → Attribute0* and *Rule1* is defined as *Attribute1→ Attribute0*. The attributes and measure are represented by the yellow circles. As we can see the *PreferenceParameters* (in green) is composed by the *supp* = 0, *conf* = 6 and the goal analysis attribute is *Attribute1*. The *Rule1* is considered a strong association rule since its performance measures [*supp* = 5; *conf* = 6] (in *Performance* in black) are greater than the ones defined in the *PreferenceParameters* and the *Rule1* also contains the goal analysis attribute (*Attribute1*). The *Rule0* contains the same performance measures values than *Rule1*, but it does not contain the goal analysis attribute. In the end, the *Rule0* is discarded and the attributes of the strong association rule *Rule1* are used to form the preferences and suggest them to the user, in this case, *Attribute1* (the goal analysis attribute) and *Attribute0*.

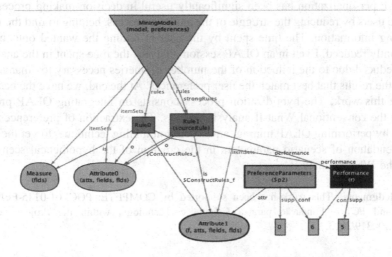

Fig. 1. A an example of a consistent instance obtained by the Alloy Analyzer

5 Conclusions and Future Work

In this paper, the authors overviewed some of the methods of OLAP personalization and how they have been used in the research community. The main goal of the OLAP personalization is to help the user providing recommendations in the analysis based on his/her preferences. The content of this paper will help the authors to choose the most adequate technique to use in the authors' developed hybridization process.

This hybridization process was developed to help overcome the pitfalls of the conventional What-If analysis. The lack of experience of the user could be one of them. The authors' hybridization process helps the user by suggesting parameters to be added in the scenario to perform the What-If analysis process, according to his needs and goals. Hence, there is a need to use some kind of technology for helping users to identify and select the most adequate scenario parameters according to their analysis goals. OLAP preferences are appropriate in this situation. Preferences suggest to the user business variables that are strongly related to the previously defined goal analysis business variable in the What-If question.

The OLAP mining process, the OLAP-based association, which consists in applying a data mining technique on a multidimensional structure, is one of many possible solutions that can be used to extract preferences and find out which are the "preferred" and "non-preferred" business variables. In this case, using an association rules algorithm as the basis of the mining process it is possible to discover which are the business variables that are related to the goal analysis business variable. Through the interpretation of the outcome of the mining algorithm, it is possible to discover the "preferred" set of parameters by pointing out the business variables that are strongly related to the goal analysis business variable.

OLAP personalization has been significantly useful in decision making process. It helps the users by reducing the struggle of the analysis process, helping to find the most interesting information. The time spent by the user in finding the wanted outcome is significantly reduced. Even in an OLAP session analysis, the time spent in the analysis can be reduced due to the reduction of the number of queries necessary to "manually" retrieve the results that best match the user preferences. At the end, we have the basis to continue this work. The hybridization process consists on integrating OLAP preferences in the conventional What-If analysis process. The extraction of preferences can be done by performing OLAP mining, an association mining technique, to get the best recommendation of scenario parameters in the creation of the hypothetical scenarios during the What-If analysis process.

Acknowledgments. This work has been supported by COMPETE: POCI-01-0145-FEDER-007043 and FCT - Fundação para a Ciência e Tecnologia within the Project Scope: UID/CEC/00319/2013.

References

1. Harinarayan, V., Rajaraman, A., Ullman, J.D.: Implementing data cubes efficiently. In: ACM SIGMOD Record, vol. 25, no. 2, pp. 205–216. ACM (1996)
2. Golfarelli, M., Rizzi, S., Proli, A.: Designing What-If analysis: towards a methodology. In: Proceedings of the 9th ACM International Workshop on Data Warehousing and OLAP, pp. 51–58. ACM (2006)
3. Golfarelli, M., Rizzi, S.: Expressing OLAP preferences. In: Winslett, M. (ed.) SSDBM 2009. LNCS, vol. 5566, pp. 83–91. Springer, Heidelberg (2009). https://doi.org/10.1007/978-3-642-02279-1_7
4. Carvalho, M., Belo, O.: Enriching What-If scenarios with OLAP usage preferences. In: Proceedings of the 8th International Conference on Knowledge Discovery and Information Retrieval (KDIR 2016), Porto, Portugal, 9–11 November 2016, pp. 213–220 (2016)
5. Lu, J., Wu, D., Mao, M., Wang, W., Zhang, G.: Recommender system application developments: a survey. Decis. Support Syst. **74**, 12–32 (2015)
6. Ricci, F., Rokach, L., Shapira, B.: Recommender systems: introduction and challenges. In: Ricci, F., Rokach, L., Shapira, B. (eds.) Recommender Systems Handbook, pp. 1–34. Springer, Boston, MA (2015). https://doi.org/10.1007/978-1-4899-7637-6_1
7. Beel, J., Gipp, B., Langer, S., Breitinger, C.: Paper recommender systems: a literature survey. Int. J. Digit. Libr. **17**(4), 305–338 (2016)
8. Aligon, J., Golfarelli, M., Marcel, P., Rizzi, S., Turricchia, E.: Mining preferences from OLAP query logs for proactive personalization. In: Eder, J., Bielikova, M., Tjoa, A.M. (eds.) ADBIS 2011. LNCS, vol. 6909, pp. 84–97. Springer, Heidelberg (2011). https://doi.org/10.1007/978-3-642-23737-9_7
9. Golfarelli, M., Rizzi, S., Biondi, P.: myOLAP: an approach to express and evaluate OLAP preferences. IEEE Trans. Knowl. Data Eng. **23**(7), 1050–1064 (2011)
10. Kozmina, N., Niedrite, L.: Research directions of OLAP personalization. In: Pokorny, J., et al. (eds.) Information Systems Development, pp. 345–356. Springer, New York (2011). https://doi.org/10.1007/978-1-4419-9790-6_28
11. Garrigós, I., Pardillo, J., Mazón, J.-N., Trujillo, J.: A conceptual modeling approach for OLAP personalization. In: Laender, A.H.F., Castano, S., Dayal, U., Casati, F., de Oliveira, J. P.M. (eds.) ER 2009. LNCS, vol. 5829, pp. 401–414. Springer, Heidelberg (2009). https://doi.org/10.1007/978-3-642-04840-1_30
12. Ravat, F., Teste, O.: Personalization and OLAP databases. In: Kozielski, S., Wrembel, R. (eds.) New Trends in Data Warehousing and Data Analysis. Annals of Information Systems, vol. 3, pp. 1–22. Springer, Boston (2009). https://doi.org/10.1007/978-0-387-87431-9_4
13. Giacometti, A., Marcel, P., Negre, E., Soulet, A.: Query recommendations for OLAP discovery driven analysis. In: Proceedings of 12th ACM International Workshop on Data Warehousing and OLAP (DOLAP 2009), Hong Kong, 6 November 2009, pp. 81–88 (2009)
14. Jerbi, H., Ravat, F., Teste, O., Zurfluh, G.: Applying recommendation technology in OLAP systems. In: Filipe, J., Cordeiro, J. (eds.) ICEIS 2009. LNBIP, vol. 24, pp. 220–233. Springer, Heidelberg (2009). https://doi.org/10.1007/978-3-642-01347-8_19
15. Kießling, W.: Foundations of preferences in database systems. In: VLDB 2002: Proceedings of the 28th International Conference on Very Large Databases, pp. 311–322 (2002)
16. Han, J. OLAP mining: an integration of OLAP with data mining. In: Proceedings of the 7th IFIP, vol. 2, pp. 1–9 (1997)
17. Quinlan, J.R.: C4.5: Programs for empirical learning (1993)

18. Carvalho, M., Macedo, N., Belo, O.: Checking the correctness of What-If scenarios. In: 11th IFIP WG 8.9 Working Conference – CONFENIS 2017. Crowne Plaza Shanghai Fudan, Shanghai, China, 18th–20th October 2017

19. Alloytools.org. http://alloytools.org/. Accessed 24 Apr 2019

20. Agrawal, R., Srikant, R.: Fast algorithms for mining association rules. In: Proceedings of 20th International Conference on Very Large Data Bases, VLDB, vol. 1215, pp. 487–499 (1994)

Sibilant Consonants Classification with Deep Neural Networks

Ivo Anjos[1]([✉])[iD], Nuno Marques[1][iD], Margarida Grilo[2][iD], Isabel Guimarães[2][iD], João Magalhães[1][iD], and Sofia Cavaco[1][iD]

[1] NOVA LINCS, Department of Computer Science, Faculdade de Ciências e Tecnologia, Universidade NOVA de Lisboa, 2829-516 Caparica, Portugal
i.anjos@campus.fct.unl.pt
[2] Escola Superior de Saúde do Alcoitão,
Rua Conde Barão, Alcoitão, 2649-506 Alcabideche, Portugal

Abstract. Many children suffering from speech sound disorders cannot pronounce the sibilant consonants correctly. We have developed a serious game that is controlled by the children's voices in real time and that allows children to practice the European Portuguese sibilant consonants. For this, the game uses a sibilant consonant classifier. Since the game does not require any type of adult supervision, children can practice the production of these sounds more often, which may lead to faster improvements of their speech.

Recently, the use of deep neural networks has given considerable improvements in classification for a variety of use cases, from image classification to speech and language processing. Here we propose to use deep convolutional neural networks to classify sibilant phonemes of European Portuguese in our serious game for speech and language therapy.

We compared the performance of several different artificial neural networks that used Mel frequency cepstral coefficients or log Mel filterbanks. Our best deep learning model achieves classification scores of 95.48% using a 2D convolutional model with log Mel filterbanks as input features.

Keywords: Deep learning · Sibilant consonants · Speech and language therapy

1 Introduction

The sibilant sounds are a subgroup of the consonant sounds that are produced by letting the air flow through a very narrow channel in the direction of the teeth [12]. These include sounds like [s] in serpent and [z] in zipper. Sigmatism, the distortion of sibilant sounds production, is a very common speech sound disorder in European Portuguese (EP) children [10,22]. Depending on the age of the child and the degree of the distortion, the speech problem can disappear naturally as the child grows up and his/her speech organ develop. Yet, in many cases these problems do not disappear naturally, and it is important that the child attends speech and language therapy to treat the disorder.

© Springer Nature Switzerland AG 2019
P. Moura Oliveira et al. (Eds.): EPIA 2019, LNAI 11805, pp. 435–447, 2019.
https://doi.org/10.1007/978-3-030-30244-3_36

In order to help children to surpass sigmatism, speech and language patholo-
gists (SLPs) start by teaching the child to produce these isolated sibilant sounds
before progressing to the production of the sounds within words. SLPs use multiple and repeated tasks to allow the child to practice the sounds and learn how
to produce them correctly. Yet, the repetition of the tasks can lead to the child's
lack of interest and motivation on doing the exercises. In order to keep children
motivated and collaborative during the therapy sessions, SLPs need to turn the
speech and language monotonous tasks into fun and appealing activities.

As a contribution to overcome the children's lack of motivation to repeat
productions of the sibilants, we have developed the *isolated sibilants game*, a
serious game that allows children to practice the isolated sibilants exercise while
playing a computer game [2]. An important characteristic of the game is that it
is controlled by the child's voice. That is, instead of using a keyboard or other
usual input device, the child must use his voice to play the game. To make this
possible, at its core, the game uses a sibilant consonant classifier that processes
the child's speech productions. This classifier was trained to distinguish the EP
sibilant consonants, but can be adapted to other languages.

In addition to being appropriate for speech therapy sessions, the game can
also be used for home training. Since the game has the ability to automatically classify the child's speech productions, it does not depend on the parents
supervision, whose free time may be limited. Allowing children to practice the
sounds often at home during their free time may contribute to faster speech
improvements [3,5,9].

While traditional automatic speech recognition (ASR) systems typically use
hidden Markov models (HMM) [11,14], the classification of isolated phonemes
and words can be successful with support vector machines (SVMs) [7,26,28]. As
for the input features, statistical measures of Mel frequency cepstral coefficients
(MFCCs) are commonly used as input to the ASR classification stages [8,13,
19,27]. MFCCs are a spectral representation of the sounds based on the Mel
scale [11]. We have previously used a less common approach to classify sibilant
consonants. We used the MFCCs as a raw feature [2], that is, without statistical
measures over the MFCCs. This approach has also been successfully used by
Carvalho *et al.* to classify the five EP vowels [6].

The classification of sibilant sounds is not a novelty. Benselama *et al.* focused
on the sibilants that are mispronounced by people with Arabic occlusive sigmatism [4]. They used MFCCs in artificial neural networks for classifying Arabic
sibilants, along with HMM with Gaussian mixture models (GMM) for segmenting these phonemes. Valenini-Botinhao *et al.* use MFCCs along with other features to construct a GMM to classify German sibilants [30]. Miodońska *et al.*
use MFCCs and other acoustic features on a SVM for the classification of Polish
sibilants [18].

Currently, there has been a tendency to substitute the more traditional
speech classifiers with deep learning models, which have proven to be quite
robust [1,24,31]. The most common features for this type of models are log
Mel filterbanks, which, like with MFCCs, are a spectral representation of the

sounds based on the Mel scale [23]. More recently, some studies also tested the use of convolutional neural networks (CNN) on the raw waveform [20,25].

The sibilant classifier in the first version of our isolated sibilants game used a simple SVM model with the raw MFCCs. That simple classifier achieved an accuracy of 90.72% [2], with an average false negative rate of 8.73%. While the score of this sibilant classifier is already high, we were able to improve it by using deep learning techniques. We compared multiple artificial neural network (ANN) models, from simpler neural network models with one to three hidden layers, to convolutional models. We also compared using MFCCs and log Mel filterbanks as input features to these models. In the end we were able to develop models with CNN that surpassed the classification scores obtained by the game's previous SVM classifier.

The purpose of these classification models is to classify EP child sibilant consonants in a serious game for sigmatism. Therefore, the false negative rate of the models must be taken into account. A low false negative rate is important to ensure that patients receive suitable feedback when their speech productions are correct. It is important that the game does not misclassify correct speech productions so that it does not lead the child into error and ensures that the child does not loose motivation in playing due to the models' incorrect classifications. Our CNN models obtained high classification scores (95.48%) combined with low false negative rates (4.35%), which shows that the models are suitable to be used in the proposed game for training the EP sibilants.

In summary, the main novelty of this paper is the use deep learning models to classify EP sibilant sounds from child speech productions, to be used in tools for speech and language therapy.

2   Sibilant Consonants and Sigmatism

Different sibilant sounds can be produced by using different parts of the vocal tract. There are two types of EP sibilant consonants: the alveolar sibilants, which are produced with the tongue nearly touching the alveolar region of the mouth, and the palato-alveolar sibilants, which are produced by positioning the tongue towards the palatal region of the mouth (Fig. 1). The vocal folds can either be used or not, resulting in a voiced or a voiceless sibilant, respectively.

There are four different sibilant consonant sounds in EP: [z] as in zebra, [s] as in snake, [ʃ] as the *sh* sound in sheep, and [ʒ] as the *s* sound in Asia. [z], and [s] are both alveolar sibilants, while [ʃ], and [ʒ] are palato-alveolar sibilants. Both [z] and [ʒ] are voiced sibilants, and [s] and [ʃ] are voiceless sibilants.

Most children with sigmatism cannot produce some sibilant sounds correctly either because they do not use the correct region of the vocal tract or because they exchange the voiced and voiceless sounds [21]. To correct these distortion errors, SLPs use different exercises and usually start with the *isolated sibilants exercise*, which consists of producing the sibilant sounds for a few seconds.

The continuous repetition and practice of the exercise is essential to master the isolated sibilant sounds. However this can be very demanding and wearing for

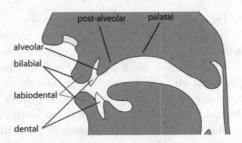

Fig. 1. Main places of articulation in the vocal tract (Adapted from: The Mimic Method - Place of Articulation, https://www.mimicmethod.com/ft101/place-of-articulation (retrieved April/2019)).

Fig. 2. Scenarios for (a) the [z] consonant, and for (b) the [s] consonant.

children, who can feel tired of repeating the exercise and thus stop collaborating with the SLP. In order to motivate the children on practicing the exercise as often as required, it is necessary to turn it into a fun activity. To this end, SLPs usually resort to rewards and make the exercise look like a game.

3   Serious Game for Training Sibilant Consonants

In order to motivate children on doing the isolated sibilants exercise and repeating it as often as necessary, and to help SLPs on turning this into a fun activity, our isolated sibilants game uses this exercise [2]. The game was designed for children from five to nine years old, because usually at these ages the regular phonological development exchange errors have already disappeared [17].

The game consists of leading the main character to a target. To make the main character move the child must use his voice. More specifically, the child has to produce one of the four EP sibilant consonants. An important characteristic of the game is that it processes the child's speech productions in real time. Thus, unlike with other speech and language therapy computer games that are manually controlled by the SLP, in this game the main character is controlled by the child's voice. The character moves towards the target if the child produces the sibilant consonant correctly. In this way, the movement of the character gives real time visual feedback about the sound production, which is an intuitive way of pointing out to the child whether his/her sound productions are correct.

The game includes a different scenario and main character for each of the four EP sibilant consonants (Fig. 2). These scenarios were created with the help of a visual artist and with images from *Freepik*[1]. In each scenario, the main character or game goal is related to the addressed sibilant sound, which is an additional visual cue that helps the child understand what sound she should produce: The main character for the [z] sibilant scenario is a bumblebee as the EP word for bumblebee, *zangão*, starts with the [z] sibilant (Fig. 2a). The main characters for the [s] and [ʒ] sibilants are a snake (Fig. 2b) and a ladybug, because the EP words for snake and ladybug, which are *serpente* and *joaninha*, start with the [s] and [ʒ] sibilants, respectively. In the [ʃ] sibilant scenario there is a boy who must run away from the rain to reach the end of the road. The EP word for rain, *chuva*, starts with the [ʃ] sibilant.

4   Data Collection and Data Representation

In order to train our EP sibilant models we used sibilant sound productions from children. The sounds were collected in three schools in the greater Lisbon area. There was always a SLP present in the recording sessions. 145 children from 4 to 11 years old participated in the recordings, from which there were 83 girls and 62 boys (Table 1). We recorded short and long versions of the four EP sibilants consonants (that is, a version that lasts less than a couple of seconds and another that last a few seconds), giving a total of over 1500 sound productions. These were manually labeled and the correct productions were used for training the models. Table 2 shows the number of correct sound productions for each sibilant.

In our previous work we used the raw MFCCs as input to the SVMs, that is, we used the columns of the MFCCs matrix (which were 13×1 MFCCs vectors) directly as feature vectors (and no statistical measure over the whole matrix) [2]. Given the good classification scores obtained using these input features, here we experimented to maintain the same type of features, that is, the raw MFCCs.

To extract the MFCCs we use a 25 ms window with a 10 ms shift. We extract the first 13 MFCCs. Therefore, each sound production is represented by a $13 \times t$ matrix, where t depends on the duration of the sound. Each column vector of this matrix consists of the 13 MFCCs of a 25 ms window. We also tried with log Mel filterbanks as input features. We use the first 40 filters to represent the data, and kept the same window and shift sizes of 25 ms and 10 ms, respectively.

5   Models for Sibilant Consonants

As explained above, here we propose to use ANN models to classify children's EP sibilant productions in a serious game for speech and language therapy for

---

[1] Freepik, http://www.freepik.com.

Table 1. Age and gender of children participating in the recordings

Age	Girl	Boy	Total
4	0	1	1
5	8	3	11
6	8	8	16
7	19	9	28
8	21	20	41
9	23	19	42
10	3	2	5
11	1	0	1
Total	83	62	145

Table 2. Number of correct sound productions for each sibilant.

Sibilant	# correct productions
ʃ	276
ʒ	257
s	278
z	264

sigmatism. We compared multiple neural network models, from simple one hidden layer ANNs to more complex CNNs. As a base support for the comparison between all our models, we kept the input features as similar as possible. We used the Adam optimizer as our loss function in all networks and we also used the stochastic gradient descent (SGD) in our CNNs [15]. Below we discuss each of these models in detail.

We started by experimenting with simple feed-forward ANN consisting of multilayer perceptrons. The input layer of these networks receives the raw 13×1 column-vectors of the MFCCs matrix. We used the rectified linear unit (ReLU) [16] as the activation function for our neurons, and applied dropout to the hidden layers, with a drop rate of 40% [29].

The simplest model has just one hidden layer with 50 neurons and an output layer with 4 neurons. The goal of training this model was to test if such a simple network can achieve a good separation of the four sounds. We observed that while the model can distinguish the sounds, it shows worse results than those achieved by our previous SVM-based model used in the first version of our game (more details in Sect. 6).

After experimenting increasing the number of hidden layers to two, and having no significant improvements, we further increased the number of hidden layers to four layers also with limited improvements. The first hidden layer has 100 neurons, and the second, third and fourth layers have 50, 25 and 10 neurons, respectively. In both models, we used 200 epochs for training.

As it will be discussed in Sect. 6, while these models provide good results, their classification scores are lower than those achieved by our previous SVM-based model. Thus, we then proceeded to create more complex models with the goal of surpassing our previous SVM scores.

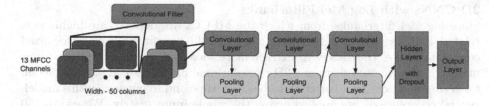

Fig. 3. Representation of our 1D CNN.

5.1   Convolutional Models

Since convolutional layers have the potential to extract relevant local information, we explored using CNN to classify the EP child sibilant productions, to see if this type of knowledge helps improving our previous classification score. Here, instead of having 13×1 column input vectors, the input to our CNNs is given in the form of a matrix. We experimented using MFCCs matrices and log Mel filterbank matrices as input features to our CNNs.

1D CNNs with MFCCs

The input to our CNNs consists of sub-matrices of the $13 \times t$ original MFCC matrix. To build these matrices we fetch sets of 50 consecutive columns of the original MFCCs matrix with a step of 5 columns (and 45 columns overlap). In other words, we extract 50 consecutive columns (that is, 13×1 vectors), then skip 5 consecutive columns, and extract another 50 columns that have some overlap with the previous matrix. We then repeat the process until we reach the end of the original MFCCs matrix, obtaining matrices of size 13×50 for each sound production. Hereafter these matrices are considered as our data samples.

Our approach here consists of applying one dimensional convolutions to the data. We do this by considering the 50 columns as our width, and having our 13 MFCCs as channels (like with the RGB channels in images). In other words, we apply temporal convolutions to each of the 13 MFCCs receptive field (Fig. 3).

Our convolutional model has three convolutional layers, each followed by the corresponding pooling layer. In the end, we flatten the output from the convolutional layers and use a fully connect layer with dropout, followed by another fully connect layer for the output (Fig. 3). We used the ReLU as the activation functions of the convolutional and hidden layers, and we trained the model for 100 epochs.

For the loss function, we performed multiple tests with both the Adam optimizer, and the SGD. The biggest advantage of using the Adam optimizer, was that it allowed the model to reach local minima considerably faster than SGD. However, with the Adam optimizer the models had a tendency to overfit. So, in the end, we used SGD, since it helped to prevent overfitting, and we were able to reach similar results as with the Adam optimizer.

2D CNNs with Log Mel Filterbanks

Since log Mel filterbanks, from which the MFCCs are derived, are highly correlated both in time and frequency, they should benefit from more localized convolutions, i.e. they allow to extract more localized features from the input matrix. Thus, we used them in a 2D convolutional model instead of a 1D model, for trying to model joint correlations between time and frequency. In this model, spacial convolutions are applied across the whole input matrix. We use the 50 columns as our width, and 40 filters as our height, with just one channel. The main architecture of this network is the same as above for our 1D CNN, but using 2D convolutional layers, instead of 1D layers.

Following the 1D model results, we started with the SGD optimizer for the 2D model. Again this optimizer easily allowed us to prevent overfitting. However, the model appeared to be converging to a local minimum. On the other hand, while it introduced some overfitting, the Adam optimizer reduced the number of epochs needed to reach the same results, and in some cases improved the results.

6 Results

The EP sibilant classifier of the game's first version used one SVM with a radial basis function kernel for each of the four EP sibilant sounds [2]. It used 13×1 MFCC vectors as input and was able to reach average accuracy test scores of 90.72% between all four SVM models. We also trained a SVM using the same 13×50 input matrix as in our convolutional models (Sect. 5.1). Yet, with this input matrix, the SVM did not learn how to separate the four sibilant sounds. Indeed, unlike with CNN models, the MFCC input vectors high dimension and strong correlation makes this data representation less appropriated for SVM classifiers.

In order to train our neural networks, we divided the data set described in Sect. 4 into training, validation and test sets. We randomly separated the data into these three sets, but to avoid any bias in the results, we were careful to put all productions of each child c either in the training, validation or the test set. Thus, while we have several feature vectors from each child, all the vectors from each child belong to the same data set. This way we avoid the insertion of bias in our results, since samples from the same sibilant of a particular child are likely to have some correlation. We used the productions of 20% of all children as the test set, 10% as the validation set and the remaining 70% productions form the training set. This type of split remained equal for all models.

This way, for the simple ANN models, we have around 250000 MFCC vectors for the training set, 30000 for the validation, and 70000 for the test set. We trained the simple ANN models for 200 epochs, using a batch size of 500 samples, and shuffling the dataset at every epoch.

While the data was split into training and test sets in the same manner for our previous SVM-based model, we did not use the whole MFCC matrices with these models due to the temporal learning complexity of the models. For these models, we used around 20000 MFCC vectors (more details in [2]).

Table 3. Accuracy test scores of all our models.

Model	Test accuracy	FNR
SVM	90.72%	8.73%
simple ANN	88.76%	11.15%
1D CNN	94.04%	5.56%
2D CNN	95.48%	4.35%

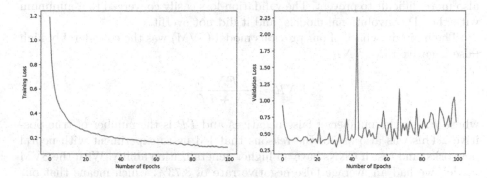

Fig. 4. 2D convolutional model. (Left) Training loss. (Right) Validation loss.

Using the matrices approach for the convolutional models reduces the total of data input samples. Nonetheless, we still have around 45000 samples for training, 5000 for validation, and 13000 samples for testing the convolutional models.

Table 3 shows the results achieved with the different models. It shows that simple ANN models for classifying EP sibilants can achieve very satisfactory results but not as high as our previous SVM-based model. A single hidden layer ANN model achieved an average classification score of 86.54%. Further increasing the number of hidden layers resulted in marginal improvements to the test score. Our best simple ANN model had three hidden layers and gave us a score of 88.76%, which was still lower than the score obtained with the SVM-based model.

The 1D convolutional model was able to increase the score to 94.04%, which is almost 6% higher than the score of our 4-hidden layer ANN model, and around 3% higher than the SVM score. This could be expected, since the convolutional layers have the ability to extract localized information that can contribute for a better classification than that of simpler ANN models. In particular, there may be relevant localized information in the 13×50 CNN input matrices that is not present in the 13×1 ANN input vectors. Using the concatenation of 50 MFCC columns as input to the CNN, can contribute for a better prediction of the sound.

The 2D convolutional model, which uses the highly correlated log Mel filterbanks, can be expected to achieve at least the same scores as our 1D model, or even to overcome them. Our experiments with the 2D CNN reached a test score of 95.48%, surpassing our 1D convolutional model. This shows that the convolutional layers were able to extract more significant information from the log Mel filterbanks than from the MFCCs.

Figure 4 shows the training and validation loss of the best 2D convolutional model. As we can see from the training loss graph, the model quickly converges. The validation graph shows that there is a lot of variation between epochs, and the model never reached a stable validation loss. For our final model, we chose the one that provided the lowest validation loss, which was at epoch 32, with a value of 0.29. After this epoch the model continued to adapt to our training set, but as can be seen by the validation loss, the model started to overfit. In our testing, the overfitting was more severe with the 2D convolutional models, and also more difficult to prevent. The validation loss easily converged to a minimum with the 1D convolutional models, and it did not overfit.

The main drawback of our previous model (SVM) was the considerably high false negative rate (FNR):

$$FNR = \frac{FN}{FN + TP},$$

where FN is the number of false negatives and TP is the number of true positives. This was also one of the reasons that led us to experiment with neural networks, and test if CNNs have an higher generalization ability. With the SVM model, we had an average false negative rate of 8.73%, which means that our model classifies a considerable amount of correct sounds as false productions. This type of misclassifications can be very prejudicial to children, since they are producing a correct sound, and the game, by considering the sound incorrect, can induce them into error. In addition, these misclassifications can be very frustrating for children. Our CNN model has provided us with a great improvement in reducing the number of false negatives. With the CNN model, we now have an average false negative rate of 4.35%, a reduction of over 4% from the false negative rate obtained by our previous model.

7   Conclusion and Future Work

Here we proposed deep CNN models to automatize the classification of child EP sibilant productions in a serious game for speech and language therapy for sigmatism. We compared the performances of different networks using either MFCCs or log Mel filterbanks. Our best model uses matrices of log Mel filterbanks as input and have three 2D convolutional layers. This model achieved a classification score of 95.48% and surpassed the classification scores obtained with our simple ANN model, and 1D model with MFFCs, and also our previous SVM-based model [2].

In addition to a higher classification score, the proposed model has a low average false negative rate, 4.35%. Taking into account that the purpose of the proposed models is to classify child speech productions in a serious game for speech and language therapy, their false negative rate is an important factor to ensure that patients do not loose motivation in playing due to the models' incorrect classifications. Since the models have high classification scores and low false negative rates, they are suitable for use in speech and language therapy games for sigmatism.

As future work it will be interesting to experiment with other input features to our CNN, such as features that have been used in other state of the art models, like delta and delta-delta features, and the raw input sound data. A thorough study on the number of layers, and the choice of hyper parameters for all the layers, can help to further improve the classification scores.

Acknowledgements. This work was supported by the Portuguese Foundation for Science and Technology under projects BioVisualSpeech (CMUP-ERI/TIC/0033/2014) and NOVA-LINCS (PEest/UID/CEC/04516/2019). We thank Mariana Ascensão and the postgraduate SLP students from Escola Superior de Saúde do Alcoitão who collaborated in the data collection task. Finally, we thank Agrupamento de Escolas de Almeida Garrett, and the children who participated in the recordings.

References

1. Amodei, D., et al.: Deep speech 2: end-to-end speech recognition in English and Mandarin. In: Proceedings of The 33rd International Conference on Machine Learning, vol. 48, pp. 173–182. PMLR (2016)
2. Anjos, I., Grilo, M., Ascensão, M., Guimarães, I., Magalhães, J., Cavaco, S.: A serious mobile game with visual feedback for training sibilant consonants. In: Cheok, A.D., Inami, M., Romão, T. (eds.) ACE 2017. LNCS, vol. 10714, pp. 430–450. Springer, Cham (2018). https://doi.org/10.1007/978-3-319-76270-8_30
3. Barratt, J., Littlejohns, P., Thompson, J.: Trial of intensive compared with weekly speech therapy in preschool children. Arch. Dis. Child. **67**(1), 106–108 (1992)
4. Benselama, Z., Guerti, M., Bencherif, M.: Arabic speech pathology therapy computer aided system. J. Comput. Sci. **3**(9), 685–692 (2007)
5. Bhogal, S.K., Teasell, R., Speechley, M.: Intensity of aphasia therapy, impact on recovery. Stroke **34**(4), 987–993 (2003)
6. Carvalho, M.I.P., Ferreira, A.: Interactive game for the training of Portuguese vowels. Master's thesis. Faculdade de Engenharia da Universidade do Porto (2008)
7. Clarkson, P., Moreno, P.J.: On the use of support vector machines for phonetic classification. In: Proceedings of the IEEE International Conference on Acoustics, Speech, and Signal Processing, vol. 2, pp. 585–588 (1999)
8. Davis, S.B., Mermelstein, P.: Comparison of parametric representations for monosyllabic word recognition in continuously spoken sentences. In: Readings in Speech Recognition, pp. 65–74. Elsevier (1990)
9. Denes, G., Perazzolo, C., Piani, A., Piccione, F.: Intensive versus regular speech therapy in global aphasia: a controlled study. Aphasiology **10**(4), 385–394 (1996)
10. Figueiredo, A.C.: Análise acústica dos fonemas /ʃ/ e /ʒ/ produzidos por crianças com desempenho articulatório alterado. Master's thesis. Escola Superior de Saúde de Alcoitão (2017)
11. Gold, B., Morgan, N., Ellis, D.: Speech and Audio Signal Processing: Processing and Perception of Speech and Music, 2nd edn. Wiley-Interscience, Hoboken (2011)
12. Guimarães, I.: A Ciência e a Arte da Voz Humana. ESSA - Escola Superior de Saúde do Alcoitão (2007)

13. Hsu, C.W., Lee, L.S.: Higher order cepstral moment normalization for improved robust speech recognition. IEEE Trans. Audio Speech Lang. Process. **17**(2), 205–220 (2009)
14. Huang, X., Acero, A., Hon, H.W.: Spoken Language Processing: A Guide to Theory, Algorithm, and System Development, 1st edn. Prentice Hall PTR, Upper Saddle River (2001)
15. Kingma, D.P., Ba, J.: Adam: a method for stochastic optimization. In: Proceedings of the International Conference on Learning Representations (ICLR) (2015)
16. Krizhevsky, A., Sutskever, I., Hinton, G.E.: ImageNet classification with deep convolutional neural networks. In: Advances in Neural Information Processing Systems, pp. 1097–1105 (2012)
17. Mestre, I.: Sibilantes e motricidade orofacial em crianças portuguesas dos 5:00 aos 9:11 anos de idade. Master's thesis. Escola Superior de Saúde do Alcoitão (2018)
18. Miodońska, Z., Kręcichwost, M., Szymańska, A.: Computer-aided evaluation of sibilants in preschool children sigmatism diagnosis. In: Piętka, E., Badura, P., Kawa, J., Wieclawek, W. (eds.) Information Technologies in Medicine. AISC, vol. 471, pp. 367–376. Springer, Cham (2016). https://doi.org/10.1007/978-3-319-39796-2_30
19. Muda, L., Begam, M., Elamvazuthi, I.: Voice recognition algorithms using mel frequency cepstral coefficient and dynamic time warping techniques. Computing Research Repository (CoRR) abs/1003.4083 (2010)
20. Palaz, D., Magimai-Doss, M., Collobert, R.: Analysis of CNN-based speech recognition system using raw speech as input. In: Proceedings of Interspeech, pp. 11–15 (2015)
21. Preston, J., Edwards, M.L.: Phonological awareness and types of sound errors in preschoolers with speech sound disorders. J. Speech Lang. Hear. Res. **53**(1), 44–60 (2010)
22. Rua, M.: Caraterização do desempenho articulatório e oromotor de crianças com alterações da fala. Master's thesis. Escola Superior de Saúde de Alcoitão (2015)
23. Sainath, T.N., Kingsbury, B., Mohamed, A.R., Saon, G., Ramabhadran, B.: Improvements to filterbank and delta learning within a deep neural network framework. In: Proceedings of the IEEE International Conference on Acoustics, Speech and Signal Processing (ICASSP), pp. 6839–6843 (2014)
24. Sainath, T.N., Kingsbury, B., Ramabhadran, B., Fousek, P., Novak, P., Mohamed, A.R.: Making deep belief networks effective for large vocabulary continuous speech recognition. In: Proceedings of the IEEE Workshop on Automatic Speech Recognition and Understanding (ASRU), pp. 30–35 (2011)
25. Sainath, T.N., Weiss, R.J., Senior, A., Wilson, K.W., Vinyals, O.: Learning the speech front-end with raw waveform CLDNNs. In: Proceedings of the Annual Conference of the International Speech Communication Association (2015)
26. Salomon, J., King, S., Salomon, J.: Framewise phone classification using support vector machines. In: Proceedings of the International Conference on Spoken Language Processing (2002)
27. Schuller, B., Steidl, S., Batliner, A.: The INTERSPEECH 2009 emotion challenge. In: Proceedings of Interspeech (2009)
28. Solera-Ureña, R., Padrell-Sendra, J., Martín-Iglesias, D., Gallardo-Antolín, A., Peláez-Moreno, C., Díaz-de-María, F.: SVMs for automatic speech recognition: a survey. In: Stylianou, Y., Faundez-Zanuy, M., Esposito, A. (eds.) Progress in Nonlinear Speech Processing. LNCS, vol. 4391, pp. 190–216. Springer, Heidelberg (2007). https://doi.org/10.1007/978-3-540-71505-4_11

29. Srivastava, N., Hinton, G., Krizhevsky, A., Sutskever, I., Salakhutdinov, R.: Dropout: a simple way to prevent neural networks from overfitting. J. Mach. Learn. Res. **15**(1), 1929–1958 (2014)
30. Valentini-Botinhao, C., Degenkolb-Weyers, S., Maier, A., Nöth, E., Eysholdt, U., Bocklet, T.: Automatic detection of sigmatism in children. In: Proceedings of the Workshop on Child, Computer Interaction (WOCCI) (2012)
31. Zhang, Y., Chan, W., Jaitly, N.: Very deep convolutional networks for end-to-end speech recognition. In: 2017 IEEE International Conference on Acoustics, Speech and Signal Processing (ICASSP), pp. 4845–4849 (2017)

Online Clustering for Novelty Detection and Concept Drift in Data Streams

Kemilly Dearo Garcia[1,2]([✉]), Mannes Poel[1], Joost N. Kok[1],
and André C. P. L. F. de Carvalho[2]

[1] University of Twente, Enschede, The Netherlands
{k.dearogarcia,m.poel,j.n.kok}@utwente.nl
[2] ICMC, University of São Paulo, São Paulo, Brazil
andre@icmc.usp.br

Abstract. Data streams are related to large amounts of data that can continuously arrive with a probability distribution that may change over time. Depending on the changes in the data distribution, different phenomena can occur, like new classes can appear or concept drift can occur in existing classes. Machine Learning algorithms have been often used to model this data. New classes are patterns that were not seen during the training of the current classification model, but appear after some time. Concept drift occurs when the concepts associated with a dataset change as new data arrive. This paper proposes a new algorithm based on kNN that uses micro-clusters as prototypes and incrementally updates the micro-clusters or creates new micro-clusters when novelties are detected. In the online phase, each instance close to a micro-cluster is considered an extension of the micro-cluster, being used to adapt the model to concept drift. The proposed algorithm is experimentally compared with a state-of-the-art classifier from the data stream literature and one baseline. According to the experimental results, the proposed algorithm increases the predictive performance over time by incrementally learning changes in the data distribution.

Keywords: Data stream · Concept drift · Novelty detection · Online learning

1 Introduction

Data streams are known as data that can continuously arrive in streams, with a probability distribution that can change over time [14]. As new data arrive, models previously induced can become outdated [6]. In addition, due to the great amount of data generated, it is not feasible to store all incoming data in the main memory, requiring the removal of previous outdated data and online processing of incoming data [12,16].

Depending on the changes in the data distribution, different phenomena can occur, like concept drifts [14,25] and novelties [12,20]. Concept drift refers to

© Springer Nature Switzerland AG 2019
P. Moura Oliveira et al. (Eds.): EPIA 2019, LNAI 11805, pp. 448–459, 2019.
https://doi.org/10.1007/978-3-030-30244-3_37

changes in the concept definitions of a normal class [15]. Novelties concepts are
are patterns that were not present during the training of the classification model,
but appear later on in the data stream [12]. In these situations, it is important
to adapt the classification model to the current data distribution, otherwise its
predictive performance can decrease along the time.

In this work, normal concepts are a set of *normal classes* used to train the
classification model and novelties concepts are the *new classes* that emerge in a
data stream along the time [12].

Novelty detection is a Machine Learning (ML) task based on the identification
of novelties in the data [11]. In data streams, the novelty detection can be divided
in two phases: *offline* and *online phase.* In the offline phase, a classification model
is trained using an initial, static, labeled dataset. In the online phase, the model
is updated using unlabeled data arriving in streams. The update occurs when
the predictive performance of the model decreases, usually because of change in
the data distribution. Thus, the model can be continuously updated [15].

One of the strategies to deal with novelty detection and concept drift is by
explicitly detecting changes in parts of the stream, comparing the current concept with previous concepts from time to time [19]. An example of this strategy
is to continuously calculate the model classification error. This strategy assumes
that the data arriving in the stream are labeled.

Another strategy is to store in a buffer the potential novelty classes instances.
However, the use of a buffer with fixed size may ignore instances with relevant
information about persistent concepts. Furthermore, the size of the buffer affects
its efficient use when the degree and speed of changes vary in the data stream.
Another deficiency of updating the model using a buffer with fixed size is the
possibility to forget old, but relevant, information.

There are two problems in assuming that the arriving data is labeled. First,
the process of labeling an instance usually has a cost, which increases with the
complexity and need of domain expertise. Second, if the data arrives in high
speed, there will not be enough time to label them. Thus, in this paper we
assume that the instances in a data stream come unlabeled.

Due to the lack of labeled data in a data streams, the update of the model
can rely only on the predictive attribute values. To deal with this limitation
it is possible to use clustering algorithms. Clusters can summarize the main
data profiles present in a data stream and be updated to incorporate changes
in class profiles and detect the appearance of novelties [2]. When clustering
algorithms are applied to data streams, micro-clusters can be used as a strategy
to summarize data present in different periods of time [3]. Each micro-cluster
can be structured as a temporal extension of a CF (Cluster Feature Vector) [24],
which is a compact statistical representation of a set of instances.

In this paper we propose *Higia*, a novelty detection algorithm based on kNN
(k-Nearest Neighbor) that uses *micro-clusters* [3] as prototypes and incrementally updates the micro-clusters or creates new micro-clusters when a novelty
is detected. *Higia* training is divided into offline learning and online learning.
During the offline learning phase, we assume that there is data from one or more

normal classes. The instances from each normal class are summarized into a set of micro-clusters. Each micro-cluster has instances from the same normal class label. In the online learning phase, each instance close to a micro-cluster is considered an extension of the micro-cluster, a concept drift. This instance is then used to adapt the predictive model to this concept drift. However, if a set of new instances are close together in a dense region, they are considered representative of new classes, named novelties.

This paper is structured as follows. Section 2, presents previous related works for novelty and concept drift detection in data streams. Data stream, novelty, concept drift and micro-clusters are introduced in Section 3. The proposed algorithm, Higia, is described in Sect. 4. Section 5 presents the experimental setup and analyses the results obtained. Finally, Sect. 6 has the main conclusions from this study and points out future work directions.

2   Related Work

This section briefly presents previous works using ML-based approaches for novelty and concept drift detection in data streams. Most of these studies use supervised ML algorithms, classification algorithms, to induce classifiers.

Most of the classification algorithms proposed for data stream mining are based on online learning [9,12,15,19]. Some of them continuously update the classification model using true labeled data [1,4,21]. However, as previously mentioned, true labels are not always available at feasible time, delaying the updating of the classification model. Assuming the absence of labels in the online phase, others apply clustering algorithms in the arriving data. Thus, the clusters are representatives of normal and new classes [5,12,17,23].

One of the first algorithms to use clusters for novelty detection in data streams is OLINDDA (OnLIne Novelty and Drift Detection Algorithm) [23], [22]. During the offline phase a single model is build by a set of clusters with data from the normal classes. After, in the online phase, whenever a new instance arrives, it is calculated the distance between it and the closest cluster from the normal model. When the distance is large, according to a threshold value, the instance is stored in a buffer, where it can later be defined as a novelty after a clustering step.

ECSMiner [21] (Enhanced Classifier for Data Streams with novel class Miner) is an ensemble of models, each model is represented by a set of clusters created using the clustering algorithm k-means. ECSMiner also stores in a buffer the instances that are distant from the normal clusters. The ensemble is updated when the instances stored in the buffer receive their true label. Afterwards, the ensemble predictive accuracy is calculated. The model with the lowest accuracy is updated with the novelties found in the buffer. While waiting for labeled data, the model can wait for a long period of time to be updated, which could reduce the accuracy of the ensemble. Besides, it is not always guaranteed that all data will be labeled, since it may be application dependent.

Another novelty detection algorithm, MINAS (MultI-class learNing Algorithm for data Streams) [12], also uses an offline phase followed by an online phase. In its offline phase, the data is separated by labels in subsets. From each subset it is generated a set of micro-clusters representing each class. In the online phase, the incoming data is stored in a buffer if is not identified by the model. When the buffer reaches a certain size, a clustering algorithm is applied in the data stored in the buffer. Valid micro-clusters are marked as extension of a known class or as novelty, and are incorporated into the classification model.

3 Problem Formalization

A data stream is a sequence of instances, potentially of infinity size, that can be formally represented by [12,15,16]: $D_{tr} = \{(X_1, y_1), (X_2, y_2), ..., (X_{tr}, y_{tr})\}$, where X_{tr} is an instance arriving in time tr and y_{tr} is the target class of this instance. Due to finite resources, each instance must be processed only once.

Concept drift is a change in the distribution probability of a problem target classes [15]. Formally, the joint probability distribution $P_{tr+1}(X, y)$ over instances X and label y can change over time, defined by tr, so that $P_{tr}(X, y) \neq P_{tr+1}(X, y)$.

Assuming that in the offline phase a dataset has m classes, the set $Y^{Nor} = \{y_1, y_2, ..., y_m\}$ represents the set of Normal Classes. These classes are used to build the initial classification model. Afterwards, during the online phase, a novel class, y_{m+1}, has the following property: $y_{m+1} \notin Y^{Nor}$ i.e., y_{m+1} was not used in the training of the classification model, but emerges during the online phase. Therefore, for any given new set of novel classes, $Y^{New} = \{y_{m+1}, y_{m+2}, ..., y_n\}$ any novelty detection approach must be able to fast detect novelties as they appear [12,16]. Considering the sets of normal classes and new classes, the total set of classes is simply defined as $Y = Y^{Nor} \cup Y^{New}$.

Micro-clustering [3] is a strategy commonly used to summarize data coming from a stream in different periods of time. Each micro-cluster $C_j = (n, \boldsymbol{LS}, \boldsymbol{SS}, t)$ stores four components: the number of its instances n, the linear sum of its instances $\boldsymbol{LS}$, the square sum of its instances $\boldsymbol{SS}$ and the timestamp, t, of when the last instance was incorporated in the micro-cluster. By using these values, it is possible to calculate the centroid ($c_j = \boldsymbol{LS}/n$) and the radius ($r_{C_j} = 2 \times (\boldsymbol{SS} \times n/n^2 + \boldsymbol{SS}/n^2)$) of a micro-cluster, which can be used to classify new instances.

4 Methodology

The proposed algorithm, Higia, is based on the assumption that in a data stream, an ideal classifier should be able to learn the current concept in feasible time without forgetting relevant past information [9].

Higia induces a classification model using unsupervised online learning. Its training also occurs by an offline phase followed by an online phase. In the offline phase, a predictive model, illustrated by Fig. 1, is induced from a batch containing labelled data. As in [12], the model is composed by micro-clusters created using the CluStream algorithm [3].

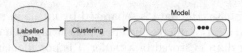

Fig. 1. Higia offline phase.

In the online phase, illustrated by Fig. 2, as new data arrives, the model classify each new instance as *normal, extension* or *unknown*. For the classification, the model calculates the euclidean distance between each instance and the centroids of the micro-clusters from the *normal* classes.

Algorithm 1. Higia: Online Phase

1: **input:** X_{tr}, T, k
2: Let ψ_k be a list of the k nearest micro-clusters to X_{tr}
3: **if** majority of ψ_k have the same label **then**
4:     Let C_j be the nearest micro-cluster to X_{tr}
5:     Let c_j be the centroid of C_j
6:     Let $radius\,(C_j)$ be the radius of C_j
7:     $dist \leftarrow EuclidianDistance(X_{tr}, C_j)$
8:     **if** dist $\leq radius\,(C_j)$ **then**
9:         update C_j with X_{tr}
10:         classify X_{tr} with the same label of C_j
11:     **else if** $dist \leq (radius\,(C_j) \times T)$ **then**
12:         create extension of C_j with centroid X_{tr} and radius 0.5
13:         classify X_{tr} with the same label of C_j
14: **else**
15:     add X_{tr} to buffer
16:     classify X_{tr} as unknown

Algorithm 1 describes how Higia works in the online learning phase when a new instance, X_{tr}, arrives. First, Higia finds the k micro-clusters closest to X_{tr}. If the majority of these micro-clusters have the same label and if the smallest distance is less than the radius of the nearest micro-cluster C_j, the instance is classified with the label of C_j. Besides, C_j is updated with X_{tr}. If the distance is larger than the radius of C_j, but is smaller than a given threshold T, the instance is added to the model as an extension. The threshold is multiplied by the radius of C_j and indicates the maximum drift of C_j.

If the distance is larger than the radius of C_j and T, then X_{tr} is labeled as *unknown* and stored in a buffer. The instances stored in the buffer are incrementally forming micro-clusters. When a micro-cluster has a given amount of instances, defined by a hyperparameter, a novelty is found and the new micro-cluster is added to the model as a new class.

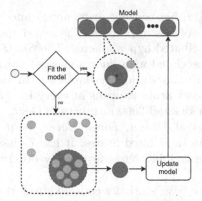

Fig. 2. Higia online phase.

5   Experimental Evaluation

In this section, we present the experiments carried out to assess the predictive performance of Higia. In this experiments, Higia was compared with two other algorithms, MINAS and the kNN algorithm. From the algorithms described in Sect. 2, MINAS is the only unsupervised algorithm for multiclass novelty detection. The kNN algorithm from the MOA framework [8] was used as a baseline. In the offline phase, all three algorithms are initialized with the same batch of labeled data representing 10% of the dataset. We assume that the instances in the training data are from the normal classes and that new classes can continuously appear during the online phase.

We adopted the accuracy measure to evaluate the predictive performance of the models over time. The accuracy is the amount of correctly classified data divided by the amount of total data in a window of 1000 instances. We also use the total accuracy measure to evaluate the performance for the whole dataset.

For a more detailed analyses we used the evaluation approach proposed in [21]. This evaluation approach has 3 measures: M_{New} = the percentage of instances from the new classes misclassified as existing class, F_{New} = the percentage of instances from the normal classes classified as novelties, and Err = average misclassification error.

The accuracy counts as mistake the instances classified as *unknown*. To analyse the algorithms in terms of misclassification of the total classes, (Y), without the influence of *unknown*, we used the Err measure.

5.1   Datasets

The experiments were performed on both synthetic and real datasets, commonly used in novelty detection studies [3,4,10,13,18,21]. The synthetic datasets are: MOA, SynD, CDT, UG and Gear. The real dataset used was the Forest Cover dataset.

The *MOA* dataset [12] has concept drift, appearance of new classes, recurrence and disappearance of existing classes. The real shape of the clusters in this dataset is normally distributed hyper-spheres. The *SynD* [4,13,21] has no novelty, but the concept associated with known classes changes over time. Finally, *CDT, UG* and *Gear* are non stationary datasets[1]. In these datasets, a single novelty occurs and concept drifts happens at every interval of 400 instances in CDT, 1000 instances in UG and 2000 instances in Gear.

Regarding the only real dataset, *Forest Cover* [7], it contains observations from 7 types of forest in the United States. It has 7 classes and 54 attributes. In the experiments, the training set is formed by observations from 3 normal classes.

Table 1 presents some basic statistics collected from these datasets: the number of normal and new classes, number of attributes, number of instances in the minority and majority classes.

Table 1. Statistical information for each dataset

Statistics	1CDT	MOA	Gear	UG	SynD	Forest Cover
Attributes	2	4	2	2	10	54
Classes	2	4	2	2	2	7
Normal classes	1	2	2	1	2	3
New classes	1	2	0	1	0	4
Instances MinCla	7199	9987	99935	44999	124660	587
Instances MajCla	7200	18180	100065	45000	125340	18350

5.2   Results and Discussion

In these experiments we used the default parameters of MINAS. Because MINAS uses the label of the nearest micro-cluster to classify a new instance, we set $k = 1$ in the Higia algorithm. As for the other parameter of Higia, the *threshold*, we set it to *threshold* $= 1.1$ as in MINAS [12]. Also for Higia, we experimentally defined the parameter *radius* $= 0.5$. The kNN has the default parameters, $k = 1$ and window size ($w = 1000$), and there is no online training. It is used to understand how the model looses predictive accuracy over time without its update to the changes in the data stream.

Next, we present the predictive accuracy over time of the 3 algorithms. As can be seen in Fig. 3, the predictive performance of Higia was better than those obtained by MINAS and the kNN baseline. Higia incrementally updates the normal and the new micro-clusters in the classification model. As consequence, model represents the current probability distribution of the data streams better

---

[1] https://www.sites.google.com/site/nonstationaryarchive/.

than MINAS. The model induced and updated by the MINAS algorithm is sensitive to the buffer size, i.e., the model needs to wait until the buffer is full of *unknown* instances to be updated. Thus, by not being able to quickly adapt to the changes in the data stream, the model loose accuracy along the time.

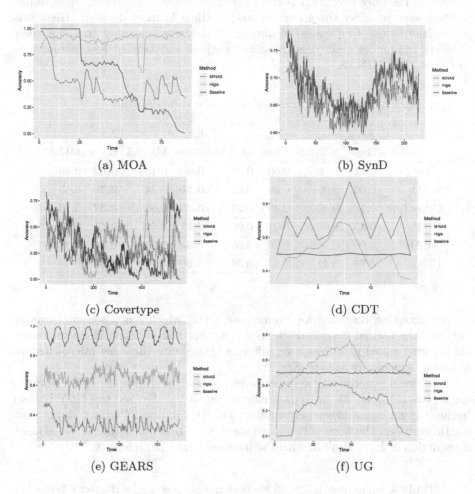

Fig. 3. Predictive accuracy over time

The baseline, kNN, presented the worst predictive performance in most of the datasets. This is somewhat expected, since it does not learn along the time. However, we can see from Fig. 3e that, for one of the datasets, the baseline had the best predictive accuracy. A possible reason is that the training set of this dataset has data from all classes. Meanwhile, for this dataset, different from the baseline, the generalization of the models induced by MINAS and Higia was not able to capture the behavior of the data. This indicates the importance of the initial training even in data stream scenarios with concept drift.

Table 2 summarizes the predictive performance obtained by the Higia and MINAS algorithms in all datasets. According to these results, for the datasets *MOA, CDT and UG*, Higia had the lowest F_{New}, but the highest M_{New}. This shows that Higia models gave more relevance to the normal classes than to the novelties. The only exception is the *CoverType* dataset. However, these results did not seem to affect the accuracy, *Acc*, of Higia in most datasets. Higia presented the lowest *Err* values in almost all datasets, meaning that, for these datasets the model made less missclassifications and labeled less instances as *unknown* than MINAS.

Table 2. Performance metrics for each algorithm

	M_{New}		F_{New}		Err		Acc	
	Higia	MINAS	Higia	MINAS	Higia	MINAS	Higia	MINAS
MOA	0.11	0.00	0.00	0.46	**0.08**	0.48	**0.62**	0.46
SynD	0.00	0.00	0.00	0.00	**0.30**	0.34	**0.70**	0.66
CoverType	0.18	0.46	0.49	0.24	**0.49**	0.54	**0.37**	0.23
CDT	0.43	0.00	0.01	0.00	0.46	**0.03**	0.47	**0.68**
GEARS	0.00	0.00	0.00	0.00	**0.34**	0.66	**0.66**	0.34
UG	0.78	0.41	0.03	0.36	**0.60**	0.70	**0.68**	0.24

An exception occurred for the dataset *CDT*, which has a seasonal overlap between the normal class and the new class. For this dataset, Higia incremental learning mixed instances from different classes into the same micro-clusters, reducing *Acc* and increasing *Err*.

Additional experiments were performed to analyse the impact of the parameter k ($k = 1, 3, 5, 10, 20$) in Higia predictive accuracy. We used the *CDT* dataset because Higia had a lower performance with this dataset. Figure 4 shows that, for this dataset, the accuracy is more stable over time for higher k. We also see a reduction of *Err*, Table 3, with the increase of the parameter k.

Table 3. Higia ($k = 1, 3, 5, 10, 20$) performance metrics for dataset CDT

	M_{New}	F_{New}	Err	ACC
1NN	0.43	0.01	0.46	0.47
3NN	0.42	0.01	0.41	0.51
5NN	0.38	0.01	0.32	0.54
10NN	0.32	0.02	0.32	0.47
20NN	0.45	0.02	0.35	0.60

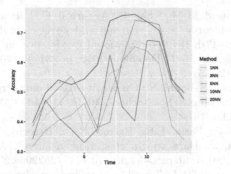

Fig. 4. Higia accuracy over time in CDT dataset varying k.

6 Conclusions and Future Work

Data stream mining has gained a great deal of attention in the last decades. Novelty detection algorithms have been successfully applied to many applications. However, most of the proposed algorithms assume that instances arriving in a stream are labeled, which is often not the case.

This paper presented Higia, a new unsupervised learning algorithm based on micro-clusters for novelty and concept drift detection in data streams. The micro-clusters are incrementally updated every time a new instance arrives from a data stream. When a novelty is detected, Higia creates new micro-clusters to represent the new class.

Considering several performance metrics, Higia was compared with MINAS, a state-of-the-art unsupervised novelty detection algorithm, and a k-NN-based baseline. According to the experimental results, Higia presented a better predictive performance than these other algorithms. Besides, Higia labeled less instances as *unknown* because it can faster adapt the model to the current concept than the compared algorithms.

As future work, the authors want to study alternatives to discard outdated information and the inclusion of an unsupervised concept drift tracker.

References

1. Abdallah, Z.S., Gaber, M.M., Srinivasan, B., Krishnaswamy, S.: Anynovel: detection of novel concepts in evolving data streams. Evol. Syst. **7**(2), 73–93 (2016). https://doi.org/10.1007/s12530-016-9147-7
2. Aggarwal, C.C.: Data Streams: Models and Algorithms, vol. 31. Springer, Heidelberg (2007). https://doi.org/10.1007/978-0-387-47534-9
3. Aggarwal, C.C., Han, J., Wang, J., Yu, P.S.: A framework for clustering evolving data streams. In: VLDB 2003, Proceedings of 29th International Conference on Very Large Data Bases, Berlin, Germany, 9–12 September 2003, pp. 81–92 (2003)

4. Al-Khateeb, T., Masud, M.M., Khan, L., Aggarwal, C.C., Han, J., Thuraisingham, B.M.: Stream classification with recurring and novel class detection using class-based ensemble. In: 12th IEEE International Conference on Data Mining, ICDM 2012, Brussels, Belgium, 10–13 December 2012, pp. 31–40 (2012). https://doi.org/10.1109/ICDM.2012.125

5. Amini, A., Teh, Y.W., Saboohi, H.: On density-based data streams clustering algorithms: a survey. J. Comput. Sci. Technol. **29**(1), 116–141 (2014). https://doi.org/10.1007/s11390-014-1416-y

6. de Andrade Silva, J., Faria, E.R., Barros, R.C., Hruschka, E.R., de Carvalho, A.C.P.L.F., Gama, J.: Data stream clustering: a survey. ACM Comput. Surv. **46**(1), 13:1–13:31 (2013). https://doi.org/10.1145/2522968.2522981

7. Asuncion, A., Newman, D.: UCI machine learning repository (2007). http://www.ics.uci.edu/~mlearn/MLRepository.html

8. Bifet, A., et al.: MOA: massive online analysis, a framework for stream classification and clustering. In: Proceedings of the First Workshop on Applications of Pattern Analysis, WAPA 2010, Cumberland Lodge, Windsor, UK, 1–3 September 2010, pp. 44–50 (2010). http://www.jmlr.org/proceedings/papers/v11/bifet10a.html

9. Bifet, A., Pfahringer, B., Read, J., Holmes, G.: Efficient data stream classification via probabilistic adaptive windows. In: Proceedings of the 28th Annual ACM Symposium on Applied Computing, SAC 2013, Coimbra, Portugal, 18–22 March 2013, pp. 801–806 (2013). https://doi.org/10.1145/2480362.2480516

10. Cao, F., Ester, M., Qian, W., Zhou, A.: Density-based clustering over an evolving data stream with noise. In: Proceedings of the Sixth SIAM International Conference on Data Mining, Bethesda, MD, USA, 20–22 April 2006, pp. 328–339 (2006). https://doi.org/10.1137/1.9781611972764.29

11. Ding, X., Li, Y., Belatreche, A., Maguire, L.P.: An experimental evaluation of novelty detection methods. Neurocomputing **135**, 313–327 (2014). https://doi.org/10.1016/j.neucom.2013.12.002

12. Faria, E.R., Gama, J., de Carvalho, A.C.P.L.F.: Novelty detection algorithm for data streams multi-class problems. In: Proceedings of the 28th Annual ACM Symposium on Applied Computing, SAC 2013, Coimbra, Portugal, 18–22 March 2013, pp. 795–800 (2013). https://doi.org/10.1145/2480362.2480515

13. Faria, E.R., Gonçalves, I.J.C.R., de Carvalho, A.C.P.L.F., Gama, J.: Novelty detection in data streams. Artif. Intell. Rev. **45**(2), 235–269 (2016). https://doi.org/10.1007/s10462-015-9444-8

14. Gama, J.: Knowledge Discovery from Data Streams. Chapman and Hall/CRC Data Mining and Knowledge Discovery Series. CRC Press, Boca Raton (2010)

15. Gama, J., Zliobaite, I., Bifet, A., Pechenizkiy, M., Bouchachia, A.: A survey on concept drift adaptation. ACM Comput. Surv. **46**(4), 44:1–44:37 (2014). https://doi.org/10.1145/2523813

16. Garcia, K.D., de Carvalho, A.C.P.L.F., Mendes-Moreira, J.: A cluster-based prototype reduction for online classification. In: Yin, H., Camacho, D., Novais, P., Tallón-Ballesteros, A.J. (eds.) IDEAL 2018. LNCS, vol. 11314, pp. 603–610. Springer, Cham (2018). https://doi.org/10.1007/978-3-030-03493-1_63

17. Hayat, M.Z., Hashemi, M.R.: A DCT based approach for detecting novelty and concept drift in data streams. In: Second International Conference of Soft Computing and Pattern Recognition, SoCPaR 2010, Cergy Pontoise/Paris, France, 7–10 December 2010, pp. 373–378 (2010). https://doi.org/10.1109/SOCPAR.2010.5686734

18. Ienco, D., Zliobaite, I., Pfahringer, B.: High density-focused uncertainty sampling for active learning over evolving stream data. In: Proceedings of the 3rd International Workshop on Big Data, Streams and Heterogeneous Source Mining: Algorithms, Systems, Programming Models and Applications, BigMine 2014, New York City, USA, 24 August 2014, pp. 133–148 (2014). http://jmlr.org/proceedings/papers/v36/ienco14.html

19. Losing, V., Hammer, B., Wersing, H.: KNN classifier with self adjusting memory for heterogeneous concept drift. In: IEEE 16th International Conference on Data Mining, ICDM 2016, Barcelona, Spain, 12–15 December 2016, pp. 291–300 (2016). https://doi.org/10.1109/ICDM.2016.0040

20. Markou, M., Singh, S.: Novelty detection: a review - part 1: statistical approaches. Sig. Process. **83**(12), 2481–2497 (2003). https://doi.org/10.1016/j.sigpro.2003.07.018

21. Masud, M.M., Gao, J., Khan, L., Han, J., Thuraisingham, B.M.: Classification and novel class detection in concept-drifting data streams under time constraints. IEEE Trans. Knowl. Data Eng. **23**(6), 859–874 (2011). https://doi.org/10.1109/TKDE.2010.61

22. Spinosa, E.J., de Carvalho, A.C.P.L.F., Gama, J.: Cluster-based novel concept detection in data streams applied to intrusion detection in computer networks. In: Proceedings of the 2008 ACM Symposium on Applied Computing (SAC), Fortaleza, Ceara, Brazil, 16–20 March 2008, pp. 976–980 (2008)

23. Spinosa, E.J., de Carvalho, A.C.P.L.F., Gama, J.: Novelty detection with application to data streams. Intell. Data Anal. **13**(3), 405–422 (2009). https://doi.org/10.3233/IDA-2009-0373

24. Zhang, T., Ramakrishnan, R., Livny, M.: BIRCH: an efficient data clustering method for very large databases. In: Proceedings of the 1996 ACM SIGMOD International Conference on Management of Data, Montreal, Quebec, Canada, 4–6 June 1996, pp. 103–114 (1996). https://doi.org/10.1145/233269.233324

25. Zliobaite, I., Bifet, A., Pfahringer, B., Holmes, G.: Active learning with drifting streaming data. IEEE Trans. Neural Netw. Learn. Syst. **25**(1), 27–39 (2014). https://doi.org/10.1109/TNNLS.2012.2236570

Mining Exceptional Social Behaviour

Carolina Centeio Jorge[1,2]([✉]), Martin Atzmueller[3], Behzad M. Heravi[4],
Jenny L. Gibson[5], Cláudio Rebelo de Sá[2], and Rosaldo J. F. Rossetti[1]

[1] University of Porto, Porto, Portugal
carolina.centeio@fe.up.pt
[2] University of Twente, Enschede, The Netherlands
[3] University of Tilburg, Tilburg, The Netherlands
[4] University College London, London, UK
[5] University of Cambridge, Cambridge, UK

Abstract. Essentially, our lives are made of social interactions. These can be recorded through personal gadgets as well as sensors adequately attached to people for research purposes. In particular, such sensors may record real time location of people. This location data can then be used to infer interactions, which may be translated into behavioural patterns. In this paper, we focus on the automatic discovery of exceptional social behaviour from spatio-temporal data. For that, we propose a method for Exceptional Behaviour Discovery (EBD). The proposed method combines Subgroup Discovery and Network Science techniques for finding social behaviour that deviates from the norm. In particular, it transforms movement and demographic data into attributed social interaction networks, and returns descriptive subgroups. We applied the proposed method on two real datasets containing location data from children playing in the school playground. Our results indicate that this is a valid approach which is able to obtain meaningful knowledge from the data.

Keywords: Subgroup discovery · Network science ·
Social interactions

1 Introduction

People interact everyday through verbal and non-verbal communication. These interactions allow us to study human beings as social entities [10]. From that, some phenomenons may emerge [6], such as homophily [25], the tendency of people for interacting more with those who are more similar to them, and so forth. This suggests that socio-demographic characteristics, as well as behavioural patterns, tend to be localized [25]. Thus, the automatic detection of patterns and unusual behaviour can be valuable to the understanding and discovery of the interactions in marketing [11], education [1], security [22], and health [28].

Furthermore, as people make more and more use of new technology, a great amount of data from their behaviour is being collected [33]. In addition, deliberately gathering data from social and ubiquitous environments through sensors

© Springer Nature Switzerland AG 2019
P. Moura Oliveira et al. (Eds.): EPIA 2019, LNAI 11805, pp. 460–472, 2019.
https://doi.org/10.1007/978-3-030-30244-3_38

(of proximity or geo-localization) is also being used to study the behaviour of people without interfering with their actions [16], e.g., *movement data* [23], on a more naturalistic basis. More specifically, it was applied to the domain of social interactions [26], where the authors analyze the properties (mainly focusing on gender phenomena) of five-year-old kids' social interactions.

Interactions may follow patterns, sequences of behaviours, or be expressed with verbal and non-verbal gestures which we do not even notice [14]. In particular, there may be some patterns which do not follow the norm, making them unusual, leading to *Exceptional Behaviour Discovery* (EBD). In that context, the automatic extraction of descriptive knowledge from the data, such as subgroups, can help and support the analysis and decisions of social sciences experts.

We propose a method for *Exceptional Behaviour Discovery* which is a combination of Data Mining approaches. In particular, we propose the combination of Subgroup Discovery and Network Science methods for the automatic detection of the characteristics that can better describe unusual social interactions. The main goal of the proposed method is to find subgroups from movement data, making use of a graph structure. Thus, we focus on descriptive subgroup discovery on such (extended) graph data structures. On the one hand, Subgroup Discovery [20] is a descriptive data mining technique that provides easy-to-understand results to the expert. It finds subgroups of objects in the data that share the same characteristics with respect to a property of interest (target) [17]. On the other hand, interactions can be represented as a set of complex networks, namely *social interaction networks* which capture interactions between the subjects involved in the study [4]. In this case, people are represented by nodes and the interactions are represented by edges.

When considering social interaction data, however, people interact on the move and over time; therefore, the sequence of locations of a person can be related to the demographic properties of the subjects involved, and modeled as attributed social interaction networks. Eventual behavioural patterns thus might not be captured in snapshots of the network, but rather in the evolution of it. Building upon compositional subgroup discovery on such attributed social interaction networks [6], we created different Subgroup Discovery quality measures to find subgroups of people whose interactions deviate from the norm.

We tested the proposed approaches on two sets of data with locations and personal attributes of children in the playground of the school. The data was collected with the use of location sensors during the school breaks. One dataset, *playgroundA* [16], has the geographic position of 18 children over time, in 10 different sessions and personal attributes (gender, age, emotional stability etc). The other dataset, *playgroundB* [26] has the position of 16 children and socio-demographic attributes, such as gender and age. The results were mostly expected, when analyzed by experts [26] in the domain, and similar between the two datasets. This shows it is a valid approach. Also, the results added meaningful information to the expected scenario.

The remainder of this paper is structured as follows: in Sect. 2 we present the background, in which we explain the underlying concepts and literature review;

in Sect. 3 we present our contributions for the state of the art, testing it with a case study presented in Sect. 4; we finally conclude in Sect. 5.

2   Preliminaries

Many domains in which we can potentially use data mining techniques are placed in a temporal or spatial scenario. Therefore, to learn from the data, it is important to take into account its temporal and spatial properties [29]. With spatial properties providing information about objects' location, also known as *movement data* [23].

2.1   Subgroup Discovery

Subgroup Discovery (SD) is a descriptive and exploratory data mining technique to identify interesting patterns, the so-called subgroups, that deviate from the norm [20]. These patterns show an unusual distribution when compared to the overall population [3]. This interesting behaviour is typically based on some criteria which balances their relevance between their size and unusualness. We can find SD applications on medical [13], marketing [8], education [30], socio-demographic [21] and social domains [6].

As in [12], we define a dataset as a bag of n records given in the form of $x = (a_1, \ldots, a_m, t_1, \ldots, t_l)$, where a_i is a descriptor and t_i is a target. Subgroups are usually described with a description language, $\mathcal{D}$, and are induced by a *pattern*. A *pattern*, p, is a function $p : \mathcal{A} \rightarrow \{0, 1\}$ and *covers* a record x iff $p(a_1, \ldots, a_m) = 1$. A *subgroup* corresponding to a pattern p is the bag of records, S_p, that p covers: $S_p = \{x \in D \mid p(a_1, \ldots, a_m) = 1\}$. $\mathcal{D}$ is typically a conjunction of conditions on attributes, such as: Gender = F $\wedge$ Age $\leq$ 22.

The interestingness of subgroups is measured by *quality measures* according to the different types of targets. Given a subgroup discovery algorithm, a set of subgroups is identified and scored by the quality function [24]: $\varphi : \mathcal{D} \rightarrow \mathbb{R}$. Quality measures are a key factor for the extraction of knowledge because the interest obtained depends directly on them [17]. Many have been proposed for identifying different deviations in different targets. Targets can be binary [35], nominal [8], numeric [15], ranked [31] or as a distribution [18].

2.2   Network Science

Network Science combines ideas from several domains of knowledge so as to address questions about networks [27]. A network is a collection of *nodes* connected with *edges*. This simple representation allows one to translate many events into the form of networks, which can often lead to new and useful insights [27].

The key concepts of Network Science are centrality measures, which measure the nodes that are the most important or central in a network. Centrality gathers a wide range of metrics and measures that can allow us to better understand the data. For example, *degree* of centrality (based on the number of links of a node), *closeness* (based on the average length of the shortest path between the node and all other nodes in the graph), *betweeness* (based on how many shortest paths of the graph go through a node) and *pagerank* (measured by the links to a node). More recently proposed metrics are *hubs* and *authorities* [19]. A hub is a node with many outgoing links to authorities, whereas an authority is a node with many links from hubs. Another network concept of practical importance is provided by communities [27] in networks. Communities are tightly knit groups within a larger, looser network.

A particular case of networks are social interaction networks [34] which focus on interactions between people as the corresponding actors. In this case, the nodes represent the actors and the edges, the links between actors, model a interaction or event. These edges may have properties, such as frequency of occurrence or duration. Furthermore, edges and nodes may have other labels, leading to attributed networks. From these attributed networks, we can extract and characterize subgroups [6].

A complex network can be represented by a graph [9]. A graph G is an ordered triple $(V(G), E(G), \psi_G)$, where $V(G)$ represents the set of vertices, $E(G)$, the edges and ψ_G is the function that associates to each edge of G a pair of vertices of $V(G)$. For example: $V(G) = \{v_1, v_2, \ldots, v_n\}$, $E(G) = \{e_1, e_2, \ldots, e_n\}$ and $\psi_G(e_1) = (v_1, v_2)$. A graph can be *directed* or *undirected*. In the case of G being directed, the output of the function $\psi_G(e_i)$, (v_j, v_k) is ordered and it is known as a *digraph* [27]. Moreover, the graph can have multiple edges, in the same direction, if directed, between two nodes. In this case, the graph is referred to as *multigraph*. The function ψ_{MG} of a multigraph returns the same pair of vertices for more than one edge.

Some approaches combine Subgroup Discovery and Network Science. In 2013, Atzmueller [2] gave an overview of data mining in social interaction networks, specifically human behavioural (offline) networks. Methods and approaches for describing and characterizing networks and their properties were proposed. In terms of community detection, Škrlj et al. [32] introduced the Community-Based Semantic Subgroup Discovery (CBSSD), an algorithm that identifies classes of instances based on structural properties of complex networks. Atzmueller [5] also presented an overview of research in subgroup discovery and community detection on attributed graphs. In 2018, Atzmueller [6] also proposed quality measures and targets based on interaction network properties for subgroup discovery in attributed social networks, as compositional subgroup discovery.

3   Exceptional Behaviour Discovery

In this paper we propose *Exceptional behaviour discovery (EBD)*. The aim of EBD is to look for social behaviour which deviates from the norm. In order to recognize unusual social behaviour among individuals (in social interactions), we adapted an existing subgroup discovery technique to deal with spatio-temporal data. We focus on the study of Subgroup Discovery methods and metrics of social networks analysis. This work extends the work proposed in [6] which combined Subgroup Discovery with social interaction networks and is referred as *Compositional Subgroup Discovery*.

3.1 Compositional Subgroup Discovery

Compositional Subgroup Discovery can be divided into two steps. First, the network is represented by means of a graph, where each subject is represented by a node and each interaction is represented by an edge between two nodes. In this graph representation, both nodes and edges can be characterized by attributes. Finally, these can be used to find subgroups and to explain some observed behavioural patterns.

Quality Measures. To measure the interestingness, the duration of the interactions and frequency are considered. The target, t_p, is numeric and corresponds to the observed number of edges normalized by the expectation.

Two different quality measures were proposed. The first measure uses simple attributed graphs where the duration of the interactions is used to weight the edges. The second one also includes the interaction frequency information in an attributed multigraph representation of the network (each edge represents an interaction).

In the first approach, the simple attributed graph, the weights of all the edges, E_p, covered by a *pattern*, are summed, normalized by the number of possible edges, n_E, among the nodes covered by the *pattern*, n_{Ep}. Then, r samples of n_E edges, where $n_E = \frac{n_{Ep}(n_{Ep} - 1)}{2}$, are considered as well as are their normalized sum of weights. Finally, a Z-score is calculated estimating the significance of the obtained value (t_P) among the samples. For a *pattern* p, the quality function, q_S, is:

$$q_S(P) = Z(\frac{1}{n_E} \cdot \sum_{e \in E_P} w(e)) \tag{1}$$

In the multigraph version, the frequency (apart from the duration) of interaction is also taken into account. Thus, for normalizing the sum of weights of a pattern p, we have to consider the multiple edges that exist between two nodes. In this case, instead of dividing by n_E, the author divides by $n_e + m_E$, where $m_E = \sum_{i=1}^{n_E}(m_i - 1)$ and m_i is the observed multiplicity of an edge. For the Z-score, all the edges are considered.

3.2 Proposed Extension

In this work, we propose to use *digraphs* to represent the interactions of the subjects. For that, we need to define proximity and when a subject is approaching another subject. If a subject approaches another within a certain proximity, a directed edge is created from the node of the subject approaching to the node of the subject approached.

This approach combines *movement data* and *social data* of the subjects and returns subgroups, according to the desired quality function. The *movement data* consists of a timestamp of the event, the *id* and position (*x* and *y*) for each subject. From that, there is a function that computes the speed, *velX* and *velY*, relatively to *x* and *y*, respectively. The *social data*, has the ids and socio-demographic data corresponding to the subjects in the *movement data*. Any numeric attributes are discretized in equal frequency bins.

Generating the Interaction Digraph. To create the interaction digraph, or multidigraph, we first need to define interactions. We consider an interaction between two subjects when their relative distance is within a certain proximity and one of the subjects approaches the other. Therefore, given a maximum distance threshold between subjects, *maxdist*, we start with an empty digraph G.

At each time step t, a matrix of distances, D, between every two subjects is calculated. Then, for each distance $d_{i,j} \in D : d_{i,j} \leq maxdist$ we compute a vector from i to j as $r_{i,j} = (x_j - x_i, y_j - y_i)$. We then verify the speed vector of i, $vel_i = (velX_i, velY_i)$, and calculate the cosine between the vectors $r_{i,j}$ and vel_i. If the cosine be positive, we consider that the subject i *approached* (or *reached*) subject j.

In the simple digraph, a directed edge, from node i to node j, is added to G and $w_{i,j} \in W$ is incremented one unit of time, where W is the matrix of weights and $w_{i,j}$ is the number of times that the subject i approaches the subject j. In the multidigraph version, a directed edge is added to G at moment t if subject i approached subject j, given that it was not interacting in $t - 1$, with $w_{i,j} \in W$, where $w_{i,j}$ is the total time that the subject i approaches the subject j without interruption.

Quality Measures. We propose two quality measures with two variations.

Simple Attributed Digraph. This quality measure takes into account the duration of the interactions between two subjects. A new directed edge (or arrow) is considered every time an interaction is observed and not clear.

For the quality function, we use the same measure as q_S (Eq. 1). However, since we have the double of the edges (because this is a directed version), we use $n_E = n_{Ep}(n_{Ep} - 1)$.

Directed Attributed Multidigraph. This quality measure considers both the duration and frequency of the interactions between two subjects. In this case, one directed edge is created every time an interaction is observed.

To-node *and* From-node *variants.* These two variants, *To-node* and *From-node*, extend the quality measures mentioned above. In the *To-node* and *From-node*, the attributes of the edges are only based on the attributes of the *head* node or the *tail* node, respectively. With these variants we hope to find valuable information about the attributes of the subjects that look for interactions (*From-node*) and the subjects that are reached the most (*To-node*).

3.3 Subgroup Discovery

The edges of the graph G are associated with features, which are based on the attributes of the nodes of that edge. Numeric attributes in the nodes are represented as *equal* (or same), *greater* or *lower* in the features of the edges in the comparison versions (Simple attributed digraph and Directed attributed multidigraph). In the *To-node* and *From-node* variants, the numeric attributes of the nodes are represented as *equal* (or same), *high* or *low* as the features of the edges. After assigning attributes to the edges, there is a function to run the SD-Map algorithm [7] on the graph. The output is a list of subgroups and their characteristics, namely pattern description, the number of edges and nodes covered by the pattern, the mean weight of those edges and the score (quality function result).

We also propose to add automatically generated features to the nodes' attributes and, consequently, to the edges' with the use of complex networks' metrics. For example, degree (also in-degree and out-degree), centrality measures (eigen, closeness, betweenness), authority and hub values.

4 A Case Study in Playground Social Interactions

Analyzing social interactions in the playground can be of utmost importance. Social group structure and dynamics are believed to be strongly related to the child well-being and yet has been poorly understood and studied [16].

4.1 Data

To test the approach explained in Sect. 3.2, we used two datasets with locations of children in the school playground. The data was collected with the use of location sensors during the school breaks.

One dataset, *playgroundA* [16], has the geographic position of 18 7–8 year-old children (9 girls) over time, during approximately 45 min. It also includes the personal attributes (gender, age, emotional stability etc). The kids were playing outdoors, without toys, during a normal day of Primary School. They had a head-mounted sensor with IMU and GNSS for precise positioning a shoe-mounted IMU sensor for activity monitoring. The following social and psychological measures were collected from a teacher:

ProSoc the higher the score the highest the social skills are
Conduct a high value represents behaviour problems
Emotion the higher the score the more emotional difficulties
Peer high scores indicate that the child has issues making friends
Hyper the higher the more hyperactive the child is.

The other dataset, *playgroundB* [26] has the position of 14 children (8 girls) around 5 years-old and socio-demographic attributes, such as gender and age. The data was collected through a real time location system that used UWB sensors. The data was collected during 1 h.

4.2   Assessment Approach

The first dataset already had ids, positions, and speeds in two dimensions. For the *social data* of this dataset, we transformed the numeric values in 3 bins. The second dataset did not include speed values, so we created them. Then, we created the graphs and experimented the 6 approaches for each: comparison, to-node and from-node attributed edges for both simple and multidigraph versions. Furthermore, we also looked for subgroups based on Network Science metrics in the *playgroundB* dataset.

4.3   Results and Discussion

In this section, we analyze some of the results of our approach with both *playgroundA* and *playgroundB* datasets. An adapted version of SD-Map [7] is used for subgroup discovery.

PlaygroundA. Table 1 shows the ranked subgroups found with the dataset *playgroundA*. We present three versions: a comparison version with simple attributed digraphs (comp in the column V, in the Table 1), and a to-node and from-node version with attributed multidigraph version (to and from in the column V, in the Table 1, respectively). For each subgroup, we show its pattern, number of nodes (children) belonging to the subgroup, N, number of edges (interactions), E, the mean time of an interactions between children in the subgroup, $|C|$, and the Z-score based on the comparison between the total duration of the interactions in the subgroup and the null model, Z.

The top-2 ranked subgroups (Table 1) obtained with the comparison version are $Gender = M \rightarrow Gender = M$ and $Gender = F \rightarrow Gender = F$. This means that boys follow other boys and girls follow other girls, much more than what would be expected. We note that these subgroups have much higher score than the others, which goes in line with the observations already discussed in [26]. This seems to confirm the homophily regarding the gender, meaning that children interact more with children of the same gender.

The subgroup $Emotion = higher \rightarrow Emotion = lower$ seems to indicate that children with more emotional problems tend to look for interactions with children with less emotional issues. The 4th best subgroup $Hyper = same \rightarrow Hyper = same$ suggests that children prefer to look for other children with similar levels of peer relations. This is also indicated by the 8th subgroup, since it connotes that similar social skills can also motivate more interactions.

Some subgroups exhibit opposite behaviour. For example, the subgroups 3 and 7 from the comparison in Table 1. However, when we visualize the graphs associated with the subgroups in Fig. 1 we can conclude that they are representing distinct behaviours. The shades in blue represent the weight of the edge: the lighter the blue the lower the weight. It is possible to observe that the subgroup ranked higher, in position 3, "Emotion=higher → Emotion 5=lower", presents edges with bigger weights. This makes sense since the quality function is based on the sum of the weights of the edges. In other words, a subgroup is more interesting if the sum of the weights of its graph are bigger than the graph of all the interactions.

Results of the to-node and from-node versions can add valuable information to the results found in the comparison version. For these results, we conclude that the multidigraph version presents better results than the simple version. The results show that there is a tendency for older children to go after interactions, whereas average aged children are the ones reached the most. Children with a low 'Peer' score, meaning they present a better quality in peer relation, as well as low 'Hyper' and 'Emotion' scores, which means they do not present hyperactivity or emotional issues, both look for interactions and are reached by other peers. Furthermore, children with low social skills ("ProSoc") tend to reach for interactions whereas children with average social skills are more reached.

Table 1. Ranking of subgroups (comp, to-node and from-node attributed multidigraph versions) according to the total duration of interactions between every two children in the dataset *playgroundA*.

Rank	V	Pattern	N	E	$|C|$	Z
1	comp	Gender=M → Gender=M	9	51	21.1	28.6
2	comp	Gender=F → Gender=F	9	50	15.4	19.5
3	comp	Emotion=higher → Emotion=lower	18	73	7.4	3.9
4	comp	Hyper=same → Hyper=same	18	72	7.3	3.7
5	comp	Conduct=lower → Conduct=higher	18	74	7.2	3.4
6	comp	Age=higher → Age=lower	18	85	7.9	3.2
7	comp	Emotion=lower → Emotion=higher	18	74	7.0	3.1
8	comp	ProSoc=same → ProSoc=same	18	69	6.5	2.8
9	comp	Conduct=higher → Conduct=lower	18	75	6.8	2.8
10	comp	Peer=same → Peer=same	18	105	9.0	2.8
1	to	Conduct=low ∧ Peer=low ∧ Hyper=low	18	174	1.5	2.0
2	to	Age=Medium ∧ ProSoc=Medium ∧ Emotion=low	17	184	1.6	2.0
3	to	Age=Medium ∧ Emotion=low	17	184	1.6	1.9
4	to	Age=Medium ∧ Conduct=low	16	157	1.4	1.7
1	from	Peer=low ∧ Age=high ∧ Hyper=low	18	135	1.3	2.8
2	from	Peer=low ∧ Emotion=low ∧ ProSoc=low	18	158	1.4	2.4
3	from	Age=high ∧ Hyper=low	18	135	1.3	2.2
4	from	Gender = M ∧ Emotion=low ∧ Hyper=low	18	147	1.3	2.2

PlaygroundB. For the dataset *playgroundB*, we analyze the attributed multidigraph approach. When analyzing the results we can also conclude that children in this dataset interact more with peers of the same gender. Moreover, we can see that boys tend to look for interactions with older boys, whereas girls show more interactions with girls with the same age.

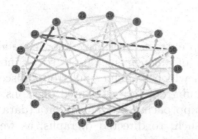   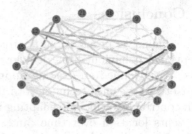

Emotion=higher → Emotion=lower   Emotion=lower → Emotion=higher

Fig. 1. Plots of graph representation of the subgroups 3 and 7, comparison version, in Table 1.

If we focus on the to-node version of *playgroundB*, we can see that boys (Gender=M) are the most reached, regardless of their age. Nevertheless, the pattern with the highest score is "Gender=M ∧ Age=low". The oldest children, however, are the ones looking for more interactions according to the from-node multidigraph version. In this version, all top-3 patterns include "Age=high", despite the gender, with small differences in the scores (11.9, 10.0 and 9.7).

Since we only have two attributes in this dataset (gender and age) we generated extra features based on the networks' metrics (Sect. 3.3). The results of the comparison version of simple attributed digraph are presented in Table 2. We can observe that boys tend to look for boys with a similar hub score and that girls look for girls with similar closeness. We can associate the hub score to interactions with popular kids and conclude that boys prefer to interact with boys with a similar level of interactions with popular peers. Closeness, on the other hand, may imply many interactions in general, which suggests that girls prefer to interact with girls that interact with a similar amount of peers. In general, we observed that children reach peers with similar centrality measures.

Table 2. Top-4 subgroups (comparison version of simple attributed digraph) according to the total duration of interactions between every two children, considering Network Science metrics in the dataset *playgroundB*.

Rank	Pattern	N	E	$|C|$	Z
1	Gender=M → Gender=M	6	25	0.2	21.7
2	Gender=M ∧ hubs=same → Gender=M ∧ hubs=same	4	12	0.2	11.7
3	Gender=F ∧ closeness=same → Gender=F ∧ closeness=same	6	12	0.1	7.7
4	Gender=F → Gender=F	8	22	0.1	7.0

5 Conclusions

In this paper we proposed an approach to extract descriptive knowledge about exceptional behaviour from demographic and movement data of social interactions. We extended an existing approach which combines Subgroup Discovery and Network Science techniques to find subgroups in attributed digraphs. Our main contributions include adapting this approach to movement data (data that represents location over time) and, as such, to directed digraphs, as well as adding Network Science metrics to the attributes of the graph. Accordingly, we developed a pipeline that receives spatio-temporal data of tracked objects (people) along with some personal and social characteristics of the individuals. Then it transforms the data into attributed directed digraphs (simple and/or multidigraphs) and returns subgroups. To test our approach we used two datasets of children interacting in the school playground. The results were as expected by the experts in the domain and similar in both datasets. Nevertheless, they can add some valuable information for further social interaction analysis.

For future work, an interesting direction is given by further alternative quality measures that might be more refined to specific interaction contexts regarding the detection of subgroups of interactions. Furthermore, we also aim to compare the presented method with further approaches and to apply more datasets.

Acknowledgements. This work has been partially supported by the German Research Foundation (DFG) project "MODUS" (under grant AT 88/4-1). Furthermore, the research leading to these results has received funding (JG) from ESRC grant ES/N006577/1. This work was financed by the project Kids First, project number 68639.

References

1. Altman, I.: The Environment and Social Behavior: Privacy, Personal Space, Territory, and Crowding. Brooks/Cole Publishing Company, Belmont (1975)
2. Atzmueller, M.: Data mining on social interaction networks. JDMDH **1** (2014)
3. Atzmueller, M.: Subgroup discovery. WIREs DMKD **5**(1), 35–49 (2015)
4. Atzmueller, M.: Local exceptionality detection on social interaction networks. In: Berendt, B., Bringmann, B., Fromont, É., Garriga, G., Miettinen, P., Tatti, N., Tresp, V. (eds.) ECML PKDD 2016. LNCS, vol. 9853, pp. 298–302. Springer, Cham (2016). https://doi.org/10.1007/978-3-319-46131-1_39
5. Atzmueller, M.: Descriptive community detection. In: Missaoui, R., Kuznetsov, S.O., Obiedkov, S. (eds.) Formal Concept Analysis of Social Networks. LNSN, pp. 41–58. Springer, Cham (2017). https://doi.org/10.1007/978-3-319-64167-6_3
6. Atzmueller, M.: Compositional subgroup discovery on attributed social interaction networks. In: Soldatova, L., Vanschoren, J., Papadopoulos, G., Ceci, M. (eds.) DS 2018. LNCS, vol. 11198, pp. 259–275. Springer, Cham (2018). https://doi.org/10.1007/978-3-030-01771-2_17
7. Atzmueller, M., Puppe, F.: SD-Map – a fast algorithm for exhaustive subgroup discovery. In: Fürnkranz, J., Scheffer, T., Spiliopoulou, M. (eds.) PKDD 2006. LNCS, vol. 4213, pp. 6–17. Springer, Heidelberg (2006). https://doi.org/10.1007/11871637_6

8. Berlanga, F., del Jesus, M.J., González, P., Herrera, F., Mesonero, M.: Multiobjective evolutionary induction of subgroup discovery fuzzy rules: a case study in marketing. In: Perner, P. (ed.) ICDM 2006. LNCS, vol. 4065, pp. 337–349. Springer, Heidelberg (2006). https://doi.org/10.1007/11790853_27
9. Bondy, J.A., Murty, U.S.R.: Graph Theory with Applications, vol. 290. Elsevier Science Ltd., North-Holland (1976)
10. Cabrera-Quiros, L., Demetriou, A., Gedik, E., van der Meij, L., Hung, H.: The matchNMingle dataset: a novel multi-sensor resource for the analysis of social interactions and group dynamics in-the-wild during free-standing conversations and speed dates. IEEE Trans. Affect. Comput. **99**, 1–17 (2018)
11. Delener, N.: Religious contrasts in consumer decision behaviour patterns: their dimensions and marketing implications. Eur. J. Mark. **28**(5), 36–53 (1994)
12. Duivesteijn, W., Knobbe, A.J.: Exploiting false discoveries - statistical validation of patterns and quality measures in subgroup discovery. In: ICDM, pp. 151–160. IEEE Computer Society (2011)
13. Gamberger, D., Lavrac, N.: Expert-guided subgroup discovery: methodology and application. J. Artif. Intell. Res. **17**, 501–527 (2002)
14. Goffman, E. (ed.): Interaction Ritual: Essays in Face to Face Behavior. Piscataway, Aldine-Transactions (1967)
15. Grosskreutz, H., Rüping, S.: On subgroup discovery in numerical domains. In: Buntine, W., Grobelnik, M., Mladenić, D., Shawe-Taylor, J. (eds.) ECML PKDD 2009. LNCS, vol. 5781, p. 30. Springer, Heidelberg (2009). https://doi.org/10.1007/978-3-642-04180-8_15
16. Heravi, B.M., Gibson, J.L., Hailes, S., Skuse, D.: Playground social interaction analysis using bespoke wearable sensors for tracking and motion capture. In: Proceedings of the 5th International Conference on Movement and Computing, MOCO 2018, pp. 21:1–21:8. ACM (2018)
17. Herrera, F., Carmona, C.J., González, P., del Jesús, M.J.: An overview on subgroup discovery: foundations and applications. Knowl. Inf. Syst. **29**(3), 495–525 (2011)
18. Jorge, A.M., Pereira, F., Azevedo, P.J.: Visual interactive subgroup discovery with numerical properties of interest. In: Todorovski, L., Lavrač, N., Jantke, K.P. (eds.) DS 2006. LNCS, vol. 4265, pp. 301–305. Springer, Heidelberg (2006). https://doi.org/10.1007/11893318_31
19. Kleinberg, J.M.: Hubs, authorities, and communities. ACM Comput. Surv. **31**(4es), 5 (1999)
20. Klösgen, W.: Handbook of Data Mining and Knowledge Discovery. Oxford University Press Inc., New York (2002)
21. Klösgen, W., May, M.: Spatial subgroup mining integrated in an object-relational spatial database. In: Elomaa, T., Mannila, H., Toivonen, H. (eds.) PKDD 2002. LNCS, vol. 2431, pp. 275–286. Springer, Heidelberg (2002). https://doi.org/10.1007/3-540-45681-3_23
22. Ko, T.: A survey on behavior analysis in video surveillance for homeland security applications. In: Proceedings of the 37th IEEE Applied Imagery Pattern Recognition Workshop, AIPR 2008, Washington, DC, USA, 15–17 October 2008, pp. 1–8 (2008)
23. Lauw, H.W., Lim, E., Pang, H., Tan, T.: Stevent: spatio-temporal event model for social network discovery. ACM Trans. Inf. Syst. **28**(3), 15:1–15:32 (2010)
24. Leman, D., Feelders, A., Knobbe, A.: Exceptional model mining. In: Daelemans, W., Goethals, B., Morik, K. (eds.) ECML PKDD 2008. LNCS, vol. 5212, pp. 1–16. Springer, Heidelberg (2008). https://doi.org/10.1007/978-3-540-87481-2_1

25. McPherson, M., Smith-Lovin, L., Cook, J.M.: Birds of a feather: homophily in social networks. Annu. Rev. Sociol. **27**(1), 415–444 (2001)
26. Messinger, D.S., et al.: Continuous measurement of dynamic classroom social interactions. Int. J. Behav. Dev. **43**(3), 263–270 (2019)
27. Newman, M.: Networks: an introduction. In: Introduction: A Short Introduction to Networks and Why We Study Them. Oxford University Press, Inc., New York (2010). Chap
28. Owen, N., Healy, G.N., Matthews, C.E., Dunstan, D.W.: Too much sitting: the population health science of sedentary behavior. Exerc. Sport Sci. Rev. **38**(3), 182–196 (2010)
29. Roddick, J.F., Spiliopoulou, M.: A bibliography of temporal, spatial and spatio-temporal data mining research. SIGKDD Explor. **1**(1), 34–38 (1999)
30. Romero, C., González, P., Ventura, S., del Jesús, M.J., Herrera, F.: Evolution-ary algorithms for subgroup discovery in E-learning: a practical application using moodle data. Expert Syst. Appl. **36**(2), 1632–1644 (2009)
31. Rebelo de Sá, C., Duivesteijn, W., Soares, C., Knobbe, A.: Exceptional preferences mining. In: Calders, T., Ceci, M., Malerba, D. (eds.) DS 2016. LNCS, vol. 9956, pp. 3–18. Springer, Cham (2016). https://doi.org/10.1007/978-3-319-46307-0_1
32. Škrlj, B., Kralj, J., Vavpetič, A., Lavrač, N.: Community-based semantic subgroup discovery. In: Appice, A., Loglisci, C., Manco, G., Masciari, E., Ras, Z.W. (eds.) NFMCP 2017. LNCS, vol. 10785, pp. 182–196. Springer, Cham (2018). https://doi.org/10.1007/978-3-319-78680-3_13
33. Terry, M.A., Mynatt, E.D., Ryall, K., Leigh, D.: Social net: using patterns of physical proximity over time to infer shared interests. In: CHI Extended Abstracts, pp. 816–817. ACM (2002)
34. Wasserman, S., Faust, K.: Social Network Analysis: Methods and Applications. Structural Analysis in the Social Sciences. Cambridge University Press, Cambridge (1994)
35. Wrobel, S.: An algorithm for multi-relational discovery of subgroups. In: Komorowski, J., Zytkow, J. (eds.) PKDD 1997. LNCS, vol. 1263, pp. 78–87. Springer, Heidelberg (1997). https://doi.org/10.1007/3-540-63223-9_108

Visual Interpretation of Regression Error

Inês Areosa[1]([✉]) and Luís Torgo[1,2]

[1] LIAAD, INESC TEC, Porto, Portugal
inesareosa@gmail.com, ltorgo@dal.ca
[2] Faculty of Computer Science, Dalhousie University, Halifax, Canada

Abstract. Numerous sophisticated machine learning tools (e.g. ensembles or deep networks) have shown outstanding performance in terms of accuracy on different numeric forecasting tasks. In many real world application domains the numeric predictions of the models drive important and costly decisions. Frequently, decision makers require more than a black box model to be able to "trust" the predictions up to the point that they base their decisions on them. In this context, understanding these black boxes has become one of the hot topics in Machine Learning and Data Mining research. This paper proposes a series of visualisation tools that help in understanding the predictive performance of non-interpretable regression models. More specifically, these tools allow the user to relate the expected error of any model to the values of the predictor variables. This type of information allows end-users to correctly assess the risks associated with the use of the models, by showing how concrete values of the predictors may affect the performance of the models. Our illustrations with different real world data sets and learning algorithms provide insights on the type of usage and information these tools bring to both the data analyst and the end-user.

1 Introduction

Interpretability and accountability has become a key issue on Machine Learning (ML) and Data Mining (DM) research (e.g. [14]). With the widespread usage of ML and DM in different areas of human society, several interest groups have been raising important questions on the accountability and responsibility of the decisions taken based on the models' predictions (e.g. [2]).

A few definitions have appeared in the literature on what is meant by interpretability. Two that we consider particularly enlightening are: (i) "interpretability is the degree to which a human can understand the cause of a decision" [16]; and (ii) "interpretability is the degree to which a human can consistently predict the model's result" [10]. These definitions stress two different, but equality important, aspects of interpretability: (i) being able to justify the decisions of a model; and (ii) being able to anticipate these decisions.

Although interpretability has been a concern of ML and DM researchers for a long time (e.g. [11]), it has gained a strong momentum as we witness the success of new ML/DM approaches like Deep Learning. These methodologies have been

© Springer Nature Switzerland AG 2019
P. Moura Oliveira et al. (Eds.): EPIA 2019, LNAI 11805, pp. 473–485, 2019.
https://doi.org/10.1007/978-3-030-30244-3_39

the focus of many news and projects, and this exposure just increased the need for thinking about interpretability and accountability (e.g. [9]).

There are many aspects and perspectives one can focus when trying to increase the ability of end users to understand the behaviour of ML/DM models. In this paper, we focus on one particular aspect: helping end users to understand the reasons or causes for the errors committed by the models. This is an important question for end-users of many relevant applications as it allows them to better understand the risks associated with trusting the prediction of a model for any concrete test case. The performance of any model will vary with different test cases. Looking only at an overall average performance score may hinder some particular difficulties of the models for some subset of cases. Being able to inform the user on the expected error of a model (or models) for a test case with certain characteristics, can be of great help when deciding whether or not to trust these models. We propose visual tools that help the end-user in understanding the relationship between the prediction error of regression models and the values of the predictor variables of the problem. These tools are important for the users to accurately access the risk associated with the usage of a certain model. Although these tools do not provide a full answer to all aspects related with interpretability and accountability, we claim that they help in understanding the risks of using some regression model, and also in explaining the reasons that may be causing some performance degradation of these models.

This paper is organised as follows. In Sect. 2 we provide an overview of related work. Our proposals are described in Sect. 3 and the results of an extensive experimental evaluation are discussed in Sect. 4. Finally, Sect. 5 presents the main conclusions.

2   Related Work

Existing work focuses on different aspects of interpretability and approaches the problem from different perspectives. For instance, distillation methods (e.g. [9, 12]) try to provide a global explanation of a non-interpretable model, while other methods are concentrated on explaining individual predictions of the models (e.g. [17]). Other proposals try to provide insights on the relationship between the predictors' values and the output of the model. That is the case of the Partial Dependence Plot (PDP) [5], where a graph is produced to show the relationship between the domain of a (continuous) predictor variable and the output of a model. These plots can be extended to bi-variate plots that highlight the interaction between the domains of two predictors and the output of the model. While PDPs show the expected average effect of the values of a numeric predictor on the output of a model, Individual Conditional Expectation (ICE) plots [6], show this effect for each instance, thus increasing the level of detail on this type of analysis.

One common feature of most existing work is the focus on analysing the output (predictions) of the models. While this is very important for end-users, we claim that providing similar analysis for the expected error of the model predictions is also of high relevance, particularly when the predictions drive costly decisions by the end-user. Being able to have an idea of the expected prediction error for a particular test case will empower the end-user with an estimate of the risk incurred when the model is trusted, and decide if the risk is acceptable. Our work is focused on this aspect of model interpretability.

The analysis of the expected error of a model is a well-studied subject within predictive analytics. Most existing approaches focus on providing (reliable) estimates of the expected average error of any model (e.g. error rate, mean squared error, etc.), often named scalar metrics. On the other hand, graphical-based metrics provide a different analysis perspective of the models' performance. They focus on providing feedback on the performance across different "operating conditions". Examples of graphical-based metrics include ROC curves (e.g. [15]), Brier curves [4], among several others. While these curves are focused on classification tasks (nominal target variable), comparable methods have been proposed for regression problems (numeric targets), like for instance the work on RROC space [8], REC plots [1] or REC surfaces [18]. Nevertheless, all these works focus on the analysis of the error behaviour of the models, and not on the relationship of this behaviour with the predictors' values, i.e. they are not focused on explaining the reasons for the behaviour. This is the main distinguishing factor of our proposals. Our work is strongly related with approaches like PDPs and ICEs, as we also focus on explaining the consequences of changes across the domain of the predictor variables, but instead of illustrating the impact of these changes on the predicted values we focus on the impact on the expected error, which means that there are also relationships with graphical-based regression error plots.

3   Explaining the Error of Regression Models

In this section we describe a series of visual tools that provide insights on the expected performance of regression models as a function of the values of the predictor variables. These tools help end users to understand why some prediction errors may have occurred. Overall, these tools provide a better assessment of the risks associated with trusting non-interpretable models for a given test case.

The tools we will describe in this section relate the values of the predictors with the expected error of the models. Even if these are non-interpretable models the tools will allow the user to better understand the relationship between the values of the predictors and what to expect from the model in terms of error. We call these graphs Error Dependence Plots (EDPs). They show the distribution of the estimated error against the values of the predictor variables. We use box-plots as graphical elements to display this distribution. Box-plots are one of the most informative and robust graphical representations of the distribution of a continuous variable (in our case the expected error). Error Dependence Plots have some similarities with PDPs [5] and ICEs [6]. However, contrary to these plots, EDPs have the expected error ($\hat{Err}$) on the Y-axis, instead of the expected prediction ($\hat{Y}$). This apparently small difference, brings considerable challenges in terms of how to obtain EDPs. PDPs are obtained with a very clever algorithm that given a feature X^k, estimates a function whose result is the expected prediction of the model for a certain value of X^k, i.e. $\hat{Y}_{X^k} = f(X^k)$. PDPs show this estimated Y value across the range of values of X^k. The function $f(X^k)$ is approximated by a simple procedure. For each value of $X^k = v_x$ we create n test cases by merging this with the n available training cases (except for the feature X^k that will have the value v_x). The black box model is queried with these n test cases and we get n predictions. The average of these n predictions is the value of $f(X^k)$, i.e. $\hat{Y}_{X^k=v_x}$. By repeating this procedure across the domain of the variable X^k we get the PDP of feature X^k. ICEs are obtained in a similar way but instead of plotting the average of the prediction for each value of X^k, we actually plot the n lines thus given a more detailed idea on the possible predictions for each value of the predictor.

The problem with applying the same general algorithm to EDPs is that we are not interested in estimating the predicted value ($\hat{Y}$). Instead we want to plot the estimated error and for calculating an error we need not only the value predicted by the model, but also the true value. Unfortunately, this true value is not available for the test cases generated through the PDP algorithm, briefly described above. We only know the true value of Y for the training cases, and not for the cases generated by the PDP algorithm. This means that the PDP algorithm can not be used to generate EDPs.

Another important consideration is how the errors are estimated. If we want EDPs to be useful we need to make sure we show reliable estimates of the error. Error estimation is a well studied subject. It is a well know fact that testing the algorithms on the same data used to obtain them will lead to unreliable and overly optimistic estimates of the error. In this context, our proposal uses Cross Validation (CV) to obtain reliable estimates of the error of the model for each of the available data observations. More specifically, we use 10-fold CV to obtain the prediction of the target model for each case. According to the CV method each of the cases of the available data set will belong to one of the test sets in the k folds. This means that for each of these cases we can obtain a prediction using a model that was not trained with that case. We compare this prediction to the true value and we obtain a reliable estimate of the error the model makes for each of case. Algorithm 1 describes this process in more detail.

3.1   Error Dependence Plots

Error Dependence Plots (EDPs) show the distribution of the expected error of a black box regression model across the domain of one of the predictor variables. The plots have in the Y-axis the expected error estimated using Algorithm 1, and on the X-axis the domain of some predictor variable.

Showing the distribution of the error for each possible value of a numeric predictor is difficult because each value will not repeat very often in the available data, particularly in small data sets. To overcome this difficulty we discretize the numerical predictor variables into meaningful bins. This process will allow us to collect several error values for each bin and thus approximate the distribution of the error using these values. Ideally, these bins should be selected by a

Algorithm 1. Obtaining reliable Cross validation Error Estimates.

---

input : data set $\mathcal{D}$
input : algorithm $\mathcal{A}$
input : nr. folds k
input : error metric Err
output: error estimates $\hat{E}$

$\mathcal{D}' \leftarrow$ Permute($\mathcal{D}$) // randomly permute the data
$P \leftarrow$ Partition($\mathcal{D}'$, k) // create k equal-size partitions
$\hat{E} \leftarrow \{\}$
foreach p *in* P **do**
    $M \leftarrow$ Train($\mathcal{A}$, $\mathcal{D}' \setminus \mathcal{D}'_p$) // train $\mathcal{A}$ on all but the partition p
    cases
    $\hat{e}_p \leftarrow \{$ Err($\hat{y}$, y) $\mid \langle \mathbf{x}, y \rangle \in \mathcal{D}'_p \wedge \hat{y} =$ Predict(M,$\mathbf{x}$) $\}$ // error of the
    model predictions for the partition p cases
    $\hat{E} \leftarrow \hat{E} \cup \hat{e}_p$

return $\hat{E}$

---

domain expert that is interested in understanding the performance of the model in a set of specific ranges of the variables. In case this know-how is unavailable, the bins can be selected using the quantiles of the distribution of the variables. In the absence of knowledge concerning the domain, we here suggest a division of values with the following quantiles: [0−10%] (extremely low values); [10%−35%] (low values); [35%−65%] (central values) [65%−90%] (high values); and [90%−100%] (extremely high values). In the case of nominal predictors this process is obviously not necessary as the variables are already discrete. However, features encompassing a large number of categories might compromise visualisation. For such cases we recommend either prioritising some of the categories and merging all the remaining or grouping the categories into larger categories, with the help of a domain expert.

Having these bins for all predictors we can obtain the absolute error of the black box model for all training cases that fall in each bin. Specifically, given the output of Algorithm 1 ($\hat{E}$) and a bin b of a predictor variable X^k, we estimate the distribution of the error using the values $e \in E$ of the training cases that have a value of X^k inside the bin b. Our proposed EDPs show this distribution of the errors by means of a box plot for each bin of the predictor variable.

Figure 1 shows two examples of such EDPs for the data set *a1* (c.f. Table 1). The leftmost plot is an example with a nominal predictor (*size*), in this case with 3 possible values shown in the X-axis of the plot. For each of these values we see the prediction error distribution of a Gradient Boosting Machine (GBM). From this simple example we can observe that this model performance varies considerably depending on the value of *size*. More specifically, the GBM is expected to have worse performance on test cases where the value of the predictor is *small*. For the value *medium* the performance seems considerably better. For comparison, EDPs also show on the right side the overall performance of the model,

---

Algorithm 2. Obtaining the EDP of a predictor.

---

input : data set $\mathcal{D}$
input : error estimates $\hat{E}$ for the cases in $\mathcal{D}$
input : bins B of the predictor X^p

if B *is empty and* X^p *is numeric* **then**
   | $B \leftarrow$ `DefaultBins`(X^p) // `get the bins of` X^p `using quantiles`

foreach $\langle \mathbf{x}_i, y_i \rangle$ *in* $\mathcal{D}$ **do**
   | $b \leftarrow$ `FindBin`(X^p_i, B) // `get the bin of the value of` X^p
   | $E_b \leftarrow E_b \cup e_i$ // $e_i \in \hat{E}$ `is the estimated error of this case`

foreach b *in* B **do**
   | `DrawBoxPlot`(E_b)

---

i.e. without any conditioning on the value of the predictor under analysis[1]. The rightmost plot of the figure shows another example for the same data set, this time with the *Cl* numeric predictor that was discretized into several bins according to the quantiles, as described above. Here we observe that the GBM performs considerably worse on lower values of *Cl*, while for extremely high values of this variable the performance is much better.

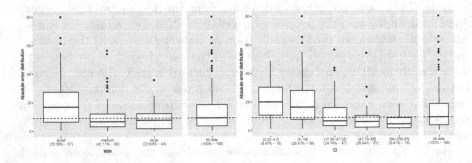

Fig. 1. Single model performance plot for dataset *a1* trained with GBM.

Algorithm 2 describes the process for obtaining the EDP of a predictor variable. It assumes as input the error estimates for the training data that can be obtained using Algorithm 1. Essentially, this algorithm partitions the error estimates $\hat{E}$ according to the bin to which the respective value of the predictor belongs, and draws the respective box-plot with these error values.

In some situations some of the bins of a predictor may have an estimated error that can be regarded as an outlier when compared to the most common errors of the model. This may distort the Y-axis scale of the EDP hiding some of the

---

[1] Please note that below each bin we provide the number of training cases belonging to each bin and the respective percentage of the full data set.

information that allows the effective comparison between the bins. In these cases we recommend the use of the log scale in the Y-axis. Such situation is illustrated in Fig. 2. As you can seen with the normal scale (left plot) the presence of some outlying errors makes the comparison among the bins very hard. The right side graph shows the same error distributions using a log scale, where we can better observe some considerable differences between the bins.

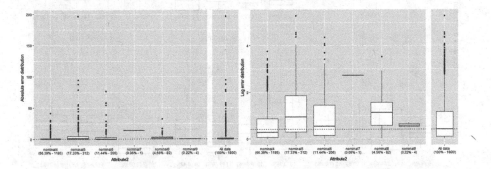

Fig. 2. EDP for dataset *maxTorque* trained with RF for feature *Attribute2* (Left: Absolute Error, Right: Log Error).

3.2   Bivariate Error Dependence Plots

EDPs (as PDPs or ICEs) ignore interactions among the predictors that may have an impact on the performance of the models. In order to try to capture some of these potential interactions we propose to use bivariate EDPs. These graphs are conceptually the same as the EDPs described in the previous section, but they show the error distribution for all combinations of the bins of two predictors. This means that they are obtained using a procedure similar to the one described by Algorithm 2 but the partitioning of the errors is made across all combinations of the bins of the two predictors, instead of a single predictor.

Figure 3 shows an example with the data set *a7* (c.f. Table 4) for an SVM model. In this case we explore the impact of the predictors *season* and *PO4* on the error of the SVM. The top left graph is the overall error distribution of the model without any conditioning on the two predictors. The remaining panels show the error distribution across the different bins of *PO4*. For each bin of *PO4*, we show the box-plots of the bins of *season*. This small example allows us to observe that the SVM has a considerably different behaviour for *season = autumn* when *PO4* is in the range [169−285.71] (high values of *PO4*). We can also observe that for the lowest values of *PO4* the performance is generally much better, independently of the season.

Bivariate EDPs have some presentation differences compared to EDPs. If a combination of values of the two variables does not occur in the data, the respective box plot is not shown, like for instance on the bottom right panel of Fig. 3 where we do not see Autumn. Moreover, the percentage and absolute

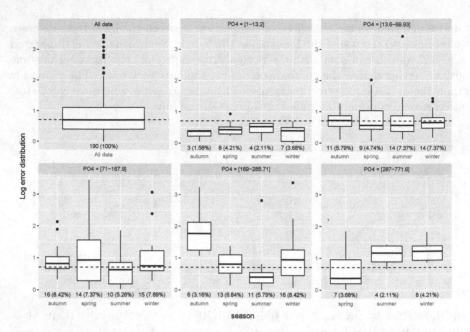

Fig. 3. Bivariate EDP for data set *a7* trained with SVM for features *season* and *PO4*

numbers of the bins are shown differently. The numbers that are shown are calculated with respect to the full data set. For instance, from the top rightmost panel we can infer that there are 9 cases with *season* = *spring* ∧ *PO4* ∈ [13.6 − 69.93], which correspond to 4.74% of the data set size.

4   Use Case Illustrations

In this section we provide some illustrative examples of the use of EDPs to try to understand the error behaviour of black box regression models. We have used 18 regression data sets whose properties are described in Table 1. For each of these data sets we have estimated the error of the black box models shown in Table 2, using the Cross Validation procedure described in Algorithm 1.

Given the number of data sets, predictors and models, we can not show all the resulting EDPs and bivariate EDPs. In this section we show a few examples that illustrate the power of EDPs. The full graphs can be seen in the web page http://github.com/ltorgo/EDP. The same web page contains all code used to obtain EDPs and bivariate EDPs, as well as the code to obtain all figures in the paper. As we have used the R open source implementations of the black box models, this ensures full reproducibility of our results and analysis.

Figure 4 depicts the EDP of a Neural Network for the bins of feature *NH4* of data set *a2*. The box plot on right part of the graph shows the overall estimated error, allowing for a visual comparison with the estimated error in each

Table 1. Used data sets (*Inst*: nr of instances; *Pred*: nr predictors).

Data set	Inst	Pred	Data set	Inst	Pred
a1	198	11	a2	198	11
a3	198	11	a4	198	11
a6	198	11	a7	198	11
Abalone	4177	8	acceleration	1732	14
availPwr	1802	15	bank8FM	4499	8
cpuSm	8192	12	fuelCons	1764	37
boston	506	13	maxTorque	1802	32
servo	167	4	airfoil	1503	5
concreteStrength	1030	8	machineCpu	209	6

Table 2. Regression algorithms, parameter variants, and respective used R packages.

Learner	Parameter variants	R package
NN	$size = 10, decay = 0.1, maxit = 1000$	**nnet** [19]
SVM	$cost = 10, gamma = 0.01$	**e1071** [3]
RF	$ntree = 1000$	**randomForest** [13]
GBM	$distribution = "gaussian", n.trees = 5000,$ $interaction.depth = 3$	**gbm** [7]

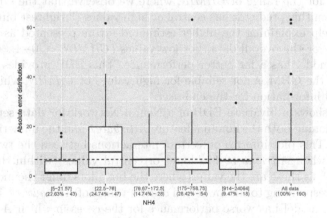

Fig. 4. EDP of a NN for feature *NH4* of data set *a2*.

bin. For all central and higher values of *NH4* ([76.67−172.75], [175−758.75] and [914−24064]), the neural network appears to have a performance similar to the global one. However, this EDP shows that for the test cases in which *NH4* is within the range [22.6−76] the model presents a slightly worse performance,

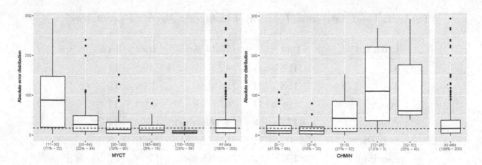

Fig. 5. EDP of a GBM for features *MYCT* (Left) and *CHMIN* (Right) of data set *machineCpu*.

while for extremely low values of the predictor variable ($NH4 = [5{-}22.7]$), the neural network performs significantly better than on the overall test set.

Figure 5 shows two EDPs of a Gradient Boosting Machine (GBM) for two numerical features of data set *machineCpu*: *MYCT* (on the left) and *CHMIN* (on the right). For *MYCT*, one can observe that the performance improves with higher values of this feature, as lower values of the predictor variable show higher expected median error than globally, whereas in high and extremely high values ($MYCT = [185{-}600]$ and $MYCT = [700{-}1500]$) the opposite occurs, with the box plots indicating lower expected errors. The right plot dissects the model performance for the range of *CHMIN*, where we observe that the GBM underperforms when this predictor has central or high values (3 rightest bins). In fact, these bins help explaining the higher estimated errors presented as outliers in the box plot for the overall data. For low values ($CHMIN = [0{-}1]$, $CHMIN = [2{-}4]$), the model has a far better performance. This EDP provides clear indications that the GBM is not reliable for high values of *CHMIN*, which may be a very useful information for the end user.

Figure 6 shows a bivariate EDP of a Neural Network for data set *fuelCons*, when conditioning both the nominal feature *Attribute1* and the numerical feature *Attribute12*. This plot informs on certain interactions between the two features, particularly when *Attribute12* has lower or central values (within the range of $[4200{-}6000]$), as these are the values where the box plots differ the most. In all 3 subplots corresponding to the lower and central values of *Attribute12*, it is noticeable that the model has worse performance for the cases in which *Attribute1* is either *nominal1* or *nominal3*. Therefore, the EDP shows a particular set of conditions where the NN model is not as trustworthy.

Overall, in our experiments with EDPs and bivariate EDPs (both the examples shown in the paper as well as the remaining graphs available at https:// ltorgo.github.io/EDP/), we have confirmed the usefulness of these tools. In effect, they provide a level of detail in terms of understanding the reasons or conditions leading to the performance of the models, that are not available with other existing tools. We claim that this type of feedback on the performance

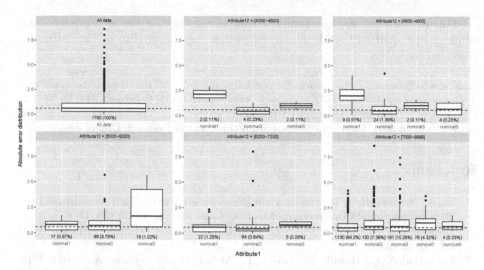

Fig. 6. Bivariate EDP of a NN in data set *fuelCons* for *Attribute1* and *Attribute12*.

of regression models is particularly useful when the predictions of black box models are driving important decisions, for which end-users are interested in understanding the risks associated with these predictions.

5 Conclusions

In this paper we described a novel approach to interpret black box regression models. This is an important topic in Machine Learning and Data Mining given the increasing usage of sophisticated modelling tools to drive important decisions. Being able to anticipate the model outcomes and the risks associated with trusting these models has become extremely important for many organisations.

Our work has focused on one aspect of model interpretability - trying to understand the relationship between the expected error of a regression tool and the values of the predictor variables. We proposed Error Dependence Plots (EDPs) that allow the visualisation of the expected distribution of the error of a model against the range of a predictor variable (bivariate EDPs extend this concept to two predictors). These plots provide important information on the risk incurred when trusting the models for predicting a certain test case. Using the information provided by EDPs the end-user may decide whether this risk is acceptable or not, and proceed accordingly.

We have shown several examples of applying EDPs and bivariate EDPs to several real world data sets, and using different black box regression algorithms. These examples illustrate the utility of these plots for better estimating the risk associated with these models. All code and tools presented in this paper are freely available to the research community.

484   I. Areosa and L. Torgo

Future work will explore forms of comparing the risk between models on a single graph, and will study means of evaluating the quality of the estimates provided by EDPs.

Acknowledgments. This work is partially funded by Portuguese Science and Technology Foundation (FCT) through the NITROLIMIT project (PTDC/CTA-AMB/30997/2017) and the project UID/EEA/50014/2019. The work of L. Torgo was undertaken, in part, thanks to funding from the Canada Research Chairs program.

References

1. Bi, J., Bennett, K.P.: Regression error characteristic curves. In: Proceedings of the 20th International Conference on Machine Learning, pp. 43–50 (2003)
2. Diakopoulos, N.: Accountability in algorithmic decision making. Commun. ACM **59**, 56–62 (2016)
3. Dimitriadou, E., Hornik, K., Leisch, F., Meyer, D., Weingessel, A.: e1071: Misc Functions of the Department of Statistics (e1071). TU Wien (2011)
4. Ferri, C., Hernández-orallo, J., Flach, P.A.: Brier curves: a new cost-based visualisation of classifier performance. In: Proceedings of the 28th International Conference on Machine Learning (ICML-11), pp. 585–592 (2011)
5. Friedman, J.: Greedy function approximation: a gradient boosting machine. Ann. Stat. **29**(5), 1189–1232 (2001)
6. Goldstein, A., Kapelner, A., Bleich, J., Pitkin, E.: Peeking inside the black box: visualizing statistical learning with plots of individual conditional expectation. J. Comput. Graph. Stat. **24**(1), 44–65 (2015)
7. Greenwell, B., Boehmke, B., Cunningham, J., Developers, G.: GBM: Generalized Boosted Regression Models (2018). https://CRAN.R-project.org/package=gbm
8. Hernández-Orallo, J.: ROC curves for regression. Pattern Recogn. **46**(12), 3395–3411 (2013)
9. Hinton, G., Dean, J., Vinyals, O.: Distilling the knowledge in a neural network. arXiv:1503.02531v1, 1–9 (2014)
10. Kim, B., Khanna, R., Koyejo, O.: Examples are not enough, learn to criticize! criticism for interpretability. In: AAdvances in Neural Information Processing Systems (NIPS 2016), pp. 2288–2296 (2016)
11. Kodratoff, Y., Nédellec, C.: Machine learning and comprehensibility. In: Proceedings of IJCAI 1995 (1995)
12. Lakkaraju, H., Bach, S., Leskovec, J.: Interpretable decision sets: a joint framework for description and prediction. In: Proceedings of ACM KDD 2016, pp. 1675–1684 (2016)
13. Liaw, A., Wiener, M.: Classification and regression by randomForest. R News **2**(3), 18–22 (2002)
14. Lipton, Z.C.: The mythos of model interpretability. ACM Queue **16**(3), 30:31–30:57 (2018). https://doi.org/10.1145/3236386.3241340
15. Metz, C.E.: Basic principles of ROC analysis. Semin. Nucl. Med. **8**, 283–298 (1978)
16. Miller, T.: Explanation in artificial intelligence: insights from the social sciences. arXiv:1706.07269 (2017)
17. Ribeiro, M., Singh, S., Guestrin, C.: Why should i trust you? Explaining the predictions of any classifier. In: Proceedings of ACM KDD 2016, pp. 1135–1144 (2016)

18. Torgo, L.: Regression error characteristic surfaces. In: KDD 2005: Proceedings of the 11th ACM SIGKDD, pp. 697–702 (2005)
19. Venables, W.N., Ripley, B.D.: Modern Applied Statistics with S, 4th edn. Springer, Heidelberg (2002). https://doi.org/10.1007/978-0-387-21706-2

Semantic Segmentation
of High-Resolution Aerial Imagery
with W-Net Models

Maria Dias[1,2(✉)], João Monteiro[1,2], Jacinto Estima[2,3], Joel Silva[2],
and Bruno Martins[1,2]

[1] Instituto Superior Técnico, Universidade de Lisboa, Lisbon, Portugal
{maria.l.dias,joao.miguel.monteiro}@tecnico.ulisboa.pt,
bruno.g.martins@ist.utl.pt
[2] INESC-ID, Lisbon, Portugal
jacinto.estima@gmail.com, dinis.joel@gmail.com
[3] Instituto Politécnico de Setúbal, Setúbal, Portugal

Abstract. The semantic segmentation of high-resolution aerial images
concerns the task of determining, for each pixel, the most likely class label
from a finite set of possible labels (e.g., discriminating pixels referring
to roads, buildings, or vegetation, in high-resolution images depicting
urban areas). Following recent work in the area related to the use of
fully-convolutional neural networks for semantic segmentation, we evaluated the performance of an adapted version of the W-Net architecture,
which has achieved very good results on other types of image segmentation tasks. Through experiments with two distinct datasets frequently
used in previous studies in the area, we show that the proposed W-Net architecture is quite effective in this task, outperforming a baseline
corresponding to the U-Net model, and also some of the other recently
proposed approaches.

Keywords: Semantic segmentation of satellite imagery ·
Fully-convolutional neural networks · W-Net architecture

1 Introduction

Large amounts of high-resolution remote sensing images are acquired daily
through satellites and aerial vehicles, and used as base data for mapping and
Earth observation activities. An intermediate step for converting these raw
images into map layers in vector format is semantic image segmentation, which
aims at determining, for each pixel, the most likely class label from a finite set
of possible labels, corresponding to the desired object categories to map (i.e.,
discriminating pixels referring to roads, buildings, or vegetation). In the particular case of urban areas, semantic segmentation is quite challenging, given
that objects in cities can be small, composed of many different materials, and

© Springer Nature Switzerland AG 2019
P. Moura Oliveira et al. (Eds.): EPIA 2019, LNAI 11805, pp. 486–498, 2019.
https://doi.org/10.1007/978-3-030-30244-3_40

have interactions with each other through occlusions, cast shadows, and inter-reflections. One can easily formulate the segmentation task as a pixel classification problem, to be addressed through supervised learning (i.e., given some labeled training data, infer the parameters of a model that estimates the conditional probabilities of the different classes, with basis on pixel intensities in the different color channels), although high within-class variability of the image intensities, and low inter-class differences, can be simultaneously expected.

In this paper, following on recent work in the area, we explore the potential of deep neural networks for semantic segmentation of high-resolution aerial images depicting urban regions. We propose to perform the segmentation using an adapted version of recent neural network architectures that have achieved very good results on other image segmentation tasks, namely W-Net architectures [1,2]. Through experiments with distinct datasets used in previous studies and competitions, we compared the performance of our particular W-Net architecture against simpler baselines, including the standard U-Net architecture. The obtained results attest to the effectiveness of the proposed method, which outperforms the baseline on the considered datasets, and also other recently proposed methods.

The rest of this document is organized as follows: Sect. 2 presents previous research in the area. Section 3 presents the deep learning method that was considered for aerial image segmentation, specifically detailing the adaptations implemented over previous W-Net approaches, as well as the hyper-parameters and the model training strategy. Section 4 details the evaluation methodology, including the selected datasets and evaluation metrics, and discusses the obtained results. Finally, Sect. 5 summarizes our conclusions and discusses possible directions for future work.

2   Related Work

Several previous studies have addressed the semantic segmentation of high-resolution aerial images through deep neural networks. For instance, Audebert et al. adapted previous deep learning models to use with multi-modal remote sensing data, i.e., multispectral imagery and digital surface model data [3]. In particular, the authors combined SegNet [4], an encoder-decoder architecture, and ResNet [5], a general convolutional architecture for image classification, that uses residual blocks as base models. Audebert et al. also proposed early and late fusion strategies for the multi-modal data. Early fusion is a strategy that learns fused feature maps of multi-modal features during the encoding process, whereas late fusion considers a separate network for each modality and fuses predictions after the decoding process. The proposed architectures were validated on multi-label datasets from previous challenges, particularly the ISPRS Vaihingen[1] and the ISPRS Potsdam[2] datasets, also used in our study.

---

[1] http://www2.isprs.org/commissions/comm3/wg4/2d-sem-label-vaihingen.html.
[2] http://www2.isprs.org/commissions/comm3/wg4/2d-sem-label-potsdam.html.

Mou and Zhu advanced a model named RiFCN for semantic segmentation of high-resolution remote sensing imagery [6], based on what can be captured by the feature maps outputted at different depths of a deep neural network, as suggested in previous studies [7,8] that argued that shallower layers can capture low-level features such as object boundaries, while deeper layers are capable of learning high-level features. The RiFCN architecture is based on a bidirectional network that has a forward stream to extract multi-level feature maps and a backward stream that uses recurrent connections to fuse these multi-level feature maps from both streams. The forward stream is inspired by VGG-16 [9], a model with convolution blocks composed of multiple convolutional and max-pooling layers. In turn, the backward stream has autoregressive recurrent connections to embed the multi-level feature maps hierarchically. The authors demonstrated the effectiveness of the RiFCN architecture on the multi-label ISPRS Potsdam dataset, and on a binary dataset named INRIA Aerial Image Labeling[3].

In turn, Chen et al. proposed two similar encoder-decoder architectures with shortcut blocks [10], based on deep fully convolutional networks [11]. The short-cut block employed by the authors has two branches, namely a main branch with three convolutional layers, and a shortcut branch with one convolutional layer to help the direct gradient propagation. Both branches are merged in the complete network, and a ReLU activation function is applied to the result. The encoder is also composed of max-pooling layers, whereas the decoder has trans-pose convolutional layers. Leveraging the previous ideas, the authors propose two encoder-decoder architectures with convolutional and shortcut blocks, namely a symmetrical normal-shortcut fully convolutional network (SNFCN) and a sym-metrical dense-shortcut fully convolutional network (SDFCN). The latter differs because it has three additional identity mappings between symmetrical pairs of the encoder and the decoder parts of the network. For validation, tests were conducted with the ISPRS Vaihingen and ISPRS Potsdam datasets.

Liu et al. described a self-cascaded convolutional neural network (Scas-Net) [12], which corresponds to an architecture that has an encoder with mul-tiple convolutional layers to extract features based on previous works, such as a 16-layer VGG-Net [9] and a 101-layer ResNet [5]. Dilated convolutions with different rates are applied in the last layer of the encoder to capture multi-level contexts. These contexts are sequentially aggregated from global to local in a self-cascaded approach to maintain the information about hierarchical depen-dencies. Then, to obtain an output with the same dimensionality of the input, corresponding to the segmentation mask, upsampling is performed, while shal-low layers of the encoder are reused to identify low-level details of objects. The authors conducted experiments in two multi-label datasets, i.e. ISPRS Vaihin-gen and ISPRS Potsdam, and in a binary dataset, namely the Massachusetts Buildings Dataset [13], verifying the advantages of ScasNet.

---

[3] http://project.inria.fr/aerialimagelabeling.

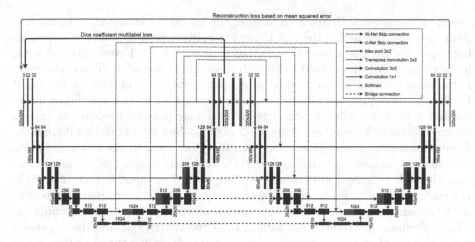

Fig. 1. Graphical representation for the considered W-Net network architecture.

3   The Proposed Segmentation Method

This section details the segmentation method used in our experiments. First, Sect. 3.1 presents the fully-convolutional neural network architecture adapted from previously proposed W-Net models [1,2]. Then, Sect. 3.2 presents the training and hyper-parameter tuning strategies that were considered.

3.1   The W-Net Neural Architecture

The neural network architecture used in our experiments borrows on ideas from previously proposed W-Net models, used for instance in the context of unsupervised image segmentation [1], or in the context of supervised medical image segmentation [2]. These models extend the typical U-shaped architecture (also commonly referred to as an hour-glass architecture) of the U-Net model [14]. Our network architecture is illustrated in Fig. 1, stacking/bridging together encoder (on the left-side) and decoder (on the right) U-Nets that, together, form a W-shaped architecture. The model is trained to simultaneously reconstruct the original input images from intermediate representations, and to predict the segmentation maps for the input aerial images. The input images are provided to the model in the LAB colour space, due to the fact that this representation is better at capturing human perceptual differences, important for segmentation and image reconstruction problems [15].

In total, our W-Net model has 44 convolutional layers which are structured into 22 modules. Each module consists of two 3 × 3 convolutional layers, each followed by a Leaky ReLU non-linearity [16] and batch normalization [17] operations. The first eleven modules form the dense prediction base of the network, and the second eleven modules correspond to a reconstruction decoder.

As in the regular U-Net architecture, the encoder consists of a contracting path (i.e., the first half of the first U-Net) to capture context, and a corresponding expansive path (the second half) that ends with a 1×1 convolutional layer, followed by a fully-connected layer with a softmax activation. The contracting path starts with an initial module which performs a convolution on the input images. In the figure, the output sizes are reported for an example input image resolution of 320×320 (i.e., the size of the image patches used in our experiments). Modules are connected via 2×2 max-pooling layers, and we double the number of feature channels at each down-sampling step. In the expansive path, modules are connected via transposed 2D convolution layers. The number of feature channels is halved at each up-sampling step. The input of each module in the contracting path is also bypassed to the output of its corresponding module in the expansive path, to recover lost spatial information due to down-sampling. The combination of the representations from the contractive and the expansive paths is made through a concatenation operation, following the ideas from Chen et al. [2]. The final 1×1 convolution maps each 32-component feature vector to the desired number of segmentation classes K, and then the softmax activation re-scales the values so that the elements of the K-dimensional output lie in the range $[0, 1]$ and sum to 1, thus forming a probability distribution over the segmentation classes.

The architecture of the decoder U-Net is similar to that of the encoder, in this case reading the output of the encoder with a dimensionality of $320 \times 320 \times K$. The final 1×1 convolutional layer of the decoder, considering a sigmoid activation function, maps a 32-component feature vector back to a reconstruction of the original input, with the 3 channels of the LAB colour model.

The W-Net proposal from Xia et al. [1] considered the task of unsupervised image segmentation, using a soft normalized cut loss as a global criterion for the segmentation [18], which measures both the total dissimilarity between different classes and the total similarity within the same classes. We instead consider a supervised setting, in which the output semantic segmentation classes are pre-established, and having the ground-truth segmentation labels informing the training of the encoder part of the W-Net. We specifically used the Dice coefficient loss function [19]. When considering multi-class segmentation problems, the Dice coefficient loss is computed for each class separately, and then summed (i.e., all the classes contribute equally to the final loss, thus addressing issues of class imbalance in the training images).

In turn, the decoder part of the W-Net is trained to minimize a reconstruction loss (i.e., the mean squared error between the predicted and the true LAB values for the images), forcing the encoded representations to contain as much information of the original inputs as possible. In our specific context, the model promotes the idea that semantic categories relate to how one can perceive and distinguish colors and pixel intensities on the images, jointly optimizing a semantic segmentation loss and a reconstruction loss for the input coloured images.

3.2 Hyper-parameters and Model Training Strategy

The selection of hyper-parameters and model training strategies relied on the general guidelines discussed by Xie et al. [20]. The last layer of the first U-Net features a number of nodes compatible with the number of classes in the segmentation task. If considering a binary segmentation mask, this last layer would consist of a single channel with a sigmoid activation function, and the model training would involve minimizing a binary cross-entropy loss or the standard Dice coefficient. The tests reported on this paper always considered multiple classes, and the last layer of the first U-Net consists of multiple channels. In this case, training involves a softmax activation function together with the multi-class Dice coefficient loss. An initial set of tests verified that this loss function always outperformed the traditional categorical cross-entropy loss. Moreover, also through initial tests, we verified that the LAB colour space lead to slightly better results than those obtained with the standard RGB colour space, in terms of both the reconstruction and segmentation quality. Besides converting the input images to the LAB colour space, we also applied a contrast enhancement procedure, analyzing the distribution of pixel intensities and re-scaling the representation to include all intensities that fall within the 2nd and 98th percentiles. This simple pre-processing procedure was also found to improve the results.

Training relied on the Adam [21] optimization algorithm together with a Cyclical Learning Rate (CLR) update procedure, as described by Smith [22]. In more detail, the learning rate varied between 10^{-5} and 10^{-4}, according to a triangular policy that decreases the cycle amplitude by half after each period (i.e., annealing the learning rate), while keeping the base learning rate constant. We used mini-batches of 5 image patches with dimensionality $320 \times 320 \times 3$, created through a generator that considered simple real-time data augmentation procedures (i.e., randomly flipping the input images horizontally, vertically or diagonally when providing them as input to the training algorithm). The loss function regulating the training of the complete network corresponds to a weighted combination of the segmentation (i.e., with a weight of 0.95) and reconstruction (i.e., with a weight of 0.05) losses.

Model training proceeded for up to a maximum of 50 epochs. However, a small validation set was used to define an early stopping criterion, and the training stopped if the validation loss (i.e., the weighted sum of the segmentation and reconstruction losses over the validation data) did not decrease for 5 consecutive epochs. The final model weights were taken from the training epoch with the smallest value for the validation loss.

4 Experimental Evaluation

This section presents the experimental evaluation of the proposed method, comparing it against a standard U-Net model, and also against other proposals in the literature. Section 4.1 starts by presenting the datasets and the experimental methodology, and then Sect. 4.2 discusses the obtained results. The model was

Table 1. Characterization of the aerial imagery datasets.

Dataset	Size (pixels)	Number (train/test)	Resolution (cm/pixel)
ISPRS Vaihingen	2100×2100	16/17	9
ISPRS Potsdam	6000×6000	24/14	5

implemented through a Python deep learning library named Keras[4], and the corresponding source code is available online[5].

4.1 Datasets and Evaluation Metrics

We conducted experiments on two datasets from a previous challenge focused on semantic segmentation of high resolution aerial imagery, namely from the ISPRS 2D Semantic Labeling Contest, with images of the cities of Potsdam and Vaihingen. These datasets have been extensively used within previous studies in the area, as discussed in Sect. 2. The task proposed in the context of both datasets is to classify each pixel in the image with a given class from a fixed set of six classes: impervious surface, car, building, background, low vegetation, and tree. Overall, the Vaihingen dataset has 33 images with different sizes, approximately with 2100×2100 pixels each and a Ground Sample Distance (GSD) of 9 cm. We used 12 images for training, 4 for validation, and 17 for testing. The Potsdam dataset has 38 images of 6000×6000 pixels each and a GSD of 5 cm. For this dataset, we used a split of 18 images for training, 6 for validation, and 14 for testing. Table 1 features a characterization of both datasets. In both cases, the data splits that we considered are common to those used in most previous studies. All images were initially converted from the RGB to the LAB colour space [15], and we also pre-processed them with a contrast enhancement procedure based on the distribution of pixel intensities, as described in Sect. 3.2.

To assess the quantitative performance of the segmentation methods, we computed the precision, recall, and F1 scores over each segmentation class, macro-averages and class-weighted averages for precision, recall, and F1 scores, and the overall accuracy (OA). Following the practice of other studies leveraging the datasets used in our tests, all the evaluation scores were computed over just five classes, ignoring the background pixels. Additionally, as suggested by the challenge organizers that made available the datasets, we evaluated the results on an alternative ground truth with the borders of the objects eroded by a radius of 3 pixels, to reduce the impact of ambiguous boundaries in the evaluation results.

4.2 Experimental Results

Table 2 features a comparison between the results of state-of-the-art methods in the selected datasets, against our U-Net and W-Net models, specifically considering the overall accuracy. Additionally, Table 3 presents the per-class metrics

---

[4] http://keras.io.

[5] http://github.com/martamaria96/deep-wnet.

that were used to assess the quantitative performance, together with the percentage of pixels, in each dataset, associated to each of the classes (not considering
the background class). Summarizing the results, Table 3 also presents macro-
averaged results and a weighted average of the metrics that takes into account
the percentage of pixels belonging to each class. Notice that the results presented
for previous models are merely indicative, given that we are directly reporting
the values given in previous publications, obtained from the author's own tests,
and not all those studies used exactly the same experimental protocol.

The results show that the classes corresponding to impervious surfaces, cars,
and buildings achieved better results than the other classes. The results also
show that the proposed W-Net model outperformed a standard U-Net (i.e., a
model using just the first U-Net from Fig. 1, relying just on the loss function corresponding to the Dice coefficient) on both datasets, at the same time achieving comparable results to some of the previous state-of-the-art approaches. A
more detailed analysis of previous results is available online, in the leader-boards

Table 2. Comparison in terms of the overall accuracy for different methods over the
ISPRS Potsdam and ISPRS Vaihingen test datasets.

Model	Overall accuracy	
	Vaihingen	Potsdam
RiFCN [6]	-	86.6
CONC_2 [23]	86.5	-
ScasNet [12]	91.1	91.1
UOA [24]	87.6	-
SegNet-RC [3]	89.8	89.0
SDFCN [10]	88.3	89.0
UFMG_4 [25]	89.4	87.9
U-Net (ours)	87.05	89.12
W-Net (ours)	88.08	89.14

Table 3. Per-class precision, recall, and F1 metrics over the ISPRS Potsdam and
ISPRS Vaihingen test datasets, with the W-Net model.

Class	Potsdam				Vaihingen			
	Percentage	Precision	Recall	F1-score	Percentage	Precision	Recall	F1-score
Impervious	31.07	92.88	90.59	91.69	30.87	89.82	90.04	89.79
Car	1.88	98.26	90.56	94.22	1.84	73.19	83.66	76.37
Building	26.99	95.29	94.73	94.98	26.94	93.77	91.95	92.75
Low vegetation	23.75	77.13	90.97	83.29	23.63	81.33	73.00	76.66
Tree	16.30	89.91	78.52	83.48	16.72	81.32	92.42	86.08
Macro-average	-	90.69	89.07	89.53	-	83.89	86.22	84.33
Weighted average	-	89.41	89.83	89.29	-	87.15	86.81	86.62

associated to the Potsdam[6] and Vaihingen[7] datasets. Many of the ideas advanced in state-of-the-art models for the task can also be combined with our W-Net approach, perhaps further improving the results. For instance, the state-of-the-art model named UFMG_4 [25] uses convolutional blocks inspired by the DenseNet architecture, i.e. an idea that can be easily combined with our W-Net [26,27].

Figure 2 illustrates the segmentation results for an example image taken from each dataset, where the third column presents the results of the W-Net model, and the fourth column compares our results with the ground truth, highlighting in red the pixels corresponding to incorrect predictions.

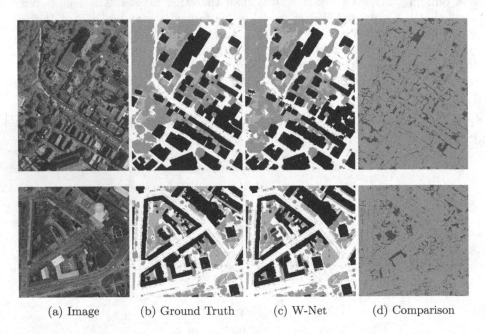

(a) Image   (b) Ground Truth   (c) W-Net   (d) Comparison

Fig. 2. Qualitative results on the ISPRS Vaihingen (first row) and Potsdam (second row) datasets. The mask has six categories: impervious surface (white), building (blue), low vegetation (cyan), tree (green), car (yellow) and background/clutter (red). The columns correspond to (i) the original image, (ii) the W-Net results, (iii) the ground truth mask, and (iv) an indication of pixels corresponding to wrong predictions. (A color version of the figure is given in the online version)

5   Conclusions and Future Work

This paper reported on a set of experiments for evaluating the performance of an adapted version of the recently proposed W-Net neural network architecture,

---

[6] http://www2.isprs.org/commissions/comm2/wg4/potsdam-2d-semantic-labeling.html.

[7] http://www2.isprs.org/commissions/comm2/wg4/vaihingen-2d-semantic-labeling-contest.html.

originally proposed for the segmentation of medical images, on the semantic segmentation of high-resolution satellite images. Through experiments with several distinct datasets used in previous studies and in competitions, we showed that the W-Net architecture is quite effective in this task, outperforming the standard U-Net model and other approaches on common datasets in the area.

Despite the interesting results, there are also many ideas for future work. Several previous studies have proposed alternative connectivity patterns for U-Nets, which we could also explore. Besides the two W-Net architectures that inspired the model used in our tests, other studies have also proposed to stack/bridge multiple U-Nets together [28–30], with features going sequentially from the first U-Net to the last in an attempt to better capture high-order spatial relationships. Several ideas from these other approaches can also be borrowed, e.g. related to the use of residuals [31] or other intermediate supervisions. Other authors still have proposed to combine dense connectivity with the original U-Net architecture, following the general design of DenseNets for image classification [26, 27]. In particular, each top-down or bottom-up module can feature a dense block with densely connected convolutional layers. Besides dense connections in the encoder and decoder blocks, one can also consider dense connections across both these parts [32]. Tang et al. proposed the coupled U-Net model, i.e. a hybrid of the dense U-Net and the stacked U-Net that integrates the merits of both dense connectivity and multi-stage top-down and bottom-up refinement [33]. Given several stacked U-Nets, these authors proposed to add shortcut connections for each U-Net pair, thus generating the coupled U-Net. Similar ideas can easily be considered as extensions to our model.

Besides taking ideas from previous developments in fully-convolutional networks for image segmentation, other recent developments in CNNs for image classification can also be integrated into the proposed approach. Examples include octave convolutions [34] or attention augmented CNNs [35].

Currently ongoing experiments relate to the use of W-Net model variants for the semantic segmentation of historical aerial photos available as gray-scale images. The segmentation of historical aerial photos can have many interesting practical applications, and we are interested in exploring the segmentation of building footprints for dasymetric disaggregation [36] of historical census data. In particular, we are studying the application of W-Net models for jointly coloring and segmenting the aerial photos, in which the first fully-convolutional part performs semantic segmentation from gray-scale inputs, and the second part returns a colored version of the original image. The entire model can be trained with modern datasets of colored aerial photos, such as the ones used in the experiments reported on this paper, ignoring the color information from the input images in the encoder part, and instead using the color information for computing the loss function from the second part of the model.

Acknowledgements. This research was supported through Fundação para a Ciência e Tecnologia (FCT), through the project grants with references PTDC/EEI-SCR/ 1743/2014 (Saturn), PTDC/CTA-OHR/29360/2017 (RiverCure), and PTDC/CCI-CIF/32607/2017 (MIMU), as well as through the INESC-ID multi-annual funding from the PIDDAC programme (UID/CEC/50021/2019). We also gratefully acknowledge the support of NVIDIA Corporation, with the donation of two Titan Xp GPUs used in the experiments reported on the paper.

References

1. Xia, X., Kulis, B.: W-Net: a deep model for fully unsupervised image segmentation. arXiv preprint arXiv:1711.08506 (2017)
2. Chen, W., et al.: W-Net: Bridged U-Net for 2D medical image segmentation. arXiv preprint arXiv:1807.04459 (2018)
3. Audebert, N., Le Saux, B., Lefèvre, S.: Beyond RGB: very high resolution urban remote sensing with multimodal deep networks. ISPRS J. Photogramm. Remote Sens. **140**, 20–32 (2018)
4. Badrinarayanan, V., Kendall, A., Cipolla, R.: SegNet: a deep convolutional encoder-decoder architecture for image segmentation. IEEE Trans. Pattern Anal. Mach. Intell. **39**(12), 2481–2495 (2017)
5. He, K., Zhang, X., Ren, S., Sun, J.: Deep residual learning for image recognition. In: Proceedings of the IEEE Conference on Computer Vision and Pattern Recognition, pp. 770–778 (2016)
6. Mou, L., Zhu, X.X.: RiFCN: recurrent network in fully convolutional network for semantic segmentation of high resolution remote sensing images. arXiv preprint arXiv:1805.02091 (2018)
7. Zeiler, M.D., Fergus, R.: Visualizing and understanding convolutional networks. In: Fleet, D., Pajdla, T., Schiele, B., Tuytelaars, T. (eds.) ECCV 2014. LNCS, vol. 8689, pp. 818–833. Springer, Cham (2014). https://doi.org/10.1007/978-3-319-10590-1_53
8. Mahendran, A., Vedaldi, A.: Understanding deep image representations by inverting them. In: Proceedings of the IEEE Conference on Computer Vision and Pattern Recognition, pp. 5188–5196 (2015)
9. Simonyan, K., Zisserman, A.: Very deep convolutional networks for large-scale image recognition. In: Proceedings of the International Conference on Learning Representations (2015)
10. Chen, G., Zhang, X., Wang, Q., Dai, F., Gong, Y., Zhu, K.: Symmetrical dense-shortcut deep fully convolutional networks for semantic segmentation of very-high-resolution remote sensing images. IEEE J. Sel. Top. Appl. Earth Obs. Remote Sens. **11**(5), 1633–1644 (2018)
11. Long, J., Shelhamer, E., Darrell, T.: Fully convolutional networks for semantic segmentation. In: Proceedings of the IEEE Conference on Computer Vision and Pattern Recognition, pp. 3431–3440 (2015)
12. Liu, Y., Fan, B., Wang, L., Bai, J., Xiang, S., Pan, C.: Semantic labeling in very high resolution images via a self-cascaded convolutional neural network. ISPRS J. Photogramm. Remote Sens. **145**, 78–95 (2018)
13. Mnih, V.: Machine learning for aerial image labeling. Ph.D. thesis, University of Toronto (2013)
14. Ronneberger, O., Fischer, P., Brox, T.: U-Net: convolutional networks for biomedical image segmentation. In: Navab, N., Hornegger, J., Wells, W.M., Frangi, A.F. (eds.) MICCAI 2015. LNCS, vol. 9351, pp. 234–241. Springer, Cham (2015). https://doi.org/10.1007/978-3-319-24574-4_28
15. Jain, A.K.: Fundamentals of Digital Image Processing. Prentice Hall, Upper Saddle River (1989)

16. Xu, B., Huang, R., Li, M.: Revise saturated activation functions. arXiv preprint arXiv:1602.05980 (2016)
17. Ioffe, S., Szegedy, C.: Batch normalization: accelerating deep network training by reducing internal covariate shift. In: Proceedings of the International Conference on Machine Learning, pp. 448–456 (2015)
18. Shi, J., Malik, J.: Normalized cuts and image segmentation. IEEE Trans. Pattern Anal. Mach. Intell. **22**(8), 888–905 (2000)
19. Sudre, C.H., Li, W., Vercauteren, T., Ourselin, S., Jorge Cardoso, M.: Generalised dice overlap as a deep learning loss function for highly unbalanced segmentations. In: Cardoso, M.J., et al. (eds.) DLMIA/ML-CDS -2017. LNCS, vol. 10553, pp. 240–248. Springer, Cham (2017). https://doi.org/10.1007/978-3-319-67558-9_28
20. Xie, J., He, T., Zhang, Z., Zhang, H., Zhang, Z., Li, M.: Bag of tricks for image classification with convolutional neural networks. arXiv preprint arXiv:1812.01187 (2018)
21. Kingma, D.P., Ba, J.: Adam: a method for stochastic optimization. In: Proceedings of the International Conference on Learning Representations (2014)
22. Smith, L.N.: Cyclical learning rates for training neural networks. In: Proceeedings of the IEEE Winter Conference on Applications of Computer Vision, pp. 464–472 (20170
23. Forbes, T., He, Y., Mudur, S., Poullis, C.: Aggregated residual convolutional neural network for multi-label pixel wise classification of geospatial features. In: Online Abstracts of the ISPRS Benchmark on Urban Object Classification and 3D Building Reconstruction (2018)
24. Lin, G., Shen, C., van den Hengel, A., Reid, I.: Efficient piecewise training of deep structured models for semantic segmentation. In: Proceedings of the IEEE Conference on Computer Vision and Pattern Recognition, pp. 3194–3203 (2016)
25. Nogueira, K., Mura, M.D., Chanussot, J., Schwartz, W.R., Santos, J.A.: Dynamic multi-scale segmentation of remote sensing images based on convolutional networks. arXiv preprint arXiv:1804.04020 (2018)
26. Jégou, S., Drozdzal, M., Vazquez, D., Romero, A., Bengio, Y.: The one hundred layers tiramisu: fully convolutional densenets for semantic segmentation. In: Proceedings of the Workshops at the IEEE Conference on Computer Vision and Pattern Recognition, pp. 1175–1183 (2017)
27. Li, X., Chen, H., Qi, X., Dou, Q., Fu, C.-W., Heng, P.-A.: H-DenseUNet: Hybrid densely connected UNet for liver and tumor segmentation from CT volumes. IEEE Trans. Med. Imaging **37**(12), 2663–2674 (2018)
28. Newell, A., Yang, K., Deng, J.: Stacked Hourglass networks for human pose estimation. In: Leibe, B., Matas, J., Sebe, N., Welling, M. (eds.) ECCV 2016. LNCS, vol. 9912, pp. 483–499. Springer, Cham (2016). https://doi.org/10.1007/978-3-319-46484-8_29
29. Sun, T., Chen, Z., Yang, W., Wang, Y.: Stacked U-Nets with multi-output for road extraction. In: Proceedings of the Workshops at the IEEE/CVF Conference on Computer Vision and Pattern Recognition, pp. 187–192 (2018)
30. Khalel, A., El-Saban, M.: Automatic pixelwise object labeling for aerial imagery using stacked U-Nets. arXiv preprint arXiv:1803.04953 (2018)
31. Zhang, Z., Liu, Q., Wang, Y.: Road extraction by deep residual U-Net. IEEE Geosci. Remote Sens. Lett. **15**(5), 749–753 (2018)
32. Zhang, J., Jin, Y., Xu, J., Xu, X., Zhang, Y.: MDU-Net: multi-scale densely connected U-Net for biomedical image segmentation. arXiv preprint arXiv:1812.00352 (2018)

33. Tang, Z., Peng, X., Geng, S., Zhu, Y., Metaxas, D.: CU-Net: coupled U-Nets. In: Proceedings of the British Machine Vision Conference, pp. 305–316 (2018)
34. Chen, Y., et al.: Drop an octave: reducing spatial redundancy in convolutional neural networks with octave convolution. arXiv preprint arXiv:1904.05049 (2019)
35. Bello, I., Zoph, B., Vaswani, A., Shlens, J., Le, Q.V.: Attention augmented convolutional networks. arXiv preprint arXiv:904.09925 (2019)
36. Monteiro, J., Martins, B., Pires, J.M.: A hybrid approach for the spatial disaggregation of socio-economic indicators. Int. J. Data Sci. Anal. 5(2–3), 189–211 (2018)

Knowledge Representation and Reasoning

On Unordered BDDs and Quantified Boolean Formulas

Mikoláš Janota[✉]

IST/INESC-ID, Lisbon, Portugal
mikolas.janota@gmail.com

Abstract. This paper proposes to study the synthesis of unordered binary decision diagrams (BDDs) using solvers for Quantified Boolean Formulas (QBF). The synthesis of a BDD falls naturally in the realm of quantified formulas as we are typically looking for a BDD satisfying a certain specification. This means that we ask whether there exists a BDD such that for all inputs the specification is satisfied. We show that this query can be encoded naturally into QBF and experimentally evaluate these queries for the minority function.

The short paper should be seen as a challenge for further research on QBF solving.

1 Introduction

Reduced and ordered BDD (ROBDDs) [1,2] are well studied and appear often in practice due to their canonicity and ease of manipulation. At the same time, exponential lower bounds for ROBDDs are well-known [17]. In that aspect, BDDs (also called branching programs) are interesting because there are no known exponential lower bounds.[1] This means that BDDs are likely to give us small representations of Boolean functions while preserving some of the advantageous properties of ROBDDs. Namely, they can be naturally represented in hardware, where each node corresponds to a 2 to 1 multiplexer.

This short paper has the following two contributions.

1. We show that synthesizing a BDD can be naturally formulated as a quantified Boolean formula (QBF).
2. We perform preliminary evaluation of state-of-the-art QBF solvers on this formulation.

The preliminary evaluation shows that the nowadays solvers scale poorly. In some sense this is not surprising because synthesis of functions is inherently a hard problem. Already in the case of the synthesis of the disjunctive normal form (DNF) minimization is Σ_2^P-complete [18]. It is only to be expected to be harder for BDDs. Limitations of QBF solvers have also been observed in other related works on *synthesis of circuits* or *reactive systems* [3,4,7,10,11].

We believe that these poor results should not be seen as a deterrent but rather as a challenge for further QBF research.

---

[1] For existing lower bounds for BDD see a survey by Razborov [14].

© Springer Nature Switzerland AG 2019
P. Moura Oliveira et al. (Eds.): EPIA 2019, LNAI 11805, pp. 501–507, 2019.
https://doi.org/10.1007/978-3-030-30244-3_41

2   Preliminaries

Standard concepts from propositional logic are assumed. Propositional formulas are built from variables, negation ($\neg$), and conjunction ($\wedge$). For convenience we also consider the constants $0, 1$ representing false and true, respectively. The results immediately extend to other connectives, e.g., $(\phi \Rightarrow \psi) = \neg(\phi \wedge \neg\psi)$, $(\phi \vee \psi) = \neg(\neg\phi \wedge \neg\psi)$. A *literal* is either a variable or its negation. An *assignment* is a mapping from variables to $\{0,1\}$. Assignments are represented as sets of literals, i.e., $\{x, \neg y\}$ corresponds to $\{x \mapsto 1, y \mapsto 0\}$. For a formula ϕ and an assignment σ, the expression $\phi|_\sigma$ denotes *substitution*, i.e., the simultaneous replacement of variables with their corresponding value.

Quantified Boolean Formulas (QBF). QBFs [9] extend propositional logic by quantifiers over Boolean variables. Any propositional formula ϕ is also a QBF with all variables *free*. If Φ is a QBF with a free variable x, the formulas $\exists x.\,\Phi$ and $\forall x.\,\Phi$ are QBFs with x *bound*, i.e. not free. Note that we disallow expressions such as $\exists x.\exists x.\,x$. Whenever possible, we write $\exists x_1 \ldots x_k$ instead of $\exists x_1 \ldots \exists x_k$; analogously for $\forall$. Semantically a QBF corresponds to a compact representation of a propositional formula. In particular, the formula $\forall x.\,\Psi$ is satisfied by the same truth assignments as $\Psi|_{\{\neg x\}} \wedge \Psi|_{\{x\}}$ and $\exists x.\,\Psi$ by $\Psi|_{\{\neg x\}} \vee \Psi|_{\{x\}}$. Since $\forall x \forall y.\,\Phi$ and $\forall y \forall x.\,\Phi$ are semantically equivalent, we allow writing $\forall X$ for a set of variables X; analogously for $\exists$. A QBF with no free variables is *false* (resp. *true*), iff it is semantically equivalent to the constant 0 (resp. 1).

Binary Decision Diagrams (BDD). A BDD [2] is a rooted directed acyclic graph where each node has two outgoing edges except for two sinks. Each node is labeled by a Boolean variable and the outgoing edges are labeled by 1 and 0, respectively. The two sinks are labeled by 1 and 0, respectively. A BDD unequivocally represents a Boolean function: starting at the root take the 1 edge if the variable labeling the current node is true and take the 0 edge otherwise. Respond "true", if the 1-sink is reached; respond "false", if the 0-sink is reached.

3   Encoding

We assume that we are given N nodes $\mathcal{N} = \{n_1, \ldots, n_N\}$ and additionally the sink nodes $\mathsf{sink}_1, \mathsf{sink}_0$. Further, there is a finite set of input variables $\mathcal{I}$. The desired semantics of the resulting BDD is assumed to be specified as a Boolean formula on the input variables. Hence, the objective is to construct a BDD of size N representing the same function as the given Boolean formula. For the purpose of this paper we focus on the minority function, i.e. the formula $\phi(i_1, \ldots, i_m)$ that is true if and only if a minority of the input variables are set to 1.[2]

---

[2] The majority function is obtained by swapping the semantics of 0 and 1, which is easy to do in BDDs.

We present the encoding in three conceptually separate steps: (1) encoding of topology (Sect. 3.1), (2) encoding of BDD's semantics (Sect. 3.2), (3) encoding of specification (Sect. 3.3). This section is concluded by Sect. 3.3, which discusses some of the technical details of the encoding.

3.1   Topology

To avoid cycles in the constructed BDD we apply the following trick. Without a loss of generality, we assume that a node n_i can be only connected to a node m if $m = n_j$ for $j < i$ or m is one of the sinks. Like so we ensure there is a topological ordering on the resulting graph and at the same time, we are not losing any graphs because a topological ordering has to exist (there are no cycles). For convenience, we define the notation $\text{neighbors}(n_i)$ to denote the set $\{n_j \mid j \in 1..i-1\} \cup \{\text{sink}_0, \text{sink}_1\}$.

The space of BDDs is modeled by two sets of Boolean variables. The variables $l_{n,x}$ represent that the node $n \in \mathcal{N}$ is labeled by the input variable $x \in \mathcal{I}$. The variables $c^e_{n,m}$ represent that there is an edge from n to m labeled by $e \in \{0,1\}$. To ensure that each node is labeled by one and only one input variable and that each edge goes into one and only one node we output the following constraints.

$$\sum_{x \in \mathcal{I}} l_{n,x} = 1, \text{for}\quad \text{each } n \in \mathcal{N}$$

$$\sum_{m \in \text{neighbors}(n)} c^e_{n,m} = 1, \text{for}\quad \text{each } n \in \mathcal{N}, e \in \{0,1\}$$

These constraints together with the restriction that a node can only connect to a sink or one of the preceding nodes yield BDDs with the correct topology.

3.2   Semantics

The semantics of the BDD under a given input is captured by assigning a value to each sub-BDD. This is done recursively as follows. The sink_0 is false, the sink_1 is true. A node n labeled by x is true iff the corresponding neighbor is true.

We introduce the following auxiliary formulas. For a node $n \in \mathcal{N}$ the formula $\mathcal{V}_n$ represents the value of the labeled variable, i.e. the formula is true if the node is labeled by one of the variables x and that variable is true at the same time. Formally defined as:

$$\mathcal{V}_n \triangleq \bigvee_{x \in \mathcal{I}} (l_{n,x} \wedge x)$$

For each sub-BDD rooted in some node $n \in \mathcal{N} \cup \{\text{sink}_0, \text{sink}_1\}$ the formula $\mathcal{T}_n$ represents the truth value of that sub-BDD. For each node $n \in \mathcal{N}$ the formula $\mathcal{B}^e_n$ represents the truth value of the neighbor of n on the edge e.

$$\mathcal{T}_{\text{sink}_0} \triangleq 0$$

$$\mathcal{T}_{\text{sink}_1} \triangleq 1$$

$$\mathcal{B}_n^e \triangleq \bigvee_{m \in \text{neighbors}(n)} (c_{n,m}^e \wedge \mathcal{T}_m)$$

$$\mathcal{T}_n \triangleq (\neg \mathcal{V}_n \wedge \mathcal{B}_n^0) \vee (\mathcal{V}_n \wedge \mathcal{B}_n^1)$$

3.3   Specification

We assume that we are given a formula ϕ on the input variables $\mathcal{I}$ that specifies the behavior of the BDD that we wish to construct, i.e. the constructed BDD should be true if and only if ϕ is true on any given input. This is now easily expressed as a QBF with two levels of quantification where the first level is over the labeling and connecting variables and the second level is over the input variables. In the parlance of the above-defined concepts, we need to ensure that the truth value of the root node is equal to the truth value of ϕ for any input.

To formalize, let $\mathcal{C}$ be the set of variables $c_{n,m}^e$ and let $\mathcal{L}$ be the set of variables $l_{n,x}$. The resulting QBF is defined as follows.

$$\exists \mathcal{C} \mathcal{L} \forall \mathcal{I}. \ \mathcal{T}_{n_N} \Leftrightarrow \phi$$

In particular, to obtain the minority function over the inputs, we output the following QBF.

$$\exists \mathcal{C} \mathcal{L} \forall \mathcal{I}. \mathcal{T}_{n_N} \Leftrightarrow \left(\sum_{x \in \mathcal{I}} x \leq \lfloor |\mathcal{I}|/2 \rfloor \right)$$

3.4   Technical Details of the Encoding

The above-defined formulas contain some constructs that are typically not supported by QBF solvers. In the implementation, we use the circuit-like language $QCIR$ supported by a number of tools [8]. QCIR supports only typical Boolean connectives. This means that the language does not have native support for the constructs $\sum_{x \in s} x = 1$ or $\sum_{x \in s} x \leq k$. These constraints can be converted to a circuit form in a number of ways. Since we are dealing with rather modest numbers we use the pairwise (quadratic) encoding for "exactly one" and sequential counter [15] for at-most$_k()$.

$$\sum_{x \in x_1, \dots, x_n} x = 1 \triangleq \bigvee_i x_i \vee \bigwedge_{i<j} \neg x_i \vee \neg x_j$$

$$\text{at-most}_0(S) \triangleq \bigwedge_{x \in S} \neg x_i$$

$$\text{at-most}_k(x_1, \dots, x_n) \triangleq x_1 \wedge \text{at-most}_{k-1}(x_2, \dots, x_n) \vee \neg x_1 \wedge \text{at-most}_k(x_2, \dots, x_n)$$

3.5 Experimental Evaluation

The encoding to QBF was implemented as a Python script allowing for different QBF solvers to be used as the back-end. The script uses encoding given in Sect. 3 with an increasing N (the number of nodes). Consequently, the majority of the QBF calls are UNSAT and the synthesized BDD is guaranteed to be the smallest in number of nodes (if found).

The targeted function was the minority function, in fact a special case of at-most$_k$() constraint, with $k = \lfloor |\mathcal{I}|/2 \rfloor$.[3] Figure 1 shows one of the synthesized BDDs for $|\mathcal{I}| = 5$, $k = 2$ with 9 BDD nodes (plus the sinks). Interestingly, this BDD is in fact ordered, but to our best knowledge, it is not known whether the smallest BDD for the minority function can be always ordered.

The following QBF solvers were used: Qute [12]; QFUN [5]; QuAbS [16]; and RAReQS [6]. The tables in Fig. 2 summarize the results. Figure 2(a) shows the running times (with the timeout 30 min). Figure 2(b) shows the lower bound for number of nodes. The solvers QFUN and RAReQS go up to 5 inputs while the solvers Qute and QuAbS stop already on 4 inputs. Interestingly enough, QFUN and RAReQS are still quite fast on 5 inputs.

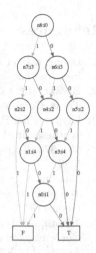

Fig. 1. Example BDD

$|\mathcal{I}|/k$	rareqs	qfun	qute	quabs
3/1	0.04	**0.02**	0.18	0.32
4/2	**0.11**	**0.11**	2.28	3.34
5/2	22.55	**17.35**	T/O	T/O
6/3	T/O	T/O	T/O	T/O

(a) Times in seconds

$|\mathcal{I}|/k$	rareqs	qfun	qute	quabs
3/1	4	4	4	4
4/2	6	6	6	6
5/2	9	9	7	8
6/3	10	10	6	7

(b) Lowerbounds for #nodes

Fig. 2. Results and example BDD

4 Future Work

We hope that this study will motivate the investigation of other methods for QBF solving; possibly based on more stochastic approaches. The study should also be carried out for other types of functions. Functions from real world, which are typically not symmetrical, might give better picture of the performance and also might be a better target for BDDs.

---

[3] Pudlák gives a $\Omega(n \lg n)$ lower-bound for this function [13].

Acknowledgments. This work was supported by national funds through FCT - Fundação para a Ciência e a Tecnologia with reference UID/CEC/50021/2019 and the project INFOCOS with reference PTDC/CCI-COM/32378/2017.

References

1. Bahar, R.I., et al.: Algebraic decision diagrams and their applications. In: Proceedings International Conference on Computer-Aided Design, pp. 188–191 (1993)
2. Bryant, R.E.: Graph-based algorithms for Boolean function manipulation. IEEE Trans. Comput. **100**(8), 677–691 (1986)
3. Faymonville, P., Finkbeiner, B., Rabe, M.N., Tentrup, L.: Encodings of bounded synthesis. In: Legay, A., Margaria, T. (eds.) TACAS 2017. LNCS, vol. 10205, pp. 354–370. Springer, Heidelberg (2017). https://doi.org/10.1007/978-3-662-54577-5_20
4. Gascón, A., Subramanyan, P., Dutertre, B., Tiwari, A., Jovanovic, D., Malik, S.: Template-based circuit understanding. In: Formal Methods in Computer-Aided Design (FMCAD) (2014)
5. Janota, M.: Towards generalization in QBF solving via machine learning. In: AAAI Conference on Artificial Intelligence (2018)
6. Janota, M., Klieber, W., Marques-Silva, J., Clarke, E.: Solving QBF with counterexample guided refinement. Artif. Intell. **234**, 1–25 (2016)
7. Jo, S., Matsumoto, T., Fujita, M.: SAT-based automatic rectification and debugging of combinational circuits with LUT insertions. In: Asian Test Symposium, pp. 19–24 (2012)
8. Jordan, C., Klieber, W., Seidl, M.: Non-CNF QBF solving with QCIR. In: Proceedings of BNP (Workshop) (2016)
9. Kleine Büning, H., Bubeck, U.: Theory of quantified Boolean formulas. In: Biere, A., Heule, M., van Maaren, H., Walsh, T. (eds.) Handbook of Satisfiability, Frontiers in Artificial Intelligence and Applications, vol. 185, pp. 735–760. IOS Press (2009)
10. Maksimovic, D., Le, B., Veneris, A.G.: Multiple clock domain synchronization in a QBF-based verification environment. In: International Conference on Computer-aided Design (ICCAD) (2014)
11. Narodytska, N., Legg, A., Bacchus, F., Ryzhyk, L., Walker, A.: Solving games without controllable predecessor. In: Biere, A., Bloem, R. (eds.) CAV 2014. LNCS, vol. 8559, pp. 533–540. Springer, Cham (2014). https://doi.org/10.1007/978-3-319-08867-9_35
12. Peitl, T., Slivovsky, F., Szeider, S.: Dependency learning for QBF. In: Theory and Applications of Satisfiability Testing (SAT), pp. 298–313 (2017)
13. Pudlák, P.: A lower bound on complexity of branching programs. In: Chytil, M.P., Koubek, V. (eds.) MFCS 1984. LNCS, vol. 176, pp. 480–489. Springer, Heidelberg (1984). https://doi.org/10.1007/BFb0030331
14. Razborov, A.A.: Lower bounds for deterministic and nondeterministic branching programs. In: Budach, L. (ed.) FCT 1991. LNCS, vol. 529, pp. 47–60. Springer, Heidelberg (1991). https://doi.org/10.1007/3-540-54458-5_49
15. Sinz, C.: Towards an optimal CNF encoding of Boolean cardinality constraints. In: van Beek, P. (ed.) CP 2005. LNCS, vol. 3709, pp. 827–831. Springer, Heidelberg (2005). https://doi.org/10.1007/11564751_73

16. Tentrup, L.: Non-prenex QBF solving using abstraction. In: Creignou, N., Le Berre, D. (eds.) SAT 2016. LNCS, vol. 9710, pp. 393–401. Springer, Cham (2016). https://doi.org/10.1007/978-3-319-40970-2_24

17. Tveretina, O., Sinz, C., Zantema, H.: An exponential lower bound on OBDD refutations for pigeonhole formulas. In: Athens Colloquium on Algorithms and Complexity, ACAC, pp. 13–21 (2009). https://doi.org/10.4204/EPTCS.4.2

18. Umans, C., Villa, T., Sangiovanni-Vincentelli, A.L.: Complexity of two-level logic minimization. IEEE Trans. CAD Integr. Circ. Syst. **25**(7), 1230–1246 (2006). https://doi.org/10.1109/TCAD.2005.855944

Using Summarization Techniques on Patent Database Through Computational Intelligence

Cinthia M. Souza[1], Matheus E. Santos[1], Magali R. G. Meireles[1(✉)], and Paulo E. M. Almeida[2]

[1] Pontifical Catholic University of Minas Gerais, Belo Horizonte, MG, Brazil
{cinthia.mikaela,matheus.1004060.santos}@sga.pucminas.br,
magali@pucminas.br
[2] Federal Center for Technological Education of Minas Gerais,
Belo Horizonte, MG, Brazil
pema@lsi.cefetmg.br

Abstract. Patents are an important source of information for measuring the technological advancement of a specific knowledge domain. The volume of patents available in digital databases has grown rapidly and, in order to take advantage of existing patent knowledge, it is essential to organize information in an accessible and simple format. The classification systems groups, made available by patent offices, were given names capable of representing them and facilitating the process of searching for the information associated with its content. The purpose of this paper is to use automatic text summarization techniques to develop an automatic methodology to help the examiner to name new patent groups created by the categorization systems. We used three summarization strategies with two different approaches to choose the most representative sentence for each subgroup. The experiments were performed on the basis of abstracts and descriptions of patent documents, in order to evaluate the performance of the methodology proposed in different sections of the patent document. Validation experiments were conducted using four subgroups of the United States Patent and Trademark Office, which uses the Cooperative Patent Classification system.

Keywords: Computational intelligence · Knowledge representation · Information systems · Automatic text summarization · Patent databases

1 Introduction

Patents are complex legal documents with a significant number of technical and descriptive details which relate to results of valuable research for the industry, companies and for researchers [1]. One of the objectives of granting patents is to facilitate the dissemination of scientific knowledge [2]. For this, the government

P. Moura Oliveira et al. (Eds.): EPIA 2019, LNAI 11805, pp. 508–519, 2019.
https://doi.org/10.1007/978-3-030-30244-3_42

grants the inventor the right to exclude others for a limited time from making, using or selling this invention, in exchange for full disclosure of an invention [3].

Patents are a source of inspiration. The efficient analysis of these documents allows monitoring technological trends, defining business models, securing market share, decreasing the time to develop new products and reducing the possibility of patent infringement [4–6]. Camus and Brancaleon [7] highlighted the importance of information contained in patent analysis, revealing risks and opportunities and gaining insight into business activities. Markellos [8] and Leydesdorff [9] explore the patent databases, showing how the production of scientific knowledge may be related to the economy. However, in order to be useful for the decision-making task, the information contained in a patent database must be in an understandable format [10].

Patent documents have idiosyncrasies that relate to the structure of the patent document, the vocabulary of the patent and the length of the sentences [4]. In this context, conventional approaches to information retrieval are difficult to apply and therefore the in-depth study of patents and their consequences still needs to be made more accessible to users and researchers.

The information contained in the patents is distributed in sections, defined by the patent office. The formatting of the patent text is controlled by laws and regulations of the country or the patent authority in which the inventor applied for the patent. In general, patents have title, abstract, claims and description. The abstract is characterized by having complex syntactic constructs and a generic vocabulary. The claims section has a hierarchical structure, with independent and dependent claims. The independent claims present a general idea of the invention whereas the dependent claims present more specific information about the invention. Each claim is composed by a single sentence. This leads to the appearance of very long sentences and significant complexity. The section of the description is characterized by having distinctive information of the inventions [4, 11].

Patent offices name the groups in the classification systems in order to facilitate the process of searching the information associated with the content of these documents. The growth of the number of patents in certain categories generates the need to reclassify the categories and divide them into subcategories. Consequently, new subgroups need to be named. Because these subgroups belong to a restricted knowledge domain, the naming task can be extremely laborious. In this context, it is necessary to look for techniques that facilitate this naming process, to assist the examiners in their task.

This paper aims to investigate how the automatic text summarization process can generate sentences directly associated with the content of patents, making it easier to identify these documents in searches and providing support to the patent management process. The experiments will be conducted in two sections of patent documents, abstract and descriptions, using two different approaches. The obtained results will be compared quantitatively, using semantic similarity analysis, and qualitatively. The work is divided into five sections. Section 2 presents the theoretical background and related works. Section 3 describes the database used and the methodological steps of the work. Sections 4 and 5 show the results, analysis and final considerations.

2   Theoretical Background

Automatic text summarization aims to construct a simple and descriptive summary of the original text from sections of the text. Thus, the process identifies the significant aspects of one or more documents to represent them consistently [12].

In general, there are two main approaches to automatic summarization: extractive and abstractive. The extractive summarization selects the main sections of the original text to generate a summary. The extractive summarization systems are usually based on the sentence/topic extraction technique and attempt to identify the set of sentences that are most important for the general understanding of a particular document. In order to identify these sentences, many approaches use the keywords as a criterion for choosing the sentences and, thus, extract the sentences that have the highest number of keywords [13].

Abstractive summarization tries to develop an understanding of the main sections of the text and, from an internal semantic representation, expresses the knowledge obtained in natural language. For this, it uses linguistic methods to interpret and describe the text, thus generating a summary with the main information of this text [13]. Because it requires extensive processing of natural language, abstractive summarization is much more complex than extractive and therefore less explored [14].

In this work, three extractive summarization strategies were implemented. The first one is based on the LexRank algorithm, the second is based on the Latent Semantic Analysis (LSA) algorithm and the third one is based on the Term Frequency-Inverse Document Frequency (TF-IDF) algorithm. Subsects. 2.1, 2.2 and 2.3 present the description of the implemented algorithms. Subsection 2.4 presents a description of the semantic similarity analysis algorithm that was used to choose the sentence that best represents the set of documents.

2.1   LexRank

LexRank is an extractive summarization algorithm, developed by Erkan and Radev. This algorithm assigns a weight to each sentence of a document, which represents the importance of the sentence for the document [15].

Initially, the method performs sentence grouping, by calculating the similarity between them. The calculation of similarity uses a bag-of-words model where each sentence is represented by a N-dimensional vector, and N is the number of all occurring words in the sentence. The documents are represented by a matrix where each cell presents the value of the cosine similarity between sentence pairs [15].

Then, the results of the similarity calculation are allocated in a non-directed graph, where the vertices are the sentences of each group and the weight of the edges is the similarity between the vertices. In order to choose the most representative sentence of each document, one evaluates the centrality of each sentence in a cluster, and draws the most important ones [15].

2.2 LSA

Deerwester et al. [16] described the LSA as a method for information retrieval. However, in 1998, Landauer, Foltz and Laham suggested using this method to find relationships between words. The main idea of this method is to reduce the number of dimensions, consequently reducing noise, and emphasizing strong indirect relationships between entities.

In this work, the LSA is used to generate a summary of a document. The method was based on the work of Dokun and Celebi [17] and consists of making an extractive summary, in which an algorithm extracts a single sentence from the document, identifying it as the sentence that best represents the document. For this, the algorithm receives as input a preprocessed document and generates a sentence-term matrix, usually sparse, in which a column vector represents the weighted frequency of the sentence in the document.

From the semantic point of view, Singular Value Decomposition (SVD) derives the latent semantic structure from the document represented by a matrix, reflecting a breakdown of the original document into linearly-independent base vectors or concepts. Each term and sentence from the document is jointly indexed by these base vectors/concepts. Beside this, if a word combination pattern is recurring in document, this pattern will be represented by one of the singular vectors. The magnitude of the corresponding singular value indicates the importance degree of this pattern within the document. Any sentences containing this word combination pattern will be projected along this singular vector, and the sentence that best represents this pattern will have the largest index value with this vector [18].

2.3 TF-IDF

The TF-IDF algorithm is an unsupervised method, which is based on the local (TF) and global (IDF) frequencies of the set or database items. TF-IDF algorithm is a numerical statistic that shows how important a word is to a document, or to a set of documents. When a word number increases in a given document, the value of TF-IDF increases proportionally. However, depending on the number of times this word occurs in the set of documents, the value of TF-IDF decreases [19].

The frequency of a term $f(i,j)$ corresponds to the number of occurrences of the term i in the document j. The inverse frequency of the document measures the amount of information a word provides, that is, whether the term is common or rare in all documents. It is a logarithmically obtained value. Thus, the total number of documents in the collection is divided by the number of documents that contain the term [19].

TF-IDF algorithm was developed based on the IDF proposed by Sparck Jones [20] and is defined by Eqs. (1) to (3). Equation (1) calculates the importance of a term, $f_{i,j}$, in terms of a document, by the quotient between the frequency of the term i in the document j and the frequency of the term that occurs the most in the document.

$$f_{i,j} = \frac{f(i,j)}{max(frequency_{i,j})} \tag{1}$$

Equation (2) calculates the importance of the term for the collection of documents by the logarithm of the quotient between the total number of documents (N) and the number of documents that have the term i under analysis (n_i).

$$idf_i = log\frac{N}{n_i} \tag{2}$$

Finally, Eq. (3) calculates the weight of the term, combining both those importance measures.

$$w_{ij} = f_{i,j} \times idf_i \tag{3}$$

There are several variations of the TF-IDF algorithm for the task of automatic text summarization. Previous experiments were carried out with the purpose of evaluating the performance of three of these variations applied to patent documents. The first variation of the TF-IDF algorithm calculates the TF-IDF considering all words as terms. The second considers only nouns as terms. The third considers only the nouns as terms and the sentence position in the paragraph is used as weight. The calculation of the sentence weight is performed based on Eq. (4), proposed by Singh et al. [21]. The results of the experiments showed that the third variation of the TF-IDF presented a result superior to the others and, therefore, will be used in this work.

$$p = \frac{1}{4}(\frac{1}{N_{pa}} + \frac{1}{N_{se}})^2 \tag{4}$$

in which N_{pa} is the paragraph number where the analyzed sentence is found and N_{se} is the position of the sentence in the paragraph. The weight p is added to the TF-IDF value of the sentence.

2.4   Analysis of Semantic Similarity

Semantic similarity is a measure that verifies the similarity between sentences and texts, also defined as semantic entities. This similarity is measured using the distance between terms based on their meaning or semantic content. The semantic similarity index between the semantic entities is a numerical estimation obtained with the semantic information of the entities terms [22].

In this work, the semantic similarity analysis method proposed by Al-Natsheh et al. was used [23]. This method consists of two phases, the first is the extraction of characteristic pairs and the second is the regression estimator. For the extraction of feature pairs, the algorithm uses attributes such as part-of-speech (PoS), which is a category of words with similar lexical properties, named-entities (NE) such as people, organizations and sites, and the representation of sentences in Bag-of-Words (BoW), which is weighted by TF-IDF. For the regression estimation, the Random Forests (RF) method is used, which is a classifier that constructs decision trees during training. This method takes two sentences and assigns to them a score between 0 and 5, so that a high score represents a large similarity between the sentences.

3   Proposed Approach

This section has been divided into two subsections. The first presents the database used in the experiments, while the second one presents the methodology used to extract the most significant sentence from the patent groups.

3.1   Database

The database used in the experiment is provided by the United States Patent and Trademark Office (USPTO). The classification system used, classifies patents into sections, classes, subclasses, groups and subgroups as illustrates in Fig. 1. For this work, four subgroups, G06K 7/1443, G06K 7/1447, G06K 7/1452 and G06K 7/1456 were randomly selected. This is a prototype to validate the proposed methodology. These subgroups belong to the G06K subclass, named "recognition of data, presentation of data, record carriers, handling record carriers" by USPTO.

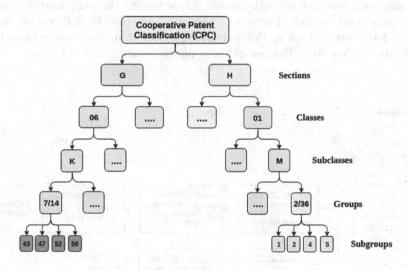

Fig. 1. Hierarchical organization of CPC system.

The database used is composed of 733 patents. Table 1 shows the patent code in the CPC classification system, the subgroup name and the distribution of the patents in each of them.

Table 1. Database.

CPC Codes	Subgroups names	Number of patents
G06K 7/1443	Locating of the code in an image	348
G06K 7/1447	Extracting optical codes from image or text carrying said optical code	198
G06K 7/1452	Detecting bar code edges	68
G06K 7/1456	Determining the orientation of the optical code with respect to the reader and correcting therefore	119

3.2   Methodological Steps

The methodology used to find the sentence that best describes the group created can be divided into three steps. The first step is the segmentation of patent documents. The algorithms used in all the methodological steps were implemented in Python language. This paper performs segmentation of two sections of a patent document, the abstract and the description. It was decided not to use the claims section because of its particularities, due to the size of sentences and their complexity. To create the basis of the description, only the first 300 words of each document were selected for each patent. According to the classification experiments performed by Fall, Törcsvári, Benzineb and Karetka [24], results using the first 300 words of each section performed better than those using the whole text. Figure 2 presents a diagram of the proposed scheme.

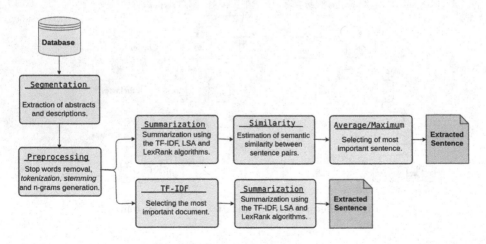

Fig. 2. Sentence extraction scheme.

In the second step, the documents were preprocessed. The used algorithm removes stop words, special characters, stemming and generates n-grams. For each of the patents, the algorithm generates a new file containing the preprocessed text and an occurrence matrix.

In the third step, the most representative sentence of each subgroup was selected. To obtain this sentence, two different approaches were used. They will be detailed in the next two paragraphs.

The first approach is divided into three phases. The first phase consisted of the summarization of each of the documents of the four subgroups using LexRank, LSA and TF-IDF algorithms. These algorithms receive as input a preprocessed text and return the phrase best ranked by the algorithm. The second phase of the process analyzes the similarity between the extracted sentences, using the method proposed by Al-Natsheh et al. [23]. The semantic similarity of each sentence in relation to the other sentences of the subgroup was calculated, creating a list of sentence pairs, and their respective indexes of similarity. In the third phase, two metrics were used, **maximum** and **mean**, to select the sentence that has the greatest similarity to the other sentences. The **maximum** metric selects the sentence that most frequently presents the highest similarity index. The **mean** metric selects the sentence with the highest mean index of similarity.

The second approach is divided into two phases. In the first phase, the most important document of each subgroup was identified. For this, the algorithm receives as input a matrix of occurrences, generated by the pre-processing algorithm, and calculates the importance of each word in the documents using the TF-IDF algorithm. Then, the sum of the scores of each document is made and the document that has the highest score is defined as the most important of the subgroup. In the second phase, the document was summarized using the LexRank, LSA and TF-IDF algorithms. These algorithms receive as input a preprocessed text and return the phrase best ranked by the algorithm.

After all, the validation of the experiments was performed, using 4 subgroups of USPTO, which already have their names designated by specialists. The selected sentences were evaluated quantitatively, analyzing the semantic similarity between the name of the subgroup and the chosen sentences as the most representative of each subgroup. In addition, a qualitative analysis was performed, with the name of the subgroup. The hypothesis is that if the selected sentence is semantically similar to the subgroup name, it will provide a meaningful description for the subgroup. From this analysis, it was possible to identify which of the approaches associated to each one of the algorithms obtained the best result applied to the abstracts and the descriptions.

4   Experiments

Initially, the experiments were performed using the first approach proposed in the methodology. To validate the obtained results, an analysis of the semantic similarity between the name of the subgroup and the sentence chosen by each one of the strategies associated with the two metrics was performed. The names of the subgroups selected to validate the proposed methodology are presented in Table 1. Tables 2 and 3 show the semantic similarity index between the sentence chosen for each metric and the name of the subgroup, using the abstracts database and descriptions, respectively. In these tables, the subgroups were only represented with their finalization, 43, 47, 52, 56. The first column shows the metric used to choose the best sentence in the group, the second column presents the strategies, which is the sentence extraction method used to choose the best sentence and the last four columns present the semantic similarity indexes for each of the four subgroups.

Table 2. Semantic similarity index using abstracts - First approach.

Metrics	Strategies	Subgroups			
		43	47	52	56
Mean	Lex	2.98	2.18	3.09	2.14
	LSA	2.98	1.66	3.09	2.63
	TF-IDF	2.98	1.75	2.85	2.82
Maximum	Lex	2.98	1.04	2.85	2.14
	LSA	**3.00**	**1.66**	**3.09**	**3.07**
	TF-IDF	2.98	1.42	2.88	2.10

Table 3. Semantic similarity index using descriptions - First approach.

Metrics	Strategies	Subgroups			
		43	47	52	56
Mean	Lex	2.89	1.44	2.83	2.78
	LSA	2.91	1.07	2.92	2.78
	TF-IDF	3.14	2.01	2.92	2.02
Maximum	Lex	2.89	2.03	2.84	2.78
	LSA	2.91	1.96	1.58	2.06
	TF-IDF	2.35	2.01	1.92	2.02

Afterwards, the experiments were performed using the second approach described in the methodology. The occurrence matrix generated by preprocessing was used as input for the TF-IDF algorithm. The TF-IDF algorithm, in this case, was used to choose the most representative document of each subgroup. Then, for each document, the most representative sentence was chosen using each of the three proposed strategies.

To validate the results obtained, each sentence was compared semantically with the subgroup name presented in Table 1. Tables 4 and 5 show the semantic similarity index between the sentence chosen for each metric and the name of the subgroup, using the abstracts database and descriptions, respectively. The first column shows the metric used to choose the best sentence in the group, the second column presents the strategies, which is the sentence extraction method used to choose the best sentence and the last four columns present the semantic similarity indexes for each of the four subgroups.

Table 4. Semantic similarity index using abstracts - Second approach.

Strategies	Subgroups			
	43	47	52	56
Lex	2.22	1.16	1.86	1.63
LSA	2.22	1.16	2.00	1.63
TF-IDF	2.22	1.44	1.90	1.02

Table 5. Semantic similarity index using descriptions - Second approach.

Strategies	Subgroups			
	43	47	52	56
Lex	1.30	0.99	0.98	0.81
LSA	1.81	1.62	1.44	1.11
TF-IDF	1.81	1.00	2.61	2.34

By analyzing the results of the two proposed approaches, it is clear to verify that LSA algorithm with **maximum** metric performs better than the other algorithms for the majority of the experiments. Figure 3 shows an example of the result obtained using the proposed scheme. For this case, the summarization method achieved a semantic similarity index equal to 3.00, which can be considered as good in a scale from 0 to 5. The word cloud, shown in Fig. 3, is a graphical representation that helps evaluating the existing similarity between the original text and the summarized phrase. It was created using Python coding.

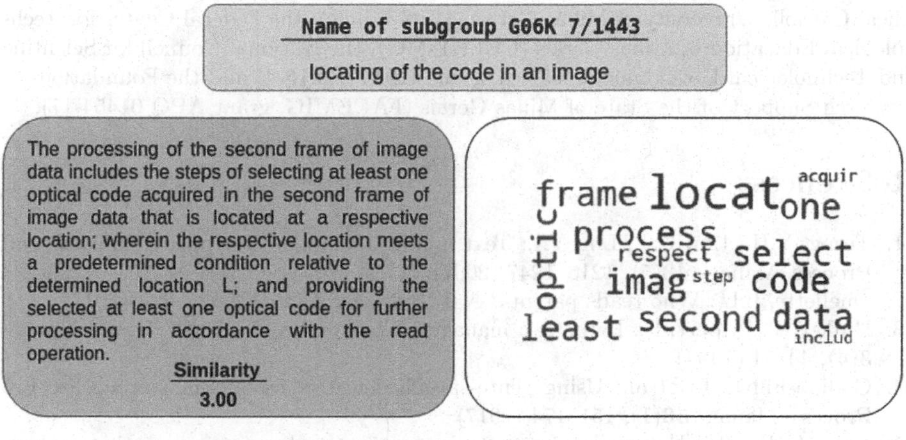

Fig. 3. Sentence extracted using LSA and metric **maximum** for the subgroup G06K7/1443.

5 Conclusions

Patent classification systems help offices categorize, classify, and subsequently retrieve patents in their state-of-the-art search processes. With the increasing number of patents and the development of new technologies, the classification systems should be constantly reviewed to avoid accumulation of patents on certain subgroups. Consequently, there is a need to reclassify the categories and subdivide them into subcategories. However, the task of naming the generated subcategories can be extremely laborious. In this context, it is necessary to look for techniques that facilitate this naming process, to assist the examiner in his task.

The main contribution of this work is the suggestion of an efficient approach to extract the most significant sentence from patent groups, in order to assist the examiners when naming new groups/subgroups. The experiments were carried out using extractive summarization strategies and semantic analysis, in an area of interest to the academic and industrial community. As a continuation of this work, the four subgroups used will be categorized and the new groups identified will be named using the proposed methodology. Another proposal of continuity is the application of an abstractive summarization methodology to be compared with the extractive summarization used in this work. Patent office professionals and researchers in the domain of information retrieval and applied machine learning have evaluated USPTO database to investigate the accessibility of the knowledge embedded in patents. Most of them deal with the upper levels of classification hierarchies (class and subclass levels), and only some have tracked the problem on a more fine-grained classification (group and subgroup levels), as it was done in this work.

Acknowledgment. The authors would like to thank the financial support of the Pontifical Catholic University of Minas Gerais (PUC Minas), the Federal Center for Technological Education of Minas Gerais (CEFET-MG), the National Council for Scientific and Technological Development (CNPq, grant 429144/2016-4) and the Foundation for Research Support of the State of Minas Gerais (FAPEMIG, grant APQ 01454-17).

References

1. Tseng, Y.H., Lin, C.J., Lin, Y.I.: Text mining techniques for patent analysis. Inf. Process. Manag. **43**(5), 1216–1247 (2007)
2. Ouellette, L.L.: Who reads patents? Nat. Biotechnol. **35**(5), 421–424 (2017)
3. Hufker, T., Alpert, F.: Patents: a managerial perspective. J. Prod. Brand Manag. **3**(4), 44–54 (1994)
4. Codina-Filbà, J., et al.: Using genre-specific features for patent summaries. Inf. Process. Manag. **53**(1), 151–174 (2017)
5. Kim, J., Lee, S.: Patent databases for innovation studies: a comparative analysis of USPTO, EPO, JPO and KIPO. Technol. Forecast. Soc. Change **92**, 332–345 (2015)
6. Trappey, A.J., Trappey, C.V., Wu, C.Y.: Automatic patent document summarization for collaborative knowledge systems and services. J. Syst. Sci. Syst. Eng. **18**(1), 71–94 (2009)
7. Camus, C., Brancaleon, R.: Intellectual assets management: from patents to knowledge. World Pat. Inf. **25**, 155–159 (2003)
8. Markellos, K., Perdikuri, K., Markellou, P., Sirmakessis, S., Mayritsakis, G., Tsakalidis, A.: Knowledge discovery in patent databases. In: Proceedings of the eleventh International Conference on Information and Knowledge Management (CIKM 2002), pp. 672–674. ACM (2002)
9. Leydesdorff, L.: The university-industry knowledge relationship: analyzing patents and the science base of technologies. J. Am. Soc. Inf. Sci. Technol. **55**(11), 991–1001 (2004)
10. Madani, F., Weber, C.: The evolution of patent mining: applying bibliometrics-analysis and keyword network analysis. World Pat. Inf. **46**, 32–48 (2016)
11. Mille, S., Wanner, L.: Multilingual summarization in practice: the case of patent claims. In: Proceedings of the 12th European Association of Machine Translation Conference (2008)
12. Allahyari, M., et al.: A brief survey of text mining: classification, clustering and extraction techniques. arXiv preprint arXiv:1707.02919 (2017)
13. Wang, D., Zhu, S., Li, T., Chi, Y., Gong, Y.: Integrating document clustering and multidocument summarization. ACM Trans. Knowl. Discov. Data (TKDD) **5**(3), 14 (2011)

14. Gambhir, M., Gupta, V.: Recent automatic text summarization techniques: a survey. Artif. Intell. Rev. **47**(1), 1–66 (2017)
15. Erkan, G., Radev, D.R.: Graph-based lexical centrality as salience in text summarization. J. Artif. Intell. Res. **22**, 457–479 (2004)
16. Deerwester, S., Dumais, S.T., Furnas, G.W., Landauer, T.K., Harshman, R.: Indexing by latent semantic analysis. J. Am. Soc. Inf. Sci. **41**(6), 391–407 (1990)
17. Dokun, O., Celebi, E.: Single-document summarization using latent semantic analysis. Int. J. Sci. Res. Inf. Syst. Eng. (IJSRISE) **1**(2), 57–64 (2015)
18. Froud, H., Lachkar, A., Ouatik, S.A.: Arabic text summarization based on latent semantic analysis to enhance Arabic documents clustering. Int. J. Data Min. Knowl. Manag. Process **3**(1), 79–95 (2013)
19. Savyanavar, P., Mehta, B., Marathe, V., Padvi, P., Shewale, M.: Multi-document summarization using TF-IDF Algorithm. Int. J. Eng. Comput. Sci. **5**(4), 16253–16256 (2016)
20. Sparck Jones, K.: A statistical interpretation of term specificity and its application in retrieval. J. Doc. **28**(1), 11–21 (1972)
21. Singh, S.P., Kumar, A., Mangal, A., Singhal, S.: Bilingual automatic text summarization using unsupervised deep learning. In: 2016 International Conference on Electrical, Electronics, and Optimization Techniques (ICEEOT), pp. 1195–1200 (2016)
22. Harispe, S., Ranwez, S., Janaqi, S., Montmain, J.: Semantic Similarity from natural language and ontology analysis. Synth. Lect. Hum. Lang. Technol. **8**(1), 1–254 (2015)
23. Al-Natsheh, H.T., Martinet, L., Muhlenbach, F., Zighed, D.A.: UdL at SemEval-2017 task 1: semantic textual similarity estimation of English sentence pairs using regression model over pairwise features. In: Proceedings of the 11th International Workshop on Semantic Evaluation (SemEval-2017), pp. 115–119 (2017)
24. Fall, C.J., Törcsvári, A., Benzineb, K., Karetka, G.: Automated categorization in the international patent classification. ACM SIGIR Forum **37**(1), 10–25 (2003)

A Complete Planner for Temporal Answer Set Programming

Pedro Cabalar[✉], Manuel Rey, and Concepción Vidal

Department of Computer Science, Universidade da Coruña, A Coruña, Spain
{cabalar,j.manuel.rey,concepcion.vidalm}@udc.es

Abstract. In this paper we present `tasplan`, a complete planner for temporal logic programs. The planner receives a planning specification as input, having the form of a temporal ASP program, and obtains as output one or several alternative (shortest) plans, if the problem is solvable, or answers that no solution exists, otherwise. The tool allows different search strategies, including informed search algorithms if the user defines a domain-dependent heuristics with additional program rules.

1 Introduction

The paradigm *Answer Set Programming* (ASP [11,12]) has become a popular approach for practical Knowledge Representation and problem solving thanks to its simple semantics based on stable models [9], the availability of efficient solvers and their application in a wide spectrum of diverse domains [7]. Although the ASP modelling language and its associated solvers are designed for static combinatorial search problems, many ASP applications require handling a dynamic component, normally, dealing with transition systems over discrete time. An extension of ASP for temporal reasoning was proposed with the introduction of *Temporal Equilibrium Logic* (TEL) [1,4], a combination of *Equilibrium Logic* [13] (the logical characterisation of stable models) with the usual modal temporal operators from *Linear-time Temporal Logic* (LTL [10,14]). The first tools for TEL inference were based on model checking [2] and automata transformation methods [5]. Although these implementations were convenient for studying system properties or strong equivalence under the assumption of infinite traces, they were highly inefficient for solving planning problems. A more practical orientation came with the recent definition of TEL for finite traces [6]. This led to the implementation of system `telingo` [3], a temporal extension of the popular ASP solver `clingo` that relies on the same incremental solving strategy for finding the shortest plan in an efficient way.

The usual strategy in ASP planning is based on an iterative deepening search, incrementally increasing the length n of the searched plan until a solution is found [8]. This kind of planners are obviously *incomplete*: when the problem

This work was partially supported by MINECO, Spain, grant TIC2017-84453-P, Xunta de Galicia, Spain (GPC ED431B 2019/03 and 2016-2019 ED431G/01, CITIC).

P. Moura Oliveira et al. (Eds.): EPIA 2019, LNAI 11805, pp. 520–525, 2019.
https://doi.org/10.1007/978-3-030-30244-3_43

has no solution, the planner is trapped in an infinite loop, trying new values for n indefinitely[1]. On the other hand, the model checking tools [2,5] mentioned before can detect non-existence of a plan, but they are not tailored for planning problems and result rather inefficient.

In this paper, we describe `tasplan`[2], a complete planner for temporal logic programs. `tasplan` receives a temporal logic program as an input. This temporal program describes the fluents that configure the states of the system, the actions that can be executed and the restrictions that have to be fulfilled. It will also determine the behaviour of the state transition system, the initial state and the goal state to be reached. The output will consist of one or several plans (sequences of actions) or the answer that there is no possible plan, so `tasplan` is the first complete planner for ASP. The strategy followed by `tasplan` consists in a classical search algorithm (we follow the pseudocode in [15]) maintaining a hash table and a fringe containing the next states to be explored (reaching an empty fringe is a guarantee that there exists no solution). The main distinctive feature in our search algorithm is that the generation of successor states relies on multiple calls to `clingo`[3] that is kept running in the background and is used through its Python API. Finally, `tasplan` can use different (uninformed and informed) search algorithms that can be selected through the command line call. Informed search incorporates the possibility of specifying a heuristic function that can be used to prune the search, when the planning problem is solvable. This heuristic is included in the specification of the problem as one more regular rule, something that provides a natural and declarative method for defining different heuristics.

2   Architecture

The proposed architecture (see Fig. 1) has the form of a pipeline: `tasplan` receives as input a file with the specification of the problem to solve, which must be written in ASP. The problem formalisation must be fragmented in five `#program` blocks named as `types(t)`, `static`, `initial`, `dynamic` and `final(t)`. The input file is grounded using tool `gringo` to obtain a ground program. No further grounding will be required afterwards. In order to avoid that the grounder makes assumptions on dynamic atoms (representing actions and fluents), for instance, assuming that non-occurring actions are false, we precede those atoms by the grounder directive `#external`. This will let us manipulate the ground program on the fly, adding and removing (ground) dynamic atoms without the need of grounding again. After that, the solving module implements the planning algorithm that explores the state space and decides the existence of a plan. Each time a non-goal state S is picked from the fringe, the algorithm computes its possible successor states by a call to `clasp` on the ground program extended

---

[1] An interesting topic for future study would be determining integer bounds for the required number of steps n to obtain a plan.

[2] https://github.com/jmanuelrey/T-ASPlan/.

[3] Systems `clingo`, `gringo` and `clasp` are available at https://potassco.org.

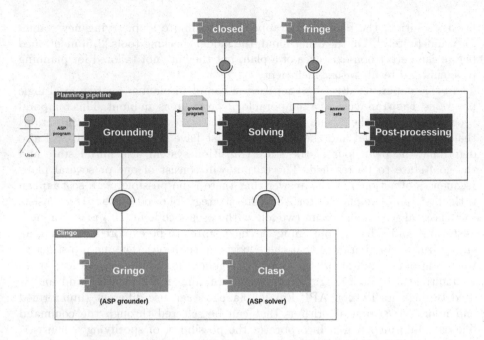

Fig. 1. tasplan architecture based on "Pipe and filter".

with the facts corresponding to S. The possible successor states are obtained as the multiple stable models. This process is repeated as many times as transition computations needed by the search algorithm. If any successor state matches with the goal specified in the problem formalisation, the solver ends, and the goal is passed to the last module. Otherwise, if tasplan explores the complete state space and no new state is generated, the tool determines the non existence of plan. The post-processing module prepares the data so it can be printed in a comfortable way for the user.

To conclude this section, we show in Fig. 2 an example of input specification for tasplan. The program represents the well-known 8-puzzle problem, where a grid of 3 × 3 cells contains 8 tiles (from 1 to 8) and a hole (represented by 0). The possible actions are moving an adjacent tile to the hole, creating a new hole in its previous position. We assume some familiarity with clingo language. The time instant is represented here by the constant terms t and t-1. Perhaps the most relevant feature is the special predicate heuristics(N, t) that is used to specify a domain-specific heuristic function N for each state at time point t. In this particular case, the heuristics corresponds to the Manhattan distance of each tile to its goal position, and uses a #sum aggregate for all tiles.

3   Evaluation

We have performed a preliminary evaluation of tasplan efficiency in comparison to the incremental solving strategy. Table 1 shows the time results obtained

```
#program types(t).
action(move(X,t)) :- dir(X).
fluent(pos(X,Y,Z,t)) :- tile(X), row(Y), col(Z).
fluent(goal(t)).

#program static.
row(1..3).
col(1..3).
tile(0..8).
cell(X,Y) :- row(X), col(Y).
% goal state
goalpos(1,1,1). goalpos(2,1,2). goalpos(3,1,3).
goalpos(4,2,1). goalpos(5,2,2). goalpos(6,2,3).
goalpos(7,3,1). goalpos(8,3,2). goalpos(0,3,3).
dir(up;down;right;left).
adj(X,Y,up,   X-1,Y) :- row(X),row(X-1),col(Y).
adj(X,Y,down, X+1,Y) :- row(X),row(X+1),col(Y).
adj(X,Y,left, X,Y-1) :- row(X),col(Y-1),col(Y).
adj(X,Y,right,X,Y+1) :- row(X),col(Y+1),col(Y).

#program initial.
pos(8,1,1,0). pos(6,1,2,0). pos(7,1,3,0).
pos(2,2,1,0). pos(5,2,2,0). pos(4,2,3,0).
pos(3,3,1,0). pos(0,3,2,0). pos(1,3,3,0).

#program dynamic(t).
% Manhattan heuristic
heuristics(N,t) :- N = #sum{ M,F : tile(F), F!=0, pos(F,X,Y,t),
     goalpos(F,X2,Y2), M=|X-X2|+|Y-Y2|}.
1 {move(D,t) : dir(D)} 1.
pos(0,Z,T,t) :- move(D,t), pos(0,X,Y,t-1), adj(X,Y,D,Z,T).
pos(P,X,Y,t) :- move(D,t), pos(0,X,Y,t-1), adj(X,Y,D,Z,T),
     pos(P,Z,T,t-1).
% Inertia
pos(P,Z,T,t) :- pos(P,Z,T,t-1), not -pos(P,Z,T,t).
-pos(P,Z,T,t) :- pos(P,X,Y,t), (X,Y)!=(Z,T), row(Z), col(T).

#program final(t).
goal(t) :- #count{X,Y: pos(P,X,Y,t), not goalpos(P,X,Y)} = 0.
```

Fig. 2. Encoding of an instance of the 8-puzzle problem in `tasplan` input language.

for different instances of the classical 8-puzzle problem. The measurements have been taken on a computer with seven Intel© Xeon© E5504 processors with 4M cache, 2 GHz processor frequency, 4.80 GT/s, 4 Intel© QPI Core CPUs, 16 GB RAM, and 3 TB of external storage. Each instance has been classified by the length (number of steps) of the shortest plan. This is represented in the leftmost column: the last line, with value ∞, corresponds to a scenario with no solution. The time values are organised in three columns: the first one corresponds to

Table 1. Time measurements for different scenarios of 8-puzzle.Time measurements for different scenarios of 8-puzzle.

Plan length	tasplan (A*)	tasplan (breadth)	telingo
5	0.044 s	0.409 s	0.024 s
9	0.068 s	2.575 s	0.036 s
12	0.108 s	13.809 s	0.104 s
15	0.634 s	75.154 s	0.282 s
17	1.259 s	143.978 s	0.865 s
20	3.615 s	289.900 s	0.868 s
25	17.732 s	551.520 s	12.341 s
28	47.271 s	860.446 s	44.203 s
30	49.485 s	951.516 s	64.537 s
31	155.139 s	1326.927 s	187.962 s
∞	1438.047 s	2294.307 s	∞

tasplan with an A* algorithm (using Manhattan distance as heuristics), the second is tasplan using an uninformed breadth search and the third one is the result of telingo with an analogous encoding (telingo does not allow heuristics specification). As we can see, telingo does not (and cannot) provide an answer to the last (unsolvable) scenario, whereas both versions of tasplan allow eventually deciding that there is no possible solution. In the rest of cases, telingo is clearly faster than breadth search in tasplan. When we allow domain specific heuristics, however, tasplan with A* has a similar performance to telingo and is even slightly better for longer plans. This comparison is not completely fair, in the sense that telingo does not use domain specific heuristics like the Manhattan distance. However, the truth is that the addition of such information to telingo could not be exploited anyway due to its iterative deepening strategy. This preliminary experiment shows the potential interest of exploiting user-defined domain heuristics for ASP planning.

4   Final Conclusions

We have presented tasplan, a complete planner for temporal Answer Set Programming. For a temporal logic program specifying a planning scenario, tasplan is capable of deciding the non-existence of a plan when the problem is unsolvable, outperforming previous tools based on model checking. When the problem has a plan, tasplan is still slower than current ASP incremental solvers, but its performance is comparable if we allow the introduction of domain specific heuristics, that can be exploited using standard informed search algorithms such as A*. For future work, we plan to modify the tasplan input language to accept telingo logic programs, so that both planners can be applied on the same specification. We also plan to study automated computation of domain-independent heuristics.

References

1. Aguado, F., Cabalar, P., Diéguez, M., Pérez, G., Vidal, C.: Temporal equilibrium logic: a survey. J. Appl. Non-Class. Log. **23**(1–2), 2–24 (2013)
2. Cabalar, P., Diéguez, M.: STELP – a tool for temporal answer set programming. In: Delgrande, J.P., Faber, W. (eds.) LPNMR 2011. LNCS, vol. 6645, pp. 370–375. Springer, Heidelberg (2011). https://doi.org/10.1007/978-3-642-20895-9_43
3. Cabalar, P., Kaminski, R., Morkisch, P., Schaub, T.: *telingo* = ASP + Time. In: Balduccini, M., Lierler, Y., Woltran, S. (eds.) LPNMR 2019. LNCS, vol. 11481, pp. 256–269. Springer, Cham (2019)
4. Cabalar, P., Pérez Vega, G.: Temporal equilibrium logic: a first approach. In: Moreno Díaz, R., Pichler, F., Quesada Arencibia, A. (eds.) EUROCAST 2007. LNCS, vol. 4739, pp. 241–248. Springer, Heidelberg (2007). https://doi.org/10.1007/978-3-540-75867-9_31
5. Cabalar, P., Diéguez, M.: Strong equivalence of non-monotonic temporal theories. In: Proceedings of the 14th International Conference on Principles of Knowledge Representation and Reasoning (KR 2014), Vienna, Austria (2014)
6. Cabalar, P., Kaminski, R., Schaub, T., Schuhmann, A.: Temporal answer set programming on finite traces. TPLP **18**(3–4), 406–420 (2018)
7. Erdem, E., Gelfond, M., Leone, N.: Applications of answer set programming. AI Mag. **37**(3), 53–68 (2016)
8. Gebser, M., Kaufmann, B., Kaminski, R., Ostrowski, M., Schaub, T., Schneider, M.T.: Potassco: the potsdam answer set solving collection. AI Commun. **24**(2), 107–124 (2011)
9. Gelfond, M., Lifschitz, V.: The stable model semantics for logic programming. In: Proceedings of the 5th International Conference on Logic Programming (ICLP 1988), pp. 1070–1080, Seattle, Washington (1988)
10. Kamp, H.: Tense logic and the theory of linear order. Ph.D. thesis, UCLA (1968)
11. Marek, V., Truszczyński, M.: Stable models and an alternative logic programming paradigm. In: Apt, K.R., Marek, V.W., Truszczynski, M., Warren, D.S. (eds.) The Logic Programming Paradigm. Artificial Intelligence, pp. 375–398. Springer, Heidelberg (1999). https://doi.org/10.1007/978-3-642-60085-2_17
12. Niemelä, I.: Logic programs with stable model semantics as a constraint programming paradigm. Ann. Math. Artif. Intell. **25**(3–4), 241–273 (1999)
13. Pearce, D.: A new logical characterisation of stable models and answer sets. In: Dix, J., Pereira, L.M., Przymusinski, T.C. (eds.) NMELP 1996. LNCS, vol. 1216, pp. 57–70. Springer, Heidelberg (1997). https://doi.org/10.1007/BFb0023801
14. Pnueli, A.: The temporal logic of programs. In: Proceedings of the 18th Annual Symposium on Foundations of Computer Science, SFCS 2077, pp. 46–57. IEEE Computer Society, Washington, DC, USA (1977)
15. Russell, S.J., Norvig, P.: Artificial Intelligence - A Modern Approach, 3. internat. edn. Pearson Education, London (2010)

An Argumentative Characterization of Disjunctive Logic Programming

Jesse Heyninck[1] and Ofer Arieli[2(✉)]

[1] Institute of Philosophy II, Ruhr University Bochum, Bochum, Germany
[2] School of Computer Science, The Academic College of Tel-Aviv,
Tel Aviv-Yafo, Israel
oarieli@mta.ac.il

Abstract. This paper extends the result of Caminada and Schulz [6,7] by showing that assumption-based argumentation can represent not only normal logic programs, but also disjunctive logic programs. For this, we incorporate a previous work of ours (see [19,20]), in which reasoning with assumption-based argumentation frameworks is based on certain core *logics* and the strict/defeasible assumptions may be arbitrary formulas in those logics. In our case, the core logic respects some inference rules for disjunction, which allows disjunctions in the heads of the programs' rules to be handled properly.

Keywords: Knowledge representation and reasoning ·
Non-monotonic reasoning · Computational models of argument ·
Disjunctive logic programming · Structured argumentation

1 Introduction

Logic programming (LP) and assumption-based argumentation (ABA) are two primary methods for knowledge representation and non-monotonic reasoning, originated from similar intuitions and applied in different contexts. In fact, to a large extent, the introduction of ABA systems was motivated by an argumentative interpretation of LP semantics [4]. The former provides a Dung-style representation [11] of coherent sets of formulas that admits other sets of formulas as their contraries, and the latter combines reasoning based on strict inference rules with an interpretation of negation as 'failure to prove the converse' [21].

The similar ground of LP and ABA calls upon translation methods for revealing the exact relations between them, and for importing reasoning methods from one formalism to the other. For example, argumentative characterizations of

This work is supported by the Israel Science Foundation (grant number 817/15). The first author is also partially supported by the Sofja Kovalevskaja award of the Alexander von Humboldt Foundation, funded by the German Ministry for Education and Research, the FCT projects RIVER (PTDC/CCI-COM/30952/2017) and NOVA LINCS (UID/CEC/04516/2013).

© Springer Nature Switzerland AG 2019
P. Moura Oliveira et al. (Eds.): EPIA 2019, LNAI 11805, pp. 526–538, 2019.
https://doi.org/10.1007/978-3-030-30244-3_44

logic programming have been proven useful for explanation [27,28] and visualization [26] of inferences in logic programming. Among the works that translate LP and ABA we recall the one of Schulz and Toni [29,30] that provides a one-to-one correspondence between the 3-valued stable models for normal logic programs [23] and complete labelings for ABA frameworks. Recent works of Caminada and Schulz [6,7] show the equivalence between ABA semantics and normal logic programs. Their research is restricted to normal logic programs, where negations may occur in the bodies of the rules but only atoms are allowed in the head of the rules. Yet, a faithful modeling of real-world problems often requires to cope with *incomplete knowledge*, which is not possible in the scope of normal logic programs. This is a primary motivation in the introduction of *disjunctive logic programming*, where disjunctions are allowed in the heads of the rules and negation may occur in their bodies.

Under usual complexity assumptions, disjunctive logic programs were shown to be strictly more expressive than normal logic programs [14,18]. Moreover, in the last decades they have been efficiently implemented and widely applied, thus became a key technology in knowledge representation (see, e.g., [31]). Therefore, in this paper we set out to generalize the argumentative characterization of logic programming for disjunctive logic programs. For this, we incorporate the ideas of [19,20], extending ABA frameworks to propositional formulas (as the defeasible or strict assumption at hand), expressed in Tarskian logics. This allows to augment the core logic of the ABA frameworks with inference rules for handling disjunctive assertions, and so associate the stable extensions of such frameworks with the stable models of the corresponding disjunctive logic programs.

2   Preliminaries

We denote by $\mathcal{L}$ a propositional language. Atomic formulas in $\mathcal{L}$ are denoted by p, q, r, s (possibly indexed), compound formulas are denoted by ψ, ϕ, σ, and sets of formulas in $\mathcal{L}$ are denoted by $\Gamma, \Delta, \Theta, \Lambda$. We shall assume that $\mathcal{L}$ contains a conjunction (denoted as usual in logic programing by a comma), disjunction $\vee$, implication $\rightarrow$, a negation operator $\sim$, and a propositional constant T for truth. Also, we denote $\sim \Gamma = \{\sim \gamma \mid \gamma \in \Gamma\}$. The powerset of $\mathcal{L}$ is denoted $\wp(\mathcal{L})$.

2.1   Assumption-Based Argumentation

Definition 1. A (propositional) *logic* for a language $\mathcal{L}$ is a pair $\mathfrak{L} = \langle \mathcal{L}, \vdash \rangle$, where $\vdash$ is a (Tarskian) consequence relation for $\mathcal{L}$, that is, a binary relation between sets of formulas and formulas in $\mathcal{L}$, which is reflexive (if $\psi \in \Gamma$ then $\Gamma \vdash \psi$), monotonic (if $\Gamma \vdash \psi$ and $\Gamma \subseteq \Gamma'$, then $\Gamma' \vdash \psi$), and transitive (if $\Gamma \vdash \psi$ and $\Gamma', \psi \vdash \phi$, then $\Gamma, \Gamma' \vdash \phi$).

The next definition, adapted from [19], generalizes the definition in [4] of assumption-based frameworks.

Definition 2. An *assumption-based framework* is a tuple $\mathbf{ABF} = \langle \mathfrak{L}, \Gamma, \Lambda, - \rangle$, where:

- $\mathfrak{L} = \langle \mathcal{L}, \vdash \rangle$ is a propositional Tarskian logic
- Γ (the *strict assumptions*) and Λ (the *candidate or defeasible assumptions*) are distinct countable sets of $\mathcal{L}$-formulas where Λ is assumed to be nonempty.
- $- : \Lambda \to \wp(\mathcal{L})$ is a contrariness operator, assigning a finite set of $\mathcal{L}$-formulas to every defeasible assumption in Λ.

Note 1. Unlike the setting of [4], an ABF may be based on *any* Tarskian logic $\mathfrak{L}$. Also, the strict as well as the candidate assumptions are formulas that may not be just atomic. Concerning the contrariness operator, note that it is not a connective of the language $\mathcal{L}$, as it is restricted only to the candidate assumptions.

Defeasible assertions in an ABF may be attacked by counterarguments.

Definition 3. Let $\mathbf{ABF} = \langle \mathfrak{L}, \Gamma, \Lambda, - \rangle$ be an assumption-based framework, $\Delta, \Theta \subseteq \Lambda$, and $\psi \in \Lambda$. We say that Δ *attacks* ψ iff $\Gamma, \Delta \vdash \phi$ for some $\phi \in -\psi$. Accordingly, Δ attacks Θ if Δ attacks some $\psi \in \Theta$.

The last definition gives rise to the following adaptation to ABFs of the usual semantics for abstract argumentation frameworks [11].

Definition 4 ([4]). Let $\mathbf{ABF} = \langle \mathfrak{L}, \Gamma, \Lambda, - \rangle$ be an assumption-based framework, and let $\Delta \subseteq \Lambda$. Then Δ is *conflict-free* iff there is no $\Delta' \subseteq \Delta$ that attacks some $\psi \in \Delta$. We say that Δ is *stable* iff it is conflict-free and attacks every $\psi \in \Lambda \setminus \Delta$. The set of stable extensions of $\mathbf{ABF}$ is denoted by $\text{Stb}(\mathbf{ABF})$.[1]

2.2   Disjunctive Logic Programs

Definition 5. A *disjunctive logic program* π is a finite set of expressions (rules) of the form $q_1, \ldots, q_m, \sim r_1, \ldots, \sim r_k \to p_1 \vee \ldots \vee p_n$, where $p_1 \vee \ldots \vee p_n$ is called the *head* of the rule, and $q_1, \ldots, q_m, \sim r_1, \ldots, \sim r_k$ is its *body*. When each head of a rule in π is either empty or consists of an atomic formula (i.e., $n \leq 1$), we say that π is a *normal logic program*. A logic program π is *positive* if $k = 0$ for every rule in π. We denote by $\mathcal{A}(\pi)$ the set of atomic formulas that appear in π.

In what follows, unless otherwise stated, when referring to a logic program we shall mean that it is disjunctive. The semantics of a logic program π is defined as follows:

Definition 6. A set $M \subseteq \mathcal{A}(\pi)$ *satisfies* a rule $q_1, \ldots, q_m, \sim r_1, \ldots, \sim r_k \to p_1 \vee \ldots \vee p_n$ in π iff either $q_i \notin M$ for some $1 \leq i \leq m$, or $r_i \in M$ for some $1 \leq i \leq k$, or $p_i \in M$ for some $1 \leq i \leq n$. We say that M is a *model* of π if it satisfies every rule in π.

---

[1] In many presentations of assumption-based argumentation, extensions are required to be closed, i.e. they should contain any assumption they imply. Since the translation below will always give rise to the so-called *flat* ABFs (that is, ABFs for which a set of assumptions can never imply assumptions outside the set; See Note 3 below), closure of extensions is trivially satisfied.

Definition 7. Let π be a disjunctive logic program and let $M \subseteq \mathcal{A}(\pi)$.

- The *Gelfond-Lifschitz reduct* [16] of π with respect to M is the disjunctive logic program π^M, where $q_1, \ldots, q_m \to p_1 \vee \ldots \vee p_n \in \pi^M$ iff there is a rule $q_1, \ldots, q_m, \sim r_1, \ldots, \sim r_k \to p_1 \vee \ldots \vee p_n \in \pi$ and $r_i \notin M$ for every $1 \leqslant i \leqslant k$.
- M is a *stable model* of π iff it is a $\subseteq$-minimal model of π^M.

3 From DLP to ABA

Given a disjunctive logic program π, we show a one-to-one correspondence between the stable models of π and the the stable extensions of an ABA framework that is induced from π. First, we describe and motivate the translation, then we prove its correctness.

3.1 The Translation

All the ABA frameworks that are induced from disjunctive logic programs will be based on the same core logic, which is constructed by three inference rules: Modus Ponens (MP), Resolution (Res) and Reasoning by Cases (RBC):

$$[\text{MP}] \quad \frac{\phi_1, \ldots, \phi_n \to \psi \quad \phi_1 \quad \phi_2 \quad \cdots \quad \phi_n}{\psi}$$

$$[\text{Res}] \quad \frac{\psi_1' \vee \ldots \vee \psi_m' \vee \phi_1 \vee \ldots \vee \phi_n \vee \psi_1'' \vee \ldots \vee \psi_k'' \quad \sim \phi_1 \quad \cdots \quad \sim \phi_n}{\psi_1' \vee \ldots \vee \psi_m' \vee \ldots \vee \psi_1'' \vee \ldots \vee \psi_k''}$$

$$[\text{RBC}] \quad \frac{\begin{matrix} \phi_1 & \phi_2 & & \phi_n & \\ \vdots & \vdots & & \vdots & \\ \psi & \psi & \cdots & \psi & \phi_1 \vee \ldots \vee \phi_n \end{matrix}}{\psi}$$

In what follows we denote by $\mathfrak{L} = \langle \mathcal{L}, \vdash \rangle$ the logic based on the language $\mathcal{L}$ which consists of disjunctions of atoms ($p_1 \vee \ldots \vee p_n$ for $n \geq 1$), negated atoms ($\sim p$), or formulas of the forms of the program rules in Definition 5. Accordingly, we shall use only fragments of the inference rules above, in which in [Res] and [RBC] the formulas ψ, ψ_i are disjunctions of atomic formulas and ϕ_i are atomic formulas. In [MP], ψ is a disjunction of atomic formulas and $\phi_i \in \{p_i, \sim p_i\}$ are literals. Now, $\Delta \vdash \phi$ iff ϕ is either in Δ or is derivable from Δ using the inference rules above. In other words, $\Delta \vdash \phi$ iff $\phi \in \mathsf{Cn}_{\mathfrak{L}}(\Delta)$, where $\mathsf{Cn}_{\mathfrak{L}}(\Delta)$ is the $\mathfrak{L}$-based transitive closure of Δ (namely, the $\subseteq$-smallest set that contains Δ and is closed under [MP], [Res] and [RBC]). Notice that for any $\phi \in \mathsf{Cn}_{\mathfrak{L}}(\Delta)$, if ϕ is not of the form $p_1 \vee \ldots \vee p_n$ then $\phi \in \Delta$.

Note 2. Since $\to \psi$ is identified with $\mathsf{T} \to \psi$, [MP] implies Reflexivity: $[\text{Ref}] \dfrac{\to \psi}{\psi}$.

Definition 8. The ABF that is *induced* by a disjunctive logic program π is defined by: $\mathbf{ABF}(\pi) = \langle \mathfrak{L}, \pi, \sim \mathcal{A}(\pi), - \rangle$, where $- \sim p = \{p\}$ for every $p \in \mathcal{A}(\pi)$.

Example 1. Let $\pi_1 = \{\rightarrow p \vee q;\ p \rightarrow q;\ q \rightarrow p\}$. The attack diagram of the induced framework $\mathbf{ABF}(\pi_1)$ is shown in Fig. 1a. Note that in this case $\{p, q\}$ is the stable model of π_1 and $\emptyset$ is the stable extension of $\mathbf{ABF}(\pi_1)$.

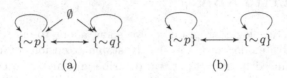

(a)   (b)

Fig. 1. Attack diagrams for Examples 1, 3c (left) and b (right)

Definition 9. Let π be a disjunctive logic program and $\Theta \subseteq \mathcal{A}(\pi)$. We denote:

- $\lfloor \sim \Theta \rfloor = \Theta$ (Thus, $\lfloor \cdot \rfloor$ eliminates the leading $\sim$ from the formulas).
- If $\Delta \subseteq \sim \mathcal{A}(\pi)$ then $\underline{\Delta} = \mathcal{A}(\pi) \setminus \lfloor \Delta \rfloor$.
- If $\Delta \subseteq \mathcal{A}(\pi)$ then $\overline{\Delta} = \sim (\mathcal{A}(\pi) \setminus \Delta)$.

In other words, $\underline{\Delta}$ (respectively, $\overline{\Delta}$) takes the complementary set of Δ and removes (respectively, adds) the negation-as-failure operator from (respectively, to) the prefix of its formulas.

Example 2. Consider again the program π_1 of Example 1, and let $\Delta = \sim \mathcal{A}(\pi_1) = \{\sim p, \sim q\}$. Then $\underline{\Delta} = \emptyset$ and $\overline{\emptyset} = \Delta$.

The semantic correspondence between a logic program and the induced ABF is obtained by the following result:

1. If Δ is a stable extension of $\mathbf{ABF}(\pi)$ then $\underline{\Delta}$ is a stable model of π, and
2. If Δ is a stable model of π then $\overline{\Delta}$ is a stable extension of $\mathbf{ABF}(\pi)$.

First, we provide some examples and notes concerning related results.

Example 3. Caminada and Schulz [6,7] consider the correspondence between ABA systems and normal logic programs. In our notations, the ABF that they associate with a normal logic program π is $\mathbf{ABF}_{\mathsf{Norm}}(\pi) = \langle \mathfrak{L}_{\mathsf{MP}}, \pi, \sim \mathcal{A}(\pi), - \rangle$ constructed as in Definition 8, except that $\mathfrak{L}_{\mathsf{MP}}$ is defined by Modus Ponens only.

(a) To see that $\mathbf{ABF}_{\mathsf{Norm}}$ is not adequate for disjunctive logic programs, consider the program $\pi_2 = \{\rightarrow p \vee q\}$. This program has two stable models: $\{p\}$ and $\{q\}$. However, the only stable extension of $\mathbf{ABF}_{\mathsf{Norm}}(\pi_2)$ is $\{\sim p, \sim q\}$. We can enforce $\{\sim p\}$ and $\{\sim q\}$ being stable models by requiring that $\pi_2 \cup \{\sim p\} \vdash q$ and vice versa. For this, we need resolution [Res].

(b) Adding only [Res] to $\mathcal{L}_{\mathsf{MP}}$ (i.e, without [RBC]) as the inference rules for the logic is yet not sufficient. To see this consider again the program π_1 from Example 1. Recall that $\{p, q\}$ is the sole stable model of π_1. The attack graph of the ABF based on [MP] and [Res] is shown in Fig. 1b. In the notations of Definition 2, we have: $\Gamma = \pi_2$ and $\Lambda = \{\sim p, \sim q\}$, thus by [MP] on $\rightarrow p \vee q$ we conclude $\Gamma \vdash p \vee q$, and by [Res] it holds that $\Gamma, \sim p \vdash q$. Thus, since $q \rightarrow p \in \Gamma$, by [MP] we get $\Gamma, \sim p \vdash p$. It follows that $\sim p$ attacks itself, (similarly $\sim q$ attacks itself), thus there is no stable extension in this case.

(c) Example 1 shows that for the ABF that is induced from π_1 according to Definition 8 (using all the three inference rules considered at the beginning of this section) the correspondence between the stable model of π_1 and the stable extension of $\mathbf{ABF}(\pi_1)$ is preserved and thus the translation is adequate for π_1. This is not a coincidence, as we show in the next section.

Note 3. The translation in Definition 8 always gives rise to a so-called *flat* ABF, that is, an ABF for which there is no $\Delta \subseteq \Lambda$ and $\psi \in \Lambda \setminus \Delta$ such that $\Gamma, \Delta \vdash \psi$:

Proposition 1. *For every disjunctive logic program π and the induced* $\mathbf{ABF}(\pi) = \langle \mathcal{L}, \Gamma, \Lambda, - \rangle = \langle \mathcal{L}, \pi, \sim \mathcal{A}(\pi), - \rangle$, *if $\Delta \subseteq \Lambda$ and $\Gamma, \Delta \vdash \psi$, then* $\psi \notin \Lambda \setminus \Delta$.

Proof. Suppose that $\Gamma, \Delta \vdash \psi$ for some $\Delta \subseteq \Lambda$. Since Λ contains only formulas of the form $\sim p$, and since $\Gamma = \pi$, then if $\Gamma, \Delta \vdash \sim p$, necessarily $\sim p \in \Delta$.   □

3.2 Proof of Correctness

The correctness of the translation follows from Propositions 2 and 3 below. First, we need some definitions and lemmas. The proofs of Lemmas 2, 3 and 5 are omitted due to space restrictions. In what follows $\mathcal{L}$ denotes the logic defined in Sect. 3.1, and π is an arbitrary (disjunctive) logic program.

Definition 10. Let M be set of atomic formulas, p, p_i, q_j atomic formulas, and $l_j \in \{q_j, \sim q_j\}$ literals. We denote:

- $M \models p$ iff $p \in M$,
- $M \models \sim p$ iff $p \notin M$,
- $M \models p_1 \vee \ldots \vee p_n$ iff $M \models p_i$ for some $1 \leq i \leq n$,
- $M \models l_1, \ldots, l_m$ iff $M \models l_j$ for every $1 \leq j \leq m$,
- $M \models l_1, \ldots, l_m \rightarrow p_1 \vee \ldots \vee p_n$ iff either $M \models p_1 \vee \ldots \vee p_n$, or $M \not\models l_1, \ldots, l_m$ (the latter means that it is *not the case* that $M \models l_1, \ldots, l_m$).

Given a set $\mathcal{S}$ of $\mathcal{L}$-formulas, we denote by $M \models \mathcal{S}$ that $M \models \psi$ for every $\psi \in \mathcal{S}$.[2]

---

[2] Since the underlying language consists only of negated atoms or formulas of the form of program rules (see Definition 5), this definition indeed covers all the possible sets $\mathcal{S}$ of $\mathcal{L}$-formulas.

Lemma 1. *Let Δ be a set of $\mathcal{L}$-formulas that are either of the form $\sim p$ or of the form $r_1, \ldots, r_m, \sim q_1, \ldots, \sim q_k \to p_1 \vee \ldots \vee p_n$. Then:*

(a) If $\psi \in \mathsf{Cn}_{\mathcal{L}}(\Delta)$ then $M \models \psi$ for every M such that $M \models \Delta$.
(b) If $\psi = s_1 \vee \ldots \vee s_l$ and $M \models \psi$ for every M s.t. $M \models \Delta$, then $\psi \in \mathsf{Cn}_{\mathcal{L}}(\Delta)$.

Note 4. Part (b) of Lemma 1 does not hold for *any* formula ψ, but only for a disjunction of atoms. To see this, let $\Delta = \{\sim s, \; p \to s\}$. The only $M \subseteq \{p, s\}$ such that $M \models \Delta$ is $M = \emptyset$. Thus, for every M such that $M \models \Delta$ it holds that $M \models \sim p$. However, $\sim p$ cannot be derived from Δ using [MP], [Res] and [RBC].

Proof. We prove Part (a) of the lemma by induction on the number of applications of the inference rules in the derivation of $\psi \in \mathsf{Cn}_{\mathcal{L}}(\Delta)$.

For the base step, no inference rule is applied in the derivation of ψ, thus $\psi \in \Delta$. Since $M \models \Delta$, we have that $M \models \psi$.

For the induction step, we consider three cases, each one corresponds to an application of a different inference rule in the last step of the derivation of ψ:

1. Suppose that the last step in the derivation of ψ is an application of Resolution. Then $\psi = p'_1 \vee \ldots \vee p'_m \vee \ldots \vee p''_1 \vee \ldots \vee p''_k$ is obtained by [Res] from $p'_1 \vee \ldots \vee p'_m \vee q_1 \vee \ldots \vee q_n \vee p''_1 \vee \ldots \vee p''_k$ and $\sim q_i$ $(i = 1, \ldots, n)$. Suppose that $M \models \Delta$. Since $\sim q_i \in \mathsf{Cn}_{\mathcal{L}}(\Delta)$ iff $\sim q_i \in \Delta$ and since $M \models \Delta$, $M \models \sim q_i$ $(i = 1, \ldots, n)$, thus $M \not\models q_i$ $(i = 1, \ldots, n)$. By the induction hypothesis, $M \models p'_1 \vee \ldots \vee p'_m \vee q_1 \vee \ldots \vee q_n \vee p''_1 \vee \ldots \vee p''_k$. By Definition 10, then, $M \models p'_i$ for some $1 \le i \le m$, or $M \models p''_j$ for some $1 \le j \le k$. By Definition 10 again, $M \models \psi$.
2. Suppose that the last step in the derivation of ψ is an application of Reasoning by Cases, and let $M \models \Delta$. By induction hypothesis, $M \models p_1 \vee \ldots \vee p_n$, and $M \models \psi$ in case that $M \models p_j$ for some $1 \le j \le n$. But by Definition 10 the former assumption means that there is some $1 \le j \le n$ for which $M \models p_j$, therefore $M \models \psi$.
3. Suppose that the last step in the derivation of ψ is an application of Modus Ponens, and let $M \models \Delta$. By induction hypothesis $M \models l_i$, where $l_i \in \{p_i, \sim p_i\}$ for $i = 1, \ldots, n$. Thus, by Definition 10, $M \models l_1, \ldots, l_n$. On the other hand, by induction hypothesis again, $M \models l_1, \ldots, l_n \to \psi$. By Definition 10 this is possible only if $M \models \psi$.

We now turn to Part (b) of the lemma. If there is no M such that $M \models \Delta$ the claim is trivially satisfied.

Suppose then that $M \models \psi$ for every M such that $M \models \Delta$, yet $\psi \notin \mathsf{Cn}_{\mathcal{L}}(\Delta)$ (where $\psi = r_1 \vee \ldots \vee r_m$ for some $m \geqslant 1$). We show that this leads to a contradiction by constructing an M' for which $M' \models \Delta$ but $M' \not\models \psi$. For this, we consider the following set of the minimal disjunctions of a set of formulas $\mathcal{S}$:

$$\mathsf{MD}(\mathcal{S}) = \{q_1 \vee \ldots \vee q_n \in \mathcal{S} \mid \nexists \{i_1, \ldots, i_m\} \subsetneq \{1, \ldots, n\} \text{ s.t. } q_{i_1} \vee \ldots \vee q_{i_m} \in \mathcal{S}\}.$$

We first show that if $q_1 \vee \ldots \vee q_n \in \mathsf{MD}(\mathsf{Cn}_{\mathcal{L}}(\Delta))$ then there is an $1 \leqslant i \leqslant n$ such that $q_i \notin \{r_1, \ldots, r_m\}$ and $\sim q_i \notin \Delta$. Indeed, suppose first for a contradiction that $q_1 \vee \ldots \vee q_n \in \mathsf{MD}(\mathsf{Cn}_{\mathcal{L}}(\Delta))$, yet for every $1 < i \leqslant n$ either $q_i \in \{r_1, \ldots, r_m\}$ or $\sim q_i \in \Delta$. In that case, by [Res], $r_1 \vee \ldots \vee r_m \in \mathsf{Cn}_{\mathcal{L}}(\Delta)$, contradicting the original supposition that $r_1 \vee \ldots \vee r_m \notin \mathsf{Cn}_{\mathcal{L}}(\Delta)$. Suppose now, again towards a contradiction, that $q_1 \vee \ldots \vee q_n \in \mathsf{MD}(\mathsf{Cn}_{\mathcal{L}}(\Delta))$, yet for every $1 \leqslant i \leqslant n$, $\sim q_i \in \Delta$. In that case, by [Res] again, $q_i \in \mathsf{Cn}_{\mathcal{L}}(\Delta)$ (for every i), but this, together with the assumption the $\sim q_i \in \Delta$ (for every i), contradicts the assumption that there is an M such that $M \models \Delta$.

We thus showed that in any case, if $q_1 \vee \ldots \vee q_n \in \mathsf{MD}(\mathsf{Cn}_{\mathcal{L}}(\Delta))$, then there is an $1 \leqslant i \leqslant n$ such that $q_i \notin \{r_1, \ldots, r_m\}$ and $\sim q_i \notin \Delta$.

We now construct the model M' such that $M' \models \Delta$ and $M' \not\models r_1 \vee \ldots \vee r_m$. In more detail, let M' contain exactly one q_i with $1 \leqslant i \leqslant n$ and $q_i \notin \{r_1, \ldots, r_m\}$ and $\sim q_i \notin \Delta$ for every $q_1 \vee \ldots \vee q_n \in \mathsf{MD}(\mathsf{Cn}_{\mathcal{L}}(\Delta))$. (If there is more than one such i, take i which is minimal among $1 \leqslant i \leqslant n$.) As shown above, there is at least one such i for every formula $q_1 \vee \ldots \vee q_n \in \mathsf{MD}(\mathsf{Cn}_{\mathcal{L}}(\Delta))$.

We now show that (1) $M' \models \Delta$ and (2) $M' \not\models r_1 \vee \ldots \vee r_m$.

Item (1): Suppose that $\phi \in \mathsf{Cn}_{\mathcal{L}}(\Delta)$. We have to consider two possibilities: $\phi = \sim s$ or $\phi = q_1 \vee \ldots \vee q_n$. In the first case, by construction, $s \notin M'$ and thus $M' \models \sim s$. In the second case, there is a $q_{i_1} \vee \ldots \vee q_{i_m} \in \mathsf{MD}(\mathsf{Cn}_{\mathcal{L}}(\Delta))$ such that $\{i_1, \ldots, i_m\} \subseteq \{1, \ldots, n\}$. By construction, there is a $1 \leqslant j \leqslant m$ such that $q_{i_j} \in M'$. Thus, $M \models q_1 \vee \ldots \vee q_n$.

Item (2): By construction $r_i \notin M'$ ($i = 1, \leqslant, m$), thus $M' \not\models r_1 \vee \ldots \vee r_m$. $\square$

Lemma 2. *For every sets M, N of literals, if $N \setminus M \neq \emptyset$ then $N \not\models \mathsf{Cn}_{\mathcal{L}}(\overline{M} \cup \pi)$.*

Lemma 3. *Given a logic program π, if M is a minimal model of a logic program $\pi' \subseteq \pi^M$, then for every $N \subset M$, $N \not\models \mathsf{Cn}_{\mathcal{L}}(\overline{M} \cup \pi)$.*

Lemma 4. *Let M be a stable model of π. Then it is the (unique) minimal subset N of $\mathcal{A}(\pi)$ such that $N \models \mathsf{Cn}_{\mathcal{L}}(\pi \cup \overline{M})$.*

Proof. Let M be a stable model of π. We first show that $M \models \mathsf{Cn}_{\mathcal{L}}(\overline{M} \cup \pi)$. Let $\psi \in \mathsf{Cn}_{\mathcal{L}}(\overline{M} \cup \pi)$. Then it has an $\mathcal{L}$-derivation $\mathsf{D}_{\mathcal{L}}(\psi)$. We show by induction on the size of $\mathsf{D}_{\mathcal{L}}(\psi)$ that $M \models \psi$.

For the base step, no inference rule is applied in $\mathsf{D}_{\mathcal{L}}(\psi)$, thus $\psi = \sim \phi \in \overline{M}$. Since this means that $\phi \notin M$, we have that $M \models \psi$.

For the induction step, we consider three cases, each one corresponds to an application of a different inference rule in the last step of $\mathsf{D}_{\mathcal{L}}(\psi)$:

1. Suppose that the last step in $\mathsf{D}_{\mathcal{L}}(\psi)$ is an application of Resolution. Then $\psi = p'_1 \vee \ldots \vee p'_m \vee p''_1 \vee \ldots \vee p''_k$ is obtained by [Res] from $p'_1 \vee \ldots \vee p'_m \vee q_1 \vee \ldots \vee q_n \vee p''_1 \vee \ldots \vee p''_k$ and $\sim q_i$ ($i = 1, \ldots, n$). Since $\sim q_i \in \mathsf{Cn}_{\mathcal{L}}(\overline{M} \cup \pi)$ means that $\sim q_i \in \overline{M}$, we have $q_i \notin M$ for every $1, \ldots, n$. By the inductive hypothesis, $M \models p'_1 \vee \ldots \vee p'_m \vee q_1 \vee \ldots \vee q_n \vee p''_1 \vee \ldots \vee p''_k$. Thus, by Definition 10, $M \models p'_i$ for some $1 \leq i \leq m$, or $M \models p''_j$ for some $1 \leq j \leq k$. By Definition 10 again, $M \models \psi$.
2. Suppose that the last step in $\mathsf{D}_{\mathcal{L}}(\psi)$ is an application of Reasoning by Cases. By induction hypothesis we know that $M \models p_1 \vee \ldots \vee p_n$, and that $M \models \psi$

in case that $M \models p_j$ for some $1 \le j \le n$. But by Definition 10 the former assumption means that there is some $1 \le j \le n$ for which $M \models p_j$, therefore $M \models \psi$.

3. Suppose that the last step in $D_{\mathcal{L}}(\psi)$ is an application of Modus Ponens on the rule $p_1, \ldots, p_n, \sim q_1, \ldots, \sim q_m \to r_1 \vee \ldots \vee r_l \in \pi$. By induction hypothesis $M \models p_i$, for every $1 \le i \le n$. Also, for every $1 \le i \le m$, $\sim q_i \in \mathsf{Cn}_{\mathcal{L}}(\overline{M} \cup \pi)$ implies $q_i \notin M$. Thus, $p_1, \ldots, p_n \to r_1 \vee \ldots \vee r_l \in \pi^M$. Since M is a model of π^M, $M \models r_i$ for some $1 \le i \le l$. Thus, $M \models r_1 \vee \ldots \vee r_l$.

Thus, we have shown that $M \models \mathsf{Cn}_{\mathcal{L}}(\overline{M} \cup \pi)$. By Lemma 2, for no $N \subseteq \mathcal{A}(\pi)$ such that $N \setminus M \ne \emptyset$ it holds that $N \models \mathsf{Cn}_{\mathcal{L}}(\overline{M} \cup \pi)$. Thus, if there is some $N \subseteq \mathcal{A}(\pi)$ such that $N \models Cn_{\mathcal{L}}(\overline{M} \cup \pi)$, then $N \subseteq M$. But if $N \subset M$, by Lemma 3 we have that $N \not\models \mathsf{Cn}_{\mathcal{L}}(\overline{M} \cup \pi)$. Thus, M is the unique set of literals that models $\mathsf{Cn}_{\mathcal{L}}(\overline{M} \cup \pi)$.   □

Corollary 1. *Let M be a stable model of π. Then $p \in M$ iff $p \in \mathsf{Cn}_{\mathcal{L}}(\overline{M} \cup \pi)$.*

Proof. Suppose first that $p \in M$. Since by Lemma 4 M is the unique model of $\mathsf{Cn}_{\mathcal{L}}(\overline{M} \cup \pi)$, by Lemma 1 it holds that $M \models p$ implies that $p \in \mathsf{Cn}_{\mathcal{L}}(\overline{M} \cup \pi)$. For the converse, suppose that $p \in \mathsf{Cn}_{\mathcal{L}}(\overline{M} \cup \pi)$. By Lemma 4, $M \models \mathsf{Cn}_{\mathcal{L}}(\overline{M} \cup \pi)$ and thus $M \models p$.   □

Lemma 5. *Let π be a disjunctive logic program, $\Delta = \{\sim p_1, \ldots, \sim p_n\}$ and $r \in \mathsf{Cn}_{\mathcal{L}}(\pi \cup \Delta)$. If M is a model of $\pi^{\lfloor \Delta \rfloor}$ and $M \subseteq \lfloor \Delta \rfloor$, then $r \in M$.*

Now we can show the main results of this section.

Proposition 2. *If M is a stable model of π, then $\overline{M}$ is a stable extension of $\mathbf{ABF}(\pi)$.*

Proof. Suppose that M is a stable model of π. We show first that $\overline{M}$ is conflict-free in $\mathbf{ABF}(\pi)$. Otherwise, there is some $\sim p \in \overline{M}$ such that $\pi, \overline{M} \vdash p$. The former implies that $p \notin M$. But since M is a model of π^M, by Lemma 5, the fat that $\pi, \overline{M} \vdash p$ implies that $p \in M$, a contradiction.

We now show that $\overline{M}$ attacks every $\sim p \in \sim \mathcal{A}(\pi) \setminus \overline{M}$. This means that we have to show that $\overline{M} \vdash p$ for every $p \in M$. This follows from Corollary 1.   □

Proposition 3. *If $\mathcal{E}$ is a stable extension of $\mathbf{ABF}(\pi)$ then $\underline{\mathcal{E}}$ is a stable model of π.*

Proof. We first show that $\underline{\mathcal{E}}$ is a model of $\pi^{\underline{\mathcal{E}}}$. Let $p_1, \ldots, p_n, \sim q_1, \ldots, \sim q_m \to r_1 \vee \ldots \vee r_k \in \pi$. If $q_j \in \underline{\mathcal{E}}$ for some $1 \le j \le m$ we are done. Otherwise, $q_1, \ldots, q_m \notin \underline{\mathcal{E}}$, and so $p_1, \ldots, p_n \to r_1 \vee \ldots \vee r_k \in \pi^{\underline{\mathcal{E}}}$. Again if $p_j \notin \underline{\mathcal{E}}$ for some $1 \le j \le n$ we are done. Thus, suppose that $p_1, \ldots, p_n \in \underline{\mathcal{E}}$. In other words, $\sim p_1, \ldots, \sim p_n \notin \mathcal{E}$ and $\sim q_1, \ldots, \sim q_m \in \mathcal{E}$. Since $\mathcal{E}$ is stable, the latter implies that $\pi, \mathcal{E} \vdash p_i$ for every $1 \le i \le n$. This means that $\pi, \mathcal{E} \vdash r_1 \vee \ldots \vee r_k$ (since $p_1, \ldots, p_n, \sim q_1, \ldots, \sim q_m \to r_1 \vee \ldots \vee r_k \in \pi$ and $\sim q_1, \ldots, \sim q_m \in \mathcal{E}$). Suppose now for a contradiction that $\sim r_i \in \mathcal{E}$ for every $1 \le i \le k$. Then by [Res],

$\pi, \mathcal{E} \vdash r_i$ for every $1 \leqslant i \leqslant k$ and thus $\mathcal{E}$ attack itself, which contradicts the fact that $\mathcal{E}$ is conflict-free. Consequently, there is at least one $1 \leqslant i \leqslant k$ such that $\sim r_i \notin \mathcal{E}$ and thus $r_i \in \underline{\mathcal{E}}$, which means that $\underline{\mathcal{E}}$ satisfies $p_1, \ldots, p_n \sim q_1, \ldots, \sim q_m \rightarrow r_1 \vee \ldots \vee r_k$.

To show the minimality of $\underline{\mathcal{E}}$, suppose that there is an $M \subsetneq \underline{\mathcal{E}}$ that is a model of $\pi^{\underline{\mathcal{E}}}$. Let $p \in \underline{\mathcal{E}} \setminus M$. Since $p \in \underline{\mathcal{E}}$, $\sim p \notin \mathcal{E}$. Since $\mathcal{E}$ is stable, this means that $\pi, \mathcal{E} \vdash p$. By Lemma 5, any model of $\pi^{\underline{\mathcal{E}}}$ satisfies p, a contradiction to $p \notin M$. □

4 From ABA to DLP

The main body of literature on ABA frameworks is concentrated on languages that consist solely of formulas of the form $p_1, \ldots, p_n \rightarrow p$ (where $p, p_1, \ldots, p_n$ are atomic formulas). For such assumption-based frameworks (or at least when the frameworks are flat) it has been shown that there is a straightforward translation into normal logic programs that preserve equivalence for all the commonly studied argumentation semantics (see [6,7]). To the best of our knowledge, the more complicated classes of ABA frameworks that are considered in this paper (and which are based on a logic allowing to reason with disjunctive rules of the form $p_1, \ldots, p_n, \sim q_1, \ldots, \sim q_m \rightarrow r_1 \vee \ldots \vee r_k$) have not been investigated for other purposes other than the translation of DLPs. We thus do not see any motivation for investigating the reverse translation from these assumption-based frameworks into disjunctive logic programs. We do believe, however, that it is interesting to see if the more general class of assumption-based frameworks that are based on an arbitrary propositional logic (as defined and studied in e.g. [19,20]) can be translated in a class of logic programs, probably more general than disjunctive ones. This is a subject for a future work.

5 Conclusion, in View of Related Work

This work generalizes translations from logic programming into assumption-based argumentation to cover also disjunctive logic programs. Somewhat surprisingly, there are only few works that investigate the representation of disjunctive defeasible reasoning by general argumentation frameworks. The most similar work to the research in this paper is probably that in [33], where a representation of DLPs by structured argumentation frameworks is proposed. In this framework, the assumptions are disjunctions of negated atoms $\sim p_1 \vee \ldots \vee \sim p_n$, instead of just negated atoms as in our translation. Furthermore, unlike [33], we define our translation in assumption-based argumentation, which means that meta-theoretical insights (e.g., complexity results [10] or results on properties of the non-monotonic consequence relations [9,19,20]), dialectical proof theories [12,13], and different implementations [8,32] can be directly used.

A representation of disjunctive logic programming by *abstract argumentation* is studied in [3]. In that translation, nodes in the argumentation framework correspond to single assumptions $\sim p$, as opposed to *sets* of such assumptions as in our translation. Because of this, the translation in [3] has to allow for attacks on *sets of nodes*, instead of just nodes, necessitating a generalization of Dung's abstract argumentation frameworks [11]. Since we work in assumption-based argumentation, where nodes in the argumentation framework correspond to sets of assumptions, the argumentation frameworks generated by our translation are normal abstract argumentation frameworks. This is important since in that way results and implementations for abstract argumentation frameworks can be straightforwardly used and applied.

Another related, but more distant line of work, is concerned with the integration of disjunctive reasoning in structured argumentation with defeasible rules (see [1,2]). We differ from this work both in the goal and the form of the knowledge bases.

In future work, we plan to generalize our results to other semantics for disjunctive logic programming, such as the disjunctive well-founded [5], extended well-founded [24], stationary [22], and possible world semantics [25]. Some of these semantics are based on ideas that are very similar to ideas underlying some well-known argumentation semantics. Likewise, For example, both the stationary semantics for disjunctive logic programming and the preferred semantics from abstract argumentation [11] can be characterized using three instead of two "truth values". Indeed, for normal logic programs the correspondence between the 3-valued stable models for normal logic programs [23] and complete labelings for ABA framework has been proven by [6,7], which further supports the conjecture that the correspondence holds for disjunctive logic programs as well. Finally, we hope to extend our results to more expressive languages, such as epistemic [15] and parametrized logic programming [17].

References

1. Beirlaen, M., Heyninck, J., Straßer, C.: Reasoning by cases in structured argumentation. In: Proceedimgs SAC 2017, pp. 989–994. ACM (2017)
2. Beirlaen, M., Heyninck, J., Straßer, C.: A critical assessment of Pollock's work on logic-based argumentation with suppositions. In: Proceedings of the NMR 2018, vol. 20, pp. 63–72 (2018)
3. Bochman, A.: Collective argumentation and disjunctive logic programming. J. Log. Comput. **13**(3), 405–428 (2003)
4. Bondarenko, A., Dung, P.M., Kowalski, R., Toni, F.: An abstract, argumentation-theoretic approach to default reasoning. Artif. Intell. **93**(1), 63–101 (1997)
5. Brass, S., Dix, J.: Characterizations of the disjunctive well-founded semantics: confluent calculi and iterated GCWA. J. Autom. Reason. **20**(1–2), 143–165 (1998)
6. Caminada, M., Schulz, C.: On the equivalence between assumption-based argumentation and logic programming. J. Artif. Intell. Res. **60**, 779–825 (2017)
7. Caminada, M., Schulz, C.: On the equivalence between assumption-based argumentation and logic programming (extended abstract). In: Proceedings IJCAI 2018, pp. 5578–5582. ijcai.org (2018)
8. Craven, R., Toni, F., Williams, M.: Graph-based dispute derivations in assumption-based argumentation. In: Black, E., Modgil, S., Oren, N. (eds.) TAFA 2013. LNCS, vol. 8306, pp. 46–62. Springer, Heidelberg (2014). https://doi.org/10.1007/978-3-642-54373-9_4

9. Čyras, K., Toni, F.: Non-monotonic inference properties for assumption-based argumentation. In: Black, E., Modgil, S., Oren, N. (eds.) TAFA 2015. LNCS, vol. 9524, pp. 92–111. Springer, Cham (2015). https://doi.org/10.1007/978-3-319-28460-6_6
10. Dimopoulos, Y., Nebel, B., Toni, F.: On the computational complexity of assumption-based argumentation for default reasoning. Artif. Intell. **141**(1–2), 57–78 (2002)
11. Dung, P.M.: On the acceptability of arguments and its fundamental role in non-monotonic reasoning, logic programming and n-person games. Artif. Intell. **77**, 321–358 (1995)
12. Dung, P.M., Kowalski, R.A., Toni, F.: Dialectic proof procedures for assumption-based, admissible argumentation. Artif. Intell. **170**(2), 114–159 (2006)
13. Dung, P.M., Mancarella, P., Toni, F.: A dialectic procedure for sceptical, assumption-based argumentation. In: Frontiers in Artificial Intelligence and Applications, vol. 144, pp. 145–156 (2006)
14. Eiter, T., Gottlob, G., Mannila, H.: Disjunctive datalog. ACM Trans. Database Syst. (TODS) **22**(3), 364–418 (1997)
15. Gelfond, M.: Logic programming and reasoning with incomplete information. Ann. Math. Artif. Intell. **12**(1–2), 89–116 (1994)
16. Gelfond, M., Lifschitz, V.: The stable model semantics for logic programming. In: Programming ICLP 1988, pp. 1070–1080. MIT Press (1988)
17. Gonçalves, R., Alferes, J.J.: Parametrized logic programming. In: Janhunen, T., Niemelä, I. (eds.) JELIA 2010. LNCS, vol. 6341, pp. 182–194. Springer, Heidelberg (2010). https://doi.org/10.1007/978-3-642-15675-5_17
18. Gottlob, G.: Complexity and expressive power of disjunctive logic programming (research overview). In: Proceedings ICLP 1994, pp. 23–42. MIT Press (1994)
19. Heyninck, J., Arieli, O.: On the semantics of simple contrapositive assumption-based argumentation frameworks. In: Proceedings COMMA 2018, Frontiers in Artificial Intelligence and Applications, vol. 305, pp. 9–20. IOS Press (2018)
20. Heyninck, J., Arieli, O.: Simple contrapositive assumption-based frameworks. In: Balduccini, M., Lierler, Y., Woltran, S. (eds.) Logic Programming and Nonmonotonic Reasoning, LPNMR 2019. LNCS, vol. 11481, pp. 75–88. Springer, Cham (2019). https://doi.org/10.1007/978-3-030-20528-7_7
21. Lloyd, J.W.: Foundations of Logic Programming. Springer, Heidelberg (1987). https://doi.org/10.1007/978-3-642-83189-8
22. Przymusinski, T.: Stationary semantics for normal and disjunctive logic programs. In: DOOD, vol. 91. Citeseer (1991)
23. Przymusinski, T.C.: The well-founded semantics coincides with the three-valued stable semantics. Fundamenta Informaticae **13**(4), 445–463 (1990)
24. Ross, K.A.: A procedural semantics for well-founded negation in logic programs. J. Log. Program. **13**(1), 1–22 (1992)
25. Sakama, C.: Possible model semantics for disjunctive databases. In: Deductive and Object-Oriented Databases, pp. 369–383 (1990)
26. Schulz, C.: Graphical representation of assumption-based argumentation. In: Proceedings AAAI 2015, pp. 4204–4205. AAAI Press (2015)
27. Schulz, C., Satoh, K., Toni, F.: Characterising and explaining inconsistency in logic programs. In: Calimeri, F., Ianni, G., Truszczynski, M. (eds.) LPNMR 2015. LNCS, vol. 9345, pp. 467–479. Springer, Cham (2015). https://doi.org/10.1007/978-3-319-23264-5_39
28. Schulz, C., Toni, F.: Justifying answer sets using argumentation. Theory Pract. Log. Program. **16**(1), 59–110 (2016)

29. Schulz, C., Toni, F.: Complete assumption labellings. In: Proceedings COMMA 2014, Frontiers in Artificial Intelligence and Applications, vol. 266, pp. 405–412. IOS Press (2017)
30. Schulz, C., Toni, F.: Labellings for assumption-based and abstract argumentation. J. Approx. Reason. **84**, 110–149 (2017)
31. Su, E.: Extensions of equilibrium logic by modal concepts. Ph.D. thesis, IRIT-Institut de recherche en informatique de Toulouse (2015)
32. Toni, F.: A generalised framework for dispute derivations in assumption-based argumentation. Artif. Intell. **195**, 1–43 (2013)
33. Wang, K.: Argumentation-based abduction in disjunctive logic programming. J. Log. Program. **45**(1–3), 105–141 (2000)

Computing Shortest Resolution Proofs

Carlos Mencía[1](✉) and Joao Marques-Silva[2]

[1] University of Oviedo, Gijón, Spain
menciacarlos@uniovi.es
[2] Faculty of Science, University of Lisbon, Lisbon, Portugal
jpms@ciencias.ulisboa.pt

Abstract. Propositional resolution is a powerful proof system for unsatisfiable propositional formulas in conjunctive normal form. Resolution proofs represent useful explanations of infeasibility, with important applications. This motivates the challenge of computing shortest resolution proofs, i.e. those with the smallest number of inference steps. This paper proposes a SAT-based approach for this problem. Concretely, the paper investigates new propositional encodings for computing shortest resolution proofs and devises a number of optimizations, including symmetry breaking, additional constraints on the structure of proofs, as well as exploiting related concepts in infeasibility analysis, such as minimal correction subsets. Experimental results show the suitability of the proposed approach.

1 Introduction

The importance of the propositional resolution proof system cannot be overstated, being at the core of modern conflict-driven clause learning (CDCL) Boolean satisfiability (SAT) solvers [19,20]. Propositional resolution can be traced to the seminal work of Davis and Putnam [11], and its formalization as a search procedure [10]. Perhaps more significantly, resolution finds fundamental applications in automated reasoning [31], representing one of the most widely used proof procedures in theorem proving [32].

Given an unsatisfiable propositional formula, a natural question is to find a shortest resolution proof, i.e. one with the fewest inference steps. Besides its theoretical interest [6,14], short refutations constitute useful certificates that explain infeasibility, and find important applications in system verification and validation (e.g. by the use of interpolation). In such settings, smaller proofs equate with smaller interpolants.

Computing shortest resolution refutations has been investigated from a theoretical perspective [1], including for restricted formulas [7,8]. From a practical

---

This research is supported by the Spanish Government under project TIN2016-79190-R and by the Principality of Asturias under grant IDI/2018/000176. This work is also supported by FCT grants ABSOLV (PTDC/CCI-COM/28986/2017) and FaultLocker (PTDC/CCI-COM/29300/2017).

© Springer Nature Switzerland AG 2019
P. Moura Oliveira et al. (Eds.): EPIA 2019, LNAI 11805, pp. 539–551, 2019.
https://doi.org/10.1007/978-3-030-30244-3_45

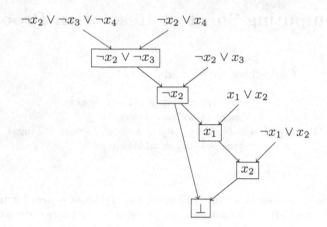

Fig. 1. Resolution proof (with 5 resolvents) for the formula in Example 1.

perspective, albeit, to our knowledge, no work has addressed the computation of shortest resolution proofs per se, the related problem of finding unsatisfiability proofs with incomplete methods has been investigated in the past [4,26,27]. In a different context, computing optimal refutations for infeasible CSPs has been studied in [15], where the notion of a refutation is related with the search tree traversed for proving infeasibility.

This paper investigates practical approaches for computing shortest resolution refutations, by iteratively solving the decision problem of whether there exists a resolution proof of size K, for increasing values of K. The straightforward solution of enumerating all possible candidate proofs of a given size is clearly unrealistic, given the sheer number of distinct proofs that need to be considered. This paper follows a different path, and proposes a SAT-based approach that uses SAT solvers in the search for such proofs. The paper builds on earlier work [27] and proposes a propositional encoding for solving the problem. However, whereas earlier work targeted encodings aiming at local search solvers, our proposed encodings target complete search algorithms. Furthermore, the paper devises a number of enhancements to the model, identifying ways to break relevant symmetries in the problem formulation and developing novel insights on how to effectively prune the search space. Experimental results show that the proposed model and its improvements enable computing shortest resolution proofs for formulas of non-trivial sizes.

The paper is organized as follows. The definitions and notation used in the paper are summarized in Sect. 2. Section 3 details a propositional model for computing shortest resolution proofs, and the enhancements to this model are described in Sect. 4. The experimental results are analyzed in Sect. 5. Finally, the paper concludes in Sect. 6.

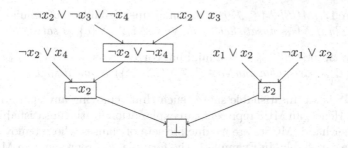

Fig. 2. A shortest resolution proof (with 4 resolvents) for the formula in Example 1.

2   Preliminaries

We consider propositional formulas in *conjunctive normal form* (CNF), defined as a conjunction, or set, of clauses $\mathcal{F} = \{c_1, c_2, ..., c_M\}$ over a set of variables $V(\mathcal{F}) = \{x_1, x_2, ..., x_N\}$, where a clause is a disjunction of literals, and a literal is a variable x or its negation $\neg x$. Throughout, for a clause $c \in \mathcal{F}$, $L^+(c)$ (resp. $L^-(c)$) denotes the positive (resp. negative) literals in c.

A formula $\mathcal{F}$ is satisfiable iff there exists a *model* for it, i.e. an assignment of truth values to the variables satisfying all the clauses. SAT is the NP-complete problem [9] of deciding the satisfiability of a formula. If no model exists for $\mathcal{F}$, proofs represent certificates of its unsatisfiability. Resolution [31] is a well-known proof system for refuting unsatisfiable CNF formulas. It relies on the application of the resolution rule:

$$\frac{\Gamma_1 \vee x \quad \Gamma_2 \vee \neg x}{\Gamma_1 \vee \Gamma_2} \tag{1}$$

In Eq. (1), clauses $\Gamma_1 \vee x$ and $\Gamma_2 \vee \neg x$, referred to as *parents*, are resolved on variable x, inferring the clause $\Gamma_1 \vee \Gamma_2$, which is referred to as *resolvent*. A *resolution proof* or *refutation* is a sequence of clauses ending with the empty clause, each of these being either a clause in $\mathcal{F}$ or a resolvent from two previous clauses in the sequence. In the general case, resolution proofs can be represented as a DAG. This paper is concerned with shortest resolution proofs (SRPs), minimizing the number of resolvents. Computing SRPs is intractable, including the case of Horn formulas [1], although it can be solved in polynomial time for 2-CNF formulas [7,8].

Example 1. Consider the formula $\mathcal{F}_{ex} = \{(x_1 \vee x_2), (\neg x_1 \vee x_2), (\neg x_2 \vee x_3), (\neg x_2 \vee x_4), (\neg x_2 \vee \neg x_3 \vee \neg x_4)\}$, with 5 clauses and 4 variables. Figure 1 shows a resolution refutation of $\mathcal{F}_{ex}$ which uses 5 resolvents (highlighted in a square). Figure 2 shows a shortest resolution proof of the unsatisfiability of $\mathcal{F}_{ex}$, with 4 resolvents.

Besides proofs, other notions have been used as a means to explaining unsatisfiability, such as minimal unsatisfiable subformulas (MUSes) or their minimal hitting set duals [18,30], known as minimal correction subsets (MCSes).

Definition 1. *[MUS]* $\mathcal{M} \subseteq \mathcal{F}$ *is a* minimal unsatisfiable subformula *(MUS) of* $\mathcal{F}$ *if and only if* $\mathcal{M}$ *is unsatisfiable and* $\forall c \in \mathcal{M}, \mathcal{M} \setminus \{c\}$ *is satisfiable.*

Definition 2. *[MCS]* $\mathcal{C} \subseteq \mathcal{F}$ *is a* minimal correction subset *(MCS) of* $\mathcal{F}$ *if and only if* $\mathcal{F} \setminus \mathcal{C}$ *is satisfiable and* $\forall c \in \mathcal{C}, \mathcal{F} \setminus (\mathcal{C} \setminus \{c\})$ *is unsatisfiable.*

An MUS is an unsatisfiable subset such that removing any clause renders it satisfiable. Hence, an MUS represents an explanation for the unsatisfiability of $\mathcal{F}$. On the other hand, MCSes are irreducible sets of clauses whose removal renders the formula satisfiable. In Example 1, the formula $\mathcal{F}_{ex}$ represents an MUS itself, and each of the clauses in $\mathcal{F}_{ex}$ represents an MCS. Despite the high complexity of computing MCSes, *efficient* algorithms exist for this task (e.g. [5,13,17,21–23,28,29]). In the worst case, there can be an exponential number of MUSes and MCSes [16,25].

3   Deciding Fixed Size Resolution Proofs

For a fixed value K, deciding the existence of a resolution proof with K resolvents can be encoded into a propositional formula [27]. This motivates a SAT-based approach for computing SRPs by solving a sequence of decision problems with varying values of K.

This section describes a propositional model that produces a CNF formula that is satisfiable if and only if the original formula has a resolution refutation involving K resolvents. The original formula $\mathcal{F} = \{c_1, \ldots, c_M\}$ is defined on variables $V(\mathcal{F}) = \{x_1, \ldots, x_N\}$, and the number of resolvents considered is K, with the new clauses indexed from $M + 1$ to $M + K$ (i.e., these being c_{M+1} to c_{M+K}).

Resolution proofs are encoded as a sequence of resolvents, preventing a node from being a parent of an earlier resolvent. The propositional model uses the following variables, where j ranges from 1 to N, r ranges from $M + 1$ to $M + K$, and s can range from 1 to $M + K$, with $s < r$:

$p_{jr} = 1$ iff there exists a positive literal on variable x_j in resolvent r.

$n_{jr} = 1$ iff there exists a negative literal on variable x_j in resolvent r.

$v_{jr} = 1$ iff variable x_j is resolved away to obtain resolvent r.

$la_{rs} = 1$ iff the left parent of resolvent r is c_s, with $s < r$.

$ra_{rs} = 1$ iff the right parent of resolvent r is c_s, with $s < r$.

$wp_{jr} = 1$ iff a positive literal on x_j is available at resolvent r.

$wn_{jr} = 1$ iff a negative literal on x_j is available at resolvent r.

Notice that the clauses in $\mathcal{F}$ are not explicitly represented in the encoding, but only the list of resolvents in the proof, with information of their parents and the variables used at each resolution step. Variables wp_{jr} and wn_{jr} are used as an intermediate step in the application of the resolution rule, indicating that the literals exist in some parent of r. These are referred to as *working literals*.

The propositional model enforces the following constraints:

1. A resolvent cannot contain a variable and its complement, which is accomplished by the following AtMost1 constraints:

$$(\neg p_{jr} \vee \neg n_{jr}) \tag{2}$$

2. Computation of working literals of resolvents from the literals in the parents: If a parent of a resolvent has a positive (negative) literal, the corresponding working literal in the resolvent is activated.

$$\begin{aligned} (la_{rs} \vee ra_{rs}) \wedge p_{js} &\rightarrow wp_{jr} \\ (la_{rs} \vee ra_{rs}) \wedge n_{js} &\rightarrow wn_{jr} \end{aligned} \tag{3}$$

3. If the working literals exist, they must also exist in the declared parents.

$$\begin{aligned} wp_{jr} &\rightarrow \bigvee_s (la_{rs} \vee ra_{rs}) \wedge p_{js} \\ wn_{jr} &\rightarrow \bigvee_s (la_{rs} \vee ra_{rs}) \wedge n_{js} \end{aligned} \tag{4}$$

4. Definition of literals in resolvents: A resolvent will include all its working literals except those on the variable resolved away.

$$\begin{aligned} p_{jr} &\leftrightarrow wp_{jr} \wedge \neg v_{jr} \\ n_{jr} &\leftrightarrow wn_{jr} \wedge \neg v_{jr} \end{aligned} \tag{5}$$

5. Definition of resolution variable given working literals:

$$v_{jr} \leftrightarrow wp_{jr} \wedge wn_{jr} \tag{6}$$

6. Resolvents have exactly one left and one right parent, chosen among earlier clauses.

$$\begin{aligned} \sum_{s=1}^{r-1} la_{rs} &= 1 \\ \sum_{s=1}^{r-1} ra_{rs} &= 1 \end{aligned} \tag{7}$$

7. Exactly one variable is resolved away for creating each resolvent.

$$\sum_{j=1}^{N} v_{jr} = 1 \tag{8}$$

8. The final resolvent, with index $M + K$, must be the empty clause.

$$\neg p_{jM+K} \wedge \neg n_{jM+K} \tag{9}$$

For the sake of clarity, in Eqs. (3) and (4) there is a slight abuse of notation. Note that p_{js} and n_{js} are not defined for $s \leq M$. In these cases, constraints are added *on demand*, without the p_{js} and n_{js} terms. For instance, in (3) the clause $c_s \in \mathcal{F}$, yields the constraints $(la_{rs} \vee ra_{rs}) \rightarrow wp_{jr}$ for $j \in L^+(c_s)$ and $(la_{rs} \vee ra_{rs}) \rightarrow wn_{jr}$ for $j \in L^-(c_s)$. The sets $L^+(c_s)$ and $L^-(c_s)$ are also exploited in (4). Besides, transforming (4) into CNF requires adding $\mathcal{O}(NK^2)$

new variables and clauses encoding the equivalences $yp_{rsj} \leftrightarrow (la_{rs} \vee ra_{rs}) \wedge p_{js}$ and $yn_{rsj} \leftrightarrow (la_{rs} \vee ra_{rs}) \wedge n_{js}$, with $s > M$.

Cardinality constraints of the form $\sum_{i=1}^{n} x_i = 1$ are encoded as the conjunction of one *at least one* constraint, represented by the single clause $\bigvee_{i=1}^{n} x_i$, and one *at most one* constraint, which is encoded using *sequential counters* [33]. For a constraint $\sum_{i=1}^{n} x_i \leq k$, sequential counters produce $\mathcal{O}(nk)$ variables and clauses. Clearly, other encodings could be considered as well (e.g. [3,24]).

The encoded formula has $\mathcal{O}(NK^2 + MK)$ variables. Regarding the number of clauses, constraints (3) and (4) result in $\mathcal{O}(NK^2 + K||\mathcal{F}||)$ clauses, with $||\mathcal{F}||$ the number of literals in $\mathcal{F}$. Constraints (2), (5), (6) and (8) result in $\mathcal{O}(NK)$ clauses (7) amounts to $\mathcal{O}(K(M + K))$ clauses and (9) yields $\mathcal{O}(N)$ clauses. The encoding has $\mathcal{O}(NK^2 + K||\mathcal{F}|| + K(M + K))$ clauses and $\mathcal{O}(NK(M + K) + K||\mathcal{F}|| + K(M + K))$ literals, the increase due to some large clauses from (4).

The encoding is related to the model proposed in [27], with several differences. In [27] the encoding targeted computing resolution proofs with local search. It used refinements to reduce its size and increase the solution density. These included not enforcing that literals in a resolvent must exist in some parent (known as the *weakening rule*) or allowing for more than two parents for a node. The resulting encoding had $\mathcal{O}(K^2 + KN + KM)$ variables and $\mathcal{O}(NK^2 + K||\mathcal{F}||)$ literals, smaller than the one herein. However, when looking for SRPs with a complete solver it is necessary to prove unsatisfiabilty for some values of K, and constraining formulas as much as possible, promoting propagation, is beneficial. So, we opted for not using the weakening rule, at the expense of a larger encoding. Anyway, the results in [27] showed that applying the weakening rule was not beneficial in practice. The proposed encoding represents proofs more explicitly than in [27], e.g. by distinguishing left and right parents, which is useful for enforcing additional constraints, as shown in the next section.

4 Enhancements to the Model

This section devises a number of enhancements to the model above. These constrain the structure of resolution proofs, remove symmetries and exploit the information given by a collection of MCSes to prune the search space.

4.1 Constraints on the Structure of the Proofs

We first enforce symmetry breaking constraints, establishing that the left parent of any resolvent must have a lower index than its right parent. Any resolution DAG can be rewritten without additional nodes to fulfill this property. Besides, for each clause $c_s \in \mathcal{F}$, we compute beforehand the set of clauses $R(c_s) \subseteq \mathcal{F}$ that can be resolved with c_s producing a valid resolvent, which restricts the selection of parents as follows:

$$la_{rs} \rightarrow \bigvee_{t \in R(c_s); t > s}^{M} ra_{rt} \vee \bigvee_{t=M+1; t > s}^{r-1} ra_{rt} \tag{10}$$

The following constraints avoid computing resolvents that are subsumed by any original clause in $\mathcal{F}$, which would not be useful in the proof. Here $s \in [1, M]$.

$$\bigvee_{j \in L^+(c_s)} \neg p_{jr} \vee \bigvee_{j \in L^-(c_s)} \neg n_{jr} \tag{11}$$

In an SRP, all resolvents but the last one are used as a parent of later resolvents [27] (otherwise, such resolvent would be useless). Imposing these constraints has the drawback that for some values of K overestimating the length of the SRPs, the encoded formula may be unsatisfiable, thus requiring the search method to iteratively refine lower bounds from 1 on. Here, $r \in [M+1, M+K-1]$.

$$\bigvee_{u=r+1}^{M+K} (la_{ur} \vee ra_{ur}) \tag{12}$$

Equations (10) and (12) entail that resolvent $K-1$ must be the right parent of K. This is enforced by setting $ra_{(M+K)(M+K-1)} = 1$. Besides, both parents of K must be unit clauses. The following constraints prevent the left parent of K from being a non-unit input clause. $U(\mathcal{F})$ denotes the unit clauses in $\mathcal{F}$.

$$\bigwedge_{s \in \mathcal{F} \setminus U(\mathcal{F})} \neg la_{(M+K)s} \tag{13}$$

In addition we add constraints enforcing the resolvent $K-1$ (the right parent of K) to be a unit clause.

$$\sum_{j=1}^{N} p_{j(M+K-1)} + n_{j(M+K-1)} = 1 \tag{14}$$

The constraints above do not increase the asymptotic number of variables and clauses of the encoding. However, the $\mathcal{O}(K(M+K))$ clauses from (10) can be large, adding in total $\mathcal{O}(K(M+K)^2)$ literals to the encoding in the worst case.

4.2   Levels in the Resolution DAG

Nodes in the resolution DAG can be associated a *level*. Original clauses have level 0, whereas the level of a resolvent is given by the maximum of the levels of its parents plus 1. We focus on the property of having level 1, indicating that both its parents are original clauses. The following result establishes bounds on the number of resolvents of each kind:

Proposition 1. *In an SRP with K resolvents, at least $\lfloor K/2 \rfloor$ resolvents do not have level 1.*

Proof. In an SRP, all resolvents but the last one are used in the proof. Hence, $K-1$ items need to be allocated at least once as a parent of other resolvent.

Nodes at level 1 have both parents as input clauses. Suppose there are $\lfloor K/2 \rfloor$ resolvents not at level 1. In the worst case K is odd, so $\lfloor K/2 \rfloor = (K-1)/2$. Each of these nodes has two parents, so there are $K-1$ positions for the $K-1$ items. This represents the limit case; if there were fewer nodes at level greater than 1, not all $K-1$ items could be used in the proof.

From these observations, we further restrict the search space. For each resolvent r, a variable is defined as $l1_r = 1$ iff resolvent r is at level 1. Then, we set that the first node has level 1, i.e. $l1_{M+1} = 1$, and that the last $\lfloor K/2 \rfloor$ nodes are not at level 1, i.e. $l1_r = 0$ for $r \in [h+1, M+K]$, where $h = M + \lceil K/2 \rceil$. The following constraints reduce the number of possible parents depending on levels and break symmetries:

1. A resolvent is at level 1 if and only if its right parent is not an earlier resolvent.

$$l1_r \leftrightarrow \bigwedge_{s=M+1}^{r-1} \neg ra_{rs} \tag{15}$$

2. All the resolvents at level 1 are computed at the beginning.

$$\begin{aligned} l1_r &\rightarrow \bigwedge_{u=M+2}^{r-1} l1_u \\ \neg l1_r &\rightarrow \bigwedge_{u=r+1}^{h} \neg l1_u \end{aligned} \tag{16}$$

3. If two consecutive resolvents are at level 1, the left parent of the first one has an index not greater than the left parent of the second one. Here $r \in [M+2, h]$.

$$(l1_r \wedge la_{rs}) \rightarrow \bigvee_{t=1}^{s} la_{(r-1)t} \tag{17}$$

Enforcing constraints (16) and (17) does not prevent from finding a shortest refutation, since any resolution DAG can be transformed to fulfill these conditions by reordering some nodes in the proof. Regarding space, the constraints above do not affect the asymptotic number of variables, clauses or literals in the encoding. Constraints (17) result in $\mathcal{O}(K(M+K)^2)$ literals, matching those analyzed previously from (10).

4.3 Exploiting Minimal Correction Subsets

The last enhancement proposed in the paper is aimed at further reducing the search space by exploiting minimal correction subsets (MCSes) in the encoding. It is based on the following result:

Proposition 2. *Let $\mathcal{C} \subsetneq \mathcal{F}$ be an MCS. All resolution proofs of $\mathcal{F}$ use some clause in $\mathcal{C}$.*

Proof. By Definition 2, $\mathcal{F} \setminus \mathcal{C}$ is satisfiable. Hence, if all the clauses in $\mathcal{C}$ were dropped, there would not exist a proof of unsatisfiability.

So, in a pre-processing step a collection of MCSes is enumerated, and for each MCS $\mathcal{C}$ we enforce that at least one of its clauses is used at least once in the proof:

$$\bigvee_{r=M+1}^{M+K} (\bigvee_{c_s \in \mathcal{C}} la_{rs} \vee ra_{rs}) \tag{18}$$

We exploit the fact that for a proof with K resolvents, at most $2K$ clauses can be used. We define, for each clause c_s, a variable $used_s = 1$ if c_s is used at least once in the proof, and add the following constraints:

1. All the resolvents, but the last one must be used for computing later resolvents in the proof.

$$\bigwedge_{r=M+1}^{M+K-1} (used_r) \tag{19}$$

2. At least one clause in each MCS must be used in the computation of some resolvent. For each MCS $\mathcal{C}$ we add a clause as the following:

$$\bigvee_{c_s \in \mathcal{C}} used_s \tag{20}$$

3. If a clause is a parent of a resolvent, it is marked as used.

$$(la_{rs} \vee ra_{rs}) \rightarrow used_s \tag{21}$$

4. At most $2K$ different clauses can be used.

$$\sum_{s=1}^{M+K-1} used_s \leq 2K \tag{22}$$

Constraints (18) produce one clause of size $\mathcal{O}(K(M+K))$ for each MCS. So, if C MCSes are considered, the encoding grows in $\mathcal{O}(C)$ clauses and $\mathcal{O}(CK(M+K))$ literals. The last constraints do not affect the asymptotic size of the model. The final encoding has $\mathcal{O}(NK^2 + MK)$ variables, $\mathcal{O}(NK^2 + K||\mathcal{F}|| + K(M+K) + C)$ clauses and $\mathcal{O}(NK(M+K) + K||\mathcal{F}|| + CK(M+K) + K(M+K)^2)$ literals.

5   Experimental Results

This section evaluates the proposed encodings for computing SRPs. For this purpose, we implemented a prototype in Python 2.7, interfacing the SAT solver minisat (v 2.2) [12]. The tool computes SRPs by iteratively refining lower bounds on the number of resolvents. Starting with $K = 1$, while the encoded formula is found unsatisfiable K is increased in one unit. The process terminates upon a satisfiable call, in which case an SRP is extracted from the computed model.

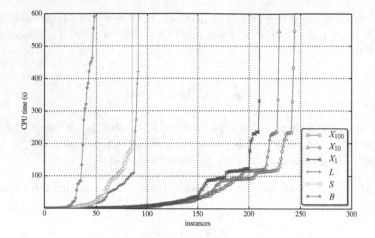

Fig. 3. Running times (s).

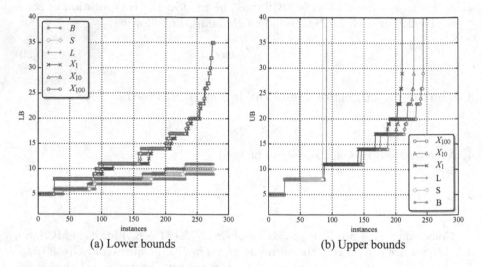

(a) Lower bounds   (b) Upper bounds

Fig. 4. Summary of results.

Notice that this procedure iteratively proves that no resolution refutation of size K exists for increasing values of K, until the last iteration where resolution proof is found. This way, the computed resolution proof is guaranteed to be an SRP.

The experiments have been carried out over a set of unsatisfiable Horn formulas (whose clauses contain at most one positive literal) derived from the domain of axiom pinpointing in lightweight description logics [2]. We considered the ones with a number of clauses in the range $[20, 594]$, making 278 instances in all. The number of variables ranges from 17 to 493. A number of these formulas have short proofs, so they represent an adequate benchmark for assessing the effectiveness of the encodings. Recall that computing SRPs for Horn formulas is intractable [1] (in contrast to 2-CNF formulas [7,8]). We distinguish different versions of the encoding: B refers to the base encoding from Sect. 3, S includes the additional constraints from Sect. 4.1, L adds the constraints related to levels from Sect. 4.2 and versions with prefix X exploit MCSes as well, as described in Sect. 4.3. X_1, X_{10} and X_{100} establish a limit on the number of MCSes enumerated to 100, 1000 and 10000 respectively. MCSes are computed with the tool mcsls [17]. All the experiments were run on a Linux cluster, with a time limit of 600 seconds. The computation of MCSes is included in the time limit. To this respect, the average (maximum) time taken for enumerating MCSes was 0.01 (0.14), 0.08 (0.58) and 0.83 (5.74) seconds for X_1, X_{10} and X_{100} respectively. Besides, complete enumeration of MCSes was possible for a number cases: Out of the 278 instances, 130, 156 and 188 have less than 100, 1000 and 10000 MCSes respectively.

Figure 3 shows the running times taken by each of the aforementioned versions of the encoding in solving the considered instances. For a given version of the encoding, a point (x, y) in the plot indicates that x instances were solved taking up to y seconds. As we can observe, the basic encoding B yields the worst results overall, solving 49 instances. The optimizations included in S and L allow for computing SRPs for more instances (87 and 93 respectively). Although L is able to solve a only few more instances than S, there is an observable gain in terms of running times. Noticeably, exploiting MCSes brings the most significant improvements, these being directly related to the number of MCSes enumerated beforehand. X_1, X_{10} and X_{100} can cope with far more challenging instances than before, solving 212, 231 and 246 instances respectively.

Figure 4 provides a more detailed view on the performance of the encodings. Figure 4a reports the best lower bounds on the size of the SRPs (LBs) computed by the time limit, and Fig. 4b shows the actual size of the SRPs (UBs) computed. For a given version of the encoding, a point (x, y) in Fig. 4a means that an LB lower than or equal to y was obtained for x instances using such encoding within the time limit. Analogously, in Fig. 4b, a point (x, y) means that the given encoding enabled computing SRPs with up to y resolvents for x instances. For the solved instances, LBs match the size of the SRPs. As we can observe, B is only able to cope with formulas with very short proofs, computing SRPs with 5 to 8 resolvents and proving LBs of at most 9 for some instances. On the other hand, S and L are capable of proving larger LBs (up to values 10 and 11 respectively), being L able to find SRPs with 11 resolvents for a few instances. Exploiting MCSes results in very significant gains, proving LBs of size 35 and computing SRPs with up to 29 resolvents.

The proposed improvements also allow for coping with larger formulas, solving several of the largest ones in the set (with more than 350 variables and near 600 clauses). These results indicate that the proposed enhancements are effective at pruning the search space and guiding the construction of resolution proofs, enabling the computation of SRPs for non-trivial formulas.

6   Conclusions

This paper addresses the problem of computing shortest resolution proofs (SRPs) of unsatisfiable CNF formulas and develops a SAT-based approach for this task. SRPs are computed by solving a sequence of decision problems encoding the computation of resolution refutations of fixed size K, with increasing values of K. Building on an initial reference propositional model, the paper devises several enhancements to the encoding, which constrain the structure of the proofs and exploit minimal correction subsets to further reduce the search space. The enhancements are shown to be very effective in practice, enabling the computation of SRPs for more challenging formulas.

References

1. Alekhnovich, M., Buss, S.R., Moran, S., Pitassi, T.: Minimum propositional proof length is NP-hard to linearly approximate. J. Symb. Log. **66**(1), 171–191 (2001)
2. Arif, M.F., Mencía, C., Marques-Silva, J.: Efficient MUS enumeration of horn formulae with applications to axiom pinpointing. In: Heule, M., Weaver, S. (eds.) SAT 2015. LNCS, vol. 9340, pp. 324–342. Springer, Cham (2015). https://doi.org/10.1007/978-3-319-24318-4_24
3. Asín, R., Nieuwenhuis, R., Oliveras, A., Rodríguez-Carbonell, E.: Cardinality networks: a theoretical and empirical study. Constraints **16**(2), 195–221 (2011)
4. Audemard, G., Simon, L.: GUNSAT: A greedy local search algorithm for unsatisfiability. In: IJCAI, pp. 2256–2261 (2007)
5. Bacchus, F., Davies, J., Tsimpoukelli, M., Katsirelos, G.: Relaxation search: a simple way of managing optional clauses. In: AAAI, pp. 835–841 (2014)
6. Ben-Sasson, E., Wigderson, A.: Short proofs are narrow - resolution made simple. J. ACM **48**(2), 149–169 (2001)
7. Buresh-Oppenheim, J., Mitchell, D.: Minimum witnesses for unsatisfiable 2CNFs. In: Biere, A., Gomes, C.P. (eds.) SAT 2006. LNCS, vol. 4121, pp. 42–47. Springer, Heidelberg (2006). https://doi.org/10.1007/11814948_6
8. Buresh-Oppenheim, J., Mitchell, D.: Minimum 2CNF resolution refutations in polynomial time. In: Marques-Silva, J., Sakallah, K.A. (eds.) SAT 2007. LNCS, vol. 4501, pp. 300–313. Springer, Heidelberg (2007). https://doi.org/10.1007/978-3-540-72788-0_29
9. Cook, S.A.: The complexity of theorem-proving procedures. In: STOC, pp. 151–158 (1971)
10. Davis, M., Logemann, G., Loveland, D.W.: A machine program for theorem-proving. Commun. ACM **5**(7), 394–397 (1962)
11. Davis, M., Putnam, H.: A computing procedure for quantification theory. J. ACM **7**(3), 201–215 (1960)
12. Eén, N., Sörensson, N.: An extensible SAT-solver. In: Giunchiglia, E., Tacchella, A. (eds.) SAT 2003. LNCS, vol. 2919, pp. 502–518. Springer, Heidelberg (2004). https://doi.org/10.1007/978-3-540-24605-3_37
13. Grégoire, É., Izza, Y., Lagniez, J.: Boosting MCSes enumeration. In: IJCAI, pp. 1309–1315 (2018)
14. Haken, A.: The intractability of resolution. Theor. Comput. Sci. **39**, 297–308 (1985)
15. Hulubei, T., O'Sullivan, B.: Optimal refutations for constraint satisfaction problems. In: IJCAI, pp. 163–168 (2005)

16. Liffiton, M.H., Sakallah, K.A.: Algorithms for computing minimal unsatisfiable subsets of constraints. J. Autom. Reason. **40**(1), 1–33 (2008)

17. Marques-Silva, J., Heras, F., Janota, M., Previti, A., Belov, A.: On computing minimal correction subsets. In: IJCAI, pp. 615–622 (2013)

18. Marques-Silva, J., Janota, M., Mencía, C.: Minimal sets on propositional formulae. Problems and reductions. Artif. Intell. **252**, 22–50 (2017)

19. Marques-Silva, J., Malik, S.: Propositional SAT solving. In: Clarke, E., Henzinger, T., Veith, H., Bloem, R. (eds.) Handbook of Model Checking, pp. 247–275. Springer, Cham (2018). https://doi.org/10.1007/978-3-319-10575-8_9

20. Marques-Silva, J., Sakallah, K.A.: GRASP - a new search algorithm for satisfiability. In: ICCAD, pp. 220–227 (1996)

21. Mencía, C., Ignatiev, A., Previti, A., Marques-Silva, J.: MCS extraction with sublinear oracle queries. In: Creignou, N., Le Berre, D. (eds.) SAT 2016. LNCS, vol. 9710, pp. 342–360. Springer, Cham (2016). https://doi.org/10.1007/978-3-319-40970-2_21

22. Mencía, C., Previti, A., Marques-Silva, J.: Literal-based MCS extraction. In: IJCAI, pp. 1973–1979 (2015)

23. Narodytska, N., Bjørner, N., Marinescu, M., Sagiv, M.: Core-guided minimal correction set and core enumeration. In: IJCAI, pp. 1353–1361 (2018)

24. Ogawa, T., Liu, Y., Hasegawa, R., Koshimura, M., Fujita, H.: Modulo based CNF encoding of cardinality constraints and its application to MaxSAT solvers. In: ICTAI, pp. 9–17 (2013)

25. O'Sullivan, B., Papadopoulos, A., Faltings, B., Pu, P.: Representative explanations for over-constrained problems. In: AAAI, pp. 323–328 (2007)

26. Pereira, D., Lynce, I., Prestwich, S.D.: On improving local search for unsatisfiability. In: LSCS, pp. 41–53 (2009)

27. Prestwich, S., Lynce, I.: Local search for unsatisfiability. In: Biere, A., Gomes, C.P. (eds.) SAT 2006. LNCS, vol. 4121, pp. 283–296. Springer, Heidelberg (2006). https://doi.org/10.1007/11814948_28

28. Previti, A., Mencía, C., Järvisalo, M., Marques-Silva, J.: Improving MCS enumeration via caching. In: Gaspers, S., Walsh, T. (eds.) SAT 2017. LNCS, vol. 10491, pp. 184–194. Springer, Cham (2017). https://doi.org/10.1007/978-3-319-66263-3_12

29. Previti, A., Mencía, C., Järvisalo, M., Marques-Silva, J.: Premise set caching for enumerating minimal correction subsets. In: AAAI, pp. 6633–6640 (2018)

30. Reiter, R.: A theory of diagnosis from first principles. Artif. Intell. **32**(1), 57–95 (1987)

31. Robinson, J.A.: A machine-oriented logic based on the resolution principle. J. ACM **12**(1), 23–41 (1965)

32. Robinson, J.A., Voronkov, A. (eds.): Handbook of Automated Reasoning. Elsevier and MIT Press, Cambridge (2001)

33. Sinz, C.: Towards an optimal CNF encoding of Boolean cardinality constraints. In: van Beek, P. (ed.) CP 2005. LNCS, vol. 3709, pp. 827–831. Springer, Heidelberg (2005). https://doi.org/10.1007/11564751_73

Forgetting in Answer Set Programming with Anonymous Cycles

Matti Berthold[1,2], Ricardo Gonçalves[3(✉)], Matthias Knorr[3], and João Leite[3]

[1] Technische Universität Dresden, Dresden, Germany
[2] Universität Leipzig, Leipzig, Germany
[3] NOVA LINCS, Departamento de Informática, Faculdade de Ciências e Tecnologia,
Universidade Nova de Lisboa, Caparica, Portugal
rjrg@fct.unl.pt

Abstract. It is now widely accepted that the operation of forgetting in the context of Answer Set Programming [10,18] is best characterized by the so-called *strong persistence*, a property that requires that all existing relations between the atoms not to be forgotten be preserved. However, it has been shown that strong persistence cannot always be satisfied. What happens if we must nevertheless forget? One possibility that has been explored before is to consider weaker versions of strong persistence, although not without a cost: some relations between the atoms not to be forgotten are broken in the process. A different alternative is to enhance the logical language so that all such relations can be maintained after the forgetting operation. In this paper, we borrow from the recently introduced notion of *fork* [1] – a conservative extension of Equilibrium Logic and its monotonic basis, the logic of Here-and-There – which has been shown to be sufficient to overcome the problems related to satisfying strong persistence. We map this notion into the language of logic programs, enhancing it with so-called anonymous cycles, and we introduce a concrete syntactical forgetting operator over this enhanced language that we show to always obey *strong persistence*.

1 Introduction

There has been a substantial interest in investigating the operation of *forgetting* in the context of Answer Set Programming (c.f. [10] for a recent survey). Intuitively, when we forget some atoms from a logic program, the goal is to come up with another program, written in a language that does not include the atoms to be forgotten, which preserves the meaning with respect to the remaining atoms.

Whereas different approaches over the years, e.g., [5–9,12,23,24], proposed different ways to semantically characterize this operation, it is now rather well accepted that *strong persistence* [16] best captures its essence. *Strong persistence* is a property that requires that all existing relations between the atoms not to be forgotten be preserved during the forgetting operation. However, it has been shown that strong persistence cannot always be satisfied [11]. There are cases where the atoms to be forgotten play such a pivotal role in the original

P. Moura Oliveira et al. (Eds.): EPIA 2019, LNAI 11805, pp. 552–565, 2019.
https://doi.org/10.1007/978-3-030-30244-3_46

program that one cannot represent its effects on the remaining atoms without them. These cases are usually associated with atoms involved in the so-called *even cycles through negation* (somehow equivalent to *choice rules*) that generate different stable models (or answer sets).

What if we are faced with a situation in which we must forget – e.g., because of a court order, or any other strong reason – but we cannot while obeying *strong persistence*? This problem was first tackled in [13], where the authors investigated different ways to weaken *strong persistence*. However, that does not come without a cost: some relations between the atoms not to be forgotten are broken in the process. This may result, for example, in the unwanted disappearance of existing stable models, or the appearance of new ones. What if we cannot afford to loose any relations between the non-forgotten atoms, but must proceed with the forgetting operation? One alternative is to enhance the logical language so that all such relations can be maintained after the forgetting operation. Recently, in [1], the authors introduced the notion of *fork* – a conservative extension of Equilibrium Logic and its monotonic basis, the logic of Here-and-There – which, in a nutshell, allows for the specification of formulas whose stable models are the union of the stable models of separate formulas. They also proved that *forks* are sufficient to overcome the problems related to satisfying strong persistence.

Inspired by the concept of *forks*, we begin this paper by enhancing the language of logic programs with so-called *anonymous cycles*, aiming at being able to specify concrete forgetting operators that satisfy strong persistence. Extending the language of logic programs with *anonymous cycles* essentially amounts to extending the alphabet with a set of anonymous atoms that can *only* be used in *anonymous cycles*, i.e., to generate and condition alternatives, which are then ignored when the stable models are considered. We then introduce a concrete forgetting operator over this enhanced language, which we show to obey *strong persistence*.

The new operator is syntactical in nature, i.e., it achieves the result by syntactically manipulating the rules of the input program – there is no need to compute any models – and it is the first concrete forgetting operator that obeys *strong persistence*, albeit for this enhanced language. One might argue, somehow cynically, that if we allow ourselves to extend the language and use new atoms, then why not simply keep the ones we were supposed to forget, perhaps renaming them to appear as if they are not the same. Even if this renaming would obey *strong persistence*, modulo these new atoms, it could hardly be classified as *forgetting*. By ensuring that all the non-forgotten atoms introduced by our forgetting operator are anonymous, thus used in a very constrained and fixed way, we ensure a clear syntactical distinction between these and the forgotten ones. Equally important is the fact that the operator is closed under the language of logic programs with anonymous cycles. This allows its iteration, admitting for any number of atoms to be forgotten from a program in any sequence, while still obeying *strong persistence*.

2   Preliminaries

In this section, we recall necessary notions on answer set programming. We assume a *propositional signature* Σ. A *logic program* P over Σ is a finite set of *rules* of the form

$$a_1 \vee \ldots \vee a_k \leftarrow b_1, \ldots, b_l, not\, c_1, \ldots, not\, c_m, not\, not\, d_1, \ldots, not\, not\, d_n, \qquad (1)$$

where all $a_1, \ldots, a_k, b_1, \ldots, b_l, c_1, \ldots, c_m$, and $d_1, \ldots, d_n$ are atoms of Σ. Such rules r are also written more succinctly as

$$H(r) \leftarrow B^+(r), not\, B^-(r), not\, not\, B^{--}(r), \qquad (2)$$

where $H(r) = \{a_1, \ldots, a_k\}$, $B^+(r) = \{b_1, \ldots, b_l\}$, $B^-(r) = \{c_1, \ldots, c_m\}$, and $B^{--}(r) = \{d_1, \ldots, d_n\}$, and we will use both forms interchangeably. Given a rule r, $H(r)$ is called the *head* of r, and $B(r) = B^+(r) \cup not\, B^-(r) \cup not\, not\, B^{--}(r)$ is called the *body* of r, where, for a set A of atoms, $not\, A = \{not\, q : q \in A\}$ and $not\, not\, A = \{not\, not\, q : q \in A\}$. We term the elements in $B(r)$ *(body) literals*. $\Sigma(P)$ and $\Sigma(r)$ denote the set of atoms appearing in P and r, respectively. Given a program P and an *interpretation*, i.e., a set $I \subseteq \Sigma$ of atoms, the *reduct* of P given I, is defined as $P^I = \{H(r) \leftarrow B^+(r) : r \in P \text{ such that } B^-(r) \cap I = \emptyset \text{ and } B^{--}(r) \subseteq I\}$.

An *HT-interpretation* is a pair $\langle X, Y \rangle$ s.t. $X \subseteq Y \subseteq \Sigma$. Given a program P, an HT-interpretation $\langle X, Y \rangle$ is an *HT-model of* P if $Y \models P$ and $X \models P^Y$, where $\models$ denotes the standard consequence relation for classical logic. We admit that the set of HT-models of a program P is restricted to $\Sigma(P)$ even if $\Sigma(P) \subset \Sigma$. We denote by $\mathcal{HT}(P)$ the set of *all HT-models of* P. A set of atoms Y is an *answer set* of P if $\langle Y, Y \rangle \in \mathcal{HT}(P)$, but there is no $X \subset Y$ such that $\langle X, Y \rangle \in \mathcal{HT}(P)$. The set of all answer sets of P is denoted by $\mathcal{AS}(P)$. Two programs P_1, P_2 are *equivalent* if $\mathcal{AS}(P_1) = \mathcal{AS}(P_2)$ and *strongly equivalent*, $P_1 \equiv P_2$, if $\mathcal{AS}(P_1 \cup R) = \mathcal{AS}(P_2 \cup R)$ for any program R. It is well-known that $P_1 \equiv P_2$ exactly when $\mathcal{HT}(P_1) = \mathcal{HT}(P_2)$ [19]. Given a set $V \subseteq \Sigma$, the *V-exclusion* of a set of answer sets (a set of HT-interpretations) $\mathcal{M}$, denoted $\mathcal{M}_{\|V}$, is $\{X \backslash V \mid X \in \mathcal{M}\}$ ($\{\langle X \backslash V, Y \backslash V \rangle \mid \langle X, Y \rangle \in \mathcal{M}\}$).

3   Forgetting with Anonymous Cycles

Forgetting in answer set programming (ASP) aims at eliminating certain elements from the language Σ, without affecting the consequences inferable for the language elements that remain. However, it is not always possible to forget in ASP [11], intuitively, because some elements of the language are crucial to preserve certain dependencies between atoms in the program. A way to avoid this problem would thus be to not remove such atoms entirely, but rather preserve them in a localized form, such that later, under certain circumstances, they could potentially be removed, e.g., after all related atoms have been forgotten. This has been tackled by proposing an extension of ASP with a new construct, called forks [1]. Here, we map this notion into the language of logic programs, but instead of extending the language with the fork constructor, we enhance the language with a set of distinguished atoms, called anonymous atoms, that can only be used in a very restricted way, namely to generate so-called anonymous cycles.

Thus, in this section, we first introduce programs with anonymous cycles and, then, we reconcile the notions of forgetting in ASP with this extension of programs. We start by extending the signature to allow for an infinite number of anonymous atoms.

Definition 1. *An* anonymous signature *is a pair* $\langle \Sigma, \Sigma_{an} \rangle$ *where* Σ *is a signature and* Σ_{an} *is an infinite set of atoms such that* $\Sigma \cap \Sigma_{an} = \emptyset$.

We use Roman letters to denote elements of Σ and Greek letters to denote elements of Σ_{an}. In what follows, we assume a fixed anonymous signature $\langle \Sigma, \Sigma_{an} \rangle$. Based on this, we now define the class of programs with anonymous cycles.

Definition 2. *A* program with anonymous cycles *(over* $\langle \Sigma, \Sigma_{an} \rangle$*) is a program* P *such that, for each* $\delta \in \Sigma_{an}$ *and* $r \in P$, *exactly one of the following conditions is true:*

- δ *does not appear in* r;
- δ *belongs only to* $B^+(r)$;
- δ *belongs only to* $B^-(r)$;
- r *is of the form* $\delta \leftarrow not\,not\,\delta$.

We term a rule r *of the latter form an* anonymous cycle.

Therefore, in a program with anonymous cycles, the atoms of Σ_{an} can only appear in a very restricted way. Namely, they can only be used to generate cycles, in anonymous cycles,[1] and, in addition, appear in the positive or negative body of rules. This means that for an anonymous atom $\delta \in \Sigma_{an}$, the rule $\delta \leftarrow not\,not\,\delta$ is the only rule in which δ is allowed to appear in the head or in the double negated body.

Since the atoms of Σ_{an} are to be seen as auxiliary, the semantics of programs with anonymous cycles over an anonymous signature $\langle \Sigma, \Sigma_{an} \rangle$ is defined as the restriction to Σ of the semantics of the program when considered as program over $\Sigma \cup \Sigma_{an}$.

Definition 3. *Let* P *be a program with anonymous cycles over* $\langle \Sigma, \Sigma_{an} \rangle$, *and* P^* *the program over* $\Sigma \cup \Sigma_{an}$ *with the same rules as* P. *Then, the set of HT-models of* P *and the set of answer sets of* P *are defined, respectively, as*

$$\mathcal{HT}(P) = \mathcal{HT}(P^*)_{\|\Sigma_{an}} \qquad \mathcal{AS}(P) = \mathcal{AS}(P^*)_{\|\Sigma_{an}}.$$

---

[1] Note that this term is due to the fact that the answer sets of such an anonymous cycle are precisely $\{\delta\}$ and $\{\}$.

Example 1. Consider the program with anonymous cycles P over $\langle \Sigma, \Sigma_{an} \rangle$:

$$a \leftarrow b, \delta \qquad\qquad c \leftarrow not\ \delta \qquad\qquad \delta \leftarrow not\ not\ \delta$$

where $a, b, c \in \Sigma$ and $\delta \in \Sigma_{an}$. If we consider program P^* over $\Sigma \cup \Sigma_{an}$ with precisely the same rules as P, we have that $\mathcal{AS}(P^*) = \{\{\delta\}, \{c\}\}$ and $\mathcal{AS}(P) = \{\emptyset, \{c\}\}$.

We are now ready to extend notions of forgetting in ASP from the literature to the class of programs with anonymous cycles.

A *forgetting operator* over a class $\mathcal{C}$ of programs with anonymous cycles[2] over $\langle \Sigma, \Sigma_{an} \rangle$ is a partial function $\mathsf{f} : \mathcal{C} \times 2^{\Sigma} \to \mathcal{C}$ s.t. the *result of forgetting about V from P*, denoted as $\mathsf{f}(P, V)$, is a program with anonymous cycles over $\langle \Sigma(P) \backslash V, \Sigma_{an} \rangle$, for each $P \in \mathcal{C}$ and $V \subseteq \Sigma$. We denote the domain of f by $\mathcal{C}(\mathsf{f})$. The operator f is called *closed* for $\mathcal{C}' \subseteq \mathcal{C}(\mathsf{f})$ if $\mathsf{f}(P, V) \in \mathcal{C}'$, for every $P \in \mathcal{C}'$ and $V \subseteq \Sigma$. A *class* F *of forgetting operators (over $\mathcal{C}$)* is a set of forgetting operators f s.t. $\mathcal{C}(\mathsf{f}) \subseteq \mathcal{C}$, commonly satisfying some definition of the class.

The notions in the remainder of the section are indeed very similar to the ones introduced for programs (without anonymous cycles). They can essentially be re-used here due to our definition of HT-models and answer sets for programs with anonymous cycles, and because we never forget anonymous atoms.

Arguably, among the many properties introduced for different classes of forgetting operators in ASP [10], *strong persistence* [16] is the one that should intuitively hold, since it imposes the preservation of all original direct and indirect dependencies between atoms not to be forgotten. In the following, F is a class of forgetting operators.

(SP) F satisfies *Strong Persistence* if, for each $\mathsf{f} \in \mathsf{F}$, $P \in \mathcal{C}(\mathsf{f})$ and $V \subseteq \Sigma$, we have $\mathcal{AS}(\mathsf{f}(P, V) \cup R) = \mathcal{AS}(P \cup R)_{\|V}$, for all programs $R \in \mathcal{C}(\mathsf{f})$ with $\Sigma(R) \subseteq \Sigma \backslash V$.

Thus, **(SP)** requires that the answer sets of $\mathsf{f}(P, V)$ correspond to those of P, no matter what programs R over $\Sigma \backslash V$ we add to both, which is closely related to the concept of strong equivalence. Among the many properties implied by **(SP)** [10], **(SI)** indicates that rules not mentioning atoms to be forgotten can be added before or after forgetting.

(SI) F satisfies *Strong (addition) Invariance* if, for each $\mathsf{f} \in \mathsf{F}$, $P \in \mathcal{C}(\mathsf{f})$ and $V \subseteq \Sigma$, we have $\mathsf{f}(P, V) \cup R \equiv \mathsf{f}(P \cup R, V)$ for all programs $R \in \mathcal{C}(\mathsf{f})$ with $\Sigma(R) \subseteq \Sigma \backslash V$.

Although **(SP)** is the central property one wants to ensure to hold when forgetting atoms from an answer set program, it was shown in [11] that this is not always possible, that is, there is no forgetting operator that satisfies **(SP)** and that is defined for all pairs $\langle P, V \rangle$, called *forgetting instances*, where P is

---

[2] In this paper, we only consider the very general class of programs introduced before, but, often, subclasses of it appear in the literature of ASP and forgetting in ASP.

a program and V is a set of atoms to be forgotten from P. Moreover, a sound and complete criterion, Ω, was presented to characterize when exactly it is not possible to forget while satisfying **(SP)**. In addition, a corresponding class of forgetting operators, $\mathsf{F_{SP}}$, was introduced. It was shown that every operator in $\mathsf{F_{SP}}$ satisfies **(SP)** for instances $\langle P, V \rangle$ that do not satisfy Ω, i.e., those instances for which it is possible to forget V from P while satisfying **(SP)**. This makes $\mathsf{F_{SP}}$ the ideal choice whenever forgetting is possible. Nevertheless, $\mathsf{F_{SP}}$ has two main problems: first, it is only defined semantically, i.e., it only specifies the HT-models that a result of forgetting a set of atoms V from program P should have; and second, for instances $\langle P, V \rangle$ that satisfy Ω, i.e., those instances for which we know that it is not possible to forget V from P while satisfying **(SP)**, the result $\mathsf{f}(P, V)$ necessarily does not have a strong connection with P as imposed by **(SP)**.

4   A Syntactic Operator

Our main result of this paper is that the impossibility result for forgetting in ASP can be overcome at the cost of introducing anonymous cycles (whenever necessary). Moreover, we do it in a syntactic way, by only manipulating the rules of the input program. Note again that this approach does not coincide with, e.g., renaming some atom, as in the end only one rule with the new anonymous atom in the head exists.

Thus, in this section, we introduce the operator f_{AC} which, by syntactical manipulation of the input, removes an atom from a program with anonymous cycles. As this operator produces in the worst case a program with anonymous cycles, we will then extend it in a straightforward way to forget any number of atoms iteratively and show that the order of doing so in fact has no effect on the correctness of the result.

To simplify the presentation and the cases that are considered in the construction, and also to reduce the size of the input, we reduce programs to a normal form, similar to [16] and previous related work [4,14,15,20]. There are two essential differences to the normal form considered in [16]. First of all, contrarily to [16], our normal form applies to programs with disjunctive heads. Moreover, we eliminate non-minimal rules [2], which further strengthens the benefits of using normal forms, since non-minimal rules do not have to be considered any longer. Formally, a rule r in P is *minimal* if there is no rule $r' \in P$ such that $H(r') \subseteq H(r) \land B(r') \subset B(r)$ or $H(r') \subset H(r) \land B(r') \subseteq B(r)$.

Definition 4. *Let P be a logic program with anonymous cycles over $\langle \Sigma, \Sigma_{an} \rangle$. We say that P is in* normal form *if the following conditions hold:*

- *for every $a \in \Sigma$ and $r \in P$, at most one of a, not a or not not a is in $B(r)$;*
- *if $a \in H(r)$, then neither a, nor not a are in $B(r)$;*
- *all rules in P are minimal.*

Note that though the restrictions on appearance of atoms in the definition of the normal form are only on non-anonymous atoms, they are met by the anonymous ones too, thanks to the restrictions within the definition of programs with anonymous cycles. The next definition shows how to transform any program into one in normal form.

Definition 5. *Let P be a logic program with anonymous cycles over $\langle \Sigma, \Sigma_{an} \rangle$. The normal form $NF(P)$ is obtained by:*

1. *removing from P all tautological rules r, i.e. rules with $H(r) \cap B^+(r) \neq \emptyset$, with $B^+(r) \cap B^-(r) \neq \emptyset$ or with $B^-(r) \cap B^{--}(r) \neq \emptyset$;*
2. *removing, from the remaining rules, occurrences of double negated atoms from the body, if the atoms appear in the positive body of the same rule;*
3. *removing, from the remaining rules r, the atoms from the head of r that also occur in the negated body of r;*
4. *finally, removing from the resulting program P' all rules r that are not minimal.*

Note that the above construction ensures that all items of Definition 4 are satisfied, namely the first item of Definition 4 is ensured by condition 1. and 2. of Definition 5, the second by conditions 1. and 3., and the third by conditions 1. and 4. Notably, not only we can show that the construction of $NF(P)$ is correct, i.e. that $NF(P)$ is in normal form, but, additionally, we can show that it is strongly equivalent to the original program P.

Proposition 1. *Let P be an logic program with anonymous cycles. Then, $NF(P)$ is in normal form and is strongly equivalent to P.*

In addition, $NF(P)$ can be computed in at most quadratic time in terms of the number of rules in P (as ensuring minimality requires comparing all n rules with each other).

Proposition 2. *Let P be an logic program with anonymous cycles. Then, the normal form $NF(P)$ can be computed in PTIME.*

Thus for the remainder of the paper, we only consider programs in normal form, as these can be efficiently computed and are syntactically equal to the original programs apart from redundancies in the rules.

Forgetting about an atom from a program while satisfying **(SP)** should imply the preservation of the implicit dependencies between the atoms that are not forgotten.

Example 2. Consider the following program P:

$$a \leftarrow q \qquad\qquad q \leftarrow c \qquad\qquad q \leftarrow d$$

Whenever c or d are true, a is indirectly implied via q. Therefore, when forgetting about q from P, the implicit relationship between a and c, and that between

a and d should be preserved. This can be expressed using the following rules without q:

$$a \leftarrow c \qquad\qquad\qquad a \leftarrow d$$

These rules correspond to replacing the positive occurrences of q in a rule body with the body of the rules in which q appears in their head.

If q is not the only atom in the head of a rule, then we need to consider these additional atoms in the head of the resulting rule.

Example 3. Consider the following program P:

$$a \leftarrow q \qquad\qquad\qquad q \vee b \leftarrow c$$

When forgetting about q from P the implicit relation between c and a must be preserved. This can be expressed by the rule:

$$a \vee b \leftarrow c$$

But what happens if the atom to be forgotten appears in the negative body of a rule?

Example 4. Consider the following program P:

$$a \leftarrow not\ q \qquad\qquad q \vee b \leftarrow c \qquad\qquad q \leftarrow d$$

In this case, there is an implicit relationship between a and the atoms b, c, and d. When forgetting about q from P such relationship must be preserved. For the literal $not\ q$ in the body of the first rule to be true we must have, for each rule r in which q appears in the head, either the body r is false (c in the case of the second rule and d in the case of the third rule), or the other atoms that appear in head of r must not be false (b in the case of the second rule). This can be represented by the following two rules:

$$a \leftarrow not\ d, not\ c \qquad\qquad a \leftarrow not\ d, not\ not\ b$$

This problem has been tackled by collecting a set of conjunctions of literals [6,16], each of which can be used to replace $not\ q$, but preserves its truth value.

Accordingly, we now generalize the notion of as-dual from [16], for which we need to introduce some auxiliary functions first. Let N be the function that applies a number of negation symbols to literals. Formally, for all $p \in \Sigma$, $N^0(p) = p$, $N^0(not\ p) = not\ p$, $N^0(not\ not\ p) = not\ not\ p$, $N^1(p) = N^1(not\ not\ p) = not\ p$, $N^1(not\ p) = not\ not\ p$, $N^2(p) = N^2(not\ not\ p) = not\ not\ p$, $N^2(not\ p) = not\ p$. For a set of literals S, $N^i(S) = \{N^i(s) : s \in S\}$. The sets $B^{\backslash q}(r)$ and $H^{\backslash q}(r)$ respectively denote the set of body and head literals after removing every occurrence of q, i.e., $B^{\backslash q}(r) = B(r) \backslash \{q, not\ q, not\ not\ q\}$ and $H^{\backslash q}(r) = H(r) \backslash \{q\}$.

To make this notion concrete, we introduce the as-dual $\mathcal{D}_{as}^q(P)$ for forgetting about q from P that collects the set of conjunctions of literals, that can be used to replace $not\ q$, the negated occurrence of the atom to be forgotten.

$$\mathcal{D}_{as}^q(P) = \{\{N^1(l_1), \ldots, N^1(l_m)\} \cup \{N^2(l_{m+1}), \ldots, N^2(l_n)\} :$$
$$l_i \in B^{\backslash q}(r_i), 1 \leq i \leq m, l_j \in H^{\backslash q}(r_j), m+1 \leq j \leq n,$$
$$\langle\{r_1, \ldots, r_m\}, \{r_{m+1}, \ldots, r_n\}\rangle \text{ is a partition of } P\}$$

The idea is to pass to the operator all the rules that have q in their head as an argument. Then, we consider the possible partitions $\langle F, T\rangle$ of P, and the sets obtained by collecting the negation of exactly one element (except q) from the body of each rule of F, thus guaranteeing that the body of every rule of F is not satisfied, together with the double negation of exactly one head atom (except q) from each rule of T, thus guaranteeing that the head of every rule of T is satisfied. This definition covers all possible cases to provide the set of all rules for a program P such that the considered q cannot be derived. In particular, there are two interesting corner cases: If there is no rule with q in its head, i.e. the input program P is empty, $\mathcal{D}_{as}^q(P) = \{\emptyset\}$, meaning that negating q requires no atom to have a particular truth value. Furthermore, if P contains q as a fact, $\mathcal{D}_{as}^q(P) = \emptyset$, because it is impossible to negate q.

In the examples above, when forgetting about q from a program P, we were able to capture the implicit relationships using rules only over the remaining atoms. As already mentioned, the impossibility results in [11] show that this is in general not possible. In fact, if the atom to be forgotten has self-cycles, it may be the case that we cannot faithfully represent the implicit relationships between the remaining atoms using only rules over these remaining atoms. In theses cases we consider the use of anonymous atoms within anonymous cycles.

Example 5. Consider the following program P:

$$q \leftarrow not\ not\ q, b \qquad\qquad a \leftarrow q \qquad\qquad c \leftarrow not\ q$$

When b is not true, the first rule does not allow us to conclude q, and therefore c must be true by the third rule. This implicit relationship between b and c can be captured by the rule $c \leftarrow not\ b$, which is obtained by the substitution pattern mentioned in the previous examples. Whenever b is true, the self-cycle on q of the first rule generates a choice between a and c. Such choice cannot be represented using only rules over a, b and c. We therefore use anonymous cycles to generate such choice. So, additionally to the rule $c \leftarrow not\ b$, the result of forgetting about q from P has also the rules:

$$a \leftarrow b, \delta_q \qquad\qquad c \leftarrow not\ \delta_q \qquad\qquad \delta_q \leftarrow not\ not\ \delta_q$$

where δ_q is a fresh anonymous atom from Σ_{an}. These rules faithfully capture the implicit relationship between a, b and c in P.

We are now ready to present the formal definition of the operator f_{AC}. As this definition is technically involved, we will first present the new operator itself that allows forgetting about a single atom from a given program and subsequently explain and illustrate its definition. Forgetting about a set of atoms iteratively is presented subsequently.

In order to guarantee the uniqueness of the construction of the operator f_{AC}, we assume a fixed enumeration $\delta_0, \delta_1, \ldots \delta_n, \ldots$ of the elements of Σ_{an}.

Definition 6. *Let P be a program with anonymous cycles over $\langle \Sigma, \Sigma_{an} \rangle$, and $q \in \Sigma$. Let $P_{nf} = NF(P)$ be the normal form of P and δ_q the anonymous atom with the lowest index that does not occur in P. Consider the sets*

$$R := \{r \in P_{nf} \mid q \notin \Sigma(r)\} \qquad R_2 := \{r \in P_{nf} \mid not\ not\ q \in B(r), q \notin H(r)\}$$
$$R_0 := \{r \in P_{nf} \mid q \in B(r)\} \qquad R_3 := \{r \in P_{nf} \mid not\ not\ q \in B(r), q \in H(r)\}$$
$$R_1 := \{r \in P_{nf} \mid not\ q \in B(r)\} \quad R_4 := \{r \in P_{nf} \mid not\ not\ q \notin B(r), q \in H(r)\}$$

The result of forgetting about q in P, $f_{AC}(P, q)$, is the normal form of the program composed of the following rules:

- *each $r \in R$*
- *for each $r_4 \in R_4$*
  1a *for each $r_0 \in R_0$*
    $H(r_0) \cup H^{\backslash q}(r_4) \leftarrow B^{\backslash q}(r_0) \cup B(r_4)$
  1b *for each $r_2 \in R_2$*
    $H(r_2) \leftarrow B^{\backslash q}(r_2) \cup N^1(H^{\backslash q}(r_4)) \cup N^2(B(r_4))$
- *for each $r' \in R_1 \cup R_4$*
  2 *for each $D \in \mathcal{D}_{as}^q(R_3 \cup R_4 \setminus \{r'\})$*
    $H^{\backslash q}(r') \leftarrow B^{\backslash q}(r') \cup D$
- *for each $r_3 \in R_3$*
  3a *for each $r_0 \in R_0$*
    $H(r_0) \cup H^{\backslash q}(r_3) \leftarrow B^{\backslash q}(r_0) \cup B^{\backslash q}(r_3) \cup \{\delta_q\}$
  3b *for each $r_2 \in R_2$*
    $H(r_2) \leftarrow B^{\backslash q}(r_2) \cup N^1(H^{\backslash q}(r_3)) \cup N^2(B^{\backslash q}(r_3)) \cup \{\delta_q\}$
- *if $R_3 \neq \emptyset$*
  4 *for each $r' \in R_1 \cup R_4$, $D \in \mathcal{D}_{as}^q(R_4 \setminus \{r'\})$*
    $H^{\backslash q}(r') \leftarrow B^{\backslash q}(r') \cup D \cup \{not\ \delta_q\}$
  AC $\delta_q \leftarrow not\ not\ \delta_q$

The first step is to obtain the normal form P_{nf} of P using Definition 5. Then, five sets of rules, R_0, R_1, R_2, R_3, and R_4, are defined over P_{nf}, in each of which q appears in the rules in a different form. In addition, R contains all rules from P_{nf} that do not mention q. These latter rules are preserved in the final result of forgetting.

In general terms, the construction is divided in two major cases: one for the rules which contain q or $not\ not\ q$ in the body (those in R_0 or R_2), and one for the rules that contain $not\ q$ in the body or q in the head (those in R_1 or R_4).

Derivation rules **1a** and **1b** connect rules in which q occurs positively in the body with non-cyclic supports of q. In the case of Examples 2 and 3 the occurrences of q in rule bodies are replaced with the body literals of rules that have q in the head.

Derivation rule **2** replaces negative occurrences of q in the body of rules by a proof that q cannot be derived, i.e., an element of $\mathcal{D}_{as}^{q}(R_3 \cup R_4)$. This is illustrated in Example 4. If P does not have rules with cyclic support on q, then only rules **1a**, **1b**, and **2** are used to obtain the result of forgetting about q from P.

If P has rules with cyclic support for q, i.e., R_3 is not empty, then f_{AC} creates an anonymous cycle with a fresh anonymous atom δ_q from Σ_{an}. This anonymous atom is then used as an arbiter between rules derived by **3a**, **3b** and **4**. The derivation rules **3a** and **3b** replace the positive occurrences of q in rule bodies by the anonymous atom δ_q, along with the body literals of the corresponding rule of R_3. Derivation rule **4** replaces negative occurrences of q in rules by a proof that there is no non-cyclic support for q, i.e., an element of $\mathcal{D}_{as}^{q}(R_4)$ and *not* δ_q. These derivation rules are illustrated in Example 5.

We now prove that our operator f_{AC} behaves in a desirable way, in the sense that it preserves the HT-models of the original program (modulo the forgotten atom), thus necessarily preserving the (direct or indirect) relationships between the remaining atoms.

Theorem 1. *Let P be a program with anonymous cycles over $\langle \Sigma, \Sigma_{an} \rangle$, and $q \in \Sigma$. Then, we have that:*

$$\mathcal{HT}(f_{AC}(P, q)) = \mathcal{HT}(P)_{\|\{q\}}$$

We have defined an operator that forgets only one atom from a given program. In order to forget a set of atoms, we need to iterate the operator. Iteration is only possible if the operator is closed under the considered class of programs. Although fundamental, this property is not satisfied by some operators in the literature, namely the one in [16], thus not allowing the iteration of the operators. In the case of f_{AC}, we can prove that it is closed for the class of programs with anonymous cycles.

Proposition 3. *Let P be a logic program with anonymous cycles over $\langle \Sigma, \Sigma_{an} \rangle$ and $q \in \Sigma$. Then $f_{AC}(P, q)$ is a logic program with anonymous cycles over $\langle \Sigma \backslash \{q\}, \Sigma_{an} \rangle$.*

When forgetting a set of atoms iteratively, although the concrete result of forgetting depends on the order by which the atoms are forgotten, the following result shows that this is not a problem, in the sense that the results are strongly equivalent.

Proposition 4. *Let P be a program with anonymous cycles over $\langle \Sigma, \Sigma_{an} \rangle$, and $q_1, q_2 \in \Sigma$. Then we have that:*

$$f_{AC}(f_{AC}(P, q_1), q_2) \equiv f_{AC}(f_{AC}(P, q_2), q_1)$$

In order to define a concrete extension of the operator f_{AC} that allows forgetting a sets of atoms, we assume a fixed linear order on Σ, which we denote by $<$.

Definition 7. *Let P be a program with anonymous cycles over $\langle \Sigma, \Sigma_{an} \rangle$ and $V = \{q_1, q_2, \ldots, q_n\} \subseteq \Sigma$ a set of atoms with $q_i < q_j$ for each $1 \leq i < j \leq n$. The result of forgetting about V from P, denoted by $f_{AC}^*(P, V)$, is defined inductively as:*

$$f_{AC}^*(P, \emptyset) = P$$
$$f_{AC}^*(P, \{q_1, q_2, \ldots, q_n\}) = f_{AC}^*(f_{AC}(P, q_1), \{q_2, \ldots, q_n\})$$

Example 6. Consider the following program P:

$$a \leftarrow q. \qquad c \leftarrow p. \qquad p \leftarrow not\ q. \qquad q \leftarrow b, not\ p.$$

In order to forget about the set $V = \{p, q\}$ from P, we start by forgetting about p from P using f_{AC}. Since there are no cycles on p, f_{AC} does not introduce anonymous cycles, and we thus obtain the rules:

$$a \leftarrow q. \qquad c \leftarrow not\ q. \qquad q \leftarrow b, not\ not\ q.$$

If we now subsequently forget also q, and since now there are cycles on the atom to be forgotten, f_{AC} introduces anonymous cycles, and thus the following program with anonymous cycles is obtained:

$$a \leftarrow b, \delta. \qquad c \leftarrow not\ \delta. \qquad c \leftarrow not\ b. \qquad \delta \leftarrow not\ not\ \delta.$$

which is the result of $f_{AC}^*(P, \{p, q\})^3$.

We can now state the main result of the paper. Namely, our new operator f_{AC}^* satisfies (**SP**), thus making it the first (syntactical) operator that satisfies (**SP**) for all forgetting instances.

Theorem 2. *The operator f_{AC}^* satisfies (SP), i.e. for each program with anonymous cycles P over $\langle \Sigma, \Sigma_{an} \rangle$, and $V \subseteq \Sigma$, we have that*

$$\mathcal{AS}(f_{AC}^*(P, V) \cup R) = \mathcal{AS}(P \cup R)_{\|V},$$

for all programs R with $\Sigma(R) \subseteq \Sigma \backslash V$.

This result guarantees that we can use the operator f_{AC}^* to forget about a set of atoms from a program, while preserving all the dependencies between the atoms that were not forgotten. Given the already mentioned impossibility results of [11], the use of anonymous cycles is essential to allow the preservation of all dependencies. An important consequence of the previous theorem is the fact that f_{AC}^* satisfies also several other properties of forgetting. In particular, f_{AC}^* satisfies (**SI**), which guarantees that all rules of a program P not mentioning the atoms to be forgotten be preserved when forgetting. It is worth noting that, although (**SI**) is a desirable property for forgetting, several classes of forgetting operators in the literature fail to satisfy this condition.

---

[3] We could have chosen a different order by which p and q are forgotten, but, according to Proposition 4, the result would be strongly equivalent.

Proposition 5. *The operator f^*_{AC} satisfies* (**SI**).

An important consequence of this result, together with the fact that f^*_{AC} is a syntactic operator, is the fact that the result of forgetting about a set of atoms from a program P according to f^*_{AC} can ben obtained by a syntactic manipulation of only those rules of P that mention the atoms to be forgotten, while the remaining rules are simply preserved in the result of forgetting.

5   Conclusions

We enhanced the language of logic programming to include anonymous cycles so that we can express relations between atoms that, under traditional logic programming semantics, were only possible to be expressed by the help of third atoms that act as arbiters. We then used this enhanced language to formulate a syntactic operator that forgets atoms from logic programs while obeying *strong persistence*, and is closed under this language, which means that it can be iterated, making it possible for any number of atoms to be forgotten from a program, in any order, while still maintaining (**SP**). This is an improvement over existing operators, which either were only defined for very restricted classes of programs [16], or did not obey most desirable properties [6,25].

Future work includes investigating syntactic operators defined over traditional logic programs for the semantics in [13], that correspond to weaker versions of (**SP**), as well as investigating how forgetting relates to other operations such as updating [21], and how it translates to hybrid knowledge representation formalisms [3,17,22].

Acknowledgments. R. Gonçalves, M. Knorr, and J. Leite were partially supported by FCT projects FORGET (PTDC/CCI-INF/32219/2017) and NOVA LINCS (UID/CEC/04516/2019).

References

1. Aguado, F., Cabalar, P., Fandinno, J., Pearce, D., Pérez, G., Vidal, C.: Forgetting auxiliary atoms in forks. In: Proceedings of the ASPOCP@LPNMR, vol. 1868. CEUR-WS.org (2017)
2. Brass, S., Dix, J.: Semantics of (disjunctive) logic programs based on partial evaluation. J. Log. Program. **40**(1), 1–46 (1999)
3. Brewka, G., Ellmauthaler, S., Gonçalves, R., Knorr, M., Leite, J., Pührer, J.: Reactive multi-context systems: heterogeneous reasoning in dynamic environments. Artif. Intell. **256**, 68–104 (2018)
4. Cabalar, P., Pearce, D., Valverde, A.: Minimal logic programs. In: Dahl, V., Niemelä, I. (eds.) ICLP 2007. LNCS, vol. 4670, pp. 104–118. Springer, Heidelberg (2007). https://doi.org/10.1007/978-3-540-74610-2_8
5. Delgrande, J.P., Wang, K.: A syntax-independent approach to forgetting in disjunctive logic programs. In: Proceedings of AAAI, pp. 1482–1488. AAAI Press (2015)

6. Eiter, T., Wang, K.: Semantic forgetting in answer set programming. Artif. Intell. **172**(14), 1644–1672 (2008)
7. Gonçalves, R., Janhunen, T., Knorr, M., Leite, J., Woltran, S.: Variable elimination for DLP-functions. In: Proceedings of KR, pp. 643–644. AAAI Press (2018)
8. Gonçalves, R., Janhunen, T., Knorr, M., Leite, J., Woltran, S.: Forgetting in modular answer set programming. In: Proceedigs of AAAI. AAAI Press (2019)
9. Gonçalves, R., Knorr, M., Leite, J.: Forgetting in ASP: the forgotten properties. In: Michael, L., Kakas, A. (eds.) JELIA 2016. LNCS (LNAI), vol. 10021, pp. 543–550. Springer, Cham (2016). https://doi.org/10.1007/978-3-319-48758-8_37
10. Goncalves, R., Knorr, M., Leite, J.: The ultimate guide to forgetting in answer set programming. In: Proceedings of KR, pp. 135–144. AAAI Press (2016)
11. Gonçalves, R., Knorr, M., Leite, J.: You can't always forget what you want: on the limits of forgetting in answer set programming. In: Proceedings of ECAI, pp. 957–965. IOS Press (2016)
12. Gonçalves, R., Knorr, M., Leite, J.: Iterative variable elimination in ASP. In: Oliveira, E., Gama, J., Vale, Z., Lopes Cardoso, H. (eds.) EPIA 2017. LNCS (LNAI), vol. 10423, pp. 643–656. Springer, Cham (2017). https://doi.org/10.1007/978-3-319-65340-2_53
13. Gonçalves, R., Knorr, M., Leite, J., Woltran, S.: When you must forget: beyond strong persistence when forgetting in answer set programming. TPLP **17**(5–6), 837–854 (2017)
14. Inoue, K., Sakama, C.: Negation as failure in the head. J. Log. Program. **35**(1), 39–78 (1998)
15. Inoue, K., Sakama, C.: Equivalence of logic programs under updates. In: Alferes, J.J., Leite, J. (eds.) JELIA 2004. LNCS (LNAI), vol. 3229, pp. 174–186. Springer, Heidelberg (2004). https://doi.org/10.1007/978-3-540-30227-8_17
16. Knorr, M., Alferes, J.J.: Preserving strong equivalence while forgetting. In: Fermé, E., Leite, J. (eds.) JELIA 2014. LNCS (LNAI), vol. 8761, pp. 412–425. Springer, Cham (2014). https://doi.org/10.1007/978-3-319-11558-0_29
17. Knorr, M., Alferes, J.J., Hitzler, P.: Local closed world reasoning with description logics under the well-founded semantics. Artif. Intell. **175**(9–10), 1528–1554 (2011)
18. Leite, J.: A bird's-eye view of forgetting in answer-set programming. In: Balduccini, M., Janhunen, T. (eds.) LPNMR 2017. LNCS (LNAI), vol. 10377, pp. 10–22. Springer, Cham (2017). https://doi.org/10.1007/978-3-319-61660-5_2
19. Lifschitz, V., Pearce, D., Valverde, A.: Strongly equivalent logic programs. ACM Trans. Comput. Log. **2**(4), 526–541 (2001)
20. Slota, M., Leite, J.: Back and forth between rules and SE-models. In: Delgrande, J.P., Faber, W. (eds.) LPNMR 2011. LNCS (LNAI), vol. 6645, pp. 174–186. Springer, Heidelberg (2011). https://doi.org/10.1007/978-3-642-20895-9_16
21. Slota, M., Leite, J.: The rise and fall of semantic rule updates based on se-models. TPLP **14**(6), 869–907 (2014)
22. Slota, M., Leite, J., Swift, T.: On updates of hybrid knowledge bases composed of ontologies and rules. Artif. Intell. **229**, 33–104 (2015)
23. Wang, Y., Wang, K., Zhang, M.: Forgetting for answer set programs revisited. In: Rossi, F. (ed.) Proceedings of IJCAI, pp. 1162–1168. IJCAI/AAAI (2013)
24. Wang, Y., Zhang, Y., Zhou, Y., Zhang, M.: Knowledge forgetting in answer set programming. J. Artif. Intell. Res. (JAIR) **50**, 31–70 (2014)
25. Zhang, Y., Foo, N.Y.: Solving logic program conflict through strong and weak forgettings. Artif. Intell. **170**(8–9), 739–778 (2006)

MultiAgent Systems: Theory and Applications

Self-adaptive Team of Aquatic Drones with a Communication Network for Aquaculture

Daniela Sousa[1,2]($\boxtimes$), Susana Sargento[1,2] ⓘ, Artur Pereira[2] ⓘ,
and Miguel Luís[1] ⓘ

[1] Instituto de Telecomunicações, 3810-193 Aveiro, Portugal
nmal@av.it.pt
[2] Departamento de Eletrónica, Telecomunicações e Informática,
University of Aveiro, 3810-193 Aveiro, Portugal
{dcsousa,susana,artur}@ua.pt

Abstract. The use of Unmanned Surface Vehicle (USV) teams, more commonly known as drones, has become increasingly common for aquaculture scenarios due to their availability and low cost. For monitoring to be feasible and in real time, it is necessary for the drones to be in constant communication so that they can organize themselves and send data to a land platform. This paper presents a cooperative navigation behavior in constant communication with the network layer to achieve a better overall performance in the coverage of a space and a better network quality between heterogeneous USVs. In conclusion, increasing the amount of USVs is beneficial as long as an Avoid or Assist does not impact the overall time.

Keywords: Unmanned Surface Vehicles ·
Cooperative perception and navigation · Target allocation

1 Introduction

Over the past years, aquaculture has taken a bigger role in the economy, and with it the need for aquatic monitoring also increased. Unmanned Surface Vehicle (USVs) have been deployed to reduce the human effort and increase efficiency in these tasks. According to Ramos et al. [19], a better overall performance can be achieved with a group of cooperative USVs. Moreover, since the aquaculture tanks can be off the coast, the platform should integrate multi-technologies (long and short-range) for a better real-time data gathering. However, we cannot plan a trajectory in advance, because the number of USVs and the map can change while the task is being completed, and furthermore, the network quality is dependent on external factors. This work proposes the development of an aquatic platform where the navigation decisions are influenced by the network, and the network takes an important role on the synchronization and transmission

ⓒ Springer Nature Switzerland AG 2019
P. Moura Oliveira et al. (Eds.): EPIA 2019, LNAI 11805, pp. 569–580, 2019.
https://doi.org/10.1007/978-3-030-30244-3_47

of navigation information. The team uses the network to cooperatively perceive the location of each USV and the obstacles, and create the map, which is then used to search a path to the allocated target. Furthermore, in order to ensure that no drone is left isolated, it is necessary for the team to be able to self-adapt, meaning that USVs must determine new positions and change their new locations considering the quality of the connection between them, while allowing the team's shape to dynamically change for a better performance on the task completion. In the course of this work, a simulation environment was also developed [22] to test the team's navigation behavior. The results show that the proposed platform is able to cover large areas while allocating the targets, which take into consideration the sensors that each USV has. From the different topologies tested for the specific scenario described here, five USVs are the optimal team topology. The remainder of this paper is organized as follows. Section 3 presents the platform architecture overview and the aquatic elements. Section 4 describes the navigation behavior of the team and each USV, and then Sect. 5 presents the evaluation of the path planning in different scenarios. Finally, Sect. 6 presents the conclusions and ideas for future work.

2   Related Work

Several USV platforms have been developed for aquatic monitoring. Ferreira et al. [9] presented a swarm of affordable USVs (FLEXUS) with WiFi capabilities for water-based Internet of Things (IoT) platforms. López et al. [13] presented a centralized approach with a master slave architecture to measure pH and temperature levels. Lloret et al. [12] proposed a platform where a coverage of 100% of the tanks can be achieved by the USVs' mobility grouped with the number of vehicles. AquaBotix developed the SwarmDiver [2], where several vehicles can work simultaneously as a single coordinated entity communicating with each other. Each vehicle contains only a pressure and a temperature sensor, and relies on a single communication technology. Paravisi et al. [17] presented a simulator with realistic environmental disturbances in order to test coordination in teams of USVs. Berger et al. [4] presented a multi-system of heterogeneous Unmanned Aerial Vehicles, where the area coverage can be maximized by dividing the area between platforms. However they do not maintain connectivity between vehicles.

By using a network and its protocols, the team can build up navigation information. An example of this communication-aided navigation mechanism is described by Ducatelle et al. [7], where all robots periodically share their navigation tables through a mobile *ad hoc* network (MANET). To maintain the formation in a team, several structures have been proposed. With centralized control topology we have the leader-follower approach [6, 10, 16, 18], and the virtual structure approach [5, 15, 23]. However, the behavior-based structure approach [3, 21] allows decentralized control. The A* algorithm [20] is one of the most popular search algorithms in graphs used in path planning algorithms. To improve the translation of the map to the graph used by the A*, some approaches like Basic Theta* and Phi* were introduced according to Duchoň et al. [8], where Basic

Theta* relies on testing the visibility between cells, and Phi* relies on defining the range in which the local predecessor of each evaluated cell can be found.

The path planning of multiple vehicles is more complex than single vehicle path planning, due to the optimization of multiple objectives [11]. Formation path planning can be categorized in two disciplines: deterministic and heuristic approaches. Heuristic approaches are strong for multi-optimization problems that require fast computational speed, and according to Liu et al. [11], these algorithms use decentralized control topologies.

3   Platform Architecture

The proposed platform, illustrated in Fig. 1, is comprised by a team of USVs with one Mobile Gateway that communicates with an Infrastructure Gateway on land. This Infrastructure Gateway is connected to a Server that stores sensed information, which is then used by end-user applications such as a real time dashboard and alert platform.

As illustrated in Fig. 2, the USV software structure is divided in three layers:

- **Sensors and Actuators:** This layer is responsible for reading the sensors through multiple protocols (I2C, SPI, 1-Wire, and others), and control the motor rotation speeds and direction according to the commands received from the Path Planning Layer.
- **Communication:** This layer comprises two technologies for communication, LoRa for long range and WiFi for short range. The team can use both technologies to connect the Mobile Gateways to the Infrastructure Gateways, however only WiFi is used in inter-USVs communications. Between them a Delay Tolerant Network (DTN) was implemented with a link quality-based routing strategy described in [22].
- **Path Planning:** This layer is responsible for the update and synchronization of the team's navigation information given by the Communication Layer and the map. It also manages the allocation of new sensing points, and calculates the trajectory avoiding obstacles. This module should maintain the connectivity between the team's members. The avoidance of mobile obstacles is made by fusing the shared USV's positions and the on-board obstacle sensor. Furthermore, this layer communicates the next waypoint to the Sensors and Actuators Layer.

4   Cooperative Navigation

4.1   Individual Path Planning

The first step of many path planning systems is to describe the environment into a map suitable for the chosen path planning algorithm. In this work, a fixed-size cell decomposition grid map is used, where well-known search algorithms can be applied, like A*. Each cell is square with side equal to the length of a USV,

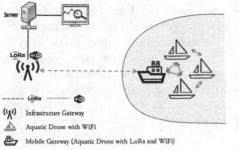 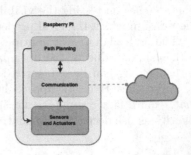

Fig. 1. Platform overview.   **Fig. 2.** USV's software architecture.

and cells occupied with USVs do not count as occupied cells when computing a path to a target. The location of each USV on the map is given by the relative difference in latitude and longitude from a given reference point shared by all USVs. An algorithm based on Basic Theta* is used (USV-A*), where a path is decomposed in fewer straight lines utilizing the Supercover Line algorithm by Andres et al. [1], to produce the intersected cells, where a line crossing two cells by the vertexes also occupies the adjacent cells. The algorithm starts from the target position and passes through all the trajectory points until the straight line drawn intersects any occupied cell. This process solves the problem of a scenario where the path does not cross an occupied cell, but the vehicle, due to its width, may cause a collision. Figure 3 presents a graphic comparison of the paths produced by a standard A* for a grid map and A* with a graph redefined at run time.

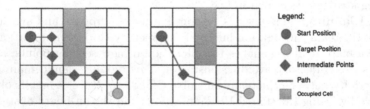

Fig. 3. Graphic comparison of the trajectories produced by the standard A* on the left, and, on the right, the proposed Path Planning algorithm.

4.2   Multiple Vehicle Path Planning

The nature of path planning of a team of unmanned vehicles is an optimization of multiple objectives, which is more complex than single path planning. Figure 4 compares the two processes.

The multiple vehicle path planning algorithm has to comply with three main objectives:

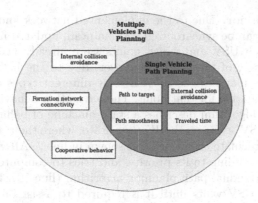

Fig. 4. Comparison of formation and single path planning inspired by [11].

- Maintain connectivity between all vehicles;
- Achieve cooperative behavior for full coverage, while minimizing traveled time;
- Avoid collisions between the vehicles.

A formation control structure similar to the *leader-follower* structure is here proposed to maintain connectivity in simple scenarios.

A ranking system is also proposed, based on a heuristic approach to deal with multi-optimization problems. This system gives a priority value to each USV, in order to choose the target that each vehicle will visit, the team's collision avoidance behavior, and each vehicle's leader-follower behavior.

Leader-Follower Behavior. Each USV on the team has a priority value, and each USV has to maintain connectivity with only one vehicle. Furthermore, if the connection's quality is weak, the USV has to follow the immediately higher ranked USV. Therefore, each vehicle is both a leader and a follower for different USVs, with the exception for the higher and lower ranked.

Priority Calculation. Two ranking systems with a different set of rules are here considered, denoted R1 and R2. **R1** sets the priorities based on a single rule: the USV closest to an available target has the highest priority. **R2** presents a more complex set of rules, where we distinguish a USV with priority 1 from the others. For the USV with priority 1, we choose the one with a minimum number of neighbors, or if there is more than one with the same score, we choose the one with the minimal path cost to a target. For the remainder USVs, we also prioritize the ones with a minimum number of neighbors, and if more than one with the same score exist, the one with minimum distance to a neighbor is chosen. If, however rarely, more than one USV with the same cost exists, then a priority is given to each one of them increasing by 1 to the next USV. For example, if there were two USVs, the first one calculated would have priority p and the other priority $p + 1$.

Navigation Behavior. Due to the implemented network and the transmitted packets, the team can be synchronized and maintain updated information about the location of each USV and which points were already visited, cooperating on the total coverage of the space. Moreover, due to the heterogeneity of the USVs, some points may have to be visited by different types of USVs in order to get all the information for that point. The navigation behavior is described in Algorithm 1. This algorithm describes a state machine of behaviors followed by each USV. Each USV starts on the *Waiting* state, where the ranking system (R1 or R2) is used to calculate the priority, as shown in line 7. Afterwards, the vessel chooses a target according to its priority, and tries to compute a path with the aforementioned individual path planning algorithm (line 10). If no more points are available, the USV waits until it is required to assist on maintaining the network connectivity (line 13). While heading towards the chosen target, if the quality of the connection to its leader passes a threshold, then the USV assumes the Assist state, following the leader towards its last known location (line 23). In a worst case scenario, all the follower USVs' trajectories can be affected, and the team starts adjusting the trajectory to follow the leader to maintain connectivity. If a USV enters the USV avoidance area, then the vehicle with lower priority stops and lets the one with higher priority pass through (line 27). Afterwards, it resumes its path to the designated target (line 42). If a static obstacle is found, then the USV stops moving, ignores the current target and changes to the Waiting state. At this time, the map already has this static obstacle included and the new path for the same point or a new one already avoids it (line 30). After each allocation of a new target, the information is passed to the communication layer to be transmitted to other USVs, using the neighbors' announcements. The team is then triggered to recalculate its priorities and change to Waiting state (line 4).

5 Evaluation

In the scope of the SmartBioR project [14], maritime biology experts concluded that a way to address the several points of interest is by evenly scattering the points to be sensed on a grid. Therefore, a scenario with a tank-like shape in accordance with these specifications was designed. In this scenario, 10 experiments with random USVs' initial positions were conducted for each test.

Several tests were conducted to evaluate both sets of priority rules and the team topology. The results of the two first tests are shown in Fig. 5, where we compare the two sets of priority rules (R1 and R2) and how they are affected by the reassignment of targets when the priority is recalculated (line 10 of Algorithm 1). This experiment uses 4 equal boats (topology F in Table 1) and shows the normalized time taken for the experiment to complete, and the normalized amount of times that an event happens. The normalized time is calculated considering the time taken for a single USV to complete an exemplary path, shown in Fig. 6. As an example, 0.5 means that the experiment took half the time of the same one with 1 single USV. The amount of events is normalized with respect to

---

Algorithm 1: Navigation Decision Logic.

```
1  status = Waiting
2  while not all points visited do
3  │   if recalculate priority triggered then
4  │   │    status = Waiting
5  │   switch status do
6  │   │   case Waiting do
7  │   │   │    p = calculate_priority()
8  │   │   │    path = null
9  │   │   │    while path == null do
                                              ▷ path not found
10 │   │   │   │   point, path = choose_next_available_point(p)
                       ▷ When path for a point is not found, the point is
                       discarded
11 │   │   │   │   if point == null then
12 │   │   │   │   │    break
13 │   │   │    if point == null then
14 │   │   │   │   if losing connection to leader then
15 │   │   │   │   │    follow_leader
16 │   │   │   │   │    status = Assist
17 │   │   │   │   else
18 │   │   │   │   │    continue
19 │   │   │    else
20 │   │   │   │   go_to(point)
21 │   │   │   │   status = Navigate
22 │   │   case Navigate do
23 │   │   │    if losing connection to leader then
24 │   │   │   │   free_point
25 │   │   │   │   follow_leader()
26 │   │   │   │   status = Assist
27 │   │   │    else if mobile_obstacle in avoidance area and it has a higher
                 priority then
28 │   │   │   │   Stop_moving
29 │   │   │   │   status = Avoid
30 │   │   │    else if static_obstacle in avoidance area then
31 │   │   │   │   Stop_moving
32 │   │   │   │   status = Waiting
33 │   │   │    else
34 │   │   │   │    go_to(point)
35 │   │   case Assist do
36 │   │   │    if good connection to leader then
37 │   │   │   │   status = Waiting
38 │   │   │    else
39 │   │   │   │    follow_leader()
40 │   │   case Avoid do
41 │   │   │    if mobile_obstacle no longer in avoidance area then
42 │   │   │   │   go_to(point)
43 │   │   │   │   status = Navigate
44 │   │   │    else
45 │   │   │   │    Stop_moving
46 │   wait new_info_entry
```

---

a maximum threshold for those events, which in the Assists case means 40 events, and for the Repeated Points and Avoids means 10 events. The results include the mean of 5 repetitions for each experiment and 95% confidence interval.

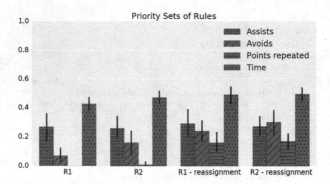

Fig. 5. Comparison between R1 and R2 with and without reassignment of targets.

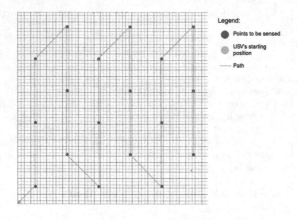

Fig. 6. Path done by a single USV.

To characterize the performance of the algorithms, only two variables are taken into account: Repeated Points and Time. The Time should be minimized and, for experiments with close Time values, minimizing the Repeated Points can provide a valuable reduction in resource use at the cost of a small Time increase. Moreover, the Avoids and Assists events, as expected, increase the Time taken to complete an experiment.

We can observe that reassigning targets every time the priority is recalculated leads to an increase of repeated points explored by different USVs. This is due to the delay on the synchronization of information among the network. When the assigned targets rapidly change, the network is unable to maintain updated information on each vehicle. This leads to multiple vehicles exploring the same target, thus increasing the repeated points and wasting resources.

R2 was proposed with the goal of promoting the network's quality and number of connections. The USVs at the edges of the network, with fewer neighbors, gain priority and will try to maintain connection through the Assist behavior. As expected, in this scenario, where the points are evenly distributed, the data gathering causes the team to spread, leading to more Assists behaviors triggered. When comparing R1 and R2, we can see that R2 takes slightly more time and has Repeated Points, making R1 more efficient.

The second experiment was conducted with R1 and no reassignment, and each test was repeated five times. Table 1 describes several topologies, comparing the number of USVs with their types, where each type considers a different set of sensors. Table 1 also contains the legend of the tests performed on this experiment.

Table 1. Teams' topologies description.

Name	Number of USVs	Type 1 IDs	Type 2 IDs
A	2	1	2
B	3	1 and 2	3
C	4	1, 2 and 4	3
D	4	1 and 3	2, 3 and 4
E	4	1 and 2	3 and 4
F	4	1, 2, 3 and 4	1, 2, 3 and 4
G	5	1, 2, 3, 4 and 5	1, 2, 3, 4 and 5
H	6	1, 2, 3, 4, 5 and 6	1, 2, 3, 4, 5 and 6

Figure 7 shows a comparison of the results of these topologies, with the goal of decreasing the time taken to complete the experiment. Each point needs to be sensed by the sensors in Type 1 and in Type 2. Some vehicles may have both types, due to the fact that it is more expensive to have two boats with different sets than to have one with all sensors.

We have observed that USVs of different types tend to group and sense the same points. We define a full set as a USV with both types (full USV), or two USVs of different types. In tests A, B and C, we can see that the time taken is directly proportional to the number of full sets that is available in the topology. When we increase the amount of USVs without increasing the amount of full sets, the number of Avoids and triggered Assists increases. In tests D and E, we compare the introduction of a full USV. When these types of USVs are introduced with an uneven number of single type USVs, the full USV tends to follow the USV that is not in a full set, thus repeating the sensed points.

In tests F, G and H, we increase the amount of full sets, with the goal of decreasing the time of the experiment and discovering the trade-off point between the time and the number of full sets. Comparing tests F and G, we can see that the time decreases, but the number of Avoids also increases. In test H, the Avoids

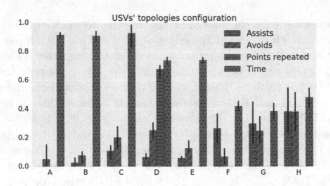

Fig. 7. Teams' topologies comparison.

are higher, which affects the time of the experiment, no longer compensating the increasing amount of USVs.

In conclusion, in this scenario the best solution with respect to the time of the experiment is G, with 5 full sets. Cheaper solutions can be found with the trade-off between the amount of full sets and the properties shown. For example, if we want to minimize the Avoids, Assists and Repeated points, solution A should be chosen. If we want to minimize the time along with the other properties, solution F is efficient.

6   Conclusions

This work aimed to outline and develop the infrastructure needed to build a self-adaptive team for aquatic monitoring, while integrating it in an already deployed platform.

A comparative assessment of the leader-follower behavior was conducted, where we concluded that the set of Rules R1 without reassignment is the most time effective for the scenario described. However, both sets of Rules can maintain network connectivity to all the USVs in the team. Lastly, we evaluated the team's topologies in the described scenario, where the most time effective solution is having five full USVs to achieve full coverage.

As future work, we plan to address multiple dynamic swarms of drones, where each drone can belong to different swarms in a dynamic approach on the path planning task.

Acknowledgements. This work was funded by the European Regional Development Fund (FEDER), through the Competitiveness and Internationalization Operational Programme (COMPETE 2020) of the Portugal 2020 by the Project MOBI-WISE, POCI-01-0145-FEDER-016426, through the Programa Integrado de IC&DT Centro2020 by the project "SmartBioR: Valorizacao Inteligente de Recursos Biologicos Marinhos Endogenos num Clima em Mudanca", Centro-01-0145-FEDER-000018, and through Urban Innovative Actions Initiative by the project AVEIRO STEAM City, UIA03-084.

References

1. Andres, E., Nehlig, P., Françon, J.: Supercover of straight lines, planes and triangles. In: Ahronovitz, E., Fiorio, C. (eds.) DGCI 1997. LNCS, vol. 1347, pp. 243–254. Springer, Heidelberg (1997). https://doi.org/10.1007/BFb0024845
2. AquaBotix: SwarmDiver Brochure. www.aquabotix.com/images/SwarmDiver%20Brochure%208.23.18.pdf. Accessed 19 Nov 2018
3. Balch, T., Arkin, R.C.: Behavior-based formation control for multirobot teams. IEEE Trans. Robot. Autom. 14(6), 926–939 (1998). https://doi.org/10.1109/70.736776
4. Berger, C., Wzorek, M., Kvarnström, J., Conte, G., Doherty, P., Eriksson, A.: Area coverage with heterogeneous UAVs using scan patterns. In: 2016 IEEE International Symposium on Safety, Security, and Rescue Robotics (SSRR), pp. 342–349, October 2016. https://doi.org/10.1109/SSRR.2016.7784325
5. Cong, B.L., Liu, X.D., Chen, Z.: Distributed attitude synchronization of formation flying via consensus-based virtual structure. Acta Astronaut. 68(11), 1973–1986 (2011). https://doi.org/10.1016/j.actaastro.2010.11.014. http://www.sciencedirect.com/science/article/pii/S0094576510004303
6. Cui, R., Ge, S.S., How, B.V.E., Choo, Y.S.: Leader-follower formation control of underactuated autonomous underwater vehicles. Ocean Eng. 37(17), 1491–1502 (2010). https://doi.org/10.1016/j.oceaneng.2010.07.006. http://www.sciencedirect.com/science/article/pii/S0029801810001678
7. Ducatelle, F., et al.: Cooperative navigation in robotic swarms. Swarm Intell. 8, 1–33 (2014). https://doi.org/10.1007/s11721-013-0089-4
8. Duchoň, F., et al.: Path planning with modified a star algorithm for a mobile robot. Procedia Eng. 96, 59–69 (2014)
9. Ferreira, B., et al.: Flexible unmanned surface vehicles enabling future internet experimentally-driven research. In: OCEANS 2017 - Aberdeen, pp. 1–6, June 2017. https://doi.org/10.1109/OCEANSE.2017.8084934
10. Kowalczyk, W., Kozlowski, K.: Leader-follower control and collision avoidance for the formation of differentially-driven mobile robots. In: 2018 23rd International Conference on Methods Models in Automation Robotics (MMAR), pp. 132–137, August 2018
11. Liu, Y., Bucknall, R.: Path planning algorithm for unmanned surface vehicle formations in a practical maritime environment. Ocean Eng. 97, 126–144 (2015). https://doi.org/10.1016/j.oceaneng.2015.01.008. http://www.sciencedirect.com/science/article/pii/S0029801815000165
12. Lloret, J., Sendra, S., Garcia, M., Lloret, G.: Group-based underwater wireless sensor network for marine fish farms. In: 2011 IEEE GLOBECOM Workshops (GC Wkshps), pp. 115–119, December 2011. https://doi.org/10.1109/GLOCOMW.2011.6162361
13. López, M., Gómez, J.M., Sabater, J., Herms, A.: IEEE 802.15.4 based wireless monitoring of pH and temperature in a fish farm. In: Melecon 2010–2010 15th IEEE Mediterranean Electrotechnical Conference, pp. 575–580, April 2010. https://doi.org/10.1109/MELCON.2010.5476024
14. MARE: SmartBioR project. http://www.mare-centre.pt/en/node/703. Accessed 19 Nov 2018
15. Mehrjerdi, H., Ghommam, J., Saad, M.: Nonlinear coordination control for a group of mobile robots using a virtual structure. Mechatronics 21(7), 1147–1155 (2011). https://doi.org/10.1016/j.mechatronics.2011.06.006. http://www.sciencedirect.com/science/article/pii/S0957415811001127

16. Morbidi, F., Bullo, F., Prattichizzo, D.: Visibility maintenance via controlled invariance for leader–follower vehicle formations. Automatica **47**(5), 1060–1067 (2011). https://doi.org/10.1016/j.automatica.2011.01.065. http://www.sciencedirect.com/science/article/pii/S000510981100080X

17. Paravisi, M., Santos, D.H., Jorge, V., Heck, G., Gonçalves, L.M., Amory, A.: Unmanned surface vehicle simulator with realistic environmental disturbances. Sensors **19**(5) (2019). https://doi.org/10.3390/s19051068. https://www.mdpi.com/1424-8220/19/5/1068

18. Peng, Z., Wen, G., Rahmani, A., Yu, Y.: Leader–follower formation control of nonholonomic mobile robots based on a bioinspired neurodynamic based approach. Robot. Auton. Syst. **61**(9), 988–996 (2013). https://doi.org/10.1016/j.robot.2013.05.004. http://www.sciencedirect.com/science/article/pii/S092188901300095X

19. Ramos, D., Oliveira, L., Almeida, L., Moreno, U.: Network interference on cooperative mobile robots consensus. Robot 2015: Second Iberian Robotics Conference. AISC, vol. 417, pp. 651–663. Springer, Cham (2016). https://doi.org/10.1007/978-3-319-27146-0_50

20. Russell, S.J., Norvig, P.: Artificial Intelligence: A Modern Approach. Pearson Education Limited, Malaysia, Kuala Lumpur (2016)

21. Shiell, N.: Behaviour-based pattern formation in a swarm of anonymous robots. Ph.D. thesis, Memorial University of Newfoundland (2017)

22. Sousa, D., Luís, M., Sargento, S., Pereira, A.: An aquatic mobile sensing USV swarm with a link quality-based delay tolerant network. Sensors **18**(10) (2018). https://doi.org/10.3390/s18103440. http://www.mdpi.com/1424-8220/18/10/3440

23. Zhou, D., Wang, Z., Schwager, M.: Agile coordination and assistive collision avoidance for quadrotor swarms using virtual structures. IEEE Trans. Robot. **34**(4), 916–923 (2018). https://doi.org/10.1109/TRO.2018.2857477

Assessment of Testability on Multiagent Systems Developed with Organizational Model Moise

Eder Mateus Gonçalves$^{(\boxtimes)}$ ⓘ, Bruno Coelho Rodrigues,
and Ricardo Arend Machado

Center for Computational Sciences, Universidade Federal do Rio Grande - FURG,
Rio Grande, RS, Brazil
edergoncalves@furg.br, brunocoelho.r@gmail.com, ricardoarend@gmail.com

Abstract. Trying to guarantee some level of correctness for multiagent systems (MAS) is a hard task once we are dealing with systems that inherently has properties such as autonomy, reactivity, pro-activity, and social skills. The social dimension of a MAS can be described with an organizational model, where agents are structured using concepts like groups, roles and must obey some norms. It would be useful to dimension how many tests are necessary to validate an organizational model as a metric for validation and verification processes. In this paper, we propose a method to assess the testability of an organizational model specified with Moise. Using a graphical process based on Coloured Petri Nets (CPN), the method indicates the number of test cases necessary to validate a Moise model. In a broad view, the obtained results are an important metric to evaluate the complexity of validation of a social dimension of a MAS.

Keywords: Testability · Moise · Organization · Petri Nets

1 Introduction

Testing in Multiagent Systems (MAS) can be framed into the verification and validation area. According to [2], the main formal method used to verify MAS is Model Checking, and its variants, when compared with other techniques such as Theorem Proving, Simulation, and even Runtime Testing and Debugging [1,4]. In [12], a mapping is proposed between testing for traditional software and its similar steps for MAS. On the other hand, Petri Nets can be seen as a solid solution for formal verification in MAS [7,19].

How to test something that naturally has some level of uncertainty? How to test software with so different levels of development?

We start to answer these questions by isolating one of these levels. The social dimension of a MAS can be specified and structured through an organizational model. An organizational structure can reduce the scope of interactions between

P. Moura Oliveira et al. (Eds.): EPIA 2019, LNAI 11805, pp. 581–592, 2019.
https://doi.org/10.1007/978-3-030-30244-3_48

agents, reduce or explicitly increase redundancy of a system, or formalize high-level system goals, of which a single agent may be not aware [20]. From another perspective, an organization can be seen as a set of behavioural constraints that a group of agents adopts in order to control the agent's autonomy and easily achieve their goals purposes [6].

One of the most referenced organizational models is $\mathcal{M}$oise, a model which proposes an organizational modelling language that explicitly decomposes a specification into structural, functional and deontic dimensions. The structural dimension describes organizations using concepts such as *roles*, *groups* and *links*. The functional dimension describes a system by global collective goals that must be achieved. The deontic dimension realize the binding between the structural and functional dimensions, where it defines *permissions* for each role and *obligations* for missions [14].

Because testing a MAS is a complex task, we propose to decompose this challenge in its different dimensions and complexity. In this paper, we propose the following research questions: how testable is the social dimension of a MAS? More specifically, *how testable is a $\mathcal{M}$oise specification?*

The goal of this paper is to propose a method to assess the testability of $\mathcal{M}$oise specifications, where testability has the same conception proposed by [21], i.e., the outcome of a testability method indicates the number of test cases necessary to validate a specification. Considering the distributed and asynchronous nature of an organizational model, the method is based on Coloured Petri Nets [15] that is able to integrate the three dimensions of a $\mathcal{M}$oise description. Employing a method that counts the different paths inside a net, the method proposed indicates the number of test cases necessary to verify a $\mathcal{M}$oise specification. We apply the method in a classical example of $\mathcal{M}$oise in the literature demonstrating that it is able to manage the most common scenarios for this kind of description.

The paper presents three main contributions: (i) a mapping of the testability method presented in [21] into a method using Ordinary Petri Nets; (ii) a method to describe a $\mathcal{M}$oise specification in Coloured Petri Nets (CPN) integrating the structural, functional and deontic specifications in a only description; and (iii) a software that reads a CPN description and transforms it into a directed graph, counting the number of paths within this graph, which represents the degree of testability of a $\mathcal{M}$oise model.

2   Testability for $\mathcal{M}$oise

The notion of *testability* used in this paper was initially proposed by WINIKOFF and CRANEFIELD [22], i.e., testability of a program is a (numerical) metric that indicates the effort required to adequately test a program. More specifically, it is the number of tests required for the satisfaction of a test adequacy criterion. It can be seen as a strategy to mitigate the testing problem, where at first is necessary to dimension the testing scenarios, and after that, to generate the necessary scenarios for validation. The method proposes an equation set that indicates the number of tests necessary to cover all edges in a control-flow graph, which corresponds to a specific BDI program.

Next subsections explain the mapping process between the one proposed at [21] in Ordinary Petri Nets and after that its application in the context of a $\mathcal{M}$oise organizational model including extensions in the mapping using Coloured Petri Nets.

2.1   The Mapping

We start describing our method proposing a mapping between that one described in [21] using a flow-control graph, and a Petri Net [18].

Figure 1 describes an example of a flow-control graph of a BDI program. It starts in the node S and has four possible actions: α_1, α_2, α_3 and α_4. If any of these actions are successfully executed, then the program executes the node Y and ends at node E. However, if action α_1 fails, the program advances for α_2, that in its turn can also fail, advancing for α_3, and so on. This program demands five tests to cover all the possibilities, one for each action being executed successfully, and one more where all the actions failed. Each test scenario can be understood as a different path inside the graph, once there are five different paths from S until E.

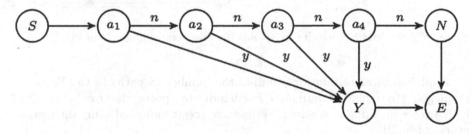

Fig. 1. A flow-control graph describing a BDI program, adapted from [21].

The equations proposed in [21] compute the least number of paths required to start a program in S and ending in E. It finds which paths are successful, going through Y, and the paths which fail, passing through N. The method defines $p(P)$ as the number of paths demanded to cover all edges in the graph corresponding to the program P, $y(P)$ for the paths that go through Y and $n(P)$ for the paths that go through N, resulting in $p(P) = y(P) + n(P)$.

A graph describing a control-flow as a state machine can be easily translated into an Ordinary Petri Net. A Petri Net is a graphical and mathematical modelling method used to model and analyze discrete event systems [5]. Thus, we formally propose a mapping Petri Net from a control-flow graph as a 6-tuple: $PNM = (P, T, F, W, M_o, M_f)$, where P is a finite set of places with dimension n which corresponds to action nodes in a control-flow graph; T is a finite set of transitions with dimension m which corresponds to edges connecting nodes in a control-flow graph; the flow relation between P and T is denoted by $F \subseteq (P \times T) \cap (T \times P)$ which corresponds to flow relations in a control-flow graph; $W : F \rightarrow \{0, 1, 2, ...\}$ is a weight function; $M_0 : P \rightarrow \{0, 1, 2, ...\}$ is the initial marking, which corresponds to an initial state, which must mark the places corresponding the initial nodes in a control-flow graph; and $M_f : P \rightarrow \{0, 1, 2, ...\}$ is the final marking, which corresponds to a final state, which must mark the final nodes in a control-flow graph. Tokens distributed in places represent the state of a system [17, 18].

Applying these mapping model, the flow-control graph presented in Fig. 1 is converted in a Petri Net as described in Fig. 2, where S is the place corresponding to the initial state and E is the final place.

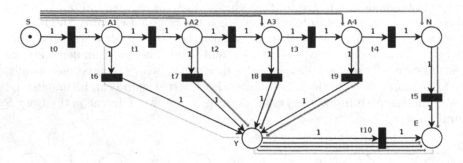

Fig. 2. Petri Net which corresponds the flow-control graph from Fig. 1.

Applying an algorithm for counting the number of paths in the Petri Net graph going from place S until place E will indicate 5 paths, that can be identified by 5 arrows with different colors, as the same result indicated using the method proposed in [21].

At this point, it is necessary to make a statement about this method using Petri Net: the goal is not to substitute the method proposed in [21] for testability on BDI programs, once it has more solid results. Applying the Petri Net model in a more general context involving BDI description demands a more meaningful investigation including results and theoretical background. The formalization of this mapping Petri Net is necessary as a first step in the sense of a mapping able to incorporate elements of a more complex model, like those in $\mathcal{M}$oise, once it has social structures integrating different dimensions of a specification.

2.2   Extending the Method: Incorporating $\mathcal{M}$oise Elements into the Mapping Petri Net

In a global view of the development of a MAS, we consider that it has three main dimensions: the social level, the communication aspects, and the agent level [9]. We understand that the work presented by [21] solves the testability question at the agent level. Here, we propose a method that constrains the testability problem to the social level of a MAS, more specifically, those systems that are specified with a $\mathcal{M}$oise organizational model.

In a MAS, an organization can be seen as a roles collection, relationships and authority structures that regulate behaviors. The organization will exist, even in an implicit and informal way, or by formal organizational models. These regulations have an influence on authority relations, data flow, resources allocation, coordination standards or any other system feature [11].

One of the most referenced organizational models is $\mathcal{M}$oise. It conceives a MAS as an organization, i.e., a normative set of rules that constrains the agent's behaviors. These organizational constraints are represented by three main concepts: roles, plans, and norms [10]. It is structured by three levels (individual, collective and social) and in three types of specification (structural, functional and deontic). The individual level defines constraints about possible actions of each agent. The collective level constrains the set of agents that can cooperate. The social level imposes constraints about the kind of interactions that the agents can perform.

Before describing the method, it is necessary to explain the reasons for the choice of Petri Nets as the main resource for this problem [8]: (i) they provide a graphically and mathematically founded modelling formalism which is a strong requirement for system development processes that need graphical as well as algorithmic tools; (ii) they are able to integrate the different levels and types of the $\mathcal{M}$oise specification as a result of its mechanisms for abstraction and hierarchical refinement; (iii) there exists a huge variety of algorithms for the design and analysis of Petri Nets and powerful tools have been developed to aid in these process; (iv) there are different variants of Petri net models that are all related by the basic formalism which they build upon. Besides the basic model, the Ordinary Petri net, there are extensions such as timed, stochastic, high-level, and others, meeting the specific needs for almost every application area.

However, the Petri Net model formalized in the previous section is not sufficient to represent a complete $\mathcal{M}$oise model, once it integrates different dimensions of representation, expressed by a Structural Specification (SS), a Functional Specification (FS), and a Deontic Specification (DS) [10]. Since it demands a more powerful representation resource, we propose an extension in the mapping procedure described in the previous subsection, using a model based on Coloured Petri Nets (CPN) [15].

A CPN is considered a high-level Petri Net once it enlarges its representation power including information in the tokens of a net, assigning a data structure for them. In CPN, this structure is named color.

We propose the Coloured Petri Net for $\mathcal{M}$oise (CPNfM) description as a nine-tuple, $CPNfM = (P, T, A, \Sigma, V, C, G, E, I)$ where P is a finite set of places with dimension n which represent goals in a $\mathcal{M}$oise organization; T is a finite set of transitions with dimension m which define plans to achieve the goals in a organization; A is a set of arcs and $A \subseteq P \times T \cup T \times P$, Σ is a finite nonempty color set which represents roles in a $\mathcal{M}$oise organization; V is a set of typed variables such that $Type[v] \in \Sigma$ for all variables $v \in V$, which define the deontic specification in a $\mathcal{M}oise$ organization; $C : P \to \Sigma$ is a set of colors functions, which assigns color sets to places, defining which roles are responsible by which goals in a $\mathcal{M}oise$ organization; $G : T \to EXPR_V$ is a guard function which assigns a guard to each transition t such that $Type[G(t)] = Bool$; and $E : A \to EXPR_V$ is a arc expression function that assigns an arc expression to each arc a such that $Type[E(a)] = C(p)_{MS}$, where p is the place connected to the arc a; and $I : P \to EXPR_\emptyset$ is an initialization function which assigns an initialization expression to each place p such that $Type[I(p)] = C(p)_{MS}$, defining an order of execution for goals in a $\mathcal{M}oise$ organization.

The method proposed by [21] uses a plan-goal tree, whose similar structure in a $\mathcal{M}oise$ specification is the goal decomposition tree which specifies a social scheme in a FS. Thereby, the testability method proposed here describes a functional specification of a $\mathcal{M}oise$ model using Petri Nets, working in the same logic presented in the previous subsection.

The method for the testability assessment of an organizational model specified by a $\mathcal{M}oise$ description has the following steps, described by the Fig. 3.

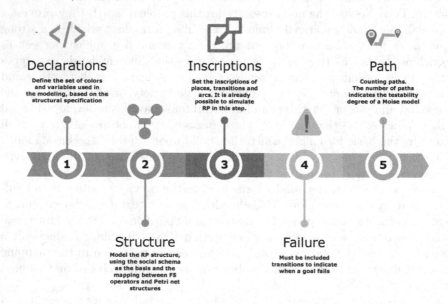

Fig. 3. Steps to asses the testability of a $\mathcal{M}oise$ model.

Declarations. The *Declarations* is based on the Structural Specification. Each role in the SS must be enumerated inside a set of colours. Herewith, it is possible to define the relationship between SS and FS, once these colours/roles will be assigned with its places/goals in the Petri net structure, to be done in the next step.

Structure. The structure of the CPNfM is made up following the *Moise* Functional Specification, identifying the basic operators (sequence, choice, and parallelism), and applying the corresponding Petri net structure, according to Fig. 4.

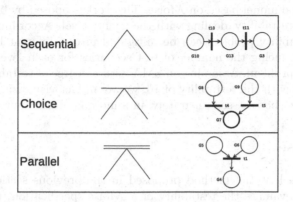

Fig. 4. A Mapping between FS operators and Petri net structures.

Inscriptions. The CPN inscriptions must obey the assignment of roles to each mission, which defines which colours must be assigned to each place in the net, according to Deontic Specification. The same logic must be used to define transitions and arc inscriptions. At this point, it is already possible to perform some simulations and is already set the complete relationship between the FS and SS.

Failure. At this step, it must be included transitions to indicate when a goal fails. It can be done including a transition and a failure place for each place existent currently in the model, and an auxiliary transition is needed to connect them with a final place.

Paths. The last step of the process is the counting of paths inside the CPNfM model. The number of paths indicates the testability degree of a *Moise* model. The number of paths founded indicates the number of test cases needed to validate a *Moise* model. To perform this job, it was developed a Web software that takes a CPN description, from CPN Tools software[1] for example, and convert it in a directed graph. The software loads a file with **.cpn** extension and convert it into a **JSON** object. This object converts places and transitions in vertices of a directed graph and arcs from the CPN model into arcs of a directed graph. The algorithm is based on [3], where a path is a alternating sequence $w = x_1 a_1 x_2 a_2 .... x_{k-1} a_{k-1} x_k$ of vertices x_i and arcs a_1, x_1 is the initial vertex and x_k is the terminal vertex, since all the vertices are distinct. The number of os paths in a graph is the total number of alternating sequences that can be generated inside a graph where all the vertices are different.

---

[1] http://cpntools.org/.

The generalization of this procedure is possible once a whole method is conceived considering the social, communication and the agent themselves dimensions of a full multiagent system. In this way, the procedure presented here represents the first level of testability, indicating the scenarios quantity to validate an organizational model based on $\mathcal{M}$oise. The work proposed by [21] indicates a second level of testability, dealing with the agents level. According to this approach, the testability problem can be mitigated in the different levels of SMA development, reducing the number of test scenarios for each level, becoming a more treatable problem. Assuming an SMA with a degree of testability of 5, and a BDI program with the testability of 10, we are in fact visualizing 50 scenarios of tests, that can be assessed separately, in a more modular approach.

3   Test Case

To demonstrate how the method proposed in the previous section works and its capacity to evaluate the testability of a $\mathcal{M}$oise specification, we present an application scenario presented in [16]: the Writing Paper. It describes an agents group that has a goal to write a paper to be published. Figure 5 describes the Structural Specification composed by a `wpgroup` group that has two roles, `writer` and `editor`, and both roles are sub-roles from `author`.

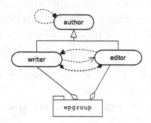

Fig. 5. Structural Specification for a Writing Paper scenario [13].

The Functional Specification for this scenario is presented in Fig. 6. According to this scheme, an agent undertake the `mMan` mission and must write a paper draft (`fdv`), which contains as sub-goals write a title (`wtitle`), an abstract (`wabs`) and section titles (`wsectitles`). These goals must be reached in sequence. The second branching named `sv`, the submission version is composed by the goals `wsec`, writing sections, and to finish the paper it is necessary to reach two goals in parallel, `wcon` writing a conclusion and `wref` writing references.

Table 1 describes the Deontic Specification defining permissions and obligations for the roles that undertake the missions. The missions are `mMan`, project general managing, that is composed of four goals; `mCol` collaborating for the writing process; and mission `mBib` for the agent which must gather and write the paper references.

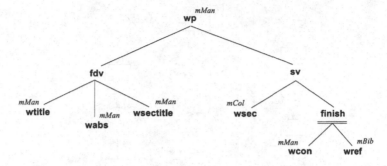

Fig. 6. Functional Specification for a Writing Paper scenario [13].

Table 1. Deontic Specification for a Writing Paper scenario [13].

Role	Deontic relationship	Mission
Editor	Permission	mMan
Writer	Obligation	mCol
Writer	Obligation	mBib

Implementing the method described in the previous section follow these steps:

Declarations. According to Structural Specification, the roles are `Editor` and `Writer`. Hence, the declarations are:

```
colset Role = with writer | editor | failure;
colset ROLES = list ROLES;
var w, e, f: ROLES;
```

Structure. The goal decomposition tree in Fig. 6 is used as reference for the main CPN structure. Following the mapping of Fig. 4, the CPN structure is presented in Fig. 7. The structure of a net is composed of places, transitions, and arcs, without the inscriptions.

Inscriptions. Gathering information from social scheme and Deontic Specification of Table 1, it is defined the CPN inscriptions, namely, the editor role is responsible for mission `mMan` and the writer role is responsible for mission `mCol` and `mBib`. An initial token must be located in places where a different agent initiates a mission, indicating that the following transition requires a new role, as seen at place `wsec` in Fig. 7.

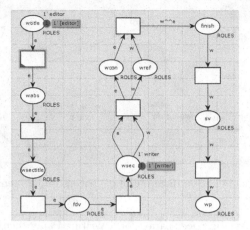

Fig. 7. CPN with inscriptions.

Failures. Figure 8 demonstrates a new version of the testability model including paths for possible failures in each goal of the Functional Specification. It is a similar approach to that proposed by [21] which includes a failure route for each action.

Paths. Once the model is considered ready, it was loaded in the Web software developed for the path counting. The CPN described in Fig. 8 presents six different paths, which indicates that this *Moise* description needs six test cases to cover all the possibilities for correction guarantee.

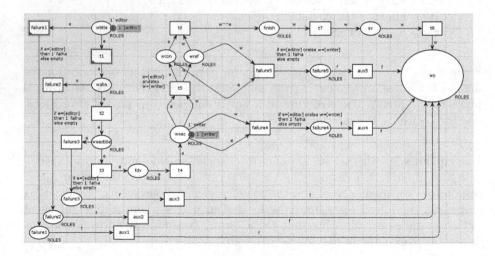

Fig. 8. CPN considering failure routes.

4   Conclusions

The contributions presented in this paper are: (i) a mapping between the method for measuring the degree of testability of a BDI program proposed in [21] and its correspondence when specified by Petri Nets; (ii) a method that adapts this mapping to measure the testability of a $\mathcal{M}$oise specification based on Coloured Petri Nets, constraining this analyses for a social dimension of a MAS; (iii) a software that transforms the CPN description of a $\mathcal{M}$oise specification into a directed graph and counts the paths within this graph, which defines the degree of testability of this specification, indicating the number of test cases necessary to validate it.

In a more general perspective of testing MAS, these contributions mitigate the testing problem into the different dimensions that compose a MAS, namely: social, communication and agents themselves.

Future works include the definition of the notion of test cases in a $\mathcal{M}$oise specification. This notion is necessary to automatically generate the test cases necessary for a complete validation of a description like this one. Besides that, the whole package for testing MAS would be closed with a similar approach applied for communication aspects.

References

1. Aminof, B., Murano, A., Rubin, S., Zuleger, F.: Automatic verification of multi-agent systems in parameterised grid-environments. In: Proceedings of the 2016 International Conference on Autonomous Agents & Multiagent Systems, pp. 1190–1199. International Foundation for Autonomous Agents and Multiagent Systems (2016)
2. Bakar, N.A., Selamat, A.: Agent systems verification: systematic literature review and mapping. Appl. Intell. **48**(5), 1251–1274 (2018)
3. Bang-Jensen, J., Gutin, G.Z.: Digraphs: Theory, Algorithms and Applications. Springer, London (2008). https://doi.org/10.1007/978-1-84800-998-1
4. Belardinelli, F., Lomuscio, A., Murano, A., Rubin, S.: Verification of multi-agent systems with imperfect information and public actions. In: Proceedings of the 16th Conference on Autonomous Agents and MultiAgent Systems, pp. 1268–1276. International Foundation for Autonomous Agents and Multiagent Systems (2017)
5. Cassandras, C.G., Lafortune, S.: Introduction to Discrete Event Systems. Springer, New York (2009). https://doi.org/10.1007/978-0-387-68612-7
6. Dignum, V., Dignum, F.: Modelling agent societies: co-ordination frameworks and institutions. In: Brazdil, P., Jorge, A. (eds.) EPIA 2001. LNCS (LNAI), vol. 2258, pp. 191–204. Springer, Heidelberg (2001). https://doi.org/10.1007/3-540-45329-6_21
7. Ermakova, V.O., Lomazova, I.A.: Verification of nested Petri nets using an unfolding approach. In: Algorithms and Tools for Petri Nets, p. 9 (2017)
8. Girault, C., Valk, R.: Petri Nets for Systems Engineering: A Guide to Modelling, Verification, and Applications. Springer, Heidelberg (2013). https://doi.org/10.1007/978-3-662-05324-9

9. Gonçalves, E.M., Quadros, C., Saldanha, J.: Uma análise comparativa da especificaçao formal em sistemas multi-agente: os desafios e as exigências uma década depois. In: Anais do X Workshop-Escola de Sistemas de Agentes, seus Ambientes e apliCaçoes, Maceio, Brazil, vol. 1 (2016)
10. Hannoun, M., Boissier, O., Sichman, J.S., Sayettat, C.: MOISE: an organizational model for multi-agent systems. In: Monard, M.C., Sichman, J.S. (eds.) IBERAMIA/SBIA -2000. LNCS (LNAI), vol. 1952, pp. 156–165. Springer, Heidelberg (2000). https://doi.org/10.1007/3-540-44399-1_17
11. Horling, B., Lesser, V.: A survey of multi-agent organizational paradigms. Knowl. Eng. Rev. **19**(4), 281–316 (2004)
12. Houhamdi, Z.: Multi-agent system testing: a survey. Int. J. Adv. Comput. **2**, 135–141 (2011)
13. Hübner, J.F., Boissier, O., Bordini, R.H.: A normative programming language for multi-agent organisations. Ann. Math. Artif. Intell. **62**(1–2), 27–53 (2011)
14. Hübner, J.F., Boissier, O., Kitio, R., Ricci, A.: Instrumenting multi-agent organisations with organisational artifacts and agents. Auton. Agent. Multi-Agent Syst. **20**(3), 369–400 (2010)
15. Jensen, K.: Coloured Petri Nets: Basic Concepts, Analysis Methods and Practical Use, vol. 1. Springer, Heidelberg (2013). https://doi.org/10.1007/978-3-662-03241-1
16. Kitio, R., Boissier, O., Hübner, J.F., Ricci, A.: Organisational artifacts and agents for open multi-agent organisations: "giving the power back to the agents". In: Sichman, J.S., Padget, J., Ossowski, S., Noriega, P. (eds.) COIN -2007. LNCS (LNAI), vol. 4870, pp. 171–186. Springer, Heidelberg (2008). https://doi.org/10.1007/978-3-540-79003-7_13
17. Liu, H.C., You, J.X., Li, Z., Tian, G.: Fuzzy Petri nets for knowledge representation and reasoning: a literature review. Eng. Appl. Artif. Intell. **60**, 45–56 (2017)
18. Murata, T.: Petri nets: properties, analysis and applications. Proc. IEEE **77**(4), 541–580 (1989)
19. Piera, M., Buil, R., Ginters, E.: State space analysis for model plausibility validation in multi-agent system simulation of urban policies. J. Simul. **10**(3), 216–226 (2016)
20. van den Broek, E.L., Jonker, C.M., Sharpanskykh, A., Treur, J., Yolum, I.: Formal modeling and analysis of organizations. In: Boissier, O., et al. (eds.) AAMAS 2005. LNCS (LNAI), vol. 3913, pp. 18–34. Springer, Heidelberg (2006). https://doi.org/10.1007/11775331_2
21. Winikoff, M.: BDI agent testability revisited (JAAMAS extended abstract). In: Proceedings of the 16th Conference on Autonomous Agents and MultiAgent Systems, pp. 260–261. International Foundation for Autonomous Agents and Multiagent Systems (2017)
22. Winikoff, M., Cranefield, S.: On the testability of BDI agent systems. J. Artif. Intell. Res. **51**, 71–131 (2014)

Fair Division Minimizing Inequality

Martin Aleksandrov[1(✉)], Cunjing Ge[2], and Toby Walsh[1]

[1] Technical University, Berlin, Germany
{martin.aleksandrov,toby.walsh}@tu-berlin.de
[2] Chinese Academy of Sciences, Beijing, China
gecj@ios.ac.cn

Abstract. Behavioural economists have shown that people are often averse to inequality and will make choices to avoid unequal outcomes. In this paper, we consider how to allocate indivisible goods fairly to agents with additive utilities, so as to minimize inequality. We consider how this interacts with axiomatic properties such as envy-freeness, Pareto efficiency and strategy-proofness. We also consider the computational complexity of computing allocations minimizing inequality. Unfortunately, this is computationally intractable in general so we consider several tractable mechanisms that minimize greedily the inequality. Finally, we run experiments to explore the performance of these mechanisms.

Keywords: Fair division · Gini index · Subjective Gini index · Envy index

1 Introduction

In resource allocation, one of the most frequently used normative measures of fairness is envy-freeness (i.e. no agent envies another agent's allocation). Unfortunately, when the resources are indivisible, envy-free allocations may *not* exist. In addition, computing an envy-free allocation when it exists is computationally intractable. Another desirable property in resource allocation is Pareto efficiency. In contrast to envy-free allocations, Pareto efficient allocations *always* exists. Moreover, with additive utilities, such allocations can be computed quickly. However, Pareto efficient allocations may not be very fair (e.g. giving all items to a single agent might be a Pareto efficient allocation). We consider here whether minimizing the inequality between agents offers an alternative to envy-freeness and Pareto efficiency. A number of different measures of inequality have been proposed in economics (e.g. Gini, Atkinson, Hoover indices [2,12,13]). However, we focus on the Gini index as it has been commonly used in many other settings.

We start our paper with a motivating example. We consider three normative inequality measures for fair division: the *Gini* index, the *subjective Gini* index and the *envy* index. These three indices measure the quality of allocations and

Funded by the European Research Council under the Horizon 2020 Programme via AMPLify 670077.

mechanisms between perfect equality (i.e. each agent values equally their own allocation) and envy-freeness. As these are numeric measures, there are *always* allocations that minimize them. We study the relationship between the Gini, subjective Gini and envy indices and axiomatic properties such as envy-freeness, Pareto efficiency and strategy-proofness. For example, we show that there are fair division problems when *none* of the envy-free allocations minimizes the inequality indices. We further study the complexity of computing allocations minimizing each of these indices. Unfortunately, most of these computational tasks are intractable in general. For this reason, we propose three tractable online mechanisms that allocate each item in a given sequence, thus greedily minimizing the three inequality indices without the knowledge of the future items in the sequence. Finally, we run experiments with these online mechanisms.

2   Formal Background

We consider a fair division problem with agents 1 to n and indivisible items o_1 to o_m. We suppose that each agent has some (private) cardinal *utility* $u_i(o_k) \in \mathbb{R}^{\geq 0}$ for each item o_k but can submit a (public) cardinal *bid* $v_i(o_k) \in \mathbb{R}^{\geq 0}$ for each item o_k. Let A be an allocation of all items to agents. We write A_i for the bundle of items allocated to agent i, and $u_i(A_j)$ for the utility of agent i for the items in the bundle A_j. We assume additive utilities. That is, $u_i(A_j) = \sum_{o_k \in A_j} u_i(o_k)$. Additivity offers an elegant compromise between simplicity and expressiveness in our model as well as in many other theoretical models of fair division (e.g. [3,7,9,14,16]). For example, in an economy, incomes and wealth are additive for the population. Also, in a food banking network, donated products accumulate additive value for the banks in the network.

We consider *responsive* mechanisms that compute actual allocations of items to agents based on their reported positive bids. We say that a mechanism is *strategy-proof* if, for each problem, no agent can increase their utility in the allocation returned by the mechanism by misreporting their bids. We are interested in welfare, fairness and efficiency properties of the allocations returned by mechanisms. The *utilitarian welfare* of A is equal to $\sum_{i \in [n]} u_i(A_i)$. The *egalitarian welfare* of A is equal to $\min_{i \in [n]} u_i(A_i)$. An allocation A is *envy-free* iff $u_i(A_i) \geq u_i(A_j)$ for every $i, j \in [n]$. An allocation A is *Pareto efficient* iff there is no allocation B such that $\forall i \in [n] : u_i(B_i) \geq u_i(A_i)$ and $\exists j \in [n] : u_j(B_j) > u_j(A_j)$.

In this paper, we study primarily how these properties are related to inequalities. One of the most frequently used measures of inequality is the *Gini* index. It is commonly used to measure inequalities in income or wealth distributions. The Gini index satisfies a number of desirable properties such as anonymity, scale independence, population independence, and the transfer principle (i.e. inequality reduces when we take from the rich and give to the poor). We will use it here to measure the inequality between agents' utilities for items in allocations. More precisely, the Gini index of an allocation equals half of the relative mean absolute difference in the utilities of the agents.

$$\text{Gini} = \frac{\sum_{i=1}^{n} \sum_{j=1}^{n} |u_i(A_i) - u_j(A_j)|}{2n \sum_{i=1}^{n} u_i(A_i)}$$

The Gini index lies in the interval $[0,1]$, taking the value 0 when all n agents get the same utility, and $1 - \frac{1}{n}$ when all agents but one agent get zero utility. In a plot of the cumulative utility distribution, the Gini index measures the ratio of the area that lies between the line of equality (i.e. all n agents get the same utility) and the Lorenz curve [10].

3   A Motivating Example

A simple example provides some motivation. Suppose Alice, Bob and Carol arrive at the car hire office and are offered to rent a Renault, a Skoda, or a Toyota car. Alice knows that Skoda's share their mechanicals with VW, and likes reliable German cars, so she prefers the Skoda most. Bob is torn between the Skoda and the more unusual Renault. And Carole loves quirky cars, so has a strong preference for the Renault. She is also an environmentalist, so dislikes VW and has a strong preference against the Skoda. Their precise utilities for the different cars are given in the following table. Who gets what car?

	Renault	Skoda	Toyota
Alice	1	8	3
Bob	8	7	1
Carol	18	1	8

There is no envy-free allocation. Bob and Carol both most prefer the Renault and only one of them can get it. The allocation with the least amount of envy (either of one person for another or in total) allocates the Renault to Carol, the Skoda to Bob and the Toyota to Alice. This is also the optimal allocation from a welfare perspective with both the greatest utilitarian and egalitarian welfare. However, Alice might not consider this allocation fair as she gets less than half the utility of Bob or Carol, as well as less than half the utility of her most preferred car, whilst Carol gets her most preferred car and Bob gets a car with value close to his greatest utility for an item.

We might decide instead that it is fairer to chose from among those allocations which minimize the inequality between Alice, Bob and Carol. For instance, allocating the Renault to Bob, the Skoda to Alice and the Toyota to Carole is one such allocation. Everyone gives their car the same 8 units of utility. This allocation is Pareto efficient and has a Gini index of 0, the minimum possible. In this allocation, only Carol envies Bob, but since she gets as much utility for her car as both Alice and Bob get for their cars, this might be acceptable.

Note that there is another allocation that minimizes inequality. Allocating the Renault to Alice, the Skoda to Carol and the Toyota to Bob gives everyone the same 1 unit of utility. This also has a Gini index of 0. However, everyone now has their least preferred car, and everyone envies everyone else. Moreover, this allocation is not Pareto efficient and has the minimal welfare possible, both from the utilitarian and egalitarian perspectives.

To sum up, this example suggests that whilst the Gini index can help in choosing between allocations, we cannot minimize inequality alone. Amongst allocations that minimize inequality, we might look to maximize welfare, minimize envy, etc. Minimizing inequality does, however, have a minor advantage over envy-freeness as a primary measure of fairness. An allocation of indivisible items minimizing inequality always exists whilst an envy-free allocation may not.

4   The Subjective Gini Index

As remarked earlier, the Gini index is typically used to measure the inequalities in income and wealth distributions. However, we are concerned here with the distribution of indivisible items that are not money, and importantly agents might have different *subjective* utilities for these items. For example, the utility you get for an item is not necessarily the same as the utility I get for it.

Should it increase the "inequality" of an allocation that someone else gets an item they value when you have little or even no value for it? To return to our motivating example, suppose Alice gets the Renault, Bob gets the Toyota, and Carol gets the Skoda. Everyone gets 1 unit of utility so this allocation has a Gini index of 0. But from everyone's subjective perspective, this is not a very equitable allocation of items. For instance, from Alice's perspective, rather than the 1 unit of utility she gets, she would get 8 units of utility for Carol's car and 3 for Bob's car. Also, from Bob's perspective, rather than the 1 unit of utility he gets, he would get 8 units of utility for Alice's car and 7 for Carol's car.

In response, we propose a *new* measure of inequality. The *subjective Gini* index takes such subjective differences into consideration. We modify the definition of the Gini index to sum the difference in utility an agent has for its allocation and the utility the *same* agent has for the allocation of items to other agents.

$$\text{subjective Gini} = \frac{\sum_{i=1}^{n} \sum_{j=1}^{n} |u_i(A_i) - u_i(A_j)|}{2 \sum_{i=1}^{n} \sum_{j=1}^{n} u_i(A_j)}$$

The subjective Gini index is between $[0, 1]$, taking the value 0 when each agent gives the same utility to each bundle of items, and $1 - \frac{1}{n}$ when one agent gets all items. Returning again to our motivating example, the allocation in which each agent gets 1 unit of utility has a Gini index of 0 but a subjective Gini index of $\frac{23}{55}$ (i.e. ≈ 0.41818181818). The allocation in which each agent gets 8 units of utility might be more preferred as it has a lower subjective Gini index of $\frac{37}{110}$ (i.e. ≈ 0.33636363636).

5   The Envy Index

Minimizing the subjective Gini index will find allocations which divide the items into bundles so that each bundle has similar utility for each agent. This reminds us of a fairness concept such as the maximin share when each agent's utility should be at least as high as the agent can guarantee by dividing the items into as many bundles as there are players and receiving their least desirable bundle [8].

On the positive side, an allocation which minimizes the subjective Gini index always exists, unlike maximin fair shares [18]. On the negative side, such an allocation may not be envy-free. To overcome this, we propose also an *envy index* whose definition is closely related to that of the subjective Gini index. Nevertheless, this index is focused only on the amount of envy in an allocation. Minimizing this index will return an envy-free allocation whenever one such exists.

$$\text{envy} = \frac{\sum_{i=1}^{n} \sum_{j=1}^{n} \max\{0, u_i(A_j) - u_i(A_i)\}}{\sum_{i=1}^{n} \sum_{j=1}^{n} u_i(A_j)}$$

The envy index lies in $[0,1]$, taking the value 0 when the allocation is envy-free, and tending towards 1 as we increase the number of agents and allocate all items to just one agent. It is easy to see that the envy index is never greater (and sometimes smaller) than the subjective Gini index. Returning to our motivating example, the unique allocation minimizing the envy with index of $\frac{6}{110}$ (i.e. ≈ 0.05454545454) allocates the Renault to Carol, the Skoda to Bob and the Toyota to Alice. As we noted, this is also the optimal allocation from a welfare perspective with both the greatest utilitarian and egalitarian welfare.

6   Relationship to Envy-Freeness

We consider how these indices relate to a fairness concept such as envy-freeness. Suppose that an envy-free allocation exists. Clearly, such an allocation minimizes the envy index. On the other hand, envy-free allocations may not minimize the Gini or subjective Gini indices.

Theorem 1. *There exist problems with envy-free allocations in which no envy-free allocation minimizes the Gini or subjective Gini index.*

Proof. For the Gini index, let us consider the following fair division problem with 2 agents, 2 items and utilities as in the below table.

	item o_1	item o_2
agent 1	1	2
agent 2	3	1

The only envy-free allocation gives o_1 to agent 2 and o_2 to agent 1. However, the unique allocation that minimizes the Gini index gives o_1 to agent 1 and o_2 to agent 2. In this allocation, both agents envy each other. For the subjective Gini index, consider another problem with 3 agents and 3 items.

	item o_1	item o_2	item o_3
agent 1	9	1	5
agent 2	5	9	1
agent 3	1	5	9

The unique envy-free allocation gives to each agent their most valued item. However, the unique allocation that minimizes the subjective Gini index gives to each agent their second most preferred item, i.e. the one they value with utility of 5. □

The proof of Theorem 1 critically depends on the agents not sharing common (i.e. identical) utilities for items. In this case, there is no incompatibility between envy-freeness and minimizing the Gini or subjective Gini indices. If an allocation is envy-free, then every agent assigns the same utility to every bundle of allocated items.

Observation 1. *With common utilities, an allocation is envy-free iff the Gini and subjective Gini indices are zero.*

7   Relationship to Pareto Efficiency

Another fundamental notion in fair division is Pareto efficiency. We would prefer allocations where no agent can improve their outcome without making others worse off. Pareto efficiency is not necessarily compatible with minimizing inequality. The first example in the proof of Theorem 1 shows that for the Gini index. This should perhaps not be surprising as other fairness properties are also incompatible with Pareto efficiency. For example, an allocation that is envy-free may not necessarily be Pareto efficient. Moreover, each envy-free allocation could be Pareto dominated only by allocations that are not envy-free [14]. It follows quickly that minimizing the envy index is not compatible with Pareto efficiency. We can show that the same is true for the subjective Gini index.

Theorem 2. *There exist problems in which no Pareto efficient allocation minimizes the subjective Gini index.*

Proof. Let us consider a problem with 2 agents and 4 items. Also, let ϵ be some very small non-negative number that is strictly less than one.

	item o_1	item o_2	item o_3	item o_4
agent 1	1	$2 - \epsilon$	1	ϵ
agent 2	$2 - \epsilon$	1	ϵ	1

The allocation that gives o_1, o_3 to agent 1 and o_2, o_4 to agent 2 minimizes the subjective Gini index. However, the only Pareto efficient allocation swaps items o_1, o_2, giving o_1 to agent 2, and o_2 to agent 1, thus increasing the agents' utilities. □

Again, with common utilities, there is no incompatibility between Pareto efficiency and minimizing the Gini, subjective Gini and envy indices. This follows because each allocation, including those that minimize these indices, is Pareto efficient.

Observation 2. *With common utilities, any allocation that minimizes the Gini, subjective Gini or envy index is Pareto efficient.*

We can measure the trade-off between Pareto efficiency and minimizing one of these indices. The *egalitarian/utilitarian price of an index* for a given welfare is the ratio between the best welfare of any Pareto efficient allocation and the worst welfare of an allocation minimizing the index.

Theorem 3. *The utilitarian and egalitarian prices of the Gini and subjective Gini indices are unbounded.*

Proof. Consider 2 agents, 2 items and let $\epsilon \in (0, \frac{1}{2})$. Suppose the first agent gives item o_1 a utility of ϵ and o_2 a utility of $1 - \epsilon$, whilst the second agent gives respectively utilities of $2 - \epsilon$ and ϵ. Then, the Pareto efficient outcome with the best utilitarian and egalitarian welfare allocates o_1 to the second agent, and o_2 to the first agent. However, the only allocation that minimizes the Gini index does the reverse. The egalitarian price of the Gini index is then $\frac{1-\epsilon}{\epsilon}$ which is unbounded as ϵ goes to zero. Its utilitarian price is $\frac{3-2\epsilon}{2\epsilon}$ which is unbounded as ϵ goes to zero. The same example demonstrates that the utilitarian and egalitarian price of the subjective Gini index are also unbounded.   □

For the envy index, we have examples where the utilitarian price grows as the number n of agents. We conjecture that this may also be an upper bound. And, we next show that the egalitarian price of this index is unbounded.

Theorem 4. *The egalitarian price of the envy index is unbounded.*

Proof. Let us consider the fair division problem with 3 agents and 3 items, in which the agents' utilities are as in the below table.

	item o_1	item o_2	item o_3
agent 1	1	1	1
agent 2	8	4	4
agent 3	8	4	4

The Pareto efficient outcome with the best egalitarian welfare allocates the item with utility 8 to the second or third agent, and each of the remaining items to a different agent. This has an egalitarian welfare of 1 unit. However, the allocation that minimizes the envy index gives the item with utility 8 to the second agent and both the other items to the third agent, or vice versa. As the first agent gets no items, this has an egalitarian welfare of zero units. Hence, the egalitarian price of the envy index is unbounded.   □

8 Relationship to Strategy-Proofness

If we use a mechanism that minimizes one of these indices, agents have an incentive to declare false utilities. Again, this should not be too surprising. We often need to choose between fairness and strategy-proofness. For example, the random priority mechanism is strategy-proof but it can return allocations which are not envy-free [4].

Theorem 5. *A mechanism which minimizes the Gini, subjective Gini or envy index is not strategy proof.*

Proof. For the Gini index, consider the first example in the proof of Theorem 1. If agents report sincerely their utilities, the first agent gets o_1 and the second agent gets o_2. If the first agent misreports their utilities as $1/2$ and 3 respectively, then the agents swap items, and both are better off. Similarly, if the second agent misreports their utilities as 2 and $1/2$ respectively, then the agents swap items and are better off.

For the subjective Gini index, consider 2 agents and 4 items. Let the first agent have utilities $u_{11} = 1, u_{12} = 3/2, u_{13} = 1, u_{14} = 1/2$ whereas the second agent have utilities $u_{21} = 3/2, u_{22} = 1, u_{23} = 1/2, u_{24} = 1$. Suppose sincere play. The mechanism that minimizes the subjective Gini index to zero gives to each agent both items for which they have utility 1, or both items for which they have utilities $3/2$ and $1/2$. The utility of each agent is then 2. Suppose next that the first agent reports strategically bids $1, 3/2, 0, 0$ for items o_1 to o_4 respectively. The mechanism now gives the first and second items to the first agent, and the third and fourth items to the second agent. The utility of the first agent is $5/2$. This is a strict improvement.

For the envy index, we can use the same problem as for the subjective Gini index.   □

9 Online Mechanisms

We next consider the computational properties of the Gini, subjective Gini and envy indices. Computing envy-free allocations is NP-hard even with just 2 agents, and common utilities [6]. It immediately follows that finding an allocation minimizing the envy index is NP-hard. By Observation 1, the same general result holds for the subjective Gini and Gini indices. Our approach to deal with the intractability of computing allocations that minimize inequality or envy is to use tractable online mechanisms. These will often return an allocation with little inequality or envy, even if there is no guarantee that it is minimal. These mechanisms can be applied to a given problem by picking a (perhaps random) sequence of the items. WLOG, let $o = (o_1, \ldots, o_m)$ be such a sequence. Each considered mechanism computes firstly a set of agents feasible for each next o_j in o given an allocation A of o_1 to o_{j-1}, and allocates secondly o_j to some feasible agent with a probability that is uniform with respect to the other feasible agents.

- GINI: this decides that $i \in [n]$ is feasible for o_j if $v_i(o_j) > 0$ and giving o_j to i minimizes the Gini index given A
- SUBJECTIVE GINI: this decides that $i \in [n]$ is feasible for o_j if $v_i(o_j) > 0$ and giving o_j to i minimizes the subjective Gini index given A
- ENVY: this decides that $i \in [n]$ is feasible for o_j if $v_i(o_j) > 0$ and giving o_j to i minimizes the envy index given A.

A powerful technique to study online mechanisms is competitive analysis [21]. Competitive analysis identifies the loss in efficiency due to the data arriving in an online fashion. We say that an online mechanism M is c-competitive for a given welfare w iff there exists a constant b such that, whatever the order o of items, we have that $w(\text{OPT}) \leq c \cdot w(M, o) + b$ holds where $w(M, o)$ is the welfare of M on o and $w(\text{OPT})$ is the optimal welfare in the offline problem. A mechanism that is c-competitive has a ratio c. Most of our mechanisms have ratios that are unbounded. For example, we can use the instance from the proof of Theorem 10 in [1] and show that both the utilitarian and egalitarian ratios of SUBJECTIVE GINI are unbounded. We next prove similar results for GINI and ENVY.

Theorem 6. *The utilitarian and egalitarian competitive ratios of* GINI *are unbounded.*

Proof. For GINI, consider the online fair division of items o_1, o_2 to agents 1,2. Further, let the utilities of the agents for the items are given in the below table in which $\epsilon \in (0, 1)$.

	item o_1	item o_2
agent 1	1	ϵ
agent 2	ϵ	1

The mechanism allocates o_1 to agent 2 and o_2 to agent 1, returning utilitarian and egalitarian welfare of 2ϵ and ϵ. The optimal offline allocation allocates o_2 to agent 2 and o_1 to agent 1, returning utilitarian and egalitarian welfare of 2 and 1. Consequently, both competitive ratios are equal to $\frac{1}{\epsilon}$ which goes to ∞ as ϵ goes to 0. □

Theorem 7. *The utilitarian competitive ratio of* ENVY *is at least* $\frac{n}{2}$ *whilst its egalitarian competitive ratio is unbounded.*

Proof. For the utilitarian ratio, consider n agents and n items. Let the first agent have utility n for each item, and each other agent have utility 1 for each item. Then, ENVY will allocate the first item to the first agent, and then each subsequent item to a new agent. The utilitarian welfare of this allocation is $2 \cdot n - 1$. The optimal utilitarian welfare is n^2, giving all items to agent 1.

For the egalitarian ratio, consider the online fair division of items o_1, o_2 to agents 1, 2. Let agent 1 have a utility 1 for each item whilst agent 2 have a utility ϵ for o_1 and 0 for o_2, where $\epsilon > 0$. The mechanism allocates the items to agent 1, and thus returns an egalitarian welfare of 0. The optimal offline allocation gives to each agent an item they like, and has egalitarian welfare of ϵ. The egalitarian ratio is ∞. □

We can also measure the price of anarchy of these online mechanisms. The *price of anarchy* is closely related to the competitive ratio but now supposing agents act strategically [15]. The *price of anarchy* of an online mechanism for a given welfare is the ratio between the best welfare of an allocation returned by the mechanism when agents are sincere and the worst welfare of an allocation returned by the mechanism when agents are strategic. Interestingly, the price of anarchy of each of our online mechanisms is at least n. We conjecture that this may also be their upper bound.

Theorem 8. *The utilitarian and egalitarian prices of anarchy of* GINI, SUB-JECTIVE GINI *and* ENVY *are at least* n.

Proof. Consider an instance with n agents and n items. For $i \in \{1, \ldots, n\}$, let agent i have utility of 1 for o_i, and utility of $\epsilon > 0$ for each other item. The optimal offline allocation gives to each agent i their most valued item. The utilitarian welfare and egalitarian welfare of this allocation are n and 1 respectively.

We start with GINI. At round 1, this mechanism gives the first item to one of the agents who likes with it ϵ. The first agent then has an incentive to report at most ϵ for this item simply because they do not know what items will arrive next. By a similar argument, at round $i \in [n]$, the optimal play for agent i is to bid at most ϵ. Given this strategic profile, at the end of the allocation, each agent gets expected utility of $\frac{1}{n} + \frac{(n-1)}{n} \cdot \epsilon$. The utilitarian welfare and egalitarian welfare of this strategic allocation go to 1 and $\frac{1}{n}$ respectively as ϵ goes to zero. Consequently, the corresponding prices of this mechanism are at least n.

We next consider SUBJECTIVE GINI. The sincere play is optimal for each agent with this mechanism because they get each item with probability $\frac{1}{n}$. The welfare values go to 1 and $\frac{1}{n}$ respectively as ϵ goes to zero. The prices are at least n.

We finally consider ENVY. This mechanism tends to allocate each item to agents with the highest utility for this item. By similar arguments as for GINI, we conclude that the optimal play of each agent is to bid 1 for each item. Each agent thus gets expected utility of $\frac{1}{n} + \frac{(n-1)}{n} \cdot \epsilon$. The utilitarian welfare and egalitarian welfare given this strategic profile go to 1 and $\frac{1}{n}$ as ϵ goes to zero. Hence, the prices are at least n. $\qquad\qquad\square$

Finally, our results in this section suggest that the considered online mechanisms have performance that cannot be bounded in the worst-case. For this purpose, we next study their performance in the average-case.

10   Experiments

We ran a simple experiment to see how these online mechanisms would perform in practice. We generated 100 instances of $n = 5$ agents, m items for $m \in \{10, 20, 30, 40, 50, 60, 70, 80, 90, 100\}$ and integer utilities drawn uniformly at random from $\{0, 1, \ldots, m\}$. For each combination of values for n and m, we computed the Gini index, the subjective Gini index, the envy index, the egalitarian welfare and the utilitarian welfare of 100,000 sampled allocations returned by the GINI, SUBJECTIVE GINI and ENVY mechanisms. We report in our graphs only the average results because their standard deviations were less than 1% of them. We further omit our results for the subjective Gini index for reasons of space.

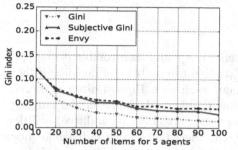

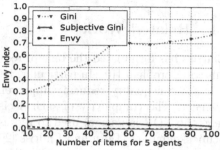

In the left graph, GINI achieves the lowest value of the Gini index for each number of items. For example, the Gini value of GINI is nearly 50% lower than the Gini values of SUBJECTIVE GINI and ENVY for 100 items. This gap actually remains similar for $m \geq 40$. Unfortunately, GINI fails to minimize envy. In the right graph, we could clearly see that ENVY outperforms GINI. In fact, ENVY achieves an envy index of almost 0 for 100 (and any other number m of) items. Interestingly, SUBJECTIVE GINI tends to favor envy-freeness to minimum inequality. By comparison, as the value of m increases, the performance of GINI diverges from envy-freeness and converges to perfect equality. Perhaps, we observe this as GINI tends to allocate items to agents with low utilities. In contrast, SUBJECTIVE GINI and ENVY tend to allocate items to agents with high utilities, thus minimizing simultaneously both the envy and inequality.

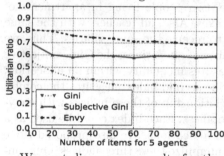

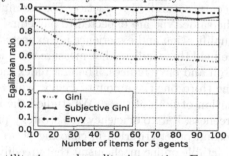

We next discuss our results for the utilitarian and egalitarian ratios. From a utilitarian perspective (the left graph), ENVY outperforms the other two mechanisms for each number of items. For example, this mechanism achieves a utilitarian ratio close to 0.7 for 100 items. This value is nearly 16% higher than the ratio of SUBJECTIVE GINI and 100% higher than the ratio of GINI for 100 items. From an egalitarian perspective (the right graph), again ENVY outperforms SUBJECTIVE GINI and GINI, followed closely by SUBJECTIVE GINI. Interestingly, for each value of m, ENVY not only minimizes the envy but also maximizes the egalitarian welfare. For 100 items, its egalitarian ratio is nearly 0.95. This value is nearly 82% higher than the value of GINI for 100 items. For both ratios, the performance of SUBJECTIVE GINI is getting closer to the performance of ENVY as the value of m increases.

Finally, our experimental results indicate that envy-freeness, (subjective) equality and welfare efficiency might often (at least approximately) be achievable in practice.

11 Related Work

Endriss has formulated the task of reducing inequality as a combinatorial optimisation problem [10]. In particular, he studied the problem of deciding if there exists an inequality reducing improvement such as a Pigou-Dalton or Lorenz transfer. The complexity of such decision problems depends on the language (e.g. the XOR-language) used to represent the (possibly non-additive) utilities. Schneckenburger, Dorn and Endriss [20] considered allocating indivisible goods to minimize inequality as measured by the Atkinson index. Their proof showing that minimizing the Atkinson index is NP-hard can be related to finding an allocation that minimizes the Gini or subjective Gini index. By comparison, we show that computing allocations with small inequalities might be fast by using online mechanisms. Other such mechanisms are used in other settings as well (e.g. [1,17]). Finally, the idea of measuring envy was firstly proposed in [11]. Moreover, there are some existing analyses of the Gini and envy indices in [5,19]. However, our idea of measuring inequality subjectively is new.

12 Conclusions

We study fair division minimizing inequality. Equitability is very important and occurs naturally in practice. For example, two people living in apartments of the same type are expected to pay equal taxes. Also, all teachers with the same qualification and experience are expected to receive the same salaries. Thus, we defined three indices that measure the quality of allocations: the Gini, subjective Gini and envy indices. The first index measures inequality within an allocation, the third one the amount of envy, whilst the second index measures the combination of both of these. We studied the relationship of these indices with envy-freeness, Pareto efficiency and strategy-proofness. Each index could be used as a second order criterion in choosing between allocations. We also proposed three tractable online mechanisms that greedily minimize these three indices. Our simple experimental results showed that, even for modest sized problems, we may be able to efficiently compute allocations with limited inequality or envy as well as with reasonably high values of the egalitarian welfare and utilitarian welfare.

References

1. Aleksandrov, M., Aziz, H., Gaspers, S., Walsh, T.: Online fair division: analysing a food bank problem. In: Proceedings of the Twenty-Fourth IJCAI 2015, Buenos Aires, Argentina, 25–31 July 2015, pp. 2540–2546 (2015)

2. Atkinson, A.: On the measurement of inequality. J. Econ. Theory **2**(3), 244–263 (1970)
3. Beviá, C.: Fair allocation in a general model with indivisible goods. Rev. Econ. Des. **3**(3), 195–213 (1998)
4. Bogomolnaia, A., Moulin, H.: A new solution to the random assignment problem. J. Econ. Theory **100**(2), 295–328 (2001)
5. Bosmans, K., Öztürk, Z.E.: An axiomatic approach to the measurement of envy. Soc. Choice Welf. **50**(2), 247–264 (2018)
6. Bouveret, S., Lang, J.: Efficiency and envy-freeness in fair division of indivisible goods: logical representation and complexity. J. Artif. Intell. Res. (JAIR) **32**, 525–564 (2008). https://doi.org/10.1613/jair.2467
7. Brams, S.J., Edelman, P.H., Fishburn, P.C.: Fair division of indivisible items. Theor. Decis. **55**(2), 147–180 (2003)
8. Budish, E.: The combinatorial assignment problem: approximate competitive equilibrium from equal incomes. J. Polit. Econ. **119**(6), 1061–1103 (2011)
9. Chevaleyre, Y., Endriss, U., Estivie, S., Maudet, N.: Multiagent resource allocation in k-additive domains: preference representation and complexity. Ann. Oper. Res. **163**(1), 49–62 (2008)
10. Endriss, U.: Reduction of economic inequality in combinatorial domains. In: Gini, M., Shehory, O., Ito, T., Jonker, C. (eds.) International conference on Autonomous Agents and Multi-Agent Systems, AAMAS 2013, IFAAMAS, pp. 175–182 (2013)
11. Feldman, A.M., Kirman, A.: Fairness and envy. Am. Econ. Rev. **64**(6), 995–1005 (1974)
12. Gini, C.: Variabilità e mutabilità. C. Cuppini, Bologna (1912)
13. Hoover, E.M.: The measurement of industrial localization. Rev. Econ. Stat. **18**(4), 162–171 (1936)
14. de Keijzer, B., Bouveret, S., Klos, T., Zhang, Y.: On the complexity of efficiency and envy-freeness in fair division of indivisible goods with additive preferences. In: Proceedings of the First ADT International Conference, Venice, Italy, 20–23 October 2009, pp. 98–110 (2009)
15. Koutsoupias, E., Papadimitriou, C.: Worst-case equilibria. In: Meinel, C., Tison, S. (eds.) STACS 1999. LNCS, vol. 1563, pp. 404–413. Springer, Heidelberg (1999). https://doi.org/10.1007/3-540-49116-3_38
16. Lesca, J., Perny, P.: LP solvable models for multiagent fair allocation problems. In: Coelho, H., Studer, R., Wooldridge, M. (eds.) 19th European Conference on Artificial Intelligence (ECAI 2010), pp. 393–398. IOS Press (2010)
17. Mehta, A.: Online matching and ad allocation. Found. Trends Theor. Comput. Sci. **8**(4), 265–368 (2013)
18. Procaccia, A., Wang, J.: Fair enough: guaranteeing approximate maximin shares. In: Babaioff, M., Conitzer, V., Easley, D. (eds.) ACM EC 2014, pp. 675–692 (2014)
19. Sanchez-Perez, J., Plata-Perez, L., Sanchez-Sanchez, F.: An elementary characterization of the Gini index. MPRA Paper, University Library of Munich, Germany (2012)
20. Schneckenburger, S., Dorn, B., Endriss, U.: The Atkinson inequality index in multiagent resource allocation. In: Larson, K., Winikoff, M., Das, S., Durfee, E. (eds.) Proceedings of the 16th AAMAS 2017, pp. 272–280. ACM (2017)
21. Sleator, D.D., Tarjan, R.E.: Amortized efficiency of list update and paging rules. Commun. ACM **28**(2), 202–208 (1985)

Semantic Web Services for Multi-Agent Systems Interoperability

Alda Canito[1]([✉]), Gabriel Santos[1], Juan M. Corchado[2],
Goreti Marreiros[1], and Zita Vale[3]

[1] Research Group on Intelligent Engineering and Computing for
Advanced Innovation and Development, Institute of Engineering -
Polytechnic of Porto (ISEP/IPP), Porto, Portugal
{alrfc,gajls,mgt}@isep.ipp.pt
[2] BISITE - Research Centre, University of Salamanca, Salamanca, Spain
corchado@usal.es
[3] Institute of Engineering - Polytechnic of Porto (ISEP/IPP), Porto, Portugal
zav@isep.ipp.pt

Abstract. Agent-based technologies are often used including existing web services. The outputs of some services are also frequently used as inputs for other services, including other MAS. However, while agent-based technologies can be used to provide services, these are not described using the same semantic web technologies web services use, which makes it difficult to discover, invoke and compose them with web services seamlessly. In this paper, we analyse different agent-based technologies and how these can be described using extensions to OWL-S. Additionally, we propose an architecture that facilitates these services' usage, where services of any kind can be registered and executed (semi-)automatically.

Keywords: Semantic web services · Multi-agent systems · OWL-S

1 Introduction

The execution of complex tasks often requires the composition of several, atomic services. While a wide variety of these are available on the web as web services, the design and development of a workflow is still very time-consuming, considering that they need to be found, they may have different interaction protocols, and proper description of their workings, inputs and outputs if often lacking [1, 2]. Semantic Web technologies have been proposed for the description of web services in order to make those descriptions richer: by providing them in a machine-readable way, the processes of discovery and composition of services by intelligent software agents become easier [2–4].

Individual agents, capable of solving specific tasks in their systems, can be seen as service providers, as well as the Multi-Agent Systems (MAS) that are able to solve more complex tasks. Both agents and MAS are capable of providing services, as is the case of decision support agent-based systems [5–7]. Additionally, existing MAS-based Decision Support Systems often execute tasks that depend on the outputs of services [5, 8], but also of other known MAS, as is the case of [6, 9–11]. These services are

© Springer Nature Switzerland AG 2019
P. Moura Oliveira et al. (Eds.): EPIA 2019, LNAI 11805, pp. 606–616, 2019.
https://doi.org/10.1007/978-3-030-30244-3_50

often not available outside of their environment for several reasons, e.g. the complexity of the network configurations required to ensure secure communications. Service providers can be shifted to different servers, and systems requiring those services need to be reconfigured. To overcome these issue, one possible solution would be to have a services' catalogue where both agents and web services could register, expose the service(s) they provide, making them publicly available for other systems that might be potentially interested in using them. On the other hand, systems interested in using services would be able to search for a type of service, and as response would receive a list of available services – considering the type of service, the service provider, the expected input(s), and the result output.

In order to overcome the necessary services' heterogeneity, we propose an architecture featuring semantic description of services that facilitates service publishing, discovery, composition and interoperability. Additionally, we present an extension to OWL-S for Agent-based services, using JADE agents as an example. Agent-based services and web services are described rather differently, with the former requiring information to be communicated with, including, but not limited to, host, port, agent identifier, performative(s), language(s) and ontology(ies). For the invocation of the later, in turn, information regarding its URI, protocol (e.g.: HTTP, HTTPS), port, technology (e.g. SOAP, REST) and method (e.g. GET, POST), among others, must be known.

This document is structured as follows: Sect. 1 exposed the problem and motivations. Section 2 presents existing approaches to semantic web services description and discusses the relevance of agent-based approaches to service composition and how intelligent agents could be described as service providers. Section 3 proposes an extension to OWL-S to allow the description of agent-based services. Section 4 proposes an architecture that would use these semantic notations to invoke MAS-based services alongside with other types of services, while Sect. 5 presents illustrative use-cases. Finally, Sect. 6 presents the final conclusions and future work.

2 Multi-Agent Systems and Semantic Web Services

Intelligent Agents are often used to solve and simulate scenarios where the involved parties have different goals and objectives which require different levels of proactivity. While using Multi-Agent Systems in these scenarios are adequate, more complex scenarios can arise, as is the case of [5], where several multi-agent systems are invoked and the outcomes of them must be processed and combined in order to generate a bigger picture. Running several agent-based simulations concurrently in order to compare results is a fairly common task to perform, especially in scenarios where different configurations have immediate impact on the results or where different systems must communicate. Similarly, it is often necessary to perform simulations sequentially, where the results of the first serve as input or influence those that follow. While in some scenarios these systems directly communicate with each other [9, 11], such is not always the case [5, 8]. This problem becomes even more complex if the data must be transformed through other processes, such as those provided by services or tools [12], whose availability must be assessed. As such, establishing which systems and services are available and how they can be combined becomes an important issue.

As proposed in [3], describing web services in a semantically rich way – not only in terms of their inputs and outputs, but also by describing the inner processes of these services themselves and the tasks they perform – allows for a bigger automation in the processes of service discovery, composition and compensation [2, 13–15]. The principles of interoperability and coordination between agents follow the same vision as the semantic web [4]; however, while web services represent atomic, mostly state-less tasks, intelligent agents are proactive entities with specific goals [16]. This proactivity manifests, among other things, in locating services and partners which will help the agent to fulfil its tasks. In [17], the importance of the semantic description of services for this task is discussed, establishing that web services and agents are similar when it comes to their discovery and that any matching to be made between different service groundings must ultimately rely on semantic abstractions.

While there are many concurrent semantic approaches to the description of web services [18–22], OWL-S includes a number of concepts and properties to allow the proper description of SOAP services, with extensions also available for the RESTful kind [23]. Additionally, with OWL-S it is possible to describe not only atomic services, but also workflows resulting of the composition of several atomic ones. In order to use OWL-S to also describe agents and multi-agent systems, new concepts must be added to the ontology. As such, we will study the properties of agent-based technologies in order to establish how these can be described, and then proposing the necessary additions to OWL-S.

3   Semantic Description of Agent-Based Services

OWL-S includes a number of concepts and properties to allow the proper description of SOAP services, with extensions also available for RESTful services [21]. Here, we propose extending this ontology to include descriptions of services that are provided by agent-based systems.

OWL-S is divided in three main components: (i) Service Profile, (ii) Process Model, and (iii) Grounding. The first is meant to be read by humans and features the name of the service, its description, provider, limitations and other relevant information. The Process Model describes how the service works, describing its inputs and outputs, pre-conditions and effects. Finally, the Grounding specifies interaction details such as the interaction protocol and message formats [24].

Agents do not expose their services through any standardized description formats like WSDL [25] or WADL [26]. And although agents can offer gateways to communicate with non-agent-based software, which allows them to be exposed on the web as web services, this might not be the best option since it may result in a bottleneck, reducing the service's performance and being a potential point a failure [27]. Agent-based systems are meant to be distributed and, whenever necessary, to be able to move from one machine to another. The use of static gateways, which must be defined programmatically beforehand [28], hinders the agent's capabilities. Therefore, agents' gateways and WSDL and WADL description formats are static. Our proposal is to enable the dynamic disclosure of unknown services provided by both software agents and web services to increase systems interoperability. In order to define the properties that an entity must know to interact with agents – in our case, specifically JADE agents [28] – an abstract agent ontology was defined, from which *JADE* agent has been extended. Figure 1 introduces the abstract *Software Agent* ontology including possible SubClasses, such as *OAA* [29], *ZEUS* [30], *Jadex* [31], *EMERALD* [32], *SeSAm* [33] and *JADE* agents.

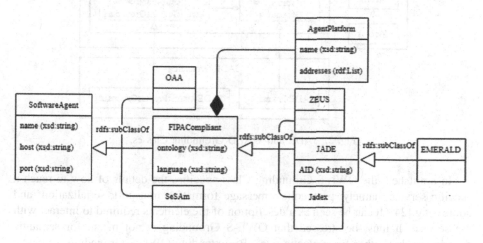

Fig. 1. The *Software Agent* ontology.

By definition, software agents run on a given host through a specific port and have a unique name for identification purposes. While additional information may be required for interaction with an agent, these basic properties are used in the *Soft-wareAgent* abstract Class. Other properties, which may be required by different agent implementations, are exposed in different SubClasses.

FIPA provides a number of standards for communication between heterogeneous agents and the services they provide [34], specifying that all agents must state which ontology they use to describe their message and the language they use (e.g.: XML, JSON, RDF/XML, TURTLE, etc.). Therefore, the *FIPACompliant* agent SubClass includes the *ontology* and *language* Data Properties for the effective communication with the agent, and the *AgentPlatform* Class which identifies the agent platform *name* and the *addresses* list. ZEUS, JADE, EMERALD, and Jadex-based agents, being FIPA compliant, are expressed though four new SubClasses, named accordingly. JADE agents, in particular, require an identification for individual agents in a given community, which is provided by the Data Property AID (agent unique identifier).

The *JADE* agent Class supplies atomic services via the *JadeAtomicService* Class. The interaction protocol for this scenario, i.e. its Grounding, is provided by the *JadeGrounding* Class.

The relationships between these entities and those supplied by the OWL-S and RESTFul Grounding are represented in Fig. 2, below:

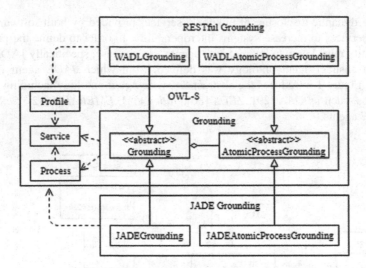

Fig. 2. JADE and WALD Grounding Classes.

In a nutshell, the OWL-S Grounding Class specifies the details of how to reach a specific service, namely: protocol(s); message format(s); transport; serialization; and addressing [24]. It can be seen as a description of the elements required to interact with the service. It must be stressed that OWL-S Grounding is not meant for semantic description, but rather for syntactic ones. By extending OWL-S Grounding, semantic meaning is given to data, with the intention of facilitating systems interoperability: by describing and exposing services semantically, and their expected inputs and outputs. Interoperability between heterogeneous systems is achieved by semantic communications [5, 8].

4 Architecture

The system's architecture is inspired in already existing architectures in the literature [3, 4, 14, 16], with the novelty of using semantic data models instead of syntactic data models, to ease the contextual searches of available services and communications between heterogeneous systems.

The proposed architecture must: (i) enable semantic services to register/deregister in/from the platform; (ii) enable client applications to search for services by different filter parameters and (iii) provide clients with machine-readable information about the available services (including services' parameterization, inputs and outputs). This way, systems will be able to perform these processes automatically when a service is required.

Figure 3 introduces the application level architecture, where three different entities are easily identified: (i) the Service's Catalogue, (ii) Service Providers (e.g. Agent-based or web service) and (iii) the Services' Clients.

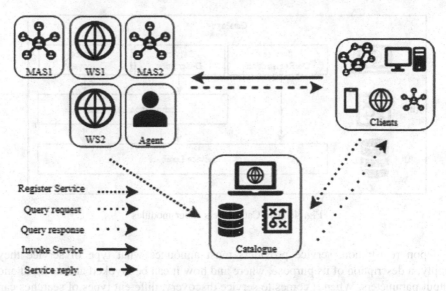

Fig. 3. Application level architecture.

Service providers can be any Agent, Multi-Agent System or Web Service that is able to execute a specific atomic task. This task must clearly specify its input and output parameters and supply a description as to what processes it entails.

Concurrently, the Services' Client represents the client applications searching for available services. These applications can use the information provided by the Services' Broker response to request for the services' execution directly to the service provider(s). It should be noticed that any registered service is also a potential service client: for instance, an agent-based service may be composed by several web-services, also available independently in the broker's application platform.

The Catalogue is the main application. It is responsible for proving semantic service's registration, deregistration and search services. The Catalogue's modules are distributed through three layers, namely: (i) Client Interface, which fulfils tasks such as Service Registration and De-Registration, supplies descriptions of services and allows Clients to search for the services they need; (ii) Composition Suggestion, which is used for supplying descriptions and services when a specific task requires more than one known service to be fulfilled, and (iii) Service Database, where the descriptions of the known services are stored and which can be queried via a SPARQL endpoint.

The layers and modules, along with the relationships between them are shown in Fig. 4, below:

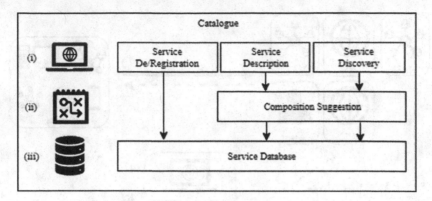

Fig. 4. The Catalogue's inner modules

Upon registration, service providers must announce what type of service they supply, a description of its purpose, where and how it can be invoked and its input and output parameters. When it comes to service discovery, different types of searches can be performed [35], allowing not only for syntactic similarity but for semantic similarity as well: e.g., by being able to compute how similar two ontological entities are or if mappings between them are available. Additionally, as single service may not be able to fulfil a certain task, but the combination of two or more known services may generate the desired outcome, the Composition Suggestion module can be invoked. As the name suggests, it will try to break down a discovery request into multiple queries and confirm that a composition can be made with those results. Different techniques of service discovery and composition will be employed in this task. If the Client agrees with the suggestion, it will be stored in the database as a composite service, with its own OWL-S description.

5   Use Case

For our example, let's consider a Forecast Service, which is provided simultaneously by a RESTFul web service and by an agent. This is a generic forecasting service based on an artificial neural network algorithm. As input, the algorithm expects to receive a training set composed of two arrays, and a testing set array to determine the output. The training set arrays are the *TrainInput* and *TrainOutput*. The *TrainInput*, is an array of arrays where each array outputs the value of the corresponding position of the *TrainOutput* array. Given the training set, the algorithm determines the output of the *TestInput* array.

Figure 5 presents the *Forecast* ontology.

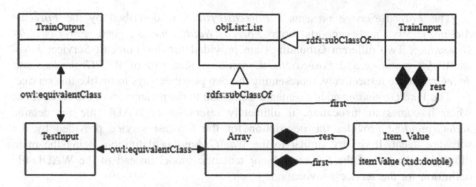

Fig. 5. The *Forecast* ontology.

The *Forecast* ontology is composed by the classes *Array*, *TestInput*, *TrainInput*, *TrainOutput* and *Item_Value*. The *Array* Class is an abstract class equivalent to the *objList:List*[1] Class in conjunction with the Object Property *first* with range *Item_Value*, and the Object Property *rest* with recursive range *Array*. The *objList:List* Class is part of the OWL-S ontology and it is used due to the need of representing lists of objects. The *Array* abstract Class has been defined to be reused in both *TestInput* and *TrainOutput* Classes, being these last equivalents to the *Array* Class. The *Item_Value* Class is defined by the Data Property *itemValue* which holds the double value of each item. Finally, the *TrainInput* Class is equivalent to the *objList:List* Class in conjunction with the Object Property *first* with range *Array*, and the Object Property *rest* with recursive range *TrainInput*.

Now that the entities regarding inputs and outputs of the service are established, a definition of the service itself is in order. Figure 6 introduces the Forecast Service definition.

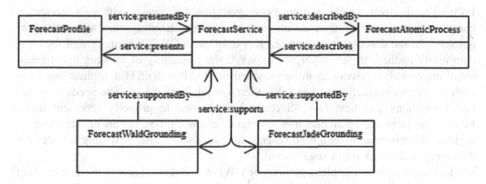

Fig. 6. Forecast Service definition.

---

[1] http://www.daml.org/services/owl-s/1.2/generic/ObjectList.owl#List.

The *ForecastService* presents a *ForecastProfile*, is described by the *Forecast AtomicProcess*, and supports both *ForecastWaldGrounding* and *ForecastJade-Grounding*. Two different Groundings are provided for this Forecast Service: *ForecastWaldGrounding* and *ForecastJadeGrounding,* instances of *WadlGrounding* and *JadeGrounding* respectively, representing the two possible ways to invoke this service.

The *WadlGrounding* adds a semantic definition to the parameters of the service, but when it comes to invocation, it ultimately refers to its WADL file for details. *JadeGrounding* provides the description for the forecast service provided by the software agent. It is very similar to the *WadlGrounding* definition, being the main difference the use of the *Software Agent* semantic model instead of the WADL file definition for the service's invocation.

The applications of the service descriptions can be further explained through another example. Consider a scheduling service provided by a given Agent A. For Agent A to be able to perform the scheduling for a given period, it needs to know which values can be expected to occur during that same period. Knowing the inputs required by Agent A (an array of values) and their meaning (a forecast's result), a search can be made for which existing services fill these criteria. The two versions of the Forecast Service provided above would be fitting, since they have the same inputs, the same outputs, and pertain to the same task – which grounding the service uses is indifferent for our problem. As such, the Catalogue Service would return a list containing the two services and either could be chosen and invoked, with the guarantee that the result could be used as input for Agent A in its scheduling task.

Due to size constraints, the complete service description, along with instantiation files, as well as the semantic data models introduced above are publicly available online[2] for appreciation.

6 Conclusions

In order to discover, invoke and compose agent-based alongside with web services, a common framework for their description is required. Existing semantic web technologies for the description of web services exist, with OWL-S being one of the most commonly applied. In this paper, we explored the possibility of viewing agent-based solutions as web services - as those provided in SOAP or RESTful applications - but with a different interaction protocol. We therefore analysed the specific needs of agent-based solutions and how OWL-S could be extended to properly represent them. Finally, we proposed an architecture that would allow entities, agents or otherwise, to register, deregister an invoke each other seamlessly, while also providing services for discovery and composition suggestion.

The most common implementations of OWL-S ontology, namely the instantiation of Grounding ontology module, end up by pointing to an XML file. In the future, it would be interesting to study the implications of using a purely semantic description for the invocation of all services, as we proposed in this paper to be done for agents, such

---

[2] http://www.gecad.isep.ipp.pt/epia/19/services/forecast/.

that no WADL or WSLD files would be necessary, especially when it comes to service definition change over time.

Acknowledgements. The present work has been developed under the PIANISM Project (ANI| P2020 40125) and has received funding from FEDER Funds through NORTE2020 program and from National Funds through Fundação para a Ciência e a Tecnologia (FCT) under the project UID/EEA/00760/2019. Gabriel Santos is supported by national funds through FCT PhD studentship with reference SFRH/BD/118487/2016.

References

1. Lemos, A.L., Daniel, F., Benatallah, B.: Web service composition. ACM Comput. Surv. **48**, 1–41 (2015)
2. Klusch, M., Kapahnke, P., Schulte, S., Lecue, F., Bernstein, A.: Semantic web service search: a brief survey. KI - Künstliche Intelligenz **30**, 139–147 (2016)
3. McIlraith, S.A., Son, T.C., Zeng, H.: Semantic web services. IEEE Intell. Syst. **16**, 46–53 (2001)
4. Huhns, M.N.: Agents as web services. IEEE Internet Comput. **6**, 93–95 (2002)
5. Teixeira, B., Pinto, T., Silva, F., Santos, G., Praça, I., Vale, Z.: Multi-agent decision support tool to enable interoperability among heterogeneous energy systems. Appl. Sci. **8**, 328 (2018)
6. Pinto, T., et al.: Adaptive portfolio optimization for multiple electricity markets participation. IEEE Trans. Neural Netw. Learn. Syst. **27**, 1720–1733 (2016)
7. Pinto, T., Vale, Z., Praça, I., Pires, E.J.S., Lopes, F.: Decision support for energy contracts negotiation with game theory and adaptive learning. Energies **8**, 9817–9842 (2015)
8. Teixeira, B., Silva, F., Pinto, T., Santos, G., Praca, I., Vale, Z.: TOOCC: enabling heterogeneous systems interoperability in the study of energy systems. In: 2017 IEEE Power and Energy Society General Meeting, pp. 1–5. IEEE (2017)
9. Santos, G., et al.: House management system with real and virtual resources: energy efficiency in residential microgrid. In: 2016 Global Information Infrastructure and Networking Symposium (GIIS), pp. 1–6. IEEE (2016)
10. Santos, G., Pinto, T., Praça, I., Vale, Z.: MASCEM: optimizing the performance of a multi-agent system. Energy **111**, 513–524 (2016)
11. Kravari, K., Bassiliades, N., Boley, H.: Cross-community interoperation between knowledge-based multi-agent systems: a study on EMERALD and rule responder. Expert Syst. Appl. **39**, 9571–9587 (2012)
12. Carneiro, J., Alves, P., Marreiros, G., Novais, P.: A multi-agent system framework for dialogue games in the group decision-making context. Presented at the (2019)
13. Klusch, M., Fries, B., Sycara, K.: Automated semantic web service discovery with OWLS-MX. In: Proceedings of the Fifth International Joint Conference on Autonomous Agents and Multiagent Systems - AAMAS 2006, p. 915. ACM Press, New York (2006)
14. Lord, P., Alper, P., Wroe, C., Goble, C.: Feta: a light-weight architecture for user oriented semantic service discovery. Presented at the (2005)
15. Rodriguez-Mier, P., Pedrinaci, C., Lama, M., Mucientes, M.: An integrated semantic web service discovery and composition framework. IEEE Trans. Serv. Comput. **9**, 537–550 (2016)

16. Greenwood, D., Calisti, M.: Engineering web service - agent integration. In: 2004 IEEE International Conference on Systems, Man and Cybernetics (IEEE Cat. No.04CH37583), pp. 1918–1925. IEEE
17. Martin, D., Burstein, M., McIlraith, S., Paolucci, M., Sycara, K.: OWL-S and agent-based systems. In: Cavedon, L., Maamar, Z., Martin, D., Benatallah, B. (eds.) Extending Web Services Technologies, pp. 53–77. Springer, New York (2004). https://doi.org/10.1007/0-387-23344-X_3
18. Web Service Modeling Language (WSML). https://www.w3.org/Submission/WSML/
19. Semantic Annotations for WSDL and XML Schema. https://www.w3.org/TR/sawsdl/
20. Pedrinaci, C., Cardoso, J., Leidig, T.: Linked USDL: a vocabulary for web-scale service trading. Presented at the (2014)
21. Kopecký, J., Gomadam, K., Vitvar, T.: hRESTS: an HTML microformat for describing RESTful web services. In: 2008 IEEE/WIC/ACM International Conference on Web Intelligence and Intelligent Agent Technology, pp. 619–625. IEEE (2008)
22. SA-REST: Semantic Annotation of Web Resources. https://www.w3.org/Submission/SA-REST/
23. Freitas, O., Filho, F., Alice, M., Varella, G.: Semantic web services : a RESTful approach. In: IADIS International Conference WWW/Internet 2009, pp. 169–180 (2009)
24. OWL-S: Semantic Markup for Web Services. http://www.ai.sri.com/∼daml/services/owl-s/1.2/overview/
25. Christensen, E., Curbera, F., Meredith, G., Weerawarana, S.: Web Service Definition Language (WSDL). https://www.w3.org/TR/2001/NOTE-wsdl-20010315
26. Hadley, M.: Web Application Description Language. https://www.w3.org/Submission/wadl/
27. Gunasekera, K., Zaslavsky, A., Krishnaswamy, S., Loke, S.W.: Service oriented context-aware software agents for greater efficiency. Presented at the (2010)
28. Bellifemine, F.L., Caire, G., Greenwood, D.: Developing Multi-agent Systems with JADE. Wiley, Hoboken (2007)
29. Martin, D.: The Open Agent Architecture
30. The Zeus Technical Manual. http://zeusagent.sourceforge.net/docs/techmanual/TOC.html
31. Braubach, L., Pokahr, A., Lamersdorf, W.: Jadex: a BDI-agent system combining middleware and reasoning. In: Unland, R., Calisti, M., Klusch, M. (eds.) Software Agent-Based Applications Platforms and Development Kits, pp. 143–168. Birkhäuser-Verlag, Basel (2005)
32. Kravari, K., Kontopoulos, E., Bassiliades, N.: EMERALD: a multi-agent system for knowledge-based reasoning interoperability in the semantic web. Presented at the (2010)
33. Klügl, F., Herrler, R., Klügl, F., Herrler, R., Fehler, M.: SeSAm: implementation of agent-based simulation using visual programming. In: Policy Agents I, II, III View project SeSAm: Implementation of Agent-Based Simulation Using Visual Programming (2006)
34. Foundation for Intelligent Physical Agents: FIPA ACL Message Structure Specification
35. Negi, A., Kaur, P.: Examination of sense significance in semantic web services discovery. Presented at the (2019)

Ising Model as a Switch Voting Mechanism in Collective Perception

Palina Bartashevich$^{(\boxtimes)}$ and Sanaz Mostaghim

Faculty of Computer Science, Otto von Guericke University, Magdeburg, Germany
{palina.bartashevich,sanaz.mostaghim}@ovgu.de
http://www.ci.ovgu.de

Abstract. This paper investigates the influence of the preferences of individuals on the process of collective perception in the collective decision-making systems. To do this, the Ising model from the context of Social Impact Theory is studied on a dynamic network of agents within an environment. This model additionally considers the mechanisms of the direct modulation of positive feedback. We propose learning rules for updating the preferences. Such rules depend on the undertaken decisions of the individuals. The experiments are evaluated on the best-of-2 collective perception problem and compared with the state-of-the-art voting mechanisms such as majority and voter models. The results show that assigning preferences to the agents allows a designer to take control over the outcome of the collective decision-making process. In addition, the agents with a right conjecture can faster reach the correct conclusion even if only 20% of the initial population holds the target opinion.

Keywords: Ising model · Collective decision making ·
Collective perception · Social impact theory

1 Introduction

The Ising model is a well-known model in statistical physics to study ferromagnetism, the property of a material to exhibit spontaneous aligned magnetic moments. Due to the emerging dynamics, it can be also used as a tool to study collective behaviors connected with opinion formation like consensus decision-making. The Ising model is always assumed to perform on a static network, where each agent keeps its neighbors. However, many natural collective decision-making systems (e.g. ant colonies, bird flocks) form dynamic networks, where the individuals move, change their local neighbors, and actively interact with each other and with the environment. The main goal of this paper is to investigate a variation of the Ising model as a potential voting mechanism in collective decision-making systems.

In recent years, there has been a surge of interest in the research on designing and validating collective decision-making approaches using robot swarms. Artificial systems make the study easier than dealing with natural collectives, giving a

© Springer Nature Switzerland AG 2019
P. Moura Oliveira et al. (Eds.): EPIA 2019, LNAI 11805, pp. 617–629, 2019.
https://doi.org/10.1007/978-3-030-30244-3_51

designer the possibility to focus on a particular decision-making phase excluding
the others. Previous studies [9,11] have mainly focused on the voting mechanisms, especially the majority voting and the voter models. However, mostly
one voting algorithm is assumed to be selected at the beginning by the designer
and it is assigned to all the individuals, and remains unchanged throughout the
whole decision-making process.

In this work, we aim to provide the individuals the capability to switch
between different voting mechanisms based on their current preferences. To do
this, we examine a family of nonlinear voter models with Ising-like criticality [5]
and couple it with the direct modulation of positive feedback [11] on a dynamic
network of agents, where each individual exerts a bias regarding a certain outcome. As the benchmark scenario, we consider collective perception [11], where
a swarm of agents explores a certain environment on the availability of particular resources (features) and has to determine which is an abundant one.
Although the local interactions here are different from [5], since they are modulated by internal (direct modulation) and external factors (changing interactions
with others), we expect to get an adaptive collective decision-making mechanism
according to [1,10]. In addition, we also study how incorporation of a learning
procedure affects the decision process and enhances the model with the preference update rules, which allow the agents to change their preferences over time
depending on the taken decisions.

In the remaining part of the paper, we draw the parallel between the Ising
model and the social impact theory along with some corresponding background.
Based on that, we then describe the considered voting mechanism together with
learning update rules. Afterwards, we provide the description of the multi-agent
simulation and the undertaken experiments. The results from the experiments
are discussed and analyzed, and, finally, the conclusion provides a brief summary,
highlighting the further research direction.

2   Related Work

2.1   Ising Model

In its original formulation, the Ising model is defined on a d-dimensional lattice,
i.e. $\mathbb{Z}^d \subseteq \mathbb{R}^d$, with all coordinates as integer numbers. Let's consider the finite
lattice $\Lambda_L \subset \mathbb{Z}^d$ of size L:

$$\Lambda_L = \{(i_1, i_2, ..., i_d) : |i_j| \leq L, j = 1, 2, ..., d\},$$

where i is a site in the lattice. One usually wants to work with the full infinite
lattice $L \to \infty$. Each site has a discrete variable σ_i, which is called spin, and
can take only two values $\sigma_i = +1$ (spin pointed "up") or $\sigma_i = -1$ (spin pointed
"down"). A spin configuration σ describes an assignment of a spin value σ_i to
each lattice site $i \in \Lambda_L$, i.e. $\sigma = \{\sigma_i\}_{i \in \Lambda_L}$. The total energy of the configuration
σ, defines the Ising model and is calculated using its Hamiltonian:

$$H(\sigma) = -\sum_{\langle ij \rangle} w_{ij}\sigma_i\sigma_j - h\sum_i \sigma_i, \tag{1}$$

where $\langle ij \rangle$ denotes a pair of sites in a finite Λ_L with Euclidean distance of 1: $\langle ij \rangle = \{i, j \in \Lambda_L : |i - j| = 1\}$. The parameter coefficient w_{ij} indicates the interaction between two spins σ_i and σ_j, where $|w_{ij}|$ is the strength of interaction, and h is an external magnetic field (if any). We consider the Ising model without an external field, therefore $h = 0$:

$$H(\sigma) = -\sum_{\langle ij \rangle} w_{ij} \sigma_i \sigma_j. \tag{2}$$

The probability that the system is in a state with configuration σ is called the configuration probability $\mu_L(\sigma)$:

$$\mu_L(\sigma) = exp(-\beta H(\sigma)) / \sum_{\sigma} exp(-\beta H(\sigma)), \tag{3}$$

where $\beta = 1/kT$ with the temperature T and Boltzmann constant k. The denominator is defined by the sum over all possible 2^L spin configurations on a finite lattice Λ_L. To simulate the Ising model, the single-spin-flip dynamics are established as follows: (1) In the current configuration σ, select a random spin with probability $1/L$ and flip its value (2) calculate the energy $H(\sigma')$ of a new configuration σ' (3) if $H(\sigma') < H(\sigma)$ accept the flip, else accept it only with probability $exp(-\beta(H(\sigma') - H(\sigma)))$ (4) repeat the process until all the spins become aligned, i.e. the lattice becomes ferromagnetic. It is stated that the system converges in $d \geq 2$. To quantify the level of magnetization, one can calculate the average value of all the spins: $M(\sigma) = (1/L) \sum_{i=1}^{L} \sigma_i$. Although the system dynamics are studied in the thermodynamic limit $(L \rightarrow \infty)$, Peierls [2] has shown that spontaneous magnetization already occurs in a relative small lattices but with the smoothed singularities due to the finite size.

2.2 Social Impact Theory

Theory of social impact is based on psychosocial laws and describes how individuals are affected by their social environment [8]. It is defined by microlevel rules (i.e. in individual level) expressed for each individual i via social force field I_i, which depends on the total number of individuals in the group N, strength of their assertiveness s_i, and either spatial or abstract (e.g. personal relations) distance between its members d_{ij}. Therefore, the social impact is considered as a multiplicative function of the described above parameters: $I = f(N \cdot s \cdot d)$.

The impact of a group with N members on the i-th individual, I_i, is calculated as follows:

$$I_i = \Big[\sum_{j=1}^{N} \frac{p_{ij}}{d_{ij}^{\alpha}} (1 - \sigma_i \sigma_j)\Big] - \Big[\sum_{j=1}^{N} \frac{s_{ij}}{d_{ij}^{\alpha}} (1 + \sigma_i \sigma_j)\Big], \tag{4}$$

$\sigma_i \in \{-1, +1\}$ is the binary opinion (e.g. yes/no) of the individual i; $\alpha \geq 0$ indicates the speed of the distance influence decline with the increase of the distance d_{ij} between the individuals. Parameter $s_{ij} \geq 0$ corresponds to the so-called supportiveness, i.e. the ability to support someone to keep the opinion and $p_{ij} \geq 0$ indicates the so-called persuasiveness, the ability to convince someone to change his opinion. Nowak and Latane [8] re-assign these parameters to some positive random values every time an individual has changed his opinion. In case, $\beta = 0$ and we have no noise in the system, the opinion σ_i changes for $I_i > 0$, and remains the same for $I_i < 0$: $\sigma_i(t+1) = -\sigma_i(t)sgn(I_i(t))$. For $\beta > 0$ (noise in the system), the probability to switch the opinion is proportional to $exp(\beta I_i(t))$.

As the result of using the above operations, a collective behavior such as polarization or fragmentation [6], can be observed on the macro-level, depending on the initial conditions. Both the social impact theory and the Ising model consider that the agents do not move in a physical space and evaluate them on a cellular automata. In comparison to statistical physics, a finite number of individuals brings difficulties into the analysis of the sociophysical models [3], since the singular behavior (i.e. order-disorder phase transition) can emerge only in the thermodynamic limit of the system ($N \to \infty$).

3   Proposed Model and Learning Process

Similar to the Ising model, we consider a swarm of N interacting individuals (instead of sites in the lattice, we take individuals), which move in a search space and explore for certain features (Fig. 1). The goal of the swarm is to collectively find the most occurring feature in the environment. In this work, we concentrate on the estimation of two environmental features, so that each individual holds its own opinion, $\sigma_i = \pm 1$, similar to the "up" and "down" spins. Different from previous approaches [11], we additionally assume that each individual has its own internal preference for a certain overall outcome, $\sigma(i) = \pm 1$. This strengthens the influence of the neighbors whose opinion correlates with own preference. In this case, the strength of the preference impact, $w_i \in \mathbb{R}_+^2$, will act similar to the supportiveness parameter in Eq. (4).

Now, we redefine Eq. (2) in a more convenient form for the z-th individual:

$$I_z = -\sum_{\langle zj \rangle} w_{zj}\sigma_z\sigma_j = \frac{1}{2}\sum_{\langle zj \rangle} w_{zj}(1 - \sigma_z\sigma_j) - \frac{1}{2}\sum_{\langle zj \rangle} w_{zj}(1 + \sigma_z\sigma_j), \quad (5)$$

where $\langle zj \rangle$ indicates the pair of the individual z and its neighbor j. The parameter $|w_{zj}|$ is the intensity of the influence of z on j. The first term in Eq. (5) contributes if the individuals j and z have opposite opinions. The second term is non zero if the individual j holds the same opinion as the individual z and is zero otherwise. In this case, if the preference of the individual z is $\sigma_z = +1$, then it means that if there are any agents in the neighborhood with opinion $\sigma_j = +1$, the second part of the Eq. (5) has to be $|w_{zj}|$ times stronger than the first part. And vice versa, if the preference of the individual z is $\sigma_z = -1$, the first part of Eq. (5) should take an advantage over the second one. In this sense, the value of $|w_{zj}|$ represents the relation of weight between neighbors with contradiction opinion to the zth individual's preference and those with the consistent one. Assuming that individual z has the same impact on all his neighbors, i.e. $w_{zj} = w_z$ for any j, we can write the following:

$$I_z = \sum_{j=1}^{N_z} w_z \sigma(z)(1 + \sigma_z \sigma_j) - \sum_{j=1}^{N_z} \sigma(z)(1 - \sigma_z \sigma_j) \tag{6}$$

$$= \begin{cases} w_z n_z^+ - n_z^-, & \text{if } \sigma(z) = +1 \\ n_z^+ - w_z n_z^-, & \text{if } \sigma(z) = -1 \end{cases}$$

$$= w_z' n_z^+ - n_z^-, \text{ where } w_z' = \begin{cases} w_z, & \text{if } \sigma(z) = +1 \\ \frac{1}{w_z}, & \text{if } \sigma(z) = -1, \end{cases}$$

where $\sigma(z)$ is the preference opinion of individual z, $|w_z| > 1$ is the strength of the preference and σ_z is the opinion holding by z. If $w_z' = 1$, the individual is considered as not biased, i.e. without any preference, while $w_z' \in (0,1)$ and $w_z' > 1$ corresponds to $\sigma(z) = -1$ and $\sigma(z) = +1$ respectively. The parameters n_z^+ and n_z^- indicate the amount of the neighboring individuals with opinion $\sigma_j = +1$ and $\sigma_j = -1$ accordingly.

If we take the spatial distances between the individuals into account, we can combine Eq. (4) and Eq. (6):

$$I_z = w_z' \sum_{j \in \mathcal{N}_z^+} (1/d_{zj}^\alpha) - \sum_{j \in \mathcal{N}_z^-} (1/d_{zj}^\alpha), \tag{7}$$

where $\mathcal{N}_z^+$ and $\mathcal{N}_z^-$ correspond to the neighbors of z-th individual, which are holding opinions $\sigma_j = +1$ and $\sigma_j = -1$ respectively. In this way, the distances between z and j influence the value for I_z. Considering two individuals with different distances to z, the influence of the closer one to z is greater than the other.

The opinion dynamics are defined probabilistically using the following sigmoid function as in [5]:

$$p(\beta I_z) = \frac{1}{2} \left(1 + \frac{tanh(\beta I_z)}{tanh(\beta)} \right) \in [0,1], \tag{8}$$

where a social field I_z is normalized, i.e. $I_z = \dfrac{w_z' \sum\limits_{j \in \mathcal{N}_z^+} (1/d_{zj}^\alpha) - \sum\limits_{j \in \mathcal{N}_z^-} (1/d_{zj}^\alpha)}{w_z' \sum\limits_{j \in \mathcal{N}_z^+} (1/d_{zj}^\alpha) + \sum\limits_{j \in \mathcal{N}_z^-} (1/d_{zj}^\alpha)} \in [-1, 1]$,

and β acts as a noise parameter. Varying β values from 0 to ∞ allows observing a spectrum of voting mechanisms from the voter ($\beta \to 0$) to majority models ($\beta \to \infty$) and everything in between [4]. The transitions from the state $\sigma_z^t = -1$ at time t to $\sigma_z^{t+1} = +1$ at $t+1$ occur with $p(\beta I_z)$ probability, and from $\sigma_z^t = +1$ to $\sigma_z^{t+1} = -1$ with probability $1 - p(\beta I_z)$ respectively, for all swarm members.

In the following, we introduce a learning process for updating the preferences (see Algorithm 1). The main idea is based on the fact that the current opinion of the individual σ_z^t and its preference $\sigma(z)$ can be in conflict with each other (e.g. $w_z > 1$ corresponds to $\sigma(z) = +1$, while the holding opinion is $\sigma_z^t = -1$). However, when due to the interactions with the others and the environment the individual changes his opinion, so that it becomes in agreement with its preference $\sigma(z)$, we reinforce the preference strength on Δw either in a positive or in a negative side depending on the current sign of the preference (i.e. we add if $w_z > 1$ and subtract if $w_z < 1$). In case if the agent keeps its opinion in conflict with its own preference, we make a double reinforcement (i.e. $w_z \pm 2\Delta w$) in order to change the preference to the side of this opinion (e.g. (5+6) and (9+11) lines in Algorithm 1). If there is no conflict between the individual's preference and the current opinion, we keep the preference strength w_z unchangeable (lines (1+3) and (12+14) in Algorithm 1). In this way both opinions and preferences are evolved as the result of the interactions between the individuals and the environment.

Algorithm 1 Preference Update Rules

1: **if** $w_z > 1$ & $\sigma_z^t = +1$	9: **if** $w_z < 1$ & $\sigma_z^t = +1$
2: **if** $\sigma_z^{t+1} = -1$, $w_z = w_z - \Delta w$;	10: **if** $\sigma_z^{t+1} = -1$, $w_z = w_z - \Delta w$;
3: **if** $\sigma_z^{t+1} = +1$, $w_z = w_z$;	11: **if** $\sigma_z^{t+1} = +1$, $w_z = w_z + 2\Delta w$;
4: **end**	12: **end**
5: **if** $w_z > 1$ & $\sigma_z^t = -1$	13: **if** $w_z < 1$ & $\sigma_z^t = -1$
6: **if** $\sigma_z^{t+1} = -1$, $w_z = w_z - 2\Delta w$;	14: **if** $\sigma_z^{t+1} = -1$, $w_z = w_z$;
7: **if** $\sigma_z^{t+1} = +1$, $w_z = w_z + \Delta w$;	15: **if** $\sigma_z^{t+1} = +1$, $w_z = w_z + \Delta w$;
8: **end**	16: **end**

3.1   Multi-Agent Simulation

The environment is defined by a square grid of 20×20 cells 1×1 unit each, painted in black and white. Without loss of generality, we consider that in all environments the white color is prevailing. We consider 100 iterations in simulation as 1 s, and we plot the simulation environment every 10 iterations (i.e. 0.1 s) as it was done in previous research [9]. We use a swarm of 20 agents, initially assigned with half for opinion white ($\sigma_i = -1$) and half for black ($\sigma_i = +1$). The preferences of the individuals coincides with their initial opinions. We keep the other parameters similar to [11].

The size (diameter) of an agent is proportional to the size of the grid cells and is equal to 0.7 units (considering 1 unit = 10 cm). The agents move in the environment using a random walk executed along with collision avoidance to other agents and the borders of the grid. The random walk is performed by alternating periods of the straight linear motion and rotation on the spot for random periods of time taken from normal distribution with mean 40 s and uniform distribution between 0 and 4.5 s respectively. The linear velocity v is set to 1.6 units/s and the angular velocity ω is 7.5 rad/s. If agents collide with each other or with the borders of the grid, they randomly rotate on the spot (equally likely clockwise or counterclockwise) until their bearings will not allow them to go freely further resuming a straight motion.

Besides different movement phases, each agent i can be also in either one of the two following states going one after another: (1) *exploration* E_i, where it moves and only estimates the quality of its current opinion $\hat{\rho}_i$, or

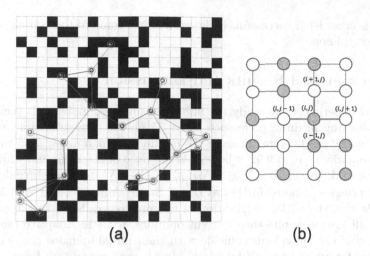

Fig. 1. Dissemination of opinions: (a) in multi-agent simulation; (b) on static lattice. Colors represent agents opinions (red for black, blue for white). Lines indicate possible connections at the current time step. Bold lines (magenta) show agents in communication with each other. The agents in (a), while moving, perceive the environment consisting of black and white cells. (Color figure online)

(2) *dissemination D_i*, when it moves and only exchanges its own opinion with the others, making at the end a decision on either to keep or to switch its current opinion i. The communication between agents is set only pair-wise, and only if both of them are in dissemination state, for each 10 iterations (0.1 s) in a random order within the communication distance of $d_{max} = 5$ units. The duration of exploration state for each individual i is the same and takes $tE = 10$ s, while the dissemination state is biased and proportional to the quality of the current opinion, i.e. $tD_i = tE * \hat{\rho}_i$, so that the less quality opinions promotes the shorter periods of time. The quality $\hat{\rho}_i$ is calculated as the ratio of time when the agent observed the color related with its current opinion i during tE. Each agent logs the opinions of its neighbors during the last 30 iterations of its dissemination state as in [11] and takes the last $\mathcal{N}$ opinions to decide based on one of the three DM strategies with $\mathcal{N} = 2$: In DMMD, the agent takes opinion which is preferred by the majority out of $\mathcal{N}$ including its own opinion. In DMVD, it adopts the opinion of a random agent from $\mathcal{N}$ excluding itself. In DC, time tD is unbiased ($tD_i = tE \; \forall i$) and at the end of tD_i each agent directly compares the quality of its own opinion i with a randomly chosen neighbor's j, and if $\hat{\rho}_j > \hat{\rho}_i$, then it switches its opinion $i \to j$ and starts E_j. The agents also transmit their individual IDs and save the received ones, so that in case, if the agent was perceiving the opinion of one and the same neighbor for two consecutive steps, only the first one is saved in the log. To validate the performance of DMs we consider two commonly used metrics: (1) *Exit probability* (E_N) to measure the ratio of successful runs among all simulations and (2) *Consensus time* ($T_N^{correct}$) as the number of iterations until all the agents converge to the correct opinion.

The run is considered successful, if the swarm has come to the consensus with the correct opinion.

4   Experimental Results and Discussion

In the first experiment, we study the impact of unbiased individuals (i.e. which do not have any intrinsic preference $w_z = 1$) on the consensus time and the exit probability for different values of the nonlinearity parameter β on the most difficult scenario, i.e $\rho_b^* = 0.92$, where ρ_b^* is the ratio of black N_{bl} and white N_{wh} cells in the grid, considering $N_{wh} > N_{bl}$: $\rho_b^* = \frac{N_{bl}}{N_{wh}}$. We examine three decision-making strategies (denoted further as DMs): Static, Adaptive, and W-Adaptive. In W-Adaptive the initial distribution of the preferences is set to the range of $(0, 1)$ for all agents despite their current opinions, while in Adaptive the initial preferences of the individuals coincide with their initial opinions (i.e. half with preferences for white and half for black). In all the experiments below, we set $\Delta w = 0.1$ in Algorithm 1 and $\alpha = 0$ in the Eq. (7), unless otherwise stated.

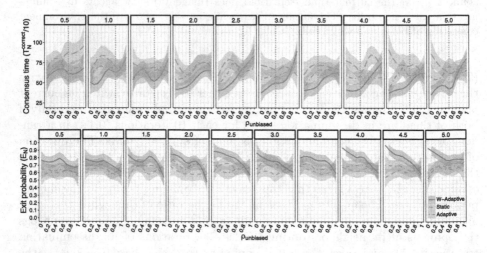

Fig. 2. Consensus time ($T_N^{correct}$) and exit probability (E_N) as a function of the proportion of unbiased individuals in the swarm (i.e. $\{0, 0.1, ..., 1.0\}$) for each value of the noise level $\beta \in \{0.5, 1.0, 1.5, 2.0, 2.5, 3.0, 3.5, 4.0, 4.5, 5.0\}$ (top headings). Task difficulty: $\rho_b^* = 0.92$. Dashed (pink), solid (blue) and dotdashed (red) lines correspond to the Static, W-Adaptive and Adaptive strategies respectively. (Color figure online)

Figure 2 shows the estimated smoothed conditional means of the consensus time calculated only among successful runs and the exit probability with shading areas of 95% confidence interval for the described above experiment. For all noise levels, there is a clear trend of the performance deterioration in all of the considered DMs with the increase of unbiased individuals in the population. The best performance in terms of consensus time as well as in the accuracy is mostly

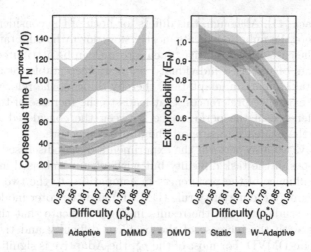

Fig. 3. Consensus time $(T_N^{correct})$ and exit probability (E_N) as a function of the task difficulty ρ_b^*. Parameter configurations: $\rho_{un} = 0$, $\beta = 4.5$. Solid (red), longdashed (khaki), dotdashed (green), twodashed (pink) and dashed (blue) lines correspond to the Adaptive, DMMD, DMVD, Static and W-Adaptive strategies respectively. (Color figure online)

at $\rho_{un} = 0$ for both adaptive strategies with $\beta \in (2.0, 5.0)$. The performance of W-Adaptive suggests that when the whole population is initially biased to the white (i.e. $\rho_{un} = 0$), the agents are able to gain a momentum and to keep their weights in $(0, 1)$ range during the adaptation process, thereby leading the collective to the fastest and the most accurate (almost 100% success rate) collective decisions among the others (see Fig. 2). However, with the introduction of unbiased individuals into W-Adaptive population, the accuracy starts decreasing at any values of β, while for Static and adaptive strategies it keeps almost stable at around $(0.65, 0.7)$ exit probability. For the consensus time, at $\beta = 4.0$, we observe a stable rate for both W-Adaptive and Adaptive until $\rho_{un} = 0.4$ along with a significant drop for Static. At other noise levels, the consensus time for W-Adaptive and Adaptive mostly increases with the increase of unbiased individuals along with a few non-significant drops at the lower values of noise, i.e. $\beta \in (0.5, 1.5)$ at $\rho_{un} = 0.6$. While for the Static, the presence of unbiased individuals promotes a significant decrease in the consensus time without compromising the accuracy for most levels of β, i.e. at $\rho_{un} = 0.4$ and $\rho_{un} = 0.5$ for $\beta = \{2.0, 4.0\}$ and $\beta = \{4.5, 5.0\}$ respectively.

The obtained results for the Static are in agreement with findings in [5], which showed that the individuals without a preference (unbiased) help to minimize the time to achieve the consensus but on the 2D square lattice. In our case with Static strategy, this finding goes further in its understanding as our results indicate that an unbiased sub-population aids to propagate exactly the *correct opinions* (i.e. with the highest quality) in the dynamic network coupled with the environment within the concept of a direct modulation mechanism of positive feedback [11]. Although, this differs for both of the considered adaptive strategies, where the unbiased agents mostly slow down the adaptation process, especially in the case of W-Adaptive. Such a result can be attributed to the fact that the weights of unbiased individuals, $w_z = 1$, keep stable for all period of time without taking part in adaptation, thereby diluting the reforming process of the already existence preferences, that leads to the increase of the consensus time. The difference in the performance between the considered strategies in Fig. 2 provide the evidence to support the above conjecture.

Additionally, we also perform the experiments of the discussed above DMs on all eight types of the task difficulty but without any unbiased individuals to examine the influence of the preferences in comparison to the two well-studied DMs in [11], namely the majority rule (DMMD) and the voter model (DMVD). As in previous studies of [11], the results in Fig. 3 indicate that the consensus time increases with the increase of the problem difficulty and the DMMD is much faster than DMVD. For most of the ρ_b^*, the Adaptive is significantly faster than DMMD but evens out with it at higher $\rho_b^* = 0.92$. The W-Adaptive is the fastest among the others with a slight acceleration in the consensus time after $\rho_b^* = 0.72$. It is approximately three times faster than the DMMD for all ρ_b^*. The Static shows the intermediate performance between the DMMD and the Adaptive with an increase in consensus time after $\rho_b^* = 0.72$. It is significantly worse than Adaptive for higher ρ_b^* (i.e. after $\rho_b^* = 0.72$). For the exit probability, the difficulty of $\rho_b^* = 0.72$ is a breaking point for the preference-based DMs. That is, until $\rho_b^* = 0.72$, Static and W-Adaptive indicate the similar accuracy trend in $(0.9, 1.0)$ range along with almost 1.0 stable rate until $\rho_b^* = 0.67$ for Adaptive. After $\rho_b^* = 0.72$, the performance of Static and Adaptive is decreasing until $(0.6, 0.7)$ exit probability, while W-Adaptive keeps the highest accuracy (i.e. $0.9 - 1.0$) also for higher ρ_b^*. The accuracy of the DMMD is lower than for the preference-based DMs starting from $\rho_b^* = 0.67$ and decreasing until the chance level at higher ρ_b^*. While the exit probability of the preference-based DMs is always higher than by the chance, the DMVD accuracy is almost always in $(0.5, 0.6)$ range despite the problem difficulty.

Altogether, these results suggest that the Ising model performs mostly similar to the majority rule in the context of the direct modulation of the positive feedback. However, the existence of preferences allows taking control over the decision-making process by manipulating the influence of neighbors whose opinions are in agreement with an individual's preference (as it is done in W-Adaptive and Adaptive).

4.1 Influence of Initial Preferences

In the following, we study the performance of the preference-based DMs *without unbiased individuals* depending on the initial number of the agents $E_a(0)$ favoring the incorrect opinion a (black), and compare it with the DMMD and the DMVD strategies. Taking into account that the total number of agents $N = 20$, we varied $E_a(0)$ from 1 to 19 with all the values in between and performed 40 simulation runs for each configuration. Figure 4-left shows that in a simple scenario $\rho_b^* = $

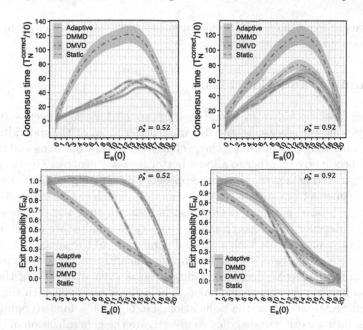

Fig. 4. Consensus time ($T_N^{correct}$) and exit probability (E_N) as a function of the initial number $E_a(0)$ of individuals with opinion a (black) in the swarm (while prevailing color in the environment is b, i.e. white). The values of initial preference bias of an individual are in accordance with its initial opinion. Parameter configurations: $\rho_b^* \in \{0.52, 0.92\}$, $\beta = 4.5$, $\rho_{un} = 0$, $N = 20$. Solid (red), longdashed (khaki), dotdashed (green) and twodashed (pink) lines correspond to the Adaptive, DMMD, DMVD and Static strategies respectively. (Color figure online)

0.52, Adaptive is the fastest strategy for all initial conditions $E_a(0)$ than the others, along with the highest accuracy holding $(0.9, 1.0)$ exit probability even with 80% of the initial population targeting the wrong opinion (i.e $E_a(0) = 16$), while the DMMD starts already degrading from $E_a(0) = 9$ (i.e. 45%). For the difficult scenario, in Fig. 4-right, the DMMD and Adaptive have similar consensus speed followed by the Static and the DMVD. Although, the decision accuracy of the Adaptive strategy decreases more slowly than the DMMD with increase of $E_a(0)$.

4.2 Matter of Distance Dependency

We have also performed the experiments incorporating the influence of the moments α of the *spatial* Euclidean distance d_{ij} between the individuals (see Eq. 7) with $\alpha \in \{-1, 0, 1, 2\}$. The obtained results (not reported here) indicate no significant impact of the *spatial distance* dependencies on the overall decision-making process, independently on the parameter α. This can be explained by the fact that agents communicate with each other in a very limited radius of max 5 units, which resulted in a small numbers not affecting the outcome of Eq. (8).

However, more experiments with unlimited interactions, i.e. global communication, are needed to support this claim.

5   Summary and Conclusion

In this work, we provided an Ising-based approach for the collective decision-making systems incorporating the dynamic preferences of the individuals. We proposed a learning procedure for the preferences, so that opinions and the preferences can co-evolve together to allow a better decision process. The Ising model can be considered as a general voting approach, integrating in itself the variety of the mechanisms from voter to majority models, which can be controlled by its non-linearity (noise) parameter. Our results indicate that the preferences give an external observer (a designer) an opportunity to manipulate the undertaken decisions of the individuals with an initial conjecture of the suggested outcome. With the right conjecture, the latter can significantly increase the speed and accuracy of the collective decision-making process even with 80% of the initial population holding the opposite opinion. The same is observed with the equally distributed preferences over the population, i.e. 50%–50% for two opinions. As part of the future work, we are going to investigate the generalization of the Ising model, which is called the Potts model [7], to explore the case of the best-of-n problem with $n > 2$.

References

1. Berdahl, A., Torney, C.J., Ioannou, C.C., Faria, J.J., Couzin, I.D.: Emergent sensing of complex environments by mobile animal groups. Science **339**, 574–576 (2013)
2. Bonati, C.: The Peierls argument for higher dimensional Ising models. Eur. J. Phys. **35**(3), 035002 (2014)
3. Castellano, C., Fortunato, S., Loreto, V.: Statistical physics of social dynamics. Rev. Mod. Phys. **81**, 591–646 (2009)
4. Drouffe, J.M., Godrèche, C.: Phase ordering and persistence in a class of stochastic processes interpolating between the Ising and voter models. J. Phys. A: Math. Gen. **32**(2), 249–261 (1999)
5. Hartnett, A.T., Schertzer, E., Levin, S.A., Couzin, I.D.: Heterogeneous preference and local nonlinearity in consensus decision making. Phys. Rev. Lett. **116**, 038701 (2016)
6. Holyst, J.A., Kacperski, K., Schweitzer, F.: Social impact models of opinion dynamics. Annual Rev. Comput. Phys. **IX**, 253–272 (2001)
7. Martin, P.: Potts Models and Related Problems in Statistical Mechanics. Series on Advances in Statistical Mechanics. World Scientific, Singapore (1991)
8. Nowak, A., Latane, B., Szamrej, J.: From private attitude to public opinion: a dynamic theory of social impact. Psychol. Rev. **97**(3), 362–376 (1990)
9. Strobel, V., Castelló Ferrer, E., Dorigo, M.: Managing byzantine robots via blockchain technology in a swarm robotics collective decision making scenario. In: Proceedings of the 17th International Conference on AAMAS, pp. 541–549 (2018)

10. Torney, C., Neufeld, Z., Couzin, I.D.: Context-dependent interaction leads to emergent search behavior in social aggregates. Proc. Natl. Acad. Sci. **106**(52), 22055–22060 (2009)
11. Valentini, G.: Achieving Consensus in Robot Swarms. SCI, vol. 706. Springer, Cham (2017). https://doi.org/10.1007/978-3-319-53609-5

Social Simulation and Modelling

Reflections on Social Simulation and Complexity

Helder Coelho$^{(\boxtimes)}$ iD

MAS-BioISI and Mind-Brain College, FC, ULisbon, Lisbon, Portugal
hmcoelho@ciencias.ulisboa.pt

Abstract. After the involvement with a huge collection of case studies, where the experimentation may distinguish between luck and skill, our motivation was directed to see how agent-based modeling and model thinking were applied to general problem solving and case studies on complexity. Also, the development of models was directed to show the efficacy of diversity in attacking new scenarios and landscapes. And, even we avoided often Nassim Taleb's mantra, "we tend to learn the overall precise and not the general", the desire was to get realism (avoid embellished depiction of nature and behavior). This direction of research forced our attention upon the calibration of parameters, the validation, the use of mechanisms, the use of big data, and the activity of scaling up to check the plausibility of the outcomes.

Keywords: Multi-agent systems · Sociality · Social simulation · Complexity · ABM

1 Introduction

The exercise of reflection about a line of research (e.g. use of ABM (Agent-Based Modeling) to make experiments on complex social systems), from the 90's, implies some prudence, an open mind and a deconstructive criticism by increasing the scope of what is questionable. Starting by referring back to the subject of innovation, either related to a technology park or to street violence (Lisbon, Kiev, Madrid, Cairo, London, Paris), there was a reconsideration of the results, in order to review the limits of this research [1].

Dismantling and unbuilding through a step back is necessary to show the outline of a future possibility, to find questions about behavior where others found only certainties, and to open new controversies with rational thought. Social simulation allows us to understand precisely how conflicts are built and how we can regulate them.

We live in a complex world with diverse people, enterprises, and governments whose behaviors aggregate to produce new and unexpected phenomena. We see a never-ending array of social trends, but the degree to which individuals tend to associate in social groups, exploring sociality, is not often a worry. Yet, how do we make sense of it in social simulation [2]? The answer is quite common, with models, which help us to better organize the information and to make accurate forecasts. Also, they help us make better decisions and select more effective strategies. They even improve our ability to design institutions and procedures with a great care. How is behavior

© Springer Nature Switzerland AG 2019
P. Moura Oliveira et al. (Eds.): EPIA 2019, LNAI 11805, pp. 633–641, 2019.
https://doi.org/10.1007/978-3-030-30244-3_52

generated? Agents need to be simple, but they are driven by goals, beliefs and desires (mentality), cognition, emotions (affective computing) and social concerns.

Beyond models, we need also big data, simulation tools (NetLogo, MASON, Repast, AnyLogic, Jade), languages (Python, Java) in order to define sound agent-based modeling, to capture individuality and rich behaviors. With micro motives we stimulate collective actions and replicate different sorts of social dynamics (coordination, cooperation, collaboration, grouping, crowding, interacting). We start with a bunch of assumptions to produce results, which are later on evaluated and validated carefully [3].

Models help us to understand, predict, strategize, and re-design our would-be worlds. But, we need to follow our intuitions to test those models with more rigour. For example, Thomas Schelling's segregation model represents people as agents on a checkboard, the segregation of neighborhoods based on race, ethnicity or income, and this is not a very rich environment, yet nice results were produced.

Evidence show that people who think with models outperform those who don't. By exploring several models, critiquing them, finding each model' limits, its strength and weakness, we build and deepen our overall comprehension.

We used always many surveys by interrogating the people concerned with the situational conditions, inspected also videos about protests (in the Internet), which were helpful to understand actions of uncertainty and to explain sophisticated cutting-edge research with a concrete clarity.

2   Some Applications and Case Studies

Along three decades, several applications were developed to present a diversity of constructions and to experiment the intricacies of this approach to problem solving. The following list presents only some examples:

2004: Interactions (innovation and foresight) in Tagus Park, Lisbon (Portugal) for generating new policies to involve people and be creative, with Schilperoord [17].
2007: Tax Evasion in Portugal, to check how honesty stance is adopted (against deceive taxes, modify data), with Antunes and Balsa [19].
2009: Vip-Serious Game for Water Management, São Paulo (Brazil), to study how local authorities are sensible to popular desires, with Adamatti and Sichman [18].
2016: Social Conflicts (street protests), Lisbon (Portugal), to check how political tensions are liberated with calls for freedom, with Lemos and Lopes [1, 4–6].
2017: Electricity Markets, in Portugal and within Iberian region, to exchange and negotiate potency, with Lopes [20].
2018: Risk management and the banking antifragility index, São Paulo (Brazil), to see how institutions are resilient and deal with pression, with Passos and Sarti [21].
2019: Sentiment Analysis for UK Brexit Referendum (also Trump USA 2016 and Bolsonaro Brazil 2018 elections), the abuse of faked news to manipulate the final results, with Santos and Louçã [22].

The interesting thing about this collection of cases is the exploitation of a diversity of models along a large spectrum of problematic situations and some ones involving complexity. We found points in common concerning honest behaviors, disruption, shifts and surprises, and they can serve to think better and in an open style about "innovation" and bad characters.

3 Model Thinking

The world today is uncertain, random, fragile, unexpected and global. Model thinking is today an important asset [8] for exploring ideas and intuitions, a new kind of science. The tool kit is suitable for test hypothesis, represent the world with persuasive narratives, think through the logic of any given situation, evaluate a battery of models, design new or modified models when appropriate, or distinguish a complex set of important facts with their interrelationships and behaviors of multiple agents.

The ODD (Overview, Design concepts, and Details) protocol for agent models [9] is suitable to evaluate how well fitted it is to adopt social simulation to look into behaviors. Such shared protocols can facilitate model review and help to descibe with precision many intrincacies. The framework holds promise as a standard communication mechanism. The goal is to evaluate how well fitted it is to make social simulations and how successful it might be in increasing communication between individual and agent-based modelers.

Models improve our abilities to make accurate forecasts, to fix tailored decisions and adopt more effective strategies. As a matter of fact, models make us better thinkers, by organizing information, identifying relationships, understanding classes of outcomes and giving good sense to big data.

4 ProtestLab and Complexity

The environment (dashboard) of any simulation is a matter to be carefully designed [1]: all the variables able to set up the dynamics to be later observed, the windows to follow particular events, the main scene where the drama is to be controlled, and the operation of certain mechanisms and circuits. In social conflicts, where street violence may occur, we need to choose the two models of violence, say, fear linked to the jail mechanism, defined by the Epstein formula (in our case the formula was enlarged [10]), and the anger with tensions, drives, and the causality of conflict/crisis, tuned by the legitimacy feedback (focus upon austerity, inequality and corruption). Government and its credibility depend on the economy versus sociality, and may be covered by surveys done during the protests (manifs, demos).

Sociality, interference (contagion), time and complexity are four topics that need a careful attention when we try to study them within real urban areas, such as street protests. Often, we arrange the tools (ABM, Laboratories) with big data to make simulations able to envisage spatial and temporal realistic behaviors. Yet, models are always far from the truth and experiments suffer from being too weak even when scaling-up is taken into account. The use of videos, observed user data, taken from the streets where protests are happening, may be added to the systematic coverage with micro surveys on the spot, interviews and reports. And, a strange feeling harasses our tests. What can be done moreover?

The need of more empirical studies, done with big data, follows every experiment. Many times, we find easily something extra that explains why the real thing (reality) is forgotten by social simulation. Using data alone is not sufficient, and we need machine learning to explore forecasting to get deep understanding. Removing gatekeepers is important for innovation. Also, taking risks, observing errors and failures are the best ways to ensure a try has a future. It is not an experiment if you know already the outcome. Measure and learn. If things fail, they can still be successful if the lessons you learn drive the next try. Follow your curiosity and find something new, different or weird which contradicts what you believe.

The social conflict is a phenomenon able to show the "no free lunch theorem". Scale diversity, entities and mechanisms are so large that each type of conflict requires a different model. Machine learning models may provide recommendations, behavioral analytics and insights. Intelligent tasks, such as activity recognition, mood detection and move prediction, are also suitable for follow how street protests go on.

Agent model (abstract, middle-range, fac-simile) was the first theme to be attacked when a sense of unrealism was brought up. There are other alternatives, and Agent_Zero [11] was the one with more traits, including social and emotional issues. The old BDI (Beliefs, Desires, Intentions) model was thought as the solution because mental states were present and the whole idea of mind was interesting. An alternative is the adoption of PECS (Physical conditions, Emotional states, Cognitive capabilities, Social status) model [12], a kind of BDI adopted many times by crowd dynamics.

The modeling of social conflicts may be greatly improved with all the knowledge coming from crowd safety and risk analysis [13], in order to take into account origi- nality and avoid some pitfalls. For example, when we reach a high score of 40% of the crowd, in the jail, we cannot refer only violence recruit as the explanation. Then, we may, take contagion or imitation as two possible reasons. Adopting behavior based upon goals implies some changes, and to think more about adopting attraction and repulsion points. Variable density is rather important for movement patterns during emergency, police charges and accidents.

All the discussions (and controversy) about sociality [14] are associated to a variety of ways able to assemble individuals into groups (of protesters) and to the movement of groups into different confrontation spaces. The fights among hard protesters and policemen are dependent on the available leadership of the protesters. The side of policemen gains also with the existence of some trusted leader. The real time explo- ration of ProtestLab needs to include decision frequency and degrees to which indi- viduals tend to associate.

The inclusion of informal media agents (with smartphones) apart of current media (newspapers and radio/television) is the way to cover feedback links, and it is mandatory to allow a measure of legitimacy (associated with the aggressors and victims).

The search for realism can be done through scaling up the number of agents: 100, 1000, 2000, 5000 or 10000. There are difficulties to process data when enlarging the number of agents, and also, we need to enhance the power (GPU) of social simulation.

There are two quantities that trade off against each other, things that are about complexity (motion, patterns) and others about scale (weights, repetition). Both divided into a diversity of categories: endurance, strength, balance and flexibility. Solving social problems is a matter to be solved in the space of possibilities. How does an agent make decisions? Considering preferences and options. Does he try to make choices before acting with emotions? What about the bad choices (constrained by negative emotions)? And, when occur errors and failures? Can he correct them? Does he evaluate risks? And, what about the agent's profile? Is it necessary to include identity, character and personality in every agent? Easily, we start with simple agents and by upgrading we close the experiments with heavier agents.

Check the outcome distributions in order to constrain the simulation in many issues/dimensions/scales. Moreover, look to the empirical models in the absence of good data sets (pattern-oriented modeling): there is a need to find surveys to better calibrate the agents' behaviors and experiment/simulate at local level. Yet, be careful with the variables: some make no difference and others have a large influence, Attention to sensible patterns generated by the model. Use alternative case studies to test the model in general and to find weak parts. Compare the model outcome to different measures. Look at interesting events' to check whether the model is able to capture these. Confirm the model logic through peer review and be attentive to sweeps/Monte-Carlo testing of model.

Use un-validated exploratory models as a way to inspect social dynamics, feel (no way to validate) the model or the mechanisms driving it. There is not an only way to get an insight into the real dynamics of the system. Validation is stronger when trying to make forecasts.

5 Simulation

Simulation is a mix of cinema and animation, a device to support voyages and generating effects. On one side, the screen window of the dashboard shows a sequence of images, a time line, and, on the other side, the experimenter is pushed by the movement and works hard with his mind to imagine things and to understand them, like a spectator. Yet, there are no flashbacks, and the images are not so clear as in the cinema. Also, simulation has no sound, which is rather important in movies and television. Sound creates the layers of the minds, and any film is a mental labyrinth of the main character. In cinema, sound and images are necessary to produce chaos and labyrinths (of a city), and all of that is inside the mind of each spectator.

Simulation is a poor means, where there are no mix of movie set and real scenery. However, the importance of the mystery is still reinforced, and the experimenter is always thinking about what is shown (visible and non-visible). Characters are not so complex like in the movies, but the subjectivity of the viewer is part of the game.

Cinema is a powerful device, able to combine light and shadows, memory and silence, to cover secrets and to enhance the mysteries. The power to show is bigger, and there are more things to reveal. Cinema is a stronger experience for viewers, something more than storytelling, and associated to the inner layers of human nature.

Can a film or a simulation explain what happens? A story can be difficult to access, but every viewer can think about it, pose questions, re-do experiences, discover new relations, backtrack, and oppose causes (reasons, motives) to effects (ends).

6 Further Research

Premonitions, intromissions, suspicions, or even infections affect society, constrain diverse choices and the whole decision process, provoking severe disruptions. Among social circles, exchanging arguments with persuasion, along conversations, enhance our ability to make predictions about future changes.

Along COSI Project on Innovation (2003–2005) we did empirical experimentation around Tagus Technological Park (Portugal), using the Interactions platform [17] to find innovation bursts due to new policies and the enhancement of the environment design. We found urban choices made to attract people together (to socialize), examples of failures, impeaching friendly interactions, and able to push innovation and creativity. Also, the encounters were difficult to organize because suitable space (large rooms, halls) were not available. Innovation request always diverse sorts of interactions.

Polite conversations, within circles, may help to discuss politics at large, exchange many arguments, and enhance our ability to make predictions about changes in society. Asking people about their friends improve voting behavior. Mind pressing causes a different outcome, based upon infections through social nets (addition of fake news). The use of Deep Learning may add new capabilities to agents, to predict new moves of the opponents, or even measure changes of their behavior.

Individuals participate in multiple networks with similar features. Class, wealth, amount of time, affinity, friendship, collaboration, and spatial distance are present, and the question is whether there is any plausible set of metrics. There are differents types of measures that can be exploited, such as the Manhattan distance (the sum of the horizontal and vertical distances between points on a grid). The selection of a metric must be adapted to the particular problem.

Theorists must develop a model that describes the observed phenomenon; the new theory inspires an empirical study to see if the concept holds and vice-versa. Each approach informing the other, but it seems there isn't much overlap. However theoretical and empirical research are more tightly connected than generally thought, avenues exist to further increase this integration.

Early on, SFI (Santa Fe Institute) had a reputation for doing very abstract, blue-sky, theoretical thinking. But recently, that is been changing drastically. They are embracing messy, real-world data sets and finding ways to ground theory in data. We are going toward a unified theory of decision-making in humans and animals. Therefore, access to data banks is needed with the help of R tool and due to network science. Big data banks, such as SCAD (Social Conflict Analysis Database) and FSI (Financial Soundness Indicators – IMF), are suitable to be inspected with network science, and such exercise may complement the experimentation based upon ABM.

How do we perceive time during social simulation trials? The sense of time influences complex behavior and it is responsible for the adaptation to the demands of the external environment. It adds also noise. Agent minds with clocks influence feelings which are critical for decisions (choices) and actions.

We do not so much perceive time itself, but changes in or the passage of time, or what might be described as "events in time". In particular, we are aware of the temporal relations between events, and we perceive events as being either simultaneous or successive. We also have a perception of the sequence or the order of such events.

World is too complex and dynamic, near a constant change. In order to face a decision, we need to consider thousands of variables. Then, it is necessary to choose more real environments [15]. Realistic simulations are a very interesting target, because static worlds lack the complexity. Then, we need to avoid losing complexity: computer-constructed worlds make research more reproducible.

A general rule is to use a cascade of multiple layers of nonlinear processing units for feature extraction and transformation. Each successive layer uses the output from the previous layer as input. Two directions are possible. First, learn in supervised (classification) and/or unsupervised (pattern analysis) manners. Second, learn multiple levels of representations that correspond to different levels of abstraction. The levels form a coherent hierarchy of concepts.

Finally, the complete understanding of behavior [16] is far to be attained. The known parts, to be the key needed to its generation, are far to be considered in artificial worlds, and more research is requested to calculate with great rigour.

7 Conclusions

Processes and mechanisms are behind complexity and we need to face it with better tools. Prototypes/demos are fragile and there is a strong need to focus on realism increase. Seamless realism uses narrative structures and the film techniques are able to create a reality effect to maintain authenticity. Realism usually attempts to represent subject matter truthfully without artificiality and avoiding artistic conventions. The use of social simulation may also explore a kind of movie, within the screen window, where interactions play a new kind of cinema.

There is a need to sense the complexity requests, and the possible limits to attain (the so-called red lines). Before starting the design of a model, it is necessary to isolate a phenomenon. There are many side effects between variables and parameters, and with scale and weight we are pushed to extend experiments.

Attention is due to augment scaling up and the structure of the interactions. We know that the classes and the complexity of all entities is a matter to be followed closely. Enlarging the number of agents is a matter of equilibrium, because there are also desires to give more power and abilities (identity, character, affection, sociality) in order to enhance agent behaviors (see Epstein suggestions) [11].

The mental construction of alternatives to past or future events ("What if", "If I had only..."), causal thinking skills, pose a lot of doubts and controversy, because there is a general idea that simplicity is a good bet and an advice to avoid troubles. The abuse of heuristics and intuitions, in playing games and social simulation, may help to evaluate the strength of moves. Causation is part of intuition, and by causal thinking (and reasoning programmed on computer) we may depict cause-effects relations on diagrams. And, the use of imagination helps to build new models of the world, generating hypothesis and alternatives to the past.

Acknowledgments. I am very indebted to my colleagues Carlos Lemos and João Balsa for the discussion of several themes of this paper, and during recent years. Social simulation and modeling is an area of AI research important to many fields in Portugal (and world wide), namely for the health care, where we need to be very careful. This research was funded by BioISI, FCT funding UID/MULTI04046/2019.

References

1. Lemos, C.M., Coelho, H., Lopes, R.J.: ProtestLab: a computational laboratory for studying street protests. In: Nemiche, M., Essaaidi, M. (eds.) Advances in Complex Societal, Environmental and Engineered Systems. NSC, vol. 18, pp. 3–29. Springer, Cham (2017). https://doi.org/10.1007/978-3-319-46164-9_1
2. Gilbert, N., Troitzsch, K.G.: Simulation for the Social Scientist. Open University Press, London (2005)
3. Thiele, J.C., Kurth, W., Grimm, V.: Facilitating parameter estimation and sensitivity analysis of agent-based models: a cookbook using NetLogo and R. JASSS **17**(3), 11 (2014)
4. Lemos, C., Lopes, R.J., Coelho, H.: On legitimacy feedback mechanisms in agent-based modelling of civil violence. Int. J. Intell. Syst. **31**(2), 106–127 (2015)
5. Lemos, C., Lopes, R.J., Coelho, H.: Quantitative measures of crowd patterns in agent-based models of street protests. In: IEEE Xplore Digital Library, Best Paper, IEEE 3rd World Conference on Complex Systems (WCCS15), Marrakech (Marocco), pp. 23–25, November 2015
6. Lemos, C., Lopes, R.J., Coelho, H.: Analysis of the decision rule in Epstein's agent-based model of civil violence. In: IEEE Xplore Digital Library, IEEE 3rd World Conference on Complex Systems (WCCS15), Marrakech (Marocco), pp. 23–25. Best Paper Award, November 2015
7. Grimm, V., Railsback, S.F.: Individual-based Modeling and Ecology. Princeton University Press, Princeton (2005)
8. Page, S.F.: The Model Thinker: What You Need to Make Data Work for You. Basic Books, New York (2018)
9. Grimm, V., Berger, U., DeAngelis, D.L., Polhill, J.G., Giske, J., Railsback, S.F.: The ODD protocol: a review and first update. Ecol. Model. **221**(23), 2760–2768 (2010)
10. Epstein, J.M.: Why model? JASSS **11**(4), 12 (2008)
11. Epstein, J.M.: Agent_Zero, Toward Neurocognitive for Generative Social Science. Princeton University Press, Princeton (2014)
12. Schmidt, B.: Modelling human behavior, the pecs reference manual. In: Verbraeck, A., Krug, W. (eds.) Proceedings of the 14th European Simulation Symposium, SCS Europe BVBA (2003)
13. Still, G.K.: Introduction to Crowd Science. CRC Press, Boca Raton (2014)
14. Galesic, M., de Bruin, W.B., Dumas, M., Kapteyn, A., Darling, J., Meijer, E.: Asking about social circles improves election predictions. Nat. Hum. Behav. **2**(3), 187 (2018)
15. Pineau, J.: Reproducible, reusable and robust. In: YouTube Invited Talk December 14, Invited Talk at the Conference on Neural Information Processing Systems in Montreal (NeurIPS 2018) (2018)

16. Sapolsky, R.M.: Behave, The Biology of Humans at our Best and Worst. Vintage, New York (2018)
17. Coelho, H., Schilperoord, M.: Intersections: experiments and enhancements. In: Coelho, H., Espinasse, E. (eds.) Proceedings of the 5th workshop on Agent-Based Simulation. SCS Publishing House, Erlangen (2004)
18. Adamatti, D.F., Sichman, J.S., Coelho, H.: An analysis of the insertion of virtual players in GMABS methodology using the Vip-JogoMan prototype. J. Artif. Soc. Soc. Simul. **12**(3), 7 (2009)
19. Antunes, L., Balsa, J., Coelho, H.: Agents that collude to evade taxes. In: Proceedings of the 6th International Joint Conference on Autonomous Agents and Multiagent Systems – AAMAS (2007)
20. Lopes, F., Coelho, H. (eds.): Electricity Markets with Increasing Levels of Renewable Generation: Structure, Operation, Agent-based Simulation, and Emerging Designs. SSDC, vol. 144. Springer, Cham (2018). https://doi.org/10.1007/978-3-319-74263-2
21. Passos, D.S., Coelho, H., Sarti, F.M.: Measuring banks' antifragility via fuzzy logic. World Acad. Sci. Eng. Technol. Int. Sci. Index Comput. Syst. Eng. **12**(7), 153 (2018)
22. Santos, T., Louçã, J., Coelho, H.: Measuring agenda-setting effects on Twitter during the 2016 UK EU Referendum. In: Proceedings of the WCCS 2019, 22-24 April 2019

Emergency Evacuation Simulation in Open Air Events Using a Floor Field Cellular Automata Model

Dionysios Strongylis$^{(\boxtimes)}$, Charalampos S. Kouzinopoulos,
Georgios Stavropoulos, Konstantinos Votis, and Dimitrios Tzovaras

Information Technologies Institute, Centre for Research and Technology Hellas,
Thessaloniki, Greece
{dionstro,kouzinopoulos,stavrop,kvotis,dimitrios.tzovaras}@iti.gr

Abstract. In order to enhance human safety in open air events and simulate evacuation scenarios, a two dimensional cellular automata model
is proposed based on human behavior. To make the model more reasonable, human behavior effects like inertial, group effect, friction, pedestrian velocity, wall repulsion and panic behavior were included. A demo
scenario of the proposed system in Pützchens Markt's fair in Bonn with
different numerical results is also discussed.

Keywords: Cellular automata · Floor field · Evacuation simulation

1 Introduction

Open air events such as concerts, festivals and carnivals usually involve a large
number of people gather to a given, usually confined space. Crowds can vary
from a few hundreds to several thousand pedestrians. However, due to unpre-
dictable and often hazardous events, such as fires, explosions and earthquakes, an
emergency evacuation of the area can be deemed necessary. The unpredictability
of the exact incident, in addition to the human behavior in these overcrowded
events can lead to injuries and even deaths. In most cases, these types of inci-
dents can happen due to the lack of proper planning or effective spectator control. Maintaining a high level of safety for the participants can be challenging.
To enhance safety during an evacuation, it is very important to perform an adequate initial planning in order to determine exit pathways, the configuration of
obstacles in the area, the maximum number of humans allowed to enter simultaneously, as well as possible congestion points. Most major disasters involving
evacuating crowds can be effectively avoided by understanding risks and human
behavior and by designing open air events accordingly.

To determine proper security measures to be taken in open air events during
an emergency evacuation and evaluate their efficiency, an evacuation simulation is performed before such events using different models to detect potential
issues and take appropriate measures. These models are the product of research

© Springer Nature Switzerland AG 2019
P. Moura Oliveira et al. (Eds.): EPIA 2019, LNAI 11805, pp. 642–653, 2019.
https://doi.org/10.1007/978-3-030-30244-3_53

on crowd psychology and evacuation dynamics and aim to replicate pedestrian movement.

This paper proposes a customizable floor field cellular automata model that combines different parameters to simulate pedestrian movement during an evacuation. The proposed model can be used for crowd management in large, open air settings. The aim of this research is to provide event coordinators with a tool that can help in the decision making process regarding the safety of spectators. The model is evaluated in such an event for different scenarios.

The paper is structured as follows: Sect. 2 presents past research on the simulation of the motion of pedestrians during an emergency evacuation. Section 3 discusses the proposed floor field cellular automata model. Section 4 presents preliminary experimental results for open air evacuation in the Pützchens Markt fair in Bonn, Germany. Finally, Sect. 5 discusses the conclusions of this research and presents ideas for future work.

2   Related Work

Simulating the motion of pedestrians during an emergency evacuation in the presence of a hazard or threat is an ongoing research topic in the literature. A number of studies have already been published that model human movement, based on a variety of fundamental theories, such as fluid dynamics [5], game theory [11], animal behavior [4], cellular automata [17] and agent-based models [3]. A general comparison between these methods is described in [21].

Studies that employ cellular automata for the evacuation of pedestrians, commonly divide the target area into a grid of fixed-size cells. In such cells, people, empty space, walls and obstacles are represented using different states. The interaction between pedestrians is frequently modelled using different force fields, such as a static or a dynamic [7,19].

Implementation in evacuation sites with obstacles is included in a number of the aforementioned models [7,17,19]. Obstacle inclusion provides a diagnostic tool for simulation purposes with significant more case scenarios. Thus, the outcome of an emergency situation can be differentiated by allocating barriers in a variety of ways, in an effort to approach the best object placing in space.

Characteristics of human behavior and social models have also been studied [12]. People in general, tend to exhibit panic during emergency situations [8]. In these settings, there is a tendency for pedestrians to move away from obstacles and other people, hence wall repulsion and conflict resolution mechanisms were introduced [1]. Furthermore, due to the inevitable crowd congestion (primarily on the exits), friction and other slowdown factors were also described [16]. Several simulations also included an inertia effect to pedestrians' mobility, in order to create more realistic scenarios [20].

Although there is significant research on the use of evacuation models during emergency situations, the incorporation of various variables of human behavior is limited. To the best of our knowledge, this is the first time that a cellular automata evacuation model with parameters such as pedestrian velocity, friction and repulsion, inertia, panic and random slowdown has been used to model emergency evacuation in open air events.

3   Cellular Automata Model

This Section details the proposed cellular automata model for evacuation. A floor field is defined as a total of variable values describing certain properties of each cell in a grid, such as distances. The model uses two such floor fields, a static floor field and a dynamic, both enabling pedestrian interactions through long-range forces. Moreover, different aspects of human behavior in evacuation scenarios are also incorporated into the model, as discussed below. The model parameters were defined based on the Pützchens Markt fair site, described in Sect. 4.

An outdoors area, such as the grounds for a concert, a carnival or a sporting event, can be represented using cellular automata. For this, a grid of cells is superimposed on top of the area with the dimension of each cell being $0.4\,m^2$, the surface typically occupied by a person in a dense situation [2]. Each cell can be in an "empty" state, indicating an area space that can be occupied by a pedestrian or an obstacle, a "pedestrian" state that represents an area where a pedestrian is currently located or an "obstacle" state that indicates an area where no pedestrian or other obstacle can move into.

Time step $t = 0$ is marked as the beginning of the evacuation and is selected as the initial state of the automaton. At every subsequent time step t, a pedestrian or obstacle can potentially move from an *origin* cell with coordinates (i, j) to a neighbor, *destination* cell with coordinates (i', j'). In that case, the state of the origin cell will be set to "empty" while the state of the destination cell will be modified to "pedestrian" or "obstacle" accordingly. For the model of this paper, a Moore neighborhood is used, which for a given cell consists of all its 8 adjacent cells. Note how the distance to the diagonally adjacent cells is greater than that to orthogonal adjacent ones, hence the longer arrows.

The probability of a pedestrian moving to a neighbor cell at t is given by:

$$P_{i',j'} = N \times \exp(P_S \times P_D \times P_w \times P_I) \tag{1}$$

where N is a parameter used for normalizing all probabilities to 1. The probabilities P_S, P_D, P_w and P_I are defined below.

3.1   Static Floor Field

The goal of an evacuation process is to lead pedestrians away from a given area with safety. A primary motive of people in case of emergency is to move towards the nearest exit in the most direct possible way. Exit points are usually known to participants, as escape routes are frequently illustrated along with proper staff guidance. This motivation can be represented by a static floor field S, defined as the shortest distance, Euclidian, Manhattan, Dijkstra or any other proper metric [1], between each cell of the grid and an exit of the area. It is a force applied to any pedestrian occupying a given cell, increasing the probability to move to a neighbor cell that is located spatially closer to the exit. Pedestrians will always prefer to move towards cells with a lower static field value. A parameter $k_S \in [0, \infty]$ is used to define the magnitude of S. As discussed in [8] and [13], k_S ranges usually between 2 and 3. In the proposed model of this paper, $k_S = 2.5$ is used.

For a given area, the static field is calculated initially and its value is updated during the simulation only if an obstacle is introduced, removed or moves between cells. The floor field is then calculated as follows:

1. For every cell marked as an exit, $S = 0$
2. For every cell without a static field value that is adjacent to a cell with a value of K, a value is assigned according to the following rules:
   - Orthogonally adjacent cells are assigned a value of $K + \lambda$.
   - Diagonally adjacent cells are assigned a value of $K + \mu$, where $\mu > \lambda$. For the floor field cellular automata model of this paper, the values of $\mu = 0.14$ and $\lambda = 0.1$ have been chosen.
   - If multiple values are to be assigned to a cell on the same time step, the minimum value is selected.
3. After the calculation of the field, cells that are difficult to access have their static field value increased by 0.5.
4. All obstacles, such as walls, are also considered when defining the grid. Cells that are impassable are marked as out of bounds while cells that contain difficult terrain are given very high values of the floor field so that it will be less probable to be occupied by pedestrians.

The probability of movement due to the static field is given by:

$$P_S = k_S S_{i',j'} k_{scale} \tag{2}$$

Note that the exponential function is used to enhance the effect of each parameter as it deviates from 0. However, since its value ranges from 0 to $+\infty$, it is possible for the outcome of Eq. (1) to reach very high values and overflow the variables of the simulation, which will result in the immobility of pedestrians. For this reason, a single scaling parameter $k_{scale} \in (0, 1]$ has been introduced that applies to the static field and all subsequent parameters to reduce their effect.

3.2 Dynamic Floor Field

The dynamic floor field D represents a virtual trace left by moving pedestrians. People that move towards an exit during an evacuation process have the tendency to mimic the behavior of other people in front or around them, usually by following them. The personality of each pedestrian influences their predisposition; some people are more likely to follow others and less likely to detour when they encounter another individual while other people will be more likely to ignore the behavior of their surrounding people. This phenomenon can be

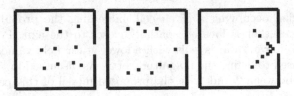

Fig. 1. Impact of the k_D parameter to pedestrian movement for $k_D = 1$ (left), $k_D = 4$ (middle) and $k_D = 8$ (right).

reflected by increasing the probability of certain groups of pedestrians to move towards cells with a higher dynamic field [9].

The dynamic floor field has a parameter $k_D \in [0, \infty]$ to modify its impact in the simulation. As can be seen in Fig. 1, low values of k_D make pedestrians move independently from each other, while high values force them to move in straight lines which is not observed in practice. For the proposed model, $k_D = 4$ to maintain a realistic behavior for open air spaces.

In most models proposed, this field has also its own dynamics, specifically diffusion and decay, similar to the process of chemotaxis [15] used by ants. The dynamics are controlled by parameters $\alpha \in [0, 1]$ and $\delta \in [0, 1]$ accordingly, that describe the broadening and dilution of the trace. At each t of the simulation, every single cell of the whole dynamic field decays with a probability of α and diffuses with a probability of δ to its adjacent cells, as shown in Fig. 2. For the proposed model, $\alpha = 0.2$ and $\delta = 0.2$ were used, similar to [13]. Since there is no limit to the maximum value of the dynamic field, it can be considered as a bosonic field [7]. Every moving pedestrian creates a D-particle at their origin cell (i, j). When a person moves to an adjacent destination cell, the value of the D-particle is subsequently incremented. Given parameters α and δ, the development of the dynamic field for $t + 1$ over t can be computed as:

$$D_{i,j}^{t+1} = (1 - \alpha)(1 - \delta)D_{i,j}^t + \frac{\alpha(1 - \delta)}{8}(D_{i-1,j-1}^t + D_{i-1,j}^t + \tag{3}$$
$$D_{i-1,j+1}^t + D_{i,j-1}^t + D_{i,j+1}^t + D_{i+1,j-1}^t + D_{i+1,j}^t + D_{i+1,j+1}^t)$$

The probability P_D of the dynamic field is given by:

$$P_D = k_D D_{i',j'} k_{scale} \tag{4}$$

3.3 Wall Repulsion

People attending open air events usually avoid walking close to walls and various obstacles such as dance stages or stands [1]. This is taken into consideration in the proposed model by using a repulsive force P_w, inversely proportional to the wall distance:

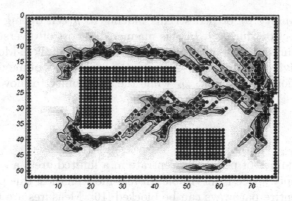

Fig. 2. A contour plot of the dynamic floor field. The darkness of shading is proportional to the field

$$P_w = k_w min(d_{max}, d_{k,l})k_{scale}) \tag{5}$$

where d is the minimum distance from all the walls for the current cell (k, l), $k_w \in [0, 1]$ is a sensitivity parameter that determines the magnitude of P_w and d_{max} is the maximum range in cells in which the effect of the walls affects the peoples movement. d_{max} is commonly set in the literature between 1 and 10 cells.

Given that the Pützchens Markt fair is located in a residential area with wide roads and empty spaces, a big value of $d_{max} = 10$ was selected, as pedestrians have the required maneuverability to stay away from walls. However, due to the existence of numerous obstacles (from buildings to businesses to fair amusements), pedestrians cannot be significantly affected by walls. This is shown in the right block of Fig. 3 and leads to an improbable behavior. Based on our experiments, values ranging around approximately $k_w = 0.3$ seem to model human behavior more accurately.

Fig. 3. Impact of the k_w parameter to pedestrian movement for $k_w = 0.1$ (left), $k_w = 0.3$ (middle) and $k_w = 0.7$ (right) with $d_{max} = 5$.

3.4 Inertia

People tend to maintain the same direction as they move towards an exit [10]. This behavior is introduced into the proposed model of this paper with an increased probability p_I of pedestrians moving to a cell during $t + 1$ according to their direction during t. In this manner, the cost of diversion from one's path is also minimized and a concept of acceleration is entailed. More specifically and for a sensitivity parameter $k_I \in [0, \infty]$, the probability of moving to a cell in the same direction is $P_I = k_I k_{scale}$ while the probability to move to any other cell is $P_I = 1$.

3.5   Friction

When a vast number of people concentrate in a limited area, a contest of individuals over empty space is inevitable. In real-life scenarios, this phenomenon is so severe that entire pathways can be blocked [16]. Measures are usually implemented in order for people to behave accordingly during their exit from an event, although their effectiveness during emergency situations is limited. In the model presented in this paper, this behavior has been simulated by a friction parameter μ. When two or more pedestrians attempt to move to a given cell during t, each has a probability of $\frac{1-\mu}{\text{number of pedestrians}}$ to move to that cell, while there is a probability of $\mu \in [0, 1]$ that no pedestrian will actually move. For the model of this paper, $\mu = 0.2$, based on the literature [13].

3.6   Panic

In emergency situations, the behavior of people often deviates from normal patterns. In these scenarios, it is often observed (i) random movement with no specific target and (ii) panic that usually manifests as initial immobility during the first minutes of an evacuation procedure. Studies have shown that only an approximately 21% of the total population can stay calm in cases of emergency [18]. Typical panic times can range from a few seconds to minutes. The time required for people in panic to start an evacuation procedure also depends on a number of variables such as the area size, the type of emergency or the type of the event. Receiving guidance through a voice communication system or directly by staff can shorten this period, as detailed in [14]. In the model presented in this paper, the panic of pedestrians has been simulated by an initial immobility period, randomly set per pedestrian between 10 s to 2 min.

3.7   Velocity

Participants in open air events can have a different maximum walking or running speed due to age, gender, health conditions, alcohol consumption and other characteristics. Therefore, some pedestrians can move faster than others. The average walking speed of pedestrians during emergencies is approximately 1.419 m/s [6]. Furthermore, those in the age group of 20–40 (1.505 m/s) were found to be 11% faster than younger individuals (1.349 m/s) and 7% faster than elders (1.402 m/s). Males (1.606 m/s) tend to walk 10% faster than females (1.448 m/s). The velocity of handicapped individuals is significantly lower (1.103 m/s). These numbers where included in the simulation as the speed of different pedestrian groups. This is accounted in the proposed model by increasing the granularity of the time steps. Faster individuals move during more time steps comparing to slower ones. The percentage difference in time step is proportional to the velocity of each pedestrian group. Another aspect taken into consideration, is the probability for a velocity deviation, since the velocity of a person doesn't stay the same during an emergency evacuation. In the proposed model and for each time step, the velocity of an individual can either stay the same, increase or decrease, with a probability of 0.8, 0.1 and 0.1 respectively.

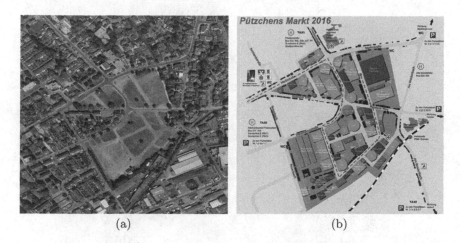

(a)   (b)

Fig. 4. Pützchens Markt in (a) satellite imagery and (b) site plan of the event area

4   Experimental Results

To evaluate the proposed evacuation model of this paper, the Pützchens Markt fair in Bonn, Germany was used. The event is held during the second weekend of September at the Market Meadows in front of Bonn-Pützchen. Around 550 businesses and fairground amusements cover the area. Numerous takeaways, bars and confectionery stalls open at the premises just for the event. Visitors can access the festival from six different open entrances. The fair spans an $80.000 \, m^2$ area, however the total evacuation area also includes roads that lead to the event, adjacent buildings and obstacles spanning approximately $360.000 \, m^2$. As described in Sect. 3, each cell has a size of $0.16 \, m^2$, therefore the simulation area consists of a grid of 1500×1500 cells.

Pützchens Markt was chosen for a variety of reasons. To begin with, the event spans a large area, containing a big amount of obstacles, such as vehicles, stages, outdoor bars and stands, that help to simulate different, complex scenarios. A vast amount of people attend the fair each year. Numbers during rush hours can reach up to thousands of visitors simultaneously, therefore different congestion simulations can be performed. Lastly, the event is held in a residential area, so initial planing, roads that lead to the area and their condition (open, closed or used as path for emergency services) and city planning in general can also help to simulate various scenarios. A satellite image of the event along with the site plan can be seen in Fig. 4. For the proposed model, a series of simulations have been performed for the Pützchens Markt's area with different inputs. A snapshot of the running model for different time steps can be seen in Fig. 5 for 6 exits and 6000 pedestrians.

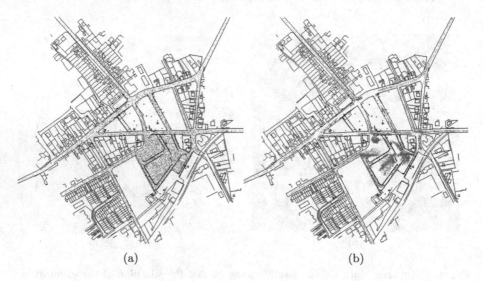

(a)   (b)

Fig. 5. Pützchens Markt evacuation with 6000 people (a) for t = 0 and (b) t = 100

A comparison of the total evacuation time for different groups of people is depicted in Fig. 6. The simulation involves all 6 exits of the event and 8000 pedestrians. The different groups, that include both male and female from different age categories, can be seen in Table 1.

Table 1. Percentages of individuals in each group

Groups	Categories			
	Ages 1–16	Ages 16–45	Ages 45 plus	Handicapped
A	15%	60%	23%	2%
B	2%	90%	7%	1%
C	2%	8%	85%	5%
D	69%	27%	3%	1%

As demonstrated in Fig. 6, every group of pedestrians has different characteristics; it is evident that there is a significant difference in the evacuation times
of the same number of pedestrians in the same area. Slower individuals require
more time to move towards the exit. Moreover, they create congestion points,
especially in narrow pathways, thus leading to additional delay.

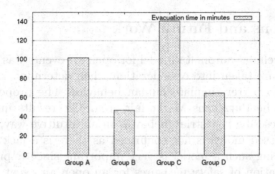

Fig. 6. Evacuation times of different pedestrian compositions

The results for a different amount of people, consisting of pedestrians between the age of 16–45 and for different number of exits can be seen in Fig. 7. On
the left part of the Figure can be seen that the evacuation time grows exponentially with the increase in the number of pedestrians. Initially, as the population
increases, the time necessary for people to arrive at the exits rises slowly. This
is expected, due to the fact that the area is not congested and people can move
freely and fast. When approximately 8000 people or more are present in the area,
the time needed to complete the evacuation starts growing rapidly suggesting
that pathways are overcrowded and measures should be taken, especially if crowd
levels estimation is even higher.

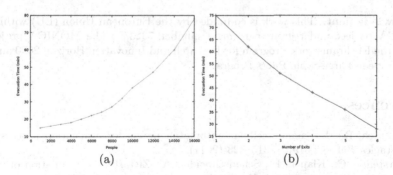

Fig. 7. Evacuation times for the model in accordance to (a) initial population and (b)
number of exits

On the right part is depicted the impact of the number exits to the total evacuation time for a fixed population of 8000 pedestrians. It approaches a reverse exponential curve, meaning that the lower the number of exits, the greater the time for pedestrians to evacuate the area. The existence of enough exit points becomes critical, as suggested by the significant increase in the evacuation time, especially for the study cases of only 1 and 2 exits.

5   Conclusions and Future Work

In this paper, a cellular automata model for open air events was described. Various parameters are taken into consideration when determining the evacuation route, in order to better simulate human behavior. The proposed model was evaluated using the Pützchens Markt fair area. The results indicate that the simulation can describe pedestrian behavior in an intuitive way. Still, the accuracy of the proposed model is not confirmed as there is a lack of actual data. However, producing such a model is very important since it provides a useful tool in the evaluation of safety measures for an open air event. It is especially helpful when testing different scenarios that include different exit plans, obstacle positioning and number of people.

Future work for the model introduced in this paper includes the evaluation of the proposed simulation based on real data and a sensitivity analysis of its key parameters. The MONICA project participates in a programme of collaboration called the IoT European Large-Scale Pilots Programme (LSP) with access to data from open air events from six major European cities. Comparison between pedestrian groups with different behavioral characteristics can also be examined. Moreover, to further speed up the execution of the simulation, especially for dense areas or large-sized events, parallel processing of the model can be considered, giving focus on the static and dynamic fields calculation. Finally, the presented model can be expanded to handle additional scenarios including guided evacuations, and the introduction of hazards such as fire, smoke or chemicals and their repercussions.

Acknowledgment. This work is co-funded by the European Union (EU) within the MONICA project under grant agreement number 732350. The MONICA project is part of the EU Framework Program for Research and Innovation Horizon 2020 and the IoT European Large-Scale Pilots Program.

References

1. Alizadeh, R.: A dynamic cellular automaton model for evacuation process with obstacles. Saf. Sci. **49**(2), 315–323 (2011)
2. Burstedde, C., Klauck, K., Schadschneider, A., Zittartz, J.: Simulation of pedestrian dynamics using a two-dimensional cellular automaton. Phys. A: Stat. Mech. Appl. **295**(3–4), 507–525 (2001)
3. Chooramun, N., Lawrence, P.J., Galea, E.R.: An agent based evacuation model utilising hybrid space discretisation. Saf. Sci. **50**(8), 1685–1694 (2012)

4. Fang, Z., Zong, X., Li, Q., Li, Q., Xiong, S.: Hierarchical multi-objective evacuation routing in stadium using ant colony optimization approach. J. Transp. Geogr. **19**(3), 443–451 (2011)
5. Helbing, D., Farkas, I.J., Molnar, P., Vicsek, T.: Simulation of pedestrian crowds in normal and evacuation situations. Pedestr. Evacuation Dyn. **21**(2), 21–58 (2002)
6. Kemal, B., Putra, H., et al.: An observation of the walking speed of evacuees during a simulated tsunami evacuation in Padang, Indonesia. In: IOP Conference Series: Earth and Environmental Science, vol. 140, p. 012090. IOP Publishing (2018)
7. Kirchner, A., Nishinari, K., Schadschneider, A.: Friction effects and clogging in a cellular automaton model for pedestrian dynamics. Phys. Rev. E **67**(5), 056122 (2003)
8. Kirchner, A., Schadschneider, A.: Simulation of evacuation processes using a bionics-inspired cellular automaton model for pedestrian dynamics. Phys. A: Stat. Mech. Appl. **312**(1–2), 260–276 (2002)
9. Li, D., Han, B.: Behavioral effect on pedestrian evacuation simulation using cellular automata. Saf. Sci. **80**, 41–55 (2015)
10. Liu, M., Zheng, X., Cheng, Y.: Determining the effective distance of emergency evacuation signs. Fire Saf. J. **46**(6), 364–369 (2011)
11. Lo, S.M., Huang, H.C., Wang, P., Yuen, K.: A game theory based exit selection model for evacuation. Fire Saf. J. **41**(5), 364–369 (2006)
12. Moussaïd, M., Perozo, N., Garnier, S., Helbing, D., Theraulaz, G.: The walking behaviour of pedestrian social groups and its impact on crowd dynamics. PloS one **5**(4), e10047 (2010)
13. Nishinari, K., Kirchner, A., Namazi, A., Schadschneider, A.: Extended floor field ca model for evacuation dynamics. IEICE Trans. Inf. Syst. **87**(3), 726–732 (2004)
14. Proulx, G.: Occupant behaviour and evacuation. In: Proceedings of the 9th International Fire Protection Symposium, pp. 219–232 (2001)
15. Schadschneider, A., Kirchner, A., Nishinari, K.: From ant trails to pedestrian dynamics. Appl. Bionics Biomech. **1**(1), 11–19 (2003)
16. Song, W., Yu, Y., Fan, W., Zhang, H.: A cellular automata evacuation model considering friction and repulsion. Sci. China Ser. E: Eng. & Mater. Sci. **48**(4), 403–413 (2005)
17. Varas, A., et al.: Cellular automaton model for evacuation process with obstacles. Phys. A: Stat. Mech. Appl. **382**(2), 631–642 (2007)
18. Wang, J.H., Yan, W.Y., Zhi, Y.R., Jiang, J.C.: Investigation of the panic psychology and behaviors of evacuation crowds in subway emergencies. Procedia Eng. **135**, 128–137 (2016)
19. Yanagisawa, D., Nishinari, K.: Mean-field theory for pedestrian outflow through an exit. Phys. Rev. E **76**(6), 061117 (2007)
20. Yuan, W., Tan, K.H.: An evacuation model using cellular automata. Phys. A: Stat. Mech. Appl. **384**(2), 549–566 (2007)
21. Zheng, X., Zhong, T., Liu, M.: Modeling crowd evacuation of a building based on seven methodological approaches. Build. Environ. **44**(3), 437–445 (2009)

Agent-Based Simulation of Local Soy Value Chains in Ghana

Tim Verwaart, Youri Dijkxhoorn[✉], Christine Plaisier,
and Coen van Wagenberg

Wageningen University and Research, Wageningen, The Netherlands
`youri.dijkxhoorn@wur.nl`

Abstract. The assessment of changes in the relationships between supply chain agents is considered fundamental for market transformation. This paper reports on the application of a Value Chain Lab that supports the measurement of behavioral change in vertically structured supply-chain relationships. A participative gaming approach is used that enables to identify changes in mutual trust, transaction costs and risk behavior that result from value chain support and co-operation. The Value Chain Lab comprises value chain analysis, value chain games and multi-agent simulation. The paper describes the multi-agent simulation of a soy value chain in northern Ghana. The research was conducted in the context of the 2SCALE program, aiming to improve rural livelihoods and food and nutrition security in a number of African countries by developing agricultural supply chains including local smallholder farmers. The study confirms the positive effects of trust and loyalty in value chain relationships. Furthermore, it demonstrates the usefulness of agent-based simulations for exploring potential consequences of alternative interventions.

Keywords: Value chain · Assessment · Trust · Risk attitude

1 Introduction

This research was conducted in the context of a program called 2SCALE that started in June 2012 (see https://www.2scale.org/).

The goal of 2SCALE is to improve rural livelihoods and food and nutrition security in a number of African countries. To this end 2SCALE forges public-private partnerships, with private partners varying from local producer organizations and SMEs to large-scale companies such as seed companies, processors, and trading companies. The approach is based on:

- formation of agribusiness clusters (local networks between the producers themselves and with service providers) to improve competitive intelligence and bargaining power,
- integrating the agribusiness clusters in value chains, with backward linkages to input supply chains and forward linkages to food supply chains, and
- enabling fair business environments with better access to information and finance, in particular for the weaker actors.

© Springer Nature Switzerland AG 2019
P. Moura Oliveira et al. (Eds.): EPIA 2019, LNAI 11805, pp. 654–666, 2019.
https://doi.org/10.1007/978-3-030-30244-3_54

The research objective was to validate key assumptions that underlie the change pathways to establish integrated agribusiness clusters with a fair business environment, including trust, risk attitude and transaction cost. The 2SCALE program has developed an extensive Theory of Change that underpins the market transformation and its assumptions. We applied a responsive assessment and learning framework that supports the understanding of the key behavioral assumptions and helps to assess changes in the relational relationships: the Value Chain Lab [5]. The Value Chain Lab comprises three tools: Value Chain Analysis (VCA), Value Chain Games (VCG), and Multi-Agent Simulation (MAS).

The present paper focusses on the MAS for the case of soy produced and supplied to a co-operative (APEX) in northern Ghana. The MAS is based on data from the VCA, the VCG, and key indicators taken from an impact study conducted by African Research Solutions (ARS). The paper is structured as follows. Section 2 describes the Value Chain Lab approach applied to the 2SCALE intervention in the soy value chain in northern Ghana, including results from the VCA and the VCG. Section 3 presents the agent-based simulation model in ODD format. Section 4 presents examples of simulation outcomes. Section 5 discusses the outcomes and policy conclusions for the Ghana case.

2   The Soy Value Chain in Northern Ghana

It is hard for smallholder farmers in Ghana to get access to the market. The 2SCALE program intends to support the incorporation of smallholder farmers in soy clusters or agriculture APEX organization (farmers' co-operatives). A large problem in the functioning of the value chains can be distrust between the partners. The 2SCALE program aims to include the smallholder farmers in a strong value chain, and reduce distrust. At the time of the research, four soy clusters were supported in northern Ghana, each including approximately 2000 farmers, and one was under negotiation. Two of the supported clusters were used as treatment groups and the one under negotiation was used as control group. The present section reports results from the VCA and outcomes of the VCG that were used to build the MAS.

2.1   Value Chain Analysis

The value chain analysis or mapping (VCA) is the first step of the Value Chain approach. During a 5-day field mission the key actors are interviewed: farmers, traders, input suppliers, and various service providers. For the interviews with the farmers a Focus Group Discussion approach was used, without presence of other stakeholders. A desk review of literature and additional data sources was conducted in addition to the field mission, in order to understand the sector and its dynamics. The results are summarized here.

Northern Ghana is relatively poor, isolated, dry, and politically unstable when compared to the rapidly developing and urbanizing South. However, in recent years the northern regions above the 8th parallel have received much government and donor attention in the form of agricultural subsidies and social programs. This so-called Breadbasket Initiative aims to transform the North into a more stable and prosperous area, with a focus on smallholder production of staple grains and legumes, particularly maize, rice, and soybean [6].

Soybean is a relatively new crop in Ghana [1], but is playing an increasingly important role in the rural economy. Currently, modest expansion of local production, processed in existing facilities, can substitute the imported soybean meal demanded by the poultry industry. Ghana's Council for Scientific and Industrial Research, the Ministry of Food and Agriculture, and development partners have been promoting soybean production because of its potential to increase income and enhance nutritional status of households [9]. The benefits of soybean over other grain legume (such as groundnut and cow pea) include lower susceptibility to pests and diseases, better storage quality and larger leaf biomass, which translates into soil fertility benefit, to subsequent crops [10]. In northern Ghana, most agricultural interventions promote the production and use of the soybean crop mainly through value chain improvements.

Soybean Production. Ghana produces currently between 50,000 to 60,000 tonnes of soy meal and soy protein per year. A little less than that amount is imported. The northern region contributes 70% of the national soybean area and 77% of the national production in 2012 (source: MOFA/SRID). Soybean is mostly grown as a cash crop, although there seems to be little or no evidence about its profitability for smallholders. Other crops grown for cash include cotton and cow pea. Maize, rice and cassava are mostly grown for consumption. Yam and vegetables are grown for both consumption and sale.

Soy is produced once a year. Yields range from 500 kg/ha (208 kg/acre) to 2000 kg/ha (833 kg/acre), with a generally agreed-upon average of 1200 kg/ha (500 kg/acre) [6]. Application of inoculant can increase the yield by 20–30%. Smallholder producers typically cultivate 1 to 2 acres. To access high quality soybean seed is a challenge in Ghana. It is not very common to buy new seed. Local experts estimate a yield of 150 to 300 kg/acre with own seed or seed from the local market. New seed varieties are being introduced, such as Afayak. With Afayak seed, production is estimated to be 400 kg per acre.

Input cost including tractor fee, seed, inoculant, bags, transport, and APEX dues amounts to approximately 225 GHS/acre, as estimated by one of the experts in the program. Production loans from banks are limited to 2 acres and vary from 300–400 GHS/acre. Prices ranged from 0.70–1.80 GHS/kg in November 2015.

Key Actors and Their Roles. Figure 1 presents a brief overview of the main actors in the value chain. Farmers cannot supply and receive payments when they want to. The relations vary between clusters, but in general, after harvest, they must wait for payment until all group members brought their soybeans to the collector, a private warehouse, or a warehouse provided by the APEX or an NGO. When in need for cash they tend to sell part of their harvest at the local market or to brokers who pass by. Prices vary each year and are very volatile.

No pre-harvest contracts are established. Only expressions of interest are given, but without pre-defined volumes or prices. Sometimes a margin is mentioned but to agree upon prices is risky for processors. Farmers perceive it is as a risk to agree beforehand on volumes. They face several risks and do not want to commit to one buyer because no minimum price can be guaranteed. Farmers/farmer groups do not always sell all of their produce when the price is very low. Soybeans can be stored and sold when prices are favorable but the majority of farmers face urgent financial needs, so they have to sell immediately.

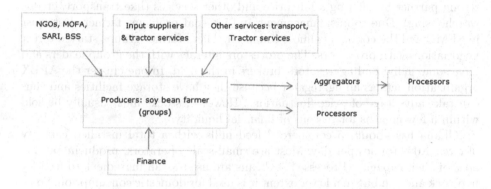

Fig. 1. Value chain overview

The number of targeted smallholders (farmers) is 18,500, of which 7,500 women. The majority is already organized in producer groups or being stimulated (by NGOs, among others) to organize. Group sizes vary from 40 to 100 members. Producer groups are again organized in APEX organizations. Buyers and banks prefer to transact with organized farmers to reach volumes and to reduce transaction costs and risk. Risk can be reduced because farmers need to stand surety for each other. Illiteracy among farmers is high, leading to a dependency on farm leaders. Thus, negotiations are done by the APEX and co-operative leaders on behalf of the members. Group assets are very low as contribution fees are minimal. Some groups can make use of an office of an NGO/Business service provider and can afford to pay an office manager.

NGOs are contracted as Business Development Service Providers to deliver group and leadership development, agronomics training, introduction and demonstration of new seed varieties and inoculant, and value chain strengthening (identification and linkage of buyers and producers, facilitate collective aggregation, value chain concepts training, facilitation of access to loans).

Various input and service suppliers act in the value chain, supplying seed, fertilizers (subsidized), agro chemicals, and soil analyses. Some provide information and extension services. There are however no contracts between farmers' organizations and input providers; deals are made individually. Seed provision and delivery of inoculant are a challenge as availability at country level is low.

The farmer groups are facilitated by the NGOs to establish new contacts with banks. Banks hesitate to provide credit due to the risk sensitiveness of agriculture. All banks have similar procedures. Farmers can apply for a fixed amount of production loan; this amount varies per year. It is only possible to apply as a group and the APEX submits a formal application on behalf of the groups. The group of farmers are together responsible for repaying the loan.

The Savanna Farmers Marketing Company (SFMC) is established by farmer groups to act on behalf of the farmers. The company is based in Tamale and geographically close to the producers. Previously it was the one and major aggregator buying from the producers and selling to processors. SFMC tried to be a strong partner by offering a fair price and other services (like transport, credit, warehousing). Due to mismanagement and internal problems farmers lost trust in SFMC and the company almost collapsed. Then, farmer groups started direct negotiations with processors. The processors interact with the group leaders and have some individual aggregators/brokers in the field. In one cluster the APEX organization acts as an aggregator because they have storage facilities and thus can take advantage of price fluctuations. However, stocks must usually be sold within a few months for reasons of financial liquidity.

Ghana has about 15 commercial feed mills with a total installed capacity of circa 1,000 tonnes per day. Most are small-scale operators, producing at 40–50% of their capacity. Processed soybeans are used as an ingredient to feed for livestock and fish but to a lower extent it is used for domestic consumption. Some local women groups and some small-scale processors make soybean products such as dawadawa or gari (used in preparing local dishes) and soy-kebabs. The farmers in the clusters mostly produce to sell for animal feed because the products for human consumption are not very profitable yet.

2.2 Value Chain Games

In the field of development economics, behavioral economics plays an increasingly important role. With data from field experiments, focusing on personal preferences and willingness to change behavior, certain economic dynamics and decision making can be better explained. For this research on trust relations and risk attitude, three behavioral economics games were played.

The trust game [3] is played in pairs. A first and a second mover send each other money. The first mover receives an amount of money from the game leader to use in a single game. The amount that the first mover sends is tripled by the game leader before it reaches an anonymous second mover. After this, the second mover can choose how much to send back to the anonymous first mover. This return is not tripled, and this procedure is explained to everyone. The revealed trust is measured as the fraction of the playing money sent by the first mover. Trustworthiness is measured as the fraction that the second mover returns.

The multiple price list method [8] was used in the risk preference game. Participants can choose between a risky option, and a certainty equivalent to

Table 1. Average trust and risk determinants

Variable	Treatment (N = 160)	Control (N = 96)	Significance (p)
Trust in group (survey)	0.86	0.93	.002
Trust in leader (survey)	0.83	0.89	.836
Trust round 1	0.49	0.47	.434
Trust round 1 group leader	0.53	0.50	.915
Group trust game	0.45	0.50	.877
Risk preference	0.18	0.17	.116
Consistency in risk game	0.08	0.09	.000

determine their risk preference. A multiple price list was used with six choices between option A, "win a certain amount of money", or option B: "flip a coin" (head means winning an amount of money, tail means winning nothing). The risk preference game was played individually.

The Voluntary Contribution Mechanism game [2] is played in a group. All players can contribute a fraction (ranging from 0 to 100%) of their playing money to a public account. The rest is stocked in a private account. Typically the public amount is then doubled or tripled. The players earn what is left on their private account, and an equal share the public account. In can be tempting to "free-ride", but in a social optimum everything is stored on the public account [4]. This game was played to measure co-operative behavior and trust in the groups.

The three games were played with randomly selected farmer groups: 11 treatment groups (participating in the 2SCALE program) and 5 control groups (not yet participating). A farmer group consists of approximately 50 persons, from which 16 participants were selected at random. A debriefing questionnaire was filled out after the gaming session, to obtain gender and age, eligibility for a production loan in the last season. Also, participants were asked to rank their trust in the group and their trust in the leadership on a Likert Scale from 1–5. At the end, all farmers were paid the amount they had won in the games.

Table 1 summarizes results from the first gaming round. Stated trust is higher than the actual behaviour: participants indicated strong trust in the survey, but most sent 3, 4 or 5 out of 10 coins in the first round.

The returns received in the previous rounds had their effects on the decision in next rounds. A negative profit leads to almost a one coin reduction in the next round, and a positive profit almost led to a one coin increase. Interesting is that this effect declines over the rounds, the trust between the two partners stabilized. Also a very high profit, does not lead to significantly more trust in the next round in comparison with a moderate but positive profit. The experience-based trust update factor can be estimated about 20%.

A large problem for smallholder farmers in Ghana is access to the market. The 2SCALE program intends to link smallholder farmers to processors in the APEX organization. A problem in the functioning of value chains is distrust between the actors. The large majority of the participants showed a high risk-aversion, by preferring GHS 1 over 50% chance on GHS 5.

The eligibility of farmers for agricultural production loans significantly correlates with the outcomes of the game data. In the field, these farmers are chosen through a personal assessment by their leaders, but it is possibly based on higher trust and risk preferences of these farmers. This same effect could work the other way around: farming on credit could affect trust and risk preference.

3 The Agent-Based Simulation Model

This section describes the simulation, following the revised ODD protocol [7]. The simulation is programmed in NetLogo. Source code and details on calibration and sensitivity analysis are published under the title "Local soy value chains in northern Ghana" in the model library at https://www.comses.net/.

Purpose. The purpose of the simulation is to evaluate value chain development projects with respect to the role of trust and opportunities to hedge risk and reduce transaction cost. The application domain is a soy supply chain in northern Ghana, where projects aim to improve rural livelihood by developing sustainable value chains for smallholder farmers.

Entities, State Variables, and Scales. The simulation models a single soy cluster. Active entities in the simulation represent plots of land, farmers who cultivate the land to produce soy, a farmers' co-operative (APEX) that sells the produce on the farmers' behalf, another aggregator, and small-scale local processing groups that contract farmers to deliver their produce. The processors which source soy from the APEX are not represented in the simulation; no data about the negotiations are available and the price is assumed to be aligned with external market prices.

A simulation typically includes approximately 2,000 farmers in groups of 64. From each group, one is given the role of group head, who decides about requesting loans for the group and distribution of the cost in case members default to redeem their loans. All farmers have a variable pointing to their group head and a variable comprising the set of group members. Farmers have personal characteristics: skills, risk avoidance, trust, and loyalty. Farmers maintain trust in the other group members. All trust is represented as an experience-based subjective probability that the others will redeem their loans. This group trust is an important factor in the decision whether or not to request a loan. Farmer agents also maintain trust in the suppliers of high quality seed. Trust in seed suppliers depends on results obtained with seed sold as "high-quality".

The APEX can have a capacity to store soy in case of low market prices. The policy implemented in the simulation is that the APEX will sell a sufficient share of the recent harvest to cover the production cost, including a compensation for labor, and that the remaining part is stored until selling prices are at a satisfactory level. Farmers deliver not only to the APEX. They can also sell to small-scale processor local groups, which buy small volumes, but pay a good price; however, this demand is still low. In addition they may sell on local markets if in urgent financial need, or, depending on their loyalty to the APEX, to other aggregators when they offer a high farm gate price.

Process Overview and Scheduling. Natural conditions affecting the harvest, such as rainfall, temperature, and pests, are represented by a single variable for which a different random value is generated for each cropping season. The value of natural conditions is equal for all farmers and thus affects the harvest of the entire cluster. The range of harvest fluctuations due to natural conditions can be set in the user interface. Similarly, market price is a system level variable that is randomly generated for each cropping season. Market price is not correlated with harvested volume in the simulation, since the external market price is assumed to be the dominant factor for price setting in the downstream value chain.

Fig. 2 represents a time step in the simulation. A simulation typically spans a period of twenty time steps, each representing a yearly soy cropping season. Seed suppliers sometimes deliver bad seed in case of shortage. A user can simulate this by using the "CHEAT WITH SEED"-button. Side-selling (delivery not to APEX) can occur when a farmer is disloyal or faces urgent financial needs.

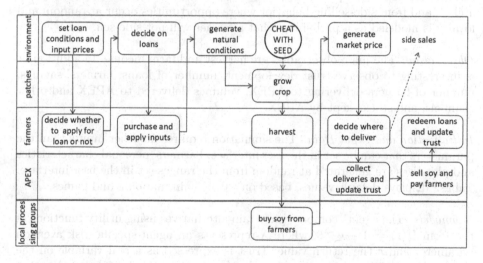

Fig. 2. Process sequence in a single time step representing a cropping season

Design Concepts: The simulation is based on value chain mapping and games conducted as part of the 2SCALE project assessment. A single soy cluster is modeled, with approximately 2000 plots of 1–2 acres, each cultivated by a farmer with personal characteristics of trust, trustworthiness, and risk avoidance in the ranges found in the value chain games. A co-operative (APEX), local food processing groups, and traveling brokers collect the harvest. The farmers are organized in groups, who can collectively apply for a bank loan to finance inputs for a next cropping season, and are collectively responsible for redemption.

Basic Principles: Crop growth depends on natural conditions, on quality of inputs, and on farmers' skills. Harvest and market price determine farm income and thus the opportunities to redeem loans and to invest in next cropping seasons. Farmers' decisions are constrained by availability of capital (loans or saving from previous seasons) and are affected by their personal risk aversion and trust. Trust is updated based on experience, and thus the farmers' decisions also depend on previous behaviors of group members and suppliers.

Emergence: Emergent features are harvests and farm incomes as indicators of livelihood and supply chain viability.

Adaptation: Agents maintain trust in fellow group members and suppliers, and update their trust based on experience.

Objectives: The farmers are assumed to optimize expected utility, taking trust and risk perception into account.

Stochasticity: Variation of outcomes results from the randomly drawn natural conditions and market prices, from trust which is modeled as a subjective probability, and from side-selling behavior where opportunities occur at random and loyalty is modeled as a probability that a farmer will not side-sell.

Observation: The main observables are harvest and farm income. In addition, it is interesting to observe trust development, number of loans, farmers' savings, number of farmers delivering to APEX, volumes delivered to APEX and other channels, and stocks kept by APEX.

Initialization and Input Data. The simulation requires no other inputs than the parameters that can be set in the user interface. Farmers' personal characteristics and plot sizes are generated at random from the ranges set in the user interface. Table 2 displays default values, based on value chain mapping and games.

Submodels. The agents compare uncertain alternatives using utility functions of the form $U(r) = 1 - e^{-\lambda r}$, where λ represents an agent-specific risk aversion parameter and r the return value. Trust is expressed as a real variable on the interval $[0, 1]$, where 1 represents the belief (subjective probability) that the other party will comply. 0 represents the belief that the other will certainly defect. In case of a positive experience, trust is updated as $\tau' = \tau + \delta_+(1 - \tau)$; in case of a negative experience, $\tau' = (1 - \delta_-)\tau$, where τ' represents the updated trust, and δ_+ and δ_- are the positive and negative trust update factors, respectively.

4   Simulation Results

This section presents examples of simulation results, using the default settings as represented in Table 2 and for some alternative interventions.

Table 2. Default parameter values

Parameter	Value	Unit	Parameter	Value	Unit
farms	2,304		min-natural-conditions	0.5	
min-farmgate-price	700	GHS/ton	savings[a]	FALSE	
max-farmgate-price	1,600	GHS/ton	min-risk-aversion	0.0025	1/GHS
local-market-price	700	GHS/ton	max-risk-aversion	0.0100	1/GHS
loan-standard	750	GHS/ha	min-initial-trust	0.8	
cost-loan-insurance	200	GHS/ha	max-initial-trust	1.0	
optimal-seed-cost	150	GHS/ha	min-loyalty	0	
inoculant-cost	50	GHS/ha	max-loyalty	1	
other-production-cost	250	GHS/ha	APEX-storage	0	tons
labour-cost	300	GHS/ton	APEX-price-advantage	5,000	%
transaction-cost-market	0	GHS	Local processing groups:		
basic-expected-yield	1.0	ton/ha	–number-of-members	34	
optimal-seed-factor	2.00		–soy-demand-per-season	8	tons
inoculant-factor	1.25		–price-local-groups	4,000	GHS/ton
min-skills-factor	0.5		pos-trust-update-factor	0.05	
farm-area	0.4–0.8	ha	neg-trust-update-factor	0.10	

[a] "savings" false: farmers are assumed to spend their revenue in the following season

Under default settings, variations in natural conditions and market price cause variations in harvest and farm income, as shown in Fig. 3a. As a consequence, some farmers default in redeeming their loans, group members must support them, lose their group trust, and then refuse to participate in group loan applications. In the long run, simulated soy supply and farm income tend to decrease by 20% and 30%, respectively (average of 30 runs).

Reliable supply and availability of high quality seed and inoculant increase soy supply on average by approximately 30…40% in the simulation; average farm income is in that case increased by approximately 50%, as shown in Fig. 3b. However, the figure also shows that still much own seed is used over a long period.

A stable farm income is required for annual purchase of high quality inputs and redemption of production loans, in order to sustainably realize the aforementioned improvements, as can be seen in the simulations underlying Fig. 3c, where long-term average price remains the same, but price fluctuations are reduced.

Another option could be price support in years with low market price. If, for instance, the minimal farm gate price is raised from 700 to 1,000 GHS per tonne, and the average price to 1,300 instead of 1,150 GHS per tonne over the simulation period, average farm income increases by another 50%, approximately.

When price support cannot be realized, the use of APEX facilities to store part of the harvest and wait for high market prices can have a positive effect on farm income. Simulations show an average income increase by approximately 20% with APEX storage capacity up to 2000 tons, when a policy is applied to sell the volume required to compensate the farmers for the production cost and postpone further sales, waiting for a good price. However, this only has its

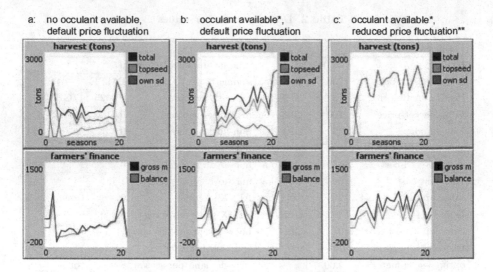

Fig. 3. Examples of NetLogo simulation output for default (a) and two alternative (b, c) scenarios, showing the evolution of harvest and the fractions produced with top quality seed and own seed, and average farmer's gross margin and financial balance (*scenarios b and c: inoculant and top seed availability = 100% and no cheating occurs; **c: reduced price fluctuation: 1100–1200 GHS/ton instead of 700–1600 GHS/ton)

effect when weaker farmers' skills are reinforced, in order to produce a sufficient volume for delayed sales. Currently, a substantial part of the harvest must be sold on short term to cover the weaker farmers' production cost.

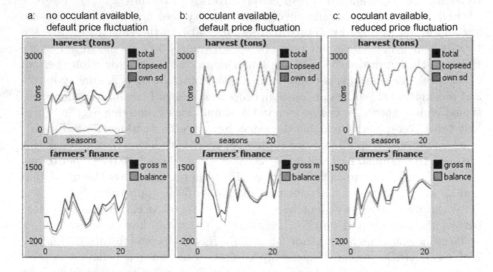

Fig. 4. Examples of NetLogo simulation output with parameter settings as in Fig. 3, but with demand from local processing groups increased from 8 to 100 tons

An effective approach to improve availability of means for purchasing of inputs for the next season is the development of local sales by developing local food processing that can offer a good, stable price. Figure 4 presents results of simulations with local demand set to 100 tons in stead of the current default of 8 tons. In the present simulations a price of 4 GSH/kg is used, as is mentioned in the value chain mapping report. However, it is questionable if such a high price can persist. The price may be assumed to converge to global market prices when local processing industry develops and sources larger volumes.

5 Conclusion

The paper reported on an agent-based simulation as part of the Value Chain Lab (VCL). The simulation is calibrated to data collected in other components of the VCL: desk research, interviews in a field mission, and behavioral economics games played with actual actors in the value chain. The results show the usefulness of agent-based simulation to explore potential consequences of interventions in value chains with many actors, with diversity in properties such as farm management skills, farm size, risk aversion, trust, and loyalty. The VCL approach is feasible in other situations where such factors play their roles [5]. However, the simulation must for each situation be adapted to the specifics of land use, products, value chain actors, their relationships, and planned interventions.

Focusing on the case of soy supply in northern Ghana, the simulation runs showed that if stable and reliable supply of high quality seed and inoculant are available, considerable soy supply and farm income improvements can be realized, under the condition that market price fluctuations can be absorbed. If prices cannot be stabilized by price support or contracts offering a good minimum price, according to the simulation, collective storage and development of small-scale local processing can be good alternatives, provided that good inputs are available and skills of weaker farmers are extended.

It should be noted that, in spite of the extensive and detailed data used, simulations are abstractions and have limited scope. For instance, in the present simulation no data is available about farmers' choices to grow soy or alternative crops. Furthermore, no data is available on negotiations or contracting by APEX/group leaders with downstream parties. For such reasons, one cannot expect simulations to provide reliable quantitative predictions of intervention consequences. However, simulations prove useful in exploring tendencies resulting from interventions in complex systems with a great diversity of actors.

References

1. Akramov, K., Malek, M.: Analyzing profitability of maize, rice, and soybean production in Ghana: results of PAM and DEA analysis. In: International Food Policy Research Institute, Ghana Strategy Support Program Working Paper 0028 (2012)
2. Andreoni, J.: Co-operation in public-goods experiments: kindness or confusion? Am. Econ. Rev. **84**(4), 891–904 (1995)

3. Berg, J., Dickhaut, J., McCabe, K.: Trust, reciprocity, and social history. Games Econ. Behav. **10**(1), 122–142 (1995)
4. Croson, R., Fatas, E., Neugebauer, T.: Reciprocity, matching and conditional co-operation in two public goods games. Econ. Lett. **87**(1), 95–101 (2005)
5. Dijkxhoorn, Y., Plaisier, C., Verwaart, T., van Wagenberg, C., Ruben, R.: Trusted sorghum: simulating interactions in the sorghum value chain in Kenya using games and agent-based modelling. J. Dev. Effect. (2019). https://doi.org/10.1080/19439342.2019.1624596
6. EAT-USAID: The market for maize, rice and soy and warehousing in Northern Ghana. USAID (2012)
7. Grimm, V., Berger, U., DeAngelis, D., Polhill, J., Giske, J., Railsback, S.: The ODD protocol: a review and first update. Ecol. Model. **221**, 2760–2768 (2010)
8. Holt, C.A., Laury, S.K.: Risk aversion and incentive effects. Am. Econ. Rev. **92**(5), 1644–1655 (2002)
9. Mbanya, W.: Assessment of the constraints in Soybean production: a case of nOrthern Region, Ghana. J. Dev. Sustain. Agric. **6**(2), 199–214 (2011)
10. Ugwu, D.S., Ugwu, H.C.: Soybean production, processing and marketing in Nigeria. J. Appl. Sci. Dev. **1**(1), 45–61 (2010)

Text Mining and Applications

Exploring Textual Features for Multi-label Classification of Portuguese Film Synopses

Giuseppe Portolese[✉], Marcos Aurélio Domingues, and Valéria Delisandra Feltrim

State University of Maringá, Av. Colombo 5790, Maringá, PR 87020-900, Brazil
giuportolese@gmail.com

Abstract. The multi-label classification of film genres by using features extracted from their synopses has recently gained some attention from the scientific community, however, the number of studies is still limited. These studies are even scarcer for languages other than English. In this work we present the P-TMDb dataset, which contains $13,394$ Portuguese film synopses, and explore the film genre classification by experimenting with nine different groups of textual features and four multi-label algorithms. As our dataset is unbalanced, we also conducted experiments with an oversampled version of the dataset. The best result obtained for the original dataset was achieved by a TF-IDF based classifier, presenting an average F1 score of 0.478, while the best result for the oversampled dataset was achieved by a combination of several feature groups and presented an average F1 score of 0.611.

Keywords: Multi-label classification · Film genre · Textual features · Natural Language Processing

1 Introduction

In recent years, the access to a large number of information about audiovisual media has become commonplace with websites like The Movie Database (TMDb) providing free access to meta-data from hundreds of thousands of titles. Such databases need to be correctly classified within a number of genres, since genre is an important information for retrieval and recommendation systems. Nevertheless, genre classification is often done manually, demanding not only significant time and resource but also allowing a high subjective and error margins, since the categorization is done by individuals with their own biases and usually without formal definitions for each genre.

There are a number of studies about automatically film genre classification. Their majority relies on audiovisual features or a combination of audiovisual and text features that are, usually, extracted from closed caption. However, few studies have tackled such classification problem by analyzing film synopses,

P. Moura Oliveira et al. (Eds.): EPIA 2019, LNAI 11805, pp. 669–681, 2019.
https://doi.org/10.1007/978-3-030-30244-3_55

which are some of the most commonly meta-data about films available in movie databases, and even fewer have explored the effects of different textual features on synopses of a specific language.

In this paper we present a study aimed at evaluating the efficacy of different textual feature extraction methods in the task of film genre classification based on synopses written in Portuguese. We also present the P-TMDb dataset, a multi-label dataset containing 13, 394 Portuguese synopses classified within 18 genres. Experiments using multi-label classifiers showed that traditional text features performed better on the original dataset, but a combination of features improved results when we resampled the dataset to reduce its imbalance.

The remaining of this paper is organized as follows. Section 2 presents some of the literature that has been published regarding the theme. In Sect. 3 we describe the P-TMDb dataset, as well as other methodological aspects. Experimental results are presented in Sect. 5. Finally, Sect. 6 presents the conclusions of this study and directions of future work.

2   Related Works

Different studies have addressed the classification of films by genre using a variety of sources for the extraction of features, such as the ones of Rasheed et al. [20], Zhou et al. [26], Huang and Wang [11] and Wehrmann and Barros [25], that used audiovisual features; Austin et al. [1], that used musical scores; and Ivasic-Kos et al. [12], that extracted features from movie posters. It can be observed, however, that there are a limited number of studies that tackled the film classification problem by analyzing the content of synopsis.

Hoang [10] approached a similar multi-label film classification problem to ours using three classification approaches: Naive Bayes; Word2Vec+XGBoost; and Recurrent Neural Networks applied to an english dataset consisting of 255, 853 synopses from the IMDB website. The author noted that by making use of Gated Recurrent Units (GRU) they were able to achieve a F1 score of 0.56, Jaccard Index of 50, 0% and hit rate of 80, 5%.

The study of Rahman and Kadir [18] addressed film genre classification using synopses of Indian movies. The authors conducted experiments with learning algorithms such as Naive Bayes, Logistic Regression, K-Nearest Neighbors, Decision Trees and Linear SVM on a dataset containing 13, 868 synopses. The best result reported in the study was an average of 0.421 precision, 0.36 recall, and 0.386 F1 score by using the Naive Bayes algorithm.

Ho [9] approached the classification of multi-label film synopses by analyzing a 16, 000 synopses dataset from the IMDB website. The study evaluated four classification methods: One-Vs-All approach with SVM; Multi-label K-nearest neighbor (ML-KNN); Parametric mixture model (PMM); and Neural network. The best results reported by the author were 0.51205 of precision, 0.61631 of recall and 0.54999 of F1 score, achieved by a SVM classifier trained on balanced subsets of the original training set.

Our study is similar to the ones presented by [10,18] and [9] as all of them use synopses as the information source. However, none of the presented works focused on evaluating and combining different textual feature extraction methods, or used synopses written in Portuguese, which is the case of our study.

3 Methodology

In this section we present the P-TMDb dataset and its resampled version P-TMDb(+), as well the feature groups, multi-label classification algorithms, and the setup used in our experiments.

3.1 The P-TMDb Dataset

The Movie Database (TMDb)[1] is an international community-driven website established in 2008 dedicated to archiving and distributing meta-data for movies and TV shows. The website currently hosts information of over 450,000 movies and 80,000 TV shows (including over 100,000 TV show seasons and 1,600,000 episodes) in 39 languages. The data provided by the TMDb website is accessed by over 200,000 developers and companies through over 3 billion daily requests.

In this work we have used the TMDb website's API to obtain titles, synopses, and genre tags for a total of 13,394 movies, which corresponds to the Portuguese language synopses subset of the site's database currently available. The collected synopses are related to 18 genres, namely: Action, Adventure, Animation, Comedy, Crime, Documentary, Drama, Family, Fantasy, History, Horror, Music, Mystery, Romance, Science Fiction, TV Movie, Thriller, and War. The genre distribution for the extracted P-TMDb dataset[2] can be observed in Fig. 1.

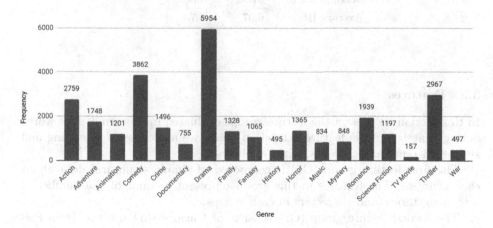

Fig. 1. Genre distribution for the P-TMDb dataset.

---

[1] https://www.themoviedb.org.

[2] P-TMDb and P-TMDb(+) datasets are available upon request.

Due to the imbalance among genre frequencies in P-TMDb, we resampled the original dataset into a new one. The P-TMDb(+) dataset was obtained by oversampling the P-TMDb with the algorithm LP-ROS (Label Powerset Random Oversampling) [4]. An increase of 25% of the original dataset's size was obtained by identifying the least frequent Label Powersets (LP) present in it and randomly replicating their entries.

Table 1 presents some metrics for both the P-TMDb and P-TMDb(+). We can observe that after the 25% resampling of the dataset, the average number of labels per synopsis (Cardinality), and the proportion of single labelled synopses (PropSingleLabel) of the datasets have not undergone significant changes as their values have been increased by 0.34 and decreased by 0.06 respectively. The most significant changes come when we analyze the imbalance ratios (IR), which show the proportion between the genre distribution for each genre and the occurrence of the most frequent genre. P-TMDb(+) shows a reduction of over 62% of the maximum IR, while the average IR has been reduced in roughly 32%, which shows that the oversampling algorithm applied to the dataset had some success in resolving the imbalance among genres.

Table 1. Metrics for the P-TMDb and P-TMDb(+) datasets.

	P-TMDb	P-TMDb(+)
Total of synopses	13,394	16,803
Cardinality	2.27	2.61
PropSingleLabel	0.30	0.24
Maximum IR	37.92	14.39
Average IR	6.97	4.73

3.2 Features

In this section we present the feature groups evaluated in this study. It is worth noting that before the feature extraction phase we made use of stemming and stop word removal techniques, when applicable.

The first feature group (G1) is composed of simple structural data about each synopsis. The features in this group represent a count of the number of sentences, terms, and characters in each synopsis.

The second feature group (G2) consists of features that use the Term Frequency - Inverse Document Frequency (TF-IDF) measure, which measures the occurrence of any given term in relation to the number of different documents in which they occur [19]. For this study, we have used the TF-IDF measure by first extracting TF-IDF values for every 1-gram, 2-gram and 3-gram in the training dataset. A table T is then constructed relating all i synopsis genres and all j possible n-grams in the training dataset, therefore $T(i, j)$ represents the sum of all TF-IDF values for the n-gram j in synopses of the i genre. We then apply the chi-squared test [16], in which the class distribution in the training dataset is used in conjunction with a normal distribution in order to identify the $1,000$ n-grams with highest probability of being statistically characteristic of the dataset. The final feature group is then given as a $1,000$ dimension vector in which each position represents the TF-IDF value for one of the identified n-grams.

The third feature group (G3) correspond to features representing the presence of each genre's name within the synopsis. Given a synopsis, this group represent it by a 18-dimensional binary vector indicating if the name of a given genre was identified within the synopsis.

The fourth feature group (G4) makes use of dictionaries of frequent terms. We constructed 18 dictionaries, one for each genre, such that for a genre i, its dictionary contains the 100 most frequent terms found in genre i synopses. In the feature extraction phase, each term in the analyzed synopsis is searched within all dictionaries and a 18-dimensional vector is constructed representing the number of terms in the synopsis that could be found in each genre dictionary.

The fifth feature group (G5) contains five features representing the frequency of verbs, nouns, adjectives, adverbs, and pronouns in the synopsis. We used the NLPNET (Natural Language Processing with neural networks) [5] for POS (Part of Speech) tagging.

The sixth feature group (G6) is composed of four features that capture linguistic aspects of the text as proposed by Zhou et al. [27] and used by Monteiro et al. [15]. These features were originally proposed with another context in mind (deception detection), however, we decided to use it as they capture aspects that can be characteristic of some genres, namely: pausality, which is defined as the proportion between the frequency of punctuation marks and number of sentences in the synopsis; emotiveness, defined by the proportion between the number of adjectives and adverbs in relation to the number of verbs and nouns; uncertainty, defined by the total number of modal verbs and uses of the passive voice; and non immediacy, measured by the total number of first and second person pronouns.

The seventh feature group (G7) makes use of the LIWC (Linguistic Inquiry and Word Count) dictionary in order to calculate the relative frequency of emotions, thinking styles, social considerations and POS in the analyzed synopses. We used a Portuguese version of LIWC [2] based on LIWC2001 [17]. The dictionary, composed of over $27,149$ terms classified in 64 semantic classes, was used to extract a 64-dimensional vector for each synopsis representing a normalized count of each class present in the dictionary.

The eighth feature group (G8) makes use of the LDA (Latent Dirichlet Allocation) probabilistic model [3], in which each entry of the dataset is assumed to be a combination of a set of topics, which in turn are composed by probabilities of term occurrences. The implementation for the LDA model extraction algorithm was made available through the Gensim toolkit [22]. This feature group consists of a 50-dimensional vector representing the probability of a synopsis to belong to each of the 50 topics modelled using LDA.

The ninth feature group (G9) is based on the use of embeddings, which as described by Hartmann et al. [6] are non-sparse numeric vectors capable of representing terms and their relations in a n-dimensional space while capturing syntactic, semantic and morphological information about them. In this study we make use of the Paragraph Vector model described by Mikolov and Le [14] to train paragraph vectors of 1, 000 dimensions on the training set. For that, we used the Doc2Vec implementation available at the Gensim framework. In the feature extraction phase, the position of the synopsis in the embedding space is calculated by the weighted average position of each of it's terms using their TF-IDF values as weight. The final 1, 000 dimensions vector of the features represents the position of the synopsis in the embedding space.

3.3 Classifiers

We evaluated four different multi-label classification methods using the implementations available at the MEKA toolkit [21], namely: Binary Relevance [23], Classifier Chains [13], RAkEL (Random k-Labelsets) [24], and Deep Back-Propagation Neural Network (DBPNN) [8]. All multi-label classifiers used J48, which is decision tree algorithm, as base classifiers, since its performance were comparable to the SVM (Support Vector Machine) classifier and it has a reduced computational cost.

The J48 classifiers were induced with the following main initializing parameters: default threshold for pruning of 0.25 and minimum number of instances per leaf of 2. The RAkEL classifier was initialized with the following parameters: number of subsets of 10 and number of labels in each subset of 3. The DBPNN classifier was initialized with the following parameters: number of restricted Boltzmann machines (RBM) of 2, number of hidden units of 10, learning rate of 0.1 and momentum of 0.1.

4   Experimental Setup

We conducted 28 experiments using different feature groups combinations on both P-TMDb and P-TMDb(+) datasets. An overview of which feature groups were used in each experiment can be found in Table 2. Experiment $E00$ was the only one which used a single feature group (G2), and it was included in the study because it achieved the best results among all individual feature groups. All other experiments used combinations of features groups as we seek to combine lexical, morphosyntactic and semantic features. It is worth mentioning that we evaluated several other combinations of groups, but due to space limitations, we have chosen to present only ones with best performance.

All experimental results were estimated using 10 fold cross-validation. The metrics used to assess classifier performance were label-based Precision, Recall and F1 score [7]. We averaged them using a micro-averaging approach, in which each label's distribution in the dataset affects its weight in the final metric's calculation. Equations 1, 2 and 3 present the formulas provided by Herrera et al. [7]

Table 2. Overview of the feature groups used in each experiment.

Ex.	G1	G2	G3	G4	G5	G6	G7	G8	G9	Ex.	G1	G2	G3	G4	G5	G6	G7	G8	G9
E00		X								E14								X	X
E01	X		X	X						E15	X		X		X				X
E02			X	X						E16					X	X			X
E03			X		X					E17							X	X	X
E04			X			X				E18	X		X		X	X	X	X	X
E05			X				X			E19	X	X	X						
E06	X		X	X	X					E20	X			X					
E07				X	X	X				E21	X					X			
E08			X			X	X			E22	X						X		
E09	X		X	X	X	X	X	X		E23	X							X	
E10	X		X						X	E24	X	X	X		X				
E11				X					X	E25	X				X	X			
E12					X				X	E26	X							X	X
E13							X		X	E27	X	X	X		X	X	X	X	

to calculate Precision, Recall and F1 score for each label, where TP_l, FP_l, TN_l and FN_l correspond, respectively, to the number of True Positives, False Positives, True Negatives, and False Negatives for a single label l in the L set of possible labels. Equation 4 presents the averaging method applied to the used metrics, where $EvalMet$ corresponds to each of the metrics presented above.

$$Precision_l = \frac{TP_l}{TP_l + FP_l} \tag{1}$$

$$Recall_l = \frac{TP_l}{TP_l + FN_l} \tag{2}$$

$$F1\text{-}Score_l = 2 \times \frac{Precision_l \times Recall_l}{Precision_l + Recall_l} \tag{3}$$

$$MicroMet = EvalMet(\sum_{l \in L} TP_l, \sum_{l \in L} FP_l, \sum_{l \in L} TN_l, \sum_{l \in L} FN_l) \tag{4}$$

5   Results

Tables 3 and 4 present the averaged precision, recall and F1 values across all cross-validation runs by each of the four classifiers.

By analyzing Table 3, we can confirm that the usage of the TF-IDF feature $E00$ was able to produce a micro F1 Score of 0.478 when classified by the Binary

Table 3. Precision, Recall and F1 Score per classifier evaluated on the P-TMDb dataset.

Experiment	BinaryRelevanceJ48			ClassifierChainsJ48			RakelJ48			DeepPropagation NeuralNetworkJ48		
	Precision	Recall	F1 Score	Precision	Recall	F1 Score	Precision	Recall	F1 Score	Precision	Recall	F1 Score
E00	0.477	0.480	0.478	0.505	0.365	0.424	0.453	0.411	0.431	0.350	0.350	0.350
E01	0.408	0.412	0.410	0.416	0.282	0.336	0.324	0.392	0.355	0.317	0.419	0.361
E02	0.402	0.411	0.406	0.408	0.261	0.319	0.303	0.393	0.342	0.317	0.419	0.361
E03	0.404	0.409	0.406	0.419	0.264	0.324	0.302	0.389	0.340	0.343	0.371	0.355
E04	0.351	0.355	0.353	0.328	0.279	0.302	0.271	0.395	0.322	0.345	0.406	0.371
E05	0.366	0.369	0.368	0.344	0.253	0.292	0.285	0.379	0.325	0.381	0.391	0.386
E06	0.404	0.406	0.405	0.404	0.289	0.337	0.315	0.397	0.352	0.317	0.419	0.361
E07	0.397	0.401	0.399	0.401	0.265	0.319	0.295	0.392	0.337	0.344	0.365	0.354
E08	0.335	0.338	0.336	0.312	0.283	0.297	0.265	0.380	0.312	0.374	0.396	0.385
E09	0.343	0.344	0.343	0.337	0.305	0.320	0.284	0.398	0.331	0.317	0.419	0.361
E10	0.341	0.348	0.344	0.334	0.256	0.290	0.246	0.349	0.288	0.317	0.419	0.361
E11	0.332	0.348	0.340	0.325	0.195	0.243	0.217	0.328	0.261	0.317	0.419	0.361
E12	0.325	0.348	0.336	0.324	0.194	0.242	0.207	0.315	0.250	0.317	0.419	0.361
E13	0.292	0.296	0.294	0.270	0.242	0.255	0.225	0.346	0.272	0.317	0.419	0.361
E14	0.328	0.337	0.333	0.302	0.237	0.265	0.236	0.350	0.282	0.317	0.419	0.361
E15	0.335	0.344	0.339	0.325	0.263	0.291	0.250	0.359	0.295	0.317	0.419	0.361
E16	0.332	0.340	0.336	0.311	0.199	0.243	0.214	0.328	0.259	0.317	0.419	0.361
E17	0.292	0.295	0.293	0.281	0.267	0.274	0.246	0.364	0.294	0.317	0.419	0.361
E18	0.324	0.325	0.324	0.322	0.301	0.311	0.270	0.387	0.318	0.317	0.419	0.361
E19	0.471	0.472	0.472	0.499	0.370	0.425	0.442	0.421	0.432	0.317	0.419	0.361
E20	0.471	0.472	0.472	0.487	0.364	0.417	0.430	0.425	0.428	0.351	0.350	0.351
E21	0.471	0.472	0.471	0.492	0.365	0.419	0.433	0.422	0.427	0.326	0.402	0.359
E22	0.433	0.437	0.435	0.431	0.374	0.400	0.384	0.452	0.415	0.317	0.419	0.361
E23	0.447	0.450	0.448	0.454	0.376	0.412	0.403	0.444	0.422	0.326	0.414	0.364
E24	0.462	0.464	0.463	0.487	0.374	0.423	0.426	0.428	0.427	0.317	0.419	0.361
E25	0.467	0.469	0.468	0.479	0.372	0.419	0.422	0.430	0.426	0.320	0.412	0.359
E26	0.426	0.429	0.428	0.417	0.382	0.399	0.377	0.457	0.413	0.318	0.420	0.362
E27	0.421	0.423	0.422	0.418	0.387	0.402	0.374	0.463	0.413	0.317	0.419	0.361

Table 4. Precision, Recall and F1 Score per classifier evaluated on the P-TMDb(+) dataset.

Experiment	BinaryRelevanceJ48			ClassifierChainsJ48			RakelJ48			DeepPropagation NeuralNetworkJ48		
	Precision	Recall	F1 Score	Precision	Recall	F1 Score	Precision	Recall	F1 Score	Precision	Recall	F1 Score
E00	0.537	0.538	0.537	0.566	0.417	0.480	0.578	0.488	0.529	0.335	0.342	0.339
E01	0.587	0.587	0.587	0.566	0.521	0.543	0.482	0.575	0.524	0.324	0.372	0.347
E02	0.582	0.584	0.583	0.559	0.505	0.530	0.466	0.578	0.516	0.324	0.372	0.347
E03	0.580	0.582	0.581	0.560	0.504	0.531	0.464	0.571	0.512	0.326	0.370	0.346
E04	0.579	0.583	0.581	0.549	0.565	0.557	0.444	0.574	0.501	0.324	0.372	0.347
E05	0.579	0.581	0.580	0.556	0.516	0.535	0.472	0.556	0.510	0.368	0.380	0.374
E06	0.590	0.592	0.591	0.564	0.536	0.550	0.476	0.577	0.522	0.324	0.372	0.347
E07	0.583	0.585	0.584	0.552	0.513	0.531	0.461	0.577	0.512	0.324	0.369	0.346
E08	0.580	0.586	0.583	0.552	0.555	0.553	0.456	0.565	0.504	0.326	0.383	0.369
E09	0.587	0.592	0.589	0.557	0.565	0.561	0.466	0.566	0.511	0.324	0.372	0.347
E10	0.549	0.554	0.551	0.522	0.534	0.528	0.421	0.549	0.477	0.324	0.372	0.347
E11	0.531	0.536	0.533	0.506	0.513	0.510	0.399	0.539	0.459	0.324	0.372	0.347
E12	0.528	0.532	0.530	0.502	0.503	0.503	0.391	0.529	0.450	0.324	0.372	0.347
E13	0.547	0.550	0.549	0.521	0.550	0.535	0.403	0.549	0.464	0.324	0.372	0.347
E14	0.548	0.553	0.551	0.528	0.528	0.528	0.428	0.541	0.478	0.324	0.372	0.347
E15	0.557	0.559	0.558	0.528	0.544	0.536	0.424	0.554	0.480	0.324	0.372	0.347
E16	0.534	0.537	0.535	0.505	0.514	0.510	0.396	0.538	0.456	0.324	0.372	0.347
E17	0.559	0.565	0.562	0.537	0.555	0.546	0.433	0.556	0.487	0.324	0.372	0.347
E18	0.574	0.580	0.577	0.550	0.567	0.558	0.451	0.566	0.502	0.324	0.372	0.347
E19	0.561	0.561	0.561	0.570	0.485	0.524	0.544	0.539	0.542	0.324	0.372	0.347
E20	0.557	0.560	0.559	0.567	0.481	0.521	0.534	0.568	0.550	0.342	0.342	0.342
E21	0.550	0.565	0.557	0.564	0.468	0.511	0.536	0.556	0.546	0.324	0.372	0.346
E22	0.604	0.607	0.606	0.580	0.594	0.587	0.501	0.599	0.546	0.324	0.372	0.347
E23	0.589	0.592	0.591	0.589	0.537	0.562	0.541	0.578	0.559	0.326	0.372	0.347
E24	0.582	0.584	0.583	0.576	0.522	0.547	0.528	0.576	0.551	0.324	0.370	0.347
E25	0.572	0.577	0.575	0.573	0.510	0.539	0.522	0.579	0.549	0.324	0.372	0.347
E26	0.608	0.613	0.610	0.586	0.596	0.591	0.519	0.596	0.555	0.325	0.372	0.347
E27	0.609	0.614	0.611	0.589	0.601	0.595	0.519	0.600	0.557	0.324	0.372	0.347

Relevance classifier, which represents the best result for P-TMDb. It is interesting to note that every other experiment among the best results also uses the TF-IDF feature group, although their results were worsened when TF-IDF were used in conjunction with others. We can conclude then that TF-IDF were successful in representing some of the genre specific information that served to improve their classifier's performance, while the addition of other feature groups may have increased the dimensionality of the feature vectors in a way that impacted their classifiers negatively.

We may also note that all of the experiments that used the embeddings feature group (G9) ranked among the lowest micro F1 scores obtained, showing that the Doc2Vec vectors created from the training sets for each experiment have failed in representing meaningful genre characteristics that would aid in their classification. We may speculate that the relatively small size and high imbalance levels of the P-TMDb dataset may have contributed in affecting the trained embedding model negatively.

The results presented in Table 4 show that the resampling of the original dataset has led to significant improvements in classifiers performance. The best overall experiment for P-TMDb(+) was $E27$, which combines the Structural Data (G1), TF-IDF (G2), Genre's Name (G3), POS frequency (G5), Linguistic Aspects (G6), Semantic Class (LIWC) frequency (G7), and LDA (G8) groups, presenting an average micro F1 Score of 0.611. It is interesting to note, however, that experiment $E22$ achieved the third highest micro F1 Score of 0.606 by using TF-IDF (G2) and Semantic Class frequency (G7), and experiment $E26$ achieved the second highest average micro F1 of 0.610 by using the same feature groups of $E22$ in addition to the LDA (G8) model group, meaning that the overall impact of all other groups improved the results only by 0.001. These results show that features that capture semantic aspects are helpful when combined with lexical features like TF-IDF.

Comparing the average micro F1 of experiments $E00$ on both P-TMDb and P-TMDb(+), 0.478 and 0.537, respectively, we can see that the resampling of the dataset led to a significant improvement in the classifiers performance. It can be speculated that the imbalance level present in the dataset, which was mitigated in P-TMDb(+) (as can be verified on Table 1), had been impacting the classifiers negatively.

Upon analyzing the combined experiments results from both datasets, we may also compare the results for each classifier individually. The overall best classifier in both cases was the Binary Relevance classifier as it was able to produce significantly better results on the experiments with P-TMDb, and marginally better results than the other classifiers on experiments with P-TMDb(+). The Classifier Chains and RAkEL classifiers produced relatively similar results for P-TMDb, with the former being able to produce slightly better results than the latter for P-TMDb(+). The Deep Propagation Neural Network based classifier presented little variation in its micro F1 Scores throughout all experiments and datasets, leading us to the conclusion that a deep neural network is not suitable for the datasets used in this study, probably due to their reduced number of samples when compared to datasets used for in studies based on deep neural networks.

By analyzing the Precision and Recall values across all experiments and datasets, we can note that, although usually comparable, their values show some discrepancy for the Classifier Chains and RAkEL classifiers, with the former presenting higher Precision values and the latter presenting higher Recall values.

6 Conclusions and Future Work

In this work we explored the use of textual features extracted from synopses written in Portuguese for the multi-label classification of film genres. We have presented the P-TMDb dataset consisting of 13, 394 film synopses, as well as a derived dataset, P-TMDBb(+), obtained through oversampling. A total of nine feature groups have been evaluated through 28 experiments per dataset. The best overall classification result for P-TMDb presented an average F1 Score of 0.478 by using TD-IDF, while the best result for P-TMDBb(+) presented an average F1 Score of 0.611 by making use of the majority of the feature groups. Both results were obtained by using the Binary Relevance classifier.

TF-IDF proved to be the most effective feature group, presenting the best F1 Score among groups when used individually. At the same time, Doc2Vec features presented the worst results among individual groups and their combinations. Regarding group combinations, they were combined in an "early fusion" manner, and since the dimensionality of the feature groups varies, it might have influenced the results. As future works, we intend to combine classifiers based on individual feature groups using "late fusion" strategies, explore other multi-label classification approaches, such as ensemble methods, as well as the learning of representations (i.e. deep learning).

Acknowledgements. This study was financed in part by the Coordenação de Aperfeiçoamento de Pessoal de Nível Superior - Brasil (CAPES) - Finance Code 001.

References

1. Austin, A., Moore, E., Gupta, U., Chordia, P.: Characterization of movie genre based on music score. In: 2010 IEEE International Conference on Acoustics, Speech and Signal Processing, pp. 421–424. IEEE (2010)
2. Balage Filho, P.P., Pardo, T.A.S., Aluísio, S.M.: An evaluation of the Brazilian Portuguese LIWC dictionary for sentiment analysis. In: Proceedings of the 9th Brazilian Symposium in Information and Human Language Technology (2013)
3. Blei, D.M., Ng, A.Y., Jordan, M.I.: Latent Dirichlet allocation. J. Mach. Learn. Res. **3**(Jan), 993–1022 (2003)
4. Charte, F., Rivera, A., del Jesus, M.J., Herrera, F.: A first approach to deal with imbalance in multi-label datasets. In: Pan, J.-S., Polycarpou, M.M., Woźniak, M., de Carvalho, A.C.P.L.F., Quintián, H., Corchado, E. (eds.) HAIS 2013. LNCS (LNAI), vol. 8073, pp. 150–160. Springer, Heidelberg (2013). https://doi.org/10. 1007/978-3-642-40846-5_16

5. Fonseca, E.R., Rosa, J.L.G.: Mac-Morpho revisited: towards robust part-of-speech tagging. In: Proceedings of the 9th Brazilian Symposium in Information and Human Language Technology (2013)
6. Hartmann, N., Fonseca, E., Shulby, C., Treviso, M., Rodrigues, J., Aluisio, S.: Portuguese word embeddings: evaluating on word analogies and natural language tasks. arXiv preprint arXiv:1708.06025 (2017)
7. Herrera, F., Charte, F., Rivera, A.J., del Jesus, M.J.: Multilabel classification. Multilabel Classification, pp. 17–31. Springer, Cham (2016). https://doi.org/10.1007/978-3-319-41111-8_2
8. Hinton, G., Salakhutdinov, R.: Reducing the dimensionality of data with neural networks. Science **313**(5786), 504–507 (2006)
9. Ho, K.W.: Movies' genres classification by synopsis (2011)
10. Hoang, Q.: Predicting movie genres based on plot summaries. arXiv preprint arXiv:1801.04813 (2018)
11. Huang, Y.-F., Wang, S.-H.: Movie genre classification using SVM with audio and video features. In: Huang, R., Ghorbani, A.A., Pasi, G., Yamaguchi, T., Yen, N.Y., Jin, B. (eds.) AMT 2012. LNCS, vol. 7669, pp. 1–10. Springer, Heidelberg (2012). https://doi.org/10.1007/978-3-642-35236-2_1
12. Ivasic-Kos, M., Pobar, M., Ipsic, I.: Automatic movie posters classification into genres. In: Bogdanova, A.M., Gjorgjevikj, D. (eds.) ICT Innovations 2014. AISC, vol. 311, pp. 319–328. Springer, Cham (2015). https://doi.org/10.1007/978-3-319-09879-1_32
13. Read, J., Pfahringer, B., Holmes, G., Frank, E.: Classifier chains for multi-label classification. Mach. Learn. J. **85**(3), 333–359 (2011)
14. Le, Q., Mikolov, T.: Distributed representations of sentences and documents. In: International Conference on Machine Learning, pp. 1188–1196 (2014)
15. Monteiro, R.A., Santos, R.L.S., Pardo, T.A.S., de Almeida, T.A., Ruiz, E.E.S., Vale, O.A.: Contributions to the study of fake news in Portuguese: new corpus and automatic detection results. In: Villavicencio, A., et al. (eds.) PROPOR 2018. LNCS (LNAI), vol. 11122, pp. 324–334. Springer, Cham (2018). https://doi.org/10.1007/978-3-319-99722-3_33
16. Pearson, K.: X. on the criterion that a given system of deviations from the probable in the case of a correlated system of variables is such that it can be reasonably supposed to have arisen from random sampling. Lond. Edinb. Dublin Philos. Mag. J. Sci. **50**(302), 157–175 (1900)
17. Pennebaker, J.W., Francis, M.E., Booth, R.J.: Linguistic inquiry and word count: LIWC 2001. Lawrence Erlbaum Associates, Mahway (2001). **71**(2001), 2001
18. Rahman, R.I., Kadir, S., et al.: Genre classification of movies using their synopsis. Ph.D. thesis, BRAC University (2017)
19. Rajaraman, A., Ullman, J.D.: Mining of Massive Datasets. Cambridge University Press, Cambridge (2011)
20. Rasheed, Z., Sheikh, Y., Shah, M.: On the use of computable features for film classification. IEEE Trans. Circuits Syst. Video Technol. **15**(1), 52–64 (2005)
21. Read, J., Reutemann, P., Pfahringer, B., Holmes, G.: MEKA: a multi-label/multi-target extension to WEKA. J. Mach. Learn. Res. **17**(21), 1–5 (2016). http://jmlr.org/papers/v17/12-164.html
22. Rehurek, R., Sojka, P.: Software framework for topic modelling with large corpora. In: Proceedings of the LREC 2010 Workshop on New Challenges for NLP Frameworks. Citeseer (2010)

23. Tsoumakas, G., Katakis, I., Vlahavas, I.: Mining multi-label data. In: Maimon, O., Rokach, L. (eds.) Data Mining and Knowledge Discovery Handbook, pp. 667–685. Springer, Boston (2009). https://doi.org/10.1007/978-0-387-09823-4_34

24. Tsoumakas, G., Katakis, I., Vlahavas, I.: Random k-labelsets for multi-label classification. IEEE Trans. Knowl. Data Eng. **23**, 1079–1089 (2010)

25. Wehrmann, J., Barros, R.C.: Convolutions through time for multi-label movie genre classification. In: Proceedings of the Symposium on Applied Computing, pp. 114–119. ACM (2017)

26. Zhou, H., Hermans, T., Karandikar, A.V., Rehg, J.M.: Movie genre classification via scene categorization. In: Proceedings of the 18th ACM International Conference on Multimedia, pp. 747–750. ACM (2010)

27. Zhou, L., Burgoon, J.K., Twitchell, D.P., Qin, T., Nunamaker Jr., J.F.: A comparison of classification methods for predicting deception in computer-mediated communication. J. Manag. Inf. Syst. **20**(4), 139–166 (2004)

Using Recurrent Neural Networks for Semantic Role Labeling in Portuguese

Daniel Henrique Mourão Falci[1,2], Marco Antônio Calijorne Soares[1,2],
Wladmir Cardoso Brandão[2,3], and Fernando Silva Parreiras[1,2]

[1] Faculty of Business Sciences,
Laboratory for Advanced Information Systems - LAIS,
FUMEC University, Belo Horizonte, MG 30310-190, Brazil
fernando.parreiras@fumec.br
[2] Liaise, P7 Criativo, Belo Horizonte, MG 30310-190, Brazil
[3] IRI Research Group, PUC Minas, Belo Horizonte, MG 30310-190, Brazil
http://www.fumec.br/lais, http://www.liaise.com.br,
http://www.iris-research.com

Abstract. Semantic Role Labeling is the task of automatically detecting the semantic role played by words or phrases in a sentence. There is a small number of studies dedicated to Semantic Role Labeling in the Portuguese language, and the obtained performance is far from that of the English language. In this article, we propose an end-to-end semantic role labeler for the Portuguese language, which leans on a deep bidirectional long short-term memory neural network architecture. The predictions are used as inputs to an inference stage that employs a global recursive neural parsing algorithm, tailored for the task. We also provide a detailed analysis of the effects of word embedding dimensionality and network depth on the overall performance of the proposed model. The proposed approach outperforms the state-of-the-art approach on the PropBank-Br corpus, while reducing the relative error in approximately 8.74%.

Keywords: Information analysis · Deep learning · Semantic parsing

1 Introduction

Semantic Role Labeling (SRL) is a Natural Language Processing (NLP) task whose goal is to capture and represent the participants and circumstances of events or situations typically expressed in human languages. These event structures are revealed by providing answers to questions such as *who did what to whom, where, when and how*. Formally, the task is to determine the semantic role played by each argument of a given predicate in a sentence.

SRL approaches are usually considered intermediary techniques that play an important role towards the natural language understanding. Previous investigations had proven its utility in a wide range of NLP tasks, such as question answering, text summarization, information extraction, machine translation, and co-reference resolution [7,19,34].

© Springer Nature Switzerland AG 2019
P. Moura Oliveira et al. (Eds.): EPIA 2019, LNAI 11805, pp. 682–694, 2019.
https://doi.org/10.1007/978-3-030-30244-3_56

However, SRL is a challenging task. A model's performance depends on its ability to deal with language aspects like syntactic alternations, selectional restrictions, and ambiguity. For the English language - the most frequently addressed language in the literature - the state-of-the-art performance reaches approximately 83 F_1-score points [16]. Regarding the Portuguese language, the research is still incipient. There is a scarcity of lexical resources and publicly available tools what hampers new research.

Earlier approaches employed statistical machine learning models that relied on the extraction of complex morphological and syntactic features, as well as on a series of declarative constraints [26,27,30]. Recently, there has been a rapid rise in the usage of neural networks, exploiting its feature induction capabilities. It reduces the overall complexity while achieving competitive results [8,16,35]. In this context, Recurrent Neural Networks (RNN) have received attention, and recent studies demonstrated that its natural ability to articulate long-range dependencies is beneficial for NLP tasks [13,21,29]. However, approaches using RNN architectures in the SRL task for the Portuguese language are lacking so far.

In this paper, we present an end-to-end semantic role labeler for the Portuguese language that address the SRL problem as a supervised sequence labeling task. Our one-step approach uses the IOB tagging schema and a word embedding model in a deep bidirectional long short-term memory neural network (deep BiLSTM). The network predictions are inputs to an inference mechanism that uses a global recursive neural parsing algorithm, specifically tailored for the SRL task. Our method requires a minimal feature engineering process and does not depend on syntactic parsing. In addition, we provide a throughout investigation on the effects of word embedding dimensionality and network depth on the overall performance of our approach. Experimental results with the PropBank-Br corpus [9] show that our SRL approach outperforms the state-of-the-art approach reported on literature for the Portuguese language.

The remainder of this article is organized as follows: in Sect. 3 section we describe our system. In Sects. 4 and 5, we describe the setup and the results of the experimental evaluation of our approach, respectively. Finally, in Sect. 6 we present our concluding remarks and directions for future research.

2   Related Work

The deep BiLSTM model does not resort to syntactic features [35]. This approach, also based on word embeddings, outperformed previous studies based on syntactic features in the English language using the CoNLL-2005 and CoNLL-2012 data sets. Unlike this work though, they employed a Conditional Random Field (CRF) layer at the inference stage and did not investigate the effects of word embedding dimensionality on the model's performance. In a similar architecture, feature templates based on part-of-speech information were added and produced a state-of-the-art labeler for the Chinese language [33]. Another BiLSTM architecture was applied in SRL task on the English language [16].

684 D. H. M. Falci et al.

They focused on network initialization, hyper-parameter optimization, and in the incorporation of recent training techniques such as highway connections and recurrent dropout. Our system may be seen as a hybrid of these approaches, considering their useful observations and experiences.

Regarding the Portuguese language, a preliminary architecture for the SRL task was proposed [2]. Their supervised approach, dependent on morphosyntactic features, consists of a pipeline that uses Naive Bayes and Decision Trees as classifiers. The system though uses an early version of PropBank-Br (v1.0) and, most importantly, relies on golden syntactic trees provided by the corpus, an inexistent condition under real-world circumstances. These factors prevent a direct comparison with our results.

The use of a fully automated semantic role labeler for the Portuguese language was already provided [2].The system (NLPNET[1]) was trained on PropBank-Br v.1.1 and is heavily based on SENNA's approach [8]. The fundamental difference between these systems regards the number of stages they employed: SENNA utilizes an one-step approach while NLPNET, after evaluating the one-step strategy, adapted its architecture transforming it into a two-step pipeline. Experiments were also conducted to verify the impact of the addition of syntactic chunks to the feature templates used in the original system. Their best single training session yielded 65.13 F_1-score points, an overall performance far inferior compared to that of SENNA (a margin of 10 F_1-score points). To the best of our knowledge, this is the only functional SRL system for the Portuguese language whose source code is publicly available and, therefore, is referred throughout this work as our baseline system.

Two approaches, [2] and [10], were compared [15] (the preliminary approach of) in a hybrid lexicon, specifically created for this task. This new corpus incorporated two subsequent versions of PropBank-Br. Their main goal was to evaluate the accuracy of these systems under revised and non-revised syntactic trees using a larger and balanced corpus for the Brazilian Portuguese. Their results indicate that NLPNET systematically yielded an inferior performance. Our results cannot be compared to this system since the new corpus is not publicly available.

Semi-supervised learning has also been investigated in the Portuguese language. An architecture based on a self-training strategy in a three-stage pipeline which uses maximum entropy classifiers was proposed [1]. In this article, however, the authors focused on the discussion of topics such as data preparation, feature extraction, and methodology, without providing practical results. The self-training strategy was materalized in a later study [5]. This article though considered only three commonly used verbs in Portuguese language (*give*, *say*, and *do*). Their results point that a supervised method must be exposed to over at least 40% more labeled arguments to achieve a comparable performance level, a promising observation considering the limited size of the PropBank-Br corpus.

---

[1] Available at http://nilc.icmc.usp.br/nlpnet/.

3   The Semantic Role Labeler Approach

This section outlines our approach[2], providing details about the relevant parts of our semantic role labeler.

3.1   Word Representations

The word representations utilized in this article were obtained by the application of the *skip-gram* model [25] on the full dump of the Brazilian Portuguese version of *Wikipedia* corpus. In this architecture, given a sliding window of words, one attempts to predict the adjacent words (the context) based on the central word (the target token). The model offers good representation for rarely seen tokens and outperformed other models in NLP tasks such as sentiment analysis and syntactic parsing [23].

After extracting the raw text from the *Wikipedia* corpus, we used the *NLTK Punkt tokenizer* [4] for sentence splitting on each of its articles. Sentences obtained were then lowercased, followed by a series of transformations that included accents removal, punctuation separation, and substitutions[3]. At last, each resulting sentence was tokenized, feeding the *skip-gram* training algorithm.

We trained three distinct word representations with 50, 100 and 150 dimensions, respectively. [24] suggest that a vector dimensionality between 50 and 150 yields the best accuracy values for extrinsic tasks and it is worthwhile to carefully choose word embedding dimensionality for such tasks. In all three models, we employed a context-window of size 5, discarding the tokens with a total frequency lower than 5. Models were trained for ten iterations with an initial learning rate of 0.025 that linearly decays until reaching the minimum learning rate of 0.0001. After traversing 10,690,000 sentences distributed in 957,206 *Wikipedia* articles for approximately 2 h of training per iteration[4], we obtained a vocabulary containing 436,190 unique tokens. This number covers more than 99% of the tokens used in PropBank-Br (we missed 138 tokens). Further analysis on the missing tokens revealed that they are primarily composed of rarely seen nouns and first-person verbs - an infrequent narrative style in *Wikipedia*, but common in journalistic and opinion texts such as those in PropBank-Br. We chose to represent these words by randomly generated vectors.

3.2   Deep Bidirectional Long Short-Term Memory (BiLSTM) Model

A recurrent neural network (RNN) is a neural network architecture designed to learn tasks whose output is not only dependent on the current input, but also from previous input events. These networks usually have a form of a chain of cell instances (also known as memory blocks) where feedback connections are

---

[2] The source code is available at https://github.com/dfalci/deep_pt_srl.

[3] Sequences of numbers were transformed into the '#' token while email addresses and URLs were replaced by the '@' token.

[4] The training time varies according to the dimensionality.

responsible for transmitting the weight of previous events throughout its structure. The standard RNN implementation suffers from exploding and vanishing gradient problems that, during the training stage, prevents the network from learning long-term dependencies [3]. To overcome the vanishing gradient problem [17], we proposed a kind of RNN architecture based on long short-term memory (LSTM) cells in its hidden units. Each LSTM cell has a gating mechanism responsible for controlling the portion of information that will be propagated to its internal structures and the rest of the chain. One of its distinctive abilities concerns preserving sequential information over long time periods.

The following equations explain the internal mechanism of each LSTM cell:

$$i_t = \sigma(x_t U^i + h_{t-1} W^i)$$

$$f_t = \sigma(x_t U^f + h_{t-1} W^f)$$

$$o_t = \sigma(x_t U^o + h_{t-1} W^o)$$

$$g_t = \tanh(x_t U^g + h_{t-1} W^g)$$

$$c_t = f_t \odot c_{t-1} + i_t \odot g_t$$

$$h_t = o_t \odot \tanh(c_t)$$

Formally, let S represent a sequence of input vectors x with an arbitrary length n, such that $S = \{x_1, x_2, ..., x_n\}$. In this case, t designates a given time step in S. Weight matrices U and W are adjusted during the training phase. The σ symbol indicates a logistic sigmoid function and $\odot$ represents an element-wise multiplication. The input gate i_t determines whether or not the current input is worth preserving while the forget gate f_t computes the proportion of the previous hidden state that must be forgotten. The cell state c_t is obtained through an operation that requires the multiplication of the new memory state g_t and input gate i_t added with the previous cell state c_{t-1} attenuated by the forget gate f_t. The hidden state h_t uses the output gate o_t to discover the part of the cell state c_t that will be exposed to the rest of the chain.

The traditional LSTM architecture (unidirectional, left-to-right or right-to-left) only considers information from the previous time steps to produce each output. Bidirectional LSTM (BiLSTM) architecture [13,14], in contrast, considers both historical and future steps in order to learn information from preceding as well as future input events. The Bidirectional LSTM (BiLSTM) architecture contains forward (left-to-right) and backward (right-to-left) LSTM layers whose outputs are merged by concatenation in a new layer that, intuitively, encodes past and future information. BiLSTM layers are typically stacked in k bidirectional layers. This arrangement, as occur in other types of multi-layer networks, enables capturing higher levels of abstraction yielding superior performance in sequence labeling tasks such as part of speech tagging, chunking, and named entity recognition [18,31].

Given a proposition expressed in natural language and its respective predicate, we start by the feature extraction stage. Our features, listed below, were inspired by [16,33,35] and are performed for each token in the proposition.

- **Token embeddings:** we capture the word representations for each token in a sentence, including the predicate. A look-up table operation is performed in an embedding matrix initialized with the word vectors computed as mentioned in Subsect. 3.1.
- **Predicate embeddings:** through a look-up table operation, the word vector for the given predicate is extracted and repeated for each token in a proposition. This time, however, to save memory, the embedding matrix contains only the predicates used by PropBank-Br.
- **Capitalization:** as our word representations are lowercased, capitalization is not naturally encoded by our model. To overcome this issue we created a set of binary features that indicate whether all characters in a given token are capitalized, contain any capital letter, or are lowercased.
- **Path to predicate:** the path to the predicate is given by the relative position of a token in a sentence with respect to the predicate position. Thereby, the token whose position coincides the predicate position is valued as 0 while the tokens that occur before and after the predicate are represented with negative and positive values, respectively. Practically, a sentence containing five tokens whose predicate occur in the fourth position would have its tokens labeled as $\{-3, -2, -1, 0, 1\}$.
- **Predicate context:** this binary feature indicates whether a given token is inside the predicate context or not. To compute the predicate context, we apply a fixed window of size five where the predicate occupies its center. If a token is inside this window, then the token is said to be a member of predicate context (the value one is assigned).

These features are concatenated and feed the deep BiLSTM network that will compute abstract representations from propositions. The output of the last BiLSTM layer is attached to a softmax layer that, for each input token contained in the original proposition, yields the probability distribution over all the possible semantic roles (39 roles), creating a probability matrix. At last, in order to obtain the final prediction for the whole proposition, this probability matrix is sent to the global recursive neural parsing algorithm, explained in more detail in the following subsection.

3.3 Global Recursive Neural Parsing

As mentioned before, BiLSTM networks can make decisions based on contextual information from previous and future input events. However, its output does not explicitly encode the functional dependencies and constraints that exist at the sentence level (global level). For instance, PropBank formalism states that core roles can occur at most once per proposition, but a network, due to its localized nature, may assign the same role for multiple tokens in the same proposition. Under these circumstances, if our final predictions are made by using only network predictions, we are exclusively relying on the model's ability to indirectly learn global dependencies. In this context, a minimal mistake may invalidate the whole sentence tagging.

Existing literature addresses such problem by applying a global inference mechanism whose objective is to find the best overall labeling for a given sentence. Dynamic programming algorithms such as Viterbi are candidates for solving this type of problem. The argument is that the usage of a transition state matrix naturally excludes violating sequences [26,30]. The inference stage can also be modeled as an Integer Linear Programming (ILP) problem where one attempts to maximize the sentence labeling probability observing the formalism constraints translated to an ILP solver [27]. At last, It is possible to rely on a re-ranking strategy that uses a second classifier which aggregates features from sentence and frame level features [32].

Our global inference stage is based on the recent work of [22] that proposed the global recursive neural parsing algorithm. It directly searches the space of all possible labels derived from the network predictions with no dynamic programming techniques. The approach may be seen as a special case of A* algorithm and was tested on Combinatory Categorial Grammar (CCG) parsing. The results point to an accurate and efficient model, finding optimal parse in 99.9% of sentences while exploring only 190 subtrees on average.

As in a standard A* search algorithm, the score function s of a partial sequence of nodes until the time step t is given by the equation $s(t) = g(t) + h(t)$ where g function is the cost of the path from starting node to node t and h function indicates an admissible heuristic for best path. Regular opening cost function g was modified by the introduction of a constraint function c that yields a non-negative score whenever the candidate sequence violates any global constraint and 0 otherwise (Eq. 1). Hence, the opening cost is given by summing over the network probabilities output (represented as $\log p$) subtracted from the violation cost from the starting node until time step t.

$$g(w, y_t) = \sum_{i=1}^{t} \log p(y_i|w) - c(w, y_i) \qquad (1)$$

The role of constraint function c is to discourage node exploring whose partial path leads to an invalid sequence of tags. The following global rules have been encoded into this function:

- **PropBank constraint:** As described in [9], core semantic roles (A0–A5) and adjunct arguments (AM) must be utilized at most once in a given proposition. Therefore, repeating semantic roles yields the violation score of 10.
- **IOB schema:** The constraints implemented here penalizes any partial sequence that does not produce a valid IOB sequence, such as the case where an inside tag (I) is not preceded by the begin tag (B). Here, the violation score is also 10.

The heuristic function h utilized in our work (see Eq. 2) is the same used by [16] and is given by the summation over the most probable labels for all times steps after t.

$$h(w, y_t) = \sum_{i=t+1}^{T} \max_{y_i \in T} \log p(y_i|w) \qquad (2)$$

4   Experimental Setup

Our models were trained using *Adam*, an efficient adaptative algorithm for gradient-based optimization of stochastic objective functions that is typically suited for high-dimensional parameter models [20]. The algorithm was initialized with the default settings suggested by the original article ($\alpha = 0.001, \beta_1 = 0.9, \beta_2 = 0.999, \epsilon = 10^{-8}$). To prevent overfitting and to improve the overall performance of our model, we used the *Dropout* technique introduced by [28]. We chose to drop 35% of the units at the input of each BiLSTM layer and another 20% between recurrent connections [12].

Each training session lasted up to a hundred epochs with an early stopping policy that ends the session after ten epochs without any improvement in the model's overall performance. We saved the network state whenever the current epoch result beats the one obtained by the previous best model.

Performance evaluation was executed after the end of each training epoch. The process was carried through the usage of the official evaluation script for the CoNLL-2005 Shared Task, dedicated to the SRL task [6]. As stated in related work (Subsect. 2), our results were compared to those reported by [10] referred to in this article as our baseline.

5   Experimental Results

Our first experiment investigates the optimal word embedding dimensionality applicable to our model. We prepared three distinct models with an almost identical setup where the only exception concerns the choice of word vector dimensionality. These model's used distinct pre-computed word vector representations with 50, 100, and 150 dimensions, respectively. Following the setup proposed by [35], the experiments in this stage used four stacked BiLSTM layers, each of them containing 300 hundred LSTM cells equally distributed between internal forward and backward layers. The remaining hyperparameters strictly followed the experimental setup described in the previous section.

In order to provide a robust evaluation, we chose to employ the cross-validation technique in a 20-fold configuration [11], what maintains the same dataset partition size used by baseline. Hence, we randomly divided the original corpus into 20 equal sized folds and performed 20 separate training sessions, each using 19 folds for training (95% of data) and 1 fold for testing (the remaining 5%). We rotate the fold selection in a way that all folds are used as the test set exactly once. Therefore, considering our experiment, in this stage we conducted 60 training sessions that took three and half days to run.

From Table 1c one may observe that the model's performance is sensitive to changes in word embedding dimensionality. Averaged results indicate a difference in performance that surpassed 4 F_1-score points. A Kruskal-Wallis H-test confirmed this observation as it rejects the null hypothesis that the population median of all the groups is equals ($p - value = 4.71 * 10^{-7}$). A post-hoc comparison using the Wilcox Mann-Whitney test points that, considering our model, the

Table 1. Main results.

(a) SRL Performance comparison

Model	Precision	Recall	F$_1$-Score
Our best	**67.62**	**68.75**	**68.18**
Ours (averaged 20-fold)			**65.63**
Baseline best (One-step)	64.41	60.34	62.31
Baseline best (Two-step)	67.06	63.31	65.13

(c) Results considering different dimensionality

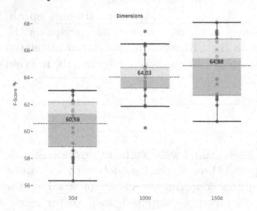

(b) Overall results for our best model

	Precision	Recall	F$_{\beta=1}$
Overall	67.62%	68.75%	68.18
A0	81.82%	86.90%	84.28
A1	71.15%	72.29%	71.71
A2	52.73%	42.03%	46.77
A3	28.57%	40.00%	33.33
A4	100.00%	50.00%	66.67
AM-ADV	42.86%	50.00%	46.15
AM-CAU	50.00%	33.33%	40.00
AM-DIS	44.44%	28.57%	34.78
AM-EXT	0.00%	0.00%	0.00
AM-LOC	54.17%	72.22%	61.90
AM-MED	0.00%	0.00%	0.00
AM-MNR	34.78%	47.06%	40.00
AM-NEG	90.00%	94.74%	92.31
AM-PNC	42.86%	66.67%	52.17
AM-PRD	100.00%	33.33%	50.00
AM-TMP	66.67%	73.47%	69.90
V	100.00%	100.00%	100.00

usage of word vectors with 50 dimensions systematically produces inferior results when compared to the other models, based on a 100 ($p - value = 2.13 * 10^{-6}$) and a 150 dimensions ($p - value = 2.27 * 10^{-6}$). Nonetheless, when directly comparing the performance of models based on word embeddings with 100 and 150 dimensions, we fail to reject the null hypothesis ($p\text{-}value = 0.11$). Thereby, despite a slightly better averaged F$_1$-score obtained by the model with 150 dimensions, there is no significant difference when compared to the result of the model based on 100 dimensions.

These results corroborate the findings of [24] that suggest that picking the optimal dimensionality is critical for obtaining the best performance on extrinsic tasks such as SRL. In our case, the optimal level of semantic expressiveness was reached using word vectors with 150 dimensions.

In the second experiment, we analyze the effect caused by the depth of stacked BiSLTM layers in the overall performance of our system. This time, we trained four identical models whose only exception regards its number of layers (1, 2, 3, and 4 layers). These models used pre-computed word embedding models with 150 dimensions (the best performance on the previous experiment) and

BiLSTM layers with 300 LSTM cells each. Once again, we used a 20-fold cross-validation technique, and the remaining hyper-parameters followed the experimental setup described in the previous section. This experiment took four days to run.

We highlight that the model based on only one BiLSTM layer yields an inferior performance when compared to the remaining models, based on more layers ($p - value = 0.01$). The accuracy reaches its peak in the model based on two layers (65.63) and, as we stack more layers, deepening the network architecture, one may observe a slight performance degradation. However, after comparing results from groups based on 2, 3, and 4 stacked layers, we observe that, notwithstanding the model based on two layers have achieved a slightly better averaged F_1-score, there is no significant difference on the accuracy of these groups ($p - value = 0.65$).

These observations converged into our **final model** that uses word vector representations of 150 dimensions and a neural network architecture composed by two stacked BiLSTM layers.

Table 1a provides a comparison of our final model with the baseline system based on one-step and two-step frameworks [10]. When we confront the one-step framework from the baseline with our system, one may observe that their best result (the best performance on a single training session) was consistently outperformed by our model's best result (62.31 vs 68.18), creating a margin of almost 6 F_1-score points. Even if we compare the baseline best model with our averaged score, the margin is still consistent, yielding a difference of 3.32 F_1-score points.

Our model also produced superior results when compared to the two-stage model of the baseline, albeit with a smaller margin. This time, the difference between the best models was 3.05 points, what points to a reduction on relative error of 8.74%. Again, our averaged result surpassed their best single model by a margin of 0.5 points.

We highlight that the baseline article [10] reported results only for their best single training sessions. For this reason, we could not produce a direct comparison based on k-fold cross-validation, that would possibly produce a more robust evaluation.

Finally, the results of our best single model are detailed in Table 1b. As expected, the system was more performant in well-defined and numerous semantic roles such as A0, A1, AM-TMP, and AM-NEG. Nevertheless, roles such as A2 and A3 yielded inferior results. This reduction may be due to the lack of standardization in the semantic role definitions. Only A0 and A1 exhibit a shared the meaning across different predicates. The meaning of the remaining core roles varies according to the predicate and its senses and can be even fused with adjunctive roles. This ambiguity may act as a noise factor for the neural network consequently causing a performance drop in the remaining roles.

6   Conclusion

In this article, we described an end-to-end semantic role labeler for the Portuguese language. The one-step approach was built on top of a BiLSTM neural network architecture tied to an inference stage based on a global recursive neural parsing algorithm that was specifically tailored for the SRL task. Seeking an optimal structure, we also conducted an extensive investigation about the effects of two crucial factors on our structure: the depth of network architecture and the proper word embedding dimensionality.

Our approach outperformed the previous state-of-the-art on the Portuguese language by 3.05 F_1-score points, reducing the relative error in 8.74%. We also confirmed the hypothesis that picking the optimal embedding dimensionality is critical for obtaining the best accuracy on SRL task. Our final model was based on word vectors with 150 dimensions passing through a deep network with two BiLSTM layers.

Future research may invest in the automated expansion of PropBank-Br corpus what, in our point of view, is an encouraging alternative for reaching a competitive performance on the task. Moreover, we believe that a promising direction point to the study of an architecture designed to attenuate the impact of ambiguity in semantic role definitions of PropBank formalism.

Acknowledgment. This work was partially funded by ANEEL Brazil R&D Project CEMIG GT641.

References

1. Alva-Manchego, F.E., Rosa, J.L.G.: Towards semi-supervised brazilian portuguese semantic role labeling: building a benchmark. In: Caseli, H., Villavicencio, A., Teixeira, A., Perdigão, F. (eds.) PROPOR 2012. LNCS (LNAI), vol. 7243, pp. 210–217. Springer, Heidelberg (2012). https://doi.org/10.1007/978-3-642-28885-2_24

2. Alva-Manchego, F.E., Rosa, J.L.G.: Semantic role labeling for Brazilian Portuguese: a benchmark. In: Pavón, J., Duque-Méndez, N.D., Fuentes-Fernández, R. (eds.) IBERAMIA 2012. LNCS (LNAI), vol. 7637, pp. 481–490. Springer, Heidelberg (2012). https://doi.org/10.1007/978-3-642-34654-5_49

3. Bengio, Y., Simard, P., Frasconi, P.: Learning long-term dependencies with gradient descent is difficult. IEEE Trans. Neural Netw. **5**(2), 157–166 (1994)

4. Bird, S., Klein, E., Loper, E.: Natural Language Processing with Python: Analyzing Text with the Natural Language Toolkit. O'Reilly Media, Inc. (2009)

5. Carneiro, M.G., Cupertino, T.H., Zhao, L., Rosa, J.L.: Semi-supervised semantic role labeling for Brazilian Portuguese. J. Inf. Data Manag. **8**(2), 117 (2017)

6. Carreras, X., Màrquez, L.: Introduction to the CoNLL-2005 shared task: semantic role labeling. In: Proceedings of the CoNLL 2005, pp. 152–164. ACL (2005)

7. Christensen, J., Soderland, S., Etzioni, O., et al.: Semantic role labeling for open information extraction. In: Proceedings of the NAACL-HLT 2010, pp. 52–60. ACL (2010)

8. Collobert, R., Weston, J., Bottou, L., Karlen, M., Kavukcuoglu, K., Kuksa, P.: Natural language processing (almost) from scratch. J. Mach. Learn. Res. **12**(Aug), 2493–2537 (2011)
9. Duran, M.S., Aluísio, S.M.: Propbank-Br: a Brazilian Treebank annotated with semantic role labels. In: LREC, pp. 1862–1867 (2012)
10. Fonseca, E.R., Rosa, J.L.G.: A two-step convolutional neural network approach for semantic role labeling. In: The 2013 International Joint Conference on Neural Networks (IJCNN), pp. 1–7. IEEE (2013)
11. Fushiki, T.: Estimation of prediction error by using k-fold cross-validation. Stat. Comput. **21**(2), 137–146 (2011)
12. Gal, Y., Ghahramani, Z.: A theoretically grounded application of dropout in recurrent neural networks. In: Advances in Neural Information Processing Systems, pp. 1019–1027 (2016)
13. Graves, A., Mohamed, A.R., Hinton, G.: Speech recognition with deep recurrent neural networks. In: Proceedings of the Acoustics, Speech and Signal Processing Conference (ICASSP 2013), pp. 6645–6649. IEEE (2013)
14. Graves, A., Schmidhuber, J.: Framewise phoneme classification with bidirectional LSTM and other neural network architectures. Neural Netw. **18**(5), 602–610 (2005)
15. Hartmann, N.S., Duran, M.S., Aluísio, S.M.: Automatic semantic role labeling on non-revised syntactic trees of journalistic texts. In: Silva, J., Ribeiro, R., Quaresma, P., Adami, A., Branco, A. (eds.) PROPOR 2016. LNCS (LNAI), vol. 9727, pp. 202–212. Springer, Cham (2016). https://doi.org/10.1007/978-3-319-41552-9_20
16. He, L., Lee, K., Lewis, M., Zettlemoyer, L.: Deep semantic role labeling: what works and what's next. In: Proceedings of the ACL 2017 (2017)
17. Hochreiter, S., Schmidhuber, J.: Long short-term memory. Neural Comput. **9**(8), 1735–1780 (1997)
18. Huang, Z., Xu, W., Yu, K.: Bidirectional LSTM-CRF models for sequence tagging. arXiv preprint arXiv:1508.01991 (2015)
19. Khan, A., Salim, N., Kumar, Y.J.: A framework for multi-document abstractive summarization based on semantic role labelling. Appl. Soft Comput. **30**, 737–747 (2015)
20. Kingma, D., Ba, J.: Adam: a method for stochastic optimization. arXiv preprint arXiv:1412.6980 (2014)
21. Kumar, A., et al.: Ask me anything: dynamic memory networks for natural language processing. In: International Conference on Machine Learning, pp. 1378–1387 (2016)
22. Lee, K., Lewis, M., Zettlemoyer, L.: Global neural CCG parsing with optimality guarantees. arXiv preprint arXiv:1607.01432 (2016)
23. Levy, O., Goldberg, Y., Dagan, I.: Improving distributional similarity with lessons learned from word embeddings. Trans. ACL **3**, 211–225 (2015)
24. Melamud, O., McClosky, D., Patwardhan, S., Bansal, M.: The role of context types and dimensionality in learning word embeddings. In: Proceedings of NAACL-HLT 2016, pp. 1030–1040 (2016)
25. Mikolov, T., Sutskever, I., Chen, K., Corrado, G.S., Dean, J.: Distributed representations of words and phrases and their compositionality. In: Advances in Neural Information Processing Systems, pp. 3111–3119 (2013)
26. Pradhan, S., Ward, W., Hacioglu, K., Martin, J.H., Jurafsky, D.: Semantic role labeling using different syntactic views. In: Proceedings of the ACL 2005, ACL 2005, Stroudsburg, PA, USA, pp. 581–588. ACL (2005)
27. Punyakanok, V., Roth, D., Yih, W.T.: The importance of syntactic parsing and inference in semantic role labeling. Comput. Linguist. **34**(2), 257–287 (2008)

28. Srivastava, N., Hinton, G.E., Krizhevsky, A., Sutskever, I., Salakhutdinov, R.: Dropout: a simple way to prevent neural networks from overfitting. J. Mach. Learn. Res. **15**(1), 1929–1958 (2014)
29. Sutskever, I., Vinyals, O., Le, Q.V.: Sequence to sequence learning with neural networks. In: Advances in Neural Information Processing Systems, pp. 3104–3112 (2014)
30. Täckström, O., Ganchev, K., Das, D.: Efficient inference and structured learning for semantic role labeling. Trans. ACL **3**, 29–41 (2015)
31. Tai, K.S., Socher, R., Manning, C.D.: Improved semantic representations from tree-structured long short-term memory networks. arXiv preprint arXiv:1503.00075 (2015)
32. Toutanova, K., Haghighi, A., Manning, C.D.: Joint learning improves semantic role labeling. In: Proceedings of the ACL 2005, pp. 589–596. ACL (2005)
33. Wang, Z., Jiang, T., Chang, B., Sui, Z.: Chinese semantic role labeling with bidirectional recurrent neural networks. In: Proceedings of the EMNLP 2015, pp. 1626–1631 (2015)
34. Wu, D., Fung, P.: Can semantic role labeling improve SMT. In: Proceedings of the EAMT 2009, pp. 218–225 (2009)
35. Zhou, J., Xu, W.: End-to-end learning of semantic role labeling using recurrent neural networks. In: Proceedings of the ACL 2015, pp. 1127–1137 (2015)

Evaluating Active Learning Sampling Strategies for Opinion Mining in Brazilian Politics Corpora

Douglas Vitório[1,2]($\boxtimes$), Ellen Souza[2], and Adriano L. I. Oliveira[1]

[1] Center of Informatics, Federal University of Pernambuco, Recife, PE, Brazil
{damsv,alio}@cin.ufpe.br
[2] MiningBR Research Group, Federal Rural University of Penambuco,
Serra Talhada, PE, Brazil
ellen.ramos@ufrpe.br

Abstract. Politics is a commonly used domain in Opinion Mining applications, in which opinions may change over time. Nevertheless, the usual approaches for Opinion Mining are not able to deal with the characteristics and the challenges brought by continuous *data streams*; so, an alternative is the use of techniques such as Active Learning, which labels selected data rather than the entire data set. The Active Learning approach requires the choice of a sampling strategy to select the most valuable instances. However, no study has performed an analysis in order to identify the best strategies for Opinion Mining. In this sense, we evaluated eight Active Learning sampling strategies, from which *Entropy* achieved the best results. In addition, due to the lack of publicly available stream data sets written in Portuguese, we created and evaluated corpora from Twitter and Facebook about the 2018 Brazilian presidential elections.

Keywords: Opinion Mining · Active Learning · Brazilian corpora

1 Introduction

The Web 2.0 and the exponential growth of social media and user-generated content (UGC) on the Internet provides a huge quantity of information, which has made understanding people's thoughts and opinions fundamental for decision making, in particular when the users share their comments voluntarily [8]. However, it is impossible for humans to fully understand UGC efficiently, which increased the scientific community's interest in developing systems capable of extracting information from this kind of data [5].

The most common approaches to solve this problem are based on Opinion Mining (OM), also known in the literature as Sentiment Analysis, which is the field of study that analyzes people's sentiments and opinions about entities, such as products and services, expressed in textual input [13]. This analysis is

© Springer Nature Switzerland AG 2019
P. Moura Oliveira et al. (Eds.): EPIA 2019, LNAI 11805, pp. 695–707, 2019.
https://doi.org/10.1007/978-3-030-30244-3_57

commonly made by the classification of opinions contained in a document into categories, such as *positive*, *negative*, or *neutral*. In this way, OM has collaborated with the goals of companies and organizations, supporting them to observe the public's reactions and customer's satisfaction [15].

Understanding opinions has also proved important in other domains, such as Politics [14]. Recent reviews [20,21] show an increasing interest for OM applications to be used in political campaigns, especially with regard to the use of data written in Portuguese. Additionally, it is estimated that social media had a great impact on the 2016 US presidential election [2].

Previously, OM applications have had their focus on static and well-known domains, such as movie reviews, and not able to deal efficiently with the characteristics of continuous *data streams* and the challenges brought by them [10]. The analysis of *data streams* from social media, also known as *social streams*, is important because people's opinions about certain entities may change as new information arrives [23].

In Machine Learning, the change in a given concept that occurs over time is known as *concept drift* [24]. In a similar way and according to Wang et al. [23], a change in an opinion that occurs over time may be considered an *opinion drift* and the detection of these drifts are relevant for the OM results. Silva et al. [18], in their turn, named this change as *sentiment drift* and explained that either the sentiment distribution or the characteristics related to certain sentiments may change and make the predictions less accurate as time passes.

Drift-sensitive and *data streams* applications face two main obstacles: the limited availability of labeled data and the need to constantly update the learning model, due to the *data streams* evolutionary nature. So, it is a problem that the most commonly used OM models are strongly based on Supervised Learning [15], because of its need for labeled data; whereas the second challenge lies in the vocabulary changes that occur in UGC [16] and, mainly, in the aforementioned nature of the *data streams* [10].

Due to these problems, an alternative is the use of Semi-supervised Learning, which does not require that all data is labeled, but only a part of it. A common semi-supervised approach in data mining is the Active Learning (AL) [26], which can deal well with problems where labeled data is costly to obtain [27], labeling only the most valuable data rather than the entire data set. However, a sampling strategy is needed to decide whether the label of an instance should be requested or not, so it can be used to feed the model's training set [28].

Only a few recent papers were found applying Opinion Mining with AL [1,11,19,27], and they used different strategies to select the instances. Also, they did not provide a complete comparison between these strategies, so, there is not a consensus of the best techniques to use. Thus, this study presents an evaluation of eight Active Learning sampling strategies in the Opinion Mining scenario. Two are proposed by the authors, inspired by other strategies found in the literature: *Variable Entropy* and *Variable Randomized Entropy*.

Furthermore, none of the found studies used Portuguese language data sets. Also, it is known that there is a lack of benchmark Portuguese corpora [20], and no publicly available corpus containing *data streams* written in this language was found. So, another contribution of this paper is the creation and evaluation of manually annotated Portuguese corpora containing *tweets* and Facebook comments about the 2018 Brazilian presidential election.

The rest of this paper is structured as follows: Sect. 2 discusses the related work. Section 3 explains Active Learning and the sampling strategies evaluated. Section 4 presents the Brazilian corpora. Section 5 details the experimental setup. In Sect. 6, the findings are reported and discussed. Finally, Sect. 7 draws the conclusions.

2 Related Work

Two new Active Learning strategies were proposed by Žliobaitė et al. [28]. They are based on uncertainty, dynamic allocation of labeling efforts over time and randomization of the search space, which, according to the authors, can explicitly handle *concept drift*. Benchmark stream prediction data sets, as well as textual data from the IMDb and Reuters, were used to carry out experiments and evaluate the techniques; however, the authors did not perform Sentiment Analysis.

As mentioned in Sect. 1, only a few studies using Active Learning in OM applications were found, and none of them used data sets written in Portuguese. Smailović et al. [19] used an SVM classifier and combined the advantages of two sampling strategies: *Uncertainty* and *Random Sampling*, besides using them separately. The authors' goal was to find the best querying strategy for Active Learning to Sentiment Analysis on financial Twitter *data streams*, concluding that, by using the AL approach, the prediction power of the sentiment classifier in the stock market application was improved.

The *Uncertainty* strategy was also used by Zimmermann et al. [27] to select the documents (*tweets* and product reviews) that will update the model and the words added to the vocabulary. In addition, they proposed a strategy based on the information gain provided by the document. These two techniques were compared with the *Random Sampling* strategy, with an incremental approach that requires all arriving document labels, and a non-adaptive method. The AL sampling strategies performed better than the others, and the *Information Gain* showed good performance on all data sets, considering the *kappa* statistic measure.

Kranjc et al. [11] created a framework for Sentiment Analysis with AL, using *Uncertainty* and *Random Sampling* strategies, although they did not evaluate or compare the strategies performances. Finally, Aldoğan and Yaslan [1] used the *Query By Committee* (QBC) AL strategy, evaluating three approaches to built the committee: random choice, Shannon Entropy, and Maximum Disagreement. They performed experiments in movie-review and product-review corpora, concluding that the Shannon Entropy approach was the best for QBC in the evaluated scenarios.

3   Active Learning Sampling Strategies

The Active Learning method uses an initial seed of labeled documents as the first training set of the model, then, a sampling strategy is used to occasionally request the label of the most suitable documents that are not presented in the training set, in order to update the model with these new instances [27]. In this paper, this process was iterative, so, each time a new instance was selected, the model was updated.

Eight sampling strategies were evaluated in this study: *Random Sampling*; *Uncertainty*, based on [28]; *Variable Uncertainty* [28]; *Variable Randomized Uncertainty* [28]; *Information Gain* [27]; *Entropy* [12]; *Variable Entropy*; and *Variable Randomized Entropy*. These strategies were chosen due to their utilization on Opinion Mining and Text Mining studies.

3.1   Random Sampling

The *Random Sampling* selects the instances at random, based on a probability B, where B is the budget. In this study, we used $B = 0.3$, so, about 30% of the instances were added to the model; the papers researched [27,28] evaluated different values of B, then, we choose 0.3 as an average value.

3.2   Uncertainty, Variable Uncertainty, and Variable Randomized Uncertainty

The *Uncertainty* strategy selects the instances for which the current classifier is less certain. The implementation of Žliobaitė et al. [28], which uses a threshold (θ) value, was adopted in our study. In this case, an instance is selected if the classifier's certainty for it is below $1 - \theta$. We also used $\theta = 0.3$, so, the instances with a classifier's confidence below than 70% were selected.

Žliobaitė et al. [28] also made two modifications in the *Uncertainty* technique. The first one, called *Variable Uncertainty*, changes the threshold using an adjusting step (s), to adapt it depending on the incoming data, expanding and contracting the threshold. The second one, called *Variable Randomized Uncertainty*, also uses the adjusting step, besides randomizing the threshold for every instance, multiplying it by a normally distributed random variable that follows $\mathcal{N}(1, \delta)$. As stated by the authors, these strategies react well to changes (*drifts*) that can occur anywhere in the instance space, being suitable for *data streams*. In this study, as in [28], we used $s = 0.01$ and $\delta = 1$.

3.3   Information Gain

The *Information Gain* sampling strategy was proposed by Zimmermann et al. [27]. This strategy is specific for Text Mining, since it uses the word-class distribution of the words of a document and the distribution after considering the predicted label for that document. So, the documents which provide a gain in information, considering the actual model, are selected.

3.4 Entropy, Variable Entropy, and Variable Randomized Entropy

According to Yang and Loog [25], the entropy can be used as a measure of uncertainty. Then, in this study, the *Entropy* implementation from Lewis and Gale [12] was used in the same way as the *Uncertainty* strategy detailed above and with the same threshold value. In this case, a document is selected if its entropy is greater than 0.3.

Therefore, inspired by the above statement and the strategies brought by Žliobaitė et al. [28], we proposed two other techniques: *Variable Entropy* and *Variable Randomized Entropy*, which are basically the same presented in [28], but using the entropy measure instead of the classifier's certainty.

The goal is to investigate whether the benefits of randomization and the use of a variable threshold for *drift* reaction appear also with different uncertainty measures. And, to compare with the strategies presented in Subsect. 3.2, the parameters used were also the same: $s = 0.01$ and $\delta = 1$.

4 The Brazilian Presidential Election Data Set

Due to the lack of stream data sets written in Portuguese and the importance of OM in the politics domain, we built corpora containing *tweets* and Facebook comments about the second round of 2018 Brazilian presidential elections, which involved Jair Bolsonaro (PSL) and Fernando Haddad (PT) on October 28.

The next subsections detail the process used to create the corpora, which are publicly available[1].

4.1 Data Extraction

During the second round of presidential election in Brazil, six debates were scheduled between the two candidates on the following days: 11, 14, 15, 17, 21 and 26 October 2018. We planned to collect *tweets* and Facebook comments during the debates, but they did not occur because of unforeseen circumstances.

However, we decided to collect opinions on the days scheduled for the debates. On Twitter, we collected opinions that contained mentions and *hashtags* with the names of the candidates. On Facebook, we collect the comments from news about the candidates, totaling over 20,000 opinions. Both collection processes were performed automatically.

4.2 Manual Annotation

We randomly selected 2,000 Facebook comments and 1,500 *tweets*. Then, the opinions were classified according to which candidate they were referring to by candidate name, or by political party, or both. After that, each comment had its opinion, regarding to each candidate, classified in *positive* or *negative*.

---

[1] http://miningbrgroup.com.br/index.php/resources/.

The classification was done by three annotators, in a way that two different annotators were responsible for each opinion. In the cases where the two annotators disagreed, i.e., each one classified the opinion as a different polarity, they discussed the annotation in order to reach a consensus. We also computed the Cohen's Kappa coefficient [6] of each corpora, in order to discover the agreement between the annotators.

Finally, we obtained six corpora, which differ by the source of data: Twitter or Facebook; and the candidate: Jair Bolsonaro, Fernando Haddad, or both. However, the opinions that refer to both candidates at the same time were excluded from the *both* corpora, because we are not dealing with multi-class classification in this study. Table 1 presents the details of the corpora created.

Table 1. Details of the created corpora.

#	Candidate	Source	Size	#positive	#negative	Cohen's Kappa
1.	Jair Bolsonaro	Facebook	1,047	817	230	0.9439
2.	Jair Bolsonaro	Twitter	861	484	377	0.7404
3.	Fernando Haddad	Facebook	1,046	440	606	0.9528
4.	Fernando Haddad	Twitter	762	298	464	0.8370
5.	Both	Facebook	1,907	1,167	740	0.9579
6.	Both	Twitter	1,377	675	702	0.7805

5   Experimental Setup

To achieve the goal of this study, the eight sampling strategies presented in Sect. 3 were evaluated on the same scenarios, which are explained in the following subsections.

5.1   Data Sets

Besides the use of the created corpora detailed in Sect. 4, we also used two other publicly available English Twitter stream data sets: Sentiment140 [9] and Sanders [17]. The studies from [19,22,27] performed OM with *data streams* using the former, while [3,4] used the latter.

The Sentiment140 *training* data set contains 1,600,000 automatically annotated *tweets*, which would be extremely costly to process; so, we took subsets of 10,000, 5,000, 2,500, and 1,000 *tweets* from two different points of the stream, in order to evaluate the strategies on different sized corpora and under the effect of different *drifts*, having the second point been inspired by Zimmermann et al. [27]. In addition, we also used the Sentiment140 *test* data set, which contains 497 *tweets* manually annotated.

The Sanders data set, in its turn, contains *tweets* about four different companies, so we used the *tweets* about each company as a subset, besides the *full* corpus, containing all *tweets*. This partition provided a bigger number of corpora in which we could evaluate the strategies; additionally, a *data stream* usually refers to only one entity.

Then, we had a total of 14 extra corpora (in addition to the six created), whose details are presented in Table 2. As can be observed, the corpora differ from each other by size, number of classes, domain, and unbalance.

Table 2. Details of the used corpora.

#	Corpus	Size	#positive	#negative	#neutral	Details
7.	Sentiment140_test	497	182	177	138	-
8.	Sentiment140_10000_1	10,000	5,812	4,188	-	*tweets* 25,000–35,000
9.	Sentiment140_5000_1	5,000	2,970	2,030	-	*tweets* 35,000–40,000
10.	Sentiment140_2500_1	2,500	1,461	1,039	-	*tweets* 40,000–42,500
11.	Sentiment140_1000_1	1,000	579	421	-	*tweets* 42,500–43,500
12.	Sentiment140_10000_2	10,000	5,602	4,398	-	*tweets* 1,235,000–1,245,000
13.	Sentiment140_5000_2	5,000	2,821	2,179	-	*tweets* 1,245,000–1,250,000
14.	Sentiment140_2500_2	2,500	1,421	1,079	-	*tweets* 1,250,000–1,252,500
15.	Sentiment140_1000_2	1,000	572	428	-	*tweets* 1,252,500–1,253,500
16.	Sanders_apple	1,002	164	316	522	-
17.	Sanders_google	838	202	57	579	-
18.	Sanders_microsoft	864	91	132	641	-
19.	Sanders_twitter	719	62	67	590	-
20.	Sanders_all	3,423	519	572	2,332	-

5.2 Pre-processing

The implementation was done using the Python programming language, and the Natural Language Toolkit (NLTK)[2] and Scikit-learn[3] libraries. To structure the data into a Vector Space Model (VSM), we used the CountVectorizer from the Scikit-learn library. The TweetTokenizer, from the NLTK, was chosen to perform the tokenization of the documents, due to its specificity; as Facebook has incorporated features from Twitter, such as *hashtags*, the TweetTokenizer was used for both sources of data. We opted to use simple pre-processing techniques and focus only on the evaluation of the AL strategies.

5.3 Processing

The classifier chosen for this study was the Multinomial Naïve Bayes (MNB), which is particularly suitable for *opinion streams*, since it adjusts to changes in the probabilities of the words [22]. Besides that, the MNB proved to be the most efficient in the paper of Žliobaitė et al. [28], which used Active Learning

---

[2] https://www.nltk.org.
[3] https://scikit-learn.org.

with textual data. The MNB was also used in the study of Zimmermann et al. [27] and, according to Souza et al. [21], it is one of the most used classifiers for Opinion Mining. We have used the Scikit-learn MNB implementation.

Finally, to implement the Active Learning sampling strategies, we used the modAL Python library [7]. This library has the implementation of the *Uncertainty* and *Entropy* measures. We adapted the strategies based on these two measures using the algorithms presented in Žliobaitė et al. [28]. The *Random Sampling* strategy was manually implemented, as well as the *Information Gain*, which followed the details as demonstrated in the paper of Zimmermann et al. [27].

5.4   Evaluation

Due to the continuous nature of the streams, we opted not to use the *cross-validation* technique in the evaluation step. Instead, we used the *holdout* technique, separating the last 30% of the stream to test the performance of the classifier and the others 70% for training. The performance measure used was *accuracy*.

For all the techniques, we started with an initial seed containing the first 10% of the stream, while the sampling strategies decided which of the documents, from the remaining 60% separated for training, would be used to update the model.

6   Results and Discussion

Table 3 shows the accuracy of each sampling strategy: *Random Sampling* (RAND), *Uncertainty* (UNC), *Variable Uncertainty* (UNCV), *Variable Randomized Uncertainty* (UNCVR), *Information Gain* (IG), *Entropy* (ENT), *Variable Entropy* (ENTV), and *Variable Randomized Entropy* (ENTVR).

The Friedman and the Nemenyi post-hoc tests were applied. The Friedman test was used to observe whether the strategies performance presented a statistical difference (considering a p-value = 0.05); the test resulted in a p-value = 8.779×10^{-8}, demonstrating that there is a statistical difference between some of the strategies. Then, the Nemenyi post-hoc test was used to determine which techniques show this difference; Fig. 1 presents the Critical Difference (CD) diagram obtained from the post-hoc test, in which the strategies connected with a black bar are statistically similar. The SciPy[4] Python library was used for the former test and the Orange[5] library for the latter.

The experiments demonstrated that the *Entropy* technique showed the best numerical results, achieving the best accuracy in seven of the 20 data sets and being the best ranked strategy (although ENTV had the best mean). This result was similar to Yang and Loog [25], which performed a comparison between AL strategies for logistic regression, and showed that the usage of entropy as a

---

[4] docs.scipy.org/doc/scipy-0.14.0/reference/index.html.
[5] http://docs.orange.biolab.si/3/data-mining-library/index.html.

Table 3. The accuracy of each sampling strategy.

#	Data set	RAND	UNC	UNCV	UNCVR	IG	ENT	ENTV	ENTVR
1.	Bolsonaro_facebook	**0.898**	0.850	0.863	**0.898**	0.796	0.878	0.875	**0.898**
2.	Bolsonaro_twitter	0.705	0.511	0.744	0.732	0.441	0.759	**0.786**	0.721
3.	Haddad_facebook	0.840	0.600	**0.878**	0.862	0.754	0.731	0.859	**0.878**
4.	Haddad_twitter	0.706	0.671	0.745	0.732	0.627	0.732	**0.754**	0.714
5.	Both_facebook	0.888	0.868	**0.931**	0.914	0.634	0.904	0.924	0.895
6.	Both_twitter	0.711	0.721	0.753	0.762	0.728	**0.770**	0.736	0.757
7.	Sentiment140_test	0.604	0.584	0.590	0.617	0.402	**0.637**	0.610	0.570
8.	Sentiment140_1000_1	0.580	0.570	0.663	0.663	0.656	**0.676**	0.670	0.616
9.	Sentiment140_2500_1	0.730	0.729	**0.749**	0.737	0.692	0.742	0.716	0.740
10.	Sentiment140_5000_1	0.681	0.680	0.703	**0.710**	0.674	0.708	0.700	0.694
11.	Sentiment140_10000_1	0.719	0.710	0.724	0.723	0.704	0.725	0.712	**0.729**
12.	Sentiment140_1000_2	0.570	0.550	0.606	0.630	0.543	0.586	**0.636**	0.596
13.	Sentiment140_2500_2	0.669	0.656	0.691	0.680	0.652	0.696	**0.698**	0.678
14.	Sentiment140_5000_2	0.695	0.708	0.703	0.700	0.682	**0.712**	0.711	0.707
15.	Sentiment140_10000_2	0.726	0.726	0.723	0.730	0.707	**0.736**	0.725	0.728
16.	Sanders_apple	0.583	0.583	0.613	0.620	0.560	**0.626**	0.623	0.603
17.	Sanders_google	**0.793**	0.741	0.773	0.777	**0.793**	0.757	**0.793**	0.765
18.	Sanders_microsoft	**0.703**	0.687	0.683	0.683	0.687	0.687	0.695	0.679
19.	Sanders_twitter	0.758	**0.763**	0.758	0.753	0.753	**0.763**	0.758	0.749
20.	Sanders_all	0.748	0.720	0.721	0.694	**0.750**	0.727	0.710	0.718
-	Mean	0.715	0.681	0.730	0.731	0.662	0.728	**0.735**	0.722
-	Average ranking	4.75	6.05	3.60	3.55	6.60	**2.65**	3.25	4.55
-	Win counts	3	1	3	2	2	**7**	5	3

measure of uncertainty can produce the best accuracy in a large number of non textual and non stream data sets; and may also support the findings of Aldoğan and Yaslan [1], that an entropy-based approach for the *Query By Committee* strategy is a good opinion for Opinion Mining with movie and product reviews.

Although the *Information Gain* strategy achieved the best results in [27], it proved to be the worst technique in our experiments, reaching results statistically worse than four of the seven other strategies. This difference may be explained by the size of corpora used: Zimmermann et al. [27] performed experiments with a data set containing 250,000 *tweets*, while the larger corpus used in this study contained 10,000 *tweets*. Besides that, it was the most complex technique evaluated in this study, as it maintains the vocabulary at a high computational cost. However, differently from [27], we performed experiments with three classes (the Sanders data sets), in which the *Information Gain* had a better performance.

The changes in the *Uncertainty* strategy proposed by Žliobaitė et al. [28] have proved to be useful for OM with *social streams*; the *Variable Uncertainty* and the *Variable Randomized Uncertainty* showed largely better results than the fixed *Uncertainty* one, which was also statistically worse than four strategies. In addition, these two strategies presented equivalent performances and selected a similar number of instances in each data set. Nevertheless, this was

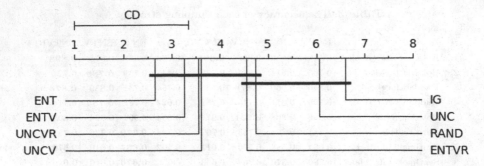

Fig. 1. Nemenyi post-hoc test comparison of the eight sampling strategies.

not observed with the entropy replacing the uncertainty measure; as aforementioned, the *Entropy* strategy without randomization and/or the adjusting step achieved the best results, although the *Variable Entropy* also reached very good ones.

Finally, during the experiments, we could observe that the fixed *Uncertainty* technique selected the smaller number of instances in almost all data sets, which may explain its poor performance. It could also be noticed that in "easy" data sets this strategy samples few instances, not enough to build a classifier that can deal well with *drifts*. In these cases, an alternative is to decrease the value of the θ threshold.

7   Conclusion

In this study, a document level sentiment analysis with *social streams* from Twitter and Facebook was performed, in order to identify the best sampling strategies for Active Learning with this kind of data. To do this, we implemented and evaluated eight AL sampling techniques, two of them proposed by us and inspired by existing strategies in the literature.

Another contribution of this paper was the creation of Twitter and Facebook stream opinion corpora about the 2018 Brazilian presidential election, which are publicly available.

According to the experiments, the *Entropy* strategy achieved the best results when compared to the other techniques, while the *Uncertainty* and *Information Gain* ones showed very poor performances.

However, the changes in the *Uncertainty* strategy presented by Žliobaitė et al. [28] proved to be useful for sentiment analysis with *social streams*, apparently bypassing the problems faced by the fixed *Uncertainty* technique. And one of the proposed techniques (*Variable Entropy*), which combines the changes from Žliobaitė et al. [28] and entropy, also achieved very good results.

As future work, an extension of the results presented in this paper is planned: measuring the impact of different parameter values and evaluating the AL strategies in other scenarios. The decrease of the θ threshold value, for instance, may improve the *Uncertainty* accuracy, besides the s and δ parameters present in the Žliobaitė et al. [28] algorithms.

Finally, we plan to evaluate the strategies in scenarios such as: (1) with a fixed number of selected instances; (2) with a stopping criteria; and (3) by selecting all instances before updating the model, rather than updating it every time a new instance is selected. And further analysis evaluating other classifier models, such as SVM or Logistic Regression, might be useful as well.

Acknowledgment. Douglas Vitório and Adriano L. I. Oliveira are supported by CNPq (Brazilian Council for Scientific and Technological Development).

References

1. Aldoğan, D., Yaslan, Y.: A comparison study on active learning integrated ensemble approaches in sentiment analysis. Comput. Electr. Eng. **57**, 311–323 (2017). https://doi.org/10.1016/j.compeleceng.2016.11.015
2. Allcott, H., Gentzkow, M.: Social media and fake news in the 2016 election. J. Econ. Perspect. **31**(2), 211–236 (2017)
3. Aston, N., Liddle, J., Hu, W.: Twitter sentiment in data streams with perceptron. J. Comput. Commun. **2**(03), 11 (2014)
4. Aston, N., Munson, T., Liddle, J., Hartshaw, G., Livingston, D., Hu, W.: Sentiment analysis on the social networks using stream algorithms. J. Data Anal. Inf. Process. **2**(02), 60 (2014)
5. Balazs, J.A., Velásquez, J.D.: Opinion mining and information fusion: a survey. Inf. Fusion **27**, 95–110 (2016). https://doi.org/10.1016/j.inffus.2015.06.002
6. Cohen, J.: A coefficient of agreement for nominal scales. Educ. Psychol. Meas. **20**(1), 37–46 (1960)
7. Danka, T., Horvath, P.: modAL: a modular active learning framework for Python (2018). https://github.com/cosmic-cortex/modAL, arXiv at https://arxiv.org/abs/1805.00979
8. Firmino Alves, A.L., Baptista, C.D.S., Firmino, A.A., Oliveira, M.G.A.D., Paiva, A.C.D.: A comparison of SVM versus Naive-Bayes techniques for sentiment analysis in tweets: a case study with the 2013 FIFA confederations cup. In: Proceedings of the 20th Brazilian Symposium on Multimedia and the Web, pp. 123–130 (2014)
9. Go, A., Bhayani, R., Huang, L.: Twitter sentiment classification using distant supervision. CS224N Project Report, Stanford vol. 1, no. 12 (2009)
10. Guerra, P.C., Meira Jr., W., Cardie, C.: Sentiment analysis on evolving social streams: how self-report imbalances can help. In: Proceedings of the 7th ACM International Conference on Web Search and Data Mining, pp. 443–452 (2014). https://doi.org/10.1145/2556195.2556261
11. Kranjc, J., Smailović, J., Podpečan, V., Grčar, M., Žnidaršič, M., Lavrač, N.: Active learning for sentiment analysis on data streams: methodology and workflow implementation in the ClowdFlows platform. Inf. Process. Manag. **51**(2), 187–203 (2015). https://doi.org/10.1016/j.ipm.2014.04.001

12. Lewis, D.D., Gale, W.A.: A sequential algorithm for training text classifiers. In: Proceedings of the 17th Annual International ACM SIGIR Conference on Research and Development in Information Retrieval, pp. 3–12 (1994)
13. Liu, B., Zhang, L.: A survey of opinion mining and sentiment analysis. In: Aggarwal, C., Zhai, C. (eds.) Mining Text Data, pp. 415–463. Springer, Boston (2012). https://doi.org/10.1007/978-1-4614-3223-4_13
14. Pang, B., Lee, L., et al.: Opinion mining and sentiment analysis. Found. Trends® Inf. Retr. **2**(1–2), 1–135 (2008)
15. Ravi, K., Ravi, V.: A survey on opinion mining and sentiment analysis: tasks, approaches and applications. Knowl.-Based Syst. **89**, 14–46 (2015)
16. Saleiro, P., Sarmento, L., Rodrigues, E.M., Soares, C., Oliveira, E.: Learning word embeddings from the portuguese twitter stream: a study of some practical aspects. In: Oliveira, E., Gama, J., Vale, Z., Lopes Cardoso, H. (eds.) EPIA 2017. LNCS (LNAI), vol. 10423, pp. 880–891. Springer, Cham (2017). https://doi.org/10.1007/978-3-319-65340-2_71
17. Sanders, N.J.: Twitter sentiment corpus (2011)
18. Silva, I.S., Gomide, J., Veloso, A., Meira Jr., W., Ferreira, R.: Effective sentiment stream analysis with self-augmenting training and demand-driven projection. In: Proceedings of the 34th International ACM SIGIR Conference on Research and Development in Information Retrieval, pp. 475–484 (2011). https://doi.org/10.1145/2009916.2009981
19. Smailović, J., Grčar, M., Lavrač, N., Žnidaršič, M.: Stream-based active learning for sentiment analysis in the financial domain. Inf. Sci. **285**(C), 181–203 (2014). https://doi.org/10.1016/j.ins.2014.04.034
20. Souza, E., et al.: Characterising text mining: a systematic mapping review of the Portuguese language. IET Softw. **12**(2), 49–75 (2018). https://doi.org/10.1049/iet-sen.2016.0226
21. Souza, E., Vitório, D., Castro, D., Oliveira, A.L.I., Gusmão, C.: Characterizing opinion mining: a systematic mapping study of the Portuguese language. In: Silva, J., Ribeiro, R., Quaresma, P., Adami, A., Branco, A. (eds.) PROPOR 2016. LNCS (LNAI), vol. 9727, pp. 122–127. Springer, Cham (2016). https://doi.org/10.1007/978-3-319-41552-9_12
22. Wagner, S., Zimmermann, M., Ntoutsi, E., Spiliopoulou, M.: Ageing-based multinomial Naive Bayes classifiers over opinionated data streams. In: Appice, A., Rodrigues, P.P., Santos Costa, V., Soares, C., Gama, J., Jorge, A. (eds.) ECML PKDD 2015. LNCS (LNAI), vol. 9284, pp. 401–416. Springer, Cham (2015). https://doi.org/10.1007/978-3-319-23528-8_25
23. Wang, D., Feng, S., Wang, D., Yu, G.: Detecting opinion drift from Chinese web comments based on sentiment distribution computing. In: Lin, X., Manolopoulos, Y., Srivastava, D., Huang, G. (eds.) WISE 2013. LNCS, vol. 8180, pp. 72–81. Springer, Heidelberg (2013). https://doi.org/10.1007/978-3-642-41230-1_6
24. Widmer, G., Kubat, M.: Learning in the presence of concept drift and hidden contexts. Mach. Learn. **23**(1), 69–101 (1996). https://doi.org/10.1023/A:1018046501280
25. Yang, Y., Loog, M.: A benchmark and comparison of active learning for logistic regression. Pattern Recogn. **83**, 401–415 (2018). https://doi.org/10.1016/j.patcog.2018.06.004
26. Zhu, X., Zhang, P., Lin, X., Shi, Y.: Active learning from data streams. In: Seventh IEEE International Conference on Data Mining (ICDM 2007), pp. 757–762, October 2007. https://doi.org/10.1109/ICDM.2007.101

27. Zimmermann, M., Ntoutsi, E., Spiliopoulou, M.: Incremental active opinion learning over a stream of opinionated documents. arXiv preprint arXiv:1509.01288 (2015)

28. Žliobaitė, I., Bifet, A., Pfahringer, B., Holmes, G.: Active learning with evolving streaming data. In: Gunopulos, D., Hofmann, T., Malerba, D., Vazirgiannis, M. (eds.) ECML PKDD 2011. LNCS (LNAI), vol. 6913, pp. 597–612. Springer, Heidelberg (2011). https://doi.org/10.1007/978-3-642-23808-6_39

Exploring Multi-label Stacking in Natural Language Processing

Rodrigo Mansueli Nunes$^{(\boxtimes)}$, Marcos Aurélio Domingues,
and Valéria Delisandra Feltrim

State University of Maringá, Maringá, PR 87020-900, Brazil
mansueli@ualberta.ca, {madomingues,vdfeltrim}@uem.br

Abstract. The task of classification with multi-label data is an important research field in Natural Language Processing (NLP). While there have been studies using one-stage multi-label approaches for automatic text classification, there are not many that use two-stages stacking models. In this paper we explored Binary Relevance (BR) classifiers, with J48 and probabilistic Support Vector Machine (SVM), in a two-stage stacking model. We have evaluated our proposal in three textual data sets: The Movie Database (TMDB), Enron email, and EURLEX European legal text. The results showed that by using a two-stage stacking model, we can obtain better results than by using one-stage classifiers.

Keywords: Machine learning · Classification · Multi-label · Stacking

1 Introduction

There is considerably more data available today than ever before due to the advancement of technology. Because of that, for the data processing field, it has become more important to use machine learning techniques to extract, classify and evaluate information from data [5]. Many of these data are contents in natural language, and classifying this specific kind of content is known as Natural Language Processing (NLP).

Natural language data is arguably one of the most challenging to classify automatically because of limits on model abstraction [3] and the constant language evolution. While many NLP tasks can be solved through the use of knowledge that can be extracted from the surface of the text, others are dependent on deep knowledge that can not be inferred by the extraction of surface features.

Text classification is a traditional NLP task, which aims to categorize texts based on human written content. The goal of using computers to classify texts is to find patterns in the training data, usually based on features that were extracted from the surface of the texts. Then, these patterns can be properly used to classify new data that was not in the training set [1].

One way to improve text classifiers is to combine several classifiers into a stacking model [2]. Stacking models have proven to be effective for single label

© Springer Nature Switzerland AG 2019
P. Moura Oliveira et al. (Eds.): EPIA 2019, LNAI 11805, pp. 708–718, 2019.
https://doi.org/10.1007/978-3-030-30244-3_58

scenarios, where each text contains only one label. More recently, these models have also grown in popularity among multi-label problems (i.e. where there is more than one label for each text), since it can improve text classification results in this scenario. For example, Godbole and Sarawagi [4] proposed a multi-label two-stage stacking model to classify text sets, and they obtained better results than by using non-stacked models (i.e. single-stage classifiers).

In this paper we explored Binary Relevance (BR) classifiers, with J48 and probabilistic Support Vector Machine (SVM), in a two-stage stacking model. We evaluated our proposal in three textual data sets: The Movie Database (TMDB), Enron email, and EURLEX European legal text. The results showed that by using a two-stage stacking model, we can obtain better results than by using single-stage classifiers.

The rest of this paper is organised as follows. In Sect. 2, we present some works related to automatic multi-label classification. We discuss the methodology used in our work in Sect. 3. In Sect. 4, we present the empirical evaluation. Finally, in Sect. 5, we present conclusions and thoughts for future work.

2   Related Work

In this section we present works related to automatic multi-label classification, using both simple and combined classifiers.

Godbole and Sarawagi [4] proposed a two-stage stacking model by using two Support Vector Machines (SVM). They called it SVM-HF since they use a heterogeneous feature kernel. To extract features from texts they have used a Bag of Words (BoW) model. A similar approach was proposed by Marques et al. [9]. Their proposal consist of a two-stage stacking model that uses two probabilistic SVM to classify music tags.

Other studies relied on neural network models to classify multi-label text data sets. In [15], the authors proposed a neural network with back propagation to classify hierarchical multi-label data, and compared their proposal against to a rule-based classifier. Their findings were slightly worse than the ones from the rule-based classifier. Méncia and Janssen [6] proposed the use of a stacking of perceptrons to classify a data set made of European legal documents in the English language. A Recurring Neural Network (RNN) was proposed by Yang et al. [14]. In their approach, Binary Relevance models are used as neurons in the neural network.

In the literature, we can also see some works that use ensembles. Read et al. [11] proposed a few ensemble methods, voting classifier chains and ensembles of Binary Relevance. They evaluated their proposal with several data sets and by using the Sequential Minimum Optimisation (SMO) method as their basis classifier. In [13], Tsoumakas et al. proposed the method RAkEL (RAndom k labELsets), which groups the labels during the training phase, and then creates a voting ensemble between the groups of labels. They explained that such approach is not recommended for data sets with a large number of labels due to its computational complexity.

Montanes et al. [10] proposed the Dependent Binary Relevance, a hybrid method combining stacking with chains of classifiers. In [7], Méncia and Janssen classified several multi-label data sets by using Association Rules. The results with the Association Rules were worse than by using J48 or SVM as basis classifiers. Finally, Madjarov et al. [8] conducted an extensive evaluation by comparing different multi-label methods found in literature. The authors found that Binary Relevance methods with SVM provides good results in larger data sets.

In Table 1, we summarise some aspects of the works described in this section. There, it is possible to see that most works use Bag of Words instead of TF-IDF to the classification task. In addition, we can see that there is a wide range of both the number of instances found in data sets (i.e. varying from 500 to slightly over 120,000) and the number of labels (i.e. that range from 6 to over 3,900 labels).

Table 1. Summary of related work.

Related work	Domain	Methods	Type of feature	# Instances	# Labels
[14]	General	Recurring neural network	BoW	640—28,000	6—374
[7]	General	SRKDA with ML-kNN as basis classifier	BoW	590—14,000	6—174
[10]	General	DBR with C4.5 as basis classifier	BoW	590—7,100	5—159
[8]	General	BR (SVM), RAkEL (SVM), ECC (SVM), RF (PCT) and ML-kNN	BoW	590—120,000	6—983
[9]	Music	BR (probabilistic LibSVM)	n/a	500—21,000	137—174
[13]	General	RAkEL with C4.5 as basis classifier	BoW	970—21,500	6—159
[11]	General	CC with C4.5 as basis classifier	BoW	590—120,000	6—983
[6]	Text	BR (perceptron), MLPP, DMLPP	TF-IDF	19,000	201—3,900
[15]	Text/Biology	BP-NN	BoW	2400—21,500	14—135
[4]	Text	SVM stacking	BoW	21,500	114—135

3   Methodology

In this section we describe the stack implemented in this study and briefly present the metrics used to evaluate our experimental results.

3.1   Stacking

Stacking consists of combining different classifiers by using the output generated by one classifier as the input of another classifier. Stacks are usually composed of two-stages and the classifiers used in each stage may have been induced by the same learning algorithm or by different ones. Supposing that the classifiers used in the stack are probabilistic, one manner to encode the first stage output as input for the second stage is to use the class probabilities generated by the first stage classifier as features vectors to the second stage classifier.

In this study we implemented a two-stage stacking model by using Binary Relevance (BR) based classifiers in both stages. Since a BR classifier is, in fact, a combination of a set of binary classifiers, we have used two different algorithms to induce the basis classifiers, namely Support Vector Machines (SVM) and Decision Trees. We used the LibSVM implementation for the SVM classifiers and Weka's J48 implementation for the decision tree classifiers. In both cases, we use the probabilistic versions of the algorithms, so instead of predicting output classes, the learned models estimate the probabilities of each possible class. We used Mulan 1.5 to build the resulting BR classifiers.

A high-level scheme of our stack is presented in Fig. 1. The left side of the figure shows the first stage of the stack, which accepts a set of texts as its input. The texts are transformed into TF-IDF feature vectors using a BoW model. For each feature vector, $L1, L2, ..., LN$ represents the labels of the corresponding instance and $F1, F2, ..., FN$ represents the extracted features. The resulting vectors are then inputted into the BR classifier, which predicts the $P1, P2, ..., PN$ probabilities for the N possible classes. The estimated class probabilities for an instance, along with its labels, are then transformed into a new feature vector, which is used as input for the second stage of the stack. The scheme of the second stage is presented on the right side of Fig. 1. As showed, this stage is composed of a second BR classifier that, once again, predicts $P1, P2, ..., PN$ probabilities for the N possible classes. To evaluate the performance of the classifiers, for both stages, a class was considered as predicted if its estimate probability was greater or equal to 0.5.

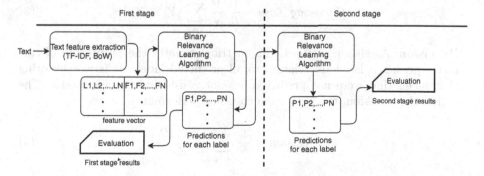

Fig. 1. The stack implemented in this work. The left side shows the first stage and the right side the second stage.

3.2   Evaluation Metrics

In this section we present some multi-label metrics that we used to evaluate our proposal.

- **Jaccard index:** Proposed by Paul Jaccard and presented in Eq. 1, this metric aims at comparing the similarity and divergence between sets [12]. In a classification context, it can be used to compare the set of labels predicted by the classification model with the set of real labels defined in the test set. In the equation, Y are the set of predicted labels and Z are the set of real labels. The higher the index, the more similar the two sets, so the better the classifier performance.

$$Jaccard\ Index = \frac{Y \cap Z}{Y \cup Z} \tag{1}$$

- **Exact match:** An exact match happens when, for a particular test instance, all the predicted labels are equal to the real ones. This metric gives the proportion of exact matches in the test set and it is calculated by Eq. 2. In this equation, N is the number of instances in the test set, and I is a function that returns 1 when the predicted label equals the real one, and 0 otherwise. The higher the value of this metric, the better the classifier performance.

$$Exact\ Match = \frac{1}{N} \sum_{i=1}^{N} I(Z_i = Y_i) \tag{2}$$

- **Hamming loss:** Hamming loss is a frequently used evaluation metric in multi-label classification tasks [5]. As shown in Eq. 3, it is calculated as the symmetric difference between the predicted label and the real one for each instance. The total number of errors are aggregated and then normalised by taking the number of labels, L, and the number of instances, N, in the test set. Ideally equal to zero, the lower the value of this metric, the better the classifier performance.

$$Hamming\ Loss = \frac{1}{L} \frac{1}{N} \sum_{i=1}^{N} Y_i\ \Delta\ Z_i \tag{3}$$

- **Precision:** As shown in Eq. 4, this metric estimates the proportion of correctly predicted labels in relation to all predicted labels. It is worth noting that labels that were not predicted are not considered by this metric. The higher the precision, the better the classifier performance.

$$Precision = \frac{1}{N} \sum_{i=1}^{N} \frac{|Y_i \cap Z_i|}{|Z_i|} \tag{4}$$

- **F1-micro:** F1 is a metric that considers both the precision estimates and the estimate of labels that should have been predicted but were not. Its calculation per label is given by Eq. 5. To estimate a single value of F1 for the test set, the values per label can be averaged, and when weighted by the label distribution on the set, it is called F1-micro.

$$F1 = \frac{1}{N} \sum_{i=1}^{N} \frac{2|Y_i \cap Z_i|}{|Z_i| + |Y_i|} \tag{5}$$

– **F1-macro:** This metric is also calculated based on Eq. 5. The difference between F1-macro and the previous one is in the way that F1 values per label are averaged. While the micro-averaged version of the metric takes the label distribution into account, F1-macro gives the same weight to all labels, so its calculation corresponds to the arithmetic mean of the F1 values. Regardless of how the metric is averaged, the higher the F1 value, the better the classifier performance.
– **Empty:** This metric estimates the proportion of instances for which no label was predicted. As presented in Eq. 6, it takes the sum of instances for which the predicted values for all labels are equal to zero and divides it by the number of instances on the test set. Assuming that all instances in the test set have a non-empty set of labels, the lower the value of this metric, the better. Ideally, it equals zero.

$$Empty = \frac{1}{N} \sum_{i=1}^{N} I(|Y_i| = 0) \tag{6}$$

4 Empirical Evaluation

In this section we evaluate our proposal. We start by presenting the data sets used in the empirical evaluation. Then, we describe the experimental setup and discuss the results of the experiments.

4.1 Data Sets

In our evaluation we used three different data sets. The first data set is the TMDB, downloaded in February 2018 by using the TMDB APIs[1]. This data set was preprocessed by removing stop words and applying stemming, and contains 159,416 instances with 1,000 TF-IDF features and 18 labels. Figure 2 shows a word cloud with the 50 most frequent terms (i.e. features) in the data set.

The second data set, called EURLEX *subject matters*, is a subset of the EURLEX data set containing legal documentation from the European Union concerning real estate, internal markets and industry. This data set was downloaded from the Mulan web site[2], and contains 19,348 instances with 5,000 TF-IDF features and 201 labels. In the rest of this paper, we will refer to EURLEX *subject matters* only as EURLEX. The word cloud with the 50 most frequent terms in this data set is presented in Fig. 3.

---

[1] https://www.themoviedb.org/documentation/api.
[2] http://mulan.sourceforge.net/datasets-mlc.html.

Fig. 2. The word cloud with the 50 most frequent terms in the TMDB data set.

Fig. 3. The word cloud with the 50 most frequent terms in the EURLEX data set.

Finally, the third data set, called Enron, is a subset from the Enron email data set which was classified by students in Berkeley, CA. This data set was also downloaded from the Mulan web site[3]. It contains 1,700 instances with 1,000 TF (Term Frequency) features and 53 labels. Figure 4 shows a word cloud with the 50 most frequent terms in the data set.

It is worth noting that with three different data sets, we expect to be able to evaluate how our proposal will behave in different scenarios. We summarize the information about the three data sets in Table 2.

Table 2. Information about the data sets.

Data set	# Instances	# Features	# Labels
TMDB	159.416	1000	18
EURLEX	19.348	5000	201
Enron	1.700	1000	53

---
[3] ibid.

Fig. 4. The word cloud with the 50 most frequent terms in the Enron data set.

4.2 Experimental Setup

As already stated, the experiments were carried out using the Mulan 1.5[4], a Java Library for Multi-Label Learning. To run the Binary Relevance with the SVM classifier, we used the following parameters "$-W, weka.classifiers.functions.$ $LibSVM, -num-decimal-places, 4, --, -S, 0, -K, 2, -D, 3, -G, 0.0, -R, 0.0,$ $-N, 0.5, -M, 40.0, -C, 0.5, -E, 0.001, -P, 0.1, -B, -seed, 1, -num-decimal-places, 4$". Note that the LibSVM is not a default weka classifier and it must be imported and adapted into the Mulan in order to run it. To run the Binary Relevance with the J48 classifier, we used "$-W, weka.classifiers.trees.J48, -output-debug-info, -num-decimal-places, 4, --, -C, 0.25, -M, 2, -A, -num-decimal-places, 4$". For each experiment and data set, we computed the metrics presented in Sect. 3.2. All results were obtained by using a 5-fold cross validation.

4.3 Results

In Tables 3, 4 and 5, we present the results of the experiments by comparing the two-stages stacking models against to the one-stage classifiers. In the tables, we separate the first stage classifier from the second one by using the symbol underline ("_"). For example, "SVM_J48" means that the probabilistic SVM was used in the first stage and the J48 classifier was used in the second stage of the stacking model. The best value for each evaluation metric is in boldface.

In Table 3, we can see for the TMDB data set that the two-stages stacking models provide better results than the one-stage classifier for the most metrics. Moreover, both stacking models that used probabilistic SVM in the first-stage showed improvements for 4 out of 7 metrics. However, there was a loss in improvement for the metrics Exact match and Hamming loss when compared to the one-stage probabilistic SVM classifier.

The results for the EURLEX data set are presented in Table 4. Again, we can see that the two-stage stacking models provide the best results for most metrics. The two-stage stacking models with the J48 on the first stage and the

---

[4] http://mulan.sourceforge.net.

Table 3. Results for the TMDB data set.

Method	Jaccard index	Exact match	Hamming loss	Precision	F1-micro	F1-macro	Empty
J48	0.349	0.151	0.107	0.575	0.437	0.314	0.087
SVM	0.411	**0.279**	**0.078**	0.469	0.471	0.280	0.191
J48_J48	0.342	0.109	0.110	0.595	0.437	0.287	**0.000**
J48_SVM	0.353	0.130	0.107	0.602	0.442	0.289	0.023
SVM_SVM	**0.451**	0.211	0.089	**0.700**	**0.533**	0.384	0.021
SVM_J48	0.448	0.212	0.092	0.691	0.529	**0.390**	0.036

probabilistic SVM on the second stage obtained the best results for this data set. It is also interesting to note that the two-stage stacking models that provided good results were the ones which used the J48 classifier in one of the stages.

Table 4. Results for the EURLEX data set.

Method	Jaccard index	Exact match	Hamming loss	Precision	F1-micro	F1-macro	Empty
J48	**0.607**	**0.361**	**0.007**	0.710	0.693	0.376	0.063
SVM	0.075	0.024	0.011	0.084	0.149	0.043	0.847
J48_J48	0.442	0.033	0.011	0.721	0.593	0.365	**0.000**
J48_SVM	0.603	0.347	**0.007**	**0.731**	**0.694**	0.381	0.068
SVM_SVM	0.342	0.087	0.012	0.512	0.466	0.107	0.012
SVM_J48	0.436	0.206	0.010	0.727	0.551	**0.514**	0.213

Finally, we see in Table 5 that the two-stage stacking models provide the best results for all metrics. The "J48_48" model was the one which provided the best results in the Enron data set.

Table 5. Results for the Enron data set.

Method	Jaccard index	Exact match	Hamming loss	Precision	F1-micro	F1-macro	Empty
J48	0.391	0.010	0.059	0.566	0.545	0.158	**0.000**
SVM	0.453	0.055	0.052	0.686	0.595	0.174	**0.000**
J48_J48	**0.556**	0.126	**0.038**	**0.788**	**0.710**	0.281	**0.000**
J48_SVM	0.423	0.079	0.058	0.585	0.552	0.164	**0.000**
SVM_SVM	0.482	**0.145**	0.052	0.651	0.594	0.218	0.007
SVM_J48	0.241	0.064	0.089	0.507	0.310	**0.327**	0.045

5   Conclusions and Future Work

In this work we explored Binary Relevance classifiers, with J48 and probabilistic Support Vector Machine, in a two-stage stacking model. We evaluated our proposal in three textual data sets: The Movie Database (TMDB), Enron email, and EURLEX European legal text. In the empirical evaluation, we compared the two-stage stacking models against the one-stage classifiers. In summary, the two-stage stacking models provided some improvements in most cases. This fact gives us evidences that by using a two-stage stacking model, we can improve the multi-label text classification.

For future work, we intend to evaluate our proposal in the Enron data set using TF-IDF instead of TF. We also intend to use some feature selection/extraction technique in order to have the same number of features in all data sets, and thus, to obtain a better understanding of our proposal in this scenario.

Acknowledgments. This study was financed in part by the Conselho Nacional de Desenvolvimento Científico e Tecnológico - Brasil (CNPq).

References

1. Aggarwal, C.: Data Classification: Algorithms and Applications. Data Mining and Knowledge Discovery Series. Chapman & Hall/CRC/Taylor & Francis (2014)
2. Džeroski, S., Ženko, B.: Is combining classifiers with stacking better than selecting the best one? Mach. Learn. **54**(3), 255–273 (2004)
3. Espinal-Enríquez, J., Mejía-Pedroza, R., Hernández-Lemus, E.: Computational approaches in precision medicine, chapter 13. In: Verma, M., Barh, D. (eds.) Progress and Challenges in Precision Medicine, pp. 233–250. Academic Press (2017)
4. Godbole, S., Sarawagi, S.: Discriminative methods for multi-labeled classification. In: Dai, H., Srikant, R., Zhang, C. (eds.) PAKDD 2004. LNCS (LNAI), vol. 3056, pp. 22–30. Springer, Heidelberg (2004). https://doi.org/10.1007/978-3-540-24775-3_5
5. Herrera, F., Charte, F., Rivera, A.J., del Jesus, M.J.: Multilabel Classification. Springer, Switzerland (2016). https://doi.org/10.1007/978-3-319-41111-8
6. Loza Mencía, E., Fürnkranz, J.: Efficient multilabel classification algorithms for large-scale problems in the legal domain. In: Francesconi, E., Montemagni, S., Peters, W., Tiscornia, D. (eds.) Semantic Processing of Legal Texts. LNCS (LNAI), vol. 6036, pp. 192–215. Springer, Heidelberg (2010). https://doi.org/10.1007/978-3-642-12837-0_11
7. Loza Mencía, E., Janssen, F.: Learning rules for multi-label classification: a stacking and a separate-and-conquer approach. Mach. Learn. **105**(1), 77–126 (2016)
8. Madjarov, G., Kocev, D., Gjorgjevikj, D., Džeroski, S.: An extensive experimental comparison of methods for multi-label learning. Pattern Recogn. **45**(9), 3084–3104 (2012)
9. Marques, G., Domingues, M.A., Langlois, T., Gouyon, F.: Three current issues in music autotagging. In: 2011 International Society for Music Information Retrieval Conference, vol. 12, Florida (2011)
10. Montañes, E., Senge, R., Barranquero, J., Quevedo, J.R., del Coz, J.J., Hüllermeier, E.: Dependent binary relevance models for multi-label classification. Pattern Recogn. **47**(3), 1494–1508 (2014)
11. Read, J., Pfahringer, B., Holmes, G., Frank, E.: Classifier chains for multi-label classification. In: Buntine, W., Grobelnik, M., Mladenić, D., Shawe-Taylor, J. (eds.) ECML PKDD 2009. LNCS (LNAI), vol. 5782, pp. 254–269. Springer, Heidelberg (2009). https://doi.org/10.1007/978-3-642-04174-7_17

12. Tan, P.N., Steinbach, M., Kumar, V.: Introduction to Data Mining, xxi. Pearson Addison Wesley, Boston (2005)
13. Tsoumakas, G., Katakis, I., Vlahavas, I.: Random k-labelsets for multilabel classification. IEEE Trans. Knowl. Data Eng. **23**(7), 1079–1089 (2011)
14. Yang, Y.Y., Lin, Y.A., Chu, H.M., Lin, H.T.: Deep learning with a rethinking structure for multi-label classification. arXiv preprint arXiv:1802.01697 (2018)
15. Zhang, M.L., Zhou, Z.H.: Multilabel neural networks with applications to functional genomics and text categorization. IEEE Trans. Knowl. Data Eng. **18**(10), 1338–1351 (2006)

Exploring Emojis for Emotion Recognition in Portuguese Text

Luis Duarte, Luís Macedo⬛, and Hugo Gonçalo Oliveira(✉)⬛

CISUC, University of Coimbra, Coimbra, Portugal
lduarte@student.dei.uc.pt, {macedo, hroliv}@dei.uc.pt

Abstract. New forms of communication, like emojis, are frequent today in social media. Having in mind their strong connection with expressed emotions, we exploit emojis towards the creation of a model for emotion recognition in Portuguese. We gather short texts from Twitter and follow a traditional text classification task, where emojis are used as labels. After the process of feature engineering, two types of Naive Bayes and SVM classifiers are trained: one for classifying emotion, based on related emojis; another for predicting emojis. Interesting but debatable results were obtained on the former task, while the latter revealed to be more challenging, mainly due to emoji similarity. Yet, this also suggests that we can rely on them as an alternative to manually labelling emotions.

Keywords: Emotion recognition · Text classification · Natural Language Processing · Emojis · Social networks

1 Introduction

Emotions have been widely studied in various areas such as Psychology, Medicine and Marketing, and are more and more a relevant aspect for human-computer interaction, in the context of Affective Computing [14]. Studies on this scope opened up a range of possibilities by improving current systems. For instance, when recommending items, recommender systems may consider the emotional state of the users [22].

There have been several attempts at the automatic classification of emotion in text, but mainly focused on English. In this paper, we report on developments towards this goal, but targeting Portuguese, a language with about 220 millions native speakers, for which there is much less work on the topic. Yet, we aim to tackle this problem in such a way that we: (i) avoid the time-consuming task of manually labelling new datasets; (ii) make this highly subjective task more

This work was developed in the scope of the SOCIALITE Project (PTDC/EEISCR/2072/2014), co-financed by COMPETE 2020, Portugal 2020 – Operational Program for Competitiveness and Internationalization (POCI), European Union's ERDF (European Regional Development Fund), and the Portuguese Foundation for Science and Technology (FCT).

P. Moura Oliveira et al. (Eds.): EPIA 2019, LNAI 11805, pp. 719–730, 2019.
https://doi.org/10.1007/978-3-030-30244-3_59

tractable, by leveraging on new forms of communication, namely emojis. We thus turn on to social networks for acquiring large quantities of real texts, written in Portuguese, where emojis are used. Given the tight relation between emotions and several emojis, emotion labels are assigned according to the presence of the latter. We further experiment on the task of emoji prediction, already explored for other languages [4] but, to our knowledge, never for Portuguese.

Briefly, with more than 1 million of posts collected from Twitter, models were trained, based on Naive Bayes and SVM classifiers. For emotion recognition, we rely on the fact there are sets of emojis adequate for expressing the six basic emotions [6]. The groups of emojis used in this work are supported by the literature [23] and, later, by our own analysis. In the end, overall results are interesting, with an average F1-score of 0.7, but this is mainly a contribution of the happiness. For most of the remaining emotions, precision is high, but recall is very low. This happens because the extracted data is imbalanced, with about two thirds of the tweets expressing happiness and a residual presence of tweets expressing some of the other emotions. The second task, emoji prediction, focuses on the automatic selection of the most suitable emoji, from a set, to use in a context. This revealed to be even more challenging, not only because there are many more emojis than emotions, but also because some of the target emojis, mainly those related to the same emotion, are used interchangeably. At the same time, this result is consistent with the assumption that the emojis used can, indeed, be used as emotion labels.

Before diving into our experiments, Sect. 2 is a brief overview of the related work, mainly on emotion classification from text. Section 3 describes the creation of the dataset used in our experiments, with focus on text processing, as well as the processes of feature extraction and training the models. Before concluding, Sect. 4 presents and discusses the obtained results. It also provides a visualisation of the considered emojis in a two-dimension space, based on their occurrences in the dataset, where emojis that express the same emotion tend to appear near each other. This supports the selection of emoji groups and opens the door for further research on emojis and emotion in Portuguese text.

2   Related Work

Emotion classification in text is a task located in the intersection of Affective Computing and Natural Language Processing. It has similarities with sentiment classification – the task of classifying a text as positive, negative or neutral, according to its contents – but adds a new layer. Emotional states are difficult to generalise due to cultural differences between distinct groups of people, in which emotions have distinct categorisations. It is also due to cultural distinctions that there are different models for emotion classification, namely Categorical and Dimensional models.

Categorical models define emotional states with labels. The most popular of this kind was proposed by Ekman [6] and considers six distinct emotions: anger, disgust, fear, happiness, sadness and surprise. According to the author, those emotions are consistent despite the cultural differences of individuals. Ekman's model is adopted in several works targeting emotion classification in text. For instance, Alm et al. [1] developed a classifier for Ekman's emotions in English stories. Even with a small dataset (185 instances), the manually labelling proved to be complex and still subjetive, with low annotator agreement ratios.

In the Dimensional models, an emotion is defined according to several dimensions. Russel's models [16,17] are the most popular of this kind. They position emotional states in a bi-dimensional model with values for valence and arousal. A third dimension, dominance, may also be considered. In this case, to assign one of the emotions, we may select the closest in this model, according to the values of the emotional state. Russel's model is adopted, for instance, in the automatic detection of emotions in song lyrics [8]. We should add that Buechel and Hahn [5] propose a method for moving from the Dimensional to the Categorical model, through valence, arousal and dominance values in text.

Most of the research on emotion classification targets English, but there is work in Portuguese. Few works focus on automatic emotion classification specifically [9], but there is much more work on sentiment analysis [13,20].

Thanks to the evolution of social media, we may leverage on new forms of communication for creating large datasets, automatically labelled, and use them, e.g., to study the connection between emojis and emotion, or for training emotion classifiers. Following this idea, both hashtags [12] and emojis [23] have been used for labelling tweets with the six basic emotions. On the latter, emotions were selected according to the name and description of the emoji used. Extracted data was then used for training an SVM classifier.

Moreover, the task of emoji prediction has recently received some interest and a shared task was organised on the topic [4]. It targeted English and Spanish, which enabled noting some cultural differences of using emojis. Barbieri et al. [2, 3] describe models developed for emoji prediction based on neural networks and LSTMs, which simulate memory between layers. They confirm the relation between certain words and emojis and add that the relation is stronger when text ends with an emoji. They also noted that emoji prediction is a challenging task, especially when there are variations (e.g., different colors) of the same emoji, or very similar emojis, often selected almost randomly. Also on emojis and emotion, Rodrigues et al. [15] created a lexicon of emojis and associated values of valence, arousal and dominance. This was based on a survey to several hundreds of Portuguese people.

Works described suggest that much can still be made, especially in non-English languages. We target Portuguese, where results may be different.

3   Methodology

This section describes the steps taken towards the development of models for emotion recognition and emoji prediction in Portuguese. They were tackled as text classification tasks, where features are extracted from the text and labels are based on the presence of emojis. We start with the creation of the dataset used for training and testing. Then, we explain how models were learned and how features were extracted. Besides typical content features (tokens), in order to take advantage of available lexicons for emotion analysis, additional features were originally considered. We used an implementation of the classification algorithms available in Scikit Learn[1], a machine learning toolkit for Python, also used for extracting the content features.

3.1 Dataset Creation

For training a model for recognising emotion in a given text, a large dataset is required. Following our initial intents, the dataset used in this work included short texts in Portuguese, extracted from the social network Twitter. This was made with Tweepy[2], a Python module for interacting with the Twitter API[3], more precisely, with the Streaming API, for extracting tweets in real time. A total of 2 million tweets was initially collected. According to the API, all of them were written in Portuguese, and all contained at least one of the emojis that, according to Wood and Ruder [23], are an indicator of one of the six basic emotions. This list is in Table 1.

Table 1. Emoji division by emotion

Hashtags	Emojis
Happiness	
Anger	
Disgust	
Fear	
Sadness	
Surprise	

To reduce noise and avoid confusion in the developed models, several tweets were removed or normalised. First, all tweets with less than three tokens and all retweets (starting with 'RT') were removed. The former do not have enough information and the latter are copies of other tweets. Then, all user mentions (i.e., tokens starting with '@') and URLs were replaced by uniform tokens, respectively @USERNAME and @URL; and elongated words (e.g., "amoooooor" instead of "amor") were reduced to their original form, as others [21] suggest.

Tweets with emotionally-contradictory emojis were also removed. Such tweets contain emojis that are related to different emotions [23], e.g., when 😊

---

[1] https://scikit-learn.org/.
[2] http://www.tweepy.org.
[3] https://dev.twitter.com.

and 😵 are in the same tweet. We noted that those are often cases of irony or sarcasm, an interesting issue for further study, but out of the scope of this work. Table 2 lists examples of emotionally-contradictory tweets, for which it is difficult to assign a suitable emotion. The last is an example of irony.

Table 2. Examples of contradictory texts

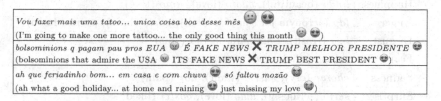

Vou fazer mais uma tatoo... unica coisa boa desse mês 😕 😵
(I'm going to make one more tattoo... the only good thing this month 😕 😵)
bolsominions q pagam pau pros EUA 😵 *É FAKE NEWS* ✖ *TRUMP MELHOR PRESIDENTE* 😵
(bolsominions that admire the USA 😵 ITS FAKE NEWS ✖ TRUMP BEST PRESIDENT 😵)
ah que feriadinho bom... em casa e com chuva 😵 *só faltou mozão* 😵
(ah what a good holiday... at home and raining 😵 just missing my love 😵)

After all the pruning, we had 1.1 million tweets, corresponding to 12.6 million tokens. Table 3 characterises the resulting dataset with the proportion of tweets per emotion, according to the used emojis, as well as an example for each.

Table 3. Distribution of texts in the dataset according to emotion.

Emotion	Quantity	Example
Happiness	770,418 (68.4%)	*Amanhã vou ao Douro!!* 😊 (Going to Douro tomorrow!! 😊)
Anger	75,521 (6.7%)	*JA ME ESTOU PASSANDO COM MINHA NET* 😡😡😡 (MY WIFI IS MAKING ME ANGRY 😡😡😡)
Disgust	1,798 (0.2%)	*@USERNAME vc nojento* 🤮🤮 (@USERNAME you are disgusting 🤮🤮)
Fear	54,621 (4.8%)	*Estou ficando com muito medo* 😨😨😨 *@URL* (I'm getting so scared 😨😨😨 @URL)
Sadness	214,801 (19.1%)	*30 dias sem vc* 😢😢 (30 days without you 😢😢)
Surprise	9,090 (0.8%)	*Estou muito surpreendido por me estar a dar tão bem com a matemática* 😮 (I'm really surprised that I'm getting along so well with maths 😮)

There is a clear predominance of the happiness class, not only due to the higher number of emojis of this class (see Table 1), but also because people tend to share more happy moments. In this context, imbalanced classes with a predominance of happiness, is something also noticed by others [12,23].

3.2 Feature Extraction

In a traditional text classification task, documents are typically represented as a bag-of-words and tokens used as features. For our experiments, tweets were also represented that way. More precisely, as a TF-IDF-weighted vector where token features are weighted according to their relevance. In the creation of this vector, Portuguese stopwords[4] and words occurring only once in the dataset

---

[4] We used the stopword list in NLTK, https://www.nltk.org.

($df = 1$) were ignored. TF-IDF was further computed for different ranges of word n-grams ($n \in \{1, 2, 3\}$). To observe which features are more relevant, a χ^2 test was performed. Table 4 reveals the top-3 word features for each class.

Table 4. Most relevant words by emotion

Emotion	Most Relevant Words
Happiness	*linda* (beautiful), *adoro* (love), *amo* (love)
Anger	*fdp* (acronym for son of a bitch), *odeio* (hate), *porra* (damn)
Disgust	*lixo* (trash), *Bolsonaro*, *merda* (shit)
Fear	*mentira* (lie), *medo* (fear), *temo* (fear)
Sadness	*chorar* (cry), *queria* (want), *dor* (pain)
Surprise	*sério* (seriously), *amo* (love), *gostei* (liked)

Besides content features, we took advantage of information in lexicons where words have emotion-related values assigned, and computed features from them. More precisely, we computed the sentiment of each tweet by averaging the polarity of each word according to SentiLex-PT [18], a lexicon that covers ≈82k Portuguese word forms and assigns them a polarity based on their sentiment when involving humans (−1, 0, or 1, respectively for negative, neutral or positive). We also computed the average valence, arousal and dominance of the tweets, this time according to ANEW-PT [19] and NRC-VAD [11] (three features for each). ANEW-PT is a Portuguese adaptation of the Affective Norms for English Words, where values for valence, arousal and dominance, between 0 and 10, are assigned to each of the 1,030 words. NRC-VAD has ≈20k English words and their values of valence, arousal and dominance, between 0 and 1, translated to more than 100 languages, including Portuguese.

Due to their potential relation to emotions in the context of social media posts, we further extracted the following features from each tweet: number of words; number of characters in the longest word (before normalisation); number of elongated words; average number of characters in the words; total count of negation words, namely *não* (no), *nem* (nor), *nunca* (never), *jamais* (never) and *nenhum* (none); number of exclamations marks; number of question marks.

3.3   Classification

Our goal was to learn a model of emotion recognition in Portuguese short texts, taking advantage of emojis. For this purpose, we took two different approaches:

- Grouping emojis according to the related emotions, as suggested by Wood and Ruder [23], and using this emotion as the class label. Given that we only considered Ekman's basic emotions [6], there are six possible classes: happiness, anger, disgust, fear, sadness, surprise.
- Predicting the emoji directly, as in SemEval's emoji prediction task [4]. The classifier has to select one out of 62 classes, corresponding to the 62 considered emojis (see Table 1). Indirectly, this would also enable to recognise emotion, if predicted emojis are then grouped according to emotion.

For both approaches, before classification, emojis were removed from the tweets and the tweets in the dataset were represented as feature vectors, based on the extracted features. Models for both approaches were validated in the full dataset, but also trained in 80% of the tweets in the dataset, selected randomly, and tested in the remaining 20%. Two different classification algorithms were used, Multinomial Naive Bayes (NB) and Support Vector Machines (SVM), significantly different but widely used for text classification. Next section reports on the results of the performed experiments.

4   Results

For each task, emotion classification and emoji prediction, this section reports on the accuracy of a 10-fold cross validation in the full dataset, and on other performance metrics when the classifiers are trained in 80% and tested in 20% of the dataset, for both NB and SVM. Reported results were achieved exclusively with TF-IDF features. Despite our focus on extracting the most information possible from the tweets, hyperparameter tests with grid search—to find the best combination of features for training, alpha values for both models and specific values for each model— showed that using just TF-IDF features was best suited for both classification tasks. Additional features, as the length of the tweet and its words, or emotion values from lexicons, proved to add confusion to the model and result in lower performance than using just TF-IDF.

A final experiment was to learn a semantic space from our dataset, which enabled to analyse emoji similarity, based on their context.

4.1   Emotion Classification

Table 5 shows the results of the models trained for the emotion classification task, obtained using 1 and 2-grams TF-IDF features. After testing different ranges of n-grams, this combination lead to the best results, which suggests that the classification of an emotion is mainly based on single words and/or two-word expressions. The most relevant words in Table 4 reinforce this point. Interesting results are obtained, especially with NB, with the best F1 score, 0.7. For this model, Table 6 has the performance by emotion and micro-averaged total.

Table 5. Results of the best classifiers for emotion classification

Model	10-Fold CV	Train 80%, Test 20%		
	Accuracy	Precision	Recall	F1
Naive Bayes	74.5% ± 1.4%	76.2%	75.7%	0.708
SVM	70.6% ± 1.4%	70.2%	71.9%	0.626

Table 6. Results obtained with the best classifier

Emotion	Precision	Recall	F1
Happiness	77%	97%	0.866
Anger	82%	8%	0.153
Disgust	93%	5%	0.078
Fear	98%	2%	0.019
Sadness	64%	44%	0.527
Surprise	87%	3%	0.021
Total	76%	75%	0.708

Distribution per emotion reveals that the model is apt for recognising happiness (F1 > 0.86), not so much for sadness (F1 0.52), and has serious difficulties with the remaining emotions. Looking at the proportion of each emotion in the dataset (Table 3), there is a positive correlation between the three most representative emotions and those for which F1 is higher, which confirms that the performance is highly affected by data imbalance. In terms of F1, these results are very similar to those of Wood and Ruder [23]'s 3-fold cross validation, in a dataset of the same nature, labelled under similar principles, but in English. It is still worth noticing that, for the classes with lower F1, precision is very high and recall very low, meaning that the classifier is not taking many risks.

These results confirm the difficulty of classification in a real-world, but imbalanced dataset. It is a conflicting issue, because the predominance of a class leads to a misclassification of the remaining. Yet, the occurrence of happy texts is, in fact, much more probable. Data balancing might increase the overall results, but the resulting classifier will no longer consider the probability of each class, leading to values that do not represent the reality of social networks.

In any case, this experiment shows that we could resort to available texts, in Portuguese, and, despite relying in common and low complexity models, classify their emotions.

4.2   Emoji Prediction

Table 7 shows the results of emoji prediction, with NB and SVM, and using the same dataset and features as for emotion classification. The main difference is that emojis were used as the labels to predict. Not grouping emojis into emotions resulted in 62 different classes, one for each considered emoji. This increases the difficulty of the task and it is one of the reasons for the obtained results, overall, much lower than those for emotion classification.

Table 7. Results of the best classifiers for emoji prediction

Model	10-Fold CV	Train 80%, Test 20%		
	Accuracy	Precision	Recall	F1
Naive Bayes	24.1% ± 2.4%	50.1%	29.3%	0.237
SVM	23.6% ± 1.3%	29.2%	22.1%	0.169

Again, the highest F1, ≈ 0.24, was achieved with Naive Bayes, this time using only 2 and 3-grams. Low performance confirms that emoji prediction is a very challenging task and that emotion classification based on emojis should start by grouping emojis according to emotions, as in the previous experiment. Table 8 shows the results for a selection of emojis.

Table 8. Results of the best classifier for predicting a selection of emojis.

Emoji	Quantity	Naive Bayes			SVM		
		Precision	Recall	F1	Precision	Recall	F1
😊	25,348 (2%)	24%	73%	0.50	23%	63%	0.33
😻	8,661 (0.7%)	28%	66%	0.46	22%	67%	0.33
😕	10,755 (0.9%)	26%	18%	0.16	20%	16%	0.18
🖤	134,288 (12%)	33%	7%	0.08	21%	10%	0.13
😌	14,843 (1%)	30%	52%	0.42	87%	3%	0.06
😍	168,534 (15%)	22%	6%	0.01	28%	3%	0.01
💜	26,754 (2%)	82%	1%	0.01	0%	0%	0.00

The best F1 score, for 😻 and 😊 , is not higher than 0.33. On the other end, F1 is 0 in the prediction of 💜 . This is influenced by the overlap of its meaning with other emojis, mainly 🖤 , but also 😍 , the most frequent emoji in the dataset, and 😻 , a variation of the previous with the face of a cat. This highlights not only that there are several similar emojis, used almost interchangeably, but also that, by focusing on emotion-relation emojis, we made the task of emoji prediction even harder. It also explains why most of our results are lower than those obtained in the SemEval 2018 task [4], for English and Spanish. There, best F1 scores were between 0.05 and 0.70, confirming that emoji prediction is a challenging task. Yet, there were less emojis to predict, not all related to emotions (e.g. flag, fire, camera, music), and not sharing as many similarities as those in our dataset. Emoji similarity is further analysed in the following section.

4.3 Emoji Similarity

For better conclusions on emoji similarity, the Gensim library[5] was used for learning a word2vec model [10] from our dataset, which enabled the representation of the $\approx$12M tokens as numerical vectors, in a n-dimensional space. Emojis were considered as any other token, which means that there is a vector for each emoji and similarity can thus be computed with the cosine of their vectors. The creation of the model considered a window size of five, given that most tweets are of short length, and tokens were represented by 300-sized vectors, a common number in this type of representation.

Among other experiments, emoji distribution can be visualised. However, for this purpose, the number of dimensions has to be reduced to two. Figure 1 represents the emojis of our dataset in a 2-dimensional space, after applying the t-SNE [7] visualisation technique.

Disgust
Fear
Anger
Happiness
Sadness
Surprise
100
75
50
25
0
−25
−50
−75
−75 −50 −25 0 25 50 75 100

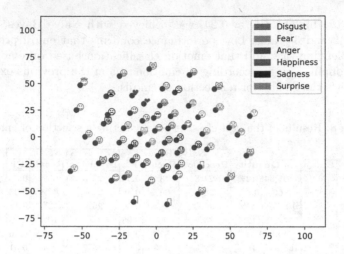

Fig. 1. Similarity between emojis in word2vec model.

No clear cluster of emojis is displayed, but a few observations are worth mentioning. Despite covering a large area, happiness-related emojis are all close, especially if 'cat-variations' are not considered. Anger and sadness emojis appear to form a single cluster, due to their negative valence. In fact, anger splits the sadness cluster in two, except for the crying and expressionless emojis, which behave as outliers. Despite some close emojis, the remaining three classes, also the least frequent in the dataset, do not look like clusters so much. Fear and surprise are more or less split into two groups, with the latter having three emojis in one boundary and another on the other. Due to technical reasons, disgusting emojis are represented with rectangles. Two of them are close, on the bottom boundary. Although our dataset is in a different language, this distribution of emojis is not too diverging from the groups of emojis according to the six emotions, proposed by others [23] and adopted in this work. Still, for stronger conclusions, in the future, emojis should be clustered automatically, for instance, with k-means.

Furthermore, emoji proximity suggests that different emojis can be used in similar texts, possibly even interchangeably, thus making emoji prediction harder than emotion classification. Figure 2 shows tweets that support this. Although text is similar, different emojis are used, even if expressing the same emotion, respectively anger and happiness.

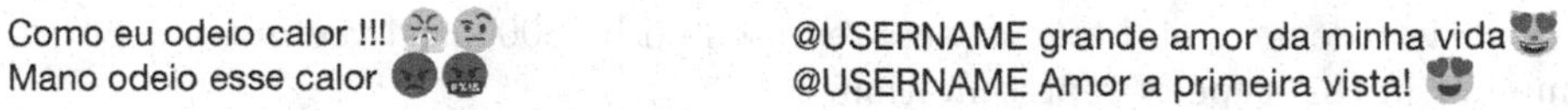

Como eu odeio calor !!!
Mano odeio esse calor
@USERNAME grande amor da minha vida
@USERNAME Amor a primeira vista!

Fig. 2. Examples of similar tweets with different emojis

[5] https://radimrehurek.com/gensim/.

5   Conclusions

Leveraging on social media text, on the presence of emojis, and on their relation with emotions, we created a dataset of tweets in Portuguese, automatically-labelled with emotions. This revealed to be an effective process and an alternative to the manual creation of such dataset.

The resulting dataset is a reflection of the cultural writing in the Portuguese speaking countries and can be the subject of many studies. Yet, in this work, we note mainly immediate observations, such as the imbalance between happy tweets and tweets conveying other emotions. To enable further studies, by other researchers, we will consider making this or a similar dataset available.

The dataset was used for emotion classification and emoji prediction, with results suggesting that there is room for improvement. A Naive Bayes classifier based on TF-IDF features and trained on 80% of the dataset could predict the emotion-based classes of emojis in the remaining 20% of the dataset with an accuracy of about 71%. Yet, results per class revealed that it is only performing well for happiness, the predominant class. On the other hand, when predicting the exact emoji, F1 is much lower, and never higher than 24%. This is due to the higher number of classes (62 emojis vs 6 emotions) and by the high similarity between several emojis, some of them used almost interchangeably.

In the future, we will use the dataset for further experiments. We plan to analyse the impact of data imbalance in our results (e.g., by comparison with results in an undersampled balanced version); and tackle emoji prediction for a smaller but more diverse set of emojis (e.g., the most predominant of each class). We also aim to test more recent and promising classification models, namely LSTM neural networks, in both tasks.

References

1. Alm, C.O., Roth, D., Sproat, R.: Emotions from text: machine learning for text-based emotion prediction. In: Proceedings of the Conference on Human Language Technology and Empirical Methods in Natural Language Processing, pp. 579–586. Association for Computational Linguistics (2005)
2. Barbieri, F., Anke, L.E., Camacho-Collados, J., Schockaert, S., Saggion, H.: Interpretable emoji prediction via label-wise attention LSTMs. In: Proceedings of 2018 Conference on Empirical Methods in Natural Language Processing (EMNLP), pp. 4766–4771. ACL Press (2018)
3. Barbieri, F., Ballesteros, M., Saggion, H.: Are emojis predictable? In: Proceedings of the 15th Conference of the European Chapter of the Association for Computational Linguistics: Volume 2, Short Papers, Valencia, Spain, pp. 105–111. Association for Computational Linguistics, April 2017
4. Barbieri, F., et al.: SemEval 2018 task 2: multilingual emoji prediction. In: Proceedings of 12th International Workshop on Semantic Evaluation, pp. 24–33. ACL Press, June 2018
5. Buechel, S., Hahn, U.: Representation mapping: a novel approach to generate high-quality multi-lingual emotion lexicons. In: Proceedings of the 11th International Conference on Language Resources and Evaluation, LREC 2018, Miyazaki, Japan, pp. 184–191, 7–12 May 2018 (2018)

6. Ekman, P.: Basic emotions. In: Handbook of Cognition and Emotion, pp. 45–60 (1999)
7. van der Maaten, L., Hinton, G.: Visualizing data using t-SNE. J. Mach. Learn. Res. **9**(Nov), 2579–2605 (2008)
8. Malheiro, R., Gonçalo Oliveira, H., Gomes, P., Paiva, R.P.: Keyword-based approach for lyrics emotion variation detection. In: 8th International Conference on Knowledge Discovery and Information Retrieval, KDIR 2016 (2016)
9. Martinazzo, B., Dosciatti, M.M., Paraiso, E.C.: Identifying emotions in short texts for Brazilian Portuguese. In: IV International Workshop on Web and Text Intelligence (WTI 2012), p. 16 (2011)
10. Mikolov, T., Chen, K., Corrado, G., Dean, J.: Efficient estimation of word representations in vector space. In: Proceedings of Workshop track of the International Conference on Learning Representations (ICLR), Scottsdale, Arizona (2013)
11. Mohammad, S.M.: Obtaining reliable human ratings of valence, arousal, and dominance for 20,000 English words. In: Proceedings of The 56th Annual Conference of the Association for Computational Linguistics (ACL), Melbourne, Australia. ACL Press (2018)
12. Mohammad, S.M., Kiritchenko, S.: Using hashtags to capture fine emotion categories from tweets. Comput. Intell. **31**(2), 301–326 (2015)
13. Nascimento, P., et al.: Análise de sentimento de tweets com foco em notícias. In: Brazilian Workshop on Social Network Analysis and Mining (2012)
14. Picard, R.W.: Affective computing for HCI. In: HCI, no. 1, pp. 829–833. Citeseer (1999)
15. Rodrigues, D., Prada, M., Gaspar, R., Garrido, M.V., Lopes, D.: Lisbon Emoji and Emoticon Database (LEED): norms for emoji and emoticons in seven evaluative dimensions. Behav. Res. Methods **50**(1), 392–405 (2018)
16. Russell, J.A.: Affective space is bipolar. J. Pers. Soc. Psychol. **37**(3), 345 (1979)
17. Russell, J.A., Lewicka, M., Niit, T.: A cross-cultural study of a circumplex model of affect. J. Pers. Soc. Psychol. **57**(5), 848 (1989)
18. Silva, M.J., Carvalho, P., Sarmento, L.: Building a sentiment lexicon for social judgement mining. In: Caseli, H., Villavicencio, A., Teixeira, A., Perdigão, F. (eds.) PROPOR 2012. LNCS (LNAI), vol. 7243, pp. 218–228. Springer, Heidelberg (2012). https://doi.org/10.1007/978-3-642-28885-2_25
19. Soares, A.P., Comesaña, M., Pinheiro, A.P., Simões, A., Frade, C.S.: The adaptation of the affective norms for English words (ANEW) for European Portuguese. Behav. Res. Methods **44**(1), 256–269 (2012)
20. Souza, M., Vieira, R.: Sentiment analysis on Twitter data for Portuguese language. In: Caseli, H., Villavicencio, A., Teixeira, A., Perdigão, F. (eds.) PROPOR 2012. LNCS (LNAI), vol. 7243, pp. 241–247. Springer, Heidelberg (2012). https://doi.org/10.1007/978-3-642-28885-2_28
21. Suttles, J., Ide, N.: Distant supervision for emotion classification with discrete binary values. In: Gelbukh, A. (ed.) CICLing 2013. LNCS, vol. 7817, pp. 121–136. Springer, Heidelberg (2013). https://doi.org/10.1007/978-3-642-37256-8_11
22. Tkalčič, M., Košir, A., Tasič, J.F.: Affective recommender systems: the role of emotions in recommender systems. In: Proceedings of RecSys 2011 Workshop Decisions, pp. 9–13. CEUR-WS.org (2011)
23. Wood, I., Ruder, S.: Emoji as emotion tags for tweets. In: Proceedings of the Emotion and Sentiment Analysis Workshop LREC 2016, Portorož, Slovenia, pp. 76–79 (2016)

Improving the Classification of Q&A Content for Android Fragmentation Using Named Entity Recognition

Adriano Mendonça Rocha$^{(\boxtimes)}$ and Marcelo de Almeida Maia

Faculty of Computing, Federal University of Uberlândia, Campus Santa Mônica,
Uberlândia, MG 38400-902, Brazil
{adriano.rocha,marcelo.maia}@ufu.br

Abstract. Despite the huge amount of high quality information available in socio-technical sites, it is still challenging to filter out relevant piece of information to a specific task in hand. Textual content classification has been used to retrieve only relevant information to solve specific problems. However, those classifiers tend to present poor performance when the target classes have similar content. We aim at developing a Named Entity Recognizer (NER) model to recognize entities related to technical elements, and to improve textual classifiers for Android fragmentation posts from Stack Overflow using the obtained NER model. The proposed NER model was trained for the entities API version, device, hardware, API element, technology and feature. The proposed classifiers were trained using the recognized entities as attributes. To evaluate the performances of these classifiers, we compared them with other three textual classifiers. The obtained results show that the constructed NER model can recognize entities efficiently, as well as discover new entities that were not present in the training data. The classifiers constructed using the NER model produced better results than the other baseline classifiers. We suggest that NER-based classifiers should be considered as a better alternative to classify technical textual context compared to generic textual classifiers.

Keywords: Q&A · NER · Textual classification ·
Android fragmentation

1 Introduction

Social-technical sites have been extensively used during developer daily routine to search for problem solutions given the rich available content related to software development. Stack Overflow is a major socio-technical site which relies on questions and answers (Q&A) to drive the collaboration among the global community of developers. Despite the possibility of asking new questions in Stack Overflow, there is already a huge number of answered questions that provides technical content that serves as solutions to recurrent problems. Surprisingly, a

© Springer Nature Switzerland AG 2019
P. Moura Oliveira et al. (Eds.): EPIA 2019, LNAI 11805, pp. 731–743, 2019.
https://doi.org/10.1007/978-3-030-30244-3_60

challenge faced by developers with a programming problem in hand is finding the desired content from the huge amount of information. Stack Overflow has almost 16 million questions, and each question can have multiple answers. In order to assist developers finding the desired piece of information, the content is organized using tags. However, there may be still a lot of information to be searched in specific tagged content. For instance, there are more than one million questions related to Android tag.

In general, previous work [2,13,15–17] uses some type of textual classifier to filter information targeting at specialized content for the generated documentation. A limitation of those classifiers arises when the textual content of the different classes to be classified are similar. In that case, classifiers struggle to produce correct classification. Our hypothesis is that these classifiers could be improved using specialized techniques related to natural language processing (NLP) to capture text semantics. One of those techniques that has been used in many areas is the Named Entity Recognizer (NER) that aims to locate and classify named entities from text into predefined categories, such as names of persons, locations, organizations, movies, bands, etc.

In this work, we aim at developing a NER model to recognize entities occurring in Stack Overflow posts to improve their classification. We focus on entities related to fragmentation problems of mobile applications, which emerge from the large variability of devices with different features, and also from the evolvability of the main APIs with different versions with possible incompatibility between them.

The contributions of this work are: (1) the construction of a NER model to recognize entities related to some problems of software engineering. This model can be used for various purposes, for example, to identify duplicate posts in question and answer sites by comparing entities present in these posts; and (2) the development of improved textual classifiers using entities recognized by the proposed NER model.

Section 2 presents the methodology to construct the proposed NER models and how this model is used to construct textual classifiers. Section 3 presents the results. Section 4 presents the related work and finally Sect. 6 presents the conclusion.

2   Study Setting

In this section, we describe the two studies to answer how accurate can be a NER model to recognize entities related to technical elements in natural language text of Q&A sites; and to answer how much can the proposed NER model improve a textual classifier for Android fragmentation posts, benefiting from the recognized entities.

2.1   A NER Model for Technical Q&A Posts

In order to train the proposed NER model, we used a suite of tools from the Stanford Natural Language Processing Group [7] to achieve a NER model able to recognize the new entities. In this work, we target specifically the identification and filtering of Android fragmentation posts, so the entities recognized by the proposed NER model are chosen in such a way to be further used to improve the classification of posts into two different classes: those posts related and not related to Android fragmentation. We trained this model to recognize the following entities: *device name, Android API version, API element, device hardware, technology* and *feature*.

To build the training dataset of the proposed NER model, we had to select Stack Overflow posts related to Android fragmentation. In order to construct that set, we used search engine queries to capture posts related to Android problems/bugs in Stack Overflow, and manually analyzed the retrieved posts, filtering those related to Android fragmentation. In total, 708 Stack Overflow threads were sequentially analyzed until we have accounted for 100 threads related to Android fragmentation.

After selecting the 100 threads for the training corpus, the next step was to conduct the established steps to train the NER model. The first required step is to label each token present in the training corpus. To get the tokens from the 100 training threads, we applied a tokenizing function that receives the textual content of these training threads and returns a list of tokens. A total of 26807 tokens were returned, and we manually labeled them with the entity names that the NER model will learn to identify. We consider the following entity names for training:

- **API_VERSION** - this entity represents an API along with its versions, for example, Android 6, Android version 5.1.1, KitKat, etc.
- **DEVICE** - this entity represents a device, for example, Samsung Galaxy S7 Edge, Motorola Moto G, Sony Xperia, etc.
- **HARDWARE** - this entity represents hardware components of devices, for example, camera, SD card, bluetooth, wifi, etc.
- **ELEM_API** - this entity represents elements of the API, i.e., methods, classes, interfaces, etc., for example, FaceDetector.isOperational(), ListView, getMinBufferSize().
- **TECH** - this entity represents technology elements, for example, JAVA, XML, HTML, LTE, etc.
- **FEATURE** - this entity represents operating system features or device features, for example, portrait mode, external storage, buffer size, among others.
- **O** - it represents the class of everything that does not belong to the classes of the other entities.

To evaluate the proposed NER model, we used the metrics: precision, recall and F-Measure.

2.2 A NER-Based Classifier for Android Fragmentation

The proposed NER model could be applied in several different tasks. In this work, we apply that model aiming at improving the performance of textual classifiers for Stack Overflow posts. To achieve that goal, we defined an approach where we combine the NER model with classifiers. To evaluate the performance of NER-based classifiers, we investigate the problem of classification of posts related to Android fragmentation, characterized a binary classification problem. In this section, we will show how we build and evaluate the NER-based classifiers.

The NER-based classifiers are defined as follows:

- The NER recognizer runs on each document to be classified, recognizing the following entities: API_VERSION, DEVICE, HARDWARE, API_ELEM, TECH, and FEATURE, accounting the number of entities in each class.
- For each document, a set of attributes is defined by the number of occurrences of the recognized entities: API_VERSION, DEVICE, HARDWARE, and API_ELEM.
- The classifiers are trained with the attributes generated in the previous step, where instances are labeled as Android fragmentation or not.

We do not consider TECH and FEATURE entities classes as attributes for the NER-based classifiers because these two classes are not related to the problem of Android fragmentation. For the classification of other types of posts, they could be considered.

We report on results for the implementations of the NER-based classifiers using Naïve Bayes, J48, and Random Forest decision trees of the WEKA.

To evaluate the NER-based classifiers, we use textual classifiers available in Mallet[1] as baselines. Those classifiers are based on Naïve Bayes, Maximum Entropy and Decision Tree. The textual documents given as inputs are transformed into feature vectors. For each document, a corresponding vector stores the frequencies of their respective words. Classifiers use these feature vectors to derive their internal parameters in the training phase. In the test phase, the classifiers use their internal parameters to classify the documents given as input.

We collected 300 debug-type Stack Overflow threads related to Android. Debug-type threads are those that the intent of the question is to get help to debug a specific issue [3,6]. Out of those 300 threads, 150 are related to Android fragmentation and 150 are not. In order to assess the effect of the training set size, we created five different data groups, containing training sets of sizes 50, 100, 150, 200, and 250. For each of these data groups, we randomly sampled 20 different data sets of the respective size, from the original 300 threads, observing that half of the threads were related to Android fragmentation, and the other half not. This sampling strategy would assess the effect of the variability of the content of threads in the outcome of the classifier.

We assessed the classifiers using 10-fold cross validation on each data group. We calculated and compared the precision, recall and accuracy mean from all classifiers.

---

[1] http://mallet.cs.umass.edu.

3   Results and Discussion

We first present the results obtained from the evaluation of the proposed NER model, and then we present the results from the comparison between the classifiers that use the proposed NER model and classifiers that do not use.

3.1   The Proposed NER Model for Technical Q&A Posts

The trained NER model was tested using a gold set of 10 threads of Stack Overflow that were not present in the set of 100 threads used in the training phase. These 10 threads have a total of 289 entities, used to calculate precision and recall. We will show the result for all entities considered together and also the results of each separate entity.

In order to assess if the size of input data used for the training the NER model was adequate to produce a realistic recognizer, we calculated precision, recall, and F-Measure varying the size of input data. We started calculating precision, recall and F-measure for a model trained with 2,000 input tokens, and then we successively added more 2,000 tokens, calculated again, and so on.

As we can see in Fig. 1 (All Entities), precision is already very high and does not vary significantly as the number of training tokens increases. This is an indication that the NER model is very precise even with few training data. Interestingly, we can also observe that precision may decay smoothly when the size of training corpus increases. A possible explanation for that phenomenon is that when new entities are included in the model, it becomes more complex and the model may try to identify new instances, and then may incorrectly identify those new elements.

Recall, differently from precision, is highly affected by a small training set. It increases as the number of training tokens increases, especially when the training set is still small. In the interval of 2,000 to 10,000 tokens, we have a substantial increase of 40.5% in the recall. The graph indicates that after 18,000 tokens the recall begins to converge, with a small increase in every 2,000 tokens added. F-Measure behaves like recall, because the precision does not vary too significantly. The number of tokens used in training (26807 tokens) can be considered adequate to recognize a reasonable number of entities correctly (83.4% of all entities) with a precision of 96.4%. The small increase in recall even after the NER model begins to converge from 18,000 tokens will be explained later when we analyze the generated graphs for each separate entity.

We now analyze each different entity in order to better understand their impact in the overall result of precision, recall and F-Measure.

Considering only the DEVICE entity, the precision for the DEVICE entity does not vary much over different training set sizes. The recall and F-Measure converge fast to a saturation point of 8,000 training tokens. This indicates that the NER model is very efficient to recognize DEVICE entities (the model trained with 26807 tokens achieved a precision of 98.6%, recall of 94.5% and F-measure of 96.5%). We can also observe that the NER model had better results for the separate DEVICE entity than considering all entities.

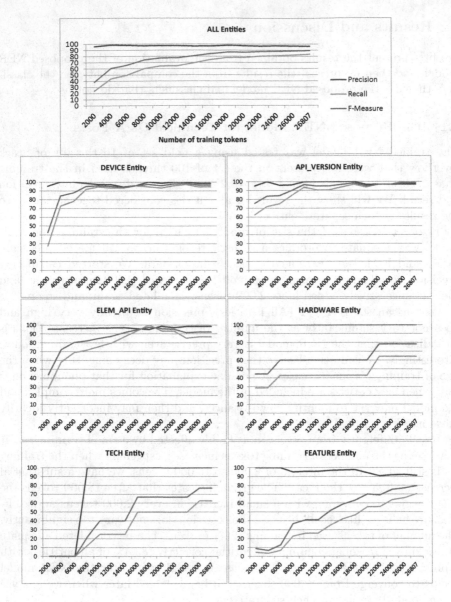

Fig. 1. Precision, recall and F-measure varying the number of training tokens

For the API_VERSION entity, precision is already high even for the smaller training sets, and that recall and F-measure also converge fast. A relevant observation is that the NER model was able to find all the entities present in the test threads in 26,000 training tokens as well as 26,807 tokens. We could find with respect to API_VERSION entities a pattern where the API name (or discriminant term) is usually followed by the version, for example, Android 6, Android

4.4.1, API level 19 and so on. As there are few different names for the Android API (but there are many versions), the NER model can recognize the name followed by the version efficiently. This model also recognizes names given to Android versions, such as KitKat, Lollipop, among others.

For the ELEM_API entity, precision is already high for small training sets, and recall and F-measure start at low rates with 2,000 tokens, but gradually converge as the number of input tokens increases. A relevant observation is that with 18,000 tokens, the NER model can recognize all API elements (100% recall). From 22,000 tokens recall begins to decrease, and then stabilizes at 26,000 tokens (about 92% of F-Measure). A possible explanation for the decrease is some noise that may have been introduced with some new tokens.

For the HARDWARE entity, recall does not increase in a similar way as the previous entities. With 20,000 tokens we still have recall just a little above 40% and maximum recall is below 65%. Interestingly, precision starts at 100% and continues stabilized. With respect to recall, from 6,000 tokens up to 20,000 tokens the model recognizes the same number of entities, that is, 22,000 tokens were necessary to recognize new HARDWARE entities. This can be explained through an analysis of the training and test data, which contains few examples of HARDWARE entities in the threads related to the Android fragmentation problem. To better understand this issue it is necessary to further study the threads related to the Android fragmentation problem, and to analyze the prevalence of fragmentation problems caused by a hardware component of devices. However, that study is beyond the scope of this work. Regarding the precision, NER model is very efficient, hitting all the entities along the increase of the training set size.

For the TECH entity, we can observe a pattern similar to the HARDWARE entity. Only with 8,000 tokens we have recognized entities. Interestingly, precision starts at 100% with this number of tokens and continues stabilized. With respect to recall, from 10,000 tokens up to 14,000 tokens the model recognizes the same number of entities, that is, it needed 16,000 tokens to recognize new TECH entities. There are few entities of this type in the training and test data.

For the FEATURE entity, recall and F-measure increases almost linearly as the number of training tokens increases. We observed in the training data that the FEATURE entity has a wide variety of names (related to the resources of the operating system or device), so it is expected a large number of training tokens to recognize this entity type more efficiently. This entity has the highest impact on the overall result because it is more prevalent than the other in the test data.

New Learned Vocabulary. We verified if the built NER model has the ability to learn new terms that are not present in the training set. We run our NER model trained with the entities ELEM_API, DEVICE, API_VERSION and HARDWARE on 7 Stack Overflow threads. A total of 50 words were recognized by the NER, and out of these 50 words, 20 were present in the training data, i.e., the built NER model recognized 30 new words (60% of the total recognized words). From those 50 recognized entities:

- 22 are ELEM_API (19 new (86.4%) and 3 in the training data (13.6%));

738   A. M. Rocha and M. A. Maia

- 20 are DEVICE - 8 new (40.0%) and 12 in the training data (60.0%);
- 7 are API_VERSION - 3 new (42.9%) and 4 in the training data (57.1%);
- 1 is HARDWARE, which was in the training data.

3.2 NER-Based Classifiers for Android Fragmentation

We present the assessment of the proposed NER-based classifiers compared to other baseline classifiers. The boxplots in Fig. 2 show the results of the accuracy of the classifier running on the 20 sampled datasets previously defined.

For example, DT_50 represents the results obtained by applying the Decision Tree classifier in the 20 data sets, constructed with 50 randomly sampled threads from the 300 threads obtained manually, as we discussed in Subsect. 2.2. ME_50, NB_50, NE+NER_50, DT_RF+NER_50 e DT_J48+NER_50 represents, respectively, the results obtained by applying the Maximum Entropy, Naïve Bayes, Naïve Bayes + NER, Random Forest(Decision Tree) + NER e J48(Decision Tree) + NER classifiers in the same 20 data sets.

We can analyze the results from two perspectives: size of training set and different classification methods.

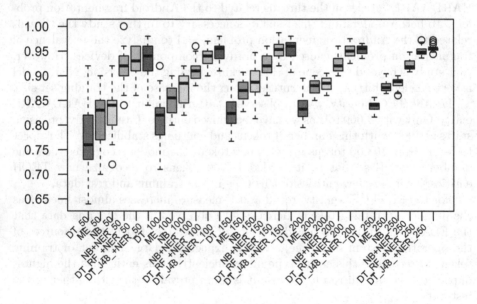

Fig. 2. Accuracy of classifiers for different size of training sets.

The first perspective is related to the performance of the classifiers with respect to the number of training threads given as input to these classifiers. For non-NER classifiers, the use of sets of size 50 produce lower accuracy classifiers. Kruskal-Wallis tests on the accuracy results showed significant difference for DT, ME and NB classifiers (p-value < 0.05). In post-hoc analysis of multiple comparisons, there was a significant difference for the 50-threads training sets where they were significantly smaller. For the NER-based classifiers, no significant difference could be observed (p-value > 0.05), indicating that NER classifiers are not significantly sensitive on the size of the training set. However, we can observe that the variability in the results in each data group decreases as the number of training threads increases. In order words, the greater the amount of training data, the greater the chance of the classifiers converge to a certain result. A good example is the results in DT_J48+NER_250, where we can observe that the results converge to around 0.95.

The second perspective is related to the comparison of the classifiers with each other. In Fig. 2, we can divide the classifiers into two groups. The first group contains the classifiers Decision Tree, Maximum Entropy and Naïve Bayes, and the second group contains the classifiers Random Forest(Decision Tree) + NER and J48(Decision Tree) + NER. The Naïve Bayes + NER classifier could be defined to be in between the two groups, except for the 50 threads training group where it is similar to the other NER classifiers. The classifiers of the second group that use the NER model with decision trees produced better results compared to the ones in the first group that are text classifiers, showed by a Kruskall-Wallis post-hoc analysis of multiple comparisons, at $\alpha = 0.05$.

Figure 3 shows the precision and recall for 250 training threads. The precision of Decision Tree Classifier (red boxplots) is higher than the recall, so it is correctly classifying more threads related to the Android fragmentation class than threads unrelated to the Android fragmentation class. The boxplots medians of precision and recall for the Maximum Entropy classifier (purple boxplots) are very close, which indicates that the classifier is classifying the two classes in a balanced way. The median recall of the Naïve Bayes classifier (yellow boxplots) is higher than the median of the precision, which indicates that this classifier is classifying more correctly threads unrelated to Android fragmentation. This is a problem for applications that aim to get only threads related to Android fragmentation. As we can see in Fig. 3, Decision Trees classifiers that use the NER model have better results for precision and recall than the other classifiers.

Threats to Validity. For external validity, our results are limited for improving classification of Android fragmentation content. For internal validity, the definition of the training set may be subject to human misclassification. We mitigated that threat by the authors discussing the cases that would be more likely to have some disagreement. Another threat is the effect that different training sets have on NER models and classifiers. For NER models, we mitigate that threat including in the study, the influence of the size of the training set in the model, in order to understand the significance of the threat. For the classifiers, we mitigate that threat, bootstrapping 20 different samples to understand the effect that different random samples would have in the result of the classifier.

4 Related Work

Some approaches to improve the use of socio-technical information would also benefit from specialized and accurate classifiers to filter the textual content.

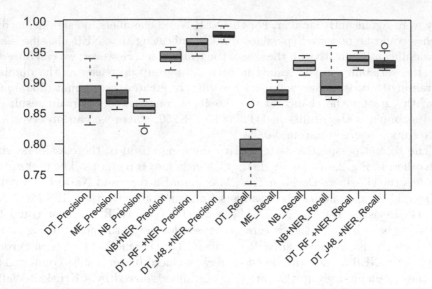

Fig. 3. Comparing precision and recall of the classifiers.

Robillard and Chhetri [12] proposed to detect and recommend fragments of documentation potentially important for a developer who is using a given API element. Head *et al.* [9] proposed language-specific routines that automatically generate context-relevant, on-demand micro-explanations of code. These routines detect explainable code in a web page, parse it, and generate in-situ natural language explanations and demonstrations of code. Zhong and Su [21] combined natural language processing and code analysis techniques to detect and report inconsistencies in API documentation. Souza *et al.* [15] and Rocha and Maia [13] proposed methodologies for automated generation of tutorials and cookbooks for APIs from the contents of the Stack Overflow filtering content using classifiers to separate how-to-do posts. Dagenais and Robillard [4] proposed a technique that automatically discovers documentation patterns.

Named Entity Recognition has been applied in several areas, corroborating with our technical choice. Liu *et al.* [10] proposed a technique for recognizing entities from tweets. Yoshida and Tsujii [20] investigated improvement of automatic biomedical named-entity recognition by applying a re-ranking method to the COLING 2004 JNLPBA shared task of bioentity recognition. Danger *et al.* [5] applied NER to recognize entity types relevant to the context of Protein-Protein Interactions. Bhasuran *et al.* [1] implemented an ensemble approach combined with fuzzy matching for biomedical named entity recognition of disease names. Yao and Sun [19] proposed a method to recognize and normalize mobile phone names from domain-specific Internet forums. Shabat, Omar and Rahem [14] developed a crime named entity recognition based on machine learning approaches that extract nationalities, weapons, and crime locations in online crime documents. Quimbaya *et al.* [11], the authors extracted information from narrative text contained within electronic health records.

Some authors [8, 18] have tried to understand, or even minimize, the problems caused by Android fragmentation. Wei *et al.* [18] built a model to check whether the use of the Android API causes issues in certain contexts (versions of Android and device models). Finding those specific threads in Stack Overflow using our classifiers to build a body of knowledge on this problem would be useful to mitigate the impact of fragmentation.

5   Conclusion and Future Work

The social-technical sites offer a lot of quality information to software developers. However, it is challenging to filter out this information due to the large amount of content available in these sites. Several works have been proposed to create alternative filters, in order to obtain only the necessary information to solve the desired problem. In this work, we proposed an alternative technique that improved the results of textual classifiers that are frequently applied in the creation of filters applied in social-technical sites.

We used NER to recognize entities related to software development technical elements in socio-technical sites. We combined this NER model with Naïve Bayes and two decision tree classifiers (Random Forest and J48). We show that decision tree classifiers obtained better results in comparison with three other raw text classifiers (Decision Tree, Maximum Entropy and Naïve Bayes).

In addition to improving the results of the textual classifiers, the NER model could also be used for other purposes. For example, we could apply this model to identify duplicate posts by recognizing entities on social-technical sites, such as Stack Overflow. This model could also be used to recognize posts that are related to problems involving new types of device models, since a major advantage of NER is to discover new entities that are not present in the training data used to train the model.

As future work, more entities related to software engineering would be included to help solving a wider range of problems in this area. New classifiers based on these models to assist solve other problems could also be developed.

Acknowledgments. We acknowledge CAPES, FAPEMIG, and CNPq for partially funding this research.

References

1. Bhasuran, B., Murugesan, G., Abdulkadhar, S., Natarajan, J.: Stacked ensemble combined with fuzzy matching for biomedical named entity recognition of diseases. J. Biomed. Inform. **64**, 1–9 (2016)
2. Campos, E.C., Souza, L.B.L., Maia, M.A.: Searching crowd knowledge to recommend solutions for API usage tasks. J. Softw.: Evol. Process. **28**(10), 863–892 (2016)

3. Campos, E.C., Maia, M.A.: Automatic categorization of questions from Q&A sites. In: Proceedings of the 29th Annual ACM SAC 2014, pp. 641–643 (2014)
4. Dagenais, B., Robillard, M.P.: Using traceability links to recommend adaptive changes for documentation evolution. IEEE TSE **40**(11), 1126–1146 (2014)
5. Danger, R., Pla, F., Molina, A., Rosso, P.: Towards a protein-protein interaction information extraction system: recognizing named entities. Know.-Based Syst. **57**, 104–118 (2014)
6. Delfim, F.M., Paixão, K.V.R., Cassou, D., Maia, M.A.: Redocumenting APIs with crowd knowledge: a coverage analysis based on question types. J. Braz. Comput. Soc. **22**(1), 9 (2016)
7. Finkel, J.R., Grenager, T., Manning, C.: Incorporating non-local information into information extraction systems by gibbs sampling. In: Proceedings of the 43rd Annual Meeting on Association for Computational Linguistics, ACL 2005, pp. 363–370 (2005)
8. Han, D., Zhang, C., Fan, X., Hindle, A., Wong, K., Stroulia, E.: Understanding Android fragmentation with topic analysis of vendor-specific bugs. In: Proceedings of the 2012 19th Working Conference on Reverse Engineering, WCRE 2012, pp. 83–92 (2012)
9. Head, A., Appachu, C., Hearst, M.A., Hartmann, B.: Tutorons: generating context-relevant, on-demand explanations and demonstrations of online code. In: Proceedings of the 2015 IEEE Symposium on Visual Languages and Human-Centric Computing, VL/HCC, pp. 3–12 (2015)
10. Liu, X., Zhang, S., Wei, F., Zhou, M.: Recognizing named entities in tweets. In: Proceedings of the 49th Annual Meeting of the Association for Computational Linguistics: Human Language Technologies, HLT 2011, vol. 1, pp. 359–367 (2011)
11. Quimbaya, A.P., et al.: Named entity recognition over electronic health records through a combined dictionary-based approach. Procedia Comput. Sci. **100**, 55–61 (2016)
12. Robillard, M.P., Chhetri, Y.B.: Recommending reference API documentation. Empir. Softw. Eng. **20**(6), 1558–1586 (2014)
13. Rocha, A.M., Maia, M.A.: Automated API documentation with tutorials generated from stack overflow. In: Proceedings of the 30th Brazilian Symposium on Software Engineering, SBES 2016, pp. 33–42 (2016)
14. Shabat, H., Omar, N., Rahem, K.: Named entity recognition in crime using machine learning approach. In: Jaafar, A., et al. (eds.) AIRS 2014. LNCS, vol. 8870, pp. 280–288. Springer, Cham (2014). https://doi.org/10.1007/978-3-319-12844-3_24
15. Souza, L., Campos, E., Madeiral, F., Paixão, K., Rocha, A., Maia, M.: Bootstrapping cookbooks for APIs from crowd knowledge on Stack Overflow. Inf. Softw. Technol. **111**, 1–16 (2019)
16. Souza, L.B.L., Campos, E.C., Maia, M.D.A.: Ranking crowd knowledge to assist software development. In: Proceedings of the 22nd International Conference on Program Comprehension, ICPC 2014, pp. 72–82 (2014)
17. Treude, C., Robillard, M.P.: Augmenting API documentation with insights from stack overflow. In: Proceedings of the 38st International Conference on Software Engineering (2016)
18. Wei, L., Liu, Y., Cheung, S.C.: Taming Android fragmentation: characterizing and detecting compatibility issues for Android Apps. In: Proceedings of the 31st IEEE/ACM International Conference on Automated Software Engineering, ASE 2016, pp. 226–237 (2016)
19. Yao, Y., Sun, A.: Mobile phone name extraction from Internet forums: a semi-supervised approach. World Wide Web **19**(5), 783–805 (2016)

20. Yoshida, K., Tsujii, J.: Reranking for biomedical named-entity recognition. In: Proceedings of the Workshop on BioNLP 2007: Biological, Translational, and Clinical Language Processing, BioNLP 2007, pp. 209–216 (2007)
21. Zhong, H., Su, Z.: Detecting API documentation errors. In: Proceedings of the ACM SIGPLAN OOPSLA 2013, pp. 803–816 (2013)

Recognizing Humor in Portuguese: First Steps

André Clemêncio[1,2], Ana Alves[1,3], and Hugo Gonçalo Oliveira[1,2(✉)]

[1] Center of Informatics and Systems of the University of Coimbra, Coimbra, Portugal
adfc@student.dei.uc.pt, {ana,hroliv}@dei.uc.pt
[2] Department of Informatics Engineering, University of Coimbra, Coimbra, Portugal
[3] ISEC, Polytechnic Institute of Coimbra, Coimbra, Portugal

Abstract. Within the domain of Artificial Intelligence, humor has been a research topic for some time, but the automatic recognition of its verbal expression has never been tackled for Portuguese. This work aims to change this scenario. We describe a set of experiments towards the development of computational models that recognize humor written in Portuguese, based on content and humor-specific features extracted. Interesting results, with F1-scores up to 0.93, are achieved when classifiers for this purpose are trained and tested on texts with a similar style (question-answers or news headlines). Yet, when the testing examples are of a different style, results are poor, which suggests that much more has to be done towards effective humor recognition.

Keywords: Natural Language Processing · Text classification · Computational Humor · Humor recognition

1 Introduction

The ultimate goal of Natural Language Processing (NLP) is to develop machines with the ability of communicating using human language. This turns out to be very challenging, because human languages use several phenomena that are hard to deal with, even for humans, such as ambiguity (at several levels), language variability, or the use of figurative language (e.g., irony, metaphor). The meaning of language is also influenced by the context, including affects or out-of-context interactions, possibly with the goal of making others laugh.

Computational Humor [3] is a field of Artificial Intelligence that uses computers for detecting, analyzing or producing humor. The automatic recognition

---

This work was partially funded by the Portuguese Foundation for Science and Technology's (FCT) INCoDe 2030 initiative, in the scope of the demonstration project AIA, "Apoio Inteligente a empreendedores (chatbots)"; and by the SOCIALITE Project (PTDC/EEISCR/2072/2014), co-financed by COMPETE 2020, Portugal 2020 – Operational Program for Competitiveness and Internationalization (POCI), European Union's ERDF (European Regional Development Fund), and FCT.

© Springer Nature Switzerland AG 2019
P. Moura Oliveira et al. (Eds.): EPIA 2019, LNAI 11805, pp. 744–756, 2019.
https://doi.org/10.1007/978-3-030-30244-3_61

of verbal humor is thus a branch of both Computational Humor and NLP. In fact, either by humans or machines, recognizing humor is a sign of fluency in the target language [20], and might result in better handling different situations. For instance, a news aggregator might gain the ability of filtering out humorous news; or a chatbot might recognize a humorous interaction and change its response, possibly ignoring it, or answering with humor as well.

Our main goal is to develop a computational model capable of recognizing humor written in Portuguese. Although there are several works on humor recognition, to our knowledge, most target English and no one tackles it in Portuguese. A long-term goal is to enable the inclusion of humor recognition capabilities in intelligent agents that use the Portuguese language. Yet, we are only taking the first steps towards it. Given the lack of studies towards such a model, the experiments described in this work will hopefully help to shake the area.

We tackle humor recognition as a traditional task of text classification. We started by collecting and organizing texts in the creation of datasets for testing our models and for reaching conclusions on the achieved progress. Such datasets had to contain both humorous and non-humorous examples of (short) texts. Two different datasets were created, including both positive and negative examples: one with questions and answers; another with news headlines. Those were used for training and testing a set of models, using different learning methods and exploiting not only content features (bag-of-words), but also some humor-specific features (e.g., incongruity, ambiguity), for which extraction procedures were adapted and applied to Portuguese. When the models are trained and tested in different parts of the same dataset (similar style), results are high, reaching F1-scores of 0.93 for humorous question-answers, using only content features, or both content and humor-specific features. However, when the model is trained in one dataset and tested on another, results are much lower, with the highest F1-score of 0.70, after training on the largest dataset and exploiting both content and humor features. Our interpretation is that the proposed approach is adequate for recognizing humor in a specific style, while recognizing it in general is much more challenging and requires additional work, especially more data. As an initial approach to the topic, we feel that interesting conclusions were achieved and doors are now open for further research on the topic.

The remainder of this paper is organized as follows: In Sect. 2, we overview the related work, with a focus on methods and approaches for humor recognition; In Sect. 3, we describe the data used, pre-processing of the data, features extracted and an initial analysis of their relevance; In Sect. 4, we describe the experiments performed and report on the results achieved; In the last section, we draw some conclusions and set directions for future work.

2   Related Work

Most studies in the field of Humor Recognition address it as a binary classification problem: humor or not. Here we analyze features explored, datasets used, and approaches adopted, previously, for this purpose.

Besides the traditional bag-of-words approach for text classification, authors have focused on specific features that might be good indicators of humor. Those include the presence of idiomatic expressions and other words typical of jokes [18]; human-centered vocabulary (e.g., "I", "you") [13]; repetition of sounds in rhymes and alliteration [14,21]; antonyms and slang [14]; length and other structural features [2]; syntactic features [11], including number of phrases by type (e.g., NP, VP) or dependency relations; ambiguity [2,18,21]; sentiment/polarity of words [2,21], including intensity [2], or focus on negative words (e.g., "wrong", "error") [13]; and, of course, incongruity [21]. Some of the previous (e.g., polarity, slang) can be acquired by looking up in specific lists or lexicons, while others have to be extracted indirectly. For instance, the amount of ambiguity can be approximated by the average number of senses that the used words have, in a dictionary or wordnet. An interesting way of approximating incongruity is considering it to be inversely-correlated with the average similarity of the used words [21].

To analyze the importance of humor-specific features, three models for humor recognition were compared [14]: one based on the presence of antonyms, alliteration and slang; another following a traditional bag-of-words approach; and one that combined both of the previous, leading to the best results. In another experiment [21], when compared to other features, incongruity, computed through distributional models of semantic similarity, lead to the best results.

Although there are many styles of humor, to simplify this task, most authors focused on a single type, generally short jokes or one-liners. Given that it is relatively easy to collect one-liners from the Web, Mihalcea and Straparava's [14] dataset, also used by others (e.g. [11,21]), includes 16,000 one-liners in English. Sjobergh and Araki [18] collected a smaller dataset with 6,100 jokes. Mihalcea and Pulman's [13] dataset included longer jokes as well. Barbieri and Saggion [2] focused on tweets and worked both on humor and irony recognition. Their dataset had 40,000 tweets, labelled with the categories of Irony, Education, Humor and Politics, according to the presence of corresponding hashtags (#irony, #education, #humor, #politics). When creating such a dataset, attention should be taken also in the selection of the negative examples. To have a fair task, the latter should be structurally and stylistically similar to the positive examples. Negative examples previously used for one-liners include other types of short texts, such as news headlines, single sentences in newspaper articles, or proverbs [14]. While the latter will have similar lengths, stylistic differences might still go beyond humor.

Work on humor recognition has mainly followed a supervised learning approach, where models were learned with the dataset and the extracted features. Classification algorithms previously used for this purpose include Naive Bayes [13,14], Support Vector Machines (SVM) [13,14], and tree-based classifiers, including Decision Tree [2] and Random Forests [2,11,21].

The aforementioned works were developed for English. There are linguistic studies on humor covering examples in Portuguese [20] but, on its recognition, we do not know of any work specifically for this language. Yet, there is work on related topics in Portuguese, such as irony [4, 7] or proverb detection [16], as well as on the automatic generation of potentially humorous riddles [9].

3   Data Preparation

Models for recognizing verbal humor in Portuguese were trained and tested in datasets created for this purpose, with examples of humor and non-humor. Besides exploiting content features, humor-specific features were also extracted. This section describes the datasets, the features extracted, and the classification algorithms used for learning binary classifiers that label Portuguese (short) texts as humorous or not.

3.1   Datasets

Since we knew of no prepared dataset of Portuguese humor, we had to create one specifically for training and testing the classification model. In this process, care must be taken, as positive and negative examples should not be too different, except in the actual features that humans rely on for discriminating between classes, here, humor and non-humor. Otherwise, we risk that the classifier learns to differentiate classes based on features that are irrelevant for our purpose, e.g., length or structure of the text, or non-relevant vocabulary differences.

With this in mind, two datasets were assembled, each with instances written in a similar style (question-answer or headline) and with a similar length, given that we only considered short texts. Since there are not many sources of Portuguese text, easily accessible and that we know, for sure, to be humorous, positive examples were first collected. Considering them, negative examples in a similar style were then selected.

All the instances in the first dataset (hereafter, D1) contained questions followed by short answers. Positive examples comprise 700 one-liners gathered from the Web—most from the collection *"Anedotário Português"*[1]; others gathered from the Facebook page *"O Sagrado Caderno das Piadas Secas"*[2]. As negative examples, D1 contained the 700 general-knowledge questions and answers in the Portuguese part of the parallel corpus MultiEight-04 [12]. Table 1 illustrates the contents of D1, including the text, in Portuguese, a rough English translation, and the label ('H' for positive examples, 'N' for negative).

The second dataset (D2) contains 4,300 news headlines: about 2,100 from the Portuguese newspaper *Público* and the remaining from *Inimigo Público*, a humoristic supplement of the previous newspaper. *Público* headlines are all from February 2019, while those from *Inimigo Público* spread from December 2018 to February 2019. Although we wanted to cover the same time periods, *Público* has much more publications. All headlines were collected from the social network Twitter, where both sources have their accounts and regularly post headlines. Before their usage, all headlines were subjected to an initial cleaning procedure,

---

[1] https://ltpf.files.wordpress.com/2011/01/omaiscompleto-anedotc3a3c2a1ri.pdf.
[2] https://www.facebook.com/CadernoDasPiadas/.

Table 1. Examples instances in dataset D1 and their labels.

Example	Label
Qual é a língua menos falada no mundo? Língua Gestual (What is the least spoken language in the World? Sign Language)	H
Porque é que os polícias não gostam de sabão? Porque preferem deter gente (Why don't cops like soap? Because they prefer to arrest people) * 'deter gente' (arrest people) sounds like detergent	H
Quem é Jean-Bertrand Aristide? O primeiro presidente do Haiti eleito democraticamente (Who is Jean-Bertrand Aristide? The first democratically elected President of Haiti)	N
Como se forma o ozono? Através de reacções fotoquímicas atmosféricas na presença de calor e luz solar (How ozone is formed? Through atmospheric photochemical reactions in the presence of heat and sunlight)	N

Table 2. Examples instances in dataset D2 and their labels.

Example	Label
Operação da GNR na estrada para fiscalizar condutores que comem carne na sexta-feira santa (GNR operation on the road to inspect drivers who eat meat on Good Friday)	H
Benfica recebeu fundos da Segurança Social para Luís Filipe Vieira gastar em gambas (Benfica received Social Security funds for Luís Filipe Vieira to spend on prawns)	H
Ministério das Finanças ainda não recebeu pedidos de pré-reforma no Estado (Ministry of Finance has not yet received pre-retirement claims in the State)	N
Nogueira acusa António Costa de tentar manipular opinião pública (Nogueira accuses António Costa of trying to manipulate public opinion)	N

where *retweets* and posts that did not correspond to headlines (e.g., "*A primeira página*", in English, "The first page") were discarded, and text frequently used in the beginning of some posts was removed (e.g. "*Hoje na edição impressa:*", "Today in the printed edition:"). Table 2 illustrates the contents of D2.

3.2 Feature Engineering

Humor recognition can be tackled as a traditional text classification task, where texts are represented as a bag-of-words. However, humor goes beyond those (content) features. Therefore, supported by the literature on the topic, we extract several humor-relevant linguistic features from Portuguese text, so that they can also be considered by the learned models.

Given that we are working on Portuguese text, once the features to extract were identified, we explored available linguistic resources for this language on which we could rely for their extraction. Pre-processing was performed with Python's Natural Language Toolkit library (NLTK), improved for Portuguese [5]. It included tokenization, for dividing the text into tokens; part-of-speech (PoS) tagging, for identifying the PoS of each word; lemmatization, for identifying the dictionary form of each word-PoS pair; and named entity recognition, for identifying named entities (NEs) and assigning them a suitable category. Features that resort to lexicons where entries are lemmatized (e.g., antonymy, ambiguity) are extracted from the lemmatized version of the text.

Next, we enumerate the humor-specific features considered and how they were extracted:

- **Sentiment** (3 features): number of words with a positive polarity, and with a negative polarity, according to SentiLex-PT [17]. Words like *beleza* (beauty) or *inteligência* (intelligence) are typically used with a positive polarity, whereas words like *engano* (mistake), *pobre* (poor) or *morrer* (to die) are typically negative. A third feature is the difference between the number of positive and negative words.
- **Slang**: number of words listed in the *Dicionário Aberto de Calão e Expressões Idiomáticas*[3] (Open Slang Dictionary). Such words include *vaca* (cow/bitch), *merda* (shit), or *cagar* (to shit), among many others.
- **Regularities in writing** (4 features): number of occurrences of the most frequent character uni/bi/tri/tetra-grams. This feature is extracted with the *ngrams()* function of NLTK and may capture the presence of alliteration.
- **Antonymy**: number of pairs of lemmas that are antonyms in at least two out of ten Portuguese lexical knowledge bases [8]. Examples of antonym pairs include *covardia-coragem* (cowardice-courage), *alegre-triste* (happy-sad), or *piorar-melhorar* (worsen-improve).
- **Ambiguity** (2 features): average number of senses per lemma and highest number of senses for a lemma, according to OpenWordNet-PT [15], a Portuguese wordnet, where words are grouped in synsets, according to their possible senses.
- **Out-of-vocabulary words**: number of words not covered by the vocabulary of a pre-trained word2vec CBOW model of word embeddings for Portuguese [10], with 300-sized vectors. This feature aims to capture words that are sometimes made-up towards a humor effect.
- **Incongruity**: average similarity of all pairs of words, according to the previous model of word embeddings. Given that incongruity is related to unexpectedness for being out of place, the lowest the value of this feature is, the higher its incongruity should be.
- **Named Entitites** (11 features): number of NEs per category, considering the 10 categories in the HAREM collection [6]. The last feature is a sum of all NEs. These features are motivated by the frequent occurrence of NEs in our dataset, mainly in general knowledge-questions and news headlines.

---

[3] http://natura.di.uminho.pt/~jj/pln/calao/calao.dic.txt.

For the extraction of the content features, datasets are previously pre-processed as well, and represented as bags-of-lemmas, with no weighting, and considering only lemmas that occur in at least three instances. This decision was based on an initial set of experiments where this configuration lead to minor improvements.

3.3   Feature Relevance Analysis

Before learning a classifier for the automatic recognition of humor, we decided to explore the datasets and compute the Information Gain of the considered features. The higher this value, the better a feature is for dividing the data into groups with low entropy, also a strong indicator of feature relevance. Table 3 lists the eight features with higher Information Gain for each dataset.

Table 3. Features with higher Information Gain in datasets D1 and D2.

D1		D2	
Incongruity	0.69	Incongruity	0.68
Avg #Senses	0.34	Avg #Senses	0.17
#NEs	0.16	Char 1-gram	0.15
Token 'um'	0.13	2-grams	0.05
Max(#Senses)	0.13	#NE 'Person'	0.05
Char 3-grams	0.11	Max(#Senses)	0.03
Char 1-gram	0.10	#NEs	0.03
Token 'porque'	0.09	Char 3-grams	0.03

Even though our incongruity feature is just an approximation through the computation of the average similarity, this analysis shows that it is the most important feature for humor recognition in both datasets. This is in line with the incongruity [1] theory of humor, which claims that *"laughter is the perception of something that violates our mental patterns and expectations"*. The second feature with highest Information Gain, also the same for both datasets, is ambiguity, here in the form of the average number of senses per word. Again, it is a feature we know to be highly related to humor (e.g., jokes may take advantage of two different senses of a word), previously exploited by other researchers for humor recognition [2,18,21]. The other ambiguity-related feature, maximum number of senses, is also in the top for both datasets, but in a different rank. The remaining top features are different for D1 and D2, and for D1 Information Gain values are higher, possibly because this dataset is smaller. Other relevant features in D1 include the number of named entities, character 1 and 3-grams, and the presence of the tokens 'um' and 'porque'. These tokens appear much more often in the positive examples of D1, so they are very relevant in the classification task. After closer inspection, we find 240 positive examples in D1 containing the word 'porque', which never occurs in the negative. In D2, the third feature with higher Information Gain is the character uni-grams, interpreted as a higher repetition of characters in the positive examples. The remaining features in D2 have lower Information Gain. One of them is the occurrence of named entities of the type person, frequent in news headlines, which is the style of both positive and negative examples.

This analysis confirmed the relevance of some of the features specifically extracted for humor recognition and helped us understand how a classifier might learn to discriminate humorous texts. Using only a subset of the most relevant features may reduce the amount of noisy features and also time complexity, with clear benefits if we aim at integrating humor recognition in a system working in real time (e.g. chatbot).

4   Experimentation

Humor recognition was tackled as a text classification problem. Our goal was to train a binary classifier for automatically labelling short texts as humorous or not, based on their features. The datasets described in the previous section were used for training and testing this classifier. Three different classification algorithms were tested for this purpose, selected for being commonly used for text classification and, specifically, humor recognition [2,13,14]. Those were Support Vector Machines (SVM), Decision Tree (DT) and Naive Bayes (NB), all available in scikit-learn[4], a machine learning toolkit in Python, used in our experiments.

This section describes the performed experiments. In the first set of experiments, we train and test on examples of the same kind, namely question-answers (D1) or news headlines (D2). Given that these results may not be valid for humor of different kinds, we refer to these experiments as the recognition of humor styles. On the second set of experiments, we analyze the results of training a classifier in one dataset and testing it on the other, to see how well the task of humor classification can be generalized. In both sets of experiments, we also compare the performance of using content features or humor-specific features exclusively, or combining both of them.

Although, in the current scenario, working with all features is still scalable[5], empirical tests suggested that results were not affected if we used only the top-200 features with higher Information Gain (see Sect. 3.3). Therefore, all reported results were obtained with those 200 features, except for experiments using only humor-specific features, which are only 24.

In all experiments, results are reported in terms of accuracy when labelling each example as humorous or not. Even though our datasets are almost balanced, given that our goal is to recognize humor, we also report the precision, recall and F1-score for the humorous class.

---

[4] https://scikit-learn.org/.
[5] A 10-fold cross validation in any dataset takes only a few seconds in a regular laptop.

4.1 Recognizing Humor "Styles"

In the first experiment, models were trained and tested in the same dataset and performance was measured with the average metrics in a stratified 10-fold cross validation. Table 4 reports the results achieved with each classifier on each dataset, when using only content features, humor-specific features, or both.

Table 4. Results of 10-fold cross validation for humor recognition in D1 and D2: exclusively with content features; exclusively with humor-specific features; with content and humor-specific features.

	D1			D2		
	SVM	DT	NB	SVM	DT	NB
Content features						
Accuracy	0.93 ± 0.04	0.88 ± 0.05	0.89 ± 0.05	0.81 ± 0.03	0.71 ± 0.03	0.72 ± 0.03
Precision	0.96 ± 0.04	0.92 ± 0.04	0.90 ± 0.06	0.85 ± 0.02	0.77 ± 0.03	0.71 ± 0.03
Recall	0.91 ± 0.08	0.84 ± 0.11	0.89 ± 0.11	0.76 ± 0.05	0.59 ± 0.06	0.77 ± 0.04
F1	0.93 ± 0.05	0.87 ± 0.06	0.89 ± 0.06	0.80 ± 0.03	0.67 ± 0.05	0.74 ± 0.03
Humor-specific features						
Accuracy	0.84 ± 0.05	0.77 ± 0.02	0.80 ± 0.04	0.80 ± 0.02	0.67 ± 0.02	0.65 ± 0.03
Precision	0.85 ± 0.06	0.79 ± 0.04	0.77 ± 0.06	0.78 ± 0.02	0.67 ± 0.03	0.66 ± 0.03
Recall	0.82 ± 0.09	0.76 ± 0.06	0.81 ± 0.03	0.75 ± 0.04	0.67 ± 0.02	0.63 ± 0.05
F1	0.83 ± 0.06	0.77 ± 0.03	0.92 ± 0.04	0.76 ± 0.02	0.67 ± 0.02	0.64 ± 0.04
Content + Humor-specific features						
Accuracy	0.94 ± 0.05	0.87 ± 0.05	0.91 ± 0.05	0.85 ± 0.03	0.72 ± 0.02	0.79 ± 0.03
Precision	0.97 ± 0.04	0.88 ± 0.05	0.92 ± 0.08	0.88 ± 0.02	0.73 ± 0.01	0.82 ± 0.03
Recall	0.90 ± 0.10	0.86 ± 0.10	0.92 ± 0.08	0.81 ± 0.04	0.70 ± 0.05	0.75 ± 0.05
F1	0.93 ± 0.06	0.87 ± 0.06	0.91 ± 0.05	0.84 ± 0.03	0.71 ± 0.03	0.79 ± 0.03

Looking at the performance of different classifiers, better results are consistently obtained with SVM. When comparing different types of features, even though the majority of features with higher Information Gain were from the humor-specific group (see Sect. 3.3), better results are obtained with content features. Looking at F1, this difference is more pronounced in D1 (0.93 vs 0.83) than in D2 (0.80 vs 0.76). Although both positive and negative examples in D1 are structured similarly, as question-answer, these results highlighted the fact that positive examples use several humor-specific tokens, not to mention the high occurrence of the pronoun 'porque' (why). Out of curiosity, those humor-specific words include 'elefante' (elephant), 'alentejano', 'lâmpada' (light bulb) or 'cúmulo' (in the extreme) with 0.026, 0.021, 0.014, 0.013 Information Gain, respectively. Still, when both types of features are used together, in D1, accuracy improves by one point (0.94), and, in D2, F1 increases four points (0.84). This suggests that combining content and humor-specific features is a good option.

Finally, the results of D1 and D2 suggest that it is easier to identify humorous questions and answers than to recognize humorous headlines. This makes sense, because recognizing the latter without additional context (e.g., recent news, political situation) can be challenging even for humans. In fact, without that specific context, many humorous and serious headlines might look very similar (see Table 2). Nevertheless, despite this difficulty, we believe that achieving a F1-score of 0.84 in D2, with an SVM and both types of features, is an interesting result. As for D1, accuracies and F1 higher than 0.9, and precision higher than 0.95 is very positive, especially when it comes to such a human characteristic as humor is. Accuracy values are in line with those reported by Mihalcea and Straparava [14], when recognizing humorous one-liners in English, among news headlines from Reuters (96%) or sentences from the British National Corpus (79%), also with Naive Bayes and SVM classifiers and using both content and a set of humor-specific features.

Despite the achieved performance, we cannot say that the learned models have successfully learned to recognize humor. Only that they have learned how to pick pontentially-humorous instances out of other textual instances written in a similar style. In the next section, we make an initial analysis of how the resulting models generalize to humor in slightly different forms.

4.2   Recognizing Humor

In order to test whether a model trained with a kind of humor would be general enough to recognize other types of humor, we trained models like the previous in one dataset and tested them on the other. Table 5 shows the results achieved with content features or humor-specific features exclusively, and Table 6 when using the top-200 relevant features, including both content and humor features.

Table 5. Results of training in one dataset and testing on the other, using different feature sets.

	Content features						Humor-specific features					
	D1 → D2			D2 → D1			D1 → D2			D2 → D1		
	SVM	DT	NB	SVM	DT	NB	SVM	DT	NB	SVM	DT	NB
Accuracy	0.52	0.51	0.55	0.69	0.40	0.49	0.53	0.55	0.46	0.63	0.55	0.46
Precision	0.66	0.52	0.55	0.68	0.40	0.50	0.55	0.56	0.44	0.77	0.57	0.42
Recall	0.11	0.25	0.66	0.72	0.41	0.90	0.41	0.49	0.25	0.37	0.40	0.20
F1	0.19	0.34	0.60	0.70	0.41	0.64	0.47	0.52	0.32	0.50	0.47	0.27

Results suggest that models learned this way are not, in fact, apt for recognizing humor expressed in different styles, other than the style they are trained with. Still, the model trained in D2 performs better in D1, regardless of the features used. However, when content features are combined with the humor-specific. F1 is considerably higher (0.70 with SVM).

754   A. Clemêncio et al.

Table 6. Results of training in one dataset and testing on the other, using all features.

	D1 → D2			D2 → D1		
	SVM	DT	NB	SVM	DT	NB
Accuracy	0.50	0.53	0.48	0.72	0.59	0.54
Precision	0.55	0.56	0.48	0.76	0.61	0.53
Recall	0.04	0.35	0.25	0.65	0.53	0.69
F1	0.07	0.42	0.33	0.70	0.57	0.60

Models trained in D1 perform poorly, with accuracies close to the random chance. Here, humor-specific features seem to generalize better, but the highest F1 is just 0.52, with DT. When using content features, recall is very low, meaning that the model is classifying most instances as non-humorous. We recall that D2 is about three times larger than D1 and, even though they cover a different style of humor, this fact should significantly affect the results achieved. Specifically, there are many content features (words) in D2 that do not occur in D1.

This experiment confirmed that recognizing humor automatically is, indeed, challenging, and it takes much more than learning on a set of examples that only cover one type of humor. Despite this fact, with more data, significantly better results could be achieved.

5   Conclusions

We tackled the problem of humor recognition in texts written in Portuguese. As far as we know, this is the first time this problem is tackled for this language. Two datasets were assembled, both with humorous and non-humorous instances, and used for training and testing models for classifying them. Besides relying on traditional bag-of-words features, we identified humor-specific features and proposed procedures for their extraction from Portuguese text.

When training and testing on texts written in the same style, results were very interesting, especially given that humor is not always trivial. These results were in line with similar work for English [14]. Yet, in the former work, models only considered one kind of humor (one-liners), written in a significantly different style than some of the negative examples (e.g. news headlines). When the training text is written in a different style than the testing, performance is much lower. This suggests that models are not learning to identify humor in general, but specific styles of humor. Nevertheless, better results are obtained when more training data is used. Results additionally point out that, with less training data, humor-specific features generalize better, but more experiments are required for confirming this finding.

This was our first approach to this topic and much more can be done. So that other researchers may tackle the same challenge, the datasets we used are available at https://github.com/andreclemencio/Recognizing-Humor-in-Portuguese.

Yet, for generalizing humor recognition, more data must be gathered, also covering different types of humor. However, in opposition to English, for which there are several large datasets with jokes, already assembled (e.g., [14]), for Portuguese, collecting such data will require additional effort. In fact, although it would be interesting to test state-of-the-art approaches for text classification (e.g., LSTM deep neural networks), with the amount of data currently available, such approaches may not be too effective. Possibly more challenging would be classifying humor into different non-trivial categories, such as adult or black humor, or take one step further, towards humor interpretation (e.g., with anchor extraction [21]).

Future versions of the developed models may also benefit from exploiting other features, such as imageability or concreteness [19]; or computing some features alternatively. For instance, instead of the average similarity between all pairs of words, incongruity could consider only the least similar pair. This kind of model may be integrated in a conversational agent, for filtering humorous interactions, or in a riddle generator [9], for ranking generated riddles according to humor potential.

References

1. Attardo, S. (ed.): Encyclopedia of Humor Studies. SAGE (2014)
2. Barbieri, F., Saggion, H.: Automatic detection of irony and humour in Twitter. In: Proceedings of 5th International Conference on Computational Creativity (ICCC), pp. 155–162 (2014)
3. Binsted, K., et al.: Computational humor. IEEE Intell. Syst. **21**(2), 59–69 (2006)
4. Carvalho, P., Sarmento, L., Silva, M.J., De Oliveira, E.: Clues for detecting irony in user-generated contents: oh...!! it's so easy;-). In: Proceedings of 1st International CIKM Workshop on Topic-Sentiment Analysis for Mass Opinion, pp. 53–56. ACM (2009)
5. Ferreira, J., Gonçalo Oliveira, H., Rodrigues, R.: Improving NLTK for processing Portuguese. In: Symposium on Languages, Applications and Technologies (SLATE 2019) (2019, in press)
6. Freitas, C., Carvalho, P., Gonçalo Oliveira, H., Mota, C., Santos, D.: Second HAREM: advancing the state of the art of named entity recognition in Portuguese. In: Proceedings of 7th International Conference on Language Resources and Evaluation, LREC 2010, ELRA, La Valleta, Malta, May 2010
7. de Freitas, L.A., Vanin, A.A., Hogetop, D.N., Bochernitsan, M.N., Vieira, R.: Pathways for irony detection in tweets. In: Proceedings of 29th Annual ACM Symposium on Applied Computing, pp. 628–633. ACM (2014)
8. Gonçalo Oliveira, H.: A survey on Portuguese lexical knowledge bases: contents, comparison and combination. Information **9**(2), 32 (2018)
9. Gonçalo Oliveira, H., Rodrigues, R.: Explorando a geração automática de adivinhas em português. Linguamática **10**(1), 3–18 (2018)
10. Hartmann, N., Fonseca, E., Shulby, C., Treviso, M., Rodrigues, J., Aluísio, S.: Portuguese word embeddings: evaluating on word analogies and natural language tasks. In: Proceedings of 11th Brazilian Symposium in Information and Human Language Technology, STIL (2017)

11. Liu, L., Zhang, D., Song, W.: Exploiting syntactic structures for humor recognition. In: Proceedings of 27th International Conference on Computational Linguistics, Santa Fe, New Mexico, USA, pp. 1875–1883. Association for Computational Linguistics, August 2018
12. Magnini, B., et al.: Overview of the CLEF 2004 multilingual question answering track. In: Peters, C., Clough, P., Gonzalo, J., Jones, G.J.F., Kluck, M., Magnini, B. (eds.) CLEF 2004. LNCS, vol. 3491, pp. 371–391. Springer, Heidelberg (2005). https://doi.org/10.1007/11519645_38
13. Mihalcea, R., Pulman, S.: Characterizing humour: an exploration of features in humorous texts. In: Gelbukh, A. (ed.) CICLing 2007. LNCS, vol. 4394, pp. 337–347. Springer, Heidelberg (2007). https://doi.org/10.1007/978-3-540-70939-8_30
14. Mihalcea, R., Strapparava, C.: Learning to laugh (automatically): computational models for humor recognition. Comput. Intell. 22(2), 126–142 (2006)
15. Paiva, V., Rademaker, A., Melo, G.: OpenWordNet-PT: an open Brazilian WordNet for reasoning. In: Proceedings of 24th International Conference on Computational Linguistics. COLING (Demo Paper) (2012)
16. Rassi, A.P., Baptista, J., Vale, O.: Automatic detection of proverbs and their variants. In: Proceedings 3rd Symposium on Languages. Applications and Technologies (SLATE 2014), Bragança, Portugal, pp. 235–249. OASICS, Schloss Dagstuhl (2014)
17. Silva, M.J., Carvalho, P., Sarmento, L.: Building a sentiment Lexicon for social judgement mining. In: Caseli, H., Villavicencio, A., Teixeira, A., Perdigão, F. (eds.) PROPOR 2012. LNCS (LNAI), vol. 7243, pp. 218–228. Springer, Heidelberg (2012). https://doi.org/10.1007/978-3-642-28885-2_25
18. Sjöbergh, J., Araki, K.: Recognizing humor without recognizing meaning. In: Masulli, F., Mitra, S., Pasi, G. (eds.) WILF 2007. LNCS (LNAI), vol. 4578, pp. 469–476. Springer, Heidelberg (2007). https://doi.org/10.1007/978-3-540-73400-0_59
19. Soares, A.P., Costa, A.S., Machado, J., Comesaña, M., Oliveira, H.M.: The Minho Word Pool: norms for imageability, concreteness, and subjective frequency for 3,800 Portuguese words. Behav. Res. Methods 49(3), 1065–1081 (2017)
20. Tagnin, S.E.: O humor como quebra da convencionalidade. Revista brasileira de linguística aplicada 5(1), 247–257 (2005)
21. Yang, D., Lavie, A., Dyer, C., Hovy, E.: Humor recognition and humor anchor extraction. In: Proceedings of the 2015 Conference on Empirical Methods in Natural Language Processing (EMNLP), pp. 2367–2376. ACL Press (2015)

The Direct Path May Not Be The Best: Portuguese-Chinese Neural Machine Translation

Rodrigo Santos[1(✉)], João Silva[1], António Branco[1], and Deyi Xiong[2]

[1] Department of Informatics, NLX—Natural Language and Speech Group,
University of Lisbon, Lisbon, Portugal
{rsdsantos,jsilva,antonio.branco}@di.fc.ul.pt
[2] College of Intelligence and Computing, Tianjin University, Tianjin, China
dyxiong@tju.edu.cn

Abstract. Machine Translation (MT) has been one of the classic AI tasks from the early days of the field. Portuguese and Chinese are languages with a very large number of native speakers, though this does not carry through to the amount of literature on their processing, or to the amount of resources available to be used, in particular when compared with English. In this paper, we address the feasibility of creating a MT system for Portuguese-Chinese, using only freely available resources, by experimenting with various approaches to pairing source and target parallel data during training. These approaches are (i) using a model for each source-target language pair, (ii) using an intermediate pivot language, and (iii) using a single model that can translate from any language seen in the source side to any language seen on the target side. We find approaches whose performance is higher than that of the strong baseline consisting of an MT service provided by an IT industry giant for the pair Portuguese-Chinese.

Keywords: Neural Machine Translation · Portuguese · Chinese

1 Introduction

Human language is the prime vehicle we use for communication. In an increasingly globalized world, language differences pose a barrier to communication, reducing the number of people we can reach, or that can reach us. Artificial Intelligence, through Machine Translation (MT), appears as a viable solution to this problem by providing an automatic way of translating between languages.

Most of the research on MT concern English and some other language, often German or French, leaving other pairs of languages underrepresented in the literature. In this paper we are concerned with the translation between Portuguese (PT) and Chinese (ZH). Both languages have a very large number of native speakers, but despite this there are few available resources with which to build an MT system for these languages.

© Springer Nature Switzerland AG 2019
P. Moura Oliveira et al. (Eds.): EPIA 2019, LNAI 11805, pp. 757–768, 2019.
https://doi.org/10.1007/978-3-030-30244-3_62

In order to determine the feasibility of creating a state-of-the-art MT system for this pair of languages, we take the current best model for MT, the Transformer deep neural encoder-decoder and, using only freely available resources, experiment with three approaches to pairing source and target parallel data for training. The results we obtain show that it is possible to develop an MT system for Portuguese-Chinese with performance surpassing that of a very strong baseline consisting of an MT service, Google Translate, provided by an IT industry giant for the pair Portuguese-Chinese.

The paper is organized as follows. Section 2 presents related work on NMT, and Portuguese-Chinese NMT in particular. Section 3 describes the approaches for pairing languages during training, and Sect. 4 covers the corpora we used. Section 5 describes the NMT model and what was done to train the system. Section 6 presents the evaluation results. Finally, Sect. 7 provides concluding remarks.

2   Related Work

This Section introduces the current state-of-the-art for NMT and the existing literature on Portuguese-Chinese NMT.

2.1   Machine Translation Models

Machine Translation (MT) has been a perennial topic in Natural Language Processing since the early days of AI research. Over the years, many approaches have been attempted, from symbolic to statistical, with varying degrees of success. Recently, beginning with sequence to sequence models based on recurrent networks [10], deep neural models have become by far the most popular approach, buttressed by the availability of large amounts of training data and hardware capable of efficient parallel computation. A clear sign of this trend can be seen in the most recent Conference on Machine Translation, WMT 2018 [2], where 33 of the 38 participating systems in the News shared task used deep neural models.

All current top-performing neural MT (NMT) models employ some variant of an attention mechanism [1,7], which allows the model to assign different weights to the different words in the input sequence. The state-of-the-art approach, the Transformer model [13], relies solely on attention and completely does without the recurrent architectures of past NMT systems.

Given its state-of-the-art performance, we will use the Transformer model in this work. The model is described in Sect. 5.

2.2   Portuguese-Chinese Machine Translation

As mentioned above, most of the research on MT involves English as one of the languages, the other often being French or German, as much of the initial research targeted these pairs and subsequent studies continued the trend in order for the results obtained to be comparable.

There is very little literature on MT for the pair Portuguese-Chinese. To the best of our knowledge, for NMT in particular, only [3] and [6] address this pair. In both cases, the authors are presenting a new parallel corpus and a system is trained in order to assess the quality of the data and show that it is feasible to use it to train a NMT system. Since both works use different test sets, their results are hardly comparable and do not allow us to establish an expected performance score for the state-of-the-art of Portuguese-Chinese NMT. Nonetheless, we return to these publications in Sect. 6 when discussing our results.

3 Approaches to Training

Given that the Transformer is currently the uncontested state-of-the-art model, what remains to determine the feasibility of creating an MT system for the pair Portuguese-Chinese is how to best use the available resources. This Section describes three approaches to how existing parallel data can be used in training.

3.1 Using a Model for Each Source-Target Language Pair

The most straightforward solution for creating an MT system for a set of languages is to use a parallel corpus for each pair of languages.

In the particular case of the current study, a Portuguese-Chinese parallel corpus would allow us to create two models, one for each translation direction, that is a PT $\rightarrow$ ZH model and a ZH $\rightarrow$ PT model.

One might expect this approach to yield the best performance, as we are training separate models, each specific to a language pair and direction. The greatest disadvantages of this approach are that the number of models that are required grows quadratically with the number of languages, which is not an issue in this study, and that for some language pairs there is little parallel data available.

3.2 Using a Pivot Language

For some pairs of languages there are few available parallel corpora. In such cases it might be more advantageous for the translation to go through an intermediate third language, the *pivot* language (p), in a two-step process, as there might be more data available for the source-pivot and pivot-target pairs.

In the particular case of the current study, four models are required, two for each translation direction.[1] The PT $\rightarrow$ p $\rightarrow$ ZH direction requires models for PT $\rightarrow$ p and p $\rightarrow$ ZH, while the ZH $\rightarrow$ p $\rightarrow$ PT direction requires models for ZH $\rightarrow$ p and p $\rightarrow$ PT.

This approach allows using more training data, but this data may be more heterogeneous since it will originate from unrelated parallel corpora, and the

---

[1] If creating an MT system for many languages, this approach only requires two models per language; a much lower number than when using a model for each language pair.

⟨pt⟩ The quick brown fox jumps over the lazy dog *(translate to Portuguese)*
⟨zh⟩ The quick brown fox jumps over the lazy dog *(translate to Chinese)*

Fig. 1. Tagging the source sentence with the target language in the corpora for the many-to-many approach

two-step process is likely to introduce detrimental translation errors in the intermediate step. Experiments need to be carried out to assess whether the increase in training data is enough to mitigate or even overcome the problematic issues.

3.3   Using a Single Model for All Pairs (Many-to-Many)

Another approach that can be attempted is to gather all available parallel data into a single corpus. This approach draws its motivation from zero-shot translation [4], which revealed that any parallel data where the source language has been seen on the source side is useful for training and, likewise, any parallel data where the target language has been seen on the target side is also useful.

Using the language pairs mentioned in the above examples, this would mean gathering in a single corpus all the parallel data for PT-ZH, ZH-PT, PT-p, ZH-p, p-PT and p-ZH.

While at first blush this may seem complicated to manage, the way it is made to work is actually quite simple. For all source-target sentence pairs, the source sentence is prefixed with a special token indicating the language of the corresponding target sentence. After the model is trained, and when a sentence is to be translated, one needs only prefix that sentence with the special token for the desired target language, as exemplified in Fig. 1.

This approach greatly increases the amount of data that can be used for training and yields a *single model* that is able to translate from any of the languages that have been seen as source to any of the languages that have been seen as target, which provides much flexibility in its use. On the flip side, the model has to contend with what is presumably a much more difficult task, which might decrease its performance, and the large amounts of data will have a negative impact on the model training time.

4   The Corpora

As mentioned in Sect. 2, there has been very little work done on NMT for the pair Portuguese-Chinese, and the publications that exist ([3] and [6]) are geared towards presenting the parallel corpora that the authors had created rather than achieving good translation performance. Therefore, each one uses different corpora for training, development and evaluation, which makes the results of those systems non comparable.

In the present work, in order to allow future comparisons, we resort to News Commentary V11, a well known corpus with good quality, non-trivial translations, which is part of the OPUS collection of corpora [12]. This corpus exists

Table 1. Corpora (UM-PCorpus) for the direct approach

Domain	Sent.
News	146,095
Legal	173,420
Subtitles	250,000
Technology	250,000
General	250,000
Total	1,069,515

for multiple pairs of language, though the textual content for a pair does not overlap with the textual content for other pairs. We take the first 1000 sentences for the PT-ZH pair as the test set for evaluation.

4.1 Corpora for the Direct Approach

In order to address the lack of quality corpora for translation between Portuguese and Chinese, both [3] and [6] created new corpora. Of these, only the UM-PCorpus [3] has been made publicly available, and only partially so, as the corpus is reported to have 6 million sentences but the authors only release 1 million of them. Still, this portion of UM-PCorpus is currently the largest publicly available parallel corpus with acceptable quality for the creation of Portuguese-Chinese MT systems, and the one that we will use for the direct approach.

The released portion of UM-PCorpus is comprised of 1 million sentences from news, legal, subtitles, technology and general domains. A detailed breakdown of the number of sentences in each domain is given in Table 1, showing a rather balanced distribution of sentences over the various domains. Alongside this corpus, meant for training, the authors also make available an extra 5000 sentences for testing, 1000 from each domain. Since we have already established News Commentary V11 PT-ZH to be the test set, we set these 5000 sentences apart to use as a development set.

4.2 Corpora for the Pivot Approach

When opting for the pivot approach, the rationale is to take advantage of the fact of there being more training data available in the source-pivot and pivot-target pairs separately than there is for the source-target pair alone.

Not surprisingly, we use English (EN) as the pivot language, as there are several parallel corpora between English and both Portuguese and Chinese that are of good quality and of large enough size to support training MT systems.

Parallel corpora for Chinese-English is abundant. We resort to the OPUS [12] collection of corpora, from where we gather close to 10 million parallel sentences for the ZH-EN pair, to which we add an additional 2.2 million sentences from the UM-Corpus [11].[2]

---

[2] UM-Corpus [11], for ZH-EN, and UM-PCorpus [3], for ZH-PT, should not be confused.

Table 2. Corpora for the pivot approach

(a) ZH-EN pair

Corpus (domain)	Sent.
News Commentary V11 (News)	0.07M
Tanzil (Religious)	0.19M
UM-Corpus (Various)	2.22M
MultiUN (UN translations)	9.56M
total	12.04M

(b) PT-EN pair

Corpus (domain)	Sent.
Tanzil (Religious)	0.1M
JRC-Acquis (Law)	1.6M
Europarl (EU Parliament)	2.0M
Paracrawl V3 (Web crawl)	3.3M
total	7.0M

Corpora for Portuguese-English is not as abundant. By again resorting to OPUS we were able to gather close to 4 million parallel sentences for the PT-EN pair, which we extend with 3.3 million sentences from version 3 of Paracrawl.[3]

The Paracrawl corpus results from a Web crawl. Consequently, its quality is not the best, and some clean-up and filtering were needed before the sentences could be added to the corpus. The sentences in Paracrawl are annotated with extra information that we use to guide the filtering. Our filtering criteria removed all sentence pairs where: (i) either sentence was shorter than 3 tokens; (ii) sentences had arabic numerals that did not match; (iii) both sentences were equal; (iv) either sentence had only numbers or symbols; and (v) where the length ratio between the sentences was larger than 3:2.

Table 2 gives a more detailed breakdown of the constituent parts of the training corpora used in the pivot approach.

For development, 5000 sentences of News Commentary V11 PT-EN were used for the PT-EN pair and the UM-Corpus test set, with also 5000 sentences, was used for the ZH-EN pair.

4.3 Corpora for the Many-to-Many Approach

For this approach, we gather in a single corpus all of the parallel corpora used for the two other approaches, that is the 1 million sentences of PT-ZH used in direct approach, and the two corpora used in the pivot approach, namely 7 million sentences of PT-EN and 12 million sentences of ZH-EN.

Note that, in the many-to-many approach, each parallel corpus can contribute to training twice, once for each translation direction. For instance, the 1 million sentences of PT-ZH can be used as an additional 1 million sentences of ZH-PT data. This results in a corpus of 40 million sentences, which turned out to be such a large amount of data as to make training unfeasible. To overcome this, we halved the amount of data.[4] For each parallel corpora, odd numbered lines are used for one translation direction while even numbered lines are used for the other translation direction (cf. Table 3), resulting in a parallel corpus with 20 million sentences, where all the sentences available to us still occur in some translation direction.

---

[3] https://paracrawl.eu/.

[4] Despite this 50% reduction in the size of the corpus, training the many-to-many model took around 808 GPU hours (more than 33 days) to converge.

Table 3. Corpora for the many-to-many approach

	$p \to$ PT	$p \to$ ZH	$p \to$ EN
PT $\to p$	—	0.5M (Even)	3.5M (Odd)
ZH $\to p$	0.5M (Odd)	—	6.0M (Even)
EN $\to p$	3.5M (Even)	6.0M (Odd)	—

5   The NMT System

This Section describes the NMT architecture, implementation framework and pre-processing steps, which were common to all approaches.

5.1   Transformer Model

The Transformer model [13] is rather recent, but it has quickly established itself as the state-of-the-art for NMT.[5] The model still follows the standard deep encoder-decoder architecture to learn a mapping between a source sequence and a target sequence. Its main innovation is in how it relies only on multiple heads of attention [1,7] and self-attention, without any of the recurrent modules of previous architectures. A high level overview of the model is shown in Fig. 2.

As per usual in neural approaches to text processing, the symbols in the source and target sequences are represented in an embedding space. Since the Transformer does not use a recurrent mechanism, information about the position of the symbols in the sequences is explicitly added through sinusoidal positional embeddings (not shown in the Figure).

The source and target sequences are then fed to a stack of encoder and decoder blocks (6 of each, in the Figure), which is the common procedure in all deep encoder-decoder architectures. These blocks begin by applying multi-head self-attention to their inputs (8 heads, in the Figure), concatenating the output of each head and running the result through a feed forward layer. Note that, for the decoder blocks, self-attention is masked in order to hide the symbols that occur after the symbol currently being predicted. For each decoder block, there is an additional multi-head attention component, this one weighing the output states of the corresponding encoder block. The output of the final decoder block is fed to linear and softmax layers in order to predict the output symbol.

The Transformer paper [13] presents variations of hyper-parameters for the model. We use the hyper-parameters of the "base" variant, with 6 encoder and decoder layers, 8 attention heads and an embedding dimension of 512. The models are trained until they converge, which is determined using a cross-entropy patience of 10 on the development corpus. That is, training stops after 10 iterations, of 5000 update steps each, with no improvement to cross-entropy.

---

[5] In the most recent WMT 2018 [2], 33 of the 38 systems used deep neural models, and 29 of these 33 were based on the Transformer model.

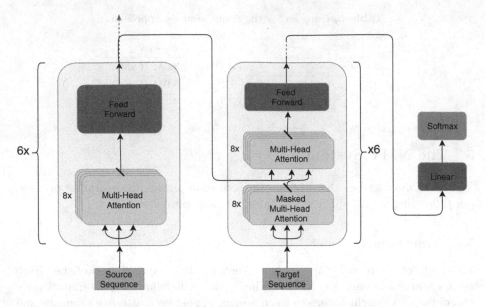

Fig. 2. The transformer - model architecture.

5.2   Training the System

To implement the system, we use the Transformer implementation that is part of the Marian framework [5], which offers an efficient runtime, good documentation and an easy API with which we built an online translation service.[6] Training was performed on a single Nvidia Tesla K40m GPU.

All data is pre-processed before being fed to the model. The pre-processing steps consist of tokenization/segmentation and sub-word vocabulary creation.

Chinese sentences were segmented using Jieba[7] and both Portuguese and English sentences were tokenized using the sacremoses[8] implementation of the Moses tokenizer.

Current NMT systems do not process texts at the word level. Since NMT models have a finite vocabulary, working at the level of words would mean that eventually the model would be faced with words that it has not encountered before, be them rare terms, neologisms or misspellings. These are known as out-of-vocabulary (OOV) words, and they have a negative impact on performance. To tackle this problem, words are split into sub-word sequences. This sub-word vocabulary is built in such a way that, for any input word, there is always some sequence of sub-words that forms the input word [9], thus eliminating the possibility of occurrence of OOV symbols while maintaining a finite vocabulary,

---

[6] https://portulanclarin.net/workbench/lx/translator.

[7] https://github.com/fxsjy/jieba.

[8] https://github.com/alvations/sacremoses.

Table 4. BLEU evaluation scores

Model	ZH → PT	PT → ZH
Google Translate	12.23	13.69
Our systems		
direct	13.38	10.72
pivot	17.79	14.84
many-to-many	14.04	11.99

at the cost of increasing the length of the sequences. For all models, a vocabulary of 32,000 sub-words was created using the implementation[9] from [9].

6 Results

This Section summarizes and discusses the results achieved in the work described in this paper. All translation quality scores are reported using the BLEU [8] metric implemented by the multi-bleu.perl script in Moses. Recall that the test corpus we use for all experiments corresponds to the first 1000 sentences from News Commentary V11 PT-ZH. The results are summarized in Table 4.

As mentioned in Sect. 2, the only other works on Portuguese-Chinese NMT are [3] and [6]. The authors of the former release a test set, which provides some common ground on which to perform a comparison, but only part (1 million out of 6 million sentences) of the training corpus they used is made available. The authors of the latter do not release the system or the corpus, making it unfeasible to compare their results to ours.

To have a competing system that we could run on the News Commentary V11 PT-ZH test set, we resorted to a popular online translation services, Google Translate.[10] To run these tests, we used an option that allows submitting to the service a file to be translated, taking care to split the work into batches as there is an unstated limit on the size of the text that the service accepts.

Google Translate is a proprietary system, but existing publications point towards it also using deep NMT, and likely a many-to-many approach [4]. Also, given the resources available to Google, it is reasonable to expect their system to have good performance and set a competitive baseline.

Evaluating the output of Google Translate raises an issue that is specific to the PT → ZH translation direction. The BLEU metric takes into account the n-gram overlap between the automatic and the reference translation, but the output of the system, being Chinese, does not separate words with whitespace. As such, it has to be segmented prior to evaluation. For this, we again use the Jieba tool, the same used for pre-processing data for our models (cf. Sect. 5.2).

---

[9] https://github.com/rsennrich/subword-nmt.
[10] https://translate.google.com/.

6.1   Direct Approach

Our direct approach gets better results than Google Translate on ZH → PT (13.38 vs. 12.23) but a worse score on PT → ZH (10.72 vs. 13.69).

Our results suggest that, when having a single parallel corpus in a direct approach, where the models are trained on the same amount of data for each direction, the PT → ZH direction performs worse than the ZH → PT direction. This is supported by the two other studies in Portuguese-Chinese NMT, namely [3] and [6], which find the same trend using different corpora and NMT systems.

Google Translate likely uses a many-to-many approach [4], and the fact that the PT → ZH direction outperforms the ZH → PT direction can be explained by there being more parallel data available where Chinese is one of the languages in the pair than there is parallel data involving Portuguese.

6.2   Pivot Approach

The results we obtained for the pivot approach corroborate the assumption that, given enough data, going through a pivot language, even if doing so introduces errors in the intermediate step, can outperform a direct approach trained with fewer data. Our system, when using the pivot approach, clearly outperform the direct approach and the Google Translate baseline on either direction, achieving a score of 17.79 for ZH → PT, against the 13.38 of the direct approach and the 12.23 of Google Translate, and 14.84 for ZH → PT, against the 10.72 of the direct approach and the 13.69 of Google Translate.

We find a similar experiment in [6], where the authors also compared a direct approach, using their (unreleased) parallel corpus, with doing a pivot approach using a greater amount of data. The results obtained, however, show the direct approach performing better than the pivot approach. This mismatch between their findings and ours can be explained by the amount of data that was used in each of the two steps of the pivot approach. For the direct approach, [6] use a corpus with nearly 1 million sentences, which is of similar size to the one we use. For the pivot approach, they use 25 million sentences for ZH-EN, which is quite larger than the 12 million we use in our work, but their corpus for PT-EN has only 2 million sentences, while ours has 7 million. The pivot approach relies on both steps having good performance, and in [6] there is not enough data for the PT-EN pair to ensure a good translation quality for the whole two-step process.

6.3   Many-to-Many Approach

Finally, the last experiment served to assess whether it was feasible to achieve good performance with the many-to-many approach given the amount of data that we used for training.

The results we obtained place the performance of the many-to-many approach between that of the direct approach and that of the pivot approach, for either direction, and above that of the Google Translate baseline for ZH → PT.

These results again highlight the extent to which neural models rely on large amounts of data to obtain good performance. The many-to-many approach gives us a single model can translate in any direction between Portuguese and Chinese (and also English, though we have not evaluated that), with better performance than that of the two direction-specific models of the direct approach. It is unable, however, to reach the performance of the pivot approach, but we believe this to be due to us having had to halve the amount of data used in training.

Although the pivot approach has to go through a presumably noisy intermediate step, its models have been trained over 7 million sentences where Portuguese is either source (PT $\rightarrow$ EN) or target (EN $\rightarrow$ PT), and 12 million sentences where Chinese is either source (ZH $\rightarrow$ EN) or target (EN $\rightarrow$ ZH); while in the many-to-many approach the amount of data for each language is much smaller (cf. Table 3).

7   Conclusion

This paper presented a study on the feasibility of creating a state-of-the-art NMT system for Portuguese-Chinese using only freely available resources. Using the state-of-the-art Transformer model, we experimented with three approaches to pairing source and target parallel data for training the system. These are (i) the direct approach, using a model for each source-target language pair; (ii) the pivot approach, translating through an intermediate language for which there is more data available; and (iii) the many-to-many approach, using a single model, trained on all available data, that can translate from any language seen as source to any language seen as target. We compare our systems against Google Translate, which we outperform when using the pivot approach for both directions, and when using the direct and many-to-many approaches for the ZH $\rightarrow$ PT direction.

The pivot approach had the best performance, but it is reasonable to expect that the many-to-many approach, given enough computational power, will be able to surpass it, as it can always make use of more data than the other two approaches since any parallel corpora where a language occurs either on the source/target sides can be used in the training of a many-to-many model that is able to translate from/to that language.

For future work, and still in keeping with the rationale of using only freely available resources, we will experiment with augmenting the training data, for all three approaches, with backtranslated monolingual texts.

An online service demonstrating the system, as well as its supporting model, may be found at https://portulanclarin.net/workbench/lx/translator.

Acknowledgements. The research results presented here were supported by FCT—Foundation for Science and Technology of Portugal, MOST—Ministry of Science and Technology of China, through the project Chinese-Portuguese Deep Machine Translation in eCommerce Domain (441.00 CHINA-BILATERAL), the PORTULAN CLARIN Infrastructure for the Science and Technology of Language, the National Infrastructure for Distributed Computing (INCD) of Portugal, and the ANI/3279/2016 grant.

Deyi Xiong was supported by National Natural Science Foundation of China (Grants No. 61622209 and 61861130364).

References

1. Bahdanau, D., Cho, K., Bengio, Y.: Neural machine translation by jointly learning to align and translate. In: Proceedings of the International Conference on Learning Representations (ICLR) (2015). arXiv preprint arXiv:1409.0473
2. Bojar, O., et al.: Findings of the 2018 conference on machine translation (WMT18). In: Proceedings of the Third Conference on Machine Translation, Volume 2: Shared Task Papers, pp. 272–307 (2018)
3. Chao, L.S., Wong, D.F., Ao, C.H., Leal, A.L.: UM-PCorpus: a large Portuguese-Chinese parallel corpus. In: Proceedings of the LREC 2018 Workshop "Belt & Road: Language Resources and Evaluation", pp. 38–43 (2018)
4. Johnson, M., et al.: Google's multilingual neural machine translation system: enabling zero-shot translation. Trans. Assoc. Comput. Linguist. **5**, 339–351 (2017)
5. Junczys-Dowmunt, M., et al.: Marian: fast neural machine translation in C++. In: Proceedings of ACL 2018, System Demonstrations, pp. 116–121 (2018)
6. Liu, S., Wang, L., Liu, C.H.: Chinese-Portuguese machine translation: a study on building parallel corpora from comparable texts. In: Proceedings of the Eleventh International Conference on Language Resources and Evaluation (LREC 2018), pp. 1485–1492 (2018)
7. Luong, M.T., Pham, H., Manning, C.D.: Effective approaches to attention-based neural machine translation. In: Proceedings of the 2015 Conference on Empirical Methods in Natural Language Processing, pp. 1412–1421 (2015)
8. Papineni, K., Roukos, S., Ward, T., Zhu, W.J.: BLEU: a method for automatic evaluation of machine translation. In: Proceedings of the 40th Annual Meeting of the Association for Computational Linguistics, pp. 311–318 (2002)
9. Sennrich, R., Haddow, B., Birch, A.: Neural machine translation of rare words with subword units. In: Proceedings of the 54th Annual Meeting of the Association for Computational Linguistics (Volume 1: Long Papers), pp. 1715–1725 (2016)
10. Sutskever, I., Vinyals, O., Le, Q.V.: Sequence to sequence learning with neural networks. In: Neural Information Processing Systems, pp. 3104–3112 (2014)
11. Tian, L., Wong, D.F., Chao, L.S., Quaresma, P., Oliveira, F., Yi, L.: UM-Corpus: a large English-Chinese parallel corpus for statistical machine translation. In: Proceedings of the Ninth International Conference on Language Resources and Evaluation (LREC 2014), pp. 1837–1842 (2014)
12. Tiedemann, J.: Parallel data, tools and interfaces in OPUS. In: Proceedings of the Eight International Conference on Language Resources and Evaluation (LREC 2012), pp. 2214–2218 (2012)
13. Vaswani, A., et al.: Attention is all you need. In: Neural Information Processing Systems, pp. 5998–6008 (2017)

Using Recurrent Neural Networks
for Toponym Resolution in Text

Ana Bárbara Cardoso[1]([✉]), Bruno Martins[1], and Jacinto Estima[2]

[1] INESC-ID and Instituto Superior Técnico, Lisbon, Portugal
barbara.inacio@tecnico.ulisboa.pt, bruno.g.martins@ist.utl.pt
[2] INESC-ID and Instituto Politécnico de Setúbal, Lisbon, Portugal
jacinto.estima@gmail.com

Abstract. Toponym resolution refers to the disambiguation of place names and other references to places present in textual documents, resolving them to unambiguous geographical identifiers (e.g., geographic coordinates of latitude and longitude). One of the major challenges in this task is that, usually, place names are highly ambiguous (e.g., there are several locations on the surface of the Earth that share the same name). In this paper, we propose to address the task through a recurrent neural network architecture with multiple inputs and outputs, specifically leveraging pre-trained contextual embeddings (ELMo) and bi-directional Long Short-Term Memory (LSTM) units, both commonly used for textual data modeling. The proposed model was tested on two datasets that were previously used to evaluate toponym resolution systems, namely the *War of the Rebellion* and the *Local-Global Lexicon* corpora. The obtained results outperform state-of-the-art results, confirming the superiority of the proposed method over other previous approaches.

Keywords: Toponym resolution · Place reference disambiguation ·
Deep learning · Recurrent neural networks · ELMo word embeddings

1 Introduction

Toponym resolution consists in the disambiguation of place references given over textual documents, so that each reference can be associated with a unique geographic location on the surface of the Earth. The process of place reference resolution has some inherent challenges, since toponyms are often ambiguous. We can distinguish three types of ambiguities that should be addressed when resolving place references in the text [19]: (1) geo/geo ambiguity, which occurs when the same place name can refer to multiple distinct locations (e.g., the name *Dallas* can be associated with either *Dallas, Texas, United States*, or with *Dallas County, Alabama, United States*); (2) geo/non-geo ambiguity, which emerges when places are named after persons or using common nouns (i.e., when a location and a non-location share the same name; for example, the word *Charlotte* can refer to a person name or to the location of *Charlotte County, Virginia*,

© Springer Nature Switzerland AG 2019
P. Moura Oliveira et al. (Eds.): EPIA 2019, LNAI 11805, pp. 769–780, 2019.
https://doi.org/10.1007/978-3-030-30244-3_63

United States); and, (3) reference ambiguity, which corresponds to when there are multiple names referring to the same place (e.g., *Big Apple* is a nickname commonly used to refer to *New York City, New York, United States*). Problem (2) should be addressed when identifying place references in textual documents, whereas Problems (1) and (3) should be addressed when attempting to unambiguously associate the recognized references to physical locations (e.g., to geospatial coordinates of latitude and longitude).

There are several possible applications relying on the results from place reference resolution, including the improvement of search engine results (e.g., by geographical indexing or ranking), as well as the classification of documents according to spatial criteria. Place reference resolution can also allow the clustering of documents into meaningful groups, or map-based visualizations of information encoded textually [19]. Another possible application is content analysis in areas such as the computational social sciences or the digital humanities [24], for example, supporting the automatic processing and analysis of geographic data encoded over large collections of textual documents (i.e., primary sources in the humanities). In addition, toponym resolution can serve as an auxiliary component for complete document geolocation [18], since toponyms can give hints about the overall document location.

Most of the previously developed systems were based on the use of heuristics (e.g., population density), relying on an external knowledge database to decide which location is more likely to correspond to the reference (i.e., place references in the text are first compared against similar entries in a gazetteer [3,17], and highly populated places are preferred given that they are more likely to be used in textual documents) [2,14]. Other studies used supervised approaches that include these types of heuristics as features in standard machine learning techniques [8, 13,15,21]. More recent methods explore the use of deep learning techniques, which that have yielded state-of-the-art results [1,11].

This article proposes a novel deep learning method for toponym resolution, corresponding to a neural model that combines multiple inputs, with two outputs and loss functions for classification and regression. Our model uses a Recurrent Neural Networks (RNN) architecture to model textual data, namely by combining pre-trained contextual word embeddings (ELMo, embeddings from language models [20]) with Long Short-Term Memory (LSTM) units.

We use the Hierarchical Equal Area isoLatitude Pixelisation (HEALPix) [10] method to model toponym resolution as a classification task. This algorithm performs a recursive partitioning of a spherical representation for the surface of the Earth, producing partitioning regions of equal-area. The proposed neural model predicts which HEALPix region concerns the place reference. Subsequently, we use the result of the classification into regions to inform and improve the prediction of geographic coordinates for each place reference, through a separate layer that directly applies the great circle distance as a loss function. This second layer produces the final result of the toponym resolution model.

We conducted experiments on two distinct corpora, both used to evaluate previously developed systems, namely the *War of the Rebellion* and the *Local-Global*

Lexicon corpora. The results achieved by our model show a clear superiority over previous studies that, at the time, demonstrated state-of-the-art results.

The rest of this paper is organized as follows: Sect. 2 presents relevant related work previously developed in this field. Section 3 describes the proposed model. Section 4 details the experimental evaluation, including the datasets that were used, the evaluation methodology, and the obtained results. Finally, Sect. 5 presents our conclusions and possible directions for future work.

2   Related Work

Gritta et al. [11] introduced a toponym resolution system, named *CamCoder*, that attempts to disambiguate location mentions by first discovering lexical clues, considering the word context surrounding location mentions. The authors introduced a sparse vector representation named *MapVec* to code the prior geographic distribution of locations (i.e., based on the coordinates of the locations and the population count). The available spatial data is projected into a 2D world map, which is then reshaped into a 1D feature vector corresponding to the *MapVec*. This allows the authors to encode additional information about spatial knowledge, normally ignored in other similar studies [11]. The *CamCoder* system combines lexical and geographic information (i.e., *MapVec*), considering four inputs: the context words (without the location mentions), the location mentions (excluding the context words), the target entity to disambiguate, and finally the feature vector corresponding to *MapVec*. The first three inputs are fed into separate convolutional layers with global maximum pooling, for detecting location-indicative words from among the context words. The fourth input is only fed into a fully dense layer, combining it with the other three inputs after the global maximum pooling. In the final layer, the system predicts a location based on a classification into regions defined by a geographic grid on the surface of the Earth. Overall, *CamCoder* is a robust model that presents state-of-art results when compared with other models tested under the same circumstances. This approach enables the consideration of geographic factors beyond lexical clues to improve the performance of toponym resolution [11].

Adams and McKenzie [1] proposed a character-level convolutional neural network model for geocoding multilingual text using any type of character set represented by the UTF-8 encoding. The proposed character level CNN uses three main transformation functions. The model receives as input a sequence of characters, each encoded as a one-hot vector, and then it passes this input trough a series of temporal convolution and temporal maximum pooling operations. Then, multiple linear transformations are applied to the result. Finally, the output layer predicts the region classification, using equal-area grid cells representing the surface of the Earth. One of the main benefits of using an approach based on character level CNNs is language independence, given that this method requires little data pre-processing operations. The authors nonetheless verified that the model did not have the best results when characters with diacritics were used, and individual words are sometimes good geographic indicators [1].

Karimzadeh et al. developed the GeoTXT geocoder [13], which offers a flexible application programming interface (API) for extracting and disambiguating toponyms in small textual documents, such as Twitter messages. GeoTXT uses standard named entity recognition tools for identifying place references, afterwards focusing on disambiguating these results. In the toponym resolution stage, for each recognized place name, the system retrieves, from a gazetteer, a ranked list of the candidate locations to the mention. This list is ranked by a combination of feature scores, including indicators and weights for independent political entities, administrative divisions, populated places, continents, regions, or point-of-interest types (e.g., buildings, schools, airports, etc.), among others [13]. Besides the options that were previously described, the system also offers the possibility of incorporating additional disambiguation mechanisms that take into account the co-occurrence of toponyms. Two such mechanisms are based on hierarchical relationships between toponyms (i.e., if two toponyms share the same containment geographic space), either applied to immediately consecutive place names (e.g., pairs consisting of *city, state*) or applied to toponyms that appear separately in the text. A third mechanism is based on spatial proximity. This last method aims to minimize the average distance between the predicted toponym location and the location for toponyms that co-occur in the text.

DeLozier et al. developed a prototype system [4] with the goal of addressing the limitations brought by the recurrent need to rely on external gazetteers when performing the task of toponym resolution. Most of these resources are incomplete, and therefore the systems that rely on them are sometimes unable to deal with unknown place names or locations. The developed system, named *TopoCluster*, aims to address this issue by modelling the geographical distribution of each word appearing in a given text (i.e., recent models showed that there are certain words with the property of being geographically indicative, so the authors used spatial statistics over multiple geo-referenced language models in order to create geographic clusters for every word). *TopoCluster* derives a smoothed geographic likelihood for each word present in the vocabulary and computes the strongest geographic point where the toponym and the context word clusters overlap. According to the authors, the most problematic words to classify were demonyms. The results show that, through the proposed approach, it is possible to obtain superior results without recurring to gazetteers. In particular, gazetteer independent models were shown to perform well on corpora based on international news, and also on historical corpora [4].

In a more recent work, DeLozier et al. [5] presented the process of annotating an historical corpus created by the authors, namely the *War of the Rebellion* (WOTR) corpus containing documents dating from the U.S. civil war. The performance of existing toponym resolution systems was evaluated on this corpus. Other corpora were also tested to compare the results, and it was concluded that the WOTR corpus was the most difficult of the ones that were surveyed, e.g. with lower scores than those obtained over the *Local-Global Lexicon* (LGL) corpus (the second most difficult corpus) from Lieberman et al. [16]. LGL was, in fact, constructed from small, geographically distributed newspapers articles,

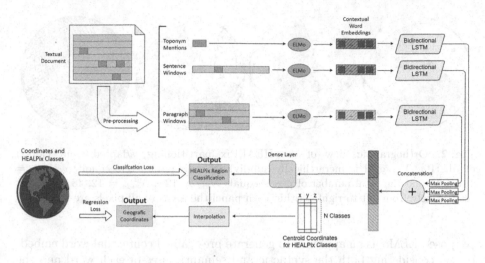

Fig. 1. Architecture of the proposed recurrent neural network model.

deliberately choosen to present difficult challenges to toponym resolution systems [16]. In Sect. 4.1, we describe in more detail the specifications for both the WOTR and LGL corpora, which were used in our experiments.

3   The Proposed Model Architecture

Our toponym resolution method receives, as input, documents with annotated place references (i.e., a separate entity recognition model, not covered in the present publication, is used to recognize place names in the text). A model based on recurrent neural networks takes three inputs from each place reference recognized in the text: (1) the place mention itself; (2) the words around the mention (i.e., a fixed window size, to the left and right sides of the focus span of the text with the toponym, totaling 50 words); and, (3) a paragraph text, also defined by a fixed window size of larger dimensions (i.e., a total of 500 words), so it can capture the text around the sentence where the toponym occurs.

When feeding the neural network with the paragraph of the mention, we are considering the general context of the document. By considering also a smaller textual window where the mention is present, we are taking into account the context closest to the entity. Other toponyms, or even common language words appearing in the surrounding text, can be characteristic of certain regions, which might provide clues about the location of the mention.

First, it is necessary to pre-process the text of the document in order to retrieve the above mentioned three textual elements that are provided to the neural network as input. Then, we apply the ELMo text representation model [20], pre-trained on a large dump of the English Wikipedia, to obtain a sequence of embeddings vectors that represent the words of each element. Petters et al.

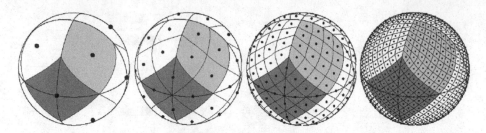

Fig. 2. Orthographic view of the HEALPix partitioning, adapted from Gorski et al. [10]. The grid is hierarchically subdivided with parameters equal to $N_{side} = 1, 2, 4, 8$, and the total number of pixels equals $N_{pix} = 12 \times N_{side}^2 = 12, 48, 192, 768$, respectively from left to right. Within each panel the areas of all pixels are identical.

proposed ELMo as an approach to generate pre-trained contextual word embeddings, considering both the syntactic and semantic uses of each word and the word use in different linguistic contexts (i.e., polysemy). The text representations produced by ELMo are composed by all the internal states of a bi-directional neural language model based on Long Short-Term Memory (LSTM) networks, where the context of the language model is extracted from left-to-right and right-to-left. The contextual representation of each token is obtained by concatenating the results from a left-to-right LSTM and a right-to-left LSTM that are independently trained to generate the representations [20].

Each one of the embedding vectors, from each of the three inputs, is provided to a separate bi-directional LSTM layer, for the purpose of modeling the word sequences. In this case, we apply the penalized hyperbolic tangent activation function in the LSTM nodes, as suggested by Eger et al. [7]. The penalized hyperbolic tangent is an improvement of the hyperbolic tangent activation function, which has been shown to achieve superior results in a variety of NLP tasks.

In brief, a LSTM module is recursively defined by a function R that receives a previous state vector as input h_{j-1}, along with the input vector of the current state x_j, and returns a new state vector h_j, as shown in Eq. 1 [9].

$$
\begin{aligned}
h_j &= o \odot \tanh(c_j) \\
\text{where,} \quad c_j &= f \odot c_{j-1} + i \odot z \\
i &= \sigma(x_j W^{xi} + h_{j-1} W^{hi}) \\
f &= \sigma(x_j W^{xf} + h_{j-1} W^{hf}) \\
o &= \sigma(x_j W^{xo} + h_{j-1} W^{ho}) \\
z &= \tanh(x_j W^{xz} + h_{j-1} W^{hz})
\end{aligned}
\tag{1}
$$

A bi-directional LSTM is composed by two LSTM modules, one that reads the input sequence from left to right and another that reads from right to left. This allows the output to be informed simultaneously by past (backward) and future (forward) states [9]. To summarize the results of processing input sequences with a biLSTM, we can use a maximum pooling operation, transforming the sequence of output states into a single vector.

In our complete model, we concatenate the resulting representations (i.e., the results of maximum pooling operations over the biLSTMs that process each of the three inputs), using this to predict the HEALPix class (first output) that corresponds to the mention, through a layer in the neural network that leverages the softmax activation function.

The HEALPix framework was proposed by Gorski et al. [10] to generate a partitioning from the surface of a sphere into cells of equal area, corresponding to different regions on the Earth's surface. The partitioning is performed hierarchically through a recursive subdivision of the cells, until the desired resolution level. Figure 2 shows the division of the HEALPix regions projected on a sphere, where it is possible to verify that the cell resolution is flexible. Throughout all experiments, we fixed the resolution $N_{side} = 256$ when calculating the HEALPix regions, which is equivalent to considering a maximum of 786432 regions (N_{pix}). In practice, the number of classes will be much smaller, given that most regions will not be associated to any data instance.

The softmax class probabilities for the HEALPix regions are also used to estimate the corresponding geographic coordinates (second and final output), through an interpolation computed from the class probability vector and a class centroid coordinate matrix (i.e., we initially build a matrix with the different classes present in the corpora, where each line represents the geographical coordinates of the class centroid, in a cartesian (x, y, z) format).

The softmax probability distribution is first raised to the power of 3 and then re-normalized, resulting in a more peaked probability distribution. The result is multiplied by the matrix with the centroids, resulting in a prediction for the geospatial coordinates. Our complete model is represented in Fig. 1.

When training, we use a regression loss based on the great circle distance (i.e., to calculate the distance between two points, namely the predicted point and the real point, on the surface of the Earth) for the output corresponding to the coordinates. For the region classification output, we use the standard cross-entropy categorical loss. We use the Adam optimization algorithm with a Cyclical Learning Rate (CLR) [22] policy, adjusting the learning rate throughout the training process, with basis on a cycle between a lower bound of 0.00001 and an upper bound of 0.0001. We also used early stopping during the training of the model, i.e. a form of regularization used to avoid overfitting when training. The training is interrupted once the model performance stops improving and, in our case, we stopped when the combined loss over the training data did not improve for 5 consecutive epochs.

4   Experimental Evaluation

This section presents the corpora that were used to support the experimental evaluation of the proposed model. In this section we also present the metrics used to analyze the results and, finally, we discuss the obtained results, in comparison with the results reported for previous model proposals.

Table 1. Statistical characterization of the corpora used in our experiments.

Statistic	WOTR	LGL
Number of documents	1644	588
Number of location references	10377	4462
Average location references per document	6.3	7.6
Average tokens per document	246	325
Average sentence per document	12.7	16.1
Vocabulary size	13386	16518
Metonyms as locations	No	Yes
Demonyms as locations	No	Yes

4.1 Datasets and Evaluation Methodology

In order to conduct experiments with the proposed model, we opted to use two well known ans publicly available datasets from previous studies in the area [2,4,5,11,12], namely the *War of Rebellion* (WOTR) corpus [5] and the *Local-Global Lexicon* (LGL) corpus [16].

DeLozier et al. developed the WOTR corpus from historical texts collected from military archives of the American Civil War. Thus, the documents are mostly military orders, reports, and government correspondence. This corpus contains 1644 documents and 10377 annotated place references.

In turn, Lieberman et al. constructed the LGL corpus from small and geographically distributed newspaper articles. This corpus was deliberately created to introduce difficult challenges to toponym resolution systems [16], as it contains articles from small newspapers based on near places with highly ambiguous names (e.g., Paris is a highly ambiguous place name, and in this collection there are articles from The Paris News (*Paris, Texas*), The Paris Post-Intelligencer (*Paris, Tennessee*), and The Paris Beacon-News (*Paris, Illinois*). This corpus includes 588 articles collected from 78 different newspapers.

Table 1 presents a statistical characterization of the textual content in both corpora, as well as some additional information about them. Note, for example, that unlike the WOTR corpus, LGL also includes annotations of metonymic expressions and demonyms. This represents an additional challenge for the toponym disambiguation task, given that these expressions must also be resolved to geographic coordinates, despite having a different textual representation (i.e., different words) from the standard location name.

To calculate the classification regions we used the Healpy Python library[1], based on the HEALPix scheme described in the previous section. Through this library it is possible to calculate the region code knowing the latitude and longitude coordinates (specifying the resolution), and vice versa.

---

[1] http://pypi.org/project/healpy/.

To evaluate the results obtained by our model, we calculated the error between the predicted and the real coordinates, by computing the distance between these two points on the surface of the Earth. Naturally, lower error values are preferred. We used Vincenty's geodetic formulae [23] (i.e., an iterative method that calculates the smallest geographical distance between two points on the surface of the Earth, with an accuracy within 0.5 mm) to calculate the distance for each individual toponym and, from these values, it is possible to calculate the mean and the median error, as well as the Accuracy@161, i.e. a measure that reflects the percentage of errors less or equal than 161 km, and that has been widely used in previous studies. Because this threshold value corresponds to a typical distance between nearby important locations, previous studies on toponym resolution and document geolocation have started to evaluate systems considering the Accuracy@161 metric.

The results obtained on the experiemnst with the WOTR corpus were performed on the train and test splits provided by the authors of the corpus [5]. This dataset was downloaded from the respective GitHub page[2]. Regarding the results presented with the LGL corpus, we split the data using 90% of the instances (i.e., place references) for training, and the remaining 10% for testing. This dataset is available from the Milan Gritta GitHub page[3].

4.2   The Obtained Results

Tables 2 and 3 present a comparison between the results obtained with our model and previous approaches, respectively over the WOTR and the LGL corpora. We can verify that our model achieved results that significantly outperformed those of previous models with state-of-the-art results.

In the case of the WOTR corpus, our model reached the lowest mean value for the distance error, with a difference of minus 281 km compared to the second best result. We obtained a mean of 164 km, followed by GeoSem with 445 km, TopoClusterGaz with 468 km, SPIDER with 482 km, and TopoCluster with 604 km. For this dataset we could not find any previous report on of median errors. Nevertheless, we indicate the obtained median of 11.48 km.

Concerning the results over the LGL dataset, our model also recorded the lowest mean value for the error distance, resulting in a median with minus 463 km of distance when compared to the best second value. We also achieved the lowest mean error with 237 km, followed by CamCoder with 700 km, Santos et al. with 742 km, SPIDER with 1233 km, GeoTxt with 1400 km, and finally TopoCluster with 1735 km. Despite these results, there are other systems that have a better performance in relation to the median error, in the LGL corpus.

Our system also achieves impressive results in the accuracy at 161 km metric, reaching 81.5% and 86.1% accuracy in WOTR and LGL, respectively. This again corresponds to a significant improvement over state-of-the-art.

---

[2] http://github.com/utcompling/WarOfTheRebellion.

[3] http://github.com/milangritta/Pragmatic-Guide-to-Geoparsing-Evaluation/blob/master/data/Corpora/lgl.xml.

Table 2. Toponym resolution results over the WOTR corpus.

	Mean (km)	Median (km)	Acc@161km (%)
SPIDER [5]	482	–	67.1
TopoCluster [5]	604	–	57.0
TopoClusterGaz [5]	468	–	72.0
GeoSem [2]	445	–	68.0
The proposed model	164	11.48	81.5

Table 3. Toponym resolution results over the LGL corpus.

	Mean (km)	Median (km)	Acc@161km (%)
GeoTxt [11]	1400	–	68.0
CamCoder [11]	700	–	76.0
SPIDER [4]	1233	16.00	68.4
TopoCluster [4]	1735	274.00	45.5
Santos et al. [21]	742	2.79	–
The proposed model	237	12.24	86.1

5   Conclusions and Future Work

In this article, we proposed a new model for the disambiguation of place name references in textual documents. Our model was implemented upon a RNN architecture leveraging ELMo (i.e., pre-trained contextual embeddings) and bidirectional LSTM units. Only textual elements (i.e., three sequences of words corresponding to the mention, sentence and paragraph text) were provided to the model as input. Experiments were conducted on the *War of the Rebellion* corpus and on the *Local-Global Lexicon* corpus, allowing us to conclude on the superiority of the proposed method over other previous approaches.

In future work, we are considering to integrate other recent contextual embedding models for text representation, namely the results from a Bidirectional Encoder Representation from Transformers (BERT) model [6], or from the recently proposed XLNet approach [25]. Furthermore, we also intend to build new corpora from English Wikipedia dumps, i.e. from a random sample of Wikipedia articles by accessing the hyperlinks contained in each of them and extracting references that correspond to locations (i.e., spans of text to which geographic coordinates are associated). Our goal is to analyze the obtained results in a scenario where the toponym resolution model is trained with more data, at the same time also seeing if models trained on large Wikipedia datasets can generalize to other domains and maintain a high accuracy.

Acknowledgments. This research was supported through Fundação para a Ciência e Tecnologia (FCT), through the project grants with references PTDC/EEI-SCR/ 1743/2014 (Saturn), T-AP HJ-253525 (DigCH), and PTDC/CCI-CIF/32607/2017 (MIMU), as well as through the INESC-ID multi-annual funding from the PIDDAC programme (UID/CEC/50021/2019). We also gratefully acknowledge the support of NVIDIA Corporation, with the donation of two Titan Xp GPUs used in the experiments reported on the paper.

References

1. Adams, B., McKenzie, G.: Crowdsourcing the character of a place: character-level convolutional networks for multilingual geographic text classification. Trans. GIS **22**(2), 394–408 (2018)
2. Ardanuy, M.C., Sporleder, C.: Toponym disambiguation in historical documents using semantic and geographic features. In: Proceedings of the International Conference on Digital Access to Textual Cultural Heritage (2017)
3. Berman, M.L., Mostern, R., Southall, H.: Placing Names: Enriching and Integrating Gazetteers. Indiana University Press (2016)
4. DeLozier, G., Baldridge, J., London, L.: Gazetteer-independent toponym resolution using geographic word profiles. In: Proceedings of the AAAI Conference on Artificial Intelligence (2015)
5. DeLozier, G., Wing, B.P., Baldridge, J., Nesbit, S.: Creating a novel geolocation corpus from historical texts. In: Proceedings of the Linguistic Annotation Workshop Held in Conjunction with the ACL Conference (2016)
6. Devlin, J., Chang, M.W., Lee, K., Toutanova, K.: BERT: pre-training of deep bidirectional transformers for language understanding. CoRR abs/1810.04805 (2018)
7. Eger, S., Youssef, P., Gurevych, I.: Is it time to swish? Comparing deep learning activation functions across NLP tasks. In: Proceedings of the Conference on Empirical Methods in Natural Language Processing (2018)
8. Freire, N., Borbinha, J.L., Calado, P., Martins, B.: A metadata geoparsing system for place name recognition and resolution in metadata records. In: Proceedings of the ACM/IEEE Joint Conference on Digital Libraries (2011)
9. Goldberg, Y.: A primer on neural network models for natural language processing. J. Artif. Intell. Res. **57**(1), 345–420 (2016)
10. Górski, K., et al.: HEALPix: a framework for high-resolution discretization and fast analysis of data distributed on the sphere. Astrophys. J. **622**(2), 759 (2005)
11. Gritta, M., Pilehvar, M.T., Collier, N.: Which Melbourne? Augmenting geocoding with maps. In: Proceedings of the Annual Meeting of the Association for Computational Linguistics (2018)
12. Gritta, M., Pilehvar, M.T., Limsopatham, N., Collier, N.: What's missing in geographical parsing? Lang. Resour. Eval. **52**(2), 603–623 (2018)
13. Karimzadeh, M., Pezanowski, S., MacEachren, A.M., Wallgrün, J.O.: GeoTxt: a scalable geoparsing system for unstructured text geolocation. Trans. GIS **23**(1), 118–136 (2019)
14. Leidner, J.L.: Toponym resolution in text: annotation, evaluation and applications of spatial grounding. In: Special Interest Group on Information Retrieval Forum, vol. 41, no. 2 (2007)
15. Lieberman, M.D., Samet, H.: Adaptive context features for toponym resolution in streaming news. In: Proceedings of the International ACM SIGIR Conference on Research and Development in Information Retrieval (2012)

16. Lieberman, M.D., Samet, H., Sankaranarayanan, J.: Geotagging with local lexicons to build indexes for textually-specified spatial data. In: Proceedings of the IEEE International Conference on Data Engineering (2010)
17. Manguinhas, H., Martins, B., Borbinha, J.L., Siabato, W.: The DIGMAP geo-temporal web gazetteer service. E-Perimetron **4**(1), 9–24 (2009)
18. Melo, F., Martins, B.: Automated geocoding of textual documents: a survey of current approaches. Trans. GIS **21**(1), 3–8 (2017)
19. Monteiro, B.R., Davis, C.A., Fonseca, F.T.: A survey on the geographic scope of textual documents. Comput. Geosci. **96**, 23–34 (2016)
20. Peters, M.E., et al.: Deep contextualized word representations. In: Proceedings of the Conference of the North American Chapter of the Association for Computational Linguistics: Human Language Technologies (2018)
21. Santos, J., Anastácio, I., Martins, B.: Using machine learning methods for disambiguating place references in textual documents. GeoJournal **80**(3), 375–392 (2015)
22. Smith, L.N.: Cyclical learning rates for training neural networks. In: Proceedings of the IEEE Winter Conference on Applications of Computer Vision (2017)
23. Vincenty, T.: Direct and inverse solutions of geodesics on the ellipsoid with application of nested equations. Surv. Rev. **23**, 88–93 (1975)
24. Wing, B.P.: Text-based document geolocation and its application to the digital humanities. Ph.D. thesis, The University of Texas at Austin (2015)
25. Yang, Z., Dai, Z., Yang, Y., Carbonell, J., Salakhutdinov, R., Le, Q.V.: XLNet: generalized autoregressive pretraining for language understanding (2019)

Author Index